SOCIETIES, NETWORKS, AND TRANSITIONS

A GLOBAL HISTORY

VOLUME I: TO 1500

CRAIG A. LOCKARD

University of Wisconsin—Green Bay

HOUGHTON MIFFLIN COMPANY   Boston   New York

Senior sponsoring editor: Nancy Blaine
Senior development editor: Julie Swasey
Senior project editor: Carol Newman
Associate project editor: Deborah Berkman
Senior art and design coordinator: Jill Haber
Senior photo researcher: Jennifer Meyer Dare
Composition buyer: Chuck Dutton
Associate manufacturing buyer: Brian Pieragostini
Senior marketing manager for history: Katherine Bates

Cover image: Machu Picchu, Cuzco, Peru. Stone/Getty Images.

Printed in the U.S.A.

Library of Congress Catalog Card Number: 2006928173

ISBN 13: 978-0-618-38612-3
ISBN 10: 0-618-38612-2

1 2 3 4 5 6 7 8 9-DOW-11 10 09 08 07

BRIEF CONTENTS

CONTENTS

SOCIETIES · NETWORKS · TRANSITIONS

Classical Blossomings in World History, 600 B.C.E.–600 C.E.

MAPS AND FEATURES

Awareness of the need for a universal view of history—for a history which transcends national and regional boundaries and comprehends the entire globe—is one of the marks of the present. Our past [is] the past of the world, our history is the first to be world history.[1]

British historian Geoffrey Barraclough wrote these words over two decades ago, yet historians are still grappling with what it means to write world history, and why it is crucial to do so. Twenty-first-century students, more than any generation before them, live in multicultural countries and an interconnected world. The world's interdependence calls for teaching a wider vision, which is the goal of this text. My intention is to create a meaningful, coherent, and stimulating presentation that conveys to students the incredible diversity of societies from earliest times to the present, as well as the ways they have been increasingly connected to other societies and shaped by these relationships. History may happen "as one darn thing after another," but the job of historians is to make it something more than facts, names, and dates. A text should provide a readable narrative, supplying a content base while also posing larger questions. The writing is as clear and thorough in its explanation of events and concepts as I can make it. No text can or should teach the course, but I hope that this text provides enough of a baseline of regional and global coverage to allow each instructor to bring her or his own talents, understandings, and particular interests to the process.

I became involved in teaching, debating, and writing world history as a result of my personal and academic experiences. My interest in other cultures was first awakened in the multicultural southern California city where I grew up. Many of my classmates or their parents had come from Asia, Latin America, or the Middle East. There was also a substantial African American community. A curious person did not have to search far to hear music, sample foods, or encounter ideas from many different cultures. I remember being enchanted by the Chinese landscape paintings at a local museum devoted to Asian art, and vowing to one day see some of those misty mountains for myself. Today many young people may be as interested as I was in learning about the world, since, thanks to immigration, many

cities and towns all over North America have taken on a cosmopolitan flavor similar to my hometown.

While experiences growing up sparked my interest in other cultures, it was my schooling that pointed the way to a career in teaching world history. When I entered college, all undergraduate students were required to take a two-semester course in Western Civilization as part of the general education requirement. Many colleges and universities in North America had similar classes that introduced students to Egyptian pyramids, Greek philosophy, medieval pageantry, Renaissance art, and the French Revolution, enriching our lives. Fortunately, my university expanded student horizons further by adding course components (albeit brief) on China, Japan, India, and Islam while also developing a study abroad program. I participated in both the study abroad in Salzburg, Austria, and the student exchange with a university in Hong Kong, which meant living with, rather than just sampling, different customs, outlooks, and histories.

Some teachers and academic historians had begun to realize that the emphasis in U.S. education on the histories of the United States and western Europe, to the near exclusion of the rest of the world, was not sufficient for understanding the realities of the mid-twentieth century. Young Americans were being sent thousands of miles away to fight wars in countries, such as Vietnam, that few Americans had ever heard of. Newspapers and television reported developments in places such as Japan and Indonesia, Egypt and Congo, Cuba and Brazil, which had increasing relevance for Americans. Graduate programs and scholarship directed toward Asian, African, Middle Eastern, Latin American, and eastern European and Russian history also grew out of the awareness of a widening world, broadening conceptions of history. I attended one of the new programs in Asian Studies for my M.A. degree, and then the first Ph.D. program in world history. Thanks to that program, I encountered the stimulating work of pioneering world historians from

North America such as Philip Curtin, Marshall Hodgson, William McNeill, and Leften S. Stavrianos. My own approach owes much to the global vision they offered.

To bring some coherence to the emerging world history field as well as to promote a global approach at all levels of education, several dozen of us teaching at the university, college, community college, and high school level in the United States came together in the early 1980s to form the World History Association (WHA), for which I served as founding secretary. The organization grew rapidly, encouraging the teaching, studying, and writing of world history not only in the United States but all over the world. The approaches to world history found among active WHA members vary widely, and my engagement in the ongoing discussions at conferences and in essays, often about the merits of varied textbooks, provided an excellent background for writing this text.

The Aims and Approach of the Text

Societies, Networks, and Transitions: A Global History provides an accessible, thought-provoking guide to students in their exploration of the landscape of the past, helping them to think about it in all its social diversity and interconnectedness and to see their lives with fresh understanding. It does this by combining clear writing, special learning features, current scholarship, and a comprehensive, global approach that does not omit the role and richness of particular regions.

There is a method behind these aims. For nearly thirty-five years I have written about and taught Asian, African, and world history at universities in the United States and Malaysia. A cumulative seven years of study, research, or teaching in Southeast Asia, East Asia, East Africa, and Europe gave me insights into a wide variety of cultures and historical perspectives. Finally, the WHA, its publications and conferences, and the more recent electronic listserv, H-WORLD, have provided active forums for vigorously discussing how best to teach world history.

The most effective approach to presenting world history in a text for undergraduate and advanced high school students, I have concluded, is one that combines the themes of connections and cultures. World history is very much about connections that transcend countries, cultures, and regions, and a text should discuss, for example, major long-distance trade networks such as the Silk Road, the spread of religions, maritime exploration, world wars, and transregional empires such as the Persian, Mongol, and British Empires. These connections are part of the broader global picture. Students need to understand that cultures, however unique, did not emerge and operate in a vacuum but faced similar challenges, shared many common experiences, and influenced each other.

The broader picture is drawn by means of several features in the text. To strengthen the presentation of the global overview, the text uses an innovative essay feature entitled "Societies, Networks, and Transitions." Appearing at the end of each of the six chronological parts, this feature analyzes and synthesizes the wider trends of the era, such as the role of long-distance trade, the spread of technologies and religions, and global climate change. The objective is to amplify the wider transregional messages already developed in the part chapters and help students to think further about the global context in which societies are enmeshed. Each "Societies, Networks, and Transitions" essay also makes comparisons, for example, between the Han Chinese, Mauryan Indian, and Roman Empires, and between Chinese, Indian, and European emigration in the nineteenth century. These comparisons help to throw further light on diverse cultures and the differences and similarities between them during the era covered. Finally, each essay is meant to show how the transitions that characterize the era lead up to the era discussed in the following part. In addition, the prologues that introduce each of the six eras treated in the text also set out the broader context, including some of the major themes and patterns of wide influence as well as those for each region. Furthermore, several chapters concentrate on global developments since 1750 C.E.

However, while a broad global overview is a strongly developed feature of this text, most chapters, while acknowledging and explaining relevant linkages, focus on a particular region or several regions. Most students learn easiest by focusing on one region or culture at a time. Students also benefit from recognizing the cultural richness and intellectual creativity of specific societies. From this text students learn, for instance, about Chinese poetry, Indonesian music, Arab science, Greek philosophy, West African arts, Indian cinema, and Anglo-American political thought. As a component of this cultural richness, this text also devotes considerable attention to the enduring religious traditions, such as Buddhism, Christianity, and Islam, and to issues of gender. The cultural richness of a region and its distinctive social patterns can get lost in an approach that minimizes regional coverage. Today most people are still mostly concerned with events in their own countries, even as their lives are reshaped by transnational economies and global cultural movements.

Also a strong part of the presentation of world history in this text is its attempt to be comprehensive and inclusive. To enhance comprehensiveness, the text balances social, economic, political, and cultural and religious history, and it also devotes some attention to geographical and environmental contexts as well as to the history of ideas and technologies. At the same time, the text also highlights features within societies, such as economic production, technological innovations, and portable ideas that had widespread or enduring influence. To ensure inclusiveness, the text recognizes the contributions of many societies, including some often neglected in texts, such as sub-Saharan Africa, pre-Columbian America, and Oceania. In particular, this text offers strong coverage of the diverse Asian societies. Throughout history, as today, the great majority of the world's population have lived in Asia.

All textbook authors struggle with how to organize the material. To keep the number of chapters corresponding to the twenty-eight or thirty weeks of most academic calendars in North America, and roughly equal in length, I have often had to combine several regions into a single chapter in order to be comprehensive, sometimes making decisions for convenience sake. For example, unlike texts that may have only one chapter on sub-Saharan Africa covering the centuries from ancient times to 1500 C.E., this text discusses Africa in six chronological eras, devoting three chapters to the centuries prior to 1500 C.E. and three to the years since 1450 C.E. But this sometimes necessitated grouping Africa, depending on the era, with Europe, the Middle East, or the Americas. The material is divided into eras so that students can understand how all regions were part of world history from earliest times. I believe that a chronological structure aids students in grasping the changes over time while helping to organize the material.

Distinguishing Features

Several features of *Societies, Networks, Transitions: A Global History* will help students better understand, assimilate, and appreciate the material they are about to encounter. Those unique to this text include the following.

Introducing World History World history may be the first and possibly the only history course many undergraduates will take in college. The text opens with a short essay that introduces students to the nature of history, the special challenges posed by studying world history, and why we need to study it.

Balancing Themes Three broad themes—uniqueness, interdependence, and change—have shaped the text. They are discussed throughout in terms of three related concepts—societies, networks, and transitions. These concepts, discussed in more detail in "Introducing World History," can be summarized as follows:

- **Societies** Influenced by environmental and geographical factors, people have formed and maintained societies defined by distinctive but often changing cultures, beliefs, social forms, institutions, and material traits.
- **Networks** Over the centuries societies have generally been connected to other societies by growing networks forged by phenomena such as migration, long-distance trade, exploration, military expansion, colonization, the spread of ideas and technologies, and webs of communication. These growing networks modified individual societies, created regional systems, and eventually led to a global system.
- **Transitions** Each major historical era has been marked by one or more great transitions sparked by events or innovations, such as settled agriculture, Mongol imperialism, industrial revolution, or world war, that have had profound and enduring influences on many societies, gradually reshaping the world. At the same time, societies and regions have experienced transitions of regional rather than global scope that have generated new ways of thinking or doing things, such as the expansion of Islam into India or the European colonization of East Africa and Mexico.

Through exposure to these three ideas integrated throughout the text, students learn of the rich cultural mosaic of the world. They are also introduced to its patterns of connections and unity as well as of continuity and change.

"Societies, Networks, and Transitions" Minichapters A short feature at the end of each part assists the student in backing up from the stories of societies and regions to see the larger historical patterns of change and the wider links among distant peoples. This comparative analysis allows students to identify experiences and transitions common to several regions or the entire world and to reflect further on the text themes. These features can also help students review key developments from the preceding chapters.

Historical Controversies Since one of the common misconceptions about history is that it is about the "dead" past, included in each "Societies, Networks, and Transitions" feature is a brief account of a debate among historians over how an issue in the past should be interpreted and what it means to us today. For example, why are the major societies dominated by males, and has this always been true? Why and when did Europe begin its "great divergence" from China and other Asian societies? How do historians evaluate contemporary globalization? Reappraisal is at the heart of history, and many historical questions are never completely answered. Yet most textbooks ignore this dimension of historical study; this text is innovative in including it. The Historical Controversy essays will help show students that historical facts are anything but dead; they live and change their meaning as new questions are asked by each new generation.

Profiles It is impossible to recount the human story without using broad generalizations, but it is also difficult to understand that story without seeing historical events reflected in the lives of men and women, prominent but also ordinary people. Each chapter contains a profile that focuses on the experiences or accomplishments of a woman or man, to convey the flavor of life of the period, to embellish the chapter narrative with interesting personalities, and to integrate gender into the historical account. The profiles try to show how gender affected the individual, shaping her or his opportunities and involvement in society. Several focus questions ask the student to reflect on the profile. For instance, students will examine a historian in early China, look at the spread of Christianity as seen through the life of a pagan female philosopher in Egypt, relive the experience of a female slave in colonial Brazil, and envision modern Indian life through a sketch of a film star.

Special Coverage This text also treats often-neglected areas and subjects. For example:

- It focuses on several regions with considerable historical importance but often marginalized or even omitted in many texts, including sub-Saharan Africa, Southeast Asia, Korea, Central Asia, pre-Columbian North America, ancient South America, the Caribbean, Polynesia, Australia, Canada, and the United States.
- It includes discussions of significant groups that transcend regional boundaries, such as the caravan travelers of the Silk Road, Mongol empire builders, the Indian Ocean maritime traders, and contemporary humanitarian organizations such as Amnesty International and Doctors Without Borders.
- It features extensive coverage of the roots, rise, reshaping, and enduring influence of the great religious and philosophical traditions.
- It blends coverage of gender, particularly the experiences of women, and of social history generally, into the larger narrative.
- It devotes the first chapter of the text to the roots of human history. After a brief introduction to the shaping of our planet, human evolution, and the spread of people around the world, the chapter examines the birth of agriculture, cities, and states, which set the stage for everything to come.
- It includes strong coverage of the world since 1945, a focus of great interest to many students.

Witness to the Past Many texts incorporate excerpts from primary sources, but this text also keeps student needs in mind by using up-to-date translations and addressing a wide range of topics. Included are excerpts from important Buddhist, Hindu, Confucian, Zoroastrian, and Islamic works that helped shape great traditions. Readings such as a collection of Roman graffiti, a thirteenth-century tourist description of a Chinese city, a report on an Aztec market, and a manifesto for modern Egyptian women reveal something of people's lives and concerns. Also offered are materials that shed light on the politics of the time, such as an African king's plea to end the slave trade, Karl Marx's *Communist Manifesto*, and the recent *Arab Human Development Report*. The wide selection of document excerpts is also designed to illustrate how historians work with original documents. Unlike most texts, chapters are also enlivened by brief but numerous excerpts of statements, writings, or songs from people of the era that are effectively interspersed in the chapter narrative so that students can better see the vantage points and opinions of the people of that era.

Learning Aids

The carefully designed learning aids are meant to help faculty teach world history and students actively learn and appreciate it. A number of aids have been created, including some that distinguish this text from others in use.

Part Prologue and Map Each part opens with a prologue that previews the major themes and topics—global and regional—covered in the part chapters. An accompanying world map shows some of the key societies discussed in the part.

Chapter Outline, Primary Source Quotation, and Vignette A chapter outline shows the chapter contents at a glance. Chapter text then opens with a quotation from a primary source pertinent to chapter topics. An interest-grabbing vignette or sketch then funnels students' attention toward the chapter themes they are about to explore.

Focus Questions To prepare students for thinking about the main themes and topics of the chapter, a short list of thoughtfully prepared questions begins each chapter narrative. These questions are then repeated before each major section. The points they deal with are then revisited in the Chapter Summary.

Special Boxed Features Each chapter contains a Witness to the Past drawn from a primary source, and a Profile highlighting a man or woman from that era. The Historical Controversy boxes, which focus on issues of interpretation, are included in each "Societies, Networks, and Transitions" essay. Questions are also placed at the end of the primary source readings, historical controversies, and profiles to help students comprehend the material.

Maps and Other Visuals Maps, photos, chronologies, and tables are amply interspersed throughout the chapters, illustrating and unifying coverage and themes.

Section Summaries At the end of each major section within a chapter, a bulleted summary helps students to review the key topics.

Chapter Summary At the end of each chapter, a concise summary invites students to sum up the chapter content and review its major points.

Annotated Suggested Readings and Endnotes Short lists of annotated suggested readings, mostly recent, and websites providing additional information are also found at the end of each chapter. These lists acknowledge some of the more important works used in writing as well as sources of particular value for undergraduate students. Direct quotes in the text are attributed to their sources in endnotes, which are located at the end of the book.

Key Terms and Pronunciation Guides Important terms likely to be new to the student are boldfaced in the text and immediately defined. These key terms are also listed at the end of the chapter and then listed with their definitions at the end of the text. The pronunciation of foreign and other difficult terms is shown parenthetically where the terms are introduced to help students with the terminology.

Ancillaries

A wide array of supplements accompany this text to help students better master the material and to help instructors in teaching from the book:

- Online Study Center student website

  Online Study Center

- Online Teaching Center instructor website

  Online Teaching Center

- HM Testing CD-ROM (powered by Diploma)
- Online Instructor's Resource Manual
- PowerPoint maps, images, and lecture outlines
- PowerPoint questions for personal response systems
- Blackboard™ and WebCT™ course cartridges
- Eduspace™ (powered by Blackboard™)
- Interactive ebook

The *Online Study Center* is a companion website for students that features a wide array of resources to help students master the subject matter. The website, prepared by Robert Shannon Sumner of the University of West Georgia, is divided into three major sections:

- "Prepare for Class" includes material such as learning objectives, chapter outlines, and preclass quizzes for a student to consult before going to class.
- "Improve Your Grade" includes practice review material like interactive flashcards, chronological ordering exercises, audio mp3 files of chapter summaries, primary sources, and interactive map exercises.
- "ACE the Test" features our successful ACE brand of practice tests as well as other self-testing materials.

Students can also find additional text resources such as an online glossary, an audio pronunciation guide, and material on how to study more effectively in the General Resources section. Throughout the text, icons direct students to relevant exercises and self-testing material located on the *Online Study Center*. Access the *Online Study Center* for this text by visiting **college.hmco.com/pic/lockard1e.**

The *Online Teaching Center* is a companion website for instructors. It features all of the material on the student site plus additional password-protected resources that help instructors teach the course, such as an electronic version of the *Instructor's Resource Manual,* blank maps of world history, and PowerPoint slides. Access the *Online Teaching Center* for this text by visiting **college.hmco.com/pic/lockard1e.**

HM Testing (powered by *Diploma*) offers instructors a flexible and powerful tool for test generation and test management. Now supported by the Brownstone Research Group's market-leading *Diploma* software, this new version of *HM Testing* significantly improves functionality and ease of use by offering all the tools needed to create, author, deliver, and customize multiple types of tests. *Diploma* is currently in use at thousands of college and university campuses throughout the United States and Canada. The *HM Testing* content was developed by Candace Gregory-Abbott of California State University, Sacramento, and Timothy Furnish of Georgia Perimeter College and offers key term identification, multiple-choice questions (with page references to the correct responses), short-answer questions, and essay questions (with sample answers) as well as unit examination questions, for a total of approximately two thousand test items.

The *Instructor's Resource Manual,* prepared by Siamak Adhami of Saddleback Community College and Doug T. McGetchin of Florida Atlantic University, contains advice on teaching the World History course, suggestions on how to utilize the book's boxed feature program, instructional objectives, chapter outlines and summaries, lecture suggestions, suggested debate topics, writing assignments with sample answers, and cooperative learning activities.

We are pleased to offer a collection of world history PowerPoint lecture outlines, maps, and images for use in classroom presentations. Detailed lecture outlines correspond to the book's chapters and make it easier for instructors to cover the major topics in class. The art collection includes all of the photos and maps in the text, as well as numerous other images from our world history titles. PowerPoint questions and answers for use with personal response system software are also offered to adopters free of charge.

A variety of assignable homework and testing material has been developed to work with the *Blackboard*™ and *WebCT*™ course management systems, as well as with *Eduspace*™: Houghton Mifflin's online learning tool (powered by *Blackboard*™). *Eduspace*™ is a web-based online learning environment that provides instructors with a gradebook and communication capabilities such as synchronous and asynchronous chats and announcement postings. It offers access to assignments, such as over 650 gradable homework exercises, writing assignments, interactive maps with questions, primary sources, discussion questions for online discussion boards, and tests, all ready to use. Instructors can choose to use the content as is, modify it, or even add their own. *Eduspace*™ also contains an interactive ebook that contains in-text links to interactive maps, primary sources, audio pronunciation files, and review and self-testing material for students.

Formats

The text is available in a one-volume hard cover edition, a two-volume paperback edition, a three-volume paperback edition, and as an interactive ebook. *Volume 1: To 1500* includes Chapters 1–14; *Volume 2: Since 1450* includes Chapters 15–31; *Volume A: To 600* includes Chapters 1–9; *Volume B: From 600 to 1750* includes Chapters 10–18; and *Volume C: Since 1750* includes Chapters 19–31.

Acknowledgments

The author would like to thank the following community of instructors who, by sharing their teaching experiences and insightful feedback, helped shape the final textbook and ancillary program:

Siamak Adhami, Saddleback Community College

Sanjam Ahluwalia, Northern Arizona University

David G. Atwill, Pennsylvania State University

Ewa K. Bacon, Lewis University

Bradford C. Brown, Bradley University

Gayle K. Brunelle, California State University–Fullerton

Rainer Buschmann, California State University, Channel Islands

Jorge Canizares-Esguerra, State University of New York–Buffalo

Bruce A. Castleman, San Diego State University

Harold B. Cline, Jr., Middle Georgia College

Simon Cordery, Monmouth College

Dale Crandall-Bear, Solano Community College

Cole Dawson, Warner Pacific College

Hilde De Weerdt, University of Tennessee, Knoxville

Anna Dronzek, University of Minnesota, Morris

James R. Evans, Southeastern Community College

Robert Fish, Japan Society of New York

Robert J. Flynn, Portland Community College

Gladys Frantz-Murphy, Regis University

Timothy Furnish, Georgia Perimeter College

James E. Genova, Ohio State University

Deborah Gerish, Emporia State University

Kurt A. Gingrich, Radford University

Candace Gregory-Abbott, California State University, Sacramento

Paul L. Hanson, California Lutheran University

A. Katie Harris, Georgia State University

Gregory M. Havrilcsak, University of Michigan–Flint

Timothy Hawkins, Indiana State University

Don Holsinger, Seattle Pacific University

Mary N. Hovanec, Cuyahoga Community College

Jonathan Judaken, University of Memphis

Thomas E. Kaiser, University of Arkansas at Little Rock

Carol Keller, San Antonio College

Patricia A. Kennedy, Leeward Community College-University of Hawaii

Jonathan Lee, San Antonio College

Thomas Lide, San Diego State University

Derek S. Linton, Hobart and William Smith Colleges

David L. Longfellow, Baylor University

Erik C. Maiershofer, Point Loma Nazarene University

Afshin Marashi, California State University, Sacramento

Robert B. McCormick, University of South Carolina Upstate

Doug T. McGetchin, Florida Atlantic University

Kerry Muhlestein, Brigham Young University–Hawaii

Peter Ngwafu, Albany State University

Monique O'Connell, Wake Forest University

Annette Palmer, Morgan State University

Nicholas C. J. Pappas, Sam Houston State University

Patricia M. Pelley, Texas Tech University

John Pesda, Camden County College

Pamela Roseman, Georgia Perimeter College

Paul Salstrom, St. Mary-of-the-Woods

Sharlene Sayegh, California State University, Long Beach

Michael Seth, James Madison University

David Simonelli, Youngstown State University

Peter Von Sivers, University of Utah

Anthony J. Steinhoff, University of Tennessee–Chattanooga

Nancy L. Stockdale, University of Central Florida

Robert Shannon Sumner, University of West Georgia

Kate Transchel, California State University, Chico

Sally N. Vaughn, University of Houston

Thomas G. Velek, Mississippi University for Women

Kenneth Wilburn, East Carolina University

The author has incurred many intellectual debts in developing his expertise in world history, as well as in preparing this text. To begin with, I cannot find words to express my gratitude to the wonderful editors and staff at Houghton Mifflin—Nancy Blaine, Julie Swasey, Carol Newman, and Jean Woy—who had enough faith in this project to tolerate my missed deadlines and sometimes grumpy responses to editorial decisions or some other crisis. I also owe an incalculable debt to my development editor, Phil Herbst, who prodded and pampered, and helped me write for a student, rather than scholarly, audience. Carole Frohlich, Jessyca Broekman, Susan Zorn, and Jake Kawatski ably handled the photos, maps, copyediting, and indexes, respectively. Sandi McGuire and Katherine Bates provided great help with marketing. I also owe a great debt to Pam Gordon, whose interest and encouragement got this project started. Ken Wolf of Murray State University prepared the initial drafts of several of the early chapters and in other ways gave me useful criticism and advice. I would also like to acknowledge the inspiring mentors who helped me at various stages of my academic preparation: Bill Goldmann, who introduced me to world history at Pasadena High School in California; Charles Hobart and David Poston, University of Redlands professors who sparked my interest in Asia; George Wong, Bart Stoodley, and especially Andrew and Margaret Roy, my mentors at Chung Chi College in Hong Kong; Walter Vella and Danny Kwok, who taught me Asian studies at Hawaii; and John Smail and Phil Curtin, under whom I studied comparative world history in the immensely exciting Ph.D. program at Wisconsin. My various sojourns in East Asia,

Southeast Asia, and East Africa allowed me to meet and learn from many inspiring and knowledgeable scholars. I have also been greatly stimulated and influenced in my approach by the writings of many fine global historians, but I would single out Phil Curtin, Marshall Hodgson, L. S. Stavrianos, William McNeill, Fernand Braudel, Eric Hobsbawm, Immanuel Wallerstein, and Peter Stearns. Curtin, Hobsbawm, and McNeill also gave me personal encouragement concerning my writing in the field, for which I am very grateful.

Colleagues at the various universities where I taught have been supportive of my explorations in world and comparative history. Most especially I acknowledge the friendship, support, and intellectual collaboration over three decades of my colleagues in the Social Change and Development Department at the University of Wisconsin–Green Bay (UWGB), especially Harvey Kaye, Tony Galt, Lynn Walter, Larry Smith, Andy Kersten, Kim Nielsen, and Andrew Austin. I have also benefited immeasurably as a world historian from the visiting lecture series sponsored by UWGB's Center for History and Social Change, directed by Harvey Kaye, which over the years has brought in dozens of outstanding scholars. My students at UWGB and elsewhere have also taught me much.

I also thank my colleagues in the World History Association, who have generously shared their knowledge, encouraged my work, and otherwise provided an exceptional opportunity for learning and an exchange of ideas. I am proud to have helped establish this organization, which incorporates world history teachers at all levels of education and in many nations. Among many others, I want to express a special thank-you to several longtime friends, early officers and members of the WHA from whom I have learned so much and with whom I have shared many wonderful meals and conversations: Ross Dunn, Lynda Shaffer, Kevin Reilly, Jerry Bentley, Heidi Roupp, Mark Gilbert, Steve Gosch, Judy Zinsser, and Anand Yang.

Finally, I need to acknowledge the loving support of my wife Kathy and our two sons, Chris and Colin, who patiently, although not always without complaint, put up for the ten years of the project with my hectic work schedule and the ever-growing piles of research materials, books, and chapter drafts scattered around our cluttered den and sometimes colonizing other space around the house. Now perhaps we shall have a chance to once again smell the roses and marvel at the sunsets without my obsessing about a chapter revision to complete, after I clear away the clutter.

About the Author

Craig A. Lockard is Ben and Joyce Rosenberg Professor of History in the Social Change and Development Department at the University of Wisconsin–Green Bay, where since 1975 he has taught courses on Asian, African, comparative, and world history. He has also taught at SUNY-Buffalo, SUNY-Stony Brook, and the University of Bridgeport, and twice served as a Fulbright-Hays professor at the University of Malaya in Malaysia. After undergraduate studies in Austria, Hong Kong, and the University of Redlands, he earned an M.A. in Asian Studies at the University of Hawaii and a Ph.D. in Comparative World and Southeast Asian History at the University of Wisconsin–Madison. His published books, articles, essays, and reviews range over a wide spectrum of topics: world history; Southeast Asian history, politics, and society; Asian emigration; the Vietnam War; and folk, popular, and world music. Among his major books are *Lands of Green, Waters of Blue: Southeast Asia in World History* (forthcoming); *Dance of Life: Popular Music and Politics in Modern Southeast Asia* (1998); and *From Kampung to City: A Social History of Kuching, Malaysia, 1820–1970* (1987). He was also part of the task force that prepared revisions to the U.S. National Standards in World History (1996). Professor Lockard has served on various editorial advisory boards, including the *Journal of World History* and *The History Teacher,* and as book review editor for the *Journal of Asian Studies* and the *World History Bulletin.* He was one of the founders of the World History Association and served as the organization's first secretary. He has lived and traveled widely in Asia, Africa, and Europe.

NOTE ON SPELLING AND USAGE

Transforming foreign words and names, especially those from non-European languages, into spellings usable for English-speaking readers presents a challenge. Sometimes, as with Chinese, Thai, and Malay/Indonesian, several romanized spelling systems have developed. Generally I have chosen user-friendly spellings that are widely used in other Western writings (such as *Aksum* for the classical Ethiopian state and *Ashoka* for the classical Indian king). For Chinese, I generally use the *pinyin* system developed in the People's Republic over the past few decades (such as *Qin* and *Qing* rather than the older *Chin* and *Ching* for these dynasties, and *Beijing* instead of *Peking*), but for a few terms and names (such as the twentieth-century political leaders *Sun Yat-sen* and *Chiang Kai-shek*) I have retained an older spelling more familiar to Western readers and easier to pronounce. The same strategy is used for some other terms or names from Afro-Asian societies, such as *Cairo* instead of *al-Cahira* (the Arabic name) for the Egyptian city, *Bombay* instead of *Mumbai* (the current Indian usage) for India's largest city, and *Burma* instead of *Myanmar*. In some cases I have favored a newer spelling widely used in a region and modern scholarship but not perhaps well known in the West. For example, in discussing Southeast Asia I follow contemporary scholarship and use *Melaka* instead of *Malacca* for the Malayan city and *Maluku* rather than *Moluccas* for the Indonesian islands. Similarly, like Africa specialists I have opted to use some newer spellings, such as *Gikuyu* rather than *Kikuyu* for the Kenyan people. To simplify things for the reader I have tried to avoid using diacritical marks within words. Sometimes their use is unavoidable, such as for the premodern Chinese city of *Chang'an;* the two syllables here are pronounced separately. I also follow the East Asian custom of rendering Chinese, Japanese, and Korean names with the surname (family name) first (e.g., *Mao Zedong, Tokugawa Ieyasu*). The reader is also referred to the opening essay, "Introducing World History," for explanations of the dating system used (such as the Common Era and the Intermediate Era) and geographical concepts (such as Eurasia for Europe and Asia, and Oceania for Australia, New Zealand, and the Pacific islands).

A journey of a thousand miles begins with the first step.

CHINESE PROVERB

This introduction is designed to help you take the important "first step" toward understanding the scope and challenge of studying world history. By presenting the main concepts and themes of world history, it will serve as your guide in exploring the story of the world presented in the rest of the book. The introduction will also give you a foretaste of the lively ongoing debates in which historians engage as they try to make sense of the past, especially how societies change and how their contacts with one another have created the interconnected world we know today. By examining world history, you can better understand not only how this connection happened, but also why.

What Do Historians Do?

History is the study of the past that looks at all of human life, thought, and behavior and includes both a record and an interpretation of events, people, and the societies they developed. Therefore, the job of the historian is to both describe *and* interpret the past. Both tasks are important. Although beginning students generally see history as the story of "what happened," most professional historians regard the attempt to make sense of historical events as the more exciting part of their work. Two general concepts help historians in these efforts. When they look at humans in all their historical complexity, historians see both changes and continuity. The legal system in the United States, for example, is unlike any other in the world, and yet it has been shaped in part by both English and ancient Roman legal practices.

Historians face their greatest challenges in their role as interpreters of the past. Although historians agree on the need for extensive evidence to support their generalizations, they often disagree on how an event should be interpreted. Often the disagreements reflect differences in political points of view. In 1992 a widely publicized disagreement took place on the occasion of the 500-year anniversary of the first cross-Atlantic voyage of Christopher Columbus to the Western Hemisphere in 1492. Depending on their political biases, historians used the well-known records of this event in different ways. Some historians pictured Columbus as a farsighted pioneer who made possible communication between the hemispheres, while others saw him as an immoral villain who mistreated the local American peoples, beginning a pattern of exploitation by Europeans. Similar debates have raged about whether it was necessary for the United States to drop atomic bombs on Japan in 1945, a deadly decision that killed thousands of Japanese civilians but nevertheless ended World War II.

While the events of the past do not change, our understanding of them does, as historians both acquire new information and use the old information to answer new questions. Only within the past fifty years, for example, have historians studied the diaries and journals that reveal the important role of women on the home front during the American Civil War. Even more recently historians have used long neglected sources to conclude that, a millennium ago, China had the world's most dynamic economy and sophisticated technology. Similarly, historians have recently discovered, in the West African city of Timbuktu, thousands of old books written in African languages, forcing a rethinking of literacy and scholarship in West African societies hundreds of years ago.

What history "tells us" is constantly evolving. New evidence, changing interests, and the asking of new questions all add up to seeing things in a new light. As you read the text, remember that no text contains the whole or final truth. **Historical revision**, or changing understanding of the past, is at the heart of historical scholarship. This revision and the difficulties of interpretation also make history controversial. In recent years heated debates about what schools should teach about history have erupted in many countries, including Japan, India, and the United States.

Historians bridge the gap between the humanities and the social sciences. As humanists, historians study the philosophies, religions, literatures, and arts that people have generated over the ages. As social scientists, historians examine political, social, and economic patterns, though frequently asking questions different from those asked by anthropologists, economists, political scientists, and sociologists; the last three groups especially are generally more concerned with the present and often more interested in theoretical questions. Because they study people in their many roles and stations in life—the accomplishments of the rich and famous as well as the struggles and dreams of common women and men—historians must be familiar with the findings of other relevant academic disciplines.

Why Study World History?

World history is the broadest field of history. It studies the human record as a whole and the experiences of people in all the world's inhabited regions: Africa, the Americas, Asia, Europe, and the Pacific Basin. World history helps us better understand individual societies and their traditions by making it easier to look at them comparatively. Studying history on a global scale also brings out patterns of life, cultural traditions, and connections between societies that go beyond a particular region, such as the spread of long-distance trade and Buddhism, which followed the trade routes throughout southern and eastern Asia nearly two thousand years ago. World, or global, history takes us through the forest of history in which the individual societies represent the individual trees. World history helps us comprehend both the trees and the forest, allowing us to situate ourselves in a broader context.

The study of world history helps us understand our increasingly connected world. Decisions made in Washington, D.C., Paris, or Tokyo influence citizens in Argentina, Senegal, and Malaysia, just as events in Africa, the Middle East, or Latin America often affect the lives of people in Europe, North America, and Australia. World historians use the widest angle of vision possible to comprehend a world in which diverse local traditions and international trends intermingle. International trends spread from many directions. Western phenomena such as McDonald's, Hard Rock Cafes, French wines, Hollywood films, churches, the Internet, and cell phones have spread around the world. Non-Western products and ideas, however, have also gained global followings; among these are Mexican soap operas, Chinese food, Japanese cars, Indonesian arts, African rhythms, and the Islamic religion. While it is important to study the histories of individual nations, we must remember that, for all their idiosyncrasies, each nation develops in the context of a wider world.

Along with the growing interconnectedness of the world, a global perspective highlights the past achievements of all peoples. The history of science, for example, shows that key inventions—printing, sternpost rudders, the compass, the wheelbarrow, gunpowder—originated in China and that the modern system of numbering came from India, reaching Europe from the Middle East as "Arabic" numerals. Indeed, various peoples—Mesopotamians, Egyptians, Greeks, Chinese, Indians, Arabs—built the early foundation for modern science and technology, and their discoveries moved along the trade routes. The importers of technology and ideas often modified or improved on them. For example, Europeans made good use of Chinese, Indian, and Arab technologies, as well as their own inventions, in their quest to explore the world in the fifteenth and sixteenth centuries. The interdependence among and exchanges between peoples is a historical as well as a present reality.

The World History Challenge

When we study world history, we see other countries and peoples, past and present. We do not, however, always see them accurately. Nevertheless, by studying the unfamiliar, world history helps us to recognize how some of the attitudes we absorb from the particular society and era we live in shape, and may distort, our understanding of the world and of history. Coming to terms with this mental baggage means examining such things as maps and geographical concepts and acquiring intellectual tools for comprehending other cultures.

Broadening the Scope of Our Histories

During much of the twentieth century, high school and college students in English-speaking countries were often taught some version of a course, usually called Western Civilization, that emphasized the rise of western Europe and the European contributions to modern North American societies. The Western Civilization course recognized the undeniably influential role of Western nations, technologies, and ideas in the modern world, but it was also a reflection of historians' extensive acquisition of data on Europe and North America compared with the rest of the world. This approach exaggerated the role that Europe played in world history before the sixteenth century, pushing Asian, African, and Native American peoples and their accomplishments into the background while underplaying the contributions these peoples made to Europe. Students usually learned little about China, India, or Islam, and even less about Africa, Southeast Asia, or Latin America.

In the 1960s the teaching of history began to change, particularly in North America. The political independence of most African nations from Western nations and the civil rights movement in the United States, which demanded equality between blacks and whites, forced a reappraisal of African history that was less influenced by colonialism and racism. By the 1970s the academic study of not only African but also Asian, Latin American, Native American, and Pacific island history in North America and Europe had become far more sophisticated. The increased knowledge has made it easier to write a world history that takes into its scope the entire globe. As a result, world history courses, rare before the 1960s, became increasingly common in U.S. universities, colleges, and high schools by the late twentieth century and have been proliferating in several other countries, such as Australia, Canada, South Africa, China, and the Netherlands.

Revising Maps and Geography

Maps not only tell us where places are; they also create a mental image of the world, revealing how peoples perceive themselves and others. For example, Chinese maps once portrayed China as the "Middle Kingdom," the center of

Mercator Projection

the world surrounded by "barbarians." This image reflected and deepened the Chinese sense of superiority over neighboring peoples. Similarly, 2,500 years ago, the Greeks developed a map that showed Greece at the center of the inhabited world known to them.

Even in modern times, maps can be misleading. For example, the Mercator projection (or spatial presentation), a map still used in many schools in North America and elsewhere and standard in most atlases, is based on a sixteenth-century European model that distorts the relative size of landmasses, greatly exaggerating Europe, North America, and Greenland while diminishing the lands around the equator and in the Southern Hemisphere. In this projection, Africa, India, Southeast Asia, China, and South America look much smaller than they actually are. In the United States, maps using a Mercator projection have often tellingly placed the Americas in the middle of the map, cutting Asia in half. The implicit message is that the United States, appearing larger than it actually is, plays the central role in the world.

Alternative maps have emerged that give a more accurate view of relative size. For example, the Eckert projection is an oval-shaped projection using an ellipse that shows a better balance of size and shape while minimizing distortion of continental areas. A comparison between the Mercator and Eckert world maps is shown on this page and the next.

The same shaping of mental images of geography found in maps is also seen in concepts of geographical features and divisions, such as continents, the large landmasses on which most people live. The classical Greeks were probably the first to use the terms *Europe*, *Africa*, and *Asia* in defining their world 2,500 years ago, and later Europeans transformed these terms into the names for continents. For centuries Western peoples have taken for granted that Europe is a continent. Actually, however, Europe is not a separate landmass, and the physical barriers between it and Asia are not that significant. If mountains and other geographical barriers define a continent, one can make a better case for India (blocked off by truly formidable mountains) or Southeast Asia than for Europe. At the same time, seeing Asia as a single continent is also a problem, given its spectacular size and geographical diversity. Today world geographers and historians usually consider Europe and Asia to constitute one huge continent, Eurasia, containing several subcontinental regions, such as Europe, South Asia, and East Asia.

Popular terms such as *Near East*, *Middle East*, or *Far East* are also misleading. They were originally formulated to describe regions as Westerners saw them in relationship to Europe. Much depends on the viewer's position; Australians, for example, often label nearby Southeast and East Asia as the "Near North." But, rejecting a Europe-centered approach, few Western scholars of China or Japan today refer to the "Far East," preferring the more neutral term *East Asia*. This text considers the term *Near East*, long used for western Asia, as outdated, but it refers to Southwest Asia and North Africa, closely linked historically (especially after the rise of Islam 1,400 years ago), as the Middle East, since that term is more convenient than the alternatives. The text also uses the term *Oceania* to refer to Australia, New Zealand, and the Pacific islands.

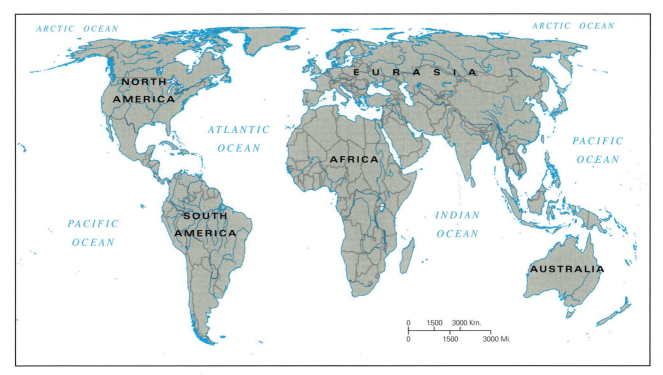

Eckert Projection

Rethinking the Dating System

A critical feature of historical study is the dating of events. World history challenges us by making us aware that all dating systems are based on the assumptions of a particular culture. Many Asian peoples saw history as moving in great cycles of birth, maturation, and decay (sometimes involving millions of years), while Westerners saw history as moving in a straight line from past to future (as can be seen in the chronologies within each chapter). Calendars were often tied to myths about the world's creation or about a people's or country's origins. Hence, the ancient Roman calendar was based on the founding of the city of Rome around 2,700 years ago, reflecting the Romans' claim to the territory in which they had recently settled.

The dating system used throughout the Western world today is based on the Gregorian Christian calendar, created by a sixteenth-century Roman Catholic pope, Gregory XIII. It uses the birth of Christianity's founder, Jesus of Nazareth, 2,000 years ago as the turning point. Dates for events prior to the Christian era were identified as B.C. (before Christ); years in the Christian era were labeled A.D. (for the Latin *anno domini*, "in the year of the Lord"). Many history books published in Europe and North America still employ this system, which has spread around the world in recent centuries.

The notion of Christian and pre-Christian eras has no longer been satisfactory for studies of world history because it is rooted in the viewpoint of only one religious tradition, whereas there are many in the world, usually with different calendars. The Christian calendar has little relevance for the non-Christian majority of the world's people. Muslims, for example, who consider the revelations of the prophet Muhammad to be the central event in history, begin their dating system with Muhammad's journey, within Arabia, from the city of Mecca to Medina in 622 A.D. Many Buddhists use a calendar beginning with the death of Buddha around 2,500 years ago. The Chinese chronological system divides history into cycles stretching over 24 million years. The Chinese are now in the fifth millennium of the current cycle, and their system corresponds more accurately than does the Gregorian calendar to the beginning of the world's oldest cities and states, between 5,000 and 6,000 years ago. Many other alternative dating systems exist. Selecting one over the others constitutes favoritism for a particular society or cultural tradition.

Therefore, in recent years most world historians and an increasing number of specialists in Asian, African, and European history have moved toward a more secular, or nonreligious, concept, the Common Era. This system still accepts as familiar, at least to Western and Latin American readers, the dates used in the Western calendar, but it calls the period after the transition, identified by Christians with the birth of Jesus, a "common" era, since many influential, dynamic societies existed two millennia ago in various parts of the world, not only in the Judeo-Christian Holy Land. Around two millennia ago, the beginning of the Common Era, the Roman Empire in the West was at its height while Chinese and Indian empires ruled large chunks of Asia. At the beginning of the Common Era many peoples in the Eastern Hemisphere were also linked by trade and religion to a greater extent than ever before. At the same time, several African societies flourished, and states and cities had long before developed in the Americas. Hence this period makes a useful and familiar benchmark.

In the new system, events are dated as B.C.E. (before the Common Era) and as C.E. (Common Era, which begins in year 1 of the Christian calendar). This change is an attempt at a method of dating that includes all the world's people and avoids favoring any particular religious tradition.

Rethinking the Division of History into Periods

To make world history more comprehensible, historians divide long periods of time into smaller segments, such as "the ancient world" or "modern history," each marked by certain key events or turning points. Historians call this process of dividing time **periodization**. For example, scholars of European, Islamic, Chinese, Indonesian, or United States history generally agree among themselves on the major eras and turning points for the region they study, but world historians need a system that can encompass all parts of the world. Finding such a system, however, presents difficulties, since most historic events did not affect all regions of the world. For instance, developments that were key to the eastern half of Eurasia, such as the spread of Buddhism, or to western Eurasia and North Africa, such as the spread of Christianity, did not always affect southern Africa, and both the Western Hemisphere, or the Americas, and some Pacific peoples remained isolated from the Eastern Hemisphere for centuries.

Given the need for a chronological pattern that is inclusive, this book divides history into periods, each of which is notable for significant changes around the world:

1. **Ancient (100,000–600 B.C.E.)** The Ancient Era, during which the foundations for world history were built, can be divided into two distinct periods. During the long centuries known as Prehistory (ca. 100,000–4000 B.C.E.), Stone Age peoples, living in small groups, survived by hunting and gathering food. Eventually some of them began simple farming and living in villages, launching the second period, the era of agrarian societies. Between 4000 and 600 B.C.E., agriculture became more productive, the first cities and states were established in both hemispheres, and some societies invented writing, allowing historians to study their experiences and ideas.

2. **Classical (600 B.C.E.–600 C.E.)** The Classical Era is marked by the creation of more states and complex agrarian societies, the birth of major religions and philosophies, the formation of the first large empires, often encompassing entire regions, and the expansion of long-distance trade, which linked distant peoples.

3. **Intermediate (600–1500 C.E.)** The Intermediate Era comprises a long middle period of expanding horizons that modified or displaced the classical societies.

It was marked by increasing trade connections between distant peoples within the same hemisphere, the growth and spread of several older religions, the rapid rise of a new religion, Islam, and oceanic exploration by Asians and Europeans.

4. **Early Modern (1450–1750 C.E.)** During the Early Modern Era, the whole globe became intertwined as European exploration and conquests in the Americas, Africa, and southern Asia fostered the rise of a global economy, capitalism, and a trans-Atlantic slave trade; undermined American and African societies; and enriched Europe.

5. **Modern (1750–1945 C.E.)** The Modern Era was characterized by industrialization and empire building on an unprecedented scale. These centuries featured rapid technological and economic change in Europe and North America, Western colonization of many Asian and African societies, the rise of nationalism and socialism, political revolutions, world wars, and a widening gap between rich and poor societies.

6. **Contemporary (1945–present)** The Contemporary Era has been marked by a more closely interlinked world, including the global spread of commercial markets, cultures, and communications, the collapse of Western colonial empires, international organizations, new technologies, struggles by poor nations to develop economically, environmental destruction, and conflict between powerful nations.

Understanding Cultural and Historical Differences

The study of world history challenges us to understand peoples and ideas very different from our own. The past is, as one writer has put it, "a foreign country; they do things differently there."[1] As human behavior changes with the times, sometimes dramatically, so do people's beliefs. Even moral and ethical standards have changed. For example, in Asia centuries ago, Assyrians and Mongols sometimes killed everyone in cities that resisted their conquest. Some European Christians seven hundred years ago burned suspected heretics and witches at the stake and enjoyed watching blind beggars fight. Across the Atlantic, American peoples such as the Aztecs and Incas engaged in human sacrifice. None of these behaviors would be morally acceptable today in most societies.

Differences in customs complicate efforts to understand people of earlier centuries. We need not approve of empire builders and plunderers, human sacrifice and witch burning, but we should be careful about applying our current standards of behavior and thought to people who lived in different times and places. There is always the danger of **ethnocentrism**, viewing others narrowly through the lens of one's own society and its values. Historians are careful in using value-loaded words such as *primitive, barbarian, civilized,* or *progress.* Such words carry negative meanings and are often matters of judgment rather than fact. For instance, soldiers facing each other on the battlefield may consider themselves civilized and their opponents barbarians. And progress, such as industrialization, often brings negative developments, such as pollution, along with the positive.

Today anthropologists use the term **cultural relativism** to remind us that, while all people have much in common, societies are diverse and unique, embodying different standards of correct behavior. For instance, cultures may have very different ideas about children's obligations to their parents, what happens to people's souls when they die, or what constitutes music pleasing to the ear. Cultural relativism still allows us to say that the Mongol empire builders in Eurasia some eight hundred years ago were brutal, or that the mid-twentieth-century Nazi German dictator, Adolph Hitler, was a murderous tyrant, or that laws in some societies today that blame and penalize women who are raped are wrong and should be protested. But cultural relativism discourages us from criticizing other cultures or ancient peoples just because they are or were different from us. Studying world history can make us more aware of our ethnocentric biases.

The Major Themes

Determining major themes is yet another challenge in presenting world history. This text uses certain themes to take maximum advantage of world history's power to illuminate both change and continuity as we move from the past to the present. Specifically, in preparing the text, the author asked himself: What do educated students today need to know about world history to understand the globalizing era in which they live?

Three broad themes help you comprehend how today's world emerged. These themes are shaped around three concepts: societies, networks, and transitions.

1. **Societies** are broad groups of people that have common traditions, institutions and organized patterns of relationships with each other. The societies that people have organized and maintained, influenced by environmental factors, were defined by distinctive but often changing cultures, beliefs, social forms, governments, economies, and ways of life.

2. **Networks** are arrangements or collections of links between different societies, such as the routes over which traders, goods, diplomats, armies, ideas, and information travel. Over the centuries societies were increasingly connected to other societies by growing networks forged by phenomena such as population movement, long-distance trade, exploration, military expansion, colonization, the diffusion of ideas and technologies, and communication links. These growing networks modified individual societies, connected societies within the same and nearby regions, and eventually led to a global system in which distant peoples came into frequent contact.

3. **Transitions** are passages, changes, events, or movements that reshape societies and regions. Each major historical era was marked by one or more great transitions that were sparked by events or innovations that had profound, enduring influences on many societies and that fostered a gradual reshaping of the world.

The first theme, based on societies, recognizes the importance in world history of the distinctiveness of societies. Cultural traditions and social patterns differed greatly. For example, societies in Eurasia fostered several influential philosophical and religious traditions, from Confucianism in eastern Asia to Christianity, born in the Middle East and nourished both there and in Europe. Historians often identify unique traditions in a society that go back hundreds or even thousands of years.

The second theme, based on networks, acknowledges the way societies have contacted and engaged with each other to create the interdependent world we know today. The spread of technologies and ideas, exploration and colonization, and the growth of global trade across Eurasia and Africa and then into the Western Hemisphere are largely responsible for setting this interlinking process in motion. Today networks such as the World Wide Web, airline routes, multinational corporations, and terrorist organizations operate on a global scale. As this list shows, many networks are welcome, but some are dangerous.

The third theme, transitions, helps to emphasize major developments that shaped world history. The most important include, roughly in chronological order, the beginning of agriculture, the rise of cities and states, the birth and spread of philosophical and religious traditions, the forming of great empires, the linking of Eurasia by the Mongols, the European seafaring explorations and conquests, the Industrial Revolution, the forging and dismantling of Western colonial empires, world wars, and the invention of electronic technologies that allow for instantaneous communication around the world.

With these themes in mind, the text constructs the rich story of world history. The intellectual experience of studying world history is exciting and will give you a clearer understanding of how the world as you know it came to be.

Online Study Center
Improve Your Grade Flashcards

Key Terms

history	cultural relativism
historical revision	societies
periodization	networks
ethnocentrism	transitions

Suggested Reading

After each chapter and essay, you will find a short list of valuable books and useful websites to help you explore history beyond the text. The general books and websites listed below will be of particular value to beginning students of world history.

Books and Journals

Bender, Thomas. *A Nation Among Nations: America's Place in World History*. New York: Hill and Wang, 2006. Looks at the history of the United States as part of modern world history.

Bentley, Jerry H. *Shapes of World History in 20th Century Scholarship*. Washington, D.C.: American Historical Association, 1996. A brief presentation of the scholarly study of world history.

Christian, David. *Maps of Time: An Introduction to Big History*. Berkeley: University of California Press, 2004. A detailed but path-breaking study mixing scientific understandings into the study of world history.

Dunn, Ross, ed. *The New World History: A Teacher's Companion*. Boston: Bedford/St. Martin's, 2000. A valuable collection of essays on various aspects of world history and how it can be studied. Useful for students as well as teachers.

Hodgson, Marshall G. S. *Rethinking World History: Essays on Europe, Islam, and World History*. Edited by Edmund Burke, III. New York: Cambridge University Press, 1993. Written by one of the most influential world historians for teachers and scholars but also offering many insights for students.

McNeill, J. R., and William H. McNeill. *The Human Web: A Bird's-Eye View of World History*. New York: W.W. Norton, 2003. A stimulating overview of world history using the concept of human webs to examine interactions between peoples.

McNeill, William H., et al., eds. *Berkshire Encyclopedia of World History*, 5 vols. Great Barrington, Mass.: Berkshire, 2005. One of the best of several fine encyclopedias, with many essays on varied aspects of world history.

Stavrianos, Leften S. *Lifelines from Our Past: A New World History*. Rev. ed. Armonk, N.Y.: M. E. Sharpe, 1997. A brief but stimulating reflection on world history by a leading scholar.

Stearns, Peter N. *Western Civilization in World History*. New York: Routledge, 2003. A brief examination of how Western civilization fits into the study of world history.

Wiesner-Hanks, Merry E. *Gender in World History*. Malden, Mass.: Blackwell, 2001. A pioneering thematic survey of a long-neglected subject.

Websites

The Encyclopedia of World History (**http://www.bartleby.com/67/**). A valuable collection of thousands of entries spanning the centuries from prehistory spanning the centuries to 2000.

Internet Global History Sourcebook (**http://www.fordham.edu/halsall/global/globalsbook.html**). An excellent set of links on world history from ancient to modern times.

Women in World History (**http://chnm.gmu.edu/wwh/**). Invaluable collection of links covering many societies and all eras.

World Civilizations (**http://www.wsu.edu/~dee/MAIN/HTM**). An internet anthology maintained at Washington State University.

World History for Us All (**http://worldhistoryforusall.sdsu.edu**). A growing site with useful essays and other materials, sponsored by San Diego State University.

World History Sources (**http://worldhistorymatters.org**). Valuable annotated links on different subjects, based at George Mason University.

PART I

Foundations: Ancient Societies, to 600 B.C.E.

Most of us carry pictures in our minds of the world's ancient peoples and their ways of life: prehistoric cave dwellers huddling around a fire, wandering desert tribes, towering pyramids, and spectacular ruins of cities and temples. In fact, the centuries between 100,000 and 600 B.C.E. saw the evolution of these and many other social and cultural phenomena, more complex and often more significant to us today than these mental pictures convey. These centuries also saw humans take the first steps in establishing regular contacts and exchanges, often those of trade, with one another, creating the networks that linked many societies over wide areas.

Human societies have emerged only recently in earth's long history. Simple life began on earth over 3 billion years ago. Several million years ago in Africa the earliest near ancestors of humans began to walk upright and use simple tools. Gradually they evolved into modern humans who commanded language, controlled fire, and eventually populated the entire world. For thousands of years, small bands of people, carrying their stone and wood tools as they moved from campsite to campsite, lived by hunting and gathering. With the first great transition in human history, the introduction of agriculture some 10,000 years ago, people began to deliberately cultivate plants and raise draft animals. Although some societies remained hunters and gatherers or herders, most people around the world shifted eventually to farming. Congregating in villages and towns and farming the neighboring fields with their simple hoes and plows, they experienced profound changes in their ways of life. For some societies, the production of an agricultural surplus—more food than was needed by the farmers—and growing commercial activity provided the economic and labor support that enabled the development of formal governments and religious institutions. Farming, town life, trade, and more advanced technology set the stage for the second great transition, the building of cities and the forming of states.

The world's first societies emerged in various parts of the world, and each society gradually created its own distinctive traditions. The first cities and states arose between 5,500 and 4,000 years ago in the lands stretching from southern Europe and northern Africa eastward through western and southern Asia to China. For most of history the vast majority of the

Cuneiform Tablet This letter, impressed on a clay tablet in Mesopotamia around 1900 B.C.E., records a merchant's complaint that a shipment of copper that he had paid for contained too little metal. Mesopotamian letters, written chiefly by merchants and officials, were enclosed in envelopes made of clay and marked with the sender's private seal. (Courtesy of the Trustees of the British Museum)

world's people lived in these regions of Africa and Eurasia. Between 5,000 and 3,000 years ago cities and states also developed in the Americas. The most densely populated ancient societies emerged where agriculture, aided by irrigation, flourished: in large river valleys, particularly the floodplains of the Nile in Egypt, the Tigris-Euphrates in Mesopotamia, the Indus in India, and the Yellow in China. The ancient world also benefited from great advances in metalworking, especially of copper, bronze, and iron, which spread widely. Growing networks of trade and transportation increasingly connected many societies to each other by land and sea. Although they exchanged ideas, products, and technologies with others, each ancient society created unique religions, cultural values, social structures, and systems for recording information. These traditions sometimes continued over several thousand years, even though modified with time. A few traditions, such as the ancient Hebrew and Indian religions, have survived into the present.

Contacts between peoples in different regions had already begun to increase greatly with the appearance of farming. Societies traded agricultural and hunting tools, as well as minerals, wood, clothing, and food. Between 2500 and 600 B.C.E. the Eastern Hemisphere experienced much more active trading networks. Improved transportation, including seaworthy sailing vessels, horse-drawn chariots, and camel caravans, fostered trade by shrinking distances. Long-distance trade served to spread ideas and expand horizons. Some peoples migrated far from their ancestral homes, with major movements into the Pacific islands (Oceana) and the southern half of Africa. Like trade, other encounters between societies, friendly or hostile, often became major forces for change.

Most ancient societies, such as Egypt and Mesopotamia, have long since disappeared, leaving only crumbling ruins or long-buried artifacts to remind us of their achievements. In their ancient forms, these societies never survived through the centuries, although their religions and values often influenced the societies that displaced them, and many of their descendants still live in the region. On the other hand, the Chinese and Indian societies persisted in some recognizable form and are familiar to us today. The Ancient Era built the framework for much that came later.

NORTH AND CENTRAL AMERICA
The ancestors of Native Americans migrated into North America from Asia thousands of years ago. They gradually occupied the Americas, working out ways of life compatible with the environments they lived in. While many remained hunters and gatherers, the first American farming began in Mexico and spread to various North American regions. The Olmecs of Mexico built cities atop huge artificial mounds and created an alphabet and religious traditions that influenced nearby peoples. Other North Americans also built settlements around large mounds.

SOUTH AMERICA
Some Native Americans reached South America thousands of years ago. Farming developed early along the Pacific coast and in the Andes Mountains region. The first cities, such as Caral in coastal Peru, arose around the same time as early cities in Egypt and India. Cities were later established in the Andes Mountains. The major Andean states influenced the art and religion of many other South American societies.

EUROPE
Ancient cities and states formed on the Mediterranean island of Crete and in Greece. Minoans, the residents of Crete, were successful maritime traders. After their collapse, the Mycenaeans of mainland Greece traded widely and exercised regional power until they declined. Migrants into Greece mixed with the Mycenaeans to form the foundation for later Greek society. These southern European societies worked bronze and participated in trade networks linking them to North Africa, eastern Europe, and western Asia.

WESTERN ASIA
The world's first farmers probably lived in western Asia, east of the Mediterranean Sea, where the oldest known cities and states also arose. The diverse societies that formed in the Tigris-Euphrates River Valley in Mesopotamia developed bronzeworking, writing, science, and mathematics, and they also traded with India and Egypt. Western Asians perfected iron technology, which eventually spread around Eurasia. The Phoenicians were the greatest traders of the Mediterranean region and also invented an alphabet later adopted by the Greeks. Another notable people, the Hebrews, introduced a monotheistic religion, Judaism.

EASTERN ASIA
Farming developed very early in the Yellow and Yangzi River Basins in China, fostering the region's first cities and states. Chinese culture then expanded into southern China. The Chinese invented a writing system and worked bronze and iron. Mixing Chinese influences with their own traditions, Koreans took up farming and metalworking. Some Koreans migrated into Japan, where they and the local peoples mixed their traditions to produce the Japanese culture.

ARCTIC OCEAN

EUROPE

Danube

ASIA

GREECE

Carthage

CRETE
ISRAEL   MESOPOTAMIA

EGYPT

Nile

NUBIA

AFRICA

SUDAN
Niger R.

Harappa

H I M A L A Y A S

Ganges R.

INDIA

CHINA

JAPAN

Mekong R.

Congo R.

ATLANTIC
OCEAN

INDIAN OCEAN

AUSTRALIA

AFRICA
Farming appeared very early in North, West, and East Africa. Africa's earliest cities and states formed along the Nile River Valley in Egypt. The Egyptians invented a writing system and flourished from productive agriculture and trade with other African societies and Eurasia. Cities and states also arose in Nubia, just south of Egypt. Africans south of the Sahara Desert developed ironworking technology very early, and iron tools and weapons helped the Bantu-speaking peoples gradually expand from West Africa into Central and East Africa.

SOUTHERN ASIA AND OCEANIA
Farming and metalworking developed early in South and Southeast Asia. The people of the Harappan cities in the Indus River Basin grew cotton, made textiles, and traded with western and Central Asia. After the Harappan society collapsed, Aryan peoples from western Asia moved into India, and the mixing of Aryan and local traditions formed the basis for the Hindu religion. Meanwhile, Austronesian peoples migrated from Taiwan into the Southeast Asian and Pacific islands. Southeast Asians pioneered in maritime trade and formed their first states. Hunters and gatherers flourished in Australia.

CHAPTER **1**

The Origins of Human Societies, to ca. 2000 B.C.E.

CHAPTER OUTLINE

- Before Prehistory: The Cosmos, Earth, and Life
- The Roots of Humanity
- The Odyssey of Early Human Societies
- The Agricultural Transformation, 10,000–4000 B.C.E.
- The Emergence of Cities and States

■ **PROFILE**
  The !Kung Hunters and Gatherers

■ **WITNESS TO THE PAST**
  Food and Farming in Ancient Cultural Traditions

Online Study Center

This icon will direct you to interactive activities and study materials on the website: college.hmco.com/pic/lockard1e

Tassili Archers Thousands of ancient paintings on rock surfaces and cave walls record the activities of African hunters, gatherers, and pastoralists. This painting of archers on a hunt was made in a rock shelter on the Tassili plateau of what is today Algeria, probably long before the Sahara region had dried up and become a harsh desert. (Kazuyoshi Nomachi/Pacific Press Photo)

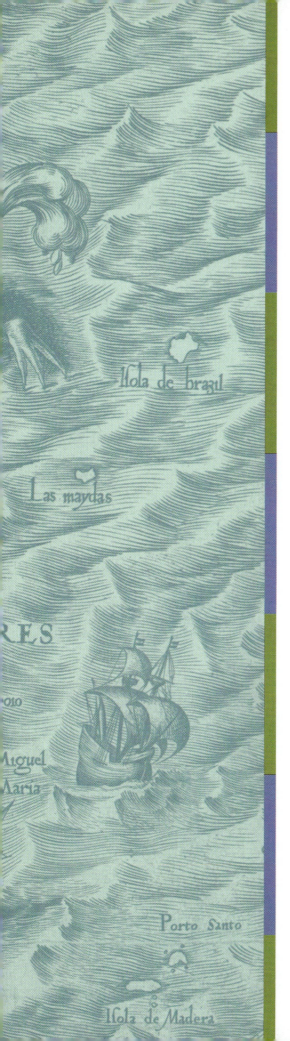

We are long past the time when we could deal with the human story apart from the life story, or the earth story, or the universe story.

COSMOLOGIST BRIAN SWIMME AND HISTORIAN THOMAS BERRY[1]

The human story was already old and the life story far older when, at Abu Hureyra (AH-boo hoo-RAY-rah) in the Euphrates (you-FRAY-teez) River Valley of what is now Syria, a group of villagers began to change their way of life. They became some of humankind's first farmers, thus taking a large step in shaping world history. People who hunted game and gathered vegetables and nuts had occupied Abu Hureyra perhaps 13,000 years ago, when the area was wetter than it is today and blessed with many edible wild plants and large herds of Persian gazelles. But their good life eventually encountered a formidable challenge. A long cold spell brought a drought, and, to survive, the Abu Hureyra villagers began to cultivate the most easily grown grains. At first they still hunted gazelle, but gradually, along with cultivating grains, they also raised domesticated sheep and goats. By 7600 B.C.E. they had shifted completely to farming and animal herding.

The Abu Hureyra farmers pursued a life that would be familiar to rural folk for millennia. Several hundred people crowded into a village of narrow lanes and courtyards. Families dwelled in rectangular, one-story, multiroom mud houses with polished black plaster floors, some decorated with red designs. At night family members studied the sky and pondered the mysteries of the universe. During the day men did much of the farm work while women carried heavy loads on their heads, prepared meals, and ground grain in a kneeling position, an activity that was hard on arms, knees, and toes. Work for both women and men involved repetitive tasks and called for muscle power. In fact, many villagers suffered from arthritis and lower back injuries. Early farming life was not easy. Eventually Abu Hureyra was abandoned: the last villagers had left by 5000 B.C.E.

Prehistory includes a vast span of time, from the earliest humans to the beginnings of agriculture and the emergence of complex societies with cities and states. Much of what we know about these millennia comes from archaeologists, who study the material remains of past cultures, and anthropologists, who study human biology and culture in relation to the physical and social environment. As was noted in Introducing World History, societies are broad groups of people that share common traditions, institutions, and organized patterns of relationships. Sometime during the long saga of our planet, during which all living creatures appeared and developed, human societies also emerged. Over many millennia humans evolved physically, mentally, and culturally, learning to make simple tools and then spreading throughout the world.

Later most societies, like the villagers at Abu Hureyra, made the first great historical transition from hunting and gathering to farming and animal herding.

This transition profoundly changed the relationship between people and the environment and prompted the working of metals for better tools. The rise of agriculture all over the world made possible another important transition, the emergence of larger societies with cities and states. In turn this stimulated long-distance trade and the rise of social, cultural, and economic networks linking distant societies.

FOCUS QUESTIONS

1. How have various human societies sought to understand the formation of the universe, earth, and humanity?
2. According to most scientists, what were the various stages of human evolution?
3. How did hunting and gathering shape life during the long Stone Age?
4. What environmental factors explain the transition to agriculture?
5. How did farming and metallurgy establish the foundations for the rise of cities, states, and trade networks?

Before Prehistory: The Cosmos, Earth, and Life

How have various human societies sought to understand the formation of the universe, earth, and humanity?

While most historians restrict their attention to the five or six millennia that can be examined through documentary sources, oral traditions, and archaeological findings, some scholars have promoted a "big history" that places the development of human societies and networks in a much longer and more comprehensive framework, the "universe story." Just as we cannot understand recent centuries without a sense of earlier history, these scholars argue, so we cannot comprehend the rise of complex societies without a knowledge of prefarming peoples. Going back further in time, we can also consider the ancestors of humans and, before that, the beginning of life on earth, and finally the formation of our planet within the larger cosmic order. We see that recurring patterns of balance and imbalance and of order and disorder in the natural world, such as global warming and cooling, have always played a role in human history. Inspired by such large forces around them, people have speculated about the origins of the cosmos, earth, life, and humanity for countless generations. Over the years their views have been integrated into religions.

Perceptions of Cosmic Mysteries

Human development on earth constitutes only a tiny fraction of the long history of the universe, which most astronomers think began in a cosmic Big Bang explosion some 14 billion years ago. As the universe expanded, matter coalesced into stars, and stars formed into billions of galaxies spread over vast distances. Our solar system emerged about 4.5 billion years ago out of clouds of gas. On our planet, earth, the developing atmosphere kept the surface warm enough for organic compounds to coalesce into life forms. This is the story presented by modern science.

Over the centuries most human societies have crafted stories to explain their existence. Many earlier societies believed that the movement of the stars influenced human actions, and astrological notions are still popular today. Societies developed creation stories and cosmologies, systematic expressions of their views on the natural and supernatural worlds. These explanations varied greatly from one society to another, but they usually involved myths or legends of some divine creator or multiple creators. The earliest known creation story, from Mesopotamia, claimed that heaven and earth were created as one in a primeval sea and then separated by the gods, human-like beings unperceivable to but far more powerful than mere mortals. Mesopotamian beliefs influenced the seven-day creation story in the Hebrew book of Genesis.

Many cosmological traditions, however, were very different. Ancient Hindu holy books, for example, describe the creation of a universe out of nothingness: "There was neither non-existence or existence then; there was neither the realm of space nor the sky which is beyond. Darkness was hidden by darkness in the beginning, emptiness."[2] Then a Big Bang–like heat formed the cosmos and generated life. Hindus also speculated, as do some astrophysicists, that other universes exist.

Online Study Center **Improve Your Grade**
Primary Source: The Rig Veda

The ancient Chinese believed that the universe was created out of chaos and darkness and that the creator Pan Ku fashioned the sun, moon, and stars to put everything in proper order. The result was a unifying force in the universe, known as the "way," or *dao* (DOW). A related Chinese theory, *feng shui*

C H R O N O L O G Y		
Cosmos	**Human Evolution**	**Prehistory Transitions**
14 billion years Big Bang		
4.5 billion years ago Solar system and earth	**5–6 million years ago** Earliest proto-humans **400,000–200,000 B.C.E.** *Homo sapiens* **135,000–100,000 B.C.E.** Modern humans	
	100,000 B.C.E. Modern humans in Eurasia	**100,000–9500 B.C.E.** Stone Age **9500–8000 B.C.E.** Beginning of agriculture **3500–3200 B.C.E.** First cities in western Asia **3000 B.C.E.** Introduction of bronze **1500 B.C.E.** Introduction of iron

Left-margin scale: **14 billion years ago** / **400,000 B.C.E.** / **100,000 B.C.E.**

(fung-SHWAY), suggests that the earth itself contains natural forces that people must comprehend in order to properly situate buildings and graves. Some ideas from the feng shui tradition have recently gained a following in Western countries. One 2,500-year-old Chinese school of thought saw the cosmos as a sphere, infinite in size, with a round earth within it.

The Dogon (DOUGH-ghun) people of West Africa developed an exceptionally complex speculation on the mysteries of the universe. In their view, the original germ of life emerged from a world egg and then expanded through the universe. Furthermore, the cosmic order is simply a projection, infinitely expanded, of phenomena, occurring at the smallest level of existence. The Dogon organized their society to reflect the working of the cosmic order as they perceived it.

The Natural Environment and Early Life

"Life," meaning organisms that are able to consume food, grow, and reproduce with a genetic code, has a long history. Simple, single-celled life emerged by perhaps 3.5 to 3.8 billion years ago, thrived 2 billion years ago, and remained dominant until about a half billion years ago, when life forms became increasingly complex and proliferated in incredible variety. Animal life colonized the land between 400 and 500 million years ago and evolved into many species.

Throughout its long history, life has been influenced by natural forces such as geology and climate. Geological activity has created diversity. A dozen or more large plates lie under the planet's surface and shift slightly each year. Over the ages this moving of plates and the spread or contraction of sea floors reconfigured the land surface into continents. Eventually the massive movement of landmasses created the present shapes and positions of continents, each with its unique plants and animals. Since the process is ongoing, millions of years from now world maps may look very different than they do today. Volcanic and earthquake activity caused by plate movements has influenced human history, and sometimes intense volcanic eruptions have dramatically altered regional climates. As we will see, warmer or cooler climates helped shape human societies and also sometimes undermined them.

Evolutionary Change

Most natural scientists agree that living things change over many generations through evolution, the process by which they modify their genetic composition to adapt to their environment. In the nineteenth century the British biologist Charles Darwin, after observing the great variety of species around the world, explained the process with his theory of natural selection. He believed individuals developed variations that helped them compete for food and domination within their own species and to triumph over rival species. Those who competed successfully then passed on their genes to their descendants. Scientists still debate evolution's precise mechanisms, and some have modified Darwin's ideas, but modern biology has mostly confirmed Darwin's basic insights. Most scientists also agree that species, including humans, are shaped by their changing biological and physical environment.

Another force for change has been mass extinctions. A half dozen massive species extinctions have occurred in the past 400 million years. For example, 250 million years ago gigantic volcanic eruptions produced enough climate-changing gases to almost wipe out all life. The best-known extinction involved the dinosaurs, which flourished for 150 million years before dying out about 65 million years ago. It is believed that environmental changes caused their demise: the cooling of the planet from increasing volcanic activity, the cataclysmic impact of one or several large asteroids or comets smashing into the earth, or both. The resulting toxic acid rain and long winter destroyed food sources, thus killing off about 70 percent of all species.

Such species extinctions can dramatically change life on earth. The demise of the dinosaurs opened the door for mammals to rise and flourish. One group of these mammals eventually evolved into humans. So far humans have been lucky. Scientists estimate that some 30 billion species have appeared over the past 500 million years, but only 30 million populate the planet today. Hence 99 percent eventually became extinct. Conditions can change dramatically, as they did for the dinosaurs. In our own time, species have been dying rapidly over the past two hundred years, most likely because of environmental changes such as pollution, habitat removal, and global warming generated by human activity.

Eventually, after several billion years, evolutionary changes among one branch of mammals led to the immediate ancestors of humans. Humans are part of the primate order, the mammal category that includes the apes. Our closeness to the apes is shown by the fact that over 98 percent of human DNA is the same as that of chimpanzees. Today's two hundred primate species probably evolved from one common ancestor that lived some 20 million years ago. Human–chimp lines diverged sometime before 5 or 6 million years ago.

Humans ultimately became dominant among large animal species by using their superior brain to gain an evolutionary edge. One key to their success was the ability to form *complex* social organizations that emphasized cooperation for mutual benefit. Humans also developed tools, mastered fire, and learned how to use speech, all of which gave them great advantages. Ultimately they began using a more complex technology that enabled them to manipulate the physical environment in many ways to meet their needs.

SECTION SUMMARY

- To fully understand human history, it is helpful to first examine the origins of our planet, the beginning of life on earth, and our prehuman ancestors.

- Throughout the millennia, various peoples have developed stories of creation and universal order.

- The constant changes in geology influence what forms of life survive.

- In order to survive, species must adapt to their changing environments.

- Humans are closely related to chimpanzees and other great apes; they eventually became dominant because of their use of intelligence.

 # The Roots of Humanity

According to most scientists, what were the various stages of human evolution?

The history of humans is hardly a wink in the long history of earth and even modest compared to the long tenure of the dinosaurs. **Hominids** (HOM-uh-nids), a family including humans and their immediate ancestors, first evolved 5 to 6 million years ago from more primitive primates. The first chapters of the human story began in Africa, where the span of human prehistory is much longer than anywhere else. Most scientists agree that hominids evolved exclusively in eastern and southern Africa until at least 2 million years ago. Various evolutionary stages led up to modern humans and spurred their spread around the globe.

The Earliest Hominids

Though scientists agree on Africa, there is debate over the details. The most extensive fossil evidence comes from the southern African plateau and the Great Rift Valley of East Africa, a wide, deep chasm stretching from Ethiopia south to Tanzania. The discovery in 2003 of possible hominid bones in Chad, in west-central Africa, challenged the consensus that hominids only evolved in eastern and southern Africa, and it may mean that hominids evolved earlier and over a larger range than has been assumed. But critics think the Chad bones came from a great ape. The heated disagreements over these bones illustrate that there is controversy over how to interpret the available evidence and that the archaeological record is full of gaps. Various methods are used to date fossil and artifact remains, but scientists disagree on which techniques are most accurate. Nor is there consensus on whether particular remains of teeth, skulls, and bones belong to ancestors of humans or of apes.

Fossil discoveries point to several stages and branches in early human evolution (see Chronology: Hominid Evolution). According to the available evidence, a common ancestral, ape-like group lived in the woodlands and savannahs of East Africa. One division (the ancestors of most apes) began specializing in forest dwelling and climbing with all four limbs. Another division developed occasional and then permanent bipedalism, walking upright on two feet. This made more activity possible because it left the hands free for holding food or babies, manipulating objects, and carrying food back to camp. Bipeds, being higher off the ground, could also scan the horizon for predators or prey. These bipedal apelike forms became the first hominids.

Several hominid groups apparently coexisted at the same time, but only one led to modern humans. Beginning about 4 or 5 million years ago, several branches of early hominids

---

hominids A family including humans and their immediate ancestors.

CHRONOLOGY

Hominid Evolution

20 MILLION B.C.E.	Common ancestor to humans and Apes (Africa)
5–6 MILLION B.C.E.	Earliest Proto-Humans
4–5 MILLION B.C.E.	Australopithecines
2.5 MILLION B.C.E.	*Homo Habilis*
2.2–1.8 MILLION B.C.E.	*Homo Erectus/Homo Ergaster*
400,000–200,000 B.C.E.	*Homo Sapiens* (archaic humans)
135,000–100,000 B.C.E.	*Homo Sapiens Sapiens* (modern humans)

The Laetoli Footprints Some 4 million years ago in Tanzania, three Australopithecines walked across a muddy field covered in ash from a nearby volcanic eruption. When the mud dried, their tracks were permanently preserved, providing evidence of some of the earliest upright hominids. (John Reader/Photo Researchers, Inc.)

known as **australopithecines** (aw-strah-lo-PITH-uh-seens) lived in eastern and southern Africa. The brains of these erect bipeds, or proto-humans, were about one-third the size of our brains. One example was found in Ethiopia, where archaeologists unearthed the bones of a small female, named Lucy by anthropologists, who lived some 20 years and probably walked mostly on her feet. Scholars disagree as to whether these hominids used simple tools and which of them might be the ancestors to modern humans.

Some 2.5 million years ago one branch of australopithecines evolved into our direct ancestor, a transition probably due to environmental change and the resulting imbalances. The Earth cooled, fostering the first of a series of Ice Ages, which covered large areas of northern Eurasia and North America with deep ice sheets and glaciers. This cooling pattern also affected Africa and its hominid inhabitants, bringing a drier climate and more open habitats. Natural selection favored increased intelligence to deal with the challenges posed by this climate change. **Homo habilis** (HOH-moh HAB-uh-luhs) ("handy human") was so named because of this species' larger brain size and its ability to make and use simple stone tools for hunting and gathering. Stone choppers and later hand axes made possible a more varied diet, more successful hunting, and larger groups that could cooperate to share food. The other branches of australopithecines died out, losing the competition to *Homo habilis*.

As hominid societies developed, males increasingly became the hunters or scavengers for meat and females the gatherers of nuts and vegetables. The receding of the forests and their food sources may have made meat a more crucial protein

source. Nonetheless, gathering still probably brought more food than hunting or scavenging. Indeed, these early humans were probably mainly vegetarians, like many primates today. In any case, cooperation between the sexes and group members was the key to survival and probably involved communication through gestures and vocal cries.

Homo Erectus and Migrations Out of Africa

Probably between 1.8 and 2.2 million years ago, some more advanced hominids evolved from *Homo habilis* in East Africa. Most scholars have termed these hominids **Homo erectus** (HOH-moh ee-REK-tuhs) ("erect human"). Others label them *Homo ergaster* (HOH-mo er-GAS-tuhr) ("work man") and argue that *Homo erectus* was a modification that developed later

australopithecines Early hominids living in eastern and southern Africa 3 to 4 million years ago.

Homo habilis ("handy human") A direct ancestor of humans, so named because of its increased brain size and ability to make and use simple stone tools for hunting and gathering.

Homo erectus ("erect human") A hominid that emerged in East Africa probably between 1.8 and 2.2 million years ago.

only in eastern Eurasia. Whether these were the same species or just closely related remains unclear, but their achievements were remarkable. They were larger than *Homo habilis* and had a brain about two-thirds the size of ours. These people eventually developed a more complex and widespread tool culture that included hand axes, cleavers, and scrapers. They spread to other parts of Africa, preferring the open savannah.

Between 1 and 2 million years ago, as southern Eurasia developed a warmer climate, some *Homo erectus* bands began migrating out of Africa, carrying with them refined tools, more effective hunting skills, and an ability to adapt to new environments. Perhaps the first migrants were following game herds. This was the first great migration in human history, and it corresponded to the ebb and flow of the Ice Ages as well as the periodic drying out of the Sahara region. Over thousands of years these hominids came to occupy northern Africa, the Middle East, South and Southeast Asia, China, Europe, and, although the evidence is thin, perhaps Australia.

Migrants spread widely. Some of the earliest non-African sites, perhaps 1.8 million years old, have been found in the Caucasus (KAW-kuh-suhs) Mountains of western Asia. Farther east, bones and tools discovered in Chinese caves and skulls from the island of Java in Indonesia have been dated (by controversial methods) at 1.6 to 1.9 million years ago (at that time western Indonesia, including Java, was connected to mainland Southeast Asia by land). These finds suggest that *Homo erectus* may have been widespread in East and Southeast Asia by 1,500,000 years ago. Fossils from eastern Siberia date back 300,000 years, indicating how adaptable and resourceful the species had become if it could survive in that brutal climate. Europe has proved a bigger puzzle. These hominids lived in Spain by 800,000 B.C.E., and in England and Germany by around 500,000 B.C.E. The hominid tool cultures of China and Europe, although equally complex, show different features, indicating cultural diversity.

We are learning more about *Homo erectus* life. By 500,000 years ago *Homo erectus* in China lived in closely knit groups, engaged in cooperative hunting, and probably used both wood and bamboo for containers and weapons. Most lived in caves, but some built simple wooden huts for shelter. The oldest hut so far found, in Japan, is 500,000 years old. Their hand axes were the Swiss army knives of their time, with a tip for piercing, thin edges for cutting, and thick edges for scraping and chipping. Scientists debate whether *Homo erectus* could use speech.

One of the key discoveries, how to start and control fire, was perhaps the most significant human invention ever. But we do not yet know precisely where or when people first used fire or how many millennia it took for knowledge of fire to spread widely. Fire opened up many possibilities: it provided warmth and light after sunset, frightened away predators, and made possible a more varied diet of cooked food, which tasted better and encouraged people to gather together. In addition, control of fire fostered group living and cooperation as people gathered together around campfires and hearths. Fire also enabled ancestral humans to spread to cooler regions, such as Europe and eastern Asia.

The Evolution and Diversity of *Homo Sapiens*

The transition from *Homo erectus* to archaic forms of **Homo sapiens** (HOH-moh SAY-pee-enz) ("thinking human"), a species that was physically close to modern humans, began around 400,000 or 500,000 years ago in Africa. By 200,000 years ago a more complex tool culture was widespread, evidence for *Homo sapiens* occupation. With this development humanity became a single species, despite some superficial differences. Eventually members of *Homo sapiens* were the only surviving hominids, in contrast to the earlier diverse species.

Members of *Homo sapiens* had many advantages over *Homo erectus*. With a larger brain they were more adaptive and intelligent, able to think conceptually. Archaic *Homo sapiens* may have used language, lived in fairly large organized groups, built temporary shelters, created crude lunar calendars, and killed whole herds of animals. They also raised more children to adulthood. Possession of symbolic language gave *Homo sapiens* an advantage over earlier hominids and all other creatures, allowing them to share information over the generations. Language enabled people to adjust to their environment and overcome challenges not just individually but collectively.

Origins of a New Species   Scientists debate precisely how and where *Homo erectus* evolved into *Homo sapiens*, and several competing theories explain the transition. Some scholars, known as multiregionalists, argue that the evolution into *Homo sapiens* occurred in different parts of the Afro-Eurasian zone and that frequent interbreeding ensured that genes were exchanged and spread widely. This might, for example, explain a modern-looking and puzzling 60,000-year-old fossil from Australia. An alternative and more widely supported scenario, known as the African Origins theory, suggests that *Homo sapiens* evolved only in East Africa and then spread throughout Afro-Eurasia, displacing and ultimately dooming the remaining *Homo erectus* groups. The evidence for this theory includes the fact that (so far, anyway) the earliest *Homo sapiens* remains have been found in East Africa and that some *Homo erectus* fossils in Java may be only around 40,000 years old.

The most controversial tool in tracing human evolution is the study of genetic codes. The mutation history of mitochondrial (MY-tuh-CON-dree-uhl) DNA (DNA passed through generations by mothers) points to a common maternal ancestor to all present-day humans who lived in East Africa some 150,000 to 200,000 years ago. Other DNA studies also mostly support the African Origins theory. Recent analysis of older fossil discoveries suggest that the fossil record and genetic studies are generally consistent on the antiquity of *Homo sapiens*.

However, some mysteries remain for scientists to ponder. In 2004 scholars were shocked by the discovery, on the small

---

Homo sapiens ("thinking human")   A hominid who evolved around 400,000 or 500,000 years ago and from whom anatomically modern humans (*Homo sapiens sapiens*) evolved around 100,000 years ago.

and remote Indonesian island of Flores, of the 18,000 year old bones of diminutive hominids, 3 to 3 1/2 feet tall as adults, a discovery that sparked a debate as to where these fossils fit into the human family tree. The Flores people may have been miniature versions of *Homo erectus* or of *Homo sapiens,* or perhaps constituted some unknown hominid species. They had apparently reached the island thousands of years earlier. Although the folklore of some modern Flores societies suggests that "little people" still lived in hard to reach caves in the recent past, scholars suspect the prehistoric inhabitants may have been wiped out in a massive volcanic explosion around 12,000 years ago.

Species Diversity Whether the evolution into *Homo sapiens* occurred only in Africa or on several continents, all humans came to constitute one species that could interbreed and communicate with each other. There were a few differences in physical features, such as skin and hair color and eye and face shape, but it remains unclear whether these developed earlier or later in *Homo sapiens* evolution. One theory suggests that tropical peoples developed dark skins to protect themselves from the blistering sun and relatively little body hair because hair slows down heat loss, while others developed lighter skins and acquired more body hair as they moved into cooler climates. However, this theory is controversial.

The diverse groupings that evolved from *Homo sapiens* were once labeled "races," meaning large groups that shared distinctive genetic traits and physical characteristics. But the race concept is for good reasons often dismissed by experts for its inability to classify human populations. Observable physical attributes such as skin color and eye shape reflect a tiny portion of one's genetic makeup and thus cannot always predict whether two groups are genetically similar or different. For this reason, most anthropologists argue that the idea of "race" is based not on biological facts but on social ideas and myths about the existence of real divisions between groups based only on the fact that they "look" different. In fact, however, there has been much genetic intermixing between human populations, and many people are difficult to classify. Humans are much more similar than different, and the human species as a whole has much less genetic variation than chimpanzees. This may suggest that sometime in prehistory some unknown catastrophe such as an epidemic wiped out a portion of humanity, reducing genetic diversity. Perhaps humans have been on the brink of extinction at least once.

The Emergence of Modern Humans

Sometime between 130,000 and 100,000 years ago in Africa, anatomically modern humans, known as *Homo sapiens sapiens,* developed out of *Homo sapiens.* The brains of these modern humans were slightly larger than those of archaic *Homo sapiens.* With this biological change, language and culture expanded in new directions and developed many variations. Scholars debate whether creativity, intelligence, and even language abilities were innate to *Homo sapiens sapiens* or arose only some 50,000 years ago, possibly as a result of a genetic

mutation. Whenever it occurred, with this great transition humanity reached its present level of intellectual and physical development, and established the foundation for the constant expansion of information networks to a global level.

Scholars have long debated the relative influence of "nature" and "nurture" in shaping human behavior. Some stress biology, maintaining that our genetic heritage as primates "hardwired" our brains with certain tendencies. Others say that the cultures we have formed have allowed us to modify our environments and develop social restraints to channel behavior. No doubt human activity reflects the interplay of these two forces.

Modern humans eventually developed their languages in ways that made possible complex cultures which shared learning. Spoken language was the main method of communication for much of history; writing was used by only a small minority of people before modern times. Perhaps there was one original language used by all humans. But eventually, with expansion around the globe, some 5,000 or 6,000 languages emerged. Some languages, such as English and German, have a clear common ancestry, but scholars debate the relationships and origins of most of the world's languages.

Human intellectual development also included abstract, symbolic thought, which was revealed early in decoration and art. Ocher (O-ker), for example, a natural red iron oxide, was mined in various African locations and probably used for body decoration. The gorgeous cave art of southwestern Europe, northern Africa, and western Asia has been traced back 30,000 to 40,000 years. The splendid rock art tradition found in southern Africa began by 30,000 B.C.E., and some recent discoveries suggest it may even be 75,000 years old. Indeed, several thousand engraved circles in rocks in northwestern Australia may be 60,000 to 75,000 years old. These creations reveal a genuine aesthetic sensibility. They probably had magical, religious, or ritual purposes, such as the celebration of spirits or valued animals. Finely polished bone tools made in South Africa 70,000 years ago also point to early creativity.

The Globalization of Human Settlement

Between 50,000 and 12,000 years ago much of the world was settled by restless modern humans. As people spread, genetic differences grew and *Homo sapiens sapiens* proved able to adapt to many environments all over the world. By 100,000 years ago some had already left Africa to settle in Palestine. Some scholars think that *Homo sapiens sapiens* settlement might not have expanded much beyond Africa and extreme southwestern Asia until 50,000 years ago. But rising sea levels at the end of the last Ice Age may also have covered evidence that might allow us to trace migration routes along the southern Asian coasts. Eventually modern humans reached eastern Eurasia, from where some moved on to Australia and the Americas and Europe (see Chronology: The Spread of Modern Humans).

Modern humans crossed to the eastern fringe of Asia before they populated Europe (see Map 1.1). They lived in India and Southeast Asia between 50,000 and 40,000 years ago, in

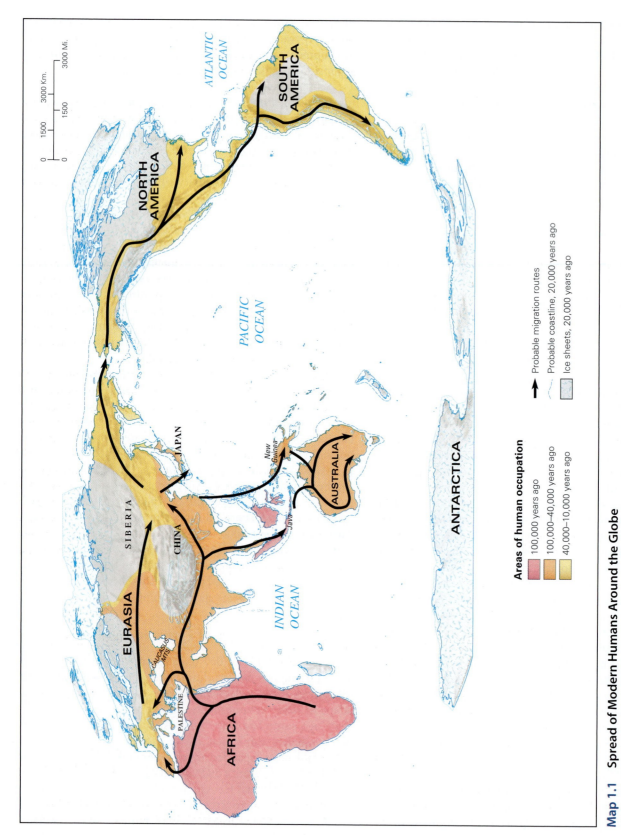

Map 1.1 Spread of Modern Humans Around the Globe

Most scholars believe that modern humans originated in Africa and some of them began leaving Africa around 100,000 years ago. Gradually they spread out through Eurasia. From Eastern Asia some crossed to the Americas.

Areas of human occupation

- 100,000 years ago
- 100,000–40,000 years ago
- 40,000–10,000 years ago

→ Probable migration routes

---- Probable coastline, 20,000 years ago

▨ Ice sheets, 20,000 years ago

CHRONOLOGY

The Spread of Modern Humans

135,000–100,000 B.C.E.	Eastern and Southern Africa
100,000 B.C.E.	Palestine
50,000–45,000 B.C.E.	Australia
50,000–40,000 B.C.E.	India, Southeast Asia
50,000–35,000 B.C.E.	China
45,000–35,000 B.C.E.	Europe
40,000 B.C.E.	Japan, Americas (disputed)
35,000–30,000 B.C.E.	New Guinea
20,000 B.C.E.	Siberia
15,000–12,000 B.C.E.	Americas (traditional view)
2000 B.C.E.	Western Pacific Islands
1500 B.C.E.	Samoa
200 B.C.E.	Marquesas Islands
400–500 C.E.	Hawaii
1000 C.E.	New Zealand

China between 35,000 and 50,000 years ago, and in Europe between 35,000 and 45,000 years ago. Dates for settlement in frigid eastern Siberia range from 28,000 to 14,000 B.C.E. By 40,000 years ago they had migrated to Japan, which could then be reached by land bridges. To reach Australia from Southeast Asia across a very shallow sea required rafts or boats, but, according to controversial findings, modern humans had settled in Australia between 50,000 and 45,000 B.C.E. While New Guinea and the nearby Solomon Islands had human settlers between 35,000 and 30,000 years ago, the peopling of the Pacific Islands to the east began much later, around 2000 B.C.E.

Beginning around 200,000 years ago, a vibrant new tool culture developed in Europe that has been identified with the **Neanderthals** (nee-AN-der-thals), hominids who were probably descended from *Homo erectus* populations. By 100,000 B.C.E. this culture was well developed. The Neanderthals gradually spread to inhabit a wide region stretching from Spain and Germany to western and Central Asia; fossils have also been found in North Africa. Neanderthals were committed to social values, burying their dead, and caring for the sick and injured. In general, their cranial capacity equaled or even exceeded that

of *Homo sapiens*, and they had larger bodies. Although they probably lacked spoken language, they were capable of communication. They also used tools, made bone flutes, and wore jewelry. They were skillful hunters, and their dietary protein came mainly from meat.

The relationship of the Neanderthals to *Homo sapiens sapiens* is unclear. By 70,000 years ago both Neanderthals and modern humans lived in Palestine, and the two species apparently resided in the same areas for many centuries. When the modern, tool-using humans known as **Cro-Magnons** (krow-MAG-nuns) arrived in Europe, probably from western Asia, they also coexisted with Neanderthals for several millennia. DNA studies suggest that Neanderthals were a rather different species from Cro-Magnons. Although there is little convincing evidence of interbreeding, a few fossil discoveries hint that it may have occurred at least occasionally. The two species seem to have both traded and fought. Around 28,000 years ago, the last Neanderthals died out or disappeared as a recognizable group. Whether they were ultimately annihilated, outnumbered, outcompeted, or assimilated by the more resourceful and adaptable *Homo sapiens sapiens*, who had better technology and warmer clothing, remains unknown.

Archaeologists long thought that the peopling of the Americas came very late and that the earliest migration into North America occurred only 12,000 to 15,000 years ago. But recent discoveries have led a few scholars to speculate that the pioneer arrivals may have crossed from Northeast Asia as early as 20,000 or possibly even 30,000 or 40,000 years ago. The scientific community is deeply divided on the antiquity of the first Americans (see Chapter 4). At various times a wide Ice Age land bridge connected Alaska and Siberia across today's Bering Strait, and the evidence for a migration chiefly from Asia over thousands of years is strong. The first settlers moved by land, or by boat along the coast. Gradually people of Asian ancestry settled throughout the Western Hemisphere, becoming the ancestors of today's Native Americans.

SECTION SUMMARY

- Early hominids first evolved in Africa (most likely East Africa) 4 to 6 million years ago.
- Of the early hominids, our direct ancestor *Homo habilis* was most successful because it used simple stone tools.
- *Homo erectus* developed more refined tools and migrated to Eurasia and throughout Africa.
- *Homo sapiens* had larger brains and evolved into modern humans, who developed language and spread throughout the world.
- Though humans from different parts of the world may have different appearances, their genetic differences are insignificant.

Neanderthals Hominids who were probably descended from *Homo erectus* populations in Europe and who later spread into western and Central Asia.

Cro-Magnons The first modern, tool-using humans in Europe.

⬥ The Odyssey of Early Human Societies

How did hunting and gathering shape life during the long Stone Age?

For thousands of years humans lived at a very basic level during what is often called the Stone Age, although they also used other materials, such as wood and bone, to help them sustain life. The Stone Age included three distinct periods, each showing evidence of more efficient tools and stoneworking. The long **Paleolithic** (pay-lee-oh-LITH-ik) period (or Old Stone Age) began about 100,000 years ago. The **Mesolithic** (mez-oh-LITH-ik) period (Middle Stone Age) began around 15,000 years ago, when the glaciers from the final Ice Age receded. With this warming trend, the vast herds of large mammals that had flourished on the grasslands of Eurasia and North America began to thin rapidly. Major meat sources that were adapted to Ice Age climates, such as the woolly mammoth and mastodon, died out from warming climates, catastrophic disease, or zealous hunting by humans. The **Neolithic** (nee-oh-LITH-ik) period (New Stone Age) began between 9500 and 8000 B.C.E. in Eurasia, with the transition from hunting and gathering to simple farming. During the many centuries of the Paleolithic and Mesolithic eras the various peoples organized themselves into small, usually mobile, family-based societies.

Hunting and Gathering

Small groups of twenty to sixty members were the earliest and simplest forms of society. Their subsistence life depended on fishing, hunting live animals, scavenging for dead or dying animals, and gathering edible plants, a way of life that depended on naturally occurring resources. Members cooperated in gathering or hunting to obtain food, and usually they obtained just enough food to ensure the group's survival. Improved tools made possible both more food options and better weapons against predators or rivals. Whether early humans obtained their meat primarily through hunting or scavenging is unclear. Hunting became more important when the bow and arrow were invented in Africa, Europe, and southwestern Asia at least 15,000 years ago. Now hunters could kill large animals at a safer distance. Although men gained prestige from being the main hunters, meat was usually a small part of the diet.

The gathering by women of edible vegetation such as fruits and nuts was probably more essential for group survival than obtaining meat, and it gave women status and influence.

Paleolithic The Old Stone Age, which began 100,000 years ago with the first modern humans and lasted for many millennia.

Mesolithic The Middle Stone Age, which began around 15,000 years ago as the glaciers from the final Ice Age began to recede.

Neolithic The New Stone Age, which began between 10,000 and 11,500 years ago with the transition to simple farming.

Ethnographic studies indicate that this is still true among many of the remaining hunting and gathering peoples today. Furthermore, women probably helped develop new technologies such as grinding stones, bone needles, nets (possibly used to catch small animals like rabbits and foxes), baskets, and primitive cloth. The oldest known woven cloth clothing was made in eastern Europe some 28,000 years ago.

The hunting and gathering way of life may not have been as impoverished and unfulfilling as we sometimes imagine it was, with people continually searching for food in harsh environments. Many societies were creative, inventing fishhooks, harpoons, fuel lamps, dugout boats and canoes, and perhaps even beer. Studies over the past fifty years of groups who still hunt and gather, such as the Mbuti (em-BOO-tee) of the Congo rain forest and the !Kung of the Kalahari Desert, have found that they enjoy varied, healthy diets, surprisingly long life expectancies, considerable economic security, and a rich communal life. Many spend only ten to twenty hours a week in collecting food and establishing camps. Work itself, often done cooperatively, is fully integrated into daily life. Generally these people have plenty of time for activities such as music, dance, and socializing. The Mbuti live in a symbiotic and mystical relationship with the forest and possess an intimate knowledge of the natural world, trying to work with rather than against their surroundings. Although we cannot know for sure, the hunting and gathering life millennia ago may have offered similar pleasures.

On the other hand, hunters and gatherers have always faced serious challenges. Early humans had to make their own weapons and clothing and construct temporary huts. For some groups, life remained precarious and many died young, since not all enjoyed access to adequate food resources. Some, like the Inuit Eskimos who live along the Arctic Rim of North America and Greenland, had to survive in harsh climates with few plants. The Inuit of today, like their Stone Age ancestors, are mostly hunters.

Communities of Kinship and Cooperation

Hunting and gathering generally encouraged cooperation, which led to more closely knit communities based on kinship. Community members were able to communicate with one another, and, as language developed, they also passed information from one generation to another, conveying a sense of the past and traditions. Gradually humans increased in numbers, and societies, still based on kinship, became more complex. In societies founded on family ties, personal relationships were paramount, while little value was given to obtaining material wealth. The mostly nomadic way of life made individual accumulation of material possessions impractical. These small groups shared food resources among the immediate family and friends, thus helping to ensure success and hence ultimate survival for both the individual and the group. Cooperative work and food sharing promoted the intense social life that is still common among hunting and gathering peoples today. But living close to others did not always result in harmony and mutual affection. Those who violated group customs could be killed or banished, temporarily or permanently, and sometimes groups split apart because of conflicts.

Most hunters and gatherers lived in small bands that had no system of government or leader. In these egalitarian social structures, all members in good standing often had equal access to resources. Everyone played a needed role, and social responsibilities linked people together. At the same time, groups often tended to reward the most resourceful members, and some societies had a headman who was chosen for his favored personal qualities. However, these headmen had limited authority over other group members, and early European explorers in the Americas and Australia were amazed at the degree to which many of the hunting and gathering peoples they encountered belittled or insulted their own leaders and could not comprehend the notion of high rank.

Women and men probably enjoyed a comparable status, as they do in many hunting and gathering societies today. As key providers of food, women may have participated alongside men in group decision making. They also likely held a special place in religious practice as bearers of life. Midwives were highly respected. **Matrilineal** (mat-ruh-LIN-ee-uhl) **kinship** patterns, which trace descent and inheritance through the female line, were probably common, as they are today in these societies. But these societies mostly maintain a clear sexual division of labor and give men some advantages over women. Sometimes men could have more than one wife.

Although childbearing influenced women's roles, women were not constantly pregnant. Since it was necessary to limit group size to avoid depleting resources from the environment, most hunting and gathering societies practiced birth control. The practice of breastfeeding an infant for several years suppressed ovulation and created longer intervals between pregnancies. Many groups also imposed ritual taboos against intercourse after childbirth or during specified periods. Plants and herbs were used as contraceptives or to induce abortions. If these schemes failed, unwanted babies might be killed. Paleolithic populations grew slowly, perhaps by only 10 percent a century.

Cultural Life and Violence

Some aspects of culture that we might recognize today were taking shape, such as religious belief. As people sought to understand dreams, death, and natural phenomena, they developed a perspective known as **animism** (ANN-uh-miz-um), the belief that all creatures, as well as inanimate objects and natural phenomena, have souls and can influence human well-being. For many hunting and gathering peoples today, for example, animals have souls and often play an important role in folktales. Many early peoples also practiced **polytheism** (PAUL-e-thee-ism), the belief in many spirits or deities. Since spirits were thought capable of helping or harming a person, **shamans** (SHAW-mans), specialists in communicating with or manipulating the supernatural realm, became important members of the group. Many shamans were women. The widespread practice of burying the dead suggests that many people believed in an afterlife.

Like many hunters and gatherers today, these societies may have had ample time for leisure, engaging in such group-oriented activities as story-telling. Some scholars think some of them may have enjoyed an early form of wine, slurping the juice of naturally fermented wild grapes from crude wooden bowls or animal-skin pouches. Some activities with a social function that we might consider essential for enjoyment developed early, including music, dance, and painting on rocks and cave walls. Primitive flutes can be traced back 45,000 years. Dancing and singing may have promoted feelings of togetherness and lessened personal rivalries. They may also have led to nonviolent competition.

Egalitarian, self-sufficient societies enriched by spirituality and leisure activities may sound appealing to many modern people, but this was not the complete story. Violence between and within different societies has been a part of human culture throughout history, and the seeds were planted in the Paleolithic period. People were hunters, but they were also hunted by predators such as bears, wolves, and lions. This reality may have instilled in early societies not only a terror of dangerous animals, apparent in myths and folklore, but also a tendency to justify violence. Men were often expected to prove their bravery to attract females. And some prehistoric peoples may have practiced cannibalism.

Anthropologists disagree about whether humans are inherently aggressive and warlike or peaceful and cooperative. The experiences of societies still based on hunting and gathering or simple agriculture suggest that both patterns are common. Some peoples, such as the Hopi and Zuni Indians of the American Southwest, the Penan of Borneo, and many Australian Aborigines, have generally avoided armed conflict. But most societies have engaged in at least occasional violence, such as when their survival or food supply was threatened. Some societies admired military prowess and male bravado. For example, the Dani of New Guinea, who engaged in frequent conflict with their neighbors, lost a third of their men to war-related death.

Social and cultural patterns that promoted certain behaviors, such as violence against neighboring groups, arose in response to environmental conditions. Despite their carnivorous diets and primate origins, humans may not be genetically programmed for either violence or cooperation. They have a capacity but not a compulsion for aggressive behavior. Some primate species find ways to avoid conflict, and most engage in forms of reconciliation after fights. Humans may naturally seek self-preservation, but the influence of cultural patterns

---

matrilineal kinship   A pattern of kinship that traces descent and inheritance through the female line.

animism   The belief that all creatures as well as inanimate objects and natural phenomena have souls and can influence human well-being.

polytheism   A belief in many spirits or deities.

---

shamans   Specialists in communicating with or manipulating the supernatural realm.

Cave Paintings in Europe   This Ice Age painting of bison is from a cave at Altamira, Spain. Many paintings on cave walls have been found in France and Iberia. Paleolithic peoples all over the world painted pictures of the animals they hunted or feared as well as of each other, suggesting an increasing self-awareness. (Jean Cottes)

can channel behavior in one direction or another. Changing contexts can alter behavior too. For example, the normally gentle and nonviolent Semai (Se-MY) of the Malayan mountains can be transformed into enthusiastic soldiers when drafted into the Malaysian military and removed from their home communities.

The Heritage of Hunting and Gathering

Hunting and gathering never completely disappeared. Throughout history some peoples have found this way of life the most realistic strategy for survival. Although not environmentalists in the modern sense, most recent hunting and gathering societies have made only a marginal impact on the surrounding environment because of their small numbers and limited technology. Since they have learned to live within environmental constraints, these peoples could be seen as highly successful adapters. Although it has generated little material wealth, hunting and gathering has remained viable for many societies, such as Australian Aborigines, until modern times. Indeed, Australia was the only inhabitable continent where agriculture never developed before modern times, largely because populations remained small, much of the continent was harsh desert, and the Aborigines were such skillful hunters and gatherers. But trade routes spanned the continent, and many Aborigines developed detailed notions of land management as

well as rich mythologies about their origins and their relationship to the fragile environment.

As already mentioned, some version of hunting and gathering is practiced even in modern times. Although we must be cautious in comparing modern hunters and gatherers to peoples who lived several millennia ago, today's few remaining hunting and gathering peoples, to the extent that they have not yet been significantly changed by the outside world, can probably reveal much about ancient societies (see Profile: The !Kung Hunters and Gatherers). Prehistoric peoples undoubtedly developed a wide range of behaviors and values, adapting to differing environments just as hunting and gathering societies do today.

But this way of life, which has survived for many millennia, may disappear during the twenty-first century. In recent decades many hunters and gatherers have seen their lives disrupted or destroyed by logging, commercial fishing, plantation development, dam building, tourism, and other activities that exploit their environments. For example, revenue-hungry governments lease the Borneo rain forests inhabited by the reclusive Penan to timber companies for logging. In the Amazon Basin, the burning of rain forests and opening of new land for farming or mining overwhelms many Native American groups. In the end these peoples, defenseless against modern technology, may have to make the same transition to new survival strategies as other peoples did millennia ago.

THE !KUNG HUNTERS AND GATHERERS

Although we need to remember that all societies change over time, often in response to environmental conditions, the remaining hunting and gathering peoples today may give us a glimpse of how some prehistoric peoples lived. The !Kung, a subgroup of the San people (once known as Bushmen), live in the inhospitable Kalahari Desert in southwestern Africa, chiefly in what is today Botswana and Namibia. Several thousand years ago they were widespread in the southern half of Africa, and some probably adapted to desert life a long time ago.

The !Kung became skilled hunters and gatherers. Women obtain between 60 and 80 percent of the food, collecting nuts, berries, bulbs, beans, leafy greens, roots, and bird eggs, as well as catching tortoises, small mammals, snakes, insects, termites, and caterpillars. While the women gather, the men hunt animals, snare birds, and extract honey from beehives. These hunters are skilled trackers who can follow animal tracks and other clues for many miles without rest. The !Kung utilize some fifty species of plants and animals for food, medicine, cosmetics, and poisons. Although Western peoples may disregard many of the food sources because of cultural biases, these sources are in fact highly nutritious. Termites, for example, are about half protein.

The !Kung have adapted well to a harsh environment. Even during periodic drought conditions that devastate the more vulnerable farmers, the diversity of !Kung food sources ensures a steady supply. Furthermore, their diet is low in salt, carbohydrates, and saturated fats, and high in vitamins and roughage. Their diet, combined with a relatively unstressful life, helps them avoid modern health problems like high blood pressure, ulcers, obesity, and heart disease. But because they live far from clinics, they die more easily from accidents and malaria, and some scholars doubt that their diet is nutritionally sound. Nonetheless, !Kung life expectancy is similar to that in many industrialized countries.

Since they spend only about fifteen to twenty hours a week in maintaining their livelihood, the !Kung have ample free time for resting, conversing, visiting friends, and playing games. Children have few responsibilities because their labor is not needed for the !Kungs' survival. The !Kung value interdependence between the genders and are willing to do the work normally associated with the opposite sex. For example, fathers take an active role in child rearing. The intense social life is symbolized by a large communal space in the midst of the camp surrounded by family sleeping huts; they prefer companionship to privacy. The !Kung strongly discourage aggressiveness. Their folk stories praise the animal tricksters who evade the use of force.

Throughout history farming peoples have affected hunters and collectors. The !Kung faced many challenges in recent decades that have altered the lives of many bands. Most are no longer completely self-sufficient. They trade desert products to nearby farming villages for tools and food. Others have been drafted into the military, have taken up wage labor, or have been displaced because their territory has been claimed by governments or business interests. Today, forced or induced to abandon their traditional ways of life, some disoriented !Kung have moved to dilapidated, impoverished villages on the edges of towns. The future for their ancestral lifestyle is unpromising.

THINKING ABOUT THE PROFILE

1. What role does the gathering by women play in the !Kung economy?
2. How does the traditional !Kung way of life promote leisure activity?
3. What problems do the !Kung face today?

!Kung Women Returning to Camp
These !Kung women in the Kalahari Desert of southwestern Africa are returning to camp after gathering wild berries and vegetables, sometimes by using digging sticks. Many Stone Age societies were sustained by such activity. (M. Shostak/Anthro-Photo)

SECTION SUMMARY

■ During the Paleolithic and Mesolithic eras, people lived in small groups of hunters and gatherers.

■ In general, women gathered fruits and nuts, which provided the majority of the food, while men hunted game.

■ Hunting and gathering groups were usually close-knit and egalitarian, though violence was not unknown.

■ Anthropologists are undecided as to whether humans have a natural tendency toward violence or peace.

■ Some hunting and gathering groups still exist, but they are threatened by modernity.

The Agricultural Transformation, 10,000–4000 B.C.E.

What environmental factors explain the transition to agriculture?

Between 10,000 and 11,500 years ago, people who had survived largely by hunting and gathering during the Mesolithic period began to develop simple agriculture. This momentous change marked the beginning of the Neolithic period, a time when humans began to master the environment and change natural biological relationships in unprecedented ways. As agriculturalists, people now deliberately altered the ecological system by cultivating the soil, selecting seeds, and breeding animals that could help them survive. The often-used term *Agricultural Revolution* is misleading, because the development did not involve rapid, electrifying discoveries but occurred over hundreds of years. Nonetheless, the shift from hunting and gathering to farming was one of the greatest transitions in history, and it changed human life all over the world. The earth's surface was also transformed as trees and grass were cleared from one-tenth of the planet for plowing. The production of a food surplus set the stage for everything that came later, including cities, states, social classes, and long-distance trade.

Environmental Change and the Roots of Agriculture

Agriculture started with small preliminary steps. Even before farming began, some people were preparing themselves for permanent village life. Some, like the villagers at Abu Hureyra in Syria, were settling alongside lakes or in valleys rich in wild grains that were easy to collect. Around the world, archaeologists have discovered clay-walled houses from the Neolithic Period, as well as baskets, pottery, pits for storing grain, and

equipment for hunting, fishing, and grain preparation. Probably the first farmers did not even see themselves as pioneers forging a new way of life. As will be discussed shortly, they were probably reacting to environmental changes that were dooming the old ways.

However, documenting the steps taken in the transition to agriculture and settled life is not easy. For the earliest periods we have no written sources, since writing appeared only around 3500 B.C.E. Many material artifacts still lie buried, while others have long since turned to dust or were covered by rising sea levels. Historical reconstruction depends largely on archaeological evidence such as bones, artifacts, seeds, wild plants, tools, buildings, campsites, and the radiocarbon dating of the soils where these things are discovered.

Climate change was probably one key factor in triggering the shift to agriculture. After the last great Ice Age, the earth entered a long period of unusual warmth, which still persists. The melting glaciers caused rising sea levels, covering about a fifth of previously available land. Some scholars contend that the spread of the Persian Gulf, the Black Sea, and the Mediterranean onto once occupied lowlands may have led to legends in the Middle East of a great flood and human expulsion from a "garden of Eden." Rising sea levels also covered over many land links, including those connecting the British Isles to continental Europe and Japan to Asia.

Another factor was probably population growth. Around 10,000 B.C.E., the world population had grown to perhaps 5 or 10 million, and in some regions hunting and gathering could no longer meet the basic needs of everyone, especially as good land was submerged. Neighboring lands were already occupied by other bands of people. But the warmer climate encouraged the spread of grasses such as barley and wild wheat, which attracted grazing animals. Soon food gatherers gravitated to these areas, some of them abandoning their nomadic ways to live permanently near these rich food sources.

The Great Transition to Settled Agriculture

The environment continued to change, posing new challenges. The earth cooled again briefly about 9000 B.C.E., reducing food supplies, and a drought in the Middle East presented a crisis for some food-gathering societies because they had no real concept of saving or storing for the future. Eventually it was no longer enough to just exploit local resources more efficiently. Responding to the challenges, hunters and gatherers like those at Abu Hureyra began to store food and learn how to cultivate their own fields. Some people experimented with new foods, especially cereal grains collected in a wild state. These grains were generally most plentiful in mountain areas, where many settled. Others planted the grains after migrating to the plains in search of better prospects. Former hunters and gatherers began to pioneer **horticulture** (HORE-tee-kuhl-chur), the growing of crops with simple methods and tools,

---

horticulture   The growing of crops with simple methods and tools.

Ruins of Abu Hureyra The site of this ancient village overlooks the floodplain of the Euphrates River in northeastern Syria. The earliest settlement included intersecting pits that were turned into huts by roofs of reeds, branches, and poles. (Courtesy, Andrew M.T. Moore)

such as the hoe or digging stick. These efforts eventually resulted in a profound reorganization of human society.

Women may well have taken the lead in domesticating plants and some animals and in molding clay for storage and cooking pots. People in southwest Asia made pottery by 7500 B.C.E. to serve as waterproof containers. As the chief gatherers, women knew how plants grew in certain types of soil and sprouted from seeds, and they also knew the amount of water and sunshine needed to sustain plants. Women are generally the main food producers in horticultural societies today.

One major food-producing strategy was shifting cultivation, a method still practiced today by millions of people, especially in Southeast Asia, Africa, and Latin America. Shifting cultivation was especially adaptable in wooded areas, where people could clear trees and underbrush by chopping and burning (hence the common term *slash and burn*). Once the area was cleared, they loosened the soil with digging sticks and finally scattered seeds around the area. Natural moisture such as rain helped the crops mature. But since the soil became eroded after a few years, shifting cultivators moved periodically to fresh land, returning to the original area only after the soil had recovered its fertility. Most shifting cultivators still rely on men to supply protein by hunting and fishing.

The Consequences of Settled Agriculture

Farming promoted many radical changes in the way humans lived and connected with their environments. Whether agriculture made life more secure, predictable, and healthy than hunting and gathering remains subject to debate. But the domestication of plants and animals increased the production of food in a given amount of land. A farmer could not necessarily grow more food than might be collected from the wild in a favorable setting with ample land, but agriculture could produce a much higher yield per acre and thus could support much denser populations in the same area. Permanent settlements also made possible the storage of food for future use, since the pots and buildings did not have to be moved periodically. Most people apparently believed farming was necessary for survival.

But farmers faced new problems. Since they depended on fewer plant foods than food gatherers, they were in some ways more vulnerable to disaster from drought or other natural catastrophes. Food shortages may have become more rather than less common with farming. The earliest farmers could probably grow enough to feed themselves and their families with three or four hours of work a day. But as they required more food to feed growing populations, they were forced to exploit

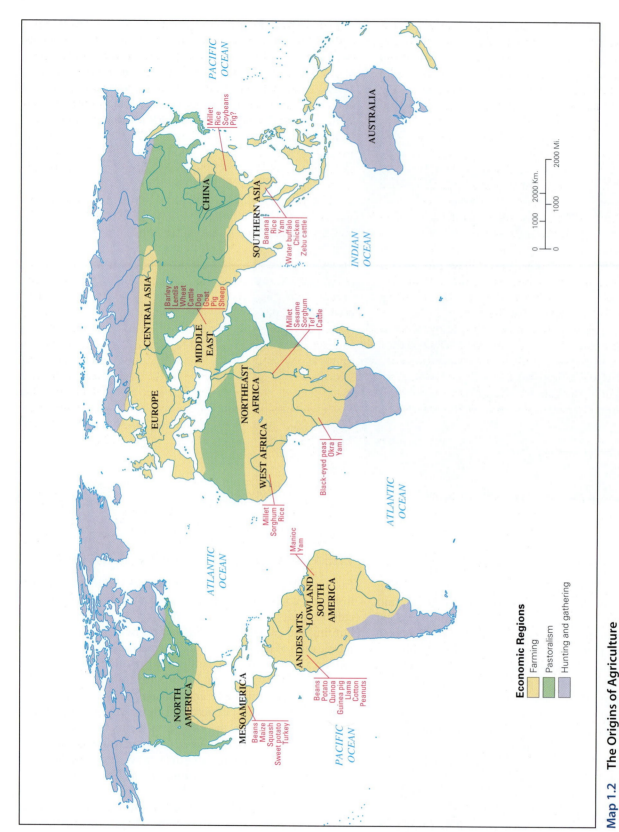

Map 1.2   The Origins of Agriculture
Between 11,500 and 7000 years ago, people in western Asia, North and sub-Saharan Africa, southern Asia, East Asia, New Guinea, Mesoamerica, and South America developed agriculture independently and domesticated available animals. Later most of these crops and some of the animals spread into other regions.

Online Study Center   Improve Your Grade   Interactive Map: River-Valley Civilizations, 3500–1500 B.C.E.

local resources more intensively and to work harder in their fields. And some domesticated foods, like corn and bread, caused more dental problems and gum diseases than their wild counterparts. Some people complained. The Hebrew writer who recorded the biblical garden of Eden story blamed women for the hard work of farming: "Cursed is the ground for your sake; in toil you shall eat of it all the days of your life. In the sweat of your face you shall eat bread til you return to the ground."[3] Agriculture eventually depended on peasants, mostly poor farmers who worked small plots of land that were often owned by others. Although most lived at little better than subsistence levels, they had to share some of their crop with their landlords. Hard-working peasants were the backbone of most societies before the Industrial Revolution.

Whether for spiritual reasons or because of a new understanding of natural forces, some early farming peoples all over the world constructed megaliths, huge stone monuments. For example, Stonehenge was built in southern England in stages between 3100 and 1800 B.C.E. Some of the stone, weighing several tons, was obtained up to 140 miles away. Many scholars think Stonehenge was a temple for shamanistic religious rites. It may also have been a secular ceremonial center, where the community gathered at special times. It clearly served as an astronomical observatory, because its axis aligns with the summer solstice sunrise, an important time for Neolithic farmers.

The Globalization and Diversity of Agriculture

The agricultural transformation eventually reached across the globe. Agriculture came first to Eurasia, where geography favored the movement of people to the east or west along the same general latitude, without abrupt climatic changes. By contrast, the Americas are constructed along a north-south axis, and northern and southern temperate regions are linked only through a huge tropical zone stretching from southern Mexico to northern and eastern South America. Some peoples, such as those in Australia and the Arctic, did not or could not make the transition from food gathering because of environmental and geographical constraints. Nonetheless, the different regions all contributed significantly to the discovery and production of the food resources we use today.

The Multiple Origins of Farming Where did agriculture begin? Although some controversial evidence points to mainland Southeast Asia, most archaeologists believe the earliest transition to farming occurred in the area of southwestern Asia known as the "Fertile Crescent." This includes what is today Iraq, Syria, central and eastern Turkey, and the Jordan River Valley. This region had many fast-growing plants with high nutritional value, such as wheat, barley, chickpeas, and peas. The breakthrough came between 9500 and 8000 B.C.E.. There is good evidence for the growing of grain crops by 8000 B.C.E., and scattered evidence for even earlier farming at a few sites such as Abu Hureya.

Food growing also began independently in several other parts of the world, although we still do not know precisely when (see Map 1.2). Hot, humid climates such as those in Southeast Asia, tropical Africa, and Central America are poor for preserving plant, animal, and human remains, so archaeologists may never learn the full story. But clearly several Asian peoples were among the earliest farmers. A few scholars think farming began in northern Vietnam by 8000 B.C.E.. Crop cultivation began around 7000 B.C.E. in China and New Guinea, 7000 or 6000 B.C.E. in India, 5000 or 4000 B.C.E. in Thailand, and 3000 B.C.E. in Island Southeast Asia.

Elsewhere the dates varied considerably (see Chronology: The Transition to Agriculture, 10,000–500 B.C.E.). In the Mediterranean region, farming began in the Nile Valley by at least 6000 B.C.E., if not earlier, and in Greece by 6500 B.C.E. Agriculture reached northward to Britain and Scandinavia between 4000 and 3000 B.C.E. Farming may have spread into Europe with migrants from western Asia who intermarried with local people. While some historians suspect that farming in the southeast Sahara is very ancient, dating to between 8000 and 6000 B.C.E., others doubt it began that early. People in Ethiopia were farming by 4500 B.C.E. In the Americas cultivation apparently began in central Mexico between 7000 and 5500 B.C.E. and in the Andes (ANN-deez) highlands by 6000 B.C.E., if not earlier. Farming reached Panama by 4900 B.C.E., the Amazon Basin by 1500 B.C.E., Colorado by 1000 B.C.E., and the southeastern part of North America by 500 B.C.E.

CHRONOLOGY	
The Transition to Agriculture, 10,000–500 B.C.E.	
9500–8000	Southwestern Asia (Fertile Crescent)
8000	Vietnam (date disputed)
7000	Nubia (date disputed), China, Mexico, New Guinea
6500	Greece
6000	Northwestern India, Egypt, Andes, West Africa (disputed)
5000	Thailand (traditional)
4900	Panama
4500	Ethiopia
4000	Britain, Scandinavia
3000	Island Southeast Asia, Tropical West Africa
1500	Amazon Basin
1000	Colorado
500	Southeast North America

Food and Farming in Ancient Cultural Traditions

As agriculture became an essential foundation for survival, it became increasingly important in the traditions and mindsets of societies around the world. The following excerpts show three examples of how food and farming were reflected in the cultural traditions of ancient societies. The first, an Andean ritual chant many centuries old, is a prayer for successful harvests addressed to an ancient deity. The second is from a farmer's almanac from eighteenth-century B.C.E. Mesopotamia that offers guidance on cultivating a successful grain crop; this excerpt deals with preparing the field and seeding. The third reading, a song collected in China around 3,000 years ago, celebrates a successful harvest and explains how some of the bounty will be used.

Andean Chant

Oh Viracocha, ancient Viracocha, skilled creator,
who makes and establishes
"on the earth below may they eat, may they drink" you say;
for those you have established, those you have made
may food be plentiful.
"Potatoes, maize, all kinds of food may there be"

Excerpt from Farmer's Almanac

Keep a sharp eye on the openings of the dikes, ditches and mounds [so that] when you flood the field the water will not rise too high in it. . . . Let shod oxen trample it for you; after having its weeds ripped out [by them and] the field made level ground, dress it evenly with narrow axes weighing [no more than] two thirds of a pound each. . . . Keep your eye on the man who puts in the barley seed. Let him drop the grain uniformly two fingers deep. . . . If the barley seed does not sink in properly, change your share. . . . Harvest it at the moment [of its fill strength].

Chinese Harvest Song

Abundant is the year, with much millet, much rice;
But we have tall granaries,
To hold . . . many myriads and millions of grain.
We make wine, make sweet liquor,
We offer it to ancestor, to ancestress,
We use it to fulfill all the [religious] rites,
To bring down blessings upon each and all.

THINKING ABOUT THE READING

1. Who did the Andeans believe determined the success of their harvest?

2. How did Mesopotamian farming depend on draft animals and cooperation?

3. How did ancient Chinese farmers use surplus grain and rice to fulfill obligations?

Sources: Brian M. Fagan, *Kingdoms of Gold, Kingdoms of Jade* (London: Thames and Hudson, 1991), p. 88; Samuel Noah Kramer, *Cradle of Civilization* (New York: Time-Life, 1967), p. 84; *The Book of Songs*, translated by Arthur Waley (London: George Allen and Unwin, 1954), p. 161. © 1954 by permission of the Arthur Waley Estate.

Varieties of Crops and Methods The earliest crops that were grown varied according to local environments and needs. Millet dominated in cold North China, rice in tropical Southeast Asia, wheat and barley in the dry Middle East, yams and sorghum in West Africa, corn in upland Mesoamerica, and potatoes in the high Andes. Food, however, was not the only concern. Some crops such as flax were grown for fiber to make clothing. Other plants had medicinal properties. Chinese were mixing herbs, acids, rice, and beeswax together to make a potent fermented alcoholic beverage by 7000 B.C.E. Southwest Asians began making wine from grapes and beer from barley between 6000 and 3000 B.C.E. The growing of fruits and nuts added variety to the diet. Over time farming became deeply ingrained in the psychology, social life, and traditions of many societies (see Witness to the Past: Food and Farming in Ancient Cultural Traditions).

Farming technology gradually improved. People living in highlands where slopes are steep, such as in Peru, Indonesia, China, or Greece, made their fields on terraces, which were laborious to construct and maintain. Then, as more people moved from highlands into valleys, they needed new techniques. Some people used water from nearby marshes or wells. On less well watered plains, they built large-scale water projects such as irrigation canals.

Animal Domestication

The domestication of animals for human use developed in close association with crop raising and brought many advantages. As they continued to be bred in captivity, animals were gradually modified from their wild ancestors. Men may have tamed and looked after the larger animals such as oxen and cattle, while women may have taken charge of smaller species such as sheep and pigs. Wild boars were domesticated into pigs in several different regions. Animals were raised to supply meat and leather, to aid in farming, to produce fertilizer, or to supply transportation. For example, horses and camels made long-distance travel and communication easier. Plows, probably developed from hoes, became more efficient tools when pulled by oxen or cattle. The oldest cart wheels so far discovered date back over 5,000 years. One disadvantage was that domesticated animals passed on diseases to humans, although this eventually led to immunities among peoples in Eurasia.

Much remains unclear about the chronology and location of animal domestication. For example, dogs may have been domesticated from gray wolves by 15,000 years ago in East Asia, but some scholars think this change came much earlier. Dogs were welcome for companionship, guarding, assistance in hunting, and sometimes food. Migrants took Asian dogs to the Americas. Sheep, goats, pigs, and cattle were all domesticated in the Middle East between 9000 and 7000 B.C.E., but it is possible that cattle and pigs were exploited during the same period in southern Asia, where chickens were domesticated. Some contested evidence also suggests cattle domestication in East Africa around 13,000 B.C.E. and in the Sahara region between 9000 and 8000 B.C.E. Indeed, cows were used in several parts of Africa by 7000 B.C.E. The first domesticated horses and donkeys, which date back to around 4000 B.C.E., enabled the improved transportation that stimulated long-distance trade networks. In some places animals may have been domesticated for herding even before the shift to farming occurred.

Zoological differences among the continents were crucial to the evolution of advanced agriculture. Eurasia contained many species of large, plant-eating, herding mammals whose habits and mild dispositions made their domestication into draft animals possible. But outside Eurasia, the lack of draft animals hindered the development of agriculture. Africa (except for cattle) and Australia lacked such animals, and most of the candidates in the Americas, such as the horse and camel, were extinct by 10,000 B.C.E. The only American possibilities were the gentle llamas and alpacas of the South American highlands. Though Andean people used them as pack animals by 3500 B.C.E., they were not well suited for farming.

Agriculture and Its Environmental Consequences

At the same time that the environment influenced farming, the resulting population growth also contributed to environmental changes, some with negative consequences. Human activities have had an impact on environments since the time of *Homo habilis*. Indeed, Stone Age hunters in both hemispheres may have contributed to the extinction of many animal species. But most hunters and gatherers, with limited technology and small numbers, left only a modest impact on their physical environment. Intensive agriculture more radically altered the ecology, especially as technology improved.

Technological innovation solved some problems for a while, but it did not always prove advantageous in the long run. For example, the invention of the plowshare made it easier to loosen dirt and eliminate weeds so that seeds could be planted deeper in nutrient-rich soil. But it also exposed topsoils to water and wind erosion. Similarly, vast irrigation networks provided the economic foundations for flourishing agriculture and denser settlement. But irrigation requires more labor than dry farming, and it also tends to foster centralized governments that can allocate the water resources among the people, with the result that more controls are placed on people's behavior. In addition, adding water to poor soils can produce waterlogged land and also change the mineral content of the soil, eventually producing a thick salt surface that ruins farming. In Mesopotamia and the Americas, where irrigation ultimately created deserts, it helped account for the rise and fall of entire societies.

Various activities contributed to environmental destruction. Farming and animal raising placed new demands on the land. Goats, for example, caused considerable damage as they browsed on shrubs, tree branches, and seedlings, thus preventing forest regeneration. Cattle required much pasture. People exploited nearby forests for lumber to build wagons, tools, houses, furniture, and boats. As early as 2700 B.C.E. Egyptians were ravaging the famed cedar forests of nearby Lebanon for wood to build their fleets, and the seafaring Phoenicians of Lebanon soon did the same. Contemporary observers were aware of the deforestation. For example, twenty-four centuries ago the philosopher Plato bemoaned the deforestation of the Greek mountains, which he called "a mere relic of the original country. What remains is like the skeleton of a body emaciated by disease. All the rich soil has melted away, leaving a country of skin and bone."[4] Overgrazing and deforestation in the mountains feeding the main rivers produced silt that contained harmful salt and gypsum, which moved downstream to the sea, clogging canals and dams. Water evaporated in the hot sun, leaving a salt residue. Later, much once fertile land in the Tigris-Euphrates and Indus River Basins of Mesopotamia and India became a salt desert.

The changing relationship of humans to their environment with farming generated new religious ideas. Early sacred and philosophical texts often justified human domination over nature. For example, the authors of the Hebrew book of Genesis believed God told humans to "be fruitful and multiply; fill

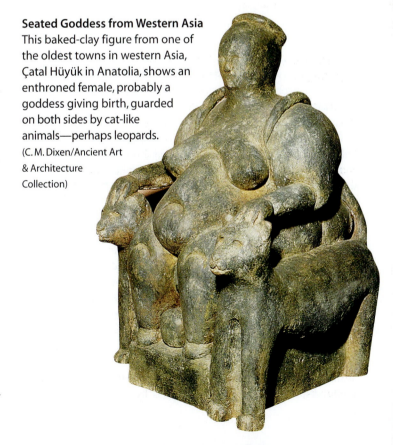

Seated Goddess from Western Asia This baked-clay figure from one of the oldest towns in western Asia, Çatal Hüyük in Anatolia, shows an enthroned female, probably a goddess giving birth, guarded on both sides by cat-like animals—perhaps leopards. (C. M. Dixen/Ancient Art & Architecture Collection)

the earth and subdue it; have dominion over the fish of the sea, over the birds of the air, and over every living thing that moves upon the earth."[5] Similarly, the Greek thinker Socrates argued that the gods were careful to provide everything in the natural world for human benefit. Many ancient thinkers saw an ordered world in which every part had a role and purpose in a divine plan, with humans the ultimate beneficiaries.

SECTION SUMMARY

■ The shift from hunting and gathering to farming had tremendous consequences, but it occurred gradually, over hundreds of years.

■ The end of the last great Ice Age and increased population density led people to shift from hunting and gathering to farming.

■ Settled farming could support much denser populations and allowed for food storage, but it also led to some new health problems.

■ Farming probably began in the area of southwestern Asia known as the "Fertile Crescent."

■ Irrigation and other technological advances led to larger crops but also caused great environmental damage.

The Emergence of Cities and States

How did farming and metallurgy establish the foundations for the rise of cities, states, and trade networks?

The cause-and-effect link between farming and more complex societies can be described in the following scenario. Given the prospects for ample food, some western Asian people moved to fertile areas to farm. They unloaded their stone tools, clay pots, and plant seeds and built flimsy huts of mud and reeds. Families formed small villages, and, with the food surpluses that were produced, they had more children to help in the fields. They built houses with a sleeping platform, bread oven, grain silo, and a corral for their domesticated animals. Older women served as religious specialists, acting as midwives, reciting myths, and composing verses and incantations. Over time hamlets grew into larger villages, and people began to see themselves as part of larger communities. To honor a special deity the villagers built a temple, not just brick and mortar but a holy place. Eventually these villages with their temples grew into the first cities. In turn, cities established a foundation for the rise of states, trade networks, and writing.

The Rise of New Technologies

While making possible such complex societies, agriculture also fostered new technology. Many times in history people came up against a serious resource problem, such as lack of food and water, and had to overcome the problem or perish. Often their solution was to develop some new technology, and many of these had long-lasting value. One innovation, metalworking, made possible a new level of human control over resources supplied by the environment.

The first metalworking was done with copper. Copper was being used in Europe for making weapons and tools as early as 7000 B.C.E. and in the Middle East by 4500 B.C.E. In fact, copper mining may have been the first real industry of the ancient world; for example, the Egyptians maintained substantial mining operations in the Sinai Peninsula. Traded over considerable distances, copper also became perhaps the first major commodity to enjoy a world market. Gold was also used and valued very early. These two soft metals could be fairly easily cut and shaped with stones.

Soon specialist craftsmen emerged to mine and work metals. By 3000 B.C.E. some of these specialists in western Asia had developed heating processes by which they could blend copper together with either tin or arsenic to create bronze. The bronze trade became a major spur to commerce in early Mesopotamia. By 1500 B.C.E. the technology for making usable iron had also been invented, although it took many centuries for people to perfect the new alloy for practical use. Bronze and iron made better, more helpful, and more durable tools (such as plows), but also more deadly weapons, and their use shaped many societies of the ancient and classical worlds (see "Societies, Networks, Transitions," page 101).

Urbanization and the First Cities

Agriculture also fostered population growth. By using cow's milk and grain meal for infant's food, women could now breast-feed for a shorter period and consequently bear children more frequently. In the Middle East the population is believed to have grown in the space of 4,000 years (some 160 generations) from less than 100,000 in 8000 B.C.E. to over 3 million by 4000 B.C.E.

In more densely populated areas, farming villages grew into substantial, often prosperous towns. In one of the oldest towns, Çatal Hüyük (cha-TAHL hoo-YOOK) in central Turkey, roughly 10,000 residents lived in cramped mud-brick buildings from 6700 to 5700 B.C.E. The residents decorated the white plaster walls of their houses with paintings. The town's wealth derived from volcanic obsidian, which people converted into polished mirrors and traded around the region. Çatal Hüyük and similar towns became centers of long-distance trade and the basis for the first cities. For example, by around 3700 B.C.E. Tell Hamoukar (Tell HAM-oo-kar) in northeastern Syria had grown from a village into a town enclosed by a defensive wall. It contained both a bakery and a brewery, evidence of some residents organizing people and resources, and seems to have had some occupational divisions and a growing bureaucracy, perhaps even a king. By 3500 B.C.E. Tell Hamoukar had grown into a city, which later traded with the cities of southern Mesopotamia. Road networks linked the various cities of the Tigris-Euphrates Basin.

Çatal Hüyük   A view of rooms and walls in one of the first known towns, Çatal Hüyük in eastern Turkey. The ruins contained many art objects, murals, wall sculpture, and woven cloth.   (Courtesy Arlene Mellaart)

As people grouped together, they pioneered new ways of living. Through the process of urbanization permanent settlements became larger and more complex, dominating nearby villages and farms. A city is a permanent settlement with a greater size, population, and importance than a town or village, and it usually contains many shops, public markets, government buildings, and religious centers. Cities emerged only where farmers produced more food than they needed for themselves and so could be taxed or coerced to share their excess crops. This surplus was critical to sustain people with no time or land for farming, and priests, scribes, carpenters, and merchants increasingly congregated in the larger settlements that eventually became cities.

What some call the urban revolution constituted a major achievement in different parts of the world, perhaps as significant as the agricultural transformation. In southwest Asia the first small cities were formed between 3500 and 3200 B.C.E.; they were administered by governments and dominated by new social hierarchies. Soon cities appeared elsewhere (see Chronology: The Rise of Cities). Many were surrounded by walls, which the Greek philosopher Aristotle later called a city's "greatest protector [and] best military measure."[6] City people enjoyed many new amenities. Many streets were lined by small shops and crowded with makeshift stalls selling foodstuffs, household items, or folk medicines. Hawkers peddled their wares from door to door, some announcing their presence with calls or songs. Craftsmen in workshops fashioned the items used in daily life, such as pottery, tools, and jewelry. Some of the goods made, mined, or grown locally were traded by land or sea to distant cities. Thus the rise of cities reshaped societies and fostered networks of communication and exchange.

CHRONOLOGY	
The Rise of Cities	
3500–3200 B.C.E.	Western Asia
3100–3000 B.C.E.	Egypt
3500–3000 B.C.E.	Northwestern India
3000–2500 B.C.E.	Peru
2000 B.C.E.	Northern China
1800 B.C.E.	Nubia
1600 B.C.E.	Crete
1200 B.C.E.	Mesoamerica (Mexico)
100 C.E.	West Africa

The Rise of States, Economies, and Recordkeeping

Food production and urbanization eventually led to the formation of states: formal political organizations or governments that controlled a recognized territory and exercised power over both people and things. The people within them, often from diverse ethnic and cultural backgrounds, did not necessarily share all the same values or allegiances. Furthermore, they exchanged influences with neighboring peoples. Complex urban societies organized into states developed at least 3,000 years ago on all the inhabited continents except Australia, and by 1,000 years ago they were widespread around the world.

These urban societies relied on diversified economies that generated enough wealth to permit a substantial division of labor and to support a social, cultural, and religious hierarchy. Farmers, laborers, craftsmen, merchants, priests, soldiers, bureaucrats, and scholars served specialized functions. The priests served the religious institutions that emerged as societies organized and standardized their beliefs. Some states constructed monumental architecture, such as large temples, palaces, and city walls. While men dominated most of the hierarchies and heavy labor, women also played key economic roles. In all of the ancient urban societies, women made the cloth. They prepared the raw materials; spun the yarn; wove the yarn into fabrics; and fashioned and sewed the clothing, blankets, and other useful items, passing along their knowledge from mother to daughter.

Most urban societies were connected to elaborate trade networks extending well beyond the immediate region. The earliest known long-distance trade, by dugout canoes in Europe, dates to around 9000 B.C.E. By 4000 B.C.E. a network of merchant contacts linked India and Mesopotamia, 1,250 miles apart. Very crude mathematical calculations were being etched in bones by people in western Asia by 15,000 or 10,000 B.C.E., and clay counting tokens used for trade had appeared by 3100 B.C.E., if not earlier. By 5000 B.C.E. the first seafaring vessels had been built around the Persian Gulf to serve increased long-distance trade, and by 3500 B.C.E. these and other developments had set the foundation for more extensive networks linking diverse societies.

The early urban societies also introduced cultural innovations such as recordkeeping and literature. A system of recordkeeping could involve a written language, such as those developed by the Egyptians, Greeks, Arabs, Chinese, and Mayans, among others. Or records could be kept by a class of memory experts, such as the professional "rememberers" that lived among some South American peoples and were common in Africa. In most literate societies writing was usually reserved for the privileged few until recent centuries, so knowledge of literature was not widespread unless it was passed on orally. Both nonliterate and literate societies created rich oral traditions of stories, legends, historical accounts, and poems, often nourished by specialists, that could be shared with all the people.

Some historians apply the term *civilization* to larger, more complex societies such as ancient Egypt and China, but this is a controversial concept with a long history of abuse. From ancient times up to today, some peoples have seen themselves as "civilized" and dismissed or criticized their neighbors, or any people unfamiliar to them, as "barbarians." Another problem is that modern historians may focus too much on societies, such as Egypt, that left more of an archaeological and written record, giving lesser attention to those societies that did not. The historian can cast a wide or narrow net in choosing which societies to consider "civilized." The term could refer to a large grouping of people with a common history and traditions, such as the Chinese, Mayans, Arabs, Bantu Africans, Brazilians,

or western Europeans. Or it could be restricted to those large, complex urban societies that developed or borrowed certain useful patterns such as bureaucratic governments, monumental architecture, and writing. Thus the term is too subjective to have much value in understanding world history, and many historians refuse to use it altogether. It is not used in this text.

The Rise of Pastoral Nomadism

Some societies adopted an alternative to agriculture and cities known as **pastoral nomadism**, an economy based on breeding, rearing, and harvesting livestock. The interaction between pastoral nomads and settled farmers was a major theme in history for many centuries. On the marginal land unsuitable for farming, some people began specializing in herding, moving their camps and animals seasonally in search of pasture. They traded meat, hides, or livestock to nearby farmers for grain. Both trade and conflict between the two contrasting groups, farmers and herders, became common. Pastoral nomadism was a highly specialized and developed way of life involving dispersed rather than concentrated populations. Yet some pastoral nomads exercised a strong influence on societies with much greater populations.

Pastoral Societies   Pastoral nomads mostly concentrated in grasslands and deserts, which could sustain only small populations. Grasslands covered much of central and western Asia from Mongolia to southern Russia, as well as large parts of eastern and southern Africa. An even more inhospitable area was the Sahara region of northern Africa, which was part of a great arid zone stretching from the western tip of Africa eastward through Arabia into western Asia and then to the frontiers of China. By 2500 B.C.E. a long drought had intensified the drying out of the Sahara region, and by 2000 B.C.E. it had become a huge, inhospitable desert habitable only by pastoralists.

Living along or beyond the frontiers of settled farming, the pastoralists lived very differently than farmers, but they were not culturally "unsophisticated." For example, they domesticated horses in Central Asia around 4300 B.C.E. (Horses reached western Asia by 2000 B.C.E. Although camels were domesticated around 3000 or 2500 B.C.E. in Arabia, they were not widely used in western Asia until sometime after 1500 B.C.E.) Pastoralists were also capable of undertaking ambitious projects. Around 5000 B.C.E. Sahara cattle herders built a remarkable megalithic ceremonial center of large stones to mark astronomical changes. Like other societies, pastoralists had humane values and a rich cultural life, and many were connected to other peoples by various networks.

The nomadic pastoral life had many similarities regardless of the region. Since a large area was needed to support each animal, herds had to be kept small and separated some distance from other herds to prevent overgrazing. As a result, the herders lived in small, dispersed groups, generally organized by extended families that were often part of **tribes**, associations of clans that traced descent from a common ancestor; sometimes they were

pastoral nomadism   An economy based on breeding, rearing, and harvesting livestock.

part of federations of tribes. While most pastoralists had few material possessions, they did not necessarily envy the settled peoples. For example, the pastoral nomads who today herd yak, sheep, and goats across the windswept high plateaus of northern Tibet enjoy ample leisure time and believe, despite the harsh conditions, that they have an easier life than farmers.

There were also many differences among pastoralists. While some societies maintained egalitarian social structures, others were headed by chiefs. In some of the pastoral societies of Central Asia women seem to have held a high status and to even have served as warriors. Burial mounds in Turkestan contain the remains of what may be female warriors from 2,500 years ago. These women, unusually tall, were buried with daggers, swords, and bronze-tipped arrows. Some pastoralists became tough, martial peoples who were greatly feared by the farmers. As discussed in later chapters, Central Asian pastoralists like the Huns and Mongols played a central role in world history before modern times.

The Indo-Europeans Among the pastoral nomads who had a great influence on world history were the various tribes known collectively as the **Indo-Europeans** (IN-dough-YUR-uh-PEE-uns). Historians derive this term from the original common tongue that spawned the many related languages spoken today by these peoples' descendants. All these languages have many similar geographic, climatic, botanical, and zoological terms. Scholars have long debated where the original Indo-European homeland was located. Many think these societies arose either in the Caucasus Mountains or in the adjacent plains to the north, in what is now southern Russia. Others place them in eastern Anatolia (modern Turkey). Eventually, because of the spread of these seminomadic and strongly patriarchal tribes and their languages, most people in Europe, Iran, and northern India came to speak Indo-European languages.

Indo-European expansion apparently occurred in several waves. According to recent studies, some Indo-Europeans may have moved into Europe and central Asia as early as 6500 or 7000 B.C.E., perhaps carrying with them not only their language but also farming technology, both of which they shared with, or imposed on, the local peoples. The culturally mixed people who resulted may have been the ancestors of, among others, the Celts and Greeks. Sometime between 3000 and 2000 B.C.E. many of the Indo-Europeans remaining in Anatolia and the Caucasus, most of them pastoralists, were driven from their homeland by some disaster, perhaps drought, prolonged frost, overpopulation, plague, or invasions by even more warlike peoples. The various tribes dispersed in every direction, splitting up into smaller, more cohesive units and driving their herds of cattle, sheep, goats, and horses with them. As they encountered farming peoples, they turned to conquest in order to occupy the land (see Map 1.3).

This dispersal of peoples from the Indo-European heartland set the stage for profound changes across Eurasia. The

Hittites gained dominance in Anatolia and then, around 2000 B.C.E., expanded their empire into Mesopotamia. Other tribes pushed on between 2500 and 1500 B.C.E., some to the west across Anatolia into Greece, some to the east as far as the western fringe of China, some south into Persia. From Persia some tribes moved southeast through the mountain passes into northwestern India. Everywhere they went the Indo-Europeans spread their languages and imposed their military power, eventually absorbing or subduing the peoples they encountered. Most eventually abandoned pastoral nomadism for farming, but their spread opened a new chapter in the history of Europe, the Middle East, and India.

SECTION SUMMARY

- Metals such as bronze and iron helped improve farming tools and weaponry.
- Highly productive farming allowed for the formation of the first cities, which became centers of trade.
- People in cities developed forms of recordkeeping and writing.
- Pastoral nomads, or herders, kept their animals in areas that were unsuitable for farming.
- Herders played an important role in spreading culture across Eurasia, though most eventually took up farming.

 *Online Study Center* **ACE the Test**

Chapter Summary

The story of humans and their societies constitutes only a tiny part of the broader 4.5-billion-year history of the Earth. Some 4 million years ago our hominid ancestors emerged in Africa, learning to walk upright, to make and use tools, and to control fire. Eventually, after several stages, evolution produced modern humans, who developed language and more complex social structures. For thousands of years, during the long Paleolithic age, all humans, using simple technologies and living in small groups, hunted wild animals and gathered wild plants. Hunters and gatherers survived and even flourished by maintaining a balance with their environment. While many such societies survived over the millennia, eventually environmental changes and other factors encouraged most peoples to adopt farming.

Beginning between 10,000 and 11,500 years ago, the climate began to warm and populations increased. In response some people gradually began to grow their own food. The great transition from hunting and gathering to a farming-based economy also involved the domestication of wild animals. Farming probably emerged first in southwestern Asia or possibly Southeast Asia. Over the next few thousand years various peoples in Eurasia, Africa, and the Americas began farming. By 2000 B.C.E. agriculture had been established widely

---

tribes Associations of clans that traced descent from a common ancestor.

Indo-Europeans Various tribes who all spoke related languages deriving from some original common tongue and who eventually settled Europe, Iran, and northern India.

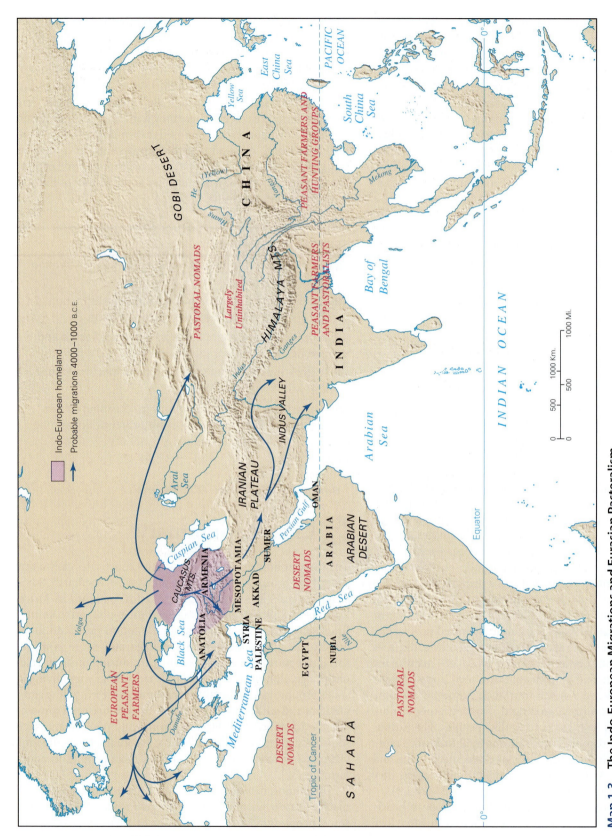

Map 1.3   The Indo-European Migrations and Eurasian Pastoralism
Some societies, especially in parts of Africa and Asia, adapted to environmental contexts by developing a pastoral, or animal herding, economy. One large pastoral group, the Indo-Europeans, eventually expanded from their home area into Europe, southwestern Asia, Central Asia, and India.

Indo-European homeland

Probable migrations 4000–1000 B.C.E.

PACIFIC OCEAN

East China Sea

Yellow Sea

South China Sea

GOBI DESERT

C H I N A

PEASANT FARMERS AND HUNTING GROUPS

He (Yellow)

Yangzi

Mekong

PASTORAL NOMADS

Largely Uninhabited

HIMALAYA MTS.

PEASANT FARMERS AND PASTORALISTS

Bay of Bengal

Ganges

I N D I A

INDUS VALLEY

Indus

Aral Sea

IRANIAN PLATEAU

INDIAN OCEAN

1000 Mi.

1000 Km.

500

500

0

0

Caspian Sea

Arabian Sea

OMAN

Persian Gulf

Volga

CAUCASUS MTS.

ARMENIA

MESOPOTAMIA

SUMER

AKKAD

A R A B I A

ARABIAN DESERT

DESERT NOMADS

Equator

Black Sea

ANATOLIA

SYRIA

PALESTINE

Mediterranean Sea

Red Sea

EUROPEAN PEASANT FARMERS

EGYPT

NUBIA

Nile

Tropic of Cancer

Danube

PASTORAL NOMADS

DESERT NOMADS

S A H A R A

0°

around the world. Agriculture led to larger populations and changed people's relationship to the environment. It also set the stage for another transition, the emergence of the first societies with cities, states, social classes, and recordkeeping. In the Afro-Eurasian zone, where many peoples were in contact with others, these societies first developed between 3000 and 3500 B.C.E. Early trade and transportation networks linked some of them together. The first cities and states formed in sub-Saharan Africa and the Americas between 3000 and 1000 B.C.E. At the same time, some people living in the grasslands and deserts became nomadic pastoralists and interacted with settled farmers. The formation of distinctive societies and increased contact between peoples inaugurated a new era of human history.

 **Online Study Center** **Improve Your Grade** Flashcards

Key Terms

hominids	Paleolithic	polytheism
australopithecines	Mesolithic	shamans
Homo habilis	Neolithic	horticulture
Homo erectus	matrilineal	pastoral nomadism
Homo sapiens	kinship	tribes
Neanderthals	animism	Indo-Europeans
Cro-Magnons		

Suggested Reading

Books

Bellwood, Peter. *First Farmers: The Origins of Agricultural Societies.* Malden, M.A.: Blackwell, 2005. A detailed scholarly account summarizing recent knowledge.

Bogucki, Peter. *The Origins of Human Society.* Malden, Mass.: Blackwell, 1999. A detailed and up-to-date scholarly study of human prehistory.

Christian, David. *Maps of Time: An Introduction to "Big History."* Berkeley: University of California Press, 2004. The most extensive presentation of the "big history" approach.

Clark, Robert B. *The Global Imperative: An Interpretive History of the Spread of Humankind.* Boulder, Colo.: Westview, 1997. A well-written, brief overview of human expansion and the development of agriculture.

Diamond, Jared. *Guns, Germs and Steel: The Fates of Human Societies.* New York: W.W. Norton, 1997. A fascinating interpretation of early human societies, with emphasis on environmental influences.

Fagan, Brian. *People of the Earth: An Introduction to World Prehistory.* 11th ed. Upper Saddle River, N.J.: Prentice-Hall, 2003. A standard overview of human evolution and prehistory, from early hominids through the Neolithic.

Fagan, Brian. *The Long Summer: How Climate Changed Civilization.* New York: Basic Books, 2004. An up-to-date assessment of the connection between history and climate over the past 5,000 years.

Goudsblom, Johan. *Fire and Civilization.* London: Penguin, 1992. Examines the impact of fire use on prehistorical and early farming societies.

Lewin, Roger. *The Origin of Modern Humans.* New York: Scientific American Library, 1998. A well-illustrated survey of human evolution and early society.

Manning, Patrick. *Migration in World History.* New York: Routledge, 2005. Provocative study of human migrations, with much on prehistory and ancient history.

Megarry, Tim. *Society in Prehistory: The Origins of Human Culture.* New York: New York University Press, 1995. A sociological study of human evolution and Stone Age societies.

Mithen, Steven, *After the Ice: A Global Human History, 20,000-5000 BC.* Cambridge: Harvard University Press, 2004. an unorthodox but fascinating portrayal, based on the latest research, of 15,000 years of prehistory.

Smith, Bruce D. *The Emergence of Agriculture.* New York: Scientific American Library, 1994. An account for the general reader of the origins of food production.

Websites

About Archaeology
(http://archaeology.about.com/science/archaeology).
Contains much material on archaeology and ancient societies.

ArchNet Home Page
(http://archnet.asu.edu/). This Arizona State University site contains links to information on human origins, prehistory, and archaeology.

Evolution of Modern Humans
(http://anthro.palomar.edu/homo2/default.htm).
Valuable site maintained by Palomar College.

Internet Ancient History Sourcebook
(http://www.fordham.edu/halsall/ancient/asbook.htm).
Good collection of essays and links on prehistory.

The Internet Public Library: Archaeology
(http://www.ipl.org/div/subject/browse/soc06.00.00/).
Extensive collection of links on the ancient world and prehistory.

World Civilizations
(http://www.wsu.edu/~dee/TITLE.HTM).
A useful collection of materials on prehistory and ancient history, operated by Washington State University.

CHAPTER 2

Ancient Societies in Mesopotamia, India, and Central Asia, 5000–600 B.C.E.

Online Study Center

This icon will direct you to interactive activities and study materials on the website: college.hmco. com/pic/lockard1e

Bull's Head from Sumerian Lyre   This bull's head is part of the soundbox of a wooden harp. The harp, made in Sumeria around 2600 B.C.E., is covered with gold and lapis lazuli and reflects the popularity of music in Mesopotamian society.   (Michael Holford)

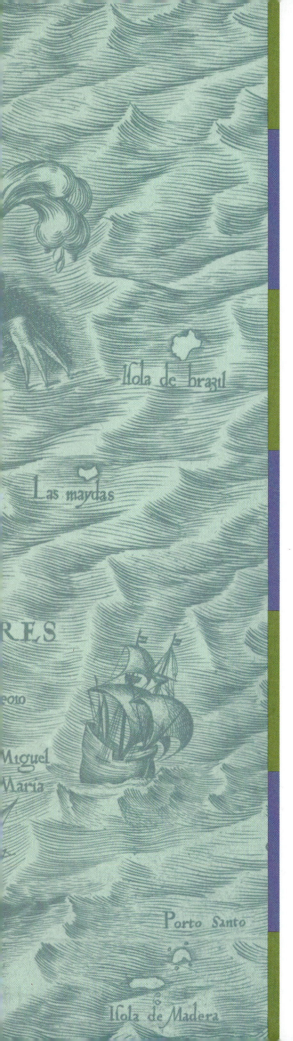

Inanna filled Agade [a Mesopotamian city], her home, with gold. She filled the storerooms with barley, bronze, and lumps of lapis lazuli [a stone used in jewelry]. The ships at the wharves were an awesome sight. All the lands around rested in security.

POEM PRAISING THE GODDESS OF LOVE AND GENEROSITY, WRITTEN IN 2250 B.C.E.[1]

Some 5,000 years ago in the Mesopotamian (MESS-uh-puh-TAIM-ee-an) city of Uruk (OO-rook), an unknown artist carved a beautiful narrative relief on a large stone-pedestaled vase, the first such sculpture known in history, and donated it to the city's temple for the goddess of love, Inanna (ih-NON-a), the first known goddess in recorded history. The scenes of domestic and religious life celebrate a festival honoring the goddess. The artist divided the vase into three bands, each illustrating different aspects of Uruk life and traditions. The lowest band presents an agricultural scene, with ewes and rams, barley and flax, and water, the staples of the area's economy. Inanna, the sculptor believed, had blessed Uruk's people with growing herds and good crops. The central band portrays a procession of naked men carrying jars and baskets overflowing with foodstuffs that they will present as gifts of gratitude to Inanna. Finally, the uppermost band features a female figure wearing a tall horned headdress, perhaps Inanna or her priestess. The Warka vase, as it is known today, reflects the artistic skill of a fine craftsman and also pictures for us the social order and rituals of one of the world's earliest cities.

Sometime after the people in southwest Asia and India had become comfortable with the farming technology necessary for successful living, they began to make the next great transition by founding the first cities, like Uruk and Agade (uh-GAH-duh), and the first states. Various urban societies eventually formed in the Indus Valley in northwestern India and all along the **Fertile Crescent**, a large semicircle of fertile land that included the valleys of the Tigris (TIE-gris) and Euphrates (you-FRAY-teez) Rivers stretching northwest from the Persian Gulf, the eastern shores of the Mediterranean Sea, and, to some historians, the banks of the Nile River in Egypt. The Mesopotamians in the Fertile Crescent divided their labor into specialized tasks assigned to full-time farmers, professional soldiers, government officials, artisans, and priests. To the east, the people in ancient India also divided their society into social classes and established the foundations for several religions of wide and enduring appeal.

Fertile Crescent   A large semicircular fertile region that included the valleys of the Tigris and Euphrates Rivers stretching northwest from the Persian Gulf, the eastern shores of the Mediterranean Sea, and, to some scholars, the banks of the Nile River in North Africa.

Among the Mesopotamians and Indians, the first dramatic changes in human life arose from contact through trade and migration networks or warfare. Various Afro-Eurasian peoples built the foundations to sustain large populations. For at least three millennia a large majority of the world's population has lived in an arc stretching from Egypt and Mesopotamia eastward through India and China to Japan. The people of western Asia created many innovations: the first systematic use of writing for both business transactions and literature, the first working of bronze, the first large state structures and empires, and the first institutionalized religions to worship deities like Inanna. These societies also constructed networks to exchange products and information over long distances by land and sea. Agade, the hub for such a network, was visited by traders from near and far. Over time the Middle East, which includes North Africa and western Asia, became a crossroads or bridge between Europe, Africa, and southern Asia. And Mesopotamia was for centuries a great hub for trade and communication networks extending to distant lands.

FOCUS QUESTIONS

1. Why did farming, cities, and states develop first in the Fertile Crescent?
2. What were some of the main features of Mesopotamian societies?
3. What were some of the distinctive features of the Harappan cities?
4. How did the Aryan migrations reshape Indian society?
5. How did Indian society and the Hindu religion emerge from the mixing of Aryan and local cultures?

Early Mesopotamian Urbanized Societies, to 2000 B.C.E.

Why did farming, cities, and states develop first in the Fertile Crescent?

The creation of small city-states around 5,000 years ago made Mesopotamia, and especially the southern part of the Tigris-Euphrates Valley, the home of some of the world's earliest urban societies. Geography played a key role in this region's transition to farming and then to urbanization and state building. Even in these early millennia, the connections between diverse peoples helped cultures change and grow. Over the centuries various peoples moved into the area, each adopting and building on the achievements of their predecessors. They built the first great cities and developed a written language. The cities were dominated by religious temples and had elaborate social class structures. As conquerors combined various city-states into a series of ever larger states, empires were formed, and Mesopotamian societies were soon linked by trade to the Mediterranean and North Africa.

Western Asian Environments

Life in these early societies owed much to the geographic features that brought people together. Most early urban societies began first in wide river valleys such as the Tigris-Euphrates, Indus, and Nile Valleys because such places provided life-giving irrigation for the crops that supported larger populations. In the case of Mesopotamia (the Greek word for the "land between the rivers"), the flooding of the Tigris and Euphrates Rivers made possible a flourishing society. The first known cities and states arose in the Tigris-Euphrates Basin, a region stretching from the western edge of the Persian Gulf through today's Iraq into Syria and southeastern Turkey. The long river valley promoted interaction between peoples, both friendly and hostile. For example, it invited frequent invasions through mountain passes by people living to the north and east. To the northwest the mountainous Anatolia (ANN-uh-TOE-lee-uh) Peninsula (modern Turkey) provided the key link between Asia and Europe. East of Mesopotamia lay Iran (known through most of history as Persia), a land of mountains and deserts and the pathway to India and Central Asia. To the south the Arabian peninsula, largely desert, was characterized by oasis agriculture and nomadic pastoralism.

Although the rivers provided water, other characteristics of this region and its climate were not so generous. Ancient

CHRONOLOGY

	Mesopotamia	India and Central Asia
3000 B.C.E.	3000–2300 B.C.E. Sumerian city-states	
2500 B.C.E.	2350–2160 B.C.E. Akkadian Empire	2600–1750 B.C.E. Harappan city-states 2200–1800 B.C.E. Oxus cities
2000 B.C.E.	1800–1595 B.C.E. Old Babylonian Empire	1600–1400 B.C.E. Aryan migrations 1500–1000 B.C.E. Aryan Age
1000 B.C.E.	1115–605 B.C.E. Assyrian Empire	

Mesopotamia had a climate similar to southern California today. Most rain fell in the winter, and summer temperatures in some places reached 120 degrees Fahrenheit. During the long and incredibly hot summer, the land, mostly composed of clay soils, baked stone-hard. Under a scorching sun searing winds blew up a choking dust. Vegetation withered. The winter was little more comfortable, as winds, clouds, and the occasional rains made for stormy and bleak days. In spring the green was welcome, but the rains and melting snows in the nearby mountains swelled the rivers to flood level, sometimes submerging the plains for miles around. Still, the annual but unpredictable floods created natural levees that could be drained and planted, and the nearby swamps contained abundant fish and wildlife.

Diverse peoples and languages contributed to the history and identity of western Asia. Many different peoples settled the region, some of them speaking Semitic languages, including Arabic and Hebrew, which are related to some African tongues. Speakers of Turkic and of Indo-European languages such as Persian, Armenian, and Kurdish arrived later. The various names given by outsiders to these lands hint at other influences and concepts. Two millennia ago the Romans called the lands from the eastern shores of the Mediterranean Sea to the Persian Gulf the "Orient" ("east"). Later Europeans referred to southwestern Asia as Asia Minor or the Near East (since it was part of the "East" nearest to them), and to the region along the eastern Mediterranean coast (today's Israel, Lebanon, and Syria) as the Levant (luh-VANT) ("rising of the sun"). Geographers today use the label "southwest Asia," and often lump the region together with Islamic North Africa under the broader concept of the "Middle East," since Europeans saw it as midway between East Asia (the "Far East") and themselves ("the West").

Mesopotamian Foundations

Despite its harsh geography and climate, Mesopotamia saw the first transitions to settled agriculture and then to urbanization. Long before Sumerians built the first cities at the head of the

Persian Gulf, the transition to farming had taken place in various places of the Tigris-Euphrates Basin as well as in Palestine. For example, by 9000 B.C.E. Jericho (JER-ah-ko), located near the Jordan River, was an agricultural community that had some 2,000 people at its height. Excavated storage rooms, town walls, and a round storage tower indicate a complex town organization. Towns like Jericho in Palestine and Çatal Hüyük in south central Anatolia foreshadowed the beginnings of urban society in Mesopotamia.

The Tigris and Euphrates Rivers fostered several Mesopotamian societies. Both rivers begin in eastern Anatolia and flow southeast over a thousand miles to the Persian Gulf. The modern city of Baghdad is midway up the Tigris, and the ancient city of Babylon was only a few miles away on the Euphrates where the two rivers flow closest to each other. Sometime after 6500 B.C.E., the population of farmers and herders in the fertile hills on either side of these rivers increased. Because of their greater need for food, and possibly pushed by a cooler climate between 6200-5800 B.C.E, they left the hill country and created the first towns in the marshy but fertile areas near the head of the Persian Gulf. Although these people had been raising cattle and sheep and growing wheat and barley for several thousand years, after moving to the river valleys they worked together to build elaborate irrigation canals so they could grow food after the annual floods. Thus irrigation had significant historical consequences, for it necessitated the cooperation that laid the foundations for organized societies and then cities. Yet, irrigation also slowly degraded the soil, the salts it added eventually creating infertile desert.

The Pioneering Sumerians

People built the first Mesopotamian cities and states in Sumer (soo-MUHR), the lower part of the Tigris-Euphrates Valley in southern Iraq (see Map 2.1). Historians think the Sumerians originally came from the north or the east and that they settled in southern Mesopotamia about 5500 B.C.E. Over time villages grew into towns. By 3500 B.C.E. Uruk had grown into a city,

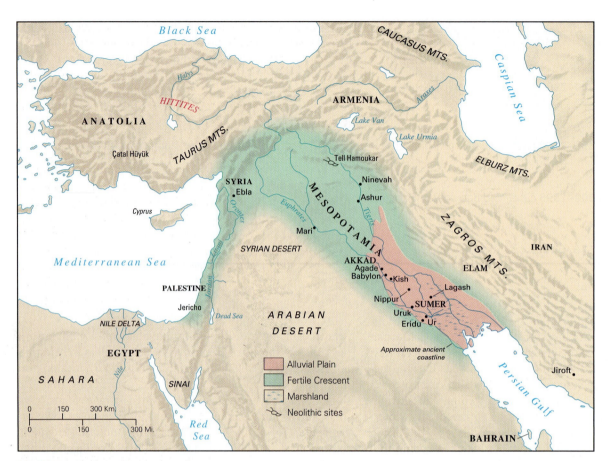

Map 2.1   Ancient Mesopotamia
The people of Mesopotamia and the adjacent regions of the Fertile Crescent pioneered farming. The Mesopotamians also built the first cities and formed the first states. The Sumerian cities dominated southern Mesopotamia for over a millennium, only to lose power to societies from northern Mesopotamia.

Online Study Center   **Improve Your Grade**   Interactive Map: Ancient Mesopotamia Through the Persian Empire

eventually reaching a population of 50,000. From the archaeological discoveries at Tell Hamoukar, on the northern fringe of the Tigris-Euphrates Valley in modern Syria, some scholars suspect that other peoples may have been as important as the Sumerians in forging the first states. But our knowledge of the Sumerians is much more extensive.

The various settlers created elaborate canal systems and, by 3000, a network of city-states, urban centers surrounded by agricultural land controlled by the city and used to support its citizens. These earliest territorial political units allowed Sumerian societies to grow, to perhaps several million people, by 2500 B.C.E. For example, Uruk was surrounded by 5 miles of fortified walls and had extended its influence through trade as far north as modern Turkey by 3500 B.C.E. An attack by Uruk on the city of Tell Hamoukar in northern Mesopotamia is the world's oldest known example of large-scale organized warfare. Uruk also exercised regional power. A document from the era reported that Uruk was obsessed with weapons and used them to conquer the nearby city of Ur (see Chronology: Mesopotamia, 5500–330 B.C.E.).

Sumerians had little sense of being citizens, as we understand that term, but they were clearly proud of their cities. A Sumerian myth begins with the lines "Behold the bond of Heaven and Earth, the city. Behold the kindly wall, the city, its pure river, its quay where the boats stand. Behold its well of good water. Behold its pure canal."[2] The Sumerians felt that city life made them superior to others and referred scornfully to the various desert peoples and tribes living to the west and south of the valley as "people who have never known a city." The city-dwellers lived in mud-baked brick houses constructed around courtyards. The largest building in any Sumerian city was the temple, or **ziggurat** (ZIG-uh-rat), a stepped, pyramidal-shaped building (almost an artificial mountain) that was seen as the home of that city's chief god. One of these temples may have inspired the later Hebrew story of the tower of Babel (BAY-buhl/BAH-buhl).

---

ziggurat   A stepped, pyramidal-shaped temple building in Sumerian cities, seen as the home of the chief god of the city.

Mesopotamia, 5500–330 B.C.E.

5500	First Sumerian settlements
3200	First cuneiform writing
3000–2300	Sumerian city-states
2750	Model for legendary Gilgamesh rules Uruk
ca. 2500–2100	Jiroft
ca. 2350–2160	Akkadian Empire unified Mesopotamia
ca. 2100–2000	Neo-Sumerian Empire led by city of Ur
ca. 2000	*Epic of Gilgamesh* written in cuneiform
ca. 1800–1595	Old Babylonian Empire
ca. 1790–1780	Hammurabi's Law Code
ca. 1600–1200	Hittite Empire
ca. 1115–605	Assyrian Empire
745–626	Height of Assyrian Empire
ca. 626–539	Chaldean (Neo-Babylonian) Empire
ca. 539–330	Persian Empire

Sumerian Society and Economy

The social, political, and economic structures of Sumerian society became hierarchical, with some people having higher ranks than others. In the early years, decision-making assemblies of leading citizens governed the cities. Scholars have long debated whether these assemblies, which included elders and other free citizens, amounted to a kind of democratic government. The assemblies seem to have appointed a city leader, sometimes a woman, with both secular and religious authority. However, with the waging of wars, rulers, priests, and nobles came to dominate large numbers of lower-class people, workers, and slaves. Women lost the right to be elected leader and serve in the assemblies. War leaders became kings, or hereditary monarchs. By increasing their power and forming large armies, they weakened the power of the assemblies and priests. Either the nobility or the priests controlled most of the land in and around the city, which was tilled by tenant farmers or slaves, and many of these common people became dependent on the nobles or priests for their survival. A Sumerian proverb claimed that "the poor man is better dead than alive; if he has bread, he has no salt; if he has salt, he has no bread."[3] The many slaves, who included captives taken in battles and criminals, were treated as personal property but allowed to marry. If a slave married a free woman, the children were free. Eventually royal officials, nobility, and priests controlled most of the economic life of the cities. In many places, for example, temple priests distributed seed for planting and planned crop distribution.

As the first of many male-governed societies, Sumeria introduced **patriarchy**, a system in which men largely control women and children and also shape ideas about appropriate gender behavior. Sumerian women were generally subservient to men and excluded from government, but they could inherit property, run their own businesses, and serve as witnesses in court. A queen enjoyed much respect as the wife of the king. Sumerian religion also allowed a woman to be the high priestess if the city divinity was female. Sumerians treasured the family; a proverb said: "Friendship lasts a day; kinship endures forever." Another proverb suggested the importance of women in the family but also the stereotypes they faced: "The wife is a man's future; the son is a man's refuge; the daughter is a man's salvation; the daughter-in-law is a man's devil."[4]

The trade networks involving Sumeria may have been some of the first in world history with significant consequences. Because of their location and lack of natural resources, the Sumerian cities engaged in extensive trade, which helped form networks with neighboring societies. Even today satellite images reveal the outlines of the 5,000-year-old road system that linked Mesopotamian cities. Sumerians imported copper from Armenia in the Caucasus Mountains and then discovered how to mix it with tin to make bronze. This alloy made for stronger weapons, which they often used against each other. Thus the Bronze Age originated in western Asia, and later the use of bronze helped shape other societies in Eurasia and North Africa. The Sumerians also imported gold, ivory, obsidian, and other necessities from Anatolia, the Nile Valley, Ethiopia, India, the Caspian Sea, and the eastern shore of the Mediterranean.

The Persian Gulf became a major waterway, with many trading ports. Bahrain (Bah-RAIN) Island served as a transshipment point for goods flowing in from all directions and as a hub where various traders and travelers met. Mesopotamian merchants traveled to this port of exchange carrying cargoes of textiles, leather objects, wool, and olive oil, and they returned with copper bars, copper objects, ivory, precious objects, and rare woods from various Western Asian societies and India. Some Mesopotamian traders lived in central Iran and others traveled widely. Already this early in history, trade helped people learn and profit from each other's skills and surplus goods.

The Sumerians also seem to have had some trade and other connections with another urban-based farming society known as Jiroft [JEER-oft], located in southeastern Iran. Scholars debate where the still sparsely documented Jiroft fits into the development of the most ancient urban societies. Jiroft seems to have emerged sometime between 3000 and 2500 B.C.E., with a rural economy based on cultivating date palms.

patriarchy A system in which men largely control women and children and shape ideas about appropriate gender behavior.

Overview of Early City of Uruk　This photo shows the ruins of one of the earliest Mesopotamian cities, a rich source of art objects and fine architecture. The best-known king of Uruk was the legendary Gilgamesh.　(Hirmer Verlag Munchen)

Some scholars think inscribed lines and images on seals constituted a form of writing. Mesopotamian texts describe a state they called Aratta, a possible reference to Jiroft. Aratta's gaily decorated capital city had lofty red brick towers, and the rulers supplied artisans and craftsmen to Uruk. The ruins of the main Jiroft city, a regional commercial center, include a two-story citadel and a Sumerian-like ziggurat. Archaeologists have found the world's oldest known board games and staggering numbers of decorated vases, goblets, cups, and boxes. The people adorned their products with precious stones from India and Afghanistan. Some decorations on Jiroft pottery resemble the gods, plants, and beasts of Sumeria.

Sumerian Writing and Technology

The Sumerians were innovators in many areas. Although a few scholars think the Egyptians, Indians, or Chinese might have developed a simple writing system at least as early as the Sumerians, most still credit the Sumerians with producing the first written records. Trade and the need to keep accurate records of agricultural production and public and private business dealings led around 3200 B.C.E. to one of the most significant Sumerian contributions. This was their **cuneiform** (kyoo-NEE-uh-form) (Latin for "wedge-shaped") writing system, in which temple recordkeepers, or scribes, began to keep records

of financial transactions by making rough pictures (say, of an animal or fish) on soft clay with a stylus that made wedges in the clay. They then baked the bricks on which these pictograms were scratched. Archaeologists have discovered hundreds of thousands of such bricks intact. Sumerian scribes soon let a stylized version of the pictogram stand for an idea, and later they converted an even more abstract version into a phonetic sign describing a speech sound.

Writing provided a way of communicating with people over long distances and allowed rulers to administer larger states. Those who controlled the written word, like those who master electronic communication in our day, had power, prestige, and a monopoly over a society's official history. Writing also gave temple scribes and other religious leaders the power to determine how written texts attributed to the gods or political authorities should be interpreted.

Since writing required mastery of at least three hundred symbols, few people learned to write, and those that did largely came from the upper class. In part to produce scribes, the Sumerians created the world's first schools, where strict instructors beat students for misbehavior or sloppy work. A clay tablet from the eighteenth century B.C.E. describes the life of a pupil who spent twenty-four days a month in school and was frequently beaten: "The fellow in charge of Sumerian said: 'Why didn't you speak Sumerian?' [He] caned me. My teacher said: 'Your hand [writing] is unsatisfactory.' [He] caned me. I [begin to hate] the scribal art."[5] However, because cuneiform eventually transformed pictures into phonetic sounds, it made

---

cuneiform ("wedge-shaped")　Latin term used to describe the writing system invented by the Sumerians.

the written word more accessible, even for people whose only goal was a good recipe for a meal of red broth and meat.

Writing became crucial in human history for a number of reasons. First, written language made it easier to express abstract ideas and create an intellectual life based on a body of literature. The oldest known signed poetry was composed by Enheduanna (en-who-DWAHN-ah), a Sumerian priestess and princess living around 2300 B.C.E. Since some of her poems dealt with religious issues, some consider her the first theologian. Royal women were often authors. Eventually writing also helped explain the physical world in rational instead of magical terms. In addition, a written language based on clearly understood symbols, whether phonetic or pictographic, allowed communication among people who spoke different languages but understood the same written symbols. For example, the number 5 is understood today the same way by Spanish speakers, who pronounce it "cinco," and German speakers, who say "funf." Finally, writing was one key to the interaction among societies. It not only gave a strong sense of identity to all who shared the language but also eventually encouraged the spread of trade and culture, including religion, to those outside a particular homeland. Through this process some people became, by choice or necessity, multilingual.

These first city builders were innovative in many areas. They pioneered the first use of the wheel, glass, and fertilizer, inventions that we still live with today. Sumerians also created some of the earliest calendars, which were based on their observations of the movements of various celestial bodies, and one of the first mathematical systems, based on the number 60. Remnants of this system can be seen today in our 60-minute hours and 60-second minutes. Later the Babylonians improved Sumerian mathematics by developing a simple calculator with tables of squares, cubes, reciprocals, square roots, and cube roots. Many other peoples eventually adopted all of these inventions. They were also used by the Sumerians who became the world's first known accountants. Humanity also owes to the Sumerians the decision to divide night and day into twelve hours each. In leisure-time endeavors, the Sumerians were innovative as well. Although they were not the first to convert barley into beer, they designated a special goddess to supervise its production, called Ninkasi or "the lady who fills the mouth." The many taverns fostered early drinking songs: "I will summon brewers and cupbearers to serve us floods of beer and keep it passing round! Our hearts enchanted and our souls radiant."[6]

The Akkadian Empire and Its Rivals

Eventually the political structure of the region changed. In the beginning the Sumerian cities were related by a common culture and not a common ruler. Each city had its own king who ruled the people in the name of the city's god. This independence ended about 2350 B.C.E. when Sargon (SAHR-gone), the ruler of Akkad (AH-kahd), a region just north of Sumer whose capital was Agade, conquered Uruk as a prelude to uniting the other Sumerian cities under the rule of his family. Sargon formed the world's first known empire, a large state controlling other societies through conquest or domination. He claimed a

humble origin, boasting that "in secret [my mother] bore me. She set me in a basket in the river which rose not over me." Later, he said, "I conquered the land, and the sea three times I circled."[7] The Akkadians enslaved many other people in addition to the Sumerians; in fact, slaves constituted perhaps a third of the empire's population in 2300 B.C.E. Under Sargon trade between Mesopotamia and India reached a peak. Indeed, Akkad became the major center for regional trade, and merchant ships from as far as Oman (O-mahn) in eastern Arabia docked at the wharves, carrying copper and various exotic products.

Struggles between rival cities became endemic, generating frequent warfare. Sargon's empire soon came into conflict with one created by another imperial city, Ebla (EBB-luh), in northern Mesopotamia. Ebla had a population of 30,000 and subject peoples totaling another 200,000 or more. It had created a large empire based on trade that stretched from eastern Turkey to the ancient city of Mari (MAH-ree), several hundred miles north of Akkad.

The Akkadian Empire was destroyed by the twenty-first century B.C.E., probably from a combination of internal conflicts, external attacks, and climate change. Less rainfall may have prompted many to migrate. Mesopotamian societies such as Sumer and Akkad were powerless against abrupt climate change which could reduce rainfall dramatically. Sumerian legends celebrated years of plenty: "Behold, now, everything on earth. The harvest was heaped up in granaries and hills." But they also expressed dread of the periodic droughts: "The famine was severe, nothing was produced. The fields are not watered. In all the lands there was no vegetation [and] only weeds grew."[8] A disastrous drought began in 2200 B.C.E., affecting much of Eurasia, and lasted for 300 years. Irrigation canals silted up and settlements became ghost towns.

As the Akkadian Empire collapsed, a new Sumerian dynasty led by Ur took over much of the lower valley between 2100 and 2000 B.C.E., forming what historians term the Neo-Sumerian Empire. Some Ur kings boasted of their commitment to art and intellectual life, one ordering that the places of learning should never be closed. But Ur was devastated by a coalition of enemies and sacked and burned along with other Sumerian cities. Its temples were destroyed, its populations killed or enslaved, and its treasures plundered. These horrific events may have left an enduring mark on the cultures of these cities. A surviving lamentation describes the destruction of Ur in graphic detail: "Ur is destroyed, bitter is its lament. The country's blood now fills its holes like hot bronze in a mould. Our temple is destroyed, the gods have abandoned us, like migrating birds. Smoke lies on our city like a shroud."[9]

The Akkadians, Eblaites, and the later Sumerians established the first empires in history, even though their creations were short-lived and were not the large bureaucratic organizations we see in later empires. They were largely collections of city-states that acknowledged one city as overlord, especially when the ruler's troops were present. However, once the pattern of one city dominating others was established, it soon became clear that whoever had the best army would dominate Mesopotamia.

The Royal Standard of Ur   This mosaic from around 2500 B.C.E., made of inlaid shells and limestone, was found in a royal tomb. It depicts various aspects of life in the Mesopotamian city-state of Ur. The bottom panel shows a four-wheeled battle wagon drawn by a horselike animal. The middle panel features soldiers wearing armor and helmets. The top panel shows war prisoners being brought before the king.   (British Museum/Michael Holford)

SECTION SUMMARY

- The first urban societies of Mesopotamia developed in the Tigris-Euphrates Basin.
- The ziggurat, or temple, was the largest building in Sumerian cities.
- Sumerian society was hierarchical and patriarchal.
- The earliest writing system was the cuneiform system.
- The world's first empire, the Akkadian Empire, was founded by Sargon.

✦ Later Mesopotamian Societies and Their Legacies, 2000–600 B.C.E.

What were some of the main features of Mesopotamian societies?

The Sumerians and Akkadians established a pattern of city living, state building, and imperial expansion. From 2000 B.C.E. and continuing for the next 1,500 years, a series of peoples, coming mainly from the north, successively dominated Mesopotamia and created new empires. The most important of these peoples were the Babylonians, Hittites, and Assyrians. Each made important contributions to the politics, laws, culture, and thought of the region. This pattern changed only when the entire area was incorporated into the Persian Empire in 539 B.C.E., an event that inaugurated a new era in the history of the region.

The Babylonians and Hittites

Several states dominated Mesopotamia during the second millennium B.C.E., beginning with the Amorite kingdom of Babylon (BAB-uh-lawn). In 1800 B.C.E. the Amorites (AM-uh-rites), a Semitic people, conquered Babylon, a city about 300 miles north of the Persian Gulf on the Euphrates, and gradually extended their control in the region. Babylon's most famous king, Hammurabi (HAM-uh-rah-bee), who ruled from 1792 to 1750 B.C.E., reunified Mesopotamia. Hammurabi had nearly three hundred laws collected and "published" on a black basalt pillar erected near the modern city of Baghdad. These laws were designed, he said, "to make justice appear in the land, to destroy the evil and the wicked [so] that the strong might not oppress the weak."[10] Hammurabi's law code was really a collection of earlier Sumerian concepts and practices. It remains famous today because some of its principles appeared later in the laws of the Hebrews and also because of its most noted principle, the law of retaliation: an eye for an eye and a tooth for a tooth. Hammurabi's successors were able to hold his empire together for little over a century.

By 1595 B.C.E., the Babylonian Empire had disintegrated in the face of attacks by the Hittites (HIT-ites), an Indo-European people who moved into Mesopotamia from their base in central Anatolia. The Hittites were most famous for their later use of iron weapons, which were superior to those made of bronze, but these had not yet been invented when the Hittites invaded Mesopotamia. Iron technology was introduced around 1500 B.C.E., although it took several centuries to perfect. Whether the Hittites invented ironworking or obtained the technology from nearby people in Anatolia, with iron weapons they expanded their power until they met the equally strong Egyptians in Syria and Palestine. The Hittites may also have used the first known biological weapons, since one of their tactics was to send plague victims into enemy lands. The Hittite Empire dominated various parts of western Asia from 1600 to 1200 B.C.E. The Hittites treated their subjects less harshly than the Babylonians. They followed a tolerant attitude toward other religions and adopted many Mesopotamian gods, establishing a tradition of tolerance in the region.

The Assyrian Empire and Regional Supremacy

For several centuries after Hittite power declined, no one group dominated Mesopotamia for long. In 1115 B.C.E., however, the Assyrians (uh-SEER-e-uhns), named for their major city, Ashur, created an empire in western Asia larger than any before, the first that was more than a collection of city-states. They did this in three ways: by creating a large, well-organized, and balanced military; by systematically using terror against enemies; and by devising methods of bureaucratic organization that later empires, especially the Persian, imitated. One of the greatest kings, Tiglath-pileser (TIG-lath-pih-LEE-zuhr) III (745–727 B.C.E.), conquered the entire eastern shore of the Mediterranean as far south as Gaza. Later Assyrian rulers added much of Egypt to the empire. One Assyrian king described himself with some accuracy as "obedient to his gods and receiving the tribute of the four corners of the world."[11]

Assyrian armies made war serious business. Using iron weapons while their enemies still relied on softer bronze ones, the Assyrians launched armies of over 50,000 men that were carefully divided into a core of infantrymen aided by cavalry and horse-drawn chariots. In addition to fighting traditional battles in the open, the Assyrians conducted sieges in which they used battering rams and tunnels against the city walls of their enemies. They also employed guerrilla, or irregular hit-and-run, tactics when fighting in the forests or mountains.

Assyrian kings created a systematic bureaucracy by increasing the number of administrative districts and making local officials responsible only to the kings. They ruled over several million people in the Tigris-Euphrates heartland alone. To improve their administrative control, the rulers used horsemen to create an early version of the "pony express," which allowed them to send messages hundreds of miles within a week. Some kings were both brutal, and learned. Ashurbanipal (ah-shur-BAH-nugh-pahl) (680–627 B.C.E.) founded a great library to collect tablets from all over the country, and boasted of his learning. He noted that, in school, he learned to solve complex mathematical problems and discovered the "hidden treasure" of writing, enabling him to read tablets in Sumerian and Akkadian.

Violence and the Fall of the Assyrians

The Assyrians were most remembered, and deplored, for their brutality, which ultimately contributed to their downfall. King Ashurbanipal bragged about mutilating and burning prisoners. After destroying the state of Elam, he boasted that "like the onset of a terrible hurricane I overwhelmed Elam [a state in southwestern Iran]. I cut off the head of Teumman, their braggart king. In countless numbers I killed his warriors." As to the capital city, "I destroyed it, I devastated it, I burned it with fire."[12] Soldiers routinely looted cities, destroyed crops, and both flailed and impaled their enemies. To prevent revolts, the Assyrians often simply moved people to another part of the vast empire. For example, according to legends, inhabitants of one of the two Hebrew kingdoms were sent to Mesopotamia, where they disappeared from history (see Chapter 3). The rulers sent thousands of people from Syria to the mountains east of the Tigris, and many Mesopotamians to the Mediterranean coast. And yet the Assyrians also tolerated other religions, a policy that allowed the Hebrew faith to survive the conquest of their state.

The terror tactics understandably undermined Assyrian popularity. In 612 B.C.E., a coalition including the Chaldeans (kal-DEE-uhns) (also known as neo-Babylonians) captured the Assyrian capital at Nineveh (NIN-uh-vuh). Soon the Assyrian Empire collapsed, but the Chaldeans, who formed the last Mesopotamian empire, adopted the Assyrian administrative system. The Chaldeans retained most of the Assyrian territories and flourished from 626 B.C.E. until they were conquered by the much larger Persian Empire in 539 B.C.E. Their most memorable ruler, Nebuchadnezzar (NAB-oo-kuhd-nez-uhr) II (r. 605–562 B.C.E.), a brutal strongman, rebuilt Babylon and adorned it with magnificent palaces and the elaborate terraced "hanging gardens," which were built to please one of his wives and which became famous throughout the ancient world. Nebuchadnezzar led the conquest of the remaining Hebrew kingdom in 586 B.C.E.

Not all of these ancient peoples disappeared from history. Although most scholars consider their direct ancestry doubtful, today several million people, mostly Christians in Syria and Iraq, identify themselves as Assyrians or Chaldeans, and they speak an ancient Semitic language. Many emigrated in recent decades to North America and Australia.

Mesopotamian Law

Several very different documents tell us much about Mesopotamian life and beliefs. The eighteenth-century B.C.E. law code of Hammurabi gives us a good look at the social structures of this early urban society (see Profile: Hammurabi the Lawgiver). Hammurabi's code makes clear both what people valued and the value of people, and it also reveals much about society. The code is also one of the earliest systematic records we have of how ancient peoples viewed laws, government, and social norms.

The code probably reflected a high crime rate in the cities, no doubt because of the tremendous gap between rich and

HAMMURABI
THE LAWGIVER

No person personifies Mesopotamian society better than Hammurabi, a Babylonian king (r. 1792–1750 B.C.E.) who was also at times a diplomat, warrior, builder of temples, digger of canals, and, most famously, lawgiver. Many surviving tablets, inscriptions, and letters, some from Hammurabi himself, made the king and his era the best documented in Mesopotamian history. He seems to have been a good administrator and able general who governed fairly and efficiently. Like other Mesopotamian kings, Hammurabi probably had a chief queen and various concubines, as well as several sons and daughters.

When Hammurabi became king, Babylon (which meant "gateway of the gods" in Akkadian) was an insignificant city-state. To expand its power, Hammurabi shrewdly allied with the powerful king of Ashur, probably by becoming a vassal, and allowed him to conquer some nearby cities. For some years Hammurabi's small domain remained one of many rival states, as noted by one of his officials: "There is no king who by himself is strongest. Ten or fifteen kings follow Hammurabi." Like other kings, Hammurabi had intelligence agents in other cities keeping him abreast of important developments such as pending alliances and troop movements. A spy for another king became close to him, writing that "whenever Hammurabi is perturbed by some matter, he always sends for me. He tells me whatever is troubling him, and all of the important information I continually report to my lord." After his army repulsed an invasion by a coalition of rivals, a confident Hammurabi engaged in a long series of wars that added all of southern Mesopotamia and then much of the north to his kingdom. Finally he conquered the strongest power, his former ally Ashur.

Kingship brought responsibilities. His letters reveal Hammurabi sitting in an office at his palace, dictating to a secretary who recorded his orders or thoughts with a reed stylus on a clay tablet. Most letters conveyed commands to governors. Messengers brought letters from officials, which the secretary read aloud. In his replies, Hammurabi tried to resolve problems, for example, suggesting ways to clear a flooded shipping channel, warning delinquent tax collectors of their obligations, punishing corrupt officials, improving agricultural productivity, or protecting frontiers. He also held daily audiences for petitioners seeking justice. Many decisions concerned temple property and administration, indicating the link between church and state.

Hammurabi realized the need to have uniform laws in his diverse country. He compiled older laws, recent legal decisions, and social customs, arranged them systematically, and placed them on an 8-foot block of basalt stone in the temple of Babylon's patron god, Marduk. At the top, an artist pictured Hammurabi receiving the symbols of kingship from Shamash, the sun-god and lawgiver. The code of 282 laws informed citizens of their rights and demonstrated to both gods and people that the king was doing his job to uphold justice in a moral universe.

For close to four millennia, the principles of this ancient Mesopotamian law code have intrigued us. The code reflected the harsh views of the era. It mandated two kinds of punishments, a

Hammurabi Receiving the Law Code   The top of this stela, which is 7 feet high, shows the powerful sun-god, Shamash, on his throne bestowing the famous law code to King Hammurabi.
(Hirmer Verlag Munchen)

monetary penalty and a retribution in kind, and the harshness of the punishment depended on the class of the people involved. The code recognized three social classes: nobles and landowners, commoners, and slaves. Many of Hammurabi's laws discouraged burglary by prescribing instant death for those caught. This emphasis may have reflected the fact that mud-brick homes were not very secure. On the other hand, prostitution was legal. Some laws protected women and children from abuse and arbitrary treatment. For example, a husband who divorced his wife because she bore no sons had to return the dowry she brought into the marriage and forfeited the money he had given her parents for a bridal price. Since the Hebrews borrowed some of these laws, often in modified form, and passed them into Christian and Islamic traditions, Hammurabi's legacy remains influential today.

THINKING ABOUT THE PROFILE

1. How did Hammurabi increase the power of Babylon?
2. What were the purposes of his great law code?

Note: Quotations from William H. Stiebing, Jr., *Ancient Near Eastern History and Culture* (New York: Longman, 2003), pp. 88–89.

poor, but it also addressed violations of social custom. Families were responsible for the crimes of any of their members. To keep lines of inheritance clear, Hammurabi prescribed harsh punishments for sexual infidelity and incest, as did many societies. Women who violated social norms generally suffered harsher punishments than men, just as the eyes and teeth of poor men or slaves were worth less than the same body parts among the upper classes. The code tells us that if someone put out the eye of a free man, he had his eye put out; but a person who put out the eye of a dependent tenant could make things right by paying the tenant's landlord about one pound of silver. Each slave was branded with the owner's symbol, and some endured harsh lives of forced labor. Hammurabi's laws made clear that slaves could expect little sympathy. And yet, while it may seem contradictory to their status as property, some slaves also owned their own assets, carried on business, and even acquired their own slaves.

The code also addressed economic issues. In this class-conscious society, a surgeon could lose his hand if his patient was a free man who failed to survive the operation, certainly a disincentive to take up medicine. If the patient was a slave, however, the surgeon had only to replace him with another. If a builder's house collapsed and killed its inhabitants, the builder could be executed. The existence of a thriving commercial class is confirmed by the existence of high interest rates on loans. One law limited the interest rate on loans of grain or silver to only 20 percent. In general, the punishments in Hammurabi's law code tell us how precarious life must have been in this society, where even a single small break in an irrigation canal wall could spell disaster.

Mesopotamian Religion and Literature

Like most early people, the Mesopotamians believed in a host of gods and goddesses, such as Inanna, later called Ishtar (ISH-tar), the beautiful goddess of love who created desire. But this polytheistic religion imposed no moral demands. These divinities represented heavenly bodies or natural forces and came with human weaknesses, yet they were powerful enough to punish humans, who were created to serve them. People saw themselves as subject to the gods' whims. A Sumerian wrote that mere mortals must accept that their days are numbered and whatever they do, "they are just wind." The gods were housed in massive and opulent temples, where ritual ceremonies were held. The Babylonians and later the Assyrians changed the names of some of the earlier Sumerian gods but maintained the basic Sumerian view of the universe.

The *Epic of Gilgamesh* (GILL-guh-mesh), first composed late in the third millennium B.C.E. but revised and retold by Mesopotamians for 1,500 years, reveals some of their religious values and attitudes. Perhaps humanity's first epic adventure story, *Gilgamesh* echoes Hammurabi's view of the world as a dangerous place in which happiness is hard to find. Although only one part of a very rich legacy of imaginative literature and mythology from Mesopotamia, *Gilgamesh* probably had the most enduring and widespread influence, enriching the traditions of varied Eurasian societies. The stories probably originated in Sumerian times and were eventually written down around 2000 B.C.E.

Online Study Center Improve Your Grade
Primary Source: The Epic of Gilgamesh

In one version of the Gilgamesh story, the hero, modeled after a real king in Uruk about 2750 B.C.E. and created to be two-thirds god and one-third man, engages in a series of adventures involving both the gods and men. With his friend Enkidu, Gilgamesh challenges and defeats the evil but divine giant who guards a mysterious cedar forest. Following this adventure, Gilgamesh rejects a proposal from Ishtar, the goddess of love, telling her that she is fickle and recounting the disagreeable things she has done to her previous lovers, such as turning one of them into a wolf. In revenge at being snubbed, Ishtar causes the death of Enkidu.

Reflecting on the death of his friend, Gilgamesh decides to search for the key to eternal life, an ultimately futile quest that reflects the general pessimism of Mesopotamian culture. Despite problems caused by a great flood, Gilgamesh eventually discovers a prickly but sweet underwater plant that keeps people young and prevents death. After securing the plant from the bottom of the sea, Gilgamesh, tired from his labors, takes a nap before taking the plant back to his city. While he is sleeping, a snake eats the plant, sloughs off its skin, and disappears, depriving humans of immortality. A Uruk master scribe lamented around 1300 B.C.E.: "Gilgamesh, what you seek you will never find. For when the Gods created Man they let death be his lot, eternal life they withheld. Let your every day be full of joy, love the child that holds your hand, let your wife delight in your embrace, for these alone are concerns of humanity."[13]

Scholars have noted the similarities between this story and stories found in the later Hebrew book of Genesis. In both there is a paradise: the Garden of Eden for the Hebrews, Dilmun for the Mesopotamians. In both a great flood destroys humankind. In both a man challenges the god(s). And in both a serpent comes between a man and immortality. However, although these two stories may have derived from an earlier one and the writer or writers of Genesis may been influenced by *Gilgamesh*, there are some differences in tone and attitude between the Babylonian and Hebrew versions. In the Hebrew story, God sends a flood to punish humans for evil living. In more urban Mesopotamia, where floods were frequent and destructive, the gods "decide to exterminate mankind" because humans are too noisy, and "the uproar of mankind is intolerable and sleep is no longer possible by reason of the babel."[14] But a dissenting god causes his favorite mortal to survive by building a boat and loading it with his family and "the seed of all living creatures, the game of the field, and all the craftsmen."

The parallels between the Gilgamesh legend and Genesis remind us that the Gilgamesh story became widely known far beyond Mesopotamia. Some motifs can be found in the literature of the Greeks, such as the Homeric epics. They also reappear in the much later Islamic period, such as the stories of Aladdin and Sinbad. Gilgamesh and other myths remained common in some parts of western Asia down to at least the tenth century C.E., and they are still found in the folk cultures of some villages. The Gilgamesh epic became one of the many unique traditions that shaped the societies of southwestern Asia and made them different from other early societies such as India and Egypt.

SECTION SUMMARY

■ The Babylonians, Hittites, Assyrians, and Chaldeans created empires in Mesopotamia.

■ Hammurabi's code provided a legal framework that included harsh punishments.

■ The Assyrian Empire, known for its brutality, dominated a large region.

■ The *Epic of Gilgamesh* reflected Mesopotamian values and perspectives, including a pessimistic view of life.

The Earliest Indian and Central Asian Societies, 6000–1500 B.C.E.

What were some of the distinctive features of the Harappan cities?

India developed a society with cultural features vastly different from those of the Middle East, Europe, or China. Aided by environmental factors, some Indians made the transition to farming very early, in 7000 to 6000 B.C.E., and the first cities and states east of Mesopotamia were founded around 2600 B.C.E. (see Chronology: Ancient India and Central Asia, 7000–600 B.C.E.). The antiquity of Indian urban society is debated, but most scholars trace its foundations to the city-states and the widespread Bronze Age culture they shared, often called **Harappan** (huh-RAP-un) that were centered in the Indus (IN-duhs) River Valley and nearby rivers in what is now Pakistan and northwest India. Harappan culture eventually covered some 300,000 square miles, the largest in geographical extent of the ancient societies. Although the Harappans built no pyramids like the Egyptians or ziggurats like the Sumerians, they developed a remarkable society. To the north, an urban society also developed in Central Asia.

South Asian Environments and the Rise of Farming

River valley environments strongly shaped the early societies of India, just as they did Mesopotamia, Egypt, and China. The Indian subcontinent, about half the size of Europe, is rimmed by the Indian Ocean to the south and the Himalayan Mountains to the north, which boast the half dozen highest peaks in the world,

Harappan Name given to the city-states and the widespread Bronze Age culture they shared that were centered in the Indus River Valley and nearby rivers in northwest India.

including Mt. Everest at nearly 30,000 feet. The Himalayas, which stretch some 1,500 miles from east to west, inhibited regular communication between China and India. Just north of the Himalayas, the Tibetan Plateau is the source of great rivers, including the Indus and Ganges in India, the Yellow and Yangzi in China, and the Irrawaddy and Mekong in Southeast Asia, which eventually reach great plains and deltas. The land proved highly fertile in these river basins, allowing for productive farming and dense settlement. Rice and wheat became the staple crops for most peoples in both South and East Asia, and scavenging animals like chickens and pigs were more important food sources than beef cattle, which requires extensive pasture.

As with all societies, India's distinctive features resulted in part from its physical environment and climate. The fertile north Indian plains, watered by the Indus and Ganges Rivers, are relatively flat and so encouraged cultural unity and the formation of cities and kingdoms. By contrast, mountainous south India developed more cultural diversity. The southern peoples and languages differ greatly from those of north India, and south Indians have strong regional feelings. Other regions with highly distinctive local cultures include Bengal, framed by the delta of the Ganges River, and the fertile island of Sri Lanka (once known as Ceylon), just a few miles off India's southern tip.

The tropical climate affected Indian life. Some areas enjoy high rainfall, especially in the south and northeast, but much of the northwest is today desert. The annual rains, which usually fall in torrents within a period of two or three months, sustain life. But seasonal flooding can be a chronic problem. Water has been an especially sacred commodity in Indian life and thought, and a frequent subject of literature. Extensive rain forests once covered large sections of India and the island of Sri Lanka, but they have rapidly diminished in recent centuries.

The early Harappan farmers lived in mud houses and raised domesticated sheep, goats, and oxen. Because they had many domesticated cattle, most Indians also learned to con-

CHRONOLOGY	
Ancient India and Central Asia, 7000–600 B.C.E.	
7000–6000	Agriculture begins in Indus River Basin
2600–2500	Harappan cities established
2300–1900	Harappan cities at height
2200–1800	Oxus cities in Central Asia
1900–1750	Harappan society collapses in Indus Basin
1600–1400	Beginning of Aryan migrations into India
1500–1000	Aryan age of conquest and settlement
1000–700	Compilation of Brahmanas
1000–450	Height of Indo-Aryan synthesis
800–600	Compilation of Upanishads

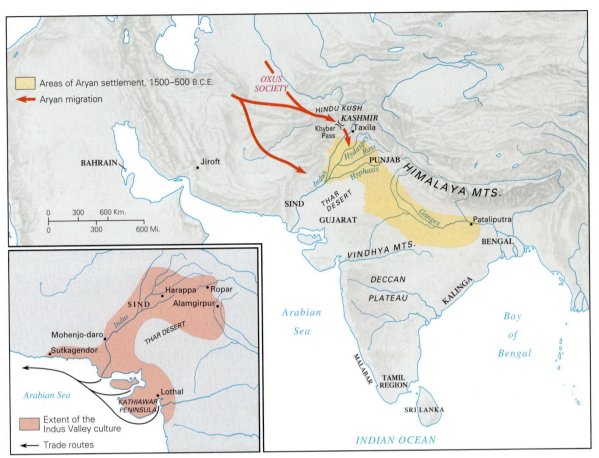

Map 2.2   **Harappan Culture and Aryan Migrations**
The Harappan culture emerged in the city-states of the Indus River Basin. They had collapsed by the time the Aryan peoples began migrating into India from Iran around 1500 B.C.E. and setting up states.

sume dairy products, including yogurt, a local invention. Thanks to surpluses of wheat and barley, by 3000 B.C.E. the population of the Indus Valley may have reached 1 million, and regional trading networks emerged, setting the stage for the emergence of cities.

Harappan Cities

Around 2600 B.C.E., nearly a millennium after the rise of Sumer), the first Indian urban society emerged from regional cultures in the Indus River Valley, a semiarid region similar ecologically to the Nile and Tigris-Euphrates Valleys. Along the banks of the Indus, which later inspired the English term *India*, a vibrant urban-based culture thrived for hundreds of years and planted some seeds for the rich Indian culture that endures to the present. Silt spread by regular river floods served as a natural fertilizer, while nearby forests provided enough wood for baking the bricks used in building cities. Like the Nile in Egypt, the flat, easily navigable Indus and its tributary rivers gave Harappan society considerable uniformity.

Over time cities grew up around the northwestern rivers, as well as along the coast (see Map 2.2). Most of the Harappan cities were in the Punjab (PUHN-jab) and Sind provinces of modern Pakistan, a crossroads of major trading routes, but

some were hundreds of miles to the west or east. The two major Indus cities, called by archaeologists Harappa and Mohenjo-Daro (moe-hen-joe-DAHR-oh), stood 400 miles apart. Over 1,500 cities and towns contained a total population of perhaps 5 million people at the zenith of Harappan society.

All the cities had many common features, in construction as well as in society, government, religion, and culture. The uniformity among Harappan cities suggests that the same central planning board designed them, and it reveals a society that valued order, organization, and cleanliness. As cities were re-built every half century or so, administrators used the same pattern as their predecessors, carefully laying them out using a north-south grid pattern with wide streets and large rectangular city blocks. They built most buildings of sturdy baked brick molded to a standardized size. Residential and commercial districts were separated from a smaller area for public affairs. Shops probably lined the main streets. The Harappan cities were broken up into large blocks, which may have separated occupational or kinship groups. This enclave pattern still characterized Indian cities in later centuries.

The cities offered many amenities. The largest city, Harappa, some 3⅓ miles in circumference, contained perhaps 80,000 people at its height. Massive brick ramparts 40 feet thick at their base partially protected it from the river waters

Ruins of Mohenjo-Daro The photo shows the great bath at Mohenjo-Daro. Like modern Indians, the Harappans valued bathing for hygienic and possibly religious reasons. (Josephine Powell)

and any potential human attackers. Large granaries provide evidence of wealth. These ventilated warehouses could store voluminous supplies, perhaps of wheat for the local population, or goods to be shipped downstream or imported from Mohenjo-Daro or even Sumeria. People in all the cities had exceptional housing for ancient times. Some blocks housed more affluent residents, who lived in spacious homes constructed on strong brick foundations with interior courtyards that provided considerable privacy, in a manner similar to elite Indian homes today. But even the common people enjoyed well-built accommodations.

The urban Harappans enjoyed the most advanced sanitation system in the ancient world and many strategically located public wells. Most houses had a bathroom as well as drains to carry away the wastewater. The covered drains, both inside homes and along the city streets, were a technological masterpiece and more sanitary than those found in many modern cities. Indeed, not until modern times did urban sanitation anywhere duplicate and then exceed Harappan models. The close attention to providing and carrying away water and the huge public baths suggest an emphasis on washing and personal cleanliness for ritual purity, which later became important in Indian religion.

Harappan Society and Its Beliefs

The Harappan governments, social system, and religious beliefs remain a puzzle. Clearly the people met the challenges of unruly rivers and unpredictable rains through cooperation, especially at the community level. Perhaps, like their trading partners in Sumer, the Harappan cities were ruled by priests or kings who were believed to communicate with divine forces. But the available evidence for an organized monarchy is thin, and there were no elaborate palaces or temples. Nonetheless, we have some hints of how the society was structured.

Political and Social Patterns Each city was probably independent, perhaps governed by some powerful guild of merchants or a council of commercial, landowning, and religious leaders who maintained peace with neighbors. There is no Harappan counterpart to the glorification of Egyptian kings and little evidence for much warfare or militarism. The ruins contain few weapons, suggesting that, in contrast to Mesopotamia, peace was the norm. But excavations reveal a privileged elite: some people owned beautiful objects of personal adornment, such as necklaces and beads, while others apparently lacked such valuable possessions. The ruins also contain many toys made from clay or wood, indicating a prosperous society that valued leisure for children.

Harappan society had unusual gender relations for that era, different from the rigid patriarchies that characterized Mesopotamia or China as governments grew more powerful. Apparently Harappan husbands moved into their wives' households after marriage, a practice that suggests a matrilineal system. Yet, some practices harmed women. One set of double graves suggests that at least some Harappans practiced a form of *sati* (suh-TEE), the custom of a widow killing herself by jumping onto the funeral pyre as her dead husband is being cremated.

Scholars debate the identity of the Harappan people. Most believe that those who created the society spoke a **Dravidian** (druh-VID-ee-uhn) language, although speakers of Iranian and possibly Indo-European languages may also have lived there. The term *Dravidian* refers to a specific language family, as well as to the people who speak these languages. Most modern Dravidian speakers live in southern India, where they are the great majority of the population.

Culture and Religion Harappan city-dwellers developed an artistic appreciation, mixing art with religion and even commerce. Harappans made small, square, clay seals, possibly used by merchants for branding their wares. Some of the seals contain brilliant portraits of indigenous animals, including bulls and water buffaloes as well as the tigers, elephants, and rhinoceros that inhabited the forests in ancient times. Pottery shows animal and geometric motifs. Small bronze statues of dancers suggest the Harappans enjoyed dance.

Most scholars argue that the Harappans created a written language by at least 2600 B.C.E., although a few believe abstract symbols or graffiti on pots may indicate an even more ancient writing. There are also some historians who question whether the Harappans had a true writing system comparable to the Mesopotamians and ancient Chinese. By Harappan times the seals, pottery, and various clay tablets contained some four hundred different signs that were completely unrelated to the scripts of Mesopotamia and Egypt. Perhaps the writing represents a mix of images representing concepts and phonetic symbols. Unfortunately, modern scholars have not been able to decipher the Indus language. Most likely many of the signs represent the personal or business names of merchants, and perhaps the commodities being sold.

Some Harappan religious notions contributed to Hinduism (HIN-doo-ism), a religion that developed after Harappan times. For example, one of the seals features a human figure sitting in a yogalike position, surrounded by various animals. He wears a horned headdress, an apparent tiger skin on his torso, and bangles on his arms. The figure also appears to have multiple faces, a regular feature of later Hindu icons, and may depict what later became the great Hindu god **Shiva** (SHEEV-uh) in one of his major roles as "Lord of the Beasts."

Harappan Seal The seal from Mohenjo-Daro features a humped bull. The writing at the top has yet to be deciphered. (J. M. Kenoyer/Courtesy, Department of Archaeology and Museums, Government of Pakistan)

Harappans apparently already worshiped Shiva in his dual role as god of destruction and of fertility and the harvest. Possibly the later Hindu notions of reincarnation and the endless wheel of life derived from Harappan beliefs.

Mother-goddess worship seems also to have been prominent in Harappan religious life, as it was in the Fertile Crescent and ancient Europe. Many small clay figurines have a female theme, and some figurines with exaggerated breasts and hips may have represented the mother goddess. Such artistic representations of voluptuous female deities remain common today in India. The goddesses symbolized earth and the life-bearing nature of women. Whereas a female orientation largely disappeared or became a minor element in the religions of many other societies, it remained prominent in India as Hinduism evolved over the centuries.

The Harappan Economy and the Wider World

The Harappan cities were hubs tied to surrounding regions, especially southwestern and Central Asia, through trade and transportation networks that fostered extensive contact. This foreign trade grew out of a vibrant and diverse local economy based on the cultivation of the staples barley and wheat and the production of cotton and metal products. Harappans were also among the pioneers in using animals for economic support. These innovations helped Harappan society to remain stable and prosperous for hundreds of years.

A highly sophisticated irrigation system and animal husbandry aided farming. Harappans or their ancestors domesticated the camel, zebu (oxen), elephant, and, perhaps most importantly, the chicken and water buffalo. The raising of fowl enriched the diet, and water buffalo and zebu greatly aided farming as draft animals. Possibly the Harappans worshiped

---

Dravidian A language family whose speakers are the great majority of the population in southern India.

Shiva The Hindu god of destruction and of fertility and the harvest.

these two animals; if they did, this worship may have been the basis for the later respect accorded cows in Hinduism.

Harappans invented cotton cloth and learned to produce cotton textiles for clothing, one of ancient India's major gifts to the world. For many centuries, cotton spinning and weaving remained the most significant Indian industry, producing materials for eager markets both at home and abroad. Cotton was probably a chief item in the interregional trading system, and it was shipped in bulk to Mesopotamia. Since there were few metals in the Indus Basin, the Harappans had to develop external sources of supply. With the metals obtained in exchange for cotton and other products, metallurgists made tools and art works of copper, bronze, and stone.

The desirable Harappan agricultural and manufactured products led to extensive foreign trade that linked India with the wider world of western and Central Asia. A huge dock, massive granaries, and specialized factories at the coastal port of Lothal reflected a high-volume maritime trade. Some Harappan trade outposts have been found along the Indian Ocean coast as far west as today's Iran-Pakistan border. The Harappans traded with Jiroft in Iran. A continuous trade with Sumer was particularly brisk when the dynamic king Sargon of Akkad ruled that land. Many Harappan seals found at the Mesopotamian city of Ur suggest a steady trade for over 300 years, between 2300 and 2000 B.C.E. Bahrain Island in the Persian Gulf functioned as a major crossroads for the Harappan-Sumerian trade. Indeed, the Persian Gulf was a major contact zone where ancient communication networks linked with each other and where ideas, technologies, and products from a wide area were exchanged.

Many different products were traded through these networks. The Harappans exported surplus food, cotton, timber products, copper, and gold, as well as luxury items such as pearls, precious stone products, ivory combs, beads, spices, peacock feathers, and inlay goods made from shell or bone. Many of these items found their way as far west as Palestine. The Harappans imported precious stones from southern India and silver, turquoise, and tin from Persia and Afghanistan. The imports from Mesopotamia probably included various perishable commodities.

The Decline and Collapse of Harappan Society

Eventually, Harappan society declined, for reasons not altogether clear. Sometime between 1900 and 1750 B.C.E. a combination of factors disrupted the urban environment and diminished the quality of life of this once wealthy, highly efficient, and powerful society. By 1700 B.C.E. most of the Harappan cities had been destroyed or abandoned, although a considerable rural population remained. The decay is obvious in the archaeological excavations. Seals and writing began to disappear around 1900 B.C.E. The careful grid pattern for city streets was abandoned, the drainage systems deteriorated, and even home sizes were reduced. Some evidence points to plundering and banditry. Squatters from elsewhere may have occupied the declining cities.

Harappan decline may have resulted from several factors. Perhaps the Harappans overextended their economic net-

works, putting too much pressure on the land and exhausting their resources. Some evidence points to ecological catastrophes resulting from climate change, deforestation, increased flooding, excessive irrigation of marginal lands, and soil deterioration. Apparently rainfall decreased significantly between 2000 and 1500 B.C.E., and one major river seems to have dried up entirely. These catastrophes probably led to economic breakdown. The crop surpluses that had long sustained the cities disappeared, and people abandoned farms. Perhaps disease epidemics weakened the population.

The end of some of the Indus Valley cities may have been sudden, the result perhaps of a disastrous flood. Some scholars think that sometime between 1900 and 1700 B.C.E., volcanic or earthquake activity in the mountains to the north generated a mud slide that may have temporarily dammed the Indus River or one of its tributaries, changing its course and unleashing an awesome flood that quickly overwhelmed low-lying cities and their surrounding farms. The hoards of jewelry, skeletons buried in debris, and cooking pots found strewn across kitchens indicate hastily abandoned homes. Floods were not unusual, and many people may have been trapped by such a catastrophe. Some centuries later a Greek visitor reported seeing a land with more than a thousand cities and villages abandoned after the Indus shifted to a new riverbed. The rising floodwaters may have been accompanied by more earthquakes, a double blow. The chaos of the last days spread rapidly along the river. Harappa, located on higher ground, and some other cities survived a while longer, although with much reduced populations.

The fate of the Harappan people and their cultures is unclear. Many remained in the area, and some Harappan material technology and symbolism survive there today. Some cities well east of the Indus Valley remained populated for several more centuries, practicing modified but diverse forms of Harappan culture until around 1300 B.C.E. Many Harappans may have migrated into central and southern India, mixing with local Dravidian populations. They carried with them a culture, technology, and agriculture that contributed to the Indian society to come. Whatever the causes of their decline, the calamities left the remaining Indus peoples weak and unable to resist later migrations of peoples from outside.

Central Asian Environments and Oxus Cities

Central Asia is the vast area of plains (**steppes**), deserts, and mountains that stretches from the Ural Mountains and Caspian Sea eastward to Tibet, western China, and Mongolia. Before modern times Central Asians played a role in history far greater than their relatively small populations would suggest, not only as invaders and sometimes conquerors but also as middlemen in the long-distance trade that developed on the land routes between China, India, the Middle East, and Europe.

Much of Central Asia offered a harsh living environment suitable only for the nomadic way of life. It was inhabited largely by people speaking Ural-Altaic languages, including various Turkish and Mongol tongues. Many different peoples speaking

steppes The plains of Central Asia.

Turkish or Persian languages lived in the region known as Turkestan, from east of the Caspian Sea to Xinjiang (SIN-john) on China's western frontier. Because of the geography and harsh living conditions, large-scale population movements and frequent warfare between competing tribal confederations became common. Most of the steppe societies were led by warrior chieftains, and many peoples were skilled horsemen and famous warriors, who used bronze and gold to make weapons and ornaments. The area's strategic location also promoted contact, and often conflict, with India and China. Some Central Asian peoples attacked and occasionally conquered northern China, and over the centuries various Central Asian peoples also migrated through the mountain ranges into northwest India.

Although much of Central Asia was steppe lands, some areas did support city life. We know much about most of the earliest urban societies such as Mesopotamia, Egypt, and China, and some about others such as the Olmecs of Mexico and the Harappans. These peoples have been restored to memory by many years of research. But archaeologists regularly find previously unknown sites, such as Jiroft in southern Iran, to expand our knowledge. In recent years these discoveries have revealed an early urban society in Central Asia, which some call the Oxus (OX-uhs), after the river that runs through the area.

The Oxus society apparently thrived between 2200 and 1800 B.C.E., about the time that the Harappan culture was at its height. The Oxus people built a number of walled cities with mud-brick buildings and possibly temples or palaces around desert oases in what is now Uzbekistan and Turkmenistan. Since they had a somewhat wetter climate than now, the people grew wheat and barley. They also forged bronze axes, carved figurines of women from stone and ivory, and decorated pottery with elaborate designs. A tiny stamp seal with letter-like symbols dated to 2300 B.C.E. is evidence for writing, and so far the writing has not been linked to any other society.

The Oxus society may have spread over a wide area. The cities, perhaps independent city-states, were situated along the "Silk Road" trade routes between India and China, suggesting that this trade may be older than is often thought. But the relationship of the Oxus cities to China, India, and Mesopotamia is unknown. Some scholars think they were closely linked to the Harappans and probably traded with China, Jiroft, and Mesopotamia. Eventually the cities were abandoned and, over the centuries, buried by sand.

SECTION SUMMARY
- The earliest Indian urban society emerged in the Indus River Valley around 2600 B.C.E.
- The Harappans had well-planned cities with advanced sanitation, a culture that gave women high status, and a written language.
- The Harappans invented cotton cloth
- Harappan cities enjoyed extensive foreign trade with western and Central Asia.
- The steppes of Central Asia were home to mostly horsemen, but evidence of an urban society has been discovered on the Oxus River.

The Aryans and a New Indian Society, 1500–1000 B.C.E.

How did the Aryan migrations reshape Indian society?

Throughout India's long history, many people migrated from elsewhere into the subcontinent, some of them conquering parts of India, and the assimilation of these various newcomers resulted in an increasingly diverse Indian society. One such group of invaders were the **Aryans** (AIR-ee-unzs), Indo-European-speaking nomadic pastoralists who migrated from Iran into northwest India, expanded across northern India, and introduced new traditions to the area. The Aryan Age, which lasted from around 1500 to 1000 B.C.E., built the foundation for a new society that mixed Aryan culture with the traditions of the indigenous peoples, including the Dravidians. Despite regular contact with western, Central, and Southeast Asia, the patterns that developed in the Aryan Age and the centuries which followed were so distinctive and enduring that India even today is unlike any other society.

The Aryan Peoples and the Vedas

Most scholars believe that the Aryans began migrating by horse-drawn chariot from Iran (the Persian word for "Aryan") or Central Asia into northwestern India between 1600 and 1400 B.C.E., after the collapse of the Harappan cities. Other Indo-Europeans had already settled in Iran and Mesopotamia. The earliest arrivals were probably pastoralists, but later migrants might have been farmers. The migration to India came when rainfall in the Indus region was increasing again, improving economic conditions. Some modern historians and Indian nationalists argue that Aryan settlement in India was far older, dating perhaps to 4000 B.C.E., and that the Harappans may have been Aryans, but most historians remain skeptical of this view.

In the conventional view favored by most historians, the Aryans arrived in small groups over several centuries, bringing with them a rich oral literature and unusual ideas about government, society, and religion. For the next 500 years, the Aryans expanded throughout northern India as more arrived from Iran and perhaps Central Asia. But archaeologists have found little material evidence, such as pots or weapons, that might tell us more about Aryan migration and settlement. Furthermore, unlike the Chinese and Greeks, ancient Indians never developed a tradition of historiography, the study and writing of history, perhaps because their conceptions of time and the relationship of human society to universal forces emphasized the temporary nature of existence.

Much of what we know about the ancient Aryans comes from their literature, the **Vedas** (VAY-duhs) ("books of knowledge"). A

Aryans Indo-European-speaking nomadic pastoralists who migrated from Iran into northwest India.

Vedas The Aryans' "books of knowledge," the principal source of religious belief for Hindus: a vast collection of sacred hymns to the gods and thoughts about religion, philosophy, and magic.

vast collection of sacred hymns to the gods and thoughts about religion, philosophy, and magic, the Vedas were based on oral accounts carefully preserved by bards, the memory experts of each Indo-European tribe, through a vibrant oral tradition. The Vedas reflected the worldview of the priestly class and were already old when written down. They are the principal early source of Hindu religious belief.

From the Vedas we can infer that the Aryans were organized into tribes that frequently moved their settlements. Their class system consisted of warriors, priests, and commoners. Unlike the Harappans, before settling in India the Aryans apparently never fashioned sewer systems, baked bricks, developed writing, or crafted figurines. They were a cattle-raising people, as is reflected in one of the hymns: "A bard am I, my father a leech, And my mother a grinder of corn. Diverse in means, but all wishing wealth, Alike for cattle we strive."[15] They were also a militaristic people who harnessed horses to chariots and skillfully wielded bows and arrows and bronze axes. They had fought and trekked their way through blistering deserts and snowy mountains to reach India. Some Vedas celebrate Aryan victories against fortified settlements inhabited by peoples of inferior military technology, probably including Dravidians, many of whom had darker skins than the Aryans: "For fear of thee fled the dark-hued races, scattered abroad, deserting their possessions."[16] The various Aryan tribes could unite against a common enemy, but most of the time they fought against each other.

In India the Aryans mixed their language with those of local people, creating **Sanskrit** (SAN-skrit), the classical written and spoken language of north India, through which the Vedas were preserved during the first millennium B.C.E. By the fourth century B.C.E., however, vernacular (everyday) Indo-European spoken languages like Hindi and Bengali had become dominant in north India, and Sanskrit gradually became mostly a written language for religious and literary works. Since few Indians today learn to write or speak Sanskrit, some fear the language may eventually become extinct.

Early Aryan Government, Gender Relations, and Social Life

The early Aryan political and social structure was tribal and patriarchal, and marked by persistent conflict. Each tribe was governed by an autocratic male, known as a *raja*, who sought as much power for himself and his group as possible. The most powerful tribe seems to have been the Bharata (BAA-ray-tuh), which is also the official Sanskrit name for India today. Later the *Mahabharata* (MA-huh-BAA-ray-tuh) ("Great Bharata"), an Aryan epic and the world's longest poem, spun a complex and entertaining tale of many cousins and their titanic battles for supremacy.

Sanskrit The classical language of north India, originally both written and spoken but now reserved for religious and literary writing.
Mahabharata ("Great Bharata") An Aryan epic and the world's longest poem.

The Vedas suggest that Aryan family structure, like the tribal organization, was patriarchal, with the father dominating his wives and children. In the centuries to follow, both male supremacy and a hierarchy based on age became the standard Indian family pattern. The Aryans developed a living pattern known as the joint family, also common in China, in which the wives of all the sons moved into the larger patriarchal household, which included members from three or even four generations. The Vedas praised heroic sons who gained honor through battle. The status of Aryan women changed with time. The early Aryans educated both daughters and sons in the Vedas. One Vedic hymn encouraged women to speak publicly, and women may have composed some of the hymns. Several centuries later women became more restricted and daughters less valued. They needed to obtain dowries (gifts for the prospective in-laws) in order to marry, could not participate in the sacrifices to gods, and did not inherit property.

The Vedas also reveal something of Aryan recreational interests. The leading sports seem to have been horse-drawn chariot racing and gambling. Both dice and chess were invented in India, and many dice carved out of nuts have been found in the ruins of Mohenjo-Daro. Gambling features prominently in the *Mahabharata*; one raja loses his kingdom through his fondness for games of chance. The Aryans may also have used drugs like hashish, perhaps mixed into drinks, and were fond of wine. They loved music and used such instruments as lutes, flutes, and drums. Some Vedas were especially designed for singing. In the centuries that have followed, song and dance have been an integral component of Indian religious worship and ritual.

Aryan Religion

As sacred texts, the Vedas contained considerable information about Aryan religion, the significance of various gods, and the role of priests. They confirm that Aryan religious views were similar to those of the Aryans' Hittite cousins in western Asia. Each Aryan tribe boasted its own bards, poets who were also priests. Because they alone had memorized the Vedic hymns, these bards presided over sacrifices and rituals. The oldest and most important Veda, the *Rig Veda* ("Verses of Knowledge"), was probably composed between 1500 and 1000 B.C.E. It contains over 1,000 poems written in Sanskrit, most of them soliciting the favor of Aryan gods. The *Rig Veda* is the world's earliest surviving example of literature by any Indo-European people.

The Aryans worshiped a pantheon of nature gods, to whom they offered sacrifices. The *Rig Veda* describes some thirty-three deities, several of which are prominent. They are led by the thunderbolt-wielding war-god Indra (INN-druh), who is ever youthful, heroic, and victorious and who is credited with defeating a demon, who probably symbolizes the power of those the Aryans defeated in their conquests. There were also powerful gods of universal order and justice, fire, and immortality. Many poems celebrate the awesome power of the deities, as in the following tribute to the storm-gods:

You are terrible and powerful, O storm gods. You bring everlasting rain in the desert. Dark rain clouds shroud the sky, Turning day into night, drenching the earth. And when the storm gods shout, the earth trembles. Men reel and shudder. The song is in my mouth! It praises the storm gods! They are beautiful and terrible. Their glory is everlasting.[17]

Like the Hinduism that later developed, Aryan religion also included speculations on the deepest mysteries of existence. One poem, the "Hymn of Creation," is one of the most ancient expressions of doubt or at least questions about the creation of the universe and the nature of knowledge: "Who really knows? Who will here proclaim it? Whence was this creation? The gods came afterwards, with the creation of the universe. Who then really knows whence it has arisen?"[18] This hymn also suggests a time before time when there was no space or sky, night or day, life or death. Then, in a kind of Big Bang, the cosmos was created by the power of heat (see Chapter 1).

It is unclear when or why many Indians began to consider the cow forbidden as food, but the earlier Harappans seem to have worshiped bulls. Early Aryan views were completely different. Although cows were highly prized and kept as currency, the Aryans of the Vedas also consumed beef and held little reverence for these animals. Eventually, however, the practice of worshiping cows and avoiding beef became widespread even among Aryans.

Aryan Expansion and State Building in North India

The Aryans eventually moved eastward, building kingdoms and mixing with local peoples. As the Indus region once again entered a cycle of reduced rainfall, many Aryans migrated into the wetter Ganges (GAN-geez) Valley. During this time they changed through conflict, cooperation, and assimilation with the peoples they encountered. The Aryan occupation of the Ganges and adjacent areas of north India took half a millennium, from 1000 to around 450 B.C.E. As the Aryans spread out and settled down, they eventually adopted Dravidian systems of farming, land tenure and taxation, village structure, and some religious concepts, but they also contributed their language, social system, and many religious beliefs to the mix.

Throughout north India, city development and economic growth encouraged political consolidation. The tribes of early times became kingdoms. By the sixth century B.C.E. sixteen major Aryan kingdoms stretched from Bengal westward to the fringes of Afghanistan, and power had shifted from the Indus Basin to the central Ganges region, where most kingdoms were located. However, kings did not have unlimited power; though Vedic writings describe their growing power and their elaborate court rituals, they were still advised by councils of warriors. Thus no kingdom was yet strong enough to conquer all the others and create a unified government for all north India. That unity would not come until the establishment of the Mauryan Empire by a Ganges state in 321 B.C.E. (see Chapter 7).

The ancient Aryans never ceased engaging in military conflict. The *Mahabharata*, written down around 400 B.C.E. but reflecting life around 1000 B.C.E., was, like Homer's *Iliad* and Mayan records, drenched in the blood of endless struggles over succession and for supremacy between two rival kingdoms and their leaders. These epic battles suggest that states were continuously expanding and consolidating their control of nearby territories, which the rulers administered from their capital cities. The *Ramayana* (ruh-MA-yawn-uh) ("The Story of Rama"), another old Aryan epic written down sometime around 500 B.C.E., may be an allegory about the conflicts resulting from the extension of Aryan power into southern India.

Aryan Warfare Vedic stories remain popular in modern India. This scene from an old temple wall of Aryan warfare depicts embattled gods and demons from the *Mahabharata*.
(Eliot Elisofon/Getty Images)

SECTION SUMMARY

■ The Indo-European Aryans, a cattle-raising tribal people, migrated into north India 3,500 years ago.

■ The Vedas, written in Sanskrit, are religious writings that reveal information on the Aryan religion and their patriarchal culture.

■ Aryan priests supervised the worship of the religion's many nature gods.

■ Eventually Aryans built kingdoms in the Ganges River Basin.

✦ The Mixing of Dravidian and Aryan Cultures, 1000–600 B.C.E.

How did Indian society and the Hindu religion emerge from the mixing of Aryan and local cultures?

The encounters that resulted from Aryan migration brought together several very different peoples and cultures, reconfiguring Indian society. Over many centuries a fusion of Aryan and Dravidian cultures occurred, a complex process that historians have labeled the **Indo-Aryan synthesis**. The mixing explains why many aspects of Aryan culture, such as the joyous and lusty consumption of beef and liquor, differed dramatically from the traits of later Indian society. The mixing forged a distinctive new social system and Hinduism, a religion of diverse beliefs and traditions. To be sure, the Aryans had a greater impact in the north. The mostly Dravidian south, where society was organized around rice farming, retained its own languages and adopted writing systems very different from Sanskrit. However, enough cultural exchange between north and south took place so that Indian society, despite great regional variety, developed many common features and considerable cultural unity.

The Roots of the Caste System

The Indo-Aryan synthesis modified the social structure, which became increasingly complex as the expanding Aryans integrated diverse peoples into their network. A four-tiered class division emerged that comprised the **brahmans** (BRAH-munz), or priests; the **kshatriyas** (kuh-SHOT-ree-uhs), the warriors and landowners, who were headed by the rajas; the

vaisyas (VIGH-shuhs), or merchants and artisans; and the **sudras** (SOO-druhs), mostly poorer farmers, farm workers, and menial laborers. The Aryans allocated the three highest categories to themselves. In fact, genetic studies suggest that upper-class Indians are more closely related to Europeans and Persians than to lower-class Indians. The top class, the priests, enjoyed many special privileges as guardians and interpreters of sacred knowledge. Over time the lowest tier, the sudras, mostly of non-Aryan origins, were locked into a permanent low status and were prohibited from reading or even studying the magically potent Vedic hymns.

The system was based on prejudice and religion. The Sanskrit term for a class division, or, in Hindu terms, ritual status, was *varna* (VARN-uh), which meant "[skin] color." The term suggests that the lighter-skinned Aryans wanted to maintain their domination over, and purity from "pollution" by, the darker-skinned indigenous people, whom they originally viewed as slaves. Many centuries later, Portuguese visitors referred to the system as *castas* ("pure"); hence the origin of the Western term *caste*. Aryans used religion to justify this class system. One of the hymns in the *Rig Veda* attributed the classes to the Lord of Beings, the originator of the universe:

> When they divided the Man, into how many parts did they divide him? What was his mouth, what were his arms, what were his thighs and his feet called? The brahman was his mouth, of his arms was made the kshatriya. His thighs became the vaisya, of his feet were born the sudra.[19]

Gradually, over many centuries, this four-tiered class hierarchy evolved into the immensely complex **caste system**. Each hereditary social class was restricted to certain occupations, and members of a class were also restricted in their relations with members of other castes. For example, only members of closely allied groups could intermarry, a practice that probably reflected the Aryan fear of losing power. Below the caste system were a large group of outcasts (**pariahs**) or untouchables, labeled such because the higher castes considered their touch defiling. The pariahs performed tasks considered "unclean," such as tanning animal hides and removing manure. This four-tiered system differed in many respects from the modern-caste system and remained weak in some regions, but the basic caste structure was firmly in place by around 500 B.C.E. Although the system was never rigid and changed over time, the division of most Indians into castes with different functions and status provided the basic structure of Hindu society for several millennia.

Indo-Aryan synthesis   The fusion of Aryan and Dravidian cultures in India over many centuries.

brahmans   The priests, the highest-ranking caste in Hindu society.

kshatriyas   Warriors and landowners headed by the rajas in the Hindu class system.

vaisyas   The merchants and artisans in the Hindu class system.

sudras   The poorer farmers, farm workers, and menial laborers in the Hindu class system.

caste system   The four-tiered Hindu social system comprising hereditary social classes that restrict the occupation of members and their relations with members of other castes.

pariahs   The large group of outcasts or untouchables below the official Hindu castes.

Hindu Values in the Bhagavad Gita

The *Bhagavad Gita*, a philosophical poem in the *Mahabharata*, helped shape the ethical traditions of India while providing Hindus with a practical guide to everyday life. The following excerpt is part of a dialogue between the god Krishna (Vishnu) and the poem's conflicted hero, the warrior Arjuna (are-JUNE-ah), on the eve of a great battle in which Arjuna will slaughter his uncles, cousins, teachers, and friends. The reading summarizes some of Krishna's advice in justifying the battle. Krishna suggests that Arjuna must follow his destiny, for while the physical body is impermanent, the soul is eternal. The slain will be reborn. Furthermore, humans are responsible for their own destiny through their behavior and mental discipline. They also, like Arjuna, need to fulfill their obligations to society.

The wise grieve neither for the living nor for the dead. There has never been a time when you and I and the kings gathered here have not existed, nor will there ever be a time when we will cease to exist. As the same person inhabits the body through childhood, youth, and old age, so too at the time of death he attains another body. The wise are not deluded by these changes.

When the senses contact sense objects, a person experiences cold or heat, pleasure or pain. These experiences are fleeting; they come and go. Bear them patiently.... Those who are not affected by these changes, who are the same in pleasure and pain, are truly wise and fit for immortality. Assert your strength and realize this!

The impermanent has no reality; reality lies in the eternal. Those who have seen the boundary between these two have attained the end of all knowledge. Realize that which pervades the universe and is indestructible; no power can affect this unchanging, imperishable reality. The body is mortal but he who dwells in the body is immortal and immeasurable.... As a man abandons worn-out clothes and acquires new ones, so when the body is worn out a new one is acquired by the Self, who lives within.... Death is inevitable for the living; birth is inevitable for the dead. Since these are unavoidable, you should not sorrow....

Now listen to the principles of yoga [mental and physical discipline to free the soul]. By practicing these you can break through the bonds of karma. On this path effort never goes to waste, and there is no failure.... When you keep thinking about sense objects, attachment comes. Attachment breeds desire, the lust of possession that burns to anger....

They are forever free who renounce all selfish desires and break free from the ego-cage of "I," "me," and "mine" to be united with the Lord. This is the supreme state. Attain to this, and pass from death to immortality.... Strive constantly to serve the welfare of the world; by devotion to selfless work one attains the supreme goal of life. Do your work with the welfare of others always in mind.

THINKING ABOUT THE READING

1. What key aspects of Hindu thought are revealed in the poem?
2. How do the attitudes toward life, death, and desire influence the behavior of individuals?
3. What are some of the viewpoints in this ancient poem that might be considered universal in their appeal?

Source: Lynn H. Nelson and Patrick Peebles, eds., *Classics of Eastern Thought* (San Diego: Harcourt Brace Jovanovich, 1991), pp. 43–47. From *The Bhagavad Gita*, trans. by Eknath Easwaran, founder of the Blue Mountain Center of Meditation, copyright 1855. Reprinted by permission of the Nilgiri Press: www.easwaran.org.

Indo-Aryan Social Life and Gender Relations

The Vedas reveal some of the expectations and attitudes of ancient Indian society. For example, contained within the *Mahabharata* is a philosophical poem called the **Bhagavad Gita** (BAA-guh-vad GEE-tuh) ("Lord's Song"), the most treasured piece of ancient Hindu literature (see Witness to the Past: Hindu Values in the *Bhagavad Gita*). It encourages people to do their duty to their superiors and kinsmen resolutely and unselfishly. It also explains that death is not a time of grief because the soul is indestructible. The other great ancient epic, the *Ramayana,* resembles the *Odyssey* of Homer in that it tells of a hero's wanderings while his wife remains chaste and loyal. The *Ramayana* conveys insights into the character of court life, which apparently involved endless intrigues.

We know something also of gender relations in Indo-Aryan society. The *Ramayana* illustrates the early Hindu notion of perfect manhood and womanhood through the main characters: Rama, the husband, and Sita (SEE-tuh), his wife. The couple demonstrate mutual loyalty, devotion, truthfulness, and self-sacrifice. But Sita is also patient, faithful, and pure in supporting her husband and family. The Sita ideal strongly influenced cultural expectations of womanhood, and Sita became a familiar figure of strength and affection, especially in north India.

Compared to the Aryan-dominated north, women seem to have enjoyed a higher status in mostly Dravidian south India. There both matriarchal and matrilineal traditions persisted for centuries, and goddesses remained especially central to religious life. Dravidian women also exercised some economic power and owned property. But even in the north during the Vedic Age, some women mastered the Vedas and mixed freely with men.

Bhagavad Gita ("Lord's Song") A poem in the *Mahabharata* that is the most treasured piece of ancient Hindu literature.

Indo-Aryan Technology and Economy

Indo-Aryan technology derived from both foreign and local developments. The Hittites might have passed iron technology along to fresh waves of Indo-Europeans migrating into India. Certainly the Aryans used iron, initially for weapons and horse harnesses, once they reached iron-rich districts in the Ganges region around 1000 B.C.E. But some metalworking derived from pre-Aryan cultures, which worked bronze and used gold in jewelry and ritual sacrifices.

Soon after they arrived in India the Aryans made the transition from a largely nomadic pastoral economy to a combination of pastoral and agricultural pursuits that emphasized grains like barley and wheat. One Veda prays: "Successfully let the good ploughshares' thrust part the earth, successfully let the ploughman follow the beasts of draft."[20] The use of plows and the expansion of irrigated agriculture greatly increased the available food supply and thus fostered population growth. India's population in 500 B.C.E. has been estimated at 25 million, including 15 million in the Ganges Valley.

Hinduism: A New Religion of Diverse Roots

Although Indian religion has changed much since the Harappans, it has remained unique. Nothing in the Middle East or Europe remotely resembles basic Indian beliefs such as reincarnation. These are part of the bedrock of Indian society, molding thought and daily lives. What modern Indians would clearly recognize as Hinduism had probably not fully formed until the second half of the first millennium B.C.E., and perhaps not until the early centuries of the Common Era. But the foundations were clearly established in ancient times. Hinduism can be seen historically as a synthesis of Aryan beliefs with Harappan and other Dravidian traditions that developed over many centuries. As the religion became more complex, it probed ever more deeply into cosmic mysteries. Eventually this spiritual quest resulted in a period of ferment and questioning.

Religious Synthesis   The religious system became one of the richest and most complex in the world, with gods, devotions, and celebrations drawn from various regional and village cultures. The Aryans gradually turned from their old tribal gods to deities of probable Harappan origin such as Shiva. Hence the rise of the great gods of Hinduism: *Brahma* (BRA-ma) (the Creator of life); *Vishnu* (VISH-noo)(the Preserver of life); and *Shiva* (among other functions, the destroyer of life). In popular worship Vishnu and Shiva have had the most devotees. Vishnu is a benevolent deity who works continually for the welfare of the world. Shiva personifies the life force and embodies both constructive and destructive power.

Earlier Aryan nature worship was soon transformed by a relentless desire to understand and control the larger cosmic forces. Hinduism never developed a rigid core of beliefs uniting all followers; instead, it loosely linked together diverse practices and cults that shared a reverence for the Vedas. For over 3,000 years ago Indians posed questions and offered possible answers to cosmic mysteries that even today remain little understood. The Vedic thinkers were influenced by pre-Aryan meditation techniques and mystical practices of possible Harappan origin, such as those that were later known as *yoga*. In the eternal quest for divine favor, the Hindus came to believe that everyone must behave properly so that the universe can function in an orderly manner. They came to see human existence as temporary and fleeting and only the realm of the gods as eternal.

Religious Explorations   The Vedas underwent three major stages of development to become accepted as revealed literature. The earliest stage included the poems and hymns in the *Rig Veda* and several other collections. A half millennium later, from around 1000 to 700 B.C.E., a series of prose commentaries on the earlier Vedas appeared. They elaborated on the meaning of the Vedic literature and also prescribed proper procedures for sacrificing to and worshiping the gods. These commentaries are called the **Brahmanas** (BRA-ma-nus), since they emphasize the central role of the priests, or brahmans ("those who chant the sacred words"). At this time, the prevailing religion can be termed Brahmanism. The authors of the *Ramayana* portrayed the powerful force of religious law in dictating proper behavior, even for the monarch.

Later still, between 800 and 600 B.C.E., a third group of more philosophical writings appeared, mostly in the form of 108 poetic dialogues known as the **Upanishads** (oo-PAHN-ih-shahds)("sitting around a teacher"). These writings, which speculated on the ultimate truth about the creation of life, offered a striking contrast to the emphasis on ritual, devotion, and ethics in the older works. One mystic pleaded, "From the unreal lead me to the real. From the darkness lead me to light. From death lead me to immortality."[21] These writings also gave women more importance; for example, the dialogues include the story of an exceptionally learned female. The *Upanishads* probably came out of the same atmosphere of questioning, ferment, and rebellion against priestly power that produced the great religious teacher Buddha in the sixth century B.C.E.

The religious atmosphere of ancient India seems to have been dynamic, with growing tensions between competing ideas about the nature of existence and appropriate human behavior. The *Ramayana* contrasts the luxury-filled decadence of the royal courts with the austere existence of hermit-sages dwelling in the forest and practicing forms of meditation and mysticism. By the middle of the first millennium B.C.E. the debate and disenchantment that produced the *Upanishads* resulted in much more far-reaching critiques of the brahman-led system. The movements that developed out of this ferment transformed the framework of Indian religion, fostering both Buddhism and the modified form of Brahmanism known today as Hinduism, as we shall see in Chapter 7.

Brahmanas   Commentaries on the Vedas that emphasize the role of priests (brahmans).

Upanishads   Ancient Indian philosophical writings that speculated on the ultimate truth about the creation of life.

SECTION SUMMARY

■ Aryan and local cultures mixed together over the centuries and eventually produced a unique four-tiered caste system.

■ The *Bhagavad Gita,* which emphasizes one's earthly duty and the soul's immortality, became the most treasured piece of Indian literature.

■ Hinduism developed over many centuries but never became a rigid belief structure.

■ The philosophical *Upanishads* represented a departure from the emphasis on priestly ritual.

Online Study Center ACE the Test

Chapter Summary

Mesopotamian society and early Indian society were two of humankind's first experiments with farming, cities, and states. While varying in size, complexity, and duration, both used technologies that were unheard of in Neolithic times. These ancient societies also developed different religious notions, social systems, and political structures. They were shaped, at least in part, by the challenges and opportunities of flood-prone river valleys: Mesopotamian society arose in the Fertile Crescent between the Tigris and Euphrates Rivers, and Harappan society arose in the Indus River Valley. Mesopotamians introduced the first cities and states, the cuneiform system of writing, bronze metalworking, mathematics, and science. Their many kingdoms were united under several different empires. Mesopotamia was also part of the early trade networks linking the Mediterranean Basin with India. Such connections among societies were a crucial and continuing part of history.

One of the oldest Eurasian urban societies emerged in northwest India, where the Harappan people built peaceful, bustling, and well-planned cities. They produced cotton products and developed sophisticated sanitation systems. The Harappans also participated in a trading network that reached into the Fertile Crescent and Central Asia, where the Oxus cities flourished for several centuries. After the Harappan collapse, Aryan migrants established political control. The mixing of Harappan and Aryan cultures shaped a new Indian society. This Indo-Aryan synthesis established the foundation for a caste system and for the religion of Hinduism, whose holy books interweaved many Harappan gods with Aryan stories and poems.

Online Study Center
Improve Your Grade Flashcards

Key Terms

Fertile Crescent	Harappan	Aryans
ziggurat	Dravidian	Vedas
patriarchy	Shiva	Sanskrit
cuneiform	steppes	*Mahabharata*

Indo-Aryan synthesis	vaisyas	*Bhagavad Gita*
brahmans	sudras	*Brahmanas*
kshatriyas	caste system	*Upanishads*
	pariahs	

Suggested Reading

Books

Allchin, F. R. *The Archaeology of Early Historic South Asia: The Emergence of Cities and States.* Cambridge: Cambridge University Press, 1995. A scholarly overview.

Basham, A. L. *The Wonder That Was India.* 3rd ed. London: Macmillan, 1968 (reprinted 1999 by Rupa and Company, New Delhi). An older study but still the best survey of premodern India.

Bottero, Jean. *Everyday Life in Ancient Mesopotamia.* Baltimore: Johns Hopkins University Press, 2001. Summarizes recent discoveries about Mesopotamian social and cultural life.

Crawfurd, Harriet. *Sumer and the Sumerians.* 2nd ed. Cambridge: Cambridge University Press, 2004. An up-to-date and interdisciplinary summary of the achievements of the Sumerians.

Dunstan, William E. *The Ancient Near East.* New York: Harcourt Brace, 1998. Designed for the general reader, this work makes sense of the confusing array of states and empires in western Asia.

Kenoyer, Jonathan Mark. *Ancient Cities of the Indus Valley Civilization.* New York: Oxford University Press, 1998. A valuable, well-illustrated summary of the most recent discoveries.

McIntosh, Jane. *A Peaceful Realm: The Rise and Fall of the Indus River Civilization.* Boulder, Colo.: Westview, 2001. A comprehensive, well-illustrated survey of the Harappans, based on recent archaeological research.

Sandars, N. K. (translator). *The Epic of Gilgamesh.* New York: Penguin Books, 1972. Easy introduction to the ancient Mesopotamian world view.

Stiebing, William H. *Ancient Near Eastern History and Culture.* New York: Longman, 2003. An up-to-date survey of ancient western Asia, Egypt, and the eastern Mediterranean.

Thapar, Romila. *Early India from the Origins to AD 1300.* Berkeley: University of California Press, 2002. A valuable revision of the standard history of early India, detailed and comprehensive.

Wolpert, Stanley. *A New History of India.* 7th ed. New York: Oxford University Press, 2003. One of the most readable survey texts.

Websites

Exploring Ancient World Cultures (http://eawe.evansville.edu/index/htm). Excellent site run by Evansville University, with essays and links on the ancient Near East and Europe.

Indus Valley Civilization (http://ancienthistory.about.com/cs/indusvalleyciv/). Gives access to many sites and links on ancient India, run by About.com.

Internet Ancient History Sourcebook (http://www.fordham.edu/halsall/ancient/asbook.html). Exceptionally rich collection of links and primary source readings.

Internet Indian History Sourcebook (http://www.fordham.edu/halsall/india/indiasbook.html). An invaluable collection of sources and links on ancient India.

CHAPTER 3

Ancient Societies in Africa and the Mediterranean, 5000–600 B.C.E.

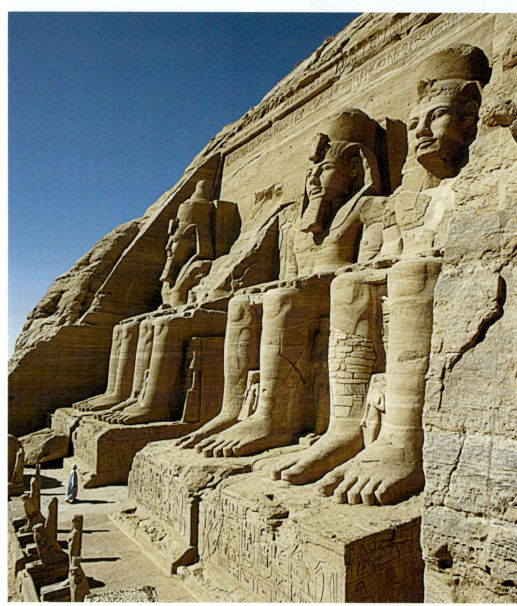

Online Study Center

This icon will direct you to interactive activities and study materials on the website: college.hmco.com/pic/lockard1e

Abu Simbel The great temple with its colossal statues at Abu Simel overlooking the Nile River in Egypt was built as a monument to honor the powerful thirteenth century B.C.E. pharaoh Rameses the Great, who presided over empire building and economic prosperity. (George Holton/Photo Researcher, Inc.)

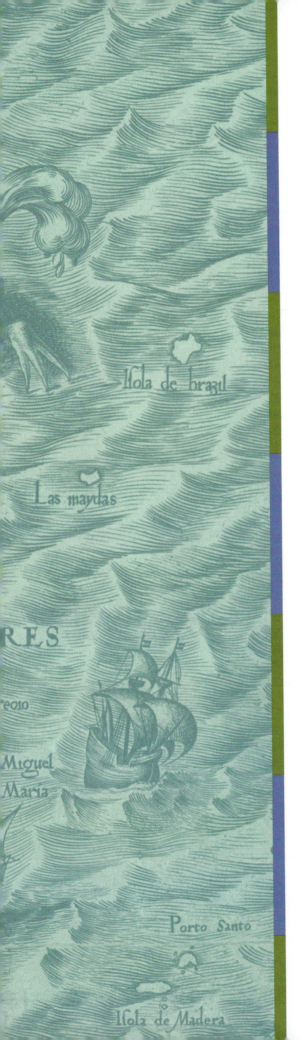

Behold, the heart of his majesty was satisfied with making a very great monument; never has happened the like since the beginning. He made it as an everlasting fortress. It is wrought with gold and many costly stones.

TEMPLE INSCRIPTION AT THEBES, EGYPT, FOURTEENTH CENTURY B.C.E.[1]

Around 1460 B.C.E. Queen Hatshepsut (hat-SHEP-soot), the powerful and gifted ruler of Egypt, issued a decree to build a temple in the city of Thebes on the banks of the Nile River for the glory of the highest god, Amon-Re (AH-muhn-RAY). The temple would be like none before it, with terraced gardens planted with fragrant myrrh. But no such trees grew in Egypt. To obtain them, the queen ordered an expedition to be sent down the Red Sea to the fabled land of Punt (poont) on the coast of northeast Africa, probably modern Somalia (so-MAH-lee-uh). Egyptian ships had previously visited Punt at various times, including 500 years earlier. On that journey, three thousand men, mostly slaves, carried building materials 90 miles from the Nile to the Red Sea, where they constructed a ship. With no charts to guide it, the ship sailed through unfamiliar seas to Punt and returned with riches. Now Hatshepsut, for reasons of commerce, religion, and personal ambition, ordered that contact with Punt to be renewed.

The new expedition was extremely successful, returning with myrrh trees for the temple, jewels, incense, and other treasures. Like other rulers before and after her, Queen Hatshepsut commemorated her achievements with inscriptions and pictures, in this case by summarizing the results of the trading expedition on the walls of her magnificent new temple:

> *The loading of the cargo-boats with great marvels of the Land of Punt, with all the good woods of the divine land, with ebony, with pure ivory, with pure gold, with apes, monkeys, hounds, with skins of leopards, with inhabitants of the country and their children. Never were brought such things to any king, since the world was.*[2]

To obtain such luxury products, Egyptians became shipbuilders and sailors, and with their frequent sea-going voyages they became connected to a much wider world. Foreign trade made Egypt the ancient world's wealthiest society.

Among the Egyptians and some other African and eastern Mediterranean societies—including the Hebrews, Minoans (mih-NO-uhns), Mycenaeans (my-suh-NEE-uhns), Phoenicians (fo-NEE-shuhns), and early Greeks—we see the same kind of dramatic changes resulting from contact among different peoples that fostered urban life in Mesopotamia and India. A major ancient society, Egypt greatly influenced neighboring peoples. In turn it was influenced by societies such as Kush (koosh) to the south and the Phoenicians of Lebanon, both societies known for their commercial riches. This interaction among neighbors promoted cultural development in the Nile valley and the Mediterranean, much as it did in Mesopotamia and Harappa. Like the large river valleys of the Tigris-Euphrates and Indus, the Nile valley also made possible the population growth and social organization necessary for people to expand their domination over nature and to create large state structures and elaborate religious systems.

Ancient peoples also created unique and complex societies elsewhere in Africa and the eastern Mediterranean. Diverse sub-Saharan African societies developed or borrowed farming and metal technologies, and some built cities. However, unlike Egypt's spectacular pyramids, over the centuries many of the sub-Saharan people's monuments and buildings were covered by rain forest, blowing sand, or wayward rivers. This was not the case on the islands and shores of the eastern Mediterranean, where various peoples traded widely, built cities whose ruins still interest visitors, and developed religious concepts that endure to this day.

FOCUS QUESTIONS

1. How did the environment shape ancient Egypt?
2. What were some unique features of Egyptian society?
3. How did environmental factors help shape ancient sub-Saharan African history?
4. What were some achievements of the ancient Nubian, Sudanic, and Bantu peoples?
5. What were the contributions of the Hebrews, Minoans, Mycenaeans, Phoenicians, and Dorian Greeks to later societies in the region?

 # The Rise of Egyptian Society

How did the environment shape ancient Egypt?

As in Mesopotamia, the formation of Egyptian society was a rich and complex process involving interactions among many different peoples. Egypt became a mixed society with multiple roots, and it was so successful that it survived in more or less its basic form for nearly 2,000 years. The ancient Greek historian Herodotus (heh-ROD-uh-tuhs) called Egypt the "gift of the Nile" because it owed its existence to the Nile River. The river valley's African location allowed the Egyptians to develop many traditions and ideas that were completely different from those in nearby Mesopotamia, Palestine, and Crete.

North African Environments

North Africa, a region stretching from Morocco to the Red Sea, has been shaped by several environmental features. In ancient times maritime routes in the Mediterranean Sea linked societies along its shores and islands and enabled the spread of products, ideas, technologies, and peoples. These routes invited both peaceful traders and brutal pirates or invaders. Just

to the southeast, the Red Sea connected Egypt to northeast Africa, Arabia, and India. Agriculture, then and now, is mainly possible only in a narrow fertile plain in Egypt nourished by the Nile River, which runs on a north-south axis just west of the Red Sea. To the west and east of this plain lies the vast Sahara Desert, which stretches all the way to the western coast of Africa on one end and the Red Sea and Ethiopian highlands on the other. In northwestern Africa (today's Tunisia, Algeria, and Morocco) mountain ranges separate the desert from the Mediterranean and Atlantic coastal plains, where farming is also possible.

The Nile River is the key to understanding the formation of Egyptian society (see Map 3.1 on page 58). The settlers in the northern Nile valley enjoyed many centuries of uninterrupted development thanks to the deserts on both sides of the valley. The Egyptians referred to the small belt of fertile soil along the Nile as "the black land" and to the inhospitable deserts on either side as "the red land." This physical environment allowed Egypt to thrive for a thousand years without significant outside challenge. Since the Nile was navigable and slow moving, boats drifted northward with the current and used southerly winds to move south; thus the river was a great highway that promoted political stability and uniformity. Although the Nile valley was grassland and rain forest in prehis-

C H R O N O L O G Y

...pt	Sub-Saharan Africa	Eastern Mediterranean
...E.		
...0 B.C.E. ...Kingdom	2000 B.C.E.–1000 C.E. Bantu migrations	2000–1400 B.C.E. Minoan Crete
1550–1064 B.C.E. New Kingdom	1800–1500 B.C.E. Nubian kingdom of Kerma	1600–1200 B.C.E. Mycenaea
		1500–650 B.C.E. Phoenicia
1000 B.C.E.	900 B.C.E. Rise of Kush	1000–722 B.C.E. Hebrew kingdoms

toric times, by the fourth millennium the grassland had turned to desert and "the black land" was fertile only because of the silt deposited by the fall flooding of the Nile.

Foundations of Egyptian Society

The same process that transformed farming societies into urban societies in Mesopotamia took place a few centuries later, around 3100 or 3000 B.C.E., in the Nile valley and also attracted a diverse population. Here too, with little rainfall, irrigation works were necessary to take advantage of the rich silt. A temple inscription acknowledged the river's value: "I know the Nile. When he is introduced in the fields, his introduction gives life to every nostril."[3] But the river valley here was 10 miles wide, instead of 100 miles wide as in Mesopotamia. Therefore in Egypt, the deserts isolated people more from outside contact than in Mesopotamia and concentrated them in a smaller area.

Nonetheless, the Nile valley began attracting immigrants well before the birth of cities, and it continued to be shaped by the arrival of new peoples. Many of the earliest settlers were migrants from a Sahara region that had been fertile but began drying out some 6,000 to 7,000 years ago. This environmental change forced the peoples living there to move to the south, to the grasslands of western Africa, to the northern coast, or east into the Nile valley. Other early migrants came from western Asia, including the Arabian peninsula, and from the Horn of Africa, southeast of Egypt.

The Egyptian population eventually included peoples of Semitic (suh-MIT-ik), Berber (BUHR-bur), Ethiopian, Somali, black African, and, later, Greek origins. Egypt also enjoyed close relationships with the Nubians, black African peoples living along the Nile in what is today southern Egypt and northern Sudan. The ancient Egyptian language belonged to the Afro-Asiatic family, which included not only Semitic languages but also many African tongues spoken in a wide area from Nigeria to Somalia. Before 600 C.E. most of the people in northwest Africa were Berbers, who spoke languages related to Egyptian.

The Rise of Egyptian States

Because the floods came on an exact schedule, Egyptians formed a central government to organize large numbers of people to prepare the cropland in time to take best advantage of the flooding, for example, by building dikes to contain the floodwater used in irrigation. This pattern differed from that in Mesopotamia, where the flooding was less predictable. In Egypt, as in Mesopotamia, it took much hard work to irrigate the fields. The backbreaking work required to maintain the irrigation canals reminds us that, for peasants at least, a complex society was a mixed blessing.

The Egyptian state arose through the need to control the Nile waters and maintain stability. If the floodwaters were not carefully channeled, little would grow. In periods of political disorder, when weak central governments left the dikes untended, the desert spread and famine struck the land. When order prevailed and the dikes were maintained, the valley could support a high population. By 1000 B.C.E., the population had reached 3 or 4 million. Protected by the desert from foreign invasion until about 1500 B.C.E., Egyptians understandably worried more about domestic disorder. Given their general good fortune, it is not surprising that Egyptians were more ethnocentric than their Mesopotamian neighbors. They saw themselves as the center of the world. As far as they knew for many centuries, they were.

Most of Egypt's people lived along the Mediterranean coast or on the Nile River down to Aswan (AS-wahn), some 750 miles south at the river's first large waterfall (see Map 3.1). The 100-mile-long area from the modern city of Cairo down the Nile to the sea was considered Lower Egypt or the northern kingdom, at the end of which was the fertile Nile Delta. The area from Cairo south to Aswan was Upper Egypt or the southern kingdom. These two states were united by the legendary Upper Egyptian King Menes (MEH-neez) in about 3000 B.C.E.

Egyptian history from 3000 to 1075 B.C.E. is divided into periods called the Old Kingdom, the Middle Kingdom, and the New Kingdom. During each period various dynasties ruled

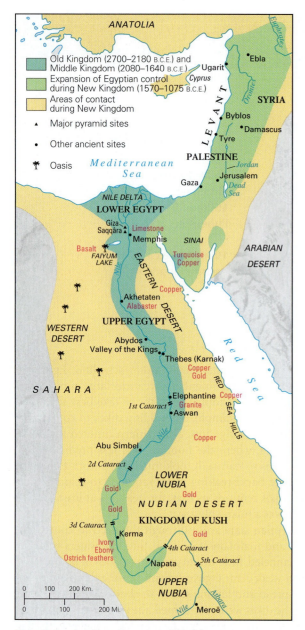

Map 3.1 **Ancient Egypt and Nubia**
The Egyptian and Nubian societies developed along the Nile River. Egypt traded with, and sometimes controlled, the peoples of the Levant on the eastern Mediterranean coast.

Online Study Center **Improve Your Grade**
Interactive Map: Ancient Egypt to the Levant

Egypt, and the intermediate periods were marked by disorder or foreign conquest. After 1075 B.C.E. Egypt increasingly fell victim to the empire building of western Asian, Mediterranean, and other African peoples.

The Old Kingdom: Egypt's Golden Age

When we think of ancient Egypt, most of us picture the Old Kingdom because of the pyramids built in this splendid era. Indeed, nothing better illustrates the Egyptian self-confidence

CHRONOLOGY	
Ancient Egypt, 3100–525 B.C.E.	
3100 B.C.E.—3000 B.C.E.	Upper and Lower Egypt unified
2663 B.C.E.—2195 B.C.E.	Old Kingdom and Age of Pyramids
2195 B.C.E.—2066 B.C.E.	First Intermediate Period
2066 B.C.E.—1650 B.C.E.	Middle Kingdom
1650 B.C.E.—1550 B.C.E.	Second Intermediate Period
1550 B.C.E.—1064 B.C.E.	New Kingdom
1064 B.C.E.—525 B.C.E.	Third Intermediate Period

of this period than the pyramids, which have awed visitors for thousands of years. The Old Kingdom lasted from 2663 to 2195 B.C.E., and the first large pyramid tombs near Giza were built between 2600 and 2100 B.C.E. They reflected a powerful government, unsurpassed organizing talent, a prosperous society, and unique values and beliefs (see Chronology: Ancient Egypt, 3000–525 B.C.E.).

Pharaohs, Pyramids, and Trade The pyramids, perhaps the greatest, most enduring of the ancient world's construction projects, derived from the Egyptian political system and beliefs. The largest pyramid, that of the twenty-fifth-century Pharaoh Cheops at Giza, near modern Cairo, is nearly 500 feet high, covers an area of nearly 200 square yards, is almost exactly level, and remained the tallest building in the world until the twentieth century. It was built with nearly 6 million tons of limestone. All the limestone was moved into place on ramps and wooden rollers by tens of thousands of workers without the benefit of winches, pulleys, or scaffolds. Most of the workers were not slaves, and many were highly skilled artisans. Work on the pyramids and other royal tombs took place in the fall, when the Nile flooded, and the workers and their families lived in villages where the government supplied them with ample food and good housing. This did not prevent complaints, however. One disgruntled draftsman wrote to his superior: "If there is some beer, you do not look for me, but if there is work, you do look for me. I am a man who has no beer in his house."[4] The flood allowed workers to use barges to float the stones close to the construction site.

Only a ruler with immense power could command the resources necessary for such a project. The rulers of Egypt, who were eventually known as **pharaohs** (FAIR-os) (from *per-o* or "great house"), had that power because their subjects believed them to be the divine offspring of the sun-god Re, the creator of heaven, earth, and humans. The great Giza pyramids were

---

pharaohs Rulers of ancient Egypt.

Great Pyramid at Giza Three Egyptian pharaohs from the twenty-sixth century B.C.E. were buried in these magnificent pyramids, which symbolized the power of Old Kingdom Egypt. The rearmost pyramid, built for Pharaoh Cheops, remains the largest all-stone building ever constructed anywhere. (Michael Holford)

symbols of the sun. Pharaohs also had soldiers as well as the authority of priests and religion to support their rule. Writing, invented perhaps as early as 3200 B.C.E. and certainly by 3000 B.C.E., enabled the administration to function smoothly. The Egyptian writing system of **hieroglyphics** (hi-ruh-GLIF-iks), like Sumerian cuneiform, evolved from pictograms into stylized pictures expressing ideas. The surviving records give us a detailed view of ancient Egyptian society.

These pharaohs, who were considered the owners of all the land and people in Egypt, governed a highly centralized state from the city of Memphis, strategically located where the Nile valley met the delta. From Memphis the ruler, officially called "King of Upper and Lower Egypt," could control both parts of his kingdom. Egypt was divided into about forty provinces, each headed by a governor appointed by the king. A chief minister supervised the administrative structure and ensured that taxes were collected, grain properly stored in government warehouses, and salaries paid to government officials. Most ministers came from noble families, but occasionally

hieroglyphics The Egyptian writing system, which evolved from pictograms into stylized pictures expressing ideas.

pharaohs recruited for talent. One advised his son: "Do not distinguish the son of a noble man from a poor man, but take to thyself a man because of the work of his hands."[5]

During the Old Kingdom, the royal government also expanded trade through regional networks. The pharaohs dispatched expeditions east to Arabia, south to Nubia (NOO-bee-ah), and northeast to Lebanon, Syria, and Anatolia. Although the Egyptians may not have invented international maritime trade, the records from the Pharaoh Snefru (SNEF-roo) around 2600 B.C.E. provide the first known written accounts of this activity. They describe the arrival of forty ships filled with cedar logs, probably from today's Lebanon, to make the cedar wood doors of the royal palace. It was a prosperous time, despite the great wealth spent on the royal tombs.

The End of the Old Kingdom

Some historians believe that the expense of the great royal tombs eventually impoverished the country during the final decades of the twenty-second century B.C.E. Whether or not this was true, we do know that at this time the governors became more independent of the ruler at Memphis, whose authority was thereby weakened. Egyptian beliefs led people to accept this development. The Egyptian term for justice was **ma'at** (muh-AHT), which referred to the correct order of things, the way the universe and human society are supposed to be. Many peasants reasoned that if the power of the ruler was weakened, it must mean that the gods were displeased. But environmental change may also have undermined the government. A dramatic and sudden drop in rainfall led to many years of poor harvests and starvation in Upper Egypt.

The demise of the Old Kingdom led to a century of social disorder during which thieves ransacked some royal tombs. One scribe lamented the consequences of this upheaval:

> The son of the high-born is no longer to be recognized. The child of his lady is become the son of his handmaid. Men do not sail to Byblos (BIB-loss) [Phoenicia] today. Gold is diminished. To what purpose is a treasure without its revenues? Laughter hath perished. It is grief that walketh through the land.[6]

The Middle Kingdom and Foreign Conquest

Around 2080 B.C.E., the pharaohs of the Twelfth Dynasty restored strong government. They moved the capital from Memphis to the city of Thebes in the south and established stronger control over the governors. This Middle Kingdom lasted for 400 years and saw Egyptian influence extend to Palestine in the north and, briefly, to Nubia in the south. Amon-Re, a fusion of two great gods, now became Egypt's chief god and was proclaimed the ancestor of the divine pharaoh.

However, foreign conquest and domestic disorder brought an end to the Middle Kingdom in 1640. The Hyksos (HICK-soes), an iron-using Semitic people from Syria and Palestine, conquered a portion of the Nile Delta region and established an independent kingdom. Hyksos rule led to further divisions: a separate dynasty began to rule Upper Egypt from Thebes, and the Nubians established yet a third state. Although regarded by Egyptians as invading barbarians, the Hyksos adopted Egyptian customs and brought several improvements to Egypt that would later pay dividends for the strong rulers of the New Kingdom. These benefits included increased trade with the Semitic and Indo-European peoples of the eastern Mediterranean and Mesopotamia, and new methods of working bronze and making pottery. Most significant were the military innovations, including the use of iron and the practice of using smaller shields, body armor, the compound bow (much more powerful than the single bow), and, especially, horse-drawn chariots.

The New Kingdom and Egyptian Expansion

In 1570 B.C.E. a dynamic new set of rulers reestablished Egypt's regional power and presided over social and religious changes. Using the new military technology, the pharaohs began the most expansionist period of ancient Egyptian history. During the New Kingdom, Egypt abandoned its former policy of isolation and became more active in the western Asian and Mediterranean worlds. By 1500 B.C.E. its rulers were leading armies on repeated campaigns into Palestine and Syria and as far east as the Euphrates River. At the same time they expanded south into Nubia. Foreigners from Libya in the west and from as far away as Babylon in the east came to serve in the Egyptian court. During this time Egypt's power derived partly from its position as the major regional supplier of gold, which it obtained mostly from Nubia and Punt. One allied king whose sister had married the pharaoh remarked that gold was like "dust" in Egypt.

For a certain period Egypt was ruled by the female pharaoh introduced earlier. Hatshepsut (r. ca. 1479–1458), the daughter of Pharaoh Tuthmosis (tuth-MOE-sis) I, was the wife of another pharaoh and ruled in her own name between 1473 and 1458. The Egyptians had no word for a female ruler and described a queen only as the "king's wife." To ensure that she looked like a proper pharaoh, Hatshepsut apparently wore male clothing and the headdress and false beard that were symbols of royalty. During this time, Hatshepsut supervised military campaigns in both the north and south and also sponsored the marine expedition to Punt to collect luxury goods.

Another New Kingdom pharaoh, Amenophis (AH-men-o-fis) IV (r. 1353–1333), rebelled against the priests of Amon-Re and promoted the worship of a new sun-god, Aton, who he claimed was the only god (other than the pharaoh himself). Amenophis changed his name to Akhenaton (AH-ke-NAH-tin) ("servant of Aton") and wrote a famous hymn to Aton: "Beginner of Life. How manifold are thy works? They are hidden from the sight of men, O Sole God. Thou didst fashion the earth according to thy desire."[7] His experiment with **monotheism**, the belief in a single, all-powerful god, has long intrigued historians because it occurred at roughly the same time that the Hebrews were developing their belief in a single god. Some scholars see cross-cultural influences at work, since Hebrews were within the Egyptian sphere of influence and some may have lived in the kingdom. As evidence for cultural mixing, they note that some Hebrew psalms and proverbs are clearly derived, sometimes nearly word for word, from Egyptian writings, including Akhenaton's hymn to Aton. At Akhenaton's death, however, the priests successfully pressured his successor to return to Amon-Re worship.

Despite this domestic dispute, the New Kingdom continued its military successes for a while before faltering. In the thirteenth century the high point of Egyptian empire building was reached when Rameses (ram-ih-SEEZ) II (r. 1290–1224) signed a treaty with the Hittites dividing Syria and Palestine between them. In 1208 B.C.E. Libyan tribes invaded the Nile Delta, probably to escape famine; a temple inscription reported that people came to Egypt to seek the necessities of their "mouths." Although they were pushed out, starting in about 1075 B.C.E. Egypt began its long decline as a power in the eastern Mediterranean. From about 750 to 650 B.C.E., a dynasty of pharaohs from the kingdom of Kush in Nubia ruled Egypt.

---

ma'at   Ancient Egyptian term for justice, the correct order of things.

monotheism   The belief in a single, all-powerful god.

They adopted Egyptian customs and wrote their language in hieroglyphics. Finally, Egypt was conquered by the Assyrians in the seventh century and by the Persians in the late sixth century B.C.E.

SECTION SUMMARY

■ The regular flooding of the Nile River provided the ancient Egyptians with a highly fertile valley and a dependable growing season.

■ A strong central government allowed the Egyptians to make the most of their agricultural system.

■ The pyramids were built by the Egyptian pharaohs of the Old Kingdom, thought to be descendants of the sun-god.

■ During the Middle Kingdom, the Egyptian capital moved from Memphis to Thebes.

■ The New Kingdom was a time of Egyptian expansion into western Asia and the Mediterranean, but it ended with the decline of Egyptian dominance.

Egyptian Society, Economy, and Culture

What were some unique features of Egyptian society?

Like other ancient societies, the Egyptians had many distinctive customs, technologies, and beliefs. Compared to most places, Egypt was a generally tolerable place to live. Perhaps because of the Nile inundation each fall, Egyptians of all social classes, blessed with many centuries of good crops, seemed to view themselves as favored. One writer celebrated the Nile Delta as "full of everything good—its ponds with fish and its lakes with birds. Its meadows are verdant, its melons abundant. Its granaries are so full of barley that they come near to the sky."[8] Although many peasants and workers worked very hard and had far fewer comforts than those in the upper classes, they at least had a life that was secure and a routine that was predictable. In addition, women enjoyed considerable freedom. Finally, although Egyptian cities had few close neighbors that could attack them, they could grow rich by trading with many distant suppliers and markets.

Social Life and Organization

Like other societies with cities and states, Egypt was divided into classes. During the Old Kingdom members of each social class had different responsibilities and roles. The head of this social hierarchy, the pharaoh, theoretically owned everything in the kingdom and had particular estates reserved for him in each of the provinces. The priests and nobles owned 80 to 90 percent of all the usable land (see Profile: Hekanakhte, an Egyptian Priest). However, the scribe, or "writing man," held the most honored upper-class occupation. "Be a scribe," a young man was advised in one

source. "Your limbs will be sleek. Your hands will grow soft. You will go forth in white clothes with courtiers saluting you."[9]

Not all enjoyed such amenities. Peasants maintained the irrigation works and paid taxes that could be as high as 20 percent of their crop. At the bottom of society were slaves, perhaps 10 or 15 percent of the population. They were mostly [prisoners] of war and foreigners, including Nubians and [Syro-]Palestine, among them some Hebrews. Mos[t worked in] homes of the wealthy, in the palaces, or [... .] Some helped build pyramids and monum[ents.]

Influenced by the Nile environme[nt ... se-]curity and regularity more than soci[... It was rel-]atively easy to plant in the soft soil l[eft behind and did] not need heavy plows. After harvesti[ng ... hunted] in the marshes. Despite occasional grueling [construc-]tion projects, peasants showed little discontent ex[cept in] the troubled intermediate periods. Although the rich ate m[eat] and the poor had beer, bread, and beans ("beer and bread" was an ancient Egyptian greeting, much like "have a good day"), most people thought themselves lucky. Their massive tombs and mummies may seem gloomy to us today, but their temples were once bright with paint and gold, and people seemingly enjoyed life so much they wished to perpetuate it in tombs equipped with the trappings for everyday life.

Numerous temple paintings show people at work and play. Egyptians told bawdy stories (often about their gods), played musical instruments such as flutes, pipes, and harps, got drunk, and gave boring lectures to children. Both men and women used cosmetics to enhance their physical attractions, massaging themselves with scented oils and decorating their eyes with colorful eyeliners. In seeking beauty aids, Egyptians became the world's first chemists. Young people wrote sentimental poems to sweethearts. One love poem by a girl reported on a swim with her lover:

> Diving and swimming with you here,
> Gives me the chance I've been waiting for,
> To show my looks,
> Before an appreciative eye.
> My bathing suit of the best material.
> Nothing can keep me from my love,
> Standing on the other shore.[10]

Scholars debate whether stone carvings in a tomb that show two men embracing and kissing indicates a homosexual relationship or instead portrays identical or conjoined ("Siamese") twins.

Gender roles were flexible, and women had more independence and rights, especially in law, than women in any other ancient society. Hatshepsut was the most famous of at least four women pharaohs. By the New Kingdom the status of Egyptian women was higher than that of women in Mesopotamia or later in classical Greek and Roman society, and legal distinctions among persons seemed to be based more on class than on gender. A woman could inherit, bequeath, and administer property, conclude legal settlements, take cases to court, initiate divorce, and testify. She could bring a lawsuit against another woman or a man and have a real chance of winning. Some women could probably read and write. Many were

HEKANAKHTE,
AN EGYPTIAN PRIEST

Hekanakhte (Heh-KHAN-akt) who lived about 2000 B.C.E., was the *ka*-priest of a chief government minister who had died a generation earlier. As a *ka*-priest, it was his duty to tend the tomb of his patron, near the city of Thebes, in order to protect the deceased individual's guardian spirit or soul (*ka*). Wealthy individuals, like the great minister Ipi whom Hekanakhte served, left money or other resources to support a priest who would perform these duties. If the *ka* were not honored with these ceremonial offerings, Egyptians feared that it would die a "second death" or be annihilated.

In this case, the minister Ipi had left a large estate to support Hekanakhte and his family. Hekanakhte also supervised other properties left to his care, and he had to be gone visiting them much of the year. We know much about him because during his absences he wrote many letters to his eldest son, Mersu. Mersu read and eventually discarded them in a local tomb, where they were forgotten but where the dry desert climate preserved them until they were discovered by an archaeologist in 1922. These letters give us an interesting picture of family life in the Middle Kingdom. We discover that Hekanakhte had a large family that included five sons, two of them married, and all of them living at home. He also supported his mother, a poor female relative, and a widowed daughter.

Perhaps because he had such a large household, Hekanakhte's letters to Mersu give advice on cultivating and tending the grain crops. Some of the letters were written during a bad year, when harvests were slim because of inadequate Nile flooding. The priest tells his son that he is sending some food, but he carefully lists what each family member is to receive. He tells Mersu to remind family members not to complain, since "half life is better than dying together." Hekanakhte orders that only those who work should get food and urges Mersu to "make the most of my

land, strive to the uttermost, dig the ground deep with your noses." He also tells his son exactly what seeds to plant and where to plant them. And he warns his son not to overpay the help, saying that if he does, his own personal funds will be reduced. Trust between father and son seems to have been in short supply.

Family disputes in Hekanakhte's household were a frequent topic in these letters. Apparently Hekanakhte had spoiled Mersu's younger brother, Snerfu, because he constantly reminds Mersu to give this youngest son things he wants. In addition, Hekanakhte apparently decided late in life, after his wife died, to take a young concubine, Iutenhab (YOU-ten-hob), who disrupted the household with her many requests. In one letter, the priest tells his son to fire a maid who had offended Iutenhab. Given the nagging tone of many of Hekanakhte's letters to his long-suffering son, it may not surprise us that one of the letters found in the debris of the tomb had been left unopened.

THINKING ABOUT THE PROFILE

1. What were the duties of a *ka*-priest?
2. What do these letters tell us about family relationships in this social class?

Note: Quotations from Barbara Mertz, *Red Land, Black Land: Daily Life in Ancient Egypt* (New York: Dodd, Mead, 1978), p. 127.

Measuring and Recording the Egyptian Harvest This wall painting from a tomb in the city of Thebes shows officials and peasants figuring the size of the annual harvest. (Michael Holford)

involved in well-paying economic activities, and they were paid the same as men for the same work. Women weavers produced some of the finest cloth in world history. Wives also enjoyed rough equality with husbands and assumed the public and family responsibilities of their deceased spouses. Women served as doctors and priestesses, and a few women even held administrative positions. Despite all these exceptions, however, most women were wives and mothers, and public duties were normally reserved for men. An Old Kingdom sage advised men to "love your wife at home, as is proper. Fill her belly and clothe her back. Make her heart glad as long as you live. You should not judge her, or let her gain control."[11]

Cities, Trade, and Regional Networks

Mesopotamian cities had been trading centers almost from their beginnings. Egyptian cities, by contrast, were largely administrative centers created by the pharaoh to house tax collectors, artisans in government workshops, shopkeepers, and the priests who cared for the local temple. Even the larger cities such as Memphis and Thebes did not begin as centers for long-distance trade and commerce, since most trade involved the import of luxury goods by the wealthy. Also, Egyptian city-dwellers, unlike their Mesopotamian counterparts, did not think of themselves as attached to the city. They were, like all Egyptians, subjects of the pharaoh. Since the Nile floods were more predictable than those along the unruly Euphrates, fewer people were needed to manage the irrigation system. Therefore, more Egyptians lived in villages, and market towns were scattered up and down the river.

Yet, although the cities were not commercial centers, the Egyptians' long-distance trade systems were more wide-ranging than those of the Mesopotamians. Either directly or through intermediaries, Egyptians traded with sub-Saharan Africans as far south as the Congo River Basin, with the Berber peoples of Libya and Algeria to the west, with the societies along the Red Sea to the east, with Palestine, Phoenicia, and Mesopotamia to the northeast, and with southeastern Europe. Gold, semiprecious stones, and such exotic things as frankincense, myrrh, ivory, ostrich feathers, and monkeys came from sub-Saharan Africa through Nubia or via the Red Sea and were exchanged for furniture, silver, tools, paper, and linen. Egyptians mined copper in the nearby Sinai (SIGH-nigh) Peninsula and along the Red Sea coast, and the Nile Delta provided papyrus as well as waterfowl.

Science and Technology

The geometrical precision of the pyramids tells us that the ancient Egyptians understood some mathematics and physics. They knew enough to make the pyramids level and to match the corners of each pyramid with the four points of the compass. The Egyptians also used a solar calendar that divided the year into 365 days, using twelve months of thirty days each and adding five days at the end. This was more accurate than the Sumerian lunar calendar. Egyptian arithmetic, however, was less sophisticated than their calendar might suggest. They understood fractions, but they had no concept of zero and dealt with numbers only by adding them. In medicine, Egyptians used both surgery and herbal remedies to treat illnesses. They recognized that the heart

was a pump, were able to cure some eye diseases, and did some dental work. In science and mathematics generally, however, they had much technical skill but little theoretical understanding.

Modern observers still admire Egyptian technical skill in treating the dead. If pyramids are the first things that come to mind when we think of ancient Egypt, mummies are probably the second. Using a form of salt found abundantly in Egypt, and taking advantage of the extremely dry climate (which probably created the first mummies in the Nile valley by accident), Egyptian morticians were able to preserve human tissue well enough that the distinct features of individuals could be seen 4,000 years later.

Religion

Egyptian religious and moral beliefs included some two thousand gods and goddesses, most of them benevolent, many myths, and unique views of death. Like their Mesopotamian counterparts, the Egyptian gods were created to explain nature, but were also made in the image of humans and shared human weaknesses. Eventually they were seen as responsive to human needs. For instance, the twelfth-century B.C.E. pharaoh Rameses IV asked the gods to give him good health, a long reign, and strength to all his limbs.

The emphasis on preserving bodies indicates another chief feature of Egyptian religion, the belief that a person's soul could be united with his or her body after death, but only if the body was properly preserved. In the Old Kingdom, only pharaohs could expect this afterlife, which mirrored life on earth. By the Middle Kingdom, however, all who could afford some form of mummification and whose souls passed a final moral judgment after death were candidates for immortality. As a result, people devoted vast resources to this quest.

The most dramatic and long-lived of the Egyptian myths is the story of Osiris (oh-SIGH-ris) and his wife Isis (EYE-sis). One version describes Osiris as the god-king who originally established peace and justice on earth. By this act he incurred the jealousy of his brother Set, who murdered him by sealing him in a box and throwing it into the sea. Isis, grief-stricken, found the body of her husband washed ashore. With the help of other gods, she revived Osiris long enough for him to impregnate her. Their son Horus later took revenge on Set, and Osiris descended to the underworld, where he established justice there as he had done on earth. A famous Egyptian drawing from the *Book of the Dead*, which depicts the afterlife, shows Osiris weighing the heart of a dead princess against the symbol

Online Study Center Improve Your Grade
Primary Source: Egyptian Book of the Dead

The *Book of the Dead* describes a confession that the dead person is to repeat as part of this judgment by Osiris. This confession includes statements by the deceased indicating that he or she has not murdered or cheated anyone. The following affirmations by the person facing judgment also show the practical side of Egyptian religion:

I have not stolen temple property.
I have not harmed the food of the gods [left in temples].

I have not held up water in its season.
I have not dammed running water.
I have not put out a fire that should have stayed alight.[12]

Because of the *Book of the Dead,* the durability of the pyramids, other Egyptian tombs, and mummified remains, some scholars have viewed the ancient Egyptians as people preoccupied with death and the afterlife. However, the tombs are the only artifacts that remain because they were made of stone. The less durable mud-brick houses of most Egyptians, in which a great deal of activity took place, were washed away or dissolved into mud long ago. Thus the Egyptians were probably not as preoccupied with death as the physical remains suggest. They no doubt enjoyed life as much or more than other people and, like the hero in one Egyptian tale, considered their homeland the only place where they could be happy. Many wall paintings suggest that even the lower classes accepted their lot as part of the natural order of things and found ways to cope. They show farmers and herders telling jokes, women bringing them their lunches, children squabbling, and shepherds asleep under a tree, a dog or flask of beer beside them. If conditions became too harsh, the peasants and workers might move elsewhere or go on strike. They could find solace in religion and awe of the pharaoh who sat, as the gods ordained, at the apex of the social pyramid.

SECTION SUMMARY

- Though Egyptian society was divided into classes, with the rich enjoying lavish lifestyles, even the poor were relatively comfortable.

- Women had greater independence and rights in Egypt than in any other ancient society, but their roles were still quite limited.

- Ancient Egyptians had great technical skill in architecture, medicine, and preserving the dead, but little theoretical understanding of science and mathematics.

- Ancient Egyptians believed they could obtain immortality if their bodies were mummified and if they passed a moral judgment after death.

- Ancient Egyptians traded widely with societies in sub-Saharan Africa and western Asia.

The Roots of Sub-Saharan African Societies

How did environmental factors help shape ancient sub-Saharan African history?

Africa is the original homeland for all of humanity, and Egypt was only the best-known of the early farming societies and states which emerged on the continent. Africans fostered varied societies, some of which also built cities,

formed states, and became linked to each other and the wider world by growing networks. Just as the annual Nile floods fostered Egypt's distinctive development, so the environment also influenced the varied traditions of sub-Saharan Africans and helped or hindered their early development of farming and technology.

African Environments

Both geography and climate have shaped African history. Africa, with one-fifth of the earth's landmass, is the second-largest continent after Eurasia and occupies more space than the United States, Europe (excluding Russia), China, and India combined. The equator almost exactly bisects Africa, giving most of the continent a tropical climate. Lush rain forests have flourished along West Africa's Guinea coast and in the vast Congo River Basin in the heart of the continent. These forests and other areas near the equator are home to many insects, parasites, and bacteria that cause debilitating diseases like malaria, yellow fever, and sleeping sickness. Since the last is deadly to cattle and horses, it was impractical to use a plow or wheel in much of ancient Africa. Despite the common image of Africa as a vast jungle, most of the continent has long been parched desert or savannah grasslands. African weather can be erratic, with fluctuating and often unpredictable rains. In addition, rain quickly diminishes north and south of the equator, producing a huge dry zone that receives less than 10 inches of rain a year. The deserts and some of the grasslands have largely been occupied by pastoral societies and herds of large wild animals. In some regions the poor-quality soil has been easily eroded by overuse, and erosion has fostered low agricultural productivity. Nonetheless, early farmers cultivated the grassland-covered region known as the **Sudan** (soo-DAN), which stretches along the southern fringe of the Sahara Desert from the western tip of Africa to the Nile Basin, where the modern nation of Sudan is located south of Egypt.

Geography has often hindered communication. The eastern third of Africa includes extensive plateau and mountain regions, which in Ethiopia rise to 15,000 feet. Deep valleys and gorges complicate travel. Even so, in some plateau districts great lakes and volcanic soils have permitted denser populations. The eastern highlands also produced great river systems, including the Nile, the Congo (which drains the vast central African rain forests), and, in the south, the Zambezi (zam-BEE-zee). but all these rivers have numerous rapids and waterfalls that have limited boat travel. Only the Niger (NIGH-jer) River, which flows mostly through the flat West African plains, is navigable over large distances. Nor was maritime transportation easy in the past. Prevailing winds made it difficult to sail along the West African coast, and much of the African coast has sandbars that create great swells, making it difficult to land a boat. Furthermore, much of Africa's coastline is unbroken by bays, gulfs, and inland seas. Hence, along

---

Sudan   A grassland region stretching along the southern fringe of the Sahara Desert from the western tip of Africa to the Nile valley.

the entire Atlantic coast, historically there have been no great natural harbors to serve as maritime hubs. Only along the eastern, Red Sea, and Mediterranean coasts did a few protected bays and prevailing winds favor seagoing trade.

The Expanding Sahara Desert

The catastrophic climatic change that created and expanded the Sahara Desert strongly shaped early African societies. The Sahara region was once a rich grazing land with lakes and rivers, occupied by a large human population that flourished from hunting, gathering, fishing, and some farming. Ancient rock art portrays people dancing, worshiping, riding chariots, and tending horses and cattle. The paintings endow women with dignity as they raise children, gather plants, and make baskets, pottery, and jewelry. The history of rainfall explains why **desertification**, the process by which productive land is transformed into mostly useless desert, set in. For several millennia the region became relatively wet. This pattern reached a peak in 3500 B.C.E., making settlement more attractive. Then, as rain patterns shifted southward again, the gradual "drying out" of the continent began. By 2000 B.C.E. the Sahara region was harsh desert, and animals and plants had disappeared along with the water. People contributed to this process by overgrazing marginal lands and burning forests to create grasslands. The same desertification processes continue today on the Sahara's southern fringe.

Desertification influenced societies. The Sahara was left largely to nomadic herders of cattle and other animals, and most other inhabitants migrated to the north and south or into the lower Nile valley. This migration may have helped generate ancient Egyptian development. Eventually the Sahara marked a general boundary between the Berber and Semitic peoples along the southern Mediterranean coast and the darker-skinned peoples in the rest of Africa. But the desert barrier did not prevent considerable social, cultural, and genetic intermixing and exchange. For example, several West African spoken languages are closely related to Arabic.

The Origins of African Agriculture

Africa's geographical disadvantages did not prevent agriculture from developing early as the result of both local and imported discoveries. Recent discoveries suggest that, some 12,000 or 13,000 years ago, people in the eastern Sahara were perhaps the first in the world to make pottery, probably for storing food and water, two centuries earlier than Middle Eastern people. Between 8000 and 5000 B.C.E., people in the north-central Nile (Nubia) and the Sahara region had become among the world's first farmers (see Chronology: Ancient Sub-Saharan Africa, 8000 B.C.E.–350 C.E.). People in the Ethiopian highlands domesticated *teff* (tef) (a nutritious grain) and the banana-like *ensete* (en-SET-ay/en-SET-ee), probably between

---

desertification   The process by which productive land is transformed into mostly useless desert.

CHRONOLOGY	
Ancient Sub-Saharan Africa, 8000 B.C.E.–350 C.E.	
8000–5000	Earliest agriculture in the Sahara and Nubia
5000–4000	Earliest agriculture in Ethiopia
3100–2800	First Nubian kingdom (disputed)
2500	Widespread agriculture in West, Central, and East Africa
2000	Beginning of Bantu migrations
1800–1500	Kerma kingdom in Nubia
1200	Early urbanization in western Sudan
1000–500	Bantu settlement of Great Lakes region
1000–500	Beginning of trans-Saharan trade
1000–500	Early ironworking technology
900–800	Mande towns
900–350 C.E.	Early Kush

5000 and 4000 B.C.E. By 2500 B.C.E. farming was widespread in West, Central, and East Africa. In West Africa and the Sahara almost all food crops developed from local wild African plants like sorghum, millet, yams, and African rice. Probably domesticated in the Niger River region, rice gradually spread south to become a major crop in the rain forest zone of the west coast. People in the eastern Sahara had also domesticated cotton and worked it into fabrics using spindles of baked clay, perhaps as early as 5000 B.C.E. Other crops came later from outside Africa, including wheat, barley, and chickpeas from the Middle East and bananas from Southeast Asia. But the movement went in both directions. Crops domesticated in West Africa such as sorghum and sesame reached India and China well before 2000 B.C.E.

Animal domestication presented a great challenge to sub-Saharan Africans. Cattle were probably domesticated from local sources in what is now the southern Sahara Desert and East Africa. Some scholars think this came as early as 9000 B.C.E., while others favor later dates. But no other African animals were suitable for domestication, and some were dangerous predators. Rock art and other evidence reveal possible attempts to domesticate giraffes, antelopes, and elephants. Failure to do so meant that most draft animals would have to come from North Africa and Eurasia. Goats and sheep were brought in from the Middle East by 6000 B.C.E. and were adopted in the Saharan region by both farmers and pastoralists.

African peoples overcame geographical challenges in many ways. The major response to difficult climate and soils was to create a subsistence economy, rather than the high-productivity agriculture possible in Egypt, China, India, Southeast Asia, or southern Europe. One such subsistence strategy, pastoral nomadism, became the specialty of some groups in dry regions. Others chose farming by shifting cultivation, a creative adaptation to prevailing conditions. As explained earlier, shifting cultivators moved their fields around every few years, letting recently used land lie fallow for a while to regain its nutrients. If not abused, this system worked well for centuries. Only in a few fertile areas was intensive sedentary agriculture possible, especially around the Great Lakes region of Central and East Africa and in the Ethiopian highlands.

Ancient African Metallurgy

Most sub-Saharan peoples learned to make metal tools and weapons, but unlike in Egypt and Eurasia, they probably used iron first. Copper may have been mined in the Sahara by 1500 B.C.E. and in the Niger valley between 600 and 400 B.C.E. But there was no pronounced bronze age, and generally the use of bronze, copper, and gold came around the same time or later than iron. Sub-Saharan Africans were among the world's earliest ironworkers, probably making iron by at least 1000 B.C.E. on the northern fringe of the Congo Basin rain forests. Iron smelters were built around 900 B.C.E. in the Great Lakes region of East Africa—modern Burundi, Rwanda, and Tanzania (TAN-zeh-NEE-uh). This date makes them slightly older than the earliest Egyptian works. Between 600 and 300 B.C.E., iron was being mined, smelted, and forged in West, East, and North Africa, and by around 500 B.C.E. true steel was being made in Tanzania. Iron and bronze metallurgy established on the North African coast after 700 B.C.E., especially at the Phoenician colony of Carthage (KAR-thage), may have influenced West Africans. Since most of the major iron ore deposits were located in far western Africa and Ethiopia, ore and iron artifacts had to be transported over long distances.

Mining and working iron were both difficult operations, and those who did them probably occupied a special position in the community. Sometimes blacksmiths were ranked with the priests and nobility. According to the oral traditions of the Haya (HI-uh) people in Tanzania, when a new king was installed on the throne, one important ritual was to visit the hut of the blacksmiths which symbolized the special relationship between the king and the iron workers.

The technology gradually improved and the number of products increased. Although some iron ore could be easily obtained from surface outcrops or riverbeds, in many places miners had to dig open pits and trenches or even put down vertical shafts to reach deposits deep underground. Furnaces for smelting ranged from simple open holes in the ground to elaborate clay structures 6 or 8 feet high with blower systems that used animal skin bellows. The craftsmen made spear blades and arrowheads for warriors and hunters; hoes, axes, machetes, and knives for farmers and traders; bangles and rings for jewelry; gongs to produce music; hammers, hinges, and nails for household use; and iron bells for ceremonies and rituals. The iron industry and its workers became a central feature of African life.

Recent discoveries show how some early farmers and metal-users lived. The ruins of a 2800-year-old village in Eritrea in the northeastern highlands revealed a people who lived in stone houses, drank beer, and ate cow and goat meat. They made gold earrings, bracelets, and rings as well as copper and bronze daggers and pottery jugs. Villagers also carved stone figurines, possibly for religious purposes.

Agriculture and metallurgy came to various African regions at different times, depending on circumstances, and they spread to the southern half of the continent last. Originally much of this region was inhabited by expert hunters and gatherers such as the !Kung (see Chapter 1), successful adapters to their environment who had little incentive to develop agriculture or ironworking. Gradually most of these groups were pushed farther south by iron-using farmers.

SECTION SUMMARY

- African geography is extremely varied, ranging from jungles with abundant rainfall to deserts with practically no rainfall.
- The area now covered by the Sahara Desert was once lush and fertile, but it gradually dried out as rain patterns shifted southward.
- Small-scale agriculture flourished in Africa, though widespread disease made it difficult to domesticate animals.
- Sub-Saharan Africans worked with iron at the same time or before they worked with bronze or gold.
- Ironworkers held a special position in sub-Saharan society.

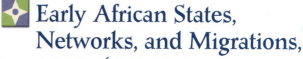

Early African States, Networks, and Migrations, 1800–600 B.C.E.

What were some achievements of the ancient Nubian, Sudanic, and Bantu peoples?

Historians tend to emphasize state building and the rise of political leaders, and some Africans formed states in this era, but the establishment of royal or centralized government did not always improve people's lives. Unlike the Egyptians and Nubians, many Africans rejected political centralization. Before the twentieth century, millions of people in sub-Saharan Africa, and many other parts of the world, remained by choice within loosely organized political structures, without kings, chiefs, or bureaucracies. In contrast to the citizens of most premodern kingdoms, these societies often enjoyed considerable democratic decision making and little tyranny.

However, some sub-Saharan peoples were linked, regularly or sporadically, to societies in North Africa and western Asia, and thus participated in the iron and commercial revolutions of

Afro-Eurasia. Most early sub-Saharan states probably developed around trading centers. As demonstrated by the expeditions to Punt, the Egyptians traded extensively with some of the peoples in northeastern Africa, and this trade probably helped foster the rise of states, especially of Nubia in the central Nile basin just south of Egypt. But the complex societies in the Sudan, some of which may have fostered kingship by 600 B.C.E., probably owed less to Egyptian connections. Meanwhile, migrating **Bantu** (BAN-too)—African people who developed traditions based on farming and iron metallurgy (the name is also used for the large family of African languages these people speak)—spread their languages, cultures, and technologies widely in the southern half of the continent. This migration brought farming and metallurgy to once remote regions.

Early Urban Societies in Nubia

The first known urban African state after Egypt emerged in the region known in ancient times as Nubia (see Map 3.1). The Nubians occupied the land that today is the northern half of the country of Sudan and far southern Egypt. Like Egyptians, Nubians turned to the Nile for survival. Today the region is mostly desert, and even several millennia ago it presented a difficult environment. But a thin area along the Nile was fertile, and copper and gold could be mined nearby. By 6000 B.C.E. villages in the region were among the world's earliest pottery makers. The first Nubian kingdom may have formed as early as 3100 B.C.E.

Egypt enjoyed a long connection with Nubia and dominated the region for many centuries, occasionally through military occupations. Many Nubians served willingly or unwillingly in the Egyptian army. Egypt and Nubia also established a two-way trade, with Egypt exporting materials such as pottery and copper items to Nubia and importing ivory, ebony, ostrich feathers, and slaves from the Nubians. This trade provided an economic incentive for local state building.

An independent Nubian kingdom, Kerma (CARE-ma), appeared between 1800 and 1600 B.C.E., as Egyptian power temporarily waned. Immigrants to this kingdom arrived from the Sahara and the south. Extensive ruins of massive cemeteries and large towers, as well as of a fortified city with stone and mud brick buildings, testify to a prosperous and well-organized society. Kerma was also distinguished for painted pottery and copper vessels and weapons. The Kerma religion mixed Egyptian and local African elements. Around 1500 B.C.E. Egyptian forces once again occupied Nubia and destroyed the Kerma state.

The Rise of Kush

When Egyptian power declined around 900 B.C.E., after the end of the New Kingdom, a larger Nubian state known as Kush (koosh) emerged, laying the foundations for a golden age of trade, culture, and metallurgy. The remains of many Kushite

towns and cities have been found. The Kushites conquered Egypt in the eighth century B.C.E. but were pushed out by the Assyrians after nearly a century of occupation. Kush became a major regional trading hub, connected to growing networks of communication. Overland caravan routes linked Kush with the Niger Basin, the Congo Basin, and the Ethiopian highlands. This enterprising society provided goods from central and southern Africa to the Mediterranean and Red Sea regions, as well as to markets as distant as India and China. From these places Kush imported Roman goblets and Chinese copper vessels.

Kush clearly benefited from its contacts with other societies, adding imported ideas to Nubian traditions. For example, mechanical irrigation technology imported from Egypt and western Asia made farming possible in this barren area. Kushite culture mixed Egyptian and local ideas, along with touches from Hellenistic Greece and India. In religion, Kushites worshiped both Egyptian and local gods and buried their kings in Egyptian-style pyramids. A sixth-century B.C.E. inscription tells us that King Aspelta (as-PELL-ta), as the son of the Egyptian sun-god, Ra, built for his son a pyramid of white stone and made many offerings of gold and silver. Although the Kushites welcomed these foreign influences, they also reshaped them. For example, Kushite art reflected considerable Egyptian and even sometimes Greek influence, but the overall effect remained distinctively Nubian. The unique Kushite society may have also been matrilineal, and some women held key political positions, including that of queen. Kings sometimes traced their descent back through female ancestors.

Coronation Stela of Kushite King Aspelta (ca. 600 B.C.E.). The stela and inscription celebrate the coronation of King Aspelta. Related to the royal line through his mother, he was chosen from among many candidates by high priests acting in the name of the gods. (From Derek A. Welsby, *The Kingdom of Kush* (Princeton, NJ: Markus Weiner Publishers). Reproduced with permission of the the British Museum.)

Bantu Sub-Saharan peoples who developed a cultural tradition based on farming and iron metallurgy, which they spread widely through great migrations.

Eventually Kush linked the peoples of Africa and the Mediterranean. By 600 B.C.E. Kush had become the major African producer of iron, a position that gave it an even more crucial economic influence on the ancient world. The ancient Greek poet Homer described Kushites as "the most just of men; the favorites of the gods. The lofty inhabitants of Olympus (oh-LIM-pus) (home of Greek gods) journey to them, and take part in their feasts."[13] Kush played an even more prominent historical role during the Classical Age (see Chapter 9).

The Sudanic Societies and Trade Networks

In ancient times peoples in the Sudan grasslands also began developing towns and long-distance trade routes, and perhaps a few small kingdoms. Although trade extended to Nubia and Egypt, the Nubian and Egyptian influences in this region remain unclear. Urban societies existed in the Sudan three millennia ago, and perhaps earlier. By 1200 B.C.E. farmers in Mauritania (MORE-ee-TAIN-ee-uh) had built over two hundred stone villages and towns in what is now mostly uninhabited desert. They may have been the ancestors of the Mande (MAN-da) peoples, who now occupy a large area of the western Sudan, and they probably domesticated African rice. By 900 or 800 B.C.E. the population increase had changed walled villages into large, well-constructed towns. Then, between 500 and 300 B.C.E., this flourishing society was swallowed by the expanding Sahara and the people probably moved south.

Long-distance trade, especially the caravan routes crossing the Sahara Desert, greatly aided the growth of Sudanic societies by forging enduring networks of communication. The earliest caravan activity dates back to 1000 or 500 B.C.E. Gradually trade networks formed, and some groups took up commerce as their primary activity. The trans-Saharan trade depended on pack animals introduced by Berbers from North Africa, initially mules and horses and later camels. First domesticated in parched Arabia and used in the Nile valley by 700 B.C.E., camels stimulated trans-Saharan trade because they could endure many days of caravan travel without water, and they also provided meat and milk. Eventually a large trade system spanned the Sahara, linking the Sudanic towns with the peoples of the desert and the southern Mediterranean coast as well as the forest zone to the south.

On the southern fringe of the Sudan, in what is now central Nigeria, the Nok people, mostly farmers and herders, were working iron by 500 B.C.E., and they created enduring artistic traditions. Nok artists fashioned exquisite terra cotta pottery and sculpture, including life-size and realistic human heads. The later art of several Nigerian societies shows Nok influence. The worldviews of other peoples in the region, such as the ancestors of the Igbo (EE-boh) people in what is today southeastern Nigeria, may derive in part from Nok traditions.

During the Ancient Era African societies, such as the people who later coalesced into the Mande and Igbo groups, were shaping their longstanding beliefs into complex religious traditions (see Witness to the Past: The Worldview of an African Society). While each society developed some distinctive notions of

Nok Terra Cotta Sculpture of Head   Elaborate, life-size, technically complex sculptures reveal something of Nok material life in ancient Nigeria. Some figures sit on stools, carry an axe, or wear beads.   (Werner Forman/Art Resource, NY)

the cosmic order and their place within in, there were common patterns. Many peoples, like the Mande and the Igbo, believed in one divine force or supreme being, either male or female, who created the cosmos, earth, and life, and then either completely ignored the human sphere entirely or at least remained remote from human affairs. Africans needing immediate spiritual help appealed to secondary gods and spirits. By 6,000 or 7,000 years ago some West Africans were perhaps the world's first monotheists, and a few historians wonder if their ideas influenced later Middle Eastern peoples such as the Hebrews. Sub-Saharan African religion became a mix of monotheism, polytheism, and animism.

The Bantu-Speaking Peoples and Their Migrations

The Bantu-speaking peoples, who developed a cultural tradition based on farming and iron metallurgy, spread these techniques widely by their great migrations. Today people who speak closely related Bantu languages occupy most of the continent south of a line stretching from Kenya in the northeast to Cameroon in west-central Africa. All of these societies can trace their distant ancestry back to the same location in west-

Few primary sources survive for the ancient period in sub-Saharan Africa. Although it is difficult to extrapolate the distant past from contemporary oral traditions, we can get some insight into ancient understandings of the natural and spiritual realms from such accounts. This excerpt on the worldview of the Igbo people in southeastern Nigeria was compiled by an Igbo anthropologist, who summarized Igbo thought. Many Igbo perspectives may well derive from the Nok and Bantu cultures, whose ancestral homelands are near the region where the Igbo live today.

There is the world of man peopled by all created beings and things, both animate and inanimate. The spirit world is the abode of the creator, the deities, the disembodied and malignant spirits, and the ancestral spirits. It is the future abode of the living after their death. . . . Existence for the Igbo is a dual but interrelated phenomenon involving the interaction between the material and the spiritual, the visible and the invisible, the good and the bad, the living and the dead. . . . The world of the "dead" is a world full of activities. . . . The principle of seniority makes the ancestors [in the world of the "dead"] the head of the [extended kinship system in the world of man]. . . .

The world as a natural order which inexorably goes on its ordained way according to a "master plan" is foreign to Igbo conceptions. Rather, their world is a dynamic one—a world of moving equilibrium. It is an equilibrium that is constantly threatened, and sometimes actually disturbed by natural and social calamities. . . . But the Igbo believe that these social calamities and cosmic forces which disturb their world are controllable and should be "manipulated" by them for their own purpose. The maintenance of social and cosmological balance in the world becomes . . . a dominant and pervasive theme in Igbo life. They achieve this balance . . . through divination, sacrifice, and appeal to the countervailing forces of their ancestors . . . against the powers of the malignant spirits. . . . The Igbo world is not only a world in which people strive for equality; it is one in which change is constantly expected. . . . Life on earth is a link in the chain of status hierarchy which culminates in the achievement of ancestral honor in the world of the dead. . . .

The idea of a creator of all things is focal to Igbo theology. They believe in a supreme god, a high god, who is all good. . . . The Igbo high god is a withdrawn god. He is a god who has finished all active works of creation and keeps watch over his creatures from a distance. . . . Although the Igbo feel psychologically separated from their high god, he is not too far away, he can be reached, but not as quickly as can other deities who must render their services to man to justify their demand for sacrifices. . . . Minor gods [can] be controlled, manipulated, and used to further human interests. . . . Given effective protection, the Igbo are very faithful to their gods.

THINKING ABOUT THE READING

1. How do the Igbo understand the relationship between the human and spiritual worlds?
2. What is the role of the supreme god in their polytheistic theology?
3. How might their beliefs about the relationship of the human and spiritual realms shape Igbo society?

Source: Victor C. Uchendu, *The Igbo of Southeast Nigeria* (New York: Holt, Rinehart and Winston, 1965), pp. 11–13, 15–16, 94–95. Copyright © 1965. Reprinted with permission of Wadsworth, a division of Thomson Learning: www.thomsonrights.com.

---

central Africa. The Bantus incorporated many of the peoples they encountered and modified their own cultures to suit local conditions.

The Bantu occupation of central, eastern, and southern Africa is the result of one of the great population movements in premodern world history, a saga similar to that of the sea voyages that resulted in the settlement of the Pacific islands, the Indo-European migration into western and southern Eurasia, and the Native American settlement of the Western Hemisphere. During this process, the Bantu population multiplied many times and formed networks that fostered trade and the diffusion of technology. As the Bantus spread out over a wider area, they became less cohesive and gradually divided into the over four hundred different ethnic groups that today dominate this vast region.

Archaeological and linguistic evidence allows us to reconstruct the Bantu migrations (see Map 3.2). The Bantus originated along the Benue (BAIN-way) River in what is now eastern Nigeria and western Cameroon (KAM-uh-roon). By 3000 B.C.E. they were already combining farming (especially of yams) with hunting, gathering, and fishing. But agricultural progress fostered overcrowding by 2000 B.C.E., or perhaps earlier, spurring some to migrate eastward into the lands just north of the Congo River Basin. Bantus settled the Great Lakes region of East Africa between 1000 B.C.E. and 500 B.C.E., and by 1000 B.C.E. some land-short Bantus from the Benue began moving to the south and southeast. Some moved up the Congo River, setting up small farms. Often whole family groups moved together. As they settled in new areas, Bantus mixed with the local peoples, exchanging technologies and cultural patterns.

The Bantus benefited from metallurgy and agricultural technologies. Well before the Common Era the Bantus in the Benue region had learned to smelt iron, perhaps from the

Map 3.2 Bantu Migrations and Early Africa
The Bantu-speaking peoples spread over several millennia throughout the southern half of Africa. Various societies, cities, and states emerged in West and North Africa.

nearby Nok culture. Iron spread along the Bantu communication network. But Bantus migrating eastward may also have adopted the ironworking technology developed by peoples living there. Metallurgy allowed the Bantus to use iron tools and weapons to open new land and subdue the small existing populations. They were also skilled farmers. Some adopted cattle and goat raising as a sideline, while others made these a major economic activity. By 2,000 years ago some Bantus living in northeast Africa had also learned to grow domesticated bananas and plantains (large bananas) imported from Southeast Asia, as well as sorghum (SOAR-gum) from the Nile valley. These high-yielding crops replaced yams as their primary staple food and provided a spur to population growth, encouraging new migration into southern Africa.

Early Societies and Networks of the Eastern Mediterranean

What were the contributions of the Hebrews, Minoans, Mycenaeans, Phoenicians, and Dorian Greeks to later societies in the region?

During the second millennium B.C.E., when the Egyptians and various Mesopotamian empires were growing in strength and competing with one another, smaller bronze- and then iron-using societies in the eastern half of the Mediterranean Basin were developing influential ideas or establishing cities and states. Among these, the Hebrews created the base for three major religions. The Minoans became a flourishing society and an economic bridge between western Asia and southeastern Europe, and the trade-oriented but warlike Mycenaeans built the first cities in Greece. The Phoenicians created an important new alphabet, established colonies in the western Mediterranean, and forged trade links with people as far away as England. Phoenician migration and trade fostered networks connecting many ancient societies. Greek migrants also began building an important society that eventually nourished other societies in Europe, western Asia, and North Africa.

Eastern Mediterranean Environments

The history and diet of peoples living around the eastern Mediterranean, such as the Phoenicians, Minoans, and Greeks, were influenced by the regional climate, with its cool, rainy winters and hot, dry summers, and by the Mediterranean Sea and its coastal areas. On the narrow coastal or interior plains of the northern shores, grain was planted in the late fall and harvested in the spring before the heat of summer killed it, and bread became a basic product. The many hills also encouraged the planting of olive trees and grape vines, and both olive oil and wine became export crops for Greece and Anatolia. Since the mountains and hills of Greece and Anatolia, as well as the drier lands of Lebanon and Palestine, made the development

of large herds of cattle impractical, people raised pigs, sheep, and goats. Indeed pastoralism was common inland from the Levant coast. Finally, the eastern Mediterranean Sea, a large and mostly placid body of water, fostered boat building, maritime trade, and other contacts over long distances and between diverse societies (see Map 3.3).

One of the densest populations emerged in Greece, an appendage of southern Europe located less than 100 miles from Anatolia across the Aegean (ah-JEE-uhn) Sea. The Greeks were destined to live in relatively small, independent city-states and to be a seafaring, trading people. Unlike western Asia and Egypt, where long and wide river valleys invited the creation of large political units, Greece consists of small valleys separated by numerous mountains, some 8,000 to 10,000 feet high. This physical separation encouraged political fragmentation, which meant that people with unpopular or new ideas could move from one small state to another. This mobility encouraged intellectual diversity. Greece also has an extensive coastline with many good harbors, and most Greek cities were built on or near the coast. Greeks could travel by sea east to Ionia (today western Turkey), south to Crete, or west to southern Italy more easily than they could establish connections with nearby inland towns. Thus the Mediterranean linked the societies of the Greek peninsula to other peoples such as the Minoans, Egyptians, and Phoenicians.

The Hebrews and Religious Innovation

For over a thousand years the Hebrews, a Semitic people, were one of many groups of pastoral nomads, led by powerful men known as patriarchs (from the Greek word for "rule by the father"). Their population was smaller, and their economic and technological developments less impressive, than those of many of their neighbors, and when they did organize themselves into a state, their political achievements were short-lived. The united Hebrew monarchy lasted less than a century. Yet the Hebrew contribution to religious history, especially to Christian and Islamic traditions, exceeds that of either the Mesopotamians or Egyptians.

Early Hebrew Society and Politics The various books of the Hebrew Bible contain the basic laws of the Hebrews and are the main source for their early history. The Hebrews trace their ancestry as a people back to Abraham, a patriarch who supposedly lived in Mesopotamia sometime between 2000 and 1500 B.C.E. (see Chronology: The Eastern Mediterranean, 2000–539 B.C.E. on page 73). The question of whether Abraham was a real person or, as most scholars suspect, mythical may never be resolved by archaeological research. Nevertheless, the patriarch and his two sons, Isaac and Ishmael, are considered the spiritual ancestors of three monotheistic religions—Judaism, Christianity, and Islam—which are often called the Abrahamic faiths and collectively have some 3 billion followers today.

Historians and archaeologists, among them modern Israelis, have heatedly debated the historical reliability and antiquity of the Hebrew Bible, which was probably based in part on older oral

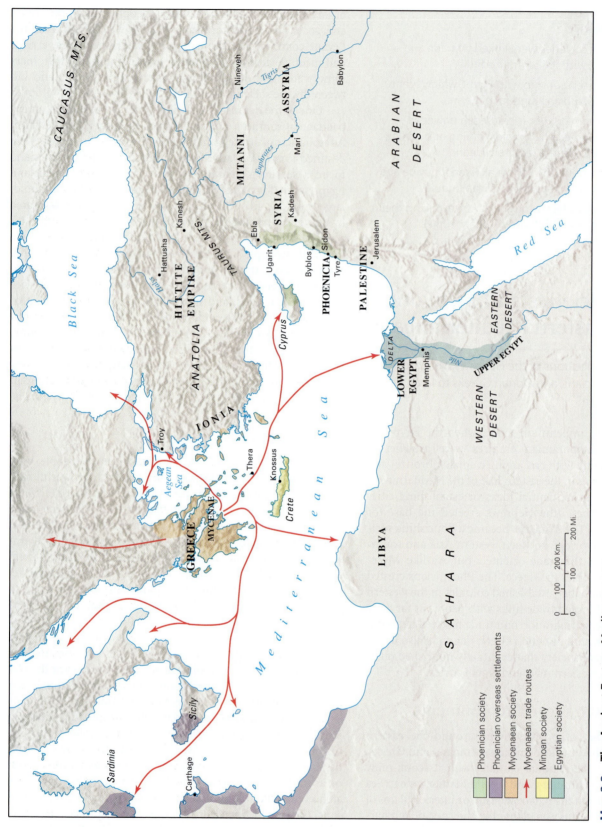

Map 3.3 The Ancient Eastern Mediterranean
The Hebrew, Minoan, Mycenaean, Phoenician, and Greek societies developed along the eastern shores of the Mediterranean Sea. They exchanged goods and ideas with each other and with other western Asians and the Egyptians.

The Eastern Mediterranean, 2000–539 B.C.E.

2000–1500	Possible time frame for Abraham (biblical account)
2000–1400	Minoan society
1630	Volcanic eruption destroys Thera (Santorini)
1600–1200	Mycenaean society
1500–650	Phoenician society
1300–1200	Hebrew Exodus from Egypt led by Moses (biblical account)
1200–800	Greek "Dark Age"
1250	Destruction of Troy, possibly by Mycenaeans
1000	First Hebrew kingdom (biblical account)
922–722	Hebrew kingdoms of Israel and Judah
750	Carthage colony established by Phoenicians
722	Assyrian conquest of Israel
586	Neo-Babylonian (Chaldean) conquest of Judah
539	End of Babylonian captivity

polytheistic world, Abraham recognized one supreme god. Peoples from Palestine, probably including some Hebrews, had migrated, either voluntarily or as slaves, to Egypt since at least 2000 B.C.E. A group of Hebrews who had gone to Egypt to escape drought and been enslaved were freed and left Egypt, probably in the thirteenth century. This "Exodus" from Egypt and eventual return to Palestine was led by Moses, whom the later Hebrews believed to be the founder of their religion. Moses gave his name to a code of laws, including the Ten Commandments, by which the Hebrews governed themselves. Egyptian and Mesopotamian ideas influenced some of the laws and religious views. The biblical account indicates that not all Hebrews were monotheists who followed the Mosaic laws, but that around 1000 B.C.E. the Hebrews had enough unity to establish a monarchy centered in the small city of Jerusalem.

Hebrew unity proved short-lived. After the death of King Solomon in 922 B.C.E., the monarchy split into a northern kingdom of Israel and a southern kingdom of Judah. In 722 the Assyrians conquered Israel and resettled its inhabitants elsewhere in their empire. When Assyria fell, the Hebrew prophet Nahum (NAY-hum) expressed the joy of many: "Nineveh [the Assyrian capital] is laid waste; who will bemoan her? All who hear the news of you will clap their hands over you."[14] In 586 the Chaldeans conquered the kingdom of Judah and moved its leaders to the Euphrates near Babylon. The bitterness of the "Babylonian Captivity" was reflected in a Hebrew psalm: "By the rivers of Babylon, there we sat down, yea, we wept when we remembered Zion."[15] This exile ended in 539 when the Persians conquered the Chaldeans and allowed the Hebrews to return to Palestine. Later Palestine became part of the Roman Empire. The Jews (from the word *Yehudin,* a term Hebrews used to describe themselves by about 500 B.C.E.) were again dispersed after a revolt against Roman rule in 70 C.E. From that time until the establishment of modern Israel in 1948 C.E., there was no Hebrew or Jewish state.

traditions. Little of it can be confirmed by nonbiblical sources such as archaeology. Some scholars think the biblical books are quite old while others argue that most or all of the books, even those offering accounts of very ancient events, were composed after 700 B.C.E. to support the claims of Hebrew political and religious factions. The earliest known material evidence for biblical passages are inscriptions found on silver scrolls dating from the late 500s B.C.E. Some bible stories seem based on Mesopotamian and Egyptian traditions, such as the great flood in the *Epic of Gilgamesh,* suggesting the spread of ideas. For example, some of the advice in the Hebrew Book of Proverbs, such as helping neighbors rather than acquiring wealth, and treating the disabled with dignity, closely echoes advice in more ancient Egyptian writings. These ongoing controversies in biblical scholarship underline the importance of Hebrew religion to later history.

In the biblical account, during the second millennium Abraham led a small group of people on a migration from southern Mesopotamia to Palestine, an area on the Mediterranean coast between Egypt and Syria. Although born into a

Hebrew Religion and World History The religious history of the Hebrews, especially their ethical code, makes them memorable in world history. Over their long history both as nomads and as settled state builders, the Hebrews developed or refined four religious concepts that made them stand out among ancient peoples and that later influenced the Western and Islamic traditions. These concepts are found in their sacred writings; they include monotheism, morality, messianism, and meaning in history.

The first concept, monotheism, developed in two stages. At first, while polytheism remained influential for some centuries among other peoples, many Hebrews worshiped a single god, *Yahweh* (YA-way). They believed Yahweh had made an agreement, or covenant, with their earliest patriarchs and reinforced it when Moses received the Ten Commandments. If they would obey him, he would protect them. This form of monotheism, similar to that proposed by the Egyptian pharaoh Akhenaton to replace the two thousand Egyptian gods, did not deny that other peoples had gods but asserted that the Hebrews had only one. Some neighboring peoples may also have adopted

The Captivity of Israeli Women at Ninevah   This relief comes from the palace of the Chaldean king Sennacherib in Ninevah. It was probably carved at the beginning of the seventh century B.C.E. (Erich Lessing/Art Resource, NY)

monotheistic views around the same time. Gradually, however, the Hebrews reshaped monotheism, asserting that there is only one God, Yahweh, for all peoples, as the prophet Isaiah proclaimed: "There is no other God besides Me, a just God. Look to Me, and be saved, all you ends of the earth!"[16]

Hebrew holy men known as prophets refined a second Hebrew religious concept, morality. Working in the troubled times between the end of the united monarchy and the fall of Israel to the Assyrians, these men emphasized that it was not enough to obey the Bible's social and ritual commandments. Following Yahweh also meant leading a moral life, that is, refraining from lying, stealing, adultery, and persecution of the poor and oppressed. For example, the prophet Amos advised his people to hate evil and love good. One of the differences between the code of Hammurabi and the law of Moses was that the latter, while accepting the belief in retaliation, also emphasized compassion for the poor, for example, by ordering that all debts be canceled every seven years. Also, unlike the Mesopotamian law, Hebrew law required that only the wrongdoer be punished, and not members of his or her family. Hebrew ethics emphasized mercy as well as justice.

The third Hebrew contribution to religious thought was **messianism**, the belief that God had given the Hebrew people

a special mission in the world. As the Hebrews faced their time of troubles after the division of Solomon's kingdom, and especially after the fall of Judah to the Chaldeans, messianism acquired a broad spiritual meaning of bringing proper ethical behavior to all peoples. This idea is found in the book of Isaiah, where the prophet refers to Israelites as models from whom other people can learn moral truth: "I will give you as a covenant to the people, as a light to the [nations]. To open blind eyes, to bring out prisoners from the prison, those who sit in darkness."[17] This idea later inspired Christian missionary work.

The final important Hebrew religious contribution is the idea that history itself has meaning and that it moves forward in a progressive, linear fashion and not in great repetitive cosmic cycles of thousands or millions of years. The Hebrews believed that Yahweh acted in history by making specific agreements with particular individuals, such as Abraham and Moses. Sanctifying a linear view of time meant that the material, time-bound world was where human beings worked out their salvation by choosing good over evil. This belief helped shape the attitudes toward the material world found in all Western religions, and it also helped give birth later to the idea of progress, the notion that the future will be better than the past. It stood in contrast to ideas enshrined in the Indian religions of Hinduism and Buddhism that the material world is illusory and that time is cyclical.

---

messianism   The Hebrew belief that their God, Yahweh, had given them a special mission in the world.

Minoan Crete and Regional Trade

An important urban society and network hub, now called Minoan (mi-NO-an), thrived on the island of Crete (kreet) between about 2000 and 1400 B.C.E. Crete lies just south of the Aegean Sea and the Greek peninsula, a strategic location that made it a logical center for sea trade between Egypt, western Asia, and southeastern Europe. Archaeologists who discovered the remains of an elaborate royal palace at Knossos (NAW-sus), on the northern shore of the island, named it Minos (MY-nus), after a Greek legend about a king who had once ruled in Crete. In the story, Minos "made himself master of the Greek waters, and for the safer conveyance of his revenues, he did all he could to suppress piracy."[18]

Historians have remained intrigued by the achievements of Minoan society. Some of the buildings had plumbing, and some towns had streets with drains and sewers, like the cities in ancient India. Paintings and sculptures show some Mesopotamian and Egyptian influences, but they are also different in style. Particularly interesting was the apparent worship of a large number of female deities, including an im-

portant mother goddess, and many paintings of flowers, animals, and bare-breasted females. The Minoans built no fortresses, and the towns lacked defensive walls. They apparently relied on their fleet alone to protect them. Around 1630 B.C.E. many cities on the island were destroyed, perhaps from earthquakes that followed a massive volcanic explosion that blew apart the nearby island of Thera (THER-uh) (today's Santorini). The sinking of most of Thera and the dispersal of the survivors may have given rise to the legend of the lost continent of Atlantis.

The first great Mediterranean sea power, the Minoans were innovators and played a very important role in regional trade. They pioneered a mixed agriculture that was well suited to the region's sunny, dry climate, growing both olives and grapes as well as grain. Already by 3000 B.C.E. they were using copper and trading intermittently with Egypt, and this trade became regular after 2000. Minoans traded extensively with Sicily, Greece, and the Aegean islands and sent wine, olives, and wool to Egypt and southwest Asia. Though their writing has not been deciphered, tablets found in the palace at Knossos appear to be written in two scripts, one of which may be related

Wall Painting from Thera, Crete The paintings in palaces and homes show slices of Minoan life. This portrays female boxers, hinting that women played many roles in Minoan society. (Julie M. Fair)

to a Mesopotamian language and the other to early forms of Greek. This suggests that ancient Crete served as a hub or meeting place connecting, through trade, western Asians and North Africans with various European societies. The Cretan ports were counterparts to the Persian Gulf ports that linked western and southern Asia.

The Mycenaeans and Regional Power

The Mycenaeans, Indo-Europeans named after the city of Mycenae (my-SEE-nee) in southern Greece, also became an important power between 1600 and 1200 B.C.E. after migrating into the Greek peninsula. Like the Hyksos then moving into Egypt, they were a warrior society. Their graves, which contain swords and armor, show that they valued fighting and had a command of bronze technology. They had a state-controlled economy that was tightly organized from the top down by the king and his scribes. By the middle of the second millennium, the Mycenaeans controlled Crete, whose Minoan society had already collapsed. The Mycenaeans also conquered all of southern Greece and the Aegean islands, forming an empire from which they collected taxes and tribute. They continued the Minoan trading networks, dispatching ships to Sicily, Italy, and Spain and into the Black Sea. This trade spread bronze technology. Mycenaeans also engaged in war with rivals, operating, unlike the Minoans, out of strong fortresses.

According to legends, around 1250 the Mycenaeans conquered Troy, a trading port along the northwestern coast of Anatolia. This event inspired Homer's epic story, the *Iliad*, some 500 years later. Scholars differ as to whether an actual Trojan War ever took place, and some suspect that the Homeric stories combine oral accounts of various conflicts. Whatever their accuracy, they strongly influenced the later Greeks and Romans.

By 1200 B.C.E., however, the Mycenaeans themselves faced collapse, although the reasons remain unclear. A prolonged drought resulting from climate change or a possible series of earthquakes, which may also have destroyed Troy, may have been factors. Many historians blame civil wars and attacks by warlike Indo-Europeans known as the Dorian Greeks, who were migrating into the peninsula. In the several centuries after 1200 various groups known as "Sea Peoples" pillaged and disrupted trade throughout the Aegean and eastern Mediterranean. In Homer's *Odyssey*, a king boasts that he "wandered and suffered much to collect these treasures and bring them home in my ships,"[19] a statement probably referring to regional piracy networks. But eventually a creative society emerged in Greece that incorporated many influences from the Dorian Greeks, Mycenaeans, Phoenicians, and Egyptians, as will be discussed below.

The Phoenicians and Their Networks

The Phoenicians, one of the greatest ancient trading societies, linked Mediterranean and southwest Asian peoples by trade networks and by their invention of a phonetic alphabet.

Between 1500 and 1000 B.C.E. this Semitic people, known to the Hebrews as the Canaanites (Kay-nan-ites), established themselves along the narrow coastal strip west of the Lebanon mountains, where they built the great trading cities of Tyre (tire), Sidon (SIDE-en), and Byblos (BIB-los). Described by Hebrew sources as the crowning city whose merchants were also princes, Tyre was a major hub, the place where luxury goods from many societies were collected and the finest artists and craftsmen worked. The Hebrew prophet Ezekial denounced the rich, vibrant city and listed the extraordinary network of mercantile connections: "Tyre, You who are situated at the entrance of the sea, merchants of the peoples on many coastlands. Your borders are in the midst of the seas. All the ships of the sea were in you to market your merchandise."[20]

Although sometimes dominated by Egypt, these cities were fiercely competitive and independent states headed by kings. Although the Phoenicians spoke a common language and worshiped the same gods, they never united to form one country. The Greek word for book, *byblos*, was taken from the name of the Phoenician city that was famous for its high-quality papyrus, which was used to make written scrolls, the ancient equivalent of our bound books. The Phoenicians' relatively rich, well-situated land was the home of the now long-gone "cedars of Lebanon" prized by the tree-starved Sumerians, Egyptians, and Hebrews. The most famous cultural achievement of the Phoenicians, their simplification of Mesopotamian cuneiform writing into an alphabet of twenty-two characters, became the basis of later European alphabets.

Only a few tablets containing information on government and religion survive, while the papyrus documents which might record their views on trade and daily life, or provide a glimpse of their stories, songs, and jokes, have mostly disappeared. As a result, most of what we know comes from Egyptian, Greek, and Hebrew sources; these peoples generally admired the Phoenicians' skills as scribes, seafarers, engineers, and artisans but also denounced them as immoral profiteers and cheaters. For example, an Egyptian report from around 1100 B.C.E. describes the difficult mission of a pharaoh's envoy, Wen-Amon, who was sent to Byblos to purchase some cedarwood for a new temple. Such trade had gone on for centuries, often with Egypt dictating the terms, but by now Byblos was strong and Egyptian power had waned. On his sea journey the hapless Wen-Amon was robbed. In Byblos he waited days for an audience with the Byblos king, Zakar-Baal, who wanted to sell timber but realized Wen-Amon now had little money left to purchase anything. After a chilly meeting, Zakar-Baal sold the demoralized Egyptian a small amount of wood. The king made clear he would deal with Egypt and any other power on his own terms. The Phoenician image as schemers, deserved or not, survives into modern times. Our term for a shameless woman, Jezebel, is derived from a princess of Tyre.

The Phoenician creation of this alphabet helped spread Phoenician influence in the Mediterranean and the networks they created. Between 1000 and 800 B.C.E., the seafaring Phoenicians began to replace the declining Mycenaeans as the leaders in Mediterranean trade with western Asia. They also may have helped spread knowledge of ironworking to Europe. In addition, the Phoenicians became experts in new methods of dyeing cloth, and they may have traveled as far as England to get supplies of tin. In the process, they established colonies or trading posts beyond the Strait of Gibraltar on the southern coast of Spain, as well as in Morocco, Sicily, and southern Italy. They fished for tuna in the Atlantic and some historians think the Phoenicians may have reached the Canary Islands and Madeira, off the coast of Morocco, and conceivably the more distant Azores, nearly a third of the way to North America. Thus the Phoenicians became the greatest mariners of the ancient Mediterranean. They also traded overland with Arabia and Syria.

Between 1000 and 500 B.C.E., the Mediterranean Sea became a major source of goods and wealth, partly because of Phoenician efforts. Although coins were probably not used widely until the seventh century B.C.E., centuries earlier solid bars of precious metals served as currency. By 1200 B.C.E., if not earlier, ships capable of carrying two hundred copper bars were sailing the Mediterranean. Using their colonies as ports for resupply and repair, the Phoenicians traveled long distances to secure iron, silver, timber, copper, gold, and tin, all valuable commodities in western Asia and Egypt during the second and first millennia B.C.E. Legends suggest that around 600 B.C.E., under the sponsorship of the Egyptian king, a Phoenician fleet may even have sailed around Africa in an expedition lasting three years, but these journeys cannot be substantiated. In 650 B.C.E. the Assyrians conquered the Phoenician home cities and brought an end to their dynamic power, but some Phoenician colonies lived on. The most famous colony was Carthage in North Africa, established around 750 B.C.E. near what is today Tunis. A legend tells of Elissa, the sister of a king in Tyre who was caught in a political feud and left with some followers in search of a new home. They eventually established the city of Carthage, which became the capital of a major trading empire and the chief competitor to the Romans in the western Mediterranean by the third century B.C.E. As great sailors the Carthaginians later explored far down the coast of West Africa.

The Eclectic Roots of Greek Society

The fall of the Phoenicians and the Mycenaeans set the stage for another seafaring people, the Greeks, to found an influential urban society. Historians have referred to the centuries from the destruction of Mycenae around 1200 B.C.E. down to around 800 B.C.E. as the Greek "Dark Age," because during this time organized states and writing disappeared and social and political conditions were chaotic on the peninsula. During these centuries the economic and social environment changed considerably, and there was great population movement. This was the period of the "Sea Peoples" mentioned earlier. Dorian Greeks, whose migrations had contributed to the fall of Mycenae, settled much of the Greek peninsula, and many Mycenaeans dispersed, some settling the offshore islands and others crossing the Aegean Sea to Ionia, where they established cities.

The Greek world, scattered, as the philosopher Plato later put it, like frogs around a pond, became a mix of Mycenaean and Dorian peoples and traditions. In the absence of strong governments, various tribes struggled for power. The Homeric epics, which were written during this period, became an integral part of the Greek tradition in an era of much political and economic change.

Although the Greeks were famous as maritime traders, they were also warriors. Their respect for military strength is reflected in the works of Homer, oral epics written down between the eleventh and the eighth centuries B.C.E. Historians disagree as to whether Homer was an actual person or the collective name for several authors who compiled these epic poems into a narrative. As mentioned earlier, they also debate whether the epics reflect actual events from the Mycenaean era or represent a composite of various stories from the past. Some scholars argue that many themes and plots in the epics reflect influences from Mesopotamian literature such as *The Epic of Gilgamesh*, indicating the spread of ideas around the eastern Mediterranean world.

The first Homeric epic, the *Iliad*, is set during an attack by some Greek cities, led by their king Agamemnon (ag-uh-MEM-non), on Troy across the Aegean in Anatolia. The poem emphasizes the aristocratic value of valor in war but also warns its readers against excessive pride. Arrogance leads the Greeks to make some nearly fatal mistakes. For example, the Greek hero Achilles (uh-KIL-eez) refuses to fight after a quarrel with Agamemnon. When the Trojans, led by Hector, try to burn the enemy ships, Achilles' friend Patroclus (puh-TROW-klus) takes Achilles' place in the battle and is killed by Hector. An angry and remorseful Achilles then kills Hector, warning that friendship between them is impossible, and there could be no truce until one of them has fallen. The poem ends when Hector's father, Priam, comes to ask Achilles for his son's body. Achilles is moved by Priam's courage, and both men share their grief. The Greek victory also costs many lives on both sides.

This poem and Homer's second epic, the *Odyssey* (ODD-eh-see), a story of the adventures of Odysseus (oh-DIS-ee-us), or Ulysses (YOU-lis-eez) returning home after the Trojan War, portrayed the Greek gods as superheroes who intervened frequently to help their human friends and hinder their enemies. The Homeric world measured virtue by success in combat. Both gods and men took more joy in competition and battle than they did in justice or mercy. Yet these great epics continue to be read, not only because of their dramatic and often brutal war scenes, but also because they tell us something about the tragedy and pathos of human life. This emphasis on both human power and suffering remained a part of Greek literature throughout the following centuries. The Homeric epics and belief in the gods that they introduced greatly influenced the emerging Greek society.

As mentioned above, Greek society eventually became a synthesis of Mycenaean and Dorian traditions. The Greeks also borrowed ideas from neighboring peoples, including the Egyptians and western Asians, although the degree of outside influence on early Greek culture is debated (see the Historical

Controversy feature in "Societies, Networks, Transitions," page 101). Certainly the Mediterranean was a zone of interaction for peoples living around its rim. Phoenician ships, which had avoided a turbulent Greece for several hundred years, began to show up again, restoring Greek contact with the eastern Mediterranean and its regional trade networks. Soon the Greeks adopted and modified the Phoenician alphabet and began trading with western Asia again as they had during the Mycenaean period. These centuries built a foundation for a dynamic Greek society in the Classical Era.

SECTION SUMMARY

- Mountainous Greece favored the development of many small, independent communities, rather than one homogenous community.

- The Hebrews were politically fragmented, but their religious writings, with their emphasis on monotheism, morality, messianism, and meaning in history, have had a tremendous impact on religious history.

- Minoan Crete was the first great Mediterranean sea power and had a well-developed urban infrastructure.

- Around 1250 B.C.E., the Mycenaeans possibly conquered Troy; this event later inspired Homer's epic, the *Iliad*.

- The Phoenicians, the region's greatest maritime traders, simplified the Mesopotamian cuneiform writing into an alphabet, which served as the basis for later European alphabets.

- The Homeric epics, the *Iliad* and the *Odyessy*, greatly influenced the emerging Greek society, which was a synthesis of Mycenaean and Dorian Greek peoples.

Online Study Center ACE the Test

Chapter Summary

Egypt is often called "the gift of the Nile" because it arose in the flood-prone Nile River valley. The Egyptian system was extraordinarily durable, lasting for several thousand years in its basic form. Like the Mesopotamians, the Egyptians developed a state led by kings and invented the hieroglyphics writing system. In their stable and predictable environment, the Egyptians developed a more optimistic worldview and culture than the Mesopotamians, who were buffeted by chronic power struggles. Egyptians also participated in trade networks linking western Asia and the Mediterranean Basin with sub-Saharan Africa and India.

Many of the peoples of sub-Saharan Africa also made the great transition to farming by inventing or adopting agriculture and metallurgy, both of which built the framework for cities and states. These societies were often modified by contacts with other peoples around them. An environment of grasslands, forests, and the expanding Sahara Desert helped to

shape their history, and the gradual drying out of the Sahara region forced many people to migrate. Cities arose early in Nubia (along the central Nile), probably stimulated by long-distance trade and contacts with Egypt. The Sudan fostered distinctive cultures. The Bantu peoples, in one of the greatest migrations in history, spread their farming and iron-based culture and languages widely in the southern half of Africa and established networks over vast distances.

The Mediterranean societies also benefited from regional connections. The trade routes of the Minoans, Mycenaeans, and especially the seafaring Phoenicians enriched the peoples of western Asia and the Mediterranean Basin by bringing them material goods, markets, cultural contacts, and a practical new alphabet. The Hebrews' evolving understanding of their mission, and of Yahweh, was influenced by their contact with Egyptians and Mesopotamians. Some of these contributions, such as the Phoenician alphabet and Hebrew religious and ethical concepts, have influenced many peoples down to the present day. Greece arose from interaction among several Mediterranean societies in a turbulent period during which Homer wrote his great epics.

Online Study Center Improve Your Grade Flashcards

Key Terms

pharaohs	Sudan
hieroglyphics	desertification
ma'at	Bantu
monotheism	messianism

Suggested Reading

Books

Castledon, Rodney. *Minoans: Life in Bronze Age Crete.* New York: Routledge, 1993. Valuable recent survey.

Connah, Graham. *African Civilization: An Archaeological Perspective.* 2nd ed. Cambridge: Cambridge University Press, 2004. A good overview of early African societies; emphasizes the rise of cities and states.

Dunstan, William E. *The Ancient Near East.* New York: Harcourt Brace, 1998. Designed for the general reader, this work makes sense of the confusing array of states and empires in western Asia and Egypt.

Ehret, Christopher. *The Civilizations of Africa: A History to 1800.* Charlottesville: University of Virginia Press, 2002. A pathbreaking introduction to African history, with nearly half devoted to the ancient period.

Grimal, Nicholas. *A History of Ancient Egypt.* Oxford: Blackwell, 1992. A clear account of this society for beginning students.

Harris, Nathaniel. *History of Ancient Egypt: The Culture and Lifestyle of the Ancient Egyptians.* New York: Barnes and Noble, 1997. A richly illustrated overview of Egyptian life.

Markoe, Glenn E. *The Phoenicians.* Berkeley: University of California Press, 2000. A fine account of the history, cities, economy, and literature of this maritime society.

McNutt, Paula M. *Restructuring the Society of Ancient Israel.* Louisville: Westminster John Knox Press, 1998. Recent survey of knowledge and scholarly debates.

Mertz, Barbara. *Red Land, Black Land: Daily Life in Ancient Egypt.* Rev. ed. New York: Peter Bedrick, 1990. A lively and readable re-creation of the lives and values of ancient Egyptians.

Newman, James L. *The Peopling of Africa: A Geographic Interpretation.* New Haven: Yale University Press, 1995. An excellent summary of what we know about the early history and migrations of Africa's people.

Niditch, Susan. *Ancient Israelite Religion.* New York: Oxford University Press, 1997. An account of the Hebrew religion that shows its debt to the Canaanites as well as those features that made it unique.

Stiebing, William H. *Ancient Near Eastern History and Culture.* New York: Longman, 2003. An up-to-date survey of ancient western Asia, Egypt, and the eastern Mediterranean.

Tyldesley, Joyce. *Hatshepsut: The Female Pharaoh.* New York: Viking, 1996. Readable biography of this remarkable leader.

Welsby, Derek A. *The Kingdom of Kush: Napatan and Meroitic Empires.* Princeton: Markus Wiener, 1996. A well-illustrated and up-to-date survey of kushite society.

Websites

African Timelines (http://web.edu/cagatucci/classes/hum211/timelines/htimelinetoc.htm). Offers many links to essays and other sources on Africa; maintained by Central Oregon Community College.

Ancient Jewish History (http://www.us-israel.org/jsources/Judaism/jewhist.html). Offers much useful information.

Exploring Ancient World Cultures (http://eawe.evansville.edu). Excellent site run by Evansville University, with essays and links on the ancient Near East and Europe.

Internet African History Sourcebook (http://www.fordham.edu/halsall/africa/africasbook.html). This site contains much useful information and documentary material on ancient Africa.

Internet Ancient History Sourcebook (http://www.fordham.edu/halsall/ancient/asbook.html). Exceptionally rich collection of links and primary source readings.

CHAPTER 4

Around the Pacific Rim: Eastern Eurasia and the Americas, 5000–600 B.C.E.

Online Study Center

This icon will direct you to interactive activities and study materials on the website: college.hmco.com/pic/lockard1e

Shang Axe Head The Shang Chinese made some of the ancient world's finest bronze tools. This axe head, decorated with a human face, may have been used to behead rivals of the Shang rulers. (Bildarchiv Preussischer Kulturbesitz/Art Resource, NY)

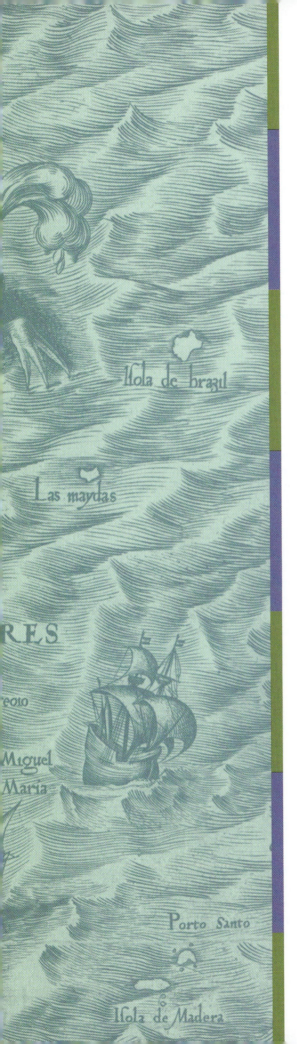

He encouraged the people and settled them. He called his superintendent of works [and] minister of instruction, and charged them with the building of the houses. Crowds brought the earth in baskets. The roll of the great drum did not overpower [the noise of the builders].

<small>CHINESE POEM FROM THE SECOND MILLENNIUM B.C.E.[1]</small>

According to Chinese tradition, around 1400 B.C.E. a ruler named Pan Keng supervised the building of a new capital city, Anyang (ahn-yahng), on a flat plain alongside the Huan River. The king and his officials supervised the citizens in the hard construction labor, which was done to the beat of a drum. Because Anyang's location had many advantages, the king had high expectations for his new capital. Thanks to the rich soil, productive farms would stretch out into the distance. The river could supply water and aid in defense. People could find timber, hunt animals, or—the king himself probably thought of this—seek relief from the summer heat in mountains a short chariot ride away. Anyang was likely China's first planned city. Surrounded by four walls facing the points of the compass, it reflected the ancient adage that without harmony nothing lasts. This basic system governed city planning for the next 3,000 years.

Three and a half millennia later archaeologists digging at Anyang found exquisite ritual bronzes and "dragon bones," animal bones carved with some of the earliest Chinese writing. For hundreds of years, local chemists, not knowing their priceless historical value, had been grinding up these bones to make folk medicine. To the archaeologists, however, they showed that ancient China, like Mesopotamia and Egypt, had both cities and a writing system. The Chinese concern for posterity is reflected in their writing. An Anyang artisan, Ts'ai Shu, had inscribed on a bronze vessel: "I myself made this. May my sons and grandsons for a myriad years treasure it and use it without limit."[2] Although Anyang's buildings crumbled with time and ruling families came and went, the legacy of early China did live on for centuries.

Cities, states, agriculture, and trade networks developed in various societies on both sides of the Pacific Ocean. On the Asian side, ancient cities like Anyang confirm that, as in India, Mesopotamia, and Egypt, distinctive urban societies appeared very early in China, developing largely from local roots. People in China, Southeast Asia, and Korea were among the first people in the world to develop farming, metalworking, and maritime technology and to establish enduring traditions. The ancient Chinese established a foundation for a society that has retained many of its original ideas and customs down to the present day. Despite formidable geographical barriers, China and Southeast Asia also became connected very early to other parts of Eurasia by trade networks. On the

American side of the Pacific, too, many peoples underwent the great transitions to farming, cities, and complex social structures, while others, less involved with urbanization or state formation, nevertheless flourished by using various strategies for survival. Although environmental factors such as mountains, deserts, and forest barriers tended to isolate North, Central, and South American societies from each other, regional networks of exchange still formed even here during the ancient period.

FOCUS QUESTIONS

1. How did an expanding Chinese society arise from diverse local traditions?
2. What were some key differences between the Shang and Zhou periods in China?
3. How did the traditions developing in Southeast and Northeast Asia differ from those in India and China?
4. How do scholars explain the settlement of the Americas and the rise of agriculture in these continents?
5. What were some of the main features of the first American societies?

The Formation of Chinese Society, 6000–1750 B.C.E.

How did an expanding Chinese society arise from diverse local traditions?

China was one of the first societies with cities and states, joining Harappa, Mesopotamia, Egypt, and Minoan Crete in pioneering new ways of life. Societies change in part through contact with each other, but this was less true for ancient China than for India, southwestern Asia, or the Mediterranean Basin. Forbidding desert and mountain barriers, including the high Tibetan (tuh-BET-en) Plateau, on China's western borders complicated travel, although they did not prevent some influences from crossing borders. This relative remoteness resulted in limited contact with the other ancient urban societies. But productive farming, creative cultures, and the rise of states laid the framework for a distinctive society, now at least 4,000 years old, that dominated a sphere of interaction in eastern Eurasia.

China and Its Regional Environments

The Chinese faced many challenges in communicating both with each other and with distant peoples. China's vast size, combined with a difficult topography, made transportation difficult and also encouraged regional cultural and political loyalties. The Chinese were often divided into competing states, especially in early times, and governments struggled to enforce centralizing policies. The Himalayas (him-uh-LAY-uhs), the Tibetan Plateau, and great deserts inhibited contact with South and West Asia. However, the ancient Chinese did

have regular exchanges, including both trade and conflict, with the various peoples in Central Asia, North Asia, Southeast Asia, and Tibet, whose cultures, languages, and ways of life were very different from the Chinese. Over the centuries the Chinese sometimes extended political control over these peoples and sometimes were invaded and even conquered by them.

China's large land area was one major factor that fostered regionalism (division into different regions). Modern China covers as much land as western and eastern Europe combined. The eastern third of the modern country, where most of the people live, is about half the size of the continental United States. Before modern times, most Chinese lived in inland river valleys rather than along the coast. As a result, maritime, or ocean, commerce was not very significant until 1000 C.E. In the interior, extensive mountains, deserts, and wetlands hindered transportation, and therefore communication, between one region and another.

China's three major river systems helped shape Chinese regionalism. The Yellow, or Huang He (hwang ho), River; the Yangzi (yahng-zeh), or Yangtze, River; and the West, or Xijiang (SHEE JYAHNG), River all flow from west to east and hence do not link the northern, central, and southern parts of China. The Yellow River, sometimes termed "China's sorrow" because of its many destructive floods, flows some 3,000 miles through north China to the Yellow Sea, but it is easily navigable only in some sections. The more navigable but also flood-prone Yangzi, the world's fourth-longest river, flows through central China, a region of moderate climate that has had the densest population for the past thousand years. The shorter West River system helps define mountainous and subtropical south China.

China's neighboring regions had diverse environments and distinctive cultures. The deserts and grasslands of Central Asia, with their blazing hot summers and long, bitterly cold winters, were unpromising for intensive agriculture except in the Oxus River Valley (see Chapter 2). The rugged, pastoralist

CHRONOLOGY

	China	Japan and Southeast Asia	The Americas
10,000 B.C.E.		**10,000–300 B.C.E.** Jomon culture	
5000 B.C.E.	**5000–3000 B.C.E.** Yangshao culture	**4000–2000 B.C.E.** Austronesian migrations	
3000 B.C.E.	**3000–2200 B.C.E.** Longshan culture		**3000–1600 B.C.E.** Peruvian cities
2000 B.C.E.	**1752–1122 B.C.E.** Shang dynasty **1122–221 B.C.E.** Zhou dynasty		**1200–300 B.C.E.** Olmecs **1200–200 B.C.E.** Chavín
1000 B.C.E.		**1000–800 B.C.E.** First Southeast Asian states	

Central Asian societies that lived there traded with, warred against, and sometimes conquered the settled farmers of China, Korea, and India. The Central Asians who most affected Chinese history included diverse Turkish-speaking peoples, some of whom still live in the dry Xinjiang (SHIN-jee-yahng) region of far western China. South of the deserts, the Tibetans of the high plateau were subsistence farmers and herders. The ancient Chinese also forged occasional relations with people in mainland Southeast Asia, Manchuria, and Korea.

Early Chinese Agriculture

Agriculture in China began around 7000 B.C.E., perhaps 1,000 years later than in Mesopotamia, and fine food became a Chinese preoccupation (see Chronology: Ancient China, 7000–600 B.C.E.). The remains of Neolithic settlements have been discovered all over China, and they have revealed various regional traditions, suggesting the diverse roots of Chinese society. The Yellow and Wei River Valleys in north China were major centers of early farming. The modest annual rainfall and tendency toward flooding made the region somewhat similar to the Nile, Tigris-Euphrates, and Indus Basins. In addition, winds blowing in from the Gobi Desert of Mongolia to the northwest deposited massive amounts of dust, known as **loess** (LESS), which enriched the soils of north China. The people planted the wheatlike, highly drought-resistant prairie grass called millet. Later, wheat, likely imported from India or Mesopotamia, became northern China's main cereal grain.

loess The dust blown in from the Mongolian deserts that enriched the soils of northern China.

Ancient songs tell us something about the farming routine:

They clear away the grass, the trees; Their ploughs open up the ground. In a thousand pairs they tug at weeds and roots, Along the low grounds, along the ridges. They sow the many sorts of grain, The seeds that hold moist life. How that blade shoots up, How sleek, the grown plant.[3]

Further south, the Chinese in the Yangzi River Basin began cultivating rice by 5000 B.C.E. Whether they were the first to grow rice or learned it from people in southern China or

CHRONOLOGY

Ancient China, 7000–600 B.C.E.

7000	Agriculture begins in Yellow River Basin
5000	Agriculture begins in Yangzi River Basin
5000–3000	Yangshao culture in northern China
3000–2200	Longshan culture in northern China
2600	Copper mining
2183–1752	Xia dynasty in northern China (disputed)
1752–1122	Shang dynasty in northern China
1400	Beginning of bronze-casting industry
1122–221	Zhou dynasty

Southeast Asia remains unclear. Thus very early two distinct agricultural traditions emerged. In the north, where the climate was cold and dry, drought-tolerant crops like wheat, millet, pears, and apricots were mainstays. In the wetter, warmer southern half of China, irrigated rice and more temperate crops came to predominate. But rice became so important that for several thousand years Chinese have greeted each other by asking, Have you eaten rice yet?, and have described losing a job as breaking one's rice bowl.

Highly productive agriculture was always a key to China's success. Making wise use of the land, the Chinese sustained reasonably adequate diets over many millennia. In part because of climate changes, famine was fairly common, as it was elsewhere, yet the Chinese people were basically well fed, well clothed, and well housed throughout much of history, beginning in ancient times. Productive farming also promoted population growth: northern and central China contained between 2 and 4 million people by 3000 B.C.E.

The Chinese ate well enough and grew enough food that they came to perceive food as more than simple fuel. Cooking became an art form, an arena for aesthetic involvement and sensory delight, and an essential component of social life. A God of the Kitchen became an important deity of folk religion. Many distinctive regional variations in cooking developed, as any traveler will see if he or she explores the Cantonese, Hunanese (hoo-nahn-eez), Mandarin, and Sichuanese (SUH-chwahn-eez) restaurants in large cities around the world. Boiling and steaming were the most common cooking methods during ancient times, but gradually stir-frying replaced roasting in preparing meat. The use of chopsticks for eating meals probably goes back 4,000 years.

The First Farming Societies

Neolithic China included several societies with distinctive regional traditions that established a foundation for Chinese cultural development. The best known of these societies is the Yangshao (YANG-shao) ("painted pottery") culture, which began in the middle Yellow River region around 5000 B.C.E. and covered an area of north China larger than Mesopotamia or Egypt. Several excavated villages from around 4000 B.C.E. tell us that people made fine painted pottery, used kilns, fashioned stone and bone tools, bred pigs and dogs, weaved thread, lived in houses constructed partly with timber, and buried their dead in cemeteries, suggesting belief in an afterlife. They also raised silkworms and fashioned the silk into clothes. In the centuries to follow silk making become a unique Chinese activity, and Chinese silk was exported all over Eurasia.

Farming life in this early society was hard, and probably much communal effort was needed to produce a small agricultural surplus. Village layouts suggest that people already were organizing themselves into larger kinship groups such as clans, a feature of Chinese life thereafter. However, there is little evidence for a ruling elite or warfare.

Neolithic Chinese developed some long-lasting cultural patterns. Music was popular; a 7,000-year-old seven-holed flute is the oldest still playable musical instrument ever found anywhere in the world. The Chinese also created the first known numerical system. Evidence for jade carving, for which the Chinese later became famous, has been found in several regions. Since floods and earthquakes were common, the early Chinese sought various ways to avert disaster. This search led to religious speculation and experimentation with techniques to predict the future.

The Growth and Spread of Chinese Culture

About 3000 B.C.E., when the Sumerians were building their cities, the exchange of ideas and technologies over the developing trade networks began to produce an expansive Chinese culture out of various regional traditions, although apparently there were not yet any true states. The Chinese in the Yellow River Basin developed a society more complex than the Yang-

Peasant Life in Zhou China   The decorations on bronze vessels from Zhou China offer information on peasant life. This decoration, from the Warring States Period, shows people in varied activities: fighting, hunting, making music, performing rituals, and preparing food.   (E. Consten, Das alte China)

shao society, with permanent settlements and irrigated farming, and there were also major achievements elsewhere. As late as 2000 B.C.E. many societies with different cultures and languages remained in China, but gradually the societies in northern and central China merged their traditions into a common social and cultural zone.

Various societies arose in river basins. The Yellow River Basin was always a major core of creativity. The Longshan (LUNG-shahn) ("black pottery") culture dominated the eastern Yellow River area between around 3000 and 2200 B.C.E. Because occupations were more specialized in this society than in the Yangshao society, a division of labor was created and social classes began to emerge. The Longshan people built strong houses, lived in walled villages and towns, had weapons for warfare, and developed farming. They also made pottery almost as hard as metal, carved high-quality jade, and created a simple pictographic writing system. Millennia before any other society, the Chinese of this era also used industrial diamonds to polish ceremonial ruby and sapphire axes, giving them a fine sheen. Societies to the south, east, and north of the Yellow River also made contributions to the emerging Chinese society. For example, the people in the Yangzi Basin produced distinctive traditions of agriculture, animal domestication, town building, and bronze metallurgy that were at least as old, if not older, than those of north China.

Later, during the first millennium B.C.E., Chinese identity and customs gradually expanded from the Yellow and Yangzi Basins into south China. The Chinese displaced or absorbed most of the indigenous (in-DIJ-uh-nuhs) peoples (the original inhabitants) in the south, although many ethnic minorities still live there. An old folk song celebrated the expansion: "We shall extend to the limits of the east, Even to the states along the sea. Tribes to the south will all proffer their allegiance."[4] This mixing of different peoples produced a Chinese culture that encompassed many regional traditions and, at times, different states, all held together by many common customs and values as well as a standardized written language. Political unity helped but was not essential to this sense of a shared cultural identity. Indeed, the political states that arose in the first two millennia never encompassed all the Chinese people.

Population growth and shared culture made possible the first states, which may have appeared during the third millennium B.C.E. The Chinese trace their political ancestry to several culture heroes who supposedly lived in north China during Longshan times. The honorable deeds of these men, real or mythical, led later Chinese philosophers to make them models of behavior for all Chinese. Chinese historians labeled this era the Xia (shya) (Hsia) dynasty (2183–1752 B.C.E.), but its existence is still debated. A possible Xia capital city, one square mile in size, was built around 2000 B.C.E. near the Yellow River. The Xia may have presided over an occupationally diverse society including scribes, metallurgists, artisans, and bureaucrats. If the Xia were the first real Chinese state, the extent of their rule remains unclear.

Ancient China built on its foundations in such an original fashion as to almost create a world apart. Some influences filtered in from Central Asia, including the horse and chariot, ironworking, and certain philosophies, but in general, the Chinese themselves developed the ideas and institutions that gave their society the ability to expand, grow, adapt, and coordinate large populations. Many of the ancient traditions remain influential even today.

SECTION SUMMARY

- Early Chinese society was concentrated inland from the sea and was frequently fragmented into various states.
- In the cold, dry Chinese north, crops such as wheat and millet were grown, while in the wetter, warmer south, rice was dominant.
- Members of the Yangshao ("painted pottery") society were skilled craftspeople who excelled at carving, weaving, and village design.
- As time passed, the widely diverse Chinese peoples began to knit themselves together in one broad society with traditions that persist to this day.

The Reshaping of Ancient Chinese Society, 1750–600 B.C.E.

What were some key differences between the Shang and Zhou periods in China?

China had clearly made the great transition to cities and states when the Shang (shahng) dynasty established a powerful state and an expanding culture based on bronze technology. The Shang were followed by a more decentralized, iron-using system under the Zhou (joe) dynasty, during which time the Chinese improved writing and developed a literature. Some religious notions of enduring influence in China also appeared in these centuries. In addition, isolation from other Eurasian states convinced the Chinese that they needed little help from others, and a feeling of cultural superiority gradually developed. They perceived themselves surrounded by less developed neighbors who either adopted Chinese customs or invaded China to enjoy its riches. There was much truth to these assumptions, since strong governments, technological developments, and writing helped make China the most influential East Asian society.

The Shang Dynasty Reshapes Northern China

The Shang (1752–1122 B.C.E.), the first Chinese dynasty that can be fully documented, began around the same time that Hammurabi ruled in Babylon and the Harappan society was

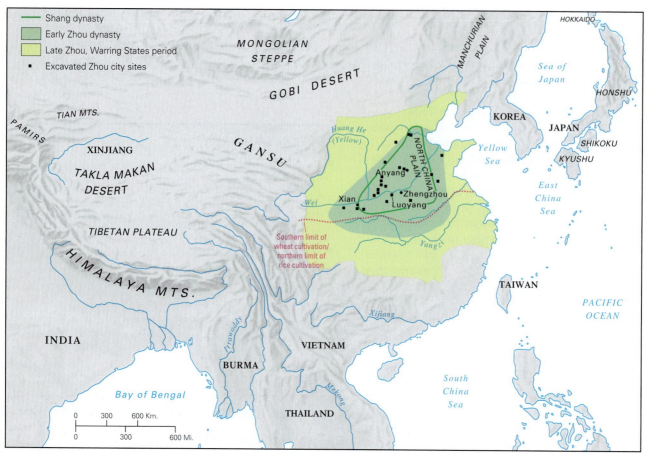

Map 4.1 Shang and Zhou China

The earliest Chinese states arose in north China along the Yellow River and its tributaries. The bronze-using Shang dynasty presided over the first documented state and were succeeded by the iron-using Zhou, who governed much of north and central China.

collapsing in India. A people from the western fringe of China, the Shang, like the Aryan migrants into India, had adopted horse-drawn chariots for warfare and owed their success partly to networks linking them with Central Asian pastoralists. They conquered the eastern Yellow River Basin and imposed a hierarchy dominated by landowning aristocrats (see Map 4.1). Shang kings presided over a growing economy and the building of more cities, and the influence of Shang culture reached far beyond their state. However, many Chinese maintained their own states and unique customs. For example, large cities with complex technology and highly developed art also flourished in places such as the western Yangzi Basin.

The Shang established an authoritarian state, perhaps in part to coordinate irrigation and dam building. Shang kingship was hereditary and was passed on to a monarch's male relative, usually a brother or son. Kings presented themselves as patriarchal and undisputed father figures who headed the country as a father did a family. The Shang made little distinction between the secular and the sacred, and their kings claimed both political and spiritual leadership. Like the Aryans who were then moving into India, they devoted much of their energy to military matters, using a lethal combination of

archers, spearmen, and charioteers. One of their concerns was defending their northern borders, a recurring theme in Chinese history. The relative prosperity of China in comparison to the marginal existence possible in the grasslands and deserts beyond the frontiers often prompted pastoral nomads to invade the Yellow River Valley.

Economically the Shang was a flourishing period. Commerce developed, and many cities were built as administrative and economic centers. The largest of the successive Shang capital cities, Anyang, was the ruler Pan Keng's new capital city discussed in the opening to this chapter. It was surrounded by a wall 30 feet high and 60 feet wide that enclosed 4 square miles; altogether, the city and its suburbs spread out over some 10 square miles. It apparently took some 10,000 workers 18 years to build Anyang, and the project reflected the considerable political and social organization of the time.

Technology improved, especially with the introduction of bronze and the earliest porcelain. The Chinese used copper by 2600 and bronze by 1400 B.C.E. This was the great age of bronze in the Afro-Eurasian Zone. The Shang and other Chinese are often considered the most skilled bronze casters the world has ever known. They used complex methods to produce flawless

Shang Bronze Pots   These bronze ritual vessels, some featuring animal designs, were made during the Shang or early Zhou period. They were used for ceremonies.   (Courtesy of the Trustees of the British Museum)

bronze arrows, spears, sculpture, pots, and especially ritual vessels for drinking wine. The Shang also produced glazed pottery that was the forerunner of the porcelain ("china") for which the Chinese would later become so famous.

Shang Society and Culture

The Shang fostered a new social organization. As already mentioned, their social hierarchy was dominated by landowning aristocrats, many of whom also served as government officials. These elite individuals enjoyed luxurious and extravagant surroundings and engaged in regular royal-sponsored hunts for tigers, bears, boars, and deer. Their residences were built on cement-like foundations in a style that closely resembled the houses of the wealthy many centuries later. Aristocratic women also enjoyed a high status. For example, Fuhao (foo-HOW), a wife of a Shang king, led military campaigns and owned large estates. These leaders and their families were buried in elaborate royal tombs surrounded by great quantities of valuable objects.

Most people were commoners or slaves. The Shang middle class consisted of skilled artisans, scribes, and merchants. The most valued artisans were the bronze casters. The scribes, most of them employed in government service, may have formulated the world's earliest simple decimal system, around 1500 B.C.E. Farmers and laborers occupied the bottom of the social hierarchy, and they were often mobilized by the powerful state for major building projects. Many of these laborers were war captives who had become slaves. The Shang were harsh masters. They practiced human and animal sacrifice as part of their religious observances, often using slaves as victims.

The Shang's momentous contribution was an elaborate writing system. Some scholars believe that 4,800-year-old inscriptions on pottery can be considered writing, but most conclude that oracle bones from Shang times provide the earliest examples of Chinese writing. In an attempt to predict the future, influential people wrote questions addressed to the gods on bones of animals and tortoise shells. The variety of subjects included the abundance of the next harvest, the outcome of a battle, the weather, or the birth of an heir. For example, one inquired "whether today there would be prolonged rain," and another asked whether "if the king hunted, whether the chase would be without mishap."[5] Some officials, probably those with great prestige, seem to have been experts in interpreting the future with these bones. The writing found on oracle bones was clearly the forerunner of today's Chinese writing. In the later Shang period, people also wrote inscriptions on bronze vases.

The Early Zhou and Their Government

As Shang power faded, the Zhou, a state on the western fringe of China, invaded and overthrew the Shang. The new rulers formed a new dynasty, the Zhou (1122–221 B.C.E.), and established a new type of government. The triumph of the Zhou occurred about the time that the Assyrian Empire was rising in western Asia and the Mycenaean society in Greece disintegrated. The Duke of Zhou, credited by early Chinese historians for completing Zhou expansion, supposedly urged that "we must go on, abjuring all idleness, until our reign is universal and from the corners of the sea and the sun rising there shall not be one who is disobedient to our rule."[6] But the decentralized Zhou system differed considerably from the Shang system. A relatively weak central government ruled over small states that had considerable autonomy but owed service obligations to the king, somewhat like the earlier Akkadian Empire in Sumeria.

The decentralized system reflected the Zhou realization that, despite their impressive military technology, Chinese culture had spread too far for them to administer the entire society effectively. The royal family directly ruled the area around their capital, the present-day city of Xian (SEE-an), but parceled out the rest to followers, relatives, and Shang collaborators. The regional leaders became local lords with much local power. This system allowed the Zhou kings to preside, however symbolically, over a much larger land area than that of the Shang, from southern Manchuria to the Yangzi Basin (see Map 4.1).

To solidify their position, the Zhou justified their triumph over the Shang with a new concept: the **Mandate of Heaven**. According to this belief, rulers had the support of the supernatural realm ("heaven") so long as conditions were good. However, when there was war, famine, or other hardships, heaven withdrew its sanction and rebellion was permissible. The decadent and cruel Shang, the Duke of Zhou argued, lost their right to rule because their last kings mocked the gods by their behavior and "did not make themselves manifest to Heaven."[7] But over time this radical new concept was used against the Zhou and all later dynasties, since it added the criterion of morality to kingship. Monarchs lost their legitimacy if their misrule led to a crisis. Ever since the Zhou, the Chinese have invoked the Mandate of Heaven to justify and explain the demise of a discredited dynasty or government.

The Mandate of Heaven was not the only enduring political idea fostered by the Zhou. In about the sixth century B.C.E., Chinese scholars began to view their political history in terms of the **dynastic cycle**. Instead of seeing a straight line of progress in history, as the Hebrews did, the Chinese focused on dynasties of ruling families, all of which more or less followed the same pattern as their predecessors. The cycle always began with a new dynasty, which brought peace and prosperity for a few decades. Then overexpansion and corruption led to increasingly costly government, bankruptcy, social decay, and rebellions. This disorder eventually resulted in a new dynasty, beginning the cycle anew. Modern scholars consider this narrative too simple because it ignored many factors, such as the continuity of government institutions from one dynasty to the next, but it shaped Chinese thinking for the next 2500 years.

The Zhou system was unstable, plagued by chronic warfare between the various substates and outsiders. Over the centuries, larger substates conquered smaller ones. The worst warfare occurred during the Era of the Warring States, beginning around 500 B.C.E. (see Chapter 5). As a result, the 1,700 substates of the early Zhou years were reduced to 7 by 400 B.C.E. These larger substates now had considerable power in counteracting the weakening Zhou kings. External pressures also threatened political order. The Central Asians were obtaining faster ponies, forcing the Chinese to erect better defenses against the relentless pressure.

Mandate of Heaven A Chinese belief that rulers had the support of the supernatural realm as long as conditions were good, but rebellion was justified when they were not.

dynastic cycle The Chinese view of their political history, which focuses on dynasties of ruling families.

Early Zhou Society and Economy

Zhou government not only brought political fragmentation and a figurehead monarchy, but it also fostered a rigid social structure. Zhou society clearly divided aristocrats, commoners, and slaves. The nobility owed allegiance to the king as vassals but governed their own realms as they liked. Most aristocratic families owned large estates that were worked by slaves, and they hired private armies to defend their property. As influential commoners, the merchants and artisans were more insulated from the aristocracy. Indeed, merchants had much freedom of action and often became rich. The majority of slaves were soldiers from rival ministates who were captured in the frequent wars. Criminals and sometimes their relatives were enslaved for their misdeeds.

Peasants, the largest group of commoners, were mostly bound to the soil on aristocracy-owned land (see the Witness to the Past: The Poetry of Peasant Life in Zhou China). Their superiors assigned them work and punished them if it was not done. Peasants were assigned houses, wore prescribed clothes to indicate their status, and had specified tax obligations. Their songs reflected resignation: "We rise at sunrise, We rest at sunset. Dig wells and drink, Till our field and eat—What is the strength of the emperor to us?"[8] Yet, there were some checks on landowner power. A major rebellion or massive desertion could ruin a landlord, so he had an incentive to develop reasonably humane policies toward the common people on his lands. The more repressive and exploitive lords did indeed lose many of their workers and slaves, who migrated or absconded, depopulating the land.

Gender roles were rigid in this patriarchal society. Both men and women were expected to marry, but all marriages were arranged by parents. A song from the times states: "How does one take a wife? Without a matchmaker she cannot be got." Whatever their class status, before or after marriage most women worked hard, and their assigned place was in the home. They prepared food, did housekeeping, and made clothes. Women at all levels were expected to be meek and submissive, and they enjoyed no official role in public affairs, although some women exercised considerable informal influence. While many elite women were literate, few peasant women or men enjoyed opportunities to learn to read and write. But some women could travel beyond their villages. Both genders valued friendship and kinship, as another song illustrates: "Of men that are now, None equals a brother. When death and mourning affright us, Brothers are very dear."[9]

Zhou social life often revolved around food: the Zhou-era Chinese clearly appreciated the culinary arts. The Chief Cook of the ruler was a high state official. Written sources describe many lavish feasts, often used to cement social ties. Indeed, the banquet was a chief tool of diplomacy at all levels of society, often lubricated by wine: "When we have got wine, we strain it; When we have got none, we buy it!"[10] The costly and complicated ceremonies enjoyed by the rich did not extend down to peasants, who had little money for anything more than basic hospitality.

The Poetry of Peasant life in Zhou China

We can learn something of the lives of ancient Chinese common folk, especially the peasants who worked the land, from *The Book of Songs*, a collection of 305 poems, hymns, and folk songs compiled between 1000 and 600 B.C.E.

Some songs address ordinary people at their labor. Men weed the fields, plant, plow, and harvest. Women and girls gather mulberry leaves for silkworms, carry hampers of food to the men in the fields for lunch, and make thread:

> *The girls take their deep baskets, And follow the path under the wall, to gather the soft mulberry-leaves.*

Some of the songs deal with courtship and love, sometimes revealing strong emotion, as in this song by a girl about a prospective sweetheart:

> *That the mere glimpse of a plain cap, Could harry me with such longing, Cause me pain so dire. . . . Enough! Take me with you to your house. . . . Let us two be one.*

Within the family, the father had nearly absolute authority over his wife and children. When the family patriarch died, his wife became the family head. Children were expected to obey their parents, but some songs reveal that mutual affection and gratitude were common:

> *My father begot me. My mother fed me, Led me, bred me, Brought me up, reared me, Kept her eye on me, tended me, At every turn aided me. Their good deeds I would requite.*

Peasant lives were filled with toil and hardship, but they could find some relief from drudgery in friendship and kinship. Entertaining relatives and friends was a major leisure activity:

> *And shall a man not seek to have his friends? He shall have harmony and peace. I have strained off my liquor in abundance, the dishes stand in rows, and none of my brethren*

are absent. Whenever we have leisure, let us drink the sparkling liquor.

Peasants faced many demands on their time and labor. Songs complain and even protest about an uncaring government and its rapacious tax collectors:

> *Big rat, big rat, Do not gobble our millet! Three years we have slaved for you. Yet you took no notice of us. At last we are going to leave you, And go to the happy land . . . where no sad songs are sung.*

Some songs record abject poverty and misery.

> *Deep is my grief. I am utterly poverty-stricken and destitute. Yet no one heeds my misfortunes. Well, all is over now. No doubt it was Heaven's [the supernatural realm's] doing. So what's the good of talking about it!*

Zhou peasants needed all the help they could get and some songs seem to be prayers to Heaven to bless their lives:

> *Good people, gentle folk—Their ways are righteous. . . . Their thoughts constrained. . . . Good people, gentle folk— Shape the people of this land. . . . And may they do so for ten thousand years!*

THINKING ABOUT THE READING

1. What do the songs tell us about the importance of families and friends to the Zhou Chinese?

2. What did peasants think about those who ruled them? Can you say why?

Source: The Book of Songs, translated by Arthur Waley (London: George Allen and Unwin, 1954), pp. 26, 316–317, 309, 305, 174. George Allen & Unwin LTD. © copyright 1954 by permission of the Arthur Waley Estate.

Online Study Center Improve Your Grade
Primary Source: The Book of Documents

Zhou China nurtured many significant technological and economic developments. Ironworking reached China over trade networks from Central Asia by around 700 B.C.E. From the Zhou states iron reached southern Chinese, who improved the technology by 500 B.C.E. Iron made much better plows and tools than bronze but also improved weaponry for the increasing warfare. Newly introduced soybeans provided a rich protein source and also enriched the soil. Chinese agriculture became so productive, and surpluses so common, that the population by 600 B.C.E. was around 20 million. Trade grew, and merchants became more prominent. Copper coins were issued as China developed a cash economy.

The Evolution of Chinese Writing

During the Shang and Zhou periods, a distinctive Chinese writing system arose to solve the special problems posed by the many spoken languages. Some six hundred dialects of Chinese are still spoken today, a heritage of many local cultures. Most of the Chinese north of the Yangzi River speak closely related Northern Mandarin dialects, but other Chinese, especially in the southern half of China, have different dialects that are often mutually unintelligible. Chinese from Guangzhou (GWAHN-Cho), Shanghai (shahng-hie), and Beijing (bay-JING) would not understand each other if they only spoke their local dialects. Another diffi-

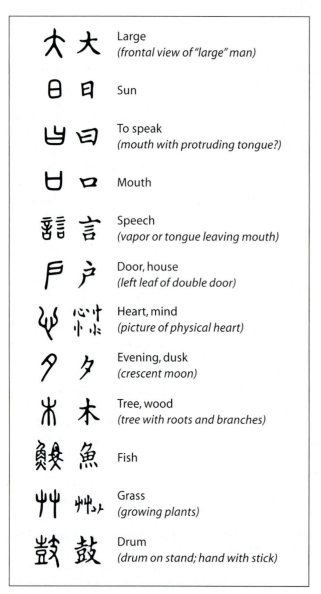

		Large (frontal view of "large" man)
		Sun
		To speak (mouth with protruding tongue?)
		Mouth
		Speech (vapor or tongue leaving mouth)
		Door, house (left leaf of double door)
		Heart, mind (picture of physical heart)
		Evening, dusk (crescent moon)
		Tree, wood (tree with roots and branches)
		Fish
		Grass (growing plants)
		Drum (drum on stand; hand with stick)

Figure 4.1 Evolution of Chinese Writing
This chart shows early and modern forms of Chinese characters, revealing how pictographs, often recognizable, matured into increasingly abstract ideographs.

culty is that the monosyllabic Chinese languages are tonal: that is, the stress or tone placed on a sound changes its meaning. For example, depending on the tone employed by the speaker, in Mandarin the sound *ma* can mean "mother," "hemp," "horse," or the verb "to curse." It can also indicate a question.

To overcome these problems, the Shang and Zhou Chinese gradually developed one written language based not on sound but on characters. The pictographs of early Shang times resemble crude pictures of an object, such as a man or bird. Over some centuries they evolved into complex ideographs, in which characters stand for ideas and concepts. Some 50,000 new characters have been created since the Shang (see Figure 4.1). The practicality of this system became apparent in modern times when Chinese linguists faced great difficulty converting tonal words into a Western-type alphabet.

As in Mesopotamia and Egypt, writing had vast social and cultural implications. The writing system promoted political and cultural unity, making possible communication between people whose dialects were often very different from each other. Without such a system, the Chinese might have split into many small countries, as occurred in India and Europe for much of history. Thus writing helped to create the largest society on earth, unifying rather than dividing peoples of diverse ancestries, regions, and languages. Chinese writing also reinforced a strong feeling of historical continuity and a deep reverence for the past and one's ancestors. The written language gained a certain mystique, giving prestige to those who mastered it. As the writing brush became the main writing instrument, writing became an art form, and every literate Chinese became something of an artist. Perhaps this written language has endured for over 3,500 years in part because it possesses so many artistic qualities.

To be sure, the demands of memorizing and mastering thousands of characters, as well as of acquiring acceptable brushwork skills, mostly limited literacy to those in the upper classes with the time and money to study writing. Those who could master the system gained special status, and education, scholarship, and literature became valued commodities. Rulers and administrators also gained legitimacy through their literacy.

Ancient Philosophy and Religion

Chinese ideas on the deeper mysteries of life and the cosmic order also developed in ancient times. The diverse Shang religion emphasized ancestor worship, magic, and mythology as well as agricultural deities and local spirits. Gradually these ideas evolved by later Zhou times into distinctive ideas, including the notion of a generalized supernatural or moral force the Chinese called *tian* (tee-an), which was believed to govern the universe. Western Christian visitors later translated this term, somewhat inaccurately, as "heaven."

The first books probably appeared during the Shang period, including the **Yijing** (Yee-CHING) (Book of Changes), an ancient collection of sixty-four mystic hexagrams and commentaries upon them that were used to predict future events. It was used regularly during the Zhou period and later became influential throughout East Asia. The *Yijing*'s main theme was that heaven and earth are in a state of continual transition. This book helped the Chinese to understand the process of change.

The *Yijing* was closely related to Chinese cosmological thinking as expressed in the theory of *yin* and *yang*, which had appeared in simple form as early as the Shang period and was elaborated in later centuries. To the Chinese, yin and yang are the two primary cosmic forces that make the universe run through their interaction. Neither one permanently triumphs;

Yijing (Book of Changes) An ancient Chinese collection of sixty-four mystic hexagrams and commentaries upon them that was used to predict future events.

rather they are balanced, in conflict and yet complementary in a kind of cosmic symphony. Many things were correlated with these principles:

Yang: bright, hot, dry, hard, active, masculine, heaven, sun
Yin: dark, cold, wet, soft, quiescent, feminine, earth, moon

Given the Chinese preference for hierarchy, yang was superior to yin, and male superior to female. Thus the philosophy justified inequalities in society.

The yin-yang dualism remains important throughout East Asia. For example, the symbol is found on the modern South Korean flag. Because China was the cultural heartland of East Asia, the Chinese strongly influenced their neighbors in Korea, Vietnam, and Japan, beginning in Shang times, and over the centuries many Chinese ideas and institutions diffused to the peoples on their fringe.

SECTION SUMMARY

- The western Shang established an authoritarian state, with the king playing the role of father to the entire country.
- Under the Shang, society became increasingly stratified, divided up into a dominant aristocracy, a middle class, farmers and laborers, and slaves.
- After a slave rebellion overthrew the Shang, the Zhou established a more widespread, less centralized empire.
- The Zhou introduced the concepts of rule by the "Mandate of Heaven," and of the dynastic cycle, which have endured to this day.
- A common written language provided a unifying link for the Chinese, who spoke hundreds of different dialects (many of which are still spoken today).
- One of the first Chinese books was the *Yijing*, which was related to the idea of the universal opposing forces, *yin* and *yang*.

Ancient Southeast and Northeast Asians

How did the traditions developing in Southeast and Northeast Asia differ from those in India and China?

While the Chinese and Indians created some of the first urban societies, the neighboring societies of Southeast and Northeast Asia also made important early contributions in farming and technology in an environment somewhat different from their large neighbors. The resulting cultures, although influenced by China or India or both, demonstrated many unique characteristics. These societies and the networks of trade and migration that formed provided the foundations for enduring traditions.

Southeast Asian Environments and Early Agriculture

While historically linked to both China and India, Southeast Asian peoples developed in distinctive ways that were shaped in part by geography and climate. Southeast Asia, which stretches from modern Burma (or Myanmar) eastward to Vietnam and the Philippines and southward through the Indonesian archipelago, is separated from the Eurasian landmass by significant mountain and water barriers. The region has a tropical climate, with long rainy seasons. Before modern times rain forests covered much of the land. But the great rivers that flow through mainland Southeast Asia, such as the Mekong (MAY-kawng), Red, and Irrawaddy (ir-uh-WAHD-ee) Rivers, also carved out broad, fertile plains and deltas that could support dense human settlement.

The topography both helped and hindered communication. Southeast Asians say that the sea unites and the land divides. The shallow oceans fostered maritime trade, encouraging seafaring and fishing. Mastery of the seas linked the peoples of large islands such as Sumatra (soo-MAH-truh), Java (JA-veh), and Borneo (also known as Kalimantan) to their neighbors. But the heavily forested interior highlands of the mainland and the islands inhibited travel and encouraged cultural diversity, including a wide variety of religions, worldviews, languages, states, and economic patterns. An old Indonesian proverb well describes the complex mosaic of cultures that resulted: different fields, different grasshoppers; different pools, different fish.

Agriculture arose early, but archaeologists still debate how early. Some think the transition to food growing began in what is today Thailand and northern Vietnam by 8000 or perhaps even 9000 B.C.E., roughly the same time as in southwest Asia, but most doubt that it began much earlier than 6000 B.C.E. Certainly farming was widespread by 5000 B.C.E. In New Guinea, the large island just east of Southeast Asia, horticulture also developed very early, sometime between 7000 and 4000 B.C.E. Rice was apparently first domesticated in northern Southeast Asia or southern-central China 6,000 or 7,000 years ago; the two areas were closely linked in Neolithic times. Between 4000 and 3000 B.C.E. rice growing became common. Southeast Asians may have been the first to cultivate bananas, yams, and taro and domesticated chickens, pigs, and perhaps even cattle (see Chronology: Northeast and Southeast Asia, 10,000–600 B.C.E.).

Southeast Asians also developed or improved technologies, some of which may have come originally from India, Mesopotamia, and China. Bronze-working appeared very early, sometime before 2000 B.C.E. By 1500 B.C.E. fine bronze was being produced in what is today northeast Thailand in villages like Ban Chiang (chang), founded around 3600 B.C.E., whose people lived in houses perched on poles above the ground, still a common pattern in Southeast Asia. Ban Chiang women made beautiful hand-painted and durable pottery. Village artists fashioned necklaces and bracelets as well as many household items of bronze and ivory.

Elsewhere in Eurasia the Bronze Age was synonymous with states, cities, kings, armies, huge temples, and defensive

CHRONOLOGY

Northeast and Southeast Asia, 10,000–600 B.C.E.

10,000–300	Jomon culture in Japan
8000–6000	Agriculture begins in Southeast Asia
7000–4000	Agriculture begins in New Guinea
5000–2000	Agriculture begins in Korea
4500–2000	Bronze Age begins in Southeast Asia
4000–2000	Austronesian migrations into Southeast Asia islands
1600–1000	Melanesian and Austronesian migrations into South Pacific
1000–800	First Southeast Asian states
1000	Austronesian settlement of Fiji and Samoa

walls, but in Southeast Asia bronze metallurgy derived from peaceful villages with few hints of warfare. Evidence for trade networks can be found in Dong Son village, Vietnam, where people made huge bronze drums that have been found all over Southeast Asia. Tin mined in Southeast Asia may have been traded to the Indus cities and Mesopotamia to be used in making bronze there; if so, this trade would suggest involvement in even larger networks. Southeast Asians worked iron by 500 B.C.E., several centuries later than northern China.

Dong Son Bronze Drum These huge Dong Son bronze drums, named for a village site in Vietnam, were produced widely in ancient Southeast Asia and confirm the extensive long-distance trade networks.
(Erich Lessing/Art Resource, NY)

Migration and New Societies in Southeast Asia and the Pacific

Gradually new societies formed from local and migrant roots. The early Southeast Asians probably included the Vietnamese, Papuans (PAH-poo-enz), Melanesians (mel-uh-NEE-zhuhns), and Negritos (Ne-GREE-tos). Several waves of migrants came into mainland Southeast Asia from China sometime before the Common Era, assimilating local peoples or prompting them to migrate eastward through the islands. Today Papuans and Melanesians are found mostly in New Guinea and the western Pacific islands, while the few thousand remaining small-statured, dark-skinned Negritos mostly live in the mountains of the Malay Peninsula and the remote Andaman and Nicobar Islands west of the peninsula. Migration fostered some of the oldest networks linking peoples over a wide area. The new-comers probably mixed their cultures and languages with those of the remaining indigenous inhabitants, shaping the region's societies. The ethnic merging produced new peoples such as the Khmers (kuh-MARE) (Cambodians), who later established states in the Mekong River Basin.

Over the course of several millennia peoples speaking Austronesian (AW-stroh-NEE-zhuhn) languages and possessing advanced agriculture entered island Southeast Asia from the large island of Taiwan, just east of China. Beginning around 4000 B.C.E., Austronesians began moving south from Taiwan into the Philippine Islands, and some later moved southward into the Indonesian archipelago (see Map 4.2). Sometime before 2000 B.C.E. they had settled Java, Borneo, and Sumatra, and by 1000 B.C.E. Austronesian languages were dominant from the northern Philippines through what is today Indonesia to the Malay Peninsula and the central Vietnam coast. Indonesian islanders were the major seafaring traders and explorers of eastern Eurasia before the Common Era.

The Austronesian migrations brought new settlers and cultures to Southeast Asia and had a profound effect on other regions as well. Melanesians migrated eastward by boat into the western Pacific islands beginning around 1500 or 1600 B.C.E., carrying Southeast Asian domesticated crops, animals, house styles, and farming technology as far east as Fiji. Traveling in outrigger canoes and, later, in large double-hulled canoes, some Austronesians also sailed east into the open Pacific, mixing their cultures, languages, and genes with those of the Melanesians. By around 1000 B.C.E. Austronesian settlers had reached Samoa and Tonga.

These voyages were intentional efforts at discovery and colonization by fearless mariners who developed remarkable navigation skills, reading the stars with their eyes and the swells with their backs as they lay down their canoes. The an-

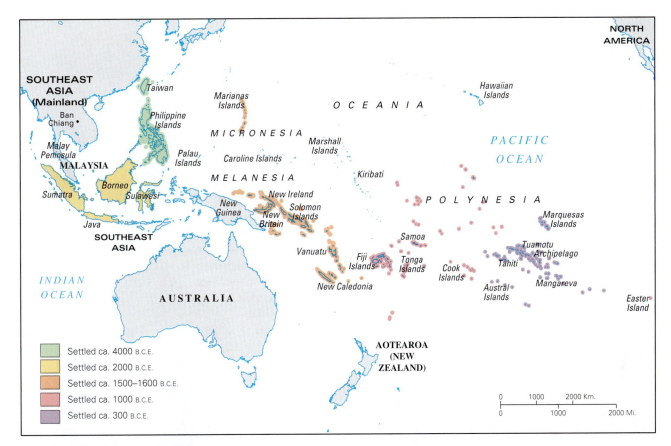

Map 4.2 The Austronesian Diaspora
Austronesians migrated from Taiwan into Southeast Asia, settling the islands. Later some of these skilled mariners moved east into the Western Pacific, settling Melanesia. Eventually some of their ancestors settled Polynesia and Micronesia.

cient western Pacific culture known as **Lapita**, stretching some 2,500 miles from just northeast of New Guinea to Samoa, was marked by a distinctive pottery style and a widespread trading network over vast distances. In Samoa and Tonga, Polynesian culture emerged from Austronesian roots. Some Polynesians eventually reached as far east as Tahiti and Hawaii, both 2,500 miles from Tonga.

The Austronesians, Vietnamese, and others established a foundation for societies based on intensive agriculture, fishing, and interregional commerce. By 1000 B.C.E. dynamic Austronesian trade networks stretched over 5,000 miles, from western Indonesia to the central Pacific, forming a commercial system unparalleled in the ancient world. Austronesians built advanced boats and carried out maritime trade with India by 500 B.C.E. Indonesian cinnamon even reached Egypt. The Vietnamese created the first known Southeast Asian states between 1000 and 800 B.C.E. and believed in a god that, according to their myths, "creates the elephants [and] the grass, is omnipresent, and has [all-seeing] eyes."[11]

Lapita The ancient western Pacific culture that stretched some 2,500 miles from just northeast of New Guinea to Samoa.

Northeast Asian Environments

The Chinese strongly influenced their neighbors in Northeast Asia, the Koreans and the Japanese, beginning in the Shang period and continuing for many centuries afterward. But the Koreans and Japanese had already established the foundations for complex societies. Over the following centuries they integrated Chinese influences with their own ideas and customs, producing unique cultures and separate ethnic identities.

Korea and Japan are neighbors, but they were shaped by different environments (see Map 4.1). The 110 miles of stormy seas that separate them at their closest point did not prevent contact between the two societies but did make it sporadic. Korea occupies a mountainous peninsula some 600 miles long and 150 miles in width. Japan, on the other hand, is a group of 3,400 islands stretching across several climatic zones. Over 90 percent of the land is on three islands: densely populated Honshu (hahn-shoo), frigid Hokkaido (haw-KAI-dow) in the north, and subtropical Kyushu (KYOO-shoo) in the south. Because mountains occupy much of Japan, only a sixth of the land is suitable for intensive agriculture. The archipelago is also weak in all metals except silver.

The Roots of Korean Society

Despite centuries of contact, the Koreans were never assimilated by the neighboring Chinese, in part because the Korean and Chinese spoken languages were very different. Korean belongs to the Ural-Altaic language family and is therefore related (although not closely) to Mongol, Turkish, and the Eastern Siberian tongues. Ural-Altaic languages are polysyllabic and nontonal, unlike Chinese.

Korean lives gradually changed as they began farming between 5000 and 2000 B.C.E., perhaps borrowing the technology from China. Later they creatively adapted rice growing, which originated in warm southern lands, to their cool climate. As Korean agriculture became more productive, the population grew rapidly, generating a persistent migration of Koreans across the straits to Japan. Growing occupational specialization led to small states based on clans. In a pattern still common today, female shamans led the animistic religion.

The ancient Koreans imported some useful ideas and also made several technological innovations. Sometime between the fifteenth and eighth century B.C.E. they adopted bronze, probably from China, and mining and metallurgy became significant activities. Ironworking reached Korea from China or Central Asia between 700 and 300 B.C.E. Shang refugees fleeing in the wake of dynastic collapse brought more Chinese culture and technology, but Koreans also created their own useful products and technology. For example, they produced some of the era's finest pottery. To contend with the frigid winters, the early Koreans invented an ingenious method of radiant floor heating, still widely used today, that circulates heat through chambers in a stone floor. Much later both the Chinese and Romans devised similar schemes.

The Roots of Japanese Society

The ancient Japanese were more isolated than the Koreans from China and no less creative. Human settlement began perhaps 40,000 years ago, before rising sea levels isolated Japan from the mainland. Pottery, for example, was produced on Kyushu by 10,700 B.C.E., earlier than in China, and this date makes Japanese pottery among the oldest in the world. The identity of these early settlers and pottery-makers is unknown, but they were probably the ancestors of the Ainu (I-noo), who are genetically close to other East Asians despite their light skin and extensive body hair, which are unusual in the region. The ancestral Ainu seem to have built seaworthy boats, for they settled the Kurile (KOO-reel) Islands north of Japan and traded with the people of eastern Siberia. Ainu relics have also been found in the Aleutian (ah-LOO-shan) Islands off Alaska, suggesting some connection there in prehistoric times. Several scholars think that ancestors of the Ainu were among the northeast Asians who settled the Americas. Today the remaining few thousand Ainu, who mostly live in their own villages on Hokkaido and Sakhalin Island, face cultural extinction.

Migration influenced Japan no less than Southeast Asia, but little is known about when the non-Ainu ancestors of most of today's Japanese arrived in the islands. Some may have come from northeastern Asia by way of Korea beginning 3,000 or

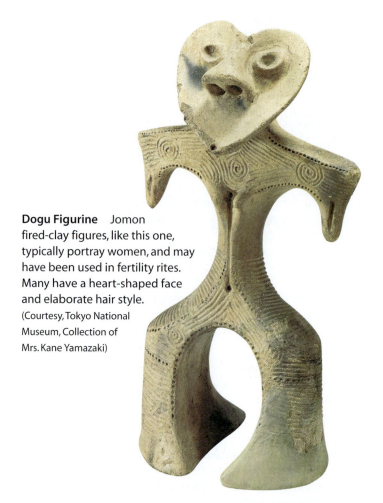

Dogu Figurine Jomon fired-clay figures, like this one, typically portray women, and may have been used in fertility rites. Many have a heart-shaped face and elaborate hair style. (Courtesy, Tokyo National Museum, Collection of Mrs. Kane Yamazaki)

4,000 years ago. Ainus and newcomers mixed over the millennia. Genetic studies link modern Japanese to the Ainu, Siberians, and especially Koreans.

Jomon Society

The best documented Japanese early society is called **Jomon** (JOE-mon) ("rope pattern"), because of the ropelike designs on their pottery. The Jomon period began around 10,000 B.C.E. and endured until 300 B.C.E. The Jomon evidently had little contact with China but did some trade with Korea and Siberia. Most scholars suspect it was a primarily Ainu culture that was divided by various languages and regional customs. The diversity may reflect the arrival of migrants from Korea, especially in southern Japan. The Jomon and other ancient islanders were only partially the ancestors of the modern Japanese. The major migrations that brought waves of iron-using settlers from Korea came later, between 500 B.C.E. and 700 C.E.

The Jomon lived primarily from hunting, gathering, and fishing, but by 5000 B.C.E. they lived in permanent wooden houses containing elaborate hearths, probably the centers for family gatherings. Scholars are impressed with the wide range of foods that made up their well-balanced, highly nutritious

Jomon The earliest documented culture in Japan, known for the ropelike design on its pottery.

diet, which included shellfish, fish, seals, deer, wild boar, and yams. The Jomon may have been better fed than the Chinese and Korean farmers. They may also have grown millet by 1000 B.C.E., but there is no evidence for more complex agriculture until around 500 B.C.E.

As in Korea, a very different spoken language helped preserve cultural distinctiveness despite much Chinese cultural influence over the centuries. Whether the Japanese language was spoken by some of the Jomon or brought by later immigrants remains uncertain. Japanese is related, but not closely, to modern Korean, and not at all to the surviving Ainu languages. At some point, probably between 500 B.C.E. and 500 C.E., most of the Ainu languages were overwhelmed by a Japanese language with diverse roots that was possibly based on a now lost Korean dialect. The environment helped shape the language. Perhaps in response to increasingly crowded conditions as Japan's population grew, the language structure and vocabulary came to promote tact and vagueness, and the Japanese became adept at nonverbal understanding and at feeling out other people's moods. It is much harder to directly insult or provoke someone in Japanese than in most languages. These tendencies, which are useful in discouraging social conflict, remain part of Japan's unique heritage.

SECTION SUMMARY

- The peoples of Southeast Asia established early maritime trading networks, while inland geographical boundaries led to the development of extremely diverse cultures.
- Extensive migration occurred among China, Southeast Asia, and the Pacific islands.
- Korea and Japan, while being strongly influenced by the Chinese, were shaped by different environments and created unique cultures and societies.
- Partly because of its distinct language, Korea was never assimilated into China and developed special technologies, such as radiant floor heating, to meet its needs.
- The ancestors of modern Japanese probably included, among others, the Ainu, the Jomon, and later the Koreans.
- Japan's language promoted tact and vagueness, probably to prevent social conflict in an increasingly populated area.

◆ Migration and Settlement in the Americas

How do scholars explain the settlement of the Americas and the rise of agriculture in these continents?

After the migrations of humans from Eurasia to the Americas thousands of years ago, American societies developed in isolation from those in the Eastern Hemisphere. Early Americans created diverse cultures that often flourished from hunting and gathering, and later Americans, in some regions, created urban societies, states, writing, and trade networks. Population movement and adaptations to differing environments shaped these varied people's most ancient history.

Diverse American Environments

Most of the land area of the Western Hemisphere is found on two continents, North and South America, which are linked by the long, thin strand of Central America. A string of fertile islands, both large and small, also rings the Caribbean Sea from Florida to Venezuela. Unlike the east-west axis of Eurasia, the Americas lie on a north-south axis, with a large forest-covered tropical zone separating more temperate regions. This meant that migrating peoples or long-distance travelers encountered very different environmental and climatic zones.

Although the total land area is smaller, the Western Hemisphere contains as much diversity of landforms and climate as the Eastern. Extensive tropical rain forests originally covered much of Central America and parts of the Caribbean islands as well as the vast Amazon and Oronoco (or-uh-NO-ko) River Basins of South America. In these tropical regions intensive farming was difficult, although some people developed simple farming. Rain-drenched forests also once covered much of the northern Pacific coast and southern Chile, while the eastern part of what is now the United States had more temperate woodlands. The long, harsh winters in much of North America made hunting and gathering the most practical subsistence option.

Great mountain ranges shaped human life by discouraging communication, while river systems encouraged it. Like the Himalayas in Asia, the high Andes (AN-deez), which stretch nearly 5,000 miles from the Caribbean coast down the western side of South America, limited human interaction. Similarly, in North America, the Rocky Mountains provided an east-west barrier from New Mexico to northwestern Canada. Mountains also run along the Pacific coast from Alaska to southern Mexico. By trapping rain clouds, these formidable coastal and Andes mountain complexes helped create huge deserts in western North America and along the Pacific coast of South America, as well as extensive grasslands in the interior of the continents. On the other hand, some of the great river systems, such as the Mississippi, drained fertile regions and fostered long-distance trade.

The Antiquity and Migration of Native Americans

The ancestry of Native Americans, and the antiquity of settlement, generate exciting debate among scholars. Most anthropologists agree that modern Native Americans are descended chiefly from stone tool–using Asians who crossed the Bering Strait from Siberia to Alaska. Most likely entered North America when Ice Age conditions lowered ocean levels and created a wide land bridge. This natural bridge is also probably how mammoths crossed from Eurasia to North America. Even today people sometimes walk the few miles across the winter ice of the Bering Sea. Some may have crossed by boat even when no land bridge existed. Seeking game like bison, caribou, and mammoths, migrants could have moved south through ice-free corridors or by boat along the Pacific coast, and gradually dispersed throughout the hemisphere. Waves of migrants from different cultural backgrounds in East and North Asia might account for the over two thousand languages among Native Americans. The last wave some 5,000 years ago brought the Inuit (IN-oo-it) and Aleuts (AH-loots).

The traditions of many Native American peoples place their origins in the Americas, usually in the areas where they lived 500 years ago, but some may have lived in these places for many centuries before that. In many North American origin stories, the first man and woman emerged from the earth and relied on the help of various animals to survive. While the stories, rich in spiritual meaning, deserve respect, much evidence supports the notion of ancient migration from Asia. The fact that no remains of any hominids earlier than modern humans have been found in the Americas suggests that all human evolution took place in the Eastern Hemisphere. Furthermore, the common ancestry of modern Native Americans is clear from the remarkable uniformity of DNA, blood, virus, and teeth types, which all connect them clearly to ancient peoples in East Asia and Siberia. For example, DNA studies link some Native Americans to the Chukchi (CHOOK-chee) people, pastoral nomads who live in the northeastern corner of Siberia. Some early American flake tools and housing styles resemble those from northern Asia, and some American languages can also be linked distantly with northeast Asian languages. As already mentioned, some evidence hints that the ancestors of the Ainu might have been early migrants. Skilled boat builders, especially of canoes, their settlements once stretched from southern Japan northward through the islands and peninsulas of eastern Siberia, and their artifacts have been discovered in the Aleutian Islands.

Recent tool and skeletal finds raise the possibility that some early immigrants may have come from someplace other than Northeast Asia. A few physical remains found in Brazil and the Pacific Northwest bear some resemblance to ancient Southeast Asians or Australian aborigines (ab-uh-RIJ-uh-neez). Several scholars have also suggested that some ancient tool cultures in eastern North America are similar to those of Stone Age peoples who lived in Spain and France several millennia earlier. Perhaps, they believe, such migrants from Europe may have used boats to skirt the edge of the ice then covering a large section of the northern Atlantic Ocean. But the evidence for possible European, Southeast Asian, or Australian migrations is sparse and controversial. If such migrants did once settle in the Americas, they likely died out or were absorbed by the peoples of Northeast Asian ancestry.

The question of when the first migrants arrived in the Americas perplexes archaeologists. For many years, most traced the migration back to the **Clovis** (KLO-vis) culture some 11,500 to 13,500 years ago, named after spear points discovered at Clovis, New Mexico (see Chronology: The Ancient

Americas, 40,000–600 B.C.E.). Clovis-type sites are widespread in North and Central America. However, human skeletons and artifacts have lately been discovered in North and South America that have much older radiocarbon dates. Monte Verde (MAWN-tee VAIR-dee), a campsite in southern Chile, which is over 10,000 miles from the Bering Strait, may be at least 12,500 years old. Monte Verde people lived in two parallel rows of rectangular houses with wooden frameworks and log foundations, and they exploited a wide variety of vegetable and animal foods. A few archaeologists think some material from Monte Verde might be as much as 33,000 years old, but many scholars doubt these are human-made artifacts.

A variety of other sites challenge the Clovis theory, but none offers conclusive evidence that convinces skeptics. Bones and diverse projectiles as old as Clovis have been found at various North American, Mexican, and Brazilian sites. A rock shelter near Pittsburgh, with possible blade knives and bone needles for sewing warm clothes, and another site in Virginia may place people in eastern North America between 17,000 and 19,000 years ago. These scattered discoveries hint at but do not prove an ancient migration somewhere between 20,000 and 40,000 years ago. The debate will rage for years to come as more sites are excavated.

C H R O N O L O G Y

The Ancient Americas, 40,000–600 B.C.E.

40,000–20,000	Possible earliest migrations to Americas (disputed)
11,500–9,500	Beginning of Clovis culture
8000	Beginning of agriculture in Mesoamerica and Andes
6000	Potato farming in Andes
4000	Early trade routes in North America
2500	Earliest mound-building cultures
3000–2500	Farming along Peruvian coast
3000–1600	Peruvian city of Caral
2500	Agriculture in lower Mississippi Valley
2000	Earliest agriculture in southwestern North America
1500	Agriculture in Amazon Basin
1200–300	Olmecs
1200–200	Chavín
1000–500	Poverty Point culture
650	Olmec writing

Clovis A Native American culture dating back some 11,500 to 13,500 years.

Hunting, Gathering, and Ancient American Life

The earliest Americans, known to scholars as Paleo-Indians, survived by hunting, fishing, and gathering while adapting to varied environments. Being skilled hunters, they may have helped bring about the extinction of large herbivore animals such as horses, mammoths, and camels, which disappeared from the Western Hemisphere between 9000 and 7000 B.C.E. But the extent to which these peoples depended on big game hunting is unclear, since they were armed only with spears and spear-throwers. A similar die-off of animals also occurred in Eurasia at the end of the Ice Age, suggesting that climate change was a factor. Most likely, the extinctions of the animals in both hemispheres was caused by some combination of over-hunting, environmental change, and perhaps an apocalyptic disease that originated with humans but then jumped to the large mammals.

In most places these trends forced a shift to hunting smaller game. But on the North American Great Plains, many peoples existed for some 10,000 years hunting bison, without benefit of horses. By 500 B.C.E. some people constructed corrals to hold captured bison. Only in the nineteenth century C.E. did this hunting way of life become impossible, as newly arrived white Americans slaughtered the bison herds on which these Native Americans depended. Abundant deer fed hunters in many other parts of North America.

Some people in favored locations flourished from hunting, fishing, and gathering for many millennia, even into modern times. This was the case in the Pacific Northwest, where coastal peoples built oceangoing boats and sturdy wood houses. Along the Peruvian coast deep-sea fishermen were exploiting the rich marine environment by 7600 B.C.E. The Monte Verde villagers, who had extensive knowledge of the available resources, used more than fifty food plants and twenty medicinal plants. In the Santa Barbara channel region of southern California beginning between 6000 and 5000 B.C.E., the Chumash (CHOO-mash) society, like the Jomon culture of Japan, lived well from a varied vegetation and meat diet that included large marine mammals such as seals. The Chumash built large, permanent villages headed by powerful chiefs, and they also used shell beads as a kind of money to distribute resources. Yet, Pacific coast peoples such as the Chumash were also subject to climate change, which periodically brought drought and hunger by altering plant and animal environments.

The eastern third of what is now the United States also provided an abundant environment for hunting and gathering, and this way of life was augmented by trade. By 4000 B.C.E. extensive long-distance trade networks linked people over several thousand miles from the Atlantic coast to the Great Plains. Dugout canoes moved copper and red ocher from Lake Superior, jasper (quartz) from Pennsylvania, obsidian from the Rocky Mountains, and seashells from both the Gulf and East Coasts. Great Lakes copper was traded as far away as New England and Florida. Indeed, copper objects made in Wisconsin around 3000 B.C.E. reached Mexico.

Early Societies and Their Cultures

Over many millennia Americans organized larger societies and developed some distinctive social and cultural patterns that emphasized cooperation within family units, animistic religion, and, for some, building huge mounds. Most people lived in egalitarian bands linked by kinship and marriage. Hunting was often a communal activity. For example, bison hunting might involve the entire village.

Americans shared with people in the Eastern Hemisphere a belief in supernatural forces, spirits, or gods. For example, perhaps like their descendants in many societies from the Amazon to the North American Great Plains, men sought a personal guardian spirit through a visionary experience induced by fasting, enduring physical pain, or taking hallucinogenic drugs. Shamans claiming command over spirits or animal souls played an important role as vehicles to connect the human and spirit worlds, often through ceremonies fueled by their showmanship. The ceremonies for such events as initiations into adult life and courtship probably included ritual dancing. Since the land furnished food, most Americans revered the earth as sacred. Some of them also adopted creation stories that were widely shared with other peoples. For example, the following Mandu creation myth from central California has much in common with the legends of some peoples a continent away on the East Coast:

> Long ago there were no stars, no moon, no sun. There was only darkness and water. A raft floated on the water, and on the raft sat a turtle. Then from the sky, a spirit came and sat on the raft. Then the spirit said that something else was needed, and he made people.[12]

Some ancient Americans organized communities around **mound building**, the construction of huge earthen mounds, often with temples on top. The oldest mound so far discovered, in Louisiana, dates to 2500 B.C.E.. Beginning around 1600 B.C.E., some peoples in the eastern woodlands and Gulf Coast of North America developed a distinctive mound-building culture. One major site, Poverty Point in northeastern Louisiana, was occupied between 1000 and 500 B.C.E., which makes it contemporary to the urban Olmec society in southern Mexico, discussed below (see Profile: The Poverty Point Mound Builders).

Occupying about three square miles, and home to perhaps five thousand people at its height, Poverty Point had the most elaborate and massive complex of earthworks in all the Americas at that time. The largest mound, an effigy of a bird that can only be seen from the air, was 70 feet high, comparable to an eight-story apartment building. It stretches nearly 700 feet from north to south and east to west. Poverty Point served as the hub of a lower Mississippi River trading system. Trade goods found there came from as far away as the Ohio and upper Mississippi River Valleys, and their exports of stone and clay products such as pendants and bowls reached what are today the states of Florida, Missouri, Oklahoma, and Tennessee.

mound building The construction of huge earthen mounds, often with temples on top, by some ancient peoples in the Americas.

THE POVERTY POINT MOUND BUILDERS

While the spectacular mounds at Poverty Point are the site's most striking legacy, the archaeological research has also revealed a remarkable community. The inhabitants did not need farming because their location, in a fertile valley nourished by annual Mississippi River floods, offered a benign hunting and gathering environment and a gentle climate. The people enjoyed a rich and varied diet that many modern people might envy. Men used simple weapons—for example, spears, spear throwers, darts, and knives—to hunt. The woods provided turkey, duck, deer, and rabbit, while the rivers offered bass, catfish, alligator, and clams. Women collected acorns, hickory nuts, walnuts, wild grapes, persimmons, sunflower seeds, squash, and gourds.

Life seems to have been agreeable. The people lived in wood houses around a central plaza and six mounds, probably governed by chiefs. In their houses men and women crafted many tools and art objects, some of which they traded hundreds of miles away. Small decorated baked-clay balls, found by the thousands in the ruins, were heated for use in cooking or boiling water. Since cooking was women's work, women probably made these clay balls, perhaps helped by their children. Each woman had her own preference for design and shape. Stoneworkers also ground and polished hard stones into ornaments and useful artifacts, and they chipped various stones into points, blades, and cutting tools. Those with an artistic bent made solid-clay female figurines, sometimes pregnant, possibly as fertility symbols. Using red jasper, they fashioned beautiful bead necklaces, bird-head pendants, and human effigies.

Located at the intersection of important waterways, Poverty Point was the central hub for a large region and was linked to trade networks that supplied the townsmen with Appalachian metal for bowls and platters, stone from the Ozarks and Oklahoma, and flint from as far away as Illinois and Ohio. The finely crafted red jasper items, often shaped like animals such as owls, have been found in distant settlements. Some of the Poverty Point men may have ventured out on trading expeditions or to bring home valuable stones from as far away as Missouri. Men and perhaps women undoubtedly arrived regularly in canoes full of trade goods to exchange.

At times the people were mobilized to build new mounds or rebuild old ones that were eroding with time. The complete earthworks contain an immense 1 million cubic yards of soil; to make them, the people probably had to transport 35 to 40 million 50-pound basket loads to the site. Several thousand people may have participated in the construction, and the project had to be carefully planned and directed so that it followed a geometric design. The mounds perhaps aided astronomical observations as a solar calendar, or perhaps served as a regional ceremonial center for social, political, or religious purposes. Some priestly or ruling class may have lived atop the mounds, as was common in some mound-building societies around the hemisphere. At least 150 smaller satellite sites, scattered along the Mississippi for several hundred miles, all contain similar artifacts, suggesting that Poverty Point was the center of both an economic and a political network.

The culture disappeared by 500 B.C.E., the people having dispersed to smaller settlements. There are no signs of war or major environmental change. Perhaps some political or religious crisis disrupted society. Whatever the case, the Poverty Point people and their culture were lost to history, leaving only the badly eroded but still impressive ruins of today.

THINKING ABOUT THE PROFILE

1. What sort of life did the Poverty Point people experience?
2. What role did Poverty Point play in the region?

Poverty Point Jasper Bead
Trade goods, such as this red jasper bead shaped like a locust, were produced at Poverty Point in Louisiana and traded over many hundreds of miles in eastern and central North America.
(Gilcrease Museum, Tulsa, Oklahoma)

SECTION SUMMARY

- The lands of the Western Hemisphere are smaller in area than those of the Eastern and are constructed on a north-south axis rather than an east-west one, but they are just as varied in terms of landforms and climate.

- Scientific evidence suggests that Native American peoples migrated from Eurasia to North America from Siberia to Alaska at least 12,000 years ago, and possibly between 20,000 and 40,000 years ago.

- Early American peoples survived by hunting, gathering, and fishing, as well as trading over large distances, but some societies clustered around huge mounds that served religious purposes.

- Mutual cooperation, earth worship, personal connections with guardian spirits, and shamanism were prominent features in early American cultural and spiritual life.

The Roots of American Urban Societies

What were some of the main features of the first American societies?

In ancient times Americans, like people in the Eastern Hemisphere, developed agriculture, trade systems, institutionalized religions, monumental architecture, and creative technologies to support them. These set the stage for more complex and highly diverse cultures, and eventually the first cities, states, and written languages. The traditions of peoples in different regions shared some common ideas, but distinctive societies also arose in various places, such as the Andes and Mexico

The Rise of American Agriculture

Americans were some of the earliest farmers, but they developed very different crops than the peoples of Afro-Eurasia. Population growth and long-distance trade were key influences sparking this great transition. The ebb and flow of weather conditions may also have contributed to the shift. Some hunting and gathering peoples were vulnerable to devastating droughts in years when the periodic weather change known today as *El Niño* (EL NEE-nyo) warmed the Pacific Ocean, shifting both rainfall patterns and the marine environment. This may have prompted them to experiment with growing food sources, and eventually several quite different agricultural traditions emerged. Some of the chief crops, such as maize (corn), were much more difficult to master than the big-seeded grains of the Fertile Crescent. Furthermore, since there were no potential draft animals, farmers needed to be creative in growing and transporting food.

Some Native Americans made the transition not long after southwest Asians had. By 8500 or 8000 B.C.E. bottle gourds and pumpkins may have been raised in **Mesoamerica**, the region stretching from central Mexico southeast into northern Central America. Avocados and chili peppers have been traced to 7000 B.C.E., and by 3500 B.C.E. some Mesoamerican farmers also grew maize, sweet potatoes, and beans. Andes people cultivated chili peppers and kidney beans by about 8000 B.C.E. Later potatoes and maize flourished there. By 3400 B.C.E. some Andeans, like early farmers in Eurasia, built elaborate irrigation canals that created artificial garden plots. By 3000 or 2500 B.C.E. societies along the Peruvian coast had also made the shift to farming, often using irrigation. They raised cotton, squash, and maize as a supplement to their still lucrative exploitation of marine resources. By 2800 B.C.E. Mound Builders in what is today Uruguay, thousands of miles from Peru, were growing corn, squash, and beans. By 1500 B.C.E. farming had spread to the Amazon Basin.

Farming later spread over trade networks to North American societies, probably influenced by environmental change with a wetter climate. Maize and squash were grown in the Southwest by 2000 or 1500 B.C.E., and beans and cotton by 500 B.C.E. The southwestern peoples were particularly ingenious in adapting farming to their poor soils and desert conditions. By 2500 B.C.E. people in the lower Mississippi Valley had discovered farming and were growing sunflowers and gourds. Eventually maize, beans, and squash became mainstays from the Southwest to the northeastern woodlands, providing a nutritionally balanced diet.

Diverse Farming Patterns and Their Consequences

Three basic farming patterns eventually shaped American societies. People in the highland and valley regions of Mesoamerica relied heavily on maize, beans, and squash. Difficult to grow, maize requires considerable labor. Another farming pattern was developed by people dwelling at the high altitudes of the Andes, who cultivated potatoes and other frost-resistant tubers. Tropical forest societies in South America evolved the third pattern, growing manioc, sweet potatoes, and root crops. The differing farming patterns proved significant for later world history because the great diversity of crops later enriched modern food supplies. Americans domesticated more different plants than had all the Eastern Hemisphere peoples combined, including three thousand varieties of potatoes, as well as chocolate, quinine, and tobacco. The shifting cultivation used in most places also limited population densities and hence fostered smaller societies.

The Americans practiced less intensive agriculture than those in the Eastern Hemisphere for one simple reason: the lack of draft animals. This fact had significant consequences. The only large herd animals available for domestication, the

Mesoamerica The region stretching from central Mexico southeast into northern Central America.

cameloids of the Andes like the llama and alpaca, were tamed by 3500 B.C.E., mostly for use as pack animals and wool sources. Americans domesticated dogs, and turkeys and guinea pigs were bred for eating in North America and the Andes, respectively. But there were no surviving counterparts to horses, cattle, and oxen. With no animals to aid in pulling, people could not use a plow or wheel. In any case, wheeled vehicles were useless in the steep Andes and the tropical rain forests. However, people made other innovations, including various ingenious irrigation schemes. For example, terracing allowed many hillsides to be farmed, and the floating gardens later developed in Central Mexico, which turned swamps into highly productive fields, provided large surpluses. To build floating gardens, farmers dug ditches to drain away water and then built long artificial islands to form planting surfaces, piling up mud and muck from the swamp bottom and organic matter to fertilize the fields. But the sort of intensive farming, aided by draft animals, that supported huge populations in China or India was not possible in the Americas.

The lack of draft animals also meant that Americans were exposed to fewer infectious diseases and epidemics. In the Eastern Hemisphere, domesticated animals passed diseases such as measles and smallpox to humans through infectious organisms such as germs and parasites, precipitating outbreaks that could kill many people and spread to adjacent regions. Historians disagree over whether, lacking these diseases, Americans may have been healthier than people across the oceans. Skeletons reveal that many of them enjoyed long lives but many people also suffered from many ailments. Furthermore, isolation from the Eastern Hemisphere left Native Americans vulnerable to the diseases brought by Europeans and Africans beginning in 1492 C.E., for which they had no immunity. These diseases eventually killed the great majority of Native Americans.

Early Farming Societies

Archaeologists are learning more about the social and cultural patterns, such as village life and religion, of early farming peoples. Permanent lakeside villages may have appeared in Mexico's fertile central valley as early as 5500 B.C.E. Communal activity was essential in these early settlements as people cooperated for survival. In the northern Andes, people fashioned the oldest known ceramics in the hemisphere between 3000 and 2500 B.C.E. By 1600 B.C.E. societies in Baja (ba-ha) California made mural paintings on rocks and in caves.

Institutionalized religions began to take shape, led by a priestly caste. Some Mesoamericans may have practiced human sacrifice by 7000 B.C.E. Later human sacrifice became common in both Mesoamerica and the Andes to honor the gods and keep the cosmos in balance. Some South American and several North American societies developed processes for mummifying the bodies of the deceased through drying. This began with the Chonchorros people in what are today southern Peru and northern Chile by 5500 B.C.E., far earlier than the more famous Egyptian mummies. Probably people noticed how bodies became naturally mummified in a dry climate and then devised techniques for deliberate preservation, perhaps because of religious beliefs about death and the afterlife.

Like the Mound Builders in North America, some societies in the Andes region and Mesoamerica began building permanent structures for religious, governmental, or recreational purposes. Pacific coast cultures in South America constructed some of the oldest monumental architecture, including stepped pyramids. Similar public buildings appeared in the Andes by the third millennium B.C.E., about the same time as monumental construction was taking place in Egypt, India, and China. Some buildings were made for recreational activities. A site in southern Mexico from 5000 B.C.E. contained a dance ground or ball court. Ceremonial ballgames involving small teams of players attempting to knock a rubber ball through a high stone hoop became a fixture of Mesoamerican life for millennia.

The Foundations of Cities and States

Agriculture, monumental construction, and long-distance trade provided a foundation for several societies to build the first cities and form the first states in the Americas (see Map 4.3). Between 3000 and 1000 B.C.E. farming people in Mesoamerica and the Andes made the technological breakthroughs and experienced the population growth that eventually led to urbanization. They worked metals like copper, gold, and silver to create tools, weapons, and jewelry, and they devised more productive farming systems, often including irrigation. Growing towns with public buildings became centers of political, economic, and religious activities. Massive ceremonial centers hundreds of feet long were constructed along the Peruvian coast, and huge mounds were erected in several places, laying the framework for the great pyramids that followed. Long-distance trade also become more common. By 1300 B.C.E. various trade routes wound around and through the Andes. Among the most valuable commodities traded over vast areas were obsidian, mirrors, seashells, and ceramics.

Growing populations and trade networks fostered the first cities. Between 4000 and 1 B.C.E. the population of the Americas grew from 1 or 2 million to around 15 million; over two-thirds of this number were concentrated in Mesoamerica and western South America. The first settlements built around massive stone structures emerged around 3100 B.C.E. in the Norte Chico region stretching from the western foothills of the Andes to the Pacific in central Peru. The largest of these settlements with some 3000 residents, and America's first known city, Caral in north-central Peru, was built perhaps as early as 2500 or 3000 B.C.E., about the same time as the Harappan cities and the Egyptian pyramids. Caral was a 150-acre complex of plazas, pyramids, and residential buildings that probably required many thousands of laborers to build. The major pyramid is 60 feet tall and covers the equivalent of four football fields. It contained a sunken amphitheater capable of seating hundreds of spectators for civic or religious events. These findings show that the local economy was able to support an elite group of priests, planners, builders, and designers. The elite seem to have lived in large, well-kept rooms atop the pyramids, the craftsmen at ground-

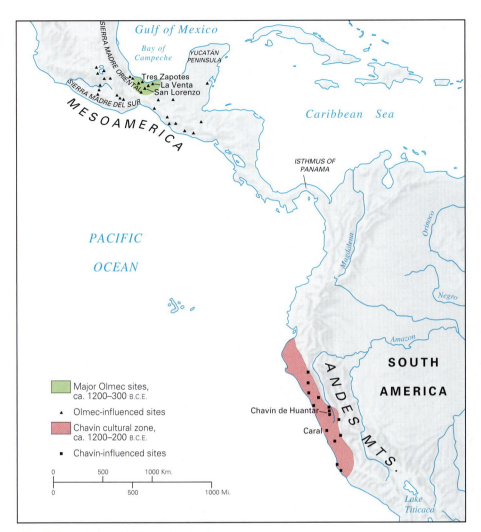

Map 4.3   Olmec and Chavín Societies
The earliest known American states arose in Mesoamerica and the Andes. The Olmecs and Chavín both endured for a millennium.

Online Study Center **Improve Your Grade**
Interactive Map: Olmec and Chavîn Civilizations

level apartments, and the workers in outlying neighborhoods. Eventually some twenty pyramid complexes occupied land for many miles around.

We know only a little of Norte Chico life. The economy was based on obtaining marine resources such as fish and growing squash, sweet potatoes, fruits, and beans as well as cotton, which they traded to coastal fishermen for making nets. The Norte Chico people do not seem to have made ceramics, unusual for a farming society, nor did they produce many arts and crafts. Caral was a major hub for trade routes extending from the Pacific coast through the Andes to the Amazonian rain forest. There is evidence for human sacrifice. The people evidently enjoyed music, and many animal bone flutes have been found in the ruins. But Caral collapsed for unknown reasons around 1600 B.C.E., several hundred years before the rise of the better-known American societies of the Olmecs and Chavín.

Mesoamerican Societies: The Olmecs

The **Olmecs** (OHL-mecks), a people who lived along the Gulf coast of Mexico, formed the earliest known urban society in Mesoamerica by 1200 or 1000 B.C.E., and they flourished until 300 B.C.E. (see Map 4.3). Each Olmec city was probably ruled by a powerful chieftain, who made alliances with chiefs in other districts. Olmec cities reflected engineering genius. The earliest city, known today as San Lorenzo, was built on an artificial dirt platform three-quarters of a mile long, half a mile wide, and 150 feet high. Home to some 2,500 people, San Lorenzo was situated above fertile but frequently flooded plains. The most famous Olmec city, La Venta, included huge earth mounds that required massive labor to build. Indeed, the mobilization of many workers was central to the construction

---

Olmecs The earliest urban society in Mesoamerica.

Olmec Head   This massive head from San Lorenzo is nearly 10 feet high. The significance of such heads (and the helmets they wear) remains unclear, but they might represent chiefs, warriors, or gods. (Nathaniel Tarn/Photo Researchers, Inc.)

of these cities. The stones for their sculptures and temples had to be brought from 60 miles away, and some of the blocks weigh more than 40 tons. The Olmecs studied astronomy in order to correctly orient their cities and monuments with the stars.

The Olmecs created remarkable architecture and art, as well as a writing system. The purpose of the huge sculptured stone heads they erected is unknown, but they might represent rulers. Olmec builders also constructed temples and pyramids in ceremonial centers and in palace complexes. The artists created a distinctive style, carving human and animal figures (especially jaguars) as well as supernatural beings in sculpture and relief. Knowing that the monuments or buildings would be a center of religious veneration and ceremonies for generations, astronomers and priests probably watched the artists work. By around 650 B.C.E. the Olmecs had also developed perhaps the first simple hieroglyphic writing in the Americas, which influenced other Mesoamerican peoples, especially the Mayan. Unlike in Mesopotamia, where writing developed from commercial needs, Mesoamerican writing kept records of kings, rituals, and the calendar, much as writing did in Egypt.

Commerce and the networks it created were a key to Olmec success and influence. The Olmecs traded with Mexico's

west coast and as far south as modern Costa Rica, importing basalt, obsidian, and iron ore. One of the major trade goods was jade, probably obtained in Guatemala, which the Olmec fashioned into ceremonial objects, masks, rings, and necklaces. The Olmecs may also have exploited cocoa trees for chocolate, later an important Mayan crop.

Extensive communication between the Olmecs and neighboring peoples contributed to some cultural homogeneity in Mesoamerica, especially in religion. Olmec religious symbols and myths emphasized a pantheon of fearsome half-human, half-animal supernatural beings, the prototypes of later Mesoamerican deities. Olmec leaders conducted great public ceremonies and honored gods feared or respected by many Mesoamerican peoples. The developing religion required precise measurement of calendar years and time cycles, which fostered the development of mathematics and writing. Although Olmec society eventually disappeared, the Olmecs established enduring patterns of life, thought, and kingship in Mesoamerica that influenced later peoples like the Maya (see Chapter 9).

South American Societies: Chavín

The earliest known Andean urban society, the **Chavín** (cha-VEEN), emerged 10,000 feet above sea level in northwestern Peru the same time as the Olmecs, around 1200 or 1000 B.C.E., and collapsed by 200 B.C.E. The Chavín created flamboyant sculpture and monumental architecture, including the large pyramid that still sits in the ruins of their major city. They also developed a highly original art focusing on real animals and anthropomorphic creatures, and they knew how to work gold and silver. As in Mesoamerica, jaguar motifs were common, but the Chavín people also seem to have venerated eagles and snakes, among other animals.

Chavín lasted for a millennium and exercised considerable influence in surrounding regions. At its height, between 860 and 200 B.C.E., the main city probably had some three thousand inhabitants. Elaborate burial sites clearly reveal a pronounced class division. The Chavín people became a major regional power, trading widely with the coast and spreading their religious cult to distant peoples. They worshiped two main deities, one of which was the "smiling god," depicted as a human body with a feline head and clawed hands and feet. Their ceremonial center became a site of pilgrimage for the faithful from a wide area. Chavín helped to establish or perpetuate some of the architectural and religious patterns that became common in the Andes.

Chavín   The earliest-known Andean urban society.

SECTION SUMMARY

- In response to the challenges posed by different climates, American peoples domesticated more different plants than all the peoples of the Eastern Hemisphere.

- Lacking draft animals, Americans came up with ingenious approaches to farming, but they could not grow the amount of food necessary to support the population levels of India or China.

- The absence of draft animals also meant that Native Americans were not exposed to many diseases before the arrival of Europeans and Africans after 1492 C.E.

- Various technological breakthroughs led to the development of urban societies in Mesoamerica and the Andes, including Caral, America's first known city.

- The Olmecs of Mesoamerica and the Chavín of South America were early urban societies that served as patterns for later American urban societies.

Online Study Center ACE the Test

◈ Chapter Summary

Some of the most ancient complex societies, among them the Chinese, emerged in river valleys, where they made the transition to agriculture, cities, and states. The Himalayan Mountains, the Tibetan Plateau, and vast deserts allowed only sporadic contact between China and most other societies. Gradually an expanding Chinese society incorporated many local traditions. The Shang, contemporaries of the Harappans and Aryans, built a powerful state while developing both bronze technology and a unique writing system. The Zhou replaced the Shang and presided over a more decentralized system that saw further technological and cultural development, including more advanced writing and literature. China's neighbors in Southeast Asia, Korea, and Japan were also creative in farming and technology, forming unique cultural identities and producing distinctive traditions. Austronesians migrating into Southeast Asia became skilled mariners, and some of them migrated eastward, settling the Western Pacific islands. Different regional environments produced varied societies, which changed as a result of both internal forces and outside influences arriving chiefly through migration and long-distance trade.

Scholars still debate the origin and antiquity of settlement in the Americas, but most believe that migrants moved from eastern Eurasia into the Americas by land or boat many millennia ago. For centuries, hunting, fishing, and gathering supported a viable way of life. The Americans did not have the rich farmland and draft animals common in Eurasia. Nonetheless, farming appeared nearly as early as in the Eastern Hemisphere, a result of population growth, climate change, and technological development. Americans domesticated a wide variety of crops and also forged long-distance trade networks, religious institutions, cities, and states.

Online Study Center **Improve Your Grade** Flashcards

Key Terms

loess
Mandate of Heaven
dynastic cycle
Yijing
Lapita
Jomon
Clovis
mound building
Mesoamerica
Olmecs
Chavín

Suggested Reading

Books

Barnes, Gina L. *China, Korea and Japan*. Rev. ed. New York: Thames and Hudson, 2000. A well-illustrated summary of the archaeology.

Coe, Michael D. *Mexico: From the Olmecs to the Aztecs*. 5th ed. London: Thames and Hudson, 2002. A readable overview of pre-Columbian Mexico, with much on the Olmecs.

Creel, Herlee G. *The Birth of China: A Survey of the Formative Period of Chinese Civilization*. New York: Frederick Ungar, 1961. This study remains one of the best introductions to the society of early China.

Ebrey, Patricia Buckley. *The Cambridge Illustrated History of China*. New York: Cambridge University Press, 1996. A readable survey incorporating recent findings.

Fagan, Brian M. *Kingdoms of Gold, Kingdoms of Jade: The Americas Before Columbus*, London and New York: Thames and Hudson, 1991. A nicely illustrated and readable introduction.

Fairbank, John K., Edwin O. Reischauer, and Albert M. Craig. *East Asia: Tradition and Transformation*. Rev. ed. Boston: Houghton Mifflin, 1989. A major text with good coverage of ancient China, Korea, and Japan.

Fiedel, Stuart J. *Prehistory of the Americas*. 2nd ed. Cambridge: Cambridge University Press, 1992. A readable introduction.

Higham, Charles. *The Archaeology of Mainland Southeast Asia*. Cambridge: Cambridge University Press, 1989. A useful and scholarly study of early Southeast Asia.

Imamura, Keiji. *Prehistoric Japan: New Perspectives on Insular East Asia*. Honolulu: University of Hawaii Press, 1996. An up-to-date introduction to what is known about early Japan.

Kirch, Patrick V. *The Lapita Peoples: Ancestors of the Oceanic World*. London: Blackwell, 1997. A recent overview of the ancient Pacific peoples.

Websites

Ancient and Lost Civilizations (http://www.crystalinks.com/ancient.html). Offers some useful essays on various world regions and ancient cultures.

Ancient Mesoamerican Civilizations (http://angelfire.com/ca/humanorigins/index.html). Links and information about the Olmecs and other premodern societies.

Internet East Asian History Sourcebook (http://www.fordham.edu/halsall/eastasia/eastasiasbook.html). An invaluable collection of sources and links .

Internet Guide for China Studies (http://www.sino.uni-heidelberg.de/igcs/). A good collection of links on premodern and modern China.

The Ancient East Asia Website (http://www.ancienteastasia.org/). Offers useful essays and other materials on China, Japan, and Korea.

Ancient Foundations of World History, 4000–600 B.C.E.

People today live in the shadow of the ancient peoples who began farming and later founded the Bronze Age cities in western Asia, Africa, South Asia, East Asia, and southern Europe. These ancient centuries, and the transitions that marked them, constructed the foundations for much that came later, including organized societies and the growing networks that connected them.

After thousands of years of prehistory, some peoples congregated in villages and began to practice agriculture. This was perhaps one of the two greatest transitions in human history, the other being the Industrial Revolution of the eighteenth and nineteenth centuries C.E. We can thank early farmers for giving us, between 10,000 and 5000 B.C.E., valuable inventions such as pottery, cloth, and the plow. Agriculture was the essential building block that stimulated other major developments, in particular the founding of cities and states and the invention of metalworking. New developments then fostered other changes. For example, better means of transportation allowed people, goods, ideas, and even diseases to travel longer distances in a shorter time. This transportation also became the basis for networks of trade and cultural exchange linking distant societies. In turn, this wider sharing of ideas helped bring about further transformations in social and cultural patterns. Today, like the ancients, we still get our food mostly from intensive agriculture and livestock raising, work metals into useful products like tools, ride in wheeled vehicles and boats that allow us to travel over long distances, worship in religious buildings, and often live in cities, where people representing several classes and many occupations work and trade. These cities are located in powerful states that are administered by bureaucratic governments and protected by military forces.

Ancient transitions happened as the result of many influences, among them environmental factors such as disease, climate change, the availability of fertile land, and the annual flooding of rivers. Local conditions helped shape such distinctive societies as Sumeria, Egypt, Nubia, Minoan Crete, Phoenicia, the Harappan cities, Shang China, and the Olmecs. At the same time, there was much contact and communication among Eurasian and northern African societies as well as long-distance migrations by peoples like the Austronesians, Bantus, and Indo-Europeans. Such movement ensured that even largely distinctive societies shared certain common features.

TECHNOLOGICAL FOUNDATIONS

We can thank the ancient peoples for inventing useful technologies such as metallurgy and for vastly improving transportation. Today we take these technologies for granted; indeed, they are basic to modern industrial life. In ancient times, however, people developed these technologies to help them solve particular problems. Once developed, they had many consequences. For example, metallurgy became a key to economic growth. Bronze and, a few centuries later, iron aided agriculture, transportation, and communication. As improvements in land and sea transportation helped move people and products over long distances, fostering trade networks. Expanded trade encouraged cities, and metal weapons and improved transportation allowed city rulers to build or expand states.

The Copper and Bronze Ages

The first metal to be worked was copper. Stoneworkers discovered that heating copper reduced it to liquid form and allowed it to be shaped in a mold. As it cooled, it could be given a good cutting edge. Many peoples in both hemispheres made copper tools and weapons, and they traded copper widely. Excavations of sunken trading ships from this era in the Mediterranean often discover large cargoes of copper. The Sumerian city-states were the first great metal-using society, followed soon after by the Egyptians, who used copper instruments to build the great pyramids. But metallurgy also led to deforestation, as forests were cut to make charcoal to fire the kilns. For example, it took 140 pounds of wood to produce 1 pound of copper.

Beginning around 3000 B.C.E. in western Asia, metalworkers figured out how to mix copper with tin or arsenic to create bronze. This discovery launched the Bronze Age in Afro-Eurasia. The Sumerians were the first society known to use bronze in commerce. Between 2600 and 2000 B.C.E. bronze technology was adopted or invented in Egypt, eastern Europe, Nubia, India, China, and Southeast Asia. The Chinese were the greatest users and mass producers of bronze. In South America, some peoples made use of another copper-arsenic alloy, as well as silver and gold.

Bronze technology affected life. Easier to make and more durable than copper, bronze was well suited for tools, drinking vessels, and weapons. In Hebrew tradition, the formidable biblical Philistine warrior Goliath had a bronze helmet, bronze armor on his legs, and a bronze javelin. Bronze making probably spurred both trade networks and warfare. Since tin deposits are less common than copper, tin was traded over great distances, and industries arose to obtain copper and tin and to manufacture bronze products. Armies were formed in part to protect mines, markets, and trade routes. Metalsmiths were so valuable that invading armies often carried them home in captivity. Finally, copper and bronze, as well as gold and silver, were used for the first coins, which gradually became the major medium of exchange.

The Iron Age

The making of iron provided the next technological breakthrough (see map). Western Asia had little tin but large quantities of iron ore. Iron was much harder to work than copper:

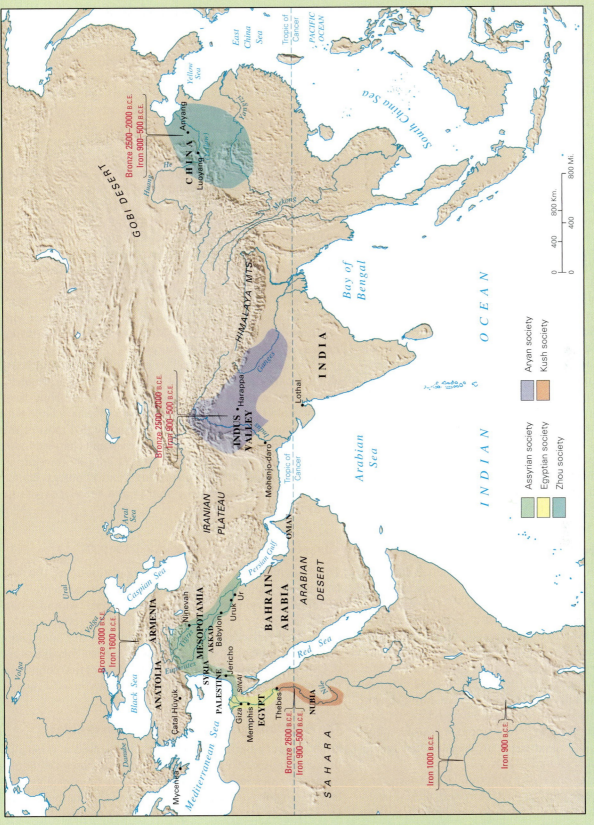

Metals and Great States ca. 1000 B.C.E.   The earliest states arose in river valleys—the Nile, Tigris-Euphrates, Indus, and Yellow— and these early states also worked metals, first bronze and then iron, to produce tools and weapons.

Legend:

Assyrian society
Egyptian society
Zhou society

Aryan society
Kush society

Map labels:

PACIFIC OCEAN
Tropic of Cancer
East China Sea
Yellow Sea
Yellow River
South China Sea
Anyang
CHINA
Luoyang
He
Huang
Yangzi
Bronze 2500–2000 B.C.E.
Iron 900–500 B.C.E.
GOBI DESERT
Mekong

HIMALAYA MTS.
Ganges
INDUS VALLEY
Harappa
Mohenjo-daro
Indus
Lothal
INDIA
Bay of Bengal
Bronze 2500–2000 B.C.E.
Iron 900–500 B.C.E.
Tropic of Cancer

INDIAN OCEAN
Arabian Sea
800 Mi.
800 Km.
0 400 800
0 400

IRANIAN PLATEAU
Aral Sea
Caspian Sea
Ural
Volga
ARMENIA
Nineveh
MESOPOTAMIA
SYRIA
AKKAD
Babylon
Tigris
Euphrates
Uruk
Ur
BAHRAIN
ARABIA
Persian Gulf
OMAN
ARABIAN DESERT
Bronze 3000 B.C.E.
Iron 1600 B.C.E.
ANATOLIA
Çatal Hüyük
Black Sea
Danube
Volga
Mycenae
Mediterranean Sea
PALESTINE
Jericho
Giza
Memphis
EGYPT
SINAI
Thebes
Red Sea
Nile
NUBIA
SAHARA
Bronze 2600 B.C.E.
Iron 900–500 B.C.E.
Iron 1000 B.C.E.
Iron 900 B.C.E.

artisans needed to produce higher temperatures, and heating produced a spongy mass rather than a liquid. Eventually inventive workers, possibly in the Hittite kingdom along the Black Sea or in Palestine, discovered a completely new but laborious technology that involved repeatedly heating and hammering the iron and plunging the result into cold water.

The Iron Age began in western Asia and Egypt by around 1600 B.C.E. Between 900 and 500 B.C.E. iron technology was also adopted or invented in Greece, India, western and central Europe, Central Asia, China, Southeast Asia, and West and East Africa. Some peoples acquired iron through trade, and others through contact with ironworking peoples like the Bantus. Since ironworking never developed in the Americas or Australia, these societies had no iron weapons or tools. Eurasians and Africans may have benefited from having societies close enough to each other to regularly exchange ideas. In contrast, many thousands of miles, much of it rain forest or desert, separated the societies of Mesoamerica from those in the Andes region, limiting contact.

Ironworking brought many advantages. The metal was both more adaptable and cheaper to make than bronze. With it people could produce better axes for cutting wood, plows for farming, wagon wheels for transport, and swords for warfare. For example, in Hebrew tradition, the Israelites could not drive the Canaanites out of the Palestinian lowland because they had iron chariots. Centuries later metalworkers learned how to add carbon to iron to make steel. But like many technologies, iron proved a mixed blessing. While it improved farming, it also made for deadlier weapons. Armies equipped with iron-tipped weapons enjoyed a strategic advantage over their neighbors. Although iron shields afforded some protection, more men may have died as warfare became more frequent.

Transportation Breakthroughs and Human Mobility

Metalworking was only one of several valuable technologies invented in ancient times. Land transport was dramatically transformed by the anonymous inventor of the wheel, to whom we owe much. Wheels were first used in pottery making, an activity that involved both men and women. But sometime between 3500 and 3200 B.C.E., probably in Mesopotamia, artisans found that fitting an axle to a cart allowed two wheels (often made of iron) to turn freely, and the wheeled cart was invented. Wagons followed rapidly, and then horse-drawn chariots. These wheeled vehicles made possible longer journeys and enabled people to carry more cargo, increasing long-distance trade. This increased travel inspired the first maps, drawn in Mesopotamia around 2300 B.C.E.

These maps, drawn onto small tablets and then baked, recognized distant relationships in portraying agricultural land, town plans, and the world as known to Babylonians. Such a map from the sixth or seventh century B.C.E. reveals how trade and communication had expanded their horizons. The map shows the Babylonian world, including rivers, canals, cities, and neighboring states, in the center of a flat earth, with the remote lands on the fringe inhabited by legendary beasts. The

mapmaker noted that his sketch showed the "four corners" of the earth.

The inventors of the first boats are unknown. The ancestors of Australian Aborigines and some of the first migrants to the Americas may have used boats, perhaps canoes or rafts, to reach their destinations many thousands of years ago. Archaeologists have discovered the remnants of 10,000-year-old boats in northwest Europe. By 5000 B.C.E. people living in Mesopotamia and along the Nile had invented square sails, and wind could then be harnessed to drive boats through the water. The use of sails spread quickly. Reed and tar boats began sailing between Kuwait, on the Persian Gulf, and India. The Greek writer Homer reported how the Mycenaeans prepared ships for voyages: "they dragged the vessel into deeper water, put the mast and sails on board, fixed the oars in leather hoops, all ship-shape, and hauled up the white sail."[1] Austronesians were probably the first to construct boats capable of sailing the deep oceans. As with land transport, better ships made it easier for distant peoples to come into contact with one another and share their ways of life. Maritime trade networks, such as those linking Pacific islands with Southeast Asia and the eastern Mediterranean with northwest Europe, stretched over vast distances.

The invention and spread of wheeled vehicles and boats also made it easier for people to migrate over longer distances. The ancient era saw several great migrations involving large numbers of people. Using seagoing boats, especially large outrigger canoes, Austronesians sailed to and settled most of the widely scattered Pacific islands. Using carts and chariots, Indo-European peoples occupied large areas of Eurasia. Traveling by foot or in canoes, and also possessing iron technology, Bantu-speaking peoples settled the forests and grasslands of the southern half of Africa.

URBAN AND ECONOMIC FOUNDATIONS

The first cities, some of them with populations over 100,000, became the cultural focal points and organizing centers for surrounding regions. The first states formed around cities, which also fostered the first writing. The urban revolution also encouraged expanded economic activities, so that merchants become prominent members of society. In turn, merchants established the first long-distance trade networks that connected people over long distances and helped spread the influence of urban societies.

The Functions and Social Organization of Cities

From the very beginning, ancient cities served a variety of functions. Some, like several Mesopotamian cities and South American cities such as Caral and Chavín, developed as centers for religious ceremonies. An Akkadian text boasted that, in Uruk, "people are resplendent in festive attire, where each day is made a holiday."[2] Cities in Egypt and China, by contrast, seem to have been founded chiefly as administrative centers to govern the surrounding territories. Many others, including the Harappan, Nubian, and Olmec cities, formed around marketplaces. Perhaps the first large city, Tell Hamoukar in

Terra Cotta Figures from Harappan Cities These terra cotta figures found in the ruins of Harappa show the diverse hairstyles and ornaments popular in the city. Archaeologists believe that these indicate the diversity of social classes and ethnic groups that inhabited Harappa. (Georg Helms/Harappa Archaeological Research Project, Courtesy Dept. of Archaeology and Museums, Govt. of Pakistan)

Mesopotamia, sat alongside a major trade route. Many cities served all these functions.

Cities produced more organized societies by fostering more elaborate class structures than could be found in the countryside. Political elites staffed the government bureaucracies such as the law courts, while religious leaders directed the temples. In Mesopotamian, Egyptian, Chinese, Harappan, and American cities, these upper-class groups generally lived in the center, around the temples and public buildings. Just outside this central zone, the middle-class merchants and skilled craftsmen lived with their families above their workshops and stores. This was true in both Sumerian Ur and Chinese Anyang. In Mesopotamia, craftsmen accounted for 20 percent of the city population. Different neighborhoods were often defined by occupation. For example, at Anyang potters apparently concentrated in one district, metalworkers in another. On the city outskirts lived the laborers, including household servants, small farmers, and slaves. Cities also attracted people from neighboring societies, and ethnically diverse populations were common. Some merchants migrated from elsewhere but probably maintained ties to their hometowns through the extensive commercial networks.

Most urban women led busy lives. As households began to stir each morning, they prepared a quick meal for husbands and sons heading out to their work, perhaps as artisans, peddlers, soldiers, or laborers. Many used pots and pans made of copper or bronze to cook and serve the food. After cleaning up the meal, many women walked through dusty streets to market stalls to buy food grown on nearby farms. As they returned home, they may have passed children playing in the narrow alleys, perhaps watched by grandparents. In some societies, the wealthier women were increasingly restricted inside walled courtyards. The poorest women and men begged, searched through trash, or offered their services to those who were better off.

Cities, Trade, and Networks of Exchange

Because trade was a major city activity, merchants became prominent members of urban society. In their shops and market stalls, they made available products from near and far. One of the most popular products was salt, which was used to preserve and add taste to food. Another was obsidian, a volcanic glass that made sharp tools and was found naturally only where volcanic activity had occurred. Diverse peoples, among them Greeks, Pacific Islanders, and Mesoamericans, actively sought obsidian. By 1500 B.C.E. long-distance traders supplied various Mediterranean and Middle Eastern societies with opium and other drugs, which were mostly used to ease the pain of disease, surgery, and childbirth. As it does today, trade could also foster disagreements. An Ur merchant, complaining about the poor quality of copper shipped from Bahrain, wrote to the sender: "Who am I that you treat me in this manner and offend me?"[3]

Growing trade required the creation of currencies, without which our modern economic life would be impossible. Simple forms of money, mostly varied weights of precious metals like silver, were invented between 3000 and 2500 B.C.E. in Mesopotamian cities. Legal codes were then written that specified fines, interest rates, and even the ideal price of some common goods. By 600 B.C.E. the first gold coins were being struck in Anatolia. Money made exchange easier, especially in cities, and it may have stimulated the development of mathematics as a tool for calculating wealth. Various ancient societies in both hemispheres developed some system of mathematics.

Trade networks moving objects of value, from raw materials to luxury goods, linked major cities and even distant societies. Between 4000 and 3000 B.C.E. traders began shipping minerals, precious stones, and other valued commodities over long distances, and Mesopotamia became a commercial hub linkng southern Asia with Egypt. Beginning around 1200 B.C.E., heavily urbanized Phoenicia, which established many trading ports around the Mediterranean, became the first known society to flourish mostly through interregional commerce rather than farming. Gradually trade routes expanded over long distances, increasing contacts between societies with different cultures and institutions. Goods traveled initially by riverboat and by donkey or horse caravans. By 2000 B.C.E., however, sea trading in the Mediterranean Sea, Persian Gulf, and Indian Ocean had become more important.

Some areas became trade centers. Mesopotamia was the center of a vast trade network, with links eastward to India and Central Asia and westward to Egypt and Italy. Its location as the hub of this network allowed it to draw ideas, produce, and people from a huge hinterland. Similarly, Egypt connected Africa and Eurasia. By 2000 B.C.E. cities like Dilmun on Bahrain Island in the Persian Gulf flourished as trade hubs located between major societies. The Persian Gulf itself has served as a contact zone for over five millennia.

Trade fostered other transitions. The need to guide ships or caravans to distant destinations, as well as the belief that the changing skies could influence human activity (astrology), sparked the study of the stars. Babylonian astrological beliefs and the zodiac may have been spread by trade to western Asia and southern Europe, where they became popular.

POLITICAL FOUNDATIONS

Closely related to urbanization was the emergence of the first states, with their bureaucratic structures and powerful ruling elites. States marked a transition to more complex and organized societies. The first known states formed in Mesopotamia around 3500 B.C.E. and in Egypt by 3000 B.C.E. Between 3000 and 1000 B.C.E. states were also established in India, China, Vietnam, Nubia, and southeastern Europe, as well as in Mesoamerica and South America. Today we take for granted the notion of large political units to whom people owe allegiance, but in the ancient world they were major innovations. Among the consequences of states was the rise of conflict between them as well as with nearby pastoral peoples, which resulted in increased warfare. Although warfare long predates state building, now it was waged on a larger scale, becoming a common pattern in world history.

Kings and Political Hierarchies

States were hierarchically organized political structures. The rulers—mostly kings and emperors, but sometimes queens, such as the Egyptian Hatshepsut—ruled over many rural peasants and city-dwellers living within the territories they controlled. These people paid taxes, in money or in agricultural products, in acknowledgment of the king's ability to keep order, promote justice, and protect his subjects from harm. The great law code associated with the Babylonian ruler Hammurabi is one illustration of this basis of ancient governments. Many kings sought the kind of support accorded the Aryan kings in the Hindu sacred writings: "Him do ye proclaim, O men as kings and father of kings, the lordly power, the suzerain of all creation, the eater of the folk, the slayer of foes, the guardian of the law."[4] Bureaucracies were formed to administer the states, including the first empires. As royal power increased, the institutions that allowed merchants and other leading citizens to participate in government, such as the assemblies in Sumerian cities, lost their importance.

The rulers of large states had to possess legal and military power to reward their supporters and punish their enemies. This required sufficient income from either taxes or the spoils of war. Some of this money was also used to build great monumental architecture, such as the Egyptian pyramids and Olmec mounds whose ruins still astonish tourists. Rulers also had to convince their subjects that they ruled, either as gods themselves (such as the pharaoh of Egypt) or with the permission of divine forces (such as the Zhou dynasty rulers in China, who claimed to rule by the "Mandate of Heaven"). We often imagine ancient pharaohs and emperors as all-powerful despots, and in many respects they were. But kingship was not always an easy job. Officials might ignore their policies, rivals could challenge them, and disenchanted groups might rebel.

After states came empires, which were generally formed by conquest. The Akkadian Sargon in Mesopotamia established the earliest known imperial state around 2350 B.C.E. Sargon's use of a standing army (with over five thousand soldiers) set the pattern that prevailed in the Fertile Crescent for the next several millennia as various states gained influence or control over their neighbors, often to secure scarce resources like silver, copper, or timber. Various ancient societies established empires, among them Assyrians, Egyptians, Mycenaeans, and Hittites. This expansion prompted states to set up forts on their frontiers to control the local population and the flow of traffic. An Egyptian inscription ordered a garrison along the Nile "to prevent any Nubian from passing northward, whether on foot or by boat," except for traders or messengers.[5]

Fragments of Egyptian-Hittite Treaty This carved stone fragment contains a treaty, signed around 1250 B.C.E., between Egypt and the Hittite kingdom in Anatolia that ended a war between the two states. The treaty is inscribed in the widely used cuneiform script of the Akkadian language. It eloquently demonstrates the reality of ancient warfare but also expresses the age-old quest for peace. (Victor Boswell/NGS)

States and Warfare

With the rise of competing states and improved military technology, warfare became more common. One of the chief tasks of the ruler was to protect and perhaps expand his state, and often rulers waged war to acquire land and capture people. More land and population meant more resources and tax revenues. As part of the rise of warfare as an institution, rulers were expected to be or honor heroic warriors. Even today people remember the legends of great ancient warriors (real or mythical) like Hercules at Troy or Arjuna in the *Bhagavad Gita*. Ancient soldiers were armed with "shock" weapons such as clubs or swords and "missiles" such as arrows or spears. Warfare by settled peoples required a powerful state. To wage war, kings had to marshal resources such as food and metals as well as recruit soldiers. They also had to discourage dissent and instill among the population a sense that warfare was worthwhile. Opposition to the ruler and his policies was viewed as treason and could mean death or imprisonment.

In Afro-Eurasia many wars matched states against pastoral nomads, who were attracted by the wealth of the farming societies and their cities. These mobile nomads, often viewed by the farming peoples as "barbarians," pioneered the development of chariot and cavalry warfare and possessed many horses or camels. Between 2000 and 1000 B.C.E. nomadic peoples occasionally conquered cities and states. Eventually many of these pastoralists, such as the Hittites in western Asia and the Aryans in India, adopted some of the ways of the conquered farmers, while the urban peoples acquired the pastoral-

ists' military technologies. Incursions into farming societies by nomadic pastoralists remained an important pattern in world history until the seventeenth century C.E.

Ancient armies, like modern ones, depended on their weapons and on soldiers who were not always enthusiastic about their job. One Egyptian text said of a soldier: "He is awakened when an hour has passed and he is driven like an ass. He works till the sun sets. He is hungry, his body is exhausted, he is dead while still alive. His body is broken with dysentery."[6] Some conscripts in Zhou China shared the disenchantment: "What plant is not wilting? What man is not taken from his wife? Alas for us soldiers!"[7] Then as now, soldiering was a dangerous activity that required bravery and self-discipline.

Warfare became increasingly lethal as weaponry and strategy improved. When the Assyrians swept through Mesopotamia in the ninth century B.C.E., their advanced cavalry and siege weaponry enabled them to level and burn the great city of Babylon. Later the Assyrians themselves experienced defeat, as their capital, Ninevah, fell to "the noise of the whip and of rattling wheels, galloping horses, clattering chariots!"[8] Even though many ancient cities were surrounded by defensive walls, they were still vulnerable to well-armed foes. But the costs of war, in treasure and people, also prompted rulers to make peace treaties with rival powers and prompted prophets to call for beating "their swords into ploughshares, their spears into pruning hooks; nation shall not lift up sword against nation."[9] The quest for peace was as old as the urge to wage war.

SOCIAL AND CULTURAL FOUNDATIONS

Beginning around 3500 B.C.E. the social forms common to hunters and gatherers began to change as more and more people settled down to farming and developed more organized societies. Metallurgy, cities, and states fostered new structures, systems, and attitudes, along with social inequality and more varied activities. Perhaps the two most significant cultural innovations were writing, which allowed for recordkeeping and improved communication, and institutionalized religion, which shaped the values and behavior of societies. The social and cultural patterns that emerged in antiquity endured because they fulfilled basic human needs for group survival and personal satisfaction.

Inequality, Conflict, and Leisure

The shift from the relatively egalitarian ethos of hunting and gathering to a more hierarchal social organization changed people's lives. Increasingly people were divided into social classes, with the wealthier groups controlling the distribution and consumption of economic resources. Ancient graves reveal the differences in social status. Some graves were elaborate, filled with offerings of material goods such as jewelry, and others were very simple. Legal codes, such as that of Hammurabi, usually favored the wealthy.

At the same time, with productive agriculture, populations grew. Between 8000 and 500 B.C.E. the world's population jumped from 5 or 10 million up to an estimated 100 million.

The great majority of these people lived in Mesopotamia (the most densely populated area), Egypt, India, China, and southeastern Europe. People were also living longer than during the Stone Age, when a third died before age twenty and only a tenth lived past forty. Bronze Age peoples lived into their early forties, and probably 5 to 10 percent lived past sixty.

With less equality but more people, the potential for social conflict increased. Most communities included haves and have-nots, landlords and landless, free citizens and slaves. The gap between rich and poor made crime a serious problem that was addressed through harsh codes like that of Hammurabi. Theft was common in major Mesopotamian and Egyptian cities. Large enslaved populations, which included debtors and prisoners of war might revolt. Slavery was more pervasive in Mesopotamia than in China, Egypt, and India, but slaveholding was common in all ancient agricultural societies.

Patriarchy was another source of inequality and remains a feature of life today (see Historical Controversy: Patriarchy and Matriarchy in the Ancient World). Men increasingly believed that women were unsuited to run governments, and few of them were allowed to do so. Social changes that required heavy physical labor in farming, warfare, and long-distance trade influenced gender and family relations. Women now became known as the "weaker sex" and were often assigned chiefly domestic tasks. An ancient Chinese saying asserted that "men plow and women weave."[10] Although women continued to produce some of the pottery and most of the cloth, they were no longer equal contributors to food needs because they now spent more time at home. In farming families, women were also encouraged to bear a larger number of children to help in the fields. Many places, men, especially rulers and the rich, had multiple wives or took concubines. In some societies, among them Sumeria, Egypt, and Shang China, the remnants of older matrilineal family systems were only fading memories, but middle-class urban women fought hard to retain their property and other rights. Sexual options became more limited for women because men wanted to ensure that their personal wealth would be passed on to their children of known paternity. Increasingly dependent on men for support, women became more preoccupied with physical appearance, hoping to attract male favor. Women used eye makeup and perfume, both invented in ancient Egypt and still popular today.

Despite the social inequality and long hours of toil, leisure activities developed that are familiar to us today. For example, the Sumerian city-dwellers enjoyed dancing and music and invented beautiful, elaborate harps and lyres for their pleasure. Zhou Chinese music lovers preferred flutes and drums, and Egyptians preferred metal horns. Music was used for worship, festivals, and work, but the oldest known love songs had also appeared by 2300 B.C.E. in Egypt. Wrestling became a popular sport in many cultures. Alcoholic drinks like beer and wine were also common, often consumed in public taverns. Drinking became an integral part of leisure and social relationships in many societies. Homer summed up the pleasures favored in early Greece: "The things in which we take a perennial delight are the feast, the lyre [a musical instrument], the dance, clean linen in plenty, a hot bath and our beds."[11] These are pleasures that most modern people share, indicating that some things have not changed much in 3,000 years.

Bell of Marquies   Music had a key function in the court life of Zhou China. This sixty-four piece bell set was found in the tomb of a regional ruler, which also contained many flutes, drums, zithers, pan pipes, and chimes. Five men using mallets and poles were needed to play this set of bells. (Cultural Relics Publishing Company)

Patriarchy and Matriarchy in the Ancient World

Today, as in the past, men generally hold political, economic, and religious power in most societies. This dominance is due to patriarchy, a system whereby men largely control women and children, shape ideas about appropriate gender behavior, and generally dominate society. Many people assume that patriarchal social organization springs from some innate characteristic of the human species, symbolized by the common expression that this is a "man's world." But the situation is more complex historically.

THE PROBLEM

The prevalence of patriarchy raises three important questions. First, was there ever a time when women held equal power and status to men? Second, was matriarchy, in which women enjoy social and political dominance, ever common? And third, assuming women once enjoyed a higher status in society, can we identify a particular period when patriarchy triumphed? These questions spark heated scholarly debates.

THE DEBATE

The first question is the easiest to answer. Historians are reasonably sure that, among many peoples, women had greater equality with men during the Stone Age. The small, closely knit societies, like the !Kung of southern Africa, were often egalitarian, had weak leaders, and had little private property to fight over. But, despite a rough equality due to women's ability, essential for a society's survival, to gather food and medicinal herbs, there is little evidence that many prefarming societies allowed women more publicly recognized authority than men. Some peoples who practiced simple farming, such as the Iroquois, Cherokee, Hopi, and Zuni in North America, gave women considerable influence within a matrilineal culture, even if men usually had ultimate decision-making power.

In response to the second question, some scholars have argued that a "golden age of matriarchy" existed before the rise of urban societies and states in Europe and the Middle East, and perhaps also in India, Japan, Southeast Asia, and the Americas. Supporters of the ancient matriarchy thesis point to the many figurines of females, many perhaps of goddesses, unearthed at archaeological sites worldwide. They believe that goddess worship correlated with high female status and that women were cherished for giving birth and nurturing the young, which gave them a connection to the earth and spirits. Patricia Monaghan identifies more than 1,500 different goddesses worldwide, representing everything from mother to warrior.

Perhaps the most debated recent studies are by Lithuanian archaeologist Marija Gimbutas, whose writings, based on discoveries at sites such as Çatal Hüyük in Turkey, the Minoan palace at Knossos, and Stonehenge, portray ancient people in Europe and Anatolia as egalitarian and peaceful farmers led by influential women. These female-oriented societies, she says, were destroyed around 3500 B.C.E. by more violent Indo-European nomads from Central Asia, who brought patriarchy with them. From then on, patriarchy spread across Europe. Similarly, Riane Eisler and Judith Lorber describe ancient, goddess-worshiping farming cultures in eastern and southern Europe, where men and women ruled equally, with no war or inequalities of wealth. And like Gimbutas, they contend that Indo-European newcomers imposed male governments on these earlier societies.

Most scholars dispute the views of Gimbutas, Eisler, and Lorber about ancient matriarchies and equal status for each gender. For example, Lotte Motz, Lucy Godison, and Christine Morris argue that goddess worship theories are unproven. Motz claims that female images are no more common in early Europe than those of men and animals. Furthermore, the figurines may have been used in fertility rites rather than revered as spiritual forces. Motz and Cynthia Eller also suggest that mother goddess theories reflect not ancient realities but modern political and cultural attitudes, including a feminism that challenges patriarchy and biases about women's roles. Nor can we assume, such critics say, that worshiping female deities, if it happened, actually gave real power to women. After all, the patriarchal ancient Mesopotamians and Greeks worshiped various female deities, including a goddess of love, and many modern patriarchal cultures, including the Chinese, Japanese, Hindu Indian, and Yoruba, have female deities in their pantheons. Many Europeans have revered the Virgin Mary over the past two millennia, but men have still dominated European society.

If the notion of ancient matriarchies transformed by force into patriarchies cannot be proven, we are still left with the third question, how and when did patriarchy emerge? Anthropologist Sherry Ortner argues for a slow but inevitable transition from the egalitarianism of food collecting to male domination in the early cities and states. To Ortner, patriarchy was a product of technological and social upheavals rather than a will to power by aggressive men. Childbearing played a role because, while women stayed home having and raising children, men could travel and engage in more paid work and governmental, leisure, and religious activities, as well as warfare. That led to the gender stereotypes of women in unpaid work at home and men at paid work elsewhere. Also arguing for a gradual change, anthropologist Elizabeth Barber contends that farming people needed products, such as metal ores, that had to be gained through long-distance trade. This gave power to the more mobile and physically stronger men, who could travel to distant places and transport the heavy cargoes home. To be sure, knowledge of cloth making and the fiber arts gave women importance in ancient societies, since men also used products such as clothing and blankets; nevertheless, patriarchy emerged

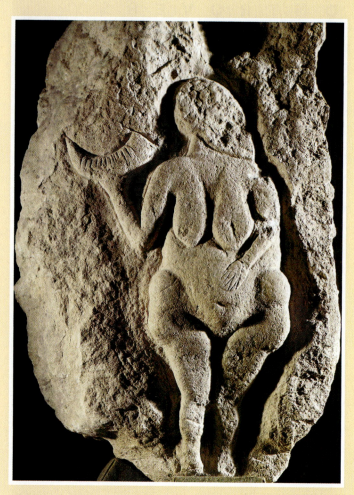

Goddess Figure　This female figure, probably a mother-goddess, found in France was probably used in fertility rights. Such figures have been found in many ancient societies studied by archaeologists.　(Erich Lessing/Art Resource, NY)

gradually as society slowly changed and began to reward strength and mobility.

There is considerable evidence that men increased their power over women in many early urban societies. Historian Gerda Lerner analyzed male power in the Mesopotamian city-states, where kings or male assemblies ruled. Law codes such as Hammurabi's favored men, and only women could be divorced or sold into slavery for adultery. Laws also restricted women's freedom of movement and treated them as private property. By this time, Lerner argues, gods had become more important than goddesses, and male power was legally recognized and sanctioned by religion.

EVALUATING THE DEBATE

What, then, was the status of women in ancient societies? The weight of scholarship favors those who doubt that full-blown matriarchal societies were once widespread. But few societies

have ever been entirely controlled by the activities or wishes of men. Until recently historians and archaeologists have neglected the role of women. When we study ancient societies, we may unknowingly be influenced by modern patriarchal attitudes, since these are prominent in today's culture. We are more likely to study kings and wars than the beginnings of herbal medicine, cloth production, and the role of women as negotiators in community disputes. We have not heard the last word from scholars on the question of ancient matriarchies and patriarchies, but their disputes have made us more aware of the role of women in history.

THINKING ABOUT THE CONTROVERSY

1. Why can worship of a mother goddess be understood in different ways?
2. Why do we need to understand patriarchy to comprehend world history?

EXPLORING THE CONTROVERSY

Some major works supporting the ancient goddess and matriarchy thesis include Marija Gimbutas, *Goddesses and Gods in Old Europe, 6500–3500 B.C.: Myths and Cult Images* (Berkeley: University of California Press, 1982); Gimbutas, *The Language of the Goddess: Unearthing the Hidden Symbols of Western Civilization* (New York: Harper and Row, 1989); Gimbutas, *The Living Goddesses* (Berkeley: University of California Press, 1999); and Riane Eisler, *The Chalice and the Blade: Our History, Our Future* (San Francisco: Harper and Row, 1995). Judith Lorber challenges basic assumptions about gender in *Paradoxes of Gender* (New Haven: Yale University Press, 1994). Patricia Monaghan, *The New Book of Goddesses and Heroines* (New York: Llewellyn Publications, 1997), provides a useful reference on mythological and legendary female deities from many lands and eras.

Strong criticism of the ancient matriarchy thesis can be found in Lucy Godison and Christine Morris, eds., *Ancient Goddesses: The Myths and the Evidence* (Madison: University of Wisconsin Press, 1999); Lotte Motz, *The Faces of the Goddess* (New York: Oxford University Press, 1997); and Cynthia Eller, *The Myth of Matriarchal Prehistory: Why an Invented Past Won't Give Women a Future* (Boston: Beacon Press, 2001). Among major books on the making of patriarchy and gender roles are Elizabeth Barber, *Woman's Work: The First 20,000 Years: Women, Cloth, and Society in Early Times* (New York: W.W. Norton, 1994); Gerda Lerner, *The Creation of Patriarchy* (New York: Oxford University Press, 1986); and Sherry Ortner, *Making Gender: The Politics and Erotics of Culture* (Boston: Beacon Press, 1997).

Writing and Its Consequences

Imagine how different our modern worlds of education and work would be without reading and writing. Although limited to a relatively small group of people for much of history, writing was a critical invention of several early societies. A Sumerian legend recalled a key discovery: "The High Priest of Kulaba formed some clay and wrote words on it as if on a tablet; with the sun's rising [to dry the clay], so it was!"[12] Writing fostered increasing occupational specialization, including the emergence of clerks, scribes, bureaucrats, and eventually teachers, scholars, and historians.

Initially developed chiefly to keep commercial accounts, codify legends and rituals, or record political proclamations, writing later gave birth to literature, historiography, sacred texts, and other forms of learning and culture that could now be transmitted and expanded. For example, writing helped spread the Sumerian epic of Gilgamesh so widely that it influenced the Hebrew book of Genesis and the *Iliad* and the *Odyssey* of the Greek Homer many centuries later. Similarly, Indian stories such as the *Ramayana* became popular in Southeast Asia. Writing also allowed rulers to communicate over long distances with district governors and foreign leaders, and it allowed merchants to make arrangements with merchants in other cities, enhancing the role of communication networks.

Writing, however, had contradictory consequences. On the one hand, it clearly stimulated creativity and intellectual growth while allowing for a spread of knowledge. But writing also often became a tool for preserving the social and political order, especially when literacy was restricted to a privileged elite such as bureaucrats, lawyers, or priests. For example, a soldier in Zhou China complained that he and his colleagues wanted to return home, but they "were in awe of the [official] orders in the tablets."[13] Sacred literature was also frequently closed to debate, since it supposedly came from the gods.

Institutionalized Religions

The rise of agriculture and then cities gradually transformed the belief that nature was alive with spiritual forces (animism) to more systematic theologies and organized religious observances. These beliefs and practices gave order and meaning to people's lives and may have promoted cooperation and a sense of community. Ideas about the fate of individual humans after death as well as notions of right and wrong differed widely as societies developed unique traditions and beliefs. While most ancient peoples were polytheists or animists, believing in many gods or spirits, a few, such as the Hebrews and some African societies, were monotheists, believing in one high god who presided over the universe.

Full-time religious specialists also evolved, often replacing the shamans, the part-time spiritual leaders associated with earlier times. With the rise of agriculture and larger communities, a priestly class arose who were seen as able to communicate with the gods and interpret their will. Because they provided essential services such as writing or calculating the time of the annual floods, priests were the first social group to be freed from direct subsistence labor. They also staffed the temples, which in some cities were massive monumental buildings serving thousands of believers.

The supernatural and natural worlds were usually explained through myths, stories about the past or about the interaction of gods with the human world. Mythology explained the birth of the universe, the progression of seasons, the uncertainties of agriculture, the flooding of rivers, and human dramas such as battlefield losses and victories. Myths and legends were included in sacred books. Several thousand years later some of these ancient books, such as the Hindu Vedas and the Hebrew Bible, are still revered by many millions of people.

Institutionalized religions influenced societies. Because religious ceremonies and ideas provided supernatural sanction for the social and political order, they became a powerful force for social control. Challenging the political or social system, which was seen as divinely inspired, now constituted blasphemy and condemned one to eternal punishment after death. Many of the ancient religions, led by men and worshiping chiefly male gods, supported patriarchal attitudes. Religious views also spread from one society to another. For example, Egyptian ideas of the afterlife and a final Day of Judgment were influential around the larger Mediterranean basin. Hebrews may have acquired their notions of a weekly Sabbath and a Garden of Eden from Mesopotamians. Many centuries later all these ideas were reflected in Christianity and Islam.

SUGGESTED READING

BOOKS

Adas, Michael, ed. *Agricultural and Pastoral Societies in Ancient and Classical History*. Philadelphia: Temple University Press, 2001. A useful collection of essays on various aspects of premodern world history.

Bogucki, Peter. *The Origins of Human Society*. Malden, Mass.: Blackwell, 1999. A detailed and up-to-date scholarly study of prehistory and the rise of ancient societies.

Casson, Lionel. *The Ancient Mariners: Seafarers and Sea Fighters of the Mediterranean in Ancient Times*. 2nd ed. Princeton, N.J.: Princeton University Press, 1991. A fascinating study of ancient maritime trade and connections.

Christian, David. *Maps of Time: An Introduction to "Big History."* Berkeley: University of California Press, 2004. The most extensive presentation of the "big history" approach, with much on the ancient era.

Curtin, Philip D. *Cross-Cultural Trade in World History*. Cambridge: Cambridge University Press, 1984. A pioneering comparative study.

Diamond, Jared. *Guns, Germs and Steel: The Fates of Human Societies*. New York: W.W. Norton, 1997. A fascinating interpretation of prehistoric and ancient human societies, with emphasis on environmental influences.

Fagan, Brian. *The Long Summer: How Climate Changed Civilization.* New York: Basic Books, 2004. An up-to-date assessment of the connection between history and climate over the past 5,000 years.

Fagan, Brian M. *People of the Earth: An Introduction to World Prehistory.* 11th ed. New York: Longman, 2003. Contains much up-to-date material on the ancient societies and prehistory.

Manning, Patrick. *Migration in World History.* New York: Routlegde, 2005. Provocative study, with much on prehistory and ancient history.

Matossian, Mary Kilbourne. *Shaping World History: Breakthroughs in Ecology, Technology, Science, and Politics.* Armonk, N.Y.: M.E. Sharpe, 1997. A general examination of science, technology, and ecology, with much material on early farmers and the ancient societies.

Snooks, Graeme D. *The Dynamic Society: Exploring the Sources of Global Change.* London: Routledge, 1996. A challenging view of world history by an economist, with much on the ancient world.

Trigger, Bruce D. *Understanding Early Civilizations.* New York: Cambridge University Press, 2003. A detailed scholarly examination of ancient societies, including Egypt, Mesopotamia, and Shang China.

Wood, Michael. *Legacy: The Search for Ancient Cultures.* New York: Sterling, 1994. A well-written survey of ancient societies for the general reader.

WEBSITES

Ancient and Lost Civilizations (http://www.crystalinks.com/ancient.html). Offers some useful essays on various world regions and ancient cultures.

Exploring Ancient World Cultures (http://eawc.evansville.edu/). Excellent site run by Evansville University, with essays and links on the ancient Near East, Egypt, India, China, and Europe.

Geology Project (http://www.unr.edu/sb204/geology). Provides brief but useful information on the history of copper, bronze, and iron technology.

Internet Ancient History Sourcebook (http://www.fordham.edu/halsall/ancient/asbook.html). An exceptionally rich collection of links and primary source readings.

Internet Global History Sourcebook (http://www.fordham.edu/halsall/global/globalsbook.html). An excellent set of links on world history from ancient to modern times.

World Civilizations (http://www.wsu.edu/~dee/TITLE.HTM). A useful collection of materials on prehistory and ancient history, operated by Washington State University.

PART II

Blossoming: The Classical Societies and Their Legacies, ca. 600 B.C.E.–ca. 600 C.E.

The Classical Era, roughly the centuries between 600 B.C.E. and 600 C.E., was a formative period that saw a flourishing of societies and networks in nearly every inhabited part of the globe. The foundations for this era had been laid with the agricultural transition and the rise of the first cities and states in both the Eastern and Western Hemispheres. The classical societies typically became more complex and often larger than their ancient predecessors. The era's art, literature, politics, and religion have had a lasting significance. Today's popular images of the Classical Era—Greek philosophers debating the meaning of existence, Roman gladiators battling in the Colosseum, and the Buddha meditating under a leafy tree—while limited, testify to the ongoing prominence this era has held in our thought.

These centuries saw innovations in thought, government, writing, and metalworking and an increase in long-distance trade aided by new transportation technologies. Improved communications between societies spread ideas and products, helping foster change. Trading zones expanded, and societies as distant from each other as Persia and China established diplomatic communication. People began to envision a larger world than their own village or kingdom, and that larger world changed them. In the increasingly cosmopolitan milieu of the Eastern Hemisphere, for example, Chinese influence began to reshape Korea and Japan, Indian religions and political ideas sparked state building in Southeast Asia, and Greek culture reached into Europe, Asia, and Africa. In the ferment sparked in the Eastern Hemisphere by local growth and contact with other societies, many of the laws, political traditions, literatures, philosophies, and religions associated with the major cultures emerged. Similarly, in both sub-Saharan Africa and the Americas, societies exchanged religious ideas, trade goods, and notions of government. Population movement into the Pacific islands (Oceana) and southern Africa continued.

The early classical centuries in Greece, Israel, Persia, India, and China were marked by philosophical speculation. This creative evolution in human thought between 600 and 250 B.C.E., often called the Axial Age, laid the groundwork for the core beliefs of some classical societies. Many of the greatest

Persian Rhyton This gilded silver drinking cup, made in Persia in the fourth or fifth century B.C.E., has the figure of the ibex, a local animal, at the base. The cup is an example of the artistic treasures produced by classical peoples. (Courtesy of the Trustees of the British Museum)

thinkers in history, such as Buddha, Confucius, and Socrates, lived at the same time or were near-contemporaries. Several billion people in Asia continue to revere the teachings of Confucius and the Buddha, Hebrew thinkers influenced later religions, and schools in North America and western Europe still introduce students to the ideas of the classical Greek philosophers.

Between 350 B.C.E. and 250 C.E. large parts of the Afro-Eurasian zone were transformed by large regional empires. During the imperial age great states dominated the Mediterranean Basin, Western Asia, India, and China. Diverse peoples, including Persians, Hellenistic Greeks, Romans, Mauryan Indians, and Han Chinese, presided over regional empires greater in scale than any that had come before. Some of the empire builders, such as the Macedonian Alexander the Great and the Roman Julius Caesar, are still famous today. Eventually, however, the empires overextended themselves territorially and collapsed. In contrast, most American and sub-Saharan African states were small and often decentralized.

The great Afro-Eurasian empires were in regular contact with each other by way of extensive trade networks. Distances narrowed. The best-known network was the overland Silk Road, named after the main commodity shipped, which linked China across Central Asia with India, the Middle East, and Europe. Caravans also linked North and West Africa across the harsh Sahara Desert, while trade routes around the Indian Ocean connected Southeast Asia and India with East Africa and Western Asia. Thanks to conquest or trade, Greek and Roman ideas and institutions permeated the Mediterranean region, and Indian cultural influences spread into Central, East, and Southeast Asia. Deadly diseases, such as plague, also moved along the trade routes, killing millions. Thus societies all over the world were increasingly altered, at times dramatically, by contact with others through various kinds of networks of trade, migration, disease, and conquest. Nonetheless, despite this contact, major societies largely remained distinct from each other.

As the Afro-Eurasian empires declined, divided, or collapsed, three religions rose in influence and enjoyed a wide appeal: Buddhism, Hinduism, and a new faith, Christianity. As these religions crossed cultural boundaries, attracting people of diverse backgrounds, they became universal religions, promoting social stability while also fostering cultural exchange. Since the Classical Era, regions have often been identified with their dominant religion, such as Hindu India or Christian Europe. These religious heritages were formed in the Classical Era.

NORTH AND CENTRAL AMERICA
The Maya established a long-lasting series of rival city-states in Mexico and Central America that flourished from creative farming, science, trade, and writing. Great cities based on trade also appeared elsewhere in Mexico. North of Mexico, town-dwelling farming societies emerged. Especially influential, the Mound Builders in eastern North America fostered long-distance trade networks stretching from the Atlantic Ocean and Gulf of Mexico to the Great Lakes.

SOUTH AMERICA
New states that used innovative agriculture emerged along the Peruvian coast and in the Andes highlands. The Moche, while warring with their neighbors, also created sophisticated pottery and art. In the Andes, Tiwanaku produced art and thought that influenced neighboring societies. Long-distance trade networks also connected various societies in South America.

116

EUROPE

Greek city-states, notably Athens, experimented with democracy and fostered philosophy and science. By conquering a large empire, Alexander the Great spread Greek culture into western Asia and Egypt. The Romans built an empire that encompassed the Mediterranean Basin and much of Europe, spreading Roman influence. By late Roman times Christianity was becoming the dominant religion in the Mediterranean, and Germanic tribes migrated into southern Europe, contributing to the collapse of Roman power. To the east, Byzantium conquered a large empire while mixing Roman, Greek, and Christian traditions.

WESTERN ASIA

The Persians established a large empire over much of western Asia and Egypt, promoting Persian thought. After their collapse the Hellenistic Greeks dominated the region and spread Greek culture. The Hellenistic Greeks were then displaced by the Romans. In Roman-ruled Palestine the teachings of a Hebrew, Jesus, sparked a new religion, Christianity, which during the later Classical Era spread around the Mediterranean Basin. With Roman decline the Persians regained power over much of western Asia.

EASTERN ASIA

Chinese philosophies emerged during a time of rapid change, and Confucianism, Daoism, and Legalism became enduring influences. The Qin dynasty reunified China, and then the Han dynasty established a huge empire and overland trade with western Asia and Rome. When the Han collapsed, Buddhism filtered in from India. Chinese science and technology during this era were innovative. Koreans and Japanese formed states and imported Confucianism, Buddhism, and political models from China.

ARCTIC OCEAN

GERMANS
EUROPE
Danube
ROMAN EMPIRE
BYZANTIUM
GREECE
Carthage
PERSIA
EGYPT
PALESTINE
KUSH
GHANA
Niger R.
AFRICA
AKSUM
Nile
ASIA
HIMALAYAS
Ganges R.
CHINA
JAPAN
INDIA
Mekong R.
CAMBODIA
Congo R.
ATLANTIC
OCEAN
INDIAN OCEAN
INDONESIA
AUSTRALIA

AFRICA

Egypt fell successively under Persian, Hellenistic Greek, and finally Roman rule. Carthage was another major North African power and trade center until the Romans conquered the region. In northeast Africa, Kush was a trade center and major iron producer, and another trading state, Aksum, adopted Christianity. Trading cities and then empires, notably Ghana, emerged in the Sudan region. Elsewhere the Bantu peoples continued their expansion, settling much of central, eastern, and southern Africa. Long-distance trade networks connected West Africans with North Africa and East Africans with India and western Asia.

SOUTHERN ASIA AND OCEANIA

Buddhism arose in India, where it was later adopted by the kings of the region's first empire, the Mauryas. However, Hinduism remained India's majority faith, and Buddhism later split into rival schools. Indians traded with western Asia, Africa, Rome, and Southeast Asia. Various groups migrated into India from Central Asia. The Gupta kingdom made India a world leader in science, and Indian influence, including Buddhism and Hinduism, spread into Southeast Asia, helping foster states. Maritime trade linked Southeast Asia with China, India, western Asia, and East Africa. During this same time Austronesians continued settling the Pacific islands and traded with each other over vast distances.

CHAPTER 5

Eurasian Connections and New Traditions in East Asia, 600 B.C.E.–600 C.E.

Online Study Center

This icon will direct you to interactive activities and study materials on the website: college.hmco.com/pic/lockard1e

Fresco from Mogao Caves   The Magao Caves, situated along the Silk Road in western China, contain many frescoes reflecting Silk Road life and the spread of Buddhism into the region. This fresco, painted in the third century C.E., shows a caravan resting at an oasis.

(Courtesy, Dunhuang Academy/ Lois Conner, photographer)

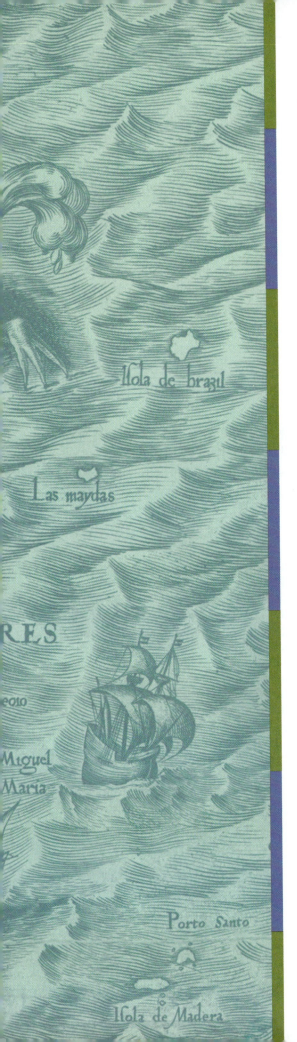

After the Han had sent its envoys to open up communications with the state of Da Xia [in today's Afghanistan], all the barbarians of the distant west craned their necks to the east and longed to catch a glimpse of China.

CHINESE DIPLOMAT ZHANG QIAN, REPORTED BY HISTORIAN SIMA QIAN, CA. 100 B.C.E.[1]

In 138 B.C.E. the Han Chinese emperor, Wu Di (woo tee), sought to make contact with a Central Asian group, the Yuezhi (yueh-chih), in order to forge an alliance against their mutual enemy, another Central Asian group known to the Chinese as the Xiongnu (SHE-OONG-noo), who were threatening China. An attendant at the imperial court, Zhang Qian (jahng chee-YEN), volunteered to undertake the dangerous diplomatic mission. Han records described Zhang as a strong man known for his generosity who inspired trust and easily made friends with non-Chinese. He set off on the lengthy overland journey west with only a small escort. Zhang was captured by the Xiongnu and held prisoner for ten years, but he finally escaped. Hoping to complete his mission, Zhang and his party made their way west, following a route that soon became known as one of the classical world's great networks of exchange. They crossed the Pamir (pah-MEER) Mountains and visited lands, in what is today Afghanistan and Turkestan, that already knew of China because they avidly imported Chinese silk, hence the name Silk Road. Although his diplomatic mission to ally with the Yuezhi failed, on his return to China after twelve years away Zhang brought back useful products, including the grape, and informed Wu Di about the lands to the west and their resources.

For over a millennium after Zhang's journey, China connected with the lands much further west by way of overland trade and travel through Central Asia. Every year merchants gathered just outside the walls of the main Chinese city and generally China's capital in these centuries, Chang'an (CHAHNG-ahn) (today's Xian (SEE-ahn)), to form a caravan. The merchants loaded bundles of metals, ceramics, spices, scrolls of paintings, seeds, and above all piles of silk on their horses and donkeys. The veteran caravaners, some Chinese, some Central Asian, were hard men who understood the dangers of the journey ahead, which could include blinding sandstorms and ruthless bandits, but also the fabulous profits that would be made from it. Once on the road they traveled west for weeks, skirting the southern side of the Great Wall of China. At the last outpost of Chinese society, marked by the Jade Gate, the horses and donkeys were exchanged for camels, which were better suited to the upcoming journey through harsh deserts. After months of travel across waterless wastes, the caravan had still to cross the snow-covered Pamir Mountains. Finally, several thousand miles from Chang'an, they arrived at the Central Asian cities of Turkestan, where the merchants traded or sold their precious commodities. Much of their cargo was then on its way to

119

India, western Asia, and even southern Europe. In spite of great distances and immense geographical barriers, this vast network of trails tied China to the world beyond and made peoples as far west as Rome aware of China.

China and its neighbors, Korea and Japan, had built their societies far away from the influence of the Middle East, India, and Europe. In doing so, and in responding to their particular environments, East Asian peoples developed many distinctive social and cultural traditions: East Asian technologies, governments, religions, and philosophies were unique. But East Asians were also influenced by peoples, ideas, and commercial goods that traveled the trade networks from far-away places such as the Afghan kingdom first visited by Zhang Qian. These were the centuries of the classical blossoming of East Asian cultures, a critical time that established some essential frameworks for the developments in these societies in the centuries to follow.

FOCUS QUESTIONS

1. What were the distinctive features of the Chinese philosophies that emerged during the late Zhou period?
2. What developments during the Han dynasty linked China to the rest of Eurasia?
3. How was Chinese society organized during the Han?
4. What outside influences helped shape China after the fall of the Han?
5. How did the Koreans and Japanese assimilate Chinese influences into their own distinctive societies?

❖ Changing China and Axial Age Thought, 600–221 B.C.E.

What were the distinctive features of the Chinese philosophies that emerged during the late Zhou period?

Chinese technology, science, and philosophical thought developed largely independently from outside influences. Yet Chinese originality was in part a response to many of the same challenges faced by other societies, especially during the Eurasian Axial Age of the early classical centuries. Like all societies, the Chinese needed ideas to explain the workings of the universe and to bring order to their lives. Such ideas appeared during the late Zhou (joe) period, when social and political conditions rapidly changed and produced unsettled conditions. Chinese philosophers seeking to restore order spawned several schools of thought that endured for several millennia.

Late Zhou Conflicts

The Zhou dynasty endured for nearly 900 years (1122–221 B.C.E.), but the later centuries, from around 600 to 221 B.C.E., experienced rapid social and economic change as well as chronic warfare (see Map 5.1 on page 122). Military technology, improved through advances in iron making, contributed

to the uncertainties and civil war of these times, a formative period for China. The era from 481 to 221 B.C.E., when the fighting was particularly intense, is known as the "Warring States Period." Local lords did not challenge the Zhou king directly but increasingly ignored him, fighting instead among themselves for supremacy. The chronic warfare between ruthless local governments generated a long crisis that fostered changes in many areas of Chinese life.

The changes during the later Zhou were apparent in many areas, and not all of them were detrimental. For example, despite the fighting, by 250 B.C.E. China had become the most populous society on earth, with 20 to 40 million people. Improving technology and communications also fostered commerce and cities. As China developed a cash economy in place of the old barter system, copper coins were issued. Political and economic power gradually shifted to the eastern part of the Yellow River Valley, while Chinese culture expanded south of the Yangzi River. The Yangzi River Basin became the major agricultural region because of its greater fertility and more favorable climate. Social mobility also increased. Many peasants and slaves abandoned their homes and moved to open land, often in the south, or to the fast-growing cities. Furthermore, the merchant class was growing in numbers and influence. A Chinese historian recorded the situation: "The law honors farmers, yet farmers have become poorer and poorer; the law degrades merchants, yet merchants have become richer and richer."[2] Merchants even bought aristocratic titles.

CHRONOLOGY

	China	Korea	Japan
1200 B.C.E.	**1122–221 B.C.E.** Zhou dynasty		
300 B.C.E.	**221–206 B.C.E.** Qin dynasty **206 B.C.E.–220 C.E.** Han dynasty	**108 B.C.E.–313 C.E.** Chinese colonization	**300 B.C.E.–552 C.E.** Yayoi culture
300 C.E.	**222–581 C.E.** Three Kingdoms and Six Dynasties	**350–668 C.E.** Koguryo Empire	
500 C.E.	**589–618 C.E.** Sui dynasty		**552–710 C.E.** Yamato state

Late Zhou Technology and Science

China joined the Iron Age during the late Zhou period. This step put the Chinese on an equal technological footing with western Asia. Chinese sources first mention iron use in 521 B.C.E., a millennium after the iron-using Hittites in western Asia and 500 years after the development of iron technology in India. Knowledge of ironworking probably filtered into China from Central Asia over trade networks and led to the production of iron-tipped ox-drawn plows, which improved agricultural productivity. By around 400 B.C.E. the Chinese became the first people to make the breakthrough to cast iron, which is much easier to shape into products. This technical advance made available superior axes, hoes, ploughshares, picks, swords, and chariots. Indeed, Chinese iron plows were the most efficient farm tools in the world before the second millennium C.E.

Iron was only one of the technological and scientific innovations of the late Zhou period. The Chinese also made major advances in water control and conservation. In 250 B.C.E., for example, a vast complex of dikes, canals, and dams was constructed to control the fickle upper Yangzi River, a huge system that worked so well that it is still used today. Soybeans, which were introduced in the seventh century B.C.E., provided a rich protein source and also enriched the soil. The late Zhou Chinese also invented the first compasses and became pioneers in mathematics, amending the Shang decimal system by adding a place for the zero in equations. Since 3600 B.C.E. the Chinese had been producing silk from strands made by a caterpillar of a moth that fed on mulberry trees, but in Zhou times they developed better methods of weaving the silk.

One Hundred Philosophical Schools

The later Zhou was the most creative period in traditional Chinese thought: it produced so many competing philosophies that it was called the era of the "hundred schools of thought" or the "hundred flowers." These diverse approaches were part of the period of widespread intellectual creativity often known as the

Axial Age because it fostered ways of thought that endured through the centuries. This age also saw new philosophies and widening intellectual horizons emerging in the Mediterranean world, western Asia, and India between 600 and 250 B.C.E. (see Chapters 6, 7, and "Societies, Networks, Transitions," page 253; see also Chronology: Classical China). During this turbulent period, philosophers across Eurasia emphasized ethical principles, criticized political conditions, and proposed new ideas, generating not only new philosophical thought but also new political ideologies. At the end of this period, powerful empires emerged in China, India, and the Mediterranean that reflected a new order of technological and organizational planning.

The Axial Age in China provoked a questioning of philosophical, religious, and political issues. The hundred schools had resulted in part from the constant conflict during the Warring

CHRONOLOGY

Classical China

1122–221 B.C.E.	Zhou dynasty
550–350 B.CE.	Height of Axial Age in China
481 B.C.E.	Beginning of Warring States Period
551–479 B.C.E.	Life of Confucius
221–206 B.C.E.	Qin dynasty
206 B.C.E.–220 C.E.	Han dynasty
141–87 B.C.E.	Reign of Wu Di
105 C.E.	Invention of paper
222–581 C.E.	Three Kingdoms and Six Dynasties Era
581–618 C.E.	Sui dynasty

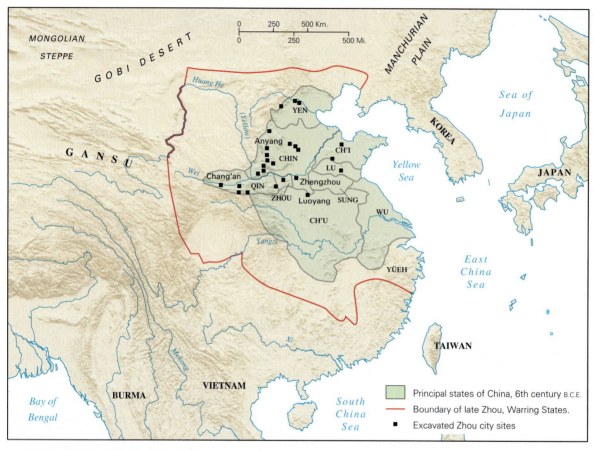

Map 5.1 China in the Sixth Century B.C.E.
During the late Zhou era China was divided into competing, often warring, states, only loosely ruled by the Zhou kings. Some, such as Ch'u and Wu, were large. In the third century B.C.E. the westernmost state, Qin, conquered the others and formed a unified empire.

States Period. Another factor may have been increased knowledge of the outside world resulting from contact with Turkish pastoralists in Central Asia, who traded horses to China for grain, wine, and silks. Instability generated a philosophical questioning that produced enduring ideas unique to China. To help explain the fighting and provide a way to restore peace and harmony, thinkers asked basic questions about government and society.

Chinese thought during the hundred schools era differed dramatically from that developed in other societies of this era. From the late Zhou period onward, Chinese philosophical interest, unlike that in, for example, India, centered on the collective and saw people as social and political creatures. Chinese philosophy also placed less emphasis on an afterlife and powerful gods than did the philosophies of many other societies. Chinese thinkers did not ignore the supernatural, and some practiced magic, meditation, or mystical techniques. But their main emphases were humanistic.

This practical, down-to-earth approach had a basis in the early Chinese philosophers' position in society. Although literate and thoughtful, these philosophers were also pragmatic men who had often served in government at various times. Some, unable to find government jobs at home, wandered from one Zhou state to another offering their services, and

thus became teachers. Their disciples collected their sayings or thoughts into the classic texts venerated by later generations. The most significant of these masters created with their followers the philosophies of Confucianism, Daoism, and Legalism, all of which ultimately stood the test of time and influenced China for the next two millennia. The divisions between the various schools were never rigid, and heated differences occurred within each school. But the core ideas of each school made each distinct.

Confucius and His Legacy

The most influential new philosophy of the late Zhou period, **Confucianism** (kun-FYOO-shu-NIZ-um), was based on the ideas of Confucius and emphasized the relations among people. Kong Fuzi (kong foo-dzu) ("Master Kung"), better known in the West as Confucius, probably lived from 551 to 479 B.C.E. (see Chronology: Classical China). As with the Buddha in India or Jesus of Nazareth in western Asia, little is known of his life and ideas except indirectly, through the writings of his

---

Confucianism A Chinese philosophy based on the ideas of Confucius emphasizing the relations among people.

followers who recorded his statements. The Chinese never considered Confucius a god, but rather a wise sage to be honored by offerings. His teachings have had a more enduring influence on East Asia than those of any other thinker and became in some form or another the official doctrine in China, Korea, Vietnam, and Japan.

Confucius and His Ideas
Confucius was born into a modest but aristocratic family in eastern China, the son of a soldier. As a young man he attempted unsuccessfully to gain appointment as a top government official of various states and then spent years as a teacher, apparently showing dazzling ability. Confucius left no direct writings, but his sayings were collected by his disciples and published a century or two after his death in a book called ***The Analects*** (see Witness to the Past: *The Analects* and Correct Confucian Behavior). Over his career he taught some three thousand students from all social classes. The sage claimed that he had "never refused to teach anyone, even though he came to me on foot, with nothing more to offer as tuition than a package of dried meat."[3] Confucius maintained that education was the key to promoting morality; he stressed the study of history, philosophy, literature, poetry, and music. Considering himself not a creator of new ideas but rather a transmitter of ancient wisdom, he revived traditional ideas and reorganized them into a coherent system of thought. Hence, he extolled the past as an example for the future.

The philosophy Confucius spawned, Confucianism, is not primarily a religion, concerned with otherworldly issues, but a philosophy of social relations, a moral and ethical code designed to promote social stability. Human-heartedness, Confucius wrote, consists in loving others. In religious terms, Confucius could best be described as an agnostic; he said little about the spiritual world, arguing that, since people know little about life, they cannot know about death. He wished to focus on humankind. Like the Ionian Greeks a world away at the same time, Confucius was developing a rationalist view opposed to superstition, although he showed little interest in the scientific analysis of nature. The sage asserted that wisdom was working to improve society and keeping one's distance from the gods and spirits while showing them reverence. The answer to the world's problems, Confucius argued, was virtue, ethics, and, above all, benevolence. Moderation in behavior was the ideal. Confucius also advised people to think about the future, contending that if they do not think about problems that are still distant, they will have to worry about them when they arrive.

In forging a new harmonious order, Confucius advocated an autocratic but paternalistic form of government in which the ruler was responsible for the welfare of the people. The family constituted the model for the state. Just as children should respect and obey their parents, a rule known as **filial piety**, so

Confucius Stone rubbing of a portrait of Confucius from an ancient temple. For 2500 years Confucius was the most honored and influential Chinese thinker, remembered in countless paintings, woodblock cuts, and carvings on walls. (Courtesy of the Trustees of the British Museum)

citizens should obey a fair government. The philosopher did not advocate a police state but advised people to play their assigned roles in a society defined by order and hierarchy: "Let the ruler be ruler, and the minister minister; let the father be father, and the son son."[4] He talked about duty and obedience of inferiors to superiors: of wife to husband, son to father, younger to older, and citizen to king. In contrast to the inferior person, who covets profits and possessions, the cultivated person practices what he preaches, preaches what he practices, cherishes virtue, and understands what is right.

In many respects Confucius was a conservative, supportive of those who hold power. But authority, he emphasized, must be wielded justly and wisely. Government was fundamentally a matter of ethics: if power was abused, it became illegitimate. The ruler, indeed any superior, must be virtuous. When asked what thought should guide the conduct of both leaders and citizens throughout life, he replied: "Do not do to others what you yourself do not desire."[5]

The Analects The book of the sayings of Confucius collected by his disciples and published a century or two after his death.

filial piety The Confucian rule that children should respect and obey their parents.

The Analects *and Correct Confucian Behavior*

The Analects is the main record of Confucius and his thought that survived the Warring States Period and the book burnings of the next dynasty. Compiled by his disciples many years after his death, it is presented largely in the form of questions from his followers and answers, short aphorisms, or long discourses by the sage. Divided into twenty chapters, the book covers many topics, mostly peoples' conduct and aspirations. It became the most important book in China from the Han dynasty down to modern times. These fragments present a few of Confucius's thoughts about the correct behavior of gentlemen (the rulers and other leaders), sons and daughters, and people in general.

About the gentleman], Confucius said, "The gentleman concerns himself with the Way [the natural order that is also a moral order]; he does not worry about his salary. Hunger may be found in plowing; wealth may be found in studying. The gentleman worries about the Way, not about poverty. . . . The gentleman reveres three things. He reveres the mandate of Heaven; he reveres great people; and he reveres the words of the sages. Petty people do not know the mandate of Heaven and so do not revere it. They are disrespectful of great people and they ridicule the words of the sages. . . . The gentleman aspires to things lofty; the petty person aspires to things base. The gentleman looks to himself; the petty person looks to other people. The gentleman feels bad when his capabilities fall short of some task. He does not feel bad if people fail to recognize him. . . ."

[About filial piety or respect for parents], Confucius said, "Nowadays, filial piety is considered to be the ability to nourish one's parents. But this obligation to nourish even extends down to the dogs and horses. Unless we have reverence for our parents, what makes us any different . . . ? Do not offend your parents. . . . When your parents are alive, serve them according to the rules of ritual and decorum. When they are deceased, give them a funeral and offer sacrifices to them according to the rules of ritual and decorum. . . . It is unacceptable not to be aware of your parents' ages. Their advancing years are a cause for joy and at the same time a cause for sorrow. . . ."

[About humanity], Confucius said, "If an individual can practice five things anywhere in the world, he is a man of humanity. . . . [These are] Reverence, generosity, truthfulness, diligence, and kindness. If a person acts with reverence, he will not be insulted. If he is generous, he will win over the people. If he is truthful, he will be trusted by the people. If he is diligent, he will have great achievements. If he is kind, he will be able to influence others. . . . When you go out, treat everyone as if you were welcoming a great guest. Employ people as if you were conducting a great sacrifice."

THINKING ABOUT THE READING

1. What are some of the main qualities expected of a gentleman?

2. How might Confucian views on respect for parents have influenced the family system?

3. How did the advice reflect on Confucius's humanistic emphasis?

Source: Patricia Buckley Ebrey, ed., *Chinese Civilization: A Sourcebook,* 2nd ed., revised and expanded (New York: Free Press, 1993), pp. 18–21. Reprinted with permission of the Free Press. All rights reserved.

The Legacy of Confucius Confucius helped set the common East Asian pattern of compromise. As a Chinese proverb advised, people should "bend like bamboo" to avoid conflict with other people. To promote harmony, Confucianism stressed strict adherence to rules of courtesy. For example, a book of etiquette from late Zhou times advised men on rules for visiting another man of equal status: "The host goes to meet the guest outside the gate, and there bows twice, answered by two bows from the guest. Then the host, with a salute, invites him to enter." The rules of courtesy continue during the visit: if the host should "yawn, stretch himself, ask the time of day, order his dinner, or change his position, then [the guest] must ask permission to [leave]."[6] The Confucian societies became noted for using ritual and etiquette to maintain stability and discipline.

Confucian ideas were designed to promote social order and continuity across generations, and, in the centuries to follow, they generally did. China became one of the most stable societies in history, and Confucianism contributed greatly to its cohesiveness. However, the ideas of Confucius were revised to some extent by his followers and became increasingly rigid in spirit and application over the centuries, leading in some cases to a conservatism and inflexibility that Confucius might have condemned.

Two of the main followers of Confucius represented opposing schools of interpretation. Both lived one and a half centuries later than their master and were contemporaries of the Greek philosopher Aristotle. Mengzi (MUNG-dze) (Mencius) (372–289 B.C.E.) advocated a liberal, even permissive government in which the ruler embraced benevolence and righteousness as his main goals. He dreamed of a united world state under a just king. Mengzi believed human nature was essentially good, and hence he was extremely optimistic about the prospects for society. He also stressed the value of education for officials, contending that those who labor with their brains govern others. Xunzi (SHOON-dze) (Hsun Tzu) (310–220 B.C.E.) disagreed; viewing human nature as essentially bad, he maintained that the state must enforce goodness and morality.

Xunzi also contributed to the authoritarian tendencies of Confucianism by claiming that Confucian writings were the source of all wisdom. But not all of his proposals were harsh. For example, Confucius had praised music, and Xunzi also argued that music was joy and produced an emotion that stirred people to find an outlet through movement and voice. Approved by sages for fostering harmony, music played a central role in court life and in village ceremonies.

Daoism and Chinese Mysticism

The second major philosophy to develop during the Hundred Flowers Period was **Daoism** (DOW-iz-um), which taught that people should adapt to nature. The main ideas of Daoism are attributed to Laozi (lou-zoe) (Lao Tzu or "Old Master"). However, we have no direct evidence such a man ever lived. According to the legends about his life, Laozi was an older contemporary of Confucius and a disillusioned bureaucrat who became a wandering teacher. If such a man existed, he probably did not write the two main Daoist texts, which were most likely composed during the third century B.C.E.

Daoism was a philosophy of withdrawal for people appalled by the warfare of the age. Daoist thinkers held that the goal of life for each individual was to follow the "way of the universe," or *dao*. Daoist teachers described the dao as "unfathomable, the ancestral progenitor of all things, everlasting. All-pervading, dao lies hidden and cannot be named. It produces all things. He who acts in accordance with dao becomes one with dao."[7] Convinced that people could never dominate their environment, Daoist philosophy urged them to ally themselves with it. This meant being simple, formless, without desire and without striving, and content with what is. An early Daoist text expressed disgust with everyday life: "To labor away one's whole lifetime but never see the result, and to be utterly worn out with toil but have no idea where it is leading, is this not lamentable?"[8] Daoists advised Chinese to conform to the great pattern of the natural world rather than, as was the emphasis of Confucians, to social expectations and governments. One of the main texts argued that the wise person prefers fishing on a remote stream to serving as emperor. To the Daoists societies were an obstacle and all governments corrupt and oppressive. Politicians were urged to rule a big country as you would fry small fish, that is, don't overdo it.

Daoism was mystical and romantic, fostering an awareness of nature and its beauties. This attitude became pronounced in Chinese poetry and landscape painting, which often recorded towering mountains, roaring waterfalls, and placid lakes. Daoists viewed nature as good; indeed, people and nature were one. This was different from the Western view growing out of the Greco-Roman and Christian traditions, where the wilderness was to be subdued. Thanks to Daoist influences, one of the main functions of a Chinese ruler was to maintain the balance between human society and nature, to govern well and follow correct rituals.

Daoism later fragmented into several traditions. Popular Daoism became a religion of countless deities and magic. Some followers sought to find the elixir of immortality, often by experimenting with a wide variety of foods. By contrast, philosophical Daoism, which appealed to the better educated, stressed mysticism, suggesting that the individual could live in harmony with nature by turning inward and experiencing oneness with the universe. Like all mystics seeking the heart of spirituality, Daoists found it difficult to express their basic ideas in words. Daoist writers claimed that "those who know do not speak; those who speak do not know."[9]

Some of the early Daoist writings contained stories such as this one, which is filled with mysticism, a sense of unity with nature, and a humbling relativism:

> One time, Chuang-tzu dreamed he was a butterfly, flitting around, enjoying what butterflies enjoy. The butterfly did not know that it was Chuang-tzu. Then Chuang-tzu started, and woke up, and he was Chuang-tzu again. And he began to wonder whether he was Chuang-tzu who had dreamed he was a butterfly or was a butterfly dreaming that he was Chuang-tzu.[10]

Balancing Confucianism, Daoism tapped a different strand of Chinese experience. It added enjoyment, reflection, and a sense of freedom. Daoists advised Confucianists to flow with the spirit and the heart rather than struggle with the intellect. The man in power was a Confucianist, but out of power became a Daoist. The active bureaucrat of the morning became the dreamy poet or nature lover of the evening. Daoism complemented Confucianism by enabling Chinese to balance the conflicting needs for social order and personal autonomy.

Legalism and the Chinese State

Among the dozens of other competing philosophies of the Warring States Period, **Legalism**, which advocated that the state maintain harsh control of people, also had an enduring influence. Borrowing ideas from the Confucian Xunzi, who believed people were inherently selfish and power hungry, the Legalists emphasized the need for an authoritarian government to secure prosperity, order, and stability. To ensure the survival of the whole, they believed, the state must control all economic resources, and people should be well disciplined, subject to military duty and harsh laws.

Taken to extremes, Legalism led to unrestrained state power. The ruler needed to be strong and to have no regard for the rights or will of the people, since the larger goal was to maintain unity and stability. One of the leading Legalists wrote that people can be controlled by means of punishments and rewards, commands and prohibitions, with force keeping them in subjection. Legalists ridiculed Confucian humanism. One Legalist, in a pointed attack on the Confucians, argued that "the intelligent ruler does not speak about deeds of humanity and righteousness, and he does not listen to the words of learned men."[11]

Daoism   A Chinese philosophy that emphasized adaptation to nature.

Legalism   A Chinese philosophy that advocated harsh control of people by the state.

Although Legalism exercised a long-term influence on Chinese politics, the Chinese always balanced it with the more humane ideas of Confucius and Mengzi, who stressed moral persuasion rather than coercion. Hence, the Chinese during the Classical Era did not follow one philosophy to the exclusion of others. In the resulting mix, leaders were to be obeyed but also ethical and benevolent. Laws were sometimes severe, but local officials had flexibility in implementing them and took into account the social context.

> **SECTION SUMMARY**
>
> ■ Despite being marred by chronic civil warfare, China became the most populous society on earth and its economy evolved rapidly.
>
> ■ The belated development of iron technologies, as well as many other breakthroughs, finally made China competitive with western Asia.
>
> ■ Instability resulting from military conflict led intellectuals to question basic tenets of society and government, thus creating the era of the "hundred schools of thought."
>
> ■ Three enduring Chinese philosophies from this period—Confucianism, Daoism, and Legalism—have influenced Chinese state and culture through two millennia.
>
> ■ Chinese philosophies emphasized humanism rather than the supernatural or gods.

✦ Chinese Imperial Systems and Eurasian Trade

What developments during the Han dynasty linked China to the rest of Eurasia?

Chinese society, more than Indian, Middle Eastern, or European societies, was characterized by cohesion and continuity, as well as by balancing and blending of diverse influences. For example, although China was often attacked and even occasionally conquered by Central Asians, the invaders maintained continuity with China's past by adopting Chinese culture, a process known as **Sinicization**. But before modern times, there was one major transition that quickly changed the face of China: the replacement of the multistate Zhou system by a centralized empire. This made China since 221 B.C.E. different from the China before it and set the pattern for the centuries to follow. The new imperial China was forged by the harsh rulers of Qin (chin). Their despotic rule was followed by the Han dynasty, which conquered a large empire, fostered foreign trade, and restored Confucianism as a guiding philosophy, establishing enduring political patterns.

Sinicization The process by which Central Asian invaders maintained continuity with China's past by adopting Chinese culture.

The Qin Dynasty

The political turmoil of late Zhou times ended when the Qin dynasty (221–206 B.C.E.) conquered the other states and implemented repressive Legalist ideas, a political change that transformed the China of many states into an empire with a powerful and highly authoritarian central government. Located on the northwest borders, the state of Qin had gradually become the strongest state within the Zhou system. Some of the Legalist scholars had moved there and been appointed to high office. Under their policies, the state controlled the economy, establishing government monopolies over many trade goods. Like Sparta in Greece around the same time, the population was regimented and militarized, the men serving as citizen-warriors. Slowly Qin began conquering other Zhou states. The prime minister, Li Si (lee SHE) (Li Ssu), a Legalist thinker, was a brutal man; he argued that those who used the past to oppose the present, the Confucians, had to be exterminated. Li Si was the chief deputy to the man who would eventually become the ruler, and first emperor, of all of China.

In 221 B.C.E. the Qin, finally defeating and absorbing all the remaining Zhou states, established a new government that ruled most of the Chinese people. The first Qin ruler assumed the new and imposing title of Shi Huangdi (SHE hwang-dee) (first emperor) and prophesied that his dynasty would last 10,000 generations. The son of a Qin prince and his concubine, he was not yet forty when he became ruler of China. This extraordinary autocrat surrounded himself with mystery and pomp to enhance his prestige, but in so doing he also concealed himself from the consequences of his decrees. Shi Huangdi lived in carefully guarded privacy, moving secretly from one apartment to another in his vast palaces. To reveal his movements was a crime that was instantly punished with death. The first emperor was also superstitious and devoted considerable resources to the search for an elixir of immortality.

The new dynasty implemented dramatic policies, including military expansion. Not content with conquering the Chinese heartland, the Qin also sent armies to incorporate much of southern China and, for a while, Vietnam, into the empire. In the following centuries many in the south were assimilated into Chinese society. The first emperor also mandated a total reordering of China along Legalist lines. In doing so, he constructed a monolithic state that sought to control all aspects of Chinese life. The growing bureaucracy that was needed to supervise these operations strengthened the centralized state system. The Qin goal of creating a unified state was accomplished once they embraced nearly all regions where Chinese society was dominant. Given this unification, the name *Qin* is quite fittingly the origin of the Western name for China.

Later Chinese historians viewed the Qin Empire as one of the most terrible periods in the country's long history. The common people hated the forced labor and strict laws. Spies, general surveillance, and thought control were paramount in the Qin police state, which closely monitored the citizenry. Intellectuals despised the Qin because the state launched attacks on all aspects of culture, including Confucianism. In the campaign to stamp out what they perceived to be subversive doctrines, the

Qin burned thousands of books, sparing only practical and scientific manuals, and executed many scholars, often by burying them alive. In so doing the Qin ended the intellectual creativity of the hundred schools. No other era could match the late Zhou for the wide range of creative thought.

The Qin Legacy

Despite the repression, Shi Huangdi's policies led to many achievements. A dazzling series of public works projects and state policies promoted communication, economic growth, and social change. The Qin standardized weights and measures, unified economic and agricultural practices, and codified laws. For example, to aid communication, roads, bridges, dams, and canals were built. They also ordered that all wheel axles be the same length so that wagons could use the ruts made by other wagons in the dusty roads. In addition, the Qin standardized the written language so that all literate Chinese anywhere in the empire could communicate easily; they also developed an "express" postal service, which conveyed documents written on slips of bamboo around the country. To foster economic growth, the Qin established state monopolies over essential commodities like salt, and ever since the Chinese have accepted a strong government role in economic matters. Taxes were high and often included devoting significant time to forced labor on government projects. The harsh Qin laws also ended crime, as a later Chinese scholar conceded: "Nothing lost on the road was picked up and pocketed, the hills were free of bandits, men avoided quarrels at home."[12] Finally, Qin land reform undermined the power of the old aristocracy, a mighty blow to the Zhou social structure.

The most famous public works project was the construction of an early and limited version of a Great Wall along China's northern borders. This wall had two purposes. First, it marked the boundary between the grasslands of the Central Asian pastoralists and the Chinese farmlands. Second, it served as a barrier to the encroachment of Central Asian warriors into China. Chinese traded with their Central Asian neighbors but also fought with and feared them, and conflict between them became more frequent during the Qin. A few partial earthen walls had already been built in Zhou times, but the Qin consolidated these into a more formidable structure, later known as the Great Wall. As part of their tax obligation, vast numbers of laborers were drafted for building the wall.

The Great Wall   This panorama from the region just north of Beijing shows a portion of the wall reconstructed in the fifteenth century C.E. The wall was an attempt to mark the northern boundary of China and keep out nomadic invaders.   (Georg Gerster/Photo Researchers, Inc.)

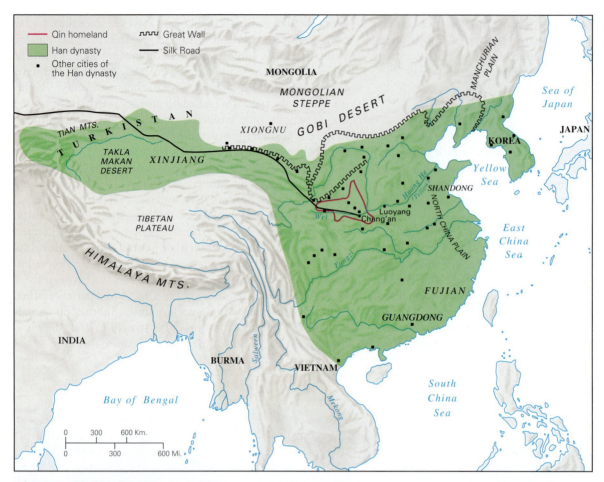

Map 5.2 The Han Empire
The Han Empire fluctuated in size but at its height controlled most of today's China, Korea, northern Vietnam, and a long corridor through Central Asia to Turkestan.

Online Study Center **Improve Your Grade** Interactive Map: Han China

The Great Wall was one of the greatest architectural feats of the ancient world. Later dynasties periodically rebuilt and added to the wall. The present brick and stone wall that so astounds tourists derives mostly from reconstruction and expansion work around 600 years ago, after which the wall stretched over 1,400 miles across north China, with watchtowers every few miles. Properly manned, it could be an effective defense, but that was an expense only the most affluent emperors could afford. The wall was seldom as successful as the Chinese had hoped in curbing invaders. Still, it was a symbolic affirmation of empire and a statement of territorial limits.

But the Qin dynasty itself was short-lived. Shi Huangdi was a tyrant who fostered much general hatred, and his expansionist policies provoked conflict with neighboring peoples. The first emperor's death in 210 B.C.E. was kept secret by his inner circle for fear of general revolt. He was buried in a huge underground mausoleum together with seven thousand astonishingly realistic life-size terra cotta horses and warriors brandishing real bronze weapons. It took 700,000 laborers to construct the final resting place and its contents. When news finally spread of Shi Huangdi's death, peasant revolts broke out. In 206 B.C.E. the Qin forces were defeated by an alliance of various rebel armies. In the chaos that followed, as the various rebel groups vied for power, a former peasant led his forces to victory, establishing a new dynasty, the Han (HAHN).

The Han Empire

The Han is the most respected dynasty in Chinese history because during these four centuries (206 B.C.E.–220 C.E.). China became a major force in the affairs of Eurasia, participating in networks of trade, diplomacy, and imperialism. The Han built a huge empire stretching far into Central Asia (see Map 5.2), and trade across this area allowed greater contact with people to the west. Like the Qin, the Han built a strong state, but they also greatly modified the Qin's harsh Legalist structure. The brilliance of the Han and the expansion of Chinese society southward led the Chinese who followed to call themselves the Sons of Han, since this classical period set the pattern for later dynasties.

Large empires like the Han were common in this era. The middle Classical Era was the age of empires, when large segments of the Eurasian landmass and North Africa were under the domination of large imperial structures. In organizing their societies, all the empires built on the ideas of the Axial Age sages, resolving the crises that had sparked their rise. But the classical empires eventually declined as their structures and finances weakened, the conquered populations revolted, and nomadic peoples invaded the imperial heartlands.

The Han and Roman Empires reached their zenith around the same time and resembled each other in population, although Rome's empire was larger in territorial size. In 2 C.E. the Han Empire contained at least 60 million people and the Roman Empire ruled some 55 million. However, unlike the situation in the Roman Empire, most of the Han subjects lived in China itself, around two-thirds of them in the Yellow and Wei River Valleys of north China. In contrast, the people in Italy were greatly outnumbered by the colonized populations.

The pinnacle of Han imperial power came under the emperor mentioned in the opening of this chapter: Wu Di, who ruled for over half a century (141–87 B.C.E.). Wu Di's imperialism came after several decades of national revival and dynastic consolidation. After he established firm control at home, Wu Di, a firm believer, like many Chinese emperors, that the best defense is a good offense, counteracted the encroaching pastoral nomads of the northern and western grasslands. In a series of bloody campaigns, Chinese forces pushed some nomads toward Europe, where they then disrupted the Roman Empire. Among the groups deflected toward the west were the Huns, who had menaced China for centuries. The branch of Huns the Chinese called Xiongnu had forged a large confederation of tribes in the third century B.C.E. that constantly threatened China. Indeed, the Qin built the Great Wall in part to deflect the Huns.

Empire building and diplomacy soon linked China to western Eurasia as well as to neighboring societies in East and Southeast Asia. In search of allies against threatening nomads, the Han used both diplomatic and military strategies. To foster diplomacy, they sent ambassadors such as Zhang Qian to distant Central Asians seeking support against common enemies. But to neutralize nearby threats, Wu Di also dispatched a series of great armies, some numbering as many as 150,000 men, into the fringe areas of China and then beyond. Within a few years they had conquered southwestern China, the Xinjiang (shin-jee-yahng) region on China's western borders, Mongolia, and parts of Turkestan. Wu Di wrote a poem about a successful military campaign in 101 B.C.E. that brought many horses as tribute: "The heavenly horses are coming from the Far West. They crossed the Flowing Sands, for the barbarians are conquered."[13] His armies also established colonial control over northern Korea and Vietnam. The Chinese ruled the former for four centuries and the latter for 1,000 years. Soon Chinese power extended even further, as states in today's Afghanistan acknowledged themselves vassals of China, sending tribute to Han emperors. By controlling the local peoples, Han military forces brought security to a narrow corridor that could be used for increased trade. But not all soldiers celebrated these achievements. One Han soldier wrote a protest song: "We fought south of the city wall. We died north of the ramparts. In the wilderness we dead lie unburied, fodder for crows. Tell the crows for us, 'We've always been brave men.'"[14]

During this time the Chinese even made contact with the Roman Empire. In later Han times a Chinese army of 90,000 men reached as far as the Caspian Sea in southeastern Russia, and a small force led by General Gan Ying apparently traveled through Parthia to the Persian Gulf in 97 C.E., the first Chinese known to reach there. On his return General Gan reported on the customs and topography of these western states and discussed the Roman Empire, noting it was a massive state ruling many smaller ones, with many large cities.

The Silk Road and Eurasian Trade

The Han presence in Central Asia allowed for the establishment of overland trade routes between China and western Asia. A lively caravan route, known as the **Silk Road** for its most valuable cargo, linked China with India, the Middle East, and southern Europe. Central Asian cities such as Kashgar (kahsh-gar), Bactra (BAK-tru), and Samarkand (SAM-mar-kahnd) grew up along the overland route to service the trade and the merchants, becoming network hubs. Indeed, the string of cities was an important contact zone between East and West. Chinese silk, porcelain, and bamboo were carried west across the deserts and mountains to Baghdad and the ports of the eastern Mediterranean. Eventually some of these Chinese goods reached Rome. Silk was the most desired product. Since it was lightweight and easily packed, large quantities were carried west by each caravan. Caravans then returned with horses and luxury goods such as Egyptian glass beads, Red Sea pearls, and Baltic amber.

The Silk Road and the trade networks that it shaped greatly influenced the peoples who participated in the trade. To pay for Chinese luxuries, the Romans dispatched considerable quantities of silver to China. A serious trade imbalance ensued that contributed to the decline of the Western Roman Empire. In such ways, the Han Empire ultimately had a political and economic impact on distant Europe. Relations with Central and West Asians during the Han and later periods also brought new products to China, such as stringed musical instruments and new foods. Imperial power and foreign trade generated an economic boom and the rapid growth of commerce in China. The Silk Road network also affected populations, even those that were not directly involved in the trade. For example, trade activities fostered a Central Asian melting pot as peoples moved, met, and mixed.

Han Government

The Han period also saw the emergence of a government structure that survived in its basic form until the early twentieth century. Whereas the Qin had sought to transform China in one brutal stroke, the Han were more pragmatic and cautious. The Han combined many elements of Qin authoritarianism but used less repression and coercion, and they retained a strong central government but also had some respect for local political power. The Han softened Legalism with Confucian

Silk Road A lively caravan route through Central Asia that linked China with India, the Middle East, and southern Europe.

humanism, demonstrating that Confucian philosophy could maintain stability in the wake of momentous change. They adopted the advice of the Confucian Mengzi, who argued that "when the personal life is cultivated, the family will be regulated; when the family is regulated, the state will be in order; and when the state is in order, there will be peace throughout the land."[15] This Han pattern of mixing Legalism with Confucianism, power with ethics, characterized the Chinese political system for the next 2,000 years.

During Han times the civil service developed. In the early Han era the bureaucracy comprised some 130,000 officials, or 1 for every 400 to 500 people. This small number in relationship to the total population was the norm throughout Chinese history and can be explained by the relatively restricted role of the imperial administration. The central government mainly existed to ensure law, order, and border defense, and its bureaucrats collected taxes, administered the legal system, and officered military forces. Han officials boasted that they did not interfere in the daily lives of the people and kept public works to a minimum. And yet, the many rebellions during Han times suggest that the reality of government often included high taxes and onerous demands on the peasants to provide the regime with military or labor service, such as rebuilding river dikes or repairing washed out roads. These demands generated occasional unrest.

The bureaucracy was staffed by educated men later called **mandarins** (MAN-duh-rinz). Chinese proverbs claimed that the country might be won by the sword but could be ruled only by the writing brush—in other words, by an educated elite. The Han Chinese invented the civil service examination system to select officials based on merit. Wu Di even established a national university, which by the late Han period trained up to 30,000 students who were studying for the exams. These exams tested knowledge of the Confucian writings, an indication that Confucianism was becoming the official ideology of the state. With its emphasis on deference, Confucianism legitimized the regime and promoted faithful service. The prestige of the scholars staffing the bureaucracy also moderated the tendency toward despotism. In their role as officials, Confucian scholars served as intermediaries between the emperor and the people.

The development of the Han bureaucracy marked the rise of the **scholar-gentry**, a social class based on learning and officeholding but also on landowning, since many of the mandarins came from wealthy landowning families. Still, the social system was somewhat fluid. Scholars could not guarantee that their sons would be competent, and some poor men did rise by passing the civil service exams. Most of the scholar-gentry lived in towns, where they had some influence on local government officials. Gentry men frequently met together in teahouses to discuss local affairs and forge common positions on government policies.

Heavenly Mandates and Dynastic Cycles

During the Han the Chinese came to view rulership in terms of the Mandate of Heaven, or sanction by the supernatural realm, and history in terms of the dynastic cycle, the rise and fall of dynasties (see Chapter 4). These concepts became ingrained in Chinese thinking. Most premodern Chinese scholars believed that emperors ruled as deputies of the cosmic forces, but only so long as they possessed the virtues of justice, benevolence, and sincerity. In each dynasty, able early rulers with these virtues were succeeded by debauched weaklings, who left government more and more to the bureaucracy while they indulged their pleasures. Emperors had vast harems of wives, concubines, and sometimes boys, and usually enjoyed fine wine and foods. When an emperor misruled, he lost the Mandate of Heaven and rebellion was justified.

The rise and fall of dynasties also correlated with economic trends. A strong new dynasty initially generated security and prosperity, which led to population increase and additional tax revenues. However, these prospects lured ambitious emperors into overextending imperial power and squandering human and financial resources, not only on wars of expansion but also on palaces and court luxury. Extraordinary art was produced for the Han elite; for example, the tomb of one princess contained a 2,000-piece jade suit that was sown with gold wire.

Overspending led to decline. Wasteful expenditures created financial difficulties and military stagnation. Governments such as the Han could no longer fund the large military commitment to protect the country, and it became vulnerable. After a century or so, decay set in, and some bureaucrats became corrupt. To meet the growing deficits the government raised taxes, forcing many poorer peasants to sell their land to large landlords, who could then evade taxes through their wealth and influence. Hence revenues further declined.

This pattern was illustrated by Han emperor Wu Di. His glorious empire came at a huge cost, straining the imperial treasury. The resulting inflation led to the world's first price stabilization board and generated a heated debate in China about the economic benefits of empire. Some Han scholars opposed military expansion as a senseless waste of lives and tax revenues. In 81 B.C.E. Wu Di's successor as emperor invited some of them to make their case before him. They did so, arguing that,

> at present, morality is discarded and reliance is placed on military force. Troops are raised for campaigns and garrisons are stationed for defense. It is the long-drawn-out campaigns and the ceaseless transportation of provisions that burden our people at home and cause our frontier soldiers to suffer from hunger and cold.[16]

But higher government officials responded that the spending was necessary to protect the country from the Xiongnu.

The Han dynasty finally collapsed in 220 C.E., not unlike the fall of Rome several centuries later. Critical factors for both empires included inadequate revenues, peasant revolts, powerful landed families contending for power, and raids by pastoralists from the borderlands. Across Eurasia the unusually

---

mandarins Educated men who staffed the Chinese bureaucracy.

scholar-gentry A Chinese social class of learned officeholders and landowners that arose in the Han dynasty.

warm conditions between 200 B.C.E. and 200 C.E. came to an end, and the colder weather affected agriculture. Both empires were also ravaged by epidemics in the second century C.E., which killed millions and thus reduced tax revenues.

SECTION SUMMARY

- Through military conquest, the Qin dynasty unified the warring states into a new centralized, imperial China.

- Legalism, with its strict authoritarianism and negative view of human nature, was the dominant philosophy of the Qin rulers.

- Both the Han dynasty and the Roman Empire reached their peaks at about the same time, with roughly similar population sizes.

- The diplomatic and military expansion under the Han rulers set the stage for expanded trade, including the development of the Silk Road linking China to western Asia and Europe.

- The structure of government established during the Han, characterized by a blending of central and local authority and a softening of Legalism with Confucian humanism, endured until the early twentieth century.

Society, Economy, and Science in Han China

How was Chinese society organized during the Han?

The Han era was formative for many aspects of Chinese life. During the Han the Chinese family matured into its basic form and the economy grew dramatically, affecting peasant life. Chinese examined their own history, looking for lessons from the past. The Han were also highly creative in technology and science, making advances, for example, in mathematics and health.

Social Life and Gender Relations

Han social life revolved around the family system, which endured for over 2,000 years because it offered many strengths. In part because of Confucian ideas, the family became an elaborate institution, the central focus of allegiance for most Chinese. Each Chinese saw himself as belonging to a large, continuing family that went backward and forward in time. They were expected to honor their ancestors while also keeping in mind the welfare of future generations. The family provided great psychological and economic security, despite the inevitable tensions that disrupted family harmony. The Chinese ideal was the joint family, that is, three or four generations living together under one roof. But only wealthy families could support the large houses and private courtyards that made the

joint family way of life possible. Most peasant families could not afford to follow this pattern.

The family was an autocratic institution that exercised considerable influence over its members. It was led by a patriarch, or senior male, who commanded respect. Chinese traced descent exclusively through the male line. Children were expected to respect not only the senior male, but also both parents, and to venerate their elders. Reflecting these obligations, Han law stated that a child who concealed a parent suspected of wrongdoing, or a wife a husband, or a grandchild a grandparent, should not to be brought to trial. Family interests always took precedence over individual ones. Because laws held the family accountable for the actions of its members, they discouraged disgraceful behavior by individuals.

The family system increasingly put most women at a disadvantage compared to men. Women were expected to be devoted first to their parents, then later to their husband, and finally to their sons; care of the family and children was their central preoccupation. A young wife joined her husband's family and was subject to the authority of his parents. Parents arranged marriages with the goal of linking families. Betrothed couples often eventually developed affection for each other, and many marriages seem to have been happy. Nonetheless, the sorrows of unhappy women became a common literary theme. Many Chinese novels and plays concerned unrequited love or lovers forced to marry others. In one small part of central China some women developed among themselves a special and secret form of writing, known as **nuxu** (nushu), to share their life experiences. It was passed down from mother to daughter. Although its origins remain obscure, some historians think it developed as early as the Han. Others believe it emerged much later.

We know much about gender roles in Chinese society and about the experiences of Han women. For example, Ban Zhao (ban chao), the most famous woman scholar in Han China and an accomplished historian, astronomer, and mathematician, wrote an influential book on women's place in society. Her advice to women stressed the Confucian obligations of selfless behavior, devotion, and obedience. Under the influence of patriarchal Confucianism reflected in Ban Zhao's advice, women's virtues became family virtues, and gender roles became more rigid than they had been a few centuries earlier. Still, many women engaged in some small-scale trade; as a Han proverb said, "To prick embroidery does not pay as much as leaning upon a market door." Most women worked long hours in the fields or the marketplace in addition to doing housework and caring for children. But they also formed groups to spin or weave together, "to economize on the expense of light and heat,"[17] as a Han source put it.

In spite of the preeminence of Confucian patterns, women's experiences were never standardized. The amount of independence and influence they enjoyed depended on their age, social class, and local practices. There were always women like Ban Zhao who achieved wide acclaim. The Han scholar

---

nuxu A secret form of writing developed by some Chinese women to share their experiences, possibly beginning in the Han period.

Liu Xiang (loo shang) wrote biographies of 125 women in antiquity who were noted for their unselfish behavior and gallant deeds, such as maintaining loyalty to the ruler or offering wise advice to husbands or fathers. Some elite women received an education, and some were celebrated for their poetry writing. The mother of the Confucian thinker Mengzi was widely esteemed as a model of astuteness and assertiveness, though these traits had not allowed her to completely overcome Confucian expectations of womanhood. She was reported by a male Han era biographer to have said that a "woman's duties are to cook the five grains, heat the wine, look after her parents-in-law, make clothes, and that is all! Therefore, she had no ambitions to manage affairs outside the house."[18] In contrast, some peasant women, who worked in the fields alongside their men, were strong-willed and exercised influence in their families and villages. Indeed, male power was strongest at the elite level and often weaker among the lower classes.

The Rural Economy

Beginning in the early Han and continuing for the next 2,000 years, China's economy was dominated by intensive farming, especially the growing of cereal crops. Peasants constituted the vast majority of the population. Although trade gradually became more significant, farming remained the basis of Chinese society, and landowning became the major goal of economic endeavor and investment. Peasants had to produce a food surplus for the 20 percent of the people living in towns and cities. The fertile Chinese land and peasant labor made this possible: Chinese peasants were able to achieve high yields, becoming some of the world's most efficient farmers. But Chinese agriculture also depended on hard physical labor, especially in growing rice. Fields had to be flooded with irrigation water and drained, and the rice had to be sown, transplanted, and harvested, all by hand.

Peasants did not lead easy lives. Most rarely went farther than the local market town to which they brought their produce. Family land and movable property were divided equally among sons, a form of inheritance that fragmented landholdings and stood in contrast to landholding patterns in pre-Han China, Japan, and Europe. In addition, a lack of capital kept many peasant families at the mercy of middlemen for advances until the crop came in. A Han scholar complained that poor peasants were left with too little land to live on and thus reduced to eating the food of pigs and dogs. As a result, many peasants were forced into tenancy to landlords. However, few were slaves. Slavery, an important feature of Shang and Zhou society, became less common during the Han.

Population pressure and land shortage posed problems to peasants and also created political stability. No great land problem existed before the Han, since virgin land was still available. By the second century B.C.E., however, practically all the good agricultural land in north and north-central China was being used. The dynastic cycle was partly a result of land shortage and population pressure, which fermented rebellion. At times of endemic unrest, caused by bad harvests, high rents, or official corruption, peasants would revolt.

Han Farmer Stone relief of Han farmer using an ox-drawn plow. These plows fostered the expansion of cultivated land during the Han. (From Patricia Buckley Ebrey, *The Cambridge Illustrated History of China,* 1996)

The labor-intensive nature of the economy was also apparent outside agriculture. Transportation meant porters with carrying poles, men pushing wheelbarrows, and men bearing the sedan chairs of the elite. Men also walked along narrow paths pulling boats upriver through the narrow gorges of the Yangzi River. Even the famous silk industry required endless labor. **Sericulture** (silk making) produced silks and brocades of the finest weave by Han times. But producing 150 pounds of silk required feeding and keeping clean the trays of 700,000 worms.

Chinese Historiography

The Chinese developed one of the greatest traditions of studying and writing about history, known as historiography, among premodern societies. The recording of history was probably inevitable among a people who looked to the past for guidance in the present. History writing in China goes back at least as far as the Zhou dynasty. One of the classics of Confucian learning, *The Spring and Autumn Annals,* attributed traditionally but probably inaccurately to Confucius, provided a largely factual and chronological recounting of political events

sericulture Silk making.

in the eastern state of Lu (loo) from 722 to 481 B.C.E. But Confucians also read into the prose a moral assessment of history.

In Han times history writing made perhaps the greatest contribution to literature. Beginning with the Han, most dynasties employed a group of professional historians, such as the Han era's Sima Qian (SI-mu tshen) (see Profile: Sima Qian, Chinese Historian). Later Chinese historians were influenced by Sima Qian's belief that past events, if not forgotten, also taught about the future. To insulate them from retribution by outraged emperors, often their work was not published until after the emperors had passed on. The Chinese historians tended to ignore social and economic history in favor of political history, concentrating on personalities, stories, wars, and the doings of emperors while neglecting long-term trends.

The greatest Chinese historians wrote monumental works and had much in common with each other. They aimed for objectivity, carefully separating their editorial comments from the narrative text, all in elegant prose. Although quoting generously from original documents, like all historians they still had to decide what to include and omit. They paid little attention to events of alleged supernatural intervention and focused more on information about human beings and their foibles. Historical literature also served as a manual for government, since it discussed the success and failure of past policies with the goal of achieving wisdom and promoting morality. The Chinese evaluated their culture by what they had done in the past.

Science and Technology

China developed one of the world's oldest and most influential scientific and technological traditions, establishing along with the Indians, Mesopotamians, Egyptians, and Greeks the foundation for modern science. The Zhou and Han are credited with many important breakthroughs. Among the inventions originating in these centuries were porcelain ("china"), rag paper, the water-powered mill, the shoulder harness for horses, the foot stirrup (possibly adapted from crude Central Asian models), the magnetic compass, the seismograph, the wheelbarrow, the stern-post rudder for boats, the spinning wheel, and certain kinds of textiles, including linen. Most of these inventions did not reach western Eurasia over the trade routes until a few centuries—in some cases a millennium—later.

Paper may have been the most significant innovation. Before paper Chinese scribes wrote with a pointed stylus on strips of wood or bamboo, but these were difficult to use and store. Then they tried woven cloth as a writing surface. Eventually an ingenious artisan tried beating the cloth into fiber and forming thin sheets. Traditionally Chinese historians attribute the invention of paper to the scholar-bureaucrat Chai Lun (tshai lun), who reported the discovery to the emperor in 105 C.E. But the first experiments had probably been done over the course of decades until paper was perfected.

The Han also made great strides in mathematics. Among the major achievements was the most accurate calculation of pi at the time. In addition, the Chinese were many centuries ahead of the rest of the world in the use of fractions, a simple decimal system, the concept of negative numbers, and in certain aspects of algebra and geometry. Han Chinese used bamboo rods, much like mini-chopsticks, to do arithmetic calculations. This system was widely used until the invention around 190 C.E. of the *abacus*, a primitive computer still used widely in Asia today, that proved an unparalleled tool for calculations. The abacus was constructed by fastening balls on wires attached to a board carved with divisions.

In the study of astronomy, the Han compiled catalogues of stars and speculated on sunspots. Around 100 C.E. the astronomer Zhang Heng (jang hoeng) explained the causes of lunar eclipses, writing that the moon reflects the sunshine and will be eclipsed when it travels into earth's shadow. Astronomy was also essential for an agricultural society, which needed accurate calendars to regulate planting and harvesting.

Chinese science, especially medicine, also owed much to the cosmological thinking exemplified in yin-yang dualism and also to Daoism, which inspired an interest in nature. To the Daoists the body was a microcosm of the universe. An influential early Han book on medicine advised readers that when yin and yang are in proper harmony, a person is filled with strength and vigor. An enduring medical discovery, *acupuncture*, also developed from the belief that good health was the result of proper yin-yang balance in the body. In this procedure, thin needles are inserted at predetermined points to alleviate pain or correct some condition. While pursuing acupuncture, Chinese experts learned the parts of the body and discovered how to read a pulse. Acupuncture is still practiced today and has spread around the world.

The Chinese made other contributions in medicine. They stressed good hygiene and preventive medicine, including proper dress, a well-balanced diet, and regular exercise. In their quest for the elixir of immortality, Daoist alchemists discovered many edible foods, herbs, and potions that improved health. They developed the greatest list of pharmaceuticals in the premodern world, which in turn promoted the study of botany and zoology. By the Han period doctors could diagnose gout and cirrhosis of the liver. The Chinese pioneered many medical innovations, and many ancient Chinese folk remedies remain popular to this day in China.

SECTION SUMMARY

- The family structure became the central social institution; its patriarchal hierarchy, codified in law, put the needs of the group above the needs of the individual.

- Despite subservience to all males in the family, some women of this period made many artistic and intellectual contributions.

- Peasant labor, as well as backbreaking labor in general, continued to be the foundation of the economy and characterized most people's existence.

- Developments in science and medicine were influenced by Daoism, which promoted the idea of a yin-yang balance in the natural world.

SIMA QIAN,
CHINESE HISTORIAN

Perhaps the greatest Han dynasty historian was Sima Qian (ca. 145–90 B.C.E.). His father, a high court official who also wrote about Chinese history, begged his son on his deathbed to continue compiling a history of China and its neighbors from earliest times. "I have failed to set forth a record of all the enlightened rulers and wise lords, the faithful ministers and gentlemen who were ready to die for duty," he conceded. His dutiful son replied, "I shall not dare to be remiss," and made the project his life's work. At the age of twenty, Sima Qian, who had grown up in the ancestral home in northwest China, began a grand tour of the empire. During the tour, he devoted time to examining historical sites, such as the tomb and family home of Confucius.

After receiving an official appointment, the Han government sent the young scholar on a mission to newly conquered territories in the southwest. Later he visited far northwestern outposts, including Mongolia, and also traveled extensively with the emperor Wu Di. Like his father, Sima Qian was appointed Grand Astrologer, a post dealing with time and the heavens, and helped to reform the calendar. But, being an honest man who spoke his mind, he alienated the emperor by defending a respected general whose brave attack against the Huns had failed for lack of support. As punishment Sima Qian was castrated.

Using his immense learning, combined with access to the vast imperial library containing the public records, Sima Qian produced his major book, *Records of the Grand Historian.* An invaluable source, *Records* covered some 2,000 years of history in 130 chapters, roughly 10,000 pages of text. Attempting to be universal, this monumental history ranges across a variety of topics, including astronomy, astrology, science, music, religious sacrifices, and economic patterns. It offers sketches of famous men from many walks of life, including political and military leaders, merchants, philosophers, scholars, comedians, assassins, rebels, bandits, and poets. *Records* also describes all foreign peoples and lands well known to the Chinese, from Korea to Afghanistan. Because it also covers rivers and canals, we know much of Wu Di's ambitious conservation and irrigation schemes. In addition, Sima Qian was the first historian to offer a comparative appraisal of China's various philosophical traditions, in which he showed particular sympathy to Daoism.

The book is strongest on the history of his times. Because Sima Qian's castration had embittered him toward Wu Di, some chapters are filled with covert satires on the emperor and warnings about his increasing power. His most original writing came in the chapters on people and contemporary affairs. Consider this criticism of those abusing their power:

We see that men whose deeds are immoral and who constantly violate the laws end their lives in luxury and wealth and their blessings pass down to their heirs with-

Sima Qian   Painting of Sima Qian. This modern painting, by an unknown artist, imagines what Han China's great historian, Sima Qian, might have looked like.   (British Library)

out end. And there are others who expend anger on what is not upright and just, and yet, in numbers too great to be reckoned, they meet with misfortune and disaster. I find myself in much perplexity.

Its vital narrative made this book popular reading among Chinese scholars for many centuries. Sima Qian's lively prose style made him an excellent storyteller. Above all, the historian was concerned with both his literary and his moral legacy. As Sima Qian concluded, in words that still stir historians everywhere: "I have assembled and arranged the ancient traditions, and if they may be handed down and communicated surely I would have no regrets," and, "those who do not forget the past are masters of the future." Sima Qian set the standard to be followed by later historians in China.

THINKING ABOUT THE PROFILE

1. How did Sima Qian become a historian?

2. What does his life tell us about the pleasures and hazards of being a high official in Han China?

3. What made his historical writing so valuable to later readers?

Note: Quotations from Ben-Ami Scharfstein, *The Mind of China: The Culture, Customs, and Beliefs of Traditional China* (New York: Dell, 1974), pp. 89–91; and Sima Qian, *Historical Records,* translated by Raymond Dawson (Oxford: Oxford University Press, 1994), p. 177.

China After the Han Empire: Continuity and Change

What outside influences helped shape China after the fall of the Han?

After the collapse of the Han in 221 C.E., China experienced three and a half centuries of disorder and political fragmentation. This period is known as the Era of the Three Kingdoms and Six Dynasties, a name that suggests its political diversity. China was divided into several states, once as many as sixteen, some ruled by Chinese and others by invaders. Just as the incursion of new peoples dominated the histories of Europe and India in the ashes of the Roman and Mauryan Empires, so this era in China was marked by frequent incursions by pastoral nomads from the north and west. By the seventh century, however, China had restored centralized government and reaffirmed the classical tradition.

Disunity, Invasion, and Cultural Mixing

The post-Han period was a troubled one. Even more than in earlier times, pastoral nomads crossed the Great Wall and attacked north China. They included the Huns, Mongols, and Turks, all of whom spoke Ural-Altaic languages and inhabited grasslands environments where livestock raising was the major economic activity. These people were not unsophisticated herders; most used bronze and iron, and some may have had written languages. However, brutal winters and keen competition for good grazing land made them martial peoples scornful of the richer life available to the agriculture Chinese. At the same time, they were attracted to that life, and one group or another regularly sought to breach the Great Wall. Sometimes they succeeded by virtue of their skills in horseback warfare, especially when they had united in confederations under strong chiefs. The Huns remained one of the major threats, and some of them had built cities in western China by the fifth century C.E.

Beginning during the Zhou and accelerating after the downfall of the Han, these invasions helped produce what historians have called the "Great Wall Complex": a natural Chinese paranoia about the security of borders and the perpetual fear of outsiders seeking to conquer. The Chinese believed that all non-Chinese were barbarians just waiting to invade and share in China's cultural glory and material wealth. This fear prompted Chinese to rally to the cause of defeating invaders. A much loved fifth-century ballad, perhaps based on an actual person, recalled the deeds of a young woman warrior, Mulan (moo-LAHN), who disguised herself as a man in order to fight invading Central Asians. Only after she distinguished herself in battle did her comrades discover her gender. The ballad recorded their shock: "Her messmates were startled out of their wits. They had marched with her for twelve years of war, And never known that Mulan was a girl." The final lines made

a case for gender equality: "For the male hare has a lilting, lolloping gait, and the female hare has a wild and roving eye; But set them both scampering side by side, And who so wise could tell you 'This is he?'."[19] These invasions also prompted many Chinese to move south, solidifying the Chinese character of the Yangzi Basin.

The Chinese learned to endure both division and invasion by outsiders. An ancient proverb reassured them by arguing that though the country may be defeated, the mountains and streams would endure. In dealing with invaders, the Chinese developed a remarkable defense mechanism: assimilation. Most of the barbarian conquerors were eventually forced to rule in a Chinese way, using the Confucian bureaucracy, while also adapting many elements of Chinese culture. As a result, the Chinese came to believe that rule by foreigners could be tolerated as long as Chinese culture itself was respected and protected. Chinese culture, social institutions, and economic patterns thus proved resilient, able to survive the shock of conquest. But the Chinese also learned from the invaders. This merging of cultures provided a foundation for the later rejuvenation of a China that would be greater than the empires of Qin and Han.

During the post-Han era China became even more connected to the world outside, fostering a vital, cosmopolitan culture. One fifth-century emperor became particularly well-known for his love of everything foreign: dress, art works, food, beds, chairs, flutes, harps, dances. Ideas and products continued to travel both directions along the Silk Road and by land and sea between China and Southeast Asia. In China, these foreign influences were reflected in post-Han art. Chinese objects from this era often showed Indian, Persian, Mesopotamian, Greek, or Roman influences, such as jade cups modeled on Roman goblets. The graves of wealthy Chinese frequently contained imported objects, such as Roman glass, Persian silver vessels, images of Greek gods, and cups made from Indonesian shells. China's openness to ideas from outside also led many Chinese to embrace an Indian religion, Buddhism.

Buddhism and Chinese Society

During the later centuries of the Classical Era, universal religions—faiths that appealed to people from many cultures—became much more prominent in Eurasia and North Africa, marking another great transition. The decline and collapse of the great Afro-Eurasian empires, from China to Rome, had produced political instability and social strife, which challenged established ways of looking at the world. In response, universal religions spread along the trade networks. Christianity spread from western Asia to Europe, where it soon became the dominant religion, Hinduism spread throughout India and into Southeast Asia, and Mahayana (Mah-HAH-YAH-nah) Buddhism became influential in Central and East Asia. Frequently these universal religions merged with or incorporated existing local beliefs, creating new hybrid artistic forms and value systems. The most pronounced synthesis took place in East Asia as Buddhism encountered earlier belief systems such as Confucianism.

Buddha Statue at Yungang This huge statue of the Buddha, created around 290 C.E., is 45 feet tall. It is one of thousands found along cliffs in western China and elsewhere along the Silk Road. (Werner Forman/Art Resource, NY)

The arrival of Buddhism was a momentous transition for East Asia, and it ultimately became a major religion there. Indeed, the fourth through the ninth centuries C.E. might well be called the Buddhist Age in both Chinese and, more generally, Asian history. Buddhism in some form became dominant in much of East, Central, and Southeast Asia as well as in portions of South Asia (see Chapter 7). The basic Buddhist beliefs about overcoming suffering through good deeds and thoughts derived from the sixth century B.C.E. teachings of the Indian sage Siddhartha Gautama, known to his followers as the Buddha ("the Enlightened One"), but the religion later split into several rival schools. One of these, Mahayana Buddhism, was carried by merchants and missionaries along the Silk Road into Central Asia. From there it spread into western China during later Han times, serving to tie China to distant India. Later the religion spread from China to Korea, Vietnam, and Japan. Buddhism, a religion of compassion and gentleness, offered meaning and hope to people experiencing hardship, warfare, and instability. People sought inner peace if they could not find external peace. Buddhism also offered the Chinese a spiritual outlook largely missing in the traditional Chinese be-

lief systems. For example, compared to Buddhism, Confucianism was intellectual, appealing to reason and practical ethics. It had little to say about the supernatural realm or life after death. The mysticism of Daoism differed from Confucianism by providing an emotional release, but the abstract philosophical underpinnings could not offer the certainty about the fate of the individual in the cosmic order that many sought. Buddhism thus appealed because of its promise of salvation in an afterlife. But Buddhism also adapted to Chinese traditions. For example, the Buddhist notion of reincarnation, which envisioned the soul passing through a long series of lives, clashed with Chinese beliefs in ancestor worship, so most Chinese never accepted this idea.

Because it had traveled from India through Central Asia, Chinese Buddhism acquired a cosmopolitan outlook. Buddhism and other outside influences fostered a China somewhat different from the country known to Confucius or Han emperor Wu Di. For example, Buddhism's peaceful spread was accompanied by Indian artistic, literary, and cultural influences, such as the huge sculptures of the Buddha found along the Silk Road and in northwestern China. Many Buddhist missionaries entered China, and several hundred Chinese pilgrims went to India, either overland or along the sea route through Southeast Asia. The most notable in this era was Faxian (fah-shee-en), a monk who spent fifteen years in India and also visited Buddhist centers in Southeast Asia in the fifth century C.E. On their return to China the pilgrims spread knowledge of the societies they encountered. Faxian's reports also provided modern historians with data on the Asia of his day.

China's Eclectic Religious Tradition

The Chinese philosophy and religion that were developing by the middle of the first millennium C.E. embraced three very different viewpoints—Buddhism, Confucianism, and Daoism—which were known as "the three ways." Over the next few centuries the three schools interacted with and tempered each other, creating a rich synthesis, and many Chinese could no longer clearly differentiate between them. An old but still popular Chinese story has Confucius, Laozi, and Buddha walking and talking together, debating the merits of their respective positions; as they cross a bridge, they are obscured in mist. When spotted again only one somewhat larger figure can be seen in the distance.

Despite the fusion of traditions, some distinctions were maintained. Only Buddhism developed a fully organized church, with monks and nuns, although there were also some Daoist orders. Confucianism, as a philosophy of social relations rather than a true religion, had no priests. In addition, many Chinese believed that people have needs that cannot be satisfied by only one set of doctrines. They sought answers in different doctrines, not identifying themselves exclusively as Buddhists, Daoists, or Confucianists. Most Chinese saw the three traditions as different roads to the same destination, personal happiness.

Gradually a gap between the relatively secular worldview of the educated elite and the popular religion of the common people widened over time. The intellectuals tended to favor a combination of Confucian humanism and Daoist naturalism, with moral perfection of humankind as the ultimate goal. This perspective emphasized moral and social concerns rather than mystical experience. For these intellectuals, Confucius and his followers had revealed a truth centered on humanity rather than on gods.

For this reason, many intellectuals viewed popular religion, with its gods, spirits, ghosts, and magic, as superstition. One Han scholar wrote that "the dead do not become disembodied spirits nor do they injure anyone. The number of persons who have died since the world began must run into thousands of millions. If everyone of them has become a spirit, there must be at least one to every yard as we walk along the road."[20] Although more Chinese at all levels may have been indifferent to religion than was common elsewhere, many peasants, artisans, and merchants believed in thousands of gods and goddesses of Buddhist, Daoist, or animist origin. Common people used shamans to communicate with the spirit realm, including ancestors. They also accepted notions of heaven and hell introduced into Chinese thought by Mahayana Buddhism. In addition, many peasants believed in astrology, ghosts, dream interpretation, and witchcraft.

Geomancy (JEE-u-MAN-see), known in Chinese as *feng shui* (fung shway) ("wind and water"), was a popular Daoist-influenced system for determining the auspicious settings of human dwellings and graves. The rationale was that humans can help improve their fate by determining the workings of nature and bringing their own actions into accord with them. Geomancy is still widely employed today in East Asia and some architects even use it to assess the auspiciousness of building modern skyscrapers in non-Asian cities, such as Chicago, Vancouver, and London. It is also used occasionally for house construction in North America and Europe.

Technology in the Post-Han Era

After the fall of the Han the Chinese continued to develop innovative technologies. Printing was particularly crucial. From early times Chinese sought ways to mass-produce writings. By the seventh century B.C.E. they were inscribing characters in bronze, and during Han times they made ink rubbings on paper from stone carvings, often of entire Buddhist books. Elementary block printing was in limited use in China by the sixth century C.E. The spur was the need to reproduce Buddhist texts and images for believers and Confucian classics for students preparing for the examinations. By the ninth century woodblock printing had become a major activity in East Asia.

Although never a great seafaring people like the Austronesians and Greeks, the Chinese became some of the world leaders in shipbuilding, and some took up maritime trade. Even in Han times, Chinese ships carried trade goods back and forth to Korea, Japan, and Southeast Asia, and perhaps sometimes to India. To increase their maritime trade activity, by at least the fifth century C.E. the Chinese had constructed oceangoing vessels with stern-post rudders for maneuvering, which permitted longer and farther journeys. Some Chinese junks carried as many as three thousand sailors. Chinese ships and navigational skills were probably adequate to even cross the vast Pacific, although there is no compelling evidence that any did so. A third century C.E. Chinese scholar wrote that he knew of no one who had crossed the Pacific. If, as a few argue, Chinese (or perhaps Japanese) ships did ever make the long voyage to the Western Hemisphere in this era, deliberately or blown by storms, this was a rare occurrence and apparently had no long-term consequences on either side of the ocean.

The Sui Reunification of China

To an observer of world history in the fourth century it might have seemed that the Roman Empire, although visibly weakening, could endure, while the Chinese empire was overrun by "barbarian" invaders, broken apart, and turning to foreign,

---

geomancy Known in Chinese as *feng shui* ("wind and water"), a system for determining the auspicious settings of human dwellings and graves.

otherworldly religions. Yet, China was eventually reunified under a powerful, centralized government, whereas Rome, facing the same kinds of challenges, fragmented and collapsed. Several factors contributed to China's reassembly. First, the high population density of the Chinese core area made reestablishment of a centralized state easier. By 400 C.E. the Chinese may have numbered 50 million, probably double the population of Europe. In addition, Chinese shared more cultural unity than the varied peoples of western Asia, India, and Europe. Finally, the nomadic invaders may have been easily absorbed in China because the newcomers were so small in number compared to the Chinese.

Culture and politics probably also played a role in Chinese reunification. Confucian ethical humanism, which did not disappear with the Han dynasty, provided cultural continuity. Chinese writing also encouraged cultural unity because it put hundreds of spoken dialects into a common system. Such linguistic unity did not exist in other regions. For example, India contained many very different spoken languages but also diverse writing systems, and in Europe, the speakers of Romance languages based on phonetic alphabets splintered into many competing countries, never to be reunited despite their cultural similarities and a shared Christian religion. Finally, in China the emphasis on rule by ethical men chosen by a merit system remained appealing and helped unify the country.

The Sui (sway) dynasty (581–618 C.E.) played the same role in history as the Qin, reuniting China after several centuries of turmoil and division. It was also nearly as ruthless. The Sui emperors were tyrants but also patrons of arts and letters, and they created the largest library at that time in the world (with 400,000 volumes). Like the Qin, the Sui were builders. For example, they mobilized 6 million forced workers to construct the Grand Canal linking the Yangzi and Yellow Rivers. At 1,200 miles long, the longest human-made channel ever constructed, this was one of the most formidable civil engineering projects in world history. The canal linked the economic power of central China with the political power of north China. By doing so, it ensured the prosperity of later dynasties, since each year huge quantities of grain could be shipped north. Tree-shaded parks and inns lined the route.

Like earlier dynasties, the Sui overreached itself and collapsed. Exhausting campaigns of conquest temporarily extended imperial frontiers into Korea and Central Asia. But the Sui drove the Chinese people too hard, resulting in overwork and food shortages. To supply food for the massive building projects, a contemporary source reported, "requisitioning was hurried and relentless; the morning's order had to be carried out by the evening. The common people sought out food with snare and net to such an extent that on land and waters, the birds and the beasts were almost extinguished."[21] Soon rebellions broke out. The victor in the ensuing struggles established the Tang (tahng) dynasty (618–907 C.E.), which launched China on its great golden age extending over many centuries and linked China more closely to Korea and Japan, whose societies we turn to now.

SECTION SUMMARY

- Spurred by invasions of nomadic peoples from the north, the population shifted south, but the invaders were assimilated by existing Chinese government structures.

- Buddhism took root in China during this tumultuous period, spreading along the trade routes from India and melding with existing Confucian thought.

- The Chinese attitude toward religion was characterized by an easy interchange of beliefs, in which individuals drew from a variety of religious or philosophical perspectives depending on their need.

- Fractured by invasions, Chinese reunification was nevertheless made easier by the population's shared written language, culture, and history.

- Like the Qin before them, the Sui rulers also reunited China using harsh measures but made lasting contributions, such as the Grand Canal.

Korea, Japan, and East Asian Networks

How did the Koreans and Japanese assimilate Chinese influences into their own distinctive societies?

Because the large, densely populated Chinese society persisted to modern times, it dominated East Asia for much of history. Consequently, eastern Asia did not develop the political diversity, with many rival states, that prevailed in India, western Asia, or Europe after classical times. To be sure, Chinese culture had only modest influence in the grasslands and deserts of North and Central Asia, where settled agriculture was difficult and societies thus maintained a pastoral nomadic life. But Korea and Japan adopted intensive farming, and thus became more receptive to Chinese cultural influence. Separated by water, Japan was able to remain the most independent of the neighboring Chinese. Although more developed than Japan for many centuries, Korea was more often in the shadow of China. Yet both Korea and Japan creatively forged distinctive societies.

Korea and China

As a close neighbor, Korea experienced regular and extensive interaction with China, which brought many advantages but also political pressures. During the first millennium B.C.E. Chinese cultural and technological influences began permeating the Korean peninsula. For example, Koreans adopted iron technology from the Chinese, including advanced weapons, and their increasing mastery of iron later fostered the rise of powerful, agriculture-based Korean states in the peninsula.

Chinese influence soon overwhelmed these states. Chinese refugees from the Zhou wars and from Qin repression migrated across the frontier, bringing with them culture and technology. Then in 108 B.C.E. Wu Di's armies, reportedly 60,000 troops strong, conquered northern Korea against fierce resistance. China ruled the territory as a colony for the next four centuries, providing models to the Koreans in government structure, architecture, and city planning (see Chronology: Classical Japan and Korea).

The end of Chinese colonization in 313 C.E. allowed Korean society to flower, and three native kingdoms emerged. These powerful states dominated Korea between the fourth and seventh centuries, occasionally warring against each other for control of fertile agricultural land. At the same time, however, Chinese cultural influences, including the writing system, spread more widely. Mahayana Buddhism, introduced from China into northern Korea in 372 C.E., had a strong influence on Korean painting, sculpture, and architecture. Confucian doctrines also became popular. But the Koreans never became carbon copies of the Chinese. For example, unlike in China, where family status rose or fell with dynastic change and civil service examination success or failure, an aristocracy of inherited position, living in considerable luxury, thrived for most of Korean history. Korean music remained distinctive even if the instruments were adapted from Chinese models. And although most Koreans eventually adopted Buddhism, the animism that had long flourished never disappeared.

Eventually one Korean kingdom, Koguryo (go-GUR-yo), became the most influential (see Map 5.3). In the fifth century, with China divided, Koguryo expanded far to the north, annexing much of Manchuria and southeastern Siberia in addition to the northern half of the Korean peninsula. In its expansion, Koguryo became one of the largest states in Eurasia at that time. The empire, which lasted from 350 to 668 C.E., also boasted a substantial population of several million people by

Map 5.3   Korea and Japan in the Fifth Century c.e. During the Classical Era Korea was often divided into several states. Koguryo in the north was the largest state, ruling part of Siberia. By the sixth century the Yamato state governed much of the main Japanese island, Honshu.

the seventh century. At the same time, several much smaller Korean states controlled the southern part of the peninsula.

Koguryo proved a strong regional force. Its army repulsed seven major Chinese invasions by the Sui and Tang dynasties between 598 and 655 C.E., when a resurgent China was the most powerful state in the world. The great Koguryo generals commanded skilled and mobile legions. In 612 C.E. they routed an invading Sui army that, according to legend, numbered at least 1 million soldiers but was probably closer to a still formidable 300,000. The huge cost of the Chinese campaigns in Korea contributed to the collapse of the Sui dynasty. Finally, in 668 C.E., Chinese armies, allied with the southern Korean state of Silla (SILL-ah or SHILL-ah), overran Koguryo and destroyed the kingdom, carrying 200,000 prisoners back to China. This event allowed for the reunification of Korea under Silla, which then flourished for several centuries.

Yayoi Japan

Like Korea across the straits, Japan experienced dramatic change between 600 B.C.E. and 600 C.E. The prehistoric, pottery-making Jomon culture (see Chapter 4) persisted until around 300 B.C.E., when a new pattern emerged that archaeologists term Yayoi (ya-YOI). This emergence correlated with the rise of an exceptionally productive wet rice-farming society

CHRONOLOGY
Classical Japan and Korea
300 B.C.E.–552 C.E.   Yayoi culture in Japan
18 B.C.E.   Rise of Koguryo in northern Korea
108 B.C.E.–313 C.E.   Han Chinese colonization of Korea
250 C.E.   Beginning of Yayoi tomb culture
350–668 C.E.   Koguryo Empire
514–935 C.E.   Silla state in southern Korea
538 C.E.   Introduction of Buddhism to Japan
552–710 C.E.   Yamato state in Japan
604 C.E.   First Japanese constitution

that established close links with Korea, a relationship that fostered migration from Korea. Hence, Japan owes its flowering in part to networks of trade and migration in Yayoi times.

During the long Yayoi era (300 B.C.E.–552 C.E.), Korea remained a source of learning and population for Japan. A relationship between people in southwestern Japan and southeastern Korea promoted a continuous flow of Korean immigrants as well as both Korean and Chinese ideas and technology from the mainland into the islands. Some Korean migrants brought horses, and the armored warrior on horseback later became a vivid feature of Japanese life. In addition, Koreans worked in Japan as skilled craftsmen, scribes, and artists. Immigration from Korea continued until the ninth century. By 600 C.E. the Japanese people as we know them today had come together from the genetic and cultural mixing over many centuries of Korean immigrants with earlier settlers and the indigenous Ainu people.

The Yayoi also traded sporadically with China. A Chinese visitor in 297 C.E. left us much information about Yayoi society. He reported that the Yayoi were much concerned with taboos, class distinctions, and especially ritual cleanliness, writing that "when [a] funeral is over, all members of the family go into the water to cleanse themselves in a bath of purification."[22] The Chinese visitor also reported that the Yayoi were fond of dancing, singing, drinking rice wine, and eating raw vegetables; experienced no theft and little other crime; revered nature; and clapped their hands in worship. All these behaviors characterize modern Japanese, suggesting that these early customs never eroded. The Chinese also noted that the Yayoi used the potter's wheel, were expert weavers, and had mastered both bronze and iron technology. Later they would fashion iron into highly effective swords and armor.

The Yayoi formed no centralized governments but did have a class structure. They were organized into a large number of clans, each ruled by a hereditary priest-chieftain. According to a Chinese source, during the second century C.E., when Japan was engulfed in war and conflict, a woman, Pimiko (pih-MEE-ko), became a powerful queen-priestess and brought peace by imposing strict laws. She lived in a palace surrounded by a tower and employed a thousand female attendants. But aside from a few women leaders such as Pimiko, the clan elites were men who governed large numbers of farmers, artisans, and a few slaves and who mobilized people to build hundreds of large earthen tombs, often surrounded by moats, all over south-central Honshu Island. The tombs housed the remains of prominent leaders, who were buried with prized possessions such as jewels, swords, and clay figurines.

Yamato: The First Japanese National State

Japan entered the light of written history in the sixth century C.E., with the beginning of the Yamato (YA-ma-toe) period (552–710 C.E.), named for the first state ruling a majority of the Japanese people. The Yamato was centered in south-central Honshu, where the cities of Kyoto (kee-YO-toe) and Osaka

(oh-SAH-kah) now stand. The Japanese population had by then probably reached 3 million. Yamato leaders exercised some control from what is today Tokyo in the north to the southern tip of Korea. Yamato was not a centralized state like Han China or Koguryo but rather a national government ruling over smaller groups based on clans and territorial control, each headed by a hereditary chief. Eventually Yamato extended its influence into southern Japan while expanding the northern frontier deep into Ainu territory.

Yamato was headed by emperors and occasionally empresses—all ancestors of the same imperial family that rules Japan today, fifteen centuries later. Political continuity under the same royal family gave the Japanese a strong sense of identity and a corresponding sense of cultural unity. The imperial family owes its longevity in part to an identification with Japanese origins. The Japanese saw their history before the sixth century C.E. in mythological terms: they believed the imperial family descended from the Sun Goddess. This beautiful spirit, *Amaterasu* (AH-mah-teh-RAH-soo), and her male consort experienced violent mood swings and periodic conflict that may have been modeled on the frequent storms, volcanic eruptions, and earthquakes that rock the islands. Despite her tantrums, a female creator deity may also have reflected a high status for women in early Japan. The Chinese reported that the Yayoi made no distinction in status between men and women, and before the eighth century C.E. around half of the imperial sovereigns were women, some of whom had charismatic personalities. But female power eventually eroded, and patriarchy became the common pattern by 1000 C.E.

Japanese Isolation and Cultural Unity

The Japanese forged a particularly distinctive society in late classical times through a mixing of the local and the foreign. Many of Japan's unique features resulted from the fact that the islands were over a hundred miles from the Eurasian mainland, which meant that communication with other societies was sporadic, mainly restricted to Korea and China, and the Japanese had to become very creative. At the same time, physical isolation severely restricted the space and resources available to the steadily growing population on the mountainous islands. The result was a tightly woven society with intense social pressures. Since personal privacy became rare in this crowded land, and since the Japanese lived in houses with thin walls, people learned how to erect psychological walls that allowed them to "tune out" the surrounding noise and activity.

Isolation made the Japanese expert at borrowing selectively from the outside during periods of intensive contact. Much of Japanese history can be understood as an interplay between the indigenous (native) and the foreign; ultimately a native element survived despite a flood of borrowing from Korea, China, and, much later, the West. The Japanese have been very conscious of borrowing, but they have always selected and adapted foreign ideas that suit their own needs. Seldom have

Prince Shotoku This painting from the eighth century C.E. shows Prince Shotoku, one of the major Yamato leaders, and his sons in the Japanese clothing style of the times. Prince Shotoku launched a period of intensive borrowing from China. (Imperial Household Collection)

they left a borrowed idea in its original form. For example, the Japanese adopted the Chinese idea of an exalted emperor but not the concept of the Mandate of Heaven, which allowed for incompetent or tyrannical dynasties to be overthrown. The Japanese imperial family had, according to their myths, been granted a permanent mandate by the Sun Goddess, which could not be withdrawn.

The Japanese also created a large proportion of their own culture. Japan has been a leading technological innovator for millennia; for instance, it developed the best tempered steel of the classical world. This creative ability is particularly striking in the traditional arts, where the Japanese created forms and styles of universal appeal, such as carefully planned gardens and *bonsai* (bon-sigh) (miniature) trees, and in social organization, where they have evolved ingenious solutions to chronic problems such as urban crowding and limited resources. Thus, the Japanese house itself, containing thick straw floor mats,

sliding paper panels rather than interior walls, a hot tub for communal bathing, and charcoal-burning braziers, conserved building materials and minimized fuel needs for heating and cooking.

Japanese Encounters with China

Japan was greatly influenced by the Chinese several times in history. The importation of Chinese ideas began on a large scale in the middle of the sixth century C.E. In this period Mahayana Buddhism was introduced around 538 and became a major medium for cultural change, bringing, for example, new forms of art and ideas about the cosmos and afterlife. Chinese teachers, artisans, and Buddhist monks crossed over to Japan, and Japanese journeyed to Korea and China, coming back as converts to Buddhism. Just as the Chinese maintained three distinct traditions of thought, in Japan Buddhism coexisted with the ancient animistic cult later known as **Shinto** (SHIN-toe) ("way of the gods"), which emphasized closeness to nature and enjoyed a rich mythology that included many deities.

During the sixth century, a growing realization among Japanese leaders that China and Korea were much stronger than Japan in the political, economic, and cultural spheres led the Japanese to embrace new ideas. The adaptation of Buddhism as well as the Chinese written language launched an era of deliberate borrowing from China to reshape Japanese society. The Yamato state was strong enough to support radical change without losing its independence. It expanded relations with Sui China and began to reorganize government structures, integrating Confucian notions of social organization and morality.

The adoption of Chinese ideas accelerated at the beginning of the seventh century under the auspices of Prince Shotoku (show-TOW-koo) (573–621 C.E.), an ardent Buddhist who sponsored the building of temples, used Buddhism to unify the politically fragmented society, and also promoted Confucian values. "Punish that which is evil and encourage that which is good," he wrote into the first Japanese constitution, issued in 604. His ideas also foreshadowed later Japanese values emphasizing group interests: "Harmony is to be cherished, and opposition for opposition's sake must be avoided as a matter of principle."[23] Shotoku became one of the most revered figures in Japanese history. His support for Buddhism has led some historians to compare Shotoku to the Indian king Asoka, who also embraced Buddhism, and the Roman emperor Constantine, who promoted Christianity. Over the next two and a half centuries many official embassies were exchanged between China and Japan, further promoting the exchange of ideas.

SECTION SUMMARY

- Like most of China, Korea and Japan were agricultural societies, a similarity that facilitated the easy transmission of Chinese culture.

- Korea's proximity to China, along with the alternating military dominance of one culture over the other, led to the adoption of Chinese writing and other technologies in Korea.

- Both Buddhism and Confucianism permeated Korean culture from China and were blended with the native belief system of animism, keeping Korean culture distinctive.

- The flow of ideas and people from Korea and China to Japan introduced Buddhism, writing, and other influences into Japan, but the Japanese culture, arts, and religion remained distinctive.

- From the beginning, Japan's small land area prompted the Japanese to deal creatively with lack of space and the social problems of overcrowding.

Shinto ("way of the gods") The ancient animistic Japanese cult that emphasized closeness to nature and enjoyed a rich mythology that included many deities.

Online Study Center ACE the Test

Chapter Summary

The classical societies that flowered in eastern Asia were distinctive in many ways. China was large, densely populated, and an innovator in government, culture, religion, science, and technology. During the late Zhou period, a time of warfare and political instability, Chinese philosophers such as Confucius as well as the Daoists and Legalists promoted ideas to restore order and promote personal happiness. Confucius promoted ethical values and suggested how people could live in harmony with each other through a well-defined and hierarchical social structure. In contrast, the Daoists advocated a life in accordance with the rhythms of the natural world. Third among these three dominant Chinese philosophies, the Legalists argued that a powerful government must harshly regulate society to preserve order. These classical ideas persisted in Chinese thought into modern times. The Legalist leaders of the Qin dynasty used brutal policies to transform China into a centralized imperial state.

Following the short-lived Qin, the great Han dynasty established a large Asian empire and traded with western Asia and Europe across the Silk Road. By constructing a centralized government and expansive empire, Han China became a major force in eastern Eurasia and traded with societies as far away as Europe. Directly or indirectly, the networks linking China with other Eurasian societies influenced all the societies involved. During the Han the social structure became more patriarchal and women were expected to be dutiful to their men. Peasant labor provided the economic foundation for the society.

After the Han collapsed, Central Asians frequently invaded and divided China politically. In this turbulent period, Mahayana Buddhism, which originated in India, became popular in China, where it mixed with Confucianism, Daoism, and animism to create various blends. At the end of this period China became reunified in an imperial state under the Sui dynasty, an achievement that contrasted with the Roman Empire in the West, which disintegrated into various fragments.

China became a model for neighboring societies. First the Koreans and then the Japanese adopted many Chinese ideas, including some technologies, writing, Confucianism, and Buddhism. But they also creatively blended them with their own unique traditions. The societies that resulted were thus a distinctive mix of the imported with the local. The East Asian societies continued to blend local creativity with foreign influences in the centuries to follow.

Online Study Center Improve Your Grade Flashcards

Key Terms

Confucianism	Sinicization	sericulture
The Analects	Silk Road	geomancy
filial piety	mandarins	Shinto
Daoism	scholar-gentry	
Legalism	nuxu	

Suggested Reading

Books

Adshead, S. A. M. *China in World History*. 3rd ed. New York: St. Martin's, 2000. A good introduction to Han China's interaction with Central Asia, western Asia, and Europe.

Clements, Jonathan. *Confucius: A Biography*. New York: Sutton, 2005. Brief study written for a popular audience.

Cotterell, Arthur. *The First Emperor of China*. New York: Penguin, 1981. A readable and fascinating study of the first emperor and his times.

Di Cosmo, Nicole. *Ancient China and Its Enemies: The Rise of Nomadic Power in East Asian History*. Cambridge: Cambridge University Press, 2002. An important study of China and the northern peoples from the Zhou through the Han dynasties.

Ebrey, Patricia Buckley, et al. *Pre-Modern East Asia: to 1800: A Cultural, Social, and Political History*. Boston: Houghton Mifflin, 2006. An excellent survey of China, Japan, and Korea.

Ebrey, Patricia Buckley. *The Cambridge Illustrated History of China*. New York: Cambridge University Press, 1996. A very readable survey with much on the classical period.

Hane, Mikiso. *Premodern Japan*. 2nd ed. Boulder, Colo.: Westview, 1991. A readable survey.

Hinsch, Bret. *Women in Early Imperial China*. Lanham, Md.: Rowman and Littlefield, 2002. A stimulating study of the factors shaping women's experiences in Qin and Han China.

Holcombe, Charles. *The Genesis of East Asia, 221 B.C.–A.D. 907*. Honolulu: University of Hawai'i Press, 2001. Provocative examination of this era.

Imamura, Kenji. *Prehistoric Japan: New Perspectives on Insular Japan*. Honolulu: University of Hawaii Press, 1996. A scholarly study of the Yayoi and Yamato periods.

Loewe, Michael. *Everyday Life in Early Imperial China: During the Han Period 202 B.C.–A.D. 220*. Indianapolis: Hackett, 2005. Reprint of classic work on Han life and society.

Mote, Frederick W. *Intellectual Foundations of China*. 2nd ed. New York: Knopf, 1989. A brief, readable introduction to classical Chinese philosophy.

Shaughnessy, Edward L. ed. *China: Empire and Civilization*. New York: Oxford University Press, 2005. Contains many short essays on premodern Chinese society and culture.

Sima Qian. *Historical Records* (translated by Raymond Dawson). New York: Oxford University Press, 1994. A brief introduction to the writings of the Han era historian.

Wright, Arthur. *The Sui Dynasty: The Unification of China, A.D. 581–617*. New York: Alfred A. Knopf, 1978. A valuable study of government and society.

Websites

History of China (http://www.chaos.umd.edu/history). Collection of essays and timelines on Chinese history maintained by the University of Maryland.

Internet East Asian History Sourcebook (http://www.fordham.edu/halsall/eastasia/eastasiasbook.html). An invaluable collection of sources and links on China, Japan, and Korea from ancient to modern times.

Internet Guide for China Studies (http://www.sino.uni-heidelberg.de/igcs/). Good collection of links on premodern and modern China, maintained at Heidelberg University.

Monks and Merchants (http://www.asiasociety.org/arts/monksandmerchants/index/html). Interesting essays, timelines, maps, and images for an Asia Society exhibition on the Silk Road as a zone of communication.

A Visual Sourcebook of Chinese Civilization (http://depts.washington.edu/chinaciv/). A wonderful collection of essays, illustrations, and other useful material on Chinese history.

CHAPTER 6

Western Asia, the Eastern Mediterranean, and Regional Systems, 600–200 B.C.E.

Online Study Center

This icon will direct you to interactive activities and study materials on the website: college.hmco.com/pic/lockard1e

Persepolis   During the height of their empire, Persian kings built a lavish capital at Persepolis, in today's Iran. This photo shows the audience hall, the part of the grand palace where the kings greeted their ministers and foreign diplomats.   (Ancient Art & Architecture Collection)

Wonders are many on earth, and the greatest of these, is man, who rides the ocean. He is master of the ageless earth. The use of language, the wind-swift motion of brain he learned; found out the laws of living together in cities. There is nothing beyond his power.

CHORUS IN *ANTIGONE,* BY THE FIFTH-CENTURY GREEK PLAYWRIGHT SOPHOCLES (SAHF-uh-kleez) [1]

The Greeks Thales (THAY-leez) and Anaximander (uh-NAK-suh-MAN-der), pioneering philosophers and scientists, had the great fortune to grow up in the prosperous city of Miletus (my-LEET-uhs), a great commercial center on the southwestern coast of Anatolia (modern Turkey). For hundreds of years Miletus had served as a crossroads for the entire region, mingling Greek and foreign cultures. Young men like Thales and Anaximander haunted the bustling docks and seaside bars, listening to the reports of sailors returning from distant shores and of travelers from foreign lands, as well as the ideas of Persian and other non-Greek residents. Milesian merchants sent ships to the far corners of the Mediterranean carrying the treasured wool developed by Miletus sheep breeders and the fine furniture produced by its cabinetmakers. Along the shores of the Black Sea Milesians established settlements that supplied fish and wheat that enriched the city's traders.

Milesians benefited from cultural cross-fertilization fostered by trade. Some sailors brought scraps of learning from older societies such as Egypt and Mesopotamia. This intermingling led to pioneering thinking about geography and cartography. Inspired by the maritime trade, Thales, around 600 C.E., worked out a geometrical system to calculate the position of a ship at sea. Fifty years later Thales' student, Anaximander, made the first map of the Mediterranean world and the first Greek chart of the heavens, and five decades after that Hecataeus (HEK-a-TAU-us) of Miletus published a map of the world known to the Greeks, from India to Spain. Miletus matured into a great intellectual center and a meeting place for the Greek and Persian worlds.

The Greeks such as those at Miletus developed not only a penchant for maritime trade and an understanding of regional geography but also a unique society on the rocky shores of the Aegean Sea. In cities such as Miletus and Athens, they introduced many ideas and institutions that endured through the centuries. The view of humanity's greatness offered by Sophocles in the opening quotation reflects an obsession with individuality and freedom that made the Greeks role models for modern democracies, where people today engage in some of the same debates as did the Greeks about the interplay between individual freedom and the community. Sophocles also shared the bias, common in classical times, that men, not women, were responsible for human progress and should dominate society. But the Greek achievements that we know today are only part of the story. Connected to a wider world through cities like Miletus, the Greeks flourished by participating in regional trade, colonizing other territories, and borrowing ideas from neighboring societies. This world included another creative society and even greater regional power, the Persian Empire, which dominated the eastern Mediterranean and western Asia and also introduced many innovations that affected the lives of many peoples. Ultimately the rival Greek and Persian societies were brought together in a political union that extended Greek culture into Asia and Africa but also added Persian culture to the mix. The resulting Hellenistic Age was an era of unprecedented cross-cultural sharing.

FOCUS QUESTIONS

1. How did the Persians acquire and maintain their empire?

2. How did democracy develop in Greece, and what were its advantages and inadequacies?

3. What were some features of Greek philosophy and science?

4. In what ways did Persians and Greeks encounter and influence each other?

5. What impact did Alexander the Great and his conquests have on world history?

 # The Persians and Their Empire

How did the Persians acquire and maintain their empire?

Although its period of greatest political influence lasted only two centuries, the Persian Empire played an important role in world history. The Persians established a larger empire than any people before them. Theirs was also the first large multicultural empire in Eurasia, encompassing Anatolian Greeks, Phoenicians, Hebrews, Egyptians, Mesopotamians, and Indians. Domination of the east-west trade routes made the empire the meeting ground of the early classical world. The Persians also tried unsuccessfully to conquer Greece. Their wars with Greece and their empire building in western Asia paved the way for the later rule of the Greek Alexander the Great and his successors. Finally, the Persians fostered an influential new religion.

Geography and the Early Persians

The Persian homeland was located on a plateau just north of the Persian Gulf (see Map 6.1 on page 148). Overland networks for traders and migrants connecting Mesopotamia and Anatolia to India and Central Asia passed through Persia, and cities emerged along the trade routes. Travelers between Mesopotamia and India encountered many mountains and deserts. For example, the area between the Black and Caspian Seas contained the Caucasus Mountains, an area of much linguistic diversity but also closely linked to Persia historically.

Various pastoral societies on the Persian plateau competed for power. Two of these, the Indo-European Medes (MEEDZ)

and the Persians, had sent tribute payments to the powerful Assyrian Empire. By 600 B.C.E. the Persians were living in southeastern Iran under their own ruling family but were subjects of the Medes, who became the dominant regional power after they joined with the Babylonians in 612 B.C.E. to overthrow the Assyrians (see Chronology: Persia, 1000–334 B.C.E.). The Median Empire extended from Anatolia in the west to Afghanistan in the east. But the Medes were soon overshadowed by the Persians.

Building a Regional Empire

The Persian Empire, usually known as **Achaemenid** (a-KEY-muh-nid) Persia after the ruling family, was an extraordinary achievement. At its peak, it extended from the Indus Valley in the east to Libya in the west and from the Black, Caspian (KASS-pee-uhn), and Aral (AR-uhl) Seas in the north to the Nile valley in the south. This empire was created by a series of four kings. Cyrus (SY-ruhs) II (r. 550–530 B.C.E.), better known as Cyrus the Great, began the expansion. Cyrus and his successors, Cambyses (kam-BY-seez) II (r. 530–522 B.C.E.), Darius (duh-RY-uhs) I (r. 521–486 B.C.E.), and Xerxes (ZUHRK-seez) I (r. 486–465 B.C.E.), conquered vast territories and created an autocratic but effective and tolerant government. They established a model for later Middle Eastern empires and challenged the Greeks in the west. But they also suffered some setbacks in this empire building.

Achaemenid The ruling family of the classical Persian Empire.

CHRONOLOGY

	Greece	Persia	Hellenistic World
600 B.C.E.	**ca. 594 B.C.E.** Solon's reforms in Athens	**550–530 B.C.E.** Kingship of Cyrus the Great **525–523 B.C.E.** Conquest of Egypt **521–486 B.C.E.** Kingship of Darius I	
500 B.C.E.	**499–479 B.C.E.** Greco-Persian Wars **460–429 B.C.E.** Periclean era in Athens **431–404 B.C.E.** Peloponnesian War		
400 B.C.E.			**338 B.C.E.** Macedonian conquest of Greece **336–323 B.C.E.** Reign of Alexander the Great **330 B.C.E.** Occupation of Persia

The Foundations of Empire

Cyrus the Great was the real founder of the Persian Empire. In 550 B.C.E. he overthrew the Median king to become the "king of the Medes and Persians." By 539 he had conquered Mesopotamia, Syria, Palestine, Lydia (LID-ee-uh) (a kingdom in the western part of Anatolia), and all the Greek cities in Anatolia that had prospered under the loose and pro-trade rule of the Lydians. In one decade Cyrus had built an empire stretching from the Aegean to Central Asia. As much diplomat as soldier, Cyrus followed moderate policies in the conquered territories, making only modest demands for tribute. After conquering Babylonia, Cyrus issued a proclamation on a cylinder, which some historians interpret as the world's first charter of human rights: "Protect this land from rancor, from foes, from falsehood, and from drought." Cyrus claimed that the main Babylonian god, Marduk (MAHR-dook), ordered him to help the Babylonians by becoming their ruler and bringing them "justice and righteousness," boasting that he and Marduk hence "saved Babylon from oppression."[2] Under Cyrus's authority, the Jews taken to Babylon by the Assyrians were allowed to return to Palestine and rebuild their temple.

Cyrus was killed in 530 B.C.E. while campaigning against nomads east of the Aral Sea. He was replaced by his son Cambyses II, who had learned to accept cultural differences while being governor of Babylonia. Cambyses II subjugated Egypt in 525 B.C.E. and wisely presented himself to the ruling class of priests as a new Egyptian ruler instead of a foreign conqueror. He carved in a granite slab that he would bring stability, good fortune, health, and gladness while ruling Egypt forever.

Cambyses' successor and distant cousin, Darius I, faced new challenges. For one thing, he was a usurper who had seized power at the age of twenty-eight. Not a modest man, he boasted that "over and above my thinking power and understanding, I am a good warrior, horseman, bowman, spear-

man."[3] Darius began his reign by crushing a revolt in Egypt. He spread Persian power east and west, even annexing the Sind region in northwestern India, and he claimed that within his territories he cherished good people, rooted out the bad, and prevented people from killing each other (see Map 6.1). To

CHRONOLOGY

Persia, 1000–334 B.C.E.

ca. 1000	Life of Zoroaster
640	Persians become vassals of Medes
550–530	Kingship of Cyrus the Great
547–546	Conquest of Lydia
530–522	Kingship of Cambyses II
525–523	Conquest of Egypt
521–486	Kingship of Darius I
518	Persian conquest of Indus Valley
499	Rebellion by Ionian Greeks against Persian rule
499–479	Greco-Persian Wars
486–465	Kingship of Xerxes
404	Egyptian independence from Persia
334	Conquest of Persian Empire by Alexander the Great

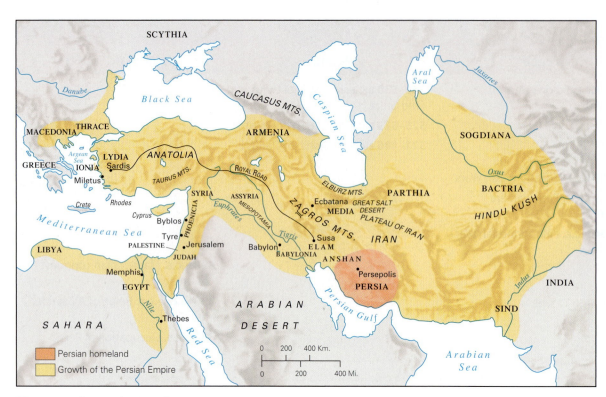

Map 6.1   The Persian Empire, ca. 500 B.C.E.
At its height around 500 B.C.E., the Persians controlled a huge empire that included northern Greece, Egypt, and most of Western Asia from the Mediterranean coast to the Indus River in India.

promote justice and ensure his posterity as a great lawgiver, Darius also supervised the organization and codification of Egyptian law. In 519 he fashioned a law code for Babylonia that basically reaffirmed Hammurabi's laws made almost 1,500 years earlier.

The Persians were among the classical world's greatest engineers and builders. For example, to forge closer links with Egypt, Darius completed the first Suez Canal, an amazing engineering achievement that briefly connected the Mediterranean and the Red Seas. The channel was 125 miles long and 150 feet wide. In 539 Darius began the building of a new capital at Persepolis (puhr-SEP-uh-luhs). This spectacular city was centered on a massive stone terrace, on which stood monumental royal buildings. The city's architecture and decoration were drawn from many traditions, including Egyptian, Mesopotamian, and Greek, and its craftsmen and workers included Egyptians, Greeks, Hittites, and Mesopotamians.

Challenges to Persian Power Darius and his successors eventually encountered some major problems. In 520 and 513 Darius campaigned unsuccessfully against the Scythians (SITH-ee-uhnz), warlike Indo-European pastoral nomads whose territory stretched from southern Ukraine and Russia eastward to Mongolia. Skilled horsemen and master workers of gold and bronze, the Scythians were among the Central Asians whose interactions with settled farmers helped shape Eurasian history. They had both fought and traded with the Greek trading cities. Later, the Scythians were one of the few peoples to defeat the formidable armies of Alexander the Great.

A more serious defeat came with the first Greco-Persian War, in which the tiny disunited Greek states turned back the world's most powerful empire. Persians and peninsular Greeks were rivals for regional power, but many Greeks lived in Persian territories, including merchants and political exiles as far east as Mesopotamia. Inspired by Scythian resistance to Darius and concerned about losing trade to rivals, at the beginning of the fifth century B.C.E. some Greek cities on the Ionian (eye-OH-nee-uhn) coast of Anatolia rebelled against Persian control (see Map 6.1). In response Darius decided to go further west and attack the cities on the Greek peninsula that supported the Ionian Greek rebels. The Greek historian Herodotus (heh-ROD-uh-tuhs) reported that a Persian general favored expansion because Europe was blessed with trees of all sorts and a very fertile soil, which only the Persian king was worthy of possessing. While the Persians failed to occupy most of peninsular Greece, they reclaimed the Ionian Greek cities, brutally punishing the most rebellious such as Miletus. Darius then turned to favoring democratic forces in Ionian cities, a tactical move he hoped would inspire democrats in the peninsula to replace anti-Persian conservatives and cooperate with Persian aims.

His hopes proved unrealistic. Xerxes, the son of Darius, tried again to conquer the Greeks in 480 B.C.E. He attacked with a huge army and naval force, and a fierce two-year struggle resulted. Perhaps Xerxes' most effective ally was Queen Artemisia (AHRT-uh-MIZH-ee-uh) of the Ionian Greek city

Bas relief of Darius and Xerxes Holding Court   This relief was carved in one of the palaces at the Persian capital of Persepolis.   (Oriental Institute, University of Chicago, Photo #P57121)

of Halicarnassus (hal-uh-kar-NASS-uhs), who was praised for her bravery, daring, and the wise counsel she gave the Persian king. But the Persian thrust failed, and Xerxes returned home. Xerxes still held a large chunk of the Greek world, including the Ionian states, and he regained control of Egypt, so he could rightly boast that he was still "the king of kings." However, defeat in this second Greco-Persian war was a turning point in Persian history.

Imperial Policies and Networks

Unlike their Assyrian and Babylonian predecessors, the Persian empire builders used laws, economic policies, and tolerance toward the conquered to rule successfully, and many people benefited from the peace that Persian rule provided for two centuries. Leading citizens came from many backgrounds. Generals might be Medes, Armenians, Greeks, Egyptians, or Kurds (curds), a people living in the mountains just north of Persia and Mesopotamia. Some of the Persian techniques were imitated by their successors, including the Greeks and Romans, when they created even larger imperial structures several centuries later.

The Persians followed and improved upon the systematic bureaucracy first used by the Assyrians. Although their power was in theory absolute, Persian kings were expected to consult with important nobles and judges. Each of the twenty-three Persian provinces was governed by a **satrap** (SAY-trap)

("protector of the kingdom"), an official who ruled according to established laws and procedures and paid a fixed amount of taxes to the king each year. The Persians had several grand capitals, including Babylon and Susa (SOO-zuh) in Mesopotamia, before Persepolis was completed. Darius also set up courts with permanent judges.

Communication between imperial officials was aided by the "royal road" stretching 1,700 miles from east to west. A messenger of the king could travel the road by horse in nineteen days by exchanging horses at a series of stations along the way. The Persians became famous for building roads and then protecting those who traveled them. Herodotus marveled at the communication network, writing that "neither snow, nor rain, nor heat, nor darkness of night prevents these couriers from completing their designated stages with utmost speed."[4] Today that is the motto of the United States Postal Service.

The highways promoted economic growth and exchange, a second Achaemenid practice that strengthened their empire. For instance, Darius minted coins, a practice derived from the Lydians. The use of standard weights and measures, along with a currency of recognized value, made trade easier throughout the empire. In addition, the Persian rulers did not steal the wealth of the lands they conquered, but allowed them to continue to engage in and benefit from the same economic activities as before. Phoenicia, for example, continued its Mediterranean trade. The Persians gained their revenue from land taxes, road tolls, and taxes on the production and consumption of goods. To open new networks for exchanging goods and technologies, Darius sent an expedition to visit India. It returned by sailing around Arabia to Suez (SOO-ez). This expedition laid the foundation for the conquest of the southern Indus River Valley and also more maritime trade.

---

satrap ("protector of the kingdom")   A Persian official who ruled according to established laws and procedures and paid a fixed amount of taxes to the emperor each year.

Perhaps most crucial to their imperial success, the Persians generally treated the people they conquered with respect, allowing them to maintain their own social and religious institutions. In Egypt, for instance, Cambyses was a pharaoh, not a Persian ruler. Similarly, Cyrus sought the approval of the local god Marduk in Babylon in claiming ancient titles, announcing that he was king of the universe and of Babylon, Sumer, and Akkad. The Persians prided themselves on their ability to unify the vastly different peoples of western Asia under the "king of kings," a title that recognized the existence of other rulers whose limited rights in their own territories were respected. For this reason, many Greeks fought for Persia in the Persian-Greek Wars.

The Persians also utilized various official languages. Eventually, Aramaic (ar-uh-MAY-ik), spoken by many peoples of western Asia, became the official language. Most official documents were written in Aramaic using the Phoenician alphabet. Greek also became widely used as a written language in the western empire. Herodotus reported of the Persians that "there is no nation which so readily adopts foreign customs. They have taken the dress of the Medes and in war they wear the Egyptian breastplate. As soon as they hear of any luxury, they instantly make it their own."[5]

Zoroaster and Persian Religion

The Persians made another distinct contribution to later world history in their promotion of **Zoroastrianism** (zo-ro-ASS-tree-uh-niz-uhm), a religion founded by Zoroaster (whose name means "With Golden Camels") that later became the state religion of Persia. Some of the key ideas in Judaism, Christianity, and Islam are foreshadowed by, and perhaps even derived from, this early Persian religion. The prophet Zoroaster was one of the first non-Hebrew religious leaders to challenge the prevailing polytheism of his day. Although he is usually thought to have lived between 630 and 550 B.C.E., at the beginning of the Eurasian Axial Age, many scholars believe he lived much earlier, between 1400 and 900 B.C.E. Zoroaster may have been a priest in the early Persian religion, which was closely related to the religion of the Aryans who migrated to India, and the language of his writings and the *Rig Veda* have much in common.

In contrast to the polytheism of other Persians, Zoroaster had a monotheistic vision. He believed in one supreme god, **Ahura Mazda** (ah-HOOR-uh-MAZZ-duh) (the "Wise Lord"), who was opposed by an evil spirit, a Satan-like figure who was the source of lies, cowardice, misery, and other forms of evil (see Witness to the Past: Good, Evil, and Monotheism in Zoroastrian Thought). Zoroaster speculated that Ahura Mazda allowed humans to freely choose between himself and evil,

between heaven and hell. By serving Ahura Mazda, men and women were serving the spirit of ultimate goodness and truth while simultaneously improving the world. At the end of time, Zoroaster believed, there would be a final judgment at which Ahura Mazda would win a final victory over the spirit of evil. At that time, even hell would come to an end.

Many core Zoroastrian ideas, especially the notion of a contest between a good God and an evil spirit or devil and the corresponding belief in heaven and hell, were developed in later Jewish scriptures, and then in the sacred writings of both Christians and Muslims. The Jews may have adopted some of their ideas about good and evil, the afterlife, and a last judgment from Zoroastrians while the Jews were held captive in Babylon (586–539 B.C.E.). The Zoroastrian watchwords of "good thoughts, good words, good deeds" became key ideas of other religions, including Christianity and Buddhism. Darius I did much to spread Zoroastrianism. He publicly attributed his victories to Ahura Mazda, whose name figured prominently in carved stone memorials honoring him for creating earth, sky, and humankind. While Zoroastrianism was displaced in western Asia by Christianity and, later, Islam, the faith lives on today among small groups in Iran as well as in the wealthy Parsee (PAR-see) minority in western India, descendants of Persian Zoroastrians.

Social Life and Gender Relations

The Persians did not develop as politically diversified a society as did the Greeks. No class of active citizens helped make political decisions at the imperial level. At the top of the system were the nobles, many of them warriors who had been granted large estates by the king, followed by priests, merchants, and bankers. In Babylonian cities ruled by Persia these citizens met in formal assemblies to make important judicial decisions, and routine administration was done by councils of twenty-five leading men. Zoroastrian priests schooled the princes of the noble families to prepare for government careers. The middle class included brewers, butchers, bakers, carpenters, potters, and coppersmiths. Affluent Persians enjoyed feasting and wine drinking.

Peasants and slaves constituted the bottom of the social structure. Over the centuries, as wealthy landowners acquired their land, more and more peasant farmers were impoverished and became poor renters or sharecroppers, bound to the land. There were also some slaves, mainly debtors, criminals, and prisoners of war. The slave population filled a variety of functions. Some were apprenticed in trades, and others were allowed to take up business.

Persian society was patriarchal. Herodotus reported that Persian men believed that the greatest proof of masculinity was to father many sons. Persian society was also polygynous: many men, especially at upper levels, had several wives. Persian women were usually kept secluded in harems and many probably veiled themselves, an ancient practice in western Asia. But some queens and other noble women exercised strong influences on their husbands, and many even controlled large estates. Herodotus commented that some queens were more outgoing and aggressive than their husbands. A few women

Zoroastrianism A monotheistic religion founded by the Persian Zoroaster, and later the state religion of Persia. Its notion of one god opposed by the devil may have influenced Judaism and later Christianity.

Ahura Mazda (the "Wise Lord") The one god of Zoroastrianism.

Good, Evil, and Monotheism in Zoroastrian Thought

The Persian thinker Zarathustra, better know today by the name given him by the Greeks, Zoroaster, offered an ethical vision that, he believed, came from God. The early Persians apparently believed in three great gods and many lesser ones, but Zoroaster preached that only one of these, *Ahura Mazda* (The Wise Lord), was the supreme deity in the universe, responsible for creation and the source of all goodness. But a rival entity, *Angra Mainyu* (Hostile Spirit), embodied evil and was the source of all misery and sin. Zoroaster asked people to join the cosmic battle for good and worship Ahura Mazda while opposing evil and Angra Mainyu, referred to as the Liar. This excerpt outlining Zoroaster's beliefs comes from one of the devotional hymns, the *Gathas*, contained within the Zoroastrian holy scriptures. It was written down in final form centuries after Zoroaster's life but was probably based on earlier writings by the prophet or his disciples.

Then shall I recognize you as strong and holy, Mazda, when by the hand in which you yourself hold the destinies that you will assign to the Liar [Angra Mainyu] and the Righteous [Ahura Mazda] . . . the might of Good Thought shall come to me.

As the holy one I recognized you, Mazda Ahura, when I saw you in the beginning at the birth of Life, when you made actions and words to have their reward—evil for the evil, a good Destiny for the good—through your wisdom when creation shall reach its goal. At which goal you will come with your holy Spirit, O Mazda, with Dominion, at the same with Good Thought, by whose action the settlements [human societies] will prosper through Right. . . .

"I am Zarathustra, a true foe to the Liar, to the utmost of my power, but a powerful support would I be to the Righteous, that I may attain the future things of the infinite Dominion, so I praise and proclaim you, Mazda. . . ."

As the holy one I recognized you, Mazda Ahura, when Good Thought [a good spirit created by Ahura Mazda] came to me, when the still mind taught me to declare what is best: "Let not

a man seek again and again to please the Liars, for they make all the righteous enemies."

And thus Zarathustra himself . . . chooses the spirit of thine that is holiest, Mazda. May Right be embodied, full of life and strength! May Piety abide in the Dominion where the sun shines! May Good Thought give destiny to men according to their works [good actions]!

This I ask you, tell me truly, Ahura. . . . Who determined the path of sun and stars? Who is it by whom the moon waxes and wanes again? . . . Who upheld the Earth beneath and the firmament from falling? Who the water and the plants? Who yoked swiftness to winds and clouds? . . .

This I ask you, tell me truly, Ahura—whether we shall drive the Lie away from us to those who being full of disobedience will not strive after fellowship with Right, nor trouble themselves with counsel of Good Thought. . . .

I will speak of that which Mazda Ahura, the all-knowing, revealed to me first in this earthly life. Those of you that put not into practice this word as I think and utter it, to them shall be woe at the end of life. I will speak of that which the Holiest declared to me as the word that is best for mortals to obey: he, Mazda Ahura said, "They who at my bidding render [Zarathustra] obedience, shall all attain Welfare and Immortality by the actions of the Good Spirit." In immortality shall the soul of the righteous be joyful, in perpetuity shall be the torments of the Liars [the followers of evil]. All this does Mazda Ahura appoint by his Dominion.

THINKING ABOUT THE READING

1. What supreme powers did Zoroaster attribute to Ahura Mazda?

2. How did Zoroaster expect individuals to work for good and combat evil?

3. What fate awaited those who chose the path of evil?

Source: Yasnas 43–45, in James Hope Moulton, *Early Zoroastrianism* (London: Williams and Norgate, 1913), 364–370.

---

became independently wealthy. For instance, one entrepreneur of commoner origins, Irdabama, was a major landowner who not only controlled a large labor force of several hundred but also operated her own grain and wine business. Egyptian women kept many of the rights they enjoyed before Persian rule, and most marriages there were monogamous.

The Decline of Achaemenid Persia

Although the Persian empire was not finally conquered until the army of Alexander the Great defeated Persian forces in 330 B.C.E., the seeds of decline were planted more than a cen-

tury earlier when the policies of Xerxes I, especially a policy of heavy taxation of the satrapies, began to weaken support for Persian rule. Vast amounts of pure silver paid as taxes were sent to the Persian capital. By 424 B.C.E. the Persian Empire was suffering from civil unrest caused by fights within the Achaemenid family, currency inflation, and difficulty collecting taxes.

Under Xerxes and his successors, the wise policies of Cyrus and Darius, which promoted trade and treated non-Persians with respect, were gradually reversed. Many merchants and landlords were ruined by having to borrow money at very high interest rates. At the same time, fewer attempts were made to include other ethnic groups in the governing of the empire.

Some regions rebelled. For example, Egypt ended Persian control in 404 B.C.E. and restored pharaonic rule. Thus support for the increasingly remote kings weakened long before the superior armies of the Macedonian conqueror Alexander brought an end to Achaemenid Persia and its once great empire.

SECTION SUMMARY

- The Persian Empire, centered on a trade crossroads, lasted for only two centuries, but it was larger than any empire that preceded it.
- The Persian Empire suffered several setbacks, including an unsuccessful campaign against the Scythians and repeated failure to completely conquer Greece.
- The Persians often won the support of peoples they had conquered through their respect for native cultures and their institution of the rule of law.
- The monotheistic Persian religion, Zoroastrianism, may have contributed some key ideas to Judaism, Christianity, and Islam.
- Though the Persian Empire was conquered by Alexander the Great in 330 B.C.E., it had begun to decline over a century earlier.

CHRONOLOGY

The Greeks, 750–338 B.C.E.

ca. 750–550	Greek colonization in Mediterranean, Black Sea
ca. 594	Solon's reforms in Athens
561–527	Peisistratus tyrant in Athens
507	Athenian democracy under Cleisthenes
499–479	Greco-Persian Wars
477	Founding of Delian League
469–399	Life of Socrates
ca. 460–429	Era of Pericles in Athens
431–404	Peloponnesian War
428–347	Life of Plato
384–322	Life of Aristotle
338	Philip of Macedonia's conquest of Greece

✦ The Emergence of the Greeks

How did democracy develop in Greece, and what were its advantages and inadequacies?

Historians of Persia's greatest rival, Greece, have tended to emphasize Greek achievements, especially the birth of democratic thought, but these were only part of a complex, often conflicted society. The Greeks had to struggle to forge democracy. How much of their culture the Greeks created and how much they adopted from others remains subject to debate. Whatever the truth, the Mediterranean was a zone of interaction for peoples living around its rim, and by 700 B.C.E. the Greeks had become active participants in maritime trade. Soon this activity led to prosperity for many Greek cities and new forms of government.

Cities and Citizenship

The Greek world was shaped by varied influences. On the Greek peninsula, a geographical context of mountains, coastal plains, and islands encouraged the development of a dozen or so major city-states rather than one centralized state. This same context also stimulated maritime trade, which was the main reason for the growth and prosperity of most Greek cities between 800 and 500 B.C.E. A growing population, a shortage of good farmland at home, and commercial interests led many Greeks to leave their home cities (see Chronology: The Greeks, 750–338 B.C.E.). In what is called the Greek diaspora

(dye-ASS-puh-ruh), meaning dispersion or spreading out, they established some 250 new settlements along the Ionian coast, around the Black Sea, in Italy, and even as far west as the Mediterranean coasts of what is today France and Spain (see Map 6.2). Trade and migration opened the Greeks to new ideas. By the sixth century B.C.E. Greeks were even visiting and living in Egypt, where they worshiped Egyptian gods under Greek names.

Prosperity led to a new conception of the city and the citizen's role in it. The result was a unique Greek political unit, the **polis** (POE-lis), a city-state that embraced nearby rural areas whose agricultural surplus helped support the urban population. The polis, whether in the peninsula or the Greek diaspora, became the major institution of classical Greek life, a living community that gave citizens a sense of personal identity and meaning. All business, from building a new temple to making war, was decided by the free male citizens meeting in an open assembly. Even loyalty to one's family or clan was less important than loyalty to the polis. The worst punishment a Greek could suffer was being asked to leave the polis. Some Greeks committed suicide rather than face ostracism.

City-states competed fiercely with each other, including in sports events. The Olympic Games, begun in the eighth century B.C.E., were associated with a religious festival to honor the god Zeus (ZOOSS). Each polis sent athletes, both men and

---

polis   A Greek city-state that embraced nearby rural areas, whose agricultural surplus then helped support the urban population.

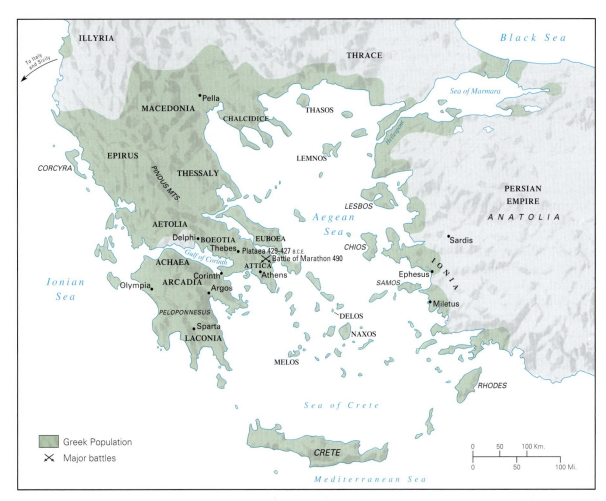

Map 6.2 Classical Greece, ca. 450 B.C.E.
Greek settlements, divided into rival city-states, occupied not only the Greek peninsula but also Crete and western Anatolia. Two alliances headed by Athens and Sparta respectively fought each other in the Peloponnesian War (431-404 B.C.E.).

Online Study Center **Improve Your Grade** Interactive Map: Ancient Greece

unmarried women, who competed naked in track and field events or personal contests of strength, such as wrestling. The idea was to win, even if it meant cheating. The Greek athlete might have viewed our modern concept of a "good loser" as somewhat bizarre.

Not all inhabitants of the polis were equal. Many cities developed **oligarchy** (AHL-uh-gar-kee), rule by a small group of wealthy leaders. As much as 80 percent of the population in most Greek cities, including women, slaves, children, and resident foreigners, were not citizens and thus had no right to participate in political life by voting or holding office. Even among the citizens, members of old, aristocratic families were treated with greater respect than others. Most Greek cities, despite their elected assemblies, were long dominated by a monarch or other executives who were supervised by a council of aristocrats.

Trade, Warfare, and Politics

By the seventh century two factors had weakened aristocratic power. One was the growth of trade. Aristocrats generally scorned trade in favor of the wealth to be gained from the land. Moreover, trade helped create wealth for other citizens, allowing them to compete with the upper class. The second factor was the development of a new battle formation that relied on infantry more than the aristocracy-dominated cavalry. By this time, the city of Sparta had perfected an infantry formation, the phalanx (FAY-langks), that was quickly adopted by other cities. The phalanx consisted of a square of soldiers eight wide and eight deep that moved in unison. Each man was protected with heavy armor and carried either a short sword or a nine-foot spear. Each soldier bought his own armor and weapons. With this development Greek armies became citizen-armies, not paid professional forces. As men other than aristocrats paid to risk their lives for their polis, they wanted a greater role in governing it.

---

oligarchy Rule by a small group of wealthy leaders.

In sum, a new military system combined with population expansion and increased wealth from trade with the Greek cities in Ionia contributed to the rise of democracy, most notably in the city-state of Athens. But the Greeks also fought many wars with each other and other enemies, and these struggles undermined some of the Greek political ideals.

Reform, Tyranny, and Democracy in Athens

Between 600 and 350 B.C.E. some Greeks tried to combine the contradictory ideas that people are politically free and that they owe their loyalty to the community. The resulting tension was not as great as it would be for citizens of modern democracies, since the Greeks did not envision anything like "perfect" liberty. Nevertheless, some Greeks discovered how people could live with each other without being controlled by gods or kings, and many cities developed notions of political freedom and equality that were radical for that era, or even for ours. Although reserved for adult male citizens only, these ideas had never been seen before.

The most dramatic political changes occurred in Athens, a polis on the eastern Greek peninsula of Attica. Athens became progressively more democratic, partly a result of a crisis. The soil on which Athenians grew wheat was wearing out, and as farmers produced less, they borrowed money and went deeply into debt. As the bad harvests continued, farmers were reduced to selling themselves and their families into slavery. The poor demanded reform.

Around 594 B.C.E. the Athenians elected Solon (SOH-luhn), a general, poet, and merchant, to lead the city and rewrite the old constitution. He canceled the debts of the poor, forbid enslavement for default of debts, and made wealth rather than birth the criterion for membership on the council of hereditary aristocrats who controlled the city. Solon also established a new Council of 400 to review issues before they came before an Assembly of Citizens, which now served as a court of appeals where people, rich or poor, could bring a case to court. Solon boasted of his attempts to gather back the common people and set straight laws alike for lowly and lords, in order to prevent mob violence and avoid civil war. While many of Solon's reforms were progressive, he also reduced the freedom of women. For example, laws now gave fathers the right to sell into slavery daughters who lost their virginity before marriage.

The Athenian path to a more democratic system came in several stages, from reform to tyranny to democracy. Solon's reforms failed to please either side in this social and economic struggle. The poor wanted him to take land from the rich and redistribute it to them, while the aristocrats resented their loss of power. After his death tensions returned, allowing Peisistratus (pie-SIS-truht-uhs) (r. 561–527 B.C.E.) to seize power as a **tyrant**, not necessarily a brutal ruler but someone who ruled outside the law. Many Greek cities were governed by tyrants in this period. Peisistratus appealed directly to the poor, giving some of them land he had confiscated from aristocratic estates. He also aided the economy and culture of Athens by launching a building program, one result of which was an aqueduct to bring water directly to the city center.

Another aristocrat, Cleisthenes (KLICE-thuh-neez), finally established genuine democracy in Athens in 507 B.C.E. Instead of emphasizing noble birth or wealth as a criterion of citizenship, Cleisthenes organized people geographically. He created geographical units that chose people by lot to serve in a new Council of 500, which submitted legislation to the Assembly for approval. The Assembly consisted of 40,000 citizens; about 6,000 generally showed up for meetings, and these selected by lot the city officials. Cleisthenes' version of Athenian democracy was extended in the mid-fifth century when the power of the aristocrats was further reduced and lower-income citizens were allowed to serve as officials. Euripides (you-RIP-uh-deez) described the system in his play, *The Suppliant Woman*: "The city is free, and ruled by no one man. The people reign, in annual succession. They do not yield power to the rich; the poor man has an equal share in it."[6]

Although the majority of people were excluded from political life, for those who were citizens, the system was more radically democratic than most modern governments. The

Narrative Drawing on Pottery The Francois vase, made around 570 B.C.E., is considered a masterpiece of narrative drawing on pottery, with fine detail and vivid coloring. It shows scenes of battle. (Scala/Art Resource, NY)

---

tyrant Someone who ruled a Greek polis outside the law, not necessarily a brutal ruler.

Athenians believed that ordinary citizens could serve in any government positions except as military officers, and they chose representatives by lot rather than by election, believing the latter was too divisive. However, only a small aristocracy of adult males enjoyed these rights. Moreover, many Greeks did not think that democracy of any type was a good thing. One disgruntled Athenian conservative, known as the Old Oligarch, complained that reforms gave more power to the poor and the common people than to the "respectable elements" of society.

The Spartan System

In the Peloponnese (PELL-eh-puh-NEESE), a peninsula that constitutes the southern half of modern Greece, the land-locked city-state of Sparta (SPART-uh) followed a course of development much different from that of Athens (see Map 6.2). In the eighth century B.C.E., when the Spartans, like other Greeks, found themselves short of land, they decided to conquer their neighbors rather than establish overseas colonies. Spartans saw military power as essential to their prestige and influence. After conquering neighboring Greeks, they made them agricultural slaves who worked the land for Spartan overlords. The slaves had no political or human rights and could be killed by a Spartan almost at will. Since slaves outnumbered Spartans ten to one, Sparta developed a rigid military state to control its subject population. Sparta's government limited participation. Spartan citizens were all male, since women had no political rights. They were led by two kings and a Council of Elders composed of twenty-eight men over age sixty who were elected for life by an Assembly of all citizens over thirty. The Assembly also elected five magistrates who controlled foreign policy, presided at the Assembly, and kept watch over the slaves. The Assembly could vote only yes or no to measures prepared for it by the Council of Elders and the king. Spartans older than thirty referred to themselves as equals and considered their system a perfect aristocratic democracy.

The Spartans discouraged independence of thought or behavior. Spartan boys who seemed physically unfit were generally taken to a remote rural area and allowed to die. The other boys were given a rigid military training in barracks from age six and taught that self-discipline and courage were the highest virtues. One famous Spartan legend tells of a young boy who found a small fox and concealed it under his shirt while engaged in military drill. While standing quietly at attention, the boy suddenly fell over dead. The fox had eaten into his vital organs, but self-discipline had kept him from crying out in pain. From ages twenty to thirty, Spartan males served in the army, and they were allowed to live at home with their wives only after this time.

Spartan women acquired a higher status than other Greek women, and their husbands' frequent absences from home allowed some of them to acquire wealth. Athenian men criticized Spartan women for their independence, portraying them as greedy and licentious. The playwright Euripides scolded the "Spartan maidens, allowed out of doors with the young men, running and wrestling in their company, with naked thighs."[7]

Male Athenian observers complained that Spartan women owned some 40 percent of all the city-state's land, giving them too much freedom from male control.

Greek Thought, Culture, and Society

What were some features of Greek philosophy and science?

When people today think of the classical Greeks, they envision the "golden age" of Athenian democracy, with philosophers debating the meaning of life and thinkers pondering the mysteries of science. The Greeks are often credited with inventing academic fields like history, biology, and geometry. Like people today, they debated how populations should be ruled, how leaders should be chosen, and how youngsters should be educated. But the Greek society modern people admire was also far from egalitarian and had many unattractive features.

Religion, Rationalism, and Science

The Greeks may have been practical people, but they were also concerned with the supernatural realm and worshiped a multitude of gods. The gods and legends introduced by the Homeric epics profoundly shaped Greek thinking and values. Greek religion was similar to that of most other early Indo-European peoples and probably also owed something to the Egyptians and Phoenicians. A group of chief gods and goddesses, along with many lesser ones, represented various natural and human activities. The leader of the traditional Greek gods was Zeus, a sky-god who guaranteed the natural and social order. His wife, Hera (HEER-uh), represented legal marriage and the family. Poseidon (puh-SIDE-uhn), the brother of Zeus, was the lord of the sea. Athena (uh-THEEN-uh), Zeus's favorite daughter and the patron of Athens, was the goddess of wisdom. Other notable deities were Apollo (uh-PAHL-oh), patron of music, philosophy, and other finer things in life; Dionysus (DIE-uh-NYE-suhs), the god of wine; and Aphrodite (af-ruh-DITE-ee), goddess of sex and fertility.

Although these gods and goddesses were portrayed in human form and were understood to have human virtues and vices, they were also seen as immortal and more powerful than humans. To defy the gods or overstep the bounds set by them was to invite disaster. The Athenian Aeschylus (ESS-kuh-luhs) warned in his play *Prometheus* (pruh-MEE-thee-uhs) *Bound* that no human councils can pass the bounds ordained by Zeus. Proper sacrifices to the gods, usually incorporated into the festivals and official ceremonies of the polis, were thought to guarantee harmony between humans and the heavens.

The Greek interest in the deeper meaning of life also led them to develop a rational approach to the search for truth, and in trying to understand the natural world, they produced some of the greatest thinkers in history. As a result, they joined the Mesopotamians, Egyptians, Indians, and Chinese in laying the ancient and classical foundation for modern science. By the sixth century B.C.E., some Greek thinkers in Ionia and the peninsula began to question supernatural explanations of natural events. The Ionian philosopher Xenophanes (zi-NAHF-uh-neez) was skeptical of the gods:

Mortals deem that the gods are begotten as they [humans] are, and have clothes like theirs and voice and form. Yes, and if oxen and horses or lions had hands, and could paint with their hands, horses would paint the forms of the gods like horses, and oxen like oxen. The Ethiopians make their gods black. The Thracians (THRAY-shuhns) say theirs have blue eyes and red hair.[8]

Creative thought erupted throughout the Greek world. Thales of Miletus (ca. 636–546), whom we met in the chapter opener, was the first person we know of to perceive the universe as orderly and rational and to seek a natural explanation of phenomena rather than attributing them to gods. For example, he asked why an earthquake or solar eclipse happened. Thales' student, Anaximander (611–547), said the first creatures lived in water. He came close to the idea, developed several millennia later, that human beings evolved from lower forms of life. He also argued that only reason could put in order what was commingled. In the fifth century, Democritus (di-MAHK-ruht-uhs) announced his belief that all matter was composed of tiny seeds known as atoms and that these moved, creating different objects. Heracleitus (HER-uh-KLITE-uhs) of Ephasus (EF-uh-suhs) in Ionia declared that the universe is in a constant state of flux and that only change was permanent. He wrote that the cosmos always existed and will exist forever, like a fire eternally smoldering. Hence, everything passes. The Ionian Pythagoras (puh-THAG-uh-ruhs) helped establish the foundations of modern mathematics by emphasizing the number 10 and developing the multiplication tables as well as major mathematical theorems.

These early thinkers laid the foundations of natural science and philosophy by emphasizing the explanatory power of human reason. In the fifth century, Protagoras (Pro-TAG-or-uhs) summarized the new understanding when he claimed that human beings are creatures of great worth and dignity and that therefore human achievements should be measured by human standards. Before that, most people believed that all human actions had to be measured against a divine standard, a belief that many still hold. However, some Greek thinkers also opened the door to the more troubling idea that human standards are relative rather than absolute. The **Sophists** (SAHF-uhsts) emphasized skepticism and the belief that there is no ultimate truth. One wrote that "since the criterion of truth has appeared to be unattainable, it is no longer possible to make positive assertions either about those things which seem to be evident and about those which are non-evident."[9] People have struggled with this twin legacy of Greek thinkers ever since.

Axial Age Philosophy and Thinkers

Views of the Greek contribution to world thought often focus on the specific ideas of three major fifth- and fourth-century Athenian thinkers. The first two, Socrates (SOCK-ruh-teez) and Plato (PLAY-toh), studied the nature of truth; the third, Aristotle (AR-uh-staht-uhl), examined the truth to be found in nature. These men were part of an outpouring of philosophical and religious genius across Eurasia between 600 and 200 B.C.E. that historians often term the Axial Age. From Greece to India to China, the Axial Age thinkers laid the groundwork for the beliefs of classical societies. The ideas of Buddha in India, Confucius in China, Hebrew prophets, Zoroaster, and various Greeks remained influential for many centuries.

Socrates The earliest Greek philosophical giant, the Athenian Socrates (469–399 B.C.E.), believed that "the unexamined life" was not worth living. Shabbily dressed, eccentric, passionate, and indifferent to money and pleasure, he spent much time asking people leading questions that helped them examine the truth of their ideas, an approach called the **Socratic Method**. He asked questions to help people see what he considered the falseness of the Sophists' idea that truth and justice were relative, changing from one polis to another. Socrates believed in absolute truths that, if lived by people, would make them virtuous. But he also was suspicious of democracy, favoring government by the chosen few who had acquired superior knowledge. Later in life Socrates challenged the scientific perspective, arguing against the study of astronomy. Although often credited as the founder of Western moral philosophy, some of his elitist views might be unpopular even today.

For asking so many, often embarrassing, questions and "corrupting the youth," Socrates was condemned to death by the citizens of Athens in 399 B.C.E. The prosecutor said of him: "Socrates is an evil doer and a curious person, searching into things under the earth and above the heavens, and making the worse appear the better, and teaching all this to others." Although he could have secured a lighter sentence or gone into exile, Socrates chose death: he drank the hemlock poison

Sophists Thinkers in classical Greece who emphasized skepticism and the belief that there is no ultimate truth.

Socratic Method The method, introduced by Socrates, of asking people leading questions to help them examine the truth of their ideas.

Socrates This statue, made several centuries after his death, celebrates the Athenian philosopher Socrates, who had a strong influence on the thinking of Greek philosophers who came after him, including his student, Plato. (HIP/Art Resource, NY)

provided for his execution and defiantly proclaimed, "I shall obey God rather than you [and] never cease from the teaching of philosophy."[10] His death made him, in modern eyes at least, a martyr for truth and free expression, although most of his contemporaries may not have viewed him in this way. He was charged with undermining the polis community by denying the common gods and hence the legitimacy of Athens, which was tantamount to treason.

Plato At the time of Socrates' death, his leading pupil, Plato (428–347 B.C.E.), was twenty-eight. Inspired by the impassioned Socrates, Plato became disillusioned with city politics after his mentor's execution. Most of what we know of Socrates comes from Plato, who interpreted and continued his teacher's explorations into the nature of truth. After a sojourn in Egypt, Plato founded a school in Athens that he called the Academy (the source of our word *academic*). Plato elaborated Socrates' belief in ultimate truth, beauty, and goodness. Most humans, he wrote in the *Republic*, are like men chained in a cave who mistake the shadows cast by a fire on the cave wall for reality. Because most of us are ruled by our emotions, we are unable to see that the fire is more real than the shadows it casts. Only a special class, the Guardians, trained to

use reason to control the emotions and will, can understand ultimate truth and goodness. Plato sought a just society in which everyone could play their proper role.

Because he thought most people could not live according to the dictates of reason or distinguish knowledge from mere opinion, Plato favored a democratic government only if the Guardians headed it. Only they, he believed, could be trusted to treat others with justice. Later in his life, Plato retreated from this elitist conception and suggested that strong laws could control democratic excesses. Nevertheless, some charge that Plato's thinking sanctioned dictatorships in which a small group of men claimed special wisdom and virtue.

Aristotle Aristotle (384–322 B.C.E.) was the Athenian philosopher whose ideas seem most similar to ours today. The son of a Greek physician working for the king of Macedonia, Aristotle came to Athens to study philosophy with Plato and eventually founded a school of his own. Like Socrates, he was charged with impiety, but he chose to go into exile. Aristotle offered many enduring insights. Although he distrusted democracy, he encouraged people to pursue their personal desires. But, he warned, a person is the best of all animals only when he has reached his full development, and the worst of all when divorced from justice and law. What makes Aristotle more attractive to many modern thinkers was his pragmatism, since he emphasized how human nature and physical nature worked, rather than exploring the ultimate truths that lay behind our actions.

Aristotle's writings spanned many fields of what we today call the social sciences, humanities, and natural sciences. For example, he was one of the first psychologists, describing human emotions like affection, anger, bravery, fear, hate, joy, and pity. Aristotle was particularly interested in classifying and analyzing the world of nature. He dissected animals, wrote about more than five hundred different animal species, and was the first to classify animals zoologically. His work was a key foundation for both the Western and Islamic scientific traditions. Aristotle also wrote works on logic and ethics, advocating moderation in personal behavior, and studied and designed political systems. In philosophy, he was one of the first people to speculate on **metaphysics**, the broad field that studies the most general concepts and categories underlying people and the world around them (such as "time" and "causation").

Online Study Center Improve Your Grade
Primary Source: Aristotle

Literature

The cultural creativity of Greece, especially of Athens, reflected an atmosphere of dynamism and freedom. Athens attracted many of the great writers and artists because the prosperity derived from a wealthy empire gave many people spending

metaphysics The broad field of philosophy that studies the most general concepts and categories underlying ourselves and the world around us.

money for entertainment. Perhaps the Athenians' most enduring contribution was in drama, which arose from annual religious festivals and was based on historical or mythological themes. Plays were usually performed in outdoor amphitheaters, accompanied by music played on flutes, trumpets, and stringed instruments. Most were tragedies. In Athens, several thousand people a year performed as actors or members of the chorus.

The dramatists had different styles. Aeschylus (525–456), who had fought in the Greco-Persian Wars, emphasized traditional values, probing the relationship of Greeks and their gods. He also explored issues of justice and portrayed the disasters brought by too much pride. Sophocles (ca. 497–406) was a humanist. In his 120 plays he treated emotional issues with restraint. Aristophanes (AR-uh-STAHF-uh-neez) (448–380) took a lighter approach, writing comedies that ridiculed Athenians and their pretensions. For example, in *The Knights*, a general tries to convince an ignorant sausage-seller to unseat the Athenian leader: "To be a leader of the people isn't for learned men, or honest men, but for the ignorant and vile. Don't miss the golden opportunity."[11] Some of his criticism reflected Athenian losses during a terrible war. Even modern readers might wonder why Athenians tolerated his mocking of the city's leaders in that critical time.

Some playwrights offered vivid images of women, especially those who refused to be silenced or abused. In *Agamemnon* (ag-uh-MEM-non), a great tragic drama by Aeschylus, the wife of Agamemnon, the hero of the Trojan War, kills him upon his return for sacrificing their daughter to the gods to get a favorable wind to sail to Troy. In *Medea* (mi-DEE-uh) by Euripides (480–406 B.C.E.), Medea is abandoned by her husband Jason and takes revenge by murdering her two sons by Jason as well as Jason's new wife and father-in-law. At the end of the play she crosses the stage in a fiery chariot, torn by inner conflict but still triumphant.

Greek lyric poets also contributed to literary life, especially in the Ionian cities. They reflected an individualistic and openly intellectual way of thinking. For example, in contrast to Spartan heroism, Archilochus (ahr-KIL-uh-kuhs) defended cowardice. Mocking the Spartan order to their soldiers to "return with your shield—or on it," Archilochus wrote: "Some lucky Thracian has my shield, For, being somewhat flurried, I dropped it by a wayside bush, As from the field I hurried. Thank God, I made it clear away. To blazes with the shield. I'll get another just as good, When next I take the field."[12] Perhaps the most intensely personal poet was Sappho (SAFF-oh), who lived on the Ionian island of Lesbos around 600 B.C.E. A director of a girl's school dedicated to Aphrodite, Sappho wrote passionate love lyrics to her students: "A host of horsemen, some say, is the loveliest sight upon the earth; some say a display of soldiery; some a fleet of ships, but I say it's whomever one loves."[13] Sappho was seen in her times as the equal of Homer as a poet, and her poems were read in the Mediterranean world for at least a thousand years after her death.

Social Life and Gender Relations

The Greeks pursued their individual lives within the larger public sphere of the polis. The differences between social classes and genders were pronounced. Only some enjoyed formal citizenship. Freedom was reserved primarily for males, although women played a larger role than we might suspect. As in other societies in which women were denied a political voice, Greek women exercised power mostly in the family.

Social Classes Greek society consisted, from top to bottom, of free men (only some of whom were citizens), resident foreigners, free women, and slaves. Most free men, if not wealthy landowners or small farmers, worked as laborers, artisans, or shopkeepers. In many Greek cities, there was a large class of resident foreigners, some from other Greek cities and some non-Greeks such as Phoenicians, Lydians, and Syrians. These noncitizens, in Athens about one-third the number of citizens, were primarily merchants, bankers, and artisans. Many acquired considerable wealth, and they were required to serve in the military. Free women could not vote, hold office, or serve on juries, and they were supposed to take no interest in public affairs. Socrates supposedly asked a colleague, Critobulus: "Is there anyone of your acquaintance with whom you have less conversation than your wife?" The reply: "Hardly anyone, I think."[14] Women from elite families generally stayed inside the home, in contrast to many less affluent women.

About one-third of the population in a Greek city consisted of slaves, many of them non-Greeks. Most slaves were captives taken in battle or debtors. Some were not badly treated, though none had any political rights. Aristotle maintained that the system was necessary as long as tools and looms did not work on their own. Slaves were often household servants or paid artisans, but many served as teachers, instructing generations of young people in how to write and play music. Slaves also built some of the great buildings and worked on agricultural plantations owned by aristocrats. Life for many slaves was harsh. They could be tortured and executed for mere suspicion of a crime. The most abused slaves in Athens were those who worked in the nearby silver mines.

Whether free or slave, the poor did most of the work in industry and agriculture. In one drama, the playwright Aristophanes argued that their efforts were needed:

If wealth should distribute equally, no one would practice a craft or skill. Who will work as a smith or a shipwright or a tailor or a wheelwright or a shoemaker or a bricklayer or plough the land or harvest the crops, if you can live in idleness and neglect all this work?[15]

Gender Relations and Families Like the nuclear family system of the modern West but unlike the extended family pattern of many African and Asian societies, most Greek families consisted of a husband, a wife, and children. The principal tasks of women were to feed and clothe their families and to bear and raise children. Every woman brought to marriage a dowry, which a husband was legally required to use to support his wife and children. While a woman did not have the same sexual freedom as men, she could own property, inherit it in the absence of male children, and divorce her husband. Women's participation was also essential in religious festivals. For example, the oracle at the temple of Delphi (DELL-fye), which many leaders consulted to determine the will of Apollo, spoke through a woman's voice.

But women also experienced strong prejudice in a patriarchal society. The misogynist, or anti-woman, views of many men were articulated by Aristotle, who saw only males as capable of perfection and described women as deformed males. In Athens a popular saying expressed male views: "Respectable women should stay at home; the street is for worthless hussies." Some women expressed their discontent, as reflected in a tragic play by Euripides: "[Men] say we lead a safe life at home. What imbeciles! I'd rather stand to arms three times than bear one child."[16] In contrast to their role in politics, in Greek literature women are often powerful and capable of great anger, humor, faithfulness, and intelligence. The last two are the chief qualities of Penelope, the wife of Ulysses in Homer's *Odyssey* who waits patiently for her husband, ruling the state wisely until his return while escaping the clutches of many men who want to marry her. Indeed, it is often the male characters, like Jason in *Medea*, for whom the audience feels contempt. Powerful women also appear in a different form in the comedy *Lysistrata* (lis-uh-STRAH-tuh) by Aristophanes. In this bawdy play, a group of women organize to end war by refusing to have sex with their husbands until the men stop fighting. Lysistrata tells her husband: "We women got together and decided we were going to save Greece. Listen to us and keep quiet, as we've had to do up to now, and we'll clear up the mess you've made."[17]

Some Greek social customs might be considered controversial today. For example, free men could have sex with slaves or prostitutes. While their wives stayed at home, men attended parties and festive gatherings, sometimes enlivened by the presence of courtesans celebrated for their wit and charm. Many courtesans were from Ionia, and some had high status as free people and probably a good education. The most famous courtesan was Aspasia (ass-PAY-zhee-uh), a vivacious, literate Milesian who migrated to Athens and then operated a meetinghouse where educated men came for sex and conversation with intellectual women. An advocate of gender equality, Aspasia was a close friend of Socrates and became the mistress of the Athenian leader Pericles (PER-eh-kleez), whose enemies accused her of writing his speeches, violating the tradition that politics was for men only. But most prostitutes were slaves whose lives were far different from Aspasia's.

Same-sex sexual relationships known today as homosexuality has existed in all societies from earliest times, but Greek men were particularly open about these relationships. Much art emphasized the human body, and artists fashioned many naturalistic statues of naked men and women. Some Greek thinkers described the perfect relationship as one between two men of different generations. Homosexual behavior between older and younger upper-class men was accepted as part of a training or mentoring relationship for career preparation, and many famous Greeks had such relationships. In Sparta some of the top military units comprised homosexual male couples. Among the elite, this tendency was encouraged by

Women Fetching Water The painting on this vase portrays everyday life in a Greek city. Women have congregated at a public fountain to fill jugs with water to be carried back home, where it will be used for drinking, cooking, and cleaning. The women's hair coverings and long robes reflect the fashion of the day. (William Francis Warden Fund. Courtesy, the Museum of Fine Arts, Boston [61.195])

the fact that boys and girls were often brought up separately, reducing heterosexual contact. But we must not assume that the concepts of same-sex or even opposite-sex relationships 2,500 years ago were precisely the same as those today. In general, men of superior status took for granted that, with or without consent, they could have intimate relations with anyone of inferior status, including servants, slaves, and foreigners. In contrast, nonelite Greeks often condemned and punished homosexual relations between two adults.

SECTION SUMMARY

- Though Greeks had a well-developed religion, they were also notable for their commitment to using reason to understand the world.
- Three of the greatest Greek philosophers were Socrates, who believed in absolute truths; Plato, who described an ideal society in the *Republic;* and Aristotle, who explored human nature and the workings of the physical world.
- Athens was a magnet for writers and artists because of its wealth.
- Greek drama tended to focus on tragedy, as in the works of Euripides, Aeschylus, and Sophocles; writers like Aristophanes wrote comedies.
- The differences among Greek social classes were pronounced, and even famed Greek thinkers tended to support slavery.
- Greek women were generally expected to stay at home and out of politics, but they were often featured as powerful characters in plays.
- Homosexual relations among men were considered acceptable and were common among the upper classes.

Greeks, Persians, and the Regional System

In what ways did Persians and Greeks encounter and influence each other?

The Greeks and Persians fought and connected with each other as well as with other societies. During the early fifth century B.C.E. Athens and allied Greek cities successfully fought a series of wars with the greatest power of western Asia, the Persian Empire. But the rival Greek states also fought ruinous wars with each other. The Greeks and Persians were also linked by trade and travel with many other societies, and both societies borrowed many ideas from neighboring peoples, including the Egyptians and western Asians. The legacy of classical Greece and Persia for the wider world, including Europe and the Middle East, is subject to debate.

The Greco-Persian Wars

The Greco-Persian conflict began in 499 B.C.E., when some Greek cities in Persian-held Anatolia rebelled against their Persian overlords. The Ionian Greeks were supported by Athens but were defeated by Persia in 494. To punish the Greeks in the peninsula, the Persian king Darius I dispatched a Persian fleet to Greece in 492, but his ships were destroyed by storms. He then sent a larger Persian force into Greece. This first Greco-Persian War ended with a Greek victory at the Battle of Marathon in northern Greece in 490 B.C.E. It was a violent conflict with many deaths on both sides. Herodotus reported that the Greeks carried out a slaughter and the Persians fell in heaps, many of them drowning in the sea.

The Persians made another attempt to conquer the Greeks in 480 B.C.E., sparking the second war. According to the Ionia-born Herodotus, who probably exaggerated the scale, Persia's King Xerxes sent a huge army of nearly 200,000 men into Greece, supported by the entire Persian navy of perhaps a thousand ships. Although some northern Greek cities surrendered, were neutral, or even joined with the Persians, the two chief southern cities, Athens and Sparta, along with their allies, continued the fight. A Spartan force of three hundred fought to the death holding a strategic pass, but they were betrayed by some Greeks who showed the Persians a path around them. Nothing could then stop the Persians from sweeping down into Athens and burning the city. Expecting final victory, the Persians attacked the Athenian fleet trapped in the Bay of Salamis (SAL-uh-muhs).

Surprisingly, the Greeks won the battle, destroying two hundred Persian ships while only losing forty of their own. Part of the reason was that the large Persian force was difficult to supply and control effectively. But the Athenians had also developed the world's most advanced fighting ship, the well-armored *trireme* (TRY-reem), which had three banks of oarsmen—two hundred crewmen in all—and deadly bronze rams. The Persians left an infantry force in Greece that was defeated at the battle of Plataea (pluh-TEE-uh) the following year (479). The Athenians reopened the Straits of Bosporus (BAH-spuh-ruhs) to Greek shipping and temporarily ended Persian rule in Ionia. Some historians argue that the Greek victory over the Persians also led to a growing divide between "Europe" and "Asia" as the Greeks increasingly viewed themselves as different from, and superior to, the people to the east who had long influenced them. But with the Persian threat ended, the old rivalries of the Greek cities reemerged.

Empire and Conflict in the Greek World

The period following the Greek victories against the Persians in the early fifth century B.C.E. was marked not only by great intellectual achievements by philosophers and playwrights but also by nearly constant warfare among Greek cities. Athens created an empire based on sea power, but its dominance led to a lengthy Peloponnesian War (431–404 B.C.E.) with Sparta during the last half of the fifth century. Sparta's defeat of Athens led to further political disunity in Greece.

The Acropolis   The Acropolis dominated the surrounding city. The marble Parthenon at the center, dedicated to Athena, was built during the time of Pericles.   (Michael Freeman Photography)

To defeat the Persians the Greek cities had organized a defensive alliance, called the **Delian** (DEE-lee-uhn) **League** because the treasury was located on the island of Delos (DEE-lahs). The richest state and largest naval power, Athens, led the league, while other cities contributed funds or ships to the alliance. But in 467 the island of Naxos (NAK-suhs) tried to withdraw from the league, and Athens refused, taking military action to stop Naxos. Some Athenians protested, prompting some leaders to worry that a democracy, which allows varied opinions, cannot manage an empire. It was now clear that the Delian League had changed from a defensive alliance to an Athenian empire. In midcentury, Athens made its imperial control explicit by moving the treasury of the league from Delos to Athens and beginning to spend some of the money on Athenian civic improvements. Thus the Delian League became as much a commercial as a military alliance. Athenian weights, measures, and coinage spread to other league members.

Athens reached what historians have considered its golden age in the mid-fifth century under Pericles (ca. 495-429 B.C.E.),

a visionary leader and spellbinding orator whose reforms brought more democracy to the legal system. Under his leadership Athenians had many reasons to be proud of their city, especially of the magnificent public buildings that reflected a strong sense of community, such as the Parthenon (PAHR-thuh-nahn), a temple dedicated to the city's patron goddess, Athena, on the hilltop known as the Acropolis (uh-KRAHP-uh-luhs). Athenians also praised their city for fostering the self-fulfillment and individualism they believed increased their happiness. But this did not mean they believed in unrestrained freedom; in fact, Athenians feared that too much pride or self-expression spelled trouble. Playwrights, poets, and historians all taught how pride or arrogance, including immodest boasting, could lead to punishment by the gods and personal disaster. They believed strongly that "pride goeth before the fall."

However, in the case of Athens the poets' and playwrights' warnings went unheeded. The Athenians' arrogance and pride in their city eventually brought disaster, as increasing resentment of Athenian power generated the long Peloponnesian War between Athens and Sparta and their respective allies, beginning in 431 B.C.E. Rivals considered Athens under its nationalistic leader Pericles too dominant. For their part, Athenians boasted of their many illustrious citizens and of the

---

Delian League   A defensive league organized by Greek cities in the fifth century B.C.E. to defeat the Persians.

magnificent public buildings designed to give people a sense of power during the Periclean Era (460–429 B.C.E.). In a famous "funeral oration" delivered in memory of dead Athenian soldiers after the first year of the war, Pericles reportedly contrasted Athenian democratic institutions and equality before the law with the "painful discipline" and lack of freedom found in Sparta:

> We do not copy our neighbors, but are an example to them. We are called a democracy, for the administration is in the hands of the many and not of the few. I say that Athens is the school of [Greece]. I have dwelt upon the greatness of Athens because I want to show you we are contending for a higher prize than those who enjoy none of these privileges. For in magnifying the city I have magnified the men whose virtues made her glorious.[18]

In this speech Pericles introduced the novel ideas that war was not just to defend hearth and home but to spread better ideas and systems, and also that citizens who enjoyed freedom had a responsibility to their community. High-minded as this sounds, the underlying assumption—that because they had such high ideals Athenians were superior to their neighbors, one of the reasons other Greek cities despised Athens—provided the spark that lit the war.

The war proved a disaster for Athens and a boon for Sparta. The Athenian strategy was to win the war at sea, fortifying themselves behind their city walls while using their navy to combat the superior land army of Sparta and its allies. But Athens was hit by a deadly plague. A third of the population died, and Pericles himself succumbed to the disease in 429 B.C.E. The Athenians also blundered in an unwise attempt to capture Syracuse, a city founded by Greek settlers on Sicily. Later the Spartans, with Persian advice, destroyed the Athenian fleet. The **Peloponnesian War** ended with a Spartan victory in 404. The Spartans disbanded the Athenian navy, destroyed the city walls, and killed or exiled thousands of Athenians.

Although the war made Sparta the most powerful Greek state, several decades of instability followed. In alliance with another democratic city, Thebes (THEEBZ), Athens weakened Spartan power. In the end, the frequent conflicts between the Greek cities proved too destructive. Less than a century after the Peloponnesian War ended, Greece was conquered and became the base for a much greater empire led by the northern state of Macedonia.

Historiography: Universal and Critical

The Greeks were perhaps the first people to develop concepts of history that are still used today, but they did so in the context of their connections to other societies. Of course, peoples before them had some sense of history. The legends passed down through oral traditions, such as the Gilgamesh epic in

Mesopotamia, the stories in the Hebrew Bible, and the Homeric epics, were narratives of history, although we cannot prove their accuracy. By the time of Confucius, the Chinese also wrote historical accounts. But the Greeks were the first to pursue critical, analytical, and universal history. The two most famous Greek historians were Herodotus and Thucydides (thyou-SID-uh-deez).

Herodotus (ca. 484–425 B.C.E.) wrote history on a scale never attempted before. Most of what we know of the Greco-Persian Wars comes from his account, which was only a part of his wide-ranging coverage. Integrating information on geography and cultural traditions, Herodotus wrote vividly about neighboring societies such as the Persian Empire and Egypt. Having been born in an Ionian city under Persian control and later traveling around the Persian Empire, he knew these subjects well. He sojourned in Egypt, which deeply impressed him, and concluded that some Greek gods could be equated with Egyptian divinities. Herodotus visited Tyre, where he learned that Phoenicians had invented the alphabet. A sophisticated man with an inquiring mind, Herodotus lived for a time in Athens, where he was a friend of Pericles, and portrayed the Athenians favorably in his books. He attributed the Greek victory over the Persians to the Greeks' free society, which gave them more incentive than the armies of the absolute Persian monarch.

Because his interests and travels went well beyond the Greek world, Herodotus might be considered the first world historian. He collected information in his travels and included his own observations. Much of his writings, however, seem incredible; he too often reported unverified hearsay and failed to subject all of his material to critical scrutiny. He also presented alternative versions of stories he could not reconcile. In his favor, however, he did not adopt Greek prejudices against other cultures, and he offered sympathetic views of the Persians and criticisms of the Greeks.

Much of what we know about Greek politics and wars during the fifth century B.C.E. comes from a single book, *The Peloponnesian War*, written by Thucydides (ca. 460–ca. 400 B.C.E.). A member of an aristocratic family that owned gold mines, Thucydides was an Athenian general who wrote his history after he was exiled from Athens for losing an important battle. Despite his exile, Thucydides objectively evaluated the strengths and weaknesses of his home city. He set an example of careful observation when he described the plague that broke out in Athens early in the war.

Unlike earlier writers, Thucydides added critical judgments to his narrative. For example, he was critical of the Athenians for ignoring the warnings of Pericles to attempt no new conquests. He also evaluated the strengths and weaknesses of democracy. Perhaps Thucydides was the first political scientist, since he asked fundamental questions about the nature of power and wondered whether humans could use it wisely. Thucydides saw history as much more than a list of names, events, and dates. He looked for patterns and moral lessons in the past. Whenever historians seek to interpret the past, they are acknowledging a debt to Thucydides, a

---

Peloponnesian War   A long war between Athens and Sparta and their respective allies in 431–404 B.C.E. that resulted in the defeat of Athens.

historian who was not just a teller of tales but also a teacher of wisdom.

Interregional Trade

The Mediterranean Basin remained a vast zone of exchange in which Greeks played the leading commercial role once dominated by Phoenicians. The geography and climate of Greece encouraged many to take up trade and travel, and from the eighth to the fourth century B.C.E. Greeks established colonies and spread Greek culture throughout the Mediterranean and the Black Sea region. The growing of grapes and olive oil trees fostered a merchant class that traded wine and olive oil throughout the eastern Mediterranean. Athens exported wine and oil in beautiful painted vases, as well as luxury items such as gold cups, jewelry, and textiles. Under Lydian and then Persian rule, Ionian port cities like Miletus also prospered as hubs of regional trade. The Ionians also helped lubricate commerce by being some of the first people to use metal coins.

Like the Greeks, the Persians welcomed foreign traders. Persian gold coins were widely used in the Mediterranean basin. Persian leaders patronized Greek traders living in their domains, and in 510 B.C.E. Scylax of Caryanda became the first known Greek visitor to India when he headed a trade mission sent by the Persian king Darius I. Tribute of various kinds flowed to the Persian capital, such as camels from Arabia and Bactria, gold from India, horses from the Scythians, bulls from Egypt, leather goods from Anatolia, and silver from Ionia.

Long-distance trade was crucial to the Mediterranean world in many ways. As the population of the Greek cities grew, merchants traveling elsewhere to trade eventually evolved into what historians call a **trade diaspora**, merchants from the same city or country who live permanently in foreign cities or countries. Most of the shipowners, traders, and moneylenders of Athens came from western Asia or from the Greek diaspora colonies such as Marseilles and the Crimea. Some Greeks specialized in carrying goods to and from Egypt, and communities of expatriate Greek merchants were established in Egypt, western Asia, and around the Black Sea.

Especially in Athens, trade contributed to the growth of a strong navy that helped the Greeks defeat the Persians. Capitalizing on this victory, Athens became the leading commercial and financial hub. Athens financed its rise to regional power through its control of rich silver mines, which were worked by over 20,000 slaves. It was fed by huge amounts of wheat from Egypt, Sicily, and southern Russia. After the Peloponnesian War, bankers and traders became increasingly prominent in Athenian politics, and Athens developed a reputation as a place where even those of humble origins, including some slaves, could achieve wealth. One Greek writer described Athens as the most profitable city to do business in; it was also safe, because its docks were protected from storms.

Cultural Mixing in the Eastern Mediterranean

The Mediterranean Basin provided a context for the intermingling of southern European, western Asian, and North African cultures. Persians, very open to outside influences, learned much from other peoples. For example, they blended Ionian Greek, Mesopotamian, and Scythian art styles and motifs with their own traditions. Reflecting the ability to endure while accepting new customs, Persian poetry throughout history extolled the cypress tree, which has deep roots and bends in strong winds, unlike the mighty oak, which can be broken by wind, or the tumbleweed, which moves every which way.

Like Persians, Greeks were both highly creative and benefited from their connections with other societies. They were especially open to influences from the Phoenicians, Egyptians, and Mesopotamians. Phoenician traders brought art forms and styles that led the Greeks to modify their columns, pottery, statues, and ceramic styles, and the music played in Greece for celebrations, labor, and even military training used many instruments and melodies from western Asia. The Greeks also adopted the Phoenician alphabet and several of their gods, and Ionian Greeks worshiped Anatolian deities and borrowed artistic motifs, coins, and fashion trends from the Lydians. In addition, many Greek colonists absorbed local influences. For example, Massalia (modern Marseilles), on the southern coast of France, had a mix of Greek and Celtic residents, forcing local Greeks to understand the Celtic customs and language.

Greeks visited, worked in, or settled in other societies, in the process learning about other cultures. For example, many Ionian merchants, such as Sappho's brother Charaxus (chuh-RAX-us), lived in Egypt. The Athenian lawgiver Solon visited Egypt as a merchant, studied with priests, and wrote poems about living at the mouth of the Nile, and the Athenian physician Hippocrates (hip-AHK-ruh-teez) was probably familiar with Egyptian medicine, since some Egyptian ideas are found in his influential writings. Some Greeks even fought as mercenaries for Egyptian kings; Greek soldiers left graffiti on monumental architecture 700 miles up the Nile. These soldiers worshiped Egyptian gods, and some Greeks brought home statues that were imitated by Greek sculptors. Other Greeks served in Mesopotamian and Persian armies. The scientist Democritus visited Babylonia and Persia and probably brought back many useful ideas, and both Plato and Aristotle knew something about Zoroastrianism.

Cosmopolitan Ionia, where Greek and Asian cultures mixed, produced pathbreaking thinking in philosophy and science, often under Persian patronage. In fact, rational thinking appeared there earlier than in Athens. Some scholars think Thales, a Lydian subject, was of Phoenician descent. He had studied in Egypt, where he learned geometry. Thales was the first Greek to inscribe a right-angled triangle and to determine the sun's course from solstice to solstice, something the Babylonians had long known how to do. The Ionian-born mathematician Pythagoras (ca. 580–ca. 500 B.C.E.) may have visited Egypt and Babylon, and he seems to have learned Egyptian.

---

trade diaspora Merchants from the same city or country who live permanently in foreign cities or countries.

The Persian and Greek Legacies

Both the Persians and Greeks influenced the peoples around them while leaving a rich legacy for later societies. Persians built not only the world's first large empire but also the first international state, bringing together diverse societies under one canopy. Rather than imposing one culture on diverse peoples, they followed flexible and tolerant policies under a king who was a symbol of unity. Persians fused traditions from many cultures while spreading learning, such as Babylonian astronomy, to peoples such as the Greeks. Two thousand years later Persians still practiced many customs from Achaemenid times and looked back to Cyrus the Great for inspiration.

Persians made a number of contributions to other cultures. Zoroastrian ideas influenced several religions, including Judaism, Christianity, and Islam. Many Persian words entered other languages. For example, the Persian word for "garden" became the English word *paradise*. English words associated with items of trade that derive from Persian include *shawl*, *sash*, *tiara*, *orange*, *lemon*, *melon*, *peace*, and *spinach*. The Persians fostered an atmosphere in which science and mathematics, especially in Mesopotamia, Babylonia, and the Ionian Greek cities, continued to develop. They may also have been the first people to play hockey.

In the past several centuries many historians have credited the Greeks with creating the Western tradition. They have admired the Greeks as the direct cultural, intellectual, and political ancestors of modern Europeans and North Americans, and perceived Greek society as culturally richer than any other before modern times. In particular the Athenian era of Pericles, Plato, and Aeschylus is viewed as the "golden age" that launched Western literature, history, philosophy, science, and the democratic ideal. Some modern historians argue that because the Greeks continue to offer many lessons about the human condition, they are worthy of a central place in Western educational systems and conceptions of world history.

However, the view of Greece as the fountainhead of Western culture has problems. Some historians argue that the Romans, who came after the Greeks, founded the Western tradition. Perhaps, they suggest, rather than being a part of Europe, the Greeks can be better understood as an extension of the western Asian and North African societies that influenced them. From a modern Western perspective, the Greeks seem both very strange and quite familiar. Many classical Greek customs and social inequalities, especially their sometimes cruel treatment of women and slaves, appall people today. Greek morality also lacked values such as compassion. To critics, Greek thinkers were not as liberal and secular as is often claimed, their democracy was elitist and flawed, and what ideas western Europe derived from the Greeks came in modified form through the Romans. Later, Europe rediscovered much of Greek thought through the Arabs. Moreover, they argue, modern science is based not only on Greek but also on Chinese, Indian, and Middle Eastern discoveries.

The debate suggests how fascinating the Greeks have been to various societies over the centuries, beginning with the Romans. Middle Eastern societies also inherited the Greek legacy, treasuring Greek thinkers and scientific understanding for many centuries. Greek philosophy strongly influenced some Islamic scholars. The debate also indicates that the Greeks, however imperfect their society, fostered ideas and institutions that were unusual for their time and that have endured for over two millennia.

SECTION SUMMARY

■ Early in the fifth century B.C.E., the Persians attacked the Greeks several times, but the Greeks, against great odds, fended them off.

■ Following the Greek victory over the Persians, Athens's growing arrogance eventually led to the Peloponnesian War between Athens and Sparta, which ended with Spartan victory.

■ Herodotus, who wrote of the Greco-Persian Wars, and Thucydides, who wrote of the Peloponnesian War, were the first historians to write critical and analytical history.

■ The eastern Mediterranean and western Asia were zones of intense trade and cultural mixing.

■ The long-held idea that the Greeks created the Western tradition is controversial, as are the merits of some Greek customs and ideas.

The Hellenistic Age and Its Afro-Eurasian Legacies

What impact did Alexander the Great and his conquests have on world history?

Between 334 and 323 B.C.E., Alexander of Macedonia (MASS-uh-DUHN-ia), a student of classical Greek ideas, created the largest empire yet seen in the Afro-Eurasian zone, revitalizing Greek society and spreading its culture over a wide area. Alexander's achievements brought about a historical transition, establishing new networks of communication, and his legacy lived on for centuries in **Hellenism** (HELL-uh-niz-uhm), a widespread culture that combined western Asian (mainly Persian) and Greek (Hellenic) characteristics. During the Hellenistic Age, Greeks ruled over large parts of western Asia and North Africa, a domination that ended only by the rise of the Roman Empire. Meanwhile, the impact of the Hellenistic Greeks spawned new empires based in Persia that continued to influence Middle Eastern history.

Hellenism A widespread culture flourishing between 359 and 100 B.C.E. that combined western Asian (mainly Persian) and Greek (Hellenic) characteristics.

Alexander the Great and World Empire

The disunity into which Greece had fallen after the Peloponnesian War opened the door to the armies of Macedonia, whose rulers then conquered a vast empire. By winning the Peloponnesian War, the Spartans ended the attempt by Athens to create an empire uniting all the Greek cities under one rule. The war itself had so weakened all the Greek cities that no one of them, not even Sparta, could unite the peninsula. That task, and the creation of a great Greek empire, was left to the state of Macedonia, on the northern fringe of Greece. Led by King Philip II (382–336 B.C.E.), who developed a paid professional army instead of one composed of citizens and devised a more effective infantry phalanx, the Macedonian army conquered the Greek cities by defeating the combined armies of Thebes and Athens in 338 B.C.E. (see Chronology: Hellenistic Age, 359–100 B.C.E.). Two years later, on the eve of an expedition to Asia, Philip was assassinated. The culprits were never identified, but the hard-living, hard-drinking Philip had many enemies among Greeks, Persians, and Macedonian nobles.

After a power struggle, Philip's twenty-year-old son, Alexander (r. 336–323 B.C.E.), a former student of Aristotle, became king. Today we might call the fearless and resolute Alexander a megalomaniac. His ambitions for conquest were evident as a child. According to his biographer Plutarch (PLOO-tahrk), when told that there were an infinite number of other countries, Alexander reportedly wept and then lamented that, with such a multitude of countries, it was a shame that he had not yet conquered even one of them. Later, when Alexander invaded Asia, he wrote to the Persian king that he was seeking vengeance on Persia for its invasions of Greece a century and half earlier.

During his thirteen-year reign from 336 to his death in 323 B.C.E., Alexander used Macedonian, Greek, and mercenary troops to conquer the world from Greece east to western India, and from the Nile valley in the south to the Caucasus Mountains and the Black and Caspian Seas in the north. He employed ruthless tactics against enemies, sometimes destroying entire cities that resisted and slaughtering the inhabitants. The powerful Persian Empire was dismantled in three major battles between 334 and 331. Alexander was a brilliant military strategist and leader of men, which he proved when, although cut off from his supply lines, he defeated a great Persian force at Issus in Syria. The last Persian emperor, Darius III, was murdered by his own troops after Alexander had burned Persepolis and taken his place as Persian ruler.

From their base in Persia, Alexander's forces moved through Afghanistan, fighting difficult battles with the tough peoples of that mountainous region. His crossing of Afghanistan's rugged Hindu Kush Mountains was arduous. The inhabitants pursued a scorched earth policy, preferring to destroy their homes and farms rather than surrender. Many of Alexander's horses died and his grain ran out, and his soldiers were reduced to eating their baggage animals. Finally reaching the Indus Valley, the Macedonian wanted to move into the heart of India, but his exhausted and homesick troops refused

Alexander Defeating Persians at Battle of Issus   In this Roman copy of an earlier Greek painting, Alexander the Great is shown on his horse in the battle that brought defeat to Persian king Darius III in 333 B.C.E.   (Scala/Art Resource, NY)

C H R O N O L O G Y

Hellenistic Age, 359–100 B.C.E.

359–336	Reign of King Philip of Macedonia
338	Philip's conquest of Greek states
336–323	Reign of Alexander the Great
332	Invasion of Egypt
330	Occupation of Persia
327–325	Invasion of India
306–30	Ptolemaic Egypt
238	Parthian state in Persia
141	Parthians' conquest of Seleucids

to go farther. Alexander and his remaining troops made a difficult desert journey back to western Asia.

Conquering everything from the central Mediterranean to the Hindu Kush Mountains, Alexander saw himself as a new world ruler. According to Plutarch, Alexander believed he came as a governor to all peoples and as a mediator for the whole world. His wide vision was extraordinary for the times. His empire incorporated the remnants of most of the major ancient Afro-Eurasian societies, including Egypt, Crete, Mycenae, Phoenicia, Mesopotamia, and the Indus Valley. It may also have been foreshadowed by the earlier Greek settlement in many cities of western Asia, North Africa, and southern Europe.

The burning of Persepolis symbolized the end of one era of cultural exchange and the beginning of another. In Egypt Alexander was accepted as a pharaoh, the physical son of god. Alexander also initially organized his empire like the Persians. Although many historians think he was bisexual or homosexual and continued to have an intimate relationship with a male advisor, Alexander, increasingly influenced by Eastern traditions, married a princess from the eastern Persian province of Bactria (northern Afghanistan). He also encouraged his soldiers to take Asian wives as well. He adopted the dress of a Persian ruler, wearing a purple and white cloak and a head ribbon previously worn by Persian royalty.

Alexander's Legacy: Hellenism and New Kingdoms

When Alexander died in Babylon at age thirty-three, his victories had already ensured that the conquered territories would retain a mixed Greek and Persian cultural flavor for centuries under the influence of Hellenism. Some at the time thought he was poisoned by rivals but he probably died from a fever

acquired after a night of heavy drinking. Alexander was gone but the Hellenistic Age in the eastern Mediterranean and western Asia lasted several centuries until these lands came under the control of the Roman Empire and a revived Persian Empire.

During this time, the legacy of classical Greece was passed on in a form that fifth-century Greeks might have found hard to understand. Among other things, Hellenistic culture placed less emphasis on individual freedom and the use of reason and more emphasis on the emotions than did earlier Greek society. Some of Alexander's soldiers settled in Afghanistan and western India, and Greek ideas had an enduring influence on the art of these regions. Even after the fall of the Hellenistic kingdoms, people as far away as Ethiopia, Nubia, and western India studied the Greek language and borrowed Greek artistic styles.

Alexander's empire soon fragmented. During his unexpected brief final illness, Alexander, when asked to whom he left his empire, was alleged to have said: "to the strongest." Whether or not this story was true, it describes what happened after his death. Within twenty years, by the end of the fourth century B.C.E., Alexander's empire had been divided by his former generals, all Macedonians. A dynasty begun by Ptolemy (TAHL-uh-mee) controlled Egypt and the eastern Mediterranean coast; the family of Seleucus (suh-LOO-kuhs) controlled Persia, Mesopotamia, and Syria; and followers of Antigonus (an-TIG-uh-nuhs) controlled the Macedonian kingdom and northern Greece (see Map 6.3).

Cities and Economic Networks

These Greek-dominated kingdoms were based in cities that differed from the polis in Golden Age Greece, but they also enjoyed an increase in transregional trade. Throughout his travels, Alexander had founded many cities named after him, the most famous of which was the still-surviving city of Alexandria on the Mediterranean coast of Egypt (see Map 6.3). Hellenistic cities were not politically independent city-states as in classical Athens but rather part of kingdoms, and their citizens did not enjoy much political freedom or participation in government. Wealthy aristocrats, professional soldiers, and bureaucrats ran the cities' governments. Although the Hellenistic cities were centers of Greek culture, they also existed in a world that was predominantly non-Greek and so were partly influenced by local traditions. For example, the Ptolemaic dynasty in Egypt ruled with the pomp of the pharaohs. Hellenistic monarchs relied on Greeks, Greek-speaking Persians, and others to rule their kingdoms, but these Greek leaders were vastly outnumbered by their Asian and African subjects.

In addition, the cities were no longer the vibrant democratic communities they had been in the time of Pericles and Plato. The population of each city had less sense of community and the urban culture glorified hedonism. The upper classes enjoyed high living, and poets celebrated activities like horse racing, lovemaking, and drinking. A satirical Egyptian poem mocked a drunken and gluttonous harpist who showed up at weddings and festivals: "He disputes with the party-goers,

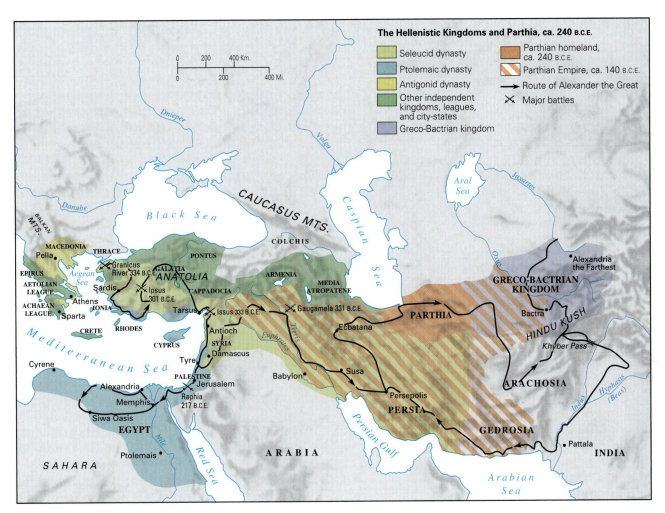

Map 6.3   The Hellenistic Kingdoms
The empire conquered by Alexander the Great was divided into rival Hellenistic kingdoms on his death in 323 B.C.E. By 140 B.C.E. the Parthians had conquered some of the eastern territories.

shouting: 'I can't sing when I'm hungry, I can't hold my harp without my fill of wine!' And he drinks wine like two people and eats the meat of three."[19]

Hellenistic cities were more cosmopolitan and ethnically diverse than their earlier Greek counterparts. Alexandria, Egypt, for example, was a city with large Egyptian, Greek, and Jewish populations. It was here that the Zoroastrian holy books and Hebrew Bible were translated into Greek, the latter to benefit Greek-speaking Jews. Alexandria was a melting pot where many religions met and new ones sprouted up. Many poets and scholars moved there. The Syrian Greek poet Meleager expressed the cosmopolitan Hellenistic attitude: "Stranger, we live in the same motherland, the world."[20]

Alexander's conquests also linked the Mediterranean and western Asia in a vast trading network. Alexander used part of the great wealth he found in the Persian capital to build and repair roads and harbors. Greek colonists introduced or expanded money-based economies. In Bactria, in northern Afghanistan, for example, bilingual bronze coins mixing Greek

and local scripts became widely used. Long-distance trade expanded rapidly as silk from China and sugar from India were traded for onions from Egypt, wood products from Macedonia, and olive oil from Athens. As caravans of vegetables and wine moved eastward, they crossed caravans of spices and other goods moving westward out of India, Arabia, and northeast Africa. This trans-Eurasian trading network remained strong long after the Hellenistic states had disappeared.

Science

Hellenistic thinkers maintained the classical Greek interest in scientific questions and made numerous contributions to our understanding of the natural world during the third and second centuries B.C.E. Although influenced by thinkers like Aristotle, Hellenistic scientists and mathematicians were more rigorous and professional in collecting and evaluating data, then offering hypotheses to explain mathematics problems, natural phenomena, and the workings of the universe.

ARCHIMEDES, HELLENISTIC MATHEMATICIAN AND ENGINEER

Archimedes was an outstanding mathematician, the greatest engineer of the Hellenistic world, and perhaps the most wide-ranging mind of his time. Some historians consider Archimedes and Aristotle the two greatest thinkers of Greek society. Born around 287 B.C.E. to an influential family—his father was apparently an astronomer—in Syracuse, a Greek city on the island of Sicily, Archimedes studied in the intellectual capital of the Hellenistic world, Alexandria in Egypt. In the Hellenistic world inquisitive souls of financial means or, like Archimedes, political connections traveled widely and learned from varied cultures. In cosmopolitan Alexandria Archimedes became acquainted with famous scientists, including the astronomer Aristarchos. Eventually Archimedes returned to Syracuse, where he spent the rest of his days. We know little of his personal life and do not know whether he ever married.

In mathematics Archimedes introduced many new ideas, some of which added to Euclid's geometry. He offered a new system of numerals to handle large numbers; calculated the value of *pi*, the ratio of the circumference to the diameter of a circle, more accurately than anyone before him; and discovered the laws for finding the centers of gravity of plane figures. A book he wrote, lost for centuries but recently rediscovered, hints that 1,800 years before anyone else he was exploring calculus, the basis for much twenty-first-century technology. Archimedes also studied astronomy and built an instrument for measuring the movements of the sun, moon, and planets. This early clock may have inspired later timekeeping inventions.

Archimedes is equally well known for his engineering innovations. His later biographer, the Greek writer Plutarch, claimed that, like Plato, Archimedes disdained practical applications. Certainly he wrote much less about his applied than his theoretical studies. Nonetheless, his contributions were immense. He discovered "Archimedes law," still tested in high school classrooms, which states that a body wholly or partly immersed in a fluid loses weight equal to the weight of the fluid displaced. This insight apparently came to him while in the public baths, as he watched water flow over the side as he entered the pool. According to Plutarch, he leaped from the pool and ran home naked, crying aloud: "Eureka!" ("I have found it!"). The public nudity would not have astonished Greeks, who were used to seeing people in public without their clothes. With such discoveries, Archimedes founded the science of hydrostatics, which involves balance and weights.

Archimedes made other practical contributions. For instance, he supervised construction of the world's first three-masted ship, a huge combination of warship, yacht, and cargo ship that had horse stalls, fish tanks, cargo holds for wheat, and luxurious cabins. He also worked out the law of the lever and the theory of mechanical advantage, using his knowledge to launch his ship with the use of compound pulleys. He solved a major problem of the time in irrigation and mining by discovering how to move great volumes of water up a steep incline by using a large pipe with a tightly fitted screw.

With Roman power on the rise, Archimedes was put in charge of Syracuse defenses. For a while Roman attackers were repulsed by his ingenious weapons, including missiles dropped from cranes that swung out over the fortified walls, and darts and balls delivered by catapults. Some legends, which many historians doubt, credit him with experimenting with mirrors to direct the sun's rays at enemy ships to set them on fire.

Eventually Romans captured Syracuse in 212 and killed the aged Archimedes—according to one legend, as the famously absent-minded scientist worked on geometrical diagrams. This Roman triumph helped end the Hellenistic Age and begin the Roman age in the central Mediterranean. The engineering and mathematical discoveries of Archimedes now became part of Roman and later world traditions.

THINKING ABOUT THE PROFILE

1. How did Archimedes' career reflect the Hellenistic Age?
2. Why was Archimedes considered one of the major classical engineers and mathematicians?

The Archimedes Palimpsest In 1889 scholars discovered a crumbling, long-lost parchment containing a copy of a major work by Archimedes, the treatise called "On Floating Bodies." This work, on buoyancy, suggests that he was centuries ahead of the rest of the world in his thinking on mathematics and physics, even suggesting ideas that did not reappear until the past several centuries. (Image taken by the Rochester Institute of Technology. Copyright resides with the owner of the Archimedes Palimpsest)

Alexandria in Egypt, with the largest library in the ancient world (700,000 papyrus scrolls), was the research center of the Ptolemaic kingdom and the Hellenistic world. Much of the work of Alexandrian thinkers and inventors initiated or anticipated the scientific, mathematical, and technological developments of the modern world. Here in the third century, for example, Euclid (YOU-klid) wrote his text on plane geometry, a book used for 2,000 years. Herophilus (hair-OFF-uh-lus) did research on the brain, improving people's understanding of the central organ of the nervous system and the seat of human intelligence. Also in Alexandria, Aristarchus (AR-uh-STAHR-kuhs) first proposed that the sun rather than the earth was the center of the universe, an idea rejected for the next 1,000 years by most Europeans. A third-century B.C.E. geographer, Eratosthenes (ER-uh-TAHS-thuh-neez), calculated the circumference of the earth within about 200 miles, and the Alexandrian inventor Hero devised a steam turbine, although it was treated only as an amazing toy. Various other major thinkers, such as the engineer and mathematician Archimedes, spent time in Alexandria (see Profile: Archimedes, a Hellenistic Mathematician and Engineer).

Philosophy and Religion

Greek philosophical and religious thought went in new directions during the Hellenistic era. Cities, now part of large empires, lacked much of the public spirit of the earlier Greek polis. Some of the new ideas put less emphasis on the power of reason to solve problems and more on the importance of resigning oneself to life in ways that often seemed fatalistic. There was a new emphasis on simplicity and taking life as it comes. The school of thought known as **Cynicism**, made famous by Ionia-born Diogenes (die-AHJ-uh-neez) (ca. 412–ca. 323 B.C.E.), emphasized living a radically simple life, shunning material things and all pretense, and remaining true to one's fundamental values. A famous legend of the meeting of Diogenes and Alexander just before the Macedonian leader's initial conquests conveys the flavor of Cynic philosophy. Diogenes asked Alexander about his greatest desire, and the Macedonian replied, "to subjugate Greece." Next he would subjugate Southwest Asia and then the world. And after that, Alexander said, "I will relax and enjoy myself," prompting Diogenes to reply: "Why not save yourself all the trouble by relaxing and enjoying yourself now?"[21]

Another Hellenistic era philosophy, **Stoicism** (STOH-uh-siz-uhm), emphasized cooperating with and accepting nature, as well as the unity and equality of all people. Founded by Zeno (ZEE-noh) (ca. 334–ca. 265 B.C.E.) in Athens in the third

century B.C.E., Stoicism, often misunderstood today as the belief in resigning oneself to fate, was actually a cosmopolitan and optimistic philosophy that accepted the ethnic diversity evident in the Hellenistic world. Stoics also taught that the law of nature governing human affairs was common to all people, was found in our minds and hearts, and transcended the limited human laws created by kings. The Stoic emphasis on basic human equality survived over the centuries to influence modern law-makers.

Hellenistic religion, like its major philosophies, stressed personal satisfaction and offered people individual happiness or salvation. The religion of Isis, originally an Egyptian fertility goddess, promised personal salvation. In addition, various mystery religions valued faith and promised their followers eternal life. A very popular mystery religion was **Mithraism** (MITH-ruh-iz-uhm), a cult that worshiped Mithra, a Persian deity associated with the sun. Worshipers of Mithra were also promised salvation, providing they were properly initiated into the community of the faith. Mystery religions were open to all, not restricted to members of a particular ethnic group or geographic area.

Some historians believe that these Hellenistic religions, which shared features with Christianity, help explain the appeal of the teachings and life of Jesus several centuries later. And some of their ideas were incorporated into various Christian cults that emerged in western Asia. For example, Christianity borrowed from Mithraism the concept of purgatory as well as the winter solstice and birthday of Mithra (December 25). Hellenistic ideas also influenced the Romans (see Chapter 8) and remained important in western Asia and the eastern Mediterranean long after the end of the Hellenistic era.

Hellenistic Asia and Persian Revival

As mentioned earlier in this section, after Alexander's death his empire was split into three parts ruled by the Ptolemies, Seleucids, and Antigonids. The dominance of the Hellenistic Seleucid kings, who governed a large territory in western Asia, including Persia and Mesopotamia, was short-lived. They were challenged by the Parthians (PAHR-thee-uhnz), originally Indo-European pastoral nomads who migrated from Central Asia into eastern Persia in the third century B.C.E. and initially became subjects of the Seleucids. In the middle of the second century B.C.E., however, the Parthians conquered large parts of Persia, Afghanistan, and Mesopotamia and seized the Seleucid capital on the Tigris River. Over the next few decades they fought off Scythian invaders in the north, expanded their empire into the Caucasus, and then crushed an invading Roman army in 53 B.C.E.

The Parthians adopted many Hellenistic traditions and institutions, and they made Greek the official language of their state. Gradually Persian influences grew stronger, and the Parthians adopted a form of Zoroastrianism. But frequent wars

Cynicism A Hellenistic philosophy, made famous by the philosopher Diogenes, that emphasized living a radically simple life, shunning material things and all pretense, and remaining true to one's fundamental values.

Stoicism A Hellenistic philosophy that emphasized the importance of cooperating with and accepting nature, as well as the unity and equality of all people.

Mithraism A Hellenistic cult that worshiped Mithra, a Persian deity associated with the sun; had some influence on Christianity.

with Rome sapped their strength. In 224 C.E. the last Parthian ruler was defeated by a new Persian power, the Sassanians (suh-SAY-nee-uhnz). The Sassanians ruled much of western Asia for the next four centuries, coming into frequent conflict with the Romans who replaced the Hellenistic kingdoms.

SECTION SUMMARY

- After the Peloponnesian War, no Greek city was strong enough to unite the rest of the Greek peninsula.
- King Philip II of Macedonia conquered several Greek cities, and, after he died, his ambitious son Alexander the Great established an empire that ranged from Egypt to India.
- Alexander's legacy included a vast trading network that linked the Mediterranean, western Asia, and India, as well as the spread of Hellenism, a mix of Greek and Persian culture.
- Hellenism was marked by rigorous scientific inquiry, philosophies such as Cynicism and Stoicism that urged people to take life as it came, and mystical religions that had some influence on Christianity.

 *Online Study Center* **ACE the Test**

Chapter Summary

Two societies, the Greeks and Persians, dominated the Mediterranean and western Asia during the early Classical Era, influencing many other peoples in the region. The Persians forged an enduring legacy by building a huge multiethnic empire. The Persian emphasis on organizing government in a large imperial state through mutual tolerance, a skillful bureaucracy, and good roads influenced the Macedonian Alexander the Great and his successors, as well as the Roman and the Muslim rulers of West Asia after them. Persian religious ideas, including Zoroastrianism, also spread to neighboring peoples such as the Hebrews.

The Greeks became a major Mediterranean society between 800 and 500 B.C.E., reaching their golden age during the fifth century. The Athenians are best remembered for practicing democracy, however imperfect the system may have been in a society where there were many slaves and where women had few legal rights. Democracy developed over some decades, partly as a result of citizens demanding a voice in the decisions that ordered them to war. The classical Greeks were pioneers in many areas, including philosophy and science. Influenced by the increasing emphasis on reason, Greek thinkers like Socrates, Plato, and especially Aristotle established a foundation for critical thinking and natural science. Their legacy influenced people in both the Middle East and Europe.

The Greeks and Persians were also fierce rivals for regional power, fighting a series of destructive wars but also exchanging trade goods and ideas. The eastern Mediterranean zone fostered cultural mixing, maritime commerce, and the sharing of knowledge and products. Alexander the Great's conquests made Greek language and culture part of the eastern Mediterranean world for several centuries after his death. By the second century B.C.E., this world, dominated by Hellenism, had developed some of the elements of a common culture, mixing Greek arts and philosophy with many Persian or western Asian ideas of government. The later Roman, Christian, and then Muslim rulers in these areas retained some of this Greco-Persian heritage.

Online Study Center **Improve Your Grade** Flashcards

Key Terms

Achaemenid	tyrant	trade diaspora
satrap	Sophists	Hellenism
Zoroastrianism	Socratic Method	Cynicism
Ahura Mazda	metaphysics	Stoicism
polis	Delian League	Mithraism
oligarchy	Peloponnesian War	

Suggested Reading

Books

Allen, Lindsay. *The Persian Empire.* Chicago: University of Chicago Press, 2005. A wonderfully illustrated recent survey of the classical Persians.

Briant, Pierre. *From Cyrus to Alexander: A History of the Persian Empire.* New York: Eisenbraun, 2001. An excellent and up-to-date survey.

Bridenthal, Renate, et al. *Becoming Visible: Women in European History,* 3rd ed. Boston: Houghton Mifflin, 1998. Contains excellent chapters on ancient and classical societies.

Brosius, Maria. *Women in Ancient Persia, 559–331 B.C.* New York: Oxford University Press, 1996. Examines women and their roles, providing a detailed picture of their lives.

Casson, Lionel. *The Ancient Mariners: Seafarers and Sea Fighters of the Mediterranean in Ancient Times,* 2nd ed. Princeton: Princeton University Press, 1991. Pathbreaking study of maritime trade, migration, and warfare.

Cook, J. M. *Persian Empire.* New York: Schocken Press, 1987. Useful scholarly survey, especially strong on political history.

Faceliere, Robert. *Daily Life in Greece at the Time of Pericles.* London: Phoenix, 2002. A detailed examination of various aspects of life in classical Athens.

Fox, Robin Lane. *Alexander the Great.* New York: Penguin, 2004. Updated edition of a readable introduction.

Levi, Peter. *The Greek World.* Oxford: Stonehenge, 1992. A comprehensive, well-illustrated, and readable survey.

Lloyd, G. E. R. *The Ambitions of Curiosity: Understanding the World in Ancient Greece and China.* New York: Cambridge University Press, 2002. An interesting scholarly study of the achievements and limitations of scientific inquiry in these two societies.

Martin, Thomas R. *Ancient Greece from Prehistoric to Hellenistic Times*. New Haven, Conn.: Yale University Press, 1996. A clear survey of Greek history, written for the general reader.

Pomeroy, Sarah B. *Goddesses, Whores, Wives and Slaves: Women in Classical Antiquity*. New York: Schocken, 1975. An excellent study of women's lives in classical Greece and Rome.

Samons, Loren J., ed. *Athenian Democracy and Imperialism*. Boston: Houghton Mifflin, 1988. Valuable collection of writings on an important theme.

Vernant, Jean-Pierre, ed. *The Greeks*, translated by Charles Lambert and Teresa Lavender Fagan. Chicago: University of Chicago Press, 1995. A collection of essays interpreting Greek political, economic, social, and religious life.

Wood, Michael. *In the Footprints of Alexander the Great: A Journey from Greece to Asia*. Berkeley: University of California Press, 1997. A fascinating recreation of Alexander the Great's route to, and experiences reaching, India.

Websites

Ancient/Classical History
(http://ancienthistory.about.com/library). Essays and timelines for many ancient civilizations and societies.

Diotima: Women and Gender in the Ancient World
(http://www.stoa.org/diotima/). Contains excellent materials on gender and women in the early Mediterranean world.

Exploring Ancient World Cultures
(http://eawc.evansville.edu/). Excellent site run by Evansville University, with essays and links on the ancient Near East and Europe.

Internet Ancient History Sourcebook
(http://www.fordham.edu/halsall/ancient/asbook.html). Exceptionally rich collection of links and primary source readings.

Livius: Articles on Ancient History
(http://www.livius.org). Very useful site with many short essays on the Greeks, Persians, Parthians, Romans, and other ancient and classical societies.

CHAPTER *7*

Classical Societies in Southern and Central Asia, 600 B.C.E.–600 C.E.

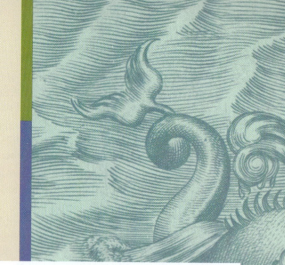

CHAPTER OUTLINE

- The Transformation of Indian Society and Its Religions
- Eurasian Exchanges, Indian Politics, and the Mauryan Empire
- South and Central Asia After the Mauryas
- The Gupta Age in India
- The Development of Southeast Asian Societies

■ **PROFILE**
The Trung Sisters, Vietnamese Rebels

■ **WITNESS TO THE PAST**
Basic Doctrines in the Buddha's First Sermon

☀ *Online Study Center*

This icon will direct you to interactive activities and study materials on the website: college.hmco. com/pic/lockard1e

Gold Coin This gold coin, showing a horseman, was made in India during the reign of King Chandragupta II, who presided over a great and prosperous Indian empire, with a dynamic economy, between 380 and 415 C.E.   (C. M. Dixon/Ancient Art & Architecture Collection)

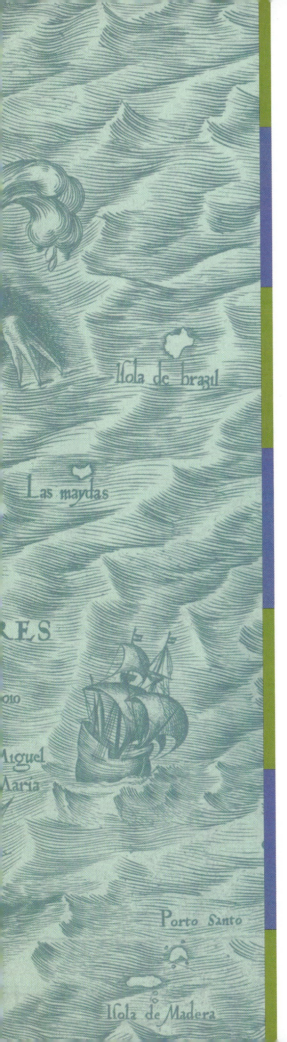

The merchants used to move about in the rivers as they wished, in the forests as if in gardens and on mountains as if in their own houses. As [the King] used to protect the earth so it too gave him gems out of mines, corns from the fields, and elephants from forests.

INDIAN WRITER KALIDASA (KAHL-I-DAHSS-UH), FIFTH CENTURY C.E.[1]

Sometime around 80 C.E. an unknown Greek boarded a trading ship that left the Egyptian port of Berenike (BER-eh-nick-y) headed for India, and he recorded his journey in writing. The ship sailed down the Red Sea and then along the coast of Arabia, braving the dangers from pirates. Eventually it reached the Indus River, where the merchants exchanged clothing, silverware, and glassware with local people for semiprecious stones from Afghanistan, Chinese silks, and Indian textiles. Then, proceeding down India's west coast, they stopped near present-day Bombay, trading silverware, Italian wine, and slave musicians for pepper. Finally the travelers reached the great port of Muziris (MOO-zir-us) in southwest India. A second-century Indian poet recorded the arrival of such ships at Muziris: "The beautiful vessels stir white foam on the river, arriving with gold and departing with pepper."[2] After a stay in the port, which allowed the sailors to haunt the waterfront dives, the ship sailed around the southern tip of India and up the east coast, stopping to collect pearls, textiles, spices, and gems, before reaching the mouth of the Ganges River. Finally the ship returned to Egypt, the merchants aboard hoping to make a fortune from their cargo.

From the west—Arabia, Egypt, Persia, East Africa, Greece, Rome—ships like this one arrived annually at Indian seaports to trade. They came to share in the fabled wealth from the cities, mines, fields, and forests of India. The merchant ships collected fabulous trade goods, such as pepper, cinnamon, cotton, and gems, for sale in distant markets, part of the long-distance trade networks linking India to other lands. India also attracted sojourners, some arriving by sea and others overland, such as varied Chinese Buddhist (BOO-dihst) pilgrims who stayed for years before returning to their homeland with new wisdom and tales of adventure. Other people came to settle permanently. For those who arrived over the mountains from windswept Central Asia, the Indian sun was a blazing fury and the drenching summer rains a shock.

To all the newcomers, whether visitors like the Greek writer or settlers, the Indian culture and religion were more unusual than the climate. Indian society was adaptable and accommodating. Most immigrants, whatever their original religious views, found themselves gradually enfolded into Indian religions, which allowed for many paths to understanding. But immigrants could also maintain their special customs while living side by side with other groups that followed their own. Hinduism was resilient, bending to meet the varying needs of dissimilar people. This adaptability also helped Indian culture to spread into Southeast Asia. India remained confidently distinctive while also engaging with the world around it.

The Classical Era was a time of flowering in South and Southeast Asia, particularly in state building, the development of new trade networks, and religious thought. Many of the patterns forged in this era endured into modern times. Several great empires brought unusual political unity to South Asia and made India a leading world power. India also remained closely connected to land and sea networks of exchange that helped reshape the society. Hinduism developed new schools of thought, while Buddhism (BOO-diz-uhm) arose to become a major faith in many parts of Asia. Meanwhile, various Central and Southeast Asian societies established states and social systems that differed greatly from those in India and China. While some Central Asian cities flourished from overland trade, Southeast Asians became major participants in international maritime trade.

FOCUS QUESTIONS

1. What ideas did Buddhism take from Hinduism, and what ideas were unique?
2. How did the Mauryas shape Indian society?
3. What were some of the ways in which classical India connected with and influenced the world beyond South Asia?
4. What were the main achievements of the Gupta era?
5. How did Southeast Asians blend indigenous and foreign influences to create unique societies?

The Transformation of Indian Society and Its Religions

What ideas did Buddhism take from Hinduism, and what ideas were unique?

The forging of a new society from the synthesis of Aryan and local traditions that began in the second millennium B.C.E. (see Chapter 2) continued for centuries, affecting many aspects of life and thought. In particular, the distinctive caste system became a key part of the framework of Indian society, and Hinduism grew even more diverse and complex. In addition, Jainism and Buddhism were born out of the religious ferment of the Axial Age, that great philosophical awakening across Eurasia during the early Classical Age that spawned many new ways of thinking from Greece to China.

Caste and Indian Society

The social configuration we know today as the caste system began to take shape early in the Classical Era, especially in North India. Members of a caste generally practiced a common occupation: some were priests, others warriors, merchants, artisans, or farmers, while still others performed the more menial tasks. Caste membership was also supported by Hindu values, including beliefs in reincarnation and ritual practices. Although the social and religious characteristics became similar throughout India over the centuries, the caste system was never uniform and unchanging. Still, it produced a social stability that allowed it to persist for several thousand years.

Characteristics of Caste　Over time the caste system became more fully developed. A third-century B.C.E. Greek visitor remarked that Indians were not allowed to marry outside their own caste or to change their occupation. A political and legal document with advice for a Hindu king, usually known as the Code of Manu (MAN-oo) and probably compiled sometime during the first or second century C.E., formalized many rules regarding caste relations. Gradually, during the first millennium of the Common Era the four main castes (*varna*) subdivided into thousands of subcastes known as *jati* ("birth group"), each with its own rules and, frequently, occupational specialization. Through the generations some subcastes moved up or down in the caste hierarchy from one varna to another.

Online Study Center **Improve Your Grade**
Primary Source: The Laws of Manu

CHRONOLOGY

	India	Southeast Asia
600 B.C.E.	563–483 B.C.E. Life of the Buddha	
400 B.C.E.	322–185 B.C.E. Mauryan Empire	
200 B.C.E.		111 B.C.E.–939 C.E. Chinese colonization of Vietnam
1 C.E.	50–250 C.E. Kushan era	ca. 75–550 C.E. Funan ca. 192–1471 C.E. Champa
200 C.E	320–550 C.E. Gupta era	

Eventually the caste system became hereditary. Each person was born into a certain caste and marked by several social and religious characteristics. For example, each caste maintained a moral code that stipulated such duties as family maintenance and which jatis could supply marriage partners. Caste members were also required to eat and drink together. Strong food regulations prescribed the types of food that could be consumed by each caste, who could cook and serve the food, and who could accompany the diner. Some castes, especially those of higher rank, became vegetarian; others could eat meat.

Gradually vegetarianism became more common among the higher castes, and cows were protected against being killed. A third-century B.C.E. book ordered that cattle should never be slaughtered. Many historians think that beef eating was common in Vedic and classical times and probably did not become completely taboo until after 500 C.E. By then pious Hindus avoided eating beef because the cow had come to be considered sacred, the symbol of life and motherhood. In Indian cities and villages cows wandered at will, eating whatever grain they found and generally enjoying a pampered existence. Foreign observers have often criticized this situation, arguing that the cows spread disease and consume scarce food resources. However, some anthropologists argue that cow tolerance was not an irrational superstition but made economic sense. For example, protecting cows ensured an ample supply of cow dung for fuel and fertilizer, as well as milk for food. Cows also bore oxen, the basis for agriculture.

The mix of social and religious notions strongly influenced a group's placement in the caste system. The Hindu doctrine of *karma* held that one's caste status in the present life was determined by deeds in past lives. Every action, whether good or evil, had repercussions, and the sum of one's karma in past lives determined one's fate in this life. The three top caste groupings were considered further along the path of reincarnation. Low-caste Indians were held responsible for their status because of their presumed past sins. Their only hope for improved caste status in future lives lay in dutifully performing their present duties and obligations. The *Bhagavad Gita* also warned that ignoring caste destroyed the family: "When lawlessness prevails, the women of the family become corrupted. And to hell does this confusion [of caste] bring the family itself."[3]

At the bottom of the social system were the untouchables, or *pariahs* (puh-RYE-uhz), who had a status below the formal caste system. Probably constituting some 10 percent of the Indian population, untouchables were generally condemned to trades and crafts regarded as undesirable (such as carrying water to village houses) or unclean because their function involved being polluted by filth (such as sweeping village paths of garbage and manure) or the taking of animal life. They also worked as hunters, fishermen, butchers, gravediggers, tanners, leather workers, and scavengers, and they lived largely in their own villages or in shabby neighborhoods in towns.

The Persistence of Caste The caste system has functioned in some form for the past 2,500 years, though not without considerable change. Social and religious sanctions helped maintain caste, but it also persisted because of what it accomplished within Indian society. For example, in several ways the caste system provided stability and security. It promoted mutual aid within each caste and regulated village life, as subcastes exchanged goods or services with other subcastes in the village. It also aided the assimilation process: new groups, such as invaders into northern India, were integrated into the larger society by becoming a new subcaste. Regional variations also developed: no single hierarchy or ranking was recognized throughout India. For example, landowning groups dominated some places, trading groups in others. In South India, Bengal, and northwestern India, caste status remained ambiguous and the system was less complex.

Village Scene, Second Century C.E. In classical times most Indians lived in villages. This drawing of a village scene is based on a relief made at Amaravati, a Buddhist temple complex built in the second century C.E. It shows members of different caste groups carrying out various village activities.
[From A.L. Balsham, *The Wonder That Was India* (London: Sidgwick and Jackson,1954)]

The caste system contributed greatly to the long-term continuity of Indian society through the centuries, providing meaning and direction to the lives of Indians, especially in the villages. Caste, along with village and family, became the pillar of Indian society, contributing to a group orientation, a passion for stability, and an acceptance of authority. Caste still remains strong in many villages of India. However, the system has been rapidly breaking down in the larger cities, as it has been undermined by the realities of modern industrial life. It is difficult to avoid close contact with members of other castes while eating in a restaurant, being confined in a hospital, or working in an office.

The Shaping of Hinduism

The religion known today as Hinduism faced increasing dissent during the Classical Era. Between around 1000 and 600 B.C.E., power was increasingly concentrated in the hands of the priestly class, the *brahmans*. They alone had mastered the scriptures and hymns for worship. Rituals presided over by priests were an essential feature of Hinduism. Enriched by gifts from the devout, many priests became wealthy landowners. Eventually, however, some Indians became resentful at what they viewed as priestly wealth and corruption and the empty rituals over which the priests presided. Out of these conflicts came new movements that emphasized spirituality, especially medita-

tion, over ritual and that fostered new approaches to worship. The critics of priestly power did not necessarily reject the Vedas or ritual, but they proposed other, complementary paths to spiritual fulfillment. Some of their writings were collected in the *Upanishads*, the final portion of the vast Hindu scriptures.

As a result of this new spirituality, the highest ideal of Hinduism came to be the escape from sensual pleasures and the material world (seen as an "illusion") and the joining of one's individual soul with **Brahman**, the Universal Soul, or Absolute Reality, that fills all space and time. To achieve this goal, some seekers turned to asceticism, rejecting society and seeking mystical unity with the divine through techniques known as *yoga* (YOH-guh) ("yoke" or "union"). Yoga was a system of physical and mental exercises that emphasized control of breathing to promote mental concentration, calmness, and a trancelike state that produced a mystical awareness of a universal soul. Holy men who abandoned worldly pleasures through such practices as yoga were greatly admired in India, even if only a tiny minority of people followed this challenging path.

Union with the Universal Soul meant ending the cycle of reincarnation, called the "wheel of life." The *Bhagavad Gita* (see Chapter 2) identified three paths for achieving release

---

Brahman The Universal Soul, or Absolute Reality, that Hindus believe fills all space and time.

from the wheel of life: devotion to God, selfless action, and knowledge achieved chiefly through intense meditation. According to these writings, believers should worship "the Imperishable, the Undefinable, the Omnipresent, the Incomprehensible, the Eternal." Selfless action meant working "for the welfare of all living things." Finally, knowledge was also praiseworthy: "To know is better than to do; To meditate than to know; And to renounce action's ends is better than to meditate. Peace comes straight from such renunciation."[4]

Whatever the path chosen, the ultimate goal was to escape from one's ego. Only by doing this could a person end the round of reincarnation and finally achieve the ultimate bliss of merging with Brahman. This bliss was described in the *Upanishads* as a deep, dreamless sleep. But achieving this state necessitated mastering oneself and abandoning the desires and actions that prevent release from earthly lives. "In thinking 'This is I' and 'That is mine,'" warns the *Upanishads*, "one binds himself to himself, as does a bird with a snare!"[5]

New forms of worship stressing devotion or prayer made salvation more accessible to the lower castes, since members of these groups did not have time for intense meditative practices. Gradually worship focused on personal devotion to specific gods such as Vishnu or Shiva, as well as to thousands of lesser deities represented by sacred stones and images. Every home had a shrine to worship such deities. Believers could also seek inspiration from many ancient stories about Hindu gods. Frequent religious festivals had mass appeal, and great throngs made annual pilgrimages to sacred places such as the River Ganges.

New Schools of Hindu Thought

Eventually the quest for spiritual experience led to the formulation of new schools of Hindu thought. Perhaps the most influential new school was **Vedanta** (vay-DAHNT-uh), meaning the "completion" of the Vedas. Vedanta offered mystical experience and a belief in the underlying unity of all reality. Members of Vedanta and similar schools found sophisticated ways of thinking about the countless gods found in popular Hinduism, a diversity often summed up by the phrase "33,000 gods." However, Vedanta thinkers have not seen their religion as polytheistic, since all of these gods and spirits are only manifestations of the single Absolute Reality that pervades everything. All creation was seen in Vedantic philosophy as ultimately unified. The *Upanishads* states that Brahman is

God, all gods, the five elements—earth, air, fire, water, ether; all beings, great or small, born of eggs, born from the womb, born from heat, born from soil; horses, cows, men, elephants, birds; everything that breathes, the beings that walk and the beings that walk not.[6]

Thanks to the great diversity of gods and beliefs, Hinduism developed a broad and tolerant approach to religious differences. Through history many invaders swept into India,

but most of them found a place in Hinduism, which incorporated a wide variety of other beliefs, even integrating some non-Hindu figures (including the Buddha) into devotional cults. In India, God may be worshiped in many forms and on many paths. As an old Indian folk song puts it: "Into the bosom of the great sea, flow streams that come from hills on every side. Their names are various as their springs. And thus in every land do men bow down, To one great God, though known by many names."[7]

From this time onwards Hinduism developed not as a cohesive, rigidly defined theology with a centralized church but as a broad collection of loosely connected sects with some common ideas but many variations of belief and practice. Indeed, before the nineteenth century C.E. Indians did not use the term *Hinduism* to refer to these sects collectively. Toleration and accommodation allowed Hinduism to retain its widespread popularity among both the better educated and the villagers, despite the clearly inequitable divisions of caste and the burdens of karma. Theology remained less important than rituals and caste duties.

Jainism and Buddhism

Two dissident ascetics during the height of the Eurasian Axial Age eventually gave up on reforming Hinduism and founded new movements that eventually became separate religions, Jainism (JINE-iz-uhm) and Buddhism. Jain ideas were organized by a famed teacher, Mahavira (MA-ha-VEER-a) ("Great Hero"), around 500 B.C.E. Mahavira grew up near Patna in north India, the pampered son of a tribal chief. At the age of thirty, he abandoned his affluent life to wander naked as an ascetic. A master of self-control, Mahavira practiced self-torture as the route to salvation, eventually starving himself to death. But his message had reached a wider audience.

The basic tenet of **Jainism** is that life in all forms must be protected because everything, including animals, insects, plants, and even sticks and stones, have a separate soul and are alive. While walking, a devout Jain sweeps the ground to avoid stepping on insects and wears a cloth over the nose to prevent inhaling insects. Nonviolence is, in Mahavira's words, "the pure, unchanging law. All things living, all beings whatever, should not be slain, or treated with violence."[8] Jains are vegetarians, but the most devout would not even eat vegetables such as carrots or potatoes because uprooting them would damage the microorganisms living in the soil. To take life, Mahavira warned, meant that the soul suffers for its carelessness and is whirled about in the universe. Jain monks beg for their food from the faithful.

Given the emphasis on austere behavior, the Jain sect never became very large; there are perhaps 1 million Jains in the world today. Only a few take up full-time the demanding life of a Jain monk, the only sure path to salvation. But Jainism had a major intellectual influence on Hindu ideas of nonviolence. Twenty-five centuries after Mahavira, Mohandas

Vedanta ("completion of the Vedas") A school of classical Indian thought that offered Hindus mystical experience and a belief in the underlying unity of all reality.

Jainism An Indian religion that believed life in all forms must be protected because everything, including animals, insects, plants, sticks, and stones, has a separate soul and is alive.

Worship of Buddhist Relics   In the first century C.E. Buddhists erected a pillar containing this frieze of a stupa housing relics of the Buddha. The stupa is surrounded by throngs of worshipers and pilgrims making music and bringing offerings to honor the Buddha. (Jean-Louis Nou/akg-images)

Gandhi, a devout Hindu, utilized Jain ideas in developing his philosophy of nonviolence, out of which passive resistance and the fast-until-death developed as strategies for generating political change. Since agriculture was difficult without killing some bugs and animals, most Jains became merchants and bankers, forming a relatively prosperous community. They are prominent today in India's economic elite.

More important in the long run than Jainism was **Buddhism**, a religion based on the teachings of a major Axial Age thinker, the Buddha. As part of a great Eurasian transition involving the growth and spread of universal religions, Buddhism eventually spread out of India to become a major faith in Central, East, and Southeast Asia and Sri Lanka. Paradoxically, Buddhism had far more influence outside its land of birth than inside, although within India the teachings of Buddhism posed a challenge to priestly Hinduism.

The religion's founder was Siddartha Gautama (si-DAHR-tuh GAUT-uh-muh) (563–483 B.C.E.), who was born a prince of a small kingdom in what is now southern Nepal. He was a contemporary of Confucius, Mahavira, and several other great Axial Age thinkers. As with Jesus of Nazareth and Confucius, his life and thought are known largely through the accounts written by his followers. As a youth, Siddartha led a privileged, carefree, and self-indulgent life, and then was shocked when he ventured from the palace and encountered the disease, sorrows, and miseries experienced by common people.

As a result of witnessing this unhappiness, Siddartha abandoned his royal life, wife, and family to search for truth as a wandering holy man. In his quest he was influenced by the

critiques of brahman prayers and sacrifices that had led to the *Upanishads*. He also rejected the Hindu caste system as immoral. For several years he lived in the forest, practicing yoga, meditating, and begging for his food, nearly dying from fasting and self-torture. He met religious skeptics who argued that there is no afterlife or god. Eventually, around 528 B.C.E., Siddartha believed he understood cosmic truths. Thereafter Siddartha Gautama was called the Buddha ("The Enlightened One"). He began traveling to teach his new religion, attracting many disciples but living simply.

Buddhist Thought

Giving his first sermon in the Ganges city of Benares around 527 B.C.E., Buddha laid out his basic insights, highlighting the Four Noble Truths (see Witness to the Past: Basic Doctrines in the Buddha's First Sermon). The first truth asserts that this life is one of suffering and ignorance. The second suggests that suffering stems from desiring what one does not have and clinging to what one already has for fear of losing it. The third truth is to stop all desire. The fourth truth provides the method of stopping desire, which is to follow the Noble Eightfold Path: correct views, intent, speech, actions, trade (or profession), effort, mindfulness, and concentration. Following this path means leading a good life that does no harm to others and realizing that one is but a tiny part of a larger chain of composite events. To Buddhists, the world is in a constant state of flux; when mortals try in vain to stop the flow of events, they suffer. Even the gods are subject to the four noble truths. Buddhism is neither monotheistic nor polytheistic, and the Buddha was ambivalent as to whether a god or gods existed. If they did, he argued, they must follow the same four truths as mortals.

Along with embracing nonviolence, moderation, and love for all creatures, Buddhists were encouraged to live morally

Buddhism   A major world religion based on the teachings of the Buddha that emphasized putting an end to desire and being compassionate to all creatures.

Basic Doctrines in the Buddha's First Sermon

Buddhist tradition holds that, after achieving enlightenment, the Buddha preached his first sermon in a deer park in the outskirts of the Ganges city of Varanasi (Benares) around 527 B.C.E. The sermon became one of the most important sources of belief for all Buddhists. It laid out the framework of Buddha's moral message, including the Middle Way between asceticism and worldly life, the Noble Eightfold Path, and the Four Noble Truths. These are the most important concepts in all branches of Buddhism.

There are two ends not to be served by a wanderer. What are these two? The pursuit of desires and of pleasure which springs from desire, which is base, common, leading to rebirth, ignoble and unprofitable; and the pursuit of pain and hardship [asceticism], which is grievous, ignoble, and unprofitable. The Middle Way of the [Buddha] avoids both of these ends. It is enlightened, it brings clear vision, it makes for wisdom, and leads to peace, insight, enlightenment, and Nirvana. What is the Middle Way? It is the Noble Eightfold path—Right Views, Right Resolve, Right Speech, Right Conduct, Right Livelihood, Right Effort, Right Mindfulness, and Right Concentration....

And this is the Noble Truth of Sorrow. Birth is sorrow, age is sorrow, disease is sorrow, death is sorrow; contact with the unpleasant is sorrow, separation from the pleasant is sorrow, every wish unfulfilled is sorrow—in short, all of the five components of individuality are sorrow.

And this is the Noble Truth of the Arising of Sorrow. It arises from craving, which leads to rebirth, which brings delight and passion, and seeks pleasure from here, now there—the craving for sensual pleasure, the craving for continued life, the craving for power.

And this is the Noble Truth of the Stopping of Sorrow. It is the complete stopping of the craving, so that no passion remains, leaving it, being emancipated from it, being released from it, giving no place to it.

And this is the Noble Truth of the Way which Leads to the Stopping of Sorrow. It is the Noble Eightfold Path....

THINKING ABOUT THE READING

1. What does the Buddha mean by the Middle Way?
2. What causes suffering, and how can people stop it?
3. What conduct do these ideas promote?

Source: William Theodore De Bary et al., eds., *Sources of Indian Tradition,* vol. 1 (New York: Columbia University Press, 1958), pp. 98–99.

---

and consider the needs of others. For example, men were urged to treat their wives with respect and to acquire wealth to benefit their family. Believers were urged to take refuge from the world's sorrows not only in wisdom but also in constructive brotherhood, bringing joy to others. Buddha advised his followers to be their own lamps and their own refuges and to hold firmly to the truth. Asked to summarize his beliefs, he replied: "Avoid doing evil deeds, cultivate doing good deeds, and purify the mind."[9] These teachings had economic consequences. The Buddha did not oppose acquiring wealth but believed that wealth alone did not bring happiness. He also condemned the irresponsible use of wealth, such as wasting it on drinking, gambling, and laziness rather than saving some for emergencies and donating some to worthy causes.

Buddha adopted many Hindu ideas but also modified them. For example, to be released from the chronic cycle of birth and rebirth, Buddhists were urged, as were Hindus, to abandon all sense of self. Buddhists, like Hindus, believed in reincarnation: the idea that the individual soul progresses through a series of lives. But the goal for Buddhists was not unity with Brahman but rather **nirvana** (neer-VAHN-uh) (literally, "the blowing out"), a kind of everlasting peace or end of suffering achieved through perfection of wisdom and compassion. Buddha also urged his followers to avoid taking animal life if possible. As a result, many Buddhists became vegetarians.

Buddha seems to have been the world's first religious leader to introduce the idea of **monasticism** (muh-NAS-tuh-siz-uhm), the pursuit of a life of penance, prayer, and meditation, either alone or in a community of other seekers. He advocated voluntarily adopting a monastic life that required chastity, poverty, and nonviolence. Joining the monastic life, usually at a temple or monastery, meant suspension of family ties. Buddha initially sanctioned only monks, but later nuns were also admitted to the order. Monks and nuns followed the rules of proper conduct and also used such techniques as yoga for concentration, thoughtful meditation, and self-discipline. They also begged for their food, which affirmed their humility; in addition, believers gained merit by giving them food and other necessities.

Buddha soon gained many followers. People believed his ideas offered a philosophical depth and ethical purity, established firm moral standards, and pointed the way to ending the suffering of life. The Buddhist opposition to caste and priestly

---

nirvana ("the blowing out") For Buddhists a kind of everlasting peace or end of suffering achieved through perfection of wisdom and compassion.

monasticism The pursuit of a life of penance, prayer, and meditation, either alone or in a community of other seekers.

power also attracted followers. Eventually Buddhism became a major influence on the first great Indian imperial state, the Mauryan Empire.

SECTION SUMMARY

- The Indian caste system, which began to take form in the Classical Era, placed limits on one's occupation, diet, religious practice, and social interactions.
- Caste became hereditary; according to the doctrine of karma, one's caste was seen as punishment or reward for one's behavior in previous lives.
- New spiritual movements within Hinduism, such as yoga and Vedanta, challenged priestly control and emphasized the goal of escaping the ego.
- Although Hinduism was extremely inclusive, the two movements of Jainism and Buddhism split off from it.
- Buddhism, which offered a set of guidelines to help people achieve nirvana, was ultimately far more influential outside of India than inside it.

CHRONOLOGY	
Classical India	
563–483 B.C.E.	Life of the Buddha
326 B.C.E.	Alexander the Great's army reaches western India
322–185 B.C.E.	Mauryan Empire
269–232 B.C.E.	Reign of Ashoka
200 B.C.E.–150 C.E.	Division of Buddhism into Theravada and Mahayana schools
ca. 50–250 C.E.	Kushan Empire in northwest India
ca. 320–550 C.E.	Gupta era

Eurasian Exchanges, Indian Politics, and the Mauryan Empire

How did the Mauryas shape Indian society?

The outstanding political development in the Classical Era was the emergence of India's first centralized empire, the Mauryan (MORE-yuhn) Empire, centered in the Ganges valley. The rise of this powerful and prosperous state was in part a response to contact with peoples to the west, including the Hellenistic Greeks. Indeed, the Mauryas were very much involved with the wider world, engaging in foreign trade and official sponsorship of Buddhist missions to neighboring societies. Like the Hellenistic Greeks and Romans, the Mauryans were linked to networks of trade, warfare, and communication. They also established a powerful army and government that brought unprecedented political unity to the subcontinent.

Indian Encounters with Persians and Greeks

For several centuries northwest India remained in close communication with societies to the west, first Persia and then Hellenistic Greece. These encounters resulted from military conflict. Under their great king, Darius, the Persians conquered much of the Indus River Valley in what is now Pakistan in 518 B.C.E. This conquest brought India to the attention of the Greek historian Herodotus, whose fabulous tales, many based

on rumor rather than fact, may have stimulated the imagination of the young Alexander the Great (see Chapter 6).

By 326 B.C.E. Alexander, whose forces had already conquered Persia, had reached the Indus River (see Chronology: Classical India). Alexander's forces soon subdued several small Aryan kingdoms east of the Indus. The Macedonian conqueror was impressed with wealthy India and its systems of thought. Being always curious, he held numerous discussions with Indian scholars about religion and philosophy, apparently dispatching his notes back to his own teacher, Aristotle. In this way some Greek thinkers became aware of some of the ideas of Buddhism and Hinduism. Faced with a rebellion by his exhausted and homesick soldiers, however, Alexander turned back before entering the Ganges Valley, and he died in Babylon in 323 B.C.E.

Alexander's legacy endured much longer than his power. Hellenistic cultural influence persisted in northwest India. For example, Greek artistic styles helped to shape Buddhist art. There was also some continuing Greek political influence, since the Greek imperialists set up a state in northern Afghanistan known as Bactria (BAK-tree-uh) as an outpost of their Persian venture. Later the local Greek rulers of Bactria declared their independence from the Hellenistic Empire, and Bactria flourished as a regional power that occasionally dispatched forces into India over the next several centuries. Some Greeks also remained behind in northwest India, intermarrying with local women. Eventually, however, they and their culture were absorbed into the Indian population.

The Imperial Mauryan State

The disruption by Alexander's invasion into western India created a political vacuum that was filled by the military forces of Chandragupta (CHUHN-druh-GOOP-tuh) Maurya, who established the first imperial Indian state, the Mauryan Empire (322–185 B.C.E.). Perhaps inspired by Alexander, Chandragupta

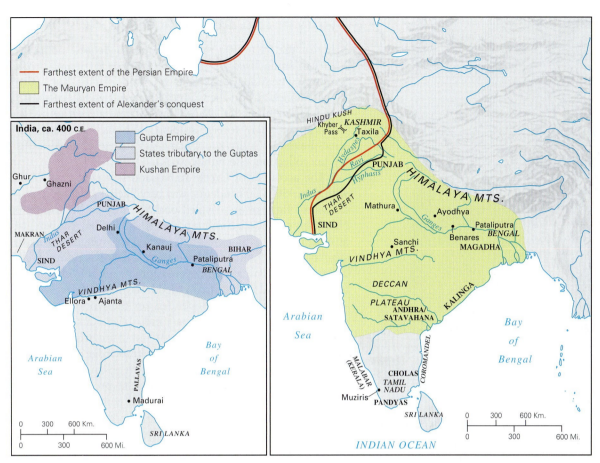

Map 7.1   The Mauryan Empire, 322–185 B.C.E.
During the Classical Era major states arose in north India, most notably the Mauryan, Kushan, and Gupta Empires. The brief encounter with the Greek forces led by Alexander the Great, which reached the Indus River Valley in 326 B.C.E., may have stimulated the Mauryas to build India's first empire.

transformed himself from the ruler of the most important Ganges state, Magadha (MAH-guh-duh), into the monarch of half the subcontinent, and he reigned from 324 to 301 B.C.E. He conquered an empire embracing the Ganges and Indus Basins and held it together with a powerful army and an efficient administration (see Map 7.1). In 305 B.C.E. Chandragupta concluded a treaty with Alexander's heir that set the mutual border along the Hindu Kush Mountains and resulted in the withdrawal of all remaining Greek forces to Persia. At its height the Mauryan Empire included parts of Afghanistan, most of north and central India, and large parts of south India. The Mauryas maintained diplomatic relations with many societies, including Greece, Syria, and Egypt.

Chandragupta was a cynical political realist who was skilled in manipulating power. He was influenced by the ideas of his chief adviser, Kautilya (cow-TILL-ya), who favored political centralization. Kautilya may have compiled the initial draft of what was to become a manual for rulers on obtaining and holding power. The manual has been compared to the works of Legalist thinkers in late Zhou China around the same time. For example, the manual elaborated the six forms of state

policy as "peace, war, neutrality, marching, alliance, and making peace with one and waging war with another.?[10]

The entire empire was ruled by a powerful state that probably offered the most efficient government in the classical world. A large army and secret police maintained order. The king closely supervised government officials, and spies kept them under constant surveillance. The Greek ambassador particularly admired the conscientious justice system, in which the king presided personally over court sessions and settled disputes. To maintain the expensive government, the state claimed between a quarter and a half of all agricultural production while also heavily taxing trade, mining, herding, and other economic activities. At the village level, councils composed of older men from leading families governed with considerable local autonomy, a pattern that became entrenched over the centuries.

The Mauryan monarch lived in great splendor, often in seclusion and surrounded by an entourage of women who cooked his food, served his wine, and in the evening carried him to his apartment, where they lulled him to sleep with music. Since Vedic times Indian rulers had claimed to be blessed

Ashoka Column This 32-feet-tall sandstone column, erected in northeast India around 240 B.C.E., weighs 50 tons. The inscriptions on the pillar outline Ashoka's achievements and offer advice on how citizens of the empire should behave. (Borromeo/Art Resource, NY)

by the gods, endowed with supernatural and magical powers. The claim had a propaganda value because it suggested that opponents would be punished even after death. Yet, checks on autocratic power existed. One was the realization that excessive taxes and forced labor might drive the people into rebellion.

Mauryan Life, Institutions, and Networks

Many of the 50 to 100 million people in densely populated Mauryan India lived in cities, the centers for a prosperous economy. The Mauryan capital city, Patna (PUHT-nuh) (then called Pataliputra) on the Ganges River, was widely celebrated for its parks, public buildings, libraries, and a great university that attracted many foreign students. Various boards administered the municipality, supervising such things as trade, industry, tax collection, and public works.

The accounts of Greek ambassadors suggest that Patna, with some 500,000 residents, was very likely the largest city in the world for that era, rivaled perhaps only by the capital of Han China. The circumference of the fortified timber wall around the city, which had 570 towers, was roughly 21 miles, suggesting that Patna was about twice as large as Rome several centuries later. Patna itself covered some 9 miles from one end to the other, and it was surrounded by a moat 900 feet wide.

Mauryan prosperity depended on the world's most advanced trading system and craft industries. Kautilya praised material gain as the most important end in life because it made possible the other two aims, religious knowledge and pleasure. Many skilled woodworkers, ivory carvers, and stonecutters populated the cities, and various cities also produced fine cotton fabrics. Well-kept highways fostered commerce. Products and merchants moved along the major east-west highway, which stretched from a seaport near present-day Calcutta (kal-KUHT-uh) through the Ganges and Indus Valleys to the borders of Afghanistan. Many foreign merchants resided in the empire, and an active exchange took place with China, Arabia, and the Middle East over trade networks.

The economy was a mix of private and public enterprise, which became a long-term pattern in India. Most cities had large merchant quarters. Artisan and merchant guilds, ruled by councils, supervised the private sector, while the government owned mines and forests and engaged in shipbuilding, arms manufacture, and textile production. Public granaries stored surplus food.

Ashoka and Buddhist Monarchy

The Mauryas reached their height under the enlightened king Ashoka (uh-SHOH-kuh) (whose name means "Sorrowless"), one of the major political and religious figures in world history. The grandson of Chandragupta, the ambitious Ashoka became a general and rose to power through a bloody campaign of eliminating rivals and expanding into frontier lands. We know much about Ashoka (r. 269–232 B.C.E.) from the many edicts he had carved in rocks and sandstone pillars. His early edicts boast of many enemies slain and captured. But this boasting of violence stopped when Ashoka underwent a spiritual experience and became a devout Buddhist. Edicts written after his religious conversion proclaim his remorse at past atrocities and conquests and his commitment to nonviolence. One edict noted that Ashoka "began to follow righteousness, to love righteousness. The greatest of all victories is the victory of righteousness."[11]

Ashoka spent his remaining years in power promoting the pacifist teachings of the Buddha. He wrote that his duty was the good of the whole world. He pledged to bear wrong without violent retribution, to look kindly on all his subjects, and to ensure the safety, happiness, and peace of mind of all living beings. To fulfill his pledge, he designed laws to encourage Buddhist virtues such as simplicity, compassion, mutual tolerance, vegetarianism, and respect for all forms of life. He also sponsored many public works, including hospitals and medical care paid for by the state. Trees were planted, parks developed, wells dug, and rest houses built along highways. Ashoka dispatched Buddhist missions to various foreign countries, spreading the religion into Sri Lanka, Southeast Asia, and Afghanistan. According to one legend, a Buddhist monk sent by Ashoka reached Greece, where he debated with Greek thinkers about the nature of being. Such contacts indicate that Eurasian networks of religious and philosophical exchange were forming.

Despite his own devotion and strong beliefs, Ashoka neither made Buddhism the state religion nor persecuted other faiths. Indeed, while Ashoka financed the building of Buddhist temples and *stupas* (STOOP-uhz) (domed shrines), government aid was distributed to all religious groups. The king argued that "all sects deserve reverence for one reason or another. By thus acting a man exalts his own sect and at the same time does service to the sects of other people."[12]

Although reflecting Buddhist attitudes, Ashoka was also a practical statesman. He sought to spread humane ideas peacefully both within and without the borders of the state while also maintaining the system of courts and a military force. Public respect for his pacifist ideals and behavior discouraged rebellion. Ashoka styled himself "Beloved of the Gods," which in practice meant he was considered at least a semi-deity. For both Hindus and Buddhists, the Mauryas created a political legacy of the universal emperor, a divinely sanctioned leader with a special role in the cosmic scheme of things.

The Decline of the Mauryas

Ashoka ruled with popular acclaim, but his successors were less able. Within a half century after his death, regions were seceding, the Mauryas were overthrown, and the empire destroyed. Perhaps Ashoka's policies had made India too peace-loving and had weakened Mauryan military forces. But difficult communications in a large empire also fostered local autonomy, and the mounting costs of a centralized bureaucracy drained the treasury. Perhaps caste divisions and ethnic and religious diversity also undermined political unity.

The end of the Mauryan Empire set a political pattern different from that of China. In China, long periods of unity were interspersed with short intervals of political fragmentation. In India, on the other hand, periods of unity were relatively brief, followed by prolonged fragmentation. But while India did not always possess political unity, it did possess a strong sense of cultural unity. This culture and mindset emphasized loyalty to the social order, including the family and caste, rather than to the state.

SECTION SUMMARY
- Through the conquests by Darius and Alexander the Great, northwest India experienced significant influence from the West.
- After Alexander's retreat, Chandragupta established the first imperial Indian state, the centralized, autocratic Mauryan Empire, which included the Indus and Ganges Basins.
- The Mauryan capital city, Patna, was among the largest in the world, and the empire excelled in crafts and trade.
- King Ashoka, Chandragupta's grandson, became a pacifist convert to Buddhism, which he helped to spread to Sri Lanka, Southeast Asia, and Afghanistan.
- Unlike those of China, India's periods of unity were relatively brief; and, several decades after Ashoka died, the Mauryan Empire broke down.

South and Central Asia After the Mauryas

What were some of the ways in which classical India connected with and influenced the world beyond South Asia?

Although the end of the Mauryas in the early second century B.C.E. was followed by 500 years of political fragmentation before the rise of the next empire, that of the Guptas, these centuries saw increasing contact between India and the outside world. This contact had strong repercussions for both sides. India's contact with peoples in Central Asia increased, and Indian cultural influence, especially Buddhism, spread into that region. Various Central and West Asian peoples swept into northwestern India from time to time, conquering the Indus Valley and mixing with local peoples, who eventually absorbed the invaders and their ways. Substantial foreign trade and Buddhist missions to neighboring societies also occurred. In world history, change has often come from contact with other peoples, and this was certainly true of India.

India, Central Asia, and the Silk Road

India's relations with Central Asia, the area stretching from Russia eastward to the borders of China, were constant and included several dimensions. Central Asia, especially the Turkestan region north of India, so known since many people spoke Turkish languages, was a key contact zone and hub for networks stretching east to China, south to India, and west to Persia and Russia. As trade between China and western Asia developed, cities developed in Central Asia along the overland route (known as the "Silk Road") through Turkestan. A Persian-speaking society, the Sogdians (SAHG-dee-uhns), mostly

Zoroastrians or Buddhists, dominated the commerce of many cities along the trade network, and they also linked the trade to India. The Sogdians, who had a written language and literature, developed a flourishing mercantile society based on their interaction with Persians, Turks, Indians, Chinese, and others. A Chinese traveler described the country around the major Sogdian city, Samarkand (SAM-uhr-kand), as "a great commercial entrepot, very fertile, abounding in trees and flowers, its inhabitants skillful craftsmen, smart and energetic."[13]

Over the centuries various pastoral groups living on China's borders, unable to penetrate China's defenses or under pressure from Chinese expansion, moved westward. Among the best known were the Huns, who developed the most effective weapon of the day, a reflex bow. Pressure from the horseback-riding Hun soldiers had long pushed various Indo-Europeans, including the Germanic peoples, into Europe. Some Huns migrated into the fertile plains of southern Russia and Hungary. In the fourth and fifth centuries C.E. Huns invaded and inflicted much damage on the weakened Roman Empire (see Chapter 8). Various other Central Asians settled in eastern Europe, southern Russia, and the Caucasus. Others moved south through Turkestan into Persia, Afghanistan, and India, helping shape developments there.

Migrations into Northwest India

Throughout the Classical Era new peoples migrated through the mountain ranges into northwest India from Central Asia and western Asia. These invasions introduced new cultural influences, adding to India's hybrid character. The newcomers were diverse. Invaders from the Hellenistic kingdom of Bactria in Afghanistan, for instance, occupied parts of the Indus Basin, reintroducing Greek influence. Bactria was a crossroads between east and west where Greek, Persian, and Indian cultures met and mixed. There Greeks and Indians exchanged knowledge of medicine and astronomy. Bactrian Greeks adopted Hinduism or Buddhism and inspired a Greek- and Roman-influenced form of Buddhist painting and sculpture, known as Gandhara after the region where it emerged west of the Indus. Gandharan art became preeminent in parts of the northwest, reaching its height in the fourth and fifth centuries C.E. Eventually the Bactrian Greeks became absorbed into the broad fold of Indian society. Various Central Asians migrated into northwest India beginning around 50 B.C.E. Like their predecessors, the new rulers adopted Hinduism and fit themselves into the caste system, mostly as warriors.

In the first century C.E. the **Kushans** (KOO-shans), an Indo-European people from Central Asia, conquered much of northwest India and western parts of the Ganges Basin, and they constructed an empire that also encompassed Afghanistan and parts of Central Asia, including many Silk Road cities. This expansion brought occasional conflicts with first the Parthians

Kushans An Indo-European people from Central Asia who conquered much of northwest India and western parts of the Ganges Basin, constructing an empire that also encompassed Afghanistan and parts of Central Asia.

and then the Sassanians, two groups who successively dominated Persia (see Chapters 6 and 8). This empire building promoted communication and extensive trade between India and China, the Middle East, and the eastern Mediterranean.

Some Kushan leaders embraced Buddhism and sought to become world leaders of the faith. Indeed, the Kushans were instrumental in spreading the religion into Central Asia, from which it then diffused to China. The Kushans also encouraged the Gandhara and other schools of Buddhist art. Hence, they promoted and spread a mix of Indian and Greco-Roman culture over a wide area. Some Kushan kings, especially the much respected Kanishka (ka-NISH-ka) (r. 78–144 C.E.), patronized artists, writers, poets, and musicians and tolerated all religions. Like invaders before them, the Kushans intermarried with local people, enhancing the hybrid character of the culture in northwestern India.

South India and Sri Lanka

The Kushan Empire lasted from 50 to 250 C.E. When it eventually faded, northern Indians replaced it with a patchwork of competing states. The political instability in northwestern India was duplicated elsewhere in the subcontinent, where there was frequent warfare between competing states. But the post-Maurya period also saw considerable political and cultural development in both south India and the large island of Sri Lanka. The culture of north India, partly rooted in Aryan traditions, spread southward. At the same time, south Indians and Sri Lankans developed distinctive cultures of their own.

South India   North Indian influence spread south in part because some Dravidian peoples extended their political power northward into the Ganges Basin. Aryan myths, values, rituals, and ideas such as divine kingship from north India appealed to south Indian rulers. South Indians also adopted the caste system, although in a less rigid form than that practiced in north India. These adaptations strengthened southern states, some of which had already flourished for centuries from maritime trade networks stretching from China to the Persian Gulf. South India was renowned as far west as Greece and Rome for its prosperity and for products such as gold.

However, Aryan influence did not destroy regional traditions in south India. For example, the Dravidians, who speak a Dravidian language and inhabit India's southeastern corner, developed a vigorous cultural tradition distinct from that of the Ganges Basin. Poetry became the Tamils' most esteemed art. The mountain city of Madurai (made-uh-RYE), the temple-filled cultural center for the Tamils, had several important colleges and developed into a major center of Hinduism, literature, and education. A Tamil poem from the second century C.E. describes Madurai's function as a religious center filled with devout people:

The great and famous city of Madurai, Is like the lotus flower of God Vishnu. Its streets are the petals of the flower. God Shiva's temple is the center. The citizens are the plentiful pollen; The poor, the crowding beetles. And

*in Madurai, we wake to the chanting of the four Vedas,
Sacred sculptures from the tongue of Brahma, born of the
lotus flower.*[14]

Sri Lankan Society Just south of India, on Sri Lanka (Ceylon), a very different south Asian society developed even before Mauryan times. In the sixth century B.C.E. an Aryan prince and his followers had established the first Sri Lankan kingdom. Over the centuries, more migrants from India intermarried with the local people, in a mixing that eventually produced the Sinhalese (sin-huh-LEEZ) people. Sri Lanka was also connected to the Indian Ocean maritime trade as a hub between Southeast Asia and the Middle East.

Beginning in the first century B.C.E. the Sinhalese began constructing one of the most intricate irrigation systems in world history to better grow rice. Over the next half millennium, to provide irrigation water, they built canals dozens of miles long and artificial lakes covering thousands of acres. The engineering required a deep understanding of trigonometry as well as complex hydraulic technology. This project transformed Sri Lanka into one of the most skilled societies in water control, comparable to ancient China and Mesopotamia.

During Ashoka's reign Buddhist missionaries converted much of the population, making Sri Lanka the first foreign land to adopt Buddhism. Buddhism became an integral part of Sinhalese identity, and Sinhalese culture contributed a great deal to Buddhist art and thought. Indeed, the Sinhalese came to view themselves as the protectors and preservers of Buddhism. But Sri Lanka was not purely Buddhist. By the beginning of the Common Era, Tamil-speaking Hindus began to cross the narrow straits and settle in the northern part of the island. For the next two millennia Sinhalese Buddhist and Tamil Hindu societies coexisted, sometimes uneasily, in Sri Lanka.

Indian Encounters with the Afro-Eurasian World

The post-Maurya era stands out as a time of unprecedented Indian communication with other cultures and connection to networks of exchange. Even merchants from the Mediterranean visited India. For example, India dispatched spices, cloth, silks, ivory, and works of art to the Roman Empire in exchange for gold coins, copper, tin, lead, and wine. The balance of trade seems to have favored India. Indeed, the Roman writer Pliny (PLIN-ee) claimed that importing Indian goods cost the Roman treasury dearly. Around 80 C.E. a Greek handbook for merchants interested in trade with India, written by the Greek traveler whose voyage was traced at the beginning of the chapter, described its sailing routes, products, and culture, suggesting the importance of the commercial relationship. For example, the author recommended a south Indian port offering a large quantity of cinnamon and pepper as well as multicolored textiles, tin, copper, gems, diamonds, sapphires, fine-quality pearls, ivory, and Chinese silk. These port societies were multilingual and the cities had special neighborhoods dominated by foreign trading communities. Another sign of these relations was the Indian

words incorporated into the Greek language, especially words for spices, such as *ginger,* and for foods, like *rice.* Trade with China continued through the Sogdian merchants along the Silk Road, while many Indian traders traveled to Southeast Asia.

Expanding foreign and domestic trade brought much wealth to the Indian commercial and artisan castes, fostering considerable economic growth in India. The increased use of gold coins prompted the emergence of banking and financial houses. But this commercial dynamism mostly occurred in the cities. Competition and business, as well as foreign products, did not often reach the villages, where the bartering of services between farmers, craftsmen, and servants continued to define social and economic relations.

Also in this post-Maurya era, Indian philosophy and religious ideas gained a foreign audience. Some Indian philosophers seem to have visited western Asia, including eastern Mediterranean coastal cities, and their ideas may have influenced some of the religious and philosophical movements then percolating in the region. The idea of monasticism also expanded from India to western Asia: some historians suspect that the Indian Buddhist pattern may have influenced the evolution of Christian monasticism. Buddhist missionaries from India continued visiting neighboring regions to spread their message. Beginning in Ashoka's reign and continuing well into the Common Era, Buddhism and Buddhist art also spread into Central Asia, especially into the Silk Road cities. Indian cultural influence thus flowed out to the world, in a manner similar to the spread of Hellenistic Greek culture throughout the eastern Mediterranean and western Asia.

Buddhist Division

The division of Buddhism into two major schools with competing visions occurred after Ashoka's reign, in the two centuries just before the Common Era. Some followers criticized the religion as it had developed during Mauryan times as being remote from the real world, atheistic in its rejection of a conventional and personal god, excessively individualistic, and requiring too much self-discipline. The detachment from emotion and the denial of any afterlife or heaven were also unappealing to many. In response to this criticism, a canon outlining monastic rules and the structure of faith attempted to maintain orthodoxy. Critics, however, viewed the canon as neglecting the spirit of the original faith. Soon reformers began to coalesce into a new school. In the second century C.E., during the Kushan domination of northern India, the division into two schools, Theravada (THERE-eh-VAH-duh) and Mahayana (MAH-HAH-YAH-nah), became complete.

Theravada, which means "Teachings of the Elders," became one of the two main branches of Buddhism. It remained closer to Buddha's original vision and clearly descended from the Buddhism promoted by Ashoka. To its followers Buddha

Theravada ("Teachings of the Elders") One of the two main branches of Buddhism, the other being Mahayana, that arose just before the Common Era. Theravada remained closer to the Buddha's original vision.

was not a god but rather a human teacher. The universe was in continuous change and had no supreme being or immortal soul. Since gods could not help or hinder humans, believers could only take refuge in the wise and compassionate Buddha, his teachings, and the community of monks who maintained them. Theravadans emphasized that each believer was responsible for acquiring merit through devotion, meditation, and good works, such as feeding monks or supporting a temple. The only sure way to dramatically improve the chances of ending rebirth and reaching nirvana was to become a monk and abide by strict monastic rules, abandoning the temptations and responsibilities of normal life. While all males were expected to spend some portion of their lives as monks, usually two years as a youth, a much smaller number made the sacrifice of a long-term commitment.

Mahayana ("the Greater Vehicle" to salvation), a more popularized and less demanding form of Buddhist belief and practice than Theravada, became the other major branch of Buddhism. Mahayana developed many sects, most of which transformed the Buddha into a god. Mahayana followers found comfort in devotional attachment to a loving deity (Buddha) and stressed charity and good works as paths toward salvation. A central feature in the faith is the **bodhisattva** (boe-dih-SUT-vuh) ("one who has the essence of Buddhahood"), a loving and ever compassionate saint who has died but postponed his or her own attainment of nirvana to help others find salvation through liberation from birth and rebirth. In China, Mahayanists converted the notion of nirvana into an appealing heaven, while the wicked were assigned to a terrifying hell.

Some historians have suggested that Mahayana ideas about achieving salvation with the help of a saint filtered across Bactria and Persia to Palestine, perhaps contributing to Jewish concepts of a messiah. Or perhaps the process worked in reverse: the news of the religious ferment in Palestine (see Chapter 8) traveled eastward along the trade routes to India, where it shaped the Mahayana understanding of a savior. Most likely, though, these were completely independent developments. Perhaps the link, if any, was Persian Zoroastrianism, which may have influenced both Mahayana Buddhism and Christianity as it had earlier provided ideas to the Hebrews.

Buddhism, Hinduism, and Christianity in South Asia

The post-Mauryan centuries saw considerable religious change, including the decline of Buddhism in India, the resurgence of Hinduism, and the arrival of both Christianity and

Judaism. Although several Buddhist monastic orders continued to exist in India and some believers remained, Buddhism was gradually absorbed into Hinduism. Some Buddhist ideas on compassion, for example, were incorporated into Hinduism. Its weaker emphasis on ritual hindered Buddhism in its competition with Hinduism and the brahman elite. Perhaps Buddhism was too pessimistic a faith, portraying life as suffering in contrast to the many life-affirming Hindu gods.

But Buddhism flourished abroad, often by providing spiritual support in times of rapid political change or instability. During the first millennium C.E. Buddhism spread widely along the trade routes, accommodating itself to local traditions and faiths. The Mahayana school eventually became the dominant form of Buddhism in Central Asia, including Tibet and Mongolia, from where it filtered into China, Korea, Vietnam, and Japan. Mahayana Buddhism was also common in Southeast Asia for many centuries. The Theravada school became entrenched in Sri Lanka. Eventually, early in the second millennium C.E., Theravada Buddhism expanded from Sri Lanka into mainland Southeast Asia, in the process mostly replacing Mahayana Buddhism (see Map 7.2).

New religions also arrived in India. According to local legends, the Christian apostle St. Thomas traveled to India around 52 C.E., establishing Christian churches and attracting many followers along the Malabar (MAL-uh-bahr) coast of southwestern India. Although the role of St. Thomas cannot be proven, such a trip along active maritime trade routes was certainly possible. Large Christian communities still flourish in the Malabar state of Kerala (KER-uh-luh), especially in the ancient coastal ports that were once the centers for maritime trade with the lands to the west. A few centuries after the arrival of Christianity, Jewish settlers also came to India's west coast, where they established permanent communities in Kerala and to the north at Bombay. The Jewish and Christian presence added two more elements to social and religious life in post-Maurya India. In the later twentieth century C.E., many Indian Jews emigrated to the new Jewish state of Israel.

Mahayana ("the Greater Vehicle" to salvation) One of the two main branches of Buddhism; a more popularized form of Buddhist belief and practice than Theravada. Mahayana Buddhism tended to make Buddha into a god and also developed the notion of the bodhisattva.

bodhisattva ("one who has the essence of Buddhahood") A loving and ever compassionate "saint" who has postponed his or her own attainment of nirvana to help others find salvation through liberation from birth and rebirth.

SECTION SUMMARY
- Various peoples, among them the Kushans from Central Asia, invaded northwest India and ended up adopting various aspects of Indian culture.
- Aspects of northern Indian culture spread to the south, including Buddhism, which was also adopted in Sri Lanka.
- During the post-Mauryan era, there was great demand for Indian goods among traders from western Asia and the Mediterranean.
- Buddhism split into Theravada, a more traditional form, and Mahayana, a more accessible form.
- Buddhism declined in popularity in India as Hinduism adopted many of its ideas, but it spread to Central Asia, China, and Southeast Asia, where it flourished.

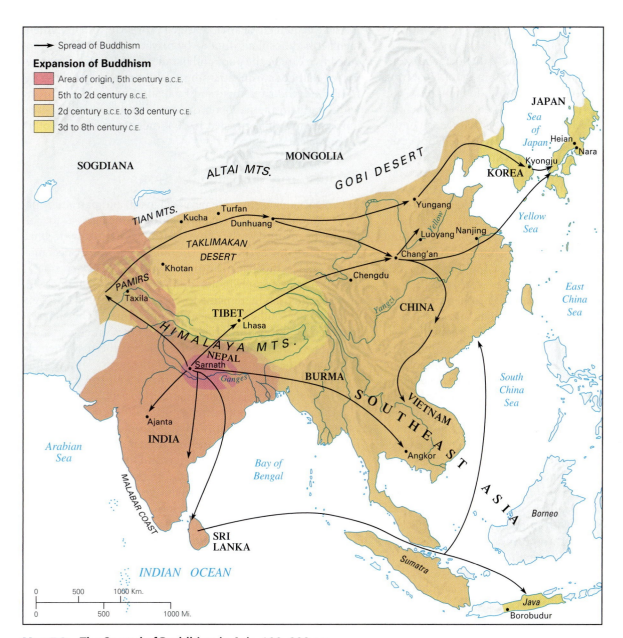

Map 7.2 The Spread of Buddhism in Asia, 100–800 C.E.
Buddhism originated in what is today Nepal and became a major religion in India during the Classical Era. From India it spread into Central Asia, China, Korea, Japan, and Southeast Asia as far east as Java.

 Online Study Center **Improve Your Grade** Interactive Map: The Spread of Buddhism

The Gupta Age in India

What were the main achievements of the Gupta era?

In the fourth century C.E. the great Gupta (GOOP-tuh) Empire was established, bringing political unity to India once again. The Gupta era (320–550 C.E.) was a brilliant period that saw the assimilation of both immigrants and the foreign cultural influences that reshaped an ancient society. Today Indians consider the Gupta their great golden age, a period of economic prosperity, tolerant government, and major developments in science, medicine, mathematics, and literature. In comparison with the Roman Empire, by then in steep decline, and China during the tumultuous centuries between the Han and the Sui, Gupta India was perhaps the most dynamic society in the world at that time, visited by travelers and pilgrims from all over Asia, including China.

Government and Economy

Between 320 and 409 C.E. the Gupta family and their allies conquered most of north India, carving out an empire covering roughly the same territory as Ashoka's domain. Like the Mauryan Empire before it, the Gupta Empire was somewhat decentralized, with relatively autonomous local rulers in outlying districts acknowledging Gupta overlordship. Gupta rule reached its height of cultural brilliance under King Chandra Gupta II (r. 375–414), who became one of the most revered figures in Indian history, praised as enlightened, bold, and resourceful. Southernmost India remained outside Gupta control, Bengal in the east maintained languages and various social and cultural patterns different from the Ganges and Indus plains, and there were many regional differences, but with these exceptions, Indian society became somewhat uniform throughout the subcontinent under Gupta rule.

Gupta India enjoyed a considerable prosperity that was marked by significant internal and external trade, the widespread use of gold and silver coins, and highly productive agriculture. The many Roman coins found in southern India confirm the extensive foreign trade. India increasingly became the textile center of the world, producing fabrics like calico, linen, wool, and cotton for export by sea and land westward to the Middle East and Europe and eastward as far as China and Indonesia. Jewels, pepper, spices, and timber were also important exports. Hence, Gupta India stood at the center of a widespread commercial network.

The Gupta government favored merchants and farmers. Taxes were relatively low, even for the peasants who traditionally bore the brunt of the land revenue. Agriculture provided Indians and foreign visitors with a rich variety of foods, including fruits such as mangos, pears, peaches, and apricots. However, forced labor for one day a month to assist public projects remained common. The Gupta rulers, like the Mauryas, operated all metal and salt mines as well as various industrial enterprises such as arms factories and textile mills.

Gupta India enjoyed a remarkable degree of domestic peace, personal freedom, tolerance for minority views, and affluence. One Chinese Buddhist pilgrim, Faxian (fah-shee-en) (Fa-hsien), who sojourned in Gupta India in the fifth century, was impressed by the general level of prosperity, the state services, and the humane justice system: "The people are very well off. The king governs without corporal punishment. Criminals are fined according to circumstances, lightly or heavily. Even in cases of repeated rebellion, they only cut off the right hand. The people kill no living thing."[15] Chinese visitors noted that, while the rulers were Hindu, there was no official discrimination against Buddhists or Jains. Indeed, Buddhist monks and temples were numerous even in the capital. The Guptas even helped build a great Buddhist monastery and university at Nalanda (Na-LAN-da), where students from all over Asia explored not only Buddhist subjects but also logic, medicine, and Hindu philosophy. In fact, the state aided all religions. However, as before the Gupta age, tolerance did not extend to the untouchables, who still occupied a degraded status.

The capital city, Patna, reflected prosperity and enlightenment. It had hospitals, funded by private donations, that provided free care to the poor and handicapped. One observer reported that he saw in Patna "the workshops thriving along the royal road, the river furrowed by boats, and maidens flirting with youths in the parks on the outskirts of town."[16] A great university in Patna attracted 10,000 students, many from other Asian societies.

Society and Gender Relations

Indian social patterns were never stagnant, and patriarchy became more dominant over time. Through the ages, as the authority of men grew, the status of women gradually declined throughout northern India. The *Mahabharata* warned men not to put "confidence in a woman or a coward, a lazybones, a violent man, a self-promoter, a thief, much less an atheist."[17] However, patriarchy remained weaker in south India. For example, many southern peoples were matrilineal, a kinship system still common in Kerala, and southern women often enjoyed more freedom and options than northern women. In contrast to the mostly male deities in the north, Hinduism in south India placed more emphasis on goddess worship, which may have given women higher status in society.

Even before the Gupta era women faced more restrictions, especially in north India. By Mauryan times women enjoyed fewer opportunities to pursue intellectual or religious leadership. While they had property rights and some worked in wage labor, increasingly the female sphere, especially for those of higher caste, was restricted to marriage and the family. A notable exception, however, to the idea that females should be submissive was found in the *Kama Sutra*, a detailed sexual handbook written in the third century C.E. that offered ideas about gender that seem almost modern. The book suggested a liberal approach to sexual freedom and viewed homosexuality with some understanding. Another Hindu book advised that honoring women pleased the gods.

These exceptions aside, the Gupta was not a golden age for women. Brahmans attempted to impose their rigid views on gender relations. The Code of Manu, devised by brahmans, tied women to the patriarchal family, urging that "in childhood a female must be subject to her father, in youth to her husband, and when her lord is dead, to her sons; a woman must never be independent."[18] The code also restricted women's property rights and recommended early marriage to preserve chastity. It became common for girls to be married well before puberty, after negotiations were made between the senior men of the two families involved. In addition, widows could no longer remarry. The ancient custom of *sati* (suh-TEE), in which wives joined their late husbands on the funeral pyre, had been uncommon but in the late Gupta became more widespread. Many Indian scholars and writers denounced it, especially since families often forced an unwilling wife to agree. In addition, some popular literature of the era extolled freethinking heroines, but even these women tended to ultimately resolve their dilemmas through self-sacrifice and marriage.

Science and Mathematics

Intellectual pursuits flourished during the Gupta era, and India became the world's leading producer of scientific knowledge, planting some of the roots of modern science. The Gupta period produced one of the world's major astronomers, mathematicians, and physicists, Aryabhata (AR-ya-BAH-ta) (ca. 476–550), who wrote his most influential work at the age of twenty-three. Aryabhata taught that the earth was round, rotated on its own axis, and revolved around the sun as one of a family of planets. He also correctly analyzed lunar eclipses, accurately calculated the moon's diameter and the circumference of the earth, and precisely determined the length of a solar year at 365.36 days. In verse, Aryabhata discussed physics, including the earth's rotation and the nature of gravity. Many of these insights did not spread outside India until many centuries later.

In mathematics the Gupta Indians surpassed all other classical peoples, except in geometry. Aryabhata analyzed quadratic equations and the value of *pi*. The greatest Gupta achievement was the formulation of the concept of zero and the consequent evolution of the decimal system. In 499 C.E. Aryabhata wrote the oldest existing text utilizing the zero. The base could have been any number; Indians probably chose 10 because it corresponded to the number of fingers. With this system, individual numbers were needed only for 0 through 9. By contrast, for the ancient Greeks each 8 in 888 was different.

And for the Romans, 888 was written as DCCCLXXXVIII, rendering multiplication and division rather difficult.

The simple and logical Indian numbering system eventually reached the Middle East. Later still it was carried to Europe by Arab merchants and scholars, and hence became known misleadingly as Arabic numerals. This immensely practical system was scorned in the West for centuries as "pagan." Only in the fifteenth century, a thousand years after Gupta times, did European scientists and mathematicians adopt "Arabic" numerals, opening the door to modern science and mathematics. The Indian formulation of the zero and decimal system compares to the invention in western Asia of the wheel and alphabet: all pathbreaking and revolutionary in their consequences.

The Guptas were also remarkably creative in industrial chemistry. They discovered how to make soap and cement, and they produced the finest tempered steel in the world at that time. India's fine dyes and fabrics were later adopted by Europe; *cotton*, *calico*, and *cashmere* are all Indian words. Another major Gupta advance was learning how to crystallize sugar, or how to transform sugar-cane juice into granulated crystals for easy storing or shipping.

Considerable innovation in medicine was yet another feature of Gupta life. The Guptas built on a long tradition. For centuries yoga had fostered an increased understanding of physiology. The ascetic practices of yoga practitioners required control of the body to promote mental and spiritual discipline.

Ajanta Cave Paintings This painting, made on a cave wall in central India during or just after the Gupta era, depicts one of the Buddha's earlier lives as a king listening to his queen. This and other wall paintings made at Ajanta were part of a complex of Buddhist shrines. (Benoy K. Behl)

To demonstrate the power of mind over body, yogis studied posture, breath control, and regulation of the pulse. Western science still cannot fully explain yoga and kindred spiritual practices. Indian physicians also discovered the function of the spinal cord and sketched out the structure of the nervous system. The new knowledge of physiology, along with refinement of herbal medicines, contributed to a better understanding of health and the writing of medical textbooks by at least the second century C.E.

Gupta India had the best medical system, drugs, and therapeutic methods in the world. Medical experimentation was common. Through their studies, doctors learned to sterilize wounds, do Caesarian deliveries, and develop plastic surgery. Drugs the Guptas discovered to control leprosy are still used today. Gupta doctors also vaccinated patients against smallpox by scratching a small amount of smallpox matter into the skin of children and inducing a mild case to give lifetime immunity. The effectiveness of the procedure is not known. By 1000 C.E. this practice had traveled the trade routes to China, and by the 1700s to Europe.

Culture and the Arts

The Gupta era was also a great period for literature and performing arts. Writing mostly in Sanskrit, Gupta writers, many of them patronized by the royal court, produced religious works, poetry, and prose. The most popular writer, Kalidasa (kahl-i-DACE-uh) (ca. 400–455), rendered ancient legends and popular tales into drama and lyrics. His works were rich in imagery, an almost timeless realism, and a sensitivity to humanity that was rare for the era. Kalidasa's famous poem, "The Cloud Messengers," uses a passing cloud surveying the panoramic landscape to capture the heartache of lovers separated by a vast distance: "I see your body in the sinuous creeper, your gaze in the startled eyes of deer, your cheek in the moon, your hair in the plumage of peacocks, and in the tiny ripples of the river I see your sidelong glances."[19]

Theater, music, and art flourished in the creative Gupta atmosphere. Theatrical presentations combined prose and poetry. Also noteworthy were music and dance, which established the basis for the Indian performing arts of today. Instruments such as the lute, or *vina* (VEE-nuh), and zither, or *sitar* (si-TAHR), were adopted after being imported from western Asia. Improvisational instrumental pieces known as *ragas* (RAHG-uhz) were designed for religious and philosophical contemplation. Gupta artists produced many religious sculptures and paintings, especially on cave or temple walls.

Decline of the Guptas

The arrival of Central Asian peoples brought an end to the Guptas and sparked many changes. In the last half of the fifth century C.E. Huns invaded the Indus Valley. Other Huns were then unsettling Europe during the fragmenting last days of the Roman Empire. The Huns conquered part of northwestern India before being blocked by Gupta power. But the Gupta state was in decline, and the cost of holding off the Huns badly depleted the treasury. Soon the empire disintegrated, and other Central Asian invaders followed the Huns into north India.

After the Gupta collapse, India lost its role as a major political power in South Asia, as the varied Hindu states could not unite. Political and intellectual leaders also lost interest in improving science, medicine, and technology. By 650 C.E. India had entered a period of fragmentation, political instability, and frequent warfare that persisted for several centuries and left Indians open to conquest by Muslim peoples.

Nevertheless, the many rival states that now constituted India remained part of the wider world. For example, several southern states took up plundering, and seafarers from the southeastern coast made regular piratical raids deep into Southeast Asia. At the same time, the maritime trade linking southern India with Southeast Asia and China intensified dramatically. Cargo-laden Indian fleets from flourishing ports sailed with the monsoon winds far to the east. Furthermore, Indian cultural influences, including Hinduism and Buddhism, diffused along the trade networks to Southeast Asia, the region we will next discuss.

SECTION SUMMARY

■ Under the decentralized Gupta Empire, based in northern India, the government attained prosperity while pursuing progressive tax policies and religious tolerance.

■ Over time, the status of Indian women declined, particularly in the north.

■ During the Gupta era, science, mathematics, literature, and the arts all thrived.

■ The Guptas formulated the concept of zero, which made the decimal system possible and made mathematical computation infinitely more powerful.

■ The Gupta Empire was greatly weakened by Hun invasion, and soon thereafter it collapsed and other Central Asian groups invaded India.

The Development of Southeast Asian Societies

How did Southeast Asians blend indigenous and foreign influences to create unique societies?

In the tropical lands east of India and south of China, many societies borrowed political, religious, and cultural ideas from the two neighboring regions, although the impact of these ideas varied greatly. When Southeast Asian states emerged, they were products of indigenous as well as outside forces. Most of the early Southeast Asian societies were centered on coastal plains and in river valleys, where they flourished from both productive agriculture and extensive foreign trade. The first cities and states were located in what is now Cambodia and Vietnam, and they established enduring patterns in government, religion, and trade.

Relief of Indonesian Ship   The Indonesians were skilled mariners. This rock carving, from a Buddhist temple in central Java, depicts a sailing vessel of the type commonly used by Indonesian traders in the Indian Ocean and South China Sea in this era. These ships also carried Indonesian colonists to East Africa and Madagascar.   (Ancient Art & Architecture Collection)

Austronesian Seafaring, Trade, and Migrations

Seafaring and maritime trade were major forces in the development of some Southeast Asian societies. As mentioned in Chapter 4, various Austronesian (AW-stroh-NEE-zhuhn) peoples were among the world's greatest mariners. Not only did they travel over hundreds of miles of ocean on trading ventures, but some also migrated thousands of miles away from Southeast Asia.

One group of Austronesians, the ancestors of the people known today as the Malays (muh-LAYZ), benefited from having a strategic position for maritime commerce and intercultural exchange. The Straits of Melaka (muh-LAK-uh), between Sumatra and Malaya (muh-LAY-a), had long served as a crossroads through which peoples, cultures, and trade passed or took root in the area. It became one of the most important contact zones of the world. The lands bordering the Straits of Melaka had for many centuries enjoyed a widespread reputation as a source of gold, tin, spices, and forest products, some of which were traded as far west as Rome. The prevailing climatic patterns in the South China Sea and Indian Ocean allowed ships sailing southwest and southeast to meet in the straits, where their goods could be exchanged.

By early in the Common Era small coastal Malay trading states had emerged in the Malay Peninsula and Sumatra. Maritime commerce was particularly crucial in enabling these societies to rise and prosper. Like the Phoenicians and Greeks in the Mediterranean, Malays specialized in maritime trade to distant shores. In the third century B.C.E., Chinese sources reported Malay ships along the coast using a sail that may have been the prototype for the revolutionary four-sided lateen (luh-TEEN) sail used soon after by Arabs and Polynesians, which allowed ships to sail directly into the wind.

Malays and other Austronesians became prominent in the expanding networks of exchange. Malays opened the maritime trade between China and India by obtaining cinnamon grown on the China coast and carrying it across the Indian Ocean to India and Sri Lanka. This cinnamon eventually reached Europe. The Austronesian sailors returned to Southeast Asia from India with pottery, beads, and small luxuries, and possibly Indian ideas about government and religion. At the same time, other Austronesians from what is today central Indonesia introduced Southeast Asian foods (especially bananas and rice), outrigger canoes, and musical instruments (including the xylophone) to East Africa, where they were adopted by people there. By the third century C.E., according to Chinese sources, Malay ships were huge and able to carry seven hundred sailors and 6,000 tons of cargo.

Between the fourth and sixth centuries C.E., instability in Central Asia disrupted the overland trading routes along the Silk Road; as a result, the Indian Ocean connection became more important. Just as various Central Asian peoples had become important because of land-based international commerce, so some Southeast Asians, among them Malays, benefited from the growth of seagoing trade between China, India, and the Middle East. But the voyages held many dangers. For example, the Chinese Buddhist pilgrim Faxian, sailing from Sri Lanka to Sumatra in 414 C.E., reported that he "set sail on a large merchant ship which carried about two hundred passengers. A small boat trailed behind, for use in case the large vessel should be wrecked, as sailing on this sea was most hazardous. [We] were caught up in a typhoon [which] lasted for thirteen days. That sea is [also] infested with pirates."[20]

Austronesian seafaring trade also led to migration. Between 100 and 700 C.E. some Austronesians from southern Borneo (BOR-nee-oh) and Sulawesi (soo-luh-WAY-see) migrated westward across the Indian Ocean. After sojourning along the East African coast, where some may have intermarried with local Africans, most of them settled on the large island of Madagascar (mad-uh-GAS-kuhr), off the southeast coast of Africa. Today their descendants account for the majority of the island's population, most of whom speak Austronesian languages. Many Austronesian cultural practices persisted in Madagascar, in part because trade and contact across the Indian Ocean remained strong for many centuries. While some Austronesian emigrants moved westward, others, beginning in ancient times, moved the other direction, from Southeast Asia into the western Pacific. Eventually the descendants of these Austronesians, known today as the Polynesians (pahl-uh-NEE-zhuhn) and Micronesians (my-kruh-NEE-zhuhn), settled nearly all of the islands of the central and eastern Pacific (see Chapter 9). As a result of these movements in different directions, Austronesian-speaking societies stretched thousands of miles from Madagascar eastward through Indonesia and the Philippines to Hawaii and Easter Island in eastern Polynesia, and many of them were linked by trade networks.

Indianization and Early Mainland States

Around the dawn of the Common Era various states also arose on the Southeast Asian mainland, especially the lands bordering the lower Mekong River in what is now Cambodia and southern Vietnam. Indian culture influenced much of mainland Southeast Asia as well as the western islands of the Indonesian archipelago. At the same time, Chinese colonization shaped a quite different society in Vietnam. Some outside influences were superficial, while others penetrated more deeply. However, many local traditions had a resilience that allowed them to survive the centuries of borrowing and change.

The Emergence of New Societies Various states developed on the Southeast Asian mainland by early in the Common Era, but their foundations had been established a few centuries earlier. Land suitable for rice growing was an enormous environmental influence on Southeast Asia. The most populous societies emerged along the fertile coastal plains or in the valleys of great rivers like the Mekong, where irrigated rice cultivation was possible. Irrigated rice provided an ecologically sound, highly productive, and labor-intensive economic mainstay that could be sustained for many generations. By promoting social cooperation, this economy led to centralized kingdoms.

By 500 B.C.E. a few small states had emerged that were based on irrigated rice agriculture as well as bronze and iron use. One of the earliest states was Van Lang in northern Vietnam. The Van Lang kings ruled through a landed aristocracy who controlled vast rice-growing estates worked by peasants. Large fourth-century B.C.E. walled villages, such as Ban Chiang in Thailand, which probably contained over two thousand people, indicate urbanization. During the third century B.C.E. the earliest cities with monumental architecture appeared, most notably Co Loa in Vietnam. Here, near modern Hanoi, King An Duong built a huge citadel surrounded by a wall 5 miles long and 10 yards wide, to allow for chariot traffic on the top of the wall. By the first century C.E. urban societies had emerged in the river valleys among peoples such as the Khmers (kuh-MEERZ) (Cambodians), who carried on complex maritime trade.

Outside influences from China and India also generated change in Southeast Asia. A major transition came in the second century B.C.E., when Han China conquered what is today northern Vietnam, imposing a colonial rule that endured for a millennium (111 B.C.E.–939 C.E.) and spreading many Chinese cultural patterns into Vietnam (see Chronology: Classical Southeast Asia). Although Chinese traders regularly visited many Southeast Asian states over the centuries, strong Chinese cultural and political influence was restricted to the Vietnamese.

Elsewhere Indian influence was paramount in fostering a transition to a very different form of society. Southeast Asian sailors had been visiting India for centuries and returning with new ideas. Around the beginning of the Common Era, Indian traders and brahman priests began regularly traveling the oceanic trade routes. They settled in some of the mainland and island states, where they married into or became advisors to influential families. They brought with them Indian concepts of religion, government, and the arts. Gupta India provided a political model for Southeast Asians.

CHRONOLOGY	
Classical Southeast Asia	
111 BCE–939 C.E.	Chinese colonization of Vietnam
39–41 C.E.	Trung Sisters' rebellion in Vietnam
ca. 75–550 C.E.	Funan
ca. 100–1200 C.E.	Era of Indianization
ca. 192–1471 C.E.	Champa
ca. 450–750 C.E.	Zhenla states

Indianization The process by which Indian ideas spread into and influenced many Southeast Asian societies is often termed **Indianization,** a mixing of Indian with indigenous ideas. This occurred about the same time as classical Greco-Roman culture was spreading around the Mediterranean. For a millennium Southeast Asian peoples such as the Khmers in the Mekong Basin, the Chams along the central coast of Vietnam, and the Javanese (JAH-vuh-NEEZ) on the fertile island of Java were closely connected to the more populous and developed India. Just as the Phoenicians spread their alphabet around the Mediterranean, and the Koreans and Japanese adopted the Chinese writing system, so Indian writing systems came to Southeast Asia, to be adapted to local spoken languages. By 500 C.E. writing was common both on the mainland and in the archipelago.

Indian influence was particularly strong in religion and government. Mahayana Buddhism and Hinduism became important in Southeast Asia, especially among the upper classes. The imported religions fused with an indigenous animism that focused on communicating with spiritual forces, benevolent and malevolent, to ensure bountiful harvests, address problems of daily life, and keep the cosmic order in balance. Many Southeast Asian peoples blended various outside and local religions rather than following one exclusively. In politics, Southeast Asian rulers anxious to control increasing and diverse populations adopted the Indian concept of powerful kings who possessed supernatural powers and were supported by religious sanction, which made their positions difficult to challenge.

Although centuries of borrowing and sometimes foreign conquest helped shape Southeast Asian cultures, Southeast Asians rarely became carbon copies of their mentors or conquerors. Like the Japanese and western Europeans, they took ideas that they wanted from outsiders and adapted them to their own use, creating a distinctive synthesis. For example, the Hindu and Buddhist architecture and temples of Burma, Cambodia, or Java differed substantially from the South Asian models as well as from each other. As a result, temple complexes in Java were often much larger than in India. The same diversity was true for the Indian heroes of Hindu epics, which Southeast Asian cultures shaped to their own liking.

Funan, Zhenla, and Champa

Productive agriculture, commerce, and Indianization helped foster most of the early mainland states. Funan (FOO-nan), founded by the first century C.E., flourished through the sixth century (ca. 75–550 C.E.). Funan was centered in the fertile Mekong Delta of what is today southern Vietnam. While the Khmer people who dominated the area for many centuries probably made up most of the population and the ruling

Map 7.3   Funan and Its Neighbors
The first large mainland Southeast Asian states emerged during the Classical Era. The major states included Vietnam, which became a Chinese colony in the second century B.C.E., Funan, Zhenla, and Champa.

group, some historians think Austronesians also lived in Funan and did most of the maritime trade. Funan was in regular contact with China, had become Indianized, valued literacy, and its people, using remarkable engineering skills, built complex irrigation systems to turn swamps into productive agricultural land. Funan apparently extended some authority over much of what is today Cambodia and southern Thailand (see Map 7.3). Chinese sources reported that Funan subdued the neighboring kingdoms, which all became vassals. With its access to major land and sea trade routes, it was part of large trading networks. Trade goods from as far as Rome, Arabia, Central Asia, and perhaps East Africa have been found in its ruins, and merchants from various countries (including India and China) lived in the major port city.

Another Khmer kingdom or grouping of city-states, Zhenla (CHEN-la), seems to have emerged inland in the Mekong River Basin around the fifth century C.E. It played a major regional role until the eighth century C.E., when it succumbed to civil war. A fertile and strategic location, a vigorous and adaptive society, and a knack for political organization soon made the Khmer-speaking peoples who founded Funan and Zhenla the most influential society of mainland Southeast Asia.

But the Khmers had rivals. Dating from the second century C.E., the coastal Cham people of central Vietnam formed an Indianized state, or possibly several states, known as

Indianization The process by which Indian ideas spread into and influenced many Southeast Asian societies; a mixing of Indian with indigenous ideas.

Champa (CHAM-pa). It was one of the oldest Indianized states and tried to control the increasingly dynamic coastal commerce between China and Southeast Asia. The Chams, who speak an Austronesian language, became renowned as sailors and merchants. Like many other maritime peoples, they sometimes resorted to piracy, and they frequently fought the Vietnamese, who continually pushed southward, forcing the Chams to shift their own settlements down the coast. Champa existed from 192 to 1471 C.E., when the Vietnamese finally conquered Champa and occupied its main city near modern Hue.

The states that emerged in these centuries, such as Funan and Champa, had much in common. They did not have fixed territorial boundaries; rather, they were fluctuating zones of influence. The central court attempted to dominate economic and human resources in outlying areas through a combination of diplomacy and military might. The kings excelled in pomp and circumstance but ruled uneasily over troublesome local chieftains.

Vietnam and Chinese Colonization

During Chinese colonial times, Vietnamese society was largely confined to what is today the northern third of Vietnam; it did not include the lands then occupied by Funan or Champa that are part of modern Vietnam. Vietnam developed a very different pattern than the Indianized kingdoms because of the long period of Chinese colonial rule. China's final conquest and annexation of Vietnam, their southern neighbor, in 111 B.C.E. ended the independent evolution of one of the earliest Southeast Asian kingdoms. A relatively dense population already lived in the Red River Valley, the heart of what is today northern Vietnam. A Han dynasty census in 2 C.E. recorded a population of around 1 million in the valley. But some Vietnamese evaded Chinese power by migrating southward.

Chinese policy was to assimilate the Vietnamese and implant Chinese values, customs, and institutions; in this process, some revolutionary changes took place. Over the centuries Chinese philosophies and religions like Confucianism, Daoism, and Mahayana Buddhism were adopted by most Vietnamese but also mixed with earlier ancestor and spirit worship. China's patriarchal family system, written language, and ideas about government also sank deep roots into Vietnamese culture.

Yet, while the Vietnamese adopted many of these Chinese patterns, they also sustained a hatred of Chinese rule and resisted cultural assimilation. The survival of the Vietnamese identity, language, and many customs during a millennium of colonialism constituted a display of national determination practically unparalleled in world history. Indeed, throughout their history the chronic question for the Vietnamese has been how they could benefit from Chinese culture without becoming Chinese themselves.

Several factors probably encouraged the Vietnamese to resist much of the assimilationist policy. Perhaps the Vietnamese were able to avoid cultural and national extinction because they already had several centuries of state building and cultural identity behind them when the Chinese colonized. A long history of resistance to the Chinese as well as a sense of nationhood also helped them resist assimilation. Some historians have noted an ancient and perhaps unprecedented sense of Vietnamese nationhood that aided resistance to absorption and stimulated rebellions against Chinese rule. It comprised a desire for independence and a collective identity that reached through all social classes right down to the villages. Chinese and later foreign conquerors such as the French in the modern era found that they had to do more than defeat or co-opt the rulers; they also had to conquer each village, one by one. The Vietnamese were formidable in resisting adversaries collectively.

Given these realities, the Chinese colonial period was punctuated by many revolts, all of them well remembered by the Vietnamese today as symbols of patriotism. The rebellions were sometimes led by women, the best known of whom are the Trung Sisters (see Profile: The Trung Sisters: Vietnamese Rebels). Rebel forces often fought for decades against hopeless odds. Chinese officials in the ninth century C.E. recommended harsh retaliation as the response to Vietnamese rebellion: "At every stream, cave, marketplace, everywhere there is stubbornness. Repression is necessary."[21] This history of resistance to foreign invaders meant frequent warfare. A Vietnamese Buddhist poet described the results: "War, no end to it, people scattered in all directions. How can a man keep his mind off it? The winds dark, the rains violent year after year, laying waste the land, over and over."[22] The Vietnamese qualities of patience, determination, and sense of a larger national community eventually generated a successful struggle for independence from the Chinese in the tenth century.

Economies, Societies, and Cultures

The social and cultural patterns established by these varied Southeast Asian societies between 100 and 600 C.E. established a framework for the centuries to come. Despite the great differences between societies like Champa, Funan, and Vietnam, there were many similarities throughout the region. For one, most of the larger Southeast Asian states were multiethnic in their population, including foreign merchants in temporary or permanent residence. For example, Malay and Indian seafaring traders were common in Funan. They were part of extended trade diasporas. Because many people in these states specialized in interregional commerce, the cities were frequently cosmopolitan.

Many Southeast Asians lived well. Chinese envoys who visited Funan around 250 C.E. described walled cities, palaces, and houses occupied by people who ate with silver utensils and paid their taxes with gold, silver, perfumes, and pearls. The Chinese envoys were also impressed with the many books available and the well-kept archives, indicating that an Indian writing system was already in use. Commerce was prevalent in most places, but rice agriculture was the basis for prosperity and survival. Funan's prominence resulted chiefly from its highly productive cultivation of the fertile land. Most Southeast Asians were farmers and fishermen living in self-

THE TRUNG SISTERS, VIETNAMESE REBELS

Some of the major anti-Chinese rebellions in Vietnamese history were led by women such as the Trung Sisters in 39 C.E. Even after 2,000 years, the Vietnamese honor the two sisters and their martyrdom with annual ceremonies at cult shrines dedicated to their memory. Our knowledge of the two sisters and their experiences is limited. Some historians consider them semimythical rather than flesh and blood. Their revolt was caused by Chinese attempts to raise taxes and consolidate their control over the indigenous landed aristocracy. The Trung Sisters became enshrined in images of brave but beautiful, sword-bearing women mounted on elephants, leading their troops against the Chinese.

The sisters are believed to have been daughters of a prominent family of landed aristocrats from near Hanoi. The older sister, Trung Trac, had married a member of another landed family. When her husband protested an increase in taxes by Chinese colonial authorities, he was apparently executed. The spirited sisters then sparked a rebellion that rapidly spread throughout the entire country and involved both the elite and the peasantry. With local Chinese officials in retreat, her followers declared Trung Trac queen of a newly independent country. Some sources suggest the sisters served as joint queens, ruling for two years. They abolished taxes, but, as traditionalists, they also sought to restore the pre-Chinese order dominated by landed aristocrats and protect local autonomy. Despite the sisters' aristocratic agenda, the common people joined the revolt because of their hostility to the authoritarian rule of the Chinese governors. Han dynasty rulers, not about to allow this valuable part of their empire to secede, dispatched their most able general and his army to destroy the rebellion. As the fighting and repression intensified, most of the sisters' upper-class supporters abandoned their cause. Eventually their remaining forces were defeated in 41 C.E., and the sisters either committed suicide or were captured and executed. China now intensified its direct control of the colony and launched a more deliberate cultural assimilation policy to integrate Vietnam politically into China proper.

Although the revolt failed to dislodge the Chinese, the Trung Sisters established a model for later rebels, some of them also women. Another famous anticolonial leader, the nineteen-year-old Lady Trieu in the third century C.E., demonstrated a similar commitment. When advised to marry rather than fight, she replied: "I want to ride the storm, tread the dangerous waves, win back the fatherland and destroy the yoke of slavery. I don't want to bow down my head working as a simple housewife." The Lady Trieu seems an almost modern figure in her patriotic and social defiance.

Even in the nineteenth and twentieth centuries, Vietnamese women inspired by the Trung Sisters and Lady Trieu took up arms alongside men to fight oppressive governments and invading forces. Although men led the movements, women were prominent in the struggle against French colonialism and in the revolution by Communist forces to overthrow the U.S.-backed government in South Vietnam in the mid-twentieth century.

THINKING ABOUT THE PROFILE

1. What sparked the rebellion led by the Trung Sisters?
2. What does the experience of the Trung Sisters tell us about Vietnamese society under Chinese rule and the role of women in that society?

Note: Quotation is from Thomas Hodgkin, *Vietnam: The Revolutionary Path* (New York: St. Martin's, 1981), p. 22.

The Trung Sisters This painting by a Vietnamese artist shows the Trung Sisters riding into battle on war elephants against the Chinese. (From Wiliam J. Duiker, Jr., *Sacred War: Nationalism and Revolution in a Divided Vietnam* (New York: McGraw-Hill, 1995) © 1995. Reproduced with permission of the McGraw Hill companies.)

sufficient villages and held together by ties of kinship and a communal spirit of cooperation for mutual survival.

The family system contrasted with those in China or India, where patrilineal and patriarchal systems prevailed. While some Southeast Asians such as the Vietnamese followed a patriarchal pattern, others developed flexible systems incorporating both paternal and maternal kin. Some matrilineal systems also existed. The matrilineal Cham society was also matriarchal, and its women enjoyed considerable political influence. Both Cham men and women could have more than one spouse. In Southeast Asia women generally enjoyed a higher status and played a more active public role than they did in China, India, the Middle East, and Europe; for example, they took charge of most village markets. Older women had considerable power in family affairs.

Most Southeast Asians also blended diverse elements into a cultural unity. For example, animism was incorporated into or coexisted quite easily with Hinduism, Buddhism, Confucianism, and other imported religions. The result was a widespread tendency, as in East Asia, for religions to be inclusive and eclectic. This pattern of inclusion and blending, along with extensive trade, made Southeast Asian societies distinctive.

SECTION SUMMARY

- The lands bordering the Straits of Melaka were rich in natural resources, and their peoples engaged in wide-ranging maritime trade.
- Austronesians settled over a wide area, from Madagascar, off the coast of Africa, to the Pacific islands of Polynesia.
- Southeast Asians were influenced by both Chinese and Indian culture, but they retained distinct aspects of their native cultures.
- Some principal states in this era were Funan, Zhenla, and Champa on the southeast Asian mainland.
- Vietnam showed great resistance in its long struggle against Chinese colonization.
- Though different from each other, Southeast Asian societies tended to be multiethnic and able to blend diverse elements into cultural unity.

 **Online Study Center** ACE the Test

 Chapter Summary

The Classical Era saw dramatic changes in India and Southeast Asia, some generated by outside influences such as migration and long-distance trade, that forged distinctive societies. India developed unique social systems and religious ideas. The caste system divided the population into categories

based on descent and occupation. Unique among the religions was Hinduism, which flowered into various schools of speculative thought. Buddhism challenged Hinduism and the caste system in the first millennium B.C.E. Hinduism and Buddhism shared many beliefs, such as reincarnation and karma, but differed in their conception of gods and the path to ending reincarnation.

India's political, economic, and intellectual life also changed during the Classical Era. The Mauryan Empire united India for the first time. Under Ashoka the empire reflected humane and peaceful Buddhist values. The Classical Era also saw the forging of deeper cultural and trade connections between India and the peoples to the north and east, and many peoples migrated into the country from Central Asia. Buddhism spread into both Central and Southeast Asia, becoming a major world religion. During the Gupta golden age, Indians achieved new knowledge in science and mathematics that later influenced the Middle East and Europe.

The states that emerged in Southeast Asia were based on maritime trade, rice agriculture, and the blending of local and foreign influences. The Austronesian sailors fostered trade networks over vast distances, and kingdoms arose in Cambodia and Vietnam. Indian religious, political, and cultural ideas had a great impact in many parts of the region, and China's conquest of Vietnam spread Chinese influence.

Online Study Center Improve Your Grade Flashcards

Key Terms

Brahman	nirvana	Mahayana
Vedanta	monasticism	bodhisattva
Jainism	Kushans	Indianization
Buddhism	Theravada	

Suggested Reading

Books

Armstrong, Karen. *Buddha*. New York: Viking Penguin, 2001. A brief and readable introduction to the Buddha's life and thought.

Auboyer, Jeannine. *Daily Life in Ancient India: From 200 BC to 700 AD*. Translated by Simon Watson Taylor. London: Phoenix, 2002. A fascinating and readable examination of classical Indian society.

Basham, A. L. *The Wonder That Was India*. 3rd ed. London: Macmillan, 1968 (reprinted 1999 by Rupa and Company, New Delhi). Although dated, this is still the best general study of pre-Islamic India.

Foltz, Richard C. *Religions of the Silk Road: Overland Trade and Cultural Exchange from Antiquity to the Fifteenth Century*. New York: St. Martin's, 1999. An introduction to trade and the spread of religions, especially Buddhism, in Central Asia.

Frye, Richard N. *The Heritage of Central Asia: From Antiquity to the Turkish Expansion*. Princeton: Markus Wiener, 1996. One of the best surveys of Central Asia in this era.

Hall, Kenneth. *Maritime Trade and State Development in Early Southeast Asia*. Honolulu: University of Hawai'i Press, 1985. Useful study of trade, politics, and international connections.

Kulke, Hermann, and Dietmar Rothermund. *History of India*. 3rd ed. London and New York: Routledge, 1998. A concise but stimulating general history that incorporates recent scholarship on the Classical Era.

Mabbett, Ian, and David Chandler. *The Khmers*. London: Blackwell, 1995. An authoritative study of early Cambodian history.

Oxtoby, Willard G. *World Religions: Eastern Traditions*. New York: Oxford University Press, 1996. Contains valuable essays on the Budhist, Hindu, and Jain traditions.

Ray, Himanshu Prabha. *The Archaeology of Seafaring in Ancient South Asia*. New York: Cambridg University Press, 2003. Scholarly study of India's maritime trade and contacts in this era.

Shaffer, Lynda Norene. *Maritime Southeast Asia to 1500*. Armonk, N.Y.: M.E. Sharpe, 1996. A very readable brief introduction to premodern Southeast Asia, including Funan and the Austronesian maritime trade.

Stein, Burton. *A History of India*. Malden, M.A.: Blackwell, 1998. A survey text especially strong on social and religious history.

Taylor, Keith Weller. *The Birth of Vietnam*. Berkeley: University of California Press, 1983. The major study on Vietnam before and during Chinese colonization.

Thapar, Romila. *A'soka and the Decline of the Mauryas*. Delhi: Oxford University Press, 1997. An update of an earlier study, with much information on the Mauryas.

Thapar, Romila. *Early India from the Origins to* AD *1300*. Berkeley: University of California Press, 2002. A valuable revision of the standard history of early India, detailed and comprehensive.

Websites

Austronesian and Other Indo-Pacific Topics (http://w3.rz-berlin.mpg.de/~wm/wm3.html). A useful collection to sources on Austronesian languages and cultures, operated by Germany-based scholars.

Internet Indian History Sourcebook (http://www.fordham.edu/halsall/india/indiasbook.html). An invaluable collection of sources and links on India from ancient to modern times.

Silk Road Narratives (http://depts.washington.edu/uwch/silkroad/texts/texts.html). Explores cultural interaction in Eurasia through excerpts from Silk Road travelers.

Virtual Religion Index (http://virtualreligion.net/vri/). An outstanding site with many links on the history of Buddhism and Hinduism.

CHAPTER 8

Empires, Networks, and the Remaking of Europe, North Africa, and Western Asia, 500 B.C.E.–600 C.E.

CHAPTER OUTLINE
- Etruscans, Carthage, Egypt, and the Romans
- Roman Society During the Imperial Era
- Celts, Germans, and Roman Decline
- Christianity: From Western Asian Sect to Transregional Religion
- Revival in the East: Byzantines, Persians, and Arabs

■PROFILE
Hypatia of Alexandria, a Pagan Philosopher

■WITNESS TO THE PAST
The Voices of Common Romans

☀ *Online Study Center*

This icon will direct you to interactive activities and study materials on the website: college.hmco.com/pic/lockard1e

Santa Sophia The magnificent Santa Sophia Church in Constantinople, rebuilt during the reign of the emperor Justinian in the sixth century C.E., had interior walls covered in gold mosaics that glowed from reflected sunlight. This mosaic from the Zoe panel shows Jesus holding a Bible. (Erich Lessing/Art Resource, NY)

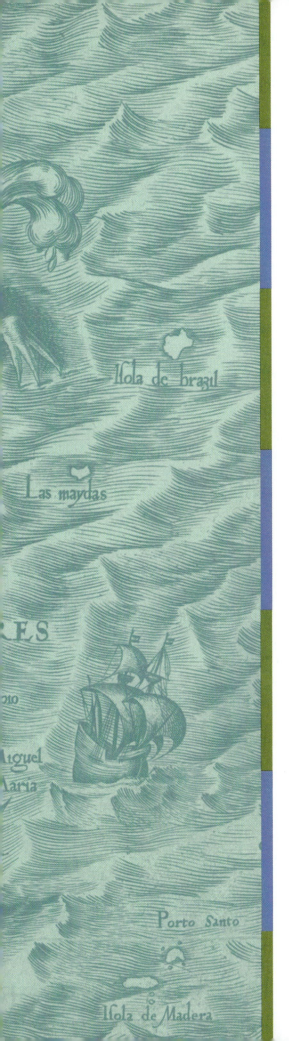

*Remember, Roman, that it is for you to rule the nations.
This shall be your task: to impose the ways of peace, to
spare the vanquished and to tame the proud by war.*

ROMAN POET VIRGIL[1]

Around 320 B.C.E. Pytheas (PITH-ee-us), a scientist from the Greek colony of Massalia (ma-SAL-ya), today's city of Marseilles (mahr-SAY) on the Mediterranean coast of France, wrote a book about his remarkable travels in Europe. A brave, curious man, some ten years earlier, according to his account, Pytheas had reached the western coast of France by sea or over land. From there he arranged to sail on a boat owned by local Celtic (KELL-tik) people to southwest England. He continued north through the Irish Sea and may have reached Iceland. He then ventured down the east coast of Britain before turning north, exploring the North Sea coast as far as Denmark before retracing his journey back to Massalia. Some of his contemporaries were awed by his daring adventure. Others called him a liar. Today some scholars consider Pytheas one of the world's great explorers because he gave Mediterranean societies their first eyewitness account of the remote northern coast and its mysterious peoples.

Pytheas's story tells us much about the western Eurasia of those times. The people of the Mediterranean knew little of the lands north of the Alps and Balkans, whose peoples they considered dangerous barbarians. Many goods were exchanged between Mediterranean and northern societies, but mostly by being passed from community to community. However, the western Mediterranean where Pytheas lived was crisscrossed by trade networks: Greeks, Etruscans (ee-TRUHS-kuhns), Carthaginians (kar-thuh-JIN-ee-uhns), and the upstart Romans competed intensely for economic resources and political power. These societies were all part of an interdependent world incorporating southern Europe, North Africa, and western Asia, where commodities flowed and ideas were exchanged. Three hundred years after Pytheas's voyage, Europe was much more closely linked, thanks largely to a people who in Pytheas's time were an ambitious but still minor power, the Romans.

By the time Pytheas wrote his book, the Romans had begun their rise to power in the region. The Roman success in creating a large empire and rich society, celebrated in the opening quote by the Roman poet Virgil, had a considerable impact on world history. As Rome flowered, many societies became its subjects. Under Rome, diverse societies were changed in many ways, and networks were expanded. Roman expansion helped reshape much of Europe, marginalizing or incorporating the northern peoples while also transforming North African and western Asian politics. In addition, when the Roman Empire finally ended after half a millennium, it left several legacies for later European, western Asian, and even African societies. The Romans passed on to later Europeans useful ideas on law and government, some of which derived from the Greeks. In addition, during Roman times Christianity emerged to form the cultural underpinning of a new, post-Roman European society while also spreading in Asia and Africa.

A version of the Roman Empire, Greek-speaking Byzantium (buh-ZANT-ee-uhm), continued to exist in the eastern Mediterranean for a thousand years, a Christian society serving as an important center of transcontinental trade and a buffer between western Europe and the states of western Asia. The Romans and their successors also had conflicts with societies in western Asia and North Africa, including a revived Persian Empire; these conflicts continued long after the Classical Age. Finally, these various struggles set the stage for the rise of another society, the Arabs.

FOCUS QUESTIONS

1. What were the main political and social features of the Roman Republic?
2. How did the Romans maintain their large empire?
3. What were the relations between Romans and other societies, including Celts and Germans?
4. How did Christianity develop and expand?
5. How did the Byzantine and Sassanian Empires reinvigorate the eastern Mediterranean world?

◆ Etruscans, Carthage, Egypt, and the Romans

What were the main political and social features of the Roman Republic?

By 300 B.C.E. the Mediterranean world was politically and culturally diverse, divided between Etruscans, Carthage, small Greek city-states, various Hellenistic kingdoms including Egypt, and the rising Romans, who eventually dominated the entire region. Roman society was built on several foundations. The Romans learned much from the older Etruscan society that they eventually absorbed, and they were influenced by Greek ideas in building their republic. The regional environment also played a part, as Roman political expansion was made possible by good access to the Mediterranean Sea. Eventually Rome conquered peoples in southern Europe and then beyond, establishing the framework of a huge empire.

Western European Geography

Geography and climate were influential in shaping Roman society. The geological spine of Italy is the Apennine mountain range running down the eastern side of the narrow peninsula. The rich agricultural Po Valley lies north of the Apennines, and smaller plains spread west from the Apennines to the Mediterranean. This topography directed the at-

tention of the early settlers to the sea, where they took up maritime trade. But the Roman newcomers had to adapt to seagoing. One Roman poet wrote in 30 B.C.E.: "Whoever first dared to float a ship on the grim sea must have had a heart of oak coated with a triple layer of bronze."[2] In addition, Italy's geography, unlike the rocky hills of Greece, offered considerable fertile land suitable for intensive agriculture, especially along the west coast. The Mediterranean climate was perfect for growing grapes and olives, and as the Roman state grew, the Romans were able to increase their export of wine and olive oil while importing grain from the nearby islands of Sicily and Sardinia (sahr-DIN-ee-uh) and from northern Africa, which is only 100 miles from Sicily. Agricultural success, and the ease of north-south contact in the peninsula, also made it easier than in Greece to develop large states. The mild climate of Italy also encouraged attacks by the Indo-European Celtic and Germanic peoples living in the forested hills and plains of western and northern Europe. Attracted to the warmer lands in the south, these northern peoples made frequent invasions using passes through the Alps, a formidable complex of mountains. By forcing the early inhabitants of the peninsula to emphasize military defense, these attacks had a significant effect on the history of Roman society and the entire region.

As the Romans themselves expanded beyond Italy, they drew upon the natural resources of the larger Mediterranean world (see Map 8.1 on page 202) and beyond. In Spain, they found a rich supply of silver, copper, and tin. Egypt provided

CHRONOLOGY

	Roman Republic	Roman Empire	Byzantium and Western Asia
500 B.C.E.	509 B.C.E. Roman Republic		
300 B.C.E.	264–146 B.C.E. Punic Wars		
100 B.C.E.		31 B.C.E.–180 C.E. *Pax Romana* 7–6 B.C.E.–30 C.E. Life of Jesus	
1 C.E.			240–272 C.E. Founding of Sassanian Empire
300 C.E.		395 C.E. Division of eastern and western empires 476 C.E. Official end of western Roman Empire	330 C.E. Founding of Constantinople
500 C.E.			527–565 C.E. Reign of Justinian

wheat. Beginning about 200 B.C.E., overland trade routes connected the Mediterranean with China along the famous Silk Road, named after the most important product acquired from East Asia, which was bartered in return for gold, silver, precious stones, and some textile products from the west.

The Etruscans and Early Rome

The Romans were greatly influenced by the Etruscans, who established the first urban society in the peninsula. A non-Indo-European people who may have come originally from western Asia, the Etruscans had founded a dozen or so city-states in central and northern Italy by the eighth century B.C.E. They were aggressive chariot warriors but also sailors who traded with the western Mediterranean islands and Spain. Eventually Etruscans expanded their territory to include more of Italy as well as the nearby island of Corsica (KOR-si-kuh). They also had considerable contact with Greeks and Phoenicians. They adopted a form of the Greek alphabet, as well as Greek craft styles and myths, and Greek craftsmen worked in some Etruscan cities. As more Greeks settled in Italy after 550 B.C.E., they had increased conflict with the Etruscans.

We do not know very much about the Etruscans. Their language is only partially understood, and none of their major literature survives. Later Roman writers portrayed them as barbarians, a view that distorted the picture of Etruscan culture. The Etruscans' huge cemeteries with impressive, well-decorated tombs show that they were skilled artists and artisans. Some of their cities, which could include as many as 35,000 people, were well planned and were linked together by a good road system. Each city apparently had its own king. The Etruscans were known for mining and working iron ore, and their excellent iron axes, sickles, and tools were carried by merchants to every region. Their rigid social system included slavery, although Etruscan women apparently had a higher social status than women in most classical societies. Etruscan women conversed openly with men in public, drove their own chariots, owned real estate, and sometimes ran businesses like pottery workshops.

Initially the relationship between the Romans and the Etruscans was peaceful. Rome began as a small city-state just south of Etruscan territory in central Italy. It was established in the eighth century B.C.E. by a group of Indo-European pastoralists known as the Latins (see Chronology: The Roman Republic, 753–58 B.C.E. on page 203). The major Latin city, Rome, built on seven hills along the Tiber (TIE-buhr) River, was originally founded as a base from which the early Romans could trade with the Etruscans.

Map 8.1 Italy and the Western Mediterranean, 600–200 B.C.E.
During the early Classical Era the Etruscan cities in the north and the Greek city-states in the south held political power in Italy. Carthage held a similar status in northeast Africa. Eventually the Latins, from their base in Rome, became the dominant political force in the entire region.

CHRONOLOGY

The Roman Republic, 753–58 B.C.E.

753	Founding of Rome (traditional date)
ca. 616–509	Etruscan kings rule over Rome
509	Beginning of Roman Republic
265	Roman control of central and southern Italy
264–241	First Punic (Roman-Carthaginian) War
218–201	Second Punic War
149–146	Third Punic War
113–105	First German-Roman conflicts
60–58	Julius Caesar completes conquest from Rhine to Atlantic

During the sixth century B.C.E. the Etruscans came to dominate Rome, and their influence was significant. The Romans adopted the twenty-six-character alphabet that the Etruscans had themselves borrowed from the Greek colonies in southern Italy and Sicily, as well as the Etruscan phalanx infantry formation originally devised by the Greeks. Skilled Etruscan engineers taught the Romans to make the weight-bearing semicircular arch, which Romans used to construct city walls, aqueducts to carry water, and doorways. Although Etruscan kings won support in Rome by building new public buildings, at the end of the sixth century B.C.E. the last Etruscan king was driven out for his brutality, and Rome became independent. Later the Romans conquered and assimilated the Etruscans.

The Roman Republic

The Romans also borrowed many political ideas from the Greeks. As the Greeks did in Athens, the Romans built a system of self-government for their city-state. While doing so, however, they also began their territorial expansion. Again like Athens, Rome then faced the challenge of how to maintain its democratic aspirations while expanding an empire. And, like the Greeks, the Romans ultimately failed to keep their fragile system of self-government alive.

A New Government System

After deposing the last Etruscan monarch, in 509 B.C.E. Romans established a republic, a state in which supreme power is held by the people or their elected representatives. Over the next three centuries, the Romans developed a system of representative government that introduced many enduring political ideas. Many modern English words taken from Latin—such as *senate, citizenship, suffrage* (the right to vote),

dictator (a man given full power for a limited time, usually during a war), *plebiscite* (PLEB-i-site), and even *republic*—remind us of the influence of the Romans on modern political life.

The system changed over time. Initially, power rested entirely in the hands of the aristocratic upper class, or **patricians** (puh-TRISH-uhnz). Patricians controlled the Senate, a small body that had previously advised the kings and later dominated foreign affairs, the army, and the legislative body made up of soldiers, known as the **Centuriate Assembly**. The Senate, composed of three hundred older men, all former government officials, claimed the right to ratify resolutions of the Centuriate Assembly before they became law. As the Republic developed, the Centuriate Assembly elected two men each year to serve as **consuls,** who had executive power. Consuls were assisted by other patrician officials, such as judges and budget directors.

The Patrician-Plebeian Conflicts

The patricians were heavily outnumbered by the commoners, or **plebeians** (pli-BEE-uhnz), who were plagued by debts owed to the patricians. Wealth flowed into Rome as a result of military expansion in the peninsula and then beyond. As the soldiers who fought to make this expansion possible, the plebeians wanted to share in this wealth. The long, hard-fought wars left many plebeians in debt because long years of service in the army had taken them away from their farms, which were now in ruin. The plebeians therefore demanded a greater political voice, hoping that by gaining access to political power they could secure economic equality. A Roman historian reported the bitterness of a plebeian leader toward those who opposed reform: "[You] realize vividly the depth of the contempt in which you are held by the aristocracy. They would rob you of the very light you see by; they grudge you the air you breathe, the words you speak."[3] Political power, the plebeians believed, would allow them to pass laws that distributed the wealth of the state more fairly.

Gradually social and political rights expanded. In 494 B.C.E. the plebeians selected two of their number, called **tribunes,** to represent their interests in the Centuriate Assembly, much as the consuls represented patrician interests. By 471 a separate Plebeian Assembly was established to elect tribunes and to conduct votes of the plebeian class, called plebiscites. In 451 the plebeians also demanded that the law code be published so that all could know the laws. The laws were carved on tablets and placed in the Forum, the public gathering place in Rome. Plebeians later gained the right to share with the patricians lands that the Roman state had won in war. In 367 B.C.E.

---

patricians   The aristocratic upper class who controlled the Roman Senate.

Centuriate Assembly   A Roman legislative body made up of soldiers.

consuls   Two patrician men, elected by the Centuriate Assembly each year, who had executive power in the Roman Republic.

plebeians   The commoner class in Rome.

tribunes   Roman men elected to represent plebeian interests in the Centuriate Assembly.

The Roman Forum　The Forum, located amidst various religious and governmental buildings, was the center of Roman political life.　(Bruce Coleman, Inc.)

plebeians also became eligible to serve as consuls, a major step that eventually led to their full acceptance into the political system. Full equality for plebeians was won by 267 B.C.E., when their assembly became the principal lawmaking body of the state.

Expanding Roman Power in Italy

In the fourth century, the Roman Republic turned to imperialism, the control or domination by one state over another, as a way of resolving some of its problems. Roman political expansion began with a major defeat at the hands of the Gauls (gawlz), a Celtic people who plundered Rome in 390 B.C.E. Shocked by this defeat, Roman leaders decided to expand their territory to keep their frontiers safely distant from the city of Rome. Their military successes were due in part to their wise decision to enlist defeated enemies as allies in future conquests.

During the rest of the fourth century, Romans successfully fought a series of wars with other Italian city-states. At the end of each successful war, they granted either full or limited Roman citizenship to the inhabitants of many of the defeated cities. Being a Roman citizen became a great honor entitling a person to special legal treatment, an honor that fathers were proud to pass on to their sons. By treating former enemies

fairly, the Romans spread their power without encouraging revolts and ensured that more men would enlist in their army. They first conquered the Etruscan cities, which had been weakened by conflicts with the Gauls. After securing their power in north and central Italy, the Romans were then able to conquer the remaining Greek cities in southern Italy and Sicily. Across the sea from Sicily, however, the Romans encountered their greatest enemy, the Carthaginians.

Carthage, Egypt, and Regional Trade

Both Carthage and Egypt played key roles in Mediterranean trade. The city-state of Carthage (KAHR-thij) was originally a Phoenician colony founded in 814 B.C.E. on the North African coast near where the city of Tunis (TOO-nis) is today. The other great power on the southern shores of the Mediterranean was Egypt, ruled by the Hellenistic Greek Ptolemaic (tawl-uh-MAY-ik) dynasty, which had fostered great prosperity for over a century.

With a fine harbor and a strategic position, Carthage rapidly grew into the wealthiest and strongest Phoenician outpost. A Greek from Sicily reported that Carthage in the third century B.C.E. had "gardens and orchards of all kinds, no end of country houses built luxuriously, land cultivated partly as vineyards and partly as olive groves, fruit trees, herds of cattle and flocks of sheep."[4] However, the autocratic city government experienced much political instability as rival leaders vied for power, and differences between the Phoenician settlers, who owned most of the wealth, and the native Berbers also created tensions. The Carthaginians also fought frequent wars with their main commercial rivals, the Greeks.

The Carthaginians were great sailors and used their maritime skills to develop trade networks. Around 425 B.C.E. an admiral, Hanno (HAN-oh), led a naval expedition through the Strait of Gibraltar and down the coast of West Africa, seeking markets and perhaps a sea route to Asia. He founded trading posts along the Morocco (muh-RAHK-oh) coast and sailed at least as far as the Senegal River. Some historians think Hanno may have sailed much further along the West African coast. Other Carthaginian expeditions apparently reached the British Isles and perhaps several of the Atlantic islands off the northwest African coast, such as Madeira and the Canary Islands.

Gradually the Carthaginians created an empire along the southern and western shores of the Mediterranean Sea. By the third century B.C.E. they controlled a large part of Spain, much of the North African coast, and the islands of Corsica and Sardinia. In 264 B.C.E. they moved troops to Sicily to aid several Greek cities allied with them against Rome.

To the east there was Egypt. Although it had long flourished, the Ptolemaic hold on that country was becoming more tenuous by the second century B.C.E. The Ptolemies were hard-headed businessmen and worked to increase agricultural and crafts production, in part by demanding more work from Egyptians. As it had been under the ancient pharaohs, Egypt remained a major producer of wheat. The Hellenistic Greeks introduced a new variety of hard wheat, popular with non-Egyptians, which made Egypt a major supplier of wheat to other Mediterranean societies. Egypt also exported papyrus, the preferred medium for scientific, philosophical, and literary texts throughout the region; textiles, including linen and woolen fabrics; and pottery and metal objects. Greeks and Phoenicians owned some of the ships which carried these goods to foreign ports. Despite the economic growth, many Egyptians tired of foreign occupation, hardship, and high taxes, and several rebellions threatened the government, including an attack on Alexandria. At the same time, the ruling Greeks gradually became somewhat Egyptianized, and the more privileged sectors of Egyptian society became relatively Hellenized.

Women had long exercised power behind the Egyptian throne, but in 180 B.C.E. Cleopatra (KLEE-oh-PA-truh) I became sole ruler, the first in a long chain of assertive queens who competed with men for the dominant position. During this time Egyptian rulers sought alliances with rising Rome in order to maintain their own independence. In 47 B.C.E., with Roman assistance, an ambitious eighteen-year-old became ruler as Queen Cleopatra VII, just as years of poor harvests and official corruption fostered more unrest. Her skills enabled the unstable state to maintain domestic peace and deflect Rome for nearly two decades.

The Punic Wars and Afro-Eurasian Empire

The result of Roman expansion southward was the Punic (PYOO-nik) Wars, which pitted the two major powers and bitter rivals of the western Mediterranean, Rome and Carthage, against each other. In 264 B.C.E. the Romans began the first of three wars against the Carthaginians. The first Punic War (264–241 B.C.E.) resulted in several Roman naval expeditions against Carthage and finally ended with Roman occupation of Sicily, Corsica, and Sardinia. In the second of the wars (218–201), the brilliant Carthaginian general Hannibal (HAN-uh-buhl) (247–182 B.C.E.) led his troops through Spain and France to invade Italy across the Alps, defeating every Roman army sent against them. Hannibal's father had instilled in him an intense hatred of the Romans, and he used every tactic at his disposal to achieve victory, including drafting Celts from Spain and southern France into his army. Modern people may have images in their mind, probably accurate, of war elephants used by Hannibal's army lumbering through the rugged mountains. The Carthaginians had carefully trained these elephants to charge and possibly terrify the enemy on the battlefield. But the elephants and Hannibal's troops were not used to the snow and ice of the mountains, and perished by the thousands.

The arrival and early military success of Hannibal's still formidable force alarmed the Romans. In a Roman play of the time, a character implored Romans to "conquer by inborn valor, as you have done before; increase resources; destroy your foes; laud and laurels gather."[5] With his supply lines overstretched, however, Hannibal could not conquer the Italian cities. Eventually the Romans drove him out and defeated Carthage, which had to surrender all its overseas possessions, including Spain. In the final Punic War (149–146), Rome laid siege to the city of Carthage and destroyed it, spreading salt on the fields around the city to make it difficult to plant crops there in the future. Northwest Africa became a Roman province, a source of copper, grain, and West African gold.

Roman victory in the wars not only destroyed Carthage but also encouraged additional Roman imperial expansion in the Mediterranean region, aimed either at punishing Carthage's allies or at restoring stability. Rome went to war with Macedonia and ended Macedonian control of the Greek cities in 197 B.C.E. When the Hellenistic Seleucid rulers in Anatolia attempted to conquer Greece, the Romans intervened in 146 B.C.E. and made Greece and Macedonia into a Roman province. Few could resist the Roman infantrymen, who were armed with swords and rectangular shields, or the armor-clad Roman archers, who rode in carts carrying large crossbows, among the era's most feared weapons.

Through these struggles, a Roman Empire was being built that eventually commanded the entire Mediterranean and its vast resources, binding together Europe, western Asia, and North Africa. By the middle of the first century B.C.E., Roman power extended throughout the entire Mediterranean basin and beyond. The empire included most of Anatolia, Syria, and Palestine, as well as much territory in northern and western Europe. The Ptolemies still controlled Egypt, but the rulers were careful to do nothing to offend the Romans. The Romans absorbed much of the Hellenistic east, with its rich web of international commerce centered on several hubs, including Alexandria in Egypt, which distributed goods from as far away as India and East Africa. But imperial success also led to major changes in Roman society.

SECTION SUMMARY

■ The agricultural plenty of Italy allowed for the development of larger states than had been possible in Greece, and the Mediterranean Sea allowed for Roman expansion.

■ The Etruscans, a non-Indo-European people most likely from western Asia, formed the first urban society in Italy; they influenced and were eventually conquered by the Romans.

■ Rome formed a republic, in which citizens rule the state; initially upper-class patricians dominated, but over time the plebeians attained increasing amounts of power.

■ After a major defeat by the Gauls, the Romans decided that the key to safety was to expand their territory so their frontiers would be safely distant from Rome.

■ Rome defeated Carthage, its primary rival, in the Punic Wars and then conquered an empire.

Roman Society During the Imperial Era

How did the Romans maintain their large empire?

Athenians had pondered whether empire and democracy were compatible, and eventually they proved incompatible. Likewise, in Rome the rise of empire, with its clash of personal ambitions and greed created by the wealth gained through conquest, had important consequences. In particular, the expanding empire led to the decline and replacement of the Republic with a more autocratic and arrogant imperial system. The Roman historian Tacitus (TASS-uh-tuhs) observed how the growth of empire increased the love of power: "It was easy to maintain equality when Rome was weak. World-wide conquest and the destruction of all rival[s] opened the way to the secure enjoyment of wealth and an overriding appetite for it."[6] This period of imperial rule saw the full development of Roman culture and of those elements of the Roman heritage, such as law, that formed a significant legacy to European society.

The Decline of the Republic

Imperial expansion provoked various crises that reshaped Roman politics and undermined the Republic, turning the representative institutions into window-dressing. Warfare gave excessive power to military leaders, weakening the influence of the Senate. In addition, growing Roman wealth increased the gap between rich and poor. As the empire expanded, upper-class families bought farmland from peasants who had become impoverished by long service in the army and the cheaper grain being imported from Sicily and North Africa. Many farmers moved to the city of Rome, where the government supported hundreds of thousands of displaced people to maintain their loyalty. Thus Roman society became polarized between the very rich and the desperately poor.

Some leaders attempted to deal with this impoverishment. With fewer farmers willing to serve in the army, the tribune Tiberius Graccus (tie-BIR-ee-uhs GRAK-uhs) proposed turning over public land to farmers who agreed to serve in the Roman legions when needed. When the poor gathered in Rome to support this measure, some wealthy Romans panicked and spurred a mob to club Tiberius and many of his followers to death. This event demonstrated both the determination of the wealthy not to give up power and the fact that many poor people could be mobilized to support one leader or another. In addition, the Senate was unable to control the military leaders.

The changing nature of military power also undermined democracy. In 107 B.C.E., Gaius Marius (GAY-uhs MER-ee-uhs), who defeated Roman enemies in North Africa and southern France, was elected consul for five straight years, despite a law that prohibited a person from holding the office more than one year. Marius set an undemocratic precedent for the future when he brought his military veterans to pressure the senators to vote for a law that gave the veterans public land. As a result, skillful military leaders thereafter used their armies to enhance their political power and outmaneuver civilian leaders and the Senate. The result was a series of civil and foreign wars. Between 78 and 31 B.C.E., several ambitious military leaders used their power to expand Roman territory in Asia and Europe while finally destroying republican institutions within Rome itself. Crassus (KRASS-uhs) gained power by putting down a great slave revolt in 71 B.C.E., and Pompey (pahm-PAY) conquered more wealthy lands in the east, including Syria and Palestine. At one point, both joined with the young Julius Caesar (SEE-zer) in an alliance to share power.

Caesar proved the most ambitious. During his years as Roman governor in Gaul (France), he completed the conquest of Europe from the Rhine River west to the Atlantic and sent the first Roman forces into Britain. These victories enhanced his influence. His power was further increased when he won a civil war against his former allies. In addition, Caesar weakened the Senate by enlarging it to nine hundred men, making it too large to be an effective governing body. Finally, in 44 B.C.E. he took charge of the state by having himself declared Perpetual Dictator (see Chronology: The Roman Empire and Its Successors, 60 B.C.E.–526 C.E.). This act led to his assassination, made famous centuries later in the play *Julius Caesar* by the English author William Shakespeare.

Caesar's death led to another civil war, the end of any pretence of democracy, and conquest of Egypt. Caesar's adopted son, Octavian (ok-TAY-vee-uhn), fought Mark Anthony, a general who had fallen in love with the Egyptian ruler Cleopatra. A

CHRONOLOGY

The Roman Empire and Its Successors, 60 B.C.E.–526 C.E.

60–44 B.C.E.	Julius Caesar rises to dominance in Roman politics
31 B.C.E.–14 C.E.	Reign of Octavian (Caesar Augustus)
31 B.C.E.–180 C.E.	*Pax Romana*
6–7 B.C.E.–30 C.E.	Jesus's life and preaching in Palestine
64 C.E.	Death of Peter (first bishop of Rome) and of Paul of Tarsus
66–73 C.E.	Jewish revolt against Rome
251 C.E.	Germans defeat Roman armies and sack Balkans
306–337 C.E.	Reign of Constantine
313 C.E.	Legalization of Christianity
325 C.E.	Council of Nicaea
354–430 C.E.	St. Augustine of Hippo
391 C.E.	Paganism banned by Emperor Theodosius I
395 C.E.	Final division of eastern and western empires
410 C.E.	Alaric and Ostrogoths sack Rome
451–452 C.E.	Huns invade western Europe
455 C.E.	Vandals sack Rome
476 C.E.	Official end of western Roman Empire
481–511 C.E.	Clovis and Franks conquer Gaul
493–526 C.E.	Ostrogoths rule Italy

remarkable personality who had borne a son by Julius Caesar, Cleopatra was described by the Greek historian Plutarch (PLOO-tark), who wrote that "her presence was irresistible; the attraction of her person, the charm of her conversation, was something bewitching. She could pass from one language to another."[7] The turmoil and the Republic itself ended when Octavian defeated Anthony and Cleopatra at the naval Battle of Actium (AK-tee-uhm), in Greece, in 31 B.C.E. Anthony and Cleopatra escaped to Egypt and eventually committed suicide. Soon their armies surrendered to Octavian, giving Rome control of Egypt. The Romans placed Egypt under a tighter grip than most of their colonies, passing laws to discourage Greek-Egyptian intermarriage, imposing heavy taxes, and encouraging more wheat production to feed the city of Rome.

Augustus and the *Pax Romana*

Rome and its empire were now ruled by emperors who controlled the military and much of the government bureaucracy. This trend was begun by Julius Caesar's nephew, Octavian (63 B.C.E.–14 C.E.), who called himself Augustus (aw-GUHS-tihs), a Latin term meaning "majestic, inspiring awe." Augustus became the empire's effective ruler in 31 B.C.E., and the Senate affirmed his exalted position in 27 B.C.E. His long reign (r. 27 B.C.E–14 C.E.) gave Augustus time to establish and consolidate a system in which he allowed the Senate to appoint governors to the peaceful provinces while he took charge of provinces where troops were stationed. Augustus gained the power to legally enact or veto legislation and to call the Senate into session. The writer Juvenal (JOO-vuhn-uhl) deplored the consequences of the lost popular voice and its replacement by entertainments to divert public attention: "The people that once bestowed commands now meddles no more and longs eagerly for just two things: bread and circuses."[8]

The period in Roman history from the beginning of the reign of Augustus through that of Emperor Marcus Aurelius (aw-REE-lee-uhs) in 180 C.E. is known as the **Pax Romana** ("Roman Peace"). For the first and last time, the entire Mediterranean world was controlled by one power and remained at peace for two centuries (see Map 8.2). During this time Rome experienced few challenges from the Germanic peoples, who for the most part remained east of the Rhine and north of the Danube Rivers. In the east the Romans faced only a weak Parthian kingdom in Persia and Mesopotamia. Whether in London or Paris, Vienna or Barcelona—all cities founded by the Romans—people lived under the same laws.

Peace and prosperity encouraged trade and population growth. Great fleets of ships moved mountains of goods across the Mediterranean Sea. Trade also flourished along the Silk Road between China and Rome through Central and western Asia. Rome governed a huge population, which has been estimated at 54 million in the first century C.E., including 6 million in Italy, 17 million in the rest of Europe, 20 million in western Asia, and 11 million in North Africa. Rome may have been the world's largest city, with a half million to 1 million inhabitants.

In this diverse empire the Roman ideal, like that of the Hellenistic Greeks, was cosmopolitan. Hence, Emperor Marcus Aurelius (r. 161–180 C.E.) wrote: "Rome is my city and country, but as a man, I am a citizen of the world."[9] Non-Romans were incorporated into the ruling class. By the second century C.E., half of the members of the Roman Senate were non-Italians from the provinces. Men of wealth and military skill, whatever their ethnic background, could rise to the highest levels in the army and civil administration. Many people from outside Italy migrated to Rome, bringing with them cultural forms such as new musical instruments and dances. As the cosmopolitan

---

Pax Romana ("Roman Peace") The period of peace and prosperity in Roman history from the reign of Augustus through that of Emperor Marcus Aurelius in 180 C.E.

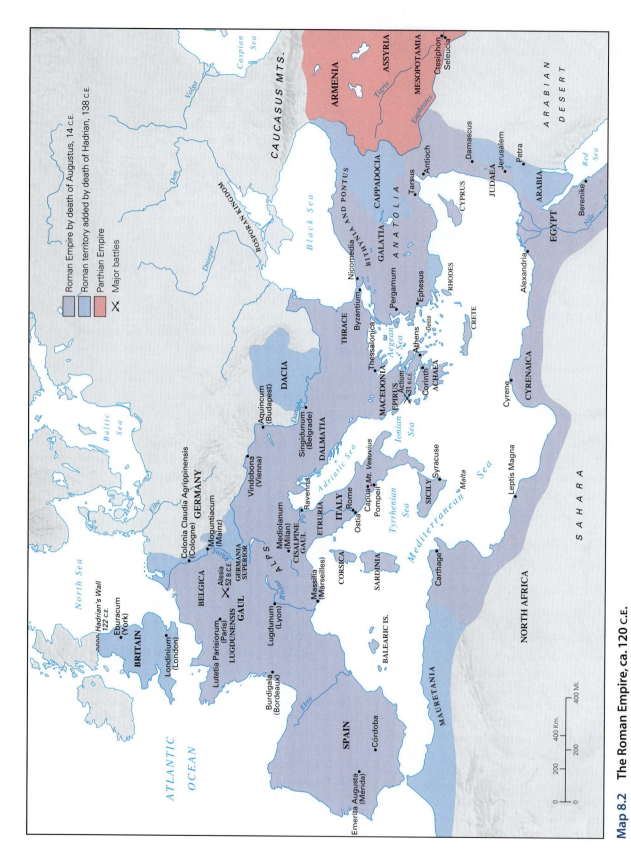

Map 8.2   The Roman Empire, ca. 120 C.E.
The Romans gradually expanded until, by 120 C.E., they controlled a huge empire stretching from Britain and Spain in the west through southern and central Europe and North Africa to Egypt, Anatolia, and the lands along the eastern Mediterranean coast.

Online Study Center   Improve Your Grade Interactive Map: The Roman World in the Republic and Early Empire

trend continued, the empire slowly changed from a possession of the people of central Italy to a multinational state that fostered diversity within unity. It was no accident that the phrase chosen as the slogan of the new United States in the eighteenth century C.E., *e pluribus unum* (EE PLUR-uh-buhs OO-nuhm), "one from many," is written in Latin.

Law, Citizenship, and Religion

Roman society owed much to other Mediterranean peoples, especially the Greeks and Etruscans. The Romans drew, for example, on the Greeks' political, ethical, and metaphysical philosophies. But the Romans also made something distinctive from this Greek legacy, going beyond the Greeks in developing a practical way of looking at the world. In particular, the Romans extended the meaning of some of the classic Greek ideas, such as citizenship, and developed a concept of civic virtue, an idea close to what people today call public duty. The Romans also developed a legal system and a polytheistic religion.

Legal Philosophy   Codified laws underpinned the Roman system and encouraged public responsibility. Roman laws were divided into two types. Civil law applied to Roman citizens. The second type of law, known as the "law of peoples," consisted of principles and practices that the Roman jurists believed were common to all peoples, such as ownership of property. Several principles of Roman law have survived the centuries to become an accepted part of the laws of most modern nations and modern international law. For example, the Romans believed that all people, regardless of wealth or position, were equal before the law. They also developed the idea of crimes against the state, what we today call treason. Perhaps most important, the Romans promoted individual responsibility; a person's family could not be held responsible for one individual's misdeeds. Roman jurists also said that the burden of proof in a trial should rest with the person making the charge, and not with the defendant.

The Roman concept of law was influenced by the Greek Stoic belief in eternal truths that lay deeper in the human mind than the particular cultural practices found among many diverse societies. Leading Roman Stoics included the philosopher Seneca (SEN-i-kuh) (4 B.C.E.–65 C.E.), the great Roman lawyer and essayist Cicero (SIS-uh-roh) (106–43 B.C.E.), and the second-century emperor Marcus Aurelius (uh-REAL-yus), famous for his humanity and justice. These thinkers believed that all people were alike in their rationality, at least to the extent that each person could use his or her reason to determine that certain things were right and others wrong. For instance, Marcus Aurelius wrote that there was a universal nature of things. Stoics promoted tolerance, moderation, and acceptance of life's travails. Because of such beliefs, the Romans generally allowed conquered cities to govern themselves. Provinces could keep their own customs and leaders so long as they paid their taxes and did not revolt. Rome, of course, made overall policy.

Religion   Roman religion comprised a pantheon of gods and goddesses, who were worshiped for practical reasons. Proper sacrifices, rituals, and prayers were crucial to ensure good fortune and to keep the gods and various spirits happy. The Romans did not pray to their gods and then hope for the best; they honored each god or goddess with precise ritual and expected favorable results. Specific gods or goddesses were associated with the agricultural tasks of hoeing, sowing seed, and weeding, and there was even a goddess for thieves and one for door hinges. A good illustration of the practical, down-to-earth, legalistic philosophy of the Romans is this prayer recorded by the Roman orator Cato (KAY-toh):

> Whether you are god or goddess to whom this grove is dedicated, it is your right to receive a sacrifice of a pig for the thinning of this sacred grove. In offering this pig to you I humbly beg that you will be gracious and merciful to me, to my house and household, and to my children.[10]

Reflecting the practical goals of Roman religion, Caesar Augustus commissioned the building in Rome of the *Ara Pacis,* or Altar of Peace, a sacrificial marble altar to celebrate the end of the wars of conquest in Gaul and Spain and, hopefully, launch a long era of peace.

Ara Pacis   The Altar of Peace, built in 9 B.C.E., resided in a large enclosure, whose walls contain relief sculptures. This scene depicts Mother Earth and her children, with the cow and sheep at her feet representing the prosperity resulting from peace.   (Scala/Art Resource, NY)

As their control of the Mediterranean world increased, the Romans did not wish to offend any divinity who might help them. Hence, they adopted the gods and goddesses of other peoples. This was especially true of the Greek deities, which the Romans equated with their own gods. For example, the Greek leader of the gods, Zeus, became the Roman Jupiter (JOO-puh-tuhr), Zeus's wife Hera became the Roman Juno (JOO-noh), and the Greek god of wine, Dionysus, became the Roman Bacchus (BAK-uhs). But in their cosmopolitan attitudes, the Romans also adopted the deities of other cultures. The Celtic goddess Sulis was seen as equal to the Roman goddess of wisdom, Minerva, and the Egyptian sun-god Amon was viewed as equivalent to Jupiter.

Roman religion was an integral part of civic life. There was no "separation of church and state" in Roman society. Priests were part-time, unpaid state officials who performed public sacrifices to please the gods and interpreted natural signs (such as the flight patterns of birds) to determine the will of the gods. The Roman priests performed ceremonies promoting the welfare of the state.

Social Life and Gender Relations

Throughout all the political changes of the Roman Empire, Roman society remained stratified into sharply defined upper and lower classes, although there was some class mobility. Romans were very class conscious, and society remained sharply divided by wealth. Below the upper classes were middle-class merchants and artisans. They ranked above the city-dwellers and peasants, who were the backbone of the Roman armies during the Republic. While many peasants became seriously impoverished, a small minority became wealthy from wealth or land gained as a result of Roman conquests. We know something of a wide range of the concerns and values of the middle and lower classes from the graffiti and tombstone memorials that they left (see Witness to the Past: The Voices of Common Romans).

As in Greece, slaves occupied the bottom of the social ladder. By the first century B.C.E., one in every three persons in Italy was a slave. Most slaves were men and women captured in the many wars, but some people were enslaved as payment for debt or as the result of a legal conviction for crime. Some slaves lived very hard lives, working in mines, on vast plantations growing cash crops such as olives and grapes, or as oarsmen of Roman ships. A Roman historian described the lives of slaves working in a silver mine in Spain: "The slaves secure for their masters riches which are almost beyond belief. They, however, are physically destroyed, their bodies worn down. Many die because of the excessive mistreatment they suffer. They are given no break from their toil."[11] Most of the gladiators who fought in the arenas to entertain the public were slaves. Gladiatorial contests were deadly, and few participants lived to old age. But the gladiators were highly skilled combatants, many of whom had studied at gladiator schools. The Romans were generous in freeing slaves after years of good service, and they could then become Roman citizens. But ex-slaves were still stigmatized socially and satirized in plays as uncultivated.

Like most classical societies, the Romans were patriarchal. Only men had a political voice, and they enjoyed extensive power over women, children, and slaves. The oldest living male in a family had the power of life and death over other family members, able even to kill his children without fear of legal problems. Wives were advised to accept the extramarital sexual exploits of their husbands: "Let the matron be subject to her husband." Yet, some women stepped outside expected bounds. For example, Seneca criticized those daring women who copied "male indulgences, they keep just as late hours, and drink as much liquor; they challenge men in carousing."[12]

Women also enjoyed some legal rights. Although they had no recourse if their husbands committed adultery, early Roman laws did give an adult woman possession of her own property, even if she was married. Some women thus came to enjoy considerable wealth, using it for such community ends as financing public monuments. Another law said a wife could escape her husband's legal control by spending three days and nights away from his house. She could also sue her husband if he abandoned her. For example, one plea to the court came from a woman whose husband had moved to Alexandria and married another woman; she asked that her husband be compelled to return the dowry she brought to the marriage. In addition to these rights, Roman women had more freedom to leave their homes and travel through the city than did their Greek sisters. Also giving them some freedom, abortion and contraception were common until they were outlawed around 200 C.E. But some Romans blamed emancipated women for Roman decline. The satirical writer Juvenal, often prone to exaggeration, denounced ambitious and assertive upper-class women for breaching moral standards, which he believed undermined the family.

The family system changed over time. In the later years of the Republic, Romans became free to choose their own spouse. By 17 B.C.E., adultery and even avoidance of marriage by both genders had become serious social problems. To attempt to halt a population decline among native Italians, a law was passed requiring men to marry. Those who stayed single paid higher taxes. But, in spite of the emphasis on procreation, views on human sexuality were diverse. Romans were generally tolerant of homosexual activity, for example, and did not view it as immoral. Acknowledged homosexuals participated openly in Roman life.

Economy and Trade Networks

Roman society flourished from expanding trade and industry. The Romans had industries, such as mining and pottery making, that produced wealth. But because the industrial work force consisted mostly of slaves, the Romans had little incentive to produce laborsaving technologies. In addition, those who acquired wealth beyond that needed for public display invested it in land, the most prestigious form of investment, rather than in business or industry.

During the *Pax Romana*, many public works projects were begun by Augustus and continued by his successors, including the Roman road system. The Romans built over 150,000 miles

As with most premodern societies, we know much more from the surviving records and literature about the prominent and wealthy Romans than about the common people who constituted most of the population. But we can learn something about the middle and lower classes from the graffiti preserved in the ruins of ancient cities like Pompeii and the epitaphs on tombstones. Romans used graffiti and epitaphs to voice frank opinions on many matters and to summarize their lives. Like modern graffiti, some of the remarks address sexual activities and bodily functions or insult rivals with profanity. The following are some examples of less profane but often humorous graffiti and epitaphs from various Roman cities.

Graffiti

I'm amazed, O wall, that you've not collapsed under the weight of so much written filth.

A bronze urn has disappeared from my tavern. Whoever returns it will get 65 sesterces reward. Whoever informs on the thief will get 20 sesterces, if we recover it.

Perarius, you're a thief.

No loiterers—scram!

Livia, to Alexander: "If you're well, I don't much care; if you're dead, I'm delighted."

Samius Cornelius, go hang yourself!

Stronnius is an ignoramus.

Crescens is a public whore.

Whoever doesn't invite me to dinner is a barbarian.

Whoever is in love, may he prosper. Whoever loves not, may he die. Whoever forbids love, may he die twice over!

Marcus loves Spendusa.

If you haven't seen the Venus that Apelles painted, take a look at my girl—she's just as beautiful.

Thraex makes the girls sigh.

All the goldsmiths support Gaius Cuspious Pansa for public works commissioner.

The mule-drivers support Gaius Julius Polybius for mayor.

Genialis supports Bruttius Balbus for mayor. He'll balance the budget.

I ask you to support Marcus Cerrinus Vatia for public works commissioner. All the late-night drunks back him.

Epitaphs

If you wish to add your sorrow to ours, come here and shed your tears. A sad parent has laid to rest his only daughter, whom he treasured with sweet love as long as the Fates permitted. Now her dear face and form are mere shadow and her bones mere ash.

For my dearest wife, with whom I lived two years, six months, three days, and ten hours. On the day she died, I gave thanks before gods and men.

I was once famous, preeminent among thousands of strong Bavarian men. I swam across the Danube in full armor. I once shot an arrow in the air and split it with a second in midair. No Roman or barbarian ever beat me with a spear, no Parthian with the bow. This tombstone preserves the story of my deeds. But I am still unique, the first to do such things as these.

THINKING ABOUT THE READING

1. What do these graffiti tell us about political life?

2. What do the graffiti and epitaphs reveal about what common people valued?

3. In what ways do the sentiments seem familiar to modern readers?

Source: James P. Holoka and Jiu-Hwa L. Upshur, eds., *Lives and Times: A World History Reader*, vol. 1 (Minneapolis: West, 1995), pp. 156–158. Copyright © 1995. Reprinted with permission of Wadsword, a division of Thomson Learning: www.thomsonrights.com.

of roads, most of them 4 feet thick. The phrase "all roads lead to Rome" reflects these accomplishments, as well as the fact that Rome became a communications center for a large area of Afro-Eurasia. The roads allowed for the movement of armies, commercial traffic, and official mail. Roads and bridges, along with many cargo ships, were components of a vast network of long-distance trade.

The Roman trade network became elaborate by the end of the Republic. Maritime trade provided a crucial foundation. Land and sea trade routes linked the Roman Empire to peoples in East Asia and sub-Saharan Africa. The Egyptian port of Berenike (BER-eh-nick-y), on the Red Sea, was a transfer point for fabrics, spices, gems, and other exotic goods from India and Southeast Asia, frankincense and myrrh from Arabia, and ivory, drugs, tortoise shells, and slaves from Somalia and Ethiopia. During the *Pax Romana* over a hundred ships a year set off

from Berenike and nearby ports for India. Merchant ships, the largest able to carry 1200 tons of grain, plied the Mediterranean between Egypt and Rome. Roman merchants may also have sailed the Indian Ocean, and Chinese records indicate that some Roman merchants may have reached Southeast Asia and even the borders of China. Roman coins have been found in the ruins of Funan, in what is now southern Vietnam.

The Romans also traded widely over land. Roman-ruled North Africa obtained gold from West African societies across the Sahara Desert. The longest land network, the Silk Road across Central and western Asia, allowed Chinese products to reach Rome. Romans shipped much gold and silver east in return for spices, jewelry, cut gems, glassware, and silk. Eventually the Roman economy was harmed by the expanding Roman appetite for Chinese goods. The historian Pliny (PLIN-ee) the Elder bemoaned the wealth shipped east and blamed it on

Roman women's fondness for silks, pearls, and perfumes: "India and China and [Arabia] together drain our empire. That is the price that our luxuries and our womankind cost us."[13] However, the criticism was misplaced, since both men and women coveted imported Asian goods.

Literature, Architecture, and Technology

As in the realm of public works and trade, the achievements of Roman literary culture during the late republic and early empire were considerable, although they mostly reflected the views of the aristocratic elite. Virgil (70–19 B.C.E.) was Rome's greatest epic poet. His *Aeneid* (i-NEE-id) described the journey of the legendary Trojan hero Aeneas (i-NEE-uhs), who, according to the poem, left Troy and eventually founded the city of Rome. This Roman counterpart to the Greek *Iliad* and *Odyssey* was designed to promote Roman greatness and honor the ruler of Virgil's day, Augustus Caesar. Less pleasing to the moralistic Augustus were the love poems of Ovid (OH-vid) (43 B.C.E.–17 C.E.), which were irreverent and erotic. For instance, Ovid's treatise on the art of love advised men to indulge their sexual cravings, for, he stated, the grass is forever greener in neighboring fields. In disgust, Augustus eventually sent Ovid into bitter exile along the Black Sea.

Historians also made substantial contributions to Roman literature. For example, Tacitus (56–117 C.E.) wrote a history of the early emperors in which he lamented the end of the Republic, which had a more open political atmosphere. He concluded that little remained of the old morality and that, deprived of equality, everyone looked up to the ruler's commands without apprehension. He also authored a description of the Germanic tribes north of the Rhine and Danube, in which he contrasted the sexual purity and other virtues of the Germans with the vices of his fellow Romans. Tacitus was blunt. For example, in describing Domitian, one of the emperors who became corrupted by power, Tacitus wrote that he "fancied that the voice of the Roman people, the liberty of the senate, the conscience of the human race were obliterated; he banished teachers of philosophy and exiled every noble pursuit, so that nothing honorable might anywhere be encountered."[14]

The Romans' quest to provide public services fostered creativity in other areas, including notable architecture. The Pantheon (PAN-thee-ahn), or temple to all the gods in Rome, provides an excellent example of why they earned a reputation as excellent engineers. The great dome of this building has no interior-supporting pillars and forms a perfect sphere, as high as it is wide. Roman buildings were also designed to impress. The famous Colosseum in Rome, for example, was the world's largest outdoor arena until the twentieth century. Aqueducts carried water hundreds of miles from the mountains of Italy and Spain into the Roman cities. In the capital, each person enjoyed a daily average of 130 gallons of fresh water pouring into the city from 1300 miles of aqueduct. This abundance of water encouraged the development of public baths, which were social centers containing gardens, exercise and game rooms, and libraries. A Roman writer observed that baths, sex, and wine ruin bodies but make life worth living.

The Romans are also remembered for some creature comforts and a practical attention to detail. For example, some of the homes of the wealthier citizens were heated from furnaces under the floor that spread heat to the house through ductwork. The Koreans at the other end of Eurasia also developed similar heating systems. In addition, Romans invented glass windowpanes, scales with weights, chemical fertilizer, the theater curtain, the door key, the heavy plow, and a primitive dental drill. Finally, Julius Caesar almost perfected the modern calendar. The Julian calendar that he set up created a year of 365 days and a few minutes. His calendar had to be reformed, but not until the sixteenth century.

SECTION SUMMARY

- With the shift from Roman Republic to empire, military leaders gained power, farmers grew impoverished, and the people had less voice in government.
- The *Pax Romana*, which began with Augustus, was a time of peace, prosperity, and cosmopolitan living, but also of imperial rule and a passive populace.
- The Romans set long-lasting legal standards and offered allegiance to a wide variety of gods, many of them borrowed from other peoples.
- Roman society was highly stratified; slaves performed much of the manual labor, and women, although accorded some significant legal rights, were generally subjugated.
- Rome served as a nexus for trade and communication, and it excelled in architecture and engineering.

Celts, Germans, and Roman Decline

What were the relations between Romans and other societies, including Celts and Germans?

The Roman Empire lasted in the west for about five hundred years and in the east for many more centuries. Its decline began when a long period of internal and external disorder challenged the *Pax Romana*. Some of this resulted from various population movements across a large part of Eurasia that put pressure on the frontiers of the Roman Empire and eventually contributed to imperial collapse. The decline of Rome also corresponded to the rise of northern European societies. Celts and Germans, both of Indo-European origin, were the two major peoples of northern Europe, and both were affected by the Romans in different ways. But the crises in succession to the imperial throne and difficulties in managing a tax-burdened society, as well as social and health problems, also sapped the Roman Empire from within. The growing problems led to the empire's division.

The Decline of the Western Roman Empire

The chief political problem causing the decline of the Roman Empire was not new. From the time of Augustus onward, Roman leaders had not found a good way to pass power on to a successor. In 211 the dying Emperor Septimius Severus (suh-VIR-uhs), a former general, advised his successor to enrich the soldiers and ignore everyone else. The reliance on the army to decide who ruled resulted in twelve soldier-emperors between 235 and 260 C.E., none of whom died peacefully in old age. Temporary political stability was restored only at the end of the third century.

Another problem was economic. To control their possessions, the Romans spent more and more of their wealth to support a growing bureaucracy and the military, pushing the state toward bankruptcy. However, paying the taxes was a particular problem in the western half of the Roman Empire, where serious inflation caused by debasement of the coinage decreased real wealth substantially. The Roman economy was stronger in the east, where the older, larger cities provided more people with work and a stronger tax base for the government. A serious "balance of payment" problem developed between the west and the east. The frontier lands west of Italy consumed more than they produced. To pay for goods and food, produced largely in the eastern half of the empire, the people of the west had to constantly find more precious metals (such as gold and silver) or more wealth in the form of slaves, which they could sell or trade to the east for manufactured products.

The early third century was a turning point. At that time, Roman rulers were forced by increasing costs and the difficulties of efficiently controlling an ever-growing empire to end further conquests and merely defend the existing frontiers. In so doing, however, they cut themselves off from the income that conquest provided, thus further impoverishing the government. To make matters worse, some gold and silver mines in the western lands became exhausted, as did some of the fertile soil in Italy. These two conditions made goods more expensive at a time when the people in the western empire had less money to pay for them. Alongside these were a steadily widening gap between rich and poor, a serious trade deficit with China, dropping levels of literacy, and growing corruption, apathy, and loss of public spirit.

Climate change and recurring epidemics brought additional challenges. A cooler climate may have diminished crop yields. Because of contacts with distant lands, Rome was also increasingly vulnerable to the spread of diseases. Epidemics that killed many thousands erupted from time to time. A plague in the empire from 251 to 266 C.E., which reached Europe from North Africa, caused dramatic population decline and weakened Roman military forces. At the height of the epidemic 5000 people were said to have died each day just in the city of Rome.

Celtic Societies and the Romans

The Celtic (KELL-tik) peoples who occupied a large area of Europe posed a challenge to the expanding Romans. The Celtic culture had developed by the twelfth century B.C.E. in the upper Danube River Basin north of the Alps. The early Celtic farmers used bronze and, around 750 B.C.E., adopted iron. Aided by these technologies, by 500 B.C.E. they had occupied large sections of central and western Europe, from Germany and France to southern Britain and Spain. Celtic migration continued westward into the British Isles and southeast into the Balkans. Fierce warriors and fine horsemen, by 400 B.C.E. Celtic tribes had raided into Italy, sacked Rome, and weakened the Etruscan states. Some Celts even settled in central Anatolia (where the Romans knew them as Galatians). The Celtic warriors terrified their opponents. A Roman writer describing the Celtic armies in Gaul said that the many trumpeters and horn blowers, as well as their war cries, presented a very frightening scene.

Roman Army Camp This carving shows a camp being built by Roman legionnaires during a military campaign. Soldiers' helmets, shields, and pikes are propped up at the right side. Some men build walls and dig ditches. (Drawing from *Atlas of the Roman World*. Reproduced with permission of Facts on File, Inc.)

We are learning more about the early Celts. Celtic society was hierarchical. Powerful chiefs ruled small states, and priests, known as *druids* (DROO-ids), organized the worship of the many gods. Many Celts lived in large fortified towns, and some had coins and writing. However, Roman conquest may have prevented the Celts from developing a thriving urban society of their own.

Celtic tribal rivalries contributed to Roman conquest, and the well-drilled, disciplined Roman legions easily overwhelmed the Celtic fighters, despite their alarming war cries. Most of the Celts were eventually colonized by the Romans or dislodged by the Germans. In 225 B.C.E. the Romans overran the Celts in northern Italy. First the Carthaginians and then the Romans crushed Celtic power in Spain. By 100 B.C.E. the Celts were caught in a vise between northward-expanding Rome and westward-expanding Germans. Julius Caesar conquered the Celts of Gaul. In 60–61 C.E., the Romans faced a temporary setback when Celts led by a warrior-queen, Boudica (boo-DIK-uh) (d. 61 C.E.), destroyed several Roman settlements in England. Boudica had good reason to despise the Romans, who had pillaged her territory, flogged Boudica, and raped her daughters. According to legends, Boudica's forces killed some 70,000 Romans. A Roman historian lamented the defeat brought by a woman, which caused the Romans great shame. In retaliation, the Romans sent in a larger force, killing 80,000 of Boudica's subjects. The queen committed suicide rather than surrender to the Romans. But in most of mainland Europe and England, Celtic culture was gradually Latinized and Germanized, although even today pockets of Celtic identity can be found in Brittany (BRIT-uhn-ee) (western France) and in northwest Spain. Eventually the Celtic language mostly died out in the Roman Empire, to be replaced by Latin or Germanic tongues.

Celtic societies remained strong mostly in Ireland, the rugged hills of Wales, and the Scottish highlands, where harsh weather, rugged mountains, and the challenge of overcoming long lines of communication kept the Romans from extending their rule. Indeed, the Roman emperor Hadrian (HAY-dree-uhn) had a remarkable 73-mile-long rock wall built across northern England to keep Celtic tribes out of Roman territory. Although Celtic culture survived in the British Isles, it was eventually modified by Christianity, which reached Ireland in the fifth century. Today the people of Ireland, Scotland, Wales, and Cornwall in southwest England still honor their Celtic heritage but few can speak the languages.

German Societies and the Romans

Another major challenge to Roman rulers was posed by the Germanic peoples who put pressure on the empire's northern borders and eventually began migrating into the empire. Organized German societies speaking closely related languages seem to have originated in Scandinavia and the northern plains of Germany sometime during the first millennium B.C.E. No known German cities or states existed. The Roman geographer Strabo (STRAY-boh) reported that one German group, the Lombards, "migrate with ease, because of the meagerness of their livelihood and because they do not till the soil and live off their flocks."[15] The Roman historian Tacitus praised the Germans for their hospitality, noting that they considered it a crime to turn any visitor away from their door.

But the Germans were already expanding to the south and west. In military conflicts beginning in 113 B.C.E., Germans inflicted several defeats on Roman legions in Gaul. Although the Romans reorganized their legions and crushed the Germans, fear of Germanic invasions was a major reason the Romans expanded northward. As a result, some Germans were brought into the Roman fold, and some served in the Roman army. However, they were prone to rebellion, and most Romans viewed the Germans as dangerous "barbarians."

Unlike the Celts, the Germans successfully resisted the Romans, and for the next several centuries Romans and Germans watched each other warily on the fringes of the empire. Contacts with Rome led to political change among the Germans between 10 and 300 C.E. Tribes joined to form confederations, whose combined strength made them a greater threat. Pushed by their own enemies such as the westward-moving Huns from Central Asia, many Germanic peoples began looking to the fertile Roman lands for new homes.

German-Roman conflict intensified as Germanic peoples began moving slowly into the empire, often encouraged by the Romans themselves, who used German troops to fight against other enemies. This migration could not have happened at a worse time for Rome, whose empire and population were declining. In 251 C.E., a group of Germans defeated a Roman army and plundered the Balkans. But the Romans were unable to field enough high-quality soldiers to defeat the invaders because their shrinking population meant that men needed to farm could not be spared for the army. In 381 the Romans began drafting men into service, but so many draftees mutilated themselves to avoid service that the government announced that those who declined military service as an honor must endure it as a forced labor. Armies were also expensive, and German military pressures were responsible for a crushing tax burden.

German Expansion and Changing Roman Society

German expansion had a major impact on Roman society. High taxes needed to support the Roman armies alienated all classes, but they fell primarily on the poor. Many of the poor peasants lost their land and threw themselves on the mercy of the wealthy, who took them in to work on their large landed estates. Sometimes whole villages placed themselves under the protection of a wealthy landlord, who would then pay their taxes for them in return for agricultural labor. This system, in which men and women worked the land of their patrons, eventually reshaped the peasant class as they gave up their freedom in exchange for protection.

The upper classes also increasingly abandoned the government. They escaped the cities, which they had earlier supported with their money and public service, and created a new private life for themselves on their country estates. To continue to work for the empire subjected them to German attack

Life on a Late Roman Empire Estate The painting, of a fortified manor house and its surroundings, shows typical farming activity for each season. (Gilles Mermet/Art Resource, NY)

or burdened them with the job of collecting the hated taxes. Neither possibility was attractive, and so the Roman cities slowly but steadily shrank in size as fewer children were born and the upper classes moved away.

The Division of the Roman Empire

The mounting problems led to the division of the empire. At the end of the third century, Emperor Diocletian (DIE-uh-KLEE-shuhn)(r. 285–305) recognized the weakness of the western empire and tried to stop the decline by dividing the empire in half, making the Adriatic Sea an east-west dividing line. He ruled the east from Nicomedia (NIK-uh-MEED-ee-uh) in Anatolia and appointed another man, Maximian, as emperor in the west. A later emperor, Constantine (r. 306–337), reunited the empire under one ruler. He also established a new eastern capital on the Straits of Bosporus (BAHS-puhr-uhs). His new city, first named New Rome and then Constantinople (cahn-stan-tih-NO-pul)—today's Istanbul (IS-tahn-BUL)—in 395 became the capital of the eastern, or Byzantine (BIZ-uhn-teen) Empire, which survived the western Roman Empire by nearly a thousand years.

The worst military defeats suffered by Roman armies occurred in the fourth and fifth centuries C.E., forcing emperors to gradually withdraw their armies and abandon claims to many territories, including Britain. In 410 the Germanic Ostrogoths (AH-truh-GAHTHS) (eastern Goths), led by their king, Alaric (AL-uh-rik) (370–410), plundered the city of Rome. Around 410 a branch of the Huns, fierce horse-riding Central Asian pastoralists who had occupied southern Russia, formed an empire in Hungary. They conquered some Germans

and pushed other Germans west into Gaul, Italy, and Spain. Led by the able warrior Attila (uh-TIL-uh) (406–453), the Huns ravaged the Balkans and Greece before plundering northern Italy in 452. After Attila's death in 453, Hun power collapsed, but Rome was again sacked by another German group, the Vandals (VAN-duhlz), in 455 C.E. The official end of the western empire came in 476, when Germans deposed the last Roman emperor.

The western Mediterranean world was now ruled by various Germanic kingdoms, including the Vandals in Northwest Africa, the Visigoths (VIZ-uh-gahths) in Spain, and the Ostrogoths in Italy. Another German group, the Franks, under their leader Clovis (KLO-vuhs), conquered what is now France and western Germany. Meanwhile, Germanic Angles and Saxons migrated into England. These Germanic peoples retained a considerable amount of Roman culture; moreover, some adopted local versions of Latin, which formed the basis for **Romance languages** such as French, Italian, and Spanish.

SECTION SUMMARY

- Beset by a range of problems, including uneasy succession, economic imbalance, overexpansion, climate change, and disease, the Roman Empire began to decline.

- The Celts, fierce warriors, posed a threat to the Romans, but they were eventually pushed back to rugged areas of the British Isles.

- The Germans, whom the Romans considered barbarians, exerted a tremendous amount of pressure on the Roman Empire.

- The Roman Empire had trouble fielding enough soldiers or gathering enough money to fend off the German threat, since many of its poor had traded their rights for protection by the rich, and many of the rich had left the cities to live on their estates.

- The Roman Empire fell in 476 C.E., but an offshoot, the Byzantine Empire, lasted for another thousand years.

Romance languages Languages that derive from Latin, such as French, Italian, and Spanish.

Christianity: From Western Asian Sect to Transregional Religion

How did Christianity develop and expand?

The one institution that was a vigorous part of the life of the Roman cities even in the final decades of the western empire was the Christian church. Christianity arose in Palestine (in western Asia) in the first century C.E. as a Jewish sect (see Map 8.3). The religious and social institutions of Christianity accompanied Greco-Roman culture into the new Germanic kingdoms, and together they defined the culture of the new societies that dominated Europe in the centuries following the Classical Age. To understand the history of the Western societies, we need to analyze the rise and values of Christianity.

Roman Palestine and Jesus of Nazareth

Christianity was founded on the teachings of Jesus of Nazareth, a Jewish teacher in first-century C.E. Roman-ruled Palestine. Palestine and the surrounding region contained a mix of several traditions. For example, most people, including the Jews, spoke Aramaic (ar-uh-MAY-ik), the official language in the later Persian Empire, and most literate people wrote in Greek, a legacy of Hellenism. Various ideas from Egyptian, Mesopotamian, Phoenician, Persian, and Greek traditions undoubtedly influenced the Jewish and then Christian faiths.

Palestine was one of the most restless Roman provinces and had a history of rebellion against Rome. Over the centuries the Hebrew prophets, such as Isaiah in the eighth century B.C.E. and Jeremiah, Ezekiel and the "Second" Isaiah during the early Axial Age, explored the relations of the Hebrews to their God and other peoples. First-century B.C.E. Jewish society was characterized by diverse beliefs and practices. Zoroastrian and Hellenistic thought influenced some Jews. In contrast, various mystical Jewish sects rejected both Hellenistic cosmopolitanism and the formal Jewish leadership. Jesus inherited these prophetic traditions and spoke of himself as the fulfillment of Jewish law.

Much uncertainty surrounds the life of Jesus. Roman records offer no help; although they confirm religious conflicts in Palestine, they make no mention of Jesus. According to Christian tradition, Jesus was a Jewish teacher and healer, a carpenter by trade, who probably lived from around 7 or 6 B.C.E. to 30 C.E. As with Buddha and Confucius, our knowledge of Jesus and his career comes from the writings of followers, primarily through the four gospel (literally "good news") accounts of the Christian New Testament. The earliest of these narratives, the Gospel of Mark, was written around 70 C.E., some forty years after the death of Jesus. Like the other three gospels in the official canon compiled in the middle of the second century C.E., Mark was written not as a historical account but as a faith statement, a "witness" to the power of God in the lives of the early followers of Jesus. Modern theologians and historians vigorously debate the accuracy of gospel accounts,

all of which were written several generations after the events described. Several dozen other gospels or fragments of gospels were not included in the Christian Bible, and some of them differ considerably from the official gospels. It is unclear whether the various gospel accounts were based largely on eyewitness testimonies, oral traditions, earlier writings that have since been lost, or a combination of all of them.

In any case, the gospels describe Jesus as, among other things, a moral reformer who confronted the Jewish leaders. He was especially critical of the *Pharisees* (FAR-uh-seez), a group that emphasized ritual purity, obeyed strict ceremonial laws, and awaited the coming of a messiah who would free them from the Romans. Jesus favored a simple life that included love of others, forgiveness of enemies, acceptance of the poor and other despised groups, and opposition to excessive legalism and ceremony. According to the Gospel of Matthew, Jesus summed up his teachings in two commandments: "Love God with all your heart, soul, and mind; and love your neighbor as yourself."[16] Matthew also reported that Jesus angered influential Jews and Romans by advising the wealthy to give their money to the poor since, according to gospel accounts, he said that rich people were unwelcome in God's kingdom. Some modern theologians argue that Jesus made no claims to be divine or a "son of God," and they note that in the earliest version of the gospels, Jesus describes himself only as a healer and wisdom teacher. Other scholars, however, emphasize that Jesus was seen as much more than a wisdom teacher by his followers.

Jesus's enemies, especially the Roman governor but also a few Jewish religious leaders, accused him of treason against Rome, and Jesus was tried, convicted, and executed by crucifixion. After his death, followers of Jesus claimed that he was revived or resurrected from death and that he "appeared to" his disciples. Although historians cannot verify such a faith claim, this belief in the continuing divine presence of Jesus probably motivated his followers to stay together, preach his message to others, and honor his teachings by gathering for worship as a special sect within the first-century C.E. Jewish community.

Paul and the Shaping of Christianity

The evolution of the religion of Jesus into Christianity was greatly affected by the activities and writings of Paul of Tarsus (TAHR-suhs), a port city in southeast Anatolia. Paul was a first-century Romanized Jew from a Pharisee family who said that he was miraculously converted to belief in Jesus as a young man, probably around 33 C.E. He then spent the rest of his life spreading this faith to non-Jews, traveling extensively from Palestine to western Asian and Greek cities before his death in a prison in Rome about 64 C.E.

Paul's teaching emphasized two things. First, he stressed that Jesus was a divine being, the "son of God" who earned forgiveness for the sins of humankind by his death on the cross. By accepting Jesus as the Christ (*Christus* meant "anointed one"), Paul taught, a person could be saved from damnation to an eternity in Hell. Second, Paul preached that a non-Jew who did not follow Jewish laws and ritual could become a follower of Jesus. By arguing that, among followers of the faith, there was nei-

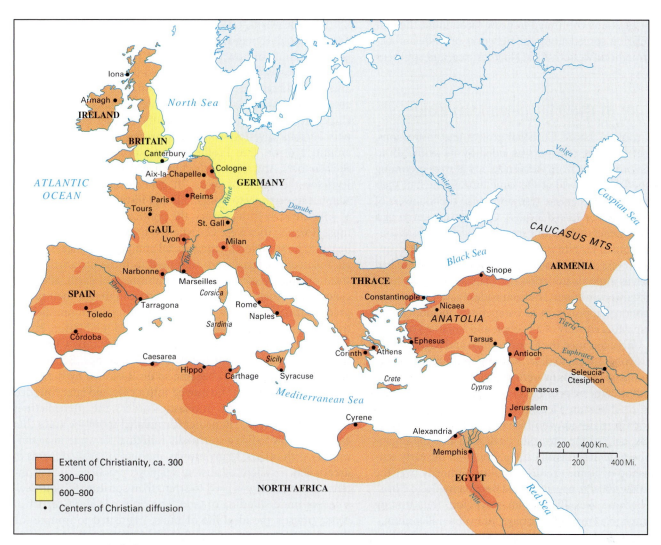

Map 8.3   Spread of Christianity
Christianity arose in Palestine in the first century C.E., and gradually gained footholds in parts of Western Asia, North Africa, and southern Europe by 300 C.E. Over the next five centuries Christianity became the dominant religion in much of western and central Europe, and expanded its influence in western Asia and North Africa.

ther Jew nor Greek, slave nor free person but instead a spiritual equality, he was challenging fundamental Roman assumptions such as those behind slavery. These kinds of beliefs prompted many otherwise broad-minded Roman citizens to regard Christians as a countercultural threat. Paul's patriarchal views also strongly influenced Christian thinking. He argued that, while man is the glory and image of God, woman is the glory of man. Paul valued celibacy above marriage and urged wives to be subject to their husbands and remain silent in church.

Paul disagreed strongly with those in Jerusalem who believed that Christians had to follow Jewish laws, thus creating something of a rift with the "Judaizers" (JOOD-uh-ize-uhrz) led by Peter, the chief disciple of Jesus who became the leader of the church. Paul's decision to exempt converts from undergoing the circumcision required by Jewish law was crucial for the success of Christianity, for, in those days before antibiotics and anesthesia, such operations would have discouraged many. Eventually, Peter agreed that God made no distinction between

Jews and others, and in Roman Catholic tradition Peter became the first bishop of Rome (and hence the first pope). Peter was probably killed in Rome during the persecution of Christians in 64. Eventually, most Christians believed they were saved by faith in Jesus, not by following any Jewish tradition.

The victory of Paul in convincing Peter to include non-Jews was crucial in establishing Christianity as a world religion (see Map 8.3). A Jewish revolt from 66 to 73 C.E. resulted in the Roman destruction of the Jewish temple in Jerusalem and the dispersion of many Jews to other lands. During the revolt the *Zealots* (ZELL-uhts), a group of Jewish rebels, held out in a hilltop fort known as Masada (muh-SAHD-uh) overlooking the Dead Sea. Although the Romans eventually took the fort, Masada stood through history as a symbol of Jewish resistance to oppression. After the Roman victory, any Jew became discredited in Roman eyes, so it was fortunate for the early Christians that they had broken with Judaism. Meanwhile, while Jews scattered across Eurasia and North Africa, the number of non-Jewish Christians continued to grow throughout the empire as the religion spread along the networks of trade and occupation throughout western Asia, North Africa, and southern Europe.

Christianity in the Mediterranean Zone

The Roman context shaped Christian growth and institutions. The spread of this new religion was aided by its similarity to "mystery religions," many from western Asia, that were becoming popular in the Roman world at the same time. Some had their roots in Persian and Hellenistic traditions. Like the followers of Mithra (MITH-ruh) or Isis (ICE-uhs), Christians believed in a life after death, a belief that became increasingly attractive as conditions in the Roman Empire worsened over the next several centuries. Like followers of the mystery religions, Christians also had practices, such as a special initiation rite (baptism), that fostered a sense of religious community. But some ideas gave Christianity a greater emotional appeal than its competitors, including their belief in the spiritual equality of all people and a marked concern for the poor. Christians used the terms heathen and pagan, which had negative connotations, to describe those who followed polytheistic or animistic religions or were irreligious.

These advantages helped Christianity gain greater acceptance. In 313 C.E. it became a legal religion by an edict of the Roman emperor Constantine, who believed he had won a battle because of the help of the Christian God. After this the organized church became more significant, although in the early centuries the bishop of Rome exercised limited authority over the wider church. By 400 C.E. paganism had been banned and Christianity had become the official Roman religion, thus uniting state and church in a troubled marriage for over a millennium.

But Christians also had to contend with theological divisions. For example, the sect of **Arianism** (AR-ee-uh-niz-uhm), especially popular among Germans, taught that Jesus was not divine but rather an exceptional human being. To combat what most Christians saw as heresies and to establish core beliefs, the emperor Constantine called a church council at Nicaea (nye-SEE-uh), in Anatolia, in 325 C.E., where he virtually ordered the bishops to resolve their doctrinal differences and determine which beliefs to follow. The **Nicene** (NYE-seen) **Creed** they produced became the official doctrine of the early church and is still recited in many denominations.

The early Christians did not live in a world of their own making but borrowed much Greco-Roman culture. They did not see themselves as enemies of the Roman Empire. Their only difference with the state was to refuse to acknowledge the emperor's official divine status, for which they sometimes were persecuted. Nevertheless, as the Christian religion spread, most Christians were left alone to worship as they wished, and they, in turn, acquired a Roman education and even celebrated traditional Roman festivals along with the new Christian ones.

The Christians' celebration of the birthday of Jesus on the date of the old Roman and Mithraist festival of the winter solstice is one example of how classical and Christian culture merged. Early Christians also generally adopted the Greco-Roman tolerance toward homosexuality, even within their own churches. Of course, there were also tensions between Christians and non-Christians, such as those that led to the murder of the philosopher Hypatia (hye-PAY-shuh) by Christian mobs in Alexandria around 416 C.E. (see Profile: Hypatia of Alexandria, a Pagan Philosopher). And some early church leaders already blamed the Jews for the death of Jesus. In general, however, Christians adapted successfully to Roman life and institutions.

By the early fifth century, the political and social leaders in most Roman cities were Christian, but some Christian leaders began to be troubled by their social and political success. After all, followers of Jesus were supposed to focus on spiritual instead of worldly success, on Heaven instead of earth, and they claimed that their moral code differed from that of their pagan predecessors. One result of this questioning was monasticism, the pursuit of a life of penance, prayer, and meditation, either alone or in a community of other seekers. For early Christians this often meant leaving the cities. For instance, Benedict of Nursia (ca. 480–ca. 543) became so disillusioned by the hedonistic life in Rome that he moved into a cave and later founded western Europe's first monastic order, the Benedictines (ben-uh-DIK-teenz). Benedict formulated monastic rules that explained how to live a spiritually fulfilling life while in a community with others. Many monks and nuns practiced forms of **asceticism**, a system of austere religious practices, such as intense prayer, that was used to strengthen spiritual life and seek a deeper understanding of God. The church leader Gregory of Nyssa praised the ideal life of nuns, "regulated to imitate the life of angels, a nature freed from human cares."[17] As part of this increasing tendency to withdraw from society, some church leaders began to reemphasize the superiority of a life of virginity over that of marriage, a value stressed in the writings of Paul earlier.

Augustine and Roman Christianity

As Christianity expanded during the first centuries of the Common Era, it developed church institutions and produced thinkers who shaped the theology. A major Christian thinker, the North African bishop Augustine of Hippo (354–430 C.E.), redefined Christianity's relation to the Roman world in the declining decades of the empire. Augustine defined Christian morality and history in a form that dominated western European culture for a thousand years.

Born in North Africa, Augustine was a seeker after truth who had tried several faiths before becoming a convinced Christian. He first taught rhetoric in Italy and then practiced the monastic life. Eventually Augustine became a priest and

Arianism A Christian sect which taught that Jesus was not divine but rather an exceptional human being.

Nicene Creed A set of beliefs, prepared by the council at Nicaea in 325 C.E., that became the official doctrine of the early Christian church.

asceticism A system of austere religious practices, such as intense prayer, that was used to strengthen spiritual life and seek a deeper understanding of god; began to be used in the Christian church in the fifth and sixth centuries C.E.

HYPATIA OF ALEXANDRIA, A PAGAN PHILOSOPHER

Hypatia was a female philosopher and mathematician in the old Hellenistic city of Alexandria in Egypt, then part of the Roman Empire. But at a time when Christianity was becoming more influential, she followed a non-Christian polytheistic religion. Thus in Christian eyes she was a "pagan." Perhaps nothing better shows the complex relationship between Christians and pagans in the late Roman Empire, and the tension within the Christian community itself, than her murder at the hands of a Christian mob in 415 C.E. To critics of religious intolerance such as the eighteenth-century English historian Edward Gibbon, Hypatia was a beautiful woman torn to pieces by a fanatic mob because she believed in the Greek spirit of reason instead of, in his view, the irrational beliefs of Christianity. But it was not that simple.

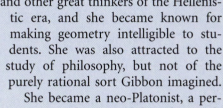

Hypatia was born around 355 C.E., the daughter of a well-educated mathematician and astronomer. As a youth she studied the works of the mathematician Euclid and other great thinkers of the Hellenistic era, and she became known for making geometry intelligible to students. She was also attracted to the study of philosophy, but not of the purely rational sort Gibbon imagined. She became a neo-Platonist, a person who saw philosophy as almost a religion, a way to discover the hidden spirit of the divine within each person. She stressed the feminine aspects of culture and argued that women benefited from honoring goddesses. Hypatia wrote commentaries on mathematical and astronomical subjects and lived quietly as a teacher, did not publicly participate in pagan worship, and, like many Christian women of her day, practiced celibacy, although she was married to another philosopher. Women philosophers were uncommon in those days, but Hypatia's wisdom and learning were celebrated. Admirers claimed she had "the spirit of Plato and the body of Aphrodite [the Greek goddess of love]." Her students were both pagan and Christian. One of them became a Christian bishop in Anatolia but remained Hypatia's lifelong friend.

Conditions in Alexandria began to change after 391 C.E., when the Roman emperor Theodosius forbade pagan worship in the empire. During the next twenty years, more and more Christians felt called to eradicate all non-Christian religions, and violent attacks on Jews and pagans became more frequent. By then Christians were a majority of the city population, though they were divided into feuding factions. Tensions grew worse in the city after the fanatic Cyril, who was generally intolerant of non-Christians, won election as bishop in 412. Since Hypatia was a close friend and supporter of Orestes, the city's Christian governor, his bitter rival Cyril spread the rumor that the widely respected Hypatia was a witch and practiced black magic. He also encouraged attacks on Jews.

In 415 a semimilitary gang of young Christians allied with Cyril dragged Hypatia from her carriage, stripped off her clothes, murdered her, and burned her body. Cyril had not ordered this, but he had created a social climate that made such a crime possible. After this event, Alexandria became a more thoroughly Christian city. The Jews, who had been a substantial community in Alexandria for over 600 years, were expelled, and Orestes returned to Rome. Cyril was never punished for his part in Hypatia's death.

Later critics were probably wrong to view Hypatia mostly as a martyr to her non-Christian beliefs. She was also, at least partly, a victim of a jealous bishop. However, Gibbon and others were correct to see her as one of the last representatives of a tolerant paganism rooted in the cosmopolitan ethos of Hellenistic and Roman culture, which was replaced by an intolerant form of Christianity. Her death also represented the displacement of philosophers from the public forum by religious men who claimed that the ideas they preached were superior because they came from God rather than from book learning.

THINKING ABOUT THE PROFILE

1. What does Hypatia's career tell us about Alexandrian society?
2. What does her experience reveal about conflicts between Christians and non-Christians in the late Roman Empire?

Note: Quotation from Maria Dzidzka, *Hypatia of Alexandria* (Cambridge: Harvard University Press, 1995), p. 5.

Statue of Hypatia This statue honors the great pagan philosopher and mathematician of fifth-century Alexandria who was murdered by Christian rivals. (Ancient Art & Architecture Collection)

then, in 395, bishop of Hippo, a city near Carthage. Like many Roman cities, Hippo had followers of many faiths, including various pagan and Persian traditions, all seen as heretical by the established church. After the sack of Rome by the Ostrogoths in 410, Augustine became especially troubled by the pagan accusation that it was the refusal of Christians to fight (many early Christians were pacifists) and the abandonment of the Roman gods that caused Roman society to wither. He felt compelled to defend his faith.

In his book, *City of God*, completed in 427, Augustine defended Christianity against its critics. He argued that the "city of God" comprised all who followed God's laws (i.e., Christians) while the "city of man" consisted of non-Christians, who ignored God's teachings and would be damned in a final judgment at the end of time. Augustine contended that all of history was in God's hands, writing that human kingdoms are established by divine providence. He promoted a view of history as a straight line of progress from past to future, in which, at the end of history, Jesus would return to judge all humanity, living and dead.

Online Study Center Improve Your Grade
Primary Source: St. Augustine Denounces Paganism and Urges Romans to Enter the City of God

In developing a moral thinking he viewed as superior to that of the tolerant Roman culture, Augustine also urged Christian men and women to remain celibate, viewing marriage as only for those with low self-control. He criticized sex outside of marriage and sanctioned sex within marriage only for procreation. He also argued that man "rules by making decisions, [while woman] is subordinate and obeys."[18] Augustine's writings reached a wide audience, and his theology strongly influenced the Roman Catholic tradition. His beliefs also helped create a clearer separation between Roman morality and the new Christian culture, which increasingly saw itself as different and superior. Christians increasingly separated themselves from hedonistic Roman traditions. For example, in 498 Christian leaders introduced an annual feast day in honor of St. Valentine to replace a holiday honoring Juno, the Roman goddess of love and marriage, and a popular, somewhat raunchy, Roman fertility festival.

Christianity filled the vacuum in the western Mediterranean as Roman government collapsed and many people left the cities in the fifth century. For example, the population of the city of Rome fell from 800,000 in 300 to 60,000 in 530. The Christian clergy often provided the only semblance of order for those who remained. Church officials also achieved a huge boost when the Franks, a Germanic people, were converted to Latin Christianity under their ruler Clovis in the 490s. Then, in the late sixth century, Europe was hit by many disasters, which were enumerated in 599 by an alarmed Pope Gregory: "as the end of the world approaches, many things menace us which never existed before: inversions of the climate, horrors from the heavens and storms contrary to the season, wars, famine, plagues, earthquakes."[19] But the widespread mood of doom proved premature. A new age was dawning in western Europe. It was largely German and Christian in tone, with a Greco-Roman overlay of language and culture.

SECTION SUMMARY

■ Christianity was born in Palestine, an area with a tradition of rebellion against Rome, and grew out of the Jewish prophetic tradition.

■ Jesus opposed excessive legalism and ceremony, but scholars debate whether he saw himself as divine, or the "son of God."

■ Paul was instrumental in spreading and shaping Christianity after Jesus's death, as well as in arguing that one did not have to be Jewish to become a Christian.

■ Aided by the popularity of mystery religions similar to it and by the decline in quality of life, Christianity took hold and became the official Roman religion.

■ In defending Christianity against its critics, Augustine distinguished between Christians, who would be saved, and non-Christians, who would be damned, and he also argued for strict standards of sexual morality that favored celibacy.

Revival in the East: Byzantines, Persians, and Arabs

How did the Byzantine and Sassanian Empires reinvigorate the eastern Mediterranean world?

A century after Roman emperor Constantine dedicated his new capital city, later known as Constantinople, in 330 C.E., the western part of the empire fell to various German groups while the eastern empire fostered a new and distinctive society, Byzantium. Byzantium saw itself as a continuation of the Roman Empire but developed a quite different political structure as well as a culture and church that was more Greek than Latin. By taking the brunt of attacks by resurgent western Asian peoples such as the Sassanian Persians, Byzantium gave the struggling new states in western Europe time to develop into a separate Latin Christian culture. The conflict between the Persians and Byzantines also helped shape the rising Arab society.

Early Byzantium and the Era of Justinian

Byzantium emerged as the most powerful state in the eastern Mediterranean region, a status it maintained for many centuries. Its capital, Constantinople, straddled the narrow waterway linking the Aegean and Black Seas and separating Europe from western Asia, symbolically linking diverse peoples and traditions. The large eastern Roman Empire initially encompassed the Balkans, Greece, Anatolia, Syria, Palestine, and Egypt, and some early Byzantine emperors expanded the borders even further. Few emperors in Rome enjoyed the power that the Byzantine government had over its people, economy, and religious institutions.

The most important early ruler of the Byzantine Empire was the Emperor Justinian (juh-STIN-ee-uhn) (r. 527–565 C.E.)

(see Chronology: Byzantium and Western Asia, 224–616 C.E.). Spurred on and advised by his powerful and ambitious wife, Theodora (THEE-uh-DOR-uh), Justinian was determined to defeat the German states in the west and reunite the old Roman Empire, announcing that God would help him to reconquer the lost lands. Justinian and his brilliant general, Belisarius (bel-uh-SAR-ee-uhs), reconquered a large part of the western territories, including the Vandal kingdom in North Africa. They defeated the Ostrogothic kingdom in Italy in 563 after long years of fighting, but repeated battles for control of Rome left the city devastated, with only a few thousand impoverished, disease-ridden inhabitants. Moreover, Justinian's victories were accomplished only at the cost of high taxes on his eastern subjects. In addition, he was barely able to defend his own domains from Huns, Persians, and various peoples migrating into Europe. During the first half of the seventh century, Justinian's successors had to turn east to fight the Sassanian Persians, and the western lands were once again lost (see Map 8.3).

Justinian also established a political pattern of despotism in which the Byzantine emperors were treated as near-gods by their subjects and thus gained absolute power over nearly every area of national life. They presided over a centralized and complex bureaucracy (hence our term *byzantine* for complicated and puzzling systems). Spies monitored the population. Justinian had many critics, among them the great Byzantine historian Procopius, who described the emperor as "at once villainous and amenable; as people say colloquially, a moron. He was never truthful with anyone, but always guileful in what he said and did. His nature was an unnatural mix of folly and wickedness."[20] But Justinian also collected all existing Roman laws into one legal code. Later, the greatest Roman legal writings and principles were published. These works and early Byzantine laws preserved Roman laws and legal principles for later generations.

Justinian's fortunes gradually declined. In 540 the Byzantines encountered one of the most terrible epidemics in world history, often known as the plague of Justinian. The sickness, probably bubonic plague, began in Egypt and spread along the trade routes into western Asia before reaching Europe. The misery hit remote villages as well as densely populated cities. At its height some 10,000 people a day perished. Ships were loaded with corpses, rowed out to sea, and abandoned. As the epidemic raged, agriculture largely halted and many communities were abandoned. A Christian bishop in Palestine wrote that "all the inhabitants, like beautiful grapes, were trampled and squeezed dry without mercy."[21] The plague returned several times until 590. When Justinian died at age eighty-three, his empire was much poorer, weaker, and less populated than it had been when he took power.

Byzantine Society, Gender Relations, and Economy

Despite its many political misfortunes, the Byzantine Empire survived for centuries because of its social and economic strengths. For example, the empire remained much more urban than western Europe. Constantinople grew to perhaps a million people and was described by a visitor as "a splendid city, how stately, how fair. It would be wearisome to tell of the abundance of all good things."[22] The rich in the cities lived in splendor, with luxury goods like silk clothes, carpets, and elegant tapestries provided by local industry. But not everyone enjoyed the benefits. As in most classical societies, a huge gap separated rich and poor, but the Byzantine peasants faced unique restrictions. By the fifth century laws required peasants who had lived many years in one place to remain there. They became bound to the soil, under the control of powerful landlords.

Byzantine society was patriarchal, and women experienced many challenges. In the early years upper-class women in the large cities enjoyed respect and influence, and some queens exercised considerable power. Women had the legal right to control their own property and the return of their dowry if their husbands divorced them. However, men enjoyed greater legal safeguards, and wife-beating was common. In an era when maternal and infant mortality rates were high, pregnancy remained hazardous and childbirth dangerous. Many women wore amulets, pre-Christian in origin, that they hoped would protect them.

The eastern lands were wealthier than the western Roman Empire, and the Byzantine economy flourished. Merchants and bankers, including many non-Greeks, were prominent members of the urban aristocracy and benefited from Constantinople's position astride the principal trade routes between Europe and Asia. It was difficult to go by land from western Asia to Europe without passing through Constantinople, where the government placed a 10 percent tax on all goods that passed through the capital. Byzantine currency was internationally recognized and retained its value for six centuries, a remarkable achievement. Byzantine coins have been found as far away as China. But most trade with China and India had to go through Persian-controlled lands, and the Persian-Byzantine relationship alternated between uneasy peace and armed conflict.

Constantinople served as a hub to which ships and caravans brought many products and resources: spices, cotton, and copper from India and Southeast Asia; jewels, silk, gold, and

CHRONOLOGY

Byzantium and Western Asia, 224–616 C.E.

224–226	Sassanians overthrow Parthians
240–272	Sassanian Empire established
306–337	Reign of Constantine
330	Founding of Constantinople
395	Final division of eastern and western empires
527–565	Reign of Justinian
540–590	Plague of Justinian
607–616	Sassanians conquer Syria, Palestine, and Egypt

Interior of Santa Sophia Cathedral
The great cathedral of Santa Sophia in Constantinople, rebuilt for Byzantine emperor Justinian, was famous for its spectacular interior. (Werner Forman/Art Resource, NY)

silver from China and Central Asia; gold, ivory, and slaves from Africa; cotton and grain from Egypt; grains, wool, and tin from northwestern Europe; olive oil and silver from Spain and Italy; timber, fur, copper, hides, and slaves from Russia and Scandinavia. These products went through many hands. For example, Indonesians and Indians brought spices from Southeast Asia to India or Sri Lanka. From there Persian, Indian, Ethiopian, or Arab boats carried some of the cargoes through the Red Sea to Suez, where they were transported overland to Alexandria. From that port, also a great regional hub, they connected with sea and land routes around the Mediterranean world.

Byzantine Religion and Culture

The Byzantine society inevitably diverged from the western Roman tradition in many ways, but especially in religion and culture. Though it saw itself as a continuation of Roman culture, Byzantine culture was fundamentally Hellenistic Greek. The Byzantines preserved and later passed on to the Latin west (often through the Muslims) the works of Plato, Aristotle, Homer, Sophocles, and other Greeks. The Christian church in the east also became separated from its Latin counterpart, over time evolving into a different branch of Christianity, the Greek Orthodox Church, which developed many customs and viewpoints quite foreign to the Roman church in western Europe.

Religion permeated all aspects of Byzantine life. The church, especially monasteries, gained control of considerable land and hence wealth derived from the peasants. From the ruler, who controlled both temporal and religious affairs, to the ordinary citizen, religious questions were avidly discussed. Emperors took the lead in proposing church reforms and calling church councils to deal with what mainstream Christians considered heresies. These heretical sects included the **Monophysites** (muh-NAHF-uh-sites), who argued that Jesus had a single divine nature rather than both a divine and human form; the Arians, who contended that Jesus was only human and not divine; and the **Nestorians**, who believed that the divine and human natures of Jesus were independent of each

other. Christianity also affected gender relations. A goddess figure who represented urban prosperity in the fourth and fifth centuries was replaced by the much beloved Christian image of the Holy Virgin Mary, which gave women moral stature. But the church also viewed women as weak and inferior, both physically and morally, and easily tempted by sin.

Over time theological disputes between the eastern and western churches grew. In general, Greek Christians came to emphasize ritual and theological disputes to a greater extent than did their Latin brethren. They also refused to accept the notion that the bishop of Rome (later known as the pope) was superior in authority to the other bishops. Conflicts over authority and doctrine contributed to the final split between the Latin and Greek churches in the eleventh century. Meanwhile, the Monophysites formed the Armenian, Coptic, and Syrian Orthodox Churches. The Nestorians migrated to Persia, becoming the basis of the modern Chaldean and Assyrian Churches. From Iran they spread their faith along the Silk Road into India and China.

Byzantine art and architecture, although quite original, reflected the cultural diversity of this huge empire and was strongly influenced by western Asian traditions. The fusion of some Persian and Greco-Roman influences can be seen, for example, in the great dome inspired by Persian models in the Church of Santa Sophia (Holy Wisdom) in Constantinople, built under Justinian. The church was designed to symbolize in-

Monophysites   A heretical sect that argued that Jesus had a single divine nature rather than both a divine and a human form.

Nestorians   A heretical Christian sect that believed that the divine and human natures of Jesus were independent of each other.

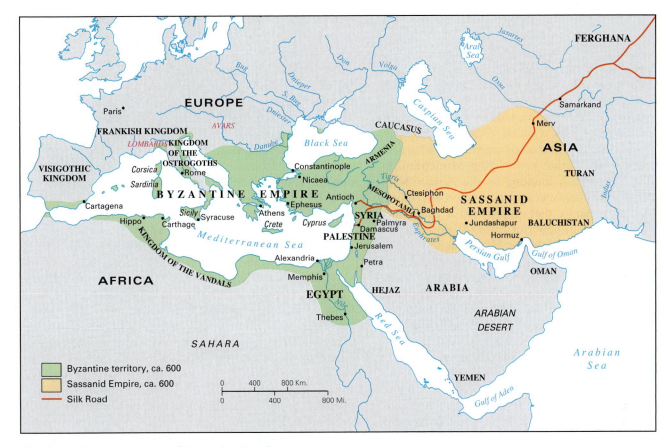

Map 8.4   The Byzantine and Sassanian Empires
By 600 C.E. the Byzantine Empire controlled much of southern Europe and the eastern end of the Mediterranean basin, and the Sassanian Empire dominated most of the rest of western Asia, part of Turkestan, and Egypt. Various Germanic kingdoms held political sway in far western Europe, northern Europe, and northeast Africa.

ner Christian spirituality in contrast to human pride. Hence, the external appearance was modest but the interior was richly decorated with mosaics, marble columns, tinted glass, and gold leaf.

Sassanian Persians and Their Networks

Both the Roman Empire and the Byzantines who replaced them in the east had to deal with a revived Persia under the Sassanian dynasty, which generated frequent conflict. The Sassanians, who took power in Persia in 224 C.E., were a high point of classical Middle Eastern history. Between 240 and 272 C.E. their rulers forged a large empire. Considering themselves the successors to the Achaemenids a half millennium earlier, they also called themselves "king of kings." At their height, the Sassanian court, based in modern Iraq, provided a focus for a brilliant culture mixing Hellenistic and Persian influences. The Sassanians ruled for over four centuries.

The Sassanians pursued empire. In the east they fought with the Kushans (KOO-shans), whose Afghanistan-based empire controlled parts of western India and Central Asia by the first century C.E. Eventually the Sassanians occupied much of Afghanistan and some of the Silk Road cities of Central Asia, but they lost these territories to the Huns in the fourth century C.E. To the west the Sassanians expanded into the Caucasus and Mesopotamia, creating chronic conflict with Rome in and around Syria. The Sassanians were usually victorious. At times they occupied parts of Arabia, including Yemen (YEM-uhn) in

the south. After their economy was revived and their army improved in the sixth and early seventh centuries the Sassanians occupied the eastern Byzantine Empire, including Syria, Palestine, and Egypt (see Map 8.4). But years of war with Byzantium weakened both societies. In 651 the last Sassanian king was murdered and Arab Muslim armies gained control of all Sassanian territories.

Controlling much of the Persian Gulf, Sassanian Persia became a contact zone for international trade. A Roman writer noted: "All along the coast [of the Persian Gulf] is a throng of cities and villages, and many ships sail to and fro."[23] Sassanian trade links stretched east as far as India, Central Asia, and China, and south as far as the Horn of Africa. Byzantine and Sassanian coins were used as currency in the Silk Road cities. Persians produced some of the world's finest pottery, silver plates, pearls, brocades, carpets, and glassware, exchanging these for gems, incense, perfume, and ivory.

Sassanian Religion and Culture

In contrast to the religiously tolerant Achaemenids, the Sassanians mandated a state religion, Zoroastrianism. The government imposed orthodoxy, supporting the priesthood and sometimes persecuting other religions. Although it was not always successful, the Sassanian example of establishing a state religion may have influenced Roman emperors to make Christianity one. However, state religions tend to decay, and Zoroastrianism was

223

no exception. The Zoroastrian establishment became corrupt and rigid, and by the fifth century the faith was losing influence and followers.

Yet Zoroastrianism spawned various religions that combined this faith with others. One of these new religions, Mithraism, became popular in the Roman Empire and spread as far west as England. Another new religion, **Manicheanism** (man-uh-KEE-uh-niz-uhm), founded by the Persian Mani (MAH-nee) (216–277 C.E.), was a blend of Zoroastrianism, Buddhism, and Christianity that emphasized a continuing struggle between the equally powerful forces of light and dark. Although Mani was executed for heresy, his faith suppressed by both the Sassanians and Christians, his religious dualism was later incorporated into Islam and some Christian sects. Augustine of Hippo's deep belief in the notion of original evil can be attributed to the fact that he was a Manichee in his youth.

As Zoroastrianism gradually lost influence, the state became more tolerant of diversity and turned the capital city, Jundishapur, into a cosmopolitan intellectual center. Christian minorities such as the Armenians of the Caucasus region were allowed freedom of religion, and the Sassanians also welcomed Nestorian Christians fleeing Byzantine repression. Foreign scholars migrated to the newly tolerant state, as did Jews and others who feared persecution in Christian Europe. The Sassanians also collected scientific and literary books from many neighboring peoples, translated Greek writings, and established a renowned hospital and medical school. Sassanian Persia's multiculturalism provided a framework that enabled later Islamic governments to rule diverse peoples and faiths. But Zoroastrianism, too closely connected to Sassanian domination, rapidly declined, becoming only a minor faith after Islam swept through the region.

Interregional Trade, Cities, and the Arabs

The ebb and flow of long-distance trade in western Asia, often influenced by the activities of the Hellenistic Greeks, Romans, Byzantines, and Sassanians, helped foster the rise of Arab culture. Diverse Semitic societies lived in the Arabian peninsula, a dusty region of mountains, dry plains, and harsh deserts stretching from the Jordan River and Sinai southeast to the Indian Ocean. Most of the Arabian peoples were pastoral nomads divided into tribes. Roman sources described these mobile people: "All alike are warriors of equal rank, ranging widely with the help of swift horses and slender camels."[24] Others lived from trade or farming. Eventually all of these groups coalesced into the Arab society.

One of the peoples out of which Arab society arose were the Nabataeans (NAB-uh-TEE-uhnz), who traded all over the Middle East by land and sea. Their trade diasporas spread as far west as Italy. The Nabataean writing system became the inspiration for the Arabic script. They also established a kingdom and built a major trading city, Petra (PE-truh), in today's Jordan, astride the overland caravan routes. Built in a narrow

gorge, Petra had a population of 30,000 at its peak. The Petra residents developed an ingenious system for collecting and storing rainwater in this arid region. The ruins of Petra's spectacular tombs, with their elaborate facades carved into rock, still astonish visitors. Beginning in the fourth century B.C.E., Petra flourished as a crossroads for goods moving between India, Arabia, Greece, and Egypt. But in 106 B.C.E. the Romans occupied Petra, and the city began a long decline as its trade shifted north to Palmyra (pal-MY-ruh), on the Euphrates River in today's Syria. Petra and Palmyra were two of the key trading cities that helped link east and west from their positions on the fringe of empires. Most Arabian peoples participated at least sporadically in these trade networks.

Palmyra thrived until 273 C.E., when the Romans crushed a revolt led by the shrewd and ambitious Queen Septimia Zenobia (zuh-NO-bee-uh). After their conquest of the prosperous and ancient trading city in 114 B.C.E., the Romans had cultivated Palmyra to protect their eastern frontier. When the Sassanians captured and killed the Roman emperor Valerian (vuh-LIR-ee-uhn) in 260 C.E., Odainat, the ruler of Palmyra and Zenobia's husband, earned Roman gratitude by defeating a Persian force. But in 267 Odainat was assassinated and the charismatic Zenobia took power. Taking advantage of Roman wars with the Goths, she sent her army into Egypt and then occupied much of Roman Asia, including much of Anatolia. As ruler she invited Greek thinkers to Palmyra and encouraged religious tolerance. However, by controlling Egypt she controlled the Roman grain supply. After fierce battles the Romans reoccupied Palmyra and took Zenobia to Rome, where she died. After another revolt the Romans destroyed Palmyra.

The farming-based kingdoms that rose and fell in Yemen in southern Arabia since the days of the fabled Queen of Sheba around 1000 B.C.E. constituted another source for Arab culture. Yemen included an area of high, cool mountains and well-watered valleys. The Yemenite people were highly skilled, especially in civil engineering and architecture. They produced an abundant harvest with the aid of elaborate dams and terraces, and they constructed splendid cities in valleys and along mountainsides. City-states emerged, among them Saba, possibly the Sheba of the Hebrew Bible. The Yemenites traded by sea with India and East Africa, as well as across Arabia by land with the eastern Mediterranean and Mesopotamia. Frankincense from the region was prized as far away as Rome.

In the sixth century C.E. Arabian conditions began to change. Political disarray, an Ethiopian invasion, and commercial depression began to undermine Yemenite society and power. To the north, renewed conflict between the Sassanians and Byzantines led both of them to actively seek allies in central Arabia. As a result, Arabia became a political pawn caught between Orthodox Byzantium, Zoroastrian Persia, and Coptic Ethiopia. This situation also increased the traffic over land trade routes and fostered the settlement of many Christian and Jewish merchants in desert towns like Mecca (MEK-uh). Some Arabs adopted these religions. In the seventh century all these trends fostered the emergence of a new Arab faith, Islam, out of classical roots. Eventually Islamic armies overran most of the Byzantine Asian territories and the Sassanian Empire.

Manicheanism   A blend of Zoroastrianism, Buddhism, and Christianity, founded by Mani, that emphasized a continuing struggle between the equal forces of light and dark.

SECTION SUMMARY

- Justinian ruled the Byzantine Empire absolutely and tried to retake the Roman Empire, with mixed results.
- More urban and wealthy than western Europe, the Byzantine Empire served as a trading hub for goods from across Europe and Asia.
- Byzantine culture became more Greek and less Roman, and the Byzantine church denied the authority of the pope and came to emphasize ritual and doctrine to a greater degree than did the Roman church.
- The Sassanians revived the strength of Persia, and adopted Zoroastrianism as a state religion.
- Arab culture began to rise out of tribes of pastoral nomads, the trading cities of Petra and Palmyra, and the farming-based kingdoms of Yemen.

Online Study Center ACE the Test

Chapter Summary

The middle and late Classical Era in the Mediterranean world and western Asia was shaped largely by the activities and cultures of the Romans, Germans, Greeks, and Persians. The Romans adopted and spread some of the values of the classical Greeks, while also making major contributions in government, law, and architecture. For several centuries they had a republic in which some of the people had a voice in government and elected Rome's leaders. To acquire more resources and preempt challengers, the Romans gradually expanded their territory until it encompassed much of Europe, North Africa, and western Asia. In the process they defeated and conquered rivals, including the Etruscans, Carthage, Egypt, and the Celts. They maintained loyalty by respecting local customs and granting Roman citizenship to prominent people. Eventually the republic was replaced by a more autocratic system led by powerful emperors. Controlling the far-flung territories was expensive, however, and the Roman forces became overextended. Soon the Romans were also defending their territories against the incursions of the Germanic peoples.

New forces also developed in the eastern end of the Mediterranean basin. Christianity arose out of Jewish society in Palestine and spread throughout the Mediterranean world, western Asia, and North Africa. The power of the Christian church rose as Roman political power declined. In the east Byzantium emerged out of the eastern Roman Empire, developing into a distinct society that incorporated Hellenistic Greek political and cultural traditions. It also fostered the Greek Orthodox Church. Meanwhile, the Sassanians reinvigorated Persian society and built an large empire, eventually putting pressure on Byzantium. These conflicts increased travel over the trade routes and generated new currents in Arab society.

Online Study Center **Improve Your Grade** Flashcards

Key Terms

patricians	*Pax Romana*	Monophysites
Centuriate Assembly	Romance languages	Nestorians
consuls	Arianism	Manicheanism
plebeians	Nicene Creed	
tribunes	asceticism	

Suggested Reading

Books

Boren, Henry C. *Roman Society*. 2nd ed. Lexington: D. C. Heath, 1992. An overview of how Roman society developed.

Chauveau, Michael. *Egypt in the Age of Cleopatra*. Ithaca: Cornell University Press, 2000. A wide-ranging, readable study by a French scholar.

Cunliffe, Barry. *The Ancient Celts*. New York: Penguin, 1997. A detailed but fascinating overview of Celtic history and culture.

Dupont, Florence. *Daily Life in Ancient Rome*. Oxford: Blackwell, 1992. Discusses material culture and social values.

Fox, Robin Lane. *Pagans and Christians*. New York: Alfred A. Knopf, 1987. Explores the early rise of Christianity.

Grant, Michael. *The Fall of the Roman Empire*. New York: Macmillan, 1990. A brief and readable account.

Pomeroy, Sarah B. *Goddesses, Whores, Wives and Slaves: Women in Classical Antiquity*. New York: Schocken, 1975. An excellent study of women's lives in classical Greece and Rome.

Taylor, Jane. *Petra and the Lost Kingdom of the Nebateans*. New York: I. B. Taurus, 2001. An overview of this pre-Arab society.

Treadgold, Warren. *A Concise History of Byzantium*. New York: Palgrave, 2001. A comprehensive recent survey.

Wiesehofer, Josef. *Ancient Persia*. London: I. B. Taurus, 2001. Scholarly essays on pre-Islamic Persia and the Sassanians.

Young, Gary K. *Rome's Eastern Trade: International Commerce and Imperial Policy, 31 BC–AD 305*. London: Routledge, 2001. A recent scholarly investigation of the Roman trading system.

Websites

Diotima: Women and Gender in the Ancient World (http://www.stoa.org/diotima/).   Contains excellent materials.

Exploring Ancient World Cultures (http://eawe.evansville.edu/index/htm).   An excellent site with essays and links on the ancient Near East and Europe.

From Jesus to Christ: The First Christians (http://www.pbs.org/wgbh/pages/frontline/shows/religion).   Valuable essays linked to a documentary series on U.S. Public Broadcasting.

Internet Ancient History Sourcebook (http://www.fordham.edu/halsall/ancient/asbook.html).   An exceptionally rich collection of links and primary source readings.

Livius: Articles on Ancient History (http://www.livius.org).   Very useful site with many short essays on the Romans.

The Roman Empire (http://www.roman-empire.net/).   Offers extensive materials and essays on the Romans.

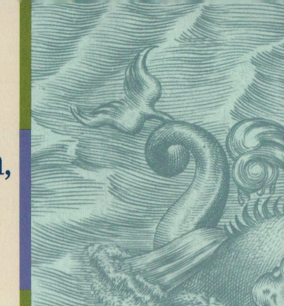

CHAPTER 9

Classical Societies and Regional Networks in Africa, the Americas, and Oceania, 600 B.C.E.–600 C.E.

CHAPTER OUTLINE
- Classical States and Connections in Northeast Africa
- The Blossoming of Sudanic and Bantu Africa
- Classical Mesoamerican Societies and Networks
- New Societies of South and North America
- Populating the Pacific: Australian and Island Societies

■ **PROFILE**
  A Moche Lord

■ **WITNESS TO THE PAST**
  A Shopper's Guide to Aksum

Online Study Center

This icon will direct you to interactive activities and study materials on the website: college.hmco.com/pic/lockard1e

Aksum Stele Early in the Common Era the kings of the African state of Aksum, in what is today Ethiopia, decorated their capital city with tall, flat-sided pillars known as steles, some nearly 70 feet high, possibly as monuments to the royal family. (Werner Forman/Art Resource, NY)

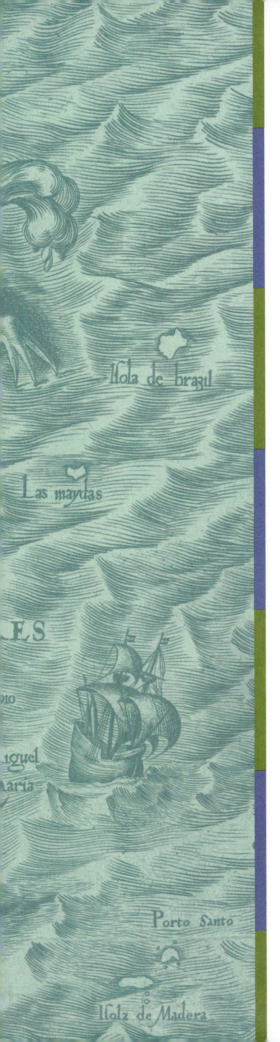

When the day dawns the trader betakes himself to his trade; the spinner takes her spindle; the warrior takes his shield; the farmer awakes, he and his hoe handle; the hunter awakes with his quiver and bow.

ANCIENT YORUBA PROVERB ABOUT DAYBREAK IN A WEST AFRICAN TOWN[1]

In the classical world, few settlements were as specialized as those serving the caravans that crossed the trackless sands of the vast Sahara Desert of Africa, a barren landscape where scorching sun and arid soil made it nearly impossible to plant crops or trees. A later traveler with these caravans commented that "the desert is haunted by demons, nothing but sand blown hither and thither by the wind."[2] The journeys were interrupted by rest stops at caravan way stations, isolated oasis towns with gardens, date palms, and flocks of sheep where weary travelers could find fresh water and restock before resuming their journeys.

The round trip of many weeks between the cities of the North African coastal zone and those on the southern fringe of the desert held many dangers besides thirst and discomfort, including fierce raiders on horseback. Camels, the major beast of burden in the caravan trade, were not always cooperative animals and often waged battles of wills with their handlers, but they could travel many days without water. On an average day camels could carry their riders and cargo some 30 miles. In the Sahara, wealth was measured more in camels than in gold. Thanks to these caravans and the brave men who led them, sub-Saharan African products reached a wider world, and goods and ideas from North Africa and Eurasia found their way along the trade networks to peoples living south of the Sahara.

The diverse societies that arose in sub-Saharan Africa, the Americas, and Oceania (the Pacific Basin) were all shaped by their environment, whether that was a desert like the Sahara, a highland, a flood-prone river valley, or a rain forest, savannah, seacoast, or small island. Societies were also influenced by their contacts—friendly, hostile, or both—with other societies, whether near and familiar or distant and alien. In Africa, for example, Egyptians, Nubians, and Ethiopians, although sometimes bitter rivals, exchanged products, ideas, and technologies with each other, with other Africans, and with Eurasian societies. Various Africans established connections with the wider world through long-distance trade, such as that carried on by the camel caravans across the bleak Sahara or by boat around the Indian Ocean. These connections ensured that few societies, regardless of where they were located, were completely isolated and unique. During the Classical Era diverse and distinctive societies developed in sub-Saharan Africa, the Americas, and Australia, and intrepid mariners settled most of the Pacific islands. These various communities worshiped their own deities, created their own artistic styles, valued some products more than others, and evolved their own political and social structures. At the same time, they had much in common. In parts of Africa and the Americas cities and states emerged that resembled each other, and in some societies there were many parallels to classical societies in Eurasia. This was truly a classical era, as societies and networks flourished and cultural influences spread over a wide area.

FOCUS QUESTIONS

1. What were some of the similarities and differences between Kush and Aksum?

2. How did the spread of the Bantus reshape sub-Saharan Africa?

3. What were the similarities and differences between the Maya and Teotihuacan?

4. How did the Mesoamerican, Andean, and North American societies compare and contrast with each other?

5. How were some of the notable features of Australian and Pacific societies shaped by their environments?

Classical States and Connections in Northeast Africa

What were some of the similarities and differences between Kush and Aksum?

In classical times tropical Africa and Eurasia were connected largely through intermediaries, including the North Africans linked to the trans-Saharan caravan trade and the maritime traders of the Indian Ocean who visited the East African coast. Two African societies, Kush (koosh) in Nubia and Aksum (AHK-soom) in Ethiopia, also served as intermediaries, becoming trading hubs and forming powerful states. Both enjoyed particularly close ties with Egypt and western Asia. Their relationship to networks of exchange strongly shaped some African societies.

Iron, Cities, and Prosperity in Kush

The kingdom of Kush, along the Nile south of Egypt, existed from about 800 B.C.E. to 350 C.E. (see Chronology: Classical Africa). From 600 to 100 B.C.E. Kush was the major African producer of iron and an important crossroads for the middle Nile region (see Map 9.1 on page 230). Its capital city, Meroë (MER-uh-wee), became an industrial powerhouse of the classical world. The Kushites acquired iron technology either from

Egypt or from the Africans who worked iron in Central and West Africa (see Chapter 3). Whatever the case, Kush had many sources of iron ore, and heaps of iron slag litter the ruins of Meroë today. Through trade networks Kush linked various peoples of sub-Saharan Africa and the Mediterranean, and hence played a central economic role in the Afro-Eurasian

C H R O N O L O G Y	
Classical Africa	
2000 B.C.E.–1000 C.E.	Bantu migrations into Central, East, and South Africa
800 B.C.E.–350 C.E.	Meroë kingdom in Kush
500 B.C.E.–600 C.E.	Garamante confederation dominates trans-Saharan trade
400 B.C.E.–800 C.E.	Aksum kingdom in Ethiopia
300 B.C.E.	Beginning of maritime trade to East African coast
200 B.C.E.	Founding of Jenne-Jenno
300 C.E.	Introduction of Christianity to Kush and Aksum
ca. 500 C.E.	Founding of kingdom of Ghana

CHRONOLOGY

	Africa	The Americas	Oceania
800 B.C.E.	**800 B.C.E.–350 C.E.** Kush		
400 B.C.E.	**400 B.C.E.–800 C.E.** Aksum		**300 B.C.E.–1200 C.E.** Polynesian settlement of Pacific
200 B.C.E.	**200 B.C.E.** Founding of Jenne-Jenno	**200 B.C.E.–600 C.E.** Hopewell Mound Builders **200 B.C.E.–700 C.E.** Moche **200 B.C.E.–750 C.E.** Teotihuacan **150 B.C.E.–800 C.E.** Flourishing of Maya society	
500 C.E.	**ca. 500 C.E.** Founding of Ghana		

zone. Kush imported pottery, fine ceramics, wine, olive oil, and honey from Egypt and western Asia, and it exported both iron and cotton cloth. Roman sources reported that Egyptian priests preferred Kushite cloth for their garments. Both the Greeks and Romans admired the Nubians. Some Nubians seem to have visited Greece and others were members of the Persian armies that attacked Greece. Roman sources report that Africans, possibly Nubians, came to Rome to trade or work, noting numerous African musicians, actors, gladiators, athletes, and day laborers in the city.

At its height Meroë was a grand city of perhaps 25,000 inhabitants. Built around a walled palace along the Nile, it contained massive temples, large brick-lined pools that may have been used for public baths, and rows of pyramids, similar to those in Egypt, where kings and queens were buried in splendor. In fact, Kush built more royal pyramids than did Egypt. The highly skilled builders used masonry, stonework, fired brick, and mud brick. As in the Indus cities, washing and sanitation facilities, with many latrines, serviced Meroë's population.

Kush Social Patterns and Culture

Although influenced by Egypt, Kushite society and the culture it produced were distinctive. At the top of the social hierarchy were absolute monarchs, including some queens, who both governed the state and served as guardians of the state religion, responsible for supporting and building the temples. In addition to worshiping some Egyptian gods, Kushites considered their monarchs, like those in Egypt, to be divine. Inscriptions testify to the piety of rulers, and Roman sources report that kings were guided by laws and traditions:

It is their custom that none of the subjects shall be executed, even if the person condemned to death appears to deserve punishment. Instead the king sends one of his servants bearing a symbol of death to the criminal. He upon seeing [it], immediately goes to his own house and kills himself.[3]

Queen mothers seem to have played an influential role in politics; some historians believe that the occasional succession of women to power indicates matrilineal succession.

Below the ruler were the military and bureaucratic elite. Kush's military officers led an army feared for both its weapons and the appearance of its soldiers. The Greek historian Herodotus described the soldiers of Kush:

[They] were clothed in panthers' and lions' skins, and carried long bows made from branches of palm trees, and on them they laced short arrows made of cane tipped with stone. Besides this they had javelins, and at the tip was an antelope horn, made sharp like a lance; they also had knotted clubs. When they were going into battle they smeared one half of their body with chalk, and the other half with red ocher.[4]

Some government officials dealt with trade, since the state dominated this activity, but the role of private merchants remains unclear. Below the bureaucratic and military elite were free peasants and slaves. Women played a variety of economic roles, working in gold mines and engaging in farming and craft production. They also served as priestesses, perhaps specializing in the honoring of female deities.

Kushites enjoyed a rich culture, as well as some activities that seem universal to all cultures. Some Greek-speaking teachers apparently lived at Meroë, perhaps immigrants or the descendants of immigrants, and at least one Kushite king studied Greek

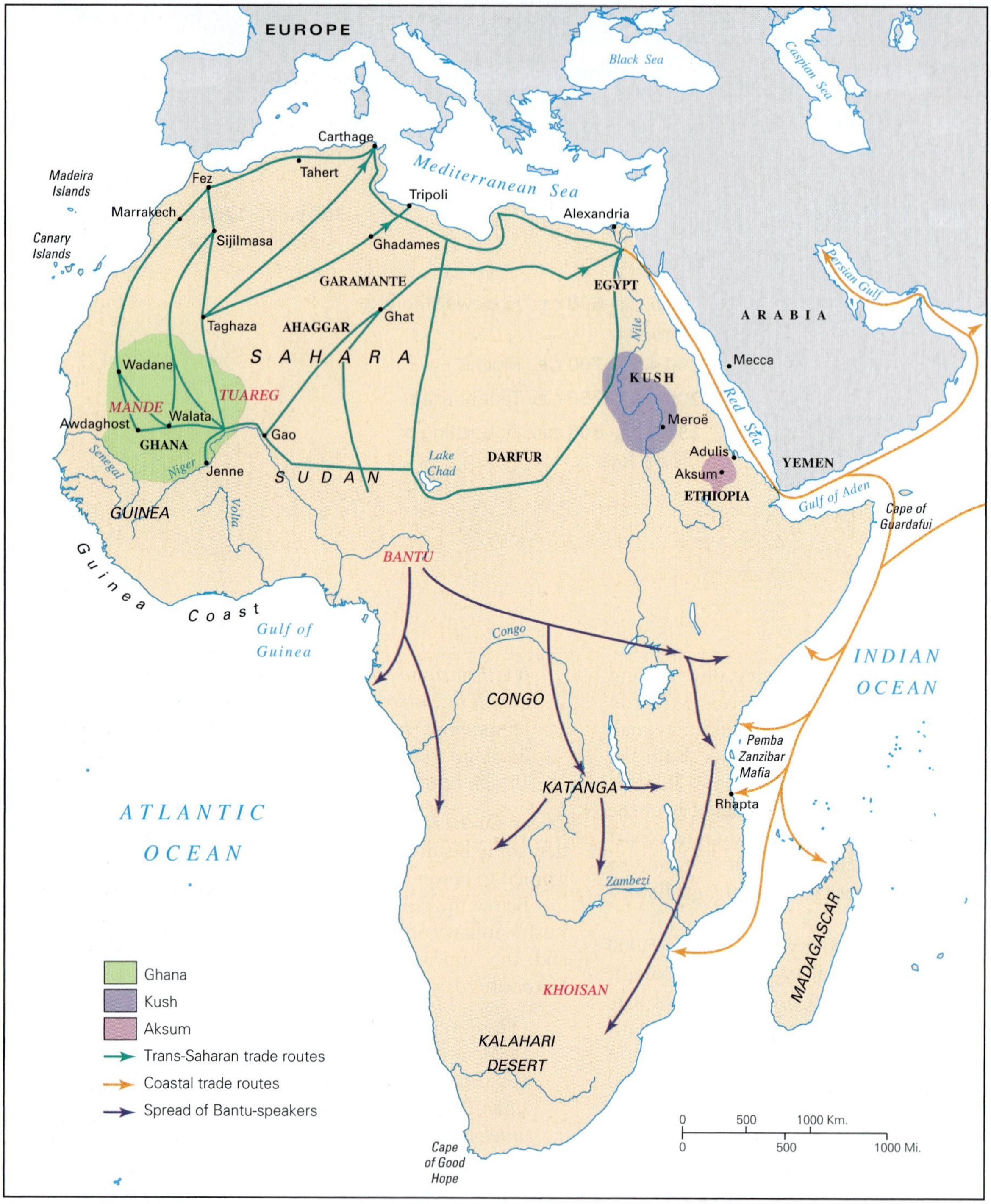

Map 9.1 Classical Africa, 1500 B.C.E.–600 C.E.
During this era, Kush, Aksum, and Jenne were major African centers of trade and government.
Trade routes crossed the vast Sahara Desert and the Bantu-speaking peoples expanded into
central, southern, and eastern Africa.

philosophy. Meroë also had artists who produced highly polished, finely carved granite statues of their monarchs, and music
played on trumpets, drums, harps, and flutes was a part of ceremonial and religious life. Some of the instruments may have been
imported from Egypt and Greece. People of all classes and both
genders wore jewelry made from gold, beads, iron, and copper alloy, and the ruins of at least one tavern have been found littered
with thousands of goblet fragments, suggesting that wine was a
popular drink. Finally, the presence of writing on numerous
tombstones as well as graffiti suggests that literacy was wide-

spread among all classes. Along with other distinctive achievements, Kushites developed their own alphabet, **Meroitic** (mer-uh-WIT-ik), a cursive script that can be only partly read today. Meroitic gradually replaced Egyptian hieroglyphics in monumental inscriptions. Indeed, over time Egyptian influence apparently faded while indigenous culture flourished.

The Legacy of Kush

After a millennium of power and prosperity, by 200 C.E. Kush was in decline, in part from environmental deterioration. Centuries of deforestation and overgrazing had helped produce a drier climate. In fact, climate change was widespread in the world at that time, and it may have also hastened the decline of the Han Chinese and Roman Empires. Chronic warfare with the Ethiopian state of Aksum also contributed to Meroë's problems. In 350 C.E. an invasion by the Aksum army destroyed what remained of the Kush kingdom.

However, the culture of Kush was kept alive in some neighboring societies. Some of its people, including the rulers, may have migrated elsewhere in Africa, spreading their iron technology and culture. Some West African societies developed political traditions not unlike those in Kush and have a folklore that identifies their origins to the northeast, though many historians doubt the connection. Nonetheless, some peoples now living a few hundred miles to the southwest of Meroë still show many signs of Kushite influence, including recreational activities (such as wrestling), fashion, body art, and material life. Indeed, like the Romans in Europe or the Han in China, the people of Kush may well have established classical patterns that still survive today.

Several new kingdoms arose from the ashes of Kush, and contacts with the outside world eventually brought a new religion, Christianity, which became dominant in Nubia between the fourth and sixth centuries C.E. Many churches were built, and ecclesiastical authorities had close ties to the monarchies. Nubian Christianity was a branch of the **Coptic** (KAHP-tik) **Church,** which followed Monophysite thought (see Chapter 8) and had become influential in Egypt. Many Copts still live in Egypt. With its patriarchal tendencies, Christianity seems to have replaced Nubian matrilineal traditions with patrilineal ones, monarchies now passing exclusively from fathers to sons. But the Christian kingdoms of Nubia, isolated from other Christians to the north by the Islamic conquest of Egypt in the seventh century C.E., gradually faded. Around 1400 C.E. Muslims conquered the last Christian Nubian state and converted most people to Islam. This religious change proved the most long-lasting transition for the societies of the middle Nile basin. Today only the ruins of Christian churches and monasteries of Nubia remain, along with the Meroite pyramids, the material legacy of Kush.

Meroitic A cursive script developed in the Classical Era by the Kushites in Nubia that can be read only partly today.

Coptic Church A branch of Christianity, based on Monophysite ideas, that had become influential in Egypt and became dominant in Nubia between the fourth and sixth centuries C.E.

Queen Amanitere Queen Amanitere ruled Meroë along with her husband, King Natakamani, around 2,000 years ago. In this relief on the Lion Temple at Naqa, Kush, she holds vanquished foes by the hair while brandishing swords, thus demonstrating the power of the royal couple and the Kushite state. (From Graham Connah, *African Civilizations*, p. 44. Reproduced by permission of Cambridge University Press.)

The Aksum Empire and Trade

Another literate urban African state, **Aksum,** emerged in the rocky but fertile Ethiopian highlands beginning around 400 B.C.E. Despite the difficult geographical terrain and the unpredictable climate of the this area, its peoples traded with Egypt from ancient times. They also benefited from proximity to the Red Sea, the major maritime route between the Mediterranean Sea and the Indian Ocean. This proximity linked northern Ethiopia to a widespread network of exchange and contact. In addition, at the Red Sea's narrowest point only 20 miles of water separates the southern tip of Arabia from northeast Africa. Many Semitic people from Arabia crossed into Ethiopia and settled among the original inhabitants. Although many deep

---

Aksum A literate, urban state that appeared in northern Ethiopia before the Common Era and grew into an empire and a crossroads for trade.

gorges inhibited communication across the plateau, the northern Ethiopians benefited greatly from accessibility to Arabia.

This accessibility may have allowed them to establish links to the Hebrews, as suggested at least in Ethiopian legends. In these legends, the Queen of Sheba who, according to biblical accounts, met the Hebrew King Solomon was in fact an early Ethiopian monarch, Queen Makeda (Ma-KAY-da), who went to Israel in search of knowledge. In the tale as reported in an old Ethiopian book, Makeda supposedly told her people:

> Let my voice be heard by all of you, my people. I am going in quest of Wisdom and Learning. My spirit impels me to go and find them out where they are to be had, for I am smitten with the love of Wisdom and I feel myself drawn as tho by a leash toward Learning. Learning is better than treasures of gold, better than all that has been created upon earth.[5]

Semitic immigrants from Yemen (YEM-uhn), the probable location of the ancient Sheba (Saba) kingdom, may have brought the story with them to Ethiopia and adapted it for local needs. The son of Solomon and Makeda, Menelik (MEN-uh-lik), supposedly founded a new kingdom, called Aksum.

The Aksum region, located on the northern edge of the Ethiopian plateau near the Red Sea, was already a center of agriculture and both bronze- and ironworking when Queen Makeda supposedly made her visit. It was inhabited by the ancestors of the Amharic (am-HAR-ik) people who today dominate central Ethiopia. Between 400 B.C.E. and 100 C.E. Aksumites built their first temples and palaces of masonry, as well as a city, dams, and reservoirs. Irrigation and terracing supported a productive farming. The Aksumites also developed an alphabet.

For centuries Aksum enjoyed close economic and cultural exchange with the peoples of both southwestern Asia and eastern Africa, becoming something of a network hub between these regions. In about 50 C.E. the Aksumites built an empire that dominated a large section of Northeast Africa and flourished chiefly from trade. One Aksumite king boasted that he compelled the nations bordering on his kingdom to live in peace and then restored their territories to them if they paid tribute to him. Soon Aksum had eclipsed Meroë and gained control of the trade between the Red Sea and the central Nile. Aksum became so well known that a Persian observer, the prophet Mani, included it with Persia, Rome, and China among the world's four great kingdoms.

The Aksumites traded all over the Middle East, eastern Mediterranean, and East Africa. A Mesopotamian poet celebrated the ships from the main Aksumite port, Adulis (A-doo-lis) on the Red Sea, whose prows cut "through the foam of the water as a gambler divides the dust with his hand."[6] The trade network also reached to Sri Lanka and India, and many Indian coins have been found at Aksum (see Witness to the Past: A Shopper's Guide to Aksum). The Aksumites exported ivory, gold, obsidian, emeralds, perfumes, and animals and imported metals, glass, fabrics, wine, and spices. A visiting Greek merchant reported that every second year the king sent agents to

an African society south of Aksum to bargain for gold. Several hundred merchants accompanied the agents, taking along iron, oxen, and lumps of salt for trade. Aksumites used the Greek language in foreign commerce and were the first sub-Saharan Africans to mint their own coins.

The Aksum empire flourished from cultural interchange with many societies. Byzantium sent envoys to the court, seeking alliances against common enemies in Arabia. In addition, the Aksumites' extensive ties with the Semitic peoples of Yemen across the Red Sea led to considerable genetic and cultural intermixing between these two peoples. The classical Amharic language, **Geez** (gee-EZ), is a mixture of African and Semitic influences. There was also much Hebrew influence on Ethiopian literature and religion. Indeed, the modern Amharic royal family, descendants of Aksumite kings, claimed ancestry from King Solomon and Queen Makeda. The Jewish communities known as *Falasha* (fuh-LAHSH-uh) have lived in northern Ethiopia for many centuries.

Aksum Society and Culture

Aksum's highly stratified social structure was dominated by kings. However, these kings had a paternalistic attitude toward their people. A fourth-century C.E. king left an inscription in which he claimed: "I will rule the people with righteousness and justice, and will not oppress them."[7] Judging from their spectacular palaces, kings also enjoyed great wealth and power. A sixth-century Byzantine ambassador reported on the royal family's pomp and ceremony, writing that the king wore

> a golden collar. He stood on a four-wheeled chariot drawn by four elephants; the body of the chariot was high and covered with gold plates. The king stood on top carrying a small gilded shield and holding in his hands two small gilded spears.[8]

Below the royal family was an aristocracy that supplied the top government officials. A substantial middle class included many merchants, and at the bottom of the social order were peasants and slaves, who could be conscripted for massive building projects.

The capital city of Aksum was a wealthy and cosmopolitan trading center, widely known for its monumental architecture. Its magnificent pillars, thin stylized representations of multi-storied buildings, were erected chiefly at burial grounds. The largest stands over 100 feet high. The city also contained many stone platforms and huge palaces. The making and transporting of the huge monoliths and stone slabs required remarkable engineering skills.

Christianity became influential just as Aksum reached its height of economic and military power in the fourth century C.E. Christian missionaries traveled the trade routes from western Asia, especially from the societies along the eastern

---

Geez The classical Amharic language of Ethiopia, a mixture of African and Semitic influences.

The following account of the trade of Aksum comes from the *Periplus of the Erythrean Sea*, written by an unknown Greek sometime in the second half of the first century C.E. The *Periplus* was a guide prepared for merchants and sailors that outlines the commercial prospects to be found in Arabia, the Indian Ocean, and the Persian Gulf. It also describes many of the bustling ports of this region. Hence, the *Periplus* is an excellent source for understanding Classical Era networks of exchange. In this excerpt, we learn about the port city of Adulis on the Red Sea. Adulis, now called Massawa (muh-SAH-wuh), was the chief Aksumite trade distribution center, where goods from the Ethiopian interior and from faraway places such as India, Egypt, and the Mediterranean were brought for sale or transshipment.

Adulis [is] a port . . . lying at the inner end of a bay. . . . Before the harbor lies the so-called Mountain Island, . . . with the shores of the mainland close to it on both sides. Ships bound for this port now anchor here because of attacks from the land [by bandits]. . . . Opposite Mountain Island, on the mainland, . . . lies Adulis, a fair-sized village, from which there is a three day's journey to Coloe, an inland town and the first market for ivory. From that place to the [capital] city of the people called Aksumites there is a five day's journey more; to that place all the ivory is brought from the country beyond the Nile. . . .

There are imported into these places [Adulis], undressed cloth made in Egypt for the Berbers; robes from . . . [modern Suez]; cloaks of poor quality dyed in colors; double-fringed linen mantles; many articles of flint glass, and others of . . . [agate] made in . . . [Thebes, Egypt]; and brass, which is used for ornament and in cut pieces instead of coin; sheets of soft copper, used for cooking utensils and cut up for bracelets and anklets for the women; iron, which is made into spears used against the elephants and other wild beasts, and in their wars. Besides these, small axes are imported, and adzes and swords; copper drinking cups, round and large; a little coin for those coming to the market; wine of Laodicea [on the Syrian coast] and Italy . . . ; olive oil . . . ; for the King, gold and silver plate made after the fashion of the country, and for clothing, military cloaks, and thin coats of skin. . . . Likewise from the district of Ariaca [on the northwest coast of India] across this sea, there are imported Indian cloth [fine-quality cotton]. . . . There are exported from these places ivory, and tortoise-shell and rhinoceros-horn. The most [cargo] from Egypt is brought to this market [Adulis] from the month of January to September.

THINKING ABOUT THE READING

1. What were some of the societies that were linked to the trade at Adulis?

2. What does this reading tell us about the networks of exchange that connected Aksum to a wider world?

Source: W. H. Schoff (trans. and ed.), *The Periplus of the Erythraen Sea: Travel and Trade in the Indian Ocean by a Merchant of the First Century* (London, Bombay & Calcutta, 1912).

Mediterranean coast with whom the Aksumites had long exchanged goods and ideas. The king adopted the new faith, making Christianity the official religion of the kingdom. According to a Roman source, the king "began to search out Roman merchants [at Aksum] who were Christian and to give them great influence and to urge them to establish [churches], supplying sites for buildings, and in every way promoting the growth of Christianity."[9] The king had political reasons for conversion, since he wanted to establish closer relations with Rome, Byzantium, and Egypt. But the Amharic population only slowly adopted the new faith. Ethiopian Christianity resembled the Coptic churches of Egypt and Nubia but also incorporated some of the long-entrenched spirit worship and various Hebrew practices, including the Jewish sabbath and kosher food.

The Aksum Legacy and Ethiopian History

Aksum eventually collapsed as a result of several forces. New challenges isolated Aksum and destroyed its dynamism. It had flourished during an era of adequate rainfall, but by 400 C.E., reduced rainfall and the resulting pressure on the land had produced an ecological crisis. Political problems added to imperial decline. The conquest of southern Arabia by Aksum's enemy, Sassanian Persia, in 575 diverted the Indian Ocean commerce from the port of Adulis. Then the rapid Islamic conquests of western Asia and North Africa beginning in the middle of the seventh century cut Aksum off from the Christian world. Aksum's trade withered, and it fell into economic stagnation, cultural decline, and political instability. By 800 C.E. the capital city was abandoned and the remnants of the kingdom had moved several hundred miles south.

Unlike Kush, however, Ethiopian society persisted in recognizable form. Indeed, the culture demonstrated a continuity for nearly 2,000 years, confirming that the Aksumite period was the Classical Age in northeast Africa. In particular, over the centuries Christianity became a deeply ingrained local religion among the Amharic and some of the neighboring peoples, producing the unique Ethiopian Christianity of today. The Ethiopian church, which became closely connected to the monarchy, benefited from owning many landed estates. Ethiopia remained relatively isolated in its mountain fastness for the next ten centuries.

SECTION SUMMARY

■ The kingdom of Kush in Nubia, with its capital city of Meroë, was a major African iron producer and crossroads of trade between sub-Saharan Africa and the Mediterranean.

■ Kush was influenced by Egypt but was also remarkable for its rich culture, its fearsome warriors and absolute monarchs, and its strong laws and traditions.

■ Aksum, in the Ethiopian highlands, had contact with Egypt and Arabia, may have forged links with the Hebrews, and after a time eclipsed Meroë as the region's primary trade center.

■ Aksum's king converted to Christianity as a means of establishing closer relationships with Rome, Byzantium, and Egypt.

■ Like Kush, Aksum may have declined in part because of climate change, but it was also hurt by the Islamic conquest of its neighbors; unlike Kush, however, the society endured for another 2,000 years.

The Blossoming of Sudanic and Bantu Africa

How did the spread of the Bantus reshape sub-Saharan Africa?

While Kush and Aksum maintained the closest connections to Eurasia, complex urban societies also arose in the Sudanic region, on the Sahara's southern fringe, among peoples like the Mande (MAHN-day). These societies were linked to North Africa and beyond by trade networks. Meanwhile, Bantu-speaking Africans, first discussed in Chapter 3, continued to spread their languages, cultures, and technologies widely, occupying the southern half of the continent. Some became connected to trade networks linked to east coast port cities.

Sudanic Societies, Farming, and Cities

In the vast but dry grassland region known as the Sudan (soo-DAN), lying between the Sahara and tropical Africa, societies composed of farmers and city-dwellers, and sharing some common features, germinated during classical times. The Sudanic peoples had long before adapted their economic life to the prevailing ecology. Most Sudanese became farmers living in small, largely self-sufficient farming villages. Cereal crops, especially millet and sorghum, mixed with vegetables, were the most basic food sources. Reliance on grains suited the dry Sudanic soils;

millet and sorghum both require little water. West Africans also grew cotton and developed richly colored cotton clothing. The fertility of a large delta region along one stretch of the Niger (NYE-juhr) River made intensive farming possible there. The food grown in the delta as well as the fish caught in the river helped to feed the people of the trading cities.

Some Sudanese congregated in large towns and cities reaching 30,000 or 40,000 in population, of which Jenne-Jenno was perhaps the major hub of a network of commercial centers along the Niger River. Located in what is now the nation of Mali (MAHL-ee), Jenne-Jenno developed as early as 200 B.C.E., with the residents building circular houses made of straw and coated with mud. By the Common Era the city's people worked copper, gold, and iron, which they obtained from mines several hundred miles away. Gold and copper had probably been brought to the city by boat for several centuries, and gold dust and small copper ingots (ING-guhts) apparently served as currency throughout the Sudan in the later Classical Era. By 400 C.E. Jenne-Jenno had

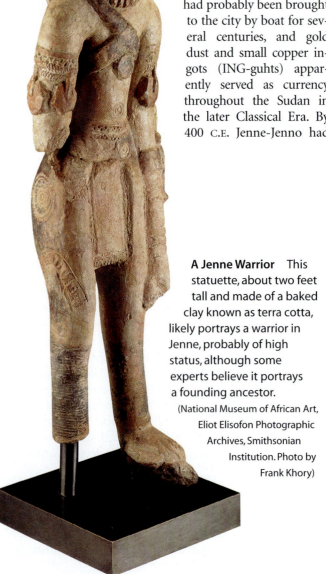

A Jenne Warrior This statuette, about two feet tall and made of a baked clay known as terra cotta, likely portrays a warrior in Jenne, probably of high status, although some experts believe it portrays a founding ancestor. (National Museum of African Art, Eliot Elisofon Photographic Archives, Smithsonian Institution. Photo by Frank Khory)

become a crucial transshipment point where goods arriving by camel or donkey caravan were exchanged for goods moved by boat along the Niger River. This position made Jenne-Jenno the major early trading city of the Sudan.

Jenne-Jenno continued to flourish as a commercial hub for many centuries, closely tied, like other Sudanic cities, to hemispheric trade by the caravans across the Sahara. Eventually a wall over a mile in circumference surrounded the city for protection of the residents, most of whom lived in houses made from dried mud. Jenne-Jenno was built upon a productive agriculture, and it exported grain, fish, and animal products in exchange for metals. States of some sort may have existed around urban centers like Jenne-Jenno, but the ruins have yielded few clues to political organization. Historians suspect that Jenne-Jenno and other Classical Age commercial centers in the Niger Valley were probably independent city-states for most of the first millennium C.E.

Large cities and states were less common in sub-Saharan Africa than in Eurasia and North Africa, in part because of the smaller population densities in Africa. The African agricultural system, mostly based on shifting cultivation, suited the soils but could not generally support the kinds of large settled populations that developed in parts of Eurasia and the northern Nile valley. At the beginning of the Common Era the African continent may have contained between 15 and 25 million people, much less than half that of China alone. About half lived in Egypt, Kush, and along the Mediterranean coast. Elsewhere in Africa, including the Sudan, small population densities meant that societies were held together by social and economic ties and did not require a powerful state to maintain order.

Trans-Saharan Trade Networks

The establishment of caravan routes crossing the Sahara, which greatly aided the growth of Sudanic societies by fostering interregional trade, began well before the Common Era. Eventually a large trade system spanned the Sahara that linked the Sudanic towns with the peoples of the desert and southern Mediterranean coastal societies such as Carthage. From ancient times Carthage sporadically carried on some trade with the Sudanic peoples, although the volume remains disputed. By the third century C.E. the gold used in coins minted in Carthage may have come from western Africa.

Salt moving south to the Sudan and gold moving north to the Mediterranean drove the complex Saharan trade. The several trade routes that crossed the barren sands eventually became one of the major trade networks of the Classical Era. However, many other goods were traded as well. Sudanic cities shipped north cotton cloth, leather goods, pepper, slaves, and most important, gold, which the merchants in North Africa then sold to Europe. The Sudanic peoples also traded meat animals to the forest societies along the West African coast, and they imported copper from the region east of the Niger. Sudanic societies were largely self-sufficient, but they needed salt mined in the central Sahara and along the West African coast.

The salt trade was mostly controlled by the *Garamante* tribal confederation, which inhabited the desert region in what is now southwestern Libya, southeastern Algeria, and northern Niger. These Berber (BUHR-buhr) people dominated the caravan trade routes as intermediaries from around 500 B.C.E. to 600 C.E., managing a vast commercial network that included trading of enslaved Africans. The Garamantes used camels as pack animals and horses to pull light chariots. The Greeks and Romans considered the Garamantes to be warlike barbarians, an ethnocentric viewpoint. As an example of this prejudice, the Roman writer Pliny complained that the Romans could not open a road to Garamante country because bandits filled up the wells with sand. Pliny underestimated the Garamantes. In fact, these Saharans made the parched desert livable by combining pastoral stock raising with irrigated farming; they constructed several thousand miles of underground canals to cultivate their farms; and they lived in walled cities and villages, built stone citadels as military outposts, and were apparently governed by royal families. Products from around West Africa, Egypt, and the Mediterranean Basin have been found in the ruins of the Garamantian capital. Their state collapsed around the same time as the Roman Empire, and the remnants were later overrun by Muslims.

Sudanic States and Peoples

As in Kush and Aksum, commerce stimulated the growth of states in the Sudan. Kingdoms apparently grew out of markets and flourished from taxing the trade in gold and other commodities. The Soninke (soh-NIN-kay) people of the middle Niger Valley formed the first known major Sudanic state, **Ghana** (GAH-nuh). Ghana existed by at least 700 C.E., but it probably formed by 500 C.E. and perhaps a century or two earlier. Excavations of the probable capital city, not far from Jenne-Jenno, show a stone town that was built sometime between 500 and 600 C.E. Ghana reached its height as a trade-based empire in the ninth century and flourished until the thirteenth.

Diverse **Mande** (MON-day) peoples may have been typical of many classical Sudanic societies. The Mande spoke closely related languages, shared many customs, and dominated the western Niger River Basin and adjacent areas. Mande speakers included such ethnic groups as the Soninke (who established Ghana), Mandinka (man-DING-goh), Malinke (muh-LING-kee), and Bambara (bam-BAHR-uh) peoples. These Mande peoples combined farming with fishing along the Niger River. The ancestors of the Mande were the likely domesticators of African rice. By 900 or 800 B.C.E. Mande farmers lived in large walled villages, and they may have built Jenne-Jenno. Later, Mande speakers dominated much of the western Sudan.

Although divided into different groups, the Mande shared many common social, political, and religious traditions. They

---

Ghana The first known major Sudanic state, formed by the Soninke people of the middle Niger valley.

Mande Diverse Sudanic peoples who spoke closely related languages, shared many customs, and dominated the western Niger River Basin and adjacent areas of West Africa.

had highly stratified societies, with aristocratic, warrior, and commoner classes, and a special group of ritual and religious specialists. Across the early Sudan political structures varied, but the Mande eventually developed a theocracy in which chiefs and village heads combined religious and secular duties. A respected class of oral historians and musicians known widely as **griots** (GREE-oh) memorized and recited the history of the community, emphasizing the deeds of leaders. The common folk had to content themselves with living in the reflected glory of their exalted leaders. Still, many Mande of all classes enjoyed considerable prosperity, often from growing cotton or making their elaborate and beautiful cotton clothing, which was traded widely. The Mande and other Sudanic peoples also developed some common ideas about religion, including animism. People believed in a distant creator god, but spirits of nature and ancestral spirits loomed large in daily life. Like many African peoples, the Mande drew no neat line between the living and the dead. They also wanted to keep the favor of good spirits and avoid the hostility of bad ones.

The Guinea Coast

Over time various peoples, including some from the Sudan, migrated into the Guinea (GIN-ee) coast just south of the Sudan, a migration made possible by new tools and agricultural techniques. The Guinea coast, which stretches some 2,000 miles from modern Senegal (sen-i-GAWL) to southeastern Nigeria (nie-JEER-ee-uh), was mainly covered by forest and swamp and had few edible plants or game animals. The mixing of Sudanic and other traditions in this area produced unique new societies.

The challenging life on the Guinea coast led to some pragmatic solutions. To survive, the people lived mostly in small, self-sufficient villages with rich social networks. They practiced subsistence agriculture, with yams and bananas as the staple crops. Although some land was privately owned, most Guinea peoples developed a tradition of cooperative labor. Furthermore, the Guinea peoples traded with the Sudanic societies, over land or by boat up the rivers such as the Niger and Volta (VAHL-tuh), and thus became linked to wider networks of economic and cultural exchange. Over time, many of the coastal societies came to practice some common customs, including Sudanese traditions such as theocratic political systems and pronounced social class divisions.

The Bantu-Speaking Peoples and Their Migrations

Over several thousand years, many iron-using speakers of Bantu languages had migrated from their original homeland in eastern Nigeria into Central and East Africa (see Chapter 3). During the Classical Era, Bantu peoples accelerated their ex-

pansion to the south and east. They carried with them many traditions of art, music, farming, and religion that had originated in the Sudan, thus spreading Sudanese influence into other areas of Africa.

Expansion of the Bantu World

Some Bantu-speaking peoples moved into the southern Congo region now known as Katanga (kuh-TAHNG-guh), which they reached by 400 B.C.E. Katanga is an area of savannah grasslands like the region they had left, but it is less fertile and more prone to drought and disease. Much of the region south of the Congo Basin rain forest is relatively arid because of irregular rainfall. Fortunately, sorghum and millet from the Sudanic region and Ethiopia spread among the Bantus, who successfully adapted these cereal crops to the dry southern climate.

From Katanga many Bantus began moving to the west, south, and east. In the east they met Bantus migrating from the Great Lakes in the East African highlands. By 200 B.C.E. Bantu culture had reached the Zambezi (zam-BEE-zee) River Basin, and by the third century C.E. the first Bantu settlers entered what is now the nation of South Africa. Networks of trade and migration spanning vast distances eventually connected the southern third of Africa to the Sudan and the East African coast.

As Bantu-speaking migrants settled in a new location, they encountered local peoples and incorporated new influences. Because they worked iron, the Bantus possessed military and agricultural technologies more effective than those of many non-Bantus, which allowed them to push some of the local peoples into marginal economic areas suitable only for hunting and gathering. For example, the Mbuti Pygmies of the Congo region moved into thick rain forests, while many of the Khoisan (KOY-sahn) peoples in southern Africa, such as the Kung! hunters and gatherers discussed in Chapter 1, became desert dwellers. But many Bantus intermingled with, and probably culturally assimilated, those they met. Sudanese cultural forms carried by the Bantus, such as drums and percussive music, woodcarving, and ancestor-focused religions, became widespread.

Cultural Mixing in Southern and Eastern Africa

The contacts also influenced the Bantu cultures, especially in southern and eastern Africa. For example, the Xhosa (KOH-sah) and Zulu (ZOO-loo) peoples, who lived along the southeastern coast of today's South Africa by the fourth century C.E., mixed their languages and cultures with the local Khoisan cattle herders. Cattle herding was incorporated into Xhosa and Zulu economic life alongside farming and trade.

The migrating Bantus also encountered and gradually absorbed various societies in East Africa, some of them pastoralists and some farmers. Various ironworking pastoralists from the eastern Sudan, known as **Nilotes** (nie-LAHT-eez) because they speak Nilotic (nie-LAHT-ik) languages very different from

---

griots A respected class of oral historians and musicians in West Africa who memorized and recited the history of the group, emphasizing the deeds of leaders.

Nilotes Ironworking pastoralists from the eastern Sudan who settled in East Africa and there had frequent interactions with the Bantus.

the Bantu tongues, were also settling in East Africa. Although their relationships to each other were not always peaceful, Bantus and Nilotes mutually modified their cultures as a result of contact. Some Bantus adopted pastoralism (cattle and goats) while others mastered new agricultural techniques and diets, including Southeast Asian foods like bananas, coconuts, sugar cane, and Asian yams available on the East African coast.

These foods, as well as domesticated chickens and possibly pigs, were brought to East Africa by Indonesian mariners and migrants in outrigger canoes early in the Common Era (see Chapter 7). Eventually these crops and domesticated animals spread throughout Africa. Some of the Indonesian mariners settled along the coast and married local people, intensifying cultural exchange. These Indonesians and later arrivals also introduced Austronesian housing styles and musical instruments, which were incorporated into local cultures. They established trading posts to barter pottery, beads, and utensils for ivory and animal products. Indonesian influences reached as far west as the Congo River Basin. Between 100 and 700 C.E. Indonesians settled the large island of Madagascar. Eventually most of the descendants of the Indonesian settlers on the East African coast relocated to that large and previously uninhabited island, implanting there a mixed Indonesian-Bantu culture and language that still survives.

Maritime Trade and the East African Coast

The East African coast, where many Bantu speakers settled, developed a cosmopolitan society based on maritime trade. The winds and currents along the coast reverse direction every six months, allowing boats from southwestern Asia to sail to East Africa and back each year. The same wind reversal is true for the Indian Ocean, making possible two-way communication between East Africa and India or Southeast Asia. A seagoing trade between Arabia and the East African coast developed even before the Common Era. The trading ports to which merchants from southern Arabia sailed were located along the coast from Somalia to present-day Tanzania. The main port city in this era, Rhapta (RAHP-ta) in Tanzania, had a large merchant community from southern Arabia.

The east coast trade grew slowly during the Classical Era and was not yet an integral component of the great trading network forming around the Indian Ocean Basin. A first-century C.E. survey of maritime trade by an Alexandria-based Greek traveler reported that ships left Egypt's Red Sea ports and then visited Adulis and various Somalian ports before sailing to East African ports such as Rhapta. The author reported that local people made sown boats, used dugout canoes (of probable Bantu origin), and behaved "each in his own place like chiefs,"[10] indicating that there were independent local communities rather than a centralized state. He and his party then headed to India rather than venturing further down the coast, avoiding what they considered the mysterious ocean stretching southward.

Growing numbers of traders came to the coastal towns. Various Roman accounts reported that East Africa exported ivory, rhinoceros horn, and tortoise shell to Egypt, India, and western Asia and imported iron goods, pottery, and glass beads. Egyptian, Roman, and West Asian coins found in the region date from 300 B.C.E. to 200 C.E., indicating trade with the Mediterranean area, and Persian pottery produced between 400 and 600 C.E. was distributed widely along the coast and inland. Eventually, the coast developed many large and flourishing port cities and a culture that mixed Bantu ideas with those of southwestern Asia. But it was many centuries before any ships ventured out into the "western seas" and established contact with the Western Hemisphere, to which we now turn.

SECTION SUMMARY

- The Sudan region included trading hubs such as Jenne-Jenno, but the population in the Classical Era was not dense enough to require a powerful state; Ghana was the first state to arise, probably around 500 C.E.

- The Garamante peoples controlled the extensive caravan routes through the Sahara Desert to bring salt from the African Mediterranean coast to Sudan, which exported gold in return.

- The Bantu peoples, equipped with iron tools, continued to migrate south and east, mixing with and sometimes pushing out other peoples, and they made their way to South Africa by the third century C.E.

- Indonesian mariners settled on the East African coast and, to a greater extent, in Madagascar, where a mixed Indonesian-Bantu culture survives to this day.

- Winds that switched direction every six months made it easy to travel back and forth between East Africa and southwestern Asia, India, and Southeast Asia.

Classical Mesoamerican Societies and Networks

What were the similarities and differences between the Maya and Teotihuacan?

As in Eurasia and Africa, the first cities and states in the Americas had developed during ancient times, including the Olmecs in Mesoamerica and the Chavín in the Andes (see Chapter 4). And in common with Eurasia and Africa, population increase helped to stimulate the growth of more American urban societies during the Classical Era. By the beginning of the Common Era there may have been around 15 million people in the Americas. Over two-thirds of them were concentrated in Mesoamerica and western South America, where the most significant developments were taking place. The most long-lasting and widespread of these societies were the **Maya**

Maya The most long-lasting and widespread of the classical Mesoamerican societies, who occupied the Yucatan Peninsula and northern Central America for almost 2,000 years.

(MIE-uh) of Mesoamerica, who forged a literate culture that excelled in some sciences and mathematics. Mesoamerica also provided a fertile environment for the rise of several cities that became the centers of prosperous states.

The Emergence of the Early Maya

To the east of the pioneering Olmecs, in the lowland rain forests of Central America and the Yucatan (YOO-kuh-TAN) Peninsula in southeast Mexico facing the Caribbean Sea, a society coalesced that became the Maya (see Map 9.2). Farming by shifting cultivation and ceramic making dates back to at least 1100 B.C.E. The Maya introduced intensive cultivation of maize (corn) and other foods into the tropical forests. Maize was the key crop. According to Maya legends, the gods had fashioned people out of corn. Maya farmers built artificial platforms and terraces on which they could grow enough crops to generate surpluses that would support a ruling elite, as well as large underground reservoirs to store groundwater where rainfall was scarce. As more productive agriculture led to more population, the Maya spread southward into the mountains and coastal zones of what is today Chiapas (chee-AHP-uhs) (Mexico), Guatemala (GWAHT-uh-MAHL-uh), Honduras (hahn-DUR-uhs), El Salvador (el SAL-vuh-DOR), and Belize (buh-LEEZ).

As their power increased, the Maya elite organized ambitious building projects. The first Maya pyramids and elaborate stone buildings were constructed by 600 B.C.E. Unlike Egyptian pyramids, which served as burial tombs for top leaders, Maya pyramids had temples on top and were built for religious worship and ceremonies. According to ancient Maya folklore, these temples housed the gods:

> There had been five generations of people since the origin of light, of continuity, of life and of humankind. And they built many houses there. And they also built houses for the gods, putting these in the center of the highest part of the citadel. They came and they stayed. After that their domains grew larger; they were more numerous and more crowded.[11]

By 100 B.C.E. notions of divine kingship became widespread, and the Maya began making stone statues and carvings of their rulers. By this time they also painted sophisticated murals on walls, illustrating Mayan myths such as their creation story.

Maya society was based on urbanization and cultural innovations such as writing. At the height of their culture, 150 B.C.E.–800 C.E., the Maya built many cities, each boasting masonry buildings, large temples, spacious plazas and pyramid complexes, and elaborate carvings (see Chronology: Classical Americas). The major early city was El Mirador, built between 150 B.C.E. and 50 C.E. In its ruins archaeologists have discovered the first examples of Maya writing, inscribed on pot fragments and sculpture. The Maya developed the most comprehensive writing system in the Americas. Their hieroglyphic script, which had phonetic as well as pictographic elements, was used for calendars, religious regulations, and many sacred books, as well as to record dynastic histories, genealogies, and

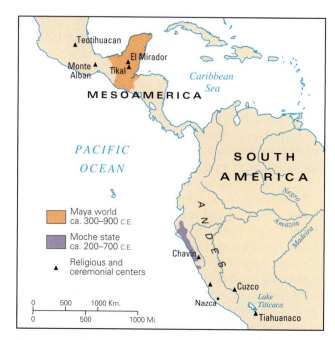

Map 9.2   Classical Societies in the Americas
The major American centers of complex agriculture, cities and states emerged in Mesoamerica, where the Mayans were the largest and longest-lasting society during the era, and the Andes regions, where Chavin, Moche, and Tiahuanaco were important societies.

Online Study Center **Improve Your Grade**
Interactive Map: Mesoamerican Civilizations

military successes. A later Spanish observer later admired "those who carried with them the black and red ink, the manuscripts and painted book, the wisdom, the annals, the books of song."[12] The heritage of the early Maya cities such as El Mirador also included a distinctive architecture, royal dynasties, and a highly stratified social system. In some cities, suburbs containing residences, markets, and workshops stretched for several miles out from the city centers. Even the Spanish who conquered the Maya lands in the 1500s marveled at the city buildings. One wrote that "the buildings and the multitude of them is remarkable. So well built are they of cut stone that it fills one with astonishment."[13]

Tikal (ti-KAHL), in what is today eastern Guatemala near the border with Belize, was one of the major Maya cities between 200 and 900 C.E. and had a population of 50,000 at its height. Tikal contained three hundred large ceremonial buildings dominated by temple pyramids 200 feet high. The pyramids were topped by temples decorated with carvings made of stucco plaster. The first ruler used the jaguar as the symbol of kingship, military bravery, and religious authority. His descendants, King Great Jaguar Paw and General Smoking Frog, led Tikal to a great victory over the rival city Uaxactun in 378 C.E., ensuring Tikal's regional supremacy for the next two hundred years.

Maya identity was more cultural than political. There was much cultural uniformity among the competing cities, proba-

women of elite status operated a mountaintop brewery that made hundreds of gallons of corn beer every week.

Tiwanaku influenced a large region of western South America. The local art and the religion, which probably involved human sacrifice, seem to have spread into neighboring societies. The lands around the capital, rich in llama herds and a center of copper technology, flourished from a system of raised field agriculture—seeds planted on long artificial ridges separated by ditches—which improved drainage, replaced nutrients in the poor soil, and protected crops such as potatoes from frost. Tiwanaku agriculture was some 400 percent more productive than the farming in the region today. The Aymara, like other Andean peoples, were skilled at using fibers. For example, they made boats to sail on the lake by weaving together reeds. But by 1100 C.E. the capital and surrounding fields were abandoned, perhaps because of climate change that generated a drought so severe that rivers dried up.

The Nazca (NAHZ-kuh), a decentralized agrarian society that flourished in the harsh desert in southern Peru from 200 B.C.E. to 600 C.E., became notable for the beautiful multicolored pottery and textiles it manufactured and the ceremonial centers it constructed. But the Nazca are most famous for creating geometric lines along their windswept plateau by clearing away surface stones to reveal the underlying rock and then laying the stones along the edges of the lines. Constructed on a huge scale, the lines depict either geometric shapes or animals such as monkeys and birds. These enigmatic markings have puzzled modern observers; scholars think they were created to mark the seasons, to communicate with gods they believed to dwell in the nearby mountains, or to mark water sources. Or they may have just been artistic expressions of shapes and animals.

Pueblo Societies of Western North America

Beginning just before the Common Era, several cultural traditions and permanent towns emerged among the desert farmers of the American Southwest, including the Hohokam (huh-HOH-kuhm), Anasazi (ah-nah-SAH-zee), and Mogollon (MOH-guh-YOHN). By around 300 B.C.E. the Hohokam of what is now southern Arizona and northwest Mexico were trading extensively with other southwestern peoples and the southern California coast. Farming success depended on water, and the peoples of this arid region sought divine help to get it, as a Yuma (YOO-muh) Indian legend of a creator spirit made clear: "When the people thirst, let them think of me, for I have the power to cover up the sun with a rain-cloud and to send rain every day."[18] Hohokam farmers used advanced irrigation, dams, terraces, and other strategies to grow maize, beans, squash, and cotton. Some of their irrigation canals extended for 10 miles.

The Hohokam survived for some 1,500 years, during which time they built large towns holding a thousand or more people. The total Hohokam population in the vicinity of present-day Phoenix may have reached 40,000. The presence in Hohokam settlements of ball courts and rubber balls, and of Mesoamerican-style platform mounds, indicates Mesoameri-

can influence over long-distance trade networks. But there is no evidence for human sacrifice or warfare, as occurred in Mesoamerica. Eventually overpopulation, deforestation, and drier climates increased conflict and put more stress on the society. By the fifteenth century the Hohokam settlements had been abandoned, though some people remained. Their modern descendants include the Pima and Papago Indians of Arizona.

The Anasazi and the closely related Mogollon culture were the direct ancestors of the Pueblo Indians in what is today Arizona and New Mexico. The Anasazi were once much more widespread and had towns in Utah and Colorado as far east as the western margins of the Great Plains. The culture arose around the first century of the Common Era but had roots that go much deeper into the past. It reached its high point between 750 and 900 C.E. The Mogollon emerged around 200 B.C.E. and covered a territory stretching from central Arizona and New Mexico into northern Mexico. Although never building towns as impressive as the Anasazi and Hohokam, they flourished from a combination of corn growing and skillful gathering until the fifteenth century C.E. All of the southwestern societies traded with and adopted material traits from each other.

The Mound Builders of Eastern North America

Another great era of mound building characterized the eastern woodlands between around 500 B.C.E. and 400 C.E. Mound-building was not new; it had begun in North America around 2500 B.C.E. (see Chapter 4). But now this new mound-building culture became even more widespread, encompassing the Mississippi, Ohio, Tennessee, and lower Missouri River Basins and their tributaries as well as the South Atlantic coast, a total area larger than India. The most prominent mound-builder tradition, known today as Hopewell, was centered in the Ohio River region and arose between 200 and 50 B.C.E. Much as the Olmecs influenced other Mesoamericans, Hopewell artistic styles, maize cultivation, religious beliefs, ceremonial traditions, and burial customs spread throughout the eastern woodlands. In spite of this widespread influence, however, there is no evidence for any large state.

The Hopewell peoples created extraordinary earthworks and other engineering projects. Elaborate geometric designs such as hexagons and circles mark their mounds. The Great Serpent Mound, built on a hilltop in Ohio around 2,000 years ago, was one of the most spectacular. Shaped like a snake, the mound ran 800 feet long from head to tail and was 4 feet tall and 20 feet wide. Some of the mounds were burial chambers. Members of the elite were buried with goods that indicated their high status. The Ortuna, a Hopewell culture in northern Florida, were also skilled engineers. They built a maze of 20-foot-wide canals that allowed them to reach both the Atlantic and Gulf Coasts by dugout canoe, thus connecting them to a trading network stretching north to Ohio.

The Hopewell and other mound-building cultures were supported by two major economic changes. First, agriculture became more intensive, especially after the spread of maize.

Second, long-distance trade, which had existed for centuries, evolved into a network spanning a large section of North America. Along the river trade routes moved obsidian from the Rocky Mountains, copper from the Great Lakes and later southern Appalachia, ceramic figurines and vessels from the lower Great Lakes, ore from Kansas, silver from Ontario, shells from the Gulf of Mexico and Florida, freshwater pearls from the Mississippi, and marine products from the Gulf Coast such as sharks' teeth and turtle shells. Thanks to this trade network, sharks' teeth have been found in Illinois, over a thousand miles from the Caribbean. Hopewell artisans created ceremonial objects, from pan pipes to mirrors, from various metals, and they also manufactured large clay cooking pots.

The Hopewell culture began to decline around 300 C.E. and collapsed by 600 C.E. Overpopulation and the resulting competition for land might have put too much stress on the environment and economic system. Trade networks may have been disrupted, perhaps by increased conflict or unsafe travel. The maize crop diminished, possibly in part because of a cooling climate. In addition, around 300 C.E. someone invented or imported the bow and arrow into the region. This new weapon may have altered the balance of power and stimulated warfare, perhaps undermining the prevailing cooperation and breaking traditional alliances.

Changing States and the Spread of Cultures

While the traditions of the earliest urban societies, the Olmecs and Chavín, remained influential in Mesoamerica and the Andes region, much change occurred in these regions over the centuries, although often on a different timeline from the Eastern Hemisphere. For example, around 200 or 300 C.E., various societies experienced a major transition. Small states such as Monte Alban, Teotihuacan, Tikal, and Tiwanaku grew into larger states, often regional empires, and many societies developed more pronounced class divisions and occupational specialization. Long-distance trade increased, merchants became more influential, and ideas (such as writing and ball games in Mesoamerica) spread more widely. Artistic culture and thought flowered. Many American peoples revered the land, seeing both physical and spiritual life as coming from and returning to the land. The land deserved reverence because of its close relationship to the supreme spirits or gods. As a result, people such as the Maya and some North American societies held maize as sacred, a gift from the gods.

Except for the exceptionally enduring Mayan and Tiwanaku, South American and Mesoamerican states, American states exhibited a pattern of rise and fall after a few centuries. These fluctuations in fortune may have been due in part to environmental and climate changes, which affected agriculture and fishing. Chronic warfare may also have played a role. Even the Maya cities were mostly abandoned long before European conquest in the sixteenth century C.E. Although the classical states established frameworks for later empires such as the *Toltec* (TOLL-tek), Aztec, and Inca, they did not survive into modern times in their original form, as the classical Chinese and Ethiopian states did.

The widespread presence of pyramids in Mesoamerica and South America has caused some observers to speculate about possible contacts across the Atlantic to North Africa and the Mediterranean long before the arrival of Norse Vikings around 1000 C.E. and, five centuries later, Spanish ships. A stray Phoenician, Egyptian, or West African boat crossing the Atlantic Ocean, perhaps swept off course by storms, cannot be ruled out. But there is no firm archaeological evidence for any ties to the Eastern Hemisphere, and most specialists are extremely skeptical such contacts were ever made. Pyramids are based on practical principles of monument construction that are probably available to builders in any culture. American pyramids actually resemble those of India and Southeast Asia more than they do Egyptian and Nubian pyramids, but the American pyramids are much older than the southern Asian pyramids, meaning they could not have been influenced by Asian traditions. And some American peoples were building mounds nearly as early as the first Egyptian pyramids.

Along the American west coast, from California to Peru, are scattered hints of trans-Pacific contacts in pottery design, artwork, and plants, leading to occasional speculation about possible Chinese, Japanese, or Polynesian voyages to the Americas. For example, some older studies argue that pottery finds and other artifacts along the Ecuador coast resemble Jomon Japanese counterparts from perhaps 2000 or 3000 B.C.E. (see Chapter 4). Other studies claim to find Olmec hieroglyphics that resemble Shang Chinese characters, Polynesian musical instruments and loan words in western South America, or Polynesian words and boat designs along the California coast. Indeed, Polynesian voyagers, the world's most skilled mariners, were capable of trips over several thousand miles of uncharted ocean, and they could have occasionally visited the American coast and then returned home. This might explain the presence of the South American sweet potato in Polynesia. However, no conclusive proof exists for any trans-Pacific contacts, and if any voyages did occur, they left no obvious long-lasting influence.

SECTION SUMMARY

■ In Peru and Ecuador, coastal and interior peoples created an interdependent trading network stretching from Mexico to Chile.

■ In the Andes, Chavín was succeeded by Moche, whose pottery depicts a violent culture of war and sacrifice but also of advanced metalwork and architecture.

■ In the desert Southwest of North America, the Hohokam people developed extensive irrigation systems, and their cultural artifacts show some Mesoamerican influence.

■ Supported by corn and expanded trade networks, mound-building cultures spread across eastern North America.

■ Though there are some similarities among pyramids of the Americas and those of Asia and Egypt, it is unlikely that this was the result of direct influence.

Agriculture never developed in part because most of the land was infertile and the rains erratic. But there were also no native plants or animals capable of domestication. Even today large-scale irrigation is needed to sustain farming in the regions settled by Europeans over the past two centuries, and, as in ancient Mesopotamia, this irrigation has increased the salt content in groundwater, endangering fresh water supplies. There was also no incentive for farming, since hunting and gathering was successful and the climate changes that fostered the transition to farming elsewhere had less impact in Australia. Instead, Aboriginal societies developed excellent patterns of land management and usage that enabled them to conserve their resources over thousands of years. They evolved a close relationship to the earth, an attachment that remained at the center of their customs and beliefs over centuries.

Many Aboriginal practices operated in tandem with the environment. For example, fire could be used to clear land to encourage regrowth of edible plants, and, of course, it could be used in cooking. Deliberately set fires may also have intentionally rejuvenated the natural ecosystem. Whether deliberate or a result of natural processes, fires have always been a regular occurrence in Australia, but they have complicated modern life for the now urbanized regions.

There were a few exceptions to hunting and gathering. At least one Aboriginal society, the Gunditjmara in southern Australia, built an ingenious artificial lake where they operated eel farms beginning around 6000 B.C.E. This activity seems to have continued down to the nineteenth century C.E., and the abundant eels raised there were traded around southern Australia. The Gunditjmara may also have lived in a permanent town with stone houses.

Aboriginal Society, Cultures, and Trade

Although they were diverse, Aboriginal societies also had many similar customs and beliefs. Since they had to move by foot with the seasons, most communities owned few possessions. Aborigines prided themselves on not loading themselves down, a stark contrast to the values of most people in Afro-Eurasia and many in the Americas. Aboriginal men carried spear throwers and spears while women carried digging sticks and baskets to hold foodstuffs. Their seasonal moves, designed to maximize food availability, were not random. Rather, they involved relocating to the same camps every year over regular trails. For example, peoples along the swampy, flood-prone northeast coast moved to high ground during the rainy season.

Aboriginal societies were divided into tribes organized either through the patrilineal or the matrilineal line. Nuclear families operated with considerable independence but regularly came together with other families. Few tribes had chiefs. However, older males exerted considerable influence in religious and social life and hence held more overall power than others. At the same time, women made critical decisions about the campsite and controlled their own ceremonial life. Relations between the genders, though varying from tribe to tribe,

Populating the Pacific: Australian and Island Societies

How were some of the notable features of Australian and Pacific societies shaped by their environments?

Although the original settlers of Australia and the Pacific islands migrated from or through Southeast Asia, the societies they developed remained largely isolated from the historical currents of Eurasia for many centuries. Australian Aborigines mastered a hostile environment, flourished from hunting and gathering, and enjoyed a highly complex mythology and ritual life. In extraordinary voyages, Austronesians migrated over thousands of miles of open ocean and were inhabiting most of the Pacific islands by the end of the Classical Era. They brought ancient Asian traditions into the Pacific but adapted them to new environments, creating diverse, distinctive cultures. The Pacific peoples organized societies that tapped island resources and developed long-distance trade networks.

Australian Geography and Aboriginal Societies

Australia was settled at least 50,000 years ago. As people spread out around this vast continent, they adapted to varied environments and organized themselves into many distinct societies. By 1000 B.C.E. most of the coastal areas, much of the arid interior, and the large offshore island of Tasmania were inhabited by Aboriginal tribes speaking some two hundred distinct languages. The environments that shaped the varied societies included the tropical, heavily forested coasts of the north and northeast, the temperate river basins and coasts of the southeast and southwest, and the deserts that dominant much of the interior.

Aboriginal life was based largely on hunting and gathering. The Aborigines were skilled at exploiting many food sources, for example, by harvesting sea life along the coast and wild plants and insects in the harsh desert interior. In the absence of written sources and firsthand visitors' accounts, to understand their lives we have to rely on their oral traditions, archaeological finds, and the descriptions by modern observers. As among other hunting and gathering peoples, Aboriginal women gathered plants and small animals, prepared meals for the family, looked after the children, made the clothing and built the huts. Men fished, hunted large animals and manufactured implements. In their food quest, Aborigines developed an intimate understanding of local weather patterns and their relationships to plants, animals, and land. This knowledge is being used by meteorologists today. In terms of nourishment, most Aborigines ate at least as well as peoples in Afro-Eurasia. Malnutrition and starvation were largely unknown.

were apparently flexible. Periodic disputes broke out between neighboring tribes and sometimes led to fighting, but they were more often settled by diplomacy involving the tribal elders.

Since most people had only to spend about three days a week in search of food, they had considerable time for ceremonial and religious matters as well as rich social interactions. The highly ritualized cultures were dominated by religion and its ceremonial expression. Most Aboriginal societies shared a belief in the mythology of the **dreamtime**, the distant past when the spiritual ancestors gave order and form to the universe at the world's creation. The dreamtime myths were remarkably consistent around the continent, as these and other traditions were passed down though countless generations by a rich oral literature. Aborigines also recognized an animistic world inhabited by many spirits and ghosts. Their art had a religious base and took various forms, including body decoration, bark paintings, and especially rock carvings and paintings.

By 1000 B.C.E. a complex trade system spanned the continent. Pearls from northwest Australia have been found hundreds of miles away, and shells from the north coast reached southern Australia. Quartz, flint, and other stones to make tools, as well as animal skins, wood products, and ornaments, were exchanged over wide areas of the continent. By classical times Indonesian trading ships probably visited the northwest coast to obtain pearls from local people. Later, Chinese ships may have also engaged in such exchanges. But these outside contacts had little influence on the lives of most Australian societies.

Today, after two centuries of change brought by European settlement and conquest, the life that sustained Australia's Aborigines for thousands of years has largely passed. Where once songs were sung about the history of the lands and the peoples, today, largely settled on rural land reserves or living in poor urban neighborhoods, they lament the loss of their traditions. Their stories still recollect tribal pasts and beliefs, but the storytellers inhabit a very different reality from their ancestors.

Austronesian Expansion

Before the Classical Era some Austronesian-speaking peoples moved from Southeast Asia into the western Pacific islands just northeast of Australia (see Chapter 4). There they encountered Melanesians (mel-uh-NEE-zhuhnz) who had earlier migrated from Southeast Asia. Over time the two traditions mixed, and Melanesians adopted Austronesian languages. Eventually some Austronesian-speaking peoples from the western Pacific sailed further east and north to colonize other islands, in the process fostering new groups later known as Polynesians (PAHL-uh-NEE-zhunz) and Micronesians (MIE-kruh-NEE-zhunz).

Sailing eastward and northward into the Pacific, and using only the stars, moon, sun, winds, and waves to guide them, the migrants endured the hardships of long open sea voyages to discover new lands and extend trade networks. Navigation and

boat-building were a science; voyagers spent many days selecting the right tree for their canoes since worm-ridden wood might prove disastrous at sea. An ancient Tahitian prayer reveals the voyagers' fears: "O gods! Lead us safely to land. Leave us not in the ocean. Give us a breeze. Let the weather be fine and the sky clear."[19]

These intentional migrations were spurred by overpopulation on islands, most of which had limited resources. Some Pacific islands were mountainous and often covered by dense rain forests, while others were flat atolls only a few feet above sea level, which left the inhabitants vulnerable to high waves due to fierce storms or tsunamis. Some islands lacked enough fresh water or fertile land to support many people. Islanders either learned to limit population growth or suffered the effects of deforestation and natural resource depletion, which generated conflict or, as an alternative to fighting, migration. Excellent naval technology made the migrations possible: each double-hulled outrigger canoe, up to 100 feet long and consisting of two hulls with a platform lashed between them for living, cooking, work space, and storage, was capable of carrying up to eighty people, along with foods, plants, and animals.

The Austronesians known today as Micronesians, who settled many central and north Pacific islands, made ingenious navigation charts from cowrie shells tied together. The Austronesian-speaking ancestors of some Micronesians, apparently originating in the Solomon Islands, eventually colonized many small islands in the central Pacific, including the Carolines. The Marianas (MAR-ee-AN-uhz), including the islands of Guam and Saipan, which in the twentieth century became territories of the United States, may have been settled directly by Austronesians sailing east from the Philippines between 1500 and 1000 B.C.E. (see Chronology: The Pacific Islands, 1500 B.C.E.–1000 C.E.). The Chamorro (cha-MOR-roe) people of the Marianas were the only Pacific society to grow Asian rice, suggesting they had continuing connections with the Philippines.

dreamtime In Aboriginal Australian mythology, the distant past when the spiritual ancestors gave order and form to the universe at the world's creation.

CHRONOLOGY

The Pacific Islands, 1500 B.C.E.–1000 C.E.

1500–1000 B.C.E.	Micronesian settlement of Marianas
1100–800 B.C.E.	Settlement of Fiji, Samoa, and Tonga
ca. 500 B.C.E.	Emergence of Polynesian culture in Fiji, Samoa, and Tonga
300–200 B.C.E.	Polynesian settlement of Marquesas and Tahiti
400–600 C.E.	Polynesian settlement of Hawaii
800–1000 C.E.	Polynesian settlement of New Zealand

Polynesian Palm-Frond Navigational Map This nautical map, made in the Marshall Islands from palm fronds, shows distances between islands as measured by time traveled. The map may have originally had bits of shell or coral to mark islands. Polynesians and Micronesians often made such maps for their ocean voyages.   (Bishop Museum)

Polynesian Migrations and Societies

Polynesian culture seems to have flowered first in the neighboring Fiji (FEE-jee), Tonga (TAHN-guh), and Samoa (suh-MO-uh) island groups around 500 B.C.E. Ancestors to the Polynesians had reached these islands between 1100 and 800 B.C.E. (see Map 9.3), and within a few centuries some were on the move again. The voyages must have involved incredible hardships, as men, women, children, animals, and precious seed plants were crammed into open canoes. By around 300 or 200 B.C.E. Polynesian mariners from Tonga may have reached the Marquesas (mar-KAY-suhs) Islands and soon thereafter Tahiti (tuh-HEE-tee), 1,500 miles east of Tonga. Sometime in the early Common Era Polynesians sailed from Samoa 1,500 miles north to the Kiribati (kear-uh-BAH-tee) Islands, and then on to the Marshall Islands. Later, between 400 and 600 C.E., mariners from the Marquesas settled Hawaii after crossing over 2,000 miles of ocean, followed around 1100 or 1200 C.E. by a migration from Tahiti. Then Tahitians journeyed some 2,500 miles east to Easter Island. Finally, between 800 and 1000 C.E., some Tahitians moved west another 2,500 miles to Aotearoa (which a Dutch explorer much later named New Zealand), the largest landmass settled by Polynesians. These settlers, the ancestors of the Maori (MAO-ree) people faced a very different climate and topography from that of the tropical Pacific islands, as well as a new mix of plants and animals. Polynesian sailors may even have visited the Peruvian coast. Such contact might

explain the presence of sweet potatoes, a South American crop, in eastern Polynesia and New Zealand for at least 1000 years.

Polynesian settlement required adapting to varied island environments. Their agriculture was based on Southeast Asian crops such as yams, taro, bananas, coconuts, and breadfruit, and animals included pigs, chickens, and dogs. But survival required some modifications. Sometimes farmers needed elaborate terracing, artificial ponds, and irrigation. Polynesians also exploited local food sources such as coconuts as well as the abundant marine life of the lagoons, coral reefs, and deep sea. Cloth made out of bark furnished clothing. But fragile island ecologies were easily unbalanced. Imported animals like pigs, dogs, and (unintentionally) rats consumed local birds. Overhunting also eliminated some species, and deforestation was also a problem. As an extreme example, Easter Island, which was heavily forested when Polynesians arrived, was completely denuded over the centuries, and the people were reduced to poverty and chronic conflict over ever scarcer resources.

Early Polynesians lived in clans that were generally dominated by hereditary chiefs who controlled the lands. Conflict between rival clans and chiefdoms over status and land led to tensions and sometimes war. Those who felt aggrieved might seek a better life by sailing to new lands. Eventually the most elaborate social hierarchies emerged in Tonga, Tahiti, and Hawaii, where paramount chiefs ruled many thousands of followers and controlled much of the economy. In these island

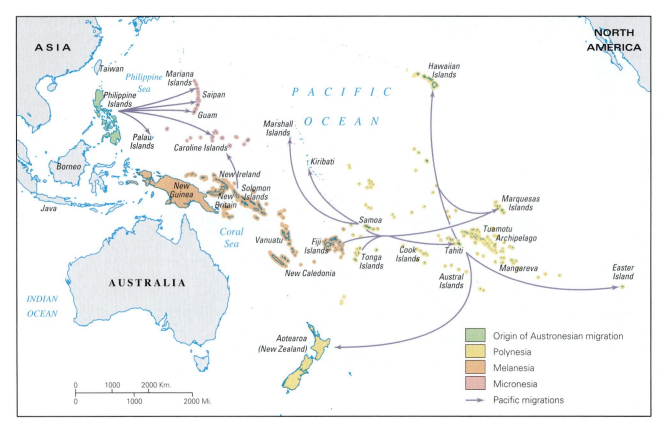

Map 9.3 Pacific Migrations in the Classical Era
During this era, Austronesian peoples scattered across the vast Pacific Basin, using ingenious canoes
and navigation techniques to settle nearly all the inhabitable islands. From bases in Tonga and Samoa in
the west, the Polynesians settled a large expanse of the basin ranging from Hawaii in the north to Easter
Island in the east and New Zealand in the south.

groups a deep divide developed between the families of the chiefs and the commoners. While men held most political power, women often enjoyed a high status. Most Micronesian and some Polynesian societies were matrilineal. In addition, Polynesian women often ranked higher than their brothers in spiritual and ritual authority and, by marrying into other clans or ruling families, could help political relations.

The Austronesian Dispersal in the Pacific and Beyond

Today some 1,200 different Austronesian languages are spoken across the huge span of space from Madagascar eastward through Indonesia, Malaysia, and the Philippines to Easter Island, a few hundred miles off the west coast of South America. All the Pacific islanders except those on and around New Guinea speak Austronesian languages. This book has elsewhere discussed the migrations of Indo-Europeans from southern Russia into Europe, western Asia, and India, as well as the long movement of Bantu-speaking peoples into the southern half of Africa. But no premodern peoples migrated over as wide an area in so short a time as did the Austronesians. The huge tri-

angle of Polynesia, anchored at the ends by Hawaii, New Zealand, and Easter Island, is one of the largest expanses of territory in the world. One of the first outsiders to explore the area, British captain James Cook, wrote in 1774 C.E.: "It is extraordinary that the same [people] should have spread themselves over all the isles in this vast Ocean, almost a fourth part of the circumference of the Globe."[20]

Migration over such vast distances did not necessarily mean isolation. The Austronesian languages may have been spread through the large maritime trading network that developed. As an example of this network, obsidian was mined on the island of New Britain, northeast of New Guinea. From there it was traded as far west as Borneo and as far east as Fiji, some 4,000 miles apart. On a smaller scale nearby island groups traded with each other and maintained social links. For example, the Tongan and Fijian chiefly families frequently intermarried. But even after sea routes were established, the sailing required remarkable observation and could be dangerous, as Captain Cook reported from Tonga in 1777: "In these Navigations the Sun is their guide by day and the Stars by night; when these are obscured they have recourse to the points from whence the Wind and waves come upon the vessel. If [these] shift, they are bewildered."[21] Even today Polynesian traditions honor great navigators of the past such as Moikeha and Pa'ao, who sailed back and forth between the Marquesas and Hawaii over a millennium ago.

Regular trade and communication ensured that the far-flung Polynesian societies shared many linguistic and cultural traits, including elaborate facial and body tattooing (the word *tattoo* is of Polynesian origin), myths, reverence for ancestors, and art forms such as woodcarving. Many of these customs were also common in Melanesia and Micronesia. And all these Pacific peoples derived not only their languages but also some of their culture, maritime prowess, and subsistence strategies from the Austronesians who ventured into Southeast Asia and then into the western Pacific in ancient times.

SECTION SUMMARY

■ Aboriginal Australians developed great understanding of natural phenomena and were very successful hunters and gatherers for thousands of years.

■ Aborigines across Australia believed in the dreamtime of the mythic past and felt that spirits and ghosts inhabited much of the physical world.

■ Austronesian peoples from Southeast Asia took to the sea and settled on various Pacific islands.

■ Polynesian culture probably began in Fiji, Tonga, and Samoa, but it spread out over a remarkable expanse of the Pacific Ocean.

■ An extensive trading network developed among the Pacific islands and, despite their isolation from each other, the islands' cultures remained quite homogenous.

Online Study Center ACE the Test

Chapter Summary

During the Classical Era some sub-Saharan Africans became more closely linked by trade with North Africa and the western half of Eurasia, and two societies, Kush and Aksum, also served as trade intermediaries. Kush, along the central Nile, became a center for iron production, and Aksum, in the Ethiopian highlands, flourished as a trading hub linked with many other societies of Africa and Eurasia. Cities and small states that emerged in the Sudanic region of West Africa participated in the growing trans-Saharan caravan trade network linking them with the Mediterranean world. Trading cities also appeared along the East African coast, which became tied by trade networks to the Mediterranean, western Asia, and India. Bantu-speaking peoples settled the southern half of Africa, carrying with them iron technology and many Sudanic influences. Many also settled on the East African coast.

Various urban societies dominated Mesoamerica and the Andes in classical times, including the Maya, Moche, Tiwanaku, Teotihuacan, and Monte Alban. The Maya forged a particularly enduring society based on competing city-states, developed a writing system, and understood much about astronomy and mathematics. The Moche on the Peruvian coast and Tiwanaku in the highlands formed empires. In Mesoamerica, Teotihuacan became the greatest city in the Americas and a major trading hub. In North America many peoples adopted farming. Southwestern peoples built permanent towns, and some societies in eastern North America took up mound building. In the Pacific, Australian Aborigines adapted well to their harsh environment, flourishing for millennia from hunting and gathering. And various Austronesian peoples, particularly the Polynesians, made spectacular migrations into the vast Pacific Ocean by using remarkable seagoing technologies and adapting to diverse island environments.

Online Study Center **Improve Your Grade** Flashcards

Key Terms

Meroitic	griots
Coptic Church	Nilotes
Aksum	Maya
Geez	Teotihuacan
Ghana	Moche
Mande	dreamtime

Suggested Reading

Books

Adams, Richard E. W. *Ancient Civilizations of the New World*. Boulder: Westview, 1997. Brief survey of Mesoamerican and South American societies before 1500 C.E.

Coe, Michael. *The Maya*. 7th ed. London and New York: Thames and Hudson, 2005. The standard overview of Maya history.

Connah, Graham. *African Civilization: An Archaeological Perspective*, 2nd ed. Cambridge: Cambridge University Press, 2001. An overview of early African societies, emphasizing the rise of cities and states.

Ehret, Christopher. *An African Classical Age: Eastern and Southern Africa in World History, 1000 B.C. to A.D. 400*. Charlottesville: University Press of Virginia, 1998. A pathbreaking study rethinking the role of classical Africa in world history.

Fagan, Brian M. *Kingdoms of Gold, Kingdoms of Jade: The Americas Before Columbus*. London and New York: Thames and Hudson, 1991. A nicely illustrated and readable introduction to the premodern American societies.

Fischer, Steven Roger. *A History of the Pacific Islands*. New York: Palgrave, 2002. Readable introduction to Pacific societies and history.

Kehoe, Alice Beck. *America Before the European Invasions*. New York: Longman, 2002. A recent overview of the North American peoples and history before 1600 C.E.

Kirch, Patrick. *On the Road of the Winds: An Archaeological History of the Pacific Islands*. Berkeley: University of California Press, 2000. The most recent and comprehensive study of the Austronesians in the Pacific.

Knight, Alan. *Mexico: From the Beginning to the Spanish Conquest.* New York: Cambridge University Press, 2002. An introduction to Mesoamerican societies.

Mann, Charles C. *1491: New Revelations of the Americas Before Columbus.* New York: Alfred A. Knopf, 2005. A readable summary of recent scholarship on the American societies.

Newman, James L. *The Peopling of Africa: A Geographic Interpretation.* New Haven, Conn.: Yale University Press, 1995. An excellent summary of what we know about the early history and migrations of Africa's people.

Nile, Richard, and Christian Clark. *Cultural Atlas of Australia, New Zealand and the South Pacific.* New York: Facts on File, 1996. A well-written overview with much on early histories and cultures.

Phillipson, David W. *African Archaeology.* 3rd ed. Cambridge: Cambridge University Press, 2005. A general study of the archaeology of premodern Africa, from prehistory into the second millennium of the Common Era.

Shillington, Kevin. *History of Africa,* revised 2nd ed. New York: Palgrave Macmillan, 2005. A recent survey text.

Welsby, Derek A. *The Kingdom of Kush: The Napatan and Meroitic Empires.* Princeton: Markus Wiener, 1996. A well-illustrated and up-to-date survey of Kushite society.

Whitlock, Ralph. *Everyday Life of the Maya.* Reprint of 1976 edition. New York: Dorset Press, 1987. Although somewhat dated, this remains an excellent introduction to Maya life.

Websites

About Archaeology (http://archaeology.about.com/library). About.com offers many essays and links relevant to early Africa and the Americas.

Africa South of the Sahara (http://www-sul.stanford.edu/depts/ssrg/africa/guide.html). Useful collection of links from Stanford University.

African Timelines (http://www.cocc.edu/cagatucci/classes/hum211/timelines/htimeline.htm). Has many links to specific periods and cultures as well as essays on controversial topics.

Ancient Mesoamerican Civilizations (www.angelfire.com/ca/humanorigins). Links and information about the premodern societies.

Austronesian and Other Indo-Pacific Topics (http://w3.rz-berlin.mpg.de/~wm/wm3.html). A useful collection of sources on Austronesian languages and cultures, operated by Germany-based scholars.

History and Cultures of Africa (http://www.columbia.edu/cu/lweb/indiv/africa/cuvl/cult.html). Extensive links provided by Columbia University.

Internet African History Sourcebook (http://www.fordham.edu/halsall/africa/africasbook.html). This site, maintained at Fordham University, contains much useful information and documentary material on African societies.

Mystery of the Maya (http://www.civilization.ca/civil/maya/nminteng.html). Canadian site offering useful essays on various aspects of Mayan history and society.

Classical Blossomings in World History, 600 B.C.E.–600 C.E.

In the second century B.C.E. a Greek historian, Polybius, recognized the expanding horizons of his time and concluded that "the world's history has been a series of unrelated episodes, but from now on history becomes an organic whole. The affairs of Europe and Africa are connected with those of Asia and all events bear a relationship and contribute to a single end."[1] In his perception of increasing connections across cultures, Polybius identified a crucial transition. During the Classical Era a vast exchange of ideas, cultures, and products grew in the Afro-Eurasian zone. For example, the Chinese sent missions into western Asia, where they met Persians and Greeks. Alexander the Great, born on the northern fringes of Greece, conquered Egypt, and later looked out on the Indus River in India, dreaming of moving on to the Ganges and even further.

The commercial exchanges that were carried out along the trade routes represented the first glimmerings of a world economy centered on Asia. Greek merchants traveled as far as south India, and one, based in the Egyptian city of Alexandria, wrote a manual describing the ports and listing the products traded in East Africa and South Asia. Warehouses in the south Indian port of Pondicherry were filled with caskets of Roman wine. Goods from Persia and Rome reached Funan in Southeast Asia, while the statue of an Indian goddess was carried to the Italian city of Pompeii. Romans craved Chinese silk, Arabian incense, and Indian spices. Merchants near Kabul, in today's Afghanistan, dealt in Greek glass, Egyptian pots, Chinese lacquer ware, and Hindu carvings.

Thanks in part to greater interregional communication over widening networks of exchange, the Classical Era was a period of flowerings of many kinds. Creative philosophies established new value systems or reinforced existing ones in the Mediterranean world and Asia. Between 350 B.C.E. and 200 C.E. the Afro-Eurasian world was also transformed by large regional empires. In the wake of these empires, universal religions such as Buddhism and Christianity crossed cultural boundaries, becoming permanent fixtures of world history. Classical peoples also refined their economic and social patterns. In this process, each society, while having its own dynamics, was also altered by contact with others.

THE AXIAL AGE OF PHILOSOPHICAL SPECULATION

Between around 600 and 400 B.C.E., several societies of Eurasia faced a remarkably similar set of crises. People in China, India, Persia, Israel, and Greece were all beset by chronic warfare, population movement, political disruption, and the breakdown of traditional values. Improved ironworking technology produced better tools but also more effective weapons. Political instability was common, as rival states competed with each other for power in China, India, the Middle East, and Greece.

These troubled conditions led to a climate of spiritual and intellectual restlessness, provoking a questioning of the old order. Because of the many influential and creative thinkers of this age, some scholars have called this an "axial period" or turning point, a crucial transition in history. This idea understates some crucial religious developments that occurred after 350 B.C.E., such as the reshaping of Hinduism, the division of Buddhism, and the rise of Christianity and Islam. Yet, the Axial Age produced enduring philosophical, religious, and scientific ideas that became the intellectual underpinning of many cultural traditions and fostered new ways of thinking.

Axial Age Thinkers

Many of the greatest thinkers in history were near-contemporaries; that is, they lived at roughly the same time, between 600 and 350 B.C.E. Laozi (credited by tradition as the inspiration for Daoism) and Confucius in China lived and taught in the sixth century around the same time as Buddha and Mahavira (the founder of the Jain faith) in India and the Greek thinkers Thales and Heracleitus. Other major Axial Age thinkers included the Hebrew prophets Jeremiah, Ezekiel, and the second Isaiah, as well as Socrates, Plato, and Aristotle in Greece. Although he may have lived much earlier, the teachings of the Persian Zoroaster also became prominent in this era. Many people today are still influenced by these thinkers: Laozi's advice to live in accordance with nature, the Confucian dream of an ordered society based on proper ethical conduct, the Buddha's rules for ending human suffering, Mahavira's belief in absolute nonviolence, the prophetic Hebrew vision of universal justice, the Greek emphasis on rational analysis, and the Zoroastrian notion of opposing forces of darkness and light still have meaning.

Some of these men were not only thinkers but also teachers. To pass along their ideas, leading intellectuals such as Confucius and Plato took on students. Confucius reflected the passion for education: "I am not someone who was born wise. I am someone who tries to learn [from the ancients]."[2] It was a time of exciting exchanges, as mystics and teachers traveled through India, dozens of philosophers spread their ideas in China, and students of Socrates competed with followers of the Stoics in the schools of Athens.

Causes and Characteristics of Axial Age Thought

In trying to identify the causes of the Axial Age, historians point to social and political instability, the effects of commercial exchanges along far-flung trade networks, economies productive enough to support a class of thinkers, and the first glimmerings of the belief that individuals have intrinsic worth apart from their role in society. Other possible causes include the increase in cultural exchanges among Afro-Asian peoples with the spread of writing, iron tools and vehicles, and

Confucius and Laozi in Conversation   This picture engraved on a stone tablet in an old Confucian temple shows Confucius visiting Laozi in the city of Loyang and amiably discussing with him views on ritual and music.   From Carl Crow, Master Kung: The Story of Confucius (New York and London: Harper and U Brothers Publishers, 1938)

improved boats. These inventions helped widen intellectual horizons and stimulated human intellect and imagination. Exactly where many of the great Axial Age ideas began, however, has led to controversy (see Historical Controversy: The Afrocentric Challenge to Historians of Antiquity).

Whatever the causes, several themes became common to Axial Age thinkers. First, especially in China and Greece, thinkers questioned the accepted myths and gods and promoted a humanistic view of life, one more concerned with the social and natural order than the supernatural order. Second, most thinkers stressed moral conduct and values, a vision that often rejected the violent, selfish pursuit of material power they saw around them. Some, like the Buddha, Mahavira, and Laozi, were pacifists who denounced all violence, the Jains going to the extreme of preventing harm even to insects. Third, Confucius, the Hebrew prophets, and several Greeks were also among the first people to think about history and its lessons for societies. Fourth, while few of these thinkers favored social equality, many argued that rulers should govern with a sense of obligation to the powerless and less fortunate. Finally, all the Axial Age thinkers believed that the world could be improved, either by the actions of ethical individuals or by the creation of an ideal social order, or both. For example, Plato devised a model government led not by kings but by a special class of wise men.

But the Axial Age thinkers disagreed as to whether truth was absolute. Socrates and Plato, for example, argued for universal concepts, Plato writing that "those who see the absolute and eternal have real knowledge and not mere opinions." Yet, some Greeks and Chinese also explored the notion that truth was relative and dependent on circumstances. As one Chinese thinker wrote: "Monkeys prefer trees: so what habitat can be said to be absolutely right? Fish flee at the sight of women whom men deem lovely. Whose is the right taste absolutely?"[3] Philosophers still struggle with the question of universal or relative truth.

The Axial Age had not only philosophical and religious but also scientific and political consequences. Across Eurasia people raised fundamental questions about many phenomena and answered them by systematic investigation. Greek thinkers such as Aristotle, who pondered and classified everything from political systems to animals, influenced European and Middle Eastern science, and their ideas inspired new discoveries by Hellenistic, Roman and, later, Islamic scientists. At the other end of Eurasia, Chinese influenced by Confucianism and Daoism also created another rich scientific tradition. Indians became some of the classical world's greatest mathematicians and astronomers. Together, the classical Greeks, Chinese, Indians, and the ancient Mesopotamians and Egyptians built the foundations for modern science. Axial Age ideas also became the basis for new political ideologies. For example, in China, Confucianism mixed with Legalism provided the ideas for building stronger states, while Romans rose to power using modified Greek ideas of democracy. As a result of strengthening state institutions and leaders, in China, India, Persia, and Greece the Axial Age ended in mighty empires that reflected a new order of technological and organizational planning.

THE AGE OF REGIONAL EMPIRES

The empires that arose in much of Eurasia during or at the end of the Axial Age were greater in size and impact than those that had flourished in ancient times. The Persian Empire set the

The Afrocentric Challenge to Historians of Antiquity

For many years the writings by Western scholars about world history emphasized Europe, a biased perspective known as Eurocentrism. In the conventional story line, history began in Egypt, Mesopotamia, and Palestine before moving to Greece and Rome and then on to northwestern Europe and finally to North America. The rest of the world, except perhaps for India and China, constituted an exotic aside to the European mainstream. The academic fields of classics (the study of the Greco-Roman world) and Egyptology specialized in the ancient Mediterranean world, excluding the rest of Africa and Asia. Before the 1970s most Western historians either ignored Africa or argued that Africa was unimportant throughout world history.

THE PROBLEM

Today a historical perspective that incorporates Africa has become common, but for much of the twentieth century many scholars openly agreed with an eminent British historian, who wrote in 1928 that Africa had no history and that most Africans had stayed stagnant and sunk in barbarism for many centuries. In reacting to racial discrimination and lingering contempt for Africa's historical legacy, many historians have made a convincing case for the importance of Africa and its critical role in world history. But questions remain. Was Africa a central part of the larger ancient and classical world? Was Egypt essentially an African or a Mediterranean society? Finally, did Egypt strongly influence classical Greece?

THE DEBATE

In dramatic contrast to Eurocentrism, an alternative approach known as Afrocentrism emphasizes Africa's, rather than Europe's, centrality in history. The more radical Afrocentrists provide a mirror image to the old Eurocentric model, dismissing the older history as a lie designed to glorify European culture and perpetuate the power of white people. They assert that Africa was the fountainhead of Mediterranean culture and that a new way of understanding world history must be developed. Afrocentrists like the Senegalese Cheikh Anta Diop and the American Molefe Asante argue that black Africans, including Egyptians, originated and developed many of the arts, philosophies, and technologies of the ancient and classical Mediterranean societies.

Critics accuse the radical Afrocentrists, like the rigid Eurocentrists, of exaggeration and selectivity in their use of historical evidence, charging that they rely on largely outdated and discredited sources. Some Afrocentrists, for example, promote the dubious notions that Egyptian queen Cleopatra (a Hellenistic Greek) and Athenian philosopher Socrates were black, or that African mariners established the Olmec society of Mexico. Such unsubstantiated theories convince few scholars, regardless of their ethnic background. The British scholar Stephen Howe even asserts that Afrocentric writings replace outmoded Eurocentric scholarship with a misleading version that offers a fictional history.

One prong of the debate is whether ancient Egypt should be seen as essentially Mediterranean or as an African society rooted in African traditions. There is some truth to both propositions. Most scholars now acknowledge extensive Egyptian connections to Africa, western Asia, and southeastern Europe. African ties were certainly extensive. For example, the ancient Egyptian language was closely related to many African tongues. In addition, historians of Africa now believe that many ideas that Egyptians shared with African peoples diffused to Eygpt from the south, including the notion and rituals of divine kingship that underpinned Egyptian royalty, various myths and gods, and much material culture. But Egypt's connections were diverse. Populated by migrants from all directions, Egypt produced people of many skin colors and physical features. As a trade crossroads, it maintained trade relations with Africans, Asians, and Europeans. People moved around and intermarried. Thus the Nile valley was a zone of contact between many groups, where there was not only considerable mingling of people but also, with that, creative cultural borrowing and invention, making it difficult for historians to precisely identify the foreign influences on Egyptian culture.

Another controversy concerns whether Egypt spread African ideas and influences to the Greek culture emerging across the Mediterranean. In his three-volume study, *Black Athena*, the British-born, U.S.-based scholar Martin Bernal contends that, until the early nineteenth century, Western historians stressed the Afro-Asiatic origins of Greek culture, acknowledging Egypt and Phoenicia as core influences. Then, in a sharp turn from that position, he argues, because of increasing racism toward black people and rising European imperialism and nationalism, Western scholars began to stress the Greeks as being a creative source of culture rather than derivative—the pure and original source of European society. African and Middle East influences, such as those from Egypt and Phoenicia, were removed from the scenario.

To argue his point, Bernal uses the myths and historical writings of the Greeks themselves, including, for example, the claims by the Greek historian Herodotus that the Egyptians invented mathematics and that the names of Greek gods originated in Egypt. Herodotus spent time in Egypt around 450 B.C.E. and admired the Egyptian heritage. Influenced by his views, Bernal agrees with Diop that a significant proportion of Greek religion, political philosophy, architecture, science, and even language was imported from Phoenicia and Egypt. For example, Bernal suggests that Athena, the Greek goddess of wisdom and patron goddess of Athens, was a transplanted version of Neith, a goddess from the Nile Delta.

Bernal's work provoked a storm of controversy. Critics accuse Bernal of misreading Greek myths and historical accounts. They suggest that the Greeks credited Egypt with these accomplishments because they wanted to legitimize their own position by connecting with the older and much respected Egyptian culture, a plausible argument. Furthermore, as most historians are aware, Herodotus often exaggerated or relied on unreliable hearsay, and so is not always a convincing source. Reliance on Herodotus, critics charge, led Bernal to unsubstantiated links, such as one tracing the origins of Greek philosophy to Egyptian literature on wisdom, despite many differences. In one of the more articulate critiques of Bernal, Mary Lefkowitz links Bernal to radical Afrocentrism (an approach he criticizes), deploring his scholarship for disputing that the Greeks invented democracy, philosophy, and science.

In this debate, few classicists disagree that the Greeks admired the Egyptians and traded with them extensively. Some leading Greek thinkers, including Herodotus, Solon, Plato, Thales, and Euclid, visited or studied in Egypt. But, like Lefkowitz, many classicists believe Bernal greatly overstates Afro-Asian influence and underestimates Greek genius. At the same time, however, many other scholars defend Bernal, while some, including the Africanist Basil Davidson and the classicist Jacques Berlinblau, take a more balanced middle view. And the controversy has also inspired more studies placing Egypt and Africa in a larger regional or world context, such as those by Schofield and Davies and by Gilbert and Reynolds.

EVALUATING THE DEBATE

Both sides of the debate have been accused of having a political agenda: to influence how the histories of Europe and Africa are taught in North American and European schools. Hence, the controversy illustrates the danger of what historians call "present-mindedness," the tendency to interpret the past largely in light of present social and political concerns. While we can never entirely escape this tendency, we can try to see the people of the past as they saw themselves. This means not using their experiences as ammunition in current social and political debates, as both Eurocentric and Afrocentric historians have often done. While many particular points made by Afrocentrists have found little favor among most historians, we can credit Bernal and others for their useful critique of Eurocentric scholarship. In any case, the sources for Greek thinking may be less important than the creative uses they made of them. Since the issues of how much Egypt contributed to Greece and how much it reflected or stimulated sub-Saharan African cultures are legitimate subjects for historical investigation, the debates will continue. But both Afrocentrism and Eurocentrism are inadequate in providing a global framework that looks at the contributions of all societies.

THINKING ABOUT THE CONTROVERSY

1. What is the argument labeled by critics as Eurocentrism?
2. What is the Afrocentric criticism of Eurocentrism?
3. What are the insights and problems of Bernal's *Black Athena*?

EXPLORING THE CONTROVERSY

Afrocentric history was pioneered by Cheikh Anta Diop in *Civilization or Barbarism: An Authentic Anthropology* (Brooklyn: Lawrence Hill, 1991) and *The African Origin of Civilization: Myth or Reality* (New York: Lawrence Hill, 1974). A more radical approach can be found in Molefe Asante's *Afrocentricity*

Athena, Greek Goddess of Wisdom. Some scholars suspect that some Greek deities, such as Athena, portrayed here in a Greek sculpture, were based on Egyptian deities.

(Trenton: Africa World Press, 1988) and *The Afrocentric Idea* (Philadelphia: Temple University Press, 1987). The most significant scholarly challenge to the views of mainstream classicists can be found in Martin Bernal, *Black Athena: The Afroasiatic Roots of Classical Civilization*, 3 vols. (New Brunswick, N.J.: Rutgers University Press, 1987, 1991, 2001). Bernal responds to his critics in *Black Athena Writes Back* (Durham, N.C.: Duke University Press, 2001). The major rebuttals to Bernal and Afrocentrism include Stephen Howe, *Afrocentrism: Mystical Pasts and Imagined Homes* (London: Verso, 1998); Mary Lefkowitz, *Not Out of Africa: How Afrocentrism Became an Excuse to Teach Myth as History* (New York: Basic Books, 1996); and Mary Lefkowitz and Guy MacLean, eds., *Black Athena Revisited* (Chapel Hill: University of North Carolina Press, 1996).

For thoughtful discussions of the Afrocentrist controversy, see Basil Davidson, *The Search for Africa: History, Culture, Politics* (New York: Times Books, 1994), and Jacques Berlinblau, *Heresy in the University: The "Black Athena" Controversy and the Responsibility of American Intellectuals* (New Brunswick, N.J.: Rutgers University Press, 1999). Useful studies of Egypt and Africa in world history include Louise Schofield and W. Vivian Davies, eds., *Egypt, the Aegean and the Levant: Interconnections in the Second Millennium* (London: Trustees of the British Museum, 1995), and Erik Gilbert and Jonathan T. Reynolds, *Africa in World History: From Prehistory to the Present* (Upper Saddle River, N.J.: Prentice-Hall, 2004).

stage, thriving for nearly three centuries. More regional empires appeared between 350 B.C.E. and 250 C.E., from China in the East to Rome in the West, that were much grander in scale than such earlier empires as the Assyrian and the Shang Chinese. In the Mediterranean Basin Rome built on the heritage of Alexander the Great. The Parthians and then the Sassanian Persians governed some of western and Central Asia, the Chinese Han Empire dominated much of East and Central Asia, and in India the Mauryan state controlled much of the subcontinent for over a century. Most of the empires built upon the ideas of classical sages and religious leaders, such as Confucius, Zoroaster, and Plato, in organizing society. In so doing they helped resolve the crises, such as political instability, that had sparked the rise of the Axial Age reformers. Empires also appeared in sub-Saharan Africa and the Americas, including Aksum, Teotihuacan, and Tiwanaku, but on a smaller scale than in Eurasia.

The Rise of Empires

The first great regional empires in the Eastern Hemisphere developed during the Axial Age. The Achaemenid Empire of Persia (550–334 B.C.E.) dwarfed its Middle Eastern predecessors and was the first large empire that ruled many diverse societies. At its height it reached from Egypt and northern Greece across western Asia to Central Asia and the Indus Basin. Persian kings had reason to brag, as did Xerxes, that they were kings of lands containing many people, of the great earth far and wide. Like many leaders, the Persian kings claimed to improve society. Darius I boasted that he had "changed many bad things that had been done to good things . . . so that people did not kill each other any more."[4] The Hellenistic Empire created by Alexander and the Macedonian Greeks built directly on the experiences of Persian imperial rule. The dynasties that succeeded Alexander dominated much of western Asia, Egypt, and southeastern Europe for the next two centuries.

By the end of the Axial Age, in the third and fourth centuries, new empires arose in Eurasia in part as a result of increased warfare, such as fighting between warring states in India, China, and the western Mediterranean. In each region one state eventually subdued its rivals; the Mauryan, Han, and Roman Empires were the results of these conflicts. Changing social and economic conditions also helped spur the rise of these empires. Rapid economic growth due to expanding long-distance trade networks made merchants more important in all of these societies, and merchants then sought more political influence and social equality. The upper classes, such as the priestly brahman caste of India and the wealthy senatorial class in Rome, protected their own privileges while increasingly exploiting the peasants. The gap between rich and poor widened, causing increased tensions. Rulers surrounded themselves with the trappings of wealth and power, enjoying lavish ceremonies and giving themselves exalted titles. But the move toward empire alleviated some social conflicts by providing large, stable environments in which resources could be acquired and distributed. During this period, the growing states required extensive administrative machinery, larger armies, standardized laws, and governing philosophies. Administrators were needed to collect taxes, organize social services, and serve as judges.

From China to Rome, provinces paid taxes and supplied soldiers to the large armies needed to sustain and expand the empires. For example, during the early Roman Empire the armed forces received 58 percent of all government revenue. At the same time the Han emperor stationed 300,000 troops along the Great Wall. Since everything was bigger and the stakes were higher, wars against competing states could be terribly destructive: after three wars with Carthage spanning more than a century, Rome razed that great city to the ground and laced salt into the soil to render it unfit for farming.

Philosophical and religious beliefs maintained community standards but were also used by rulers of these large states to sustain and legitimize their power. For example, Stoic philosophy encouraged Romans to accept their lot in life. In China Confucian ideas urged people to respect leaders, and Legalist thinkers told leaders to exercise power ruthlessly. Thus, the Confucian scholar Dong Zhongshu (ca. 179–104 B.C.E.) elevated the role of the Chinese emperor, arguing that "heaven, earth, and man are the source of all creatures. Heaven gives birth to them, earth nourishes them, and human beings complete them. Who else but a king could connect them all?"[5] In Mauryan India, Ashoka enhanced his position by using Buddhist moral injunctions emphasizing peace, tolerance, and welfare to win popular support. Ashoka recorded his goals on pillars: "All men are my children, and just as I desire for my children that they should obtain welfare and happiness, so do I desire [the same] for all men."[6]

Increasing Cultural Unity and Contact

These new regional empires imposed peace and uniformity within their boundaries. Bureaucratic structures standardized practices throughout an empire so that the weights, measures, currencies, calendars, tax codes, and official languages used throughout the far-flung provinces of an empire were the same. For example, Greek spread widely in the Hellenistic kingdoms of Asia. Latin became the common language in the Roman Empire, in the process fostering the western European "romance" languages, such as Spanish and French. Latin influences also found their way into Germanic languages such as English and German. But in Roman Asia few outside the political elite spoke or read Latin. Similarly, the northern Chinese dialect of Mandarin became China's official spoken language even though, outside of the educated class, few in the southern half of China spoke Mandarin.

By stimulating commerce and communication, the empires fostered the spread of ideas and technologies into neighboring societies and increased contact among distant peoples (see map). For example, Hellenistic Greeks and Mauryan Indians encountered each other in Afghanistan, a crossroads where Eurasian peoples both fought with each other and exchanged ideas. Spurred by imperial expansion, Roman culture and then Christianity permeated the Mediterranean Basin, Hellenistic Greek culture spread in western Asia and North Africa, while China influenced Japan, Korea, Vietnam, and Central Asia.

In Eurasia trade routes grew out of transportation systems constructed to channel resources to imperial capitals. China built canals unprecedented in scale, Achaemenid Persia and

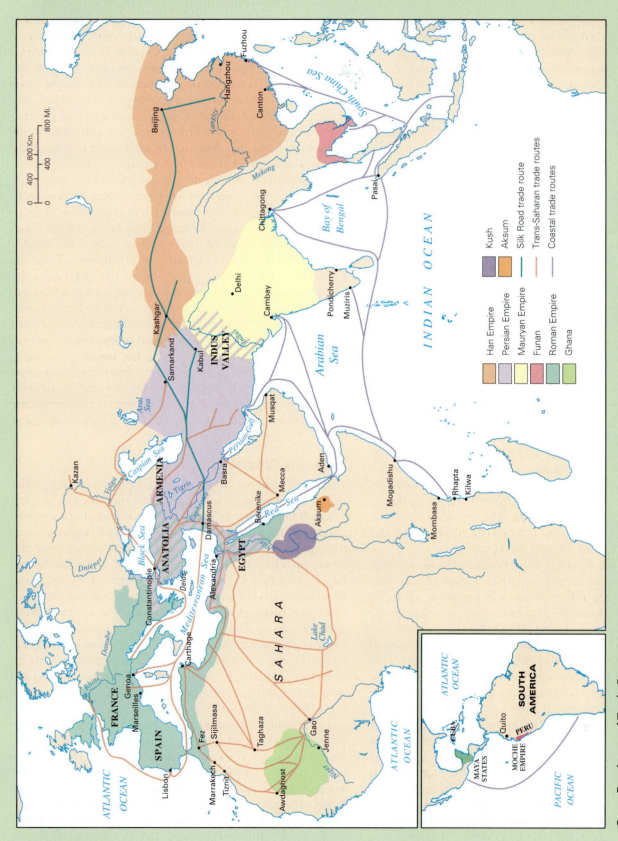

Great Empires and Trade Routes

During the Classical Era, great empires often dominated East Asia, India, western Asia, North Africa, and southern Europe. Extensive land and maritime trade routes linked East Asia with western Eurasia, West Africa with the Mediterranean, and East Africa with southern Asia.

Mauryan India constructed east-west highways, and the Romans developed 150,000 miles of paved roads. These roads and canals, along with seaports, became linked to long-distance trade networks, which brought many societies, such as the Celts and Germans in northern Europe, the Sogdians in Central Asia, the Sudanic peoples of West Africa, the East African coastal dwellers, and the Japanese and Koreans, into closer contact with major empires.

Decline of Empires

Throughout history states rise and fall, and the classical empires did as well. While each of the great regional empires declined for different reasons, the Roman and Han Chinese Empires suffered from some of the same problems. Each empire expanded beyond its ability to support itself, weakening administrative structures and finances. Some conquered territories brought wealth to the empire, but others did not. The British Isles, for example, were a net drain on the imperial Roman treasury, and it was costly to maintain Chinese control in Central Asia. Both of these empires also suffered from civil wars and growing domestic unrest. Eventually both empires, unable to acquire new wealth through further expansion, made economic cutbacks and raised taxes to sustain the imperial structure, which caused widespread resentment. Contemporary observers recorded the decline. The third-century C.E. Roman writer Cyprian argued that "the World itself testifies to its own decline by giving manifold concrete evidence of the process of decay. This loss of strength and stature must end, at least, in annihilation."[7]

Both the Han and Roman Empires were also plagued by environmental problems. Because the empires formed as the global climate was warming, they could benefit from increased food supplies. Both the Han and Rome flourished during the peak of warmth between 200 B.C.E. and 200 C.E. With the return of colder weather after 200 C.E., however, agricultural production declined and the great empires collapsed or weakened. Soil exhaustion in Italy was also a factor in Rome's declining food supply. In addition, diseases traveled along the land and sea routes, undermining Rome and China in the second century C.E. Some outbreaks, like the terrible plague identified with Justinian's Byzantium, killed millions and made life miserable over wide areas. Probably originating in Africa, the plague killed nearly half the population of Constantinople in the 540s. By the time the pandemic reached its end in the 590s, some 25 million West Asians, North Africans, and Europeans had perished.

When pastoral nomads began to put more pressure on the Roman and Chinese Empires, these states had been weakened so much by economic and environmental problems that they could no longer effectively resist. For instance, Chinese emperors could no longer afford to maintain the garrisons along the series of walls built across north China. The Germanic tribes proved a long-term threat to Rome, and various Central Asians, among them Huns, Scythians, and Turkish peoples, continuously intruded along the fringes of Persia, India, and China. By 200 C.E. population growth and climate change

pushed some of them to more aggressively seek wealth in the declining Roman and Han Empires. In the end, the imperial orders were undermined in part by forces beyond their control.

Various peoples eventually conquered or displaced the great empires, although they also usually adopted Roman, Indian, Persian, or Chinese culture. But the imperial idea never died. It proved particularly strong in Persia, where the Achaeminid, Hellenistic Seleucid, Parthian, and finally Sassanian Empires succeeded each other over a millennium. Even in India, where fragmented states were the norm, the Gupta rulers claimed kinship with the Mauryas five centuries earlier. The belief in the need for large regional empires also endured for centuries in China and served as a model for later dynasties that conquered vast territories. Hence, the China of the eighteenth century C.E., which incorporated many non-Chinese societies, clearly descended in recognizable form from the Han of 150 B.C.E. Similarly, the Byzantine Empire controlled vast European and western Asian territories once part of the old Roman Empire. After the fall of the western Roman Empire, however, western Europeans never succeeded in reviving that empire, even though some Christian German kings centuries later claimed the title of "Holy Roman Emperor." In contrast to China, where the Sui Dynasty revived much of the early Han system, western European societies were never able to restore the Roman heritage.

WORLD RELIGIONS AND THEIR INFLUENCES

During the later centuries of the Classical Era, universal religions became more prominent in Afro-Eurasia, marking another great transition that reshaped societies. Instead of the gods of the ancient world, which were local and identified with particular cities or cultures, these new religions were portable and appealed across cultural boundaries. They could be carried along trade routes, attracting believers far from their lands of birth. The Eurasian faiths with the most followers—Christianity, Buddhism, Hinduism, and Zoroastrianism—filled a vacuum created by political instability and cultural decline.

The Spread of Universal Religions

Religions spread along land and sea trade routes. Missionaries accompanied or were themselves traders, as a fourth-century C.E. Christian hymn in Syria acknowledged: "Travel like merchants, That we may gain the world. Fill creation with teaching."[8] About six centuries after its founding in India, Buddhism reached China via the Silk Road and Southeast Asia over the maritime trade routes. Christianity, with roots in the eastern Mediterranean, spread to Rome, where it became prominent by the fourth century C.E.; it permeated northern Europe beginning around 500 C.E. Christianity also established roots in western Asia, Egypt, Nubia, and Ethiopia. Other faiths also established a presence. Manicheanism, a mix of Christian and Zoroastrian influences, attracted believers from North Africa to China. Judaism also gained some converts in Arabia, the Caucasus, and Ethiopia. By 500 or 600 C.E. small Christian and Jewish communities had even been established in Central Asia, western India, and northern China. Networks of exchange helped shape religious traditions as well as spread them. For example, Zoroastrian ideas probably influenced Ionian Greek, Mahayana Buddhist, and Judeo-Christian beliefs and art forms.

The universal religions gave people hope in the face of the political and social crises that marked the decline of the great regional empires from the second through the fifth centuries C.E. Sometimes these new religions merged with or incorporated existing beliefs. In East Asia, for example, Buddhism gradually blended with or accommodated Confucianism, Daoism, and Shinto, and, in northern Europe, Christianity acquired a Germanic or Celtic flavor over the centuries. Not all the religious changes were accommodating, however. Religion could also divide families. In one case, a Roman writer told of conflict between a Christian wife and her husband, who practiced his traditional faith: "She is engaged in a fast; her husband has arranged a banquet. She celebrates the Easter Vigil throughout the entire night; her husband expects her in his bed."[9]

In sub-Saharan Africa and the Americas, some religious beliefs reached across many societies, becoming the counterparts to the organized Eurasian religions. The polytheistic beliefs of the Mande and other Sudanic peoples, for instance, gradually spread to the Guinea coast and Central Africa, and from there to eastern and southern Africa. In the Americas the Olmecs introduced gods and views of the universe that contributed to the later religious beliefs of the Maya, and some Maya ideas may have spread to other Mesoamericans. Chavín religious traditions, including gods and shamanistic practices, probably influenced the views of other Andean peoples such as the Moche and Tiwanaku. Some of the American peoples practiced human sacrifice as part of their religious devotions, as offerings to the gods. Human sacrifice was also found in some Afro-Eurasian societies, among them the Celts, Minoan Crete, ancient Egypt, and Shang China.

King David For centuries artists in the Christian Ethiopian kingdom, in the highlands of Northeast Africa, painted biblical figures on the pages of religious manuscripts. The artists often used Ethiopian motifs and this painting of the Hebrew king, David, adorned in rich robes and crown and playing a harp-type instrument, resembles that of an Ethiopian king. (Bibliotheque nationale de France)

Religion, Culture, and Society

The universal religions became a major force in shaping the societies and regions in which they became dominant, eventually creating, for example, a largely Hindu India, a Buddhist Sri Lanka, and a Christian Europe. To be sure, religion was only a part of life, and religions changed over time, dividing into varied sects such as the Mahayana and Theravada Buddhists. But after the regional empires collapsed into many rival states in the Mediterranean, India, and China, religious institutions transcended political divisions, fostering cultural unity across borders. Hindus, Buddhists, and Christians often saw themselves as part of larger communities. As a result, Chinese Buddhist pilgrims such as Faxian made the long and arduous journey to India to study with Indian Buddhists. And many Christians looked to the bishops in faraway cities such as Rome for guidance. Spirituality permeated the lives of people all over the world. Religion also offered the poor the hope that they might end their suffering and low status, if not in this life then through reincarnation or in some form of heaven.

All the universal religions, as well as the religions of urban American societies such as the Maya, had certain features, practices, and beliefs in common. They had sacred writings or scriptures, such as the Hindu Vedas and Christian Bible, strict moral codes, organized priesthoods, theologies laying out core beliefs, and some concept of existence after death. Most faiths also encouraged followers to treat others as they wanted to be treated themselves, although in practice many people ignored this advice. The devout shared a belief in the universal truth of their faith. All the religions were patriarchal to one degree or another, adding religious sanction to the growing suppression of women. Christian and Buddhist leaders also dispatched missionaries into neighboring societies, although Buddhism later lost most of its missionary zeal.

For all the spiritual comfort and insight they provided believers, these new religions, like their predecessors, were also important as forces of social control. For example, Hindu ideas of reincarnation and karma underpinned the Indian caste system, encouraging people to accept their status. Christians focused on attaining heaven and were warned that questioning religious authority and beliefs might prevent salvation. Some of the religious establishments grew intolerant of dissent. For this reason, Christian bishops established a consensus on doctrine, excluding ideas considered to be heresy. In the late Common Era those who disagreed with Christian or Zoroastrian orthodoxy might be banned or punished, and they were expected to face retribution after death in Hell, the abode of evil, an underworld for wicked people and disbelievers.

Monasticism and Its Diffusion

Some of the universal religions spawned a new social and spiritual movement, monasticism. It may have first developed as a movement within both Buddhism and Jainism. Buddha himself supposedly ordained the first monks as well as nuns, including his mother. In Theravada Buddhist societies most men spent some period as monks, bound by their rigid code of celibacy and poverty. But the concept then perhaps spread over the trade networks into western Asia. Whether or not inspired by Buddhist models, monasticism became a growing component of organized Christianity by the third century C.E.

Whether Christian or Buddhist, monasteries provided educational and charitable services while providing a focus for community religious life. In societies as far removed as England, Nubia, and China, a substantial number of men (and some women) joined monastic orders, abandoning the humdrum existence of everyday life for a focus on prayer and meditation. Most monks and nuns practiced austere religious practices to strengthen spiritual life. This could involve sexual abstinence, fasting, and solitary contemplation. In the Hindu tradition wandering holy men who abandoned the comforts of settled life and families provided a counterpart to organized monastic life.

CHANGING ECONOMIC AND SOCIAL PATTERNS

Increased migration and communication fostered major social and economic changes. Population growth encouraged migration, which led to the intermixing of peoples and the exchange of ideas. Deadly disease epidemics moving along migration networks testified to this widespread contact between distant peoples. The long-distance trade routes also spread both diseases and new ideas. The result was that certain social attitudes became more common over a wide area, including attitudes toward women and slaves that lasted for centuries. The social and economic systems of the Classical Era, some alien and some familiar to modern people, suggest both how much and how little the world has changed since the Classical Era.

The Growth and Decline of World Population

Successful agricultural systems in the great empires allowed for substantial population growth from Europe to China. In 4000 B.C.E., at the dawn of the ancient world, the world population was well under 100 million. At the beginning of the Common Era there were probably between 200 and 250 million people, over 70 percent living in Asia and about 20 million each in Africa and the Americas. China was the largest society, with some 60 million people. In addition, more people now lived in cities. In 450 B.C.E. the world's largest city was probably Babylon, with 200,000 people. By 200 B.C.E. Patna in Mauryan India had 400,000, and by 100 C.E. Rome was the largest metropolis, with at least 500,000 people and perhaps a million.

But diseases began to limit population growth in the later Classical Era. Networks of communication were often networks of contagion, port cities being the major hubs of transmission. Epidemics of smallpox and plague resulted from travelers unknowingly spreading new diseases into areas where people had not yet built up immunities to them. Epidemic diseases may have killed as many as 25 percent of the population of China and the Roman Empire during the second and third centuries C.E. Indeed, plague outbreaks contributed considerably to the decline of the classical empires; for example, they undermined the Roman state and, by producing widespread

Crossing the Pamir Mountains   The Pamir Mountains, separating the deserts of what is now western China from the deserts and grasslands of Turkestan and Afghanistan, were one of the more formidable barriers faced by camel caravans traveling the Silk Road. To avoid the blistering summer heat of the desert, the caravans often traveled in winter, forcing them to maneuver through mountain snows.
(R&S Michaud/Woodfin Camp & Associates)

misery and disillusionment, aided the spread of Christianity among demoralized or desperate Roman subjects. As a result of the various disease outbreaks, by 600 B.C.E. the world population remained between 200 and 240 million, similar to what it had been six centuries earlier.

Population growth led to increased movement, as people sought open lands and better opportunities. Responding to population pressures, Chinese migrants moved into central and southern China; Germanic and Turkish peoples spread into central Europe and western Asia, respectively; Bantu-speaking peoples occupied the southern half of Africa; and Austronesians settled remote Pacific islands. As groups migrated, they assimilated local peoples and cultures and adapted their lives to new surroundings.

Trade and Cultural Contact

The networks of trade, like those of imperial expansion and missionary activity, linked distant peoples while spreading the influence of cultures more widely. The Greeks picked up scientific and mathematical knowledge as well as some religious notions from the Egyptians and Phoenicians. Indian cultural influences, including Buddhism, spread over the trade routes into Central, East, and Southeast Asia, reaching as far as Korea, Japan, and Indonesia. Aksum was linked by commerce with the Mediterranean world and India, a link that brought Christianity to the Ethiopian highlands. Precious spices from southern Arabia, textiles from India, and gold from Malaya and West Africa found their way to the Mediterranean societies. The Roman writer Pliny was surprised at Roman demand for Indian pepper, which "has nothing in it that can plead as a recommendation [other than] a certain pungency; and yet it is for this that we import it all the way from India!"[10] Trade also connected Mesoamerica with neighboring regions and fostered networks of exchange in both eastern North America and western South America. For example, copper from the North American Great Lakes reached the Gulf Coast, and Mesoamerican ball games spread far and wide. Crops also traveled American trade routes, maize from Mexico becoming a major crop in both North and South America, and tomatoes from the Andes carried into Central America and Mexico.

The Silk Road endured as a major overland long-distance network of exchange—in effect the first transcontinental highway—and allowed people, goods, and ideas to travel thousands of miles. As a Han dynasty history put it: "Messengers come and go every season and month, foreign traders and merchants knock on the gates of the Great Wall every day."[11] In Eurasia the introduction of coinage encouraged trade by offering widely recognized tokens of value. Coins from Sassanian Persia and Byzantium as well as Chinese silk served as the network currency. Indeed, the huge amounts of gold and silver exported by Rome to pay for Chinese silk and Indian spices did some damage to the Roman economy. Overland trade expanded with the growing use of camels. After the invention of an efficient saddle allowed this pack animal to be used for longer journeys across the deserts and plains of Asia and Africa, camels became the trucks of the premodern Afro-Eurasian zone. And the merchants who used the camels carried not only bullion and products but also religions, especially Buddhism and Manicheanism, which spread along the Silk Road into Central Asia and China.

Cities grew up along the Silk Road across Central Asia to serve as suppliers and middlemen to the merchants. These cities, such as Kashgar in Xinjiang and Samarkand in Turkestan, became part of a contact zone linking many societies. Hubs at the eastern end of the Mediterranean, such as Petra, Palmyra, Alexandria, and Constantinople, served as transshipment points for goods traveling between China and Rome. This trade aided some societies. For example, Nabataean Arabs constructed a trade network linking Egypt, western Asia, and southern Europe, while the Sogdians dominated Central Asian trading cities and even had communities in western China. Chinese sources described the Sogdians as trained for trade: "At birth honey was put in their mouths and gum on their hands. They learned the trade from the age of five. On reaching twelve they were sent to do business in a neighboring state."[12]

Maritime trade also flourished during this period, enriching various ports. Hence, both trade goods and cultural influences were carried by sea between eastern and western Asia. Sailing networks connected the entire Mediterranean Basin. For several centuries one key network hub was the tiny Greek island of Delos (DEH-los) in the Aegean Sea, of which it was said, "Merchant, sail in and unload! Everything is as good as sold."[13] Merchants from all over, including Greeks from around the Mediterranean, Romans, Syrians, Jews, Phoenicians, Nabataean Arabs, and Yemenite Arabs, flocked to Delos to trade. Maritime counterparts to the overland trade diaspora of the Sogdians developed. For example, a Jewish trading community sunk roots in southwest India, Indian merchants settled in Funan (Cambodia), Indonesians and Arabs sailed to East Africa to trade or settle, and Greeks established communities all over the Mediterranean and Black Sea Basins.

Eventually a vast maritime route linked China, Vietnam, and Cambodia in the East through Malaya and the Indonesian archipelago to India and Sri Lanka, and then stretched westward to Persia, Arabia, and the East African coast. Europe and North Africa were connected to this system through the Arabs, Aksumites, and Persians. The Greek geographer Strabo wrote that since merchants from Roman-ruled Alexandria had sent trading fleets to India, "these regions have become better known to us today."[14] Some cities flourished as hubs for this maritime trade. For instance, between 100 and 500 C.E. the Egyptian port of Berenike on the Red Sea was regularly visited by ships from India. Products from as far away as Java and Cambodia reached the markets of Berenike, and eleven different written languages, including Greek and Sanskrit, were used there. Berenike was also linked through Alexandria to the Mediterranean societies.

Maritime commerce faced serious limitations, however. Because of formidable currents, only the strongest oars would allow a boat to pass through the Strait of Gibraltar separating Spain from North Africa. This problem inhibited trade between Mediterranean and Atlantic societies for many centuries. Similarly, the vast distances of the Pacific Ocean, crossed in that day only by outrigger canoes, limited the volume and type of goods carried along the trading networks there. Some people, using balsa rafts, traded along the Pacific Coast of South and Central America, while others used canoes to travel between Caribbean islands, but the volume and frequency of such maritime trade remain unclear.

Social Systems and Attitudes

The social systems and attitudes of the Classical Era set the patterns for centuries to come. In many places gender roles hardened. For example, in Greece and China, customs and laws allowed men far greater social freedom than women. Because the great empires were made through military conquest, they were very masculine in nature. In addition, patriarchal attitudes were encouraged by some of the new philosophies and religions. For example, Confucianism gave power to older men, and influential Christian leaders urged women to stay in the background. In addition, the faiths that replaced Greek and Roman religions removed goddesses as objects of worship in the Mediterranean world, although in southern Asia many Hindus continued to revere female deities.

Homosexuality existed in all classical societies and was generally tolerated in some, especially in Greece and Rome. Chinese historians reported that many emperors of the era, including the empire-builder Wu Di of the Han dynasty, had male lovers in addition to their wives and concubines. The Han era historian Sima Qian wrote numerous biographies of those men "who served the ruler and succeeded in delighting his ears and eyes, [winning] his favor and intimacy."[15] Chinese also tolerated lesbian relationships among women in polygamous households. But in many places official attitudes concerning gender roles and sexual behaviors became more rigid over time, pushing homosexuals to the margins of society.

Changing social and religious attitudes affected women. Although women had some legal protections in Greece and Rome, many also lived generally domestic and often secluded lives. For instance, when Roman women in 195 B.C.E. took to the streets to protest a law, passed during a costly war, that limited the amount of gold and finery a woman could wear, many men complained that women should stay home and out of politics. A Roman politician noted that "women cannot partake of [local office], priesthoods, [military] triumphs, badges of office, or spoils of war; elegance, finery and beautiful clothes are women's badges; in these they find joy and take pride."[16] Women faced increasing restrictions in China and north India, where they were expected to be obedient to men. Patriarchy was also common in Africa, the Americas, and the Pacific islands. While there were notable exceptions, the leaders in Aksum and in the Maya city-states were mostly men.

But wherever they lived, women had varied experiences. Some were treated as property, assigned by their fathers to husbands, and many faced permanent dependency on fathers, husbands, and sons. But those who were well loved by male relatives could perhaps gain substantial personal advantages. Only a small minority of women anywhere were educated, Hypatia of Alexandria and Ban Zhao in China being notable examples. However, a few, such as Queen Zenobia in Palmyra, Cleopatra VII in Egypt, Queen Theodora in Byzantium, and several Kushite queens, attained great power. Some women asserted their own interests, a behavior reflected in some Greek plays. Thus, in *Antigone* (an-TIG-on-ee) by Sophocles, the main female character defies King Creon, who refuses to allow her to give her dead brother the proper burial.

Like patriarchy, slavery was practiced in many classical societies around the world. Most people saw slavery as a part of the natural order of things and essential to economic life. Slaves everywhere were bought and sold at the whim of the owner, and their lives and labor were controlled. Most slaves were poor, but not all lived in misery. Some Greek and Roman slaves held high positions in society or were attached to prosperous families. In societies such as Han China, Mauryan India, Aksum, and the Maya society, slaves were only one segment of the lower class, whereas in Greece and Rome slaves constituted a large part of the population and were used in every area of the economy, from mining and construction to prostitution and domestic work. For example, in Rome it was chiefly slaves who built the Colisseum, the Forum, and the great aqueducts that so impress modern tourists. Slavery mostly died out in China and India during the first millennium C.E. and became less important in Europe after the collapse of the Roman Empire, showing that societies do change, often dramatically, over time.

SUGGESTED READING

BOOKS

Adas, Michael, ed. *Agricultural and Pastoral Societies in Ancient and Classical History*. Philadelphia: Temple University Press, 2001. A useful collection of essays on various topics.

Bentley, Jerry H. *Old World Encounters: Cross-Cultural Contacts and Exchanges in Pre-Modern Times*. New York: Oxford University Press, 1993. An up-to-date survey of trade routes and the spread of universal religions.

Bulliet, Richard W. *The Camel and the Wheel*. Cambridge: Harvard University Press, 1975. A classic study of the caravan trade in Asia and Africa.

Curtin, Philip D. *Cross-Cultural Trade in World History*. Cambridge; Cambridge University Press, 1984. Contains much material on long-distance trade in the Classical Era.

Fernandez-Armesto, Felipe. *Civilizations: Culture, Ambition, and the Transformation of Nature*. New York: Touchstone, 2001. A fascinating and wide-ranging survey across eras and regions that emphasizes adaptations to varied environments.

Foltz, Richard C. *Religions of the Silk Road: Overland Trade and Cultural Exchange from Antiquity to the Fifteenth Century*. New York: St. Martin's, 1999. Analyzes the spread of religions.

Lloyd, Geoffrey, and Nathan Sivin. *The Way and the Word: Science and Medicine in Early China and Greece*. New Haven, Conn.: Yale University Press, 2003. Compares these two great traditions of learning, arguing that modern science derives from both as well as from Indian, Islamic, and other cultures.

McClellan, James, and Harold Dorn. *Science and Technology in World History: An Introduction*. Baltimore: Johns Hopkins University Press, 1999. A survey of science and technology traditions.

Pearson, Michael. *The Indian Ocean*. New York: Routledge, 2003. A history of the maritime connections.

Prazniak, Roxann. *Dialogues Across Civilizations: Sketches in World History from the Chinese and European Experiences*. Boulder: Westview, 1996. Contains interesting comparative essays.

Smart, Ninian. *The Long Search*. Boston: Little, Brown and Co., 1977. A very readable introduction to the various universal religious traditions of Eurasia and their modern offshoots.

Super, John C. and Brian K. Turley. *Religion in World History*. New York: Routledge, 2006. Brief study of religious diffusion and change.

Wood, Frances. *The Silk Road*. Berkeley: University of California Press, 2002. Surveys 2000 years of history.

WEBSITES

Ancient and Lost Civilizations (http://www.crystalinks.com/ancient.html). Contains essays and other materials on ancient and classical societies.

Exploring Ancient World Cultures (http://eawc.evansville.edu). A very helpful collection of essays and other useful material.

Internet Ancient History Sourcebook (http://www.fordham.edu/halsall/ancient/asbook.html). An exceptionally rich collection of links and primary source readings.

Monks and Merchants (http://www.asiasociety.org/arts/monksandmerchants/index/html). Interesting essays, timelines, maps, and images for an Asia Society exhibition on the Silk Road as a zone of communication.

Silk Road Narratives (http://depts.washington.edu/uwch/silkroad/texts/texts.html). Explores cultural interaction in Eurasia through excerpts from Silk Road travelers.

PART III

Expanding Horizons: Encounters and Transformations in the Intermediate Era, ca. 600–1500

By 600 C.E. most of the great classical Eastern Hemisphere empires and states, such as Rome, Han China, Gupta India, and Kush, were only memories. The classical American societies, such as the Maya, were to flourish a few centuries longer, only to collapse. Yet vigorous new societies were emerging. Even while some classical patterns hung on or were modified to suit new needs, the Afro-Eurasian zone was in transition. During this era many societies developed a more cosmopolitan outlook. New trade networks emerged and old ones were revitalized. Though characterized by long periods of conflict, this era also saw worldwide innovations.

Historians disagree as to what this era should be called. Borrowing from European history, scholars often refer to the medieval period, a "middle ages" stretching from around 600 to 1500. The term *medieval* suggests societies with relatively weak governments, rigid social orders, and one dominating religion, a description that best fits Europe in this era and perhaps Japan and parts of India. However, the term has little relevance for China, the Islamic states, and most of Africa, Southeast Asia, and the Americas. *Intermediate Era* is a more neutral term to describe this creative transitional period, which linked the Classical Era, when contacts between distant societies were still limited, with the rise of global connections that marked the centuries after 1500.

The Intermediate Era experienced dramatic transformations of societies. The explosive rise of Islam from a local faith in Arabia in the early 600s to a hemispheric-wide religion by 1400 was one of the main transitions. The resurgence of China as a political, economic, and cultural force was another. Also during this time, Buddhism became a major influence in the eastern half of Eurasia, while Christianity became Europe's dominant faith. Mighty empires arose in Africa, Southeast Asia, and the Americas.

These nine centuries also differed from the preceding Classical Era by virtue of the increasing contacts between peoples. Contacts became more frequent and substantial beginning around 600. New interregional communications took place across Afro-Eurasia, including trade, cultural exchange, and religious links. As a result, a maritime trading network connected China and Southeast Asia

Sape Ivory Saltholder Africans had traded and carved ivory since ancient times. This magnificent ivory carving, made, probably in the fifteenth century, by an artist of the Sape people, who lived in what is today Sierra Leone in West Africa, was used to store salt. The carving reflected artistic influence brought to the region by the earliest Portuguese explorers and traders. (Courtesy, Museo Prehistorico et Etnografico, Rome)

through India and the Persian Gulf to East Africa and the Mediterranean. A growing caravan trade across the Sahara Desert brought West Africa and the Mediterranean closer together. The spread of religions also reshaped societies. For example, Arab culture expanded with Islam. The cosmopolitan Islamic world, stretching from Morocco to Indonesia, enjoyed much cultural diversity but also shared many beliefs and practices. In the Western Hemisphere, Mesoamerican cultural and agricultural influences spread deep into North and Central America.

The era was also marked by conflicts that changed societies. Spurring the rise of interregional encounters was the expansion of several Central Asian peoples. Turkish migrations and conquests in western Asia occurred throughout the period. In the thirteenth century the Mongols conquered the largest land empire in world history, stretching from Korea and China westward to Russia and eastern Europe, a momentous achievement with major consequences. For example, as a result, East Asian technology flowed along the trade routes to Europe. However, the Mongol period also witnessed the spread along these same trade routes of a catastrophic plague, known as the Black Death, that devastated societies all across Eurasia and North Africa, killing countless millions of Chinese, Persians, Arabs, and Europeans.

The Intermediate years also saw major innovations such as economic growth, technological change, the rise of new states, and maritime exploration. China became the world's most commercialized and industrialized society, often exercising influence far from its borders. In the 1400s Chinese maritime expeditions reached East Africa and the Persian Gulf. Islamic states were also dynamic, and Muslim scholars and artisans made numerous contributions to the world. West African kingdoms, East African coastal cities, and Southeast Asian states were closely tied to world trade. In the Americas, the Aztec and Inca Empires had arisen on the foundations of earlier societies. Europeans made key intellectual and technological discoveries, and they also benefited when the expansion of Islam and the Mongols introduced to Europe Asian-derived ideas, plants, and tools. In the 1400s, making good use of naval technology and weaponry from all over Eurasia and energized by economic growth and religious fervor, Europeans began voyages of discovery that set the stage for connecting the entire world after 1500.

NORTH AND CENTRAL AMERICA
The Maya city-states flourished for centuries until the cities were abandoned. The Toltecs dominated central Mexico for two hundred years. In the 1400s the Aztecs conquered a large empire in Mexico and built a huge capital city. North of Mexico, societies such as the Anasazi lived in towns and farmed in the desert for centuries. To the east the Mississippian peoples built mounds and a grand city while trading over a vast area. Farming villages also dotted the east coast.

SOUTH AMERICA
For most of the era Tiwanaku, in the Andes, and the Chimu Empire, based on the Peruvian coast, were the dominant powers in western South America. In the 1400s the Incas conquered most of the region, creating the largest empire in the history of the Americas. Skilled farmers, the Incas used a powerful but paternalistic state to rule millions of people.

EUROPE

In western Europe a rigid society, dominated by a powerful Christian church, slowly emerged, reaching its zenith around 1000 C.E. Dozens of small rival states fought each other. Urban and commercial growth, technological innovation, and the Black Death eventually undermined feudalism and church power, and political, intellectual, artistic, and religious change began reshaping western Europe in the 1400s. At the same time, imported Chinese and Arab naval and military technology helped spur maritime explorations. Meanwhile, Byzantium struggled to hold its eastern Mediterranean empire but also spread its culture to the Russians.

WESTERN ASIA

The rise of Islam in Arabia in the 600s transformed the region. Arab Muslim armies conquered much of western Asia, and most of the region's peoples eventually embraced Islam. Islam also spread west through North Africa and into Spain, as well as east to India, Central Asia, and Indonesia, linking western Asians with a vast Islamic community. Islam divided into rival Sunni and Shi'a schools. Muslim scholars fostered science and literature, and major Islamic states, especially the Abbasid Empire, dominated the region. Eventually the Ottoman Turks formed the most powerful western Asian state, conquering Byzantium.

EASTERN ASIA

China stood out for its influence and creativity. During the Tang and Song dynasties, China's economy grew rapidly and science flourished, attracting merchants and scholars from many countries. At the same time, Chinese cultural influences spread to neighboring Korea, Japan, and Vietnam. Under Mongol rule, China remained open to the world, but it later turned inward. Meanwhile, Japanese and Koreans combined Chinese influences, such as Buddhism, with their own traditions.

ARCTIC OCEAN

RUSSIA

ENGLAND

EUROPE

FRANCE
Danube

SPAIN

BYZANTIUM

OTTOMAN
EMPIRE

MOROCCO

*ABBASIDS
(IRAQ)*

EGYPT
Nile

ARABIA

*MONGOLS
(MONGOLIA)*

ASIA

JAPAN

CHINA

H I M A L A Y A S

Ganges R.

INDIA   PAGAN

Mekong R.

VIETNAM

ANGKOR

MALI

Niger R.

AFRICA

BENIN

Congo R.

KONGO

SWAHILI

INDIAN OCEAN

INDONESIA

ATLANTIC
OCEAN

ZIMBABWE

AUSTRALIA

AFRICA

Islam swept across North Africa, becoming the dominant religion north of the Sahara. It also reshaped societies as it spread into West Africa and East Africa. Sub-Saharan African peoples formed large empires, such as Mali, and flourishing states, such as Benin, Kongo, and Zimbabwe. West African kingdoms and East African coastal cities were closely tied to world trade. In the 1400s the Portuguese explored the West African coast and disrupted African states.

SOUTHERN ASIA AND OCEANIA

Although politically fragmented into diverse rival states, India remained a major commercial and manufacturing center. Muslims from West and Central Asia conquered parts of north India, spreading Islam there. In response, Hinduism became reinvigorated. Southeast Asians flourished from farming and maritime trade, and major kingdoms, notably Angkor and Pagan, emerged. Southeast Asians imported ideas from India, China, and the Middle East, and many people adopted Theravada Buddhism or Islam. Maritime trade, especially the export of spices, and the spread of Islam and Buddhism linked Southeast Asia to the wider Afro-Eurasian world. Meanwhile, Polynesians settled the last uninhabited Pacific islands, including Hawaii and New Zealand.

CHAPTER **10**

The Rise, Power, and Connections of the Islamic World, 600–1500

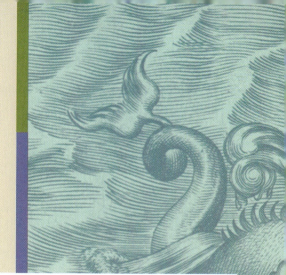

CHAPTER OUTLINE

- Early Islam: The Origins of a Continuous Tradition
- Arab Expansion and the Spread of Islam
- Early Islamic States and Empires
- Cultural Hallmarks of Islam: Theology, Society, and Science
- Globalized Islam and Middle Eastern Political Change

■ **PROFILE**
Ibn Battuta, a Muslim Traveler

■ **WITNESS TO THE PAST**
The Holy Book, God, and the Prophet in the Quran

Online Study Center

This icon will direct you to interactive activities and study materials on the website: college.hmco.com/pic/lockard1e

Pilgrimage Caravan Every year caravans of Muslim pilgrims converged on Islam's holiest city, Mecca, in Arabia. This painting shows such a caravan led by a band. Pilgrims came from as far away as Morocco and Spain in the west and Indonesia and China in the east. (Bibliotheque nationale de France)

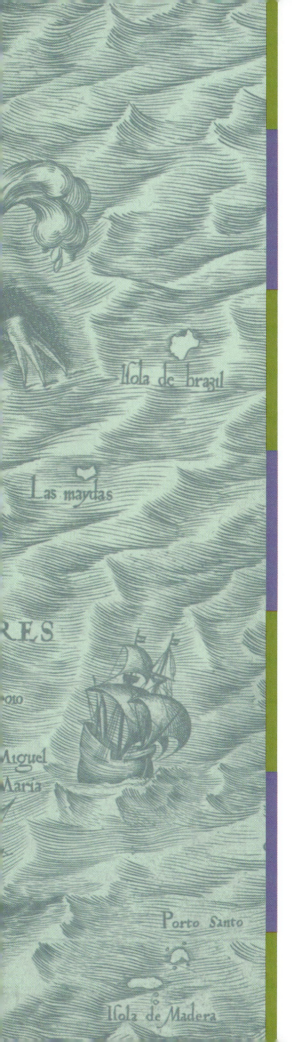

> *Then came Islam. All institutions underwent change. It distinguished [believers] from other nations and ennobled them. Islam became firmly established and securely rooted. Far-off nations accepted Islam.*
>
> IBN KHALDUN, FOURTEENTH-CENTURY ARAB HISTORIAN[1]

In 1382 the author of these words on history, the fifty-year-old Arab scholar Abd al-Rahman Ibn Khaldun (AHB-d al-ruh-MAHN ib-uhn kal-DOON), left his longtime home in Tunis in North Africa and moved east to Egypt. He was already a well-traveled man and renowned as a thinker, and his work, like his life, reflected the expansive cosmopolitan nature of Islamic society, which crossed many geographical and cultural borders. After seven years of research and writing he had recently completed his greatest work, a monumental history of the world known to educated Muslims. While writing this work, he said, ideas and words poured into his head like cream into a churn. The book was the first attempt by a historian anywhere to discover and explain the changes in societies over time, especially those shaped by Islam. Rational, analytical, and encyclopedic in coverage, it also offered a philosophy of history rooted in the scientific method.

Ibn Khaldun came from an Islamic family with ancient roots in Arabia that had later settled in Spain. Several generations later they relocated across the Mediterranean to Tunis. After growing up there, Ibn Khaldun visited and worked in various cities of North Africa and Spain. He served diverse rulers as a jurist, adviser, or diplomat. Now he was settling finally in Cairo (KYE-roh), Egypt, a city he praised as the "metropolis of the world, garden of the universe, meeting-place of nations, ant hill of peoples, high place of Islam, seat of power."[2] Cairo remained his home for the rest of his life as he served as a judge and a teacher, reading, writing voluminously, and traveling with high Egyptian officials to Palestine, Syria, and Arabia. Six centuries after his family left Arabia for the western Mediterranean, he could visit their ancestral homeland and feel at home. The Islamic world he chronicled enjoyed an extraordinary unity of time and space.

The rise of Islam that produced Ibn Khaldun and his world was a major historical turning point that led to widespread social, cultural, and political changes over the centuries. The Islamic religion originated in seventh-century Arabia and eventually spread across several continents. Today Islam is, after Christianity, the largest religion in the world, embraced by about one-fifth of the world's population. The impact of Islam on a multitude of societies and networks was complex and varied. A dynamic faith, Islam adapted to new cultures while remaining close to its founding ideals. It also had extensive dialogue with, and often tolerance toward, other traditions, establishing contacts that enriched both sides. For nearly a thousand years Islamic peoples greatly influenced or dominated much of the Eastern Hemisphere. Muslim thinkers salvaged or developed major portions of the science and mathematics that formed the basis for later industrial society, and Muslim sailors and merchants opened or extended networks that spread goods, technologies, and ideas throughout Afro-Eurasia.

FOCUS QUESTIONS

1. How did Islam arise?
2. How did Islam shape a distinctive new society from diverse sources?
3. What were the major achievements of the Islamic states and empires?
4. What were the major concerns of Muslim thinkers and writers?
5. Why do historians speak of Islam as a hemispheric culture?

Early Islam: The Origins of a Continuous Tradition

How did Islam arise?

The Islamic religion was founded in the seventh century in the Arabian peninsula, a land inhabited mainly by nomads who lived on the fringes of more powerful societies. A fervently monotheistic faith influenced by Jewish and Christian thought, Islam was inspired by the visions of a single influential man, Muhammad (moo-HAM-mad). His followers considered him to be the last of God's prophets. Islam quickly developed explosive energies that propelled it from a small Arab sect into the dominant faith of many millions of people from one end of the Eastern Hemisphere to the other.

The Middle Eastern Sources of Islam

Islam developed in a part of the Middle East known as Arabia, which occupies a peninsula in southwestern Asia. Much of the Middle East, including Arabia, is a harsh, parched land that provides a challenging environment for human settlement. Living by farming or herding, the region's peoples tamed camels, horses, donkeys, and cattle to lighten the agricultural labors or help merchants cross the deserts.

In Muhammad's day the Middle East was a region of great cultural diversity, a major factor in the rise of Islam. The peoples of Egypt, Mesopotamia, and Achaemenid Persia had produced flourishing societies in ancient times. Later the Hellenistic Greeks had conquered much of western Asia and Egypt, and later still the Byzantine Empire filled the vacuum left by the collapse of Roman control in western Asia and North Africa. Between 611 and 619 Sassanian Persia conquered Syria, Palestine, and Egypt,, and during the sixth century the

Persians, Byzantines, and Ethiopians all interfered in Arabian politics. By the end of the Classical Era many Middle Eastern people were Christians, including sects such as the Monophysites (among them the Copts of Egypt) and Nestorians, which were considered heretical by orthodox Christians. These diverse traditions eventually influenced Islam.

Islam was also the product of a distinctive Arab culture and society. The Arabs, a Semitic people, occupied the desolate Arabian peninsula, where life was sustained by scattered oases and a few areas of fertile highlands. Survival in a sparsely populated environment depended on cooperation within small groups of related peoples divided into clans and tribes. Each tribe was usually governed by a council of senior males, who selected a supreme elder respected for his generosity and bravery. Some Arabs, like the Nabataeans, became traders who ranged widely in the Middle East, and Arab trading cities and farmers flourished in Yemen in the south. But many Arab tribes were tent-dwelling nomadic pastoralists, known as **Bedouins** (BED-uh-wuhnz), who wandered in search of oases and grazing lands. Some resorted at times to raiding trade caravans.

Arab culture and literature reflected the nomadic existence of many Arabs. A pre-Muslim Arab poet wrote: "Ah, but when grief assails me, straightway I ride it off mounted on my swift, lean-flanked camel, night and day racing."[3] Poetry was so popular that, one month a year, raids and battles were halted so that poets could gather and compete. The Arab romantic poetry tradition may have been taken to Europe centuries later by Christian crusaders, and there it may have influenced the chivalric love songs of medieval European performers known as troubadours.

Arabia was saturated with ideas from diverse religious traditions, including Judaism, Christianity, and Zoroastrianism. Like their Hebrew neighbors, the Arabs believed that they were

---

Bedouins   Tent-dwelling nomadic Arab pastoralists who wandered in search of oases, grazing lands, or trade caravans to raid.

CHRONOLOGY

	Middle East	Europe	Central Asia
600	**622** Hijra of Muhammad to Medina **634–651** Arab conquests in Middle East **632–661** Rashidun Caliphate **661–750** Umayyad Caliphate		
700	**750–1258** Abbasid Caliphate	**711–1492** Muslim states in Spain	**705–715** Islamic Conquests
1000		**1096–1272** Christian Crusades in Middle East	
1200			**1218–1360** Mongol conquests in Central and western Asia
1300		**1300–1923** Ottoman Empire	**1369–1405** Reign of Tamerlane

descended from Abraham, but through his son Ishmael, not Issac, as the Hebrews claimed to be. While some Arabs had adopted Judaism or Christianity, and some practiced a monotheism similar to that of the ancient Hebrews, most were polytheistic, believing in many gods, goddesses, and spirits. Some tribes believed that the chief god was housed in a huge sacred cube-shaped stone, known as the **Ka'ba** (KAH-buh), in Mecca (MEK-uh), a bustling trading city in central Arabia near the Red Sea to which people made annual pilgrimages. Meccan merchants obtained hides, leather goods, spices, and perfumes in Yemen and exchanged them in Syria for textiles, olive oil, and weapons.

The Prophet Muhammad and His Revelations

The founder of Islam was Muhammad Ibn Abdullah (ca. 570–632). Historians debate the origins of all the major religions, and Islam is no exception. Just as historians disagree with each other about the accuracy of the historical accounts contained in the Hebrew Bible and the Christian gospels, and lack adequate sources to trace fully the lives of the Buddha and Confucius, there is controversy, especially among non-Muslim scholars, concerning Muhammad's life, how much Islamic thought arose out of older ideas, and the factors that shaped the expansion of the Arabs and Islam. The sources available for understanding early Judaism, Christianity, and Islam were compiled decades, sometimes centuries, after the events described,

Ka'ba A huge sacred cube-shaped stone in the city of Mecca to which people made annual pilgrimages.

and can be interpreted by historians in different ways, fostering disagreement.

According to the traditional accounts by both Muslim and Western historians, Muhammad was a member of the Hashimite (HASH-uh-mite) clan of the prosperous mercantile Quraysh (KUR-aysh) tribe of Mecca (see Chronology: The Islamic World, 570–1220). His father died before his birth and his mother died when he was six, so he was raised by an uncle. After becoming a merchant, Muhammad began shipping goods for a wealthy and prominent twice-widowed older woman, Khadija (kah-DEE-juh), who had capitalized on the opportunities that city life sometimes gave ambitious women. They soon married. Although Muhammad's business operating trade caravans flourished, he came to believe that Meccan merchants had become greedy and materialistic, contrary to Arab traditions of generosity.

In seeking answers to his concerns, Muhammad often retreated to meditate in the barren mountains around Mecca. His prophetic career began in 610 when he had a series of visions in the mountains in which he believed God revealed the secrets of existence. He reported that he was visited by an angel, who brought the command from God to "recite in the name of your lord who created the human."[4] Alarmed, he consulted one of his wife's cousins, a monotheist who encouraged him to accept the visions he received as revelations, or messages, from God. Fearing that he was possessed by demons, Muhammad often agonized about the visions, once even reaching a state of suicidal despair. The spiritual experiences continued over the next twenty-three years.

However, Muhammad eventually came to accept the authenticity of the messages, largely because of the support given by his wife Khadija, his closest spiritual adviser: "She believed in me when no one else did. She considered me to be truthful when the people called me a liar. She helped me with her fortune when the people had left me nothing."[5] Once convinced of the messages' truth, Muhammad began preaching the new

CHRONOLOGY

The Islamic World, 570–1220

ca. 570	Birth of Muhammad in Mecca
622	Hijra of Muhammad and followers to Medina
632	Death of Muhammad; Abu Bakr becomes first caliph
634	Muslim conquests begin
632–661	Rashidun Caliphate
636–637	Arab military victories over Byzantine and Sassanian forces
642	Arab conquest of Egypt
651	Completion of Arab conquest of Persia
661	Murder of Ali and establishment of Umayyad dynasty in Damascus
705–715	Arab conquests of Afghanistan and Central Asia
711–720	Arab conquest of Spain
732	European defeat of Arabs at Battle of Tours
750	Abbasid defeat of Umayyads and new caliphate
756–1030	Umayyad dynasty in Spain
825–900	Arab conquest of Sicily
969–1171	Fatimid dynasty in Egypt and neighboring areas
1061–1091	Norman conquest of Sicily from Arabs
1071	Beginning of Seljuk Turk conquest of Anatolia
1085	Spanish Christian seizure of Umayyad capital
1095–1272	Christian Crusades in western Asia and North Africa
1171–1193	Reign of Saladin in Egypt
1220	Beginning of Mongol conquests in Muslim Central Asia

faith of *Islam* ("submission to God's will") to a few followers. The early believers, or *Muslims* (MUZ-limz) ("those who had submitted to God's will"), were mostly drawn from among his middle-class friends and relatives and a few other Meccans, some from lower-class backgrounds. Gradually some rich members of the Quraysh tribe also joined.

In the 650s, several decades after Muhammad's death, his followers compiled his revelations into an official version, the **Quran** (kuh-RAHN), meaning "Recitation." The Quran, beloved by Muslims for its beautiful poetic verses, became Islam's holiest book, to believers the inspired word of God. A second book revered by many Muslims as a source of belief, the **Hadith** (hah-DEETH), meaning "narrative," compiled by Muslim scholars into an official version during the ninth and tenth centuries, collected the remembered words and deeds of Muhammad himself. A source of religious guidance and law, the Hadith helped explain the principles of the Quran.

Muhammad insisted that he was human, not divine, and his followers accepted him as a prophet rather than as a manifestation of God. To believers, Muhammad's visions were the last of several occasions in history during which God spoke to prophets, communicating through them from the divine to the human realm. The earlier prophets were Adam, Abraham, Moses, and Jesus, and Muhammad was considered the final voice superseding the others (see Witness to the Past: The Holy Book, God, and the Prophet in the Quran).

Muhammad's faith mixed older traditions with new understandings. Both Jews and Christians lived in Mecca, and many of the principal ideas of Islam clearly resemble some Judeo-Christian traditions. Like these traditions, Muhammad's views were strictly monotheistic. All other gods were put aside, and believers were assured of an afterlife. In contrast to the social customs dominant in Arabia at the time of Muhammad, Islam guaranteed women certain rights formerly denied them and promoted the equality of all believers. Muhammad also advocated sharing all wealth, living simply, and creating a spirit of unity. In Islam, Muhammad established principles of equality and justice.

Emigration and Triumph

Muhammad soon faced challenges that led him to leave Mecca. His ideas earned him some enemies among the Quraysh and divided the tribe, and the Mecca leaders rejected Muhammad's views and saw him and his followers as a threat to their position. He and his allies were harassed, and some enemies even plotted his murder. In 619 Khadija died, followed by the uncle who raised him, an influential tribal chief. The loss of his two most powerful supporters left Muhammad in despair. Meanwhile, the nearby city of Medina became engulfed in strife. To

Quran ("Recitation") Islam's holiest book; contains the official version of Muhammad's revelations, and to believers is the inspired word of God.

Hadith ("narrative") The remembered words and deeds of Muhammad, revered by many Muslims as a source of belief.

The Holy Book, God, and the Prophet in the Quran

The Quran is organized according to the length of individual chapters, so that early and later revelations are mixed together. That is, it does not follow a rigid organization of thoughts. In addition, the beauty of the powerful, poetic writing style is not always apparent in English translation, where most of the nuances of the Arabic language are lost. In Arabic the Quran clearly comes across as both a scripture and an elegant literature that has inspired millions. The following brief excerpts present some basic ideas about the holy book itself, the unity and power of the monotheistic God, and the recognition of Muhammad as a human prophet or apostle to God.

In the name of the Merciful and Compassionate God. That is the Book! There is no doubt therein; a guide to the pious, who believe in the unseen, and are steadfast in prayer, and of what we have given them expend in alms; who believe in what is revealed to thee, and what was revealed before thee, and of the hereafter they are sure. These are in guidance from their Lord, and these are the prosperous. . . .

God, there is no god but He, the living, the self-subsistent. Slumber takes Him not, nor sleep. His is what is in the heavens and what is in the earth. Who is it that intercedes with Him save by His permission? He knows what is before them and what behind them, and they comprehend not aught of His knowledge but of what He pleases. His throne extends over the heavens and the earth, and it tires him not to guard them both, for He is high and grand. . . . On Him is the call of truth, and those who call on others than Him shall not be answered at all, save as one who stretches out his hand to the water that it may reach his mouth, but it reaches it not! The call of the misbelievers is always in error. . . . In the name of the Merciful and Compassionate God, Say "He is God alone!"

Muhammad is but an apostle; apostles have passed away before his time; what if he die or is killed, will ye retreat upon your heels? He who retreats upon his heels does no harm to God at all; but God will recompense the thankful. . . . Muhammad is not the father of any of your men, but the Apostle of God, and the Seal of the Prophets; for God all things doth know!

THINKING ABOUT THE READING

1. What is the purpose of the Quran?
2. What are the powers of God?
3. What is the relationship between Muhammad and God?

Source: Excerpts taken from Chapters 2, 3, 13, and 33 of the Quran, as reprinted in L. S. Stavrianos, ed., *The Epic of Man to 1500* (Englewood Cliffs, N.J.: Prentice-Hall, 1970), pp. 210–211.

---

find a solution, the contending factions invited Muhammad, respected for his fairness and honesty, to come to Medina and arbitrate their disputes.

Muhammad's life changed when he accepted the offer and moved to Medina. In 622 Muhammad led seventy Muslims and their families from Mecca to Medina, an event known as the **hijra** (HIJ-ruh), or "emigration." Hence, to believers, 622, which begins the Muslim calendar, represents humanity's response to God's message. In Medina the Muslims sought to form a new community of believers, or **umma,** united around God's message. Many of the Medinans came to accept Muhammad as the true Prophet, and he built his first mosque for worship and prayers. In achieving that religious status, Muhammad was aided by his forceful personality and leadership. He also used a wise strategy of tolerating differences. For example, he accommodated Jews by respecting the stories of their past prophets.

Some historians argue that the boundaries between Muslims and Jews were not clearly defined at this time, suggesting that Muhammad saw himself as part of the Jewish prophetic tradition. They note that some late-seventh-century Christian observers outside of Arabia described Muhammad as the leader of a Jewish sect. Muslim historians generally view such accounts as mistaken. Furthermore, Muhammad also said that the original Jewish and Christian teachings had been distorted by these religions' followers. Whatever his views on the older monotheistic faiths, in Medina Muhammad also took new wives. Because frequent warfare and raiding killed off many men, Arab men often had several wives so they could protect vulnerable women and procreate more children. Concerned for the welfare of women without husbands, Muhammad urged his men to marry widows, who had no protection or support. He also required that all wives be treated equally and fairly.

Muhammad's growing popularity earned him more enemies. For example, while some Medina Jews became allies, others mocked his beliefs. Muhammad urged his followers to respect sympathetic Christians and Jews, saying, "Dispute not with the People of the Book. We believe in what has been sent down to us, and what has been sent down to you; our God and your God is One."[6] But, believing he needed strong methods to preserve his umma in Medina, he expelled two Jewish tribes and had all the men of another killed because he suspected

---

hijra The emigration of Muslims from Mecca to Medina in 622.

umma The community of Muslim believers united around God's message.

Muhammad Enters a City in Triumph   Although Islamic custom discourages painting images of the Prophet, Muslim artists, especially Persians and Turks, have done so over the centuries, emphasizing his spiritual qualities and destiny. This painting from an Islamic collection shows Muhammad leading his followers into Mecca for the first time after his exile while an angel on the gate cries, "Thou are the prophet of God."   (Courtesy, Nasser D. Khalili Collection of Islamic Art)

them of aiding his opponents. Muhammad's followers also fought and won various military skirmishes with his Meccan enemies, usually against much larger armies. The Muslims, mostly city-dwellers with urban values, quickly learned desert warfare. Muhammad insisted that war captives be treated decently rather than killed. In general Muhammad was a flexible, pragmatic leader, usually willing to negotiate and compromise rather than shed blood.

Muhammad's brilliant military victories and shrewd diplomacy made him the most powerful man in Arabia. After he was able to visit Mecca again, Muhammad pardoned most of his foes in the city, assumed power, and shared the taxes from trade with those who became Muslim. He then began building a confederacy to extend the influence and range of his umma. Gradually the Bedouin and Quraysh of the region converted to Islam. Muhammad's triumph in Mecca marked a shift of power in central Arabia.

The Appeal of Muhammad's Message

Muhammad's message of monotheism, community, equality, and justice, concepts already familiar to some peoples in the region, proved a powerful attraction because it dissolved social barriers between tribes and encouraged assimilation into a larger spiritual community. In 632, in his last sermon at Mecca, Muhammad told his audience to deal justly with each other, treat women kindly, and consider all Muslims as brothers: "Know that every Muslim is a brother to every other Muslim and that you are now one brotherhood."[7] His message empha-

sized the one and only, all-powerful God, **Allah** (AH-luh). According to the Quran: "He knows what is hidden and what is evident. He is the merciful lord of mercy. There is no God but him. He is the king, the holy, the peace, the faithkeeper, the preserver, the strong, the all-disposing."[8]

Muhammad began delivering his message at a time when social and economic changes were occurring in western Arabia. For several decades Meccan merchants had become more deeply involved in long-distance trade connecting Yemen with Syria. As the result of this trade, some Meccans had become richer and others poorer, an imbalance that led to social instability. But Muhammad, like Jesus of Nazareth six hundred years earlier, emphasized social justice and criticized class divisions between rich and poor, thus winning support among the poor.

A short time after his last sermon at Mecca, Muhammad died at age sixty-two. Islam faced a challenge with his passing. Muhammad had left little guidance on the umma's leadership after his death, and the issue provoked disagreements. The four men closest to him formed a **caliphate** (KAL-uhf-uht), an imperial state headed by an Islamic ruler, or *caliph* (KAL-uhf), considered the designated successor of the Prophet in civil affairs. In the earliest years after the Prophet's death the umma was ruled from Medina by the Arab merchant aristocracy through Muhammad's four consecutive successors, known

---

Allah   To Muslims the one and only, all-powerful God.

caliphate   An imperial state headed by an Islamic ruler, the caliph, considered the designated successor of the Prophet in civil affairs.

later as the Rashidun ("rightly guided") caliphs. These four men in succession constituted the first caliphate (632–661), but disagreements about succession continued.

Islamic Beliefs and Society

Muslims, then as now, considered their faith the last revealed religion, believing that it built on and succeeded Judaism and Christianity. As in Christianity, a strong missionary impulse also formed in the Muslim community. Muslims believed their faith should be shared with all people. But Islam offered more than a theology and a faith: the basic tenets of the religion provided a framework for a new worldview that changed history. Most influential was a sense of community in the wider brotherhood of believers.

The Beliefs of Islam Believers have clear duties, known as the five pillars. These include, first, the profession of faith. Theologically the religion is blunt: "There is no God but Allah and Muhammad is his messenger." Although Muhammad is not considered divine, he is believed to be a teacher chosen by God to spread the truth of the universe, including that of a monotheistic God said to be eternal, all powerful, all knowing, and all merciful. Second is the formal worship, which has to be performed with words and action five times daily as the worshiper faces toward Mecca. The third pillar requires giving assistance to the poor and disadvantaged, for which Muslims are expected to donate a tenth of their wealth. Muslims believe that such giving also benefits the giver. The fourth pillar, the annual fast or **Ramadan** (RAM-uh-dahn), lasts thirty days, during which time Muslims have to abstain from eating, drinking, and having sex during daylight hours, to demonstrate sacrifice for their faith and understand the hunger of the poor. The abstinence, however, is supported by lively gatherings of families and friends just before sunrise and then again following sunset. Finally, if possible, at least once in their lives believers make a pilgrimage, or **haj** (HAJ), to the holy city of Mecca, where they worship with multitudes of other believers from around the world. Among other spiritual activities, pilgrims circle the great Ka'ba shrine, as Arabs had done before Islam.

Islam places other demands on believers. A puritanical moral code prohibits adultery, gambling, usury, or the use of intoxicating liquors, the last being an attempt to curb the heavy drinking that was common among Arabs in earlier days. Like Judaism, Islam also has strict dietary laws, including a ban on eating pork. An important concept is the necessity to pursue effort, or **jihad** (ji-HAHD), to live as God intended. Most

perceive this as a spiritual, moral, and intellectual struggle to enhance personal faith and follow the Quran. In recent centuries, however, a minority has reinterpreted jihad as involving military conflict or violent struggle with nonbelievers or enemies, somewhat like the Christian crusading tradition.

Many Islamic beliefs are similar to Judeo-Christian beliefs. For example, Muslims believe in angels, heavenly servants who serve as God's messengers and helpers, and a Devil who flouts God's command. Muslims, like Christians, also anticipate a last judgment, when each individual will be accountable for his or her own actions. The good will attain Heaven, a garden paradise, while the wicked will suffer an eternity in Hell.

Online Study Center **Improve Your Grade**
Primary Source: The Quran: Call for Jihad

Islamic Social Patterns Muslims applied the idea of unity to society, seeking to build a moral and divinely guided community. To ensure moral behavior, Islam regulated how people lived together, and various rules address daily life. Many laws were more humane than those that existed before in the region. In general, people were asked to pursue justice, avoid excesses, and practice mercy.

These ideas influenced gender relations. Most scholars think that Islam improved the position of women in Arab culture. Before Islam, most Arab women had few rights, and many were kept in seclusion. Men took as many wives as they could afford, and women were considered prized booty in raids. Under Islam, men could have up to four wives as long as they could support them and treated them equally, and men had more rights under the divorce and inheritance rules than women. However, women had some legal protection, could own property and engage in business, and were considered partners before God alongside men.

Scholars debate how Muhammad viewed women's roles in society. Muhammad enjoyed the company of women, helped out with household chores, listened with interest when his wives asserted their own opinions, and emphasized that men should treat women kindly. Muhammad had taken more wives after Khadija's death and his favorite wife, A'isha, seems to have played a prominent political role, especially after his death. Muhammad also encouraged female modesty in dress, suggesting that they draw their cloaks about them when they went out. Whether this meant full veiling of the face remains a matter of dispute. Veiling was common in many earlier Middle Eastern societies going back to ancient Mesopotamia. Several generations after Muhammad veiling became expected of devout women. While this enforced modesty has restricted women, many Muslim men and women have believed the custom protects women's dignity and virtue. In practice this also separated the sexes, preventing what most Muslims considered inappropriate romantic entanglements.

Islam also served to protect the freedom to worship as one pleased. Whatever Muhammad's differences with many Medina Jews, Muslims promoted toleration of Christians and Jews as "protected peoples." The Quran stated: "Lo! those who believe [in Islam], and those who are Jews and Christians, whoever

---

Ramadan The thirty days of annual fasting when Muslims abstain from eating, drinking, and sex during daylight hours, to demonstrate sacrifice for their faith and understand the hunger of the poor.

haj The Muslim pilgrimage to the holy city of Mecca to worship with multitudes of other believers from around the world.

jihad Effort to live as God intended; a spiritual, moral and intellectual struggle to enhance personal faith and follow the Quran.

believeth in Allah on the last day and doeth right—surely their reward is with their Lord, and no fear shall come upon them, neither shall they grieve."[9] Furthermore, some Christian groups, angry with the corruption of the Byzantine Empire, aided the Muslim expansion. Many Christians viewed the Arabs as liberators.

SECTION SUMMARY

- Islam was born in Arabia, a harsh land where many people lived in cooperative tribes or clans.

- Islam's holiest book, the Quran, is believed to be a record of the divine revelations of the prophet Muhammad, who is considered the last prophet after Adam, Abraham, Moses, and Jesus.

- Facing some opposition in Mecca and drawn to resolve a dispute in Medina, Muhammad and his followers moved there and won many new converts.

- Muhammad's teachings were monotheistic (like Christianity and Judaism) and emphasized equality and mutual respect among peoples from different tribes.

- Islam is based on the five pillars: profession of faith; formal worship; charity; annual fasting, or Ramadan; and the pilgrimage, or haj, to Mecca.

Arab Expansion and the Spread of Islam

How did Islam shape a distinctive new society from diverse sources?

Within 130 years of Islam's birth, Arab armies and navies had conquered much of the hemisphere from Spain to the Indus River Valley of India, and they had also penetrated India and China, in the process implanting Islam far from its homeland. These conquests and the accompanying spread of the new religion dramatically reshaped many societies across the Afro-Eurasian zone. As part of this great transition, millions of people in the conquered regions adopted Islam. Arab language and culture spread with Islam, providing a new identity for the once diverse Middle Eastern societies. Gradually Islam encompassed many cultures, becoming a global religion.

Arab Conquests and the Making of an Islamic World

The Arabs rapidly expanded from their base in central Arabia. In 634, shortly after the Prophet's death, Muslim armies began their conquest of Iraq, Syria, Palestine, Egypt, and Persia; by 651 they controlled all these areas. Arab ships sailed into the Mediterranean, taking Cyprus (649), Carthage (698), Tunis (TOO-nuhs) (700), and then Spain (711–720). Arab forces also raided southern France, Sicily, Corsica, and Sardinia (sahr-DIN-ee-uh). In 732, exactly a century after the Prophet's death, Islamic expansion in Europe was finally stopped in southern France, at the Battle of Tours (toor), by a combined Christian force led by the Frankish general Charles Martel. Had Arab forces won that conflict, the history of Europe might have been different. Following the armies, Islam, within two centuries, had become the dominant religion in the Middle East and North Africa at the expense of Christianity and Zoroastrianism. In the centuries to follow, Islam spread across the Sahara to West Africa, down the East African coast, and north into Anatolia and then the Balkans.

Arabs also expanded eastward, carrying Islam with them. Arab armies completed the conquest of the Sassanian Empire in Persia in the mid-600s. From there, Muslim navies sailed to western India in 711, conquering Sind (sind) in the lower Indus Basin. Between 705 and 715 Arab armies seized much of Afghanistan and Central Asia (see Map 10.1). By 751 Arab armies had reached the western fringes of the Tang Empire, where they defeated the Chinese in a fierce engagement at the Talas River. This momentous battle blocked Chinese westward expansion and helped turn Central Asian Turks away from China and toward the Islamic world, a decisive turning point. Muslims now controlled most Silk Road network hubs, such as Samarkand and Bukhara. Muslim Arabs were already carrying out seaborne trade with China, and some Arab merchants settled in coastal cities there. In the eleventh century, Muslims began ruling large parts of India. Later, in the fifteenth and sixteenth centuries, Islam spread through the islands of Southeast Asia.

Historians have struggled to explain the energies involved in the rapid Arab expansion. Factors in Arabia, including long-term drought, poverty, and overpopulation, may have provided a spur to seek new lands. Arab leaders may have needed to capture lucrative trade routes and productive lands to obtain more resources to support the growing Islamic umma. In addition, the Byzantine and Sassanian Empires, exhausted from warfare and infighting, made an easy target for conquest. Byzantium was beset by dissent and squabbles over Christian doctrine, while Sassanian Persia faced power struggles and unrest. Furthermore, the Arab fighters were often motivated chiefly by religious faith. Yet, most historians agree that Muslims made no systematic attempt to impose their religion on the conquered, and some suggest that Islam was still not yet clearly differentiated from Judaism and Christianity.

The dynamics within the socially fragile Islamic community itself provided a motive for expansion. Muhammad's death confronted his followers with a crisis, since they had lost their charismatic spiritual leader. Indeed, some began to break away from the faith. Hence, by providing a common cause, war and conquest discouraged members from leaving the community. And warfare capitalized on a long tradition of tribal fighting. Under Muslim direction, Arab armies, though small, were cohesive, mobile, and well led. The methodically planned and well-executed military maneuvers were directed by a central command in Medina.

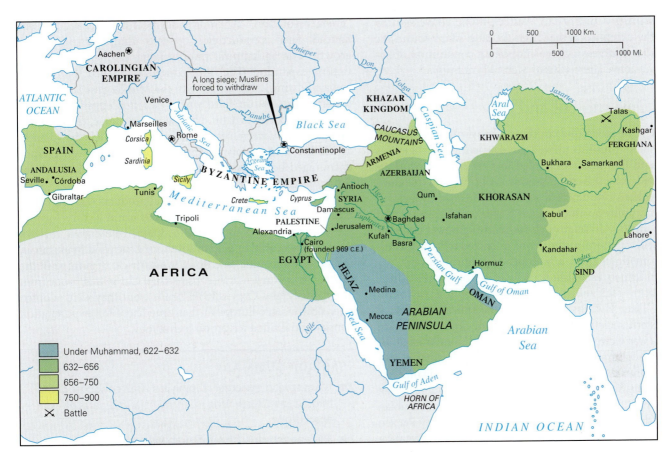

Map 10.1 Expansion of Islam, to 750 C.E.
The Arabs rapidly conquered much of western Asia, North Africa, and Spain, in the process expanding Islam into the conquered territories. By 750 their empire stretched from Morocco and Spain in the west to western India and Central Asia.

Online Study Center **Improve Your Grade** Interactive Map: Expansion of Islam to 732

To prevent the rise of rival factions, Muhammad's first successor, his best friend Abu Bakr (ab-boo BAK-uhr), forbade people from leaving the umma and declared Muhammad God's final prophet. Abu Bakr allied with other tribes, among them nomadic Bedouins. With the often feuding Bedouin tribes united behind the Muslim cause, the Bedouins' fighting spirit could be turned against non-Arab foes. Arab fighters divided up the spoils of conquest, spreading wealth within the community and thus maintaining unity. Sharing the new wealth kept the allegiance of the many Muslims who believed strongly in a radical egalitarianism, including social equality for women, that challenged those with wealth and power.

Arab expansion spread not only Islam but also Arab identity and the Arabic language to many peoples in western Asia and North Africa. This was often a gradual transition. For example, it may have taken three centuries for Arabic to completely replace the Egyptian (Coptic) and Greek languages in Egypt. Adoption of the Arabic language and Islam provided coherence by uniting diverse peoples into one cultural category, transforming many peoples into Arabs.

The Making of a Universal Religion

By the eleventh century Islam had attracted enough followers to become the dominant religion over a wide area of Afro-Eurasia, joining older universal religions such as Buddhism and Christianity. Conversion to Islam was easiest for those peoples whose own cultural ideas, attitudes, and institutions were already similar. Muslims shared animal sacrifice with animists and Zoroastrians, ritual slaughter of food animals and covering heads in worship with Jews, and circumcision with Jews and Christians. The Muslims' month-long fast followed by a festival was common in the region, and their ritual prayer resembled that of Nestorian Christians.

Late-seventh-century Muslims thought of themselves as carriers of a global movement and new religion encompassing many peoples rather than an Arab cult. They ruled over self-governing religious communities of Greek Orthodox Christians, Nestorians, Copts, Zoroastrians, Manicheans, and Jews. Rather than remaining minority rulers over non-Muslim majorities, the Arab Muslims began encouraging conversion and cultural synthesis. Contrary to Western myth, conversion by force was the exception rather than the rule. Many found the religion and the increasingly cosmopolitan community of believers an attractive alternative to their old traditions.

Islamic Government and Law

Muslims developed unique concepts of government and law. In theory many Muslims viewed government and religion as the same, and Islamic states tended to punish those Muslims who violated religious prohibitions. Political and religious power were often combined in a theocracy headed by a caliph or more commonly a **sultan** (SUHLT-uhn), a Muslim ruler of only one country. Although such far-reaching power could be easily abused, the moral authority of respected religious scholars could sometimes check any abuses of political power.

Muslim leaders established a legal code, or **Shari'a** (shah-REE-ah), for the regulation of social and economic as well as religious life. These laws institutionalized the ethical concerns of Middle Eastern societies forged over the previous 3,000 years. Since Islam was viewed as a complete way of life embracing social, political, cultural, and economic activities, the Shari'a provided a comprehensive guide, covering areas such as divorce, inheritance, debts, and morality. It was based chiefly on the Quran and the Hadith. This meant it was also rooted in central Arabian cultural traditions and customs, supplemented later by Persian and Byzantine concepts. But conflicts over the interpretation and application of the Quran led to the rise of several competing interpretative traditions that differed slightly in their emphasis on such tools as reasoning and scriptural authority.

Religious scholars played a major role in elaborating the Shari'a and in sustaining Islamic culture. Some of these scholars were judges, and others served as prayer leaders or preachers in the mosques. Some were trained in state-supported theological schools, others in informal networks of teachers. These scholars' legal decisions and writings provided cohesion and stability over the centuries, independent of the rise and fall of rulers. Muslims valued education based on studying with renowned religious and legal scholars. Their students became teachers. By the tenth century religious boarding schools, known as **madrasas** (muh-DRAH-suhz), headed by a religious scholar, began appearing. Today thousands of these schools can be found all over the Muslim world.

Agricultural Productivity and the Spread of Crops

Between the eighth and thirteenth centuries Islamic societies proved agriculturally innovative, demonstrating an expansion of production that amounted to what we today might call a

"green revolution." By improving diets and health, this enhanced farm productivity spurred dramatic population growth. The agricultural improvement resulted partly from Islamic expansion. The Arab conquests opened the door to India, allowing Arabs to bring to the Middle East South Asian crops such as cotton, hard wheat, rice, and sugar cane; fruits such as the coconut palm, banana, sour orange, lemon, lime, mango, and watermelon; and vegetables such as spinach, artichokes, and eggplant. These imports from wetter lands encouraged better irrigation, including the use of enormous water wheels to supply water.

Indeed, the spread of agricultural products was one of the Islamic peoples' major contributions to world history. Most of these crops filtered westward to Spain, where they thrived. Some crops moved by ship to southern Africa and Madagascar. Cotton became a major crop in West Africa. Beginning in the thirteenth century, many crops reached Christian Europe from Spain, Sicily, and Cyprus (SYE-pruhs), but they were adopted only slowly, since Europe at that time had a lower population density and limited irrigation technology.

SECTION SUMMARY

- Islam spread extremely rapidly via Arab conquest of the Middle East, North Africa, Central Asia, and parts of India and Europe.
- Explanations for the rapid Arab expansion include the need for resources, the weakness of other empires, and the need for a common cause to hold the Arabs together.
- Arab identity and language gradually spread to many of the conquered peoples.
- Muslim leaders imposed Shari'a, a legal code that regulated social, economic, and religious life.
- Islamic peoples helped to spread a great variety of agricultural products across Eurasia.

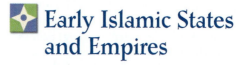

Early Islamic States and Empires

What were the major achievements of the Islamic states and empires?

Islamic expansion established a framework by which powerful states could rule millions of Muslims and non-Muslims. For over half a millennium Arabic-speaking Muslims ruled a large segment of the Eastern Hemisphere, and their leaders were courted by European and Chinese potentates. Great states and empires under strong governments dominated the Middle East, and Islamic states on the fringe of Christian Europe served as conduits of knowledge. Peoples and ideas spread widely, fostering a dynamic society mixing Arab, Persian, Indian, and Greek cultures. As new peoples were absorbed, non-Arab cultural and intellectual influences as well as leaders

---

sultan A Muslim ruler of only one country.

Shari'a The Islamic legal code for the regulation of social and economic as well as religious life.

madrasas Religious boarding schools found all over the Muslim world.

gradually became stronger in the Islamic community. But Islam also divided into rival sects, a split that created enduring tensions and that influenced Middle Eastern politics for many centuries.

Early Imperial Caliphates: Unity and Strife

Muslim political history revolved around the imperial caliphates, beginning with the Rashidun, who attempted to maintain unity but also faced challenges. After 661, the end of the Rashidun era, political power shifted outside of Arabia with two successive imperial dynasties, the Umayyad (oo-MY-ad) and the Abbasid (ah-BASS-id). Both dynasties were installed by members of Muhammad's Quraysh tribe. Arabia was the fountainhead, but power shifted elsewhere. While Mecca and Medina remained spiritual hubs, reinforced by annual pilgrimages, new cities emerged as more important political and economic centers for the Islamic world.

The sense of social and religious unity within a growing umma, achieved with the expansion of Islam and represented by the Rashidun Caliphate, did not prevent political conflict. The early conquests greatly enriched Medina and Mecca, especially their merchant clans. But some Muslims grew critical of the new materialism that enticed the young. A full revolt against the Islamic leadership erupted, and dissidents murdered the unpopular third caliph, Uthman (ooth-MAHN), and installed Ali (ah-LEE) (ca. 600–661), Muhammad's son-in-law, as the fourth caliph. Although well qualified, pious, and generous, Ali proved weak. To reform the system, he moved the capital from Medina to Kufah (KOO-fa) in what is today Iraq, but others soon challenged Ali for leadership. Muhammad's widow, A'isha, helped rally the opposition to Ali, resulting in a civil war. Ali was finally killed by Uthman's relatives, who blamed him for their leader's murder. With Ali's death, the Rashidun era ended, but the divisions generated a permanent split in the Islamic world. Centuries later, many Muslims viewed the Rashidun period as a golden age with a simple government and a righteous cause, and some called for reinstating the caliphate.

With the end of the Rashidun period the caliphate moved to Damascus (duh-MAS-kuhs), in what is today Syria, under the leadership of the Umayyad dynasty (661–750). The Islamic empire was now led by men with no direct connection to, or descent from, the Prophet. With the move to Damascus, Arab politics came to be defined by large bureaucratic states with remote leaders who passed on their rule to their sons. Military expansion continued, and the Umayyad caliphs extended the Islamic empire deep into Byzantine territory.

The Umayyad system soon experienced unrest. Although the rulers encouraged their subjects to adopt Islam, and called themselves deputies of God, they did not practice the morality that they preached. In response, devout Muslims opposed to the Umayyads emphasized Muhammad's role as God's prophet, clearly setting Islam apart from rival monotheistic religions and, some historians suggest, therefore elevated Muhammad to an even higher status as a spiritual figure. The Umayyad's laxness in religious devotion, as well as their legendary drinking and womanizing, shocked the more pious and generated civil war and division. Among the challengers was the Prophet's only remaining male heir, his grandson Husayn (hoo-SANE), who attracted support from those who believed the caliph must be a direct descendant of Muhammad. Husayn's rebellion in 680 failed, however, and he was killed in the Battle of Karbala (KAHR-buh-LAH), a city in Iraq. In death he and his father Ali, the murdered caliph, became martyrs against the Umayyads.

The Great Umayyad Mosque in Damascus
This mosque, built between 709 and 715, is the oldest surviving monumental mosque.
(Jane Taylor/Sonia Halliday Photographs)

The Sunni-Shi'a Split

After the death of Ali, the last Rashidun caliph, Islam began to split into two main branches, although this division was not fully formed for several centuries. At the heart of the split was disagreement over the nature of the umma and the full meaning of Muhammad's revelations. Both branches eventually fragmented into a variety of sects.

The main branch of Islam, **Sunni** (SOO-nee) ("The Trodden Path"), comprised those who accepted the practices of the Prophet and the historical succession of caliphs. Today about 85 percent of all Muslims, including most of those in North Africa, Turkey, the Balkans, South and Southeast Asia, and China as well as the majority of Arabs, are Sunni. Sunni embraces a wide variety of opinions and practices and was probably not named until the ninth or tenth century. It was more political than theological, suggesting adherence to one of four main schools of Islamic law and a broad view of who qualifies for political power.

The other main branch of Islam began as a dissident movement, in a dispute over the leadership of the faithful. The **Shi'a** (SHEE-uh) ("Partisans" of Ali) emphasized only the religious leaders descended from Muhammad through his son-in-law, Ali, whom they believed was the rightful successor to the Prophet. Karbala and nearby Najaf (NAH-jaf), where respectively Husayn and Ali are buried, became holy Shi'ite pilgrimage centers. Over time Shi'ites provided an alternative religious vision to Sunni Islam. By the late eighth century Shi'ism itself had divided into three rival schools, based on which leader after Ali should be followed. The main concentrations of Shi'ites are found today in Iran, where most Persians adopted the school after 1500, and also in Iraq and Lebanon. Many Shi'ites live in the Persian Gulf states, and smaller minorities are scattered across the Middle East, Central Asia, western India, and Pakistan.

Although they shared many commonalities, the differences between these two branches were deep. In general, Shi'ites followed strong religious leaders, a tradition not unknown to some Christians, ultra-Orthodox Jews, and Hindu sects. There was much antagonism between the two groups, as there would later be, for example, between Catholics and Protestants in some Western countries. Sunni majorities sometimes persecuted Shi'ite minorities. This persecution produced a Shi'ite martyrdom complex and a tradition of dissent against Sunni rulers. Over the centuries Shi'ite movements established various states, often ruling uneasily over Sunni majorities.

Arabian Nights: **The Abbasid Caliphate**

The Abbasid Caliphate (750–1258), the next dynasty after the Umayyad, enjoyed great power and fostered a dynamic society for several centuries, surviving for half a millennium. As leaders of the most powerful Islamic state between 750 and the 940s, the Abbasid caliphs embodied the unity of the Islamic umma and established a style for later Muslim rulers. The Abbasids, a Sunni branch of the Quraysh tribe descended from Muhammad's uncle, Abbas, had capitalized on dissent against the Umayyads to attract support from both Sunnis and Shi'ites, and they rallied a military force that defeated the Umayyad army. The lone Umayyad survivor fled to Spain, where he established a separate state that flourished for three centuries. The Abbasids expanded the empire to the east and maintained pressure against Byzantium in the west. By 800 the Abbasid Empire ruled some 30 million people (see Map 10.2).

In 756 the Abbasid capital was moved to Baghdad (BAG-dad), located where the Tigris and Euphrates Rivers come closest together in today's Iraq. This placed the capital strategically along major trade routes and in the middle of a farming district made fertile through irrigation. Baghdad became one of the world's greatest hubs, and its bazaars were filled with goods from as far away as China, Scandinavia, and East Africa. Steel, glass, leather, cotton, silk, and other products were manufactured or imported from other Muslim lands, and the city boasted joint-stock companies and banks. The Abbasid government employed thousands of people in public works projects, building palaces, schools, hospitals, and mosques in Baghdad. The Abbasids made a public show of their piety and generosity, such as by endowing religious buildings in the capital. Some Baghdad citizens, however, also openly flouted Islamic prohibitions against hedonistic behavior.

Baghdad reflected the cosmopolitan flavor of Islamic society. In the 1160s a rabbi from Muslim-ruled Spain, Benjamin of Tudela, visited Baghdad and wrote of the ethnically diverse city and, in particular, its large Jewish community:

> *This great Abbasid [caliph] is extremely friendly towards the Jews, many of his officers being of that nation. Baghdad contains about one thousand Jews, who enjoy peace, comfort, and much honor. Many of the Jews are good scholars and very rich. The city contains 28 Jewish synagogues.*[10]

Indeed, Islam became a far-reaching world culture because of its ability to receive and absorb culture from all parts of the Eastern Hemisphere. For example, although the Abbasids were Arabs, much of their backing came from Persia. Persian influence on the new system was strong, and many Persians came to occupy high positions in the government. The Abbasids also acquired knowledge from faraway lands. For example, Muslims first learned papermaking technology from Chinese captured in the Battle of Talas of 751. By 800 Baghdad had its first paper mill. By the twelfth century paper was also manufactured in Morocco and Spain, and then Turks spread the technology to India in the thirteenth century. Papermaking allowed for a wider distribution of the Quran, helping to spread Islam.

The height of the Abbasids in Baghdad conjures up the images of affluence and romance reported in *The Arabian Nights*, a cycle of stories probably collected from the tenth through twelfth centuries that later also influenced European writers, artists, and composers. For example, the famous

---

Sunni ("The Trodden Path")   The main branch of Islam comprising those who accept the practices of the Prophet and the historical succession of caliphs.

Shi'a ("Partisans" of Ali)   The branch of Islam emphasizing the religious leaders descended from Muhammad through his son-in-law, Ali, whom they believe was the rightful successor to the Prophet.

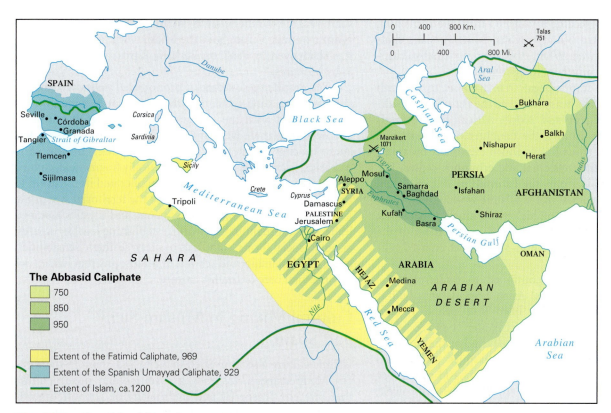

Map 10.2   The Abbasid Empire, ca. 800 C.E.
The Abbasids, a dynasty based in what is today Iraq, established the largest Muslim empire in the early Intermediate Era, ruling lands from Central Asia to Egypt before losing most of their territories. Among other major Islamic states, the Umayyads ruled Spain and northwest Africa and the Fatimids ruled Egypt and neighboring lands.

Scheherazade symphony by the nineteenth-century Russian composer Nikolai Rimsky-Korsakov (RIM-skee KAWR-suh-kawf) attempted to evoke the atmosphere of Abbasid Baghdad. Some images of old Baghdad come from fanciful children's books and films based loosely on the great literary work, where we read of flying carpets and genies in magic lamps. During the reign of the greatest Abbasid caliph, Harun al-Rashid (hah-ROON al-rah-SHEED) (786–809), there were no flying carpets, but many people enjoyed a comfortable life. Like various other caliphs, Harun had a large harem of wives, concubines, and slave girls, according to legends, some 2,000 in all. The royal harems had an image, perhaps partly true, as a secluded world of luxury, idleness, and endless plotting for royal favor. Like some other Abbasid rulers, Harun also had a reputation for heavy drinking and pursuing the temptations of the flesh.

Imperial Rule and Urbanization

As they adopted the ways of the conquered, Arabs were gradually transformed from desert herders and traders into imperial rulers. For instance, they ruled through traditional leaders, such as the Coptic Church patriarchs of Egypt. In Iraq they resolved disputes among Nestorian Christians just as the Sassanian governors had done. Like the Sassanians, the caliphs patronized a state religion, now shifted from Zoroastrianism to

Islam, and lavishly supported arts and crafts. Caliphs appointed Muslim judges and built mosques. The centralized caliphate was quite contrary to the egalitarianism of original Islam, but it worked.

The growth of cities followed Islamic conquests. New cities like Cairo and Basra, a port at the head of the Persian Gulf in modern Iraq, began as Muslim garrisons. The caliphates needed administrative centers, however, and these drew in surrounding people seeking work. Hence Baghdad, established in 756, rapidly swelled as the Abbasid capital. By 900 it contained perhaps a million people, becoming the world's largest city. The caliphs adopted the Sassanian system of dividing cities into wards marked by ethnic and occupational groups and of governing these groups through their own leaders. In doing so, they tolerated cultural diversity. Hence Muslim-ruled Toledo (tuh-LEED-oh) in Spain absorbed an influx of 10,000 Jews in the eleventh century without opposition.

Abbasid Decline and the End of Arab Empire

Like all empires, the Abbasids eventually faced mounting problems and gradually lost their grip on power by the tenth century. One factor was that Turkish soldiers, assigned to guard the caliphs, became more powerful in the government.

Furthermore, Shi'ites became disaffected from the weakening caliphate and fomented bloody revolts. Some Persians challenged the system as well. When Abbasid unity finally crumbled, the caliphate became a mere figurehead.

Soon parts of the empire began to break away. In the tenth century anti-Abbasid Shi'ites established the Fatimid (FAT-uh-mid) Caliphate in Egypt and North Africa. The Fatimids claimed descent from Fatima, the daughter of Muhammad. For their capital they chose Cairo, which eventually became a rival to Baghdad as an intellectual and economic center. The university founded in Cairo by the Fatimids in 970, Al-Azhar, became the most influential in the Islamic world. Today it remains the unrivaled center of higher learning for Muslims. Shi'ites also ruled various smaller states, where most of the population remained Sunni or non-Muslim yet enjoyed religious freedom.

Invasions and rebellions continued to undermine the Abbasids. The Mongols, Central Asian nomads who built a great regional empire stretching from East Asia to eastern Europe in the thirteenth century (see Chapter 11 and Societies, Networks, and Transitions III), were attracted by the wealth of the Abbasid realm. In 1258 Mongol armies sacked and destroyed Baghdad and executed the last Abbasid caliph (see Chronology: The Islamic World, 1095–1492). This event shattered the symbolic unity of the Muslim world and the Islamic umma. Throughout the Middle East, Arab dominance was challenged by Persians, Berbers, Kurds, and Turks as well as by Mongols.

Yet, despite these setbacks, pronounced political weakness and loss of cultural dynamism did not become evident in the Islamic world until the sixteenth and seventeenth centuries, and even then there were important exceptions. Although few later Muslim rulers could match the power of the early Abbasids, Islamic society, though politically fragmented, continued to flourish. Furthermore, Islam accelerated its diffusion to new peoples. Between 1258 and 1550 the territorial size of the Islamic world doubled. Scholars, saints, and mystics assumed leadership throughout this world, establishing legal structures, dogmas, social forms, standards of piety, aesthetic sensibilities, styles of scholarship, and schools of philosophy that helped define the vital core of Islamic culture.

Cultural Mixing in Muslim Sicily and Spain

Islamic culture also flourished in Sicily and Spain in the western Mediterranean, fostering a cosmopolitan mixed culture that brought prosperity and the sharing of scientific knowledge. Between 825 and 900 Muslim forces conquered Sicily, the largest Mediterranean island. Under Muslim rule, Sicily benefited from close ties to the Arab-dominated maritime trade system and light taxation. Muslim rulers repaired long-decayed Roman irrigation works and vastly increased agricultural production, introducing valuable new crops. Many Arabs, Berbers, Africans, Greeks, Jews, Persians, and Slavs gravitated to the island, mixing with the local peoples and creating a cosmopolitan society. At its height, the Muslim capital, Palermo (puh-LEHR-moh), was larger than any other city in Europe except Constantinople.

But by the eleventh century political divisions among Muslims left the island open to a gradual Christian reconquest. Between 1061 and 1091 the Normans, descendants of Vikings who had settled in France, had replaced a Muslim government with their own, although a Muslim minority and Arab influence remained on the island for many years. By 1200 Christian German rulers had established a Sicilian state and were persecuting Muslims and Jews on Sicily, gradually bringing to an end an era when the island blended Islamic and Christian traditions into a dynamic fusion.

A more enduring Muslim society emerged in Spain, much of which was first conquered by Islamic forces between 711 and 720. The ruling Umayyad family made their capital at Cordoba (KAWR-duh-buh), which became the largest city in Europe by 1000 C.E., home to half a million people. Under Umayyad rule, Spain was for several centuries the most powerful state in Europe and a famed center of culture and learning. Scholars and thinkers from all over Europe and the Islamic world were drawn to its schools and libraries. Cordoba's library held 400,000 volumes when libraries in Christian Europe owned only several hundred. The mood of

CHRONOLOGY	
The Islamic World, 1095–1492	
1095–1272	Christian Crusades in western Asia and North Africa
1250–1517	Mamluk rule in Egypt and Syria
1258	Mongol seizure of Baghdad and end of Abbasid Caliphate
1260	Mamluk defeat of Mongols in Battle of Ayn Jalut
1260–1360	Mongol Il-Khanid dynasty in Persia and Iraq
1300–1923	Ottoman Empire
1369–1405	Reign of Tamerlane in Central and Southwest Asia
1371	Ottoman conquest of Bulgaria and Macedonia
1396	Ottoman defeat of European forces at Battle of Nicopolis
1453	Ottoman capture of Constantinople and end of Byzantine state
1492	Christian seizure of Granada; expulsion of Muslims and Jews from Spain

Alhambra, Court of Lions
The Alhambra, or Palace of Lions, built in Granada in southern Spain in the fourteenth century, is one of the finest architectural treasures from Muslim Spain. It features a courtyard with a fountain. (Everts/Rapho/Group achette Filipacchi)

gradually pushed Muslim rule into southern Spain. By 1252 Christian princes, some of whom persecuted all non-Christians, controlled much of Spain and Portugal. Finally, in 1492, Christians took the last Muslim stronghold at Granada (gruh-NAHD-uh). The new Christian rulers, militant and intolerant, forced Muslims and Jews to either convert to Christianity or face expulsion. Thousands fled, usually to Muslim countries in North Africa or to Anatolia.

tolerance generated a productive relationship between diverse peoples and traditions. An Arab poet called Cordoba the garden of the fruits of ideas.

A great meeting of traditions occurred in Muslim Spain, with Christian, Muslim, and Jewish thinkers working together to share and advance knowledge. Intellectuals discussed ancient Greek thought and the latest astronomical discoveries, and they translated books from and into Arabic. From this cosmopolitan intellectual milieu, much of the classical Greco-Roman heritage, Islamic and Indian science and mathematics, and some Chinese technology, such as papermaking, were passed on to Europe. Both vocal and instrumental music, which were important in Islamic Arab culture for ceremonies, pleasure, and worship, also had an impact on Europe. Arab folk songs and musical instruments, such as the guitar and lute, diffused northward, influencing the courtly love songs of European troubadours and, later, Western popular music.

By 1000 decline, marked by civil wars and factionalism, had begun to set in and not everyone shared in the tolerance of the intellectual elite. Many people remained loyal to Catholicism, providing a base of support for efforts at reconquest. Much of northern Spain gradually came under Christian control. In 1085 Christian knights conquered Cordoba, the center of Islamic power. Constant Christian military pressure

SECTION SUMMARY

■ In the period of the early Rashidun Caliphate, dissidents murdered the third caliph and installed Muhammad's son-in-law Ali as fourth caliph, and after Ali's murder Islam began to split into two branches: the Sunni majority branch and the Shi'a dissident branch who believed Ali was the only successor to the Prophet.

■ Throughout history, Sunni persecution of Shi'ite minorities has created a Shi'ite martyrdom complex and a tradition of dissent against Sunni rulers.

■ The Umayyad dynasty, which succeeded the Rashidun Caliphate, was led by men with no connection to Muhammad who extended the empire into Byzantine lands.

■ Under the Abbasid Caliphate, during which *The Arabian Nights* was set, Baghdad became a cosmopolitan hub of trading and culture.

■ As they expanded, Arabs adopted the imperial ruling structures of the peoples they conquered and were targeted by numerous invaders, including the Mongols.

■ Spain and Sicily were ruled by Muslims for several centuries, though Christians gradually reclaimed them and failed to maintain the tolerance of the Muslim rulers.

✦ Cultural Hallmarks of Islam: Theology, Society, and Science

What were the major concerns of Muslim thinkers and writers?

Islamic expansion launched a thousand-year era, from the seventh to the seventeenth century, that brought many Afro-Eurasian peoples into closer contact with one another and allowed for a mixing of cultures within an Islamic framework. Muslims synthesized elements from varied traditions, including the Arab, Greek, Persian, and Indian, to produce a new hybrid culture, vital and durable, that was rooted in theology, social patterns, literature and art, science, and learning. Islamic theology continued to develop, fostering several distinct strands of thought and behavior. In western Asia and North Africa, Islamic societies fashioned a distinctive social system and a renowned cultural heritage. In addition, Islamic scholars contributed major scientific achievements and historical studies to the world.

Theology, Sufism, and Religious Practice

From the very beginning, Muslims' debates over theological questions led to divergent interpretations of the Quran. As in all religions, a variety of views about the great questions of life and death developed within Islam, reflecting the mixing of intellectual traditions. Some Muslim thinkers emphasized reason and free will, while others believed that Allah preordained everything.

Influential thinkers appeared throughout the Islamic world, some of whom had mastered several fields of knowledge. Among the greatest was Abu Yusuf al-Kindi (a-BOO YOU-suhf al-KIN-dee) (ca. 800–ca. 870), an Arab who lived in Iraq. Al-Kindi praised the search for truth and popularized Greek ideas. Although he emphasized logic and mathematics, he also published work on science, music, medicine, and psychology. Another Muslim scholar, Abu Ali al-Husain Ibn Sina (a-BOO AH-lee al-who-SANE IB-unh SEE-nah) (980–1037), known in the West as Avicenna (av-uh-SEN-uh), was both a philosopher and a medical scholar. A native of Bukhara (boo-CAR-ruh), a Silk Road city in Central Asia, he spent most of his career in Persia. Ibn Sina believed everyone could exercise a free will but that the highest goal was communion with God. Afghanistan-born Abu Hamid al-Ghazali (AH-boo HAM-id al-guh-ZAL-ee) (1058–1111), a teacher in Baghdad, used Aristotelian logic to justify Islamic beliefs. As an advocate of mysticism, he also opposed the rationalism of thinkers like Ibn Sina. The rationalistic approach remained influential in Shi'a thinking but lost support in Sunni circles from the fourteenth century onward.

Among both Sunnis and Shi'ites a variant of Islam developed and gained many followers. **Sufism** (SOO-fiz-uhm) was a mystical approach and practice that emphasized personal spiritual experience rather than nitpicking theology. Sufis stressed love and the superiority of the heart over the mind. Mysticism was suggested in the Quran: "Wherever ye turn there is the face of God."[11] Through asceticism and mysticism Sufis sought a personal, spiritual communion with God. For example, a famous Sufi poet in Persia, Baba Kuhi, saw God in everything: "In the market, in the cloister—only God I saw; In the valley and on the mountain—only God I saw. Him I have seen beside me oft in tribulation; in favor and in fortune—only God I saw."[12] Many Sufis exchanged information with Christian, Hindu, and Jewish mystics and were willing to synthesize Islam with other ideas as long as the central spirit was maintained. Indeed, many Sufis have considered their practices and beliefs universal, useful even for non-Muslims. But on the whole Sufism constituted a supplement rather than a challenge to conventional Islam.

Sufis congregated in orders led by masters who taught prescribed techniques and who attracted devoted followers. The whirling *dervishes* (DUHR-vish-iz) of Turkey are one of the most famous Sufi orders. Dervishes practiced special exercises and methods, including the trance dancing from which they get their name, to achieve a state of divine ecstasy. Several Sufi orders were renowned as peace-loving and tolerant of different views and customs. Followers credited some Sufi masters with magical powers. Later these leaders' tombs became pilgrimage destinations.

Although Sufi groups were founded all over the Muslim world, they remained a controversial movement. Some groups chiefly attracted intellectuals and others the less educated. Their tendency to minister to others and tolerate religious flexibility won them converts. However, many non-Sufis condemned the way some Sufis suspended ordinary Islamic biases against wine, drugs, and music in order to seek a state of ecstatic personal communion with God. But even today, millions of Sufis revere the Persian Sufi poet Hafez (hah-FEZ) (1326–1389), who loved God and the grape with equal devotion: "Here we are with our wine and the ascetics with their piety. Let us see which one the beloved [God] will take."[13] Sufis produced most Islamic poetry.

As the religion of Islam spread into diverse cultures, it developed three distinct patterns of practice. The adaptationists, the most liberal in defining the faith, showed a willingness to make adjustments to changing conditions. These Muslims have provided the base for reform and for secular and modernizing movements. Conservatives, on the other hand, strove to preserve established beliefs and customs, such as the rigid division of the sexes, and mistrusted innovation. The most dogmatic conservatives argued that the divine revelations channeled through Muhammad set a permanent standard to use in judging existing conditions, an unchangeable authority of universal validity. Finally, some Muslims, including many Sufis, stressed the personal aspects of the faith. These three patterns still have large followings among both Sunnis and Shi'ites, providing the basis for political and social conflict in Muslim societies. In all of them, some Muslims emphasize only the Quran while others also revere the Hadith. Some also follow the teachings of various spiritual leaders.

Sufism A mystical approach and practice within Islam that emphasized personal spiritual experience.

Social Life and Gender Relations

Most Muslims were settled farmers, craftsmen, and traders. As Islamic culture expanded and matured, the social structure became more complex and marked by clear ethnic, tribal, class-occupational, religious, and gender divisions, especially in the Middle East. Arabs generally had a higher social status than Turkish, Berber, African, and other converts. The descendants of the Prophet and members of the Hashimite clan to which he belonged held an especially honored status. Even in modern times people who can trace, or claim to trace, their ancestry to Muhammad and his family enjoy special influence in many Islamic societies around the world. Many Arabs were also members of tribes, such as Muhammad's Quraysh tribe. In addition, because the first Muslims were merchants, the religion had a special appeal for people in the commercial sector, providing spiritual sanction of their quest for wealth. This wealth could finance their pilgrimage to Mecca and also help the poor through almsgiving. Merchants and artisans established guilds that were sometimes affiliated with a particular sect or Sufi order.

Slavery was common in Islamic societies. Slaves were bureaucrats and soldiers, workers in businesses and factories, household servants and concubines, musicians, and plantation laborers. One Abbasid caliph kept 11,000 slaves in his palace. Islamic law encouraged owners to treat slaves with consideration, and many slaves were eventually freed. Many slaves were war captives and children purchased from poor families, but Christian European states like Byzantium and Venice also sold slaves to Muslims. For over a dozen centuries, but especially after 1200, perhaps 10 to 15 million African slaves were brought to the Middle East across the Sahara or up the East African coast by an Arab-dominated slave trade. African slave soldiers were common in Egypt, Persia, Iraq, Oman (oh-MAHN) in eastern Arabia, and Yemen.

The Islamic religion imposed some divisions in society. For example, Christian and Jewish communities did not always have the same rights as Muslims. They also paid higher taxes and were prohibited from owning weapons, and so were exempt from military duty. However, these non-Muslim communities did enjoy some protection under the law. Although the level of that protection varied in different societies and under different rulers, on the whole these communities were allowed to follow their own laws, customs, and beliefs and to maintain their own religious institutions.

Families were at the heart of the social system. Marriages were arranged, with the goal of cementing social or perhaps business ties between two families. As elsewhere in the world at the time, people assumed that love followed matrimony rather than the reverse. Although law allowed men to have up to four wives at a time, this situation remained fairly rare and largely restricted to the rich and powerful. Many poor men never married at all because they could not afford the large bridal gifts expected. While divorce was theoretically easy for men, marriage contracts sometimes discouraged divorce by specifying that men pay a large gift to the wife upon divorce. Parents

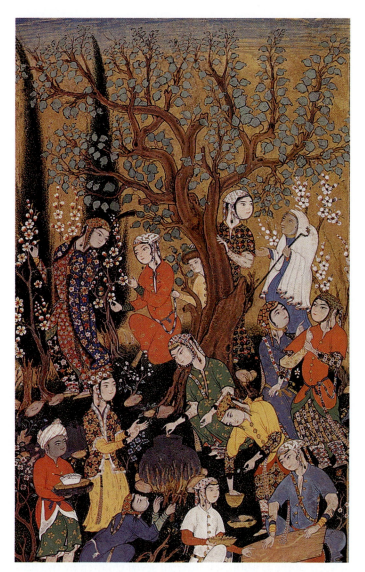

Persian Women at a Picnic This miniature from sixteenth-century Persia shows women preparing a picnic. The ability of women to venture away from home varied widely depending on social class and regional traditions. (Bodleian Library, Oxford University, MS Elliot 189)

expected children to obey and respect them, even after they became adults. Both women and men in a family entertained their friends at home. These gatherings, which were usually segregated by gender, often involved poetry recitations, musical performances, or Quran readings. Picnics were also popular family activities. Islamic law harshly punished homosexuality; yet, homosexual relationships were not uncommon, and same-sex love was often reflected in poetry and literature, most notably in Muslim Spain. European visitors were often shocked at the tolerant attitudes of Arabs, Persians, and Turks toward homosexual romantic relationships.

The status of women in Islamic society has been subject to debate by both Western and Islamic observers in modern times, and by Muslim thinkers for centuries. For example, the philosopher Ibn Rushd (IB-uhn RUSHED) (1126–1198), known in the West as Averroes (uh-VER-uh-WEEZ), attacked restrictions on women as an economic burden, arguing that "the ability of women is not known, because they are merely used for procreation [and] child-rearing."[14] Although the Quran recognized certain rights of women, prohibited female infanticide, and limited the number of wives men could have, it also accorded women only half the inheritance of men and gave women less standing in courts of law. Both Muslim and non-Muslim observers have criticized the many restrictions on women as institutionalizing their social inferiority. Many Muslim men and women have contended that these restrictions liberate women from insecurity and male harassment. Scholars have also disagreed over whether restrictions such as veiling and seclusion were based on Quranic mandates or on patriarchal pre-Islamic Arab, Middle Eastern, and Byzantine customs. Some Muslim communities in the Middle East, and many outside the region, never adopted these practices.

Women played diverse roles in Muslim societies. Muhammad's wives enjoyed great political influence. Some of the wives of Abbasid caliphs also played political roles, albeit mostly behind the scenes. For instance, Khayzuran, noted for her compassion and generosity, rose from a simple Yemenite slave girl to become the great love and wife of the Caliph Mahdi, dominating his harem, investing in land reclamation and charitable works, and giving strong support to her husband. On his death, she helped smooth the transition to the rulership of her son, Harun al-Rashid. During Abbasid times some elite women, while excluded from public life, enjoyed considerable power behind the scenes, and some exceptional women circumvented restrictions. For example, Umm Hani (also known as Mariam) in fifteenth-century Cairo studied law and religion with many famous teachers, wrote poetry, owned a large textile workshop, and became a renowned teacher and scholar of the Hadith. She also had seven children by two husbands and made thirteen pilgrimages to Mecca. While formal education for girls in the Middle East was generally limited, women monopolized certain occupations such as spinning and weaving, and they also worked in the fields or in some domestic industries beside men. And in some Muslim societies, particularly in sub-Saharan Africa and Southeast Asia, women often maintained their relative independence and were free to dress as they liked, socialize outside the home, and earn money. Turks and Mongols also seem to have been more liberal on gender issues than Arabs and Persians. In short, patterns of gender relations varied considerably.

Pen and Brush: Writing and the Visual Arts

Although Islamic societies became identified with literacy and literature, writing derived from pre-Islamic roots. The Arabic alphabet originated in South Arabia long before Muhammad's time. In Mecca the script had been used chiefly by merchants to keep their books. But Islam enhanced the script further by emphasizing literacy. The Quran stated: "Read, and thy Lord is most generous, Who taught with the pen, Taught man what he knew not."[15] Muslims adopted the Arab poetic tradition but modified romantic ideas into praise not for a lover but for the Prophet and Allah. Islamic culture also developed a written and oral prose literature, including tales of Alexander the Great.

One of the greatest writers of Abbasid times, also an astronomer and mathematician, was the Persian Omar Khayyam (OH-MAHR key-YAHM). In his famous poem *Rubaiyat* (ROO-bee-AHT), he noted the fleeting nature of life: "O, come with old Khayyam, and leave the Wise, to talk; one thing is certain, that Life flies; one thing is certain, and the rest is Lies; the flower that once has blown forever dies." This led him to regret never knowing the purpose of existence:

> *Ah, make the most of what ye yet may spend, Before we too into the Dust descend; Dust unto Dust, and under Dust to lie, [without] Wine, Song, Singer, and End! Into this Universe, and Why not knowing, Nor Whence, like Water willy-nilly flowing; And out of it, as Wind along the Waste, I know not Whither, wily-nilly blowing.*[16]

The most famous Sufi poet was the thirteenth-century Persian Jalal al-Din Rumi (ja-LAL al-DIN ROO-mee). Born in what is today Afghanistan, as a youth he lived in Central Asia and Anatolia, which reflected Islam's wide reach. Al-Din Rumi blended liberal spirituality with humor in writings about love, desire, and the human condition. His vision was optimistic, joyful, and ecumenical: "I am neither Christian, nor Jew, nor Zoroastrian, nor Muslim."[17] He often danced while reciting his poems to his disciples. At the beginning of the twenty-first century, over seven hundred years after his death, Rumi became the best-selling poet in the United States after his poems were translated into English.

Some Muslims emphasized the visual arts. For example, since Arabic is written in a flowing style, the artful writing of words, or **calligraphy** (kuh-LIG-ruh-fee), became a much admired art form. An elegant script offered not just a message but also decoration. Calligraphy appeared in manuscripts and also on the walls of public buildings. Islamic Persia, India, and Central Asia also fostered a tradition of painting, especially landscapes. In addition, Muslims produced world-class architecture, some of it monumental, that included lavishly decorated buildings such as the Taj Mahal in India. Some architecture, such as mosques with domes and towers, reflected Byzantine church influence. Muslims also produced ceramics, and then as now they were famed for weaving carpets and fabrics that were valued in many non-Muslim societies.

Science and Learning

During the Islamic golden age many creative thinkers emerged. Muslims borrowed, assimilated, and diffused Greek and Indian knowledge and were familiar with some Chinese technologies. By the seventh century certain classical and Hellenistic Greek

---

calligraphy The artful writing of words.

traditions of philosophy and science had been nearly forgotten in Europe, but they survived in the Middle East. Thanks to the mixing of ideas as cultures encountered each other, science and medicine flourished, and Muslims also made many contributions to mathematics and astronomy.

Science and Medicine Many advances in science and medicine were made in the Islamic world as experts synthesized the learning of other societies with their own insights. Some knowledge was carried into the Middle East by Nestorian Christians, who taught Greek sciences under Abbasid sponsorship and helped make Baghdad a center of world learning. The Abbasid caliphs opened the House of Wisdom in Baghdad, a research institute staffed by scholars charged with translating Greek, Syrian, Sanskrit, and Persian works into Arabic. The works included books on philosophy, medicine, astronomy, and mathematics. Aristotle's writings were particularly influential. The institute also included schools, observatories, and a huge library. Other scientific centers arose in many Muslim lands, from Spain and Morocco to Samarkand in Central Asia. For example, in the tenth and eleventh centuries the Shi'ite Fatimids built the House of Knowledge in Cairo with a massive library holding 2 million books, many on scientific subjects.

After the ninth century, Arab and Persian scholars were not just translating but also actively assimilating the imported knowledge. As the influential eleventh-century Persian philosopher Al-Biruni (al-bih-ROO-nee) wrote: "The sciences were transmitted into the Arabic language from different parts of the world; by it [the sciences] were embellished and penetrated the hearts of men, while the beauties of [Arabic] flowed in their veins and arteries."[18] For example, many Muslim intellectuals adopted the Greek idea that an underlying order underpinned the apparent chaos of reality and that this order, or laws, could be understood by human reason.

The dialogue resulting from a diversity of ideas produced an open-minded search for truth that is apparent in the work of Ibn Khaldun, Ibn Sina, al-Kindi, and Ibn Rushd. For instance, the philosopher al-Kindi wrote that Muslims should acknowledge truth from whatever source it came because nothing was more important than truth itself. Ibn Rushd (Averroes), who lived in twelfth-century Cordoba (Spain), influenced Christian thinkers with his assertion of the role of reason. In the eleventh century, Christian Europe became aware of the Muslim synthesis of Greek, Indian, and Persian knowledge from libraries in Spain.

Muslims also turned their attention to medicine, where they enjoyed considerable success. Although much influenced by Greek ideas, Muslim medical specialists did not accept ancient wisdom uncritically. Instead, they developed an empirical tradition. Baghdad hospitals were the world's most advanced. Muslim surgeons learned how to use opium for anesthesia, extract teeth and replace them with false teeth made from animal bones, remove kidney stones, and do a colostomy by creating an artificial anus. These achievements attracted attention. For example, after many Islamic medical books were translated into Latin in the twelfth century, they became the major medical texts in Europe for the next five centuries.

Two medical scientists stand out. Abu Bakr al-Razi (aboo BAH-car al-RAH-zee) (ca. 865–ca. 932) and Ibn Sina (Avicenna) compared Greek ideas with their own research. Al-Razi, a Persian, directed several hospitals and wrote more than fifty clinical studies as well as general medical works. The latter included the *Comprehensive Book,* the longest medical encyclopedia in Arabic (eighteen volumes), which was used in Europe into the 1400s. In distinguishing smallpox from measles, he added much to the clinical knowledge of infectious diseases. Al-Razi also studied what we would today call sociological and psychological aspects of medicine. A century later Ibn Sina, who was born in Central Asia, placed considerable stress on psychosomatic medicine and treated depression. He also pioneered the study of vision and eye disease and performed complicated operations on the eye. His medical encyclopedia provided about half of the medical curriculum in medieval European universities. Ibn Sina served princes as both a physician and a political adviser.

Mathematics and Astronomy As with science, Islamic mathematics moved well beyond the imitative, and it also helped spur astronomy. The scientific revolution that later occurred in Europe would have been impossible without Arab and Indian mathematics. In Baghdad the Persian Zoroastrian al-Khuwarizmi (al-KWAHR-uhz-mee) (ca. 780–ca. 850) developed the mathematical procedures he called algebra, building on Greek and Indian foundations. Omar Khayyam, the beloved Persian poet who worked at Baghdad's House of Wisdom, helped formulate trigonometry. Meanwhile, Arab thinkers also made advances in geometry. From Indian math books Muslims adopted a revolutionary system of numbers, including the concept of the zero. Today we know them as Arabic numerals because Europe acquired them from Muslim Spain. The most revolutionary innovation of Arabic numerals was not just their greater convenience but also the use of a dot to indicate an empty column. This dot eventually became the zero. Muslims also used decimal fractions. All these innovations had practical uses. Thus, advances in mathematics and physics made possible improvements in water clocks, water wheels, and other irrigation apparatus that spread well beyond the Islamic world.

The Muslim world also improved astronomical observations. Muslim astronomers combined Greek, Persian, and Indian knowledge of the stars and planets with their own observations. Applying their knowledge of mathematics to optics, Muslim scholars constructed a primitive version of the telescope, and one astronomer reportedly built an elaborate planetarium that reproduced the movement of the stars. A remarkable observatory built at Samarkand in Central Asia in 1420 produced charts for hundreds of stars. Some astronomers noted the eccentric behavior of the planet Venus, which challenged the widespread notion of an earth-centered universe. Indeed, many Muslim astronomers accepted that the world was round.

IBN BATTUTA,
A MUSLIM TRAVELER

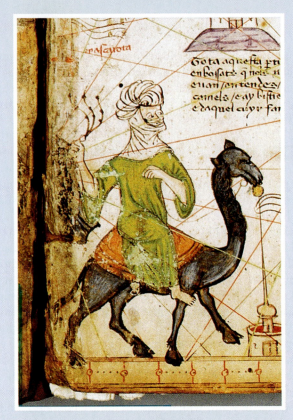

The Journey to Mali   No known paintings of Ibn Battuta exist. However, this map of Africa and the Mediterranean world, made by a Jewish cartographer in Spain in 1375, features a drawing of a camel-riding Muslim traveler that some historians think represents the journey of the Moroccan to Mali. (Bibliotheque nationale de France)

Among the Islamic travelers who journeyed to, and often sojourned in, distant lands, the most famous was Abdallah Muhammad Ibn Battuta, a gregarious and pious fourteenth-century Moroccan who spent thirty years touring the length and breadth of the Islamic world, as far east as Southeast Asia and, he claimed, the coastal ports of China. His travels demonstrated the reach of the Islamic community. He was a pilgrim, judge, scholar, Sufi, ambassador, and connoisseur of fine foods and elegant architecture. Ibn Battuta's writings about his remarkable journeys, the autobiographical *Rihla* (Book of Travels), provide detailed, often unique eyewitness accounts of many societies. A collaborator compiled the *Rihla* in a literary form near the end of the adventurer's life.

Born in Tangier, Morocco, in North Africa, to a Berber family of scholars and trained in Islamic law, Ibn Battuta left home in 1325 at the age of twenty-one to seek adventure and learning. His apparent wanderlust proved difficult to quench. Such extensive travel would have been impossible for any woman, Muslim or otherwise, in that era, since women were expected to stay close to home and family. Traveling by camel, horse, wagon, or ship, Ibn Battuta covered between 60,000 and 75,000 miles and visited dozens of countries. He never had a conventional family life and married several times for short periods, leaving children all over the hemisphere. The politically ambitious jurist often sojourned in a society for months or years; his largest career stint was seven years' service in the Delhi Sultanate of northern India. But wherever he went, Ibn Battuta made observations on a wide variety of subjects, from cuisine and botany to political practice and Sufi mystics. For example, he marveled at the "continuous series of bazaars [along the Nile] from Alexandria to Cairo. Cities and villages succeed one another without interruption." And, coming from a more patriarchal North African society, he marvelled at the "respect shown to women by the [Central Asian] Turks, for they hold a more dignified position than the men. Turkish women do not veil themselves."

Although a repeated visitor to Mecca and the Islamic heartland, his experiences in the frontier regions of Islam, such as India and the Maldive Islands, Southeast Asia, the East African coast, the western Sudan, Turkish Central Asia, Anatolia, and Mongol-ruled southern Russia, provide the most useful information for the historian. They reveal a vivid picture of an expanding, vigorous Islamic realm encountering diverse structures, peoples, and practices. For example, from him we learn about the sexual customs of the Maldive Islands, where he married the widow of a sultan, and the Arab religious scholars, Persian merchants, and Chinese painters who gathered at Delhi "like moths around a candle."

Whereas the Christian Marco Polo a century earlier was always a stranger in his travels in Asia, in most places Ibn Battuta went he encountered people who shared his worldview and social values. From Morocco to Central Asia and around the In-dian Ocean Rim, people worshiped in mosques and recognized the Shari'a as a legal framework. Far and wide, Ibn Battuta enjoyed the company of merchants, scholars, Sufis, and princes, with most of whom he could converse in Arabic on many topics, including developments in faraway lands. His knowledge of Islamic law and Arabic allowed him to work as a judge and legal scholar from Morocco to India. But, while cosmopolitan and open-minded by the standards of the day, he was clearly uncomfortable in non-Islamic societies such as China and in those frontier Islamic cultures where Islamic orthodoxy was greatly modified by local custom, such as Mali in West Africa. The traveler finally returned home to Tangier, where he died around 1368.

THINKING ABOUT THE PROFILE

1. Why was Ibn Battuta one of the great travelers of the Intermediate Era?

2. What do his travels tell us about the values and reach of Islamic religion and culture?

Notes: Quotations from Ross Dunn, *The Adventures of Ibn Battuta: A Muslim Traveller of the 14th Century* (Berkeley: University of California Press, 1986), pp. 45, 183; Nikki R. Keddie, "Women in the Middle East Since the Rise of Islam," in Bonnie G. Smith, ed., *Women's History in Global Perspective*, Vol. 3 (Urbana: University of Illinois Press, 2005), p. 81.

Social Science and Historiography

The modern study of social sciences and history owes much to Muslim research and writing. For example, Muslims made a major contribution to geography. With the expansion of Islam and Arab trading communities to the far corners of the Eastern Hemisphere, some pious Muslims were able to travel to distant lands, and many became long-distance traders. Educated Muslims enjoyed reading these travelers' accounts of other countries and peoples. Modern historians are indebted to Muslim travelers such as the Moroccan jurist Ibn Battuta (IB-uhn ba-TOO-tuh) for much of what we know today about the geography and societies of sub-Saharan Africa and Southeast Asia from the ninth to the fifteenth centuries (see Profile: Ibn Battuta, a Muslim Traveler). Aided by travel accounts, geographers and cartographers such as Al-Idrisi (al-AH-dree-see) from Muslim Spain produced atlases, globes, and maps.

Ibn Khaldun (1332–1406), the well-traveled North African introduced at the beginning of the chapter, was apparently the first scholar anywhere to look for patterns and structure in history. For example, his monumental work connected the rise of states among tribal communities with a growing feeling of solidarity between leaders and their followers, often enhanced by a coherent religion. His recognition of the role in history of "group feeling" (what today we call ethnic identity) and the powerful role of religion was pathbreaking. In studying other cultures, he advocated "critical examination":

> Know the rules of statecraft, the nature of existing things, and the difference between nations, regions and tribes in regard to way of life, qualities of character, customs, sects, schools of thought, and so on. [The historian] must distinguish the similarities and differences between the present and the past.[19]

Ibn Khaldun put the Arab expansion into the broader flow of regional history, in the process focusing on various regional cultures.

SECTION SUMMARY

- Sufism, a mystical approach to Islam that emphasized flexibility and a personal connection with God, drew both Sunni and Shi'ite followers.
- Although the Quran and most Muslim societies restricted women, some Muslim societies did not, and both Muslims and non-Muslims have debated the origins and benefits of such practices as wearing a veil.
- Literature, especially poetry, was very important in Islamic culture, as was calligraphy, the artful writing of words.
- Islamic science and medicine were very advanced and pioneered such practices as anesthesia and the replacement of false teeth.
- The Scientific Revolution would not have occurred without the help of Islamic mathematicians who passed on to Europe Indian mathematics.

Globalized Islam and Middle Eastern Political Change

Why do historians speak of Islam as a hemispheric culture?

The major theme of early Islam was the transformation of a parochial Arab culture into the first truly hemisphere-wide culture that was connected by many religious and commercial networks. Between the eighth and seventeenth centuries Islam expanded out of its Arabian heartland to become the dominant religion across a broad expanse of Africa and Eurasia, and Muslim minorities emerged in places as far afield as China and the Balkans. From this expansion was created **Dar al-Islam** (the "Abode of Islam"), the Islamic world stretching from Morocco to Indonesia and joined by both a common faith and trade. Networks fostered by Islam reached from the Atlantic eastward to the Pacific, spreading Arab words, names, social attitudes, cultural values, and the Arabic script to diverse peoples. Eventually several powerful military states rose to power and ruled over large populations of Muslims and non-Muslims. The Islamic world also faced severe challenges—expanding Turks, Christian crusaders, Mongol conquerors, and horrific pandemics—that set the stage for the rise of new political forces in the fifteenth and sixteenth centuries. Yet, the Islamic tradition was resistant and overcame factionalism and political decay to remain creative well past the 1400s.

The Global Shape of Dar al-Islam

To identify the Muslim world with the Arab world is misleading. More than half of the world's 1.3 billion Muslims today live outside the Middle East, and Arabs are significantly outnumbered by non-Arab believers. The majority of all Muslims live in South and Southeast Asia. This chapter largely focuses on the Middle East, since the spread of Islam in Africa and southern Asia is discussed in Chapters 12 and 13. But this is only a part of a larger global whole of Islam, a zone stretching from West Africa and Spain east to Indonesia and the southern Philippines.

After the destruction of the cosmopolitan Abbasid Caliphate in 1258, Arab political power diminished, but Islam grew rapidly in both Africa and South Asia. Dozens of prosperous Muslim trading cities, from Tangier in northwest Africa to Samarkand in Central Asia to Melaka in Malaya, offered goods from distant countries. Beginning in the thirteenth century, Muslims constructed a hemisphere-spanning system based not just on economic exchange but also on faith. This system, built on a shared understanding of the world and the cosmos, was linked by informal networks of Islamic scholars and saints. The Quran and its message of a righteous social order provided a framework for Dar al-Islam.

Dar al-Islam ("Abode of Islam") The Islamic world stretching from Morocco to Indonesia and joined by both a common faith and trade.

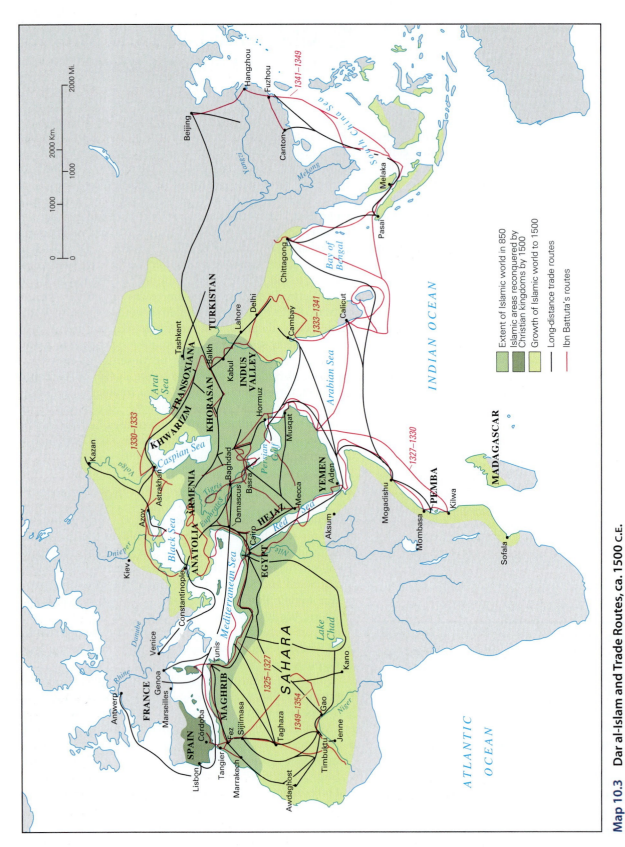

Map 10.3   Dar al-Islam and Trade Routes, ca. 1500 C.E.
By 1500 the Islamic world stretched into West Africa, East Africa, and Southeast Asia. Trade routes connected the Islamic lands and allowed Muslim traders to extend their networks to China, Russia, and Europe.

Legend:
- Extent of Islamic world in 850
- Islamic areas reconquered by Christian kingdoms by 1500
- Growth of Islamic world to 1500
- Long-distance trade routes
- Ibn Battuta's routes

The spread of Islam corresponded with the growth of Muslim-dominated long-distance trade and the travel it fostered, especially the maritime trade around the Indian Ocean Basin. Except for the Chinese, Arabs enjoyed the world's most advanced shipbuilding and navigation between 1000 and 1450. The lateen sails that Arabs devised, or perhaps adapted from classical Southeast Asians, allowed European ships to undertake long-distance voyages in the 1400s. Throughout the first millennium of the Common Era an increasingly integrated maritime trading system gradually emerged that linked the eastern Mediterranean, Middle East, East African coast, Persia, and India with the societies of East and Southeast Asia (see Map 10.3). Muslim peoples soon became the most prominent traders on this route. One Arab merchant expressed his commercial ambitions: "I want to send Persian saffron to China, where I hear that it fetches a high price, and then ship Chinese porcelain to Greece, Greek brocade to India, Indian iron to Aleppo [a Syrian port], Aleppo glass to the Yemen and Yemeni material to Persia."[20]

Between 1000 and 1500 C.E. the Straits of Melaka in Southeast Asia and Hormuz (HAWR-muhz) at the persian Gulf entrance stood at the heart of what became the key mercantile system of the Intermediate world. Over these sea routes the spices of Indonesia and East Africa, the gold and tin of Malaya, the textiles of India, the gold of southern Africa, and the silks, porcelain, and tea of China traveled to distant markets. The maritime network achieved its height in the fifteenth and sixteenth centuries, when Muslim political power was reduced but Muslim economic and cultural power remained strong. Arab and Persian merchant communities could be found as far east as the ports of Korea and south China. By intermarrying with local women and practicing their faith, Muslim merchants in these trade diasporas converted others to Islam.

Turks and Crusaders

Between the eleventh and fifteenth centuries the Muslim peoples of the Middle East faced a series of interventions by outsiders that helped reshape the region politically. The rise of the Turkish peoples in Central Asia eventually led to Turkish conquests in western Asia. During these same centuries Christian crusaders occasionally attempted to control Palestine and displace Muslim rule. The crusading thrust left a heritage of Muslim bitterness and wariness toward Christian Europe.

The Rise of the Turks The rise of the Turks is a major theme in this period of world history. The Turks were originally pastoral nomads from Central Asia who were skilled in both horse and camel travel and divided by tribe and dialect. For centuries they had intruded into Chinese, Indian, and western Asian societies, and by 550 C.E. some had established a vast confederation stretching from the Ukraine to Mongolia. Interacting with many other peoples, some Turks also adopted such religions as Nestorian Christianity, Judaism, and Buddhism. Gradually they drew closer to Middle Eastern social and cultural patterns, and most eventually embraced Islam. This conversion began when some Turkish groups sent boys to the Abbasids, where they trained to serve the Abbasids as soldiers or administrators. Other Turks were hired by the Abbasids to guard borders or to serve as mercenary soldiers.

Late in the tenth century a group of Muslim Turks, the Seljuks (SEL-jooks), achieved regional power. Beginning about 960 in Central Asia, the Seljuks expanded and recruited other Turkish tribes into their confederation. By the mid-eleventh century they had swept westward through Afghanistan and Iran into Iraq. Allied with the declining Abbasids, Seljuk forces continued to expand, conquering many Muslim and Christian societies in the Caucasus region and eventually creating a large empire stretching from Palestine to Samarkand. The weakening of an aging Byzantine state allowed the Seljuks in 1071 to seize much of Anatolia, which had for many centuries been populated largely by Greek-speaking Orthodox Christians. Now it was ruled by Turkish-speaking Muslims. Even when Seljuk power soon diminished elsewhere and their empire crumbled, they continued to govern Anatolia.

The Crusades By the eleventh century some Islamic states faced increasing challenges from European Christians. Between 1095 and 1272 Christians from various European societies launched a long series of Crusades to win back what they saw as the Judeo-Christian Holy Land from Muslim occupation (see Chapter 14). The First Crusade capitalized on Muslim weakness, since the various feuding Muslim states could not cooperate. Some states, such as Fatimid Egypt, even maintained lucrative trade ties with Europe, and parts of the Middle East still had substantial Christian and Jewish populations as well as many dissident Muslims. In the end, however, the Crusades failed to achieve their goal.

The First Crusade (1095–1099) was triggered by the encroachment of Seljuk Turks on Byzantine territory and a division of the Christian church into two rival branches in 1054. Roman popes, worried about Seljuk expansion and anxious to assert their primacy over the leaders of the breakaway Greek Orthodox Church based in Constantinople, promoted the idea of positive violence to defend the faith. Using untrue stories of Arab and Seljuk atrocities against Christians in Palestine and Syria, Pope Urban II called on Christians to reclaim the Holy Land and protect the churches and relics of Jerusalem. His plea attracted some 100,000 European volunteers, some pious, others just hungry for booty. The crusaders fought their way along the coast and reached Jerusalem in 1099. They took the city and then killed thousands of Muslims, Jews, and even local Christians. Some crusaders stayed on to guard the sites but also to colonize the surrounding territory, and four small crusader states were established in what is today Israel and Lebanon. As Muslim forces regrouped, another pope dispatched the Second Crusade (1147–1149), in which the crusaders mostly slaughtered Jews in Europe and pillaged the Byzantine Empire.

In the mid-twelfth century Muslims effectively counterattacked, pushing back Christian forces and prompting the Third Crusade (1189–1192). The Muslim armies were led by General Salah al-Din, or Saladin (SAL-uh-din) (1138–1193), an Iraqi-born Kurd who once served the Fatimid rulers of Egypt, then deposed them and became sultan, replacing Shiite with Sunni rule. Saladin's forces stopped a crusader invasion of Egypt and then, between 1187 and 1102, captured Jerusalem from the crusaders and extended his power into Syria. One of his followers, a Syrian soldier, praised Saladin as "the unifier of the faith, the vanquisher of the [Christians], the raiser of the banner of justice and benevolence."[21] He was aided by the fact that crusaders often fought each other, undermining their own power. Saladin spared the Christians who surrendered in Jerusalem. A tolerant leader, he employed the great Cordoba-born Jewish sage and legal authority Moses Maimonides (my-MAHN-uh-deez) (1135–1204) as his physician. His military exploits made Saladin a hero in Muslim eyes, and he is still revered today. The final six crusades, the last one ending in 1272, failed to wrest control of North Africa, Jerusalem, and Anatolia from Muslim hands.

Historians still debate the heritage of the Crusades. Many crusaders were undoubtedly inspired by a sincere religious zeal to preserve access to Christian holy sites, but many also looted captured cities and sacked the Orthodox Christian capital, Constantinople. Likewise, Muslim armies often showed little mercy on their enemies. Some believe that the militant Christian challenge to Islam represented by the Crusades ultimately made both religions less tolerant and more zealous, complicating relations between the two groups. For centuries afterward some Muslim rulers viewed their Christian subjects as untrustworthy while Christians persecuted the remaining Muslim populations in southern Europe. Even today, hundreds of years later, Islamic militants still capitalize on lingering resentment against Western "crusaders."

Mongol Conquests and the Black Death

Another people from outside the region, the Mongols (MAHN-guhlz), also swept into western Asia, destroying various states, creating instability, and unwittingly laying the foundation for a hemisphere-wide disease that caused much devastation and death in the Middle East. The Mongols, Central Asian pastoral nomads, constituted a much greater short-term threat to Islam than the Christian crusaders. Led by Genghis Khan (GENG-iz KAHN) (ca. 1162–1227), the Mongols, prompted perhaps by environmental stress and overpopulation, began their expansion out of their Mongolian homeland in the late twelfth century. They first extended their control over several rival Mongol and Turkish groups in Central Asia. Between 1218 and 1221 the Mongols fought their way through the lands inhabited mostly by Turkish-speaking Muslims just north of Afghanistan, destroying several great Silk Road cities.

Mongol atrocities were legendary. For example, they killed 700,000 mostly unarmed residents and even family pets in the Persian city of Merv. Their goal was to paralyze the Muslim societies with enough fear to prevent opposition. It usually worked. An Arab chronicler wrote of the Mongol invaders that "in the countries that have not yet been overrun by them, everyone spends the night afraid that they may appear there too."[22] After Genghis Khan's death in 1227, the Mongols turned to conquering China, Russia, and eastern Europe but

also put pressure on the Caucasus and Anatolia. In 1243 they defeated the remnants of the Seljuk Turks.

In 1256 a grandson of Genghis Khan, Hulegu (hoo-LAY-goo) (1217–1275), led new attacks on the Middle East that had more lasting consequences for the region. Although Hulegu had refused an offer of an alliance with Christian Europe against Islam, some Mongols were Nestorian Christians, and Christian communities in the Caucasus and western Asia often aided the Mongol forces. Crossing the mountains into Iraq, Hulegu's army, faced with fierce resistance, responded with brutal force. In 1258 the Mongols pillaged Baghdad, burning schools, libraries, mosques, and palaces, killing perhaps a million Muslims, and executing all the Abbasids. Some historians see Hulegu's destruction of Baghdad as a fateful turning point for Arab society that ended the prosperity and intellectual glory once represented by the now-gutted city. Hulegu's forces pushed on west from Baghdad, occupying Damascus and destroying the key eastern Mediterranean port of Aleppo (uh-LEP-oh). In addition to destroying cities, the pastoralist Mongols badly disrupted western Asian agriculture, returning some farms to pasture and dispersing the peasants. In some places farming never recovered.

But the Islamic tradition proved resilient. Hulegu had to return to Mongolia on the death of the Mongol emperor, Ogodei, the son of Genghis Khan. In 1260 his armies tried to invade Egypt but were defeated by the Mamluks (MAM-looks), ex-slave soldiers of Turkish origin who had taken power in Egypt. The Mamluk occupation of Palestine halted the Mongol march westward. Hulegu's Mongols, however, were content to stay in Iraq and Persia, calling themselves the Il-Khanid (il-KHAN-id) dynasty, assimilating Persian culture, and eventually adopting Islam. Many descendants of Mongol invaders in Russia, known today as Tartars, also eventually became Muslim. Hulegu's Muslim descendants practiced religious toleration and encouraged monumental architecture, learning, and a literary renaissance. Under their rule Persian scholars opened a huge library of 400,000 volumes, built a great observatory, produced enduring poetry, and wrote pathbreaking histories of the world that tell us much about the Mongol empire. Il-Khanid rule lasted a century before fragmenting in 1360.

By building a large empire across Eurasia, the Mongols fostered long-distance overland trade and travel, but in so doing they provided a path over which deadly diseases could spread. Like Europe and China, much of the Islamic world was deeply affected by the terrible fourteenth-century pandemic known in the West as the Black Death. The Black Death was a catastrophic disease, probably bubonic plague, that killed quickly and spread rapidly over the networks of exchange. Initially carried into the Black Sea region from eastern Asia by fleas infesting rats that stowed away on caravans along the Mongol-controlled Silk Road or on board trading ships, the pandemic hit the Middle East repeatedly over the course of a century.

The Black Death proved devastating. Disease reduced the population of Egypt and Syria by two-thirds. Major cities like Cairo lost half their population. Because many rural people

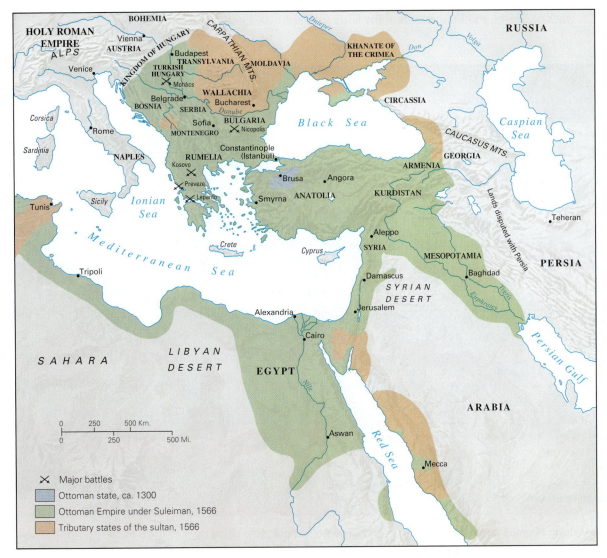

Map 10.4   The Ottoman Empire, 1566
Between 1300 and the mid-1500s the Ottoman Turks expanded out of western Anatolia to conquer a large empire in western Asia, Egypt and North Africa, and eastern Europe, making the Ottomans one of the world's largest states.

also died, food supplies were reduced. Ibn Khaldun wrote that "cities and towns were laid waste, roads and way signs were obliterated, settlements and mansions became empty. The entire inhabited world changed."[23] Ibn Khaldun felt he might be living at the end of history, but by the 1400s the Middle East had stabilized and regained some of its lost economic and cultural dynamism.

The Rise of Muslim Military States

In the thirteenth and fourteenth centuries, several powerful Muslim military states arose, including those of the Mamluks in Egypt and the Timurids in Central Asia. By this time gunpowder, a Chinese invention that filtered westward along the Silk Road during Mongol times, had reached the Middle East, where it forever changed the nature of warfare and also had an impact on politics. Between 1350 and 1450 possession of firearms gave some states and groups an advantage over rivals. Since recruiting, arming, and training soldiers to use cannons

and muskets was expensive, the use of firearms also led to the rise of stronger, more bureaucratic states.

The Mamluks, who had thwarted Mongol expansion, ruled Egypt and Syria from 1250 to 1517 and drove the crusaders out of Palestine in 1293. The Mamluks made Egypt the richest Middle Eastern state. They also extended their power into Arabia, capturing Mecca and Medina. This conquest allowed them to control and tax the flow of Muslim pilgrims. For many years the Mamluks also enjoyed an active trade with the two major Italian trading cities, Genoa and Venice, supplying valuable Asian goods to Europe. Merchants from Venice established various trading posts around the Mamluk lands, where they traded timber, metals, and gold for spices, dyes, and Indian textiles. Eventually, however, corruption grew among the Mamluk leaders. Their demands for increased taxes prompted seafaring European merchants to seek a maritime route to the East to avoid Mamluk territory, and in 1516–1517 another Turkish group, the Ottomans, defeated the Mamluks and absorbed their lands into the growing Ottoman Empire (see Map 10.4).

Venetian Ambassadors Visiting Mamluk Damascus   Venetians and Genoese merchants, fierce rivals, regularly visited the Middle East to acquire silks, spices, and other valuable products. This painting from the 1400s shows Venetians being received by the Mamluk governor of Damascus, who wears a horned hat and sits on a low platform, in today's Syria.
(Reunion des Musees Nationaux/Art Resource, NY)

To the east, in Central Asia, the Timurid state became the dominant regional power for over a century. The state's ruthless founder, Tamerlane (TAM-uhr-lane) (1336–1405), a Muslim prince of Turkish and Mongol ancestry, had been crippled by an arrow wound as a young man. Beginning his rule in 1369, Tamerlane hoped to emulate Genghis Khan. From his capital at Samarkand, Tamerlane's army rampaged through the Caucasus, southern Russia, Persia, Iraq, and Syria, killing thousands of people and destroying cities and farms. He then turned against India, wreaking havoc in the north (see Chapter 13). Only Tamerlane's death in 1405 halted his forces from invading China and Ottoman Turkey. Although Tamerlane protected merchants and Sufi mystics, his heritage was largely one of smoking ruins and pyramids of human heads. However, his successors built mosques and patronized scholars, and later his grandson established a great empire in India in the early 1500s.

The Ottoman Empire

The most powerful and enduring military state was established by the Ottoman (AHT-uh-muhn) Turks, who were the most successful Muslim people in exploiting the possibilities of gunpowder. The Ottomans originated as a small Anatolian state led by a chief, Osman (ohs-MAHN) (*Ottoman* means "followers of Osman"), who came under the influence of Sufis dedicated to the destruction of Byzantium. By the late 1200s Byzantium was reeling from temporary occupation of Constantinople by crusaders and Byzantine influence was weakening in Anatolia, where the Greek Christians were governed mostly by one of the many small Turkish states that had survived the collapse of the Seljuks. The Ottomans capitalized on this vacuum and, by 1300, began raiding and then annexing the remaining Byzantine strongholds in Anatolia. Ultimately the Ottomans conquered much of the Byzantine Empire, creating one of the most dynamic states in western Eurasia and a link between Middle Eastern Islam and European Christianity. The once great Byzantium was increasingly a shell of a state surrounding Constantinople.

Soon the Ottomans moved into the Balkans, where they challenged the strongest Christian power in southeastern Europe, Serbia (SUHR-bee-uh). In 1389, in the Serbian region of Kosovo (KOH-suh-voh), the Ottomans routed a Christian army comprising many Balkan ethnic groups, among them Serbs, Albanians, and Bulgars. The Ottomans eventually incorporated Serbia in 1459. They favored Muslims in taxes, and over the next several centuries many Albanian and Serb-speaking Christians adopted Islam, perhaps partly for economic reasons, creating a division in the Balkans between Catholic, Orthodox, and Muslim peoples that complicated politics for centuries to come.

Other battles in the fourteenth and fifteenth centuries led to eventual Ottoman triumph. At the Battle of Nicopolis (nuh-KAHP-uh-luhs) in 1396, the Ottomans defeated a Hungarian-led force drawn from throughout Europe to oppose further Ottoman expansion. Then in 1453 Sultan Mehmed (MEH-met) (1432–1481) the Conqueror finally took Constantinople and converted the city into the Ottoman capital, eventually renamed Istanbul.

The Ottoman Empire was now the major regional power, an empire of many peoples. The imperial capital, Istanbul, attracted a multiethnic and multireligious population and remained a major trade hub through which many networks passed. Mehmed the Conqueror, who patronized the arts, launched a major rebuilding project in Istanbul, even inviting some of Italy's most famous artists and architects to work in his cosmopolitan capital, which by 1500 was Europe's largest city. As in other Muslim states, Ottoman sultans used the administrative and military skills of the subject peoples and promoted men of merit regardless of their backgrounds. Through the **millet** ("nationality") system, the Ottomans allowed the leaders of religious and ethnic minorities to administer their own communities. For instance, at the national level the Greek patriarch had authority over all Orthodox Christians in Ottoman territory. Christians and Jews practiced their religions freely for the most part. Thus the millet system allowed the Turks to divide and hence rule diverse peoples and faiths.

Under a dynamic and militarily powerful state the Ottomans continued to expand. By 1500 they had solidified control over Greece and the Balkans (see Map 10.4). In the 1500s, the so-called Ottoman golden age, Ottoman rule was extended over much of western Asia as far east as Persia and also through North Africa from Egypt to Algeria. However, the Ottomans were defeated when they attempted to take Hungary in 1699. This event marked the end of Ottoman, and Islamic, expansion in western Eurasia and symbolized the decline of Islamic power, but the Ottoman Empire continued until 1923.

Islamic Contributions to World History

By linking peoples of varied cultures, ideas, religions, and languages, the Arab conquests fostered intellectual and artistic creativity. Ultimately the Arabs and the Islamic faith and culture they spread profoundly influenced the development of Indian, African, and European societies. To the east, for example, the gradual Islamic conquest of India posed an alternative to Hinduism. As Islamic influence and Arab merchants traveled west and then south across the Sahara and along the East African coast, various African societies also adopted the Islamic faith as well as some Muslim customs and technologies.

In the west, the Arabs passed on to Europe some of the fruits of the advanced science, mathematics, and technology of the Middle East, India, and even China transported over the networks of exchange. In addition, in many respects, the Arabs served as the critical link between the classical Greeks and Indians and the late medieval Europeans. The transmission of Greco-Roman and Islamic learning to Europe, where it was studied in medieval universities, came mainly through Spain and Sicily from the ninth through the eleventh centuries. Western Europeans profited from this exchange of knowledge, and eventually it helped spark not only a scientific and technological revolution in Europe but also a questioning of the entrenched Christian church that ultimately led to more diverse ideas within Western societies. But the exchange was not one way, and Muslims benefited from European knowledge of medicine, science, and art.

Mixing Arab, Persian, Turkish, Byzantine, Christian, Jewish, African, and Indian influences, Muslims created a hemispheric-wide Islamic world that connected culturally and politically diverse societies sharing a common faith and, often, values. While most people in what is today Iraq, Syria, Egypt, and North Africa adopted the Arabic language and called themselves Arabs, the Persians and Turks continued to speak their own languages, which they now wrote using the Arabic script. Indeed, for many centuries Persian remained a language of government and the elite from the Seljuk Turkish empire in Anatolia to various Muslim states in India and Central Asia. Non-Muslims played key roles in the Islamic world, especially in commerce. From the eighth through eleventh centuries Jews were the key trade middlemen between Christian Europe and the Muslim world. Hence, Jews from Narbonne in southern France traded in Spain, North Africa, and the Eastern Mediterranean, becoming fluent in Arabic. After the eleventh century the Jews lost ground as intermediaries of Muslim–non-Muslim commerce to the Italians in the west and the Armenians in the east.

Muslim scholars were proud of the intellectual cohesion of Muslim thought and the expanse of their horizons. For example, the Egyptian scholar Jalal al-Din al-Suyuti (juh-LALL al-din al-sue-YOU-tee) (1445–1505) boasted that he and his books had traveled as far as West Africa to the west and India to the east. Yet, after the defeat of the last Muslim kingdom in Spain in 1492, he also saw the Muslim world in crisis, in need of intellectual and social renewal. Although the Ottoman Turks were on the rise, al-Suyuti could not know that after 1500 Muslim states would also soon have a resurgence in Persia and India, nor that various Europeans, benefiting from the contacts with the East opened by the encounter with Islam, would become serious rivals to Muslim power and a challenge to the interconnected Islamic world.

Several powerful Islamic states, including the Ottoman Empire, continued to exercise political and economic influence in the sixteenth and seventeenth centuries. But, with the

---

millet The nationality system through which the Ottomans allowed the leaders of religious and ethnic minorities to administer their own communities.

occasional exception of Ottoman Turkey, technological innovation, scientific inquiry, and the questioning of accepted religious and cultural ideas fell off in the Middle East after 1500. The madrasas, while training Muslim clerics and providing spiritual guidance, tended to have narrow, theology-based curriculums that deemphasized secular learning. Some historians believe this undermined the humanist, tolerant tradition of Islamic scholarship, such as the open-minded approach of Baghdad's House of Wisdom and the schools in Muslim Spain. Over the next three centuries most of the Middle Eastern peoples who had boasted innovative and cosmopolitan traditions for a millennium, gradually lost military and economic power while Europeans surged.

SECTION SUMMARY

- Trade routes spread Islam throughout the hemisphere, eventually creating Dar al-Islam, an Islamic world stretching from Indonesia to Morocco, in which Arabs constituted a minority of Muslims.

- The series of Christian Crusades to win back the Judeo-Christian Holy Land from Muslims led to long-lasting resentment on the part of Muslims.

- The Mongols, led by Genghis Khan and Hulegu, one of his grandsons, ruthlessly attacked Muslims in Central Asia and sacked Baghdad, but the Islamic tradition continued throughout Mongol rule.

- The arrival of gunpowder from China allowed Muslim military states, such as the Mamluks and the Timurids, to gain power.

- The Ottoman Turks established an extremely successful empire in the territory of the former Byzantine Empire by allowing subject minorities to administer their own affairs.

- By conducting and preserving a great deal of scientific and philosophical learning, the Muslims contributed much to European culture.

Online Study Center ACE the Test

Chapter Summary

The rise of Islam in Arabia during the seventh century changed world history. Islam posed a challenge to Arab polytheism and tribalism, forging a community of believers around a set of monotheistic ideas. Muhammad and his message created a new worldview that proved so popular that, within a few decades, Muslim Arabs, inspired by Muhammad's vision, had conquered a large empire and spread Islam to many Arab and non-Arab peoples.

Islam offered a distinctive set of religious, political, and social ideas, such as pilgrimage, annual fasting, a legal code, and an emphasis on social justice, but it also was influenced by Christian, Jewish, Persian, and other traditions. Islamic societies flourished under powerful theocratic governments, such as the Umayyad and Abbasid Caliphates, while Islamic writers and scientists assimilated and developed knowledge from many societies. Muslim thinkers preserved classical Greek learning while pioneering new ideas in astronomy, mathematics, the physical sciences, and agriculture. Arab links also contributed the knowledge to medieval Europe that supplied the key for the scientific and technological rise of the West.

The Islamic world became a cosmopolitan network of peoples, linked by trade and religious scholars. While the end of the Abbasids brought some political fragmentation and other troubles, Islam still expanded, overcoming several challenges in the millennium after Muhammad. By 1500 several powerful Muslim states, especially the Ottomans, controlled vast empires, and eventually many millions embraced the religion across the Eastern Hemisphere. Stretching from western Africa and southwestern Europe eastward to Southeast Asia and western China, Islam became a hemispheric culture, even extending its influences into non-Islamic regions such as western Europe. After 1500, however, the Islamic Middle East began to fade as a political power and a center for intellectual inquiry.

Online Study Center Improve Your Grade Flashcards

Key Terms

Bedouins	caliphate	Sunni
Ka'ba	Ramadan	Shi'a
Quran	haj	Sufism
Hadith	jihad	calligraphy
hijra	sultan	Dar al-Islam
umma	Shari'a	millet
Allah	madrasas	

Suggested Reading

Books

Armstrong, Karen. *Muhammad: A Biography of the Prophet.* San Francisco: Harper, 1992. A readable and sympathetic survey of Muhammad and his life.

Aslan, Reza. *No God But God: The Origins, Evolution, and Future of Islam.* New York: Random House, 2005. An account of Islamic religion and history by a liberal, Iran-born, U.S.-based Muslim scholar.

Berkey, Jonathan P. *The Formation of Islam: Religion and Society in the Near East, 600–1800.* New York: Cambridge University Press, 2003. Fine scholarly study of the rise of Islam to 1500.

Bloom, Jonathan, and Sheila Blair. *Islam: A Thousand Years of Faith and Power.* New Haven, Conn.: Yale University Press, 2002. A well-written overview of Islamic history and society from 600 to 1700.

Dunn, Ross. *The Adventures of Ibn Battuta: A Muslim Traveller of the 14th Century.* Berkeley: University of California Press, 1986. A fascinating look at Dar al-Islam through the writings of the famed Arab traveler.

Eaton, Richard M. *Islamic History as Global History*. Washington, D.C.: American Historical Association, 1993. A valuable short pamphlet showing the significance of Islamic societies to world history.

Egger, Vernon O. *A History of the Muslim World to 1405: The Making of a Civilization*. Upper Saddle River, N.J.: Prentice-Hall, 2004. A recent and comprehensive survey.

Inalcik, Halil. *The Ottoman Empire: The Classical Age, 1300–1600*. London: Phoenix Press, 2000. A reprint of one of the best introductions to the early Ottoman Empire and society, first published in 1973.

Kennedy, Hugh. *When Baghdad Ruled the World: The Rise and Fall of Islam's Greatest Dynasty*. Cambridge, MA: Da Capo, 2005. Readable study of the Abbasid dynasty and era.

Menocal, Maria Rosa. *The Ornament of the World: How Muslims, Jews, and Christians Created a Culture of Tolerance in Medieval Spain*. Boston: Little, Brown and Co., 2002. Uses profiles of historical figures to explore the cultural flowering of Muslim Spain.

Nasr, Seyyed Hossein. *Islam: Religion, History, and Civilization*. San Francisco: HarperSanFrancisco, 2003. An insightful overview of the Islamic tradition by an Iranian-born scholar.

Risso, Patricia. *Merchants of Faith: Muslim Commerce and Culture in the Indian Ocean*. Boulder: Westview, 1995. Readable survey of Muslim trade networks.

Robinson, Francis, ed. *The Cambridge Illustrated History of the Islamic World*. Cambridge: Cambridge University Press, 1996. An authoritative, richly illustrated survey of Islamic society and history.

Walther, Wiebke. *Women in Islam from Medieval to Modern Times*. Princeton: Markus Wiener, 1999. One of the most valuable and readable studies of gender issues, by a German scholar.

Websites

History of the Middle East Database (http://www.nmhschool.org/tthornton/mehistory/database/mideastindex.htm). A fine set of essays and links on the early and modern Middle East and Islam.

Ibn Battuta's Rihla (http://www.sfusd.k12.ca.us/schwww/sch618/Ibn_Battuta/Ibn_Battuta_Rihla.html). A useful site on Ibn Battuta and his wide travels.

Internet Islamic History Sourcebook (http://www.fordham.edu/halsall/islam/islamsbook.html). A comprehensive examination of the Islamic tradition and its long history, with many useful links and source materials.

Islam and Islamic History in Arabia and the Middle East (http://www.islamicity.com/education). A comprehensive site sponsored by a moderate Muslim organization.

Islamic Studies, Islam, Arabic, and Religion (http://www.arches.uga.edu/~godlas). A comprehensive collection of links and resources maintained at the University of Georgia.

Virtual Religion Index (http://virtualreligion.net/vri/). Has many links on all major religions including Islam.

CHAPTER 11

East Asian Traditions, Transformations, and Eurasian Encounters, 600–1500

Online Study Center

This icon will direct you to interactive activities and study materials on the website: college.hmco.com/pic/lockard1e

Giant Japanese Buddha at Kamakura During this era, most Japanese adopted Buddhism, some expressing their faith in art. This gigantic statue, erected in the city of Kamakura in 1252, shows the Buddha in meditation. (Rafael Macia/Photo Researchers, Inc.)

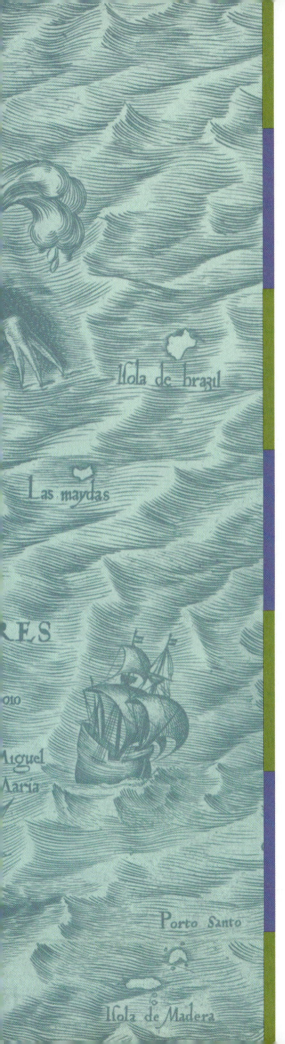

China is a sea that salts all rivers that flow into it.

ITALIAN TRAVELER MARCO POLO (1275 C.E.)[1]

Early in the twelfth century the Chinese artist Zhang Zeduan, noted for his realistic drawings, painted a massive scroll of people at work and leisure throughout the city of Kaifeng (KIE-FENG), then China's capital and home to perhaps 1 million people. The scroll, the surviving portions of which are 17 feet long, portrays a bustling city and its peoples' daily lives during one of premodern China's most creative and prosperous eras. The viewer can experience the grandeur of the city, from its riverside suburbs to the high protective walls and the towering city gates to the downtown business district. In Zhang's scroll, set during the annual spring festival, Kaifeng's streets are crowded with people (mostly men) going about their daily activities. Foreign merchants and other visitors can be seen, as well as streetside hawkers touting their goods, fortunetellers, scholars, and monks. The scroll also shows industrial activities, with people working in warehouses, iron smelters, arsenals, and shipyards. Zhang's record of Kaifeng's commercial life is particularly vivid: building material suppliers, textile firms, and drug and chemical shops, as well as hotels, food stalls, teahouses and restaurants, amenities for local people and visitors alike. Cargo barges cruise the river, while camels heavily laden with goods enter the city, some arriving from distant countries.

Much of the prosperous city life Zhang portrayed was familiar to Chinese of earlier and later generations, for Chinese society showed considerable continuity over time. The Han's eventual succession by the Sui and then by the Tang (tahng) and Song (soong) dynasties ensured that Chinese society continued along traditional lines, in contrast to the dramatic changes that took place in Japan, the Middle East, India, Southeast Asia, and Europe during the Intermediate Era. Once the Tang adopted a modified version of the Han system, the ensuing millennium, from the seventh through the eighteenth centuries, proved to be a golden age, broken only occasionally by invasion or disorder. Some scholars call the Intermediate Era in world history the "Chinese Centuries." China became and remained perhaps the world's richest and most populous society, enjoying a well-organized government and economy, a flourishing artistic and literary culture, and creativity in technology and science. Many commercial and cultural networks connected China to the rest of Eurasia. Furthermore, China's neighbors in Korea and Japan adopted many aspects of Chinese culture, though they also forged their own highly distinctive societies during this period. China did indeed, as Marco Polo recognized, influence or awe all those with whom it came into contact.

299

FOCUS QUESTIONS

1. What role did Tang China play in the Eurasian world?
2. Why might historians consider the Song dynasty the high point of China's golden age?
3. How did China change during the Yuan and Ming dynasties?
4. How did the Koreans and Japanese make use of Chinese culture in developing their own distinctive societies?
5. How did Korean and Japanese society change in the late Intermediate Era?

Tang China: The Hub of the East

What role did Tang China play in the Eurasian world?

The harsh Sui dynasty that united China after the disintegration of the Han ruled for only a short time (581–618 C.E.) before rebellions brought it to an end. The victor in the struggles between rival rebel forces established the Tang dynasty (618–907), regarded by many historians as the most splendid of all the Chinese dynasties. Many peoples admired Tang China. The three centuries of Tang rule set a high watermark in many facets of Chinese life and provided a cultural and political model for neighboring Asian societies. The only comparable power in Eurasia at that time was the expanding Muslim empire of the Abbasids; India and Europe were then divided into many small states and often threatened by invaders. The Tang made important advances in political organization, economic production, science, technology, art, literature, and philosophy, and many of these advances dominated China until the early twentieth century.

The Tang Empire and Eurasian Exchange

In the seventh and eighth centuries Tang China—an empire of some 50 or 60 million people—was the largest and most populous society on earth, and it had an immense influence in the eastern third of Eurasia (see Map 11.1 on page 302). Like the Han before them, the Tang launched a series of ambitious campaigns that brought Central Asia (as far west as the Caspian Sea), Tibet, Mongolia, Manchuria, and parts of Siberia under Chinese rule. Vietnam had already long been a colony. The Koreans became a vassal state, and the Japanese established close ties. Kingdoms as far away as Afghanistan acknowledged Chinese leadership, and Chinese garrisons protected the Silk Road, fostering the flow of goods and people across Eurasia. In western Asia, the powerful Abbasid caliph Harun al-Rashid testified to China's diplomatic clout by signing a treaty with the Tang.

The Tang were the most outward-looking of all Chinese dynasties, and during these years China became an open forum, a world market of ideas, people, and things arriving over the networks of exchange. The Silk Road, established during the Han era, remained a sort of transcontinental highway. Along this network traders, adventurers, diplomats, missionaries, and pilgrims traveled east or west, carrying goods and ideas, and many made their way to China. Nestorian Christian, Manichean, Buddhist, and Muslim missionaries arrived. Merchants from around Asia formed communities in several Chinese cities, and many arrived by sea. For example, perhaps two-thirds of the 200,000 inhabitants of the southern port of Guangzhou (gwahng-jo), also known as Canton, a great trading hub, were immigrants, including Arabs, Persians, Indians, Cambodians, and Malays. For the many Muslim residents, the city boasted both Sunni and Shi'ite mosques. Indian astronomers and mathematicians joined the Tang government as scientific officials, bringing with them Indian traditions of knowledge. Meanwhile, several hundred Chinese scholars visited or sojourned in India, most of them seeking Buddhist literature.

Tang wealth and power stimulated commerce throughout Eurasia. A lively sea trade linked China with Southeast Asia, India, Persia, and the Arabs. By land or sea, many Chinese inventions reached into western Eurasia. In 753 C.E. a Chinese craftsman reported that, in Baghdad: "As for the weavers who make light silks, the goldsmiths who work gold and silver there, and the painters; the arts which they practice were started by Chinese technicians."[2] Chinese products such as silk and porcelain were much prized in Europe and the Middle East. Because of the Tang's fame, Chinese culture also spread in this period to Korea and Japan.

This multicultural exchange also benefited China. New products appeared, most notably tea from Southeast Asia. Chinese began drinking tea, originally a medicinal substance, as a beverage, and it became the national drink. Teahouses selling boiled tea opened in every marketplace. Another new arrival was the chair, probably from the Middle East. Over the next centuries it replaced seating pads, and the Chinese became the only chair users in East Asia. Diverse societies in places such as Burma, Java, and Nepal regularly sent embassies to the Tang court bearing gifts. Renewed contacts with India and the Middle East as well as many other peoples helped foster China's creativity. But some Chinese scholars criticized the cosmopolitan attitude and complained about too much foreign culture.

The Eurasian exchange during the Tang fostered dynamic and culturally rich cities. Tang China boasted many cities larger than any contemporary cities in Europe or India, and the capital, Chang'an (CHAHNG-ahn), present-day Xi'an (SHEE-AHN),

CHRONOLOGY

	China	Korea	Japan
600	**618–907** Tang dynasty	**688–918** Silla	**710–784** Nara period **794–1184** Heian period
900	**960–1279** Song dynasty	**918–1392** Koryo	
1100	**1279–1368** Yuan dynasty		**1180–1333** Kamakura Shogunate
1300	**1368–1644** Ming dynasty	**1392–1910** Yi dynasty (Choson) **1405–1433** Voyages of Admiral Zheng He	**1338–1568** Ashikaga Shogunate

was home to 2 million inhabitants. The world's largest city, Chang'an, was also a model of urban planning, with its streets carefully laid out in a grid pattern and the city divided into quadrants. Chang'an reflected China's encounter with the wider world. The broad thoroughfares were crowded with visitors and sojourners from many lands, among them Arabs, Persians, Syrians, Jews, Turks, Koreans, Japanese, Vietnamese, Indians, and Tibetans. Many foreign artists, artisans, and merchants worked in the capital, as well as entertainers such as Indian jugglers and Afghan actors. To serve the non-Chinese, the city contained four Zoroastrian temples, two Nestorian Christian churches, and several mosques. The only contemporary cities that could nearly match its size and amenities were Baghdad, the center of the powerful Abbasid Caliphate, and Byzantine-ruled Constantinople.

Imperial Government and Economic Growth

Under the Tang, the centralized imperial structure reached a high level of efficiency and maintained one of the world's most productive economies. Despite bloody rebellions, invasions, assassinations, palace coups, and dynastic upheavals, the hallmark of China's political system for many centuries was stability, the result of mixing a strong institutional structure with innovative political ideas. Later dynasties followed the basic Tang model.

Tang China had a complex imperial structure, with the emperor standing at the top of the system. According to Confucian theory, the family was the model for the state, so the emperor was viewed as the symbolic father of the people. The Chinese believed that the country must be governed by moral example, not physical force. As during the Han, the Chinese considered the emperor the Son of Heaven—not a divine figure but the intermediary between the terrestrial and supernat-

Musicians on the Silk Road This glazed pottery figurine, one of many similar pieces from the Tang era, shows musicians playing Persian musical instruments while riding a camel on their travels along the Silk Road to China, demonstrating China's ties to the Middle East. (The National Museum of Chinese History)

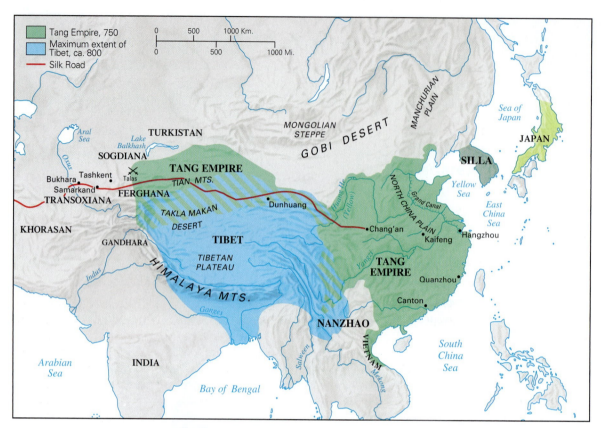

Map 11.1 The Tang Empire, ca. 700 C.E.
The Tang dynasty forged a large empire across Central Asia into Turkestan before their expansion was halted by Muslim armies at the Battle of Talas in 751. Control of Central Asia allowed the Tang to protect the Silk Road trade route. The Tang also controlled Vietnam and dominated Korea.

ural realms—and the first scholar of the land. He held daily audiences, during which diplomats from distant lands sometimes presented gifts as a symbol of their submission to his authority. In return the emperor bestowed on them a title, state robes, and gifts, a ceremony followed later by a banquet. The imperial office was masculine. While women sometimes had power behind the throne, known as "ruling from behind a screen," only one woman, the Empress Wu Zhao (woo chow) (625–705), the daughter of a Chinese general, ever officially led the government. She had become an imperial concubine at age thirteen and used her political skills and ruthless ambition eventually to displace the sickly emperor, maintaining her power for over fifty years. While Empress Wu generally ruled ably, Chinese scholars viewed her as an evil usurper and warned future generations that women should not rule the country.

In theory the emperor held absolute power, but his actual power was circumscribed in various ways. For example, he had to consider the Censorate, an agency that monitored the workings of the government, rooted out corruption, proposed changes in state policies, and criticized the government for failings. The Censorate was unique to China; such institutions appeared elsewhere only in the nineteenth century. Only the strongest emperors could punish the Censorate for criticism. Furthermore, the doctrine of the Mandate of Heaven, that people have a right to overthrow an evil, corrupt, or ineffective

government, meant that emperors had to consider the consequences of their policies and behavior.

Because administering such a large and diverse empire required a competent bureaucracy, the Tang revived the competitive civil service exams from Han times. The Chinese believed that government officials, known as mandarins, should be the wisest and ablest men in the land. The merit-based exams were intended to seek out talented individuals, regardless of birth, for government service. To help train potential officials, the government also operated a national university and hundreds of local-level academies. During the Tang and the succeeding Song periods, perhaps 15 percent of the mandarins did not come from upper-class backgrounds, indicating that the examinations led to some social mobility. The fully evolved examination system consisted of a series of exams at local, provincial, and national levels. Usually less than 5 percent of candidates passed and moved on to the next level. By passing the highest level a man received the equivalent of a Ph.D. degree, which was a prerequisite to hold office. By Tang times the exams largely tested knowledge of literary composition and the contents of the Confucian classics.

The civil service merit exam system was undoubtedly one of the greatest achievements of Chinese society. This competitive system was the single most important institution that contributed to the long duration of the political system. The educational background needed to pass gave the ruling elite a shared Confucian ideology emphasizing ethics and loyalty. The Tang bureaucracy numbered around fifteen thousand officials, an extraordinarily small number for a country as huge as China. Clearly they ruled with the cooperation of the local people. From now on whoever ruled China had to rule through and with the bureaucracy of scholars.

Tang officials had to pursue policies that maintained economic growth, especially agricultural production. A Tang official explained the system: "Grain and cloth are produced by the [peasants], natural resources are transformed by the artisan class, wealth and goods are circulated by the merchant[s], and money is managed by the ruler."[3] The 80 percent of Chinese who tilled the soil were generally able—though often just barely—to produce a food surplus for the other 20 percent in towns and cities. To feed their growing population and avert famine, the Chinese worked to achieve better yields and became one of the world's most efficient farming peoples. The Tang also attempted to circumvent the power of powerful landowning families and ensure stability by experimenting with land reform, the "equal field system." In this system officials assigned each peasant family a plot of around 19 acres, in the hope that this would provide enough for the family's needs. For a time the reforms brought the peasantry some prosperity. But powerful families used their influence with local officials to keep control of much of their land. When the Tang declined after some 120 years of prosperity, the equal field system also disintegrated. Still, throughout history some emperors and officials sought a more equitable land system.

Religion, Science, and Technology

The early Intermediate Era was the golden age for Buddhism in Central Asia, Southeast Asia, and East Asia. Under the Tang, Buddhism, which had spread into China early in the Common Era, grew to be a dominant faith, while Confucianism and Daoism remained influential. As Buddhist monks, pilgrims, and artists traveled between India and China, they drew the two societies into closer contact.

However, Buddhism presented the government with some problems. First, it divided into numerous competing sects. Furthermore, the Buddhist monasteries, which came to control vast amounts of tax-exempt land and wealth, constituted a challenge to the government as an alternative power center. In the mid-ninth century the government cracked down on Buddhism, mainly for economic reasons. Emperor Wuzong (woo-chong) (840–846), in desperate need of more revenues, closed and seized 4,600 monasteries and defrocked all monks under the age of fifty. Although Wuzong's successors reversed his policies and restored the monasteries, his actions reduced the political and economic power of the Buddhist orders enough to ensure that they never again exercised significant secular power. After this brief crackdown, Chinese Buddhism lost some of its dynamism and became absorbed into the popular art, literature, and religion.

Whereas Buddhism came from India, some new religions originated farther west and flowed east along the Silk Road.

Nestorian Christianity, a sect considered heretical in Byzantium, gained a small following, and Islam became strong in northwest China and in pockets of southwest and southern China. Jewish merchants also settled in several north China cities, founding small Jewish communities that lived there for centuries. Except for Wuzong, the Tang court generally took a tolerant, ecumenical view of religion; indeed, religious persecution is rare in Chinese history. As one Tang emperor proclaimed: "The Way [truth] has more than one name. There is more than one sage. Doctrines vary in distant lands, their benefits reach all mankind."[4]

Meanwhile, Tang scholars and craftsmen made significant scientific and technological achievements. Tang astronomers established the solar year at 365 days and studied sunspots, and some argued that the earth was round and revolved around the sun. They were also the first to analyze, record, and then predict solar eclipses. Around 600 C.E. Chinese engineers built the first load-bearing segmental arch bridge. Among other advances, Tang chemists perfected gunpowder, an elaboration of the firecracker. By using a mix of sulphur, saltpeter, and charcoal, Chinese military forces could now use primitive cannon and flaming rockets to protect their borders or resist rebels. Gunpowder also became an important medicine for skin diseases.

Paper had been developed a millennium earlier, but the Tang made great strides by inventing woodblock printing. For centuries Chinese had carved texts into stone and then taken ink rubbings for mass distribution. But demand for copies of religious and Confucian texts outpaced supply. To solve this problem, some creative men began carving texts into wooden blocks, which could be used to reproduce text on paper with ink. This invention satisfied the need to produce texts for the civil service exams, and it also spread Buddhist writings. The first known book printed on paper with this method was a Buddhist text from 868 (see Chronology: China During the Intermediate Era). The Chinese had an insatiable desire to classify

CHRONOLOGY

China During the Intermediate Era

589–618	Sui dynasty
618–907	Tang dynasty
751	Battle of Talas
868	First books from woodblocks on paper
907–960	Five Dynasties
960–1279	Song dynasty
1167–1227	Life of Genghis Khan
1279–1368	Yuan dynasty (Mongols)
1368–1644	Ming dynasty
1405–1433	Voyages of Admiral Zheng He

the wisdom of the past for use by future generations. Aided by printing, they could now compile encyclopedias to record their accumulated knowledge. Woodblock printing also gave rise to a written popular culture in the cities.

The Arts and Literature

Some of China's greatest painters and sculptors lived in Tang times. Painting, which was an activity pursued by scholars and government officials, was closely associated with calligraphy, the beautiful rendering of Chinese characters. Whereas Muslim calligraphy was used mostly for writing excerpts from the Quran, in China calligraphy was used to render a meaningful poem, quote, or passage in a refined, balanced form. Both calligraphy and painting used brush and ink on silk or paper. Chinese paintings used color sparingly and were generally restrained, understated, and philosophical in presentation. Being influenced by Daoism, many painters specialized in landscapes. An eleventh-century writer explained why: "Why does a virtuous man take delight in landscapes? It is for these reasons. That in a rustic retreat he may nourish his nature; that amid the carefree play of streams and rocks, he may take delight. Haze, mist, and the haunting spirits of the mountains are what human nature seeks, and yet can rarely find."[5] But Confucian ideas were also expressed in the people who were usually a small part of the picture.

Like Confucian philosophy, Chinese arts mainly stressed order, morality, and tradition. But there were exceptions. In Tang times, some artists were free spirits and experimented wildly; one eccentric flipped ink-soaked hair at silk, and another splashed while dancing. Artists also reflected their times. Wind-tossed bamboo and choppy water, for example, might indicate turbulent politics. Poetry and painting shared the stage with other art forms. For example, the traveler to Tang China experienced art when he sipped tea from nearly transparent porcelain cups, the most sanitary utensils in the world at that time. China also became famous for splendid lacquer ware, furniture made with mother of pearl, gold and silver inlay, fine musical instruments, and luxurious brocades.

Many of China's greatest poets also lived in this era. Poetry was highly valued: annual literary festivals were held in Chang'an to select prizewinners, and one anthology of Tang poetry contains 49,000 poems by 2,300 poets. Many poems depicted the hardships of life: poverty, war, the ups and downs of romantic love, the passing of time, the imminence of death, but many lyrical and joyful poems explored life and its wonders. Love poems were fairly rare, but friendship was a common theme. Many poems concerned the parting of close friends. Chinese poems usually contained balance and symmetry and blended emotion with restraint, reflecting their Daoist and Buddhist influences. For example, Wang Wei (wahng way) expressed a Daoist appreciation of nature: "Walking at leisure we watch laurel flowers fall. In the silence of this night the spring mountain is empty. The moon rises, the birds are startled, As they sing occasionally near the spring fountains." The poem describes a changing landscape of falling laurel leaves, a quiet spring mountain, a rising moon,

Song Landscape This painting, completed around 1000 C.E., shows a Buddhist temple dwarfed by towering mountain peaks. [The Nelson-Atkins Museum of Art, Kansas City, Missouri (Purchase Nelson Trust) #47-71. Photo: Robert Newcombe]

and birds singing, all of which create Daoist feelings of peace, detachment, and purity.

The two giant figures of Tang poetry were Li Po (lee po) and Du Fu (too foo), close friends but very different in their personalities and styles. Li (701–762) was romantic, disrespectful of authority, and humorous but often melancholy: a true free spirit. Influenced by Daoism, Li said that a good person must be carefree, maintaining the heart and mind of a child. He valued friendship above all else. Li is believed to have drowned on a boat trip when he reached out in a drunken ecstasy for the reflection of the moon in the water. Many of Li's poems were composed during drinking sessions. In "The Joys of Wine" he wrote: "Since Heaven and Earth love wine, I can love wine without shaming Heaven. With three cups I penetrate the Great Dao. Take a whole jugful and I and the world are one. Such things as I have dreamed in wine, Shall never be told to the sober."[6] Other poems struck a melancholy mood. Li also occasionally wrote about public issues. In a piece about the Tang military campaigns in Central Asia, he outlined the hardships of conscripted soldiers and wondered who would cultivate their fields.

The opposite of Li Po, Du Fu (712–770) was a Confucian humanist, the preeminent poet of social consciousness and deeply concerned with the human condition. If Li's poems reflected his eccentric personality, Du Fu's held up a mirror to his times. His antiwar poems remain powerful even a millennium later: "When will men be satisfied with building a wall against the barbarians? When will the soldiers return to their native land?" His sympathies were with the soldiers and their families rather than with imperial aims:

The war-chariots rattle, The war-horses whinny. Each man of you has a bow and quiver in his belt. Father, mother, son, wife, stare at you going. At the border where the blood of men spills like the sea. And still the heart of Emperor Wu is beating for war. Do you know that, east of China's mountains, in two hundred districts, And in thousands of villages, nothing grows but weeds? And though strong women have bent to the ploughing, East and west the furrows are all broken down.

Du was also capable of great tenderness. One of his best poems celebrated the pleasures of everyday life: "Clear waters wind, Around our village. With long summer days, Full of loveliness. My wife draws out, A chessboard on paper, While our little boys, Bend needles into fish hooks. What more could I wish for?"[7]

Changes in the Late Tang Dynasty

Significant changes took place in China between the eighth and tenth centuries. For one, the overwhelming majority of Chinese now lived in central and south China, where the fertile Yangzi Basin was the most productive economic region. For another, new crop strains were introduced from Southeast Asia that eventually made it possible to harvest two crops of rice a year. This increased productivity, combined with better transportation, led to more trade and substantial increases in the urban population. Crafts and merchant guilds and the world's first paper money appeared, and Chinese traders visited Southeast Asia to obtain luxury goods.

Eventually the Tang Empire collapsed. Like the Han, the Tang ultimately found its empire too expensive to maintain and too difficult to defend. After a bitter defeat by Arab forces at the Battle of Talas (near Samarkand) in 751, the Tang declined as a military power in Central Asia. Muslim forces filled the vacuum, and Islam became the dominant religion in Turkestan and in the Xinjiang (shin-jee-yahng) region just west of China proper. Finally the Tang lost control of China itself. The country broke apart and in 907 Chinese rebel bands, spurred by famine and drought, sacked Chang'an. The Tang demise allowed Vietnam to finally free itself from the long yoke of Chinese rule.

During the next five decades after the Tang collapse, China was divided into several competing states known as the Five Dynasties. But Chinese society was now too massive and deeply rooted to experience the centuries of anarchy that occurred between the Han and Sui, and from the Tang onward the interludes of disorder between great dynasties proved brief. Perhaps the Chinese might have remained more innovative if imperial unity had been replaced by multiple and competing political units and institutions, as happened in western Europe. But the Chinese came to deplore disunity. A proverb stated: "Just as there cannot be two suns in the sky, there cannot be two rulers in China." The centralized imperial system remained in place for nearly a millennium after the Tang.

SECTION SUMMARY
- The Tang Empire was marked by ambitious expansion, inclusion of visitors from around the world, and the spread of Chinese goods across Eurasia.
- Under the Tang, stability was maintained by keeping the emperor's authority somewhat in check and by rewarding high achievers through the civil service exam system.
- Buddhism reached its peak influence during the Tang, but it was greatly weakened when Emperor Wuzong seized Buddhist monasteries.
- During the Tang, the first book was printed using woodblocks.
- Poetry and other arts were very popular during the Tang; while usually stressing Daoist harmony, they sometimes expressed criticism of the government.

Song China and Commercial Growth

Why might historians consider the Song dynasty the high point of China's golden age?

The next great dynasty, the Song (Sung) (960–1279), founded by an able general, presided over a sophisticated period of achievement. Although lacking the Tang's grandeur, empire building, and world leadership, the Song was in many respects more refined in the arts of living and in technological development and material richness. Described by some historians as

Scroll of Kaifeng This segment from the scroll "Spring Festival on the River," discussed in the chapter opening, shows people thronging the Rainbow Bridge while boatmen lower their masts to pass under the cantilevered structure. Along the streets and bridge stalls sell their goods. (Werner Forman/Art Resource, NY)

premodern China's most exciting period, the Song was characterized by unprecedented growth, innovation, economic dynamism, urban sophistication, and cultural flowering. Late Song China contained perhaps 120 million people, with some two-thirds of them living in the Yangzi Basin or in the south. This Chinese population, between a quarter and a third of the world's total, lived in an area that stretched a thousand miles east to west and north to south, all of it linked by rivers and an extensive canal system. Clearly the Song continued the golden age begun by the Tang.

Urban Life and Economic Prosperity

During the Song, cities grew rapidly and economic growth was renewed. Song China boasted the world's largest cities. At least five cities had populations over a million, and nearly fifty other cities contained over 100,000 people. Meanwhile, once great cities in western Eurasia had fallen in population by Song times: Rome to 35,000 and Baghdad to 125,000. Chinese urban residents, such as those in the capital city of Kaifeng described earlier, enjoyed a high quality of life. A modern scholar described the vibrant activity in one of the cities:

The day started with the booming of temple bells. Peddlers began to make their way up and down the streets, calling out the foods they had for sale. Carts laden with meats and vegetables moved in toward the markets. Businesses of all kinds opened. Many of these, such as the tailors,

hairdressers, dealers in paper and brushes, and caterers, served the city's taste for luxury. As night fell, lanterns lit up taverns and restaurants, the largest of which had staffs of hundreds. In the theater district dozens of houses offered varied bills, including the latest songs, puppet shows, acrobats, wrestlers, storytellers, and comedians.[8]

In the later Song era, when the government had been pushed south of the Yangzi River by nomadic invaders, the capital was Hangzhou (hahng-jo), a city of several million on the southern end of the Grand Canal (see Witness to the Past: Life in the Chinese Capital City). A later and well-traveled visitor, Marco Polo, called it unquestionably the greatest city in the world. Social life in Hangzhou and other cities coalesced around the wine shops, restaurants, theaters, entertainment houses, and brothels. Hangzhou would be followed by Nanjing in the fifteenth century, and then Beijing from the sixteenth into the nineteenth centuries, as the world's largest cities.

The Song also marked the high point for Chinese commerce and foreign trade. The flourishing merchant class grew substantially, and tax revenues were three times higher than for the Tang. The Grand Canal, which linked the Yellow and Yangzi River Basins, provided an economic cornerstone, allowing the mass movement of goods between north and south. The Song extended the canal. China also developed the world's first fully monetized economy, putting paper money and silver coins into wide use. In addition, Song China had the world's most advanced farming, and its expanding productivity met the

The following excerpts are from a description of Hangzhou, the capital city of China during the southern Song dynasty, written by a Chinese observer in 1235. It reveals the life of urban people in China during one of its most creative eras. The writer describes the city's many amenities, including shops, restaurants, and taverns, and also its cultural and social activities. The many specialized enterprises and diverse clubs indicate a highly complex society.

During the morning hours, markets extend from . . . the palace all the way to . . . the New Boulevard. Here we find pearl, jade, talismans, exotic plants and fruits, seasonal catches from the sea, wild game—all the rarities of the world. . . . In the evening . . . the markets are as busy as during the day. . . . In the wine shops and inns business also thrives. . . . In general the capital attracts the greatest variety of goods and has the best craftsmen. For instance, the flower company at Superior Lane does a truly excellent job of flower arrangement, and its caps, hairpins, and collars are unsurpassed in craftsmanship. Some . . . famous fabric stores sell exquisite brocade and fine silk which are unsurpassed anywhere in the country.

Among the various kinds of wine shops, the tea-and-food shops sell not only wine, but also various foods to go with it. However, to get seasonal delicacies . . . one should go to the inns, for they also have a menu from which one can make selections. The pastry-and-wine shops sell pastries with duckling and goose fillings. . . . In the large teahouses there are usually paintings and calligraphies by famous artists on display. . . . Most restaurants here are operated by people from the old capital [Kaifeng], like the lamb rice shops which also serve wine. . . . There are special food shops such as meat-pie shops and vegetable-noodle shops. . . . The vegetarian restaurants cater to [Buddhist] religious banquets and vegetarian dinners. . . . There are also shops specializing in snacks. Depending on the season, they sell a variety of delicacies. . . . In the evening, food vendors of all sorts parade the streets and alleys . . . chanting their trade songs. . . .

The entertainment centers . . . are places where people gather. . . . In these centers there are schools for musicians offering thirteen different courses, among which the most significant is opera. . . . In each scene of an operatic performance there are four or five performers who first act out a short, well-known piece. . . . Then they give a performance of the opera itself. . . . The opera is usually based on history and teaches a moral lesson, which may also be a political criticism in disguise. . . . There are always various acting troupes performing, and this usually attracts a large crowd.

For men of letters, there is a unique West Lake Poetry Society. Its members include both scholars residing in the capital and visiting poets from other parts of the country; over the years, many famous poets have been associated with this society. . . . Other groups include the Physical Fitness Club, Angler's Club, Occult Club, Young Girl's Chorus, Exotic Foods Club, Plants and Fruits Club, Antique Collector's Club, Horse-Lover's Club, and Refined Music Society. . . .

There are civil and military schools inside . . . the capital. Besides lineage schools, capital schools, and country schools, there are at least one or two village schools, family schools, private studios, or learning centers in every neighborhood.

THINKING ABOUT THE READING

1. What do the main goods sold in the markets say about economic prosperity?
2. What does the reading tell us about popular pleasures and entertainments in Hangzhou?
3. What do the main recreational and educational activities available suggest about leisure time and societal values?

Source: Patricia Buckley Ebrey, ed., *Chinese Civilization and Society: A Sourcebook*, 2nd ed. (New York: Free Press, 1993), pp. 178–185. Reprinted with permission of the Free Press, a division of Simon and Schuster Adult Publishing Group. Copyright © 1993 by Patricia Buckley Ebrey. All rights reserved.

needs of a flourishing market economy for agricultural products. Song farmers doubled the rice crop and vastly increased the growing and marketing of sugar, once a minor crop.

Online Study Center Improve Your Grade
Primary Source: The Craft of Farming

Foreign trade continued to flourish, but now it was based more on maritime networks that connected China to the rest of Afro-Eurasia. Chinese merchants regularly visited Southeast Asia and traded around the Indian Ocean, and Chinese industrial and food products found a market as far away as Persia, East Africa, and Egypt. The coastal seaports of Guangzhou (Canton) and Quanzhou (Zayton) in the south, which were cosmopolitan centers for the maritime trade to southern Asia

and the Middle East, were home to thousands of foreigners, including many Arab, Indian, Persian, and even East African merchants. To accommodate these varied peoples, the cities contained numerous mosques and Hindu temples.

Industry, Technology and Science

Song China's industry was the world's most advanced, and its manufacturing sector grew dramatically. Indeed, China's continuing world leadership was reflected in its export of manufactured goods (silks, porcelain, books) and import of raw materials (spices, minerals, horses). Chinese porcelain was traded all over Asia, the Middle East, and parts of Africa, and the name *china* became synonymous with the very finest porcelain products. In addition, China's iron industry was the world's largest before the eighteenth century, producing the finest steel for tools, weapons, stoves, ploughshares, cooking equipment, nails, building materials, and bridges. Mass production and metal-casting techniques supplied standardized iron products to the world's largest internal market. The Song mined coal for fuel and produced salt for various purposes on an industrial scale. Spurred by domestic and foreign trade, Song China also developed a significant shipbuilding industry. Its huge compartmentalized ships had four decks and four to six masts and were capable of carrying five hundred sailors and extensive cargo. Many thousands of cargo ships plied the rivers and canals. This maritime technology was the world's best at that time.

The Song also maintained the Chinese technological tradition. During the Tang and Song periods, Chinese technological development outstripped that of other Afro-Eurasian societies. Some studies suggest that, between the first and fifteenth centuries C.E., the Chinese produced a majority of the world's major inventions. Song Chinese invented new agricultural and textile tools and machines, built the world's longest bridge (2.5 kilometers), and expanded the use of water-powered clocks and mills. Major Chinese inventions of the era that later spread throughout Eurasia included the magnetic compass (for naval navigation), the sternpost rudder, and the spinning wheel. Song craftsmen also made movable type, first from fired clay and then from tin or copper, an invention that greatly facilitated the printing of books. In weaponry, Song technicians developed the fire lance, a bamboo tube filled with gunpowder that was the precursor of the metal-barrel gun. Song ships were fitted with missile launchers, flamethrowers, cannon, and bombs, all used to keep the coast free of pirates. Song engineers also invented a mechanized spinning process for the reeling of silk and later hemp thread. It was the world's first industrial machinery, developed over half a millennium before the Industrial Revolution began in western Europe.

The Song had notable achievements in astronomy and medicine. Today astronomers still use data the Song collected from observation of the skies, such as on the supernova that created the Crab Nebula. A Song calendar precisely measured the solar year (365.2425 days). In medicine, Chinese doctors inoculated against smallpox, a disease that ravaged much of Afro-Eurasia. Some Chinese medical ideas reached the Middle East and Europe by the thirteenth century.

Social Life and Gender Relations

During the Song era, Chinese society changed as a common elite culture spread among the educated. Printed books fostered the spread of education, which exposed a wider audience to the values of the social and political elite. In addition, the Song government established schools in every district. Although only a small percentage of these students ever became mandarins, a degree or some educated background became a certificate of status, even if it never led to a government post. And education led many to conform their behavior and expectations to the elite culture, which was urbane and sophisticated. The cultivated gentleman, whether or not in govern-

ment service, was expected to be proficient in music (especially lute playing), chess, calligraphy, poetry, and painting.

However, while educated men enjoyed many options, women experienced more restrictions than they had known earlier. Women had been involved in public life during the Tang. Tang paintings and statues show aristocratic women in swept-up hair riding horses or standing dignified, wearing loose-fitting gowns. In some respects Song commercial growth benefited women as well as men. Women operated restaurants and sold fish and vegetables in markets. Wealthy families employed maids, dressmakers, cooks, and singing and dancing girls to entertain guests.

But during the Song era women's status began to decline. Conservatives feared that the new economic opportunities offered to women might undermine patriarchy and sought to limit women's roles. Men more often took concubines (official mistresses) in addition to their official wives, and families increasingly frowned upon remarriage for widows. Peasant wives had the most equitable position because they worked in the fields alongside men and were therefore crucial to family economic livelihood. Still, children belonged to the father's family, and the wife was ruled by her husband's mother. Divorce was possible but uncommon because it was a disgrace for the woman. In addition, old age was especially difficult for poor women, as a male Song writer sympathetically described:

> But for those destined to be poor, old age is hard to endure. For them, until about the age of fifty, the passage of twenty years seems like only ten; but after that age, ten years can feel as long as twenty. For women who live a long life, old age is especially hard to bear, because most women must rely on others for their existence. Some wives with stupid husbands are able to manage the family's finances. But the most remarkable are the women who manage a household after their husbands have died leaving them with young children. When wives themselves can read and do arithmetic then things will usually work out all right.[9]

Still another source of suffering for women was footbinding, which was introduced during the Song period among the elite and some of the common folk. Mothers tightly bound the feet of five- or six-year-old daughters to prevent normal growth. This practice crippled a girl's feet and gave her a dainty walk, which enhanced what Chinese men viewed as her beauty and eroticism. But many peasants rejected the practice as too physically debilitating, since women's labor was necessary for family survival. Footbinding was not widespread until later dynasties.

Neo-Confucianism and Chinese Thought

The Song also saw the rise of **neo-Confucianism,** a form of Confucianism that incorporated many Buddhist and Daoist metaphysical ideas. Neo-Confucianism was associated particu-

neo-Confucianism A form of Confucianism arising in China during the Song period (960–1279) that incorporated many Buddhist and Daoist metaphysical ideas.

larly with Zhu Xi (JOO shee) (1130–1200), a child prodigy and one of the most influential thinkers in Chinese history. Zhu Xi twice resigned from government service in disgust at corruption and inefficiency. He believed that the original ideas of Confucius had become rigid and altered over the centuries, and he advocated rediscovering the essence of the sage's ideas and writings. The influence of Daoism can be seen in Zhu Xi's rational and humane approach, which recognized a dualism between the material world and the energizing force thought by Chinese to pervade the universe, **qi** (ch'i). Harnessing this qi for personal centering became the goal of *tai qi* (tai ch'i), exercises to build mind and body.

Zhu offered innovative approaches. In the spirit of Confucius, he identified reason or principle as the unchanging law, and morality as the measure of all human affairs: "For every person in the society the most important thing is the cultivation of himself as an ethical being." Zhu also maintained that one should observe and investigate things outside of oneself, arguing that understanding truths required self-cultivation and unselfish behavior: "With each meal of porridge or rice, remember the hardship from whence it came."[10] Yet, Zhu was indifferent to natural science; hence, although he seemed to advocate a scientific method, his ideas did not help regenerate or sustain scientific inquiry. Over time neo-Confucianism became the dominant mindset of China's educated elite and a force for stability but not innovation.

The Song in World History

In many ways the Song could have been a turning point in Chinese and world history, but it did not foster a major transition. The profound Song economic, technological, and urban developments remind some historians of eighteenth-century Europe at the dawn of rapid industrialization. But unlike that revolution's transforming impact in the West, the Song's commercial and agricultural dynamism never revolutionized Chinese society. Instead, these developments were contained and absorbed. For example, the Chinese had the technology to sail the seas and colonize other lands, but they lacked the incentive because China was largely self-sufficient. In addition, since the highly bureaucratic empire easily adjusted to economic change, it could maintain its dominance over the merchants and keep them from disrupting China's social order and hierarchy. With an agriculture productive enough to feed a huge population, convenient transportation by water through canals, and many natural resources, the Chinese had no great need to develop additional mechanized technologies. Furthermore, the Mongol conquest of the Song, as well as a cooler climate by the thirteenth century and the Black Death pandemic in the fourteenth, undermined economic dynamism. Finally, population pressure became a growing burden as land available for farming filled up.

qi In Chinese thought, the energizing force pervading the universe.

In its domination of the merchants, the imperial government played a central role in containing economic growth. For example, the government tried to check famine by establishing granaries and taxing the wealthy to support them. Many essential commodities remained government monopolies, such as iron, grain, cloth, and salt. In part this socialist policy reflected the low esteem accorded merchants in Confucian ideology. Monopolies over essential products helped enrich the state and also protected the population from price and supply problems, but they restricted merchants to handling nonessential products. One ambitious Song prime minister with socialist leanings, Wang Anshi (wahng ahn-shee) (1021–1086), experimented unsuccessfully with guaranteed state loans to farmers, fixed commodity prices, unemployment insurance, and old age pensions. He said that every family should have enough for its needs. Thus, "the state should take the entire management of commerce, industry, and agriculture into its own hands, with a view to [preventing] the working classes from being ground into the dust by the rich."[11]

The Song government, more interested in economic than political growth and empire, devoted resources to weapons but was generally disinterested in military expansion. Prosperity, trade, and urban living made peace more attractive than conquest. Although it maintained the world's largest army, the Song, unlike the Han and Tang, took steps to reduce the power of military leaders so they could not threaten civilian authority, a chronic problem in the Tang. As a result, the Song adopted a passive attitude toward controlling the pastoral nomads across the border. They attempted not to conquer but to appease them with generous payments. Ultimately the policy failed. In the twelfth century a nomadic people, the Jin (Chin), conquered north China, forcing the Song court to move south across the Yangzi, where it continued to rule central and south China from Hangzhou until the invasion by the Mongols.

SECTION SUMMARY

- The Song dynasty was notable for its bustling urban life, its maritime trade, and its advanced economy.
- Song China made great advances in the manufacture of porcelain, ships, and bridges and in the prevention of disease.
- During the Song, the pursuit of education and cultivation became widespread among the elite.
- However, the status of women declined, and footbinding began to be practiced by the elite and some commoners.
- The Song's achievements did not lead to a major historical transition because China at this time felt self-sufficient, was not interested in conquest, and kept merchants out of important industries; it also tried to deal with neighboring pastoral nomads peacefully, a strategy that ultimately failed.

Mongol Conquest, Chinese Resurgence, and Eurasian Connections

How did China change during the Yuan and Ming dynasties?

From the thirteenth through the nineteenth centuries the Chinese way of life showed great stability. Three ruling houses—the Yuan, the Ming, and the Qing (discussed in a later chapter)— held power between the downfall of the Song and the end of the imperial system in the twentieth century. Disorder occurred chiefly only during years of dynastic decline and change. Yet this almost unprecedented record of political stability, perhaps matched only by that of the ancient Egyptian kingdoms, has a puzzling aspect, since two of the three dynasties were conquest dynasties imposed by non-Chinese nomadic peoples riding in on horseback. The two dynasties that held power between the thirteenth and seventeenth centuries were the Yuan (yu-wenn), established by invading Mongols, and the Ming, which marked a return to Chinese rule.

The Mongol Empire and the Conquest of China

For several millennia the Chinese had feared what they considered the northern "barbarian" scourge, fast-riding horsemen who came out of the Central Asian grasslands and deserts killing, looting, and taking captives. The strongest rulers could control these nomadic tribal peoples, usually by conquest or effective divide-and-rule diplomacy. But weak rulers or dynasties had to contend with the constant threat. The ever-present Central Asian influence on China's political life was based on a major geographical fact: the close proximity of the arid grasslands north and west of China, which, compared to the lush farmlands of China, were suitable only for mobile herding.

These contrasting environments had produced very different societies. In the grasslands a pastoral economy and few resources necessitated seasonal migration, chronic poverty, and small temporary settlements. The herding people were tough and self-reliant, the men skilled in martial pursuits. Because the men were not tied down working the fields, they could be easily mobilized for warfare while women tended to the herds. When China was weak, the Great Wall proved no major barrier to peoples anxious to taste the affluence of China. In the thirteenth century the Chinese realized their worst nightmare when a new confederation of warlike peoples, the Mongols, conquered all of China.

Before invading China the Mongols conquered much of Eurasia, including eastern Europe and western Asia. Traditionally divided into often feuding tribes, the Mongols became united under Temuchin (ca. 1167–1227), a ruthless but brilliant man of humble origins who defeated or co-opted his

rivals and then changed his name to Genghis Khan (GENG-iz KAHN) ("Universal Emperor"). He had simple motives: "A man's greatest pleasure is to defeat his enemies, to drive them before him, to take from them that which they possessed, to see those whom they cherished in tears, to ride their horses, to hold their wives and daughters in his arms."[12] Skilled horse soldiers, only lightly armored in horse leather but more agile than their foes, the Mongols were formidable opponents. Their well-organized fighting units possessed powerful bows that could kill at 600 feet, disc-shaped stirrups that gave the rider maneuverability, and the world's most advanced siege weaponry, including catapults.

Because of China's strength, it was one of the last countries to fall to Mongol control. Genghis Khan had conquered parts of northern China in 1215. The Mongol conquest of the rest of China, which came fifty years after the death of Genghis, was accomplished by his grandson, Khubilai Khan (koo-bluh KAHN) (r. 1260–1294). The Mongol conquest resulted in a new dynasty, which took the name Yuan (1279–1368). With this event China became, for the first and only time, part of a great world empire, one that stretched from eastern Europe to Korea and from the Black Sea to the Pacific Ocean (see Map 11.2).

Mongol Government and Chinese Culture

The Mongols under Khubilai Khan made major changes in China, imposing a distinctive government system and fostering new cultural forms. By Mongol standards Khubilai Khan was a rather enlightened ruler, far less cruel and more pragmatic than most of the Mongol leaders elsewhere in Eurasia. For example, he patronized Buddhism. The Mongols also built granaries for food storage, operated an efficient postal system, and improved the transportation network. But Chinese historians have condemned Khubilai Khan for the sins committed by the Mongols generally. One of the greatest Mongol failings in Chinese eyes was to maintain Mongol cultural identity and actively resist assimilation into Chinese society. Later Chinese viewed the Yuan as China's darkest hour, even worse than the Qin 1,500 years earlier, an intolerable rule by aliens who would not be absorbed.

In another change, Khubilai Khan moved the capital to Beijing (bay-JING) ("Northern Capital"), before this a provincial city close to the Great Wall. Beijing was a hub situated alongside the major highways leading north and west; in addition, because it was on the northern edge of the farmlands of China proper, it symbolically tied China to the borderlands. Except for brief periods since, Beijing has remained the capital of China, politically eclipsing more ancient cities like Chang'an and Hangzhou.

The Mongols did not patronize intellectuals—indeed, they mistrusted them—but they were tolerant in religious matters. They invited missionaries from all over Eurasia to come to the court for religious debates, among them Christians of various sects (including Catholics); Khubilai Khan's mother was a Nestorian Christian. In part this tolerance was because Khubilai Khan

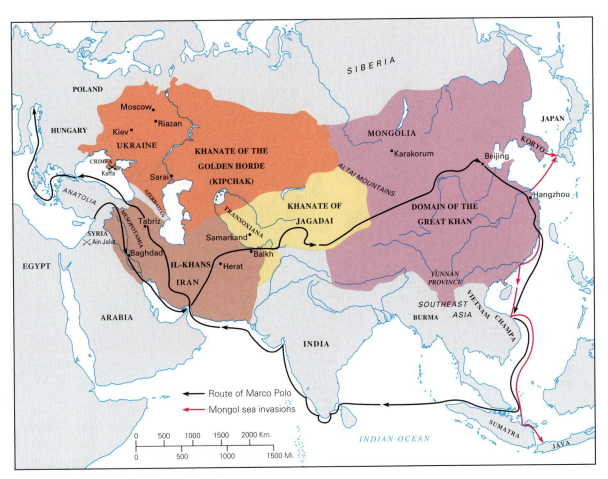

Map 11.2   China in the Mongol Empire
After the Mongols conquered much of Central Asia, western Asia, and eastern Europe, they added China and Korea to their huge empire, the largest contiguous land empire in world history. During the Mongol era many Asians and some Europeans, including the Italian Marco Polo, visited or worked in China.

and his successors ruled over a religiously diverse society and wanted to avoid conflict. Indeed, China was far more accepting of religious diversity than Christian Europe. However, the Mongols had more rigid gender expectations and marriage practices than the Chinese, and stressed the need for widows to remain chaste and dutifully serve their aging parents-in-law. In response to occasional Mongol mistreatment of Chinese women, Chinese men now also expected women to remain at home and emphasize feminine behavior, including the growing fashion of tightly bound feet to set them apart from non-Chinese women.

Culturally the Mongol period proved relatively sterile in comparison to the brilliance of the Tang and Song, but there were some innovations. Musical drama (Chinese opera) became a popular form of entertainment, appealing mostly to the Chinese common folk rather than the elite. In addition, the Chinese began writing novels, an elaboration of age-old storytelling. The first novelists were intellectuals deprived of their imperial patronage who refused to work for the Mongols. Seeking alternative sources of income, they wrote books for a popular audience.

Mongol China and Eurasian Networks

The Mongols paved the way for enhanced global communication, opening China's doors to the world. By protecting the Silk Road, which had languished for several centuries from chronic warfare between Central Asian societies, the Mongols fostered networks for the exchange of not only goods but also ideas and technology between East and West. During the Mongol era Chinese inventions like gunpowder, printing, the blast furnace for cast iron, silk-making machinery, paper money, and playing cards moved westward, as did many medical discoveries. Bubonic plague, which killed millions of Chinese during Mongol rule, probably traveled the overland trade routes, fostering the Black Death that ravaged the Middle East and Europe in the fourteenth century (see Chapters 10 and 14).

In addition, many foreigners came to Mongol China by land and sea. The Mongols encouraged them to come for a reason. Although Khubilai Khan made some determined attempts to win Chinese support by modeling his government along Chinese lines and dutifully performing Confucian rites, the Mongols failed to get the cooperation of most scholars and

Khubilai Khan and His Entourage Hunting   This painting by a Chinese artist of the time shows Khubilai Khan, dressed in ermine, and Mongol colleagues, including a woman, hunting on horseback, a popular activity among Mongols.   (National Palace Museum, Taipei, Taiwan)

bureaucrats. To rule the vast country, they were forced to rely administratively on foreigners who came to China to serve in what was effectively an international civil service. These included many Muslims from Central Asia, western Asia, and even North Africa, as well as a few Europeans who found their way to "fabled Cathay," as they called China.

One of the European visitors to Yuan China was the Italian merchant Marco Polo (ca. 1254–1324). Polo, with his brothers and father, initially went to China seeking trade goods but spent seventeen years there, mostly in government service. Eventually Polo returned to Italy and told of the wonders he had encountered (or heard about from other travelers). The Europeans, few of whom knew much or cared about the world east of Palestine, were unbelieving. When Polo's book was published, most dismissed it as full of lies, but the general accuracy of his account has been confirmed by historians. He was a keen observer and recorded the resentment of the Chinese people toward the Mongols, who imposed their rule by force and sometimes with brutality. For example, they once slaughtered a city's entire population for the killing of one drunk Mongol soldier.

Polo wrote of China's great cities, such as Beijing and Hangzhou. Standing along the shores of beautiful West Lake, Hangzhou could not help but charm the Italian, as it had fascinated other visitors. Polo wrote in the thirteenth century that "the city is beyond dispute the finest and noblest in the world in point of grandeur and beauty as well as in its abundant delights. The natives of this city are of peaceful character, thoroughly honest and truthful and accustomed to dainty living."[13] The city boasted parks, a fire department, garbage collection, a

pollution-control agency, and paved streets—all things nonexistent in Polo's much smaller Venice, then one of the major European cities.

Polo's reports seemed unbelievable to Europeans because China in this era was far more developed in many fields than the rest of Eurasia and had the world's highest standard of living. Polo noted, for example, that the Chinese had for a thousand years burned black stones (coal) for heat and that they took regular baths. According to his account: "The streets connected with the market-squares are numerous, and in some of them are many cold baths, attended by [people] of both sexes. All [residents] are in the daily practice of washing their persons, and especially before their meals."[14] This latter information was astounding, since medieval Europeans seldom if ever bathed.

While the Mongol conquests had enormous consequences for Central Asia, the Middle East, and Europe, Mongol rule in China lasted only a century and did not leave a deep imprint. Although the Mongols had a continental power and long dominated regions such as Russia and Turkestan, they failed to hold China. For one thing, they were always unpopular, even hated. In addition, their leadership deteriorated after the death of Khubilai Khan. Furthermore, the Mongols in China had a difficult time adjusting to peace: they lost their fighting toughness and came to desire luxury more than sacrifice. As Mongols in Central Asia and Persia adopted the cultures and religions of the conquered, the empire and Mongol unity fragmented, and corruption and power struggles grew rampant. Then too, a terrible plague outbreak raged and the Yellow River flooded severely, bringing famine and challenging the Mongols' claims to the Mandate of Heaven. Soon rebellions broke out all over China. The turmoil was ended by a Chinese commoner who established a new Chinese dynasty, the Ming. Mongol military forces left China and returned to Central Asia.

Ming Government and Culture

The new Ming dynasty (1368–1644) became a great period of orderly government and social stability, with a rich culture. The founder, Zhu Yuanzhang (JOO yuwen-JAHNG) (1328–1398), was a former Buddhist monk and the son of an itinerant farm worker who, like the founder of the Han, rose from abject poverty through sheer ability and ruthless behavior in a time of opportunity. Under the Ming, China's people lived for nearly three centuries in comparative peace and considerable prosperity, with living standards among the highest and mortality rates among the lowest of anywhere in the world. China more than doubled in population, from around 80 million to between 160 and 180 million.

The Ming installed a government similar to that of the Han and Tang but were somewhat more despotic. Perhaps because of the bitter experience of Mongol rule, the Ming emperors exercised more power than Song or Tang emperors and placed the bureaucracy under closer imperial scrutiny. Yet, the bureaucracy was still small, some twenty-thousand officials, of whom some 25 percent were from nonelite backgrounds. The Ming also eliminated the office of prime minister, which had been traditional since the Han. The man who filled this post had been the highest-ranking mandarin and had kept his hand on the pulse of the country. The Censorate also became more timid, reducing the checks on royal abuses. As a result of these changes, the Ming emperors became more isolated from the real world. As in previous dynasties, some Ming emperors had male lovers as well as many wives and concubines. This reflected a tolerance of same-sex relationships among many Chinese court officials and commoners.

A sense of order infused the arts, which saw several genres mature during the Ming. Theater flourished, reaching its highest level in this period. The most popular form of theater at the peasant level, Chinese opera (musical drama), included extended arias and spoken dialogue. Most operas were witty and unrealistic, often with lowbrow humor. Each performance of a play aimed at harmonizing all the elements: song, speech, costume, makeup, movement, and musical accompaniment. The stage settings were minimal, since the audience focused intently on the actors, who triggered their imagination by telling a story by word and gesture. Much Chinese music was composed for operas or for ritual and ceremonial purposes. String, wind, and percussion instruments were popular, especially the flute, lute, and zither.

Although most Ming scholars considered fiction worthless, it had a large audience. Most novels had a Confucian moral emphasizing correct behavior, but some offered social criticisms or satires. Perhaps the greatest Ming novel, *The Water Margin* (also known as *All Men Are Brothers*), presented heroes who were also bandits, Robin Hoods driven into crime by corrupt officials. Another great work, *The Golden Lotus*, re-

A Ming Imperial Workshop   Printer's shops, such as the one shown here, used movable type to publish encyclopedias with information on engineering, medicine, agriculture, and other practical topics.   [Courtesy of South China University of Technology Library, Canton (Guangzhou)]

vealed the hedonistic lives of the rich. Both these novels offered psychological depth. Ming authors also wrote some of the world's first detective stories.

Ming rulers encouraged intellectual pursuits, expanding the *Hanlin* ("Forest of Culture") Academy, which was established in the Tang. The brightest scholars were assigned there as research fellows and were paid to read and write whatever they liked. Ming scholars also compiled a 11,000-volume encyclopedia (with 20,000 chapters) and a 52-volume study of Chinese pharmacology.

Ming China and the Afro-Eurasian World

Rather than building a new empire, the Ming turned to overseas exploration, which resulted in closer political and economic relations with Southeast Asia. The early Ming rulers pursued territorial expansion, including a failed attempt to

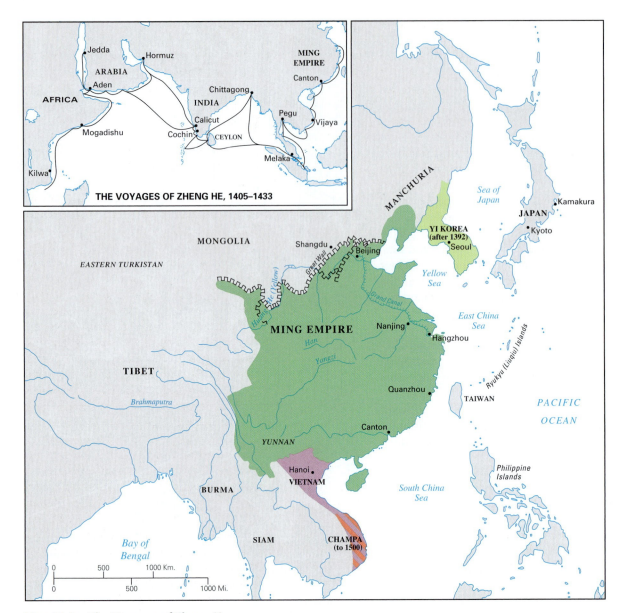

THE VOYAGES OF ZHENG HE, 1405–1433

Map 11.3   The Voyages of Zheng He

After replacing the Mongols, the Ming reestablished a strong Chinese state, attempted to recolonize Vietnam, and rebuilt the Great Wall. Ming emperors dispatched a series of grand maritime expeditions in the early 1400s that reached the Middle East and East Africa.

recolonize Vietnam. But China was now oriented more to the sea. Rather than send armies far into Central Asia, the emperor dispatched a series of grand maritime expeditions to southern Asia and beyond to reaffirm China's preeminence in the eastern half of Asia by, as official sources put it, "showing off the wealth and power of the Central Kingdom."[15] Admiral Zheng He (jung huh) (Cheng Ho) (ca. 1371–1435), a huge man and a trusted court eunuch of Muslim faith, commanded seven voyages between 1405 and 1433. The world had never before seen such a large-scale feat of seamanship: the largest fleet comprised sixty-two vessels carrying 28,000 men, and the largest "treasure ships," as they were known, weighed 1,500 tons, were

450 feet long, boasted nine masts nearly 500 feet high, and carried a crew of five hundred. Observers must have been astounded as these ships approached their harbors. A few decades later Christopher Columbus sailed from Spain in three tiny vessels carrying only about a hundred men total.

Zheng He's extraordinary voyages carried the Chinese flag through Southeast Asia to India, the Persian Gulf, and the East African coast (see Map 11.3). Had they continued, the Chinese ships had the capability of sailing around Africa to Europe or the Americas but had no incentive to do so. The expeditions expressed the exuberance of an era of great vitality. Even though the Chinese came mostly in peace and undertook only a few military actions, some thirty-six countries in southern and western Asia officially acknowledged Chinese preeminence. Even the ruler of the East African city of Malindi sent ambassadors bearing tribute, including a giraffe.

Historians still debate the reasons for Zheng He's great voyages. Some point to ideology, the desire to have so many foreign countries reaffirm the emperor's position as the Son of Heaven. Zheng He may also have sought to locate a deposed boy emperor who had disappeared, possibly fleeing into exile. Others suspect the ambitious emperor wanted to demonstrate China's military capabilities. Some historians, however, see commercial motives as primary, since these voyages occurred at a time of increased activity by Chinese merchants in Southeast Asia. During the early Ming many thousands of Chinese had settled or were sojourning in what is today the Philippines, Indonesia, Siam, and Vietnam, creating a closer commercial link to China. Chinese merchants also visited trading ports in India and forged extensive trade links across the Indian Ocean, transporting Yuan and Ming porcelain as far west as the interior of south-central Africa.

The voyages of Zheng He may also have helped revitalize the traditional tribute system. During Han and Tang times this tribute system helped shape China's relations with its neighbors. Under this system China considered the various East, Southeast, and Central Asian states as vassals or tributaries and granted them trade relations and protection. The protection was mostly symbolic, however, since the Chinese rarely intervened to support their allies, except in nearby Korea. In return the tributary states sent periodic envoys bearing gifts to the emperor, confirming his superiority in ritual form. The vassal states played along, whatever their true feelings, because they desired China's goodwill and trade goods. In Ming times tribute came regularly from states in Korea, Vietnam, Cambodia, Borneo, Indonesia, South Asia, and Central Asia. The tribute system also enabled the Chinese to benefit from trade with various countries.

Inevitably the Chinese saw themselves as the Middle Kingdom surrounded by vassal states in various degrees of barbarism. Beginning in the Han, the Chinese never recognized any other society as an equal, at least not symbolically. They developed the notion that they were superior not just materially but also culturally and that barbarians could not resist their appeal. This view was reinforced by the fact that other East Asian societies borrowed from China. For the Chinese, to be civilized was to embrace Chinese culture, and a virtuous ruler, they believed, irresistibly attracted barbarians. When a tribute mission arrived in the capital, part of the rite was the **kotow**, the tribute-bearers' act of prostrating themselves before the emperor, a practice from which we get the modern English word *kowtow*, to pander to authority. This practice, above all others, left little doubt as to who was superior and who was inferior, reflecting a Confucian sense of hierarchy.

kotow The tribute-bearers' act of prostrating themselves before the Chinese emperor.

Ming China Turns Inward

In the early Ming, China remained at the cutting edge, perhaps the world's wealthiest and most developed country. Hindu India faced Muslim conquests, the Middle Eastern societies were struggling to recover from various setbacks, and the western Europeans were just beginning to enjoy political and economic dynamism. Commercially vibrant and outward-thrusting, Ming China had the capability to open maritime communication between the continents and become the dominant world power. But world dominance never came and China turned inward. The grand voyages to the west and the commercial thrust in distant lands came to a sudden halt when the Ming emperor ordered them ended and recalled the overseas Chinese merchants from Southeast Asia. Soon the state outlawed Chinese emigration altogether. But the withdrawal was by no means total. Some Chinese continued to illegally travel abroad for trade, and foreign merchant ships still came to China. The tribute system provided cover for extensive trade and smuggling.

The causes of the stunning reversal of official Chinese engagement with the world that, in the perspective of later history, seemed so counterproductive remain subject to debate. Some causes were economic. Perhaps Zheng He's voyages were too costly even for the wealthy Ming government. The voyages were not cost-effective, since the ships mostly returned with exotic goods (such as African giraffes for the imperial zoo) rather than mineral resources and other valuable items. Other causes were cultural and ideological. Unlike Christian and Muslim societies, the Chinese lacked any missionary zeal, having little interest in spreading Chinese religion and culture except to near neighbors such as Vietnam. Furthermore, despite their flourishing guilds and frequent wealth, the merchants held a low status in the Confucian social and ideological system. Indeed, Ming leaders were even more convinced than their predecessors that profit was evil, and mercantile interests inevitably conflicted with social and political ones. Confucian officials often despised the merchants, and a later Ming scholar wrote that "one in a hundred [Chinese] is rich, while nine out of ten are impoverished. The poor cannot stand up to the rich. The lord of silver rules heaven and the god of copper cash reigns over the earth."[16] In keeping with these feelings, many mandarins opposed foreign trade.

Military and economic factors also influenced the turn inward. With the Mongols regrouping in Central Asia, the Ming court shifted its resources to defense of the northern borders and the pirate-infested Pacific coast, spending millions rebuilding and extending the Great Wall. What tourists see today of the Great Wall near Beijing is mostly work that the Ming did. But military operations along the northern border and an ill-fated invasion of Vietnam generated a fiscal crisis that weakened the government. In dealing with this crisis, the Ming began concentrating on home affairs.

Finally, the turn inward can be seen as a reaction to the Mongols. After the bitterness of the Mongol era, the Chinese became more ethnocentric and antiforeign. The early Ming maritime expeditions were an aberration, because China had always been land-based and self-centered. Ming Chinese believed that they needed nothing from outside, since the Middle Kingdom considered itself to be self-sufficient. China remained powerful, productive, and mostly prosperous, enjoying generally high living standards, well into the eighteenth century, when profits from overseas colonies and the Industrial Revolution tipped the balance in favor of northwest Europe. By the later Ming, China had entered a period of relative isolation that was ended only by the forceful intrusion of a newly developed Europe in the early 1800s.

SECTION SUMMARY

- The ancient Chinese fear of Central Asian nomads was realized when the Mongols, under Genghis and Khubilai Khan, conquered China and established the Yuan dynasty.
- Khubilai Khan made a number of improvements in China's transportation system and moved the capital to Beijing.
- Because of lack of cooperation from Chinese scholars and bureaucrats, the Mongols established an international civil service, in which Marco Polo served.
- After the decline of the Mongols, the Chinese enjoyed three centuries of prosperity under the Ming dynasty, and their sense of well-being was displayed in Zheng He's grand sailing expeditions, which enhanced China's position among its neighbors.
- The Ming dynasty received tribute from many peoples throughout Asia.
- For reasons that are still debated, the Ming emperor suddenly ordered all overseas activity halted and China turned inward, beginning an isolation that ended only in the 1800s.

Cultural Adaptation in Korea and Japan

How did the Koreans and Japanese make use of Chinese culture in developing their own distinctive societies?

As the cultural heartland of East Asia, China strongly influenced its three large neighbors of Vietnam (see Chapter 13), Korea, and Japan. Both Vietnam and Korea derived considerable culture from China, including writing systems, philosophies, and political institutions. At the same time, all these societies adapted these Chinese influences to their indigenous customs. Both Vietnamese and Koreans retained their sense of cultural identity. Although sharing many common traits with Korea, Japan produced a variant of East Asian culture even more distinctive, especially in its political and social structures.

Silla Korea and Tang China

As Korean society developed, several strong states emerged on the peninsula. In the mid-seventh century the southern Korean state of Silla (SILL-ah) defeated its main rival, Koguryo, and united all Koreans, but at the price of becoming a vassal of China. Political unity, which Koreans enjoyed into the 1900s, allowed Korean culture to became homogenized. But like earlier states, Silla also borrowed Chinese culture and institutions. Buddhism triumphed, and the Tang system became the model in government, with Confucianism used as a political ideology. Many Korean monks traveled to China, and some even visited India. But Koreans were selective in their borrowing. The Korean social structure continued to place more emphasis than the Chinese did on inherited status instead of merit, and Korean peasants faced many legal restrictions on their movements. In addition, the gap between rich and poor was much wider than in China. Yet, among Silla's rulers were three queens, two of them among the state's most effective rulers, suggesting less gender bias than in China. For instance, Queen Sondok (r. 632–647) fostered science and promoted a tolerant mixing of Buddhism and shamanism. Silla women generally shared in the social status of their menfolk, enjoyed many legal rights, and could even head families.

During the Silla era (688–918), Koreans mixed influences from Tang China with their own traditions to produce a distinctive culture. For example, they adapted Chinese writing to their own very different spoken language, though it never fit very well. Using this writing system, during the Silla era Koreans began creating a distinctive literary tradition, composing works of history, religion, and poetry. To mass-produce these works, Silla craftsmen also developed woodblock printing as early as China. The oldest still extant example of woodblock printing in the world, a Korean Buddhist writing, dates from 751. Perhaps influenced by the Chinese, Koreans also studied astronomy. A great observatory built in this era is the oldest still standing in East Asia.

While remaining culturally tied to East Asia, Korea also formed connections with the rest of the world. Buddhist pilgrims came from as far away as India, and many Arabs traded at Silla, some settling down there. One Arab wrote that "seldom has a stranger who has come there from Iraq or another country left it afterwards. So healthy is the air there, so pure the water, so fertile the soil and so plentiful of all good things."[17]

Korea During the Koryo Era

Gradually Silla declined, damaged by elite rivalries, corruption, and peasant uprisings, and it was replaced by a new state, Koryo (KAW-ree-oh), which lasted for over four centuries (918–1392). Chinese influence continued in politics and philosophy: Koreans set up an examination system like that of China and Confucian schools, and neo-Confucianism became popular. But Koreans retained a distinctive political and social system. For example, Korean kings, never as strong as Chinese emperors, were greatly influenced by the court, military, and aristocratic landowning families. In contrast to Silla, Koryo court women mainly exercised influence behind the scenes. For example, Lady Yu successfully urged her reluctant husband, Wang Kon, the founder of the Koryo dynasty, to seize power from a despotic ruler, arguing that "It is an ancient tradition to raise a banner of revolt against a tyrant. How can you, a great military leader, hesitate?"[18] While Koryo women played a lesser role in public affairs and faced more restrictions than Silla women, they took full responsibility for family affairs and farmed. Unlike in China, Korean farming relied on large estates. These patterns persisted long after the Koryo dynasty ended.

Thanks to the continued mixing of Chinese and Korean influences, substantial religious, cultural, and technological change characterized the Koryo years. Buddhism gradually became a more powerful economic and political force but also assimilated many elements from animism. The involvement of monks in political life fostered religious corruption and a more worldly orientation that alienated some believers. For the past 1,500 years Korea has been a nominally Buddhist society, but the religion gradually lost influence beginning in Koryo times. More secular artistic trends emerged, including landscape painting and some of the world's finest porcelain. Wide interest in religious and secular literature fostered a publishing industry. The first movable-type printing made of clay came from China in the eleventh century, and Koreans invented the world's first metal movable-type printing by 1234.

Like China, Korea had to occasionally fend off northern pastoralists. The Mongols conquered the peninsula in the early 1200s, making Koryo a colony in their vast empire. When Koreans resisted, the Mongols devastated the land, carrying off hundreds of thousands of captives and imposing heavy taxes on peasants. Yet, thanks to closer links to trade networks, more Chinese and western Asian learning and technology reached Korea during the Mongol era.

Nara Government and Its Challenges

Although using many Chinese and Korean influences, Japan, like Korea, produced a highly distinctive society. In the mid-sixth century the Japanese embarked on three centuries of deliberate cultural borrowing from China, and the ideas and methods they imported helped to create a robust, expansive, and sophisticated society. The changes began with the *Taika* (TIE-kah) ("Great Change") reform of 646 C.E., which the rulers hoped would transform Japan into a centralized empire on the Tang model. The country was divided into provinces that were ruled by governors who derived their power from the emperor. Japanese leaders also established a governmental system made to resemble, on the surface at least, the Chinese centralized bureaucracy. Moreover, the Japanese were now able to record their history and conduct their daily activities using the Chinese writing system. Finally, the adoption of Buddhism from China brought with it a rich constellation of art and architecture.

The height of the period of conscious borrowing from China (710–784) takes its name from Nara (NAH-rah), Japan's

CHRONOLOGY

Korea and Japan During the Intermediate Era

645	Taika reforms in Japan
688	Destruction of Koguryo
688–918	Domination of Korea by Silla
710–784	Nara period in Japan
794–1184	Heian period in Japan
918–1392	Unification of Korea by Koryo
1180–1333	Kamakura Shogunate in Japan
1274, 1281	Mongol invasions of Japan
1338–1568	Ashikaga Shogunate in Japan
1392–1910	Yi dynasty in Korea

first capital city, which was built on the model of the Tang capital, Chang'an (see Chronology: Korea and Japan During the Intermediate Era). Nara had a population of some twenty thousand, half of them government officials and their families. At that time the total Japanese population was probably 5 or 6 million. Many Buddhist temples reflected Tang influence. In addition, during the Nara period land was nationalized in the name of the emperor and, using Tang models, reallocated on an equal basis to the peasants. In return, the peasants paid a land and labor tax. This system was abandoned as unworkable after a few decades, but it illustrated that in agrarian societies land control is the key to political power, a fact demonstrated vividly throughout Japanese history.

Although these changes were designed to strengthen imperial authority, the Japanese emperor never became an unchallenged and activist Chinese-style ruler. Powerful aristocrats maintained control of the bureaucracy and also retained large tax-exempt landholdings. In practice Japan became a **dyarchy**, a form of dual government whereby one powerful family dominated the emperors, whose power was mostly symbolic. The powerful family filled the highest government posts but never aspired to the throne. The emperors passed their lives in luxurious seclusion, with the main goal of guaranteeing an unbroken succession through having sons. This dyarchical system, so different from China's, remained the pattern in Japan into the nineteenth century.

Economic unrest characterized the late Nara period. Peasants resented corvée (forced labor) and military conscription, which often resulted in economic ruin. Many abandoned their

---

dyarchy A form of dual government that began in Japan during the Nara period (710–784) whereby one powerful family ruled the country while the emperor held mostly symbolic power.

fields, becoming wandering, rootless *ronin* (ROH-neen) ("wave people"), some of whom were hired by large landowners as workers. To stop people from becoming ronin, the government abolished compulsory service and gave the responsibility for police and defense to local officials. Eventually the ronin these officials hired as troops were transformed into the provincial warrior class, whose activities reshaped Japanese life.

Nara Culture and Thought

Nara leaders promoted aspects of Chinese culture but blended them with Japanese traditions. For example, they encouraged their people to wear Chinese clothing and to construct Chinese-style buildings. The rituals and ceremonies of the imperial court, largely based on Tang Chinese models, included stately dances and orchestral music using Japanese versions of Chinese musical instruments such as the flute, lute, and zither. These ceremonial forms, which are still maintained at the Japanese court, constitute the oldest fully authenticated music and dance tradition in the world. More significantly, the Chinese written language gained great prestige, and Chinese ideographs were adapted to Japan's very different nontonal spoken language, in what must have been a difficult conversion process. Chinese literary forms, including poetry and calligraphy, became popular. One Nara collection contains 4,500 poems.

The Japanese also adopted and reshaped Chinese philosophical and religious doctrines that they found appealing. They borrowed Confucianism and modified its ethical and political doctrines to suit their own social structure. They also borrowed Mahayana Buddhism, whose worldview that all things are impermanent greatly influenced their art and literature. For example, many artists and poets focused their work on the passage of time and the changing of the seasons. They were also attracted to Buddhist ethics.

But the Japanese also retained their original animist religion known today as Shinto, a kind of nature worship. Shinto and Buddhism addressed different needs and easily blended into a synthesis. The deities of Shinto were not gods but beautiful natural phenomena such as Mt. Fuji (FOO-jee), waterfalls, thunder, or stately trees. This worship reflected the intensity with which the Japanese have loved beauty in all forms. No line separated humanity from nature. Shinto also stressed ritual purity, encouraging bathing and personal cleanliness, and the Japanese became the world's best-scrubbed people. Shinto worshiped the land and ancestors but had no coherent theology or moral doctrine, no concept of death or an afterlife. The faithful flocked to shrines, such as the famous Ise (EE-say), for festivals or to seek help from spirits.

Heian Cultural Renaissance

The period of imitation and direct cultural borrowing from China came to an end during the Heian (HAY-en) period (794–1184). After the capital moved from Nara to Heian, or Kyoto (kee-YO-toe), 28 miles north, Japan gradually returned,

over some decades, to a period of relative isolation. The leaders discontinued foreign contacts in the ninth century and set about consciously absorbing and adapting the Chinese cultural patterns imported during the Nara era under the slogan "Chinese learning, Japanese spirit." The centralized government gave way to a resurgence of aristocratic rule, and Buddhism gradually harmonized with Shinto beliefs and practices while generating new sects, art, and temple building.

A rich and uniquely Japanese court society arose, and in turn supported the development of purely Japanese art and literary styles. Heian culture fostered a distinctly Japanese writing system and worldview. The modification of Chinese influence was exemplified in the development of **kana** (KAH-nah), a phonetic script consisting of some forty-seven syllabic signs derived from Chinese characters. Now Japanese could write their language phonetically. This allowed more freedom of expression, especially when the kana letters were combined with Chinese characters. The Japanese written language of today combines the two.

Heian elite culture, a world enormously remote from us today in time, attitudes, and behavior, reached its high point around 1000 C.E. It flourished among a very small, highly inbred group of privileged families in Kyoto, which then had a population, including both the elite and commoners, of around 100,000. Many elite residents derived their incomes from bureaucratic jobs and land ownership. The Kyoto aristocracy became extraordinarily withdrawn from the realities of the outside world, creating a culture that was governed by standards of form and beauty and in which the distinction between art and life, and fact and fiction, was not clearly made. Passionately concerned with their rank and status in society, they created some of Japan's greatest literature and art. The Heian elite admired nothing so much as the ability to write in an artistic hand, compose a graceful poem, and create an elegant costume.

Guided by these priorities, the finest energies of the period went into creating beauty in a variety of forms, such as putting together harmonious syllables and lines of ink on the page or perfumes on the body. The Heian period was probably unique in world history for the careful attention spent in choosing an undergarment, or the time writing a love note, always exquisite down to the last detail, with perhaps a tastefully faded chrysanthemum to emphasize the melancholy nature of the contents. The homely, color-blind, or unromantic person would have felt terribly out of place in this culture. The Heian aristocrats were not interested in pure intellect or social morality; their value system was superficial. They were obsessed by mood, especially the sense of the transience of beauty. But they left a wonderful cultural legacy.

Women from affluent families had their highest position in Japanese history during the Heian, at least in the capital city. They were free to have romantic affairs, and sexual promiscu-

kana   A Japanese phonetic script developed in the Heian period (794–1184) that consisted of some forty-seven syllabic signs derived from Chinese characters.

LADY MURASAKI,
HEIAN NOVELIST

Women produced much of the best Heian literature. The greatest of the books was *The Tale of Genji*, the world's first psychological novel, written by a lady-in-waiting, Lady Murasaki (Murasaki Shibiku), beginning around 1008. Murasaki worked as the maid to Empress Akiko, who was a consort of the emperor and the daughter of a political leader. We know only a little of Murasaki's life, much of it from a diary she kept. She was born around 978 into a leading aristocratic family steeped in literature. Her grandfather was a famed poet and her father a provincial governor. Her father apparently lamented that she had not been a boy and allowed her to study. Murasaki's writing showed that she was familiar with Chinese history, literature, and poetry and had a considerable education. Indeed, she criticized young people who expected good jobs without undergoing the appropriate training.

Perhaps because she avidly pursued learning, she was married late, at age twenty, but her much older husband died only a few years later from illness. She had at least two children, including a daughter who later became a well-known writer. Murasaki is believed to have died sometime between 1025 and 1031, perhaps after several years as a Buddhist nun. Her self-description in her diary suggests an introverted woman:

> *Pretty yet shy, unsociable, fond of old tales, conceited, so wrapped up in poetry that other people hardly exist, spitefully looking down on the whole world—such is the unpleasant opinion that people have of me. Yet when they come to know me they say that I am strangely gentle, quite unlike what they had been led to believe.*

Murasaki's novel, *The Tale of Genji*, is much more sophisticated in language and thoughtful in sensibility than the literature that came before in Japan. In *Genji* she made contemporary language rather than the formal Chinese writing style a medium for art. Even today words and phrases from *Genji* are common in Japanese language. She also had other goals, claiming that the novel should always have "a definite and serious purpose." In focusing on the emotional and psychological interplay of her characters, her writing betrays a strongly feminine perspective. *Genji* also constitutes a treasure trove on social history, revealing much about the times.

The engaging *Genji* story chronicles the life and amorous adventures of Prince Genji, the son of an emperor and a model for all the qualities of taste and refinement admired by the Kyoto aristocracy. Genji is an accomplished poet, painter, dancer, musician, and athlete. But his supreme gift is the art most prized: "pillowing" (lovemaking). Genji and his friends devote little time to their government jobs. They spend their days largely in the search for pleasure, attend countless ceremonial functions, recite poetry endlessly, and move from one romantic affair to another. The mood of the novel is subdued melancholy and nostalgia for the passing of lovely things. Both men and women freely express their emotions. Hence, Genji shows a keen sensitivity to nature: "I hope that I shall have a little time left for things which I really enjoy—flowers, autumn leaves, the sky, all those day-to-day changes and wonders that a single year brings forth; that is what I look forward to." The novel ends with Genji making plans to give up his posts and retire to a mountain village, perhaps to continue with his poetry, music, and painting while focusing more on religious knowledge.

THINKING ABOUT THE PROFILE

1. What sort of background did Murasaki come from?
2. Why is *Genji* such an important work of literature?

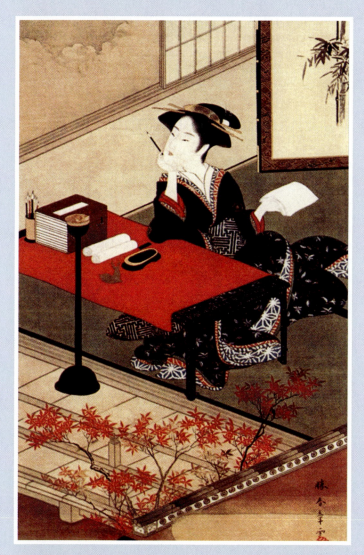

Lady Murasaki   This eighteenth-century painting of Lady Murasaki writing while observing the moon reflected the styles of the artist's times but also suggests the continuing significance of the beloved Heian era writer.   (Kyusei Atami Art Museum, Japan)

Notes: Quotations from Ivan Morris, *The World of the Shining Prince* (New York: Kodansha, 1994), p. 251; Ryusaku Tsunoda et al., eds., *Sources of Japanese Tradition*, vol. 2 (New York: Columbia University Press, 1958), pp. 178–179; and Mikiso Hane, *Japan: A Historical Survey* (New York: Charles Scribner's, 1972), p. 56.

ity was acceptable for both men and women. Aristocratic women spent their days playing games, writing diaries, listening to romantic stories, or practicing art. Some women, such as the novelist Lady Murasaki (MUR-uh-SAH-kee), gained a formal education and learned to write (see Profile: Lady Murasaki, Heian Novelist). Many elite women wrote because, without demanding jobs, they had abundant free time and could focus on their feelings. In poetry, a writer might deftly turn a scene of nature into one of emotion: "The flowers withered, their color faded away, while meaninglessly, I spent my days in the world, and the long rains were falling."[19]

The Heian aristocracy saw love as an art to be cultivated and given maximum artistic expression. People wrote poems before meeting their lover and then the next morning following their meeting. Here are two morning-after poems from the diary of a prominent woman writer, Izumi Shikibu:

> Woman: "painful though it were, to see you leave before dawn [to avoid discovery], better by far than when the dawn's grey light, so cruelly tears you from my side."
> Prince: "to leave you while the leaves are moist with dew, is bitterer by far, than if I were to say farewell at night, without a single chance to show my love."[20]

Heian standards of feminine beauty were distinctive: women wore their hair long to the ground, applied white skin powder and lipstick, plucked their eyebrows, and blackened their teeth with dye. In one novel, a lady refuses to do these things, and her attendants are disgusted: "Those eyebrows of hers, like hairy caterpillars, aren't they; and her teeth—like peeled caterpillars."[21] Men also used cosmetics and were equally concerned with their personal dress and appearance.

The Decline of Heian Japan

Heian culture was perhaps too removed from real life to survive. Only a tiny fraction of Japan's population could afford to enjoy this hedonistic way of life. The common people outside Kyoto lived vastly different lives, usually working at bare subsistence levels as farmers and craftsmen. They were mostly illiterate and saddled by unremitting work, their rural lives brightened only by the occasional festival or family activities. Most peasants knew nothing of Heian court life or Chinese literature. Likewise, aristocrats feared leaving Kyoto; they called peasants "doubtful, questionable creatures" and the provinces "uncivilized, barbarous, wretched" places.[22]

The literature written during the late Heian period shows a growing sense of pessimism. The Kyoto elite became aware that their world of aesthetic perfection was a fleeting phenomenon that might soon vanish. Such indeed was the case. While aristocrats pursued hedonism in Kyoto, social and economic changes were clearing the path for a more decentralized system. Emperors became figureheads while powerful regional families gained considerable wealth and began building up their own warrior bands to keep the peace. These bands were transformed into hierarchical military organizations based on kinship and vassal ties to lords. By the twelfth century the

Heian era had ended and Japan had moved into a new phase of its history with a much different social system.

Changing Korea and Japan

How did Korean and Japanese society change in the late Intermediate Era?

During the second half of the Intermediate Era the Koreans came under the sway of a new dynasty while the Japanese changed substantially, producing a very different way of life and outlook than they had enjoyed a few centuries earlier. For all its cultural brilliance, the Heian aristocracy was not the prototype of later Japanese society. It had grown too inward-looking to continue its dominance. Instead, it served as a transmitter of the now fully assimilated residue of Chinese culture to another vigorous group, the provincial warrior class, in whose hands the future of Japan was to lie. As a result, the post-Heian centuries constituted another important transition in East Asia.

Korea During the Early Yi Dynasty

In 1392 a new Korean dynasty took over from the Mongols, the Yi (yee), whose state was known as Choson (cho-suhn) (see Map 11.4). They lasted until 1910, an incredible longevity of 518 years. Yi rulers sought good relations with China and maintained a tribute relationship with their large neighbor. During this time Koreans learned to better use Chinese social and political models; for example, mastery of Confucian scholarship became the road to careers in government. To Koreans Confucianism provided a philosophical justification for government by a benevolent bureaucracy under a virtuous ruler. Education expanded to prepare students for the civil service exams, which tested for both Confucian and scientific knowledge, and gradually this knowledge came to define the intellectual elite. As in China, government became the main way to wealth. Confucian influence also remade Korean social institutions such as the family. The Yi believed that Korean women had too much freedom and hence behaved immorally. They introduced policies to encourage women's seclusion at home and imposed arranged marriages, veiling of the face when out in public, female chastity, and strict obedience to husbands and fathers. However, commoner women, needing to work in the fields, usually had more freedom of movement and faced less segregation from men. Today Confucianism is arguably a stronger force than Buddhism, especially in rural areas.

Aided by extensive use of movable-type printing, Yi Korea continued to develop literature, technology, and science, including mathematics and astronomy. King Sejong (say-jong) (r. 1418–1450) was a particularly strong supporter of scientific progress. Respected by his people for improving the Korean economy and military, helping poor peasants, and prohibiting cruel punishments, Sejong wrote books on agriculture and formed a scholarly think tank, the Hall of Worthies. Aided by Sejong, fifteenth-century Yi scholars invented a phonetic system for indicating Korean pronunciation of Chinese characters and for writing the Korean language. Some experts consider it the most scientific system of writing in the world. But Chinese was still used for serious scholarship. These years also saw a renaissance of intellectual activity, including a 365-volume encyclopedia of medical knowledge. In technology, Koreans created the world's first rain gauges, which were installed throughout the country to keep accurate rainfall records. In these ways, Choson was able to remain among the more creative and sophisticated of the late Intermediate Afro-Eurasian societies.

Map 11.4   Korea and Japan, ca. 1300
Japanese society developed in an archipelago, the major early cities rising in central Honshu. In 1274 and 1281 the Japanese repulsed Mongol invasions by sea. Throwing off the Mongols, Korea was unified under the Yi dynasty in 1392.

Online Study Center **Improve Your Grade**
Interactive Map: Korea and Japan Before 1500

King Sejong   This modern painting portrays the Yi dynasty King Sejong, revered by Koreans for his political, economic, and scientific achievements, observing stars, supervising book printing, and contemplating a musical instrument he commissioned. Sejong patronized learning, supported agricultural innovations that increased crop yields, introduced humane laws, and fostered economic growth.
(Courtesy, Yushin Yoo)

The Warrior Class and a New Japanese Society

When the Heian period ended, a new warrior class gradually became the dominant force in Japanese politics and society, helping to produce a very different Japanese government and culture. The warrior class triumphed for several reasons. First, Heian provincial governors, who were too fond of the refinements of Kyoto, had a growing tendency to delegate their powers and responsibilities to local subordinates. Second, rural society was changing. Powerful local families and Buddhist communities were always hungry for land and often able to seize it by force. By gaining tax exemptions, they increased the tax load on peasants, some of whom in turn fled to the north to open new land or joined roving bands of unattached ronin. Other peasants signed over themselves and their lands to lords of manors, which released the peasants from paying taxes and provided them with protection, but at the cost of becoming bound to the land and supplying food in exchange for protection. Thus the Heian era estates were replaced by a system of scattered landholdings in which a lord ruled over the villages on his parcel of land. This system led to more direct ties between peasants as vassals and the warrior class as lords.

The net result was that, by the end of the twelfth century, tax-paying land amounted to 10 percent or less of the total cultivated area, and local power had been taken over by the new aristocracy in the rural provinces. As this aristocracy expanded their landholdings, they needed military assistance. Soldiers and ronin signed on as military retainers to aristocratic families, the leaders of whom themselves became mounted warriors. Since conscription had ended earlier because it was too burdensome for the peasants, imperial forces were weak. In this way political and military power dispersed to rural areas.

As this warrior class moved to the center of the historical stage, it led Japan into a type of social and political organization more like that of Zhou China or medieval Europe than the centralized Tang state. Historians disagree as to when between the twelfth and fourteenth centuries the transition to a new, warrior-based system—Japanese called it the Age of Warriors—was completed, but it continued in some form to the nineteenth. During this time, military power absorbed into itself political and economic authority, and all three became defined in terms of rights to land and relations between lords and vassals. Although some historians have stressed the many similarities between post-Heian Japan and medieval Europe, the Japanese rulers were at times stronger than most European kings.

The warrior class, or **samurai** (SAH-moo-rie) ("one who serves"), moved gradually into a position of military supremacy over the emperor and the court. The samurai resulted from a relationship formed between the rural lords and their military retainers, based on an idealized feudal ethic later known as **Bushido** (boo-SHEE-doh) ("way of the warrior"), which was not completely developed until the seventeenth century. The samurai had two great ideals derived from Bushido: loyalty to leaders, and absolute indifference to all physical hardship. They enjoyed special legal and ceremonial rights and in return were expected to give unquestioning service to their lords. Although only a few women of the samurai class, most famously Tomoe Gozen in the twelfth century, engaged in combat, most received some martial arts training. Their main job was to run and defend the family estates.

The samurai occupied the highest level of the social system, but they were a small percentage of the population. In return for loyalty, they received material rewards and secure employment. If they failed to do their duty or achieve their purpose, suicide was a purposeful and honorable act. This act served as conclusive evidence that, although he had failed his purpose, here was a man who could be respected by friend and enemy alike for his physical courage, determination, and sincerity. Homosexuality was also common among the samurai, as among several other warrior castes in history, such as the Spartans in classical Greece, perhaps because of male bonding and an ethic extolling male values. Japanese society generally tolerated same-sex relations. Such unique cultural patterns as Zen Buddhism and the tea ceremony also rose to prominence among the samurai class.

The Shogunates

The periodic fighting of the warrior society resulted in part from overpopulation: too many people competing for control of too little good land. By the twelfth century Japan was controlled by competing bands of feudal lords, and a civil war broke out between two powerful families and their respective allies. One lord, Minamoto-no-Yoritomo (MIN-a-MO-to-no-YOR-ee-TO-mo), emerged victorious and set up a military government in Kamakura (kah-mah-KOO-rah), near Tokyo (TOE-kee-oh), which lasted from 1180 to 1333. The emperor commissioned him **shogun** (SHOW-guhn) ("barbarian-subduing generalissimo"), in effect a military dictator controlling the country in the name of the emperor, who remained in seclusion in Kyoto. The shogun was responsible for internal and external defense of the realm, and he also had the right to nominate his own successor.

Although the imperial house, which traced its origins back to the Sun Goddess in an unbroken line, had become politically impotent, no shogun seriously attempted to abolish it. To many Japanese, the emperors symbolized the people and the land. The Kamakura shoguns were nominally subordinate to the emperors but had real power in many parts of the country. However, before 1600 the system was not very centralized. In many regions, local leaders paid only nominal respect to the shoguns and governed their own districts as they liked.

---

samurai ("one who serves") A member of the Japanese warrior class, which gained power between the twelfth and fourteenth centuries and continued until the nineteenth.

Bushido ("Way of the Warrior") An idealized ethic for the Japanese samurai.

shogun ("Barbarian-subduing generalissimo") In effect a military dictator controlling the country in the name of the emperor.

During the Kamakura Shogunate the Mongols failed twice, in 1274 and 1281, to invade Japan. The 1281 Mongol attempt involved the largest force, in some accounts up to 150,000 men transported by over 4,000 conscripted Chinese ships. These ships were armed with ceramic projectile bombs, the world's first known seagoing exploding projectiles. On both occasions, the Mongol armies landed, met fierce resistance, and were destroyed when great storms scattered and shipwrecked their fleets. These divine winds, or *kamikaze* (KAHM-i-KAHZ-ee), convinced the Japanese of special protection by the gods. Japan was never successfully invaded and defeated until 1945. Any inferiority complex toward China had ended.

Japanese Society, Religion, and Culture

The new Japanese society and culture, shaped by the warrior class, differed substantially from that during the Heian era. Japanese society had always been hierarchical, but now the special status of the samurai reflected a more rigid structure than before. Inequality started in the family: children owed obedience to their parents, and the young honored the old. Each family was headed by a patriarchal male. Women now commonly moved into their husband's household, where they were considered his property and served his parents. Women were expected to be dutiful, obedient, and loyal to their menfolk. Marriages were arranged for the interest of the family, not from romantic love. Women were socialized to stay home and raise children. Yet, while women lost some freedom, marriage became more durable and divorce more difficult, giving married women more security. Furthermore, women from aristocratic families also dominated the staff of the imperial court and ran the emperor's household, giving them some political influence. As in China, the interest of the group always took precedence over that of the individual.

The Japanese developed new forms of religion and the arts between 1200 and 1500. Many Buddhist sects emerged, but three became the most significant and enduring. The largest, the *Pure Land,* emphasized prayer and faith for salvation and was very popular among the lower classes. Arising during civil war, the Pure Land school stressed the equality of all believers and minimized distinctions between monks and laypeople. It also rejected the notion of reincarnation, maintaining that believers went straight to nirvana. Another Buddhist sect, *Nicheren* (NEE-chee-ren), has sometimes been compared to Christianity and Islam because of its militant proselytizing and concern for the afterlife. Most Japanese Buddhist sects were peaceful and tolerant, but Nicheren was angry and outspoken, seeing rival views as heresy.

The third major Buddhist sect originated in China under Daoist influence. **Zen** is called the meditation sect because it emphasized individual practice and discipline, self-control, self-understanding, and intuition. Knowledge came from seeking within, deep into the mind, rather than from outside assistance. One Zen pioneer wrote, "Great is mind. Heaven's height is immeasurable but Mind goes beyond heaven; the earth's depth is unfathomable, but Mind reaches below the earth. Mind travels outside the macrocosm."[23] Zen practitioners expected enlightenment to come in a flash of understanding. The Zen culture was devised over the centuries to bring people in touch with their nonverbal, nonrational side. It stressed simplicity and restraint, contending that "great mastery is as if unskillful."[24] We might say today that "less is more."

Religious perspectives, especially Zen, affected the arts. Zen values can be seen in Japanese rock gardens, landscape gardening, and flower arrangements. Whereas the Chinese preferred their nature unspoiled, the Japanese liked it ordered. Japanese gardens, ponds, and buildings, such as the beautiful Golden Pavilion of Kyoto, built in the thirteenth century, were all constructed in harmony with their natural surroundings. The tea ceremony, which also resulted from Zen, emphasized patience, restraint, serenity, and the beauty of simple action involving the commonplace, that is, preparing and drinking tea. The highly formalized ceremony could last two hours, suggesting withdrawal from the real world. It also reflected a Japanese beverage preference. For example, a Zen monk wrote that tea was the most wonderful medicine for nourishing health and fostering a long life.

Other arts also flourished in this era. Japanese ceramics and pottery later became famous throughout the world for their subtlety and understated beauty, and they are considered by some to have been the world's greatest. Potters specialized in making cups, bowls, and vases using rough textures and irregular lines to suggest weathering and the effects of time, a Japanese preoccupation. By the fourteenth century they were mass-producing pottery. Japanese painting was also an old art and, as in other visual arts, emphasized not creativity or self-expression but skill and technique through self-discipline. Poetry too continued to be popular. The **Noh** drama, plays that presented stylized gestures and spectacular masks, also appeared in this era.

Japanese Political and Economic Change

Although a samurai-dominated hierarchical society became well established, these centuries also saw considerable political and economic change. In 1333 the Kamakura Shogunate was ended through intrigues and civil wars and replaced by a government headed by the Kyoto-based Ashikaga (ah-shee-KAH-gah) family (1338–1568). But the Ashikaga shoguns never had much power beyond the capital, although they were theoretically lords over the provincial governors. Furthermore, a growing population, which reached 5 million by the 1300s, became harder to control. Political power became increasingly decentralized, as local lords struggled to obtain more land. This

---

Zen A form of Japanese Buddhism called the meditation sect because it emphasizes individual practice and discipline, self-control, self-understanding, and intuition.

Noh Japanese plays that use stylized gestures and spectacular masks that began in the fourteenth century.

competition led to the rise of great landowning territorial magnates called **daimyo** (DIE-MYO) ("great name"), who monopolized local power. Each of the several hundred daimyo had his supporting samurai and derived income from the peasants working on their land.

By the 1400s Japan had experienced rapid change in both economic and political spheres. Agriculture became more productive, and an increasingly active merchant class lived in the fast-growing towns. The Japanese developed a new interest in foreign trade, and Japanese sailors and merchants traveled to China and Southeast Asia. The rigid political and social system strained to accommodate these new energies. In the next century civil war and the arrival of European merchants and Christian missionaries aggravated these problems and resulted in a dramatic modification of the political system.

SECTION SUMMARY

- The Yi, who ruled Korea after the Mongols, sought good relations with China and instituted the Chinese educational and civil service exam system.

- In Japan, the warrior class, or samurai, gradually attained supremacy over the emperor and the court, and an organization like that of medieval Europe, based on lords and vassals, became dominant.

- The Kamakura Shogunate began after the winner of a Japanese civil war was given the title of shogun, or military dictator, who ruled while the emperor retreated behind the scenes.

- Three enduring Buddhist sects developed in Japan: Pure Land, which stressed equality; Nicheren, which was militant; and Zen, which stressed meditation, discipline, and simplicity, qualities that are shown in the tea ceremony and such Japanese arts as gardening and flower arranging.

- The Ashikaga Shogunate, which followed the Kamakura, had little power over the provinces, which became ruled by landowning lords called daimyo.

 *Online Study Center* ACE the Test

 Chapter Summary

The Intermediate Era was in many respects a golden age for much of East Asia. With their increasingly sophisticated ways of living, the Tang and Song dynasties represented perhaps the high point of Chinese history and culture. While the Tang enjoyed great external power, the Song featured dramatic commercial growth. The Chinese continued to develop distinctive forms of literature, visual arts, philosophy, and government, as

well as new technologies and scientific understandings. Major aspects of Chinese culture, such as writing, Confucianism, and Buddhism, spread to Korea, Japan, and Vietnam. The Mongol conquest and brief period of rule weakened China's dynamism but extended overland trade routes that linked China even more closely to the outside world and promoted the spread of Chinese science and technology to western Eurasia. China became the richest segment of a vast empire spanning half of Eurasia. During the Ming, China briefly reasserted its transregional power and maintained an advanced technology. But, in part because of the experience of Mongol rule, Ming China also increasingly turned inward, becoming less involved in world affairs.

The Koreans and Japanese synthesized Chinese learning with their own native traditions to produce highly distinctive societies. Significant change occurred in Japan as it moved from the aristocratic court culture of Heian to a warrior-dominated culture based on large landowning families and their military retainers, or samurai. By the end of the 1400s the East Asian societies remained strong but faced new challenges when Europeans began to expand their power in the world.

Online Study Center **Improve Your Grade** Flashcards

Key Terms

neo-Confucianism	Bushido
qi	shogun
kotow	Zen
dyarchy	Noh
kana	daimyo
samurai	

Suggested Reading

Books

Adshead, S. A. M. *China in World History*. 3rd ed. New York: St. Martin's, 2000. A study of China's relations with the world during this era.

Adshead, S. A. M. *T'ang China: The Rise of the East in World History*. New York: Palgrave Macmillan, 2004. Provocative examination of the rise and decline of China.

Benn, Charles. *China's Golden Age: Everyday Life in the Tang Dynasty*. New York: Oxford University Press, 2002. A comprehensive look at the society, economy, and culture of Tang China.

Cohen, Warren. *East Asia at the Center: Four Thousand Years of Engagement with the World*. New York: Columbia University Press, 2000. A good summary of China, Koria, and Japan in Eurasian history.

Ebrey, Patricia Buckley, Anne Walthall, and James B. Palais. *East Asia: A Cultural, Social, and Political History*. Boston: Houghton Mifflin Company, 2006. A readable, comprehensive survey, especially strong on the Intermediate Era.

Ebrey, Patricia Buckley. *The Inner Quarters: Marriage and the Lives of Chinese Women in the Sung Period*. Berkeley: University of California Press, 1993. A fascinating study of this neglected topic.

daimyo ("Great name) Large land-owning territorial magnates who monopolized local power in Japan beginning during the Ashikaga period (1338–1568).

Gernet, Jacques. *Daily Life in China on the Eve of the Mongol Invasion 1250–1276.* Stanford: Stanford University Press, 1962. Dated but still a fascinating study of Song life.

Lee, Ki-Baik. *A New History of Korea.* Cambridge: Harvard University Press, 1984. One of the most comprehensive and readable surveys.

Levathes, Louise. *When China Ruled the Seas: The Treasure Fleet of the Dragon Throne, 1405–33.* New York: Simon and Schuster, 1994. A recent study of the Ming voyages for the general reader.

Merson, John. *The Genius That Was China: East and West in the Making of the Modern World.* Woodstock, N.Y.: Overlook Press, 1990. Lavishly illustrated with good coverage of Song and Ming China.

Morris, Ivan. *The World of the Shining Prince: Court Life in Ancient Japan.* New York: Kodansha International, 1994. A reprint of the classic 1964 study of Heian society and culture.

Rossabi, Morris. *Kublai Khan: His Life and Times.* Berkeley: University of California Press, 1987. A study of China under Mongol rule.

Shaughnessy, Edward, ed. *China: Empire and Civilization.* New York: Oxford University Press, 2005. Contains essays on many aspects of Chinese society in this era.

Souyri, Pierre F. *The World Turned Upside Down: Medieval Japanese Society,* translated by Kathe Roth. New York: Columbia University Press, 2001. A major study of later Intermediate Japan and warrior society.

Storry, Richard, and Werner Forman. *The Way of the Samurai.* London: Orbis, 1978. A nicely illustrated examination of the samurai and their culture.

Varley, Paul. *Japanese Culture,* 2nd ed. updated and expanded. Honolulu: University of Hawai'i Press, 2000. A good overview.

Websites

Ancient Japan
(http://www.wsu.edu:8080/~dee/ANCJAPAN/CONTENTS/HTM). A useful site from Washington State University offering many essays and links on premodern Japan.

A Visual Sourcebook of Chinese Civilization
(http://depts.washington.edu/chinaciv/). A wonderful collection of essays, illustrations, and other useful material on Chinese history.

East and Southeast Asia: An Annotated Directory of Internet Resources
(http://newton.uor.edu/Departments&Programs/AsianStudiesDept/index.html). Varied collection of links, maintained at University of Redlands.

Internet East Asian History Sourcebook
(http://www.fordham.edu/halsall/eastasia/eastasiasbook.html). An invaluable collection of sources and links on China, Japan, and Korea from ancient to modern times.

Internet Guide for China Studies
(http://www.sino.uni-heidelberg.de/igcs/). A good collection of links on premodern and modern China, maintained at Germany's Heidelberg University.

Silk Road Narratives
(http://depts.washington.edu/uwch/silkroad/texts/texts.html). Explores cultural interaction in Eurasia through excerpts from Silk Road travelers.

CHAPTER 12

Expanding Horizons in Africa and the Americas, 600–1500

Online Study Center

This icon will direct you to interactive activities and study materials on the website: college.hmco.com/pic/lockard1e

Feathered Shield   This brightly colored feathered mosaic shield, used for ceremonial purposes by an Aztec warrior in the fifteenth century, has an image of the Aztec water god, a monster that resembled a coyote, outlined in gold.   (Erich Lessing/Art Resource, NY)

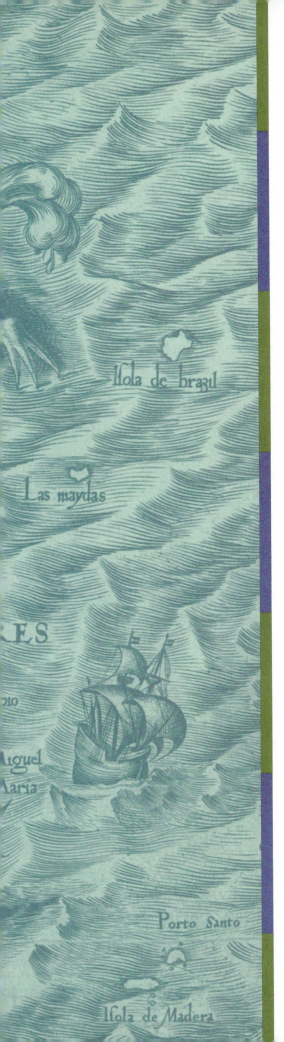

A long time ago, when the Arabs arrived in Lamu [a port in today's Kenya, East Africa], they found local people there. The Arabs were received with friendliness and they wanted to stay on. The local people offered to trade land for cloths. Before the trading was finished, the Arabs had the land, and the [local people] had the cloth.

A LAMU ORAL TRADITION[1]

Around 912 the Baghdad-born Arab geographer Abdul Hassan Ibn Ali al-Mas'udi sailed to East Africa with mariners from Oman (OH-mahn), in eastern Arabia, on their regular trading expedition to what Arabs described as *Zanj* ("the land of black people"). Al-Mas'udi discovered that the journey up and down the East African coast could be perilous, with reefs and strong winds that generated high waves that "grow into great mountains and open deep gulfs between them." Altogether al-Mas'udi spent three years traveling from port to port, venturing as far south as Sofala (so-FALL-a), a city in what is today Mozambique (moe-zam-BEEK). After further travels to Persia, India, and China, al-Mas'udi finally returned to Africa to settle in Cairo, where he wrote several scholarly books before his death around 956. His most influential book, provocatively titled *Meadows of Gold and Mines of Gems*, reported on his discoveries. He intended the book "to excite a desire and curiosity about its contents, and to make the mind eager to become acquainted with history."[2]

Al-Mas'udi's informative account pictured East African society in a key period of state formation while also recording the many links between these coastal towns and the Arabs, and through the Arabs to other Eurasian societies. He praised the energetic traders and skilled workers of the coast, reported that the Sofala region produced abundant gold for export, and provided details about the international ivory trade. Arabs carried ivory from Zanj to Oman, from where they shipped it to India and China. He wrote that "in China the Kings and military and civil officers use ivory [to decorate furniture]. In India ivory is much sought after. It is used for the handles of daggers. But the chief use of ivory is making chessmen and backgammon pieces."[3]

During the Intermediate Era many societies in East Asia, Southeast Asia, South Asia, West Asia, North Africa, and Europe benefited from extensive links across long distances over which they exchanged technologies, products, religions, and ideas. Some sub-Saharan Africans also became connected to this vast network through trade and the spread of world religions. As al-Mas'udi's description of the Zanj ports confirms, transregional trade was significant. As trade networks expanded, some African peoples, such as the gold producers near Sofala, became integral parts of hemispheric commerce while remaining part of networks within Africa. But many sub-Saharan Africans had only indirect links, and the American societies across the Atlantic Ocean had no known links at all, to these busy Afro-Eurasian networks of exchange.

Americans and many Africans had to independently address the challenges they faced. Yet, despite lack of contact with each other, Africans and Americans also shared some patterns of social and political development. Using their own creativity, some of these peoples thrived in forbidding desert, forest, or highland environments. Between 600 and 1500 African and American states rose and fell, among them a few regional empires. However, in contrast to the more densely populated areas of Eurasia, for many African and American societies politics was mainly a matter of self-governing villages rather than large, centralized governments. In the Western Hemisphere, trade routes existed over wide areas, but geography inhibited the growth of long-distance networks such as those linking, for example, East Africa to China. Only after 1492 did maritime exploration permanently connect African, American, and Eurasian peoples.

FOCUS QUESTIONS

1. How did contact with Islamic peoples help shape the societies of West Africa?
2. What networks linked East Africa and the Bantu societies to the wider world?
3. What were some distinctive patterns of government, society, thought, and economy in Intermediate Africa?
4. What factors explain the collapse of the Early Intermediate Era American societies?
5. How were the Aztec and Inca Empires different, and how were they similar?

The Power of West African States

How did contact with Islamic peoples help shape the societies of West Africa?

After 600, major changes took place in West Africa that resulted in the rise of several important kingdoms in the Sudanic region (the area stretching from west to east just below the Sahara Desert) and along the Guinea (GINN-ee) coast. As in Eurasia, empires sprouted, flourished, and decayed. Scholars studied and disputed in centers of learning, and what Chinese artists accomplished with ink and Europeans with paint, African artists achieved with bronze and wood. Networks of exchange and travel helped shape societies. The rise of great kingdoms in the Sudan coincided with the expansion of both a global religion, Islam, and a global commerce that linked West Africa with North Africa, the Mediterranean Basin, and western Asia.

Trade and the Expansion of Islam in the Sudan

For hundreds of years camel caravans had plied the trackless Sahara sands, a barren landscape where dry conditions, towering sand dunes, and searing sun conspired against crops, grasses, and trees. The caravans transported valuable products such as gold, salt, ivory, slaves, and ceramics between West and North Africa. The people benefiting the most from these networks lived in the Sudan (soo-DAN), the largely grasslands region just south of the Sahara. Because its generally flat geography and the long but sluggish Niger River allowed for easy communication, the Sudan became a meeting place of people and ideas.

Beginning in the 800s Islam filtered down the Saharan trade routes, carried peacefully by merchants, teachers, and mystics in much the same way it arrived in the islands of Southeast Asia (see Chapter 13). As Muslim merchants settled in towns involved with the trans-Saharan trade, they helped form stable governments to protect the trade and the caravans, and their religion was absorbed into the Sudanic societies.

C H R O N O L O G Y	
Africa	**The Americas**
ca. 500–1203 Ghana	700–1400 Anasazi
	800–1475 Chimu Empire
	900–1168 Toltec Empire
ca. 1000–1450 Zimbabwe	
1220–1897 Benin	
1234–1550 Mali Empire	
1464–1591 Songhai Empire	1428–1521 Aztec Empire
	1440–1532 Inca Empire

Islam introduced a complex, literate tradition to the Sudan. Many political and economic leaders of the Sudanese cities converted to the religion, and eventually most Sudanic peoples embraced Islam. Islamic influence produced changes in customs, names, dress, diet, architecture, and festivals, and Islamic schools spread literacy in the Arabic language. The Sudanic religious atmosphere promoted tolerance, by Muslims toward animists and vice versa. Still, Islamic practice was often superficial, and it took several centuries for the religion to permeate into the villages.

The First Sudanic Kingdom: Ghana

A few kingdoms with similar features already existed by the time that Islam reached the Sudan. Reflecting their peoples' animist beliefs, the kings in these societies were considered divine and enjoyed direct access to the spirits. They remained aloof from the common people and ruled through bureaucracies. But the kings' power was often limited. Many kings had to consult a council of elders, who frequently had to approve a decision to go to war, and some kings were elected by elders or chiefs. The women of the royal families also had great power, and, in a few societies, they could rule as queens. Some kingdoms became empires by either conquering neighboring peoples or linking states together through ties of kinship. States had no fixed territorial boundaries, only fluctuating spheres of influence, and they often included diverse ethnic groups. Their lack of political, ethnic, and cultural cohesion made them inherently unstable.

The earliest known Sudanic kingdom was Ghana (GON-uh), centered on the northwestern part of the Niger River (see Map 12.1). Founded by Mande speakers of the Soninke (soh-NIN-kay) ethnic group, Ghana was probably established around 500 C.E. but reached its golden age in the ninth and tenth centuries (see Chronology: Africa in the Intermediate Era). Ghana prospered from its control of the trans-Saharan gold trade between West and North Africa. Of Ghana and its

profitable commerce, the Spanish Muslim traveler Abu Hamid al-Andalusi wrote: "In the sands of that country is gold, treasure immeasurable. Merchants trade salt for it, taking the salt on camels from the salt mines. They travel on the desert as if it were a sea, having guides to pilot them by the stars or rocks."[4] For generations, gold and various tropical crops had been traded northward for salt, dates, textiles, and horses. The Ghana capital, Koumbi, was a major trade center located near gold deposits. Many of the city's 20,000 inhabitants were immigrants, including Arab and Berber merchants.

Ghana flourished for centuries before collapsing in 1203. By the tenth century Ghana's rulers, at their pinnacle of power,

C H R O N O L O G Y	
Africa in the Intermediate Era	
ca. 500–1203	Kingdom of Ghana
1000–1200	Rise of Hausa city-states
ca. 1000–1450	Zimbabwe kingdom
1200–1500	Golden age of East African coastal cities
1220–1897	Kingdom of Benin
1234–1550	Mali Empire
ca. 1275	Rise of Yoruba kingdom of Oyo
1324–1325	Mansa Musa's pilgrimage to Mecca
ca. 1375	Rise of Kongo kingdom
1464–1591	Songhai Empire
1487	Bartolomeu Dias rounds Cape of Good Hope

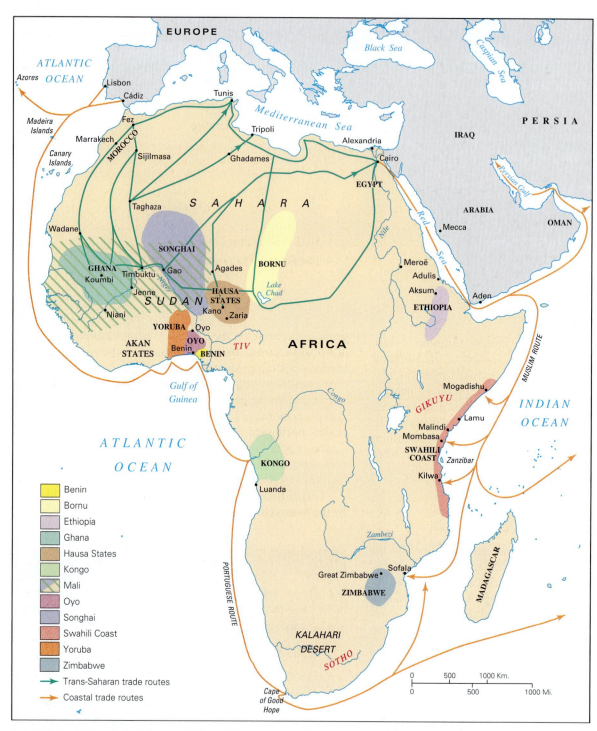

Map 12.1   Major Sub-Saharan African Kingdoms and States, 1200–1600 C.E.
Many large kingdoms and states emerged in Intermediate Africa. Large empires dominated the
Sudan in West Africa. Prosperous trading cities sharing a Swahili culture dotted the east coast.

Online Study Center   Improve Your Grade   Interactive Map: Africa Before 1500

had converted to Islam, a move that apparently increased the
wealth and splendor of the royal court. An Arab visitor in 1067
said that the king's attendants had gold-plaited hair and carried gold-mounted swords, and that even the guard dogs wore
collars of gold and silver. But early in the eleventh century a

civil war erupted and Berbers from North Africa took advantage of the turmoil to attack the kingdom. Perhaps the empire
had incorporated so many different peoples that it lost its cohesion. The court was destroyed and the merchants moved
away.

Mali: Islam and Regional Power

The next great Sudanic empire, Mali (MAHL-ee), was formed in 1234 by another Mande-speaking group, the Malinke (muh-LING-kay), led by the Keita (KAY-ee-tah) clan. The Keita leader, Sundiata (soon-JAH-tuh), became the **mansa** (MAHN-suh), or king, of Mali (see Profile: Sundiata, Imperial Founder). Famed farmers and traders, the Malinke conquered much of the western Sudan, including the territory once controlled by Ghana. The empire's total area stretched some 1,500 miles from east to west and incorporated dozens of ethnic groups. The Malinke *mansa* was both a secular and religious leader who surrounded himself with displays of wealth and ceremonial regalia and expected his subjects to approach him on their knees. This emphasis on his dignity and power helped instill respect and obedience in his people. At some point Sundiata apparently converted to Islam, perhaps to secure better relations with North Africa, but he never seriously practiced that religion. Indeed, he also made use of Malinke animism, developing a reputation as a magician.

Islamic influence, however, gradually grew stronger, expanding the networks of communication and travel. Some of the later Mali emperors made glittering pilgrimages to Mecca. When Sundiata's descendant, Mansa Musa (MAN-sa MOO-sa) (r. 1312–1337), went to Mecca in 1324 riding a white Arab horse, he took fifty slaves bearing golden staffs, one thousand followers, and one hundred camels, each loaded with 300 pounds of gold. His fabulous journey exhibited the wealth and power of his state. According to an Arab official writing of Mansa Musa's visit to Egypt en route to Arabia, he "spread upon Cairo the flood of his generosity; there was no person, officer of the court, or holder of any office who did not receive a sum of gold from him. The people of Cairo earned incalculable sums from him, whether by buying and selling or by gifts."[5] Mansa Musa reportedly spent so much money in Cairo that the Egyptian currency was devalued. An Arab observer credited Mansa Musa with being a student of religious sciences who built grand mosques in Mali and imported Islamic jurists. But whatever the attention Mansa Musa lavished on Islam, the majority of the Mali people continued to follow animism, and even the elite were lax in their Islamic practice. Mali remained an essentially secular state.

Mali's economic base included farming, commerce, and control of the gold and salt trade across the desert. The kingdom supplied most of Europe's gold reserves and about two-thirds of the world's gold supply in this era. Local Africans mined the gold in open pits or in underground passages through loose dirt along streambeds, the miners digging while crouching in waist-deep water. At the surface, women extracted the gold dust from the dirt dug out by the men. Acquiring the gold, traders then met salt merchants from the north and silently matched piles of gold and salt until a fair exchange was agreed upon. Other imports came to Mali from as far away as China and India. In the thirteenth century the Mali trading

mansa ("king") Mande term used by the Malinke people to refer to the ruler of the Mali Empire.

city of Timbuktu (tim-buk-TOO) emerged as the major southern terminus of the trans-Saharan caravan trade. Cities and towns like Timbuktu were filled with craftspeople, but most Malians lived in small villages and cultivated rice, sorghum, or millet, supplemented by herding or fishing. The wealth of rulers like Mansa Musa may have dazzled the world, but most Malians lived simply.

Mali benefited from network connections. The international links provided by Islam and the trans-Saharan commerce enticed many visitors and sojourners to the Sudan, including poets, architects, teachers, and traders from places such as Spain and Egypt. Even a few bold European Christians braved the desert to visit the area, and at least one Italian merchant reached Timbuktu. The fourteenth-century Moroccan traveler Ibn Battuta spent months in Mali and had mixed feelings about the empire. He admired the Malians' many "admirable qualities," commenting that "they are seldom unjust, and have a greater abhorrence of injustice than any other people." He also found "complete security in the country. Neither traveler nor inhabitant in it has anything to fear from robbers or men of violence."[6] But the pious Muslim frowned on what he considered the immodest dress and independent behavior of women and the custom of eating dogs.

Mali rapidly declined in the 1400s because of internal factionalism and raids by other peoples. Soon the fringes broke away, and by 1550 the Mali of former days was gone. A much smaller Mali kingdom limped into the 1600s, one of numerous small states in the western Sudan.

The Songhai Empire

The third great Sudanic empire was Songhai (song-GAH-ee), a kingdom formed by several ethnic groups that seceded from Mali in 1340. Over the next decades, Songhai increased its power, and by 1464 it was a major empire roughly as large as the former Mali Empire. Some of the Songhai rulers were nominal Muslims, and others were devout. The most revered leader was Aksia (ACK-see-a) the Great (1483–1528), a humane, pious, and tolerant man who was devoted to learning. The imperial capital at Gao (ghow) on the Niger River was a substantial city containing perhaps 100,000 people. A Moroccan visitor around 1500 wrote that Gao's rich merchants traveled continuously around the region to sell their wares, while many people came to Gao bringing gold to purchase goods from North Africa and Europe. As demand for gold and slaves increased in both North Africa and Europe, Songhai flourished from the trans-Saharan caravan trade, even more than Ghana and Mali had done before. Slaves were obtained from nearby peoples and sold in the Gao slave market, and many were taken on the arduous journey across the Sahara to the Mediterranean societies. In exchange for gold and slaves, Songhai received glass, copperware, cloth, perfumes, and horses.

Under Songhai rule, Timbuktu flourished. The city on the Niger became a major Islamic intellectual center with a famous Islamic university that specialized in teaching astronomy, astrology, medicine, history, geography, Arabic, and Quranic studies. The thousands of scholars and students in the city

SUNDIATA, IMPERIAL FOUNDER

According to tradition, the founder of the great Mali Empire was Sundiata Keita, the "Lion Prince" of the Malinke people. It is difficult to separate myth from fact about his life, but most historians believe there was a real Sundiata. Arab historians such as Ibn Khaldun mention him in their accounts. Nonetheless, any account must use oral epics, which tend to glorify his heroism and reflect a Malinke view of a glorious past.

At the time Sundiata was born in the early thirteenth century, Ghana was collapsing and various other groups were contending to fill the power vacuum. Sundiata was one of twelve sons of a Malinke king, Nare Fa Maghan, and Sogolon Conde, a hunchback. As a child Sundiata was sickly and had stiff legs that made walking difficult. Hence he was spared when a rival state, Kaniaga, under their brutal king, Sumaguru, conquered Sundiata's town, Niane, and executed all his brothers as potential threats. According to the oral epic:

> He had a slow and difficult childhood. At the age of three he still crawled along on all-fours. He had nothing of the great beauty of his father. He had a head so big that he seemed unable to support it. He was taciturn and used to spend the whole day just sitting in the middle of the house. Malicious tongues began to blab. All Niane talked of nothing but the stiff-legged son.

However, soothsayers predicted greatness for him, and eventually he overcame his physical problems so that "at the age of eighteen he had the stateliness of the lion and the strength of the buffalo."

As a young man he went into exile, and then he returned to rally his people against the tyrannical Sumaguru: "The sun will arise, the sun of Sundiata." Determined and diplomatic, he skillfully used traditional clan and kinship groups as well as a reputation for possessing knowledge of magic to build and solidify his power. Persuading other Malinke chiefs to surrender their titles to him, he became his peoples' sole king, enhancing his position in preparation for war. Sundiata put together a military force and triumphed over Sumaguru in the battle of Kirina about 1235, and then he conquered much of the old Ghana territories.

As king, Sundiata acquired the power to reshape Malinke government and society. According to the epics, "He left his mark on Mali for all time and his [rules] still guide men in their conduct [today]." As ruler for over two decades, Sundiata transformed his small state into the core of an imperial system based in his hometown of Niane, alongside the Niger River and near valuable goldfields. His rule brought peace, happiness, prosperity, and justice: "He protected the weak against the strong. The upright man was rewarded and the wicked one punished." The epic account is undoubtedly an idealized version of truth, but it also recorded that Sundiata punished his enemies. Malinke custom allowed high-status men to have

Sundiata   This modern depiction of Sundiata Keita memorializes the legendary founder of the Mali Empire. Even today, nearly a millennium after his death, Sundiata remains a hero to Africans for his political and military skills.   [From Ada Konare Ba, *Sunjiata: Le Fondateur L'Empire du Mali* (Dakar: Nouvelles Editions Africaines, 1983.)]

many wives, and Sundiata, like his father, followed this practice, leaving many descendants.

Sundiata died about 1260, but his legend lived on. As the epics retold even today put it:

> Sundiata was unique. In his time no one equaled him and after him no one had the ambition to surpass him. Men of today, how small you are beside your ancestors. Sundiata rests but his spirit lives on and today the Keitas still come and bow before the stone under which lies the father of Mali.

THINKING ABOUT THE PROFILE

1. What does Sundiata's career tell us about the personal qualities admired by the Malinke people and helpful in forging a Sudanic empire?

2. How do the epic stories told over the centuries remember Sundiata and his deeds?

Note: Quotations from D. T. Niane, *Sundiata: An Epic of Old Mali* (London: Longman, 1965), pp. 15, 40, 47, 81, 83–85.

patronized bookstores and libraries containing thousands of books, many in African languages using Arabic script. In recent years over 30,000 lost books, hundreds of years old, on many subjects have been found underneath Timbuktu's mud houses and in nearby desert caves. One North African, on visiting Timbuktu, noted many shops, some selling locally made linen and cotton cloth, and considerable wealth. Corn, cattle, milk, and butter were available in great abundance. Furthermore, the people were "of a gentle and cheerful disposition, and spend a great part of the night in singing and dancing through all the streets of the city."[7] Songhai flourished until 1591, when Moroccans destroyed its military power.

The Hausa City-States

Another dynamic area of the Sudan developed further east, in what is now northern Nigeria, eastern Niger, and southern Chad. Between 1000 and 1200 C.E. the Hausa (HOUSE-uh) people of the region erected a series of flourishing and fiercely competitive city-states, ruled by kings, that came to dominate some of the trans-Saharan trade into the eighteenth century. The prosperity of these city-states attracted many non-Hausa immigrants, including Arabs and Berbers. Over time many were assimilated into the Hausa society, which became increasingly Islamic. Hausa cities such as Kano (KAHN-oh) were centers for manufacturing cotton cloth and leatherwork, some of which was sold as far away as Europe. The Hausa were also

farmers, famed craftspeople, and skilled traders, whose pursuit of wealth ranged all over West Africa.

Hausa society combined features from several cultural traditions. For example, reflecting the trading orientation, the Hausa language mixed Arab, Berber, and West African influences. Today Hausa remains the major trading language of the central Sudan and is also the most widely-spoken African language. Like many Sudanic peoples, the Hausa possessed a strong class system. At the top were the royal families, and below them was the traditional aristocracy. Just below this group were Islamic intellectuals, such as teachers, followed by wealthy merchants, less affluent merchants, then craftspeople, and, at the bottom of the social ladder, slaves, especially in the towns. In the villages the dominant social feature was a strong sense of mutual obligation and cooperation. Hausa women enjoyed a high status compared with women in many African societies. In the fifteenth century a queen, Amina, ruled one of the major Hausa states, Zaria (zah-REE-uh). An oral poem praised her as "like the moon at its full, like the morning star. She is a lion as precious as gold among all women."[8]

Kingdoms of the Guinea Coast

West African political development was also occurring just south of the Sudan, along the Guinea coast, a region of rain forest and grasslands. Sudanic influence and trade likely fostered the growth of states among societies like the Yoruba (YORE-uh-buh). By about 1000 C.E. the Yoruba peoples of what is now western Nigeria had developed several states, each based on a large city ruled by a king or prince. The kings were powerful and considered sacred, but they were controlled by powerful elders and aristocrats. However, no united Yoruba kingdom existed: Yoruba identity was more cultural than political, based on the Yoruba language and a common culture, including complex animistic religious traditions that are still influential today. One Yoruba kingdom, Oyo (OY-oh), rose rapidly after 1275 and was soon the most

Hausa Houses in Kano Hausa towns and cities feature houses with large courtyards behind high walls. Structural beams made from local palm trees protrude from the walls. (Werner Forman/Art Resource, NY)

Benin King and Musicians This bronze plaque shows the king, preparing for war, wearing beads and royal musicians on both sides. Such plaques were hung on palace walls and pillars to glorify the ruler. (War and Attendants Plaque, Nigeria, Benin, 17th century, brass 14-3/4 x 15-1/2 inches. The Nelson-Atkins Museum of Art, Kansas City, Missouri, Purchase Nelson Trust #8.3)

included an elaborate royal palace, neat houses with verandas (porches), and neighborhoods linked by broad avenues. The king enjoyed vast wealth and had a large, lavish court, and an elite commercial class traded with the Hausa, Yoruba, and Songhai. Bini merchants dealt in woodcarvings, foodstuffs, ironwork, farm tools, weapons, and later cloth. Because they produced most of the cloth, Bini women also benefited from this trade. The upper classes dressed and dined well, consuming beef, mutton, chicken, and yams, while the poor ate yams, dried fish, beans, and bananas. However, the poor were protected from becoming beggars because an innovative welfare system supported those unable to work. A European visitor described the process: "The king being very charitable, as well as his subjects, has officers whose chief employment is, on certain days, [to carry] great quantities of provisions into the town for the use of the poor."[9] This society flourished until 1550, when it began to decline. Nonetheless, the Benin kingdom was only ended in 1897.

powerful state in the area. Oyo flourished until the late eighteenth century under able kings and a strong administrative structure.

Yoruba society had an urban and mercantile orientation. Many towns dotted Yoruba country, serving as both commercial and political centers and ruled by elaborate bureaucracies. Merchants were respected and closely connected to the north-south trade networks. Since Yoruba women were not expected to work in the fields, many developed wealth and influence as traders. Artisans worked iron, wood, leather, ivory, and cloth. The Yoruba were also famed as artists. By a thousand years ago the Yoruba at Ife (EE-fay) were already casting beautiful bronze portraits of their rulers. Since the Yoruba prized submissiveness to superiors and their culture discouraged conflict, crime was rare.

Another great Guinea kingdom, Benin (buh-NEEN), situated just east of Yoruba territory, shared some cultural traditions with the Yoruba. Benin was the state of the Bini (Bean-ee) people. It emerged around 1220, and under King Ewuare (ee-WAHR-ee) the Great it established a sizable empire in the mid-1400s. Early kings like Ewuare were warriors, but later they became more spiritual leaders, leading secluded lives but subject to influence by powerful local chiefs. Benin artists cast beautiful bronzes and carved ivory to glorify the accomplishments of the king and state.

Since Benin was located near the Atlantic coast, where Europeans began to explore in the late 1400s, it was one of the first African kingdoms to be visited by Europeans, who wrote of the prosperous society they admired. Benin city was twenty-five miles in circumference, was protected by high walls, and

SECTION SUMMARY

- The area south of the Sahara, known as the Sudan, benefited most from the Sahara caravan trade and gradually embraced Islam.
- In the kingdom of Ghana, which prospered from the trans-Saharan gold trade, councils of elders held the power of kings in check.
- The kingdom of Mali also grew fabulously wealthy because of the caravan trade, but like Ghana, it ultimately declined because of infighting and external threats.
- The Songhai, who split off from Mali, amassed great wealth from the demand for gold and slaves, and Timbuktu became a major center of Islamic learning.
- The Hausa city-states also participated in trade, and their women enjoyed high status.
- South of the Sudan, on the Guinea coast, the Yoruba developed a balance of power between kings and aristocrats and were generally peace-loving traders and artists, and the prosperous kingdom of Benin developed an innovative welfare system.

◆ Expanding Bantu Societies

What networks linked East Africa and the Bantu societies to the wider world?

African Bantu-speakers had begun migrating out of their original homeland, in west-central Africa, in deep antiquity, and this population movement continued in the Intermediate Era. As a result, Bantus settled the vast expanses of central, eastern, and southern Africa. These Africans developed many variations on Sudanic patterns, including some great kingdoms. The East African coast became a flourishing mercantile region closely linked to Eurasia, a link that allowed Islam to spread into the area. Like the Sudanic kingdoms and most Eurasian societies, some Bantu peoples built cities, kept records, engaged in extensive trade, and boasted diverse social classes.

The Bantu Diaspora

Considerable movement of Bantu peoples persisted during the Intermediate Era, bringing encounters with other groups. In East Africa and the Great Lakes region the migrating Bantus came into contact with the Nilotic-speakers, who themselves had migrated to the region from north-central Africa. Bantus and Nilotes (NAI-lots) competed over resources such as good grazing land and salt, but they also traded, coexisted, and sometimes mixed together. For example, the Bantu Gikuyu (kee-KOO-yoo), who settled in what is today Kenya, intermarried, traded, and sometimes fought with the neighboring Nilotic Masai (mah-SIE) people, who were mainly cattle herders.

Over time the Bantu peoples scattered over thousands of miles of forest, savannah, and highlands in the southern half of Africa, creating diverse cultures, languages, political systems, and economic patterns but also maintaining many common traditions. Most Bantu-speakers remained farmers, practicing shifting cultivation where necessary but using more complex methods where possible, as in the fertile East African highlands. Bananas became the staple crop of East Africa. Some Bantus lived in towns of 15,000 to 20,000 residents, such as those among the Sotho (SOO-too) and Tswana (TSWAHN-uh) of southern Africa. Some centralized kingdoms on the Sudanic model appeared, especially in the Great Lakes region. But most kings had religious and ceremonial rather than real political power, and the village usually remained supreme.

Islam, Trade, and East African Cities

Bantus began settling along the East African coast in the first millennium C.E., adapting to their new surroundings by combining fishing with agriculture. The expansion of both Islam and global commerce integrated the East African coastal peoples into Dar al-Islam and the wider world. The 1,200 miles of coast stretching from present-day Somalia down to central Mozambique was a cultural melting pot, where a growing trade network linking East Africa with the societies around the rim of the Indian Ocean and beyond brought diverse cultures, languages, and religions to the region, fostering a unique hybrid society. For hundreds of years the East African coastal peoples had been in regular contact with seafaring folk from Arabia, Persia, India, Southeast Asia, and even China. The coast was well suited to international commerce because the prevailing monsoon wind patterns made it relatively easy to sail up and down the coast.

Indeed, maritime trade had flourished along the coast from ancient times. Egyptians, Greeks, Persians, and Romans made occasional voyages. Indonesian seafarers visited East Africa for centuries, bringing with them various tropical plants such as bananas, coconuts, and yams, which proved well adapted and spread throughout tropical Africa. These nutritious crops supported large populations without needing excessive labor or complex technology. Some Indonesians also settled on the island of Madagascar. Eventually Arabs from the Persian Gulf, Oman, and Yemen came to dominate the East African coastal trade. Seafarers by tradition, Arabs came seeking products such as ivory, tortoise shell, leopard skin, and later gold and copper.

As trade increased, many city-states developed along the coast. Among the largest were Mogadishu (mo-ga-DEE-shoo), Lamu (LAH-moo), Malindi (ma-LIN-dee), Mombasa (mahm-BAHS-uh), Zanzibar (ZAN-zuh-bahr), Kilwa (KILL-wa), and Sofala. Each city-state was politically independent and governed only a small hinterland. Although rival cities sometimes attacked each other, city leaders were chiefly interested in trade, not military expansion. As the maritime networks improved, settlers came from Arabia, Persia, and India. Each city-state was dominated by a royal court, often claiming Persian or Arab ancestry, and powerful trading families. Trade networks from the coast into the interior expanded with the discovery of gold in the highlands of what is now Zimbabwe (zim-BOB-way). Because of its access to the goldfields of the interior, the port of Sofala at the mouth of the Zambezi (zam-BEE-zee) River became a major trade hub and a wealthy state.

The tenth-century Arab traveler al-Mas'udi, cited at the start of the chapter, left a record of a largely Bantu coastal society that also had many Sudanic customs. He reported that farmers grew sorghum as their chief crop, and he described the people as elegant orators with animist beliefs: "Everyone worships what he pleases, a plant, an animal, a metal." Yet, they also had a concept of a supreme deity or great god. Sofala was governed by a divine king, whom the people called the

> son of the great god because they have chosen their king to govern them with equity. As soon as he exercises a tyrannical power and departs from the rules of justice, they kill him and exclude his posterity from royal succession, because they say that in acting thus he has ceased to be the son of the great god.[10]

Two centuries later many Bantu customs had been reshaped by increasing Arab and Islamic influences.

East African Commerce

The golden age of the East African coast, which boasted royal courts, stone palaces, coral-carved mosques, and imported luxury goods, began about the ninth century and reached its peak from the twelfth through the fifteenth centuries as Islam became entrenched. Ships from Arabia, Persia, and India regularly visited the coast. One passenger, the Moroccan jurist Ibn Battuta, traveled as far south as Kilwa, a prosperous city on an island off what is today Tanzania, which he described as "one of the most beautiful and well-constructed towns in the world, elegantly built [with] good buildings of stone and mortar, entirely surrounded by a wall and towers."[11] Kilwa, which had perhaps 20,000 people, was a collection hub for goods coming in from north and south. The upper classes built three-story stone houses with indoor plumbing and lavished themselves with large quantities of gold and silver jewelry as well as Chinese silk and porcelain. Kilwa minted its own gold coins.

By Ibn Battuta's time, the coast had become largely Muslim, and the Moroccan traveler felt at home. He described the Kilwa Muslims as devout, chaste, and virtuous and its rulers, a family claiming Yemenite descent, as humble and pious. Still, he disliked some local customs. For example, he felt their daily diet was too rich and fattening. He approved of the chicken, meat, fish, vegetables, and mangoes but not the rice cooked with butter and yogurt chutney, which probably had South Asian origins. His reports show that, while East Africans had become closely linked to the Islamic world by trade and religion, they also maintained various local customs.

The East African city-states became an integral part of the greatest maritime trading network of the Intermediate world, a system of ports and trade routes that linked economies around the rim of the Indian Ocean. Stretching from Indonesia to East Africa, this network was generally dominated by seafaring Arab and Indian Muslims. Foreign traders brought pottery, Chinese porcelain, glass beads, and Indian cotton to East Africa and traded them for iron, ivory, tortoise shell, leopard skins, gold, and slaves. This trade brought the East African coastal people considerable prosperity. The beautiful homes of the coastal cities, some with tropical gardens, fountains, and pools, attested to the wealth that was available to the upper and middle classes.

Islam and Swahili Culture

Over time the blending of Bantu, Arab, and Islamic influences in the coastal cities produced a distinctive new African people, culture, and language, **Swahili** (Arab for "people of the coast"). Arab settlers had come in such numbers that they could not be absorbed into the dominant Bantu culture. Instead intermarriage and a fusion of cultures occurred. Similarly, the mixing of the Bantu and Arabic tongues created the new Swahili spoken language. The Swahili people began writing their language in

the Arabic script and produced poetry, historical legend, and religious speculation, in addition to commercial accounts. For the city-dwellers Swahili became the language of the home, but eventually it also became the major trading language of the entire coastal region. Its influence reached as far inland as the eastern Congo River Basin. Today Swahili is second only to Hausa as a first or second language in sub-Saharan Africa.

But Swahili identity involved more than language. Arab influence was pronounced in many ways. For example, the Swahili tended to favor Arab dress, including long gowns for men and modest attire for women. Yet, according to a visitor around 1500, women from wealthy families "wear many jewels of fine gold, silver too in plenty, earrings, necklaces, bangles, bracelets, and good silk garments."[12] Arab architectural styles dominated the cities. The Swahili also adopted Arab ideas of inheritance. Whereas the interior Bantu peoples practiced either patrilineal or matrilineal descent and inheritance systems, the Swahili were, like Arabs, firmly patrilineal.

Brought by Arabs and Persians, Islam became dominant along the coast by the twelfth century. However, it took many centuries for the religion to penetrate the hinterland. Islam spread in part because it was a flexible religion, willing to tolerate the incorporation of Bantu beliefs in spirits and ancestor worship. Today Muslims are numerous in all the East African countries, but five hundred years ago Islam was found mostly in the coastal towns.

Zimbabwe and International Trade

The East African trading cities were only a part of the wider Bantu diaspora, which also included various kingdoms in central and southern Africa. On the fertile plateau of south-central Africa one of the greatest kingdoms, Zimbabwe, which means "houses built of stone," emerged, and it flourished from trade with the coast. Today little remains of the kingdom's monumental buildings except for dozens of impressive stone ruins that dot the landscape for hundreds of miles. The Shona (SHO-nah) people, who still live in the area today, had lived on the plateau since at least 1000 c.e. and had constructed these buildings and a great state between the thirteenth and fifteenth centuries, eventually controlling much of the plateau.

Mining was the key to Zimbabwe's prosperity. The Shona were already advanced in mining technology, having migrated from the southern Congo River Basin, an area of many copper mines. Soon they discovered gold, copper, and iron ore on the plateau, where they extracted it from open-pit and occasionally underground mines. The Shona began trading these minerals with the Arabs and Swahili along the coast, using the Zambezi River as the route between plateau and coast. By 1500 some 10,000 Arab and Swahili traders lived inland along the river, buying and then exporting the gold to the Middle East and India through Sofala and Kilwa. The Shona mined perhaps a thousand pounds of gold annually in the early 1500s, and their exports corresponded to a rapid growth in the world demand for gold. In exchange Zimbabwe received Indian textiles and Chinese ceramics. Some residents were also skilled artists who produced copper, bronze, and gold ornaments.

Swahili   Name for a distinctive people, culture, and language, a mix of Bantu, Arab, and Islamic influences, that developed during the Intermediate Era on the East African coast.

The Great Zimbabwe Complex Great stone enclosures, most probably used as royal residences or religious sanctuaries, were built around the Zimbabwe kingdom. This one, surrounded by high walls, was at the center of the kingdom's capital city. (Visual Connection Archive)

The stone buildings, made from local granite, had various functions. Some were walls enclosing towns. Some seem to have been courts. In the heart of the capital city, which probably contained 10,000 to 20,000 people, are several large enclosures. The largest of these is an oval space surrounded by a wall 1,800 feet long, 32 feet high, and 17 feet thick. Some historians think it housed the royal family or perhaps the king's favorite wife. Others speculate it served as a sanctuary in which the royal family worshiped their patron deity.

But Zimbabwe's prosperity did not endure. In the 1400s the empire broke up into two rival states, and the capital city itself was largely abandoned by 1450. Since the Shona economy mixed farming and pastoralism, perhaps Zimbabwe was a casualty of overpopulation, soil exhaustion, and overgrazing by cattle. As Zimbabwe declined, the trade routes and then the government may have shifted north to the upper Zambezi River Valley, which was closer to main sources of gold, copper, ivory, and salt. The Zimbabwe kingdom collapsed but the Shona continued to export gold to the coast.

The Kongo Kingdom

Another great Bantu kingdom, Kongo, emerged 1,400 miles northwest of Zimbabwe, near the Atlantic coast of what is today northern Angola and western Congo. Kongo was established by the Bakongo (bah-KOHNG-goh) people in the 1300s at the hub of intersecting trade routes. Eventually its population reached 2.5 million. Because Kongo was one of the first major African states to be visited by European explorers, we know much more about it than about most African societies of the era.

The Kongo elite lived well. The king's compound, nearly a mile around, was located in the capital city of Mbanga (um-BAHN-ga). Royal musicians bearing drums and ivory trumpets announced visitors and ceremonies. The king and other high-status people wore finely woven cloth fabrics, beautifully dyed, which European visitors compared to velvet, silk, and brocade. Although in theory absolute and divine, the king faced some restrictions. To wage war he had to draft able-bodied men and risk revolt. In addition, because some provincial capitals were several hundred miles from the royal capital, communication was limited and royal power was somewhat diluted. The king was also elected by elders and governors, and he had to seek advice from a council formed by the heads of the leading clans.

Mostly dwelling in small villages, the common people lived much differently than the elite. Each village consisted of a few closely related families together with some domestic slaves, mostly war captives or lesser criminals. A village chief settled disputes but referred serious quarrels or crimes to district judges. Villagers lived in houses with walls of palm matting and thatch roofs. Each homestead had its own granary, where people stored the annual harvest of millet, the staple crop. Every day women ground this into a white flour and stirred it in boiling water to make a stiff porridge, which was eaten with peas or beans and spicy sauces made of palm oil. Meat such as chicken, fish, or game, as well as bananas, yams, and pumpkins, provided some variety. Trade flourished and people used a seashell-based currency. Local markets sold salt, colored cloth from India, palm cloth, palm belts, and animal skins.

SECTION SUMMARY

- The Bantus continued to expand across eastern and southern Africa and established numerous coastal city-states that were greatly influenced by trade with Arabs.

- The East African coast became largely Muslim, though it retained a great deal of its native African culture along with influences from such cultures as Arabia and South Asia.

- The fusion of Bantu, Arab, and Islamic culture yielded a new language, Swahili, and led to the adoption of many Arabic practices by East Africans.

- Zimbabwe rose to prosperity as a result of mining and built large granite buildings whose precise use is still debated by historians.

- The Kongo had a king who was in theory absolute and divine, though his powers were limited by logistical challenges and by other leading citizens.

African Society, Thought, and Economy

What were some distinctive patterns of government, society, thought, and economy in intermediate Africa?

Societies across Africa shared many common patterns of social organization, religion, culture, and economy. Nonetheless, African societies also varied considerably, depending partly on how closely they were connected to the Islamic world and beyond and on whether they had centralized or village-based governments. While intensive agriculture did not develop to the same extent as in Eurasia, trade was widespread. During the fifteenth century Africa's trade with the wider world attracted European explorers to the region.

Stateless Societies

The powerful kingdoms such as Mali, Benin, and Zimbabwe have usually received the most attention from historians, marking Africa as a continent of major states. But there were also many sub-Saharan Africans who lived in decentralized, village-based political systems, which modern anthropologists have called "stateless societies." These societies featured generally self-sufficient, self-governing villages, where government involved family relationships. A council of elders normally assisted the chief and applied customary law to regulate conduct. Some of these stateless societies were small and some large, but each was unique, as can be seen among the Tiv and Gikuyu peoples.

The Tiv (tihv), a West African people of what is today eastern Nigeria, developed an egalitarian society in which legal and economic rights were based on kinship. They taxed no crops and allowed no exploitation of others. Elders provided land to all according to need but allocated particular fields to families. Women controlled their own fields and did much of the farm work, but they were aided by men in harvesting and planting. Tiv politics can be described as local democracy. Although no central government existed, these were not anarchies. Village elders and family heads administered justice and organized community activities, and custom influenced the authority of leaders and the behavior of citizens.

Like the Tiv, the Gikuyu (kee-KOO-you), a Bantu people living in farming villages in the temperate, green highlands around Mt. Kenya in East Africa, had no local chiefs. Whereas most Tiv resided in multifamily villages, most Gikuyu lived in individual family homesteads, and each extended family was headed by the senior male, who represented the family to the broader Gikuyu society. Village councils elected representatives to district councils of elders, and sometimes Gikuyu leaders met together to discuss urgent matters. At the local level, younger Gikuyu formed a special council that handled military affairs. All government positions were elective, and officeholders could be dismissed. This democratic Gikuyu system relied heavily on group discussion and the power of public opinion.

Gender and Social Patterns

Although African social patterns were diverse, some commonalities also existed. Individuals were connected to others through varied social networks. The family anchored the social system, forming an economic unit and a common household that cooperated in most matters. Frequently the family consisted of several households, including all the members of living generations and their spouses and children. Various societies practiced matrilineal kinship, tracing decent and inheritance through the female line. Where matrilineal and many patrilineal societies had kings, the queen sister or queen mother was usually a highly respected figure. For example, the Bini people still revere Idia, an early-sixteenth-century queen mother who raised an army and used her magical powers to aid her son in overcoming his enemies. Queen mothers often controlled access to rulers, managed treasuries, presided over court systems, and helped enthrone or depose rulers. Some queens ruled in their own right. For instance, oral traditions suggest that the founder of the East African city-state of Mombasa was a women, Mwana Mkisi (MWAHN-a em-KEE-see).

Like family patterns, however, women's status varied widely. Older men dominated most families, even in many matrilineal societies, and powerful men often had multiple wives. Since the chief goal of marriage was children, a woman's status with her husband and the community depended on her childbearing ability. To win the highest regard as well as security meant bearing many children, and women looked to their children rather than their husbands for support in old age.

African communities were controlled by a web of associations that defined socially acceptable behavior. The family was part of a clan or lineage, which included many closely related people tracing descent to a particular ancestor. Most people lived in villages, and people related to other villagers through work or music groups, secret societies, religious cults, and age grades (groups of people about the same age, which promoted cooperation between people of the same generation). Most groups prized collective effort and responsibility instead of individual initiative.

A larger community than the clan and village was the *ethnic group,* often mistakenly called the "tribe" by modern observers. The ethnic group included people, not necessarily related by kinship ties, who had some cultural unity from speaking the same language and practicing similar customs. Most members lived in the same general territory, and some ethnic groups were quite large. For instance, both the Yoruba and Hausa numbered in the millions and were divided into various states. Distinct cultures, languages, and religions marked off groups such as the Yoruba, Hausa, Shona, and Gikuyu.

Like many societies in Eurasia, North Africa, and the Americas, some sub-Saharan peoples, especially in the kingdoms, condoned slavery and engaged in slave trading. Slaves were often war captives or debtors. Ibn Battuta wrote that, in many Sudanic cities, the wealthy "vie with one another in regard to the number of their slaves and serving-women. They never sell the educated female slaves, or but rarely and at a high price."[13] Slaves generally played a range of social and economic roles. Hausa slaves maintained city walls and grew food for the urban population; the Wolof (WOH-lohf) of Senegal assigned slaves to household work; Kongolese slaves were soldiers or plantation workers; and the Akan (ah-KAHN) in what is the modern nation of Ghana, on the Guinea coast, employed slave labor for gold mining. Some slaves, such as the palace advisers in the Hausa states, enjoyed a high social status. Some slaves were also considered members of households, and their children were often free, in which case they might be absorbed into the larger kinship system. Slaves could usually marry and have children. While slave life was often hard, among many African peoples slaves had more rights and could expect better treatment than slaves in most European, Islamic, Asian, and American societies.

Religious Traditions

African religion was diverse, including not only Muslim and Christian believers but also many millions who practiced monotheism, a rich polytheism with many gods and spirits, animism (spirit worship), or a mix of the three. Africans often recognized a supernatural world of sorcery, magic, spirits, ancestors, and multiple gods. Most African societies had shamans, male or female specialists who were skilled in curing disease and had knowledge about the spiritual realm. They were often successful as healers because they understood that many illnesses had spiritual and psychological as well as physical dimensions. Some male elders, considered sages, collected

and pondered wisdom and also challenged individuals to become better and more knowledgeable. Scholars compare these sages, who were constantly probing for truth, to classical Greek, Indian, and Chinese philosophers.

Reverence toward cosmic forces blended into a sense of worship and spirituality. Many Africans believed in a life force that was part of all living and material entities. Deceased family members and ancestors, believed to be present in spirit, were also revered. Most societies envisioned an unapproachable high god, such as the Arab traveler al-Mas'udi described for Sofala. For example, the Shona at Zimbabwe believed in a supreme being-creator, but since he held himself aloof from daily affairs, the people prayed to ancestors and spirits.

The Dogon (doh-GOHN) people, who live on a remote and arid plateau in today's nation of Mali, may represent what African society and religion were like before the formation of states and the coming of outside religions. Their society is ruled by priest-chiefs. Being group-oriented, the people work the fields collectively and center their lives on community religious festivals and arts. The Dogon order the cosmos and their society through a vast panorama of myths, and the line between reality and the spiritual world is not rigid. In their myths they perceive the cosmos as dualistic, mixing male and female, and order and change.

Literature and the Arts

Africans developed various forms of oral and written literature, as well as various arts. Most societies relied on **oral traditions,** verbal testimonies concerning the past that were passed down through the generations. Many African societies had a class of professional rememberers, known as *griots* in West Africa, who served as local historians and recordkeepers. Some griots became councilors to kings and tutors to princes. They could recount past events while also updating the story with contemporary happenings such as recent kings and wars. As a modern griot explained: "We are vessels of speech, the repositories which harbor secrets many centuries old. We are the memory of mankind."[14] These specialists were trained after a long apprenticeship, sometimes in special schools. Over time they became walking libraries, "speaking documents" who transmitted knowledge to their successors. As an Akan proverb put it, "Ancient things remain in the ear." Some griots concentrated on genealogy, remembering lists of kings or queen mothers. The top West African writers and popular musicians today often come from griot families.

Some peoples in West and East Africa had written languages and produced diverse literatures that included poetry and philosophical speculation. The most widespread written languages included Arabic, Hausa, Amharic, and Swahili. However, writing spread slowly, for two reasons. Most Africans relied on well-defined customs to maintain order and so did not need written laws, and because they had communal ownership,

---

oral traditions Verbal testimonies concerning the past; the major form of oral literature in cultures without writing.

they did not need to record facts about land use and inheritance, which generated a need for writing in some Eurasian societies. As in Mesopotamia and India, merchants in the Sudanic and East African cities found it valuable to record the buying and selling of large quantities of goods, which they could do in Arabic or Swahili. But merchants elsewhere faced serious barriers to writing. Paper deteriorates quickly in the tropical African climate, especially in the rain forest zone, which also lacks stone or clay to make writing tablets.

Africans produced a rich artistic heritage, including sculpture, dance, and music. Paleolithic Africans were among the first people anywhere to do paintings on rocks and cave walls. When farming developed, however, painting declined and sculpture became the major visual art form. Sculpting was done in wood, clay, ivory, or a metal such as bronze or gold. While the Benin and Yoruba people produced sculpture in bronze, many Africans used wood to make masks for religious festivals, as well as carvings of animal, human, and spiritual figures. In modern times African sculpture influenced artists around the world.

Perhaps the greatest cultural traditions were music and dance, both closely integrated into work, leisure, and religion and usually involving everyone's participation. Musical groups often accompanied people working in the fields. At the end of the day the farmers and musicians would return to the village for an impromptu party of dancing and singing. African musicians emphasized percussion, using many types of drums, but they also played various wind and string instruments. Later, African musical traditions spread widely and filtered into the Middle East along the trade routes, influencing Islamic music. Beginning in the 1500s African slaves carried their musical traditions to the Americas, where they blended with European and Native American styles. From these roots sprung many of the popular music styles of the twentieth century, such as blues, jazz, rock, calypso, salsa, and samba.

Agriculture and Trade

Sub-Saharan Africans successfully exploited the resources of the tropical environment, overcoming many obstacles to foster farming and trade. Whereas Eurasian societies had horses and oxen, in much of tropical Africa these animals could not be bred or survive because of various tropical diseases or insect pests that killed draft animals. Draft animals could pull a plow to cultivate more land, which was critical to agriculture in Eurasia, or pull large wheeled carts to move resources, but in Africa they could only be used in the northeast highland regions and in the dry Sudan and Sahara. For many peoples, therefore, economic production and transportation had to rely on human muscles.

Agriculture reflected African realities. Most Africans, like most Chinese, Indians, or Europeans, were peasants, small farmers who produced food primarily for their own use. With often poor soils, irregular rainfall, and no manure from draft animals for fertilizer, most Africans could not match the intensive, highly productive agriculture found in China, India, and

Europe. Hence many Africans practiced shifting cultivation, a practical adaptation to local conditions. This system worked well as long as population densities remained small. By 1500 there were probably some 40 million people in sub-Saharan Africa, compared to over 100 million in China. The land was rarely under much pressure until recent times, and new land was usually available for migrants. More sophisticated techniques such as irrigation or terracing were used where possible.

As already discussed, trading networks interlaced tropical Africa, though the extent to which they constituted a single continental economic system rather than sporadic contacts remains a matter of historical debate. Still, great markets emerged, especially in the Sudan, at cities such as Gao and Timbuktu. Here traders bought and sold ivory, ebony, and honey from the Guinea coast and books, wheat, horses, dates, cloth, and salt from the north. A visitor to the Senegal River, on the western tip of Africa, in 1455 described a regional market selling cotton, cotton thread and cloth, oil, millet, vegetables, wooden bowls, palm-leaf mats, and other articles for daily use. Throughout sub-Saharan Africa most market traders were women and most traveling merchants were men. Some peoples were renowned as long-distance traders. For example, Hausa merchants from northern Nigeria traveled to the Guinea coast to buy kola nuts, a rain forest tree crop that can be made into one of the few stimulants allowed Muslims. Likewise, Muslim Mandinka traders from Mali set up permanent operations in the Akan states, where they obtained gold in exchange for cotton, leather, and other goods. Various items, including gold, ivory, and kola nuts, were exported from tropical Africa to North Africa, Asia, and Europe. Both gold and cowry (KOW-ree) shells, collected on the Indian Ocean coast and spread around in Africa, were used as local currency.

Local trade was often more essential than international commerce. People bought and sold things needed for everyday life, such as cloth, salt, ironware, and copper. Women made cloth from such raw materials as cotton and bark. Because sources of abundant salt were rare in tropical Africa, it commanded a high price, and traders sometimes had to obtain it from hundreds of miles away. Iron ore was more common, but African miners lacked the tools to dig far underground. Smelting of iron ore took place in areas that had the best wood for making charcoal. Copper was valued from ancient times for making bangles and bracelets, but there were few good sources. The most extensive copper mining took place in the copper-belt region south of the Congo Basin and in South Africa.

Africans, Arab Slave Traders, and the Portuguese

Africa was connected to Eurasia primarily by trade across the Sahara Desert or along the East African coast. By the later Intermediate centuries the volume of this trade, especially in slaves, increased. As international trade expanded, Arab, Berber, and African traders shipped more African slaves north, where they were sold in North Africa, Muslim Iberia, Arabia,

Persia, India, and Christian Europe. Between 650 and 1500 C.E. the trans-Saharan caravans transported perhaps 2 to 4 million slaves from West Africa to the Mediterranean societies, while up to 2 million were shipped from East Africa. This was a significant number but considerably smaller in scale than the trans-Atlantic slave trade carried out by Western nations between 1500 and 1850. African slaves in the Middle East, like the slaves of European, Turkish, and other backgrounds, became domestic servants, laborers, soldiers, and even administrators. Perhaps 250,000 descendants of African slaves, traders, and sailors live in India and Pakistan today.

The trans-Saharan slave trade acquainted western Europeans, especially the Portuguese, with the prospects of eventually procuring slaves directly in West Africa. This knowledge spurred Portuguese exploration down the West African coast, which began a new era in African history. In search of Asian spices and African gold as well as slaves, the well-armed Portuguese began sailing south along the West African coastline in the early 1400s. By the later 1400s they had reached as far as the modern nation of Ghana on the west coast. As they visited more of Africa, the Portuguese became involved in African affairs, colonizing the Cape Verde (VUHRD) Islands in the Atlantic and the nearby coastal region of Guinea-Bissau (GIN-ee bis-OW) and establishing various trading forts to obtain gold, ivory, and slaves. Some West Africans picked up artistic and religious ideas from the Portuguese merchants and Christian missionaries, integrating these into their own traditions.

In 1487 a Portuguese expedition led by Bartolomeu Dias (DEE-ahsh) rounded the Cape of Good Hope at the tip of Africa and sailed into the Indian Ocean, thus opening up a whole new chapter in Western exploration and intensifying Portuguese interest both in Africa and the world to the east. Even after Christopher Columbus, sailing for Spain, announced his "discovery" of what he thought was India in 1492, the Portuguese were skeptical and concentrated on the sea route around Africa. In 1497 Portuguese ships commanded by Vasco da Gama, having rounded the Cape of Good Hope, sailed up the East African coast to the great trading city of Malindi and, engaging an Indian or Arab pilot, sailed on to southern India. Da Gama had discovered the fastest oceanic path to the great Indian Ocean maritime trading network.

In the 1480s the Portuguese began a long relationship with the Kongo kingdom, where they sent Catholic missionaries and skilled craftsmen. The resulting blend of Christian and Kongolese traditions profoundly reshaped the region. In 1491, after two court officials claimed that the Virgin Mary appeared to them in dreams and a stone shaped like a cross was discovered near the capital, the Kongolese king, Nzinga a Nkuwu (en-ZING-a ah en-KOO-WOO), and some of the aristocracy adopted Christianity and sent their children to Portugal for study. The king, who wanted Portuguese teachers, craftsmen, and weapons to use against a rival kingdom, later rejected Christianity, but in 1506 he was succeeded by his devoutly Christian son. By the early 1500s, after they realized the economic possibilities of the Americas, the Portuguese became far more interested in obtaining slaves than in helping the Kongolese economy or treating the Kongolese as equals. In 1514 they began exporting Kongolese slaves, some going to the Americas. This began a new era for Africa and a direct relationship with the peoples of Europe and the Americas, the region to which we now turn.

SECTION SUMMARY

- Many Africans lived in "stateless societies" in which family relationships, rather than rulers or governments, organized people's lives.
- Africans were part of a variety of social networks, including the family, the village, and the ethnic group, often mistakenly called the "tribe."
- In addition to Muslims and Christians, many Africans were polytheistic, believers in multiple gods and spirits.
- In Africa the oral tradition was much stronger than the written one, and writing spread slowly because African custom did not depend on recordkeeping and important knowledge was passed down orally by griots.
- African agriculture faced a number of challenges, including the difficulty of obtaining and using draft animals, poor soil, and irregular rainfall.
- Several million African slaves from across the continent were shipped to the Middle East during the Intermediate period, and the Portuguese lay the groundwork for the much larger European slave trade to the Americas.

American Societies in Transition

What factors explain the collapse of the Early Intermediate Era American societies?

As in Africa, most Americans creatively exploited their environments, whether they lived in urban societies, which had existed in the Americas for millennia, much as such societies had in Africa, or in smaller agricultural or nomadic communities. Their successes came largely from their own innovative efforts. Whereas many Africans had direct or indirect contact with Eastern Hemisphere networks, Americans remained a world apart from that interconnecting zone and the influences that flowed through it. Furthermore, these American societies were often separated from each other by great distances. In addition, like some Africans, Americans were divided by more geographical barriers—high mountains, harsh deserts, and thick forests—than was true for their counterparts in Eurasia and North Africa. Yet cultures, technologies, and trade goods spread over a wide area. At the center of some of these major networks were the powerful states and complex agricultural societies of Mesoamerica and the Andes, which supported dense populations and which arose after some longstanding American societies, such as the Maya, declined or collapsed. Less centralized or village-based governments formed elsewhere, including in North America.

The Collapse of the Classical States

Unlike their Afro-Eurasian counterparts such as Rome, Kush, Sassanian Persia, Gupta India, Han China, and Funan, most of the major American states of the Classical Era survived into the early Intermediate Era. Great cities such as Teotihuacan (teo-tee-WALK-aun) in central Mexico, Monte Alban in southern Mexico, and Tikal in the Maya lands, the Moche settlements on the northern Peruvian coast, and Tiwanaku in the southern Andes had dominated large regions and flourished for centuries. Their success was based on a combination of productive and often innovative farming, trade, and metalworking, combined, in some cases, with warfare with their neighbors.

The Ancient and Classical Era American peoples' achievements were many. For example, in their quest for good food and health, Americans became creative plant breeders, a talent that aided population growth. Maize, the main crop domesticated in Mesoamerica, is very nutritious. Combining maize with beans, squash, and fish or game provided many Americans with a well-balanced, healthy diet. Americans were also experts in pharmacology, discovering many plant drugs still used today to cure disease or alleviate pain, including quinine and coca. American medicines were comparable to those in Afro-Eurasia in many respects.

However, substantial cultural and political change occurred during the Early Intermediate Era, as older centers of religious, economic, or political power were replaced by newer ones, some of which also later collapsed. In Mesoamerica, Monte Alban, the capital of the Zapotec state, began its decline around 750 but remained inhabited for several more centuries. To the north, Teotihuacan collapsed in the eighth century, removing a unifying commercial and political hub for central Mexico. Spanning the Classical and Intermediate Eras, the Maya people had flourished beginning well before the Common Era, but by 900 they had abandoned many of their cities. In South America, Moche collapsed around 700 but Tiwanaku flourished until falling apart and being burned around 1000 (see Chronology: The Americas in the Intermediate Era).

The reasons for these rapid changes of political and economic fortunes remain somewhat unclear, but climate probably played a role. In some regions, including Mesoamerica and the Pacific coast of South America, a warming climate baked the land as rains failed and brought drought. Grassy hillsides turned brown, streams dried up, and crops withered. Coastal peoples such as the Moche in Peru and the Chumash whose southern California society goes back to ancient times, were long affected by periodic weather cycles, as marine animals used for food migrated near or far in response to cooler or warmer ocean waters.

The Zenith and Decline of the Maya

The Maya of Yucatan and northern Central America, who declined rapidly and then suddenly collapsed, reflected the transition of the era, which opened the way for new powers to rise. Maya society reached its peak between 600 and 800, with growing populations and massive monument building. The large population testified to the Maya success in mastering a marginal environment for farming. Across 36,000 square miles of territory, population densities reached a staggering 600 people per square mile, similar to China today. Several Maya cities were large. Tikal may have contained 50,000 people. At their height the lowland Maya used complex irrigation systems to cultivate their poor land, which enabled them to support a population of 3 to 5 million people between 600 and 900.

The Maya remained dynamic in the early Intermediate Era. A half dozen major Maya states existed between 300 and 800. Warfare was frequent, but victories were short-lived and resulted in no large, permanent empires. The battles were mostly for royal glory and commercial predominance, not conquest. The Maya were also in close commercial contact with the peoples of central Mexico. The largest American city, Teotihuacan had a whole neighborhood reserved for Maya merchants, who also sometimes ventured by boat to many of the larger Caribbean islands, trading jade, salt, feathers, and chocolate. Clearly the Maya and other Mesoamericans benefited from networks of exchange. Excellent sculpturers, builders, astronomers, and mathematicians, the Maya also had a well-developed writing system that could express any thought or concept. Thousands of folding-screen books called codices, made of bark paper, were produced, although only a handful survived after the Spanish arrival in the early 1500s.

Eventually this society, which had survived for so many centuries, faced the same transition as the other classical states. Between 800 and 900 most of the Maya cities in the southern lowlands were deserted, and the whole region lost perhaps two-thirds of its population over several decades. The reasons for Maya collapse are unclear. Climate change seems to have caused a drought lasting over a century, with dry weather emptying the complex system of canals and reservoirs built by the Maya to collect rainwater for farming and drinking. Overpopulation may have prompted frantic attempts to increase agricultural productivity on marginally fertile land. The resulting soil degradation and deforestation may have fostered crop failures, famine, malnutrition, starvation, epidemics, and increased warfare. Perhaps as people were drafted into military campaigns, it became even harder to maintain the agricultural economy.

Combined with military defeats and possibly natural disasters, these problems may have led to a questioning of the system and its values. Governments may have become more unstable, prompting revolts. As people abandoned the southern Maya cities, numerous changes probably occurred. Some Maya no doubt moved to fortified villages in remote areas. The political and religious hierarchy of kings, aristocrats, and priests may have disappeared, and merchants, scribes, and craftsmen ceased their work. The complex agriculture system probably then fell into disuse, and people returned to shifting cultivation.

However, these dramatic developments seem not to have affected the northern, and often newer, Maya cities such as Uxmal (oosh-MAHL), which flourished until around 1000, when they also declined. Only the northern Yucatan coast enjoyed continuity after 900. But more frequent warfare also engulfed this region, and human sacrifice increased. The city of Chichen Itza (chuh-chen uht-SAH), founded around 800, dominated the Yucatan Peninsula between 1000 and 1250 and had intensive contacts with the non-Maya peoples of central Mexico, who influenced its architecture. The state of Mayapan (MY-uh-PAHN) succeeded to power by 1250 but was itself destroyed by a rebellion in 1441. By the 1500s the Yucatan Maya were fragmented into small states in chronic conflict with each other. The remnants of the Maya people still existed over a wide area of Mesoamerica, but their once brilliant history was fading from memory.

The Toltecs and Chimu

As the older Mesoamerican and Andean states declined or collapsed, other peoples completed the transition by establishing powerful states not unlike the kingdoms that flourished in West Africa, such as Mali. In Mesoamerica, the Toltecs (TOLL-teks) moved into Mexico's central valley from the desert north and, led by King Mixcoatl (MIX-coat-el) ("Cloud Serpent"), created an empire that lasted from 900 to 1168. Since the Toltecs had writing and systematically recorded their history, we know much about them. The Toltec Empire seems to have been a loose military alliance involving newcomers from the north mixing with the local people, whose roots lay in Teotihuacan, located near today's Mexico City. The Toltecs adopted the cult of **Quetzalcoatl** (kate-zahl-CO-ah-tal), the feathered serpent, which goes back deep in Mesoamerican history and which inspired a temple at Teotihuacan. In Toltec tradition, Quetzalcoatl was a human leader who was banished to sea by the war-gods. Historians think that the story is based on Topiltzin (to-PILLT-sen) (b. ca. 947), a cult high priest who succeeded his father, Mixcoatl, as Toltec king but whose opposition to human sacrifice and promotion of peace angered more warlike leaders. Forced into exile by the militaristic faction, the man gradually blended into the god in myth. But the legend also said that the banished man-god, bearded and of fair complexion, would return to seek revenge, and this prophecy haunted later Mesoamericans.

The Toltecs achieved considerable power and influence throughout the region, even over some of the northern Maya cities. The capital city, Tula (TOO-la), built by Topiltzin, was filled with ceremonial architecture and reached a population of 30,000 to 60,000, a reflection of the Toltecs' status. The Toltecs maintained the active trade networks around the region. Tula was a center for obsidian mining and processing, and Tula craftsmen produced obsidian and copper tools. The Toltecs may have even established some contact with societies in the Andes and the southeastern part of what is now the United States, since some Toltec trade goods have been found as far north as New Mexico and Arizona. But in the twelfth century the Toltec state, weakened by long-term drought, famine, and war, collapsed and Tula was abandoned, disrupting the trade routes. Several centuries of political fragmentation followed this collapse.

A powerful new state also emerged in South America. Beginning around 800 the Chimu (chee-MOO) Empire, based at Chan Chan (CHAHN CHAHN) in the old Moche region along the Peruvian coast, began its rise to prominence. The Chimu ruling class may have descended from Moche nobles. By 1200 the Chimu controlled a sizeable empire stretching some 600 miles north to south. Chan Chan was a substantial city, filled with many adobe-walled compounds and a population of 25,000 to 50,000. The area was a center of copper manufacturing. The Chimu lords, who lived in seclusion in magnificent walled palaces up to three stories high, had elaborate funerals in which several hundred men and women were sacrificed to serve as attendants in the afterlife.

Like other Andean peoples, the Chimu were great builders. Workers drafted into the army labored on vast construction and irrigation projects. Chimu's impressive engineering skills were illustrated by its 25-foot-wide main roads. To irrigate the fields of maize, beans, cotton, gourds, squash, peanuts, and fruits, they constructed hundreds of miles of terraces and large storage reservoirs that controlled the flow of water down the mountainsides. Indeed, the Chimu linked five separate river valleys into a single agricultural complex, an amazing feat.

Quetzalcoatl The feathered serpent, a symbol that goes back deep in Mesoamerican history.

Pyramid at Tula Each figure on this pyramid at the Toltec capital is made of fitted stone sections and represents a warrior carrying a throwing stick in one hand and a bag of incense in the other. (Robert Harding World Imagery)

These activities allowed the Chimu to avoid all but the most severe droughts and to achieve two or three crops a year.

Eventually the Chimu faced challenges they could not overcome. Even with the productive farming, the Chimu faced a constant challenge from El Niño climate changes, which could disrupt irrigation. By the fourteenth century the Chimu were in decline, perhaps because of overpopulation and increased salinization of the soil. These conditions may have reduced food supplies, making the Chimu vulnerable. Around 1475 they were conquered by the Incas and incorporated into a vast Andean empire.

Pueblo Societies

While only a few American societies formed kingdoms or built large cities such as those of the Maya, Toltecs, and Chimu, many peoples creatively farmed in challenging environments and supported towns and long-distance trade. Some of the most successful societies developed in the southwestern desert of North America, where maize had been grown for many centuries. These southwestern people and their modern descendants are known as the Pueblo Indians because of their permanent towns, known as *pueblos* in Spanish. By learning to farm this dry region, they survived and sometimes flourished. To overcome a climate that was too dry for maize, the Pueblo peoples became experts at selecting just the right soils. Even today Pueblo peoples like the Zuni (ZOO-nee) celebrate maize as the basis of their existence in a hot, forbidding environment. Southwestern peoples also grew cotton and were famed for their weaving of cotton cloth. Towns were often built around riverbeds and human-made dams, terraces, irrigation canals, and reservoirs.

The Pueblo peoples also traded over long distances with societies in central Mexico and on the Pacific coast. For example, they mined turquoise and exchanged turquoise and turquoise products with Teotihuacan and the Toltecs for craft goods. Some Mesoamerican religious beliefs and customs, such as the tradition of the feathered serpent and ball courts and games, filtered north into some Pueblo communities.

Several distinct cultures emerged in the North American Southwest (see Map 12.2). By 700 the Hohokum (huh-HOH-kuhm) and Mogollon (MOH-guh-YOHN) societies dominated parts of southern Arizona, New Mexico, and northern Mexico. Hohokum artists were probably the first anywhere to etch intricate designs on shells. They also built large buildings. For instance, Casa Grande (KAH-suh GRAN-dee) in northern Mexico, three stories high, was constructed around 1325 of thick adobe atop a platform mound. The surrounding town housed some 2,200 people. By 1000 the neighboring Mogollon people had developed masonry technology for house building. But climate change caused drought in the 1300s, and both the Hohokum and Mogollon settlements were eventually abandoned.

The Anasazi (ah-nah-SAH-zee), meaning "ancient ones" in the Navaho (NAH-vuh-ho) language, flourished between 700 and 1400 and reached their height of town building and prosperity between 900 and 1250. Using huge sandstone blocks to construct masonry houses, they constructed towns over large sections of what are today the U.S. states of Arizona, Colorado, New Mexico, and Utah, including major centers at Mesa Verde and Chaco (CHAHK-oh) Canyon. Mesa Verde probably housed 2,500 people, while another 30,000 lived in the surrounding area. Even today visitors are amazed by Mesa Verde, which is ingeniously built into steep cliff walls. In Chaco Canyon, eight adobe towns sat in or on the rim of the canyon, in which multistoried houses, some six stories high, were built around central plazas. Several hundred smaller villages arose around the towns. The Anasazi constructed these pueblos with wood beams, stone, and clay carried from distant forests. Wide roads connected the Chaco pueblos with Anasazi towns a hundred miles away.

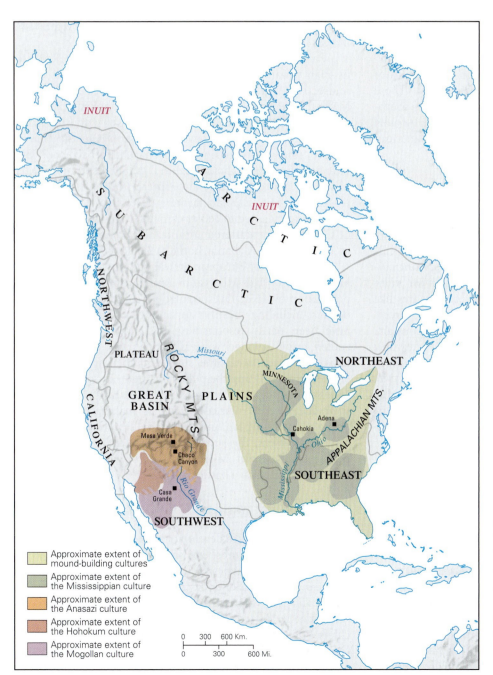

Map 12.2 Major North American Societies, 600–1500 C.E.
Farming societies were common in North America. The Pueblo peoples such as the Anasazi in the southwestern desert and the Mound Builders in the eastern half of the continent lived in towns. The city of Cahokia was the center of the widespread Mississippian culture and a vast trade network.

The total Anasazi population, dispersed over a large area, probably numbered 100,000. The Anasazi, like many Pueblo Indians, lived in egalitarian communities that practiced matrilineal kinship and matrilocal residence, with men moving into their wife's household. Women owned the houses, crops, and fields, but men dominated the council of elders who administered each town.

Environmental challenges eventually proved overwhelming for the Anasazi, precipitating collapse. By 1200 their agriculture had declined, probably because of a severe drought. Deforestation, soil erosion, disease epidemics, and invasions by outsiders may also have been factors. Hard times resulted in increased warfare between pueblos for limited resources. A few scholars suspect that some pueblos, their social order undermined, may have resorted to human sacrifice or cannibalism, perhaps to appease the gods. By 1300 many Anasazi had moved south to the Rio Grande River Valley, where they mixed with other newcomers. This merging produced the Pueblo peoples who today inhabit central and northern New Mexico. By 1400 the older Anasazi culture had collapsed and the pueblos of Chaco and Mesa Verde had long been abandoned. Those Anasazi who survived were probably the ancestors of southwestern tribes like the Hopi (HOH-pee) and Zuni. Anasazi ghost towns can be found over a wide area of the American Southwest.

The Mississippian Culture and Cahokia

In the vast Mississippi and Ohio River Basins of eastern North America, where the climate was less harsh and the land more fertile than in the southwest, a series of mound-building cultures flourished for centuries, based on trade and shifting cultivation of maize. The Mississippian culture, the most widespread between 700 and 1700, displayed urban features like those elsewhere in the world: several cities, monumental architecture, social hierarchies, ethnic diversity, and religious art. The main Mississippian center, Cahokia (kuh-HOH-kee-uh), was strategically located near the juncture of the Mississippi and Missouri Rivers, a few miles from today's St. Louis. At its peak between 1050 and 1250 the city and suburbs probably had a population of between 30,000 and 60,000. The downtown covered 200 acres, and the suburbs of thatch houses another 2,000 acres.

Cahokia was the North American counterpart to Mesoamerican cities such as Teotihuacan and Tula, and Mesoamerican influences are clear. Cahokia and most Mississippian communities were built around central plazas that included platform mounds topped by temples and elite houses, probably surrounded by markets, a pattern very similar to that in Mesoamerica. The largest pyramid, 1,000 feet long, 700 feet wide, and 100 feet long, was much larger than the great pyramids of Egypt. Indeed, in either hemisphere only two Mexican pyramids were bigger than Cahokia's. Circles of standing timbers tracked the seasons by marking the sun's position. As in Mesoamerican cities, Cahokia's priest-rulers probably presided over lavish rituals atop the pyramids. And Cahokians may have worshiped some Mesoamerican gods. For instance, the chief religious cult worshiped the sun as the guarantor of bountiful harvests. The Mississippian peoples shared a common religious symbolism of mythical creatures, which appeared in their art.

We have only limited knowledge of Cahokia society. The society was matrilineal and divided into several distinct classes. Both men and women nobles were required to marry commoners. At the death of a ruler some members of the commoner class, called "stinkards" by the elite, were sacrificed to accompany him on the voyage to the hereafter. The Cahokia state seems to have administered many other settlements over a wide area. Early Spanish explorers recorded an oral tradition in which a lord rode in a flotilla of large canoes decorated with gold objects. Warfare over territory may have been common. Cahokia had many artisans, who made baskets, pottery, shell beads, leather clothes, copper ornaments, wooden utensils, and stone tools. Like earlier Mound Builders, they carved artistic images into their buildings.

Cahokia was the major hub of a vast trade network that, at its high point, encompassed much of the North American midsection, from the Great Lakes to the Rockies, along the Mississippi, Missouri, and Ohio Rivers. Cahokians imported copper from the Great Lakes to make jewelry and other objects. The network must have reached south to the Gulf of Mexico, since many marine shells, shark, and barracuda jaws have been found at Cahokia. Cultural influences from Cahokia, including maize farming, also spread through the eastern woodlands. Mississippian farmers developed new strains of maize better adapted to cooler climates. Many smaller versions of Cahokia were scattered around the Mississippi Basin, such as Moundville in Alabama, home to 3,000 people.

By the time of European arrival, the Mississippian culture had collapsed. The Mississippi River Basin lost much of its population by 1550. Overpopulation, soil depletion, and epidemics, including the first appearance of tuberculosis, may have been partly responsible. The climate may also have cooled, bringing longer winters that damaged agriculture. Perhaps tensions between the elites and the common folk increased, undermining the political system. In some places the Mississippian culture continued until the early 1700s but was then devastated by diseases such as malaria and smallpox brought by European invaders. The last remnants of the Mound Builders, the sun-worshiping Natchez (NACH-uhz) people in the lower Mississippi valley, were wiped out by French colonizers in a battle in 1731.

The Eastern Woodlands Societies

Before 1500, few states developed in the eastern woodlands of North America, and most farming communities resembled the African stateless societies such as the Tiv and Gikuyu in their political structure. Some eastern woodlands people lived in walled villages. While warfare using bows and arrows was common, it generally led to few casualties. Individual villages had chiefs, often elected by elders, but they lacked much authority. Consensus politics was more common, with every family participating in decision making. Since most people depended on farming for survival, there were few full-time crafts specialists and only limited intergroup trade. Eastern woodland farming produced abundance. An English observer visiting what is today Massachusetts in 1614 noted that the land was "so planted with gardens and corn fields, and so well inhabited with a goodly, strong people [that] I would rather live here than any where."[15]

We know a little about woodlands society in this era. The men cleared the fields but were often gone for long periods, hunting or fighting. Women working in groups did most of the farm work. As in some African societies, since the women produced most of the food, their social and political status was high. In contrast to the arranged marriages common elsewhere in the world, the relative freedom of women resulted in a stronger emphasis on romantic courtship among some peoples. Among some tribes, women even had veto power over policies proposed by chiefs. Many societies were matrilineal, with residence based on affiliation with senior females. Women elders often had the power to approve or prohibit warfare, and often a senior clan mother known for her wisdom nominated a new chief, who would then be elected or rejected by the rest of the tribe.

SECTION SUMMARY

- American Classical states survived longer than their counterparts in Eurasia, though they ultimately declined, perhaps because of climate change.

- The Maya supported an extremely dense population, but by 900 C.E. the southern Maya had collapsed, while the northern Maya continued on fitfully before collapsing by 1500.

- The Toltecs, a loose military empire based in central Mexico, adopted the cult of Quetzalcoatl, the feathered serpent.

- The Pueblo peoples of the American Southwest thrived on maize, grew and wove cotton, and were largely egalitarian and matrilineal.

- In the Mississippi and Ohio River Basins, mound-building cultures thrived on the fertile land and built some of the largest structures in the world.

The American Empires and Their Challenges

How were the Aztec and Inca Empires different, and how were they similar?

Several rich and powerful empires formed in Mesoamerica and the Andes in the 1300s and 1400s. The transition that accompanied the collapse of the Maya and the decline of the Toltecs and Chimu had resulted in the rapid rise of the great Aztec (AZ-tek) and Inca (IN-kuh) Empires. These empires had been the products of political fragmentation and continuous military conflict in the thirteenth and fourteenth centuries. Thanks to strong armies and well-organized governments, both empires gained widespread dominance, but both also rapidly collapsed when confronted in the 1500s with the power of Spanish military forces and the epidemic diseases they brought from the Eastern Hemisphere.

The Aztec Empire, Religion, and Warfare

The Aztecs and Incas created the largest empires and most sophisticated states ever seen in the Americas before 1500 (see Map 12.3). The warlike Aztec society first developed in the 1300s out of the competition for power in Mesoamerica. The people who created the Aztec Empire were the Mexica, immigrants from the north known for their military skills. According to their legends, an early leader told them that "we shall conquer all peoples of the universe. I shall make you lords and kings of all that is in the world."[16] Many of them had served as mercenaries in other states' armies but felt mistreated. The Mexica took pride in their reputation as warriors and wrote much about their history, identifying themselves as the successor to the Toltecs and adopting many Toltec gods, rituals, and cultural forms. By 1325 they had established a strong state that soon controlled much of the Valley of Mexico, the lake-filled basin where Teotihuacan had once flourished. The city of Tenochtitlan (teh-noch-TIT-lan) became the Mexica capital. The Mexica and other Nahuatal (NAH-waht-uhl)-speaking people in the Valley of Mexico came to be known as Aztecs.

Soon the Aztecs turned to conquest. In 1428 they expanded into neighboring regions. Their greatest ruler, Moctezuma (mock-teh-ZOO-ma) I (1440–1468), was a war hero who also used diplomacy to establish the imperial foundations. He declared that war was the main Aztec preoccupation and its purpose was to gain new territories while acquiring prisoners for sacrifice to the gods. By 1519 the empire controlled much of central and southern Mexico, and it even collected tribute from people far to the south, in what is today Guatemala and El Salvador. The tribute from the conquered became an important revenue source.

Religion supported the warfare, which remained at the core of Aztec life. The Aztecs imposed a state religion that incorporated but reinterpreted many ancient Mesoamerican rituals and beliefs. The Mexica believed the sun to be a warrior-god who daily battled his way across the skies to prevent the destruction of the universe by the forces of darkness. To help the sun-god remain fit for this struggle, the Aztecs had to feed the deity with blood from non-Aztec warriors captured in their frequent fighting. These captives would be regularly sacrificed in gruesome rituals. In Aztec myths, their god Huitzilopochtli (wheat-zeel-oh-POSHT-lee) ("The Hummingbird Wizard") commanded them to feed him with human hearts torn from the recently sacrificed. The Aztec practiced human sacrifice on a greater scale than any other major society ever did, sacrificing several thousand captured warriors a year throughout the empire. Other central Mexican

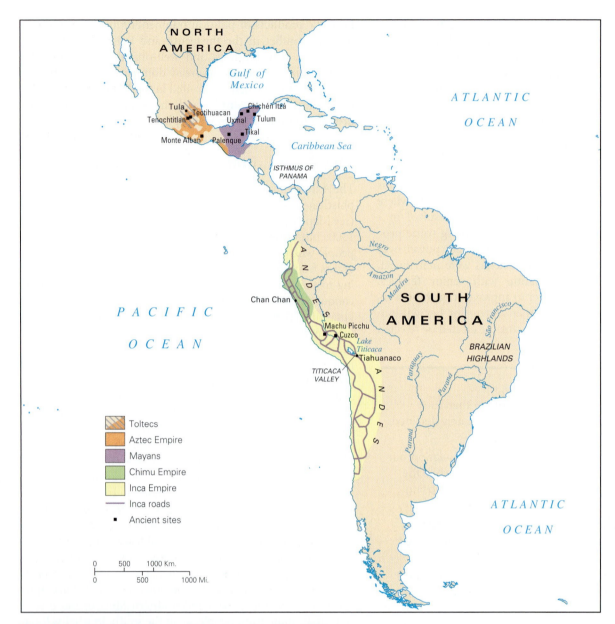

Map 12.3 South America and Mesoamerica, 900–1500 C.E.
The Mayas and Aztecs in Mesoamerica and the Incas in the Andes forged the most densely populated
societies, the most productive farming, and the best organized governments. The Incas built one of the
world's largest empires. Other urban societies also flourished in Mexico and South America.

people practiced blood sacrifice as well, sometimes with Aztec
captives.

Eventually the brutal imperialism led to collapse. The need
for a regular supply of captives fostered a permanent state of
war and terror, making for an unstable imperial system and
fierce resistance. The conquered peoples paid tribute, but
because the Aztec government ruled through local leaders, rebellions were frequent, which provided an excuse to fight and
obtain more captives. By 1500 the Aztecs faced growing economic, political, and military problems. They demanded more
tribute from colonized peoples, many of whom experienced a
decline in their living standards.

The challenge to the empire came in different forms,
largely related to the Aztec system of warfare. As a result of
their brutal policies, the Aztecs had many enemies, some
of whom were willing to cooperate with the newly arrived
Spanish in the early 1500s to invade Tenochtitlan. Even before
this, Aztec leaders seem to have had a deepening sense of insecurity and to have been haunted by bad portents. As Aztec
scribes later reported, these worries increased in 1518, when
word reached Tenochtitlan of winged towers (Spanish ships),
bearing white men with beards, landing on Mexico's east coast.
The Spanish arrival coincided with the prophesied return of
Quetzalcoatl. Seeking to explain their defeat, Aztec nobles

Aztec Warrior These drawings, made by a sixteenth-century Aztec artist, show Aztec warriors, wearing costumes that reflect their status, who have defeated their opponents and forced them to kneel in submission. Many such captives would later be sacrificed. (Bodleian Library, Oxford University, Ms. Selden A.1, fol. 64r)

claimed that fear of retribution by this god may have sapped Emperor Moctezuma II's will to resist the Spanish. Historians debate whether Moctezuma II identified the Spanish with the god. In any case, because the Aztecs had learned to make only limited use of metals, their tools and weapons were still based on sharp minerals, such as obsidian, which were no match for Spanish guns and steel swords. Although the Spanish encountered a vigorous Aztec society, it might have soon collapsed even without Spanish conquest and occupation in 1521, which ended the Aztec era.

Aztec Economy and Society

The Aztecs developed a prosperous economy and a dynamic social system. The capital city, built on a swampy island in the middle of a large lake, became a major trade center. By the early 1500s Tenochtitlan (the site of today's Mexico City) was one of the world's great cities: large palaces, temples, forty pyramids, and diverse markets served some 150,000 to 300,000 residents. The Spanish marveled at the order of the markets, where each kind of merchandise was sold in its respective street (see Witness to the Past: An Aztec Market). Traversing the city were six major canals, used daily by thousands of canoes carrying passengers or produce. Many houses were built of adobe or lava. The first Spaniards to reach the city in 1519, even those from big cities, were awed by the sight:

And when we saw all those towns and villages built in the water, and other great towns on dry land, and that straight and narrow causeway leading to Mexico [Tenochtitlan], we were astounded. These great towns and buildings rising from the water, all made of stone, seemed like an enchanted vision. Indeed, some of our soldiers asked whether it was not all a dream.[17]

The Aztec economy was based on highly productive farming and trade. The Aztecs grew their food on artificial islands, called **chinampas,** that were built on the lakes of the central valley, a technique that dated back hundreds of years before the Aztecs. An elaborate system of dikes, canals, and aqueducts increased the area available for farming. The Aztecs were also the core of a regional trade system that stretched into North America and Central America. Whole villages were devoted to the production of copper items or textiles for local use and trade, and merchants enjoyed a privileged position in Aztec society. They were organized into guilds but were careful to maintain the state's goodwill, and some probably served as spies in outlying areas. Indeed, since trading could be dangerous, merchants went armed in convoys. A Spanish observer wrote that "as they traveled the road, they went girt for war. They bore

chinampas Artificial islands built along lakeshores of the central valley of Mexico for growing food.

An Aztec Market

The Spanish conquistadors who made their first visit to the Aztec capital of Tenochtitlan in 1519, two years before their conquest, were impressed with the wealth of foods and other trade goods available in the markets in and around the city. This account by Bernal Diaz del Castillo (DEE-as del kah-STEE-yoh), a Catholic priest who observed the Spanish conquest, describes the great market of Tlatelolco, near Tenochtitlan. Every day the market was thronged with as many as 25,000 people, and special market days might have attracted twice that number.

We were astounded at the number of people and the quantity of merchandise that [the market] contained, and at the good order and control that was maintained, for we had never seen such a thing before. . . . Each kind of merchandise was kept by itself and had its fixed place marked out. Let us begin with dealers of gold, silver, and precious stones, feathers, mantles, and embroidered goods. Then there were other wares consisting of Indian slaves, both men and women. . . . Next there were other traders who sold great pieces of cloth and cotton, and articles of twisted thread. . . . There were those who shod cloths of hennequen [a tough fiber] and ropes and the sandals with which they are shod. . . .

Let us go and speak of those who sold beans and sage and other vegetables and herbs, . . . and to those who sold fowls, cocks, . . . rabbits, hares, deer, mallards, young dogs and other things of that sort in their part of the market, and let us also notice the fruiterers, and the women who sold cooked food, dough and tripe; . . . then every sort of pottery made in a thousand different forms from great water jars to little jugs; . . . then those who sold . . . lumber, boards, cradles, beams, blocks and benches. . . . Paper . . . and reeds scented with liquid [amber], and . . . tobacco, and yellow ointments. . . .

I am forgetting those who sell salt, and those who make the stone knives, . . . and the fisherwomen and others who sell some small cakes . . . [and] a bread having a flavor something like cheese. There are for sale axes of brass and copper and tin, and gourds and gaily painted jars made of wood. I could wish that I had finished telling of all the things which are sold there, but they are so numerous and of such different quality and the great market place with its surrounding arcades was so crowded with people, that one would not have been able to see and inquire about it all in two days.

THINKING ABOUT THE READING

1. What does the reading tell us about Aztec society and its material culture?

2. In what ways does the Aztec market remind you of a modern supermarket or department store?

Source: Bernard Diaz del Castillo, "The Discovery and Conquest of Mexico," trans. by A. P. Maudslay (1956). Quoted in Richard F. Townsend, *The Aztecs*, rev. ed. (New York: Thames and Hudson, 2000), pp. 182–183.

---

their shields [and] their obsidian-bladed swords, because they passed through the enemy's land."[18]

Like most centralized American states, the Aztecs had a hierarchical social structure. At the top were the emperors, true despots who were considered semigods. They were selected by a group of high officials, priests, and warriors and advised by an elected council of four princes. Then came the warrior-noble caste, whose men were divided into war lodges such as the eagle knights and jaguar knights. If captured by the enemy, they were expected to die with honor. According to an Aztec poem: "There is nothing like death in war. Far off I see it; my heart yearns for it!"[19] The warriors were followed in the hierarchy by priests and merchants. The priesthood, mostly celibate, played a key role in Aztec life. As the intellectual elite, they prepared the calendars and most of the books. An Aztec writing a few years after the Spanish conquest remembered the priests as "sages wise in words. They watch over, they read, they lay out the books. They are in charge of the writings. It is they who are in charge of us. They lead us, they tell us the way."[20] Aztec artists served the elite, creating beautiful representations of the human figure. Aztec sculpture, painted codex books, and murals influenced artists, and were traded, all over Mesoamerica.

The great number of Aztec commoners were held in contempt by the elite classes. Some were artisans and professional entertainers, and many worked as tenant farmers on land owned by nobles. While the upper classes regularly ate sumptuous meals of meat, tortillas, and tamales, followed by a chocolate drink, commoners lived on ground maize meal, beans, and vegetables, cooked with chili, and rarely ate meat. At the bottom of society were many slaves, often debtors or criminals.

Men and women led very different lives. While their menfolk served the state, elite women enjoyed wealth but faced many restrictions. Unlike men, who had public roles, women largely had two roles: childbearer and weaver. Noble fathers advised their daughters "to learn very well the task of being a woman, which is to spin and weave. It is not proper for you to learn about herbs or to sell wood, peppers, [or] salt on the streets"[21] like the commoner women. Elite girls were kept at home and closely guarded by female servants until their arranged marriage, when they moved into their husband's family. Elite women were also warned against using gaudy makeup, which was only for "shameless women." In contrast, commoner women were freer to leave the house and pursue careers such as street vendors and midwives. Many young boys of all classes went to school to learn religion, history, rhetoric, and the arts of war. In schools or at home, girls were taught domestic skills and religion, and they prepared for marriage at around age sixteen.

The Inca Imperial System

The Incas, conquerors like the Aztecs, built an empire in the Andes even larger than the Aztec Empire. The Inca society, led by warrior chiefs, came together in central Peru around 1200. In the early 1400s a new leader, Viracocha (VEE-ruh-KOH-chuh) Inca, who claimed to be a living god, launched a new era of conquest. The army, led by professional officers, was efficient and effective. Viracocha's son, the pragmatic and visionary Pachacuti (PA-cha-koo-tee) ("World Remaker"), was the major empire builder. According to legends, the sun-god told him that "you will subjugate many nations and take care to honor me and remember me in your sacrifices."[22] By 1440 the Incas under Pachacuti (r. 1438–1471) began defeating their neighbors in battle, eventually conquering the Lake Titicaca Basin and the Chimu Empire.

Thanks to Inca conquests, both the Peruvian highlands and coastal zone were united under one government for the first time in history. By 1525 the Incas dominated nearly the whole of the Andes region from what is today southern Colombia to central Chile, ruling from their capital city, Cuzco (KOO-skoh), which contained between 60,000 and 100,000 people. Their empire stretched for nearly 3,000 miles, much of it above 8,000 feet in altitude. The Inca state became the most politically integrated and dynamic in all of the Americas, geared for conquest. The Incas also treated conquered peoples much more generously than did the Aztecs, incorporating them into their armies, rewarding their service, and tolerating their religions and cultures.

Inca empire building derived in part from the Inca religion and ideas of royalty. Kings were believed to be divine, offspring of the sun and responsible for defending the order and existence of the universe. The kings enjoyed great wealth and pomp. In describing a royal procession, a Spanish observer said that the king wore a collar of huge emeralds and was borne on a sedan throne made of massive gold, lined with the feathers of tropical birds, and studded with gold and silver plates. On their death the kings' bodies were mummified and became the center of a cult. Since deceased kings were still considered the owners of their property and land, their successors had an incentive to seek new conquests so as to acquire their own property and land. Beliefs such as these supported imperial expansion.

The Incas conquered or frightened into submission nearly all the farming societies in the region but then reached their limits. Incan culture and power did not permeate into the rain forests and deserts beyond the empire, unlike Mesoamerica, where a less mountainous geography allowed influences to spread over large distances. In contrast to the brutal Aztecs, the Incas faced relatively few rebellions, in part because many non-Inca appreciated the peace imposed after several centuries of warfare. Unlike other American states, the Incas also deliberately resettled peoples to prevent rebellion or to develop new districts. To win support, the Incas encouraged sons of non-Inca leaders to attend school with the sons of Inca nobles in Cuzco, where they studied history, geometry, military tactics, and oratory. Vast quantities of maize beer were consumed at festivals and celebrations to create goodwill and cooperation among the conquered. The Incas also practiced human sacrifice on a vastly smaller scale than the Aztecs, and only on special ceremonial occasions. For example, several children from noble families of conquered peoples might be killed on top of a mountain as honored gifts to the mountain gods, and their bodies were then mummified by the cold.

But, like the Aztecs and most Eastern Hemisphere empires, the Inca system was also hierarchical and rigid. The royal family kept their bloodline undiluted by having siblings marry each other. Each ruler had a large harem of concubines but also a chief queen, his sister, who had her own magnificent palace and, like African queen mothers, often considerable power behind the scenes. She headed a cult of the moon, led ceremonies for the major goddesses, and also gave birth to the male royal heirs. The elite held anyone outside the Inca ruling caste in contempt. After some time rebellions became more frequent, and many regional leaders dreamed of independence. In addition, rivalry for the throne sometimes led to civil war. When the Spanish arrived in 1532, such a conflict had just ended, weakening the Inca resistance and allowing the Spanish to triumph militarily, replacing the Inca political system with Spanish rule.

Inca Political Economy, Society, and Technology

Although the Inca Empire was supported by the most productive agriculture and creative technology in the Americas, the Inca economy, like the imperial government, was authoritarian. While most rural people remained self-sufficient, food collected by imperial storehouses was distributed as needed to others. Trade within the empire was more limited than in Mesoamerica, though some products were exchanged between coastal, lowland, and highland peoples. In contrast to the Aztecs, who allowed merchants to trade freely, the Inca state operated the imperial economy, taking the place of merchants in collecting and distributing goods. The state also required subjects to serve in the army, work state-owned farms, or serve on public works projects. Accustomed to a strong government presence, people accepted such labor service to the rulers, traditional in the Andes, as a normal part of life. Officials regularly visited villages to monitor work productivity or to check on sanitation.

Although royal women enjoyed great influence, Inca society was patriarchal. Most Inca commoners practiced patrilineal kinship and were part of large extended families. Both men and women made pottery and worked in the fields, the men plowing and the women sowing the seeds. Peasant women also spent considerable time each day weaving and collecting fire-

Machu Picchu This dramatic mountaintop settlement in the high Andes was probably built as a spiritual retreat for Inca royalty, who enjoyed its well-constructed drains, baths, fountains, and administrative buildings. (Alison Wright/Photo Researchers, Inc.)

wood or llama dung for cooking. Women took comfort from the knowledge that the ancient Andean creator-god and chief Inca deity, Viracocha, had both male and female characteristics, and the Incas worshiped several female deities, including the Earth Mother. Separate religious orders allowed both men and women to serve the deities.

Whereas the Aztecs mainly pursued sacrificial victims, the Incas wanted control of labor and land. To secure this they built administrative centers throughout their territories. Some of these centers were retreats for the elite, such as Machu Picchu (MAH-choo PEE-choo), a spectacular collection of buildings built high atop a narrow mountain ridge above a remote river valley. The empire was divided into administrative provinces that were ruled by local families. In this way non-Inca leaders were taken into the governmental system. Because communications were a priority in ruling conquered lands, the Incas linked this vast empire with 14,000 miles of roads radiating out from Cuzco. The roads were graded and paved and had gutters for drainage. Inca engineers even tunneled through rocks and built suspension bridges across gorges and pontoon bridges of reeds across rivers. The road system

awed the Spanish, one of whom wrote, "I believe there is no account of a road as great as this, running through deep valleys, high mountains, banks of snow, torrents of water, living rock, and wild rivers. It was swept free of refuse, with lodgings, storehouses, temples, and posts along the route."[23] Along these roads relay runners, averaging some 150 miles per day, conveyed administrative messages, and llama pack trains carried supplies.

Online Study Center **Improve Your Grade**
Primary Source: Chronicles of Cieza

Unlike the Mesoamericans, the Incas had no formal writing system, but they did have an efficient and sophisticated form of recordkeeping that involved the use of differently colored knotted strings, called **quipus,** to record commercial dealings, property ownership, and census data. Since the quipus provided information on disbursements from warehouses

---

quipus Differently colored knotted strings used by the Incas to record commercial dealings, property ownerships, and census data.

or the number of subjects by age, sex, and occupation, Inca administrators knew what resources and labor were available. The Incas also created an oral literature with narrative power, including tales, prayers, and plaintive love songs, all passed down through the generations.

The Incas were particularly skilled in technology and science, paving the way for impressive material accomplishments. Although the basis for productive Andean agriculture was laid long before their time, the Incas' vast agricultural engineering projects, such as terraces and irrigation canals, generated a widespread prosperity. An extensive irrigation system for agriculture surpassed most of those in the Eastern Hemisphere, and Inca agriculture was far more productive than Peruvians can manage today. The main crops were potatoes, maize, peanuts, and cotton. Farming was a social and cooperative activity, and men and women sang and chanted while together they worked the land. Since the Incas practiced soil conservation, they rarely experienced famine.

Agriculture was not the only area for creative science and technology. The Incas developed sophisticated medicine and surgical techniques, including simple anesthesia procedures. They also fashioned beautiful metal objects using copper and bronze technology as well as gold and silver. In addition, the Incas were among the world's greatest cloth makers. Weavers wove luxurious woolen fabrics from the fleece of the alpaca, and they made bridges from cords and roofs from fibers. The Incas also developed some of the best civil engineering in the Intermediate Era world, as well as an accurate mathematical system. Engineers built fortresses and temples with great blocks of stone so perfectly joined that even a knife could not be inserted between them.

American Societies and Their Connections

The various American societies exchanged ideas and goods with each other over extended networks. As a result of trade and conquest, many people in western South America worshiped the same gods, shared mythologies, practiced human sacrifice, and made similar textiles, artworks, and metal products. Mesoamerican religious ideas, such as the cult of Quetzalcoatl, influenced the Anasazi and even reached into the Mississippi Valley. Mesoamericans traded with the Pueblo peoples for turquoise and with Central Americans for jade. But the Andean and Mesoamerican societies were separated by thousands of miles of forests and mountains, which limited direct contact. The only known direct communication between the two regions was undertaken by traders known as the Manteno, from coastal Ecuador, who for centuries had sailed large balsa rafts carrying cargo up and down the Pacific coast from Chile to Mexico.

However, geographical barriers did not prevent the Andean and Mesoamerican societies from developing some common social and political features. Gender relations, for instance, were very similar in the two regions. Unlike North America, where matrilineal patterns were common, these were patriarchal societies in which men dominated central governments

and village life, and older males led the extended family households. Generally men worked the fields, but they were assisted by women at planting and harvesting time. Women took care of food, wove cloth, and ran households. Unlike the kings and nobles, who might have several wives, most commoners practiced monogamy. Most of the empires respected local cultural practices, religions, and languages. In both regions, warfare was common but ritualized, and conflict involved much protocol, including declarations of war. Armies in close formation fought hand to hand, with the goal of capturing rather than killing opponents. Since most battles occurred far from cities, civilians, settlements, and fields were largely left alone.

The Americas, which encompassed a huge land area, had far fewer people than the Eastern Hemisphere, but even so some societies fostered relatively dense populations. Historians debate the size of the Western Hemisphere population in the late 1400s, some arguing that the population may have exceeded 100 million, more people than in Europe or Africa. Recent studies place the total population at between 60 and 75 million. Mesoamerica had the most people, perhaps 20 to 30 million, and the Caribbean islands and Central America contained around 7 to 10 million. The Andes region was home to 12 to 15 million, and another 9 to 10 million or so lived in the rest of South America. Perhaps 7 million lived in North America, two-thirds of them in the eastern woodlands and southwestern regions. Compared to the Eastern Hemisphere, Americans faced few deadly diseases, and some peoples were quite healthy. Periodic famine, often caused by climate change, was a bigger problem and could kill millions.

Eventually the American societies faced a challenge coming from the Eastern Hemisphere. The only known European visits to the Americas before the voyage led by Christopher Columbus in 1492 took place north of the eastern woodlands, in Newfoundland and Labrador. Around 1000 C.E. a small group of Greenland-based Norse (Norwegian) Vikings led by Leif Ericson visited the area and established a base camp (see Chapter 14). Ericson's Vikings alienated the local people and abandoned their settlement after a few years. But occasional Norse trading visits to the area may have continued for decades, even centuries. The isolated Norse did not publicize their discoveries to Europe, although Portuguese fishermen who visited Iceland may have picked up some information.

Five centuries later a more enduring connection between the hemispheres was forged. In search of Asia, a Spanish expedition led by an Italian mariner, Christopher Columbus, ventured out in three small ships, eventually reaching the Bahamas. In later voyages Columbus visited more parts of the Caribbean and the coast of South America. Even before 1492 some Americans had premonitions of a coming disaster. A chronicle compiled a few years earlier by the Tarascan (tuh-RAH-skuhn) people of western Mexico, rivals of the Aztecs, forecast a time when

there will be no more temples or fireplaces, everything shall become a desert because other men are coming to the earth. They will spare no end of the earth, and everywhere all the way to the edge of the sea and beyond.[24]

Despite creating technologies and ways of life that met their needs, thousands of years of isolation had left the Americans vulnerable to the devastating diseases and more effective steel weapons brought from more densely populated Afro-Eurasia. The new oceanic link altered American history forever, as epidemics wiped out millions of people, great empires fell, and Europeans colonized the hemisphere.

SECTION SUMMARY

- The Aztecs lived in a state of constant war and conquest, sacrificing thousands of enemy warriors a year, but their enemies helped the Spanish to conquer them.

- The Aztecs were productive farmers and active traders, and they had a hierarchical social structure in which priests played a central role.

- The Incas conquered a wide area in the Andes and had a hierarchical social structure, but they were far more inclusive and tolerant than the Aztecs.

- Trade in the Inca Empire was tightly controlled by the state, and an extensive irrigation system and soil conservation program yielded a consistent and abundant food supply.

- Despite extremely limited contact between Andean societies and Mesoamerican ones, they were similar in terms of gender relations and warfare protocols.

Online Study Center   ACE the Test

◆ Chapter Summary

African and American societies were separated by a vast ocean but shared certain patterns. They both formed some great centralized kingdoms and empires as well as many village-based stateless societies, and their contacts with Eurasian states and networks ranged from modest to none.

African societies varied greatly. Most peoples were settled ironworking farmers such as the Kongolese and Yoruba. The Sudanic kingdoms such as Ghana, Mali, and Songhai had a complex political, cultural, and intellectual life, as well as trade connections to the Mediterranean. The increase in long-distance trade and the widespread acceptance of Islam helped integrate West Africa, including the Sudanic kingdoms, into hemispheric networks. Similar trends reshaped the East African coast, where city-states emerged and became linked to the Middle East and the great Indian Ocean maritime trade networks, over which many slaves were transported. Some coastal Bantus blended Islam and Arab culture with their own traditions, creating a Swahili culture. Other Bantus formed great kingdoms such as Zimbabwe, which flourished from gold exports. At the same time, throughout Africa many people lived in small, relatively democratic stateless societies, in which

women had considerable independence. African religion included both polytheistic and monotheistic traditions; many people believed in diverse spirits.

Across the Atlantic in the Americas, the classical states, including the long-enduring Maya society and its cities, eventually collapsed. Climate change and chronic warfare help explain these developments. These societies were replaced by vigorous new peoples, such as the Toltecs and Chimu. When these declined, the Aztecs and Incas built the largest empires that ever existed in the Americas. While many substantial changes occurred, the Americans also showed a pattern of continuity with the past. Both the Aztecs and Incas made use of long-established religious traditions and highly efficient agricultural techniques. The Aztecs practiced human sacrifice and commerce on a much greater scale than the Incas, while the Incas were outstanding engineers and road builders. Both empires had productive agriculture and well-organized states, but neither was prepared for the diseases and iron weapons that were brought by the Spanish.

Online Study Center   **Improve Your Grade** Flashcards

Key Terms

mansa	oral traditions	chinampas
Swahili	Quetzalcoatl	quipus

Suggested Reading

Books

Connah, Graham. *African Civilization: An Archaeological Perspective.* 2nd ed. Cambridge: Cambridge University Press, 2001. An overview of early African societies, emphasizing the rise of cities and states.

D'altroy, Terence N. *The Incas.* Malden, Mass.: Blackwell, 2003. An excellent, up-to-date introduction to the Andes societies in this era.

Davidson, Basil. *The Lost Cities of Africa.* Rev. ed. Boston: Atlantic-Little, Brown, 1987. A revision of a classic and a very readable study of early African societies from the Sudan to Zimbabwe.

Ehret, Christopher. *The Civilizations of Africa: A History to 1800.* Charlottesville: University of Virginia Press, 2002. A survey text with detailed coverage.

Fagan, Brian M. *Kingdoms of Gold, Kingdoms of Jade: The Americas Before Columbus.* London and New York: Thames and Hudson, 1991. A nicely illustrated, readable introduction to the American societies.

Kehoe, Alice Beck. *America Before the European Invasions.* New York: Longman, 2002. A recent overview of the North American peoples and history before 1600 C.E.

Knight, Alan. *Mexico: From the Beginning to the Spanish Conquest.* New York: Cambridge University Press, 2002. An introduction to Mesoamerican societies through the Aztecs.

July, Robert W. *A History of the African People.* 5th ed. Prospect Heights, Ill.: Waveland Press, 1998. A very readable survey of African history.

Mann, Charles C. *1491: New Revelations of the Americas Before Columbus..* New York: Alfred A. Knopf, 2005. A readable summary of recent scholarship on the American societies.

Nurse, Derek, and Thomas Spear. *The Swahili: Reconstructing the History and Language of an African Society, 800–1500.* Philadelphia: University of Pennsylvania Press, 1985. An excellent summary of what we know about the Swahili and their early history.

Pearson, Michael. *The Indian Ocean.* New York: Routledge, 2003. Integrates east Africa into the hemispheric trading system.

Shaffer, Lynda Norene. *Native Americans Before 1492: The Mound-building Centers of the Eastern Woodlands.* Armonk, N.Y.: M. E. Sharpe, 1992. A brief overview, for the general reader, of some early North American societies.

Smith, Michael E. *The Aztecs,* 2nd ed. Malden, M.A.: Blackwell, 2003. A recent scholarly study.

Thobhani, Akbarali. *Mansa Musa: The Golden King of Ancient Mali.* Dubuque, Iowa: Kendall-Hunt, 1998. A readable introduction to Mali and its rulers.

Townsend, Richard F. *The Aztecs.* Rev. ed. New York: Thames and Hudson, 2000. A readable, well-illustrated survey of Aztec history and society.

Websites

Africa South of the Sahara
(http://www-sul.stanford.edu/depts/ssrg/africa/guide.html). Useful collection of links from Stanford University.

Ancient Mexico.com
(http://www.ancientmexico.com/). Contains useful features on art, culture, and history.

Ancient Mesoamerican Civilizations
(http://www.angelfire.com/ca/humanorigins/). Links and information about the premodern American societies.

Civilizations in Africa
(http://www.wsu.edu:8080/~dee/CIVAFRCA/CIVAFRCA.htm). Contains useful essays on premodern Africa.

History and Cultures of Africa
(http://www.columbia.edu/cu/lweb/indiv/africa/cuvl/cult/html). Provides valuable links to relevant websites on African history.

Internet African History Sourcebook
(http://www.fordham.edu/halsall/africa/africasbook.html). This site contains much useful information and documentary material on ancient Africa.

The Aztecs/Mexicas
(http://www.indians.org/welker/aztec.htm). Essays and information on the Aztecs.

South Asia, Central Asia, Southeast Asia, and Afro-Eurasian Connections, 600–1500

Online Study Center

This icon will direct you to interactive activities and study materials on the website: college.hmco. com/pic/lockard1e

Xuan Zang Arriving in China A seventh-century C.E. Buddhist Chinese pilgrim, Xuan Zang, spent many years traveling in India, collecting Buddhist wisdom and observing Indian life. This Chinese painting shows him and his caravan returning to China with pack loads of Buddhist manuscripts. (Fujita Art Museum)

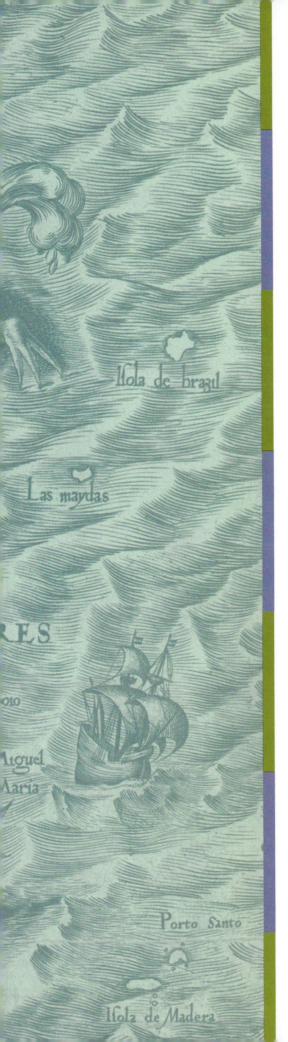

India's shape is like the half-moon. The administration of the government is founded on benign principles. The taxes on the people are light. Each one keeps his own worldly goods in peace. The merchants come and go in carrying out their transactions. Those whose duty it is sow and reap, plough and [weed], and plant; and after their labor they rest awhile.

XUAN ZANG, SEVENTH-CENTURY CHINESE VISITOR TO INDIA[1]

In 630 C.E. a brave and determined Chinese Buddhist monk, Xuan Zang (swan tsang) (ca. 600–664), traveled the Silk Road, mostly alone, to India on an extended pilgrimage to collect holy books and ended up spending fifteen years there, visiting every corner of the subcontinent. He was very observant and politically astute, but he also chafed at the perception of many Indian Buddhists that China was too remote and backward to truly claim Buddhism. In a debate at the great Nalanda (nuh-LAN-duh) Monastery, Xuan Zang told the monks that

> *Buddha established his doctrine so that it might be diffused to all lands. Who would wish to enjoy it alone? Besides, in my country the laws are everywhere respected. The emperor is virtuous and the subjects loyal, parents are loving and sons obedient, humanity and justice are highly esteemed. How then can you say that the Buddha did not go to my country because of its insignificance?[2]*

Despite Xuan Zang's Chinese pride, he found much to admire in India, including the Indian tolerance for diverse viewpoints. Even though Hinduism had become dominant, Buddhism enjoyed protection and royal patronage. Xuan Zang's writings described an Indian society that had a rigid social structure but also one that was creative and diverse and open to foreign influences, including regular contact over networks of exchange with China, Europe, the Middle East, and Indonesia. Xuan Zang was much impressed with India's high standard of living, efficient governments, and generally peaceful conditions. But some customs troubled him. Despite the bias in Indian religions against eating animals, many Indians consumed fish, venison, and mutton. He also criticized the caste restrictions, such as the practice of confining untouchables to their own neighborhoods.

357

After covering some 40,000 total miles in his many years of travel, Xuan Zang returned to China in 643, taking with him hundreds of Buddhist books to be translated into Chinese. He also became a confidant of the Tang emperor and fostered closer relations between India and China.

The cultural diversity and openness to foreign influence that Xuan Zang admired in India was due in part to the repeated invasions of Central Asian peoples, who brought with them diverse beliefs and customs. Over the centuries Hindu religion and society absorbed these newcomers and their ideas. Groups with differing customs generally lived peacefully side by side, and Indian ideals were spread through trade with neighboring peoples. But Hindu political domination and the assimilation of newcomers into Hinduism or Buddhism faced a particularly severe challenge with the arrival of Muslims, who gained control over large parts of the subcontinent. Having their own strong religious ideas, Muslims were not easily absorbed into the complex world of Hindu culture. The coming of Islam constituted a great turning point in the region's development, a transition comparable to that initiated by the Aryan migrations into India several millennia earlier.

Like Indians, Southeast Asians also adopted new political systems and religions. Powerful kingdoms emerged, some of them strongly influenced by Hindu and Buddhist culture from India. By the fifteenth century new faiths from outside, Theravada Buddhism and Islam, had reshaped the political map and created many diverse cultural and religious patterns. This diversity, as well as trade, remained a hallmark of Southeast Asian societies.

FOCUS QUESTIONS

1. What were some of the main features of Hindu society at its height?
2. How did Hinduism and Buddhism change in this era?
3. How did Islam alter the ancient Indian pattern of diversity in unity?
4. What political and religious forms shaped Southeast Asian societies in the Early Intermediate Era?
5. What was the influence of Theravada Buddhism and Islam on Southeast Asia?

◆ Hindu Politics and Indian Society

What were some of the main features of Hindu society at its height?

Political disunity and regional diversity marked the Early Intermediate Era in India. No Hindu leaders were able to recreate an empire like the earlier Maurya or Gupta, and India became a region of many states, cultures, and languages. In spite of a broad Hindu tradition and the extensive common heritage and historical continuity it created, most South Asians were split into many microcultures. Rather than a melting pot, India became a collage in which many images co-existed on the same canvas, shaping each other while retaining their own distinctive character. These pronounced regional distinctions within a widely shared Hindu culture demonstrated one of the great themes in Indian history: diversity in unity.

Unity and Disunity in Hindu Politics

The political disunity following the fall of the Gupta state in the fifth century proved to be a long-term pattern, with political fragmentation becoming the norm. King Harsha Vardhana (600–647) briefly united parts of north India, but this consolidation proved short-lived (see Chronology: South Asia, 600–1500 on page 360). Harsha came to power at the age of sixteen and ruled for forty-one years. A man of enormous energy, he put together an army that, at its strongest point,

CHRONOLOGY

	South Asia	Southeast Asia
600	**600–647** Empire of Harsha	**600–1290** Srivijaya Empire
800	**846–1216** Chola dynasty	**802–1432** Angkor Empire
1000	**1192–1526** Delhi Sultanate	**1044–1287** Pagan Kingdom
1200	**1336–1565** Vijayanagara state	**1238–1419** Sukhotai state
1400		**1403–1511** Melaka state

included 100,000 cavalry and 60,000 elephants, together with many thousands of infantrymen, a formidable force. He skillfully held together his small empire while cultivating close relations with Tang China. But his empire collapsed on his death.

We know about Harsha and his society from a biography written by a close adviser and an account by Xuan Zang, whose pilgrimage to India opened the chapter and who spent years in Harsha's domain. Much more than a warrior-king, Harsha had a fondness for philosophy and was renowned as a poet. While enjoying the pomp of kingship, he also listened patiently to the complaints of his humbler subjects. Harsha also fostered religions. A strong Buddhist like Ashoka centuries earlier, he tolerated all faiths. But Harsha opposed some practices. For example, he prevented his beloved sister, a Hindu, from committing sati at her husband's cremation.

Despite Harsha's brilliant reign, in the post-Gupta centuries dozens, and sometimes hundreds, of small states proliferated in the subcontinent. The Hindu states had varied types of government, including many absolute monarchies. Rulers owned many economic resources, such as irrigation works, forests, mines, and spinning and weaving operations. Kings tried to control outlying regions through appointed governors or patronage over local leaders. Since they occupied a precarious position of power, they attempted to buttress their rule by claiming a divine mission. The Brahmans (Hindu priests) who served as court advisers gave them legitimacy.

North and south India developed somewhat different political patterns. **Rajputs** ("King's sons"), members of a warrior caste formed by earlier Central Asian invaders who adopted Hinduism, controlled some of the north Indian states. This military aristocracy was raised in traditions of chivalry, honor,

and courage not unlike those of Japanese samurai or medieval European knights. The Rajput code emphasized respect for women, mercy toward enemies, and precise rules of conduct in warfare. However, the Rajput-led kingdoms never united and often fought wars against each other for regional power. In contrast to the north, many south Indian states were oriented to the sea and hence specialized in piracy, plunder, and foreign trade. South Indian merchants had more political influence than merchants did in north India, and various south Indians continued their lucrative maritime trade with Southeast Asia, China, and the Middle East. Indeed, many visited or settled in Southeast Asia, bringing with them lasting south Indian ideas on art, politics, and religion.

Villages and Cities

The continuity of Indian culture was reflected in village life. In an economy based mainly on agriculture, the village remained the basic unit of Indian life; even today, about 80 percent of Indians still live in villages. Farmers had to feed an Indian population that reached around 100 million by 1500. Rulers also depended on villages for income. Since ancient times land was regarded as the property of the sovereign, who was entitled to either a tax or a share of the produce. The land tax remained the main source of state revenue and the main burden on the peasant. This was a collective responsibility, since the village paid as a unit. As long as they regularly met their tax obligations, villages ran themselves and peasants had the hereditary right to use the land they farmed. A well-entrenched pattern of village government included a council, elected annually from among village elders and caste leaders, which dispensed local justice and collected taxes.

The typical Hindu village remained largely self-sufficient economically and organized itself through the caste system,

---

Rajputs ("King's sons")   An Indian warrior caste formed by earlier Central Asian invaders who adopted Hinduism.

which promoted stability. Within the village the individual served his or her caste. Members of different castes lived separately in their own neighborhoods, but all contributed to the livelihood of the larger community. Each village had a potter, carpenter, blacksmith, clerk, herdsman, teacher, astrologer, and priest as well as many farmers. These villagers with different specializations and caste levels served each other on a barter basis in what was essentially a symbiotic community. The village structure probably did not change substantially during the Intermediate Era.

Some modern Indian writers have romanticized traditional village life, portraying a society living peacefully from generation to generation. This picture contains some truth. Village life offered great psychological and economic security. Each individual had a recognized status as well as certain rights and duties, not to mention a built-in sense of community and many personal relationships. During those periods when the rulers kept the region at peace, repressed banditry, and kept the tax burden reasonable, most people were probably contented with their lot.

A large number of Indians also lived in towns and cities, many of which were commercial hubs. Urban merchants helped administer the towns, but, as in China, they were heavily taxed and not allowed to become too independent of government. Some merchant groups were immigrants. For example, during the eighth century some Zoroastrians fled to western India to escape the Islamic conquest of Persia and formed the distinctive *Parsee* (PAHR-see) (Persian) community, known for its commercial prowess in several cities of western India. Over the centuries the Parsees had adopted local languages and some Indian traditions.

Manufacturers as well as merchants lived in the cities. Indeed, India was one of the world's leading manufacturing centers. Workshops located mainly in or near cities and towns produced cloth, textiles, pottery, leather goods, and jewelry for local use or export, and some artisans spun and wove cotton to

be eventually sold as far away as China, Africa, or eastern Europe. India and China provided most of the world's industrial goods until the eighteenth century, and during this era the average per capita income for both urban and rural dwellers remained high by world standards.

Hindu Social Life and Gender Relations

The Hindu social system demonstrated great continuity over the centuries and, as in China, subordinated the individual to the group. The Indian owed an even more basic social obligation to the extended family than to the caste. An old saying described this extended family as "joint in food, worship, and property." The family, which included people of several generations, lived together in the same compound (residential area), enforced caste regulations among their members, and also collectively owned their economic assets, such as farmland. Because families helped their weaker members and shared their wealth, they constituted an effective source of social security. Most families, especially in north India, were patriarchal, headed by a senior male with strong authority, although older women held considerable influence. In a family compound children lived in close contact with many cousins, aunts, uncles, and grandparents. Child rearing became a group obligation, and children enjoyed warm support and great security.

Marriage customs reflected regional differences. In north India, parents arranged marriages for their children and hoped that love would follow marriage. Girls were married off young, sometimes by the age of seven or eight, usually to a boy in a neighboring village. Because the bride's family paid for the wedding and was expected to give lavish presents, families preferred sons. South Indians enjoyed more variation in marriage practices. Girls were more likely than in north India to marry boys whom they already knew, often a cousin. In Kerala (CARE-a-la) in southwestern India, one large group practiced **polyandry**, marriage of a woman to several husbands. However, since some male characters in the *Mahabharata* have the same wife, polyandry may have been a more common pattern in north India 3,000 years ago. Most Indian families discouraged divorce, viewing it as a humiliation.

The Indian social system of the Intermediate Era clearly favored men, who enjoyed many privileges. In ancient India, especially in merchant families, women seem to have had considerable freedom, often choosing their own husbands and circulating freely in local society. But by 600 C.E. customs had become more conservative as male leaders became obsessed with preserving social stability and controlling female sexuality. For example, from puberty females of all castes were now taught to keep a distance from all men except their closest relatives. High-caste women were expected to spend their time at home, only occasionally visiting friends or family. Low-caste and untouchable women enjoyed more mobility because they had to

---

polyandry Marriage of a woman to several husbands.

enter public society to earn the incomes needed for family survival.

Women by and large led lives marked by obedience, sacrifice, and service. From an early age they were taught to sacrifice themselves for parents, husband, and children. The stereotypical role model was the loyal and submissive wife who always followed her husband's lead. The young bride, usually much younger than her husband, moved into her husband's household and was expected to be submissive to her new mother-in-law. Yet, husbands often treated their brides indulgently and tenderly. Indians also revered motherhood and equated childbearing with success. After she bore children (especially sons), the wife's status improved considerably, and she enjoyed more freedom and respect inside and outside the household. As a woman grew older and became a mother-in-law herself, she gained even more influence, especially in domestic matters.

Women faced a complex situation. They enjoyed some legal rights, and ill-treatment of women, including physical brutality, was condemned, although it was undoubtedly common. In practice not all wives were silent and subservient. But widowhood could prove catastrophic, particularly if a woman had no son to care for her. Since Hindu custom frowned on remarriage, to be a young and childless widow was to face an especially difficult situation. This helps to explain the practice of *sati*, whether voluntary or coerced. To avoid surviving their deceased husband, some women, especially in north India, died on their husband's funeral pyre. An ancient Indian expression captures the challenge for women: "As a girl she is under the tutelage of her parents; as an adult her husband; as a widow her sons." Some women, such as actresses, singers, and prostitutes, flouted social custom and mainstream values. However, although sometimes wealthy, these women suffered from having a low status in the community.

Indians held diverse views about sex. Many books commended celibacy and advised married men to exercise their sexual prerogatives sparingly if they wanted health and virtue. Indeed, devout Hindu Brahman men frequently adopted celibacy after fathering several children. Yet, the worldly views of many, especially among the elite, are reflected in many Indian texts such as the *Kama Sutra*, a manual of lovemaking and related matters written around the third century C.E. Even the Hindu gods and goddesses were portrayed in art and writings as highly sexual beings, a view very unlike that of the virginal Madonna and celibate Jesus of Christian tradition, the image of a spiritually and morally pure Buddha, and the puritanical restrictions of Islam.

Science and Mathematics

During this era Indians made many contributions in mathematics and science. One of the greatest Indian mathematicians, Bhaskara (bas-CAR-a), lived in the twelfth century. In addition to proving that zero was infinity, he also designed a perpetual-motion machine by filling a wheel rim with quicksilver, in the process demonstrating the Hindu belief in perpetual change in

Sculpture of Two Lovers from Konarak Temple This sculpture of two embracing lovers comes from the Konarak temple in the north Indian state of Orissa. The Hindu temple, dedicated to the sun-god, was built in the thirteenth century and featured many erotic sculptures. (Benoy K. Behl)

the universe. Bhaskara's book on the subject was later translated into Arabic and reached Europe by 1200 C.E. Soon after, drawings of quicksilver wheels appeared there, generating ideas of perpetual motion that influenced modern scientific thought in the West. The first weight-driven clocks, built in Europe after 1300, may have been based in part on Bhaskara's ideas. A seventh-century Syrian astronomer said that "no words can praise strongly enough" the Hindus' discoveries in astronomy and their rational system of mathematics.[3] Some Indian astronomers and mathematicians found employment in Tang China, fostering a fruitful exchange of knowledge between the two societies.

Underlying many Indian creative investigations could be found the basis for scientific reasoning. But growing intercaste jealousy and the indifference of the higher castes to applied or practical inquiry hindered the development of science after Gupta times. The Brahmans became more powerful and controlled education, while those who pursued technical activities or physical labor sank lower in the status system. By the tenth century some visitors reported a growing ethnocentrism and disdain among Hindu thinkers for foreign ideas, including scientific ones. An astute Muslim observer wrote that "the Hindus believe that there is no country, king, religion, [or] science like theirs."[4]

SECTION SUMMARY

- In the Intermediate Era, India was fragmented into many small states; the north was influenced by earlier Central Asian invaders and the south by maritime trade with Southeast Asia.

- The village, which was based on cooperation and caste, remained the basic unit of Indian life and provided people with a sense of security.

- Indian merchants in the cities were heavily taxed, but India and China produced most of the world's manufactured goods in this era.

- In the Hindu social system, the individual was subordinate to the group and people tended to live in extended families that supported their members.

- Indian men had much more power than women, who were forced to marry early and earned respect through bearing children, particularly boys.

- The mathematician Bhaskara discovered perpetual motion, which influenced science in the West.

Hinduism and Buddhism in South and Central Asia

How did Hinduism and Buddhism change in this era?

Hinduism experienced a renaissance in the Early Intermediate centuries. Although it increasingly divided into competing schools of thought and practice, it also grew in popularity, developing into a faith that emphasized offerings and devotion. While Hinduism increasingly shaped Indian life, Buddhism faded in India but found new influence in neighboring societies. Hindu culture flourished in India for half a millennium before facing the concerted challenge from Islamic peoples and ideas.

Hindu Diversity and a Common Culture

Hinduism provided the spiritual framework for the great majority of South Asians until the coming of Islam. Its strength lay in its diversity, which could accommodate all classes, personalities, and intellects. For example, it gave the scholar and mystic an opportunity for abstract and speculative thought, while also giving the more worldly individual a wealth of ritual, art, and gods for every occasion. Because they satisfied so many needs, the values of Hinduism came to permeate the diverse Indian society.

Recognizing that individuals varied in their spiritual and intellectual capacities, Hindus tolerated many different practices and beliefs and relied on no fixed and exclusive theology or set of beliefs. As the earliest Hindu holy book, the *Rig Veda*, put it: "Reality is one; sages speak of it in different ways."[5] Concepts of spiritual power ranged from an indescribable but all-pervading, omnipotent God, to personal gods with human attributes, to demons and spirits. An Indian proverb welcomed all to sample the essence of Hindu ideas: "Life is a river; virtue is its bathing place; truth is its water; moral convictions are its banks; mercy is its wave. In such a pure river, bathe."[6] Because it had these characteristics, Hinduism remained undogmatic, a philosophy and way of life with no central institution or church to monitor the faith. Since no single leader codified their beliefs, Hindus did not even agree on which sacred writings were most important. During the Intermediate Era, Muslims introduced the collective term *Hindu*, from the Persian term for "Indians," to describe the varied Indian sects, and in the nineteenth century C.E. Europeans began referring to the diverse collection of Indian beliefs as "Hinduism."

The tradition of tolerance suggested that all approaches to God were equally valid, although mystics and intellectuals tended to consider their approaches more worthy than those of the peasantry. For example, mother goddess worship was particularly common among the lower castes living in thousands of villages, especially in south India, but was less popular among the higher castes. The many gods and goddesses were worshiped in various ways. Although India was a patriarchal society, men and women often believed that the wives and consorts (companions) of the main male gods were more responsive to their needs than the male gods themselves. For example, many cults worshiped Shiva's wife, Shakti (SHAHK-tee), who was a composite of opposites: kind and beautiful but also cruel and fearsome.

For all their diversity of beliefs, most Hindus perceived the universe as a collection of temporary living quarters inhabited by individual souls going through a succession of lives. The most devout had the ultimate goal of liberation from finite human consciousness, which freed one from the endless cycle of birth and rebirth. Yet most Hindus accepted the natural world in which people must work out their own salvation, and only a small minority seriously sought to escape from the earthly world with all its pain and pleasures. Wandering holy men were respected for their withdrawal from worldly activities but not role models for most people. Rather, Hindus were obligated to meet their social obligations to family, caste, and village. Stressing moderation and temperance, Hindu thinkers typically advised all to combine spiritual and worldly spheres.

Hinduism helped establish a common culture throughout India. Brahmans served as advisers to kings, ensuring a certain standardization of political ideas and rituals in Hindu states. While Brahmans had a monopoly on reading the Sanskrit scriptures, the Hindu classics were available to all through storytellers. Legends and traditions were also handed down through the generations by word of mouth. By around

1000 C.E. the collections of ancient prayers and hymns, the Vedas, were also being translated from Sanskrit into various regional languages. These trends in Hinduism contributed to the broader pattern of cultural unity in diversity.

The Hindu Renaissance

Many thinkers who embellished or revitalized Hindu traditions lived during the Intermediate centuries, creating what has been called the Hindu Renaissance. Perhaps the greatest was Shankara (shan-kar-uh) (788–820), a south Indian Brahman who helped refine Hindu thinking. Shankara's religious ideas harked back 1,500 years to the *Upanishads*, but he systematically organized the diffuse strands for the first time. Through his itinerant preaching, debates with rivals, and written commentaries on the *Upanishads*, Shankara revitalized the mystical *Vedanta* tradition, with its belief in the underlying unity of all reality. To Shankara, all the Hindu gods were manifestations of the impersonal, timeless, changeless, and unitary Absolute Reality, *Brahman*, and the individual soul only a tiny part of the whole unity of the universe.

Shankara tried to balance reason and intuition. While accepting the Hindu scriptures as divine revelation, he wanted to prove them through logical reasoning and debate. Yet, contradictorily, he also argued that all knowledge was inconclusive and relative, impaired because humankind's grasp of reality is warped by ignorance and illusion. The truth of existence, he believed, could only be understood through ascetic meditation. Shankara's views remain very popular among modern Indian intellectuals.

Other philosophers offered different visions of Hinduism. In the eleventh century Ramanuja (RAH-muh-NOO-ja) rejected both reliance on Brahman priests and Vedanta meditation and instead emphasized **bhakti**, devotional worship of a personal god, arguing that the gods should be accessible without priestly help. As a Hindu poet-saint put it: "The lord comes within everyone's reach."[7] A few centuries later some Christian reformers in Europe would develop a similar notion of establishing a personal relationship with God without priestly aid. Whereas Shankara had seen the human soul as identical to god, Ramanuja believed them to be quite distinct entities. To him, the goal of life was to bring communion between the two. Salvation could be achieved by pure, childlike devotion to a personal god. The bhakti tradition emphasized pilgrimage to holy places such as the city of Benares (buh-NAHR-uhs) (Varanasi), alongside the Ganges. Hindus who died in Benares, it was believed, had their sins washed away. Ramanuja and other early bhakti thinkers, most of them non-Brahmans, also opposed or downplayed the caste system. The bhakti tradition appealed particularly to women, marginalized in brahmanic worship. An early female poet, Antal, in the ninth century, urged women devotees to revere Lord Krishna (an incarnation of Vishnu). Later the bhakti movement became part of mainstream Hinduism.

The Hindu Renaissance included the building of increasingly flamboyant temples, whose sculptural art was designed to illustrate the intricate mythology of the faith. One of the best examples of such a temple was constructed in the tenth century by a prince in his home city of Khajuraho (kah-ju-RA-ho). Dedicated to Vishnu, sculptures carved into the temple walls suggested the delights enjoyed by the gods, including lovemaking. The countless erotic, sexually explicit paintings or carvings in many Hindu temples, some of them clearly presentations of sexual intercourse, reflected a rather open view about portraying sexuality.

Decline and Change in Indian Buddhism

During the first half of the Intermediate Era, while Hinduism was enjoying its resurgence, the influence of Buddhism gradually declined in much of India. However, it retained considerable support in northeast India, where many Buddhist holy sites were located. The governments there continued to patronize the religion and its institutions, such as the college at the Nalanda Monastery, which attracted religious students from around Asia, as well as the Chinese pilgrim Xuan Zang. Pilgrims from distant lands, such as Xuan Zang, showed how much Buddhism was becoming a major influence in the eastern half of Eurasia, a trend that continued throughout the Intermediate Era as the faith spread in Central Asia, Tibet, China, Korea, Japan, and Southeast Asia, adapting to different cultures.

The intellectual and cultural environment of northeast India also promoted a dialogue between Hinduism and Mahayana Buddhism that fostered new schools of Buddhist and Hindu thought. One new Buddhist school, the **Vajrayana** ("Thunderbolt"), featured female saviors and the human attainment of magical powers. It spread during the eighth century into Nepal and Tibet, where it became the predominant form of faith.

In Bengal the continued contact between Mahayana Buddhists and Hindu followers of Shiva, many of whom revered his consort, the goddess Shakti, led to a new approach called **Tantrism** (TAN-triz-uhm), which worshiped the female essence of the universe. Both the Tantric and Vajrayana schools exalted female power, as earth mother and as the highest form of divine strength. Tantric sects developed within both Hinduism and Buddhism. Some were mystical and presented male-female sexual union as an action form of worship, a symbolic unity between the earthly and cosmic worlds. Other sects promised release from life's pain in a single lifetime to those who cultivated hedonism (including drinking of alcoholic beverages), pleasure, and ecstasy. Tantric Hindus were often hostile to the caste system. Most Hindus and Buddhists denounced Tantrism as an excuse for debauchery and sexual desire, and Tantrism gradually became a minor strand in the two religions.

---

bhakti Devotional worship of a personal Hindu god.

Vajrayana ("Thunderbolt") A form of Buddhism that featured female saviors and the human attainment of magical powers.

Tantrism An approach within both Buddhism and Hinduism that worshiped the female essence of the universe.

State Building and Buddhism in Tibet

While Buddhism declined in India, the remote high plateau of Tibet became a refuge for the religion. The first known pre-Buddhist Tibetan state emerged when Songsten-gampo (SONG-sten-GOM-po) (r. 620–649 C.E.) unified several tribes. Like other Tibetan leaders during this time, he was interested in connecting to an Asian world where Buddhism was expanding. He established close relations with Tang China and married a Chinese princess, and although not a Buddhist, he allowed the religion to spread in his kingdom and tolerated Buddhist practice. Several trade routes linked Tibet to the Silk Road and China, and some young Tibetans went to China for study. Tibetans also borrowed the Sanskrit script from India and made it their written language. A Tibetan epic poem about the revered first king, one of the longest in history, eventually became a beloved part of the folk tradition in India, China, and Mongolia.

By the eighth century Buddhism had become the dominant Tibetan faith, and its monasteries enjoyed many legal protections and financial support from the government. But many Tibetans also continued to follow the ancient folk religion, *bon*. The two faiths competed for popular support and political influence for the next several centuries, and late in the ninth century violent religious conflicts destroyed the unified state.

However, both Buddhism and state building were reinvigorated in later centuries. Several factors can account for this change. In the thirteenth century many Buddhist monks fled to Tibet to escape Islamic persecution in India. Political relations with the predominantly Buddhist Mongols, who had conquered China and established loose control over parts of Tibet, also boosted Tibetan Buddhism. A unified Tibetan government was established in 1247 under the leadership of one Buddhist sect allied to the Mongols. But the end of Mongol rule in China brought a return to aristocratic lay leadership in Tibet, which persisted into the seventeenth century.

Tibetans developed a distinctive religious system in their harsh highlands environment, and many of their customs differed from those of East and Southeast Asian Buddhists. Tibetan Buddhism, which is divided into four sects, is often termed **Lamaism** (LAH-muh-iz-uhm) because of the centrality of monks, or *lamas* (LAH-muhz), and huge monasteries. Perhaps a quarter to a third of male Tibetans became career monks, and Buddhism came to permeate every aspect of Tibetan life. Believers practiced magic, chanted mantras, made pilgrimages to shrines, and provided generous support to monasteries and Buddhist teachers. Tibetans also blended Buddhism with strong beliefs in the supernatural, including evil spirits. For example, people spun hand-held or roadside prayer wheels and carved prayers into stones, seeking the help of the Buddha. Tibetan Buddhism also featured elaborate death rites to propel the soul to the next rebirth.

Lamaism The Tibetan form of Buddhism, characterized by the centrality of monks (*lamas*) and huge monasteries.

SECTION SUMMARY

- Hinduism adapted itself to the needs of a wide variety of people, from the worldly to the scholarly, and helped to establish a common culture throughout India.
- Shankara, a major thinker of the Hindu Renaissance, emphasized the importance of reason and of ascetic meditation, while Ramanuja emphasized the worship of a personal god.
- Indian Buddhism declined generally, but it remained important in the northeast, where Vajrayana and Tantrism grew out of the interplay between it and Hinduism.
- Buddhism became the dominant religion in Tibet, where it became Lamaism, and many Indian Buddhist monks took refuge there to escape Islamic persecution.

The Coming of Islam to India and Central Asia

How did Islam alter the ancient Indian pattern of diversity in unity?

The spread of Islamic religion and government in India was a major transition in Indian history, as important as the coming of the Aryans several millennia earlier. Since Muslims and Hindus were almost exact opposites in their beliefs, Islam created a great divide in South Asian society. As Al-Biruni, an eleventh-century Muslim scholar, put it: "Hindus entirely differ from us in every respect. They differ from us in every thing which other nations have in common. In all manners and usages they differ from us to such a degree as to frighten their children with us."[8] For centuries Hinduism had absorbed invaders and their faiths, but Islam, a coherent and self-confident religion, could not be assimilated. The tension between the two faiths sometimes resulted in conflict. However, Islam enriched Indian culture, establishing new connections with western Asia while also promoting the spread of Indian ideas, especially in mathematics and science, to the Middle East and Europe. Many Indians embraced the new faith, and Muslims also gained political dominance over large parts of India, though Hindu power remained strong in south India.

Early Islamic Encounters

Islamic forces reached Central Asia and India within a few decades of the religion's founding. Western Asians had long been linked to Central Asia through Silk Road trade, and they were well aware of India's riches. Arab sailors had been active in South Asia for centuries before the rise of Islam, linking India by trade to western Asia and East Africa. Initially Indian and Central Asian encounters with Islam were sporadic and often peaceful. But Islamic rulers hoped to dominate these valuable regions, and military conflict increased.

During the seventh century Arab forces expanded through Persia into what is today Afghanistan. By 673 Arab armies were moving into Silk Road cities such as Bukhara and Samarkand, dominated by the Sogdians (SOG-dee-uhnz), an ethnic group famed for their commercial skills. The rival Central Asian city-states, geared more to trade than to battle, could not easily come together against the dynamic Arabs. The Sogdians, most of whom were Zoroastrian or Buddhist, resisted and sought Chinese and Turkish help. But many merchants and landowners saw advantages in joining the powerful Arabs, and by the early eighth century Arabs had conquered most of the cities. The Arab defeat of Chinese forces at the Battle of Talas in 751 marked the end of serious resistance to Muslim dominance in Central Asia. Eventually most Central Asians adopted Islam.

In neighboring India, conflict between Hindus and Muslims began slowly, with attacks by Hindu pirates on Muslim shipping in western Asia. In 711 C.E. Indian pirates plundered an Arab ship near the mouth of the Indus River, and Arab armies responded by briefly conquering the western Indus Basin, in the first of many incursions to follow. But not all encounters were violent. Arab traders from Yemen settled in the ports of southwestern India, bringing Islam to some of the people there.

The expansion of Islam through western Asia and into Central Asia presented a challenge to India. By the eleventh century various Turkish peoples had formed independent Islamic sultanates in Afghanistan, of which Ghazni (GAHZ-nee) was the most powerful. Between 997 and 1025 Sultan Mahmud (MACH-mood) of Ghazni (r. 997–1030) led his soldiers on seventeen campaigns through the passes into India, as much for plunder as for conquest. Seeing the multitude of Hindu idols as an abomination to Islamic monotheism, the invaders destroyed Hindu temples while they looted cities. The vast wealth they took from northwestern India to Ghazni helped that city become a great center of Islamic learning and arts that attracted famed scholars such as the Persian Al-Biruni.

The Rajputs led the major Indian opposition to Muslim invaders, maintaining a spirited Hindu resistance for many decades that kept Islam from spreading into the Hindu heartland. But Rajput military tactics were outdated, based on relatively immobile war elephants, and the military forces were increasingly divided in their political loyalties. In addition, Indian wars had been fought by rulers, not by citizen-soldiers. The caste system allowed only warriors such as the Rajputs to be trained in arms, so they could not effectively mobilize other Indians to help in the fight. Eventually the Rajput armies were defeated by the more mobile, horse-riding Muslims.

The pillaging and destruction by the early Muslim invaders fostered long-term Hindu antipathy toward Muslims. Many Hindus were killed, enslaved, or robbed. For example, Mahmud's most famous exploit involved a long march across

The Kutb Minar Tower in Delhi
The 240-foot-high Kutb Minar temple in Delhi was built between the twelfth and fourteenth centuries to celebrate Muslim victory in north India. (Robert Harding World Imagery)

Map 13.1 India and the Delhi Sultanate, ca. 1300 C.E.
At its height, the Delhi Sultanate controlled much of northern India. South India was divided into many major states, with the Cholas and Pandyas the largest. Indian ports were connected by a vigorous maritime trade to the Middle East, East Africa, and Southeast Asia.

the desert to attack the revered Hindu temple of Somnath. Hindu sources reported, probably with some exaggeration, that the attack killed 50,000 Hindus. Even the Muslim scholar Al-Biruni concluded that Mahmud "utterly ruined [India's] prosperity. To Mahmud the Hindus were infidels, to be dispatched to hell as soon as they refused to be plundered."[9] The Muslim newcomers zealously persecuted Buddhists as well, destroying their monasteries and educational institutions, including the great complex at Nalanda. Thousands of monks either were killed or fled to sanctuary in the Himalayas or Tibet. This repression helped eradicate Buddhism from the land of its birth.

Islamic Expansion and the Delhi Sultanate

A new chapter in Muslim expansion began in 1191 when a Turkish prince, driven by religious fervor and lust for the region's riches, conquered most of northern India and founded the Delhi (DEL-ee) Sultanate (see Map 13.1). The sultanate (1192–1526) reached its height in the 1200s and 1300s and brought political unity to north India for the first time in centuries. Under the Delhi regime, which was administered by Turks, Afghans, and Indian Muslims, Islamic authority and religion spread throughout north India. But the Delhi system, lacking a definite rule of succession, was unstable and experienced frequent bloodshed and treachery as leaders competed for power.

The Delhi sultans had diverse ruling styles. Some were patrons of the arts, supporters of science, experts in Greek philosophy, and builders of architecturally splendid structures. Many others, however, were tyrannical and cruel, routinely killing rivals and their families. Some ruined the country with reckless spending on pet projects. All the sultans employed Persian-style ritual and royal pomp, but in some ways they also styled themselves after Hindu monarchs, even outdoing them in demanding prostration and toe-kissing from subordinates. This blending of ruling styles suggests that Muslim and Hindu cultures were mixing among the elite. Some sultans expanded Delhi's power into central India and, briefly, south India, creating an empire larger than the Gupta realm. The most militarily successful sultan, Alauddin Khalji (uh-LAH-ud-DEEN KAL-jee) (1296–1316), was also politically creative. For instance, unhappy with the high living of local officials while the poor suffered, he introduced wage and price controls to help citizens meet rising costs. Given his close relationship to a male adviser, some historians think that he may have been a homosexual or bisexual, one of the many in societies around the world who, often hiding their sexual orientation, have sat on thrones or led armies.

Two of the most able Delhi sultans were Iltutmish (il-TOOT-mish) (1211–1236), who made the Delhi Sultanate the most powerful state in north India, and his remarkable daughter, Raziya (r. 1236–1240). Iltutmish kept out the Mongol armies of Genghis Khan by skillful diplomacy and gradually followed more tolerant policies toward Hindus, allowing Hindu princes to rule their own domains as long as they paid generous taxes. During his reign, many Muslim refugees fleeing the Mongol conquest of western Asia arrived, among them scholars and artists. Their large numbers helped to abort any possibility of Hinduism gradually absorbing Islam. Iltutmish's chosen successor, Raziya, became the only female Muslim ruler in Indian history, praised by scholars of her time for her wisdom and military leadership. She proved exceptionally able, fostering trade, building roads, planting trees, supporting poets and artists, and opening schools. A male Muslim observer described her as "a great monarch, wise, just and generous. She was endowed with all the qualities befitting a king, but she was not born of the right sex, and so in the estimation of men all these virtues were worthless."[10] Raziya was resented as a female leader in a patriarchal society. She further offended Muslim conservatives by abandoning the veil, dressing in male garb, and having a close, perhaps romantic, relationship with a male personal attendant, a former slave of African origin. She died defending her position from male rivals, perhaps because they resented a female leader.

Hindu Politics and Culture

While the Delhi Sultanate governed part of India, various Hindu monarchies survived elsewhere, especially in south and east India. Like post-Heian Japan and medieval Europe, these states featured local economic self-sufficiency and political decentralization, with warriors receiving land from the monarch in exchange for military service. Although Hinduism lacked a centralized hierarchy of power, some Brahmans received tax-free land from monarchs. Commerce flourished in some places, especially in south India. For example, merchants on the southwest coast, including Jews and Arabs, maintained close ties to western Asia and North Africa and enjoyed great influence and wealth. An inscription from a merchant guild in 1055 boasted that they were "famed throughout the world, adorned with many good qualities. Born to be wanderers over many countries, the earth as their sack."[11] Ports such as Cochin (KOH-chin) and Calicut (KAL-ih-cut) in Kerala and Cambay (kam-BAY) in Gujarat (GOO-jur-ot) played major roles in Indian Ocean trade.

For many centuries the Tamil (TAA-mill) people of southeast India, controlled by a Hindu dynasty known as the Cholas (CHO-luhs) (846–1216), profited from both piracy and foreign trade. The powerful Chola navy controlled the eastern Indian Ocean and conquered both Kerala and Sri Lanka (Ceylon). Merchant castes, which played a prominent role in Chola society,

organized a dynamic maritime trade that brought great wealth to the society and revenue to the kings. Hence traders held a high status and even governed themselves. Sometimes Chola seafaring led to outright plunder and conquest as far away as Southeast Asia. But violence was not the only strategy used. Some Chola rulers established close diplomatic and trade ties to Burma, Cambodia, and China.

The Tamils developed an outstanding artistic tradition, including many fabulous Hindu temples featuring magnificent bronzes. Perhaps the greatest creation was made by some unknown tenth-century genius, a bronze figure of Shiva portrayed as "Lord of the Dance," ready to commence the cosmic dance of life and restore vitality to the world. For centuries artists and historians praised this work, one writing that

rarely has an artist achieved such perfect balance and harmony in any medium as in this metal statue, whose symbolism embraces all of Hindu civilization in its mythic power, and whose exquisite form has led to its almost infinite reproduction throughout India. The workmanship of the artists was flawless in its beauty, magically transmuting metal to fleshlike texture, imparting the breath of life to their subjects.[12]

The Cholas declined politically in the thirteenth century, and the power vacuum was eventually filled by another Hindu kingdom, Vijayanagara (Vij-uh-yuh-NUHG-uhr-uh) ("City of Victory"), established in 1336. This militarily powerful state, which eventually dominated much of south and central India, was destroyed by rivals in 1565. During its existence huge temple cities arose, including the capital, which was one of the most magnificent cities of the Intermediate Era and one of the largest in the world. The persistence of Hindu rule in southern India preserved Hindu customs and institutions, which were disappearing in some northern areas.

Shiva as Lord of the Dance This famous bronze statue of Shiva as Lord of the Dance was made by Chola artists in southeast India. Displaying himself as a god of many qualities, Shiva grasps the flame of destruction in one hand and the drum of creation in another. The small figure under his foot represents the illusions that Shiva undermines.
(The Nelson-Atkins Museum of Art, Kansas City, Missouri, Purchase Nelson Trust, #34-7. Photo: E.G. Schempf)

The Impact of Tamerlane

Eventually Delhi's power ran its course. By the mid-fourteenth century north India was humbled by severe drought and famine caused in part by climate change. The state went into a rapid decline and was devastated by increased rebellion and civil war. While conflict raged internally, a new threat appeared in the northwest, the Mongol and Turkish forces of Tamerlane (TAM-uhr-LANE) (1336–1405). Tamerlane's branch of Mongols had become Muslim. From his base in Samarkand along the Silk Road, the ruthless warrior had already conquered Central Asia and Persia, creating the Timurid Empire based at Samarkand (see Chapter 10). In 1398 his forces invaded India, looting Delhi and killing perhaps 100,000 inhabitants in the city, mostly Hindus. Thousands more were dragged away as slaves. In his memoirs, Tamerlane defended his actions, arguing that "although I was desirous of sparing them it was the will of God that this calamity should befall the city."[13] Tamerlane and his army returned to Central Asia, leaving Delhi's few surviving inhabitants to perish by plague or starvation. In 1401–1402 Tamerlane's armies invaded Egypt and Anatolia, but were repulsed. He died attempting to invade China.

Tamerlane's invasion had a great impact on India, destroying the grand city of Delhi and with it all semblance of political unity in north India. The Delhi Sultanate survived for several centuries, but in a shrunken form. Various Muslim sultans ruled small states scattered around the plains, and occasional invasions by Afghans unsettled the northwest. Some new states rose to prominence. For example, Gujarat in western India flourished from foreign trade, and its capital of Ahmadabad (AHM-uhd-uh-BAHD) was famed for its canals, mosques, and palaces. Another distinctive region, Bengal in the northeast, remained independent, incubating a unique Bengali language as well as its own forms of Islam and Hinduism. By the fifteenth century India was fragmented into dozens of Muslim and Hindu states.

Muslim Rule and the Reshaping of Indian Life

The growing number of Muslims and Islamic political power changed Indian history. Muslims and Hindus experienced a long history of conflict, the natural result of tensions created by their very different values and worldviews. To Muslims, Hinduism, with its many deities, elaborate rituals, powerful priests, fondness for images, and preference for eating pork but not beef, constituted the exact opposite of all Islam held sacred. At the same time, Hindus despised the intolerance of some Muslims and desperately resisted Muslim political control.

Although they were in control, Muslim governments could not afford to permanently alienate their Hindu subjects, who constituted a huge majority of the population. At various times repression or persecution of Hindus by zealous Muslim rulers may have contributed to the instability of Muslim regimes. This reality fostered some compromises between rulers and ruled. Although Muslim rulers often confiscated the wealth of rich Hindu nobles, the common people were less affected, and life in the villages went on largely undisturbed. While some Muslims continued to view Hindus as infidels requiring conversion, eventually many Muslim scholars and leaders came to respect Hindus and the small Zoroastrian community as peoples of the book, counterparts to Christians and Jews in western Asia. But non-Muslims still faced second-class status and special tax payments.

Over the centuries many Indians converted from Hinduism to Islam. The great majority who adopted Islam were on the periphery of India, in the Indus River Valley in the northwest and in Bengal in the northeast. A much smaller proportion of southerners embraced the new faith. Converts included rich Hindus who wanted to safeguard their positions and secure government offices in Muslim-ruled states, as well as many poor Hindus who converted to escape low or untouchable status and to avoid the heavier taxes on non-Muslims. Conversions to Islam usually resulted from peaceful means rather than coercion. Probably over 90 percent of today's Muslims in South Asia are descendants of converts from Hinduism or Buddhism rather than Muslim immigrants. Today Muslims constitute one-fourth of the South Asian population. Conversion from Islam to Hinduism was also not unknown, and some Hindu rulers in central India had been born as Muslims.

Sufi mystics, who sought personal union with god, were the key to many Hindus' conversion to Islam, especially in places like Bengal. Bengali folk tradition celebrates a Sufi who moved to a village and built a mosque: "For the whole day [he] sat under a fig tree. His fame soon spread far and wide. Everybody talked of the occult [healing and psychic] powers he possessed."[14] People respected the intensity of the Sufis' spiritual discipline and the depth of their religious understanding. Perhaps Sufi preachers and their message became popular because they closely resembled devotional bhakti Hinduism and Mahayana Buddhism, which also emphasized emotional commitment rather than dry theology. Some Sufi mystics became hermits, living much like the wandering Hindu holy men. Today many South Asian Muslims and even some Hindus still venerate Sufi mystics of earlier centuries as saints.

Some people attempted to mix the faiths, building on the similarity between Sufi mysticism and the bhakti tradition. In the later fifteenth century some Hindu and Muslim mystics came together to form a group emphasizing a love of god. Some poets of the day, honored later as saints, promoted a mixture of Sufi and bhakti ideals that appealed to mystics in both religious communities. Perhaps the most significant was Kabir (kah-BEER) (1440–1518), a member of a low-status caste of weavers from Benares (see Witness to the Past: The Songs of Kabir). Although blind and illiterate, Kabir wrote poetry that is still revered today by both Hindus and Muslims. The cultural mixing also fostered a new language, Urdu (ER-doo), a combination of Persian, Turkish, Arabic, and Indian words superimposed on a Hindi grammar and written with the Arabic script, that was used by many Muslims in north and northwest India.

Coming from a Hindu family that had recently converted to Islam, Kabir was well acquainted with both religious traditions. His mystical poems of passionate love for a monotheistic god rejected religious prejudice, rigid dogmatism, and the caste system. Modern Indian intellectuals seeking to bridge the gap between the two faiths particularly admired his attempt to see beyond the limitations of the two religions and his absolute opposition to violence. The following poem argues that individuals must experience God for themselves.

O servant, where dost thou seek Me? Lo! I am beside thee.

I am neither in temple nor in mosque; I am neither in Kaaba [Muslim shrine] nor in Kailash [abode of Shiva].

Neither am I in rites and ceremonies, nor in Yoga and renunciation.

If thou art a true seeker, thou shalt at once see Me: . . .

It is needless to ask of a saint the caste to which he belongs;

For the priest, the warrior, the tradesman, and all the thirty-six castes, alike are seeking for God.

It is but folly to ask what the caste of a saint may be; The barber has sought God, the washerwoman, and the carpenter . . .

Hindus and Muslims alike have achieved the End, where remains no mark of distinction. . . .

O brother! when I was forgetful, my true Guru [teacher] showed me the Way.

Then I left off all rites and ceremonies, I bathed no more in the holy water: . . .

From that time forth I knew no more how to roll in the dust in obeisance:

I do not ring the temple bell; I do not set the idol on its throne; I do not worship the image with flowers.

It is not the austerities that mortify the flesh which are pleasing to the Lord,

When you leave off your clothes and kill your senses, you do not please the Lord,

The man who is kind and who practices righteousness, who remains passive amidst the affairs of the world, who considers all creatures on earth as his own self,

He attains the Immortal Being, the true God is ever with him.

Kabir says: "He attains the true Name whose words are pure, and who is free from pride and conceit."

If God be within the mosque, then to whom does this world belong?

If Ram [God] be within the image which you find upon your pilgrimage, then who is there to know what happens without?

Hari [Lord Vishnu] is in the East; Allah is in the West. Look within your heart, . . .

All the men and women of the world are His Living Forms.

Kabir is the child of Allah and of Ram [God]: He is my *Guru* [Hindu teacher], He is my *Pir* [Sufi saint].

THINKING ABOUT THE READING

1. Why would someone of mixed religious background be open to questioning rigid doctrines?
2. What does Kabir think about the traditions of organized religions?
3. Where does Kabir believe that God is to be found?

Source: William Theodore De Bary, ed., *Sources of Indian Tradition*, Vol. 1 (New York: Columbia University Press, 1958), pp. 355–357. Copyright © 1958 Columbia University Press. Reprinted with permission of the publisher.

Muslims and Hindus also engaged each other culturally. For example, Muslim influences, including Persian words and Persian food, were incorporated into Hindu social life. In addition, many Hindu males adopted Muslim clothing styles, and in north India some Hindus began practicing the local Muslim custom of **purdah**, seclusion of women. Under the challenge of the new missionary faith, which was often supported by the local rulers, Hinduism became more conservative, emphasizing tradition and priestly leadership. Some intermarriage also occurred, and, at the village level, Muslims fit themselves into the caste system to some extent. Thus the Muslim society that developed in India, like the Hindu society, was not egalitarian but rather was led by an upper class who descended from immigrants. Many Muslims also adopted some Hindu religious customs, including music and dance.

However, despite some mixing, from the thirteenth century onward, the life of India became two distinct currents flowing side by side. Most Muslims refused to be assimilated into the social and religious fold of Hinduism and remain separate, disdainful of Hindus and of the caste system. Hinduism was not destroyed either. Unlike Buddhism, w was centered in vulnerable monasteries, Hinduism's dece ized structure proved stable. Thus Hindus and Muslim gled to some extent along the lines of contact but neve to form a single stream. This persistent division g fected twentieth-century India, when the British India (most of the subcontinent) was eventually separate nations, the Hindu-dominated Ind Muslim-dominated Pakistan. A third religion al

purdah   The Indian Muslim custom of secluding women.

a South Asian base, since the island of Sri Lanka remained a bastion of Theravada Buddhism.

SECTION SUMMARY

■ Hindu warriors fended off Muslim invaders for a time, but they were outmatched and eventually defeated by their aggressive opponents.

■ The destruction inflicted by Muslim invaders caused long-term Hindu resentment and also contributed to the decline of Buddhism in India.

■ The Islamic Delhi Sultanate brought unity to north India for the first time in centuries, but its rulers ranged from the enlightened to the tyrannical.

■ Various Hindu monarchies, including the Cholas, maintained power in southern and eastern India, while Hindu traditions died out in the north.

■ The Delhi Sultanate declined because of climate change and civil war, and north Indian unity was shattered by the invasion of Tamerlane.

■ Muslim and Hindu beliefs were radically opposed, but over time Muslim rulers came to tolerate Hindu subjects, many of whom eventually converted to Islam.

■ While there was some cultural interchange between Hindus and Muslims in India, for the most part, the traditions remained separate.

Cultural Adaptation and New Southeast Asian Societies

What political and religious forms shaped Southeast Asian societies in the Early Intermediate Era?

Owing partly to the stimulus from India and, to a lesser extent, China, several great Southeast Asian kingdoms developed near the end of the first millennium C.E., establishing their main centers in what is today Cambodia, Burma, the [In]nesian islands of Java and Sumatra, and Vietnam, which [manage]d to throw off the Chinese yoke in the tenth century [(Map] 13.2). These Southeast Asian states mixed outside [influences] with their own traditions to produce new societies. [While ex]perienced many changes, they also preserved [much] continuity, much as Funan and Champa had [during] the Common Era (see Chronology: Southeast [Asia]).

[From the first] century[...]

[K]ingdoms

[...] of In[dian] Common Era until around the fourteenth known[,] [S]outheast Asian societies made selective use [...] shaping their political patterns, a process [...]ion. For example, the rulers declared

CHRONOLOGY	
Southeast Asia, 600–1500	
192–1471	Kingdom of Champa
600–1290	Srivijaya Empire
802–1432	Angkor Empire
939	End of Chinese colonization in Vietnam
1044–1287	Pagan kingdom in Burma
1292–1527	Madjapahit kingdom on Java
1238–1419	Sukhotai kingdom in Siam
1350–1767	Ayuthia kingdom in Siam
1403–1511	Melaka kingdom and Sultanate
1428–1788	Le dynasty in Vietnam (founded by Le Loi)

themselves god-kings, or **devaraja**, not just China-style intermediaries between the human realm and the cosmos but rather a reincarnated Buddha or Shiva worthy of cult worship. By maintaining order in the world, they ensured cosmic harmony. In theory absolute rulers, in reality their power faded with distance from the capital cities. Kings enjoyed enormous prestige but also faced continuous threats from rivals, who often succeeded in acquiring the throne. Warfare was no less frequent in Southeast Asia than in other areas of the world as rulers sought more land and labor to supply revenues.

The Indianized kingdoms of Southeast Asia were not all alike, and the economic foundations of their prosperity differed. Some were based largely on agriculture and generally located inland. Others, including the states alongside the Straits of Melaka, depended heavily on maritime trade and international networks of exchange. In many respects these contrasting patterns represented skillful adaptations to the environment. In the agriculture-based economies, rice-growing technology improved considerably beginning in the ninth century, becoming productive enough to sustain large centralized states. But in places with large areas of swampland, such as Malaya and Sumatra, people compensated for their lack of good farmland by maximizing their access to the open frontier of the sea and becoming seafaring traders.

Indianized Social and Cultural Patterns

The migration and mixing of peoples and their cultures were significant themes in Southeast Asia, as they had been in India,

---

devaraja ("God-king") The title used by Indianized Southeast Asian rulers, who wished to be seen as a reincarnated Buddha or Shiva worthy of cult worship.

Map 13.2   Major Southeast Asian Kingdoms, ca. 1200 C.E.

By 1200 the Khmer Empire (Angkor), which once covered much of mainland Southeast Asia, had declined. Sukhothai, Pagan, Srivijaya, Champa, and Vietnam were other major states.

Online Study Center   Improve Your Grade
Interactive Map: South and Southeast Asia in the Thirteenth Century

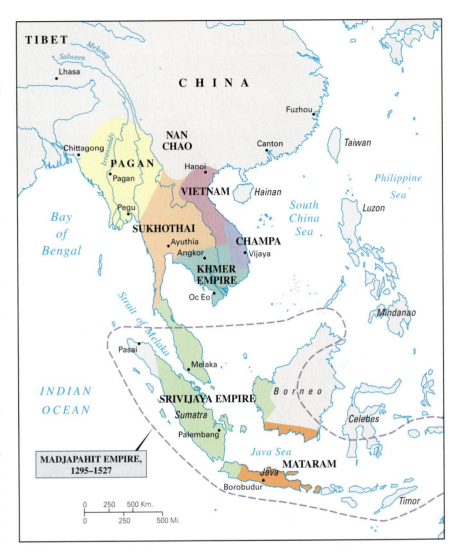

Europe, and Africa. Many influences came from immigrants. Following in the footsteps of earlier arrivals, peoples such as the Burmans (BUHR-muhnz) in the ninth century and the Tai (tie) peoples in the seventh to thirteenth centuries immigrated from Tibet and China into mainland Southeast Asia and reshaped the region. For example, the Burmans established the dynamic state of Pagan (puh-GONE) in central Burma after assimilating Buddhism and Hinduism from local people.

Religion played a central role in these states. Though the peasantry remained chiefly animist, Southeast Asian elites adopted Mahayana Buddhism and Hinduism from India. At its height in the twelfth century, the city of Pagan, the capital of a great kingdom, was one of the architectural wonders of the world, a city filled with temples and shrines for the glory of Buddhism and Hinduism. Spurred by piety, Pagan's kings and commoners alike spent as much wealth as they could spare on magnificent religious buildings, using Hindu and Buddhist sculpture and architecture from India as models. At Pagan and elsewhere religion infused government and the arts, and Hindu priests became advisers on ritual in the courts. Hindu Indian epics such as the *Ramayana* and *Mahabharata* became deeply imbedded in both the folk and elite culture, and the Hindu kings, gods, and demons animated the arts.

Southeast Asian societies shared many common features. Extensive trade networks, both land and maritime, had linked the region from earliest times, and many people specialized in local or foreign commerce. Most of the larger states were multiethnic in their population, including many foreign merchants in temporary or permanent residence. This social and ethnic diversity fostered a cosmopolitan attitude in many cities. Still, like Indians, most Southeast Asians were farmers and fishermen and lived in villages characterized by a spirit of cooperation for mutual survival. Unlike in India, however, Southeast Asian family patterns were diverse, ranging from flexible structures to a few patriarchies and matriarchies. In contrast to India and China, women held a relatively high status in most Southeast Asian societies, and some, like the Burmese queen Pwa Saw, exercised political influence behind the scenes (see Profile: Pwa Saw, a Burmese Queen).

An enduring gap separated the social and cultural traditions of the courts, including the royal families, administrations, and capital cities, and the villages. The two traditions differed significantly in religious orientations, worldviews, and ways of life. For example, Indian scripts (especially Sanskrit) became the basis for many Southeast Asian written languages, such as Khmer, Burman, and Thai, and fostered literature of various types, especially poetry, philosophical or religious speculations, and historical chronicles. These literature became an important component of Southeast Asia's elite culture but were less known among the peasantry.

The Angkor Empire

The Khmer people created the greatest Indianized st kingdom of Angkor (ANG-kor), in what is today Ca It was established by a visionary king, Jayavarma VAR-man) I (r. 802–834), in 802 C.E. The name An from the Sanskrit term meaning "holy city," and identified himself with the Hindu god Shiva. Fre extended and consolidated the kingdom, w until 1432. Angkor was notable for its sub

PWA SAW,
A BURMESE QUEEN

Women in royal families played important political roles in many Southeast Asian states, mostly behind the scenes, but few had the influence of thirteenth-century Queen Pwa Saw (pwah saw) of Pagan. Much of what we know about her life comes from a chronicle of the country's history compiled by Burmese scholars in the nineteenth century, and modern historians are divided on whether it represents more myth than fact. Whatever the accuracy, in their traditions the Burman people remember Queen Pwa Saw as witty, wise, and beautiful and as exercising political influence for forty years during one of their most difficult periods.

The girl who would become queen was born to a prosperous peasant family in a remote village around 1237. According to the legends, a deadly king cobra approached her when she was asleep but failed to attack, considered a favorable omen for a bright future, and a jasmine bush she tended astonished her neighbors by blooming in three colors. This unusual event drew the attention of the young King Uzana (r. 1249–1256), a playboy fond of hunting and drinking who was visiting the district with a large entourage of attendants. The unexpected visit of a king and his party riding on elephants spurred the villagers into frenzied preparations for a proper reception to demonstrate their respect. Infatuated with the bright, pretty, graceful, and talkative sixteen-year-old girl, Uzana took her back to Pagan as one of his many wives and appointed her a deputy queen. A short time later, Uzana died in an accident while hunting wild elephants.

With her husband's death, Pwa Saw was thrown into the schemes and rivalries of the royal court as various factions maneuvered for power. Placed in a precarious position as a young bride resented by rival queens, she quickly forged an alliance with the able and wily Chief Minister Yazathingyan (YAH-za-THING-yan), who feared the accession of the king's oldest son, the unpopular Prince Thitathu (thee-TAH-thoo), with whom he had long quarreled. Together they convinced officials to support another son, Narathihapade (NAR-a-THITH-a-PAH-dee) (r. 1256–1287), as king and make Pwa Saw chief queen. But the young king proved arrogant, quick-tempered, and ruthless, alienating many at court and earning the nickname "King Dog's Dung." While the economy declined, the king boasted that he was "the commander of 36 million soldiers, the swallower of 300 dishes of curry daily," and had 3,000 concubines. His zeal to build an expensive Buddhist pagoda fostered the proverb that "the pagoda is finished and the great country ruined." Pwa Saw remained loyal but lost respect for the king.

After her ally Yazathingyan died leading royal forces to suppress a rebellion in the south, Pwa Saw skillfully survived the king's paranoid suspicions and the constant intrigues of the court nobles, attendants, and other queens. Because the king trusted the widely revered queen, she could often overrule his destructive tendencies and talk him into making wiser state decisions. She also convinced the erratic king to appoint capable officials. But she had to maintain her wits. Increasingly paranoid, Narathihapade executed any perceived enemies and burned another queen to death. In the 1270s, anxious to prove himself a great leader, he rejected Pwa Saw's advice to meet Mongol demands for tribute and avoid conflict and instead escalated tensions, thus bringing on war, disaster, and the temporary Mongol occupation of Pagan.

Even as the Pagan state declined, Pwa Saw asserted a benevolent influence. For instance, in 1271 she donated some

---

advanced architecture, and unique social system. The magnificent temples still standing today testify to the prosperity and [orga]nization of Angkor society. By the twelfth century the [sprawling] capital city, Angkor Thom (ANG-kor tom), and its [immedia]te environs contained perhaps a million people. It [was] larger than any medieval European city and compa[rable to] but the largest Chinese and Arab cities. Trade with [many] other countries flourished, and many Chinese [li]ved in the kingdom.

[Ang]kor kings presided over a vigorous imperial sys[tem. At its] height in the twelfth and thirteenth centuries, [the] empire controlling much of what is now Cam[bodia,] of [Thai]land, and southern Vietnam. The Khmers ac[quired and] maintained their empire by a skillful combination [of] [au]tonomy, and pragmatism. The system was loosely [held together by] power, [regio]nal governors usually had considerable au[thority. The m]ost ruthless kings wielded unchallenged [power and wer]e art patrons and builders. For example, Jayavarma[n VII (r. 11]81–1219) was a devout Buddhist who

boasted of his compassion for his people. He expanded the empire, commissioned important artworks, built roads, and sponsored the construction of many monuments and temples. Zhou Daguan (joe ta-kwan), a Chinese ambassador in Angkor in 1296, left vivid descriptions of Angkor, including the system of justice presided over by the king: "Disputes of the people, however insignificant, always go to the king. Each day the king holds two audiences for affairs of state. Those of the functionaries or the people who wish to see the king, sit on the ground to wait for him."[15]

The state held much power over the population and often used that power to enrich the society. For example, the well-financed government supported substantial public services, including hospitals, schools, and libraries. It also used conscripted workers to construct an extensive canal network for efficient water distribution, exhibiting some of the most advanced civil engineering in the premodern world. Although historians debate how much farming depended on irrigation from these canals, they agree on the fact that the Khmers may

Court Life of Pwa Saw
No known paintings of Pwa Saw exist. This fresco, from the Ananda Buddhist temple at Pagan, shows rich court ladies, much like Pwa Saw herself, relaxing in an upstairs room of a magnificent Buddhist temple while, downstairs, stallholders hawk their wares to visitors.
(Robert Harding World Imagery)

of her lands and properties to a Buddhist temple, expressing hope that in future existences she would "have long life, be free from illness, have a good appearance, melodic of voice, be loved and respected by all men and gods, [and] be fully equipped with faith, wisdom, nobility." In 1287 the mad king was murdered by one of his sons. In 1289 Queen Saw and surviving ministers selected a new king, Kyawswar (kee-YAH-swar) (1287–1298). With that last effort to help her country, she retired in style to her home village.

THINKING ABOUT THE PROFILE
1. What skills did Pwa Saw use to influence the court?
2. What does this profile tell us about the relations between queens and kings at Pagan?

Notes: Quotations from D. G. E. Hall, *A History of South-East Asia,* 4th ed. (New York: St. Martin's Press, 1981), p. 169; and Michael Aung-Thwin, *Pagan: The Origins of Modern Burma* (Honolulu: University of Hawaii Press, 1985), p. 41.

have had the most productive agriculture in world history, producing three to four crops a year in a marginally fertile rice-growing region.

Angkor Religion and Society

Religion played an important political and cultural role in Angkor, and Indian influence was considerable. The Angkor government structure resembled a theocratic state: it presided over a well-developed cult for the popular worship of the god-kings, and priestly families held a privileged position. Perhaps as many 300,000 Hindu priests lived in the heart of the empire at its height, and the numerous temples controlled massive wealth. Hindu values were also reflected in many aspects of culture, including theater, art, and dance.

Many magnificent stone temples, some of them as huge as small mountains, were built during the Angkor period. They were designed to represent the Hindu conception of the cosmos centered on the abode of the gods. Built as sanctuaries and

mausoleums, these temples also provided vivid and concrete symbols of a monarch's earthly power, since the construction involved amazing engineering skills and massive amounts of conscripted labor. The most famous temple was part of the largest religious complex in the premodern world, Angkor Wat (ANG-kor waht). The complex, containing buildings, towers, and walls was built by some 70,000 workers in the twelfth century. Angkor Wat dwarfed other Intermediate Era monumental religious buildings, including the magnificent cathedrals of Europe and the grand mosques of Baghdad and Cairo. The reliefs carved into stone at Angkor Wat and other temples provide glimpses of daily life, showing fishing boats, midwives attending a childbirth, merchant stalls, festival jugglers and dancers, peasants bringing goods to market, the crowd at a cockfight, and men playing chess.

In exchange for considerable material security and the protection of a patron to whom they owed allegiance, Khmer commoners tolerated a highly inequitable distribution of wealth and power as well as substantial labor demands, such as

Angkor Wat Temple Complex This photograph shows the inner buildings of the Angkor Wat temple complex in northern Cambodia. The towers represented the Hindu view of the cosmos. Mount Meru, the home of the gods, rises 726 feet in the middle. (Robert Harding World Imagery)

the draft of workers to build Angkor Wat. Like many hierarchical societies of the era, Angkor had numerous slaves and people in some form of temporary or permanent involuntary servitude. Although no India-style caste system existed despite the strong Hindu influence, the social structure was rigid. Each class had its appointed role: below the king were the priests, and below them were the trade guilds. The vast majority of the population were of the farmer-builder-soldier class, which had some labor obligations to the sovereign. Peasants were tied to the soil they plowed, to the temples they served, and to the king's army.

Khmer women played a much more important role in society and politics than women did in most other places in the world. According to Zhou Daguan, women operated most of the retail stalls: "In this country it is the women who are concerned with commerce."[16] Some royal women were noted for intellectual or service activities. Jayarajadevi (JAI-ya-RAJ-a-deh-vee), the first wife of King Jayavarman VII, took in hundreds of abandoned girls and trained and settled them. After her death the king married Indradevi (IN-dra-deh-vee), a renowned scholar who lectured at a Buddhist monastery and was acclaimed as the chief teacher of the king. Women domi-

nated the palace staff, and some were even gladiators and warriors. Chinese visitors were shocked at the liberated behavior of Khmer women, who went out in public as they liked. Women were also active in the arts, especially as poets. Khmer society in this era was matrilineal, giving women status in the family.

Indianized Urban Societies in Java and Sumatra

Of the other important Indianized states in Southeast Asia, several developed in the Indonesian archipelago, on the large islands of Java and Sumatra. The encounters between Indian influence and local traditions produced in Java a distinctive religious and political blend known as Hindu-Javanese, which was based on an agricultural economy and which included many unique beliefs. Among the core beliefs were the notions that the earthly order mirrored and embodied the cosmic order and that, to preserve the cosmic order, people must avoid disharmony and change at all cost. The duty of the god-king was to prevent social deterioration in a turbulent human world by maintaining order. As in Angkor, the capitals and palaces of

Javanese kingdoms were built to imitate the cosmic order. Hindu-Buddhist ideas can be seen most vividly in the temple complexes of that time, such as the famous temple mountain of Borobodur (BOR-uh-buh-door) in central Java. They were also reflected in the stories and content of arts such as the shadow puppet play, or **wayang kulit** (WHY-ang KOO-leet), which was based on the Hindu epics like the *Ramayana* but had much local content as well.

The greatest Javanese kingdom of this era was Madjapahit (MAH-ja-PA-hit) (1292–1527). Madjapahit reached its peak in the fourteenth century under the fabled Prime Minister Gajah Mada, when it loosely controlled a large empire embracing much of present-day Indonesia. A court poet in 1365 described the reigning monarch, King Hayam Wuruk, as follows: "He is praised like the moon in autumn, since he fills all the world with joy. His retinue, treasures, chariots, elephants, horses are (immeasurable) like the sea. The land of Java is becoming more and more famous for its blessed state throughout the world."[17]

Social inequality permeated Hindu-Javanese society. A complex etiquette regulated the relations between those of varied status, and hence confirmed the social hierarchy. The aristocracy, who administered the realm, expected deference from commoners, most of whom lived in villages whose cultures and ways of life differed substantially from those of the royal capital. Much of village work was planned and carried out on a communal basis, following a tradition of indigenous democracy and mutual self-help. The villagers' main link with the government was through tax and labor obligations. Peasants identified more with their village community than with distant kings in their palaces.

Coastal states on Sumatra were shaped much more heavily by international trade than were the inland agricultural kingdoms of Java and Cambodia. The Straits of Melaka separating Sumatra from the Malay Peninsula was a major contact zone throughout history and a passageway for trade and religious networks. Throughout the first millennium of the Common Era a complex maritime trading system gradually emerged that linked the eastern Mediterranean, Middle East, East African coast, Persia, and India with the societies of East and Southeast Asia. A vigorously mercantile variation of Indianized culture formed to capitalize on this growing trend.

Between 600 and 1290 many of the small trading states in the Straits region came under the loose control of Srivijaya (SREE-vih-JAI-ya), a great empire based in southeastern Sumatra and a fierce rival of the Cholas in South India. Srivijaya exercised considerable power over the international commerce of the region and maintained a close trade relationship with powerful China. It was not a centralized system but rather a federation of linked trading ports held together by a naval force that both fought and engaged in piracy. Besides being a trading hub, Srivijaya was also a major international center of Buddhist study, attracting thousands of Buddhist monks and students from many countries.

wayang kulit Javanese shadow puppet play, developed during the Intermediate Era, based on Hindu epics like the *Ramayana* and local Javanese content.

International Influences and the Decline of the Indianized States

The great Indianized states of Southeast Asia came to an end between the thirteenth and fifteenth centuries, for a variety of complex reasons, but the changes were mostly gradual. Some causes of decline were internal. For example, Angkor experienced a combination of military expansion that overstretched resources; increased temple-building resulting in higher tax levies and forced labor that antagonized much of the population into rebellion; and growing breakdown of the irrigation system. But international influences also played a major role in the disintegration of Angkor and neighboring states. These included the migrations of the Tai peoples, the intervention of the Mongols, and the arrival of Theravada Buddhism and Islam.

Over several centuries various groups from mountainous southwestern China speaking Tai languages migrated into Southeast Asia. By the thirteenth century the Tai began setting up their own states in the middle Mekong valley and northern Thailand. These were the ancestors of the closely related Siamese (SYE-uh-meez), today known as the Thai, and the Lao (laow) peoples. As they moved south, the Tai conquered or absorbed the local peoples while also adopting some of their cultural traditions. Eventually they came into conflict with Angkor. By the mid-1400s they had repeatedly sacked Angkor and seized much of the empire's territory. The Khmer Empire soon disintegrated, and the Angkor capital was abandoned. The Khmers became pawns perched uneasily between the expanding Vietnamese and Siamese states.

Meanwhile, the Mongols encountered Angkor's neighbors, but their impact was smaller than that of the Tai. After conquering China, in 1288 they attacked Pagan because the Burmans refused to recognize Mongol overlordship. Although the Mongols soon withdrew, in their wake they left instability in Burma as rival groups competed for power. Elsewhere in Southeast Asia the Mongols found mostly frustration. Although an ill-fated land-and-sea invasion of Vietnam and Champa at first inflicted terrible damage, it was ultimately repelled by a temporary Vietnamese-Cham military alliance. A Mongol naval expedition to Java also proved a costly failure. Southeast Asians were among the few peoples to successfully resist Mongol conquest and power.

The third force for change was religion. By early in the second millennium of the Common Era, two new universal religions began filtering peacefully into the region from outside: Theravada Buddhism and Islam. Theravada Buddhism had been present in the region for several centuries and had been a strong influence among the Burmans at Pagan, but a revitalized form came from Sri Lanka and provided a challenge to the hierarchical order of the Indianized regimes. The Buddhist message of egalitarianism, pacifism, and individual worth proved attractive to peasants weary of war, public labor projects, and tyrannical kings. Furthermore, Theravada Buddhism was a tolerant religion able to exist alongside the rich animism of the peasants, who could honor the Buddha while worshiping local spirits. By the fourteenth century most of the Burman, Khmer, Siamese, and Lao peasants had adopted Theravada Buddhism, while the elite mixed the new faith with the older Hindu–Mahayana Buddhist traditions.

About the same time, from the thirteenth through sixteenth centuries, Sunni Islam filtered in from the Middle East via India and spread widely. Like Buddhism, Islam also offered an egalitarian message that challenged the power of traditional elites, as well as a complex theology that appealed to peasants and merchants in the coastal regions of the Malay Peninsula, Sumatra, Java, and some of the other islands. Some Southeast Asians adopted Sunni Islam in a largely orthodox form, while others mixed it with animism or Hinduism-Buddhism. The adaptable mystical Sufi ideas embedded in missionary Islam also blended well with the existing mysticism. This blending fostered conversion by promoting an emotional spirituality rather than dry, dogmatic theology.

As Theravada Buddhism and Islam spread across Southeast Asia, only a few scattered peoples maintained Indianized societies, among them the Balinese (BAH-luh-NEEZ). On the Indonesian island of Bali, Hinduism and other classical patterns remained vigorous, emphasizing arts like dancing, music, shadow plays, and woodcarving. Thus the many visitors to Bali today get a glimpse of patterns that were once widespread in the region.

SECTION SUMMARY

- Southeast Asian kingdoms were heavily influenced by India, and, as in India, their rulers considered themselves god-kings, although their power was limited in the provinces.

- Most Southeast Asian states were multiethnic and were influenced by immigrants and the migration of Mahayana Buddhism and Hinduism from India.

- The Indianized kingdom of Angkor controlled a large swath of Southeast Asia and completed advanced civil engineering projects, such as an extensive canal system and the huge temple complex of Angkor Wat.

- Hindu priests played a very important role in Angkor and the social structure was extremely rigid, though an Indian-style caste system did not take hold and women were more important in society and politics than in most places in the world.

- On Java, a highly stratified Indianized society that championed harmony developed, while on Sumatra, Srivajaya became a powerful commercial empire.

- Southeast Asians fended off the Mongols, but new peoples such as the Tai invaded and destroyed Angkor, and the gradual introduction of Theravada Buddhism and Sunni Islam challenged the hierarchical order and displaced Indian influence in many states.

Changing Southeast Asian Societies

What was the influence of Theravada Buddhism and Islam on Southeast Asia?

By the fifteenth century Southeast Asia had experienced a major transition. The Indianized kingdoms such as Angkor, Pagan, and Srivijaya had gradually been replaced by new states with less despotic governments and more dynamic economies Networks of trade and religion linked the region even more closely to wider areas of Afro-Eurasia. In these centuries the major Southeast Asian societies began to diverge in many directions from the earlier Indian and Chinese-influenced patterns, and Theravada Buddhism and Islam permeated further into the countryside. By the fifteenth century three broad but very distinctive social and cultural patterns had developed: the Theravada Buddhist, the Vietnamese, and the Malayo-Muslim or Indonesian.

Theravada Buddhist Society in Siam

The Siamese formed one of the most influential Theravada Buddhist societies, establishing several states in northern and central Thailand. The first major Siamese state, Sukhotai (SOO-ko-TAI), was founded in 1238 by former Angkor vassals and controlled much of the central plains of what is today Thailand. While some modern historians are skeptical, according to Siamese tradition, Sukhotai's glory was established by Rama Kamkheng (RA-ma KHAM-keng) ("Rama the Brave"), a shrewd diplomat who established a close tributary relationship with the dominant regional power, China. Under Rama's leadership, Siam adopted the Khmer script and experienced other Khmer influences in literature, art, and government. Siamese chronicles portray Rama as a wise and popular ruler. A temple inscription of the time tells us that

> the Lord of the country levies no tolls on his subjects. If he sees someone else's wealth he does not interfere. If he captures some enemy soldiers he neither kills them nor beats them. In the [palace] doorway a bell is suspended; if an inhabitant of the kingdom has any complaint or any matter irritates his stomach and torments his mind, and he desires to expose it to the king ring the bell.[18]

This may have exaggerated his merits, but Rama did make Theravada Buddhism the state religion and adopted laws that were humane by world standards.

By 1350 Sukhotai was eclipsed by another Siamese state that emerged in the southern Thai plains, with its capital at Ayuthia (ah-YUT-uh-yuh). While Sukhotai declined and finally collapsed in 1419, Ayuthia developed a regional empire whose influence extended into Cambodia and the small Lao states along the Mekong River. Its rivalry with the Burmans and Vietnamese for regional dominance occasionally led to war.

Buddhist states like Sukhothai and Ayuthia were monarchies. People viewed Siamese kings as semidivine reincarnated Buddhas. Kings lived in splendor and majesty and were advised by Brahman priests in ceremonial and magical practices. They had many wives and therefore many sons, all of whom could be rivals for the throne. This problem, as well as unclear or unenforceable political succession rules, meant that the top levels of government were plagued with instability. But these rivalries generally had little impact in the villages, which had substantial autonomy. Despite a bureaucratic government, royal power lessened as distance to the capital increased.

The Siamese society and culture had many similarities to those of other Theravada Buddhist peoples such as the Khmer, Burmans, and especially the Lao. Like them, the Siamese social order was divided into a small aristocracy, many commoners, and some slaves (many of them prisoners of war). Male slaves did a variety of jobs, from farming and mining to serving as trusted government officials. Slave women were often concubines, domestic servants, or entertainers. Deference to higher authority and recognition of status differences were expected among the Siamese people. In contrast to the extended families of China or India, small nuclear families were the norm. While Theravada peoples encouraged cooperation and mutual obligations within the family and village, they also valued individualism.

Although women did not enjoy absolute equality with men and were expected to show their respect for men, free women enjoyed many rights. They inherited equally with men and could initiate marriage or divorce. They also operated most of the stalls in village or town markets. Visitors from China, India, Europe, and the Middle East were often shocked at the relative freedom of Siamese women. A Muslim Persian diplomat in Ayuthia wrote that "it is common for women to engage in buying and selling in the markets and even to undertake physical labor, and they do not cover themselves with modesty. Thus you can see the women paddling to the surrounding villages where they successfully earn their daily bread with no assistance from the men."[19]

Siamese society reflected Theravada Buddhist values, such as gentleness, meditation, and reincarnation, as well as the concept of *karma*, the idea that one's actions, either in this life or a past life, determined one's destiny. To escape from the endless round of life, death, and rebirth, believers were expected to devote themselves to attaining merit by practicing merciful and generous deeds, with the ultimate goal of reaching *nirvana*, or release from pain. Many men became Buddhist monks, and monks played key roles in local affairs, operating many village schools. Hence Theravada societies had some of the highest literacy rates (especially for males) in the premodern world. Women could not gain merit as monks, although some became nuns. Despite this piety, most Siamese were tolerant of those who were less devout, believing that individuals' spiritual state was their own responsibility. Peasants moved easily between supporting their local Buddhist temple and placating the animist spirits of the fields.

Vietnamese Society

A Chinese colony for over a thousand years, Vietnam also constituted a major Southeast Asian society. In 939 C.E., with the Tang dynasty collapsing, a rebellion finally succeeded in pushing the Chinese out and establishing independence, but China remained a permanent threat. Vietnamese leaders wisely continued to borrow ideas and institutions from China and, to placate the Chinese, even became a vassal state, sending regular tribute missions to the Chinese emperor. By the fourteenth century Vietnam, still strongly influenced by Chinese political and philosophical ideas, offered a striking contrast to Theravada Buddhist societies.

Despite Vietnam's formal subservience, Chinese forces occasionally attempted a reconquest, inspiring the Vietnamese to become masters at resisting foreign invasions. In 1407 the new Ming dynasty invaded and conquered Vietnam in an attempt to restore China's control. In response to the harsh Chinese repression, Le Loi (lay lo-ee) (1385–1433), a mandarin from a landlord family, organized a Vietnamese resistance movement that struggled tenaciously for the next two decades. After it finally expelled the Chinese in 1428, Le Loi became founding emperor of a new Vietnamese dynasty, the Le (1428–1788). His efforts to launch social and economic reforms to reduce the power of the traditional elite, as well as his struggle against Chinese domination, made him one of the heroes of Vietnam's long struggle for independence and self-determination. As Le Loi told his people in his proclamation of victory: "Over the centuries, we have been sometimes strong, sometimes weak; but never yet have we been lacking in heroes. In that let our history be the proof."[20]

Some historians believe the Vietnamese also possessed a sense of national feeling centuries before such ideas developed elsewhere in the world. Over the centuries, this sense of common identity greatly aided Vietnamese survival in a sometimes dangerous regional environment. Vietnam successfully survived on the fringes of powerful China, and when the country was at peace, a cultural renaissance, including literature, poetry, and theater, flourished.

Vietnam had an imperial system modeled on China's. For example, the Vietnamese considered the emperor a "son of heaven," not a god-king but an intermediary between the terrestrial and supernatural realms, ruling through the Mandate of Heaven. As in China, emperors governed through a bureaucracy staffed by scholar-administrators (*mandarins*) chosen by civil service examinations designed to recruit men of talent. The emperor and his officials followed the official ideology of Confucianism, which stressed ethical conduct, social harmony, and social hierarchy. Vietnam also adopted the Chinese model of tributary states and sought to influence or control the peoples of the highlands as well as the neighboring Cham, Khmer, and Lao states.

Peasant society differed considerably from the Chinese-influenced culture of the imperial court and political elite. In the villages religious life mixed Mahayana Buddhism, Confucianism, and Daoism, all adopted from China, with the preexisting

Le Dynasty Ruler   This Vietnamese drawing shows the Le emperor being carried in state, accompanied by his mandarins, parasol-and fan-bearers, and a royal elephant. The drawing was printed in an eighteenth-century British book, with an English description of the procession. (From Churchill, *A Collection of Voyages and Travels,* 1732)

Vietnamese spirit and ancestor worship. Villages were self-governing and closely knit communities, and their autonomy was summarized in the peasant expression that "the authority of the emperor ends at the village gate." While individual families owned most of the land, villages also developed a built-in social security system by setting aside communal land that could be farmed by landless peasants. The Vietnamese social system was patriarchal and patrilineal, giving family and village power to senior males. But women dominated the town and village markets, doing most of the buying and selling of food and crafts, and they saw their influence increase with age.

Beginning in the tenth century some Vietnamese left the overcrowded Red River Valley and Tonkin Gulf to migrate southward along the coast in a long process known as the **Nam Tien**, or "Drive to the South." Over the centuries these Vietnamese settlers, supported by imperial forces, overran the Cham people and their states, in what is today central Vietnam. By the sixteenth century they were pushing toward the Khmer-dominated Mekong River Delta in southern Vietnam. As a result of this migration, the Vietnamese became more involved with Southeast Asia and the central and southern dialects and cultures gradually came to differ from those in the northern part of Vietnam.

Islam, Maritime Networks, and the Malay World

Southeast Asian people had excelled as seafaring traders since the beginning of their history, trading as far away as East Africa. Some Indonesians had probably even been visiting the north coast of Australia for centuries to obtain items like ornamental shells. During the Intermediate Era world trade more closely connected diverse Eurasian and African peoples, and Southeast Asian port cities became essential intermediaries in the Indian Ocean trade between China, India, and the Middle East. Peoples like the Malays and Javanese played active roles in this maritime trade.

Trade also brought Southeast Asians into contact with the Muslim traders who dominated interregional commerce. As Islamic merchants from Arabia, Persia, and India spread Islam along the Indian Ocean trading routes, Islam became a major influence in the Malay Peninsula and Indonesian archipelago. Commercial people were attracted to a religion that sanctioned the accumulation of wealth and preached cooperation among believers. By the fourteenth century Islam was well established in northern Sumatra, and some Hindu-Buddhist rulers of coastal states in the Malay Peninsula and Indonesian islands grew eager to attract Muslim traders. Impressed by the cosmopolitan universality of Islam, they adopted the new faith, converting themselves into sultans.

The increased trade fostered by the spread of Islam spurred other changes, among them the growth of cities and the increasing influence of merchants in local politics. In addition, a new type of maritime trading state emerged to handle the increased amounts of products being procured and transported. Revenue from trade became more important than agricultural tribute in many states. This transformation in the international maritime economy created an unprecedented commercial prosperity and cosmopolitan culture in Southeast Asia. At the same time, more intensive agricultural growth, including new crops and varieties of rice, spurred population increase, migration, and more bureaucratic states, some large and many small ones.

The spread of Islam in the region coincided with, and was spurred by, the rise of the great port of Melaka (muh-LACK-uh) on the southwest coast of Malaya facing the Straits of Melaka. In 1403 the Hindu ruler of the city, Parameswara,

---

Nam Tien ("Drive to the South")   A long process beginning in the tenth century in which some Vietnamese left the overcrowded north to migrate southward along the coast of Vietnam.

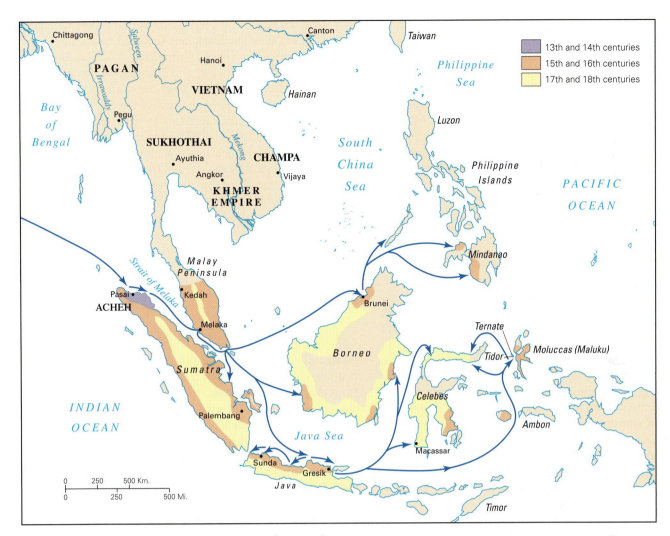

Map 13.3   The Spread of Islam in Island Southeast Asia
Carried by merchants and missionaries, Islam spread from Arabia and India to island Southeast Asia, eventually becoming the major faith on many islands and in the Malay Peninsula.

adopted Islam and transformed himself into a sultan. His motivation was probably as much political and commercial as spiritual. In Southeast Asian fashion, the Melakans blended Islamic faith and culture with the older Hindu-Buddhist (and, for peasants, animist) beliefs, creating a cultural pattern that remained eclectic for generations. Because Islam in the region was closely identified at first with the Malay people of the Melaka region, historians often refer to the Muslim Southeast Asian societies as Malayo-Muslim. Malay identity spread to many societies in Malaya, Sumatra, and Borneo who practiced Islam and spoke the Malay language.

Melaka became the main center for the spread of Islam in the peninsula and western archipelago (see Map 13.3), spurring political change and economic growth. Sultanates appeared in many districts and islands as rulers embraced the new faith for religious, political, and commercial reasons. Some Islamic states, such as Acheh (AH-chay) in northern Sumatra, became regional powers. The sultanates of Ternate

(tuhr-NAH-tay) and Tidor (TEE-door) in the Maluku (muh-LUKE-uh) (Moluccan) Islands of northeastern Indonesia prospered from the spices they produced (especially cloves and nutmeg) that were prized in Europe and the Middle East. Gradually many of the people in the region followed the example of their rulers and adopted Islam. As a result, the Malay Peninsula and Indonesian archipelago were joined to the great Islamic world. But there also remained many village-based societies, some of them still practicing animism, in more isolated or fringe areas such as the Philippine Islands, with no political authority higher than local chiefs.

As Islam was grafted onto different cultures, various patterns of Islamic belief and practice, more diverse than elsewhere in the Islamic world, emerged in the scattered island societies. In most cases Islam did not completely displace older customs. For example, on Java several religious patterns developed. While Indianized kings and courts combined Islamic beliefs with older Hindu-Buddhist ceremonies and mystical traditions, many peasants maintained their mystical animist beliefs and practices under an Islamic veneer, tolerating diverse religious views, while others (especially merchants) adopted a more orthodox Islamic faith, following prescribed Islamic practices and looking toward the Middle East for models. The complex Javanese religion mirrored a hierarchical social system. The sultans in their palaces remained aloof from the people, and the aristocracy, obsessed with practicing refined behavior rooted in mystical Hinduism, disdained the common folk. Like their pre-Muslim ancestors, Javanese of all classes placed a great value on maintaining a tranquil heart by avoiding interpersonal conflict.

Melaka: Crossroads of Trade

Melaka played a growing role in transregional trade, replacing Srivijaya as the region's political and economic power and becoming the crossroads of Asian maritime commerce. Melaka's rulers sent tributary missions to China and made their port a key way station for the series of grand Chinese voyages to the western Indian Ocean led by Admiral Zheng He (see Chapter 11), who called at the port in 1409 and 1414. In exchange for Melaka's service as a naval base, the Ming emperor supported the young state in regional disputes. Soon merchants from around Asia began coming to the new emporium, rapidly transforming the port into the archipelago's major trading hub, as well as the southeastern terminus for the Indian Ocean maritime trading network.

One of the major commercial centers in the world, Melaka rivaled other great trading ports such as Calicut, Cambay, Guangzhou (Canton), Hormuz, Alexandria, Genoa, and Venice. In 1468 Melaka sultan Mansur wrote to the king of the Ryukyu Islands, "We have learned that to master the blue oceans people must engage in commerce. All the lands within the seas are united in one body. Life has never been so affluent in preceding generations as it is today."[21] Melaka's rulers were actively involved in commerce, a pattern that became common among Muslim trading states in Southeast Asia. Gradually, Melaka became the center of a highly decentralized empire that dominated much of coastal Malaya and eastern Sumatra.

Melaka flourished until 1511 as a vital link in world trade. An early-sixteenth-century Portuguese visitor wrote that it had "no equal in the world" and extolled the importance of Melaka to peoples and trade patterns as far away as western Europe: "Melaka is a city that was made for merchandise, fitter than any other in the world. Commerce between different nations for a thousand leagues on every hand must come to Melaka."[22] Melaka had a special connection to the Indian port of Cambay, nearly 3,000 miles away. Every year trading ships from around the Middle East and South Asia gathered at Cambay and Calicut to make the long voyage to Melaka. They carried with them grain, woolens, arms, copperware, textiles, and opium for exchange. Goods from as far north as Korea also reached Melaka.

The flourishing trading port attracted merchants from many lands. By the late 1400s Melaka's 100,000 to 200,000 people included 15,000 foreign merchants, some of whom took local wives. Their diversity tells us much about Melaka's global importance. The foreigners included Arabs, Egyptians, Persians, Armenians, Jews, Ethiopians, Swahilis, Burmese, and Indians from the west, and Vietnamese, Javanese, Filipinos, Japanese, and Chinese from the east and north. Some eighty-four languages were spoken on the city's streets. Perhaps the richest Melaka merchant in the later 1400s, Naina Suradewana (NINE-a su-ROD-eh-won-a), a portly Hindu from southeast India, started as a moneylender but eventually owned a large fleet that traded with Java and the Maluku Islands. Visitors claimed that more ships crowded the Melaka harbor than in any other port in the world, attracted by a stable government and a free trade policy. City shops offered textiles from India, books from the Middle East, cloves and nutmeg from Maluku, batiks and carpets from Java, silk and porcelain from China, and sugar from the Philippines. Gold brought from various places was so plentiful that children played with it.

Southeast Asia and the Wider World

Southeast Asia had long been a cosmopolitan region where peoples, ideas, and products met, and visitors and sojourners from many lands continued to reach the region. For example, the intrepid Italian traveler Marco Polo passed through in 1292 on his way home from a long China sojourn. His writings praised the wealth and sophistication of Champa, Java, and Sumatra, arousing European interest in seeking direct trade connections with these seemingly fabulous lands. Polo wrote that "Java is of unsurpassing wealth, producing all kinds of spices, frequented by a vast amount of shipping. Indeed, the treasure of this island is so great as to be past telling."[23]

The Southeast Asia Marco Polo and other travelers such as the Moroccan Ibn Battuta encountered was one of the world's more prosperous and urbanized regions. Major cities like Ayuthia, Melaka, and Hanoi (huh-NOY) (Vietnam) each probably contained around 100,000 residents and thus were as large as the major European urban centers like Naples and Paris. But this was small by Chinese or Middle Eastern standards. By the 1400s, though having perhaps 15 to 20 million people, a fifth of them in Vietnam, Southeast Asia was dwarfed by the dense populations of nearby China and India. Still, blessed with fertile land and extensive trade, Southeast Asians often enjoyed better health, more varied diets, and adequate material resources than most peoples.

Southeast Asia's connections to the wider world, as well as its famed wealth, eventually attracted arrivals who were not welcome. By the beginning of the sixteenth century a few Portuguese explorers and adventurers, with deadly weapons, state-of-the-art ships, Christian missionary zeal, and desire for wealth, reached first India and then Southeast Asia seeking "Christians and spices." The Portuguese standard of living was probably inferior to that of Siam, Vietnam, Melaka, or Java. Yet, the Portuguese were the forerunners of what became a powerful, destabilizing European presence that gradually altered the region after 1500.

SECTION SUMMARY

- Siamese states such as Sukhotai and Ayuthia were Theravada Buddhist monarchies that valued individualism and peacefulness, offered women a fair amount of freedom, and were permeated by Buddhist values.

- Despite gaining freedom from Chinese rule, Vietnam retained a great deal of Chinese cultural influence.

- Inhabitants of the Malay and Indonesian archipelagoes embraced Islam, which arrived via increasing maritime trade, and grafted it onto Hinduism and Buddhism to create many different patterns of Islamic belief, while native animist traditions survived to some extent in the villages.

- Melaka displaced Srivajaya as the center of Southeast Asian trading power and became an international crossroads.

- Southeast Asia would eventually attract less friendly visitors, such as the Portuguese.

Online Study Center ACE the Test

Chapter Summary

Although many earlier patterns of life and thought persisted in India and Southeast Asia during the Intermediate Era, these regions also experienced tremendous changes. Islam was brought to India through violent conquest and to Southeast Asia through peaceful trade. In all cases societies adapted new ideas in different ways to their own distinctive cultures.

A constant stream of West Asian and central Asian peoples into India brought more diversity to Indian social patterns and beliefs. Although India remained politically fragmented, Hinduism enjoyed a kind of renaissance. Most people owed allegiance to their family, caste, and village. Hinduism spawned diverse ideas and cults, and gradually fostered many common cultural patterns, bringing some cultural unity. Buddhism gradually lost influence in much of India. Hindu society faced its greatest challenge from Muslim conquerors, who became politically dominant in north India. Unlike earlier ideas and peoples, Muslims would not be assimilated, although there was some mixing of Hindu and Muslim traditions. Islam added a major new strand to India's heritage, influencing the political, religious, and cultural realms but increasing diversity at the expense of unity.

Hindu and Buddhist ideas along with various other Indian traditions diffused to Southeast Asia, where they helped foster the rise of great kingdoms. The Angkor Empire dominated much of mainland Southeast Asia by mixing Indian and local patterns. New peoples, especially the Tais, and religions eventually reshaped Southeast Asia. Theravada Buddhism became a major influence of several societies, including Siam, while Islam became strong in peninsula and island societies such as Melaka and Java. International trade fostered economic dynamism, and Melaka served as a major international port in which many cultural traditions flourished.

Online Study Center **Improve Your Grade** Flashcards

Key Terms

Rajputs	Tantrism	devaraja
polyandry	Lamaism	wayang kulit
bhakti	purdah	Nam Tien
Vajrayana		

Suggested Reading

Books

Andaya, Barbara Watson, and Leonard Andaya. *A History of Malaysia.* 2nd ed. Honolulu: University of Hawaii Press, 2000. Contains an overview of Melaka and the spread of Islam in Southeast Asia.

Aung-Thwin, Michael. *Pagan: The Origins of Modern Burma.* Honolulu: University of Hawaii Press, 1985. The most comprehensive study of the Pagan society in Burma.

Basham, A. L. *The Wonder That Was India.* 3rd rev. ed. New Delhi: Rupa and Company, 1967 (reprinted 1999). Although dated, this is still the best general study of pre-Islamic India.

Chaudhuri, K. N. *Trade and Civilization in the Indian Ocean: An Economic History from the Rise of Islam to 1750.* Cambridge: Cambridge University Press, 1985. A scholarly study of trade and Islam, with much on India and Southeast Asia.

Hall, Kenneth R. *Maritime Trade and State Development in Early Southeast Asia.* Honolulu: University of Hawaii Press, 1985. One of the few studies of trade and politics in Southeast Asia before 1500 C.E.

Higham, Charles. *The Civilization of Angkor.* Berkeley: University of California Press, 2001. A scholarly but readable summary of Cambodia's early history.

Kulke, Hermann, and Dietmar Rothermund. *History of India.* 4th ed. London and New York: Routledge, 2004. A concise but stimulating general history, incorporating recent scholarship on India in this era.

Mabbett, Ian, and David Chandler. *The Khmers.* London: Blackwell, 1995. An authoritative study of Cambodian history, with much on Angkor.

Rizvi, S. A. A. *The Wonder That Was India*, Part 2. New Delhi: Rupa and Company, 1987 (reprinted 2000). A comprehensive discussion of India under the impact of Islam from 1200 to 1700.

Thapar, Romila. *Early India: From the Origins to A.D. 1300.* Berkeley: University of California Press, 2003. A recent revision of the standard work by an Indian historian.

Websites

Internet Indian History Sourcebook (http://www.fordham.edu/halsall/india/indiasbook.html). An invaluable collection of sources and links on India.

WWW Southeast Asia Guide (http://www.library.wisc.edu/guides/SEAsia/). An impressive, easy-to-use site from the University of Wisconsin-Madison.

WWW Virtual Library: South Asia (http://www.columbia.edu/cu/libraries/indiv/area/sarai/). This Columbia University site offers many useful resources.

WWW Virtual Library: Southeast Asia (http://iias.leidenuniv.nl/wwwvl/southeast.html). A Dutch site offering portals to all the countries of the region.

CHAPTER **14**

Christian Societies in Medieval Europe, Byzantium, and Russia, 600–1500

CHAPTER OUTLINE
- Forming Christian Societies in Western Europe
- Medieval Societies
- Medieval Religion, Politics, and Thought
- Eastern Europe: Byzantines, Slavs, and Mongols
- Late Medieval Europe and the Roots of Expansion

■ **PROFILE**
Heloise, a French Scholar and Nun

■ **WITNESS TO THE PAST**
A Literary View of Late Medieval People

⚡ Online Study Center

This icon will direct you to interactive activities and study materials on the website: college.hmco.com/pic/lockard1e

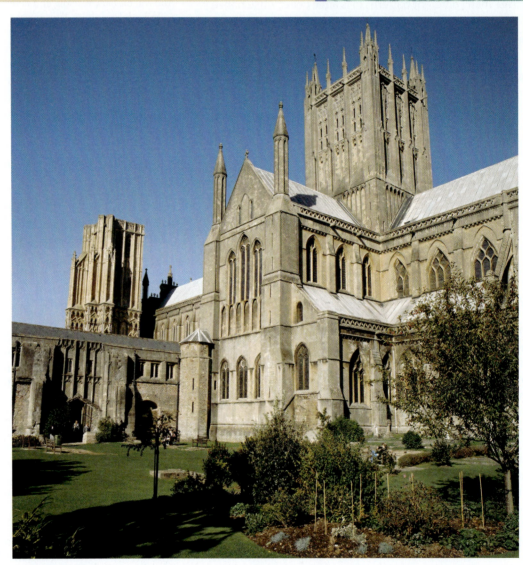

Wells Cathedral The importance of Christianity in European life was symbolized by magnificent cathedrals. This cathedral, built in the town of Wells in England in the thirteenth century C.E., was designed to reflect the glory of God. (Robert Harding World Imagery)

The most Christian man beloved by God, the glorious king of the Franks, while he was building this [Christian] monastery, wished that [its] consecration and the battles which he [waged] should not be consigned completely to oblivion.

MONASTERY DEDICATION ATTRIBUTED TO CHARLEMAGNE,
NINTH-CENTURY FRANKISH EMPEROR[1]

It was Christmas, 800 C.E., and the city of Rome, filled with magnificent buildings and monuments, still possessed majesty. Containing some three hundred Christian churches, Rome was the center of Roman Christendom. Along one of the many roads that connected the fabled metropolis to a wider Europe had come the most powerful ruler in Europe, Charlemagne (SHAHR-leh-mane), the Christian king of the Germanic people called the Franks, arriving from his capital of Aachen (AH-kuhn) some 700 miles away in what is now northwest Germany. He came to celebrate Christmas mass with Pope Leo III, the head of Christendom.

A towering man, 6 feet 4 inches tall, and wearing the Roman toga and colorful Greek cloak supplied by the pope, Charlemagne entered the spectacular St. Peter's cathedral. When the Christmas service ended, the pope placed upon Charlemagne's head a golden crown encrusted with sparkling jewels. Led by the pope, the crowd chanted, "Crowned by god, great and peace-loving Emperor of the Romans, life and victory."[2] Historians disagree as to whether Charlemagne expected to be crowned emperor of a new, church-blessed Roman Empire. But for the first time a pope had crowned an emperor and sought to shape monarchies. Indeed, for the next few centuries popes tried to influence secular affairs, while at the same time kings worked to control the church and, like Charlemagne, used religion—even the building of monasteries—for their own purposes. The complex relations between the Roman church and diverse European states helped shape the tapestry of European life in this era.

In the 1400s Italian historians first coined the term *medieval* to describe the centuries between the classical Romans and their own time. In their view, it was a superstitious and ignorant "Dark Age." But the reality of what later scholars often called the "Middle Ages" in Europe was more complex, and always in flux. Linked by networks of faith and culture, medieval western Europeans combined Christianity with practices inherited from both the Romans and Germanic groups like the Franks. The mix of religion and politics that saw Charlemagne anointed ruler by a church official and then build a monastery went back to an-

---

medieval A term first used in the 1400s by Italian historians to describe the centuries between the classical Romans and their own time.

cient times. But in both western Europe and Byzantium to the east, the strong influence of the Christian churches in all aspects of society, including politics, was an innovation. Furthermore, Christian culture also spread into northeastern Europe and Russia. Medieval people tended to think of themselves as part of Christendom rather than Europe.

The role and spread of Christianity were only one aspect of a Europe that changed considerably over the millennium between 500 and 1500. Europeans made their own history, but they also borrowed much from other cultures, especially from Muslims. In addition, the many tensions of European life, including conflicts between Christian leaders and kings for power, struggles between kings and nobles, debates over how to reconcile faith and reason, and the differing priorities of the rural-based aristocracy and urban merchants, fostered a competitive spirit that helped spur overseas exploration in the fifteenth century.

FOCUS QUESTIONS

1. How did Europeans create new societies between 500 and 1000?
2. What institutions shaped medieval European life?
3. How did the Christian church influence medieval religious, political, and intellectual life?
4. How did Byzantine society differ from that of western Europe?
5. What developments between 1300 and 1500 gave Europeans the incentive and means to begin reshaping the world after 1500?

Forming Christian Societies in Western Europe

How did Europeans create new societies between 500 and 1000?

The disintegration of the western Roman Empire in the fifth century C.E. led to political and social instability, which cleared the ground for the rise of new societies between 500 and 1000. Although classical education, building, and commerce faded in the first half of the medieval period, these were centuries of considerable creativity, spurred partly by the mixing of Roman and Germanic traditions as well as by relations with non-European peoples. While the societies of western Europe varied, they also developed many common cultural features, including a dominant Rome-based Christian church and similar social, political, and economic systems. The church helped create a unique European community of societies in this era. Economic change and technological development also set a foundation for a new Europe.

Environment and Geography

Climate change and disease were two of the factors that shaped post-Roman Europe. In contrast to the warmer weather of the middle Classical Era, a cooling climate brought shorter growing seasons between 500 and 900, after which warmer trends returned. The terrible plague that devastated Europe during Justinian's time reappeared occasionally through the eighth century. Given these challenges, it was not surprising that people turned to religion for support.

Between 200 and 800 western Europe also suffered repeated and prolonged incursions by migrating peoples. Various Germanic groups occupied much of the region, destroying forever the western Roman Empire and much of its culture. These developments prevented any imperial restoration like that in China, where classical society reemerged in stronger form during the Tang dynasty. Today few people study the Latin that was once the dominant language of the Mediterranean world.

Although classical unity was lost, Europe's favorable geography enabled many areas to develop similar religious, social, economic, and political patterns. Much of western and central Europe was blessed by fertile, well-watered plains rich in minerals, while a long coastline offered many fine harbors along the Mediterranean and Baltic Seas as well as along the Atlantic Ocean. Long navigable rivers such as the Danube (DAN-yoob) and Rhine (rine) and accessible mountain passes through the Alps made communication within the region much easier than for Asia, Africa, and South America. Hence, land and sea networks linked diverse societies, fostering the movement of ideas, products, peoples, technologies, and diseases.

CHRONOLOGY

	Early Medieval Western Europe	Later Medieval Western Europe	Byzantium and Russia
600	**750–1200** Viking attacks in Europe **768–814** Reign of Charlemagne		
800	**843** Treaty of Verdun		**988** Russian conversion to Christianity
1000		**1066** Norman conquest of England **1096–1444** Crusades	**1054** Schism between Roman and Byzantine churches
1200		**1337–1453** Hundred Years War **1348–1350** Peak of Black Death	**1237–1241** Mongol invasions
1400		**1420** Beginning of Portuguese exploration of Africa	**1453** Fall of Constantinople to Turks

Christians and Germans

As Roman power melted away, the church became the major source of authority, and local bishops and monasteries were often the only government in rural areas. Over time the bishops of Rome gained authority and prestige, eventually claiming the title of pope (Holy Father) and heading the vast church apparatus. Increasingly the papacy meant an independent church that was not controlled by any one government and that could assert its influence over kings.

The popes led a church that also included religious orders. From Christianity's earliest centuries, some men and women had tried to escape what they felt were the corruptions of cities by moving to caves or other isolated places to pray and prepare for Heaven. Many early monks were lonely hermits, but others joined monasteries, Christian communities for men who had taken holy orders, and created economic and social trends. For instance, monasteries grew their own food, and monks cleared forests for crops. Within the walls of some of the large monasteries, churchmen provided social services such as shelter for travelers, emergency food, and clothing for the poor. Some women joined convents for lives of service or prayer.

While monks tried to escape the concerns of society, they actually helped create a new culture. With the slogan "to work is to pray," monks filled their lives with activity to avoid idleness. They divided the day into periods of communal prayer and song, work in the fields, and intellectual labor such as copying manuscripts, eventually creating the bound book. By 850 one German monastery boasted a library of one thousand titles, all of them hand-copied. The willingness of monks to serve God and their neighbors with their hands as well as their hearts gave manual labor a respect that it never had in the classical Mediterranean world. Moreover, in fashioning their way of life, some monasteries almost became small towns. The abbey of St. Gall in Switzerland, for example, included churches and schools, clergy and nonclergy, workshops and granaries, and a hospital and baths, along with farm buildings.

During this time Christians also became more interested in converting "nonbelievers." The popes continued their efforts to spread the faith to those Germanic peoples who remained pagan and followed their ancient gods, such as the gods of war and weather and the goddess of love and fertility. Around 600 Pope Gregory I sanctioned turning pagan worship sites into churches rather than destroying them because "it is certainly impossible to eradicate all errors from obstinate minds at a stroke, and whoever wishes to climb to a mountaintop climbs gradually step by step, and not in one leap."[3] As a result of missionary efforts, the Anglo-Saxon kingdom of Kent in England converted and Canterbury (KAN-tuhr-bare-ee) became the headquarters of the new church in England. From there missionaries were sent to German lands. The most famous of these missionaries was Boniface (BON-uh-face) (ca. 675–754), a member of the Benedictine order who made journeys to Germany and won many converts.

But as the Christian religion spread north of the Alps, it began to change from what it had been at the time of Paul of Tarsus. Early Christians had expected the imminent second coming of Jesus and the end of the world. The passage of time undermined these beliefs but intensified the effort to convert people to Christianity. Once they had acquired key positions in governments, Christians often persecuted non-Christians by destroying their houses of worship or denying them government positions.

Christians helped spread the faith by blending German values and practices into their religion. For instance, Germans emphasized the presence of gods in nature and set up shrines in the woods where they could worship them. Christians changed these to special places where people could pray to particular holy men and women whose behavior while on earth merited their being acclaimed saints, such as the missionary Boniface. Similarly, the pagan use of special amulets or charms to ward off evil was changed to the Christian practice of wearing medals around the neck honoring Jesus or his mother. However, since the church was led by bishops who were upper-class members of the new German states, many Christian leaders began valuing warriors and fighting, which was not a prominent feature of early Christianity. Even local church leaders often were more concerned with protecting their territory and family than they were with promoting Christian values.

The Frankish and Holy Roman Empires

Between 500 and 1000 the political map of Europe changed. Muslim armies conquered North Africa, the eastern shore of the Mediterranean, and most of Spain during the seventh and early eighth centuries (see Chapter 10), and small Muslim bands raided Italy and France. The victory of the Frankish ruler Charles Martel (SHARL mahr-TEL) at the Battle of Tours (TOO-ers) in 732 finally stopped these raids (see Chronology: The Early Middle Ages, 500–1000). Following this victory, the Franks created a large state in western Europe.

In 753 Pope Stephen sought the aid of the Franks against the Germanic Lombard kingdom in northern Italy, which was threatening papal control of central Italy. He then anointed the Frankish king Pepin (PEP-in) the Short as the special protector of Italy. This blessing indicated both the sacred nature of kingship in western Christian thought and the pope's belief that he had the right to designate territorial rulers. In return for the pope sanctioning his authority, Pepin defeated the Lombards and, in 756, donated land in central Italy to the pope. This "Donation of Pepin" became the basis of the Papal States, a collection of small states surrounding Rome that remained under the political control of the popes for over 1,000 years. From this time on the attention of western Europe's chief religious leaders became divided between their spiritual and earthly concerns.

A new dynasty of Frankish rulers, known as the Carolingians (kah-roe-LIN-gee-uhnz) after their greatest ruler, Charlemagne (r. 768–814), soon controlled the Frankish kingdom. The special relationship between the popes and the Franks grew during the reign of Charlemagne, who was crowned by the pope in Rome, as dramatized in the opening of this chapter. Charlemagne spread Frankish power from France and northern Italy deep into the lands inhabited by another Germanic people, the Saxons, in north and central Germany. His Carolingian empire temporarily united the heart of west-

CHRONOLOGY	
The Early Middle Ages, 500–1000	
529	First Benedictine monastery
732	Battle of Tours
750–1200	Viking attacks in Europe
756–1492	Muslim states in Spain
768–814	Reign of Charlemagne over Franks
800	Papal crowning of Charlemagne
843	Division of Carolingian Empire in Treaty of Verdun
874	Viking settlement of Iceland
955	Defeat of Magyars
962	Revival of Holy Roman Empire by Otto the Great
986	First Norse settlements in Greenland

ern Europe (see Map 14.1). Charlemagne promoted both education and Christianity in his realm. He also used the church to strengthen his empire, since he appointed the bishops and priests, influenced the ceremonies and doctrines, and controlled the monasteries in his region. Charlemagne took great interest in the religious lives of his people, and he wanted church ritual, preaching, and presentation of scripture to be uniform throughout his lands. On one occasion, he issued instructions to the Saxons that anyone deliberately breaking the Lenten fast by eating meat should be executed. To enhance his power, Charlemagne also sent diplomatic missions to Byzantium and various Islamic states. These missions also probably involved some trade, thus creating a communications network with eastern Europe and the Middle East.

Frankish kings protected the Roman church. In 796 Charlemagne told Pope Leo III that he would defend the church from its enemies and that the pope's job was only "to assist the success of our arms with your hands raised in prayer to God."[4] In return for this protection and promotion of Christianity, however, Charlemagne and other rulers after him expected church leaders, from priests and bishops to abbots of monasteries, to be loyal to the king. When the pope crowned Charlemagne "Emperor of the Romans," he revived the Roman Empire in the west symbolically, if only temporarily. Papal relations with the Carolingian rulers also set the stage for later church-state conflict. Popes argued that lay control over church matters should only be exercised with papal approval, something that the coronation of Charlemagne seemed to signify. But later German rulers wanted some political control in Italy.

Charlemagne's empire did not long outlive him. It was divided among his three grandsons in the Treaty of Verdun (vuhr-DUN) in 843. The eldest, Lothar (LO-tar), received the

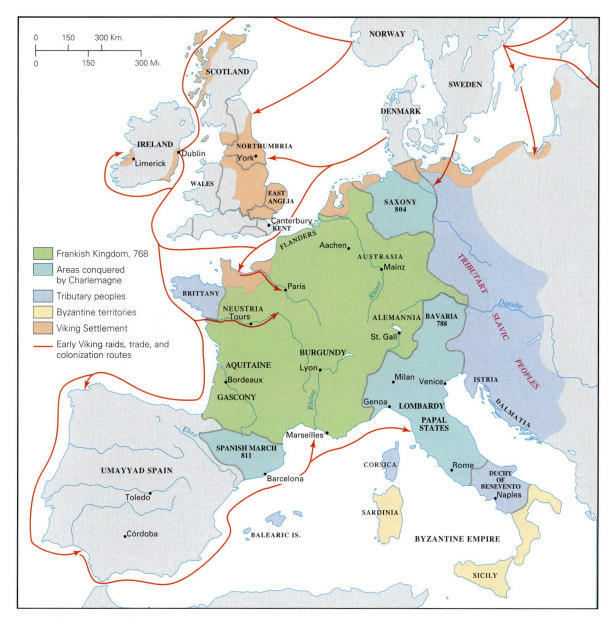

Map 14.1 Europe During the Carolingian Empire
At the height of their power under Charlemagne, the Carolingian rulers of the Franks controlled much of northwestern Europe, including what is today France, the Low Countries, western and southern Germany, and northern Italy.

imperial title and the middle portion of the empire, including the capital at Aachen, in modern-day Germany. Charles the Bald became king of West Francia, which became the heartland of modern France, and Louis the German ruled East Francia, the predominantly Saxon territory that became Germany.

Eventually other Germanic peoples challenged the Franks for influence. The Saxon ruler Otto I, known as Otto the Great (r. 936–973), a Saxon who had replaced the Frankish king in East Francia, was responsible for the creation of a new German empire. Otto established his control over rebellious princes in Germany and the next year took an army into northern Italy.

In 962 the pope, grateful for Otto's help against the Lombards, declared Otto "Roman Emperor." From this point until 1806, rulers in Germany retained this title, eventually proclaiming their lands to be the "Holy Roman Empire." But this empire had little in common with the classical Roman Empire. Much of its territory had never been under Roman control. Most Germans, Italians, Slavs, Czechs, and Hungarians within its domains had little sense of common citizenship or even much awareness of the political connections beyond the local level. Like the Carolingians before them, Otto and his successors continued to both defend and dominate the church, even appointing bishops in their lands.

Viking Longship This longship from the ninth century, excavated from a burial mound in Norway in 1904, boasted intricate decorations and carvings. Probably used for ceremonial purposes, it became the burial chamber of a royal Viking woman. (© University Museum of Cultural Heritage, University of Oslo, Norway)

Vikings and Other Invaders

The European heartland continued to attract other peoples seeking wealth. The biggest threat came from the Vikings, or Northmen, who faced population pressures that led them to launch raids out of home bases in Scandinavia, a region with limited productive farmland. Viking warriors burned and looted Christian towns and monasteries in England, France, Holland, and Ireland. While rumors may have exaggerated Viking atrocities, it was a scary time and people prayed: "From the violence of the men from the north, O Lord, deliver us."[5] In addition to being fearsome raiders, the Vikings were skilled craftsmen who built ingenious shallow-draft boats capable of both oceanic and riverine voyages.

Between 750 and 1200 various Vikings raided, traded, and settled around Europe. Some Swedish Vikings moved east into the heartland of what is today Russia, establishing several states and also sailing downriver to the Black Sea to trade with Byzantium and the Middle East. Swedes also conquered the Finns, a Ural-Altaic-speaking people from North Asia who had moved into eastern Scandinavia and northern Russia during classical times. Danish and Norse Vikings established permanent settlements in coastal England, Ireland (among them Dublin), and the islands north of Scotland. Other Vikings eventually settled down in western France, in Normandy (NOR-muhn-dee) (named after Normans or Northmen). Normans who descended from these Vikings conquered England in 1066. By 1072 other Normans had founded a kingdom in southern Italy and Sicily. Eventually the Viking peoples in Scandinavia adopted Christianity and established the kingdoms of Denmark, Norway, and Sweden.

Eventually the Vikings both at home and abroad became part of mainstream European society, giving up raiding for trade and farming. Those Vikings who settled outside Scandinavia adopted the cultures and faiths of the local Celtic, Latin, Germanic, or Slavic peoples. But their heritage remains in the many place names and words in the local languages. For example, around nine hundred English words have a Danish origin, including *dirt, egg, sky, Thursday,* and *window.*

The Vikings left other legacies too. Among the world's greatest maritime explorers, Norse Vikings began settling Iceland in 874 and founded several settlements on Greenland around 986. A century later, around 1000, a small group of Vikings based in Greenland established an outpost along the coast of eastern Canada, and Vikings made occasional trading visits to the area for the next several centuries. These Viking explorers also fostered a democratic ideal. The growing agricultural society in Iceland created an elected assembly in 930 to make and administer laws, and the Greenland Norse followed their example.

Two warlike peoples, the Bulgars (BUL-gahrz) and Magyars (MAG-yahrz), migrated from Russia into central Europe. The Slavic Bulgars created a large state between the Byzantine and Frankish empires during the ninth century. However, they were contained by Byzantine armies, and eventually they converted to Eastern Orthodox Christianity and settled in the eastern Balkan region known today as Bulgaria. The Magyars, excellent horsemen who spoke a Ural-Altaic language related to Turkish, moved from north of the Black Sea into the Hungarian plain, threatening Germany and Italy. This threat was contained when German forces under Otto the Great crushed a large Magyar army in 955. The Magyars then settled permanently in Hungary and adopted Roman Christianity.

Early Medieval Trade, the Muslim World, and Spain

Economic factors, especially trade, also shaped the new Europe. While most Europeans were peasants, growing food or raising livestock for sale at local markets, some were merchants who traded products such as wool hides, salt, fish, wine, and grain over long distances, often by sea or riverboat. As it had for centuries, trade continued briskly in the eastern Mediterranean, where it was tightly controlled by the Byzantine rulers. Trade between the Franks and Constantinople flourished at various times.

As time passed the east-west trade grew dynamic. The northeastern Italian city of Venice, built on its lagoons in the fifth century, was an active trading center throughout the Middle Ages. Venice and Genoa, on Italy's northwest coast, competed to dominate trade with the Middle East and Byzantium, negotiating agreements with Muslim rulers who distrusted most other Christian states. Other Italian cities, such as Milan and Naples, remained connected to the Byzantine economy. Even the most remote northern towns received occasional visits from merchants, and aristocrats purchased luxury goods such as silk produced in the East. By 800, multiple networks of exchange were reconnecting western Europeans to each other and to eastern Europe and the increasingly Islamic Middle East.

As trade increased, Europeans benefited from the growing connections with, and borrowings from, the Muslim world. Islamic expansion stimulated a wider movement of people, goods, and information, such as Asian science and classical Greek thought, that gradually influenced many Afro-Eurasian societies. The exchange of products and ideas between Islamic Spain and Sicily, where various cultures met, and Christian Europe proved especially fruitful for European intellectual life.

In the eighth and ninth centuries, Arab Muslims conquered Sicily and much of Spain, where they created cosmopolitan societies and several strong states (see Chapter 10). Scholars and merchants from all over the Mediterranean world gravitated to great Spanish cities such as Cordoba. For example, Jewish merchants from the Carolingian realm regularly visited Cordoba. The meeting of Christian, Jewish, and Muslim traditions in Muslim-ruled Spain and Sicily allowed the philosophical, scientific, and technological writings of many Classical Greek and Indian as well as Persian and Arab thinkers to spread among educated Europeans. In the 1140s, an Italian translator of Arabic texts wrote that "it befits us to imitate the Arabs especially, for they are our teachers and the pioneers."[6]

Technology, Agricultural Growth, and Industry

The development of new technology helped establish the economic foundations of medieval Europe, especially in farming and power generation. This technology was often borrowed from other societies, even across long distances, but it was adapted to suit local needs. Various technological improvements, some originating in Asia, came into common use in western Europe during these early centuries, laying the basis for European expansion after 1000.

Some of the major technological innovations improved agriculture. Three devices or practices spurred the higher grain yields that sparked population growth in Europe. The first was the rugged *moldboard plow,* which included a blade that dug the earth and an attached moldboard that turned over the furrow. This new plow enabled farmers to turn and drain the heavy, wet soil of northern Europe, where such difficult farming conditions had kept the populations sparse. Germans probably invented the moldboard plow after finding that the simpler Roman scratch plow used in the sandier Mediterranean soils was inadequate. The second improvement was the horseshoe, which Europeans adopted from Central Asians in the ninth century. Horseshoes allowed farmers to make greater use of horses to plow fields, especially when they were combined with the third device, the horse

"Tilling the Fields"   Most medieval Europeans were peasants growing food. This French painting from the 1400s shows peasants working land on a manor.
(The Bridgeman Art Library International)

collar. Invented in China and adopted by Germanic peoples, the horse collar distributed the weight of the burden across the animal's shoulders so that the horse could pull more weight and work longer hours.

The most crucial agricultural improvement was the three-field system, introduced in the eighth century to replace the Roman two-field system. Europeans divided their fields into three parts and let only one-third lie fallow each year; they then increased their yield by planting winter and summer wheat in the other two fields. Peasants were also learning to plant more beans and other nitrogen-fixing crops, which returned nutrition to the soil. Increased grain consumption produced a better-balanced diet. All of these measures multiplied the food supply.

Other innovations fostered the growth of industry. First invented in Roman times, watermills were built along rivers and streams to generate power. This technology spread widely in early medieval times, freeing up human and animal labor for other tasks. By 1056 there were over 5,600 watermills in England, providing power for such activities as sawing logs and grinding wheat into flour. Waterpower allowed some industries to be mechanized. For example, by the late tenth century a French mill was making beer. By the 1100s Europeans also used windmills, invented in Persia around 650, to generate power for such industries as grinding grain. By then the wheelbarrow had also reached Europe from China.

SECTION SUMMARY

- With the decline of the Roman Empire, the Christian church became a power in its own right with influence over kings, and monasteries created a new culture that respected manual labor.

- Under Germanic influence, Christians more aggressively spread their faith, assimilating pagan practices and transforming them into Christian ones and sometimes persecuting non-Christians, as well as beginning to value warfare and fighting.

- During this time the Papal States were created, Charlemagne's Carolingian empire temporarily united much of Europe, and Otto the Great began the tradition of calling Germany the "Holy Roman Empire."

- The Vikings of Scandinavia, who raided European lands for over four centuries, were also good traders and eventually settled in Iceland, Greenland, and various European territories; they also made forays to eastern Canada and experimented with democracy.

- As merchants engaged in growing networks of exchange, trade with the expanding Muslim world and contact with Muslim Spain introduced Europeans to Classical Greek, Indian, Arab, and Persian ideas.

- Technological advances such as the moldboard plow, the horseshoe, and the horse collar improved agriculture, as did the three-field system, and the watermill helped to improve European industry.

Medieval Societies

What institutions shaped medieval European life?

Medieval Europe was dominated by several institutions, three of which were paramount between 800 and 1300. The papacy, of course, was significant in religion and church-state relations. The other two institutions were feudalism in the realm of politics and social structure, and manorialism in the realm of economics. Both developed from roots that lay in the later centuries of the Roman Empire. Neither was uniform in western Europe, varying greatly across the region. Brisk economic activity also marked medieval Europe, including increasing trade encouraged in part by the growth of towns. The pluralism of religious, social, political, and economic institutions forged in early medieval Europe, combined with an unusually warm climate, spurred changes in many areas of life between 1000 and 1300, centuries historians term the "High Middle Ages."

The Emergence of Feudalism

A concept that is controversial among historians, **feudalism** was a term introduced in sixteenth-century England to describe the complex and decentralized social, political, and economic system of previous centuries. Eventually modern scholars defined feudalism as a political arrangement characterized by a weak central monarchy ruling over smaller states or influential families that were largely autonomous but owed service obligations to the monarch. In turn, these influential families, or "nobles," ruled over the warriors or farmers on their estates who owed them service. In both cases the ruler was a "lord" and his subordinates were **vassals.** Monarchs were lords to nobles, and nobles were lords to most of the common people. In medieval Europe noble families often held large estates in exchange for paying homage and offering military service or labor to the royal governments. Likewise, warriors in a landowner's service and farmers living and working on the land also owed obligations to the landowner. Church leaders supported this arrangement, arguing that "it is the will of the Creator that the higher shall always rule over the lower. Each individual and each class should stay in its place [and] perform its tasks."[7] This basic political and social formation, with its complex network of ties, was strongest in France, England, and parts of Italy.

Some historians consider the concept of feudalism to be simplistic and misleading, an overgeneralization of the complex lord-vassal relationship and land ownership patterns. But while it may be a flawed concept, feudalism can help illuminate

---

feudalism　A political arrangement characterized by a weak central monarchy ruling over smaller state or influential families that were largely autonomous but owed service obligations to the monarch.

vassal　In medieval Europe, a subordinate person owing service to a lord.

medieval life. For example, it helps explain why many monarchs of states where feudal relations prevailed had little power beyond the immediate area around their capital. Some small states were part of a larger unit, such as the Holy Roman Empire, their princes owing allegiance to the king but also exercising power in the states they ruled.

Despite the unifying role of the Christian church in creating a common culture and the accomplishments of strong rulers such as Charlemagne and Otto the Great, certain forces worked toward the decentralization and fragmentation that characterized feudalism during the early medieval period. The old Roman roads had fallen into disrepair, disrupting transportation and long-distance trade, and Europe remained sparsely populated and largely rural. Cities were few north of the Alps. The most densely populated region, France, boasted a population of only 8 or 9 million people, and, as late as 1000, England had only a million and a half. Europe as a whole was home to around 40 million by 950. By contrast, early Song China had around 100 million.

These conditions made it difficult for even a strong ruler to maintain a powerful central government. Since both money and talent were scarce and land was the source of wealth, Charlemagne often rewarded his best soldiers and administrators by giving them control over large areas of land. Vassals who held such grants of land from a lord, called **benefices**, took an oath of personal loyalty to the king and promised him military service. In return they had a virtually free hand to govern the territory, collect taxes from the people who lived on that land, and administer justice. This delegation of authority led to political fragmentation.

Historians of medieval Europe often use the concept of feudalism in a narrow sense of legal relations between lords and vassals. The term *fief* described the thing granted in a feudal contract. Although this was usually land, it could also be something such as the right to collect tolls on a bridge. The vassal might also be obliged to provide hospitality to the ruler when he traveled around his kingdom. If a fief of land were large enough, as many were, the vassal could subdivide it and have vassals of his own. Thus feudalism allowed a king to rule a large country without personally administering it through his own paid officials. This rule through subordinates, and subordinates of subordinates, was most common in England, especially after William, Duke of Normandy, conquered that island in 1066 and set up a feudal monarchy (see Chronology: The High Middle Ages, 1000–1300).

Feudal society included **knights**, armored military retainers who swore allegiance to their lord and who fought mostly on horseback. Since warhorses and elaborate armor were expensive, lords imposed this expense on their vassals. A large peasant class that was, for the most part, denied military and therefore political power, supported the warriors at the top.

---

benefices In medieval Europe, grants of land from lord to vassal.

fief In medieval Europe, the thing granted in a feudal contract, usually land.

knights In medieval Europe, armored military retainers on horseback who swore allegiance to their lord.

CHRONOLOGY

The High Middle Ages, 1000–1300

987–1328	Capetian kings in France
1066	Norman conquest of England
1095–1272	Christian Crusades to reclaim Holy Land
1198–1216	High point of medieval papacy under Innocent III
1215	Signing of Magna Carta
1231	Beginning of Inquisition
1265	First English Parliament

Knights had a rigid code of behavior, including a sense of duty and honor known as **chivalry**. A thirteenth-century French writer explained the chivalric ideal: "A knight must be hardy, courteous, generous, loyal and of fair speech; ferocious to his foe, frank and debonair to his friend. [He] has proved himself in arms and thereby won the praise of men."[8] Most of us have romantic images of medieval knights wielding lances in jousts or defending maidens from fire-breathing dragons, but the reality was usually more mundane. Knights wore 60 pounds of chain-mail armor. As a result, they often felled by heat exhaustion. The steel suits of armor seen in museums did not come into general use until the 1400s. Since states and rival lords fought each other regularly, knights were kept busy. But despite the dangers, the rewards could be great. For instance, one of the most renowned English knights, William Marshall (1145–1219), became very wealthy, an adviser to kings, and married a woman from an aristocratic family.

The mounted cavalry was medieval Europe's chief fighting force, and the innovation that made it possible was the stirrup. Central Asians probably borrowed stirrup technology from the Chinese and spread it to western Europe, where it was used by Frankish warriors when they defeated the Arabs in 732. The stirrup, which enabled the knight to stand when delivering a blow, made him much more powerful than if he delivered a blow while seated. Thus it contributed greatly to the knight's fighting power.

Manorialism and the Slave Trade

The rural economy was based on **manorialism**, a system of autonomous, nearly self-sufficient agricultural estates. The roots were laid in late Roman imperial practices. As the Roman cities

---

chivalry The rigid code of behavior, including a sense of duty and honor, of medieval European knights.

manorialism The medieval European system of autonomous, nearly self-sufficient agricultural estates.

became expensive places to live, wealthy Romans retreated to their large country estates and hired low-wage agricultural workers, who were also looking for security during dangerous times. Eventually these Roman states became the manors, the combination of farms and villages into which each territorial fief was divided. With money and trade goods in short supply, each manor was responsible for its own needs, from mills to grind the grain and press grapes for the wine to blacksmiths to shoe the horses.

The manors, often organized around a castle, were owned by nobles who had the right to the produce grown by the large class of hereditary **serfs,** peasants who were legally bound to their lord and tied to the land through the generations. Serfs tilled the lord's fields as well as their own and were given, instead of money, the use of the manor's resources, such as farming tools or crafts, and protection in the manor house or castle in case the settlement was attacked. Although serfs were not allowed to change their status or leave without permission, they were not the personal property of their lords. If they were tied to the land, the land was also tied to them. They could not be dispossessed unless they failed to live up to their obligations. Serfs were warned by lords and priests to work hard to receive their eventual reward in Heaven. Their security and stability were paid for with compliance and a lifetime of drudgery. Occasional peasant revolts, sometimes targeting the lords and ladies of the manor, indicated some dissatisfaction. But the rural life also had some pleasures. An Irish verse from the ninth century praised the "three sounds of increase: the lowing of a cow in milk; the din of the smithy; the swish of a plough."[9]

Although serfdom gradually became far more pervasive, slavery did not disappear altogether in Europe. Slaves were mostly used for farming in England, where they constituted perhaps 10 percent of the population until the eleventh century. They were also common in Italy and Spain, where many were domestic servants. Slaves worked the estates owned by the popes, and some French monasteries owned thousands of slaves to work their farms. Slavery was familiar enough that the Roman church developed rules for the humane treatment of slaves. Leading Christian thinkers like St. Thomas Aquinas argued that slavery was morally justified and an economic necessity.

Slave trading was a key part of the medieval economy. Complex networks of trade transported slaves all over Europe and the Middle East. An active Mediterranean slave trade based in Byzantium bought or seized slaves, mostly Slavs, Greeks, Turks, and Caucasus peoples, from the Black Sea region and shipped them to southern Europe and North Africa. The Carolingians and Venetians sold slaves from various European societies to the Arabs. Vikings enslaved captives and also sold English and French slaves to Byzantium and Islamic Spain. By the 1400s Arabs and Portuguese were selling some enslaved West Africans in southern Europe.

Medieval Cities and Towns

European societies experienced considerable change during the High Middle Ages, including the growth of population, towns, and cities. Compared to Byzantium, Tang China, and the Islamic world, early medieval western Europe was economically underdeveloped, a reality reflected in the size of cities: by 1000 Rome had only 35,000 people, Paris around 20,000, and London an insignificant 10,000. By contrast, Constantinople had 300,000, Kaifeng in China had 400,000, Cordoba in Muslim Spain nearly 500,000, and the world's largest city, Baghdad, a million people. However, between 1000 and 1300 the increased food resulting from the new methods of growing crops spurred Europe's population to double to about 75 million. As people from the neighboring countryside went to buy and sell agricultural produce and other goods necessary for daily life, western European cities increased in both population and importance, becoming centers of trade and industry. Milan and Paris grew to almost 100,000 during these three centuries. London had at least 30,000 people by 1300 and a problem with air pollution due to the burning of coal.

As in our own day, some medieval people thought cities were degenerate places. An eleventh-century English monk detested London:

> I do not like that city. All sorts of men crowd together there from every country under the heavens. Each race brings its own vices. No one lives in it without falling into some sort of crime. Actors, jesters, smooth-skinned lads, flatterers, effeminates, pederasts, singing and dancing girls, quacks, belly-dancers, sorceresses, extortioners, magicians, mimes, beggars, buffoons: all this tribe fill all the houses. Therefore, if you do not want to dwell with evildoers, do not live in London.[10]

Indeed, a variety of characters inhabited the medieval city. City life and the money to be made attracted many people to places such as London and Paris, then as now. A traditional German expression, "city air makes one free," referred to the fact that a serf who left the manor and was able to spend "a year and a day" in a city without being caught was considered legally free.

Cities increasingly operated outside the feudal social and political structure. City craftsmen and merchants organized themselves into **guilds,** collective fraternal organizations designed to protect the economic interests of members and to win exemptions from feudal obligations. Eventually city charters, secured from the local lord or the king, allowed the cities to have their own courts, run by local people, and other privileges of self-government. Rulers granted such privileges because of the great wealth that city commerce and payments brought them.

---

serfs In medieval Europe, peasants legally bound to their lord and tied to the land through generations.

guilds In medieval Europe, collective fraternal organizations of craftsmen and merchants designed to protect the economic interests of their members.

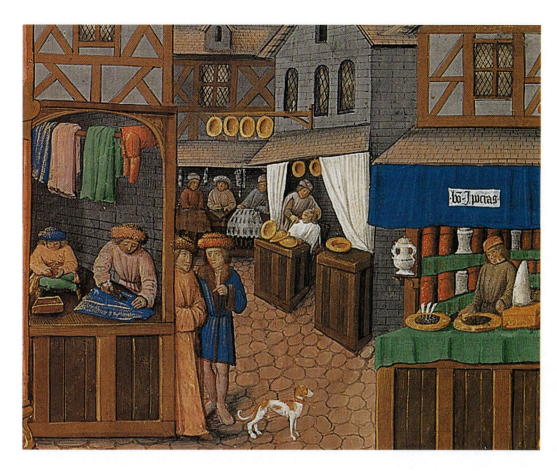

A Medieval Town This painting shows a variety of town enterprises, including a tailor's shop, barbershop, and an apothecary. (Bibliotheque nationale de France)

Merchants and Expanding Trade

The expansion of cities and commerce opened new possibilities for merchants, but they had to overcome social prejudices. In feudal society, people belonged to one of three categories, in order of importance: "those who prayed" (churchmen, priests, and monks), "those who fought" (aristocratic warriors, knights), and "those who worked" (peasants and serfs). No matter how successful, merchants and bankers had no place in this hierarchy. As an outsider, the best way for a merchant to acquire status in society was to marry the daughter of an impoverished aristocrat who needed the merchant's financial support. In this way the merchant could acquire land. But most merchants also shared society's values, including a strong Christian faith. For example, the English merchant Godric of Pinchale (ca. 1069–1170) left home as a teenager to peddle goods in nearby villages. A few years later he had enough money to travel abroad and trade goods by sea between England, Scotland, Denmark, and Holland. Eventually he owned a small fleet of vessels and became quite wealthy. Like many in that era, he never married. Godric was also deeply religious, visiting the shrines of saints and making pilgrimages to Jerusalem. Later in life he gave away all his wealth to the poor and became a hermit, writing religious poetry and gaining fame for his piety.

People resented merchants for several reasons. For one, some traveled long distances to strange places that were inhabited by foreigners who might corrupt their beliefs or morals.

For another, some merchants were aggressive in seeking wealth. Merchants sold goods for more than they paid for them. Greed was considered a serious sin, and profitmaking seemed unfair. Medieval people were particularly upset at merchants' and bankers' practice of loaning money at interest, which was regarded as **usury.** This looked like stealing because the lender was making a profit without doing any labor. As a result, usurers were accused of greed and of lacking charity. But while regarded as a sin, moneylending was necessary to commerce, and even popes borrowed money at interest on occasion. While Italians became renowned as bankers, moneylending elsewhere was left largely to Jews. In that way Christians benefited from borrowing money without committing the sin of lending at interest. Gradually using and lending money became more acceptable in later medieval times.

Long-distance trade reached its peak between 1100 and 1350. As during the Classical Era, trade in luxury goods from Byzantium and Asia flourished. Western Europeans shipped woolen textiles, flax, hemp, wines, olive oil, fruit, and timber to the East in return for luxury goods such as spices, silk, perfumes, and precious gems. Eastern Europeans exported grain, honey, fish, fur, and slaves, as well as raw materials such as iron, copper, tin, and lead.

One of the clearest signs of economic expansion, and of declining prejudice against merchants, was the growth in trade

usury The practice of loaning money at interest; considered a sin in medieval Europe, although necessary to commerce.

and commerce around Europe. Major trading centers were located on the Mediterranean (Constantinople, Venice, Genoa), in the Low Countries (Bruges [broozh] and Amsterdam), and in Strassburg in the Rhineland, Nuremberg (NOOR-uhm-burg) in south Germany, and Basel (BAHZ-uhl) in Switzerland. Italian merchants acquired goods from the Middle East and Byzantium and shipped them over the Alps to what is today Belgium and Holland in exchange for the woolen textiles manufactured there. One feudal French ruler, the Count of Champagne (shahm-PAHN-yuh), took advantage of this trade by establishing the famous "fairs of Champagne," where goods were displayed at six town fairs, each lasting seven weeks. The count provided services for the merchants, regulated weights and measures, held court in cases of disputes among fair goers, and collected tolls for his services. The Champagne fairs were ended in the 1300s when the Italian cities began to ship goods by sea to the Low Countries and England.

The wealth created in Europe through such activities as the Champagne fairs fostered a commercial revolution and made merchants and bankers more influential. By the 1200s, commerce had become more central to the European economy than agriculture. Never again would western Europe have an economy that relied primarily on farming. The broad repercussions of the commercial revolution—the rise of capitalism; new social classes, including the incorporation of merchants as a vital social class; stronger monarchies; and the weakening of both feudalism and the Christian church—became clear only centuries later. In the short term, both the popes and the political leaders of Europe seemed stronger than ever. But the merchant class gradually gained political and economic power to challenge feudal nobles and eventually the monarchies.

Family Life and Gender Relations

Medieval society was patriarchal, though family life and gender relations varied with social status and local customs. Generally, men supported the family and women ran the household and raised children. Legally, marriage existed to protect legitimate children and guarantee property rights. Sons were considered more important than daughters, since sons passed on the family line, property, and name. Parents arranged most marriages. Men were allowed to have sex outside marriage, while women were valued for their virginity and faithfulness to their husbands. Relationships between men and women reflected the tensions between the church and secular society. From the church's point of view, marriage was only a necessary evil. Marriage legitimized sex only for procreation, not pleasure. A leading theologian, St. Thomas Aquinas, contended that "woman was created to help man, but only in the act of procreation, because in all other tasks he can find far better support elsewhere." One priest even warned married people to avoid sex on the Sabbath for "monsters, cripples, and all sickly children [are] conceived on Saturday nights."[11] Rulers often flouted custom. For instance, Charlemagne enforced rigid Christian morality on his people while also marrying four times, having five mistresses, and siring eighteen children.

Today's Western middle-class model of a husband, wife, and their unmarried children living in one independent household, separate from the larger family, was the exception rather than the rule. For one thing, compared to women in much of the rest of the world, many medieval women tended to marry late, in their early twenties, and large numbers of both men and women remained unmarried. For another, childhood was short. Children often left their birth families at an early age to become apprentices in a trade, servants, or novices in religious orders. Laws favoring men encouraged many young women to join Christian convents, all-female religious communities where they could find physical and social protection and possibilities for leadership.

Medieval society had an almost contradictory view of women. On the one hand, gender stereotypes in the Bible led people to believe that women had to be subordinate to men and were depraved, leading men into sin, as Eve did Adam. Women were also considered intellectually inferior to men. On the other hand, Mary, the Virgin Mother of Jesus, became one of the most popular objects of devotion. Many cathedrals were named after Notre Dame (NO-truh DAHM) ("Our Lady"). Furthermore, women could inherit property and pass it on to their children. Women worked in many occupations, including farming, ale making, small-scale trade, glassmaking, and the textile industry. Like women in all societies, they worked less if they were rich and more if they were poor.

By the 1100s **courtly love,** a new standard of passionate but pure relationships between knights and ladies and celebrated in song by wandering troubadours, brought romance to male-female relations and elevated the status of aristocratic women. The model of courtly love probably originated in Muslim Spain, where women poets flourished, and was passed on to French and Italian authors. But whether courtly or not, romantic love existed mostly outside of marriage. Both the cult of the Virgin Mary and the great courtly love poems of the troubadours put well-born women on a pedestal as morally superior to men. In medieval tales, knights often sought the favors of fair maidens (usually the wife of another, perhaps their lord) who were unattainable. Since adultery was considered a high crime, the knight's love was usually unrequited.

The early Christian tolerance of homosexuality survived through the Early Middle Ages. Although various church leaders and some rulers, especially the Carolingians, condemned what they called "sodomites," after the immoral inhabitants of the biblical city of Sodom, public attitudes toward same sex relationships were often more accepting. Indeed, considerable homosexual fiction and poetry was published in the eleventh and twelfth centuries. Several prominent bishops and English kings, possibly including Richard I (known as Richard the Lion-Hearted) were highly respected men who were thought to be homosexuals. Beginning in the thirteenth century, however, public attitudes shifted. As states became stronger, they

---

courtly love A standard of polite relationships between knights and ladies that arose in the 1100s in medieval Europe. Courtly love was celebrated in song by wandering troubadours.

promoted uniformity in social relations and religious views, and fostered suspicion of those perceived as outside the social and religious mainstream. Furthermore, the church launched a violent campaign agains heresy and unconventional behavior that often targeted people suspected of homosexuality. In 1250 homosexual behavior was legal in most of Europe; by 1300 it had become a capital offense everywhere except Germany and south Italy.

Outsiders

Medieval society was tightly ordered but also rife with tensions. Daily life was precarious for rich and poor alike, and violent crime remained common throughout the period, with disputes often ending in murder. Many tensions, however, arose because medieval society made a major distinction between Christians and "outsiders"—pagans, Muslims, Jews, and heretics. No matter how poor or overworked medieval serfs were, they considered themselves superior to outsiders. By the High Middle Ages, Christians used the term *pagan* to describe Muslims, who reciprocated by calling Christians *infidels* (unbelievers). The drive to destroy all beliefs outside of the Christian mainstream eventually led to a long series of crusades against Islam and persecution of Jews.

Many European towns had Jewish communities. Jews worked in a variety of occupations but were best known as merchants and bankers and were welcome as moneylenders because Christians were forbidden to loan money at interest. But they often earned resentment for their commercial success and moneylending and so often became the scapegoats for misfortunes, such as epidemics, that were hard to explain. Although Christians mostly tolerated the Jews before 1150, anti-Semitism (AN-tee SEM-uh-tiz-uhm) soon increased dramatically as more Christians took up banking and marginalized Jewish rivals, and as Christians became more militant in asserting their faith. In 1182 the Jews were ordered to leave France, and this expulsion was imitated in other countries during the next three centuries. Restrictions were placed on Jewish businesses and residences. Our modern term *ghetto* was originally used to describe the part of medieval cities where the Jews were compelled to live. Numerous expelled Jews migrated to Poland and Byzantium, which developed large Jewish populations.

The disdain that was directed at Muslims and Jews was also directed at people considered to be heretics. Christians struggled with defining what was correct belief and what was heresy from the early centuries onward, and this concern intensified after 1200. Some devout Christians criticized church corruption, including ill-educated priests and arrogant bishops, but church leaders tended to view any reformers challenging their power as heretics. As a result, they organized military attacks on the Albigensians (AL-buh-JEN-shunz), a group in southern France who criticized the church's material wealth, urged clerical poverty, and wanted the Bible to be translated from Latin into the vernacular languages such as French and German so that ordinary people could read it for themselves. The church's crusade destroyed the Albigensians by killing their followers and confiscating their property.

SECTION SUMMARY

- ■ Feudalism was a medieval political arrangement in which a king gave nobles the right to rule over sections of his territory in exchange for their allegiance.
- ■ The owners of rural manors had a right to the crops of their serfs, peasants who were bound to the land, and they were protected by their knights, armored warriors on horseback.
- ■ Agricultural advances helped to fuel growing populations in European cities, though they remained smaller than cities in the Muslim world and China.
- ■ As trade in luxury goods flourished, European merchants gradually attained power, but they suffered from people's image of them as greedy and usurious.
- ■ Medieval society was patriarchal and considered women to be inferior to men; children usually left home early; and most marriages were arranged by parents to ensure property rights—the ideal of courtly love applied largely to extramarital affection or unrequited love.
- ■ In the Early Middle Ages homosexuality was widely tolerated, but by the Late Middle Ages it had become unacceptable.
- ■ Much of the tensions in medieval society were caused by the intolerance for "outsiders": non-Christians and heretics, Muslims, and Jews, all of whom were disdained and treated harshly, killed (as in the Crusades), or expelled.

Medieval Religion, Politics, and Thought

How did the Christian church influence medieval religious, political, and intellectual life?

Europeans experienced both exuberance and turmoil during the High Middle Ages. Massive cathedrals with lofty spires inspiring deep emotions were built, and the first universities were established. The power of the Roman church and its popes grew, fostering conflict with rulers and intellectuals. The earlier cooperation that had existed between church leaders and rulers changed into confrontation. European societies were beset by tensions not only between religious and lay rulers but also between Roman and Byzantine Christian leaders and between Christians and Muslims. These varied conflicts, along with the growing divergence between cities, with their merchant classes, and the traditional feudal aristocrats ruling in the countryside, helped reshape European society.

The Church as a Social and Political Force

The medieval Christian church claimed to help its members reach Heaven and avoid Hell. But the church of the High Middle Ages, contrary to today's understanding of the separation of church from state, was also a powerful social and political force. Indeed, the powerful bonds that linked people to their clergy allowed popes, for a time at least, to challenge kings.

Priests, Sacraments, and Reforms   The basis of clerical power was the sacrament, a rite believed to be a spiritual milestone and source of divine grace. Most medieval Christians measured the stages of their lives by sacraments such as baptism and matrimony. Socially, the sacraments tied the church closely to its people, since sacraments had to be administered by a priest. In the village church, people did not just receive spiritual nourishment but also did business, as in a modern courthouse. Priests certified births and marriages, and the parish church was also where people paid taxes.

Medieval priests had enormous power, since they controlled both individuals' privileges in this life and their salvation in the next. The faithful believed that a person who died in a state of serious sin (without confessing it to a priest) went straight to Hell. Priests and bishops had the power to deny someone the sacraments, which were considered necessary for salvation. They could also **excommunicate**, or expel a person from the church and its sacraments, an act that was probably more psychologically damaging than the modern act of destroying someone's social security records and thus making him or her a nonperson when it comes time to retire.

Complicating the power of priests was the fact that not all of them lived up to their responsibilities or growing expectations for celibacy. Many priests had so little education that they could barely recite the Latin necessary for the celebration of the Catholic liturgy. Some were corrupt and took bribes. Many priests and monks were married, a practice that reformist church leaders attempted to end between the eleventh and thirteenth centuries, both because they felt priests should not be distracted by families and also because they did not want priests to try to pass on their parishes to their children. Nonetheless, even after the final ban some priests were married in violation of church law, some kept mistresses, and others were either homosexual or assumed by their communities to be so. Under such conditions, it is understandable that many people had ambivalent attitudes toward the clergy. Priests were feared because of their power and ridiculed because of their shortcomings. In some societies, it was considered bad luck to meet a priest on the street, and in eleventh-century Denmark, priests were considered "bearers of bad weather, infections, and 'bodily plagues.'"[12]

In the eleventh century, reformers attempted to change the church and end abuses by priests, monks, and high officials. New religious orders tried to restore monastic life to its original purity, insisting, among other things, that all monks remain celibate. Several German rulers revived the papacy by appointing a series of reform-minded men to the position of pope. In addition to mandating clerical celibacy, these popes tried to end **simony** (SIGH-muh-nee), a common practice whereby wealthy families paid to have their sons appointed bishops. Such an appointment was desirable because bishops collected significant revenues in their territories. In an attempt to keep European rulers from interfering in papal elections, in 1059 the College of Cardinals was established to elect the pope. Churchmen made Roman law the basis of church law because Roman law referred all matters to the person at the top, in this case the pope.

Papal Controversies and Claims   The growing political power of the papacy was made clear during the eleventh and twelfth centuries, when a major church-state conflict erupted over the appointment of bishops. For centuries rulers had appointed their leading nobles to key church offices, especially that of bishop. But in 1075 Pope Gregory VII (ca. 1020–1085), hoping to change this custom, excommunicated the German emperor for appointing the archbishop of Milan (mi-LAHN) in north Italy. Gregory had a low opinion of kings, who, he said, "derive their origin from men ignorant of God who raised themselves above their fellows by pride, plunder, treachery, murder, at the instigation of the Devil."[13] The struggle was not finally resolved until 1122, when both men compromised and agreed that both emperor and pope would invest the new bishops with the symbols of authority. This dispute strengthened papal authority and weakened the German emperors by reducing their control over papal appointments. As German rulers began intervening in Italian politics to regain control over the church, they lost influence over their own princes at home. Eventually, then, the problem of papal power led to decentralized government and political warfare in the German-speaking lands.

Another pope, Innocent III (r. 1198–1216), dramatically extended papal authority over secular rulers. Innocent III used his control over the sacraments to claim victory over most of the major rulers of western Europe, for example, by forcing King John of England to accept the pope's candidate for archbishop of Canterbury and requiring the king of France to take back a wife he had divorced. This pope also received as honorary fiefs various states, among them Aragon (AR-uh-GON) (in Spain), Denmark, England, Hungary, Portugal, and Poland. Innocent III had other impacts. In 1215 he moved against non-Christians by requiring Jews to wear distinctive clothing, and he also aggressively punished "heretical depravity."

The papal drive to investigate and eliminate heresy led to the **Holy Inquisition**, a church court created in 1231. Friars

---

excommunicate   To expel a person from the Roman Catholic church and its sacraments.

simony   In medieval Europe, a practice whereby wealthy families paid to have their sons appointed bishops.

Holy Inquisition   A church court created in 1231 in medieval Europe to investigate and eliminate heresy; inquisitions continued into the 1600s.

from several religious orders tried thousands of people with views outside the mainstream, and popes sanctioned torture and starvation to induce confessions. Often it worked. For example, after a brutal spell in prison, a French doctor, Guillaume Aggase, confessed to conspiring to poison wells. Those like Aggase found guilty faced a range of punishments, including penances, banishment, prison, mutilation, and death. Over the next two centuries several thousand people were executed. The most notorious inquisition began, under state rather than church control, in Spain in 1478, and perpetrated brutal persecution of Jews and Muslims. At least 2,000 people were burned at the stake in Spain. The inquisitions continued into the 1600s and also included bans on books viewed as dangerous to the faith.

Medieval Beliefs and the Environment

Early and medieval Christians had adopted from the ancient Jewish tradition ideas about nature and history still apparent in the West today. One concept of history derived from this Jewish tradition is that of progress. Early Christian thinkers such as Augustine of Hippo had supported the notion of human society improving with time, an idea then foreign to most of the world. To think in these terms, Europeans adopted a linear rather than a cyclical concept of history. The linear view meant that history led from one point to another in a line of progressive movement. The basis for the view was found in the Bible, where, the Genesis account asserts, by gradual stages, God created light and darkness, then the earth and its plants and animals. Finally God created the highest form of life, humans.

To many Christian thinkers, God planned and ordered the world, including the natural environment, explicitly for human benefit, and human progress necessitated exploiting nature. Most medieval Christians accepted a dualism—humankind and nature—and believed that no item in the physical universe had any purpose but to serve humans. Thus, they believed, it was God's will that people improved land by clearing forests and wetlands, which some monasteries did with great enthusiasm. The crass medieval attitude toward nature gave ideological justification for the great technological and economic development to later emerge in the West but also caused environmental problems.

Some Christian and Jewish thinkers dissented from these views and affirmed that nature was also God's creation and required care and stewardship. For example, the eighth-century English theologian Bede condemned the exploitation of the land. St. Francis of Assisi (1182–1226), who renounced wealth to found a new religious order, the Franciscans (fran-SIS-kuhnz), dedicated to lives of poverty, humility, and serving the urban poor, saw all creatures as part of God's plan. In 1980 the Catholic Church named him the patron saint of ecology. And the twelfth-century Jewish philosopher and legal authority Moses Maimonides wrote that "it should not be believed that all beings exist for the sake of the existence of man."[14] Kings and lords often protected the forests where they enjoyed hunting.

New European States

Threatened by the increase in papal power, and with less need for feudal vassals as economies grew, rulers sought to gain more control over their lands (see Map 14.2). The English kings were most successful at this centralization of power in the twelfth and thirteenth centuries. After leading the Norman conquest of England in 1066, William of Normandy (1027–1087) had divided the land among his chief vassals. But by the 1100s, William's successors were taking authority away from the local nobility and shifting it to the king's representatives. Kings appointed justices and officials to collect taxes, and they closely supervised local officials. One of the strongest kings, Henry II (r. 1154–1189), expanded the power of the royal courts over feudal and church courts. He also invaded Ireland in 1171 and established English control of the eastern region centered on Dublin.

However, while seeking to strengthen royal power, some of Henry II's successors unintentionally laid the foundations for a later representative government in England. John (the Prince John of the Robin Hood legend) weakened royal power in 1215 by signing the **Magna Carta** (MAG-nuh KAHR-tuh) or "Great Charter," an agreement that limited the feudal rights of the king and his officials while protecting the rights of the church, lords, and merchants. King John promised not to tax his vassals unless the taxes were sanctioned by custom or approved by his barons. The Magna Carta was later used to support the notion that rulers had to have the consent of their subjects, one of the foundations of modern English constitutional monarchy. Henry III (r. 1216–1272) also contributed unwittingly to representative government. His incessant demand for taxes to fight foreign wars made him unpopular and, in 1265, rebellious barons called together a parliament (literally, a "speaking place") that included non-aristocrats such as middle-class townspeople and knights to air their grievances and demand that the king consider their views. This parliament became the model for later meetings called by kings to secure approval of their policies.

Online Study Center Improve Your Grade
Primary Source: Magna Carta: The Great Charter of Liberties

The Capetians (kuh-PEE-shuhnz), a dynasty that succeeded the Carolingians as kings in France (987–1328), were also trying to increase their power but under more difficult circumstances. Several Capetian kings expanded their territory and increased control over their many vassals. King Philip II (r. 1180–1223), for example, gained control over Normandy. Philip also strengthened the royal bureaucracy, replacing noblemen with paid officials who would be more loyal to the crown. Louis IX, or St. Louis (r. 1226–1270), a pious man who curbed the power of the nobility while persecuting heretics

---

Magna Carta ("Great Charter") An agreement signed by King John of England in 1215 that limited the feudal rights of the English king and his officials while protecting the rights of the church, lords, and merchants.

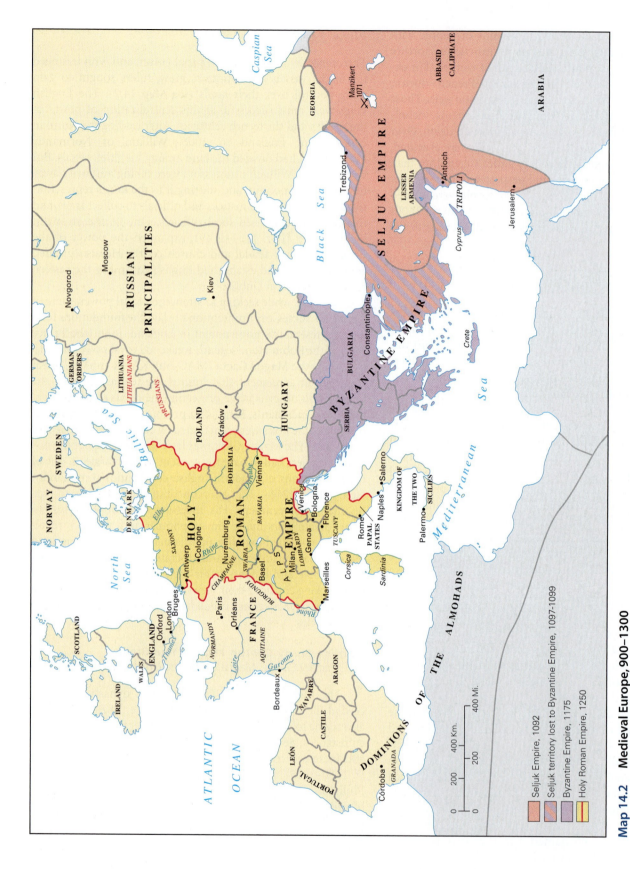

Map 14.2 **Medieval Europe, 900–1300**
During the High Middle Ages, the Holy Roman Empire, comprised of dozens of smaller states, covered much of what is today Germany, Austria, eastern France, and northern Italy. France, England, Hungary, and Poland were also major states.

Caspian Sea

ABBASID CALIPHATE

ARABIA

GEORGIA

Manzikert 1071

SELJUK EMPIRE

LESSER ARMENIA

Antioch

TRIPOLI

Trebizond

Cyprus

Jerusalem

Black Sea

BYZANTINE EMPIRE

Constantinople

BULGARIA

SERBIA

Crete

Mediterranean Sea

RUSSIAN PRINCIPALITIES

Moscow

Novgorod

Kiev

GERMAN ORDERS

LITHUANIA

LITHUANIANS

PRUSSIANS

POLAND

Kraków

HUNGARY

SWEDEN

Baltic Sea

NORWAY

DENMARK

Elbe

North Sea

HOLY ROMAN EMPIRE

SAXONY

Antwerp

Cologne

Nuremberg

Rhine

SWABIA

Basel

Danube

BOHEMIA

BAVARIA

Vienna

Venice

LOMBARDY

Milan

Genoa

A L P S

Bologna

Florence

TUSCANY

Corsica

Sardinia

Rome

PAPAL STATES

Naples

Salerno

KINGDOM OF THE TWO SICILIES

Palermo

CHAMPAGNE

BURGUNDY

Marseilles

Rhône

FRANCE

Paris

Orléans

NORMANDY

Loire

AQUITAINE

Garonne

Bordeaux

NAVARRE

ARAGON

CASTILE

LEÓN

PORTUGAL

Córdoba

GRANADA

DOMINIONS OF THE ALMOHADS

SCOTLAND

IRELAND

WALES

ENGLAND

London

Oxford

Bruges

Thames

ATLANTIC OCEAN

Seljuk Empire, 1092

Seljuk territory lost to Byzantine Empire, 1097–1099

Byzantine Empire, 1175

Holy Roman Empire, 1250

0 200 400 Km.

0 200 400 Mi.

and Jews, appointed specially paid inspectors to report to him any injustices inflicted by his officials.

Philip the Fair (r. 1285–1314) may have had the most impact on France and Europe. He added to the list of lands held directly by the French monarchy, but he is more famous for his methods of fundraising and his attack on the papacy. To raise money for his wars, he arrested all the Jews and seized their property before expelling them from the kingdom. He also had the leaders of a militant religious order, the Knights Templar (TEM-plahr), burned at the stake as heretics so that he could default on a loan they had given him. When Pope Boniface VIII (r. 1294–1303) challenged Philip's growing power, Philip accused the pope of sexual perversion and murder and sent a force to Italy to arrest him. Townspeople rescued the pope by driving French troops away, but Boniface died soon after. For the next seventy years (1305–1377), the College of Cardinals, bowing to French pressure, elected popes, most of them French, who chose to live in the papal territory of Avignon (ah-vee-NYON) in southern France. Philip's ruthless action showed that the days of papal control over European rulers were ending. By the late 1200s, France had emerged as the strongest kingdom in western Europe.

German rulers had the least success in centralizing their lands, largely because they spent too much time trying to control Italy. In addition, the feudal nobility in Germany remained powerful. Several members of the Hohenstaufen (HO-uhn-SHTOU-fuhn) dynasty, who served as Holy Roman emperors between 1152 and 1254, made the last attempt to establish a strong monarchy. Frederick I (r. 1154–1190) reasserted his authority as Holy Roman emperor over the wealthy cities in northern Italy, but this involved full-scale war with the pope, who organized an Italian coalition that defeated Frederick's forces. The Hohenstaufens' control of Sicily also involved them in struggles with the pope that weakened their control of Germany. Frederick I's successors gradually lost power to German princes, and German lands became more divided than ever. It would be seven hundred years before Italy, divided up into small papal-ruled and nonpapal states, and Germany finally achieved the territorial unity enjoyed by France and England.

The Crusading Tradition

The tensions that permeated western European religious and political life helped foster the Crusades, a series of military expeditions or holy wars between 1095 and 1272 to reclaim the Christian "Holy Land," Palestine, from Muslim control (see Chapter 10). Affluent European Christians had long made pilgrimages to Jerusalem and considered the city part of their world. The crusading began after the Byzantine emperor sought Christian help to dislodge his rivals, the Muslim Seljuk Turks, who had gained domination over much of western Asia. Medieval Christians had a militant zeal to spread their faith and destroy Islam, through the use of force if necessary, and early Christian thinkers like Augustine of Hippo had sanctioned war in defense of the faith. Except for Islam, no other world religion maintained such a strong missionary impulse to

convert the world to what its believers considered the only true faith. Many crusaders were undoubtedly motivated by sincere religious beliefs, but these often became mixed with economic motives such as lust for wealth and land. Political rivalries between European leaders also played a role.

In 1095 Pope Urban II urged Christian rulers to unite to protect the Christian holy sites, prompting the first of nine crusades by land and sea. Fabricating or exaggerating stories of Muslim atrocities against Christians, he proclaimed that the Turks "have completely destroyed some of God's churches and they have converted others to the uses of their own cult. They ruin the altars with filth and defilement. They are pleased to kill others. And what shall I say about the shocking rape of the women."[15] Various kings, nobles, and bishops joined the cause. Some crusaders temporarily occupied parts of the Holy Land, such as Jerusalem, even establishing crusader-led states, but eventually they were forced out. Other crusaders were diverted to ransacking Constantinople or Egypt.

While they looted and pillaged cities, in many cases the crusaders also slaughtered thousands of people, including Muslims, Jews, and Byzantine Christians. They burned mosques and synagogues, sometimes with hundreds of people inside. The Muslim defenders often responded by killing local Christians. The streets of Jerusalem, it was said, ran ankle-deep in blood. Crusaders even slaughtered 12,000 Jews in Germany in 1096. As a result of their depredations, they were often viewed by non-Christians as pirates and terrorists rather than the religious idealists they believed themselves to be. In the thirteenth century the crusading energies dissipated. But the long conflicts left a bitter heritage between Christian and Muslim societies that still complicates political and cross-cultural relations in the modern world.

Intellectual Life and Literature

Some of the tensions of the High Middle Ages derived from robust intellectual debates, often in universities, involving theologians, philosophers, and writers. By the twelfth century, guilds of scholars were forming centers of higher learning in some medieval cities. Universities existed earlier in India and the Islamic world but they mostly specialized in religious studies; historians debate whether they provided models for Europeans. In the European universities students gathered to study not only religion but also secular knowledge, such as the pagan ideas of Aristotle as passed on by Jewish and Arab scholars, an activity that raised eyebrows among church leaders (see Profile: Heloise, a French Scholar and Nun). The most famous European universities were at Paris, Oxford in England, and Salerno (suh-LUR-no) and Bologna (boe-LOAN-yuh) in Italy. They grew out of the old cathedral or monastic schools where students had learned the "seven liberal arts": astronomy, geometry, arithmetic, music, grammar, rhetoric, and logic. At the new universities, students learned these arts and then specialized in higher study of medicine, law, or philosophy. Of course, as today, students did not spend all of their time studying. When one student wrote home for money because "the city is expensive

HELOISE, A FRENCH SCHOLAR AND NUN

A scandalous love affair between two brilliant people, Abelard and Heloise, reveals much about the life and values of medieval times, including church politics and attitudes toward sexuality. Over the centuries the romance and its sad repercussions inspired countless works of poetry and prose. Often portrayed as a forbidden affair between a smitten schoolgirl and her unprincipled teacher, a famed but controversial theologian, the relationship between the two figures was in reality far more complex.

Heloise (1101–1164) was the niece of a high church official in Paris. Coming from a wealthy, influential family, she had more educational opportunities than most women of her time. She was educated at a well-financed convent, where she showed a keen intelligence. In 1117 her uncle Fulbert, a high-ranking cleric, arranged for the seventeen-year-old to study with Peter Abelard (1079–1142), the most famous teacher, and a nonclergyman, at the school of the Notre Dame Cathedral. Born into an aristocratic family in Brittany, Abelard had studied with renowned teachers and had taught at several schools. He was notorious for both his arrogance and his intellect and made enemies in the church by championing reason, logic, and progressive thinking on religious doctrine.

Despite a twenty-year age difference, Abelard and Heloise fell passionately in love. Abelard wrote of how they went from reading books to kissing. They composed love songs and letters to each other, but their affair also reflected a friendship and intellectual respect. Her letters reveal a good knowledge of Roman and Christian writers. The two lovers tried to keep their affair quiet and were secretly married after she became pregnant. Their romance came at a time when the church was not just encouraging but mandating that clergy as well as secular teachers, such as Abelard, and students in church schools remain celibate. Abelard realized that his marriage would end his current position and his future church career. Heloise gave birth to a son, who was raised by Abelard's sister and eventually became a church official. However, when Heloise's family learned of the affair, they sought revenge. Fulbert hired two men to beat and then castrate Abelard. Now disgraced, Abelard joined a Benedictine monastery and, at his encouragement, Heloise entered a convent. Eventually she became the community's director.

Although separated, Heloise and Abelard continued to write letters to each other. Expressing her affection, Heloise wrote him that "I seek to please thee rather than [God]. Thy command brought me, not the love of God, to the [nunnery]." Strongly influenced by the thought of Aristotle, Abelard restored his scholarly reputation by writing books and essays about the possibilities of mixing philosophy and religion, for which he was for a time condemned as a heretic. Later, as an abbot (head) of a large monastery, he helped Heloise and her nuns establish a new convent, although he maintained a personal distance from her. Her ability to gain support and funding helped her convent to flourish. She remained ambivalent

Heloise and Abelard This painting, from a fourteenth-century French manuscript, shows Heloise and Abelard (in nun's habit) in conversation, years after their torrid love affair had shocked church authorities. (Bridgeman-Giraudon/Art Resource, NY)

about her career, writing Abelard that "I am judged religious at a time when there is little in religion that is not hypocrisy." Heloise became known for her learning, and one top male cleric praised her knowledge of the liberal arts, saying, "You have surpassed all women and have gone further than almost every man." However, Heloise resented Abelard's desire to remain aloof from her, and she wrote, "Of all the wretched women I am the most wretched, for the higher the ascent, the heavier the fall." Although they died twenty years apart, the pair were buried alongside each other at the convent, a fitting conclusion to a relationship and an era. Heloise was one of the last educated churchwomen to maintain close contact with male scholars and church officials. Obsessed with celibacy, the church increasingly separated the men and women engaged in religious life.

THINKING ABOUT THE PROFILE

1. What does the love affair and its consequences tell us about life at this time?

2. How did the different ways in which Abelard and Heloise rebuilt their lives reflect the values of medieval people?

Notes: Quotations from Barbara A. Hanawalt, *The Middle Ages: An Illustrated History* (New York: Oxford University Press, 1998), p. 88; Jane Slaughter and Melissa K. Bokovoy, *Sharing the Stage: Biography and Gender in Western Civilization,* vol. 1 (Boston: Houghton Mifflin, 2003), pp. 255, 261–262; and James Burge, *Heloise and Abelard: A New Biography* (San Francisco: HarperSanFrancisco, 2003), p. 271.

and makes many demands," his father replied: "I have recently learned that you live dissolutely, preferring play to work, and strumming your guitar while others are at their studies."[16]

The medieval study of philosophy, especially the heated debates over the relative importance of faith and reason, contributed much to later Western thought. Some thinkers reclaimed the classical tradition of rational thought, often against church opposition. Leading scholars like the English Franciscan monk Roger Bacon (ca. 1220–1292) feared that church officials might ban the natural sciences. The most elaborate attempt to reconcile faith and reason was made by Thomas Aquinas (uh-KWINE-uhs) (1225–1274), an Italian monk of the Dominican (duh-MIN-i-kuhn) order and professor at the University of Paris who believed that much could be determined by reason, even the existence of God, but that at some point a believer had to accept on faith many mysteries. Reflecting medieval views, he also argued that human domination over nature was part of a divine plan and that women were passive and incapable of moral perfection. Some thinkers influenced by Aristotle argued that real knowledge came only from direct perception of individual things, a position that supported scientific inquiry.

Literature, like many other aspects of life during the High Middle Ages, was diverse and contradictory. For example, the *Song of Roland*, written down in France in the twelfth century, described the great deeds of a loyal knight who died while guarding the rear of Charlemagne's army. But the warlike and masculine tone of the epic *Song of Roland* contrasted with the many contemporary French lyric poems and stories that exalted romantic love as an ideal in a society that generally arranged marriages for distinctly nonromantic reasons. These love poems and tales of individuals who put their personal happiness ahead of the law may have reflected new notions of individualism. For example, writers all over Europe took up the Celtic legend of the British King Arthur and his court. In some versions Arthur's wife, Guinevere (GWIN-uh-veer), and his best friend, Lancelot, followed their hearts and became doomed lovers. In a lighter vein, we have this parody of the Christian Apostles' Creed written by a student more delighted by spirits than by the Spirit: "I believe in wine that's fair to see, and in the tavern of my host, More than in the Holy Ghost. The tavern will my sweetheart be, and the Holy Church is not for me."[17]

SECTION SUMMARY

■ The church and its priests had a great deal of power over people's lives, but many priests were unqualified or incompetent.

■ In some instances, popes became more powerful than kings, and they also orchestrated the Holy Inquisition, which killed thousands of "nonbelievers."

■ Christians adopted the Jewish belief in progress over time and the belief that everything in the world was for the use of humans, a view that laid the ground for later industrialization in the West.

■ While English rulers eventually consolidated their power and Philip the Fair of France ruthlessly seized power and property and even attacked the pope, German rulers had trouble centralizing their lands because they were too interested in struggling with the pope in Italy.

■ Spurred on by a mix of religious idealism and greed, Christians mounted a series of Crusades to wrest the "Holy Land" from Muslim control, thereby creating a resentment among Muslims that has lasted to today.

■ A mix of religious and secular topics were studied at urban universities, where theologians struggled to reconcile faith and reason.

Eastern Europe: Byzantines, Slavs, and Mongols

How did Byzantine society differ from that of western Europe?

Byzantium, and the eastern European societies it influenced, remained very distinct from western Europe. Despite their shared belief in the Christian religion and long-standing trade connections, deep political, economic, and religious differences separated western Europeans and Byzantines. Some cultural differences that separate eastern from western Europeans even today have their origins in the Middle Ages. Furthermore, Byzantine society demonstrated a remarkable longevity against the odds. From the sixth century onward, the Byzantine Empire fought for its life and, beginning in the eleventh century, experienced steady political decline until its final defeat by the Ottoman Turks in 1453 (see Chronology: Byzantium, Russia, and Eastern Europe, 600–1500). In the process, however, it served as a buffer zone protecting central and western Europe against Muslim, Slavic, and Mongol invaders. Most of the Slavic societies in eastern Europe adopted Eastern Orthodox Christianity, and one of these, the Russians, eventually created a powerful state.

Byzantium and Its Eurasian Rivals

Byzantium faced nearly continuous pressure from neighboring peoples. In the sixth and seventh centuries the Sassanian Persians and Byzantines fought a series of wars that weakened both empires and made Arab conquest of the Persian Empire and many of the Byzantine lands easier. The Arabs were at the walls of Constantinople in 673 and 717, but the Byzantines survived both attacks. For most of the next three and a half centuries, the Byzantines stabilized their frontier with the Arabs but were faced with other enemies. Various Slavic peoples had begun moving into eastern Europe in late Roman times. By the early Middle Ages Slavs were the dominant population in a vast region of mountains, forests, and grasslands stretching north from Greece to the eastern Baltic and eastward through Russia.

The major Slavic challenges to Byzantium came from the Bulgars and Serbs (SURBZ). One of the Byzantine rulers, known as "Basil the Bulgar-slayer," defeated a Bulgar army in 1014 and blinded 15,000 Bulgarian prisoners of war before releasing them to return home. In their homeward trek they were led in groups of ten by a soldier who was allowed to keep one eye. The defeat of the Bulgars, who had controlled considerable territory, opened the door to the Serbs, who set up several small states in the Balkans. During the eleventh century one Serbian state expanded its power, bringing it into conflict with Byzantium. After a series of wars, the Ottoman Turks conquered the Serbs in 1441.

Byzantine political fortunes began to decline seriously by the late eleventh century. In 1071, Byzantine forces were driven from southern Italy by Norman knights, and in 1091, at the Battle of Manzikert (MANZ-ih-kuhrt), they were defeated by Seljuk Turks in eastern Anatolia. From that point on, the shrunken Byzantine territories faced attacks from both east and west. Turks soon completed the conquest of Anatolia and left Constantinople a beleaguered fortress. Despite the divide between the Roman and Greek churches, the Byzantines requested the help of western knights to defend Byzantine territories against the Turks. They didn't expect crusader armies to occupy and set up states in Palestine and Syria between 1096 and 1200. Even less did the Byzantines expect the western crusaders in 1204, bribed by the Venetians, Byzantine trading rivals, to use a disputed imperial succession in the empire as an excuse to conquer Constantinople itself and govern it until forced out in 1261. Capitalizing on these disasters, the expanding Ottoman Turks finally conquered Constantinople and the surrounding territory in 1453, ending the Byzantine state and transforming the capital city into Istanbul.

Byzantine Economy, Religion, and Society

Despite its many political and military misfortunes, the Byzantine Empire survived as long as it did in part because of its economic and religious strengths. A merchant class remained a vital and accepted part of Byzantine life, since Constantinople lay astride the principal trade routes between Europe and Asia and goods from all over Eurasia and North Africa passed through the capital city. Slave traders thrived by shipping eastern European slaves, many of them Slavs from the Black Sea region, from Constantinople to be sold in the Mediterranean. Our English word for "slave" comes from the word *Slav*. Taxes from these material goods and people as well as silk production enriched the treasury, and Byzantine coins were used around Eurasia.

Church and state were intertwined, and Christianity and its rituals influenced all aspects of Byzantine society. Unlike in western Europe, governments dominated the church, and rulers regularly interfered in church affairs. The culture was artistically rich, filled with lengthy religious ceremonies and an intense prayer life, especially in the monasteries. Byzantines also engaged in hair-splitting theological disputes. For example, they bitterly disagreed on the use of icons, painted images of holy figures. Another great debate erupted over whether the Holy Spirit proceeded from God or from both God and Jesus. Byzantine Christians also refused to recognize the supreme position of the bishop of Rome over other bishops. These conflicts over theology and authority were critical issues in the final split between the Roman Catholic and Greek Orthodox Churches, which came when the pope and the patriarch of Constantinople angrily excommunicated each other in 1054.

Like the Roman church, the Byzantine church supported male power, but a few women achieved political or intellectual influence. For example, Empress Irene, an orphan who married an emperor, ruled Byzantium for two decades (780–802). Her detractors considered her cruel and ruthless, although her actions differed little from those of male Byzantine rulers. Irene fostered prosperity, made peace with Muslim states, and temporarily resolved the dispute over icons. Some women also gained an education. Byzantium's best-known historian, the princess Anna Comnena (1083–1148), studied literature, astronomy, medicine, and Greek philosophy.

Byzantium and the Slavs

The Byzantines held off political foes long enough so that Byzantine culture, stimulated by trading contacts as well as war, could spread north and east. This achievement allowed Byzantine religion and culture to survive the defeat of the empire. The differences between eastern and western versions of

Christianity gave some of the eastern European peoples a choice of which to adopt. In the ninth century, two Byzantine brothers, known later as Saints Cyril and Methodius (mi-THO-dee-uhs), traveled east of the German lands to convert the Slavs to eastern Christianity. The brothers devised an alphabet, now known as Cyrillic (suh-RILL-ik), for the Slavs, and Cyril began translating the Bible and other church writings from Greek into Slavic. Some Slavs, including the Bulgars, Serbs, Russians, and many Ukrainians, eventually adopted aspects of Byzantine culture, including Orthodox Christianity. Other Slavs, among them Croats (KRO-ATS), Czechs (checks), Lithuanians (lith-oo-ANE-ee-uhnz), Poles, Slovaks (SLO-vaks), Slovenes (SLO-veenz), and many Ukrainians, adopted Roman Catholicism.

Byzantium greatly influenced the Russians and other Slavs. For example, the Russians and other societies religiously and culturally influenced by the Russians, including the Georgians in the Caucasus, learned their Christian culture and their politics from a society in which an autocratic emperor dominated and in which church and state remained closely connected, in contrast to western Europe, where church-state conflicts remained common. Eastern and western European cultures remain distinct even today, partly because of the differences between the Greek and Roman churches of 1,000 years ago.

Russians and Mongols

The Russians descended from a people known as the Rus (roos), whose capital was at Kiev (KEE-yev), in today's Ukraine (you-CRANE). Swedish Vikings, who founded trading cities in the Slavic regions beginning around 825, had become the Rus ruling class, both trading with and raiding the Byzantines and neighboring societies. Viking trade networks connected various states situated on the great Russian and Ukrainian plains, and by the tenth century the Vikings had been assimilated by the majority Slavs. From the tenth to the twelfth centuries, the Russian people expanded, though they were not always politically unified. Their settlements went northward as far as Novgorod (NOHV-goh-rod), from which timber was shipped south through Kiev to the Black Sea. The Rus ruler Vladimir (VLAD-ih-mir) I (ca. 956–1015) in Kiev opened the doors to Byzantine influence. Vladimir had several wives and eight hundred concubines but, hoping for political advantage, sought marriage to a Byzantine princess. After she refused to marry a pagan polygamist, he agreed to accept Orthodox Christianity in 988 and make her his only wife. When Vladimir ordered his men to the Dnieper (d-NYEP-er) River in Kiev to be baptized, he unwittingly guaranteed that a large part of eastern Europe would become Eastern Orthodox.

By the time western Europeans were beginning to hear rumors about the brutal Mongols, the Russians were already encountering Mongol armies. Under their great leader Genghis Khan, Mongol armies conquered Central Asia, much of Russia, and parts of China and the Middle East (see Chapters 10 and 11 and "Societies, Networks, Transitions," page 412). Mongol armies

An Orthodox Church in Novgorod, Russia The distinctive architecture of this church represents the fusion of Slavic, Byzantine, and Viking influences. (Novosti)

repeatedly sacked Russian cities beginning in 1237. A papal envoy who visited Kiev after an attack reported, "We found lying in the fields countless heads and bones. [The city] has been reduced to nothing: barely 200 houses [still] stand there."[18] Until the fifteenth century most Russians remained subject to the Mongols, and especially to the Golden Horde, a Mongol state on the lower Volga River. Muscovy (MUSS-koe-vee), a Russian state centered on Moscow (MOS-koh), benefited from this situation, since the Golden Horde treated its ruler as the senior Russian leader.

Western Europe was fortunate to escape Mongol conquest. In 1241, several large Mongol armies moved far into Europe, crushing both Polish and Hungarian forces sent against them. Soon they stood on the banks of the Danube contemplating an invasion into German lands. But the Germans and European societies further west were spared, perhaps because Mongol generals decided to return to Mongolia when they heard of the death of the Mongol leader, Ogodei, the son of Genghis Khan. Had the Mongol conquests continued westward, the history of Europe might have been very different. But Europe was much less tempting than the far richer societies of China and Islamic western Asia.

Eventually Muscovy became the dominant Russian state as Mongol political power declined and the head of the Russian Orthodox Church, appointed by the patriarch of Constantinople, moved from Kiev to Moscow. During the reign of Ivan III (1440–1505) Muscovy escaped Mongol control and established domination over other Russian states. Ivan began to call himself *czar* (meaning "Caesar") to indicate his superiority over lesser rulers, and he married the niece of the last Byzantine emperor. The Russian Orthodox Church had broken its connection with the patriarch of Constantinople even before the fall of the Byzantine capital, and during Ivan's reign Russian clergy began referring to Moscow as the Third Rome, successor to Constantinople and Rome, and the home of the purest version of Christianity. The Russians also expanded into the territories of their most powerful rivals, the Catholic Lithuanians, adding religious antagonisms to the normal political tensions between Orthodox and Catholic states and ethnic groups in eastern Europe.

SECTION SUMMARY

■ The Byzantines were under almost constant attack by their neighbors, including Sassanian Persians, Bulgars, Slavs, and even Christians from western Europe, but Byzantium survived until it was conquered by the Turks in 1453.

■ Byzantium's culture and Orthodox Christianity survived because they were spread through war and trade to many of the eastern European peoples, including the Russians, the Bulgars, the Serbs, and many Ukrainians.

■ The Russians, who had adopted Orthodox Christianity, were attacked by the Mongols but emerged as one of the strongest societies in eastern Europe.

Late Medieval Europe and the Roots of Expansion

What developments between 1300 and 1500 gave Europeans the incentive and means to begin reshaping the world after 1500?

The Late Middle Ages, between 1300 and 1500, were a period of transition in western Europe. For a century the population shrunk dramatically as a result of famine, plague, and warfare, and this decline contributed to the gradual end of feudalism. In politics, royal power increased many places at the expense of the feudal nobility. The Roman church, including the popes, also lost influence in this era, as a profound moral crisis led to a questioning of church practices and beliefs. Many shared the pessimism of the French writer who lamented that "all mirth is lost. All hearts have been taken by storm, by sadness and melancholy."[19] Yet, the ferment fostered intellectual and cultural creativity, European trade and self-confidence rose, and brave mariners began exploring the world beyond Europe, fostering the resurgence of the West.

The Black Death and Social Change

Late medieval Europe was not a happy place, ravaged as it was by several disasters, including famine, disease, and war. Europe's climate turned colder about 1300, fostering what scholars call "the Little Ice Age." As a result, for example, the Norse farming settlements in Greenland collapsed from deforestation, expanding glaciers, and conflict with the local Inuit for scarce resources. Cooler temperatures also shortened the European growing season by several weeks, causing serious food shortages, including famine in some villages in northern Europe.

Between the mid-fourteenth and early fifteenth centuries, Europe also repeatedly suffered from the Black Death, a terrible *pandemic,* or massive epidemic that crossed many regions. The Black Death was named for the black bruises that appeared under the skin in one form of the disease. In 1347 a trading ship coming from the Black Sea limped into the harbor of Messina (mi-SEE-nuh) in Sicily with all of the crew either dead or dying. It had picked up a deadly infection spread by fleas that lived on black rats who had scampered aboard ship. Most historians believe the infection was bubonic plague, perhaps mixed with pneumonic (noo-MON-ik) plague. The pandemic caused unprecedented death and suffering as it spread along and disrupted the networks of exchange all over Eurasia and North Africa. Within a year, this plague had spread throughout southern Europe, and by 1349 it had reached the Baltic Sea (see Chronology: The Late Middle Ages, 1300–1500).

The Black Death, during its peak years from 1348 to 1350, had terrible effects, killing a third of all Europeans. Over 65 percent of the population in some congested cities (such as Venice, Florence, and Paris) died, greatly reducing commerce. Thanks to the recurring outbreaks of the Black Death and

The Late Middle Ages, 1300–1500

1309–1377	Avignon papacy
1337–1453	Hundred Years War between France and England
1348–1350	Peak of Black Death
1378–1417	Great Schism in papacy
1455–1485	Wars of the Roses in England
1455	Printing of Gutenberg Bible
1478	Beginning of Spanish Inquisition
1487	Dias arrival at Indian Ocean
1492	First voyage by Columbus to America; Spanish Christian defeat of last Muslim state

Praying for Relief   This image of survivors carrying away plague victims in Rome was commissioned by a French duke for an illuminated book in the early 1400s. It illustrates the despair and devastating loss of life caused by the Black Death, especially in cities.   (The Metropolitan Museum of Art, the Cloisters Collection, 1954 (54.1.1). Photograph © 1987 The Metropolitan Museum of Art)

other calamities, Europe's population in the fourteenth century dropped from around 70 to 75 million to some 45 to 50 million people. Many millions were killed by either a severe and fast-acting respiratory infection or by swelling and internal bleeding. Pope Clement VI wrote about the 1348 outbreak that "the living were barely sufficient to bury the dead, or so horrified as to avoid the task. So great a terror seized nearly everyone."[20] The horrors endured in nursery rhymes: "Ring around the rosies, a pocketful of posies, ashes, ashes, we all fall down." Isolated rural areas had many fewer deaths than cities. Those who survived developed some immunities: although the Black Death reoccurred for decades, up to about a century, it killed fewer people each time.

The troubles reshaped European social patterns. The plague struck all classes, but the upper classes may have suffered the greatest long-term effects. Many nobles were already weakened by royal centralization. With far fewer peasants alive to till the fields, those who were left asked for more privileges or more money or both. Peasant revolts demanding an end to serfdom increased, most notably in France in 1358 and in England in 1381. Although not successful, they demonstrated that the lower classes had some collective power. Meanwhile, some people challenged social norms. For example, in addition to writing works of history, ethics, and poetry, the French author Christine of Pasan (1364–ca. 1430) proclaimed that women were equals of men, systematically disproved all the negative stereotypes men held of women's character, such as indiscretion and loose morals, and shrewdly critiqued the patriarchal social structure. She wrote that "those who blame women out of jealousy are those wicked men who have seen many women of greater intelligence and nobler conduct than they themselves possess."[21] Some literature, such as the fiction of the

fourteenth-century English writer Geoffrey Chaucer (CHAW-suhr) (see Witness to the Past: A Literary View of Late Medieval People), reflected the changing social customs and relations.

The death and despair influenced emotional and social life. Since no one really understood the cause, many people assumed the pandemic was divine punishment. Feelings of utter hopelessness must have overwhelmed family members who vainly tried to dig graves for all the members of their family before they too succumbed to death, which usually came in a matter of days after catching the disease. Aristocrats had their own ways of responding to the environment of despair. While famine and disease raged, they regaled themselves with magnificent banquets and pageants and wore ostentatious clothing. Men wore long pointed shoes and women ornate headdresses. The poor sought escape through prayer, meditation, and self-

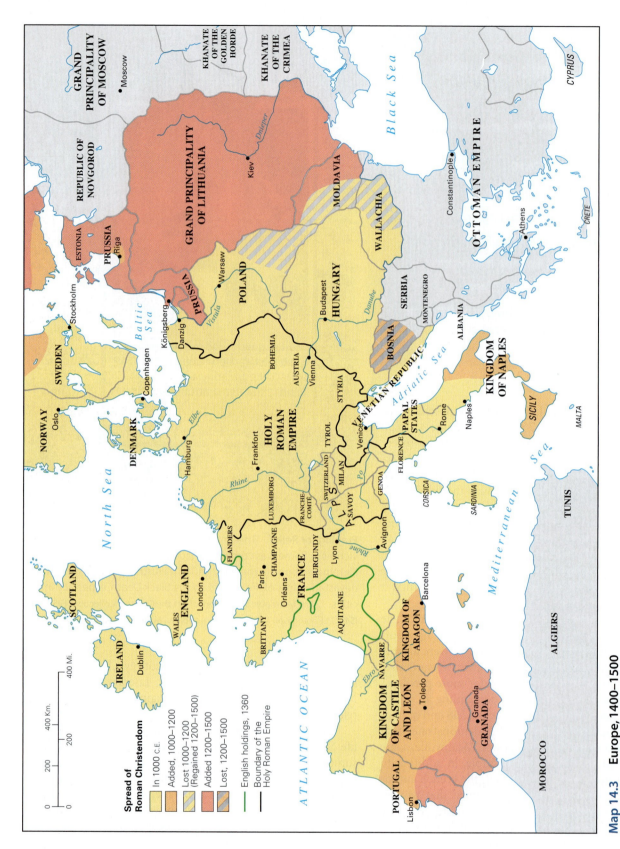

Map 14.3 Europe, 1400–1500
During this period France became western Europe's strongest kingdom but Spanish kings gradually reunified much of the Iberian peninsula. The Holy Roman empire remained decentralized. Meanwhile, Lithuania, Hungary, and Poland controlled much of eastern Europe.

Online Study Center **Improve Your Grade** Interactive Map: Europe in 1453

Spread of Roman Christendom
In 1000 C.E.
Added, 1000–1200
Lost 1000–1200 (Regained 1200–1500)
Added 1200–1500
Lost, 1200–1500
English holdings, 1360
Boundary of the Holy Roman Empire

A Literary View of Late Medieval People

The English writer Geoffrey Chaucer (ca. 1340–1400) wrote one of the best-known books of the Late Middle Ages, *The Canterbury Tales*, set in the time of the Black Death. Born in London, Chaucer was a cosmopolitan poet, soldier, and diplomat who served in the English Parliament and was familiar with French and Italian intellectual and cultural trends. His writings reflected these trends while also strongly influencing spoken and written English. *The Canterbury Tales* also offered a witty and sophisticated picture of English society. This excerpt presents stereotypical and satirical views of various pilgrims on their way to visit Canterbury, the seat of church power in England.

The knight there was, and he was a worthy man, Who, from the moment that he first began To ride about the world, loved chivalry, Truth, honor, freedom, and all courtesy . . . Of mortal battles he had fought fifteen . . . And always won he sovereign fame for prize . . . He never yet had any vileness said [about him] in all his life . . . He was a truly perfect, gentle knight. . . .

There was also a nun, a prioress, Who, in her smiling, modest was and coy . . . At table she had been well taught withal, And never from her lips let morels fall, Nor dipped her fingers deep in sauce, but ate With so much care the food upon her plate That never driblet fell upon her breast. In courtesy she had delight and zest. . . .

A monk there was, one made for mastery [and loved hunting] . . . A manly man, to be an abbot able. Full many a blooded horse had he in stable: And when he rode men might his bridle hear A-jingling in the whistling wind as clear, Aye, and as loud as does the chapel bell Where this brave monk was of the cell . . . This said monk let such lowly old things [strict old monastic rules] slowly pace And followed new world manners in their place. What? Should he study as a madman would Upon a book in cloister cell? Or yet, go labor with his hands and . . . sweat [as St. Augustine commanded]? . . .

There was a merchant with forked beard, and girt . . . Upon his head a Flemish beaver hat; His boots were fastened rather elegantly. He spoke [his opinions] pompously, Stressing the times when he had won, not lost [his profits] . . . At money-changing he could make a crown. This worthy man kept all his wits well set; There was no one could say he was in debt, So well he governed all his trade affairs. . . .

There was a good man of religion, too, A country parson, poor . . . but rich he was in holy thought and work. He was also a learned man also [a scholar] . . . who Christ's own Gospel truly sought to preach. Devoutly his parisoner's would he teach . . . Benign he was and wondrous diligent, Patient in adverse times and well content . . . But rather would he give . . . unto those poor parishioners about, Part of his income, even of his goods . . . That first he wrought and afterwords he taught [first he practiced, then he preached]. . . .

THINKING ABOUT THE READING

1. What are the various clerical stereotypes presented?
2. How is the merchant portrayed?

Source: General Prologue to Geoffrey Chaucer's *Canterbury Tales*, electronic edition prepared by Edwin Duncan (http:www.towson.edu/~duncan/chaucer/titlepage.htm)

---

flagellation, imitating the torture of Jesus by beating themselves with whips until their blood flowed.

As the Black Death took its course, and its toll, the impact on western and eastern Europe proved quite different. Because eastern Europe had fewer cities and more villages, fewer peasants died. Indeed, Poland, Lithuania, and eastern Germany experienced little labor shortage after 1350. Also, since the ruling monarchs in these eastern areas were also weaker, the aristocracy was able to impose serfdom on many of their peasants, creating large agricultural estates in northeast Europe. The eastern European nobility were actually strengthened socially and politically by the Black Death, while their western European counterparts were weakened by labor shortages and higher costs. Also for this reason, eastern Europe remained primarily an agricultural area for many centuries, while in western Europe, cities recovered and rulers continued to strengthen their central governments, since the landed aristocrats were too weak to stop them.

Warfare and Political Centralization

Warfare in late medieval Europe, which was common, generally increased the power of kings and states as opposed to the nobility (see Map 14.3). For example, the intermittent fighting between English and French troops known as the Hundred Years War (1337–1453) increased royal power in France and also, eventually, in England. This war, caused by the English kings' desire to hold on to their feudal lands in France, went through several phases before the French finally claimed victory. At first the English were victorious by using their new weapon, the longbow, which launched arrows powerful enough to pierce the armor of French mounted knights. This weapon, used by trained commoners, diminished the knights as an effective fighting force. During the war's final stage (1429–1453), the French recovered their land, aided by Jeanne d'Arc (zhahn DAHRK) (ca. 1412–1431), a sixteen-year-old peasant who believed that voices from saints told her to lead troops into battle. Led by Jeanne, the French broke the English siege of the city of Orleans (or-lay-AHN) and slowly recovered most of the English-held territory in France. Jeanne, meanwhile, was captured and tried by the English as a witch. She was burned at the stake, becoming the most famous martyr to French nationhood.

The French kings were the clearest victors in the Hundred Years War. During the conflict's final stages, the French monarchs introduced new direct taxes that lessened their dependence on the feudal nobility. Kings also reorganized the royal armies to depend less on soldiers supplied by feudal vassals and more on mercenary troops hired with the new royal tax revenues. In England, military defeat fostered a long conflict between two rival royal houses, the War of the Roses (1455–1485), which ended with Henry VII founding a new Tudor (TOO-duhr) dynasty. Henry VII sent in armies to reclaim Ireland, followed by English settlers who repressed the Celtic Irish. The Tudors established England as a world power during the 1500s.

Royal power also increased during the late 1400s in Spain. In 1085 Christians began the long reconquest of the peninsula from Muslims. By 1249 they had reclaimed Portugal, and by the 1300s Spanish Christians had displaced all of the Muslim states except for Granada (gruh-NAH-duh) in the far south. In 1469 the two largest kingdoms were united when King Ferdinand of Aragon married his cousin, Isabella of Castile (kas-TEEL). These monarchs finally crushed Granada in 1492, the same year that, obsessed with religious uniformity and heresy, they expelled the Jews from Spain. It was also the year that, hoping to increase royal wealth, they sponsored the first trans-Atlantic voyage by the Italian mariner, Christopher Columbus.

In contrast to France and England, the nobility remained strong in the Holy Roman Empire, which included much of the German-speaking lands and parts of Italy. The Habsburg (HABZ-berg) family, who took power in 1273, were unable to create a strong centralized state. In 1356 they issued an imperial edict that reduced the pope's influence over the election of Holy Roman Emperors but that also confirmed the power of the princes over the emperor. During the coming centuries imperial Habsburg rulers concentrated, not on developing a strong central state, but on increasing the personal territorial holdings of their family. In the later 1400s, by royal marriage alliances, they gained control of the Netherlands and, through their links to the Spanish throne, much of southern Italy.

Crisis in the Church

Between 1300 and 1500 papal political power and the Roman church entered a period of decline, due in part to the moral and political corruption that the church had addressed repeatedly but unsuccessfully. Some historians argue that power tends to corrupt, whether in the political or religious realms. Many within the church complained about the buying of church offices and favoritism to relatives. These led to other abuses, such as absenteeism. When a man became bishop of more than one diocese so that he could collect the extra rev-

enue, he was necessarily absent from one or other of his jobs. For instance, his detractors said that Cardinal Wolsey (WOOL-zee), archbishop of both Canterbury and York in England, entered the cathedral at York only once, for his funeral. In addition, skeptics viewed practices such as venerating holy relics associated with Jesus, Mary, or saints and going on pilgrimages as superstition that encouraged fraud. Cynics muttered that there were enough pieces of the "true cross" around to build a cathedral. Defenders argued that relics and pilgrimages gave people something tangible to cling to when seeking God's help.

Papal prestige steadily declined after the popes moved to Avignon in southern France (1309–1377). The Avignon popes increased their revenues by requiring that candidates for bishop had to pay a large sum to the papal treasury in advance. To critics, this policy was a form of extortion that reserved high church offices for the wealthy. When the papacy finally returned to Rome, two men claimed to be the rightful pope: one claimant moved back to Avignon and was supported by the French, and the other stayed in Rome, supported by the English. Europeans picked sides in this "Great Schism" (1378–1417), as the split between popes was called. Although the split ended in 1415, much damage had been done to the papacy's remaining prestige. After a council of bishops in the mid-1400s made an unsuccessful bid to replace papal monarchy with a church government by such councils, popes refused to call any further councils on church reform because they feared a council would try to seize their power.

Hemispheric Connections, the Renaissance, and Technology

The Late Middle Ages was also a time of new intellectual horizons and technologies. Some of the innovations derived partly from European contacts with Asia and Africa. The Mongols did not conquer western Europe but, by establishing an empire over a wide area, they reenergized the Silk Road and Eurasian trade, allowing many useful inventions and ideas to flow west to Europe from China and western Asia. Some of these inventions, such as printing, gunpowder, and the compass, eventually revolutionized European technology. Furthermore, Muslims and Europeans vigorously traded not only goods but also ideas and art. Europeans, especially Italians, imported spices, carpets, silks, porcelain, glassware, and even painting supplies from the bazaars of Muslim Spain, Ottoman Turkey, Mamluk Egypt, and Persia. The cosmopolitan Ottoman ruler Mehmed (MAY-met) the Conqueror (1430–1481), whose armies had seized Constantinople, read and published Greek and Latin books on history and philosophy, encouraged mapmaking, and invited Italian merchants, craftsmen, artists, and architects to work in the new Ottoman capital, Istanbul (formerly Constantinople). Some Italians, especially Venetians, were influenced by the magnificent palaces and mosques they saw in various Islamic cities such as Cairo, Damascus, and Istanbul. By the later 1400s the Portuguese brought back artworks and fabrics from West Africa and the Kongo that also influenced European artists.

Some of these imported ideas and products may have contributed to the dramatic flowering of arts and learning later known as the **Renaissance**, or "rebirth," which began in the Italian city-states around 1350 and intensified through the 1400s and 1500s, spreading to other societies. In the main Renaissance center in the 1400s, Florence, artists and thinkers rediscovered the ideas of the Classical Greeks and Romans. For emphasizing humanity, worldly concerns, and reason rather than religious ideals, Renaissance philosophy was called **humanism.** In the 1300s Italian artists and writers helped spark this cultural movement. For instance, the books of Dante Alighieri (DAHN-tay ah-lee-GYEH-ree) (1265–1321), especially *The Divine Comedy*, promoted vernacular language, in this case Italian, rather than Latin, and attacked the pope, while the writer Giovanni Boccaccio (jo-VAH-nee boh-KAH-chee-oh) (1313–1375), in his novel *Decameron*, emphasized love and reason rather than faith. In the 1400s painters in Italy, such as Sandro Botticelli (SAHN-dro BOT-i-CHEL-ee) (1445–1510), and in the Netherlands depicted space and the human figure realistically.

Scholars have long credited the Renaissance with undermining medieval worldviews by fostering the growth of individualism, secularism, and scientific inquiry. Other historians disagree, describing it as mainly a cultural movement among a small privileged elite of creative people and the political leaders who patronized them that had little impact on the larger society. Nonetheless, Renaissance artists and writers emphasized tolerance of diverse views and new ideals of beauty, and these weakened the influence of the church while helping pave the way for a more creative and secular worldview among many educated people. The Renaissance, which brought hope to a time filled with gloom, eventually spread into northern Europe in the 1500s.

Another manifestation of the dynamism of later medieval Europe was the extraordinary technological development, which was greatly aided by imports from other regions. During the twelfth and thirteenth centuries European scholars translated Arab and Greek scientific writings in Muslim Spain, while Asian and Muslim technologies reached Europe over the trade routes. For instance, the spinning wheel and loom, invented in China, arrived in the 1200s and provided the spur to improved textile manufacturing. During the fourteenth and fifteenth centuries western Europeans developed better ships, in part by improving Chinese inventions such as the compass and stern-post rudder and by adapting the Arab lateen sails. By the 1490s, thanks to these advances in navigation, sailing, and weaponry, Europeans were masters of the oceans. Europeans also devised time-measuring devices, including mechanical clocks in the 1300s, which allowed people to begin to control and standardize units of time.

Perhaps the most crucial late medieval invention was printing by movable type, which allowed information to be produced and spread in unlimited quantities. The Chinese had invented woodblock printing and then movable type made of clay centuries earlier, and in the 1200s they introduced metal type (see Chapter 11). Knowledge of Chinese techniques may have traveled the trade routes to Europe during Mongol times or after. Whatever the source, block printing was used in Europe by the 1400s for books and playing cards. In 1455 the German goldsmith Johann Gutenberg (yoh-HAHN GOO-ten-burg) (1400–1468) introduced the first known metal movable type outside of East Asia, using it to print a Bible. From then on the printed word became an essential medium of mass communication and no longer the monopoly of the few who could afford the expensive hand-copied volumes. This development undermined both feudalism and the church.

Imported technology, especially gunpowder from China, made for more lethal warfare. By the 1200s, the Chinese had developed the first flamethrowers into a primitive gun capable of ejecting flame and projectiles 40 yards, a major reason it took the Mongols so long to conquer China. This and other weapons reached Europe during the Mongol era and were then improved, making late medieval warfare far deadlier than it had been before. But gunpowder weapons, while killing many knights and nobles in European wars, also gave Europeans a huge military advantage over societies that did not have them, among them the peoples of sub-Saharan Africa and the Americas.

Population and Economic Growth

Technological advance was matched by population and economic growth. Europe's population increased by 40 to 50 percent between the tenth and fourteenth centuries. This growth rate, the highest in the world, was supported by increased agricultural development that provided more food. After the devastation of the Black Death, Europe's population again increased rapidly, grain production doubled, and many peasants moved into eastern Europe to open lands.

Commerce also grew. When feudalism and manorialism were dominant, merchants mostly dealt in luxury goods for the aristocracy. Indeed, the feudal ethic was somewhat hostile to the accumulation of wealth, and it devalued merchants. By the 1300s, however, this feudal ethic began to break down. As foreign trade became more economically important and trade networks widened, commerce became a part of everyday life. Valuable spices from India and Southeast Asia were distributed by merchants from Venice, which had trading posts all over the Middle East and around the Black Sea, as well as from Genoa. Observers were awed by the vast quality of merchandise, much of it from the East, in fifteenth-century Venice:

It seems as if the whole world flocks here. Who could count the many shops so well furnished that they seem almost warehouses, with so many cloths of every make—tapestry, brocades, carpets of every sort, silks of every kind; and so many warehouses full of spices, groceries and rugs. These things stupefy the beholder.[22]

Renaissance ("Rebirth")   A dramatic flowering in arts and learning that began in the Italian city-states around 1350 and spread through Europe through the 1500s.

humanism   The name for the European Renaissance philosophy, which emphasized humanity, worldly concerns, and reason rather than religious ideals.

Gold from West Africa, used in coins, treasuries, and jewelry, also stimulated the European economy. To keep track of their businesses, European merchants borrowed and used Arab trading practices and mathematics. For example, in the early 1200s Fibonacci (fee-bo-NACH-ee), a merchant from Pisa in Italy, wrote of the Arab and Indian numerals and calculations he had studied in Algeria, Egypt, and Syria. Soon the mathematical and commercial innovations he learned were adopted in Venice, Genoa, and Florence.

Western European cities were unique in their growing political power and autonomy. Unlike in centralized China or the Ottoman Empire, these cities existed in a politically fragmented region and thus could bargain with kings for advantages and autonomy. For example, in 1241 various North German cities expanded a trade alliance known as the Hanseatic (han-see-AT-ik) League. Eventually it had over 165 member cities, including some in Holland and Poland, and its own army and navy, making it almost an independent political power. The league existed until the end of the seventeenth century.

These developments gave European merchants a status and power unique in the world. In China, for instance, merchants, while often prosperous, had a low ranking in the Confucian social system, were heavily taxed, and faced many restrictions. By contrast, in western Europe merchants steadily gained influence and prestige, becoming mayors and political leaders in cities and towns. This meant that governments gave support to merchants and their interests. Thus, increasingly supported by a social and institutional structure that made profits possible, western European merchants gained more opportunities for profit. Not everyone approved, however. The Dutch philosopher Erasmus complained about greed, asking, "When did avarice reign more largely and less punished?"[23] Nonetheless, the late medieval Europeans laid the foundation for an economic revolution that began to fundamentally alter western European life in the 1500s and later spread its influences around the world.

The Portuguese and Maritime Exploration

In the 1400s a few Europeans, pushed by the growth of commerce, and taking advantage of the new maritime and military technologies, began to explore the world beyond Europe by sea. The first to begin pushing south in search of slaves, gold, and other trade goods were the Portuguese, who had recently been unified in a kingdom and whose standard of living was probably lower than that of many Africans and Asians. Indeed, the Portuguese were shocked at the wealth and prosperity of some of the states they encountered on their voyages. But they enjoyed the advantage of guns, better ships, and a maritime tradition, and they were moved by a missionary desire to outflank Islam and spread Christianity, as well as a compelling appetite for plunder and conquest. The Portuguese were also motivated by a larger strategic purpose: to find a way around Africa so that they could sail directly to the fabled lands of Southeast Asia, the source of the spices so valued in Europe. They also sought the sources of African gold. European legends spoke of a great Christian emperor in Africa, "Prester John," perhaps derived from the king of Ethiopia, who they believed could be a possible ally against Muslims.

Hence, in search of, in their words, "Christians and spices," the Portuguese began systematically exploring the West African coast in 1420 under the visionary sponsorship of Prince Henry the Navigator (1394–1460), an innovator in shipbuilding design and cartography. One of his officers, a Venetian, praised Henry's caravels, which were small ships that could sail both on the ocean and into shallow coastal waters and rivers: "The caravels of Portugal being the best ships that travel the seas under sail, [Prince Henry] reckoned that, provided that they were furnished with everything necessary, they could sail anywhere."[24] Soon Henry's ships discovered Madeira (muh-DEER-uh) Island and the Azores (A-zorz) and Canary Islands in the Atlantic off North Africa. By the 1480s the Portuguese had visited much of the West African coast as far as the modern African nation of Angola (see Chapter 12). In 1487 Portuguese ships led by Bartolomeu Dias (DEE-uhsh) reached the Indian Ocean, beginning a whole new chapter in Portuguese exploration and intensifying Portuguese interest both in Africa and the world to the east. One of the sailors who had manned Portuguese trading ships was a Genoese immigrant to Portugal, Christopher Columbus, who later developed an alternative strategy for reaching the East. In 1492 Columbus, under Spanish sponsorship, sailed west across the Atlantic to the Americas, changing world history forever.

SECTION SUMMARY

- The Black Death killed a third of Europe's people and reduced the power of western European nobles while increasing the power of eastern European nobles.

- French rulers increased their power in the Hundred Years War, England's Tudor dynasty later made England a world power, and Spanish Christians gradually drove out the Muslims, while in Germany and Italy the nobility remained strong.

- The church entered a decline in power and prestige as it came to be seen as corrupt, and the papacy was weakened by the Great Schism.

- During the Renaissance, artists and writers rediscovered classical influences and championed worldly concerns, individualism, and realism rather than spirituality.

- Major technological developments, influenced in part by ideas imported from China and the Muslim world, included the printing press, which further undermined the church, and guns, which killed many in European wars and were especially deadly against Africans and Americans.

- Despite the Black Death, Europe's population soared and its merchants grew increasingly successful and powerful.

- The Portuguese were the first to begin exploring the West Coast of Africa for slaves, gold, and other trade goods, and their adventures eventually led to Columbus's voyage to the Americas.

Chapter Summary

European societies changed dramatically between 600 and 1500. By mixing Greco-Roman, Christian, and Germanic legacies between 500 and 1000, western Europeans constructed new societies based upon new values and practices. These societies also acquired knowledge from and traded with the Islamic world, especially Muslim Spain. In no other major Intermediate Era society do we see as much tension between conflicting values as in medieval Europe. Feudalism, manorialism, and the papacy became the major medieval institutions, but they generated conflict between popes and kings, kings and nobles, nobles and merchants, cities and countryside, and Christians and outsiders. The church played a crucial social and political role in European societies. Priests dominated village life while popes fought heresy and spurred crusades against Muslims. The church also influenced intellectual life, including the debate over faith and reason.

European societies were diverse and shaped in part by forces from outside. The social, political, economic, and religious systems of Byzantium were different from those in western Europe. Compared to western European rulers, the Byzantine emperors were more powerful, had more control over the church, and gave more encouragement to merchants. Eventually the Byzantine church broke completely with the Roman church, becoming the Greek Orthodox Church. Byzantium also passed on many traditions to various eastern European societies such as the Russians. Russia later became a strong state with a rival Orthodox Church, adding to the societal diversity.

Western Europeans were linked by trade networks to Byzantium as well as to other societies of Eurasia and North Africa. These networks, including those formed by the Mongol expansion, allowed the movement from east to west not only of valuable goods, technologies, and ideas but also of diseases such as the Black Death. Between 1300 and 1500 western European states grew larger and, in some cases, more centralized, the church faced decline as a political force, and warfare became more deadly. Sparked in part by Afro-Asian influences, the Renaissance fostered new humanistic ideas and artistic currents. In addition, economic growth and social change enhanced the influence of merchants. In the fifteenth century, aided by Asian and Islamic seafaring technologies, western Europeans began exploring the world.

Online Study Center   Improve Your Grade   Flashcards

Key Terms

medieval	chivalry	excommunicate
feudalism	manorialism	simony
vassal	serfs	Holy Inquisition
benefices	guilds	Magna Carta
fief	usury	Renaissance
knights	courtly love	humanism

Suggested Reading

Books

Bridenthal, Renate, et al., eds. *Becoming Visible: Women in European History*, 3rd ed. Boston: Houghton Mifflin, 1998. Valuable essays.

Brotton, Jerry. *The Renaissance Bazaar: From the Silk Road to Michelangelo*. Oxford: Oxford University Press, 2002. An important revisionist interpretation by a British scholar that places European developments in a hemispheric context.

Cruz, Jo Ann, H. Moran, and Richard Gerberding. *Medieval Worlds: An Introduction to European History, 300–1492*. Boston: Houghton Mifflin, 2004. A readable and comprehensive recent text.

Davies, Norman. *Europe: A History.* New York: HarperPerennial, 1998. Fascinating examination with much on this era.

Gies, Frances, and Joseph Gies. *Marriage and the Family in the Middle Ages.* New York: Harper and Row, 1987. A thorough account of marriage and family life at all levels of society, written for the general reader.

Hanawalt, Barbara A. *The Middle Ages: An Illustrated History*. New York: Oxford University Press, 1998. A well-written overview aimed at the general reader.

Kelly, John. *The Great Mortality: An Intimate History of the Black Death, the Most Devastating Plague of All Time*. New York: HarperCollins, 2005. Very readable account of the calamity and its effects on people.

Logan, F. Donald. *The Vikings in History*. 3rd ed. London: Routledge, 2005. A wide-ranging survey that stresses the importance of the Vikings in European history.

Madden, Thomas F. *A New History of the Crusades*. Lanham, Md.: Rowman and Littlefield, 2005. A recent and well-written overview.

McCormick, Michael. *Origins of the European Economy: Communication and Commerce, A.D. 300–900*. New York: Cambridge University Press, 2001. Pathbreaking work.

Ostrowski, Donald. *Muscovy and the Mongols: Cross-Cultural Influences on the Steppe Frontier, 1304–1589*. Cambridge: Cambridge University Press, 1990. A scholarly study of Byzantine and Mongol influences on the Russians.

Treadgold, Warren. *A Concise History of Byzantium*. New York: Palgrave, 2001. A comprehensive recent survey.

Websites

Byzantium: Byzantine Studies on the Internet (http://www.fordham.edu/halsall/byzantium).   Contains useful texts, images, essays, and bibliography.

The Internet Medieval Sourcebook (http://www.fordham.edu/halsall/sbook.html).   This is one of the best, most extensive sources for texts and essays.

Lectures in Medieval History (http://www.ku/kansas/medieval/108/lectures/index.html).   Many useful essays for the general reader by a leading expert.

Medieval and Renaissance Europe: Primary Historical Documents (http://www.lib.byu.edu/~rdh/eurodocs/medren.html).   Many links to primary sources.

The WWW Virtual Library: Medieval Europe (http://www.msu.edu/-georgm1/history/medieval.htm).   Contains many links to many topical sites.

The World of the Vikings (http://www.worldofthevikings.com).   Contains many links to texts, images, and essays.

Expanding Horizons in the Intermediate Era, 600 B.C.E.–600 C.E.

Societies change largely in interaction with one another rather than in isolation, and world historians emphasize these interactions. In world history, the formation of broad connections among peoples is more crucial than the rise and fall of individual states and even great empires. World history differs from regional history primarily because the world historian stresses contacts, collisions, and networks of exchange, as well as the spread from one society to another of products, technologies, ideas, and people. From earliest times parts of Eurasia and North Africa formed an interconnecting zone, and the links continually expanded to incorporate more of Eurasia and Africa and then, after 1500, the Americas and Oceania.

These patterns can be clearly seen in the Intermediate Era, or Middle Ages between 600 and 1500 C.E., when the world changed profoundly. During this time, the Chinese, Indian, and Islamic societies stood out for their power and creativity, but by the 1400s western Europe was also emerging as a dynamic center. In the Eastern Hemisphere vigorous societies also flourished in Northeast Asia, Southeast Asia, Central Asia, and sub-Saharan Africa. Many far-flung cultures became linked as people, armies, goods, and religions moved more easily and frequently, expanding horizons. These movements and exchanges connected peoples from one end of Afro-Eurasia to the other and generated several transitions, such as the reshaping of many societies by the spread of universal religions. Connections were also growing within the Americas. Large empires such as those of the Aztecs, Incas, and their predecessors, enjoyed widespread influence, and trade networks bound societies over great distances. Thanks to European voyages of discovery, by 1500 the long divided Eastern and Western Hemispheres came into regular communication, furthering global contacts.

Today the term *globalization* refers to the increasing interconnectedness of nations and peoples around the world through international trade, investment, ideas, popular culture, and travel. Globalization is sometimes viewed as a twentieth-century phenomenon. But extensive exchanges between widespread peoples and travel over vast distances came many centuries earlier, especially in Afro-Eurasia. An English observer, William Fitzsteven, described the results of such connections in the 1170s when he noted how the markets of London carried products that reflected the cosmopolitan tastes of the city's people:

Gold from Arabia, from Sabaea [Yemen] spice
And incense; from the Scythians [Central Asians] arms of steel
Well-tempered; oil from the rich groves of palm
That spring from the fat lands of Babylon;
Fine gems from Nile, from China crimson silks;
French wines; and sable . . .
From the far lands where Rus and Northmen [Vikings] dwell.[1]

This essay examines some of these early forms of globalization during the Intermediate Era, such as long-distance trade, the spread of world religions and the social changes they fostered, the connections sparked by the Mongol expansion, and the acceleration of maritime exploration in the Late Intermediate Era.

INCREASING ECONOMIC EXCHANGE

Interregional trade was a major theme in world history, especially because it fostered other forms of exchange, including the spread of religions, cultures, and technologies over trade routes. Merchants carried with them their own traditions, and learned of other traditions in their travels. During the Intermediate Era, several trade zones developed in the Americas, while in the Eastern Hemisphere overland trade routes reached across Eurasia and Africa. Maritime trade also flourished around the rim of the Indian Ocean. Though it was dominated by Islamic merchants, who spread their faith far and wide, many peoples of various faiths engaged in long-distance commerce by land and sea, serving as links between diverse societies.

Trade and Interregional Contact

The roots of the growing commerce between societies go far back in history. Long-distance trade routes had long existed to move cargo and people by boat, camel, or horseback. The contacts between societies that occurred through trade and military expansion spread various cultural and religious ideas (see map). For instance, Indian influences, including Buddhism, were carried over the trading routes into Central Asia, Tibet, China, Japan, and Southeast Asia between 200 B.C.E. and 1500 C.E. Similarly, between 700 and 1500, Islam expanded by land and sea into West and East Africa, southern Europe, India, and Southeast Asia. Muslim-dominated trade routes ultimately reached from the Sahara to the South China Sea. Once established, these trade routes became a stimulus for travel. Indeed, the annual pilgrimage of devout Muslims proved a boon for merchants as pilgrims from all over brought their local products to Mecca, transforming it into one of the world's great fairs. In 1184 one observer marveled that "no merchandise in the world is absent from this meeting."[2]

Beginning around 200 B.C.E., the Silk Road, a 4,000-mile-long route linking China through Central Asia to India, western Asia, and the Mediterranean, provided the most outstanding example of overland trade and a symbol of east-west contacts. Cities such as Samarkand and Bukhara grew up along the overland Silk Road routes across Central Asia to service trade and merchants. The people in these cities prospered as middlemen between merchants and suppliers of caravans. Chinese silk, porcelain, and bamboo were carried west to Baghdad and the eastern Mediterranean ports, from which

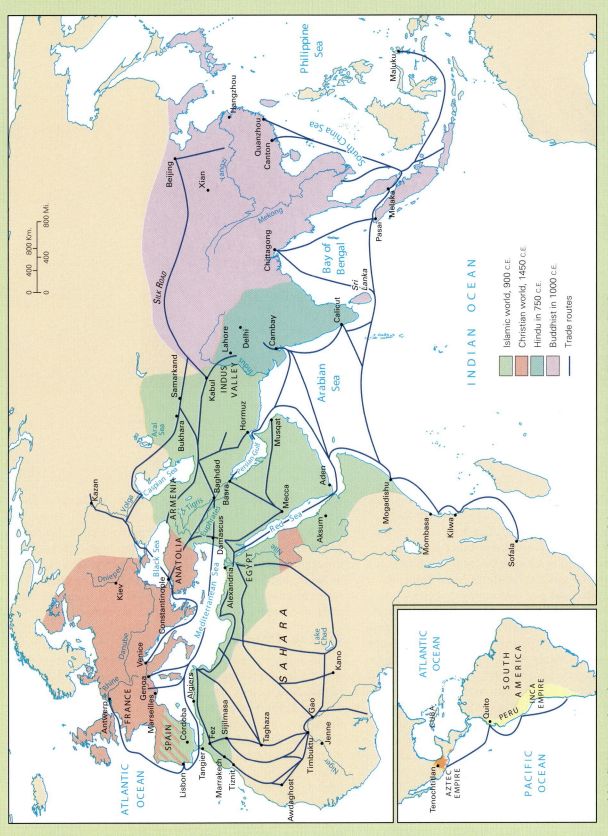

World Religions and Trade Routes, 600–1500 Much of the Eastern Hemisphere was linked by land and maritime trade routes. Along with goods and travelers, Buddhism, Christianity, and Islam spread along these trade routes, attracting believers from many societies.

Legend:
- Islamic world, 900 C.E.
- Christian world, 1450 C.E.
- Hindu in 750 C.E.
- Buddhist in 1000 C.E.
- Islam spread
- Trade routes

Silk Road Travelers   The Silk Road remained a key trade route during this era. This painting, from a fourteenth-century atlas made in Spain, shows one of the horse and camel caravans that traveled between China and Central Asia.   (Bildarchiv Preussischer Kulturbesitz/Art Resource, NY)

they were shipped by sea to Constantinople and Rome. Silk clothes were coveted by European bishops and aristocrats as well as by Mahayana Buddhist monks. The lively caravan trade that developed along the Silk Road had other consequences too. Over the centuries many Chinese inventions, such as gunpowder, wheelbarrows, and the compass, were transported westward over the Silk Road and profoundly changed Western society. The trade even influenced food preferences. Chinese noodles, for example, spread widely in Asia, and Arabs may have brought Chinese-derived pasta to Italy. But the exchange was not entirely one way. Arabs marveled at a Chinese scholar who sojourned in Baghdad around 900, learned Arabic, and made copies of important medical texts to take back to China.

The Silk Road was not the only major land trade network. Other major overland trade routes linked West Africa and the Mediterranean across the Sahara Desert, allowing the movement of commodities such as salt and gold. Land and riverine routes also tied northern and eastern Europe into the broader Eurasian trade system. For example, between 800 and 1000 Swedish Vikings established a major trading network stretching from Scandinavia through Russia to Byzantium. Persia, Mali in West Africa, Byzantium, the northern Italian city-states, and Muslim Spain also prospered from their strategic locations along major trade routes. An Arab source reported that, thanks to their extensive travels, Jewish merchants who came to Cordoba in Spain "speak Arabic, Persian, [Italian], and the language of the Franks and Slavs."[3] At about the same time that

these routes were expanding in Eurasia and Africa, in the Americas overland trade also carried Mesoamerican influences deep into North America while spreading Andean technologies, crops, and religious cults widely around South America. Although oceanic exchange in the Americas was limited, people in North and South America moved products by canoe along rivers, a lively canoe and raft trade linked the Caribbean islands, and some traders sailed along the Pacific coast on rafts.

The Rise of Maritime Trade

By 1000 an increasingly lucrative maritime trade, perhaps spurred by improving naval technology, grew in the Eastern Hemisphere, despite the dangers from pirates and storms. At one end of the Afro-Eurasian zone, much trade crisscrossed the Mediterranean, around which Venice, Genoa, Constantinople, Aleppo in Syria, Alexandria, and Algiers served as the major ports. Sailing networks along Europe's Atlantic coast later linked the Baltic and North Seas to Mediterranean ports and helped foster the Hanseatic League of Baltic ports.

Further east, the Indian Ocean routes became the heart of the most extensive maritime trade network in the Intermediate world. The Abbasid caliph al-Mansur, writing from Baghdad, boasted that "there is no obstacle to us and China; everything on the sea can come to us on it."[4] The Indian Ocean system linked China, Japan, Vietnam, and Cambodia in the east through Malaya and the Indonesian archipelago to India and Sri Lanka, and then westward to Persia, Arabia, Russia, the eastern and central Mediterranean, and the East African coast as far south as Mozambique. Over these routes the spices of Indonesia, the gold and tin of Malaya, the textiles, sugar, and cotton of India, the cinnamon of Sri Lanka, the gold and ivory of East Africa, the coffee of Arabia, the carpets of Persia, and the silks, porcelain, and tea of China moved to distant markets. Many of these products reached Europe, sparking interest there in reaching the sources of the riches of the East.

The spices, aromatic and pungent derivatives of vegetables grown in tropical lands, were among the main products moving from east to west. Black pepper was cultivated chiefly in India, Siam, and Indonesia, while cloves, nutmeg, and mace came from the Maluku (Moluccan) Islands of eastern Indonesia and cinnamon were grown in Indonesia and Sri Lanka. All of them found a market in the Middle East and Europe. Asia was not the only source for spices, since red or cayenne pepper from West Africa was traded to the Middle East and reached Europe in the 1300s. While they became ingredients in cosmetics and perfumes, spices were more commonly used as medicine or as condiments to flavor food. Intermediate Era people treated a range of illnesses and aided digestion with spices, and many cultures used copious quantities of spices in cooking. Asian spices such as almonds, ginger, saffron, cinnamon, sugar, nutmeg, and cloves improved late medieval European diets. An English book from the early 1400s reported the popularity of pepper, which helped disguise the bad taste of heavily salted preserved meat during the long European winter: "Pepper is black and has a good smack, And every man doth it buy."[5]

Various states around the Persian Gulf, Indian Ocean, and South China Sea were closely linked to maritime trade. However, no particular political power dominated the Indian Ocean trading routes. The trade dynamism depended on cosmopolitan port cities, especially hubs such as Hormuz in Persia, Kilwa in Tanzania, Cambay in northwest India, Calicut on India's southwest coast, Melaka in Malaya, and Quanzhou (chwan-cho) in southern China. These trading ports became vibrant centers of international commerce and culture, drawing populations from various societies. The thirteenth-century traveler Marco Polo was fascinated by the coming and going of ships at Quanzhou: "Here is a harbor whither all ships of India come, with much costly merchandise. It is also the port whither go the [Chinese] merchants [heading overseas]. There is such traffic of merchandise that it is a truly wonderful sight."[6]

A hemispheric trade system developed in which some people came to produce for a world market. This system was fueled by China and India, the great centers of world manufacturing in this era (see Historical Controversy: Eastern Predominance in the Intermediate World). Together China and India probably produced over three-quarters of all world industrial products before 1500. China exported iron, steel, silk, refined sugar, and ceramics, while India was the great producer of textiles. Their industrial products might be transported thousands of miles. Hence, the work of a cotton weaver in India might be sold in China or East Africa, and Chinese ceramics might reach Zimbabwe and Mali. The Muslim soldiers who resisted the Christian crusaders used steel swords smelted in India from East African iron. Merchants from all over Afro-Eurasia—Arabs,

Armenians, Chinese, Indians, Indonesians, Jews, Venetians, Genoese—traveled great distances in search of profits, often forming permanent trade diasporas. For instance, it was said of the Genoese, whose merchant networks stretched from Portugal to the Middle East and Russia, that they were so spread "throughout the world that wherever one goes and stays he makes another Genoa there."[7] One Cairo-based Jewish family firm had branches in India, Iran, and Tunisia. Most of the goods traded over vast distances were luxury items meant for the upper classes, but some goods, such as pepper and sugar, also reached consumers of more modest means.

UNIVERSAL RELIGIONS AND SOCIAL CHANGE

The power and reach of universal, or world, religions such as Buddhism, Christianity, and Islam increased during the Intermediate Era. Religion and its mandates dominated the lives of millions around the world. These religions were early agents of globalization, propagating ideas and fostering trade across regional boundaries. By 1500 the religious map of the Eastern Hemisphere looked very different than it had in 600. Millions of people had embraced ideas, beliefs, and ways of life vastly different from those of their ancestors. The religions promoted moral and ethical values that helped preserve harmony in societies that were increasingly cosmopolitan. The Christian injunction to "love thy neighbor as thyself," the Buddhist emphasis on good thoughts and actions, and the Muslim ideals of social justice and the equality of believers fostered goodwill and cooperation. Religious beliefs also spurred the emergence of new values and social forms.

The Triumph of Universal Religions

During the Intermediate Era, most people in Eurasia and many in Africa eventually embraced one or another universal religion. Islam became the most widespread, rapidly expanding through the Middle East and eventually claiming Central Asia and parts of Europe while gaining a large following in West Africa, the East African coast, South Asia, China, and Southeast Asia. Islam fostered religious, social, and economic networks that linked peoples from Morocco and Spain to Indonesia and the Philippines with a common faith, values, and trade connections. Some Muslim scholars and jurists, such as the Moroccan Ibn Battuta, traveled, sojourned, and even settled thousands of miles from their homelands.

Older faiths also spread in this era, changing societies in varied ways. Theravada Buddhism was established in Sri Lanka and then expanded into mainland Southeast Asia, where it gradually displaced earlier faiths and reshaped cultures by teaching moderation, pacifism, unselfish acts, and individualism. To the north, Mahayana Buddhism first reached Central Asia and then China early in the Common Era, and during the Intermediate Era it became entrenched in Japan, Korea, Vietnam, Mongolia, and Tibet. In most places Buddhism existed alongside rather than replacing earlier religious traditions, such as animism in Siam and Tibet, Shinto in Japan, and Confucianism in China. By 1000 a Buddhist world incorporating diverse societies and several sects stretched from India eastward to

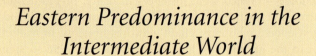

Eastern Predominance in the Intermediate World

For over a century now the prosperous and powerful nations of North America and western Europe—often known today as the West—have dominated the world economically and politically. But before 1500 the world looked very different, and various societies in Asia and North Africa were much stronger and more influential than they are today. Some Eastern societies enjoyed power and status far beyond their borders, helping to shape much of the Eastern Hemisphere in these centuries. However, historians debate to what degree we can consider this to have been an era of Eastern predominance in Afro-Eurasia.

THE PROBLEM

Some historians believe that the rise to influence and prosperity of the East, especially China, India, and various Islamic societies, was a major theme of the Intermediate Era. In their view, for most of these centuries, these Eastern peoples developed and sustained more dynamic governments, productive economies, and creative technologies than any other societies. Others disagree, contending that after 1000 the advantage shifted to western Europeans, who laid the foundations for rapid growth and eventual world dominance. These arguments are part of a vigorous scholarly debate.

THE DEBATE

Many historians identify Eastern predominance in this era, but they disagree on which society made the greatest contributions to the world. The largest number point to China as the Eurasian leader in the Intermediate Era, and they offer a variety of factors to explain China's status. S. A. M. Adshead, for example, sees Tang China as taking center-stage in the world economy and becoming the world's best-ordered state between 600 and 900. William McNeill refers to an era of Chinese predominance especially from 1000 to 1500, with China as the engine of the Eurasian economy. Various historians of Asia, among them Rhoads Murphey, describe an especially dynamic and creative Song China that had many of the conditions that would, in the later eighteenth century, foster industrialization in northwest Europe: urbanization, commercialization, widening local and overseas markets, rising demand, and mechanical invention. A few scholars such as Mary Matossian label the entire Intermediate Era the "Chinese Millennium," when China was more populous, productive, and wealthy than any other society, enjoying an orderly society and advanced technology.

There is a growing consensus among world historians that Chinese innovations and commercial expansion energized Eurasian trade and that Chinese inventions contributed much to the Intermediate world. The British scholar Robert Temple goes even further, crediting the Chinese with inventing modern agriculture, shipping, astronomical observatories, oil industries, paper money, decimal mathematics, wheelbarrows, fishing reels, multistage rockets, guns, umbrellas, hot-air balloons, chess, whiskey, and even the essential design of the steam engine. Without Chinese naval technology, he and others argue, Columbus would never have sailed to America. China and India were the two great centers of world manufacturing before 1500, and their exports fueled Afro-Eurasian trade.

But China was not the only Asian powerhouse and great source of knowledge. Indians fostered two universal religions, Buddhism and Hinduism, while inventing and exporting scientific, technological, and agricultural techniques to China, the Islamic world, and later Europe in a process the historian Lynda Shaffer terms "southernization." Such innovations as Indian granulated sugar crystals, the decimal system, "Arabic" numerals, and cotton plants had revolutionary implications for Eurasia. Then there are historians of the Middle East, such as Marshall Hodgson and Richard Eaton, who argue for the centrality of the Islamic societies. They contend that, before 1600, the Islamic culture and economy were the world's most expansive, influential, and integrating force. Islam provided a widespread, sophisticated culture as many peoples joined the Muslim-dominated hemispheric economy. Islam was cosmopolitan, egalitarian, and flexible, allowing Muslims to rebound from the Mongol conquests and Black Death and reestablish powerful states such as Ottoman Turkey.

Still other historians think China, India, and Islam all played key roles as powerhouses in an Eastern-dominated Intermediate world. For instance, Robert Marks argues that the Eastern Hemisphere in the 1300s and 1400s had three centers, with dynamic but linked regional systems based on China, India, and Islam. In the 1400s, from Ottoman Turkey eastward to Japan, agricultural efficiency, consumer goods, social welfare, and civilian and military technology were generally the equal of, and often superior to, European counterparts. British scholar John Hobson makes a strong case that the rise of the East made possible the later rise of the West. He argues that the globalization of the era allowed the advanced Eastern inventions, the products of more dynamic societies, to flow westward, where they were gradually assimilated by Europe. Many historians contend that Europe in this era was economically weak, with small, insignificant states, and did not show renewed vigor until 1400. Nor did Europe have, as some historians suggest, any unique cultural advantages. Jack Goody concludes that there were few decisive cultural differences between East and West in rationality, economic tools, family patterns, and political pluralism.

Other scholars doubt that any Eastern societies had a great advantage in this era, and they contend that medieval Europe was not backward compared to China, India, or Islam. David Landes, for example, while conceding that Europe was well behind China and Islam in many areas of life in 1000, suggests that things had changed considerably 500 years later. With what he considers many cultural and geographical advantages, Europeans, argues Landes, caught up to the East with the growth of manufacturing and trade. Landes and others describe an inventive Europe with impressive technological progress using increased nonhuman power, especially in agriculture. Toby Huff has favorably contrasted European science with its Chinese counterpart, especially after 1200. Restless human energy, influential merchants, and competing states made late medieval Europe dynamic. Rodney Stark credits the medieval Catholic Church's emphasis on reason and belief in progress for fostering economic growth, asserting that these ideas were lacking in other religions, a view many scholars have challenged. Landes and Huff also challenge the notion of Eastern leadership. They see China by 1450 as overpopulated, intellectually dormant, indifferent to technology, negating commercial success, and resistant to change. Some historians of China, such as Adshead, concur that the balance of power was shifting toward Europe in the later Intermediate Era.

If several Eastern societies, and especially China, did have some advantages and great power during much of the Intermediate Era, they lost their predominance between 1450 and 1800, raising the question of when and how the East declined. As for when, some historians believe the decline of the East preceded and made possible the rise of the West. Janet Abu-Lughod describes a well-integrated hemispheric system linking Afro-Eurasia by trade for several centuries, with no single country dominant. This network declined after 1350, reducing Europe's commercial competition. Other historians blame Eastern decline on the Mongols and their heirs, who devastated western Asia and North India and ended the creative Song dynasty.

Others credit what the historian L. S. Stavrianos termed the "Law of the Retarding Lead"—that nothing fails like success—for undermining China and helping underdeveloped Europe. This concept holds that the best-adapted, most successful societies have the most difficulty in changing and retaining their lead in a period of transition. They lose their dynamic thrust. Conversely, the less successful societies are more likely to eventually adapt and forge ahead. In the 1400s China still had an edge over other societies, with an advanced technology, efficient government, great regional power, and the world's largest commercial economy. As a result, the Chinese had a stake in preserving rather than dramatically altering their system, which seemed to work so well. Indeed, some argue that the leading Eastern societies, especially China, remained successful until overtaken by a rising West between 1600 and 1800.

EVALUATING THE DEBATE

A plausible case can be made for Eastern predominance, and most global historians now agree that, while other societies played key roles, China and the Islamic world were the two major poles of global trade and technological innovation for much of this era, at least before the 1400s. But the Eastern advantage was eventually lost. We are left with tantalizing questions. What if the Mongols or Ottomans had conquered some

Chinese Foundries By the second century B.C.E. Chinese iron masters had developed highly sophisticated techniques for producing iron and steel, including a basic blast furnace similar to those invented in Europe in the nineteenth century.
(Courtesy of South China University of Technology Library, Canton [Guangzhon])

of western Europe, or Ming admiral Zheng He had continued his voyages and headed all the way to West Africa, Europe, or the Americas? Had they occurred, these Mongol, Ottoman, or Chinese achievements might have created a world unrecognizable to us today. Perhaps China, with many prerequisites already in place and enriched by greater trade with West Africa and Europe, might have sparked an industrial revolution. It did not happen, however. Humanity stood at a crossroads in the middle of the millennium, posed between several very different futures. During the next several centuries Europe gradually forged ahead—what some historians call "the rise of the West"—partly by assimilating Eastern technologies and science, while the Islamic societies, India, and finally China struggled, making the world after 1500 very different than the world before it.

THINKING ABOUT THE CONTROVERSY

1. Why do some historians emphasize China as the predominant power in this era?
2. What role did India and the Islamic societies play in the Intermediate world?
3. What points support the argument that Europe began its rise to world power in this era?

EXPLORING THE CONTROVERSY

Among books making the case for Eastern predominance and leadership are John M. Hobson, *The Eastern Origins of Western Civilisation* (New York: Cambridge University Press, 2004); Robert B. Marks, *The Origins of the Modern World: A Global and Ecological Narrative* (Lanham, Md.: Rowman and Littlefield, 2002); and Jack Goody, *The East in the West* (Cambridge: Cambridge University Press, 1996). On China as the major power, see S. A. M. Adshead, *Tang China: The Rise of the East in World History* (New York: Palgrave, 2004); William H. McNeill, *The Pursuit of Power: Technology, Armed Force, and Society Since A.D. 1000* (Chicago: University of Chicago Press, 1982); Rhoads Murphey, *East Asia: A New History*, 3rd ed. (New York: Longman, 2004); Mary Kilbourne Matossian, *Shaping World History: Breakthroughs in Ecology, Technology, Science, and Politics* (Armonk, N.Y.: M.E. Sharpe, 1997); and Robert Temple, *The Genius of China: 3,000 Years of Science, Discovery and Invention* (London: Prion Books, 1986). For Indian and Islamic influence, see Lynda Shaffer, "Southernization," *Journal of World History*, 5/1 (Spring 1994), pp. 1–22; Marshall Hodgson, *Rethinking World History* (Cambridge: Cambridge University Press, 1993); Richard Eaton, *Islamic History as Global History* (Washington, D.C.: American Historical Association, 1993). Among books that argue for European superiority are Toby E. Huff, *The Rise of Early Modern Science: Islam, China, and the West* (Cambridge: Cambridge University Press, 1993); David S. Landes, *The Wealth and Power of Nations: Why Some Are So Rich and Some Are So Poor* (New York: Norton, 1998); and Rodney Stark, *The Victory of Reason: How Christianity Led to Freedom, Capitalism, and Western Success* (New York: Random House, 2005). For a broader study of the rise and demise of the East, see Janet L. Abu-Lughod, *Before European Hegemony: The World System A.D. 1250–1350* (New York: Oxford University Press, 1989).

Vietnam and Japan, but the temples, pagodas, and statues constructed to honor the Buddha reflected local styles and taste. Whereas many kinds of people, including merchants and jurists, moved along Islamic networks, Buddhist networks tended to facilitate the movement of pilgrims, such as the seventh-century Chinese monk Xuan Zang (swan tsang), who sojourned in India.

Christianity expanded to encompass nearly all of Europe in its fold by 1200, filtering north into the Germanic and Celtic lands and east among the Slavs. But the original Christian church divided. The Roman church dominated the west while the Orthodox church claimed Russia and much of eastern Europe. Although Christianity was pushed back by Islam in western Asia and North Africa, sizeable Christian communities grew and sometimes flourished in these regions, aided by the tolerance Muslims usually accorded Christian practice. Nonetheless, chronic tensions arose between Christian Europe and the Islamic world, derived from political and economic conflicts as well as a clash between the strong missionary impulses of both religions. Christians and Muslims often viewed each other as barbarians. A tenth-century Arab geographer argued after visiting Europe that the manners of Christian Europeans "are harsh, their understanding dull and their tongues heavy. Those of them who are furthest to the north are the most subject to stupidity, grossness and brutishness."[8] Tensions between the two rival faiths generated the European Crusades to regain the Holy Land, which left a legacy of bitterness on both sides.

All universal religions nurtured a respect for learning. An admiring Arab described a great library, the House of Knowledge, opened by the Shi'ite Fatimid caliph in Egypt in 1005: "People could visit it, and whoever wanted to copy something that interested him could do so. Lectures were held there by the Quran readers, astronomers, grammarians, philologists, and physicians."[9] The House of Wisdom in Abbasid-ruled Baghdad attracted scholars from all over the Islamic world and beyond, and scholars from Arabia and Spain even made the long journey across the Sahara to West Africa to teach or study in the university at Timbuktu. Some Buddhist centers of higher education, such as the university at Nalanda in India and the monasteries in Srivijaya, in Sumatra, attracted students from all over Asia. In Europe, various Christian orders and thinkers encouraged the preservation of knowledge, laying the foundation for universities, such as Paris and Oxford, and spurring philosophical speculation. Eventually the European universities broadened their studies, mixing theology with secular subjects such as science and logic. Confucians also revered knowledge, and Chinese rulers patronized centers of scholarship such as the Hanlin Academy. Jewish communities honored theologians and produced philosophers such as Spanish-born Moses Maimonides (971–1030), an expert on Aristotle who became a court physician in Egypt.

Gender Roles and Family Patterns

The expansion of universal religions during the Intermediate Era, combined with increasing trade, also influenced many aspects of social life, thought, and attitudes. All of the religions had patriarchal institutional structures that were led by men who promoted notions of female inferiority. For instance, even humanist Christian thinkers believed that women belonged in the home. A fifteenth-century Italian warned that "it would hardly win us [men] respect if our wife busied herself among the men in the marketplace. It also seems somewhat demeaning to me to remain shut up in the house among women when I have manly things to do among men."[10] Islam incorporated many Arab and Persian customs that constrained women, including those that prescribed female seclusion and modesty, but seclusion and veiling of women became the main pattern primarily in Muslim societies that already had a strong patriarchal tradition, such as Arabia, Egypt, north India, and the former Byzantine territories. Where pre-Islamic cultures had less rigid gender roles, as in Spain, Southeast Asia, and West Africa, Islamic patriarchy was considerably modified. The pious Arab traveler Ibn Battuta, for example, was astonished that, in his view, the Mali women wore much too revealing clothing and seemed to have a higher status than the men.

The status of women varied around the world. As Confucianism dug deeper roots in East Asia, patriarchy became a stronger force there than it had been in classical times. By Ming times it was more common to seclude upper-class Chinese women, and even bind their feet. Japanese society also became more patriarchal, as the warrior culture replaced the Heian culture in which elite women had flourished. But some Mahayana Buddhists favored gender equity, at least in principle. The Japanese Zen master Dogen (DOE-joan) argued that there was nothing special about masculinity: "The elements that make up the human body are the same for a man as for a woman. You should not waste your time in futile discussion of the superiority of one sex over another."[11] In mainland Southeast Asia, Theravada Buddhism proved a generally moderating force in gender relations, although men had more opportunity than women to acquire the merit needed to reach nirvana because only men could become monks. In societies as different as Byzantium, Carolingian France, West Africa, Southeast Asia, and the Inca Empire, individual women, such as the Burmese queen Pwa Saw, could still gain power as queens or as powers behind the throne. But in most societies religious hierarchies and military organizations remained mostly male, with priesthoods and warfare giving men more access to prestige and resources. In addition, in most places education was largely restricted to boys.

Religious values influenced family patterns and sexual attitudes. Islam allowed men to have four wives, but polygamy for some men meant that women were unavailable to others, who then could not marry. Christian teachings favored monogamy and marriage, but many men and women joined clerical orders or for other reasons never married. And European kings often flouted church teachings by having concubines and mistresses. Only a minority of western Europeans, mostly in the middle class, lived in nuclear families like those common today in the West. In many societies around the world, men of elite status, and especially in royal families, had multiple wives and concubines. Only a few societies allowed women to have more than one husband.

Attitudes toward homosexuality and gender identity varied widely. Followers of Christianity, Judaism, Islam, and Confucianism all shared an aversion to homosexual relations, in part because they did not produce children. But this sexual behavior had long been practiced and even tolerated in all these traditions. Christian tolerance turned to fierce repression only in the thirteenth century, and such repression was not a global pattern. Perhaps because there were many unmarried Muslim men, and also owing to the rigid segregation of the sexes, some Islamic societies ignored homosexual activity. Homosexual literature was common in western Asian cities under the Abbasid Caliphate. The Japanese, Chinese, and some Southeast Asian and Native American societies also tended to accept homosexuality as part of life. Gender categories could be flexible. Some Asian and American tribal peoples identified more than two genders, including homosexual or heterosexual men who lived as women and served the village as shamans.

Slavery and Feudalism

Most societies were hierarchical, and many people lived in slavery or faced severe restrictions on their freedom. Sanctioned by various religions or simply by custom or economic necessity, slavery had long been common throughout the world and remained so in the Intermediate Era, except for East Asia, where it largely died out by 1000. Islam permitted slavery but encouraged owners to treat slaves well. In Arab, Persian, and Turkish societies, the availability of slaves to do the physical work made the seclusion of elite women possible. Many Muslim African societies, and some that were non-Muslim, had slaves, including the West African kingdoms and East African city-states, although their status varied widely. Africans had been shipped north for centuries to work in the Islamic world, and some African slaves in the Persian Gulf region revolted. Slaves were also common in Southeast Asian societies such as Angkor and Siam. A Persian observer wrote that, in Indonesia, the people "reckon high rank and wealth by the quantity of slaves a person owns."[12] Various American peoples, among them the Mayas and Aztecs, enslaved prisoners of war, debtors, and criminals.

In Europe, slavery's decline after the end of the Roman Empire, and gradual replacement by serfdom, a less restrictive form of bondage, did not end the slave market there. Some slaves still labored in parts of western Europe, sometimes even on lands of Christian monasteries. An active Mediterranean slave trade shipped Slavs, Greeks, and Turks from the Black Sea region to southern Europe and North Africa. Some northwestern Europeans were also sold as slaves to Mediterranean societies. By the fifteenth century Africans appeared in southern European slave markets.

Although some scholars question the usefulness and scope of the concept of feudalism, others identify it as a major new social and political pattern in the world in the Intermediate Era. In feudal societies, relations between people of different status, especially between lords and vassals, were prescribed by agreements or law, and governments were weak or decentralized. The feudal model, which included lords and knights, independent manors, serfdom, small states, and chronic warfare, was best represented by some medieval European societies between 800 and 1300. Some historians also apply feudalism to post-Heian Japan under the warrior class and shogunates, and others to parts of India and Southeast Asia, where many small states competed for power. Feudal societies such as Norman England, the Carolingian realm, and perhaps Ashikaga Japan differed in many ways from the large centralized states such as Song China, Abbasid Iraq, Mali, or the Inca Empire, where emperors or kings exercised great power through bureaucracies.

In most hierarchical societies, whether feudal or centralized, political, military, and religious elites lived off wealth from the primary producers, such as peasants, herders, and artisans. Workers were more or less controlled by, and owed obligations to, those in power, such as Inca kings and Chinese emperors, who ruled despotically. For example, in medieval Europe the dominant Christian church encouraged people who wanted to reap rewards in Heaven to accept the social order, and some governments standardized work requirements. Hence, in 800 the Frankish king Charlemagne proclaimed that the peasant living on church and royal estates "must plow his lord's land a whole day [but not also be asked] to do handiwork service during the same week. The dependent shall not withdraw from these services and the lords shall not ask more from them."[13] In both western Europe and Japan, feudalism established a basis for future change by building up intense pressures that eventually erupted.

THE MONGOL EMPIRE AND HEMISPHERIC CONNECTIONS

The Mongol expansion, which united a large chunk of the Eurasian population and indirectly affected millions of other people, was one of the most crucial developments in world history. Between 1250 and 1350 the Mongols established the largest land empire in world history, stretching from lands on the western shores of the Black Sea east to the Pacific coast of China and Korea. The building of the Mongol Empire was a ruthless but amazing feat. Within the span of a century the Mongol armies, supported by a Mongol population of less than 2 million, swept out of their arid Central Asian grasslands to put over 200 million people under their control. By reopening Central Asian trade routes closed by political turmoil and by connecting with many different peoples and countries, the Mongols fostered communication networks and the transfer of technology between once remote parts of the Eastern Hemisphere. In doing so, they were major catalysts of change, laying a foundation for the gradual transition from the Intermediate to the Early Modern Era.

The Mongol Empire

The forces prompting the Mongols to build their empire are not altogether clear. Warfare was common among the Mongols, who were tough steppe herders of horses and camels. Historically, various other Central Asian pastoralists, including Turks, Huns, and Tibetans, had forged large but short-lived empires or confederations. Various factors in Central Asia, including

Catapults The Mongols used advanced military technology, including catapults, to conquer cities. This battle scene, painted by a Persian artist, shows the Mongols attacking a city around 1300. (Edinburgh University Library, Orms. 20, fol. 124v)

ecological instability, climate change, and population growth, may have prompted the Mongol expansion by fostering competition for limited resources. Another factor was the religions, such as Mahayana Buddhism and Nestorian Christianity, that reached remote Mongolia, which heightened awareness of the riches to be found in the world beyond the steppes. These forces led to the emergence of Genghis Khan (ca. 1162–1227), a visionary leader who effectively united the Mongol tribes. His warriors, mounted and well armed, and aided by siege weaponry and innovative military strategies of rapid attack, made a formidable fighting force.

Within a few decades Mongol armies conquered Central Asia, Tibet, Korea, Russia, part of eastern Europe, Afghanistan, and a large part of western Asia, including Persia and Anatolia. The Mongols were at the Danube, preparing to sweep through Hungary into western Europe, when Genghis Khan's successor, his son Ogodei (1185–1241), died, aborting that thrust. Thus western Europe did not suffer the ravages experienced by other peoples. In the mid-1200s the Mongols expanded their domination in western Asia, overpowering the Arab Abbasid Caliphate. The widespread destruction they caused in the Middle East and Central Asia ended the Islamic golden age and reshaped politics and agriculture in these regions. Later, China, the most formidable foe and tempting prize, and Korea were also eventually added to the Mongol-ruled realm.

Coming from a harsh environment with few resources, the Mongols, with an army of perhaps 130,000 men, sometimes used brutal methods, as had conquerors of earlier eras such as

the Assyrians and Alexander the Great. Contemporary accounts credit the Mongols with massacring hundreds of thousands, perhaps millions, of people and burning many cities. A Persian historian concluded that "it is unlikely that mankind will [ever again] see the like of this calamity."[14] The death toll, however, was probably exaggerated by both Mongols and their foes. Some historians doubt that many civilians were killed en masse, since they were needed for production and transportation.

However, the Mongol Empire proved short-lived. One reason was that the Mongols never connected with maritime commerce. They were also victims of their success. Before he died, Genghis Khan worried that his successors would forsake the rigorous life for the comforts of wealthy conquered peoples such as Arabs and Chinese, predicting that "after us, [our] people will wear garments of gold; they will eat sweet, greasy food, ride splendid coursers, and hold in their arms the loveliest women, and they will forget that they owe these things to us."[15] This warning proved prophetic. The Mongols succumbed to wealth and power, their harsh and increasingly corrupt rule provoking rebellions that would end their domination.

The Heritage of the Mongols and Their Networks

In 2000 some world historians named Genghis Khan the most crucial figure of the second millennium C.E. because, despite his brutality, the Mongol conquests he led established an early form of globalized communication characterized by technology and product transfer moving chiefly from east to west along the Silk Road. During the Mongol era, for example, Chinese inventions such as the spinning wheel, medical discoveries, and domesticated fruits and plants such as the orange and lemon reached Europe and the Middle East. People moved by way of these routes, too. A Chinese Nestorian Christian monk of Turkish ancestry, Rabban Sauma, even visited Rome, France, and England in 1287 as a diplomat for the Mongol ruler of Persia, the first known visitor to western Europe from East Asia and an early example of politics on a hemispheric scale.

Because of the Mongols, travel from one end of Eurasia to the other became easier than ever before. During Mongol times many men of talent moved from west to east. In China the Mongols relied administratively on a large number of foreigners who came to serve in the civil service. These included many Muslims from West and Central Asia and a few Europeans such as Marco Polo who found their way to the fabled land the Europeans called Cathay. Polo's reports on his travels increased European interest in Asia and inspired later explorers, such as Christopher Columbus, to seek a sea route to East Asia.

Some historians consider the Mongols the great equalizers of history by having made possible technology transfer from East Asia to western Europe and the Middle East. The Mongols unwittingly set in motion changes that allowed Europeans to acquire and improve Chinese technologies such as printing, gunpowder, and the magnetic compass while developing new inventions of their own. These Chinese inventions had a major impact in Europe. In the seventeenth century the English philosopher Francis Bacon noted that Chinese printing, gunpowder, and the magnet "changed the whole face and state of things" in European literature, warfare, and navigation.[16] Europeans improved Chinese weapons such as flamethrowers and primitive guns, making late medieval warfare far deadlier. Gunpowder and Chinese military technology, coming by way of routes opened by the Mongols, also helped reshape Middle Eastern politics and fostered the rise of the Ottoman Empire.

DISASTER AND DYNAMISM IN THE LATE INTERMEDIATE ERA

A combination of natural disasters, including a terrible pandemic and abrupt climate change, also helped reshape Eurasian societies. Increased trade by land and sea and the migration of peoples such as the Turks, Germans, and Mongols fostered the spread of diseases across the Eastern Hemisphere. Many regions also experienced much cooler climates beginning around 1300, which caused agricultural failures and with them, widespread famine. But these disasters also sparked dynamic new energies that revived trade, which in turn spurred maritime exploration.

The Spread of Diseases

Diseases have long played a major role in human life. Sometimes they have come in terrible pandemics, deadly disease outbreaks affecting millions of people in many societies.

Among the most dangerous diseases was bubonic plague, carried by fleas that infested rats. The fleas jumped from rats to humans, causing enlarged lymphatic glands in the victim's groin, armpit, or neck and a high fever, usually followed by death. The disease was sporadic, often not returning for many years. Pandemics had political consequences. A major plague epidemic from the sixth through eighth centuries, for example, weakened both Byzantium and Sassanian Persia, making it more difficult for these empires to repulse Islamic forces.

The worst pandemic in world history, known in the West as the Black Death, may have resulted from the Mongol conquests, in particular the greater contact they brought between Eurasian societies. Climate change may also have been a factor. Eurasia was unusually wet during the 1300s, perhaps increasing the number of fleas and rats. The Black Death, which most scholars think was chiefly caused by bubonic plague, apparently originated in China or Central Asia. By the mid-1300s it had been carried by merchants and soldiers along the Silk Road to southern Russia. Ships leaving the Genoese trading colony at Calfa, on the Crimean peninsula at the north end of the Black Sea, carried it unwittingly to the Middle East and Europe, where it raged through cities and towns. In the affected societies, from China to Egypt to England and even to fishing villages in remote Greenland, perhaps a third of the total population died in the first outbreak, the higher mortality being in congested cities. Surveying the damage, the Italian writer Petrarch wrote that future generations would be "incredulous, unable to imagine the empty houses, abandoned towns, the squalid countryside, the fields littered with dead, the dreadful silent solitude which seemed to hang over the whole world. Physicians were useless, philosophers could only shrug their shoulders and look wise."[17] Millions more died as the pandemic reappeared in intervals in western Eurasia over the next century.

Ultimately the Black Death disrupted the complex system of interregional trade and communication that had flourished around Eurasia in the thirteenth and fourteenth centuries. Agricultural and industrial production declined and financial crises and labor shortages wrecked economies from China to France. The pandemic also helped undermine Mongol rule in East Asia and the Middle East. Some of the problems resulted from the huge population losses. When the Black Death came to an end, a spurt of growth saw population levels soar from East Asia to Europe. By 1500 the world population had reached between 400 million and 600 million people, about twice the population of 1000. China accounted for a fourth of the total, and India for at least a fifth. Europe, including Russia, grew rapidly to 70–95 million. The Black Death did not affect sub-Saharan Africa or the Americas, each of which probably had 60 to 80 million people by 1500.

Climate Change and Societies

Climate change has helped shape, and sometimes destroyed, societies since the dawn of humankind. It spurred the transition to farming in western Asia 10,000 years ago, undermined the Mesopotamian and Indus societies 4,000 years ago, and hastened the decline of the Chinese Han and Roman Empires around 200 C.E. Eurasian weather became more erratic during the 1200s, and the fluctuations may have helped prompt the Mongol expansion. In the Americas climate change during the Intermediate Era probably contributed to the collapse of various societies, including Tiwanaku, Moche, Teotihuacan, the southern Maya, and the Anasazi.

Around 1300 an unusually warm period gave way to much cooler weather that lasted until 1850, sparking what scientists call the "Little Ice Age," with serious results for societies. Whatever the causes, which are still debated, longer and more frigid winters periodically affected Europe, North America, Central Asia, and China. Bitter cold drove the Norse Vikings out of Greenland, and Icelandic farming floundered. Severe storms and flooding in Europe were followed by drought and crop failures, causing widespread famine. Rivers and canals froze, inhibiting boat traffic. Between 1315 and 1317 perhaps 15 percent of Europe's population starved to death. Hunger apparently made northern Europeans and Chinese less resistant to the Black Death. In addition, rainfall declined in India and Africa, drying up many lakes.

In North America great droughts in the late 1200s may have contributed to Cahokia's decline and caused the dispersal of the Anasazi. Pueblo peoples responded to hard times by migrating, as they said in their songs and poems: "Survival, I know this way. It rains. Mountains and canyons and plants grow. We traveled this way."[18] The Hohokum and Mogollon societies collapsed from drought, and their people moved elsewhere in the southwest. The North Atlantic climate became even colder from the mid-1600s to mid-1700s, and such discomfort may have inspired some adventurous Europeans to seek greener pastures abroad, in the Americas.

The Roots of Oceanic Exploration

The Mongol conquests had connected distant peoples and fostered trade. With the Mongol Empire's demise, however, and the security of Silk Road travel reduced, maritime trade became more crucial and naval technology improved considerably. As a result, late in the Intermediate Era there was a trend toward oceanic exploration over vast distances. The fame of Melaka, Calicut, Hormuz, and other Asian ports as commercial hubs for valuable goods had reached Europe, and by the late fourteenth century some European merchants were beginning to dream of a sea route to the East that would enable them to trade directly with China and the Indies.

By the early 1400s the Chinese had the most advanced ships and navigational techniques, and most outward-looking attitude. The Chinese took the initiative of exploration, dispatching unprecedented voyages of discovery led by Zheng He that sailed as far as the Middle East and East Africa. Zheng's ships followed long-established maritime networks, reflecting the crucial role played in world history by Afro-Eurasian maritime commerce. This Chinese thrust did not have lasting effects on the world, however. Although they had the naval capability, the Chinese, unlike the Europeans, lacked the economic incentive and religious zeal, and hence never sailed around

Africa in search of Europe. However, some historians think a few Arabs and Indians may have. A navigation manual written by the Arab navigator Shihab al-Din Ahmad Ibn Majid (SHE-hob al-DIN AH-mad ibn MA-jeed) in the later 1400s, and probably based on earlier voyages, gives quite detailed, and mostly accurate, instructions for sailing down the East African coast, around the Cape of Good Hope, up the West African coast, and then into the Mediterranean.

The Portuguese and then the Spanish, both peoples with long maritime traditions and coastal locations, used Chinese, Arab, and European naval technology to construct ships and equip crews for successful long-distance voyages. In search of gold, spices, slaves, and other resources, Portuguese ships sailed to West and Central Africa, where they established outposts and eventually colonies. By the end of the fifteenth century the Portuguese had rounded the Cape of Good Hope to reach the Indian Ocean, the East African trading ports, and finally India. The Portuguese were not the only Europeans dazzled by Asian wealth. An historian in the early 1500s reported on another mariner and his ambitions:

> *Christopher Columbus, a Genoese, proposed to the Catholic King and Queen [of Spain] to discover the islands which touch the Indies. He asked for ships, promising not only to propagate the Christian religion, but also certainly to bring back pearls, spices and gold beyond anything imagined.*[19]

The Spanish expedition led by Columbus landed in the Americas in the 1490s. With these new networks of communication between distant societies, the history of the world was profoundly altered. An even more connected world and the Early Modern Era were at hand.

SUGGESTED READING

BOOKS

Bentley, Jerry H. *Old World Encounters: Cross-Cultural Contacts and Exchanges in Pre-Modern Times.* New York: Oxford University Press, 1993. An up-to-date survey of trade routes and the spread of universal religions.

Curtin, Philip D. *Cross-Cultural Trade in World History.* Cambridge: Cambridge University Press, 1984. A sweeping examination of world trade and cross-cultural exchange.

Fernandez-Armesto, Felipe. *Millennium: A History of the Last Thousand Years.* New York: Scribner, 1995. An idiosyncratic but interesting overview of the world over the past millennium, for the general reader.

Gilbert, Erik and Jonathan Reynolds. *Trading Tastes: Commodity and Cultural Exchange to 1750.* Upper Saddle River, N. J.: Prentice Hall, 2006. A readable survey of the salt, silk, spice, and sugar trades and their impacts.

Hobson, John M. *The Eastern Origins of Western Civilisation.* New York: Cambridge University Press, 2004. A fascinating, well-researched study offering an Asia-centric history of the era.

Larner, John. *Marco Polo and the Discovery of the World.* New Haven, Conn.: Yale University Press, 1999. A readable study of the impact of Marco Polo's writings on European exploration.

McNeill, William H. *Plagues and Peoples.* Rev. ed. Garden City, N.J.: Anchor, 1998. One of the best studies of the history and role of diseases, including the Black Death.

Morgan, David. *The Mongols.* New York: Basil Blackwell, 1986. A fine study of the Mongols and their empire.

Pacey, Arnold. *Technology in World Civilization.* Cambridge: MIT Press, 1990. Discussion of Asian and European technologies in this era.

Pearson, Michael. *The Indian Ocean.* New York: Routledge, 2000. A comprehensive look at the role this ocean played in world history.

Ringrose, David R. *Expansion and Global Interaction, 1200–1700.* New York: Longman, 2001. Explores the relationship between expansion and global interaction that began with the Mongols.

Risso, Patricia. *Merchants and Faith: Muslim Commerce and Culture in the Indian Ocean.* Boulder: Westview, 1995. A readable survey of Islam-centered commerce from the beginning through the nineteenth century.

Stearns, Peter. *Gender in World History.* New York: Routledge, 2000. A brief but general study with good material on this era.

Super, John C. and Briane K. Turley. *Religion in World History.* New York: Routledge, 2006. A brief overview of religious traditions and change.

Weatherford, Jack. *Genghis Khan and the Making of the Modern World.* New York: Crown, 2004. A readable and provocative examination of the Mongol role in world history.

Whitfield, Susan. *Life Along the Silk Road.* Berkeley: University of California Press, 1999. A readable portrait of Silk Road life through the experiences of travelers and residents.

WEBSITES

Internet Global History Sourcebook (http://www.fordham.edu/halsall/global/ globalsbook.html). An excellent set of links on world history from ancient to modern times.

Silk Road Narratives (http://depts.washington.edu/uwch/silkroad/texts/texts.html). Explores cultural interaction in Eurasia through excerpts from Silk Road travelers.

Virtual Religion Index   (http://virtualreligion.net/vri/). An outstanding site with many links on all major religions from ancient times until today.

GLOSSARY

The glossary for *Societies, Networks, and Transitions: A Global History* is for the complete text, Chapters 1 through 31.

absolutism A system of strong monarchial authority in which all power is placed in a supreme authority, a king or queen. *(p. 445)*

Achaemenid The ruling family of the Classical Persian Empire (ca. 550–450 B.C.E.). *(p. 146)*

Age of Revolution The period from the 1770s through the 1840s when revolutions rocked North America, Europe, the Caribbean, and Latin America. *(p. 566)*

Ahura Mazda (the "Wise Lord") The one god of **Zoroastrianism**. *(p. 150)*

Aksum A literate, urban state that appeared in northern Ethiopia before the Common Era and grew into an empire and a crossroads for trade. *(p. 231)*

Allah To Muslims the one and only, all-powerful God. *(p. 274)*

animism The belief that all creatures as well as inanimate objects and natural phenomena have souls and can influence human well-being. *(p.15)*

apartheid ("separate development") A South African policy to set up a police state to enforce racial separation; lasted from 1948 to 1994. *(p. 956)*

Arianism A heretical Christian sect that arose in the fourth century C.E. that taught that Jesus was not divine but rather an exceptional human being. *(p. 218)*

Aryans Indo-European-speaking nomadic pastoralists who migrated from Iran into northwest India between 1600 and 1400 B.C.E. (see **pastoral nomadism**). *(p. 47)*

asceticism A system of austere religious practices, such as intense prayer, that was used to strengthen spiritual life and seek a deeper understanding of god; began to be used in the Christian church in the fifth and sixth centuries C.E. *(p. 218)*

ASEAN (Association of Southeast Asian Nations) A regional economic and political organization formed in 1967 to promote cooperation among the non-Communist Southeast Asian nations; eventually became a major trading bloc. *(p. 993)*

Atlantic System A large network that arose with the trans-Atlantic slave trade; the network spanned western and Central Africa, the east coast and southern region of English North America, the Caribbean Basin, and the northern and eastern coastal zones of South America. *(p. 473)*

audiencias Judicial tribunals with administrative functions that served as subdivisions of viceroyalties in Spanish America. *(p. 500)*

australopithecines Early **hominids** living in eastern and southern Africa 3 to 4 million years ago. *(p. 9)*

Awami League A Bengali nationalist party that began the move from independence from West Pakistan. *(p. 975)*

Ba'ath ("Renaissance") A political party in the Middle East that favored socialism and Arab nationalism and strongly opposed Israel. *(p. 942)*

Bahai An offshoot of Persian Shi'ism that was founded in 1867; Bahai preached universal peace, the unity of all religions, and service to others. *(p. 649)*

Balfour Declaration A letter from the British foreign minister to Zionist leaders in 1917 that gave British support for the establishment of Palestine as a national home for the Jewish people. *(p. 776)*

Bantu Sub-Saharan African peoples who developed a cultural tradition based on farming and iron metallurgy, which they spread widely through great migrations. *(p. 67)*

bantustans Rural reservations in South Africa where black Africans under apartheid were required to live if they were not needed in the modern economy. *(p. 957)*

baroque An extravagant and, to many, shocking European artistic movement of the 1600s that encouraged release from restraints of thought and expression. *(p. 451)*

Bedouins Tent-dwelling nomadic Arab pastoralists of the seventh century C.E. who wandered in search of oases, grazing lands, or trade caravans to raid (see **pastoral nomadism**). *(p. 270)*

benefices In **medieval** Europe, grants of land from lord to **vassal**. *(p. 391)*

Bhagavad Gita ("Lord's Song") A poem in the *Mahabharata* that is the most treasured piece of ancient Hindu literature. *(p. 51)*

bhakti Devotional worship of a personal Hindu god. *(p. 363)*

bhangra A popular music that emerged in Britain from a blending of traditional folk songs brought by Indian immigrants with Caribbean reggae and Anglo-American styles, such as rock, hip hop, and disco. *(p. 881)*

Bharatha Janata (BJP) The major Hindu nationalist party in India. *(p. 976)*

Black Hole of Calcutta A crowded jail in India where over a hundred British prisoners of a hostile Bengali ruler died from suffocation and dehydration in 1757. This event precipitated the beginning of British use of force in India. *(p. 660)*

Black Legend The Spanish reputation for brutality toward Native Americans, including the repression of native religions, execution of rebels, and forced labor. *(p. 502)*

bodhisattva ("One who has the essence of Buddhahood") A loving and ever compassionate "saint" who has postponed his or her own attainment of **nirvana** to help others find salvation through liberation from birth and rebirth (see **Buddhism, Mahayana**). *(p. 186)*

Boers Dutch farming settlers in South Africa in the eighteenth century. *(p. 470)*

Bollywood The Bombay film industry in India. *(p. 978)*

Bolsheviks The most radical of Russia's antigovernment groups in the early twentieth century, who embraced a dogmatic form of Marxism. *(p. 722)*

bourgeoisie The urban-based, mostly commercial, middle class that arose with **capitalism** in the Early Modern Era. *(p. 435)*

Brahman The Universal Soul, or Absolute Reality, that Hindus believe fills all space and time. *(p. 176)*

Brahmanas Commentaries on the **Vedas** that emphasize the role of priests (**brahmans**). *(p. 52)*

brahmans The priests, the highest-ranking caste in Hindu society. *(p. 50)*

Brezhnev Doctrine In the late twentieth century, an assertion by Soviet leaders of Moscow's right to interfere in Soviet satellites to protect Communist governments and the Soviet bloc. *(p. 886)*

British Commonwealth of Nations A forum, established by Britain in 1931, for discussing issues of mutual interest with its former colonies. *(p. 871)*

Buddhism A major world religion based on the teachings of the Buddha that emphasized putting an end to desire and being compassionate to all creatures. *(p. 178)*

Bunraku The puppet theater of Tokugawa Japan. *(p. 543)*

Burakumin ("Hamlet people") A despised Japanese subgroup who traditionally were restricted to poor neighborhoods and performed jobs considered unclean and undignified. *(p. 706)*

Bushido ("Way of the Warrior") An idealized ethic for the Japanese **samurai**. *(p. 322)*

caliphate An imperial state headed by an Islamic ruler, the caliph, considered the designated successor of the Prophet in civil affairs. *(p. 274)*

calligraphy The artful writing of words. *(p. 286)*

calypso A song style in Trinidad that often featured lyrics addressing daily life and topical subjects. *(p. 621)*

can vuong ("Aid-the-king") Rebel groups who waged guerrilla warfare for fifteen years against the French occupation of Vietnam. *(p. 675)*

capitalism An economic system in which property, exchange, and the means of production are privately owned. *(p. 430)*

caste system The four-tiered Hindu social system comprising hereditary social classes that restrict the occupation of their members and their relations with members of other castes. *(p. 50)*

Castroism Innovative socialist policies introduced by Fidel Castro to stimulate economic development in Cuba while tightly controlling its population. *(p. 923)*

caudillos Latin American military strongmen who acquired and maintained power through force between the early nineteenth and mid-twentieth centuries. (*p. 616*)

Centuriate Assembly A Roman legislative body made up of soldiers. (*p. 203*)

Chavín The earliest-known Andean urban society. (*p. 102*)

chinampas Artificial islands built along lakeshores of the central valley of Mexico and used by the Aztecs for growing food. (*p. 349*)

Chinoiserie An eighteenth- and nineteenth-century Western vogue for artistic products of China such as painting, ceramics, lacquer ware, and decorative furniture. (*p. 688*)

chivalry The rigid code of behavior, including a sense of duty and honor, of **medieval** European knights. (*p. 391*)

Clovis A Native American culture dating back some 11,500 to 13,500 years. (*p. 96*)

Co-hong A nineteenth-century Chinese merchant's guild that had a monopoly on Guangzhou's trade with the West. (*p. 688*)

Cold War A conflict lasting from 1946 to 1989 in which the United States and the USSR competed for allies and engaged in occasional warfare against their rivals' allies rather than against each other directly. (*p. 807*)

colonialism Government by one society over another society. (*p. 474*)

Columbian Exchange The transportation of diseases, animals, and plants from one hemisphere to another that resulted from European exploration and conquest between 1492 and 1750. (*p. 499*)

commercial capitalism The economic system in which most capital was invested in commercial enterprises such as trading companies, including the world's first joint-stock companies. (*p. 435*)

communes Large agricultural units introduced in China by Mao Zedong that combined many families and villages into a common system for pooling resources and labor. (*p. 838*)

Confucianism A Chinese philosophy based on the ideas of Confucius (ca. 551–479 B.C.E.) that emphasized the correct relations among people; became the dominant philosophy of East Asia for two millennia. (*p. 122*)

conquistadors The leaders of Spanish soldiers engaged in armed conquest in the Americas. (*p. 495*)

consuls Two **patrician** men, elected by the **Centuriate Assembly** each year, who had executive power in the Roman Republic. (*p. 203*)

containment The main U.S. strategy aimed at preventing Communists from gaining power, and the USSR from getting political influence, in other nations during the **Cold War.** (*p. 905*)

Coptic Church A branch of Christianity, based on **Monophysite** ideas, that had become influential in Egypt and became dominant in Nubia between the fourth and sixth centuries C.E. (*p. 231*)

Cossacks Tough adventurers and soldiers from southern Russia who were descendants of Russians, Poles, and Lithuanians fleeing serfdom, slavery, or jail. (*p. 484*)

Counter Reformation A movement to confront Protestantism and crush dissidents within the Catholic Church (see **Protestants, Reformation**). (*p. 441*)

courtly love A standard of polite relationships between knights and ladies that arose in the 1100s in **medieval** Europe. Courtly love was celebrated in song by wandering troubadours. (*p. 394*)

creoles People of Iberian ancestry who were born in Latin America. (*p. 500*)

Cro-Magnons The first modern, tool-using humans in Europe. (*p. 13*)

cubism An early-twentieth-century form of painting that rejected visual reality and emphasized instead geometric shapes and forms that often suggested movement. (*p. 735*)

cultivation system An agricultural policy imposed by the Dutch in Java that forced Javanese farmers to grow sugar on rice land. (*p. 672*)

cultural relativism The notion that societies are diverse and unique, embodying different standards of correct behavior. (*p. xxxi*)

cuneiform ("wedge-shape") A Latin term used to describe the writing system invented by the Sumerians. (*p. 36*)

Cynicism A Hellenistic philosophy, made famous by the philosopher Diogenes (fourth century B.C.E.), that emphasized living a radically simple life, shunning material things and all pretense, and remaining true to one's fundamental values (see **Hellenism**). (*p. 169*)

daimyo ("Great name") Large landowning territorial magnates who monopolized local power in Japan beginning during the Ashikaga period (1338–1568). (*p. 324*)

Daoism A Chinese philosophy that emphasized adaptation to nature; arose in the late Zhou era. (*p. 125*)

Dar al-Islam ("Abode of Islam") The Islamic world stretching from Morocco to Indonesia and joined by both a common faith and trade; arose between the eighth and the seventeenth centuries. (*p. 289*)

Darkest Africa Those areas of the African continent least known to Europeans but, in European eyes, awaiting to be "opened" to the "light of Western civilization." (*p. 465*)

deism Belief in a benevolent God who designed the universe but does not intercede in its affairs. (*p. 454*)

Delian League A defensive league organized by Greek cities in the fifth century B.C.E. to defeat the Persians. (*p. 161*)

desertification The transformation of once productive land into useless desert. (*pp. 65 and 823*)

devaraja ("God-king") The title used by Indianized Southeast Asian rulers, who wished to be seen as a reincarnated Buddha or **Shiva** worthy of cult worship. (*p. 370*)

development Growth in a variety of economic areas that benefits the majority of people; the opposite of **monoculture.** (*p. 507*)

direct rule A method of ruling colonies whereby a largely European colonial administration supervised all activity, even down

to the local level, and native chiefs or kings were reduced to symbolic roles (see **colonialism**). (*p. 641*)

dominion A country that has autonomy but owes allegiance to the British crown; developed in the early twentieth century. (*p. 623*)

domino theory A theory that envisioned countries falling one by one to communism and that became a mainstay of U.S. policy during the **Cold War.** (*p. 904*)

Dravidian A language family whose speakers are the great majority of the population in southern India. (*p. 45*)

dreamtime In Aboriginal Australian mythology, the distant past when the spiritual ancestors gave order and form to the universe at the world's creation. (*p. 248*)

Dust Bowl Parts of the U.S. Midwest and Southwest during the 1930s where disappearing topsoil and severe drought threw agriculture badly out of balance. (*p. 733*)

dyarchy A form of dual government that began in Japan during the Nara period (710–784) whereby one powerful family ruled the country while the emperor held mostly symbolic power. (*p. 317*)

dynastic cycle The Chinese view of their political history, which focuses on dynasties of ruling families. (*p. 88*)

empiricism An approach that stresses experience and the testing of propositions rather than reason alone in acquiring knowledge. (*p. 454*)

enclosure Arising in Early Modern Europe, the pattern in which landlords fenced off common lands once used by the public for grazing livestock and collecting firewood. (*p. 455*)

encomienda ("Entrustment") The Crown's grant to a colonial Spaniard in Latin America of a certain number of Indians from whom he extracted tribute. (*p. 507*)

Enlightenment A philosophical movement based on science and reason that began in Europe in the late seventeenth century and continued through the eighteenth century. (*p. 453*)

Estado Novo ("New State") A fascist-influenced and modernizing dictatorship in Brazil led by Getulio Vargas between 1930 and 1945. (*p. 777*)

ethnocentrism Viewing others narrowly through the lenses of one's own society and its values. (*p. xxx*)

Eurocommunism A form of communism in western Europe in the later twentieth century that embraced political democracy and free elections and that rejected Soviet domination. (*p. 870*)

excommunicate To expel a person from the Roman Catholic church and its sacraments. (*p. 396*)

existentialism A philosophy, influential in post–World War II western Europe, whose speculation on the nature of reality reflects disillusionment with Europe's violent history and doubt that objectivity is possible. (*p. 882*)

extraterritoriality Freedom from local laws for foreign subjects. (*p. 690*)

fascism A twentieth-century ideology that typically involved extreme **nationalism,** hatred of ethnic minorities, ruthless repression of opposition groups, violent anticommunism, and authoritarian government. (*p. 735*)

feminism A philosophy that became strong in the twentieth century promoting political, social, and economic equality for women with men. (*p. 602*)

Fertile Crescent A large semicircular fertile region that included the valleys of the Tigris and Euphrates Rivers stretching northwest from the Persian Gulf, the eastern shores of the Mediterranean Sea, and, to some scholars, the banks of the Nile River in North Africa. (*p. 31*)

feudalism A political arrangement characterized by a weak central monarchy that ruled over smaller states or influential families that were largely autonomous but owed service obligations to the monarch; prevailed in **medieval** Europe. (*p. 390*)

fief In **medieval** Europe, the thing granted in a feudal contract, usually land (see **feudalism**). (*p. 391*)

filial piety The Confucian rule that children should respect and obey their parents (see **Confucianism**). (*p. 123*)

First World A later-twentieth-century term for the industrialized democracies of western Europe, North America, Australia-New Zealand, and Japan. (*p. 806*)

Fourth World A later-twentieth-century term for the poorest societies, with very small economies and few exploitable resources. (*p. 806*)

gauchos Cowboys in Argentina and Uruguay who worked on large ranches and were skilled horsemen and fighters. (*p. 616*)

Geez The classical Amharic written language of Ethiopia, a mixture of African and Semitic influences. (*p. 232*)

geomancy Known in Chinese as *feng shui* ("wind and water"), a system for determining the auspicious settings of human dwellings and graves that emerged in ancient times. (*p. 137*)

Ghana The first known major Sudanic state, formed by the Soninke people of the middle Niger valley around 500 C.E. (see **Sudan**). (*p. 235*)

glasnost ("openness") The policy introduced in the Soviet Union by Mikhail Gorbachev in the 1980s to democratize the political system. (*p. 889*)

global village A later-twentieth-century term for an interconnected world community in which all people, regardless of their nationality, share a common fate. (*p. 824*)

globalization A pattern in which economic, political, and cultural processes reach beyond **nation-state** boundaries. (*p. 813*)

Great Depression A collapse of the world economy that lasted in varying degrees of severity through the 1930s. (*p. 728*)

Great Leap Forward Mao Zedong's ambitious attempt in the later 1950s to industrialize China rapidly and end poverty through collective efforts. (*p. 838*)

Great Proletarian Cultural Revolution A radical movement in China between 1966 and 1976 that represented Mao Zedong's attempt to implant his vision, destroy his enemies, crush the stifling bureaucracy, and renew the revolution's vigor. (*p. 841*)

Green Revolution A later-twentieth-century term for increased agricultural output through the use of new high-yield seeds and mechanized farming. (*p. 816*)

Greens A twentieth-century political movement in western Europe that rejected militarism and heavy industry and favored environmental protection over economic growth. (*p. 870*)

griots A respected class of oral historians and musicians in West Africa who memorized and recited the history of the group, emphasizing the deeds of leaders. (*p. 236*)

guerrilla warfare An unconventional military strategy of avoiding full-scale direct confrontations in favor of small-scale skirmishes. (*p. 809*)

guilds In **medieval** Europe, collective fraternal organizations of craftsmen and merchants designed to protect the economic interests of their members. (*p. 392*)

Gulags Russian shorthand for harsh forced-labor camps in Siberia. (*p. 727*)

gunboat diplomacy The Western countries' use of superior firepower to impose their will on local populations and governments in the nineteenth century. (*p. 695*)

haciendas Vast ranches in Spanish America. (*p. 507*)

hadith The remembered words and deeds of Muhammad, revered by many Muslims as a source of belief. (*p. 272*)

haiku The seventeen-syllable poem that proved an excellent vehicle for discussing the passage of time and the change of seasons in Early Modern Japan. (*p. 544*)

haj The Muslim pilgrimage to the holy city of Mecca to worship with multitudes of other believers from around the world. (*p. 275*)

Harappan Name given to the **city-states** and the widespread Bronze Age culture they shared that were centered in the Indus River Valley and nearby rivers in northwest India between 2200 and 1800 B.C.E. (*p. 42*)

Hellenism A widespread culture flourishing between 359 and 100 B.C.E. that combined western Asian (mainly Persian) and Greek (Hellenic) characteristics. (*p. 164*)

hieroglyphics The ancient Egyptian writing system, which evolved from pictograms into stylized pictures expressing ideas. (*p. 59*)

highlife An urban-based West African musical style mixing Christian hymns, West Indian calypso, and African dance rhythms. (*p. 770*)

hijra The emigration of Muslims from Mecca to Medina in 622. (*p. 273*)

Hispanization The process by which, over nearly three centuries of Spanish colonial rule beginning in 1565, the Catholic religion and Spanish culture were imposed on the Philippine people. (*p. 529*)

history The study of the past that looks at all of human life, thought, and behavior and that includes both a record and an interpretation of events, people, and the societies they developed. (*p. xxvi*)

historical revision Changing understanding of the past. (*p. xxvi*)

Holocaust The Nazis' deliberate murder of Jews and Romany (Gypsies), one of the worst genocides in world history. (*p. 741*)

Holy Inquisition A church court created in 1231 in **medieval** Europe to investigate and eliminate heresy; inquisitions continued into the 1600s. (*p. 396*)

hominids A family including humans and their immediate ancestors. (*p. 8*)

Homo erectus ("Erect human") A **hominid** that emerged in East Africa probably between 1.8 and 2.2 million years ago. (*p. 9*)

Homo habilis ("Handy human") A direct ancestor of humans, so named because of its increased brain size and ability to make and use simple stone tools for hunting and gathering. (*p. 9*)

Homo sapiens ("Thinking human") A **hominid** who evolved around 400,000 or 500,000 years ago and from whom anatomically modern humans (*Homo sapiens sapiens*) evolved around 100,000 years ago. (*p. 10*)

horticulture The growing of crops with simple methods and tools. (*p. 18*)

humanism The name for the European **Renaissance** philosophy, which emphasized humanity, worldly concerns, and reason rather than religious ideals. (*p. 409*)

ideology A coherent, widely shared system of ideas about the nature of the social, political, and economic realm. (*p. 583*)

imperialism The control or domination, direct or indirect, of one state or people over another. (*p. 474*)

impressionism A European artistic movement of the late nineteenth century that sought to express the immediate impression aroused by momentary scenes that were bathed in light and color. (*p. 604*)

Indianization The process by which Indian ideas spread into and influenced many Southeast Asian societies; a mixing of Indian with indigenous ideas. (*p. 193*)

Indios ("Indies peoples") The Filipinos at the bottom of the Spanish colonial social structure, who faced many legal restrictions. (*p. 531*)

indirect rule A method of ruling colonies whereby districts were administered by traditional (native) leaders, who had considerable local power but were subject to European officials (see **colonialism**). (*p. 641*)

Indo-Aryan synthesis The fusion of **Aryan** and **Dravidian** cultures in India over many centuries. (*p. 50*)

Indo-Europeans Various tribes who all spoke related languages that derived from some original common tongue and who eventually settled Europe, Iran, and northern India. (*p. 27*)

Industrial Revolution A dramatic transformation in the production and transportation of goods that transformed western Europe from the 1770s to the 1870s. (*p. 577*)

international settlements Special zones in major Chinese cities set aside for foreigners in the later nineteenth century where no Chinese were allowed; arose as a result of China's defeat in the Opium and Arrow Wars. (p. 690)

Intifada ("Uprising") A resistance begun in 1987 by Palestinians against the Israeli occupation of Gaza and the West Bank. (p. 940)

Iron Rice Bowl A model of social equality in Mao's China in which the people, especially in the villages, shared resources and the peasants enjoyed status and dignity. (p. 842)

Islamic revivalism Arab movements beginning in the eighteenth century that sought to purify Islamic practices by reviving what their supporters considered to be a purer vision of Islamic society. (p. 651)

Islamists Antimodern, usually puritanical Islamic militants who seek an Islamic state. (p. 945)

Jacobins A radical faction in the French Revolution that believed civil rights had to be set aside in a crisis; the Jacobins executed thousands of French citizens. (p. 570)

Jainism An Indian religion that believes that life in all forms must be protected because everything, including animals, insects, plants, sticks, and stones, has a separate soul and is alive; arose in 500 B.C.E. as an alternative to Hinduism. (p. 177)

janissaries ("new troops") Well-armed, highly disciplined, and generally effective elite military corps of infantrymen in the Ottoman Empire. (p. 476)

Japan, Inc. The cooperative relationship between government and big business that has existed in Japan after 1945. (p. 853)

Jiangxi Soviet A revolutionary base, established in 1927 in south-central China, where Mao Zedong organized a guerrilla force to fight the Guomindang. (p. 757)

jihad Effort by a Muslim to live as God intended; a spiritual, moral, and intellectual struggle to enhance personal faith and follow the **Quran.** (p. 275)

Jomon The earliest documented culture in Japan, known for the ropelike design on its pottery. (p. 94)

Ka'ba A huge sacred cube-shaped stone in the city of Mecca to which people made annual pilgrimages. (p. 271)

Kabuki The all-male and racy drama that became the favored entertainment of the urban population in Tokugawa Japan. (p. 543)

kana A Japanese phonetic script developed in the Heian period (794–1184) that consisted of some forty-seven syllabic signs derived from Chinese characters. (p. 318)

Khmer Rouge ("Red Khmers") A Communist insurgent group that sought to overthrow the government in Cambodia during the 1960s through the mid-1990s. (p. 987)

kibbutz A Jewish collective farm in twentieth-century Palestine that stressed the sharing of wealth. (p. 654)

knights In **medieval** Europe, armored military retainers on horseback who swore allegiance to their lord. (p. 391)

kotow The tribute-bearers' act of prostrating themselves before the Chinese emperor. (p. 315)

kshatriyas Warriors and landowners headed by the rajas in the Hindu **caste system.** (p. 50)

Kushans An Indo-European people from Central Asia who conquered much of northwest India and western parts of the Ganges Basin and constructed an empire (50–250 C.E.) that also encompassed Afghanistan and parts of Central Asia. (p. 184)

laager A defensive arrangement of wagons in a circle. Used by the Boers in South Africa in the eighteenth and nineteenth centuries to guard against attacks by native Africans. (p. 638)

laissez faire Restriction of government interference in the marketplace, such as laws regulating business and profits. (p. 581)

Lamaism The Tibetan form of **Buddhism,** characterized by the centrality of monks (*lamas*) and huge monasteries. (p. 364)

Lapita The ancient western Pacific culture that stretched some 2,500 miles from just northeast of New Guinea to Samoa. (p. 93)

Legalism A Chinese philosophy that advocated harsh control of people by the state; became the dominant philosophy during the Qin dynasty (221–207 B.C.E.) and was later tempered by **Confucianism.** (p. 125)

Leninism A political system imposed by Lenin (1870–1924) in which one party holds a monopoly on power, excluding other parties from participation. Used in the Soviet Union from 1917 to the later 1980s. (p. 726)

liberalism An ideology of the Modern Era, based on **Enlightenment** ideas, that favored emancipating the individual from all restraints, whether governmental, economic, or religious. (p. 586)

liberation theology A Latin American movement that developed in the 1960s in Latin America to make Catholicism more relevant to contemporary society and to address the plight of the poor. (p. 928)

lingua franca A language widely used as a common tongue among diverse groups with different languages. (p. 766)

Little Dragons South Korea, Taiwan, Singapore, and Hong Kong, which were strongly influenced by Chinese culture and built rapidly growing, industrializing economies in the twentieth century. (p. 858)

loess The dust blown in from the Mongolian deserts that enriched the soils of northern China. (p. 83)

Long March An epic journey, full of hardship, in which Mao Zedong's Red Army fought their way 6,000 miles on foot and horseback through eleven Chinese provinces in the mid-1930s to establish a safe base of operation. (p. 757)

Luddites Antiindustrialization activists in Britain who destroyed machines in a mass protest against the effects of mechanization (see **Industrial Revolution**). (p. 579)

ma'at Ancient Egyptian term for justice, the correct order of things. (p. 60)

madrasas Religious boarding schools found all over the Muslim world. (p. 278)

Magna Carta ("Great Charter") An agreement signed by King John of England in 1215 that limited the feudal rights of the English king and his officials while protecting the rights of the church, lords, and merchants. (p. 397)

Mahabharata ("Great Bharata") An **Aryan** epic and the world's longest poem. (p. 48)

Mahayana ("the Greater Vehicle to salvation") One of the two main branches of **Buddhism;** a more popularized form of Buddhist belief and practice than **Theravada.** Mahayana Buddhism tended to make Buddha into a god and also developed the notion of the **bodhisattva.** (p. 186)

mandarins Educated men who staffed the imperial Chinese bureaucracy from the Han dynasty until the early twentieth century. (p. 130)

Mandate of Heaven A Chinese belief from ancient times that rulers had the support of the supernatural realm as long as conditions were good, but rebellion was justified when they were not. (p. 88)

Mande Diverse Sudanic peoples who spoke closely related languages, shared many customs, and dominated the western Niger River Basin and adjacent areas of West Africa (see **Sudan**). (p. 235)

Manicheanism A blend of **Zoroastrianism, Buddhism,** and Christianity, founded by Mani (216–277 C.E.), that emphasized a continuing struggle between the equal forces of light and dark. (p. 224)

Manifest Destiny Americans' conviction that their country's institutions and culture, regarded as unmatched, gave them a God-given right to take over the land. (p. 607)

manorialism The **medieval** European system of autonomous, nearly self-sufficient agricultural estates. (p. 391)

mansa ("King") Mande term used by the Malinke people to refer to the ruler of the Mali Empire (1234–1550). (p. 331)

Maoism An ideology promoted by Mao Zedong that mixed ideas from Chinese tradition with Marxist-Leninist ideas from the Soviet Union. (p. 759)

Marathas A loosely knit confederacy led by Hindu warriors from west-central India; one of several groups that challenged British domination after the decline of the Mughals. (p. 659)

market Leninism A policy followed after the Beijing Massacre in 1989 whereby the Chinese Communist state asserted more power over society while also fostering an even stronger market orientation in the economy than had existed under **market socialism.** (p. 845)

market socialism A Chinese economic program used between 1978 and 1989 that mixed free enterprise, economic liberalization, and state controls and that produced economic dynamism in China. (p. 844)

maroons Slaves who escaped from plantations and set up African-type societies in the interior of several American colonies. (p. 511)

Marshall Plan A recovery program proposed for western Europe by the United States that aimed to prevent Communist expansion and to spread liberal economic principles. (*p. 868*)

Marxism-Leninism The basis for Soviet communism, a mix of **socialism** (collective ownership of the economy) and **Leninism.** (*p. 726*)

matrilineal kinship A pattern of kinship that traces descent and inheritance through the female line. (*p. 15*)

Mau Mau Rebellion An eight-year uprising in the 1950s by the Gikuyu people in Kenya against British rule. (*p. 952*)

May Fourth Movement A radical nationalist resurgence in China in 1919 that opposed **imperialism** and the ineffective, warlord-controlled Chinese government. (*p. 755*)

Maya The most long-lasting and widespread of the classical Mesoamerican societies, who occupied the Yucatan Peninsula and northern Central America for almost 2,000 years. (*p. 237*)

medieval A term first used in the 1400s by Italian historians to describe the centuries between the classical Romans and their own time. (*p. 383*)

Meiji Restoration A revolution against the Tokugawa shogunate in Japan in 1867–1868, carried out in the name of the Meiji emperor; led to the successful modernization of Japan. (*p. 704*)

mercantilism An economic approach that emerged in Early Modern Europe based on a government policy of building a nation's wealth by expanding its reserves of precious metals. (*p. 436*)

Meroitic A cursive script developed in the Classical Era by the Kushites in Nubia that can be read only partly today. (*p. 231*)

Mesoamerica The region stretching from central Mexico southeast into northern Central America. (*p. 99*)

Mesolithic The Middle Stone Age, which began around 15,000 years ago as the glaciers from the final Ice Age began to recede. (*p. 14*)

messianism The Hebrew belief that their God, Yahweh, had given them a special mission in the world. (*p. 74*)

mestizos Groups in Latin America that blended white and Indian ancestry. (*p. 500*)

metaphysics The broad field of philosophy that studies the most general concepts and categories underlying ourselves and the world around us. (*p. 157*)

Metis People in Canada of mixed French and Indian descent. (*p. 505*)

Middle Passage The slave's journey by ship from Africa to the Americas. (*p. 472*)

millet The nationality system through which the Ottomans allowed the leaders of religious and ethnic minorities to administer their own communities. (*p. 295*)

Mithraism A Hellenistic cult that worshiped Mithra, a Persian deity associated with the sun; had some influence on Christianity. (*p. 169*)

Moche A prosperous, powerful state that formed along the northern Peruvian coast from 200 B.C.E. to 700 C.E. (*p. 243*)

modernism A Western cultural trend that openly broke with **romanticism** and other traditions by embracing progress and welcoming the future. (*p. 603*)

monasticism The pursuit of a religious life of penance, prayer, and meditation, either alone or in a community of other seekers. (*p. 179*)

monoculture An economy dependent on the production and export of one chief commodity. (*p. 507*)

Monophysites A heretical sect in the fourth century C.E. that argued that Jesus had a single divine nature rather than both a divine and a human form. (*p. 222*)

monotheism The belief in a single, all-powerful god. (*p. 60*)

Moros The Spanish term for the Muslim peoples of the southern Philippines. (*p. 529*)

mound building The construction of huge earthen mounds, often with temples on top, by some peoples in the Americas from ancient times to the fifteenth century C.E. (*p. 97*)

mujahidin ("Holy warriors") Conservative Islamic rebels who rebelled against the pro-Soviet regime in Afghanistan in the 1970s and 1980s. (*p. 948*)

mulattos Groups in Latin America that blend African ancestry with white and Indian ancestry. (*p. 500*)

multilateralism In the twentieth and twenty-first centuries, a foreign policy in which the United States sought a common front and a coordination of foreign policies with allies in western Europe, Japan, and Canada, avoiding activities that might enflame world opinion against the United States. (*p. 904*)

multinational corporations Giant business enterprises that operate all over the world; multinationals have gained a leading role in the global marketplace. (*p. 814*)

Muslim Brotherhood An Egyptian religious movement founded in 1928 that expressed popular Arab reaction to **Westernization.** (*p. 776*)

Mutually Assured Destruction A policy, known as MAD, in which the United States and the USSR used the fear of nuclear weapons to deter each other during the **Cold War.** (*p. 905*)

Nam Tien ("Drive to the South") A long process beginning in the tenth century in which some Vietnamese left the overcrowded north to migrate southward along the coast of Vietnam. (*p. 378*)

National Liberation Front (NLF) Often known as the Viet Cong, a Communist-led revolutionary movement in South Vietnam that resisted American intervention in the American-Vietnamese War. (*p. 984*)

nationalism A primary loyalty to, and identity with, a nation bound by a common culture, government, and shared territory. (*p. 583*)

nation-states Politically centralized countries with defined territorial boundaries. (*p. 584*)

NATO (North Atlantic Treaty Organization) A military alliance, formed in 1949, that linked nine western European countries with the United States and Canada. (*p. 871*)

Neanderthals Hominids who were probably descended from *Homo erectus* populations in Europe and who later spread into western and Central Asia. (*p. 13*)

negritude A twentieth-century literary and philosophical movement to forge distinctively African views. (*p. 964*)

neo-Confucianism A form of **Confucianism** arising in China during the Song period (960–1279) that incorporated many Buddhist and Daoist metaphysical ideas (see **Buddhism, Daoism**). (*p. 308*)

neoliberalism An economic model encouraged by the United States in the developing world that promoted free markets, privatization, and Western investment. (*p. 927*)

Neolithic The New Stone Age, which began between 10,000 and 11,500 years ago with the transition to simple farming. (*p. 14*)

Nestorians A heretical Christian sect in the fourth century C.E. that believed that the divine and human natures of Jesus were independent of each other. (*p. 222*)

networks Arrangements or collections of links between different societies, such as the routes over which traders, goods, diplomats, armies, ideas, and information travel. (*p. xxxi*)

New Culture Movement A movement of Chinese intellectuals started in 1915 that sought to wash away the discredited past and sprout a literary revival. (*p. 754*)

New Deal A new U.S. government program of liberal reform within a democratic framework introduced by President Franklin Roosevelt to alleviate suffering caused by the **Great Depression.** (*p. 734*)

New Economic Policy (NEP) Lenin's pragmatic approach to economic development, which mixed **capitalism** and **socialism.** (*p. 726*)

New Order The Indonesian government headed by President Suharto from 1966 to 1998, which mixed military and civilian leadership. (*p. 993*)

New Song A Latin American musical movement based chiefly on local folk music and closely tied to progressive politics and protest; became popular in the 1960s and 1970s, especially in Chile. (*p. 929*)

Nicene Creed A set of beliefs, prepared by the council at Nicaea in 325 C.E., that became the official doctrine of the early Christian church. (*p. 218*)

Nilotes Ironworking pastoralists from the eastern **Sudan** who settled in East Africa in the classical era and there had frequent interactions with the **Bantus** (see **pastoral nomadism**). (*p. 236*)

nirvana ("the blowing out") A kind of everlasting peace or end of suffering achieved through perfection of wisdom and compassion (see **Buddhism**). (*p.179*)

Noh Japanese plays that use stylized gestures and spectacular masks; began in the fourteenth century C.E. (*p. 323*)

nonviolent resistance Noncooperation with unjust laws and peaceful confrontation with illegitimate authority, pursued by Mohandas Gandhi in India. (*p. 762*)

nuclear weapons Explosive devices that owe their destructive power to the energy released by either splitting or fusing atoms. *(p. 809)*

nuxu A secret form of writing developed by some Chinese women to share their experiences, possibly beginning as early as the Han period. *(p. 131)*

oligarchs Well-placed former Communists who amassed enough wealth to gain control of major segments of the post-Soviet Russian economy. *(p. 892)*

oligarchy Rule by a small group of wealthy leaders. *(p. 153)*

Olmecs The earliest urban society in Mesoamerica. *(p. 101)*

OPEC (Organization of Petroleum Exporting Countries) A cartel formed in 1960 to give producers more power over the price of oil and leverage with the consuming nations. *(p. 943)*

oral traditions Verbal testimonies concerning the past; the major form of oral literature in cultures without writing. *(p. 339)*

Orientalism An eighteenth- and nineteenth-century scholarly interest among British officials in India that prompted some to rediscover the Hindu classical age. *(p. 664)*

ostpolitik ("Eastern politics") A West German policy, promoted by Chancellor Willy Brandt, that sought a reconciliation between West and East Germany and an expanded dialogue with the USSR. *(p. 873)*

Pacific Century The possible shift of global economic power from Europe and North America to the **Pacific Rim** in the twenty-first century. *(p. 836)*

Pacific Rim The economically dynamic Asian countries on the western edge of the Pacific Basin: China, Japan, South Korea, Taiwan, and several Southeast Asian nations. *(p. 836)*

Paleolithic The Old Stone Age, which began 100,000 years ago with the first modern humans and lasted for many millennia. *(p. 14)*

pan-Africanism The dream, originating in the early twentieth century, that all Africans would cooperate to eventually form some sort of united states of the continent. *(p. 952)*

pariahs The large group of outcasts or untouchables below the official Hindu castes. *(p. 50)*

parliamentary democracy Government by representatives elected by the people. *(p. 586)*

pastoral nomadism An economy based on breeding, rearing, and harvesting livestock. *(p. 26)*

Pathet Lao Revolutionary Laotian nationalists allied with North Vietnam during the American-Vietnamese War. *(p. 986)*

patriarchy A system in which men largely control women and children and shape ideas about appropriate gender behavior. *(p. 35)*

patricians The aristocratic upper class who controlled the Roman Senate. *(p. 203)*

Paulistas Portuguese slavers from the southern Brazilian settlement at Sao Paulo. *(p. 497)*

Pax Romana ("Roman Peace") The period of peace and prosperity in Roman history from the reign of Augustus through that of Emperor Marcus Aurelius in 180 C.E. *(p. 207)*

Peloponnesian War A long war between Athens and Sparta and their respective allies in 431–404 B.C.E. that resulted in the defeat of Athens. *(p. 162)*

people's war An unconventional struggle that combined military action and political recruitment, formulated by Mao Zedong in China. *(p. 758)*

Perestroika ("Restructuring") Mikhail Gorbachev's policy to liberalize the Soviet economy using market mechanisms. *(p. 890)*

periodization Dividing long periods of historical time into smaller segments such as "the ancient world" or "modern history." *(p. xxx)*

pharaohs Rulers of ancient Egypt. *(p. 58)*

philosophes The intellectuals who fostered the French **Enlightenment.** *(p. 455)*

pidgin English The form of broken English that developed in Africa during the colonial era. *(p. 770)*

plantation zone A group of societies with economies that relied on enslaved African labor; the plantation zone stretched from Virginia and Kentucky southward through the West Indies and the east coast of Central America to central Brazil and the Pacific coast of Colombia. *(p. 507)*

plebeians The commoner class in Rome. *(p. 203)*

plural society A medley of peoples who mix but do not blend, instead maintaining their own cultures, religions, languages, and customs. *(p. 674)*

polis A **city-state** in Classical Greece; each polis embraced nearby rural areas, whose agricultural surplus then helped support the urban population. *(p. 152)*

polyandry Marriage of a woman to several husbands. *(p. 360)*

polytheism A belief in many spirits or deities. *(p. 15)*

postmodernism A European intellectual approach contending that truth is not absolute but constructed by people according to their society's beliefs. *(p. 882)*

preemptive war A U.S. doctrine, triggered by the 2001 terrorist attacks, that sanctioned unilateral military action against potential threats (see **terrorism, unilateralism**). *(p. 909)*

proletariat The industrial working class. *(p. 588)*

protectionism Use of trade barriers to shield local industries from foreign competition. *(p. 605)*

Protestants Groups that broke completely with the Roman Catholic Church as the result of the **Reformation.** *(p. 439)*

purdah The Indian Muslim custom of secluding women. *(p. 369)*

qi In Chinese thought, the energizing force pervading the universe. *(p. 309)*

Quetzalcoatl The feathered serpent, a symbol that goes back deep in Mesoamerican history. *(p. 343)*

quipus Differently colored knotted strings used by the Incas to record commercial dealings, property ownerships, and census data. *(p. 352)*

Quran ("Recitation") Islam's holiest book; contains the official version of Muhammad's revelations, and to believers is the inspired word of God. *(p. 272)*

racism A set of beliefs, practices, and institutions based on devaluing groups that are supposedly biologically different. *(p. 471)*

rai ("opinion") A twentieth-century pop music of Algeria based on local Bedouin chants, Spanish flamenco, French café songs, Egyptian pop, and other influences and featuring improvised lyrics that often deal with forbidden themes of sex and alcohol. *(p. 947)*

Rajputs ("King's sons") An Indian warrior caste formed by earlier Central Asian invaders who adopted Hinduism. *(p. 359)*

Ramadan The thirty days of annual fasting when Muslims abstain from eating, drinking, and sex during daylight hours, to demonstrate sacrifice for their faith and understand the hunger of the poor. *(p. 275)*

Rastafarianism A religion from Jamaica that arose in 1930 and that mixed Christian, African, and local influences; Rastafarianism attracted urban slum dwellers and the rural poor by preaching a return of black people to Africa. *(p. 931)*

Red Guards Young workers and students who were the major supporters of the **Great Proletarian Cultural Revolution** in Mao's China. *(p. 841)*

Reformation The movement to reform Christianity that was begun by Martin Luther in the sixteenth century. *(p. 437)*

reggae A popular music style that began in Jamaica in the 1960s and that blended North American rhythm and blues with Afro-Jamaican traditions; reggae is marked by a distinctive beat maintained by the bass guitar. *(p. 931)*

Renaissance ("Rebirth") A dramatic flowering in arts and learning that began in the Italian city-states around 1350 and spread through Europe through the 1500s. *(p. 409)*

Romance languages Languages that derive from Latin, such as French, Italian, and Spanish. *(p. 215)*

romanticism A philosophical, literary, artistic, and musical movement that questioned the **Enlightenment's** rationalist values and instead glorified emotions, individual imagination, and heroism. *(p. 603)*

Russification A czarist policy in the nineteenth century that promoted Russian language and culture for non-Russian peoples; created resentment among many Muslims in Central Asia and the Caucasus. *(p. 711)*

salaryman A Japanese urban middle-class male business employee who commits his energies and soul to the company, accepts assignments without complaint, and takes few vacations. *(p. 854)*

samba A Brazilian popular music and dance that arose in the early twentieth century. *(p. 621)*

samurai ("One who serves") A member of the Japanese warrior class, which gained power between the twelfth and fourteenth centuries and continued until the nineteenth. (p. 322)

Sanskrit The classical language of north India, originally both written and spoken but now reserved for religious and literary writing. (p. 48)

satrap ("Protector of the kingdom") An official in the Classical Persian Empire (ca. 550–450 B.C.E.) who ruled according to established laws and procedures and paid a fixed amount of taxes to the emperor each year. (p. 149)

scholar-gentry A Chinese social class of learned officeholders and landowners that arose in the Han dynasty and continued until the early twentieth century. (p. 130)

Scientific Revolution An era of rapid European advance in knowledge, particularly in mathematics and astronomy, that occurred between 1600 and 1750. (p. 392)

Second World A later-twentieth-century term for the Communist nations, led by the USSR and China. (p. 806)

sepoys Mercenary soldiers recruited among the warrior and peasant castes by the British in India. (p. 661)

serfs In **medieval** Europe, peasants legally bound to their lord and tied to the land through generations. (p. 392)

sericulture Silk making, which arose in ancient China. (p. 132)

shamans Specialists in communicating with or manipulating the supernatural realm. (p. 15)

Shari'a The Islamic legal code for the regulation of social, economic, and religious life. (p. 278)

Shi'a The branch of Islam that emphasizes the religious leaders descended from Muhammad through his son-in-law, Ali, whom they believe was the rightful successor to the Prophet. (p. 280)

Shinto ("Way of the gods") The ancient animistic Japanese cult that emphasized closeness to nature; enjoyed a rich mythology that included many deities (see **animism**). (p. 142)

Shiva The Hindu god of destruction and of fertility and the harvest. (p. 45)

shogun ("Barbarian-subduing generalissimo") In effect a Japanese military dictator who controlled the country in the name of the emperor; the first shogun took power in 1185, and the last one fell in 1868. (p. 322)

Sikhs ("Disciples") Members of an Indian religion founded in the Early Modern Era that adopted elements from both Hinduism and Islam, including mysticism. (p. 522)

Silk Road A lively caravan route through Central Asia that linked China with India, the Middle East, and southern Europe that began during the Han dynasty (207 B.C.E.– 221 C.E.) and continued for many centuries. (p. 129)

simony In **medieval** Europe, a practice whereby wealthy families paid to have their sons appointed bishops. (p. 396)

Sinicization The process by which Central Asian invaders maintained continuity with China's past by adopting Chinese culture. (p. 126)

Slavophiles Nineteenth-century Russians who emphasized Russia's unique culture and rejected Western models. (p. 712)

socialism An ideology arising in nineteenth-century Europe offering a vision of social equality and the common, or public, ownership of economic institutions such as factories. (p. 587)

socialist realism Literary and artistic works that depicted life from a revolutionary perspective, a style first introduced in Stalin's Russia. (p. 727)

societies Broad groups of people that have common traditions, institutions, and organized patterns of relationships with each other. (p. xxxi)

Socratic Method A method of asking people leading questions to help them examine the truth of their ideas; introduced by the Greek philosopher Socrates (469–399 B.C.E.). (p. 156)

Sophists Thinkers in Classical Greece (fifth century B.C.E.) who emphasized skepticism and the belief that there is no ultimate truth. (p. 156)

soukous ("to shake") A Congolese popular music of the later twentieth century that was shaped by dance rhythms from Cuba and Brazil. (p. 964)

Soviet bloc In the twentieth century, the Soviet Union and the communist states allied with it. (p. 871)

soviets Local action councils formed by Russian radicals before the 1917 Russian Revolution that enlisted workers and soldiers to fight the factory owners and military officers. (p. 724)

sphere of interest An area in which one great power assumes exclusive responsibility for maintaining peace and attempts to monopolize the area's resources. (p. 610)

Stalinism Joseph Stalin's system of government, which included state ownership of all property, such as lands and businesses, a planned economy, and one-man rule. (p. 726)

state capitalism An economic system in which the state takes a leading role in supporting business and industrial enterprises; introduced by the Meiji government in Japan. (p. 705)

steppes The plains of Central Asia. (p. 46)

Stoicism A Hellenistic philosophy begun by Zeno in the third century B.C.E. that emphasized the importance of cooperating with and accepting nature, as well as the unity and equality of all people (see **Hellenism**). (p. 169)

Sudan A grassland region stretching along the southern fringe of the Sahara Desert from the western tip of Africa to the Nile valley. (p. 64)

sudras The mostly poorer farmers, farm workers, and menial laborers in the Hindu **caste system.** (p. 50)

suffragettes Women who press for the same voting rights as men. (p. 602)

Sufism A mystical approach and practice within Islam that emphasized personal spiritual experience. (p. 284)

sultan A Muslim ruler of only one country. (p. 278)

Sunni The main branch of Islam comprising those who accept the practices of the Prophet and the historical succession of caliphs. (p. 280)

Swahili Name for a distinctive people, culture, and language, a mix of **Bantu**, Arab, and Islamic influences, that developed during the Intermediate Era on the East African coast. (p. 336)

Taliban ("Students") A group of Pashtun religious students who organized a military force in the 1980s to fight what they considered immorality and corruption and to impose order in Afghanistan. (p. 948)

Tantrism An approach within both **Buddhism** and Hinduism that worshiped the female essence of the universe; developed in the Intermediate Era. (p. 363)

Teotihuacan ("the City of the Gods") The largest city in the Americas and the capital of an empire in central Mexico during Classical times. (p. 241)

terrorism Small-scale but violent attacks aimed at undermining a government or demoralizing a population. (p. 830)

Tet Offensive Communist attacks on major South Vietnamese cities in 1968, a turning point in the American-Vietnamese War. (p. 986)

The Analects The book of the sayings of Confucius (ca. 551–479 B.C.E.), collected by his disciples and published a century or two after his death (see **Confucianism**). (p. 123)

Theosophy A nineteenth-century North American and European movement that blended Hindu thought with Western spiritualist and scientific ideas. (p. 669)

Theravada ("Teachings of the Elders") One of the two main branches of **Buddhism,** the other being **Mahayana,** that arose just before the Common Era. Theravada remained closer to the Buddha's original vision. (p. 185)

Third Industrial Revolution The creation since 1945 of unprecedented scientific knowledge of new technologies more powerful than any invented before. (p. 815)

Third World A later-twentieth-century term for the societies in Asia, Africa, Latin America, and the Caribbean, which were shaped by mass poverty and a legacy of colonization or neocolonialism. (p. 806)

trade diaspora Merchants from the same city or country who live permanently in foreign cities or countries. (p. 163)

transitions Passages, changes, events, or movements that reshape societies and regions. (p. xxxi)

trekking The migrations of **Boer** settlers in cattle-drawn wagons into the interior of South Africa whenever they wanted to flee government restraints. (p. 470)

tribes Associations of clans that traced descent from a common ancestor. (p. 27)

tribunes Roman men elected to represent **plebeian** interests in the **Centuriate Assembly.** (p. 203)

Truman Doctrine A policy formed in 1947 that asserted that the United States was the leader of the free world and was charged with protecting countries like Greece and Turkey from communism. *(p. 871)*

tyrant Someone who ruled a Greek **polis** outside the law, not necessarily a brutal ruler. *(p. 154)*

ukiyo-e Colorful Japanese woodblock prints that celebrated the life of the "floating world," the urban entertainment districts of Tokogawa Japan. *(p. 543)*

umma The community of Muslim believers united around God's message. *(p. 273)*

UMNO United Malays National Organization, the main Malay political party in Malaysia. *(p. 991)*

unilateralism In the twentieth and twenty-first centuries, a foreign policy in which the United States acted alone in its own perceived national interest even if key allies disapproved. *(p. 905)*

Upanishads Ancient Indian philosophical writings that speculated on the ultimate truth about the creation of life. *(p. 52)*

Urdu A language developed in Mughal India that mixed Hindi, Arabic, and Persian and was written in the Persian script. *(p. 519)*

usury The practice of loaning money at interest; considered a sin in **medieval** Europe, although necessary to commerce. *(p. 393)*

vaisyas The merchants and artisans in the Hindu **caste system.** *(p. 50)*

Vajrayana ("Thunderbolt") A form of **Buddhism** that featured female saviors and the human attainment of magical powers; developed in the Intermediate Era and became the main form of Buddhism in Nepal and Tibet. *(p. 363)*

vassal In **medieval** Europe, a subordinate person who owed service to a lord. *(p. 390)*

Vedanta ("Completion of the **Vedas**") A school of Classical Indian thought that offered Hindus mystical experience and a belief in the underlying unity of all reality. *(p. 177)*

Vedas The **Aryans'** "books of knowledge," the principal source of religious belief for Hindus: a vast collection of sacred hymns to the gods and thoughts about religion, philosophy, and magic. *(p. 47)*

Viet Minh The Vietnamese Independence League, a coalition of anti-French groups established by Ho Chi Minh in 1941 that waged war against both the French and the Japanese. *(p. 766)*

voyageurs French explorers and trappers in North America. *(p. 498)*

Wabenzi ("People who drive a Mercedes Benz") A privileged urban class in Africa since the mid-twentieth century of politicians, high bureaucrats, professionals, military officers, and businessmen who manipulate their connections to amass wealth. *(p. 955)*

Wahhabism A militant Islamic revivalist movement founded in Arabia in the eighteenth century. *(p. 651)*

warlords Local political leaders with their own armies. *(p. 754)*

Warsaw Pact A defense alliance formed in 1955 that linked the Communist-ruled eastern European countries with the USSR. *(p. 871)*

wayang kulit Javanese shadow puppet play, developed during the Intermediate Era, based on Hindu epics like the *Ramayana* and local Javanese content. *(p. 375)*

welfare states Government systems that offer their citizens a range of state-subsidized health, education, and social service benefits; adopted by western European nations after World War II. *(p. 876)*

Westernization A deliberate attempt to spread Western culture and ideas. *(p. 664)*

Yijing The Book of Changes, an ancient Chinese collection of sixty-four mystic hexagrams and commentaries upon them that was used to predict future events. *(p. 90)*

Young Turks A modernizing group in Ottoman Turkey that promoted a national identity and that gained power in the early twentieth century. *(p. 647)*

zaibatsu The most powerful Japanese corporations that dominated the national economy beginning during the Meiji regime and maintained an especially close relationship to the government. *(p. 705)*

zamindars Mughal revenue collectors that the British turned into landlords who were given the rights to buy and sell land. *(p. 665)*

Zen A form of Japanese **Buddhism** that emerged in the Intermediate Era; called the meditation sect because it emphasizes individual practice and discipline, self-control, self-understanding, and intuition. *(p. 323)*

ziggurat A stepped, pyramidal-shaped temple building in Sumerian cities, seen as the home of the chief god of the city. *(p. 34)*

Zionism A movement arising in late nineteenth century Europe that sought a Jewish homeland. *(p. 585)*

Zoroastrianism A monotheistic religion founded by the Persian Zoroaster that later became the state religion of Persia. Its notion of one god opposed by the Devil may have influenced Judaism and later Christianity (see **monotheism**). *(p. 150)*

NOTES

Preface

1. Geoffrey Barraclough, *Main Trends in History* (New York: Holmes and Meier, 1979), p. 153.

Introducing World History

1. P. L. Hartley, quoted in David Lowenthal, *The Past is a Foreign Country* (Cambridge: Cambridge University Press, 1985), p. xvi.

Chapter 1 The Origins of Human Societies, to ca. 2000 B.C.E.

1. Swimme and Berry, *The Universe Story* (San Francisco: Harper, 1992), p. 2.
2. From the *Rig Veda*, quoted in Carolyn Brown Heinz, *Asian Cultural Traditions* (Prospect Heights, Ill.: Waveland, 1999), p. 132.
3. Genesis 3:17–19, *The Holy Bible*, New King James Version (Chicago: Thomas Nelson, 1983), p. 3.
4. From Plato's *Critias*, quoted in L. S. Stavrianos, *Lifelines from Our Past: A New World History*, rev. ed. (Armonk, NY: M.E. Sharpe, 1997), p. 65.
5. Genesis 1:28, *Holy Bible*, p. 2.
6. Quoted in Rodney Castledon, *The Minoans: Life in Bronze Age Crete* (New York: Routledge, 1993), p. 67.

Chapter 2 Ancient Societies in Mesopotamia, India, and Central Asia, 5000–600 B.C.E.

1. The quote is from the Oriental Institute, the University of Chicago.
2. The quote is from the Oriental Institute, the University of Chicago.
3. Quoted in Frederick Gentels and Melvin Steinfield, *Hangups from Way Back: Historical Myths and Canons*, vol. 1, 2nd ed. (San Francisco: Canfield, 1974), p. 64.
4. The quotes are from William H. Stiebing, Jr., *Ancient Near Eastern History and Culture* (New York: Longman, 2003), p. 48.
5. Quoted in Samuel Noah Kramer, *Cradle of Civilization* (New York: Time-Life Books, 1967), p. 122.
6. Quoted in Jean Bottero, *Everyday Life in Ancient Mesopotamia* (Baltimore: Johns Hopkins University Press, 2001), p. 71.
7. Quoted in R. de Rohan Barondes, *China: Lore, Legend and Lyrics* (New York: Philosophical Library, 1960), p. 3.
8. The quotes are from Brian Fagan, *The Long Summer: How Climate Changed Civilization* (New York: Basic Books, 2004), p. 138.
9. Quoted in Michael Wood, *Legacy: The Search for Ancient Cultures* (New York: Sterling, 1994), p. 34.
10. Quoted in G. R. Driver and John C. Miles, eds., *The Babylonian Laws,* vol. II (Oxford: Clarendon Press), 1952, p. 7.
11. Quoted in N. B. Jankowska, "Asshur, Mitanni, and Arrapkhe," in I. M. Diakonoff, ed., *Early Antiquity* (Chicago: University of Chicago Press, 1991), p. 256.
12. Quoted in Kramer, *Cradle of Civilization*, p. 75.

13. Quoted in Wood, *Legacy*, p. 32.
14. *The Epic of Gilgamesh*, trans. by N. K. Sandars (New York: Penguin Books, 1960), p. 108.
15. Quoted in John Keay, *India: A History* (New York: Atlantic Monthly Press, 2000), p. 35.
16. Quoted in Hermann Kulke and Dietmar Rothermund, *History of India*, 3rd ed. (New York: Routledge, 1998), p. 35.
17. William McNaughton, ed., *Light from the East* (New York: Laurel, 1978), p. 398.
18. Quoted in Burton Stein, *A History of India* (Malden, Mass.: Blackwell, 1998), p. 53.
19. Quoted in A. L. Basham, *The Wonder That Was India* (New York: Grove Press, 1959), p. 241.
20. Quoted in Romila Thapar, *Early India from the Origins to AD 1300* (Berkeley: University of California Press, 2002), p. 116.
21. Quoted in Stanley Wolpert, *A New History of India*, 6th ed. (New York: Oxford University Press, 2000), p. 44.

Chapter 3 Ancient Societies in Africa and the Mediterranean, 5000–600 B.C.E.

1. Quoted in Lionel Casson, *Ancient Egypt* (New York: Time Incorporated, 1965), p. 120.
2. Quoted in David Phillipson, *African Archaeology*, 2nd ed. (Cambridge: Cambridge University Press, 1993), p. 152.
3. Quoted in Felipe Fernandez-Armesto, *Civilizations: Culture, Ambition, and the Transformation of Nature* (New York: Simon and Schuster, 2001), p. 171.
4. Quoted in *Egypt: Land of the Pharaohs* (Alexandria, Va.: Time-Life Books, 1992), p. 142.
5. Quoted in Casson, *Ancient Egypt*, p. 95.
6. Quoted in Carl Roebuck, *The World of Ancient Times* (New York: Charles Scribner's Sons, 1966), p. 72.
7. Quoted in *Egypt: Land of Pharaohs*, p. 89.
8. Quoted in Fernandez-Armesto, *Civilizations*, p. 195.
9. Quoted in Brian M. Fagan, *People of the Earth: An Introduction to World Prehistory*, 9th ed. (New York: Longmans, 1998), p. 407.
10. Quoted in Ezra Pound and Noel Stock, *Love Poems of Ancient Egypt* (Norfolk, Conn.: New Directions, 1962).
11. Quoted in Barbara Mertz, *Red Land, Black Land: Daily Life in Ancient Egypt*, rev. ed. (New York: Dodd, Mead and Company, 1978), p. 56.
12. J. B. Pritchard, ed., *Ancient Near Eastern Texts Relating to the Old Testament*, 2nd ed. (Princeton: Princeton University Press, 1955), pp. 34–35.
13. Quoted in *Africa's Glorious Legacy* (Alexandria, Va.: Time-Life Books, 1996), p. 18.
14. Nahum 3:7, 19, *The Holy Bible*, New King James Version (Chicago: Thomas Nelson, 1983), p. 908.
15. Psalm 137:1, *Holy Bible*, p. 639.
16. Isaiah 45:21–22, *Holy Bible*, p. 721.

17. Isaiah 42:6–7, *Holy Bible*, p. 717.
18. Quoted in Rodney Castledon, *Minoans: Life in Bronze Age Crete* (New York: Routledge, 1993), p. 116.
19. From Homer's *Odyssey*, quoted in Lionel Casson, *The Ancient Mariners: Seafarers and Sea Fighters of the Mediterranean in Ancient Times*, 2nd ed. (Princeton: Princeton University Press, 1991), p. 46.
20. Ezekiel 27:3–4, 9, *Holy Bible*, p. 835.

Chapter 4 Around the Pacific Rim: Eastern Eurasia and the Americas, 5000–600 B.C.E.

1. From the ancient Chinese *Book of Songs*, quoted in Herlee Glessner Creel, *The Birth of China: A Survey of the Formative Period of Chinese Civilization* (New York: Frederick Unger, 1937), p. 64.
2. Quoted in Michael Wood, *Legacy: The Search for Ancient Cultures* (New York: Sterling, 1994), p. 96.
3. *The Book of Songs*, translated by Arthur Waley (London: George Unwin, 1954), p. 162.
4. Quoted in Felipe Fernandez-Armesto, *Civilizations: Culture, Ambition, and the Transformation of Nature* (New York: Simon and Schuster, 2001), p. 214.
5. The quotes are in John Minford and Joseph S. M. Lau, eds., *Classical Chinese Literature: An Anthology of Translations*, vol. 1 (New York: Columbia University Press, 2000), pp. 16–17, 20.
6. Quoted in Creel, *Birth of China*, pp. 228–229.
7. Quoted in Benjamin I. Schwartz, *The World of Thought in Ancient China* (Cambridge: Harvard University Press, 1985), p. 39.
8. In Minford and Lau, *Classical Chinese Literature*, p. 150.
9. The two songs come from Waley, *Book of Songs*, pp. 68, 203.
10. Waley, *Book of Songs*, p. 205.
11. Quoted in Nguyen Ngoc Bich, "The Power and Relevance of Vietnamese Myths," in David P. Elliott et al., eds., *Vietnam: Essays on History, Culture and Society* (New York: Asia Society, 1985), p. 62.
12. Quoted in Brian M. Fagan, *Kingdoms of Gold, Kingdoms of Jade: The Americas Before Columbus* (New York: Thames and Hudson, 1991), p. 55.

Societies, Networks, Transitions: Ancient Foundations of World History, 4000–600 B.C.E.

1. From Homer's *The Odyssey*, quoted in Rodney Castledon, *Minoans: Life in Bronze Age Crete* (New York: Routledge, 1993), p. 111.
2. Quoted in Lewis Mumford, *The City in History: Its Origins, Its Transformations, and Its Prospects* (New York: Harcourt, Brace and World, 1961), p. 68.
3. Quoted in Lionel Casson, *The Ancient Mariners: Seafarers and Sea Fighters of the*

Mediterranean in Ancient Times, 2nd ed. (Princeton: Princeton University Press, 1991), p. 9.

4. From the *Brahmanas*, quoted in F. R. Allchin, *The Archaeology of Historic South Asia: The Emergence of Cities and States* (New York: Cambridge University Press, 1995), pp. 86–87.

5. Quoted in John Keegan, *A History of Warfare* (New York: Alfred A. Knopf, 1993), p. 143.

6. Quoted in Barbara Mertz, *Red Land, Black Land: Daily Life in Ancient Egypt*, rev. ed. (New York: Dodd Mead, and Company, 1978), pp. 135–136.

7. *The Book of Songs*, translated by Arthur Waley (London: George Allen and Unwin, 1954), p. 121.

8. Nahum 3:2–3, *Holy Bible*, p. 907.

9. Isaiah 2:4, *Holy Bible*, p. 683.

10. Quoted in Merry E. Wiesner-Hanks, *Gender in History* (Malden, Mass.: Blackwell, 2001), p. 61.

11. From Homer's *The Odyssey*, quoted in Castledon, *Minoans*, p. 9.

12. Quoted in Stephen L. Sass, *The Substance of Civilization: Material and Human History from the Stone Age to the Age of Silicon* (New York: Arcade, 1998), p. 13.

13. Quoted in Herlee Glessner Creel, *The Birth of China: A Survey of the Formative Period of Chinese Civilization* (New York: Frederick Ungar, 1961), p. 256.

Chapter 5 Eurasian Connections and New Traditions in East Asia, 600 B.C.E.–600 C.E.

1. *Records of the Historian: Chapters from the Shih Chi of Ssu-ma Ch'ien*, translated by Burton Watson (New York: Columbia University Press, 1969), p. 274.

2. Quoted in Arthur Cotterell and David Morgan, *China's Civilization: A Survey of Its History, Arts, and Technology* (New York: Praeger, 1975), p. 58.

3. Quoted in H. G. Creel, *Chinese Thought from Confucius to Mao Tse-Tung* (New York: Mentor, 1953), p. 32.

4. Quoted in Ch'u Chai and Winberg Chai, *Confucianism* (Woodbury, N.Y.: Barron's, 1973), p. 45.

5. Quoted in Dun J. Li, ed., *The Essence of Chinese Civilization* (Princeton: D. Van Nostrand, 1967), p. 6.

6. The quotes are from Patricia Buckley Ebrey, ed., *Chinese Civilization: A Sourcebook*, 2nd ed., revised and expanded (New York: Free Press, 1993), pp. 43–44.

7. The quotes are from Lionel Giles, *The Sayings of Lao Tzu* (New York: E.P. Dutton, 1908), pp. 19, 22, 25.

8. Quoted in Creel, *Chinese Thought*, p. 85.

9. Quoted in Arthur Waley, *The Way and Its Power: A Study of the Tao Te Ching and Its Place in Chinese Thought* (New York: Grove Press, 1958), p. 210.

10. Quoted in William McNaughton, ed., *Light from the East: An Anthology of Asian Literature* (New York: Laurel, 1978), p. 132.

11. Quoted in Leon Hellerman and Alan L. Stein, eds., *China: Readings on the Middle Kingdom* (New York: Washington Square Press, 1973), pp. 49–50.

12. Sima Qian, quoted in Arthur Cotterell, *The First Emperor of China* (New York: Penguin, 1988), p. 106.

13. Quoted in Frances Wood, *The Silk Road: Two Thousand Years in the Heart of Asia* (Berkeley: University of California Press, 2002), p. 55.

14. From John Minford and Joseph S. M. Lau, eds., *Classical Chinese Literature: An Anthology of Translations*, vol. 1 (New York: Columbia University Press, 2000), p. 387.

15. Quoted in Conrad Schirokauer, *A Brief History of Chinese and Japanese Civilizations*, 2nd ed. (San Diego: Harcourt Brace Jovanovich, 1989), p. 41.

16. Ebrey, *Chinese Civilization*, pp. 61–62.

17. The quotes are from Bret Hinsch, *Women in Early Imperial China* (Lanham, Md.: Rowman and Littlefield, 2002), pp. 72, 70.

18. Quoted in Ebrey, *Chinese Civilization*, p. 73.

19. Quoted in Robin R. Wang, ed., *Images of Women in Chinese Thought and Culture: Writings from the Pre-Qin Period Through the Song Dynasty* (Indianapolis: Hackett, 2003), p. 254.

20. Quoted in Robin R. Wang, ed., *Images of Women in Chinese Thought and Culture: Writings from the Pre-Qin Period Through the Song Dynasty* (Indianapolis: Hackett, 2003), p. 254.

21. Quoted in Arthur E. Wright, *The Sui Dynasty: The Unification of China, A.D. 581–617* (New York: Alfred A. Knopf, 1978), p. 180.

22. Quoted in George Samson, *A History of Japan to 1334* (Stanford, Calif.: Stanford University Press, 1958), p. 23.

23. The quotes are from David John Lu, ed., *Sources of Japanese History*, vol. 1 (New York: McGraw-Hill, 1974), pp. 21–22.

Chapter 6 Western Asia, the Eastern Mediterranean, and Regional Systems, 600–200 B.C.E.

1. Quoted in Norman Davies, *Europe: A History* (New York: Harper, 1996), p. 117.

2. Quoted in Lindsay Allen, *The Persian Empire* (Chicago: University of Chicago Press, 2005), p. 27.

3. Quoted in A.T. Olmstead, *History of the Persian Empire* (Chicago: University of Chicago Press, 1959), p. 125.

4. Quoted in William H. Stiebing, *Ancient Near Eastern History and Culture* (New York: Longman, 2003), p. 303.

5. From George Rawlinson, trans., *The Histories of Herodotus* (London: Dent, 1910), I, 131–140.

6. From Loren J. Samons III, ed., *Athenian Democracy and Imperialism* (Boston: Houghton Mifflin, 1998), pp. 216–217.

7. Quoted in Robert Flaceliere, *Daily Life in Greece at the Time of Pericles* (London: Phoenix, 2002), p. 56.

8. Quoted in Rex Warner, *The Greek Philosophers* (New York: New American Library, 1958), p. 24.

9. From Sextus Empiricus, *Outlines of Pyrrhonism*, trans. by R. G. Bury (Cambridge: Harvard University Press, 1933), vol. I, p. 213.

10. The quotes are from Martyn Oliver, *History of Philosophy: Great Thinkers from 600 B.C. to the Present Day* (New York: MetroBooks, 1997), pp. 16–17.

11. Quoted in Mortimer Chambers et al., *The Western Experience*, vol. 1, 5th ed. (New York: McGraw-Hill, 1987), p. 96.

12. Quoted in C. Warren Hollister, *Roots of the Western Tradition: A Short History of the Ancient World*, 5th ed. (New York: McGraw-Hill, 1991), p. 109.

13. From Barbara Hughes Fowler, *Archaic Greek Poetry: An Anthology* (Madison: University of Wisconsin Press, 1992), p. 131.

14. Quoted in Robert Flaceliere, "Women, Marriage and the Family," in Allan Mitchell and Istvan Deak, eds., *Everyman in Europe: Essays in Social History*, vol. 1 (Englewood Cliffs, N.J.: Prentice-Hall, 1974), p. 53.

15. Quoted in L. S. Stavrianos, ed., *The Epic of Man to 1500* (Englewood Cliffs, N.J.: Prentice-Hall, 1970), p. 133.

16. From *Medea*, quoted in Frank J. Frost, *Greek Society*, 2nd ed. (Lexington, Mass: D.C. Heath, 1980), p. 94.

17. From Aristophanes, *Lysistrata and Other Plays*, trans. Alan H. Sommerstein (New York: Penguin, 1973), pp. 200–208.

18. Reported by Thucydides, quoted in Stavrianos, *Epic of Man*, pp. 120–122.

19. Quoted in Michael Chauveau, *Egypt in the Age of Cleopatra: History and Society Under the Ptolemies* (Ithaca: Cornell University Press, 2000), p. 188.

20. Quoted in Francis Chanoux, *Hellenistic Civilization* (Malden, Mass.: Blackwell, 2003), p. 319.

21. "Diogenes," in *Biographical Encyclopedia of Philosophy* (Garden City, N.Y.: Doubleday, 1965), p. 76.

Chapter 7 Classical Societies in Southern and Central Asia, 600 B.C.E.–600 C.E.

1. Quoted in Jeannine Auboyer, *Daily Life in Ancient India: From 200 BC to 700 AD* (London: Phoenix, 2002), p. 62.

2. Quoted in Lionel Casson, *The Ancient Mariners: Seafarers and Sea Fighters of the Mediterranean in Ancient Times*, 2nd ed. (Princeton: Princeton University Press, 1991), p. 202.

3. Quoted in Susan Bayly, *Caste, Society and Politics in India from the Eighteenth Century to the Modern Age* (New York: Cambridge University Press, 1999), p. 14.

4. From William McNaughton, ed., *Light from the East* (New York: Laurel, 1978), pp. 401–402.

5. Quoted in Stanley Wolpert, *A New History of India*, 5th ed. (New York: Oxford University Press, 1997), p. 48.

6. From Swami Prabhavananda and Frederick Manchester, eds., *The Upanishads: Breath of the Eternal* (New York: Mentor, 1957), p. 62.

7. C. E. Gover, *The Folk-Songs of Southern India* (London: Trubner and Co., 1872), p. 165.

8. Quoted in Wolpert, *New History*, p. 54.

9. Quoted in Roy C. Amore and Julia Ching, "The Buddhist Tradition," in Willard

G. Oxtoby, ed., *World Religions: Eastern Traditions* (New York: Oxford University Press, 1996), p. 230.

10. From "Kautilya's 'Artha-Sastra,'" in O. L. Chavarria-Aguilar, ed., *Traditional India* (Englewood Cliffs, N.J.: Prentice-Hall, 1964), p. 125.

11. Quoted in Rhoads Murphy, *A History of Asia*, 4th ed. (New York: HarperCollins, 2003), p. 74.

12. Quoted in Lucille Schulberg, *Historic India* (New York: Time-Life Books, 1968), p. 80.

13. Xuan Zang, quoted in David Christian, *A History of Russia, Central Asia, and Mongolia*, vol. 1 (Malden, Mass.: Blackwell, 1998), p. 254.

14. From McNaughton, *Light from East*, p. 377.

15. Quoted in John Keay, *India: A History* (New York: Atlantic Monthly Press, 2000), p. 145.

16. Kalidasa, quoted in Auboyer, *Daily Life*, p. 117.

17. Quoted in Stephanie W. Jamison, *Sacrificed Wife/Sacrificer's Wife: Women, Ritual, and Hospitality in Ancient India* (New York: Oxford University Press, 1996), p. 13.

18. Quoted in Barbara N. Ramusack, "Women in South and Southeast Asia," in *Restoring Women to History* (Bloomington, Ind.: Organization of American Historians, 1988), p. 9.

19. Quoted in A. L. Basham, *The Wonder That Was India: A Survey of the History and Culture of the Indian Sub-continent Before the Coming of the Muslims*, 3rd. revised ed. (New Delhi: Rupa and Company, 1967), p. 420.

20. From Harry J. Benda and John A. Larkin, eds., *The World of Southeast Asia: Selected Historical Readings* (New York: Harper and Row, 1967), pp. 3–4.

21. Quoted in Keith Taylor, "The Rise of Dai Viet and the Establishment of Thanglong," in Kenneth R. Hall and John K. Whitmore, eds., *Explorations in Early Southeast Asian History: The Origins of Southeast Asian Statecraft* (Ann Arbor: University of Michigan Center for South and Southeast Asian Studies, 1976), p. 153.

22. From Nguyen Ngoc Bich, ed., *A Thousand Years of Vietnamese Poetry* (New York: Knopf, 1975), p. 89.

Chapter 8 Empires, Networks, and the Remaking of Europe, North Africa, and Western Asia, 500 B.C.E.–600 C.E.

1. Quoted in Tim Cornell and John Matthews, *The Roman World* (Alexandria, Va.: Stonehenge, 1991), p. 51.

2. Quoted in Felipe Fernandez-Armesto, *Civilizations: Culture, Ambition, and the Transformation of Nature* (New York: Simon and Schuster, 2001), p. 365.

3. Livy, quoted in Frederick Gentles and Melvin Steinfield, eds. *Hangups from Way Back: Historical Myths and Canons*, vol. 1 (San Francisco: Canfield, 1974), p. 173.

4. Diodorus, quoted in Barry Cunliffe, *The Extraordinary Voyage of Pytheas the Greek* (New York: Penguin, 2002), p. 52.

5. From Plautus, *The Casket*, quoted in Henry C. Boren, *Roman Society: A Social,*

Economic and Cultural History, 2nd ed. (Lexington: D.C. Heath, 1992), p. 88.

6. Frederick Gentles and Melvin Steinfield, eds., *Hangups from Way Back: Historical Myths and Canons*, Vol. 1, 2nd ed. (San Francisco: Canfield Press, 1974), p. 167.

7. From Plutarch, *Life of Antony*, in William S. Davis, ed., *Readings in Ancient History*, Vol. 2 (Boston: Allyn and Bacon, 1913), pp. 163–164.

8. Quoted in Jerome Carcopino, *Daily Life in Ancient Rome*, 2nd ed. (New Haven, Conn.: Yale University Press, 1968), p. 202.

9. Quoted in Norman Davies, *Europe: A History* (New York: Harper, 1998), p. 193.

10. Quoted in Lesley Adkins and Roy A. Adkins, *Handbook to Life in Ancient Rome* (New York: Oxford University Press, 1998), p. 276.

11. Diodorus Siculus, in Jo Ann Shelton, *As the Romans Did: A Sourcebook in Roman Social History* (New York: Oxford University Press, 1988), p. 175.

12. The quotes are from Boren, *Roman Society*, pp. 279, 219.

13. Quoted in Susan Whitfield, *Life Along the Silk Road* (Berkeley: University of California Press, 1999), p. 21.

14. Tacitus, *Agricola*, quoted in Moses Hadas, ed., *A History of Rome from Its Origins to 529 A.D. as Told by the Roman Historians* (Garden City, N.Y.: Doubleday Anchor, 1956), pp. 126–127.

15. Quoted in Neil Christie, *The Lombards* (Malden, Mass.: Blackwell, 1998), p. 2.

16. Matthew 22: 37–39, in *The Holy Bible*, King James Version (Chicago: Thomas Nelson, 1982), p. 957.

17. Quoted in Bonnie S. Anderson and Judith P. Zinsser, *A History of Their Own: Women in Europe from Prehistory to the Present*, vol. 1 (New York: Harper and Row, 1988), p. 76.

18. Quoted in Gillian Clark, *Women in Late Antiquity: Pagan and Christian Lifestyles* (Oxford: Clarendon, 1994), p. 124.

19. Quoted in Michael McCormick, *Origins of the European Economy: Communication and Commerce, A.D. 300–900* (New York: Cambridge University Press, 2001), p. 27.

20. From A. Atwater, trans., *Procopius: The Secret History* (Ann Arbor: University of Michigan Press, 1963), p. 8.

21. Quoted in Daniel Del Castillo, "A Long-Ignored Plague Gets Its Due," *Chronicle of Higher Education*, February 15, 2002, p. A22.

22. Quoted in Philip Sharrard, *Byzantium* (New York: Time-Life, 1966), p. 36.

23. Quoted in Touraj Daryaee, "The Persian Gulf Trade in Late Antiquity," *Journal of World History*, 14/1 (March 2003): p. 9.

24. Quoted in Patricia Crone, "The Rise of Islam in the World," in Francis Robinson, ed., *The Cambridge Illustrated History of the Islamic World* (New York: Cambridge University Press, 1996), pp. 4–5.

Chapter 9 Classical Societies and Regional Networks in Africa, the Americas, and Oceania, 600 B.C.E.–600 C.E.

1. From *The Horizon History of Africa* (New York: American Heritage, 1971), p. 207.

2. Ibn Battuta, quoted in Robert W. July, *Precolonial Africa: An Economic and Social History* (New York: Charles Scribner's, 1975), p. 183.

3. Quoted in Stanley Burstein, ed., *Ancient African Civilizations: Kush and Axum* (Princeton, N.J.: Markus Wiener, 1998), p. 41.

4. Quoted in Derek A. Welsby, *The Kingdom of Kush: The Napatan and Meroitic Empires* (Princeton: Markus Wiener, 1996), p. 40.

5. From *Horizon History*, p. 78.

6. Quoted in Basil Davidson, *African Kingdoms* (New York: Time-Life, 1966), p. 42.

7. Quoted in Graham Connah, *African Civilization. Precolonial Cities and States in Tropical Africa: An Archaeological Perspective* (Cambridge: Cambridge University Press, 1987), p. 78.

8. Quoted in Robert W. July, *A History of the African People*, 5th ed. (Prospect Heights, Ill.: Waveland, 1998), p. 45.

9. Rufinus, quoted in Burstein, *Ancient African Civilizations*, p. 95.

10. Quoted in Christopher Ehret, *An African Classical Age: Eastern and Southern Africa in World History, 1000 B.C. to A.D. 400* (Charlottesville: University of Virginia Press, 1998), p. 275.

11. From the *Popul Vuh*, quoted in Brian M. Fagan, *Kingdoms of Gold, Kingdoms of Jade: The Americas Before Columbus* (London and New York: Thames and Hudson, 1991), p. 94.

12. Father Bernardino de Sahagun, quoted in Richard E. W. Adams, *Prehistoric Mesoamerica* (Boston: Little, Brown, 1977), p. 110.

13. Frey Diego de Landa, quoted in T. Patrick Culbert, *Maya Civilization* (Washington, D.C.: Smithsonian, 1993), p. 23.

14. Quoted in Michael Wood, *Legacy: The Search for Ancient Cultures* (New York: Sterling, 1994), p. 166.

15. Frey Diego de Landa, quoted in Culbert, *Maya Civilization*, p. 22.

16. Fra Bernardino de Sahagun, quoted in Juan Schobinger, *The First Americans* (Grand Rapids, Mich.: William B. Eerdmans, 1994), p. 97.

17. Cieza de Leon, quoted in Fagan, *Kingdoms of Gold*, p. 192.

18. Quoted in Brian Fagan, *The Long Summer: How Climate Changed Civilization* (New York: Basic Books, 2004), p. 213.

19. Quoted in Judy Thompson and Allan Taylor, *Polynesian Canoes and Navigation* (Laie, Hawaii: Institute of Polynesian Studies, 1980), p. 32.

20. Quoted in Peter Bellwood, *The Polynesians: Prehistory of an Island People*, revised ed. (London: Thames and Hudson, 1997), p. 7.

21. Quoted in Peter Bellwood, *Man's Conquest of the Pacific: The Prehistory of Southeast Asia and Oceania* (New York: Oxford University Press, 1979), p. 300.

Societies, Networks, Transitions: Classical Blossomings in World History, 600 B.C.E – 600 C.E.

1. Quoted in Michael Wood, *Legacy: The Search for Ancient Cultures* (New York: Sterling, 1994), p. 192.

2. Quoted in Patricia Buckley Ebrey, *The Cambridge Illustrated History of China* (New York: Cambridge University Press, 1996), p. 46.

3. The quotes are from Felipe Fernandez-Armesto, *Ideas That Changed the World* (New York: DK, 2003), pp. 117, 119.

4. Quoted in Lindsay Allen, *The Persian Empire* (Chicago: University of Chicago Press, 2005), p. 43.

5. From Patricia Buckley Ebrey, ed., *Chinese Civilization: A Sourcebook*, 2nd ed., revised and expanded (New York: Free Press, 1993), pp. 57–58.

6. Quoted in Romila Thapar, *Asoka and the Decline of the Mauryas* (Delhi: Oxford University Press, 1997), p. 147.

7. Quoted in Robert P. Clark, *The Global Imperative: An Interpretive History of the Spread of Humankind* (Boulder: Westview, 1997), p. 3.

8. Quoted in Richard C. Foltz, *Religions of the Silk Road: Overland Trade and Cultural Exchange from Antiquity to the Fifteenth Century* (New York: St. Martin's, 1999), p. 62.

9. Tertullian, quoted in Erik Gilbert and Jonathan T. Reynolds, *Africa in World History: From Prehistory to the Present* (Upper Saddle River, N.J.: Prentice-Hall, 2004), p. 74.

10. Quoted in Kenneth R. Hall, *Maritime Trade and State Development in Early Southeast Asia* (Honolulu: University of Hawaii Press, 1985), p. 29.

11. Hou Han Shu, quoted in *Monks and Merchants: Silk Road Treasures from Northwest China* (http://www.asiasociety.org/arts/monksandmerchants/index/html).

12. Quoted in Frances Wood, *The Silk Road: Two Thousand Years in the Heart of Asia* (Berkeley: University of California Press, 2001), p. 66.

13. Quoted in Lionel Casson, *The Ancient Mariners: Seafarers and Sea Fighters of the Mediterranean in Ancient Times*, 2nd ed. (Princeton: Princeton University Press, 1991), p. 166.

14. From Basil Davidson, *African Civilization Revisited: From Antiquity to Modern Times* (Trenton, N.J.: Africa World Press, 1991), p. 64.

15. Quoted in Louis Crompton, *Homosexuality and Civilization* (Cambridge: Harvard University Press, 2003), p. 218.

16. Quoted in Peter N. Sterns, *Gender in World History* (New York: Routledge, 2000), p. 28

Chapter 10 The Rise, Power, and Connections of the Islamic World, 600–1500

1. From *The Muqaddimah: An Introduction to History*, translated by Franz Rosenthal and edited by N. J. Dawood (Princeton: Princeton University Press, 1967), pp. 25–27.

2. Quoted in Albert Hourani, *A History of the Arab Peoples* (Cambridge: Belknap Press, 1991), p. 3.

3. Quoted in Mohammed Munir, "The Birth of Islam in the Arabian Desert," in Claire Swisher, ed., *The Spread of Islam* (San Diego, Calif.: Greenhaven Press, 1999), p. 40.

4. Quoted in Jonathan Bloom and Sheila Blair, *Islam: A Thousand Years of Faith and Power* (New Haven, Conn.: Yale University Press, 2002), p. 29.

5. Quoted in Wiebke Walther, *Women in Islam* (Princeton: Markus Wiener, 1993), p. 104.

6. Quoted in Karen Armstrong, *Muhammad: A Biography of the Prophet* (San Francisco: HarperSanFrancisco, 1992), p. 160.

7. Quoted in Arthur Goldschmidt, Jr., *A Concise History of the Middle East*, 4th ed. revised (Boulder: Westview, 1991), p. 37.

8. Quoted in Francis Robinson, *The Cultural Atlas of the Islamic World Since 1500* (Oxford: Stonehenge, 1992), p. 180.

9. Quoted in Henry Bucher, *Middle East* (Guilford, Conn.: Dushkin, 1984), p. 19.

10. Quoted in Manuel Komroff, ed., *Contemporaries of Marco Polo* (New York: Horace Liveright, 1928), pp. 286–292.

11. Quoted in Alfred Guillaume, "Islamic Mysticism and the Sufi Sect," in Swisher, ed., *Spread*, p. 153.

12. "Baba Kuhi of Shiraz," translated by Reynold A. Nicholson. Quoted in Mary Ann Frese Witt et al., *The Humanities: Cultural Roots and Continuities*, vol. 1, 7th ed. (Boston: Houghton Mifflin, 2005), p. 270.

13. Quoted in Adam Goodheart, "Pilgrims from the Great Satan," *New York Times*, March 10, 2002, p. A12.

14. Quoted in Walther, *Women in Islam*, p. 40.

15. Quoted in Mervyn Hiskett, "Islamic Literature and Art," in Swisher, ed., *Spread*, p. 120.

16. Excerpted in John Yohannan, ed., *A Treasury of Asian Literature* (New York: New American Library, 1965), pp. 261–262.

17. Quoted in Jonathan P. Berkey, *The Formation of Islam: Religion and Society in the Near East, 600–1800* (New York: Cambridge University Press, 2003), p. 233.

18. Quoted in Bernard Lewis, *The Arabs in History* (New York: Harper and Row, 1960), p. 131.

19. Quoted in Hourani, *History of Arab Peoples*, p. 201.

20. Hariri, quoted in Fernand Braudel, *A History of Civilizations* (New York: Penguin, 1995), p. 71.

21. From *An Arab-Syrian Gentleman and Warrior in the Period of the Crusades: Memoirs of Usamah Ibn-Munqidh*, translated by Philip K. Hitti (Princeton: Princeton University Press, 1987), p. 195.

22. Ibn Al Athir, quoted in Mike Edwards, "Genghis Khan," *National Geographic* (December, 1996): p. 9.

23. Quoted in Francis Robinson, *The Cambridge Illustrated History of the Islamic World* (Cambridge: Cambridge University Press, 1996), p. 198.

Chapter 11 East Asian Traditions, Transformations, and Eurasian Encounters, 600–1500

1. Quoted in John Merson, *The Genius That Was China: East and West in the Making of the Modern World* (Woodstock, N.Y.: Overlook Press, 1990), p. 14.

2. Quoted in John A. Harrison, *The Chinese Empire* (New York: Harcourt Brace Jovanovich, 1972), p. 239.

3. Po Chu-I, quoted in William H. McNeill, *The Pursuit of Power: Technology, Armed Force, and Society Since A.D. 1000* (Chicago: University of Chicago Press, 1982), p. 28.

4. Quoted in C. P. Fitzgerald, *China: A Short Cultural History* (New York: Praeger, 1961), p. 336.

5. Quoted in Derk Bodde, *China's Cultural Tradition: What and Whither?* (New York: Holt, Rinehart and Winston, 1957), p. 31.

6. The Wang and Li poems are from Robert Payne, ed., *The White Pony: An Anthology of Chinese Poetry* (New York: Mentor, 1960), pp. 154, 174.

7. Du's poems are from Cyril Birch, ed., *Anthology of Chinese Literature from Early Times to the Fourteenth Century* (New York: Grove Press, 1965), pp. 240–241; and *Tu Fu: Selected Poems* (Peking: Foreign Languages Press, 1962), p. 100.

8. John Meskill, "History of China," in Meskill, ed., *An Introduction to Chinese Civilization* (Lexington, Mass.: D.C. Heath, 1973), pp. 127–128.

9. Yuan Tsai, from Patricia Buckley Ebrey, ed., *Chinese Civilization and Society: A Sourcebook* (New York: The Free Press, 1981), p. 96.

10. The quotes are from Dun J. Li, ed., *The Essence of Chinese Civilization* (Princeton, N.J.: Van Nostrand, 1967), p. 88; and James Zee-Min Lee, *Chinese Potpourri* (Hong Kong: Oriental Publishers, 1950), p. 319.

11. Quoted in H. H. Gowen and J. W. Hall, *An Outline History of China* (New York: D. Appleton, 1926), p. 142.

12. Quoted in H. D. Martin, *The Rise of Chingis Khan and His Conquest of North China* (Baltimore: Johns Hopkins University Press, 1950), p. 5.

13. R. E. Latham, trans., *The Travels of Marco Polo* (Baltimore: Penguin Books, 1958), pp. 184–187.

14. Quoted in Arthur Cotterell and David Morgan, *China's Civilization: A Survey of Its History, Arts, and Technology* (New York: Praeger, 1973), p. 190.

15. Quoted in Dun J. Li, *The Ageless Chinese: A History*, 2nd ed. (New York: Charles Scribner's, 1971), p. 283.

16. Zhang Tao, quoted in Timothy Brook, *The Confusions of Pleasure: Commerce and Culture in the Ming* (Berkeley: University of California Press, 1998), p. vii.

17. Quoted in Bruce Cumings, *Korea's Place in the Sun: A Modern History* (New York: W.W. Norton, 1997), p. 37.

18. Quoted in Yung Chung Kim, ed. and translator, *Women of Korea: A History from Ancient Times to 1945* (Seoul: Ehwa Women's University Press, 1977), p. 32

19. Quoted in Donald Keene, "Literature," in Arthur E. Tiedemann, ed., *An Introduction to Japanese Civilization* (Lexington, Mass.: D.C. Heath, 1974), p. 395.

20. Quoted in Ivan Morris, *The World of the Shining Prince: Court Life in Ancient Japan* (New York: Kodansha, 1994), p. 229.
21. Quoted in ibid., p. 204.
22. Quoted in Mikiso Hane, *Japan: A Historical Survey* (New York: Charles Scribner's, 1972), p. 56.
23. From Ryusaku Tsunoda et al., eds., *Sources of Japanese Tradition*, vol. 2 (New York: Columbia University Press, 1958), p. 236.
24. Quoted in Noel F. Busch, *The Horizon Concise History of Japan* (New York: American Heritage, 1972), p. 58.

Chapter 12 Expanding Horizons in Africa and the Americas, 600–1500

1. Quoted in Patricia W. Romero, *Lamu: History, Society, and Family in an East African Port City* (Princeton: Markus Wiener, 1997), p. 14.
2. The quotes are from Basil Davidson, *The Lost Cities of Africa* (Boston: Little, Brown, 1959), p. 151.
3. Quoted in Esmond Bradley Martin and Chryssee Perry Martin, *Cargoes of the East: The Ports, Trade and Culture of the Arabian Seas and Western Indian Ocean* (London: Elm Tree Books, 1978), p. 9.
4. Quoted in *Africa's Glorious Legacy* (Arlington, Va.: Time-Life Books, 1994), p. 90.
5. Quoted in E. Jefferson Murphy, *History of African Civilization* (New York: Dell, 1972), p. 120.
6. The quotes are from E. W. Bovill, *The Golden Trade of the Moors*, 2nd ed. (London: Oxford University Press, 1970), p. 95.
7. Leo Africanus, quoted in Kevin Shillington, *History of Africa*, rev. ed. (New York: St. Martin's, 1995), p. 105.
8. Quoted in Constance B. Hilliard, ed., *Intellectual Traditions of Pre-Colonial Africa* (New York: McGraw-Hill, 1998), pp. 311–312.
9. Quoted in John Iliffe, *Africans: The History of a Continent* (Cambridge: Cambridge University Press, 1995), p. 93.
10. The quotes are from Davidson, *Lost Cities of Africa*, p. 156.
11. Quoted in John Middleton, *The World of the Swahili* (New Haven, Conn.: Yale University Press, 1992), p. 40.
12. Duarte Barbosa, quoted in Derek Nurse and Thomas Spear, *The Swahili: Reconstructing the History and Language of an African Society, 800–1500* (Philadelphia: University of Pennsylvania Press, 1985), p. 83.
13. Quoted in Bovill, *Golden Trade*, p. 96.
14. Djeli Mamoudou Kouyate, quoted in D. T. Niane, *Sundiata: An Epic of Old Mali* (London: Longman, 1965), p. 1.
15. John Smith, quoted in Charles Mann, "The Pristine Myth," *The Atlantic Online*, March 7, 2002 (http://www.theatlantic.com/ unbound/ interviews/ int2002-03-07.htm).
16. Quoted in Richard F. Townsend, *The Aztecs*, rev. ed. (New York: Thames and Hudson, 2000), p. 59.
17. Quoted in Brian M. Fagan, *Kingdoms of Gold, Kingdoms of Jade: The Americas Before Columbus* (London: Thames and Hudson, 1991), p. 7.

18. Friar Bernardino de Sahagun, quoted in Michael E. Smith, *The Aztecs*, 2nd ed. (Malden, Mass.: Blackwell, 2003), p. 113.
19. Quoted in Fagan, *Kingdoms of Gold*, p. 224.
20. Quoted in Robert M. Carnack et al., *The Legacy of Mesoamerica: History and Culture of a Native American Civilization* (Upper Saddle River, N.J.: Prentice-Hall, 1996), p. 415.
21. Quoted in Marysa Navarro, "Women in Pre-Columbian and Colonial Latin America," in *Restoring Women to History* (Bloomington, Ind.: Organization of American Historians, 1988), p. 6.
22. Quoted in *Incas: Lords of Gold and Glory* (Alexandria, Va.: Time-Life Books, 1992), p. 52.
23. Pedro Cieza de Leon, quoted in Terence N. D'Altroy, *The Incas* (Malden, Mass.: Blackwell, 2002), p. 3.

Chapter 13 South Asia, Central Asia, Southeast Asia, and Afro-Eurasian Connections, 600–1500

1. From L. S. Stavrianos, *The Epic of Man to 1500* (Englewood Cliffs, N.J.: Prentice-Hall, 1970), pp. 160, 162–163.
2. Quoted in Tansen Sen, *Buddhism, Diplomacy, and Trade: The Realignment of Sino-Indian Relations, 600–1400* (Honolulu: University of Hawaii Press, 2003), p. 11.
3. Quoted in A. L. Basham, *The Wonder That Was India* (New York: Grove Press, 1959), p. vi.
4. Al-Biruni, quoted in Romila Thapar, *Early India: From the Origins to AD 1300* (Berkeley: University of California Press, 2002), p. 437.
5. Quoted in Paul Thomas Welty, *The Asians: Their Evolving Heritage*, 6th ed. (New York: Harper and Row, 1984), p. 68.
6. Narenda K. Sethi, *Hindu Proverbs and Wisdom* (Mount Vernon, N.Y.: Peter Pauper Press, 1962), p. 5.
7. Nammalvar, quoted in Roberta Smith, "Where Gods Set Bronze in Motion," *New York Times*, December 6, 2002, p. B3.
8. Quoted in Lucille Schulberg, *Historic India* (New York: Time-Life Books, 1968), pp. 11–12.
9. Quoted in Debiprasad Chattopadhyana, *History of Science and Technology in Ancient India*, vol. 3 (Calcutta: Firma KLM Private Ltd., 1996), p. 60.
10. Minhaju-s Siraj, quoted in John Keay, *A History of India* (New York: Atlantic Monthly Press, 2000), p. 245.
11. Quoted in Hermann Kulke and Dietmar Rothermund, *History of India*, 3rd ed. (New York: Routledge, 1998), p. 119.
12. Stanley Wolpert, *A New History of India*, 5th ed. (New York: Oxford University Press, 1997), p. 113.
13. Quoted in Keay, *History of India*, p. 274.
14. Quoted in Richard Eaton, "Islamic History as Global History," in Michael Adas, ed., *Islamic and European Expansion: The Forging of a Global Order* (Philadelphia: Temple University Press, 1993), p. 21.

15. Quoted in Christopher Pym, *The Ancient Civilization of Angkor* (New York: New American Library, 1968), p. 118.
16. Quoted in David Chandler, *A History of Cambodia*, 2nd ed. updated (Boulder, Colo.: Westview Press, 1996), p. 74.
17. From Harry J. Benda and John A. Larkin, eds., *The World of Southeast Asia: Selected Historical Readings* (New York: Harper and Row, 1967), pp. 45–46.
18. From ibid., p. 41.
19. Ibn Muhammad Ibrahim, from Michael Smithies, *Descriptions of Old Siam* (Kuala Lumpur: Oxford University Press, 1995), p. 91.
20. Quoted in Ralph Smith, *Viet-Nam and the West* (Ithaca, N.Y.: Cornell University Press, 1971), p. 9.
21. Quoted in Anthony Reid, *Southeast Asia in the Age of Commerce, 1450–1680*, vol. 2 (New Haven: Yale University Press, 1993), p. 10.
22. Tome' Pires, quoted in Paul Wheatley, *The Golden Khersonese* (Kuala Lumpur: University of Malaya Press, 1961), p. 313.
23. Quoted in Kenneth R. Hall, *Maritime Trade and State Development in Early Southeast Asia* (Honolulu: University of Hawaii Press, 1985), p. 210.

Chapter 14 Christian Societies in Medieval Europe, Byzantium, and Russia, 600–1500

1. From a fourteenth-century legend, quoted in Amy G. Remensnyder, "Topographies of Memory: Center and Periphery in High Medieval France," in Gerd Althoff et al., eds., *Medieval Concepts of the Past: Ritual, Memory, Historiography* (New York: Cambridge University Press, 2002), p. 214.
2. Quoted in *What Life Was Like in the Age of Chivalry: Medieval Europe, AD 800–1500* (Alexandria, Va.: Time-Life Books, 1997), p. 17.
3. Quoted in James C. Russell, *The Germanization of Early Medieval Christianity* (Oxford: Oxford University Press, 1994), p. 186.
4. "Charlemagne's letter to Pope Leo III, 796," from C. Warren Hollister et al., *Medieval Europe: A Short Sourcebook*, 2nd ed. (New York: McGraw-Hill, 1992), p. 78.
5. Quoted in F. Donald Logan, *The Vikings in History*, 2nd ed. (New York: Routledge, 1991), p. 15.
6. Hugo of Santalla, quoted in Jerry Brotton, *The Renaissance Bazaar: From the Silk Road to Michelangelo* (Oxford: Oxford University Press, 2002), p. 195.
7. Quoted in John M. Hobson, *The Eastern Origins of Western Civilization* (New York: Cambridge University Press, 2004), p. 113.
8. Quoted in Jo Ann H. Moran Cruz and Richard Gerberding, *Medieval Worlds: An Introduction to European History, 300–1492* (Boston: Houghton Mifflin, 2004), p. 388.
9. Quoted in Eileen Power, *Medieval People*, new rev. ed. (New York: Barnes and Noble, 1963), p. 18.
10. Richard of Devizes, quoted in Jacques Le Goff, ed., *The Medieval World* (London: Postgate Books, 1997), p. 139.

11. The quotes are from Frederic Delouche, et al., *Illustrated History of Europe: A Unique Portrait of Europe's Common History* (New York: Barnes and Noble, 2001), p. 170; and Georges Duby, "Marriage in Early Medieval Society," in *Love and Marriage: The Middle Ages*, translated by Jane Dunnett (Chicago: University of Chicago Press, 1994), p. 11.

12. Quoted in Carolly Erickson, *The Medieval Vision: Essays in History and Perception* (New York: Oxford University Press, 1976), p. 73.

13. Quoted in Cruz and Gerberding, *Medieval Worlds*, p. 277.

14. Quoted in Clive Ponting, *A Green History of the World: The Environment and the Collapse of Great Civilizations* (New York: Penguin, 1991), p. 144.

15. Quoted in Thomas F. Madden, *A Concise History of the Crusades* (Lanham, Md.: Rowman and Littlefield, 1999), pp. 8–9.

16. Quoted in C. Warren Hollister, *Medieval Europe: A Short History,* 8th ed. (Boston: McGraw-Hill, 1998), p. 296.

17. Quoted in ibid., p. 273.

18. Quoted in Nicholas V. Riasanovsky, *A History of Russia*, 5th ed. (New York: Oxford University Press, 1993), p. 72.

19. Eustache Deschamps, quoted in J. Huizinga, *The Waning of the Middle Ages* (Garden City, N.Y.: Doubleday Anchor, 1954), p. 33.

20. Quoted in Delouche, *Illustrated History*, p. 168.

21. Quoted in Brotton, *Renaissance Bazaar*, p. 75.

22. Canon Pietro Casola, quoted in ibid., p. 38.

23. Quoted in Edith Simon, *The Reformation* (New York: Time-Life Books, 1966), p. 71.

24. Cadamosto, quoted in Peter Russell, *Prince Henry "the Navigator": A Life* (New Haven, Conn.: Yale University Press, 2000), p. 225.

Societies, Networks, Transitions: Expanding Horizons in the Intermediate Era, 600 B.C.E – 600 C.E.

1. Quoted in Jack Turner, *Spice: The History of a Temptation* (New York: Vintage, 2004), p. 103.

2. Quoted in Fernand Braudel, *The Wheels of Commerce* (New York: Harper and Row, 1979), p. 127.

3. Abdul Kassim ibn Khordadbeh, quoted in Elmer Bendiner, *The Rise and Fall of Paradise* (New York: Dorset Press, 1983), p. 101.

4. Quoted in John M. Hobson, *The Eastern Origins of Western Civilisation* (New York: Cambridge University Press, 2004), p. 40.

5. Quoted in M. N. Pearson, "Introduction," in Pearson, ed., *Spices in the Indian Ocean World* (Aldershot, U.K.: Valiorum, 1996), p. xv.

6. Quoted in Philip D. Curtin, *Cross-Cultural Trade in World History* (New York: Cambridge University Press, 1984), p. 125.

7. Quoted in John Kelley, *The Great Mortality* (New York: HarperCollins, 2005), p. 2

8. Quoted in Peter N. Stearns, *Western Civilization in World History* (New York: Routledge, 2003), p. 52.

9. Al-Musabbihi, quoted in Heinz Halm, *The Fatimids and Their Traditions of Learning* (New York: I.B. Taurus, 1997), p. 73.

10. Leon Battista Alberti, quoted in Jeremy Brotton, *The Renaissance Bazaar: From the Silk Road to Michelangelo* (London: Oxford University Press, 2002), pp. 73-74.

11. Quoted in Peter N. Stearns, *Gender in World History* (New York: Routledge, 2000), p. 52.

12. Quoted in Anthony Reid, *Southeast Asia in the Age of Commerce, 1450–1680*, vol 1 (New Haven: Yale University Press, 1988), p. 1.

13. Quoted in Adriaan Verhulst, *The Carolingian Economy* (New York: Cambridge University Press, 2002), p. 48.

14. Ibn al-Athir, quoted in David R. Ringrose, *Expansion and Global Interaction, 1200–1700* (New York: Longman, 2001), p. 22.

15. Quoted in Rene Grousset, *The Empire of the Steppes: A History of Central Asia* (New Brunswick: Rutgers University Press, 1970), p. 249.

16. Quoted in L. S. Stavrianos, *Lifelines from Our Past: A New World History*, revised ed. (Armonk, N.Y.: M. E. Sharpe, 1997), p. 58.

17. Quoted in Frederick F. Cartwright, *Disease and History: The Influence of Disease in Shaping the Great Events of History* (New York: Thomas Y. Crowell, 1972), p. 37.

18. Quoted in Brian Fagan, *The Long Summer: How Climate Changed Civilization* (New York: Basic Books, 2004), p. 224.

19. Peter Martyr, quoted in Turner, *Spice*, p. xi.

INDEX

House of Wisdom (Baghdad), 287, 296, 419
Housing. *See also* Construction materials and
  techniques; Abu Hureyra, 5, 18, 19 *(illus.)*;
  early humans, 10; urbanization and, 24, 25
  (illus.); in Mesopotamia, 34; in Egypt, 64; in
  Harappa (India), 43, 44 *and illus.*; Native
  American, 96, 97; Japanese, 141; in Sudanic
  towns, 234; in Africa, 333 *and illus.*, 334,
  336, 337; Pueblo Indian, 345
Howe, Stephen (historian), 255
Huang He (Yellow) River, 84, 120; flooding of,
  82, 312
Huang He (Yellow) River Valley, 84, 85,
  86*(map)*
Hue (Vietnam), 194
Huff, Toby (historian), 417
Huitzilopochtli (Aztec god), 347
Hulegu Khan, 292
Human evolution, 8–11, 96
Humanism, 254; in ancient Greece, 156, 159;
  Confucian, 122, 125, 126, 130, 137, 138, 305;
  Islamic, 296; Italian Renaissance and, 409;
  Christian, 419
Humanity, roots of, 8–13. *See also under*
  Homo; hominids, 8–11; chronology
  (135,000 B.C.E.–1000 C.E.), 13; evolution and
  diversity of, 7, 10–11, 96; globalization of,
  11–13 *and map*
Human sacrifice, 260; Aztecs and, 347–348,
  349*(illus.)*; at Cahokia, 346; in Chimu, 343;
  in early Americas, 100, 101; in early China,
  87; Maya, 240, 343; Moche, 243, 244;
  Inca, 351
Hundred Flowers Period (China), 121, 125
Hundred Years War (1387–1453), 407–408
Hungary (Hungarians), 184, 215, 396,
  406*(map)*; Ottoman Empire and, 295;
  Magyars in, 388; Mongols and, 404
Huns, 27, 221; China and, 129, 135; India and,
  184, 190; Rome and, 184, 214, 215
Hunter-gatherers, 9, 14–17. *See also* Hunting;
  cultural life and violence of, 15–16; kinship
  and cooperation in, 14–15; !Kung people,
  14, 17 *and illus.*; shifting cultivation and, 19;
  species extinction and, 23; in early Japan,
  94–95; Native Americans as, 97, 98; transition
  to farming and, 5–6, 69, 109; by Australian
  Aborigines, 247
Hunting: in Stone Age, 14; of bison by Native
  Americans, 97; by Mongols, 312*(illus.)*; by
  North American Indians, 347
Husayn (grandson of Muhammad), 279, 280
Hydraulic technology, 185. *See also* Water
  control systems
Hyksos (Semitic people), 60
"Hymn of Creation," 49
Hypatia (Pagan philosopher), 218, 219 *and
  illus.*, 264

Iberian peninsula, reunification of, 406*(map)*
Ibn Battuta, Abdallah Muhammad (Muslim
  traveler), 288, 289, 380; in East Africa, 336;
  in Mali, 288*(illus.)*, 331, 419; routes of,
  290*(map)*; in Sudanic Africa, 339
Ibn Khaldun, Abd al-Rahman (Arab scholar),
  269, 287, 289, 293, 332
Ibn Majid, Shihab al-Din Ahmad (Arab
  navigator), 423

Ibn Rushd (Muslim philosopher), 286, 287
Ibn Sina, Abu Ali al-Husain (Muslim scholar),
  284, 287
Ice Ages, 9, 10, 14, 16*(illus.)*. *See also* Stone
  Age; Bering land bridge in, 95; "Little," 404,
  423
Iceland, 423; Vikings in, 388
Icons (religious paintings), 402
Ideas: *See also* Intellectual life (intellectuals);
  Political thought; exchange of, 106; spread
  of, 120
Ideographs, Chinese, 90*(illus.)*
Igbo people of Nigeria, 68, 69
Iliad (Homer), 76, 77, 113, 212
Il-Khanid Persia, 292, 311*(map)*
Iltutmish, Sultan (Delhi India), 366–367
Imperialism. *See* Colonies (colonization);
  Expansion
Imports. *See* Trade
Inanna (Mesopotamian goddess), 31, 32
Inca Empire, 246, 348*(map)*, 351–353,
  413*(map)*, 420; Chimu and, 344, 351;
  Machu Picchu, 352 *and illus.*; political
  economy, 351; society and technology of,
  351–352
Incense, myrrh and, 55
Independence, of Vietnam, 377
India, 31–32, 338. *See also* Hinduism (Hindus);
  earliest humans in, 11; agriculture in, 21;
  Indo-Europeans in, 27, 28*(map)*; chronology
  (2600–1000 B.C.E.), 33; view of time in, 74;
  early cities in, 43–44; economy and trade,
  45–46; farming and environment of, 42–43;
  Harappa in, 42–46; chronology (7000–600
  B.C.E.), 42; decline and collapse, 46; Indo-
  Aryan synthesis, 50–52; caste and society of,
  174–176, 177, 261; Chinese Buddhists
  (Faxian) in, 137, 188, 192, 261; languages of,
  138; gold coins in, 172*(illus.)*, 185; Greco-
  Bactrian kingdom in, 167 *and map*, 180;
  Gupta Empire, 181*(map)*, 187–190, 259;
  epic literature of, 190; marriage in, 174, 175,
  188; mathematics in, 189; Mauryan Empire,
  180–183; merchant class in, 173, 182, 185,
  188, 263; Persian expedition to, 149, 163;
  science and medicine in, 188, 189–190; trade
  in, 173; Kushan Empire, 181*(map)*, 184;
  Islam in, 276, 295; Tang China and, 300;
  Chinese pilgrims in, 356*(illus.)*, 357; Delhi
  Sultanate, 365 *(illus.)*, 366–367 *and map*,
  368; manufacturing in, 416
India, religion in, 31, 150. *See also* Hinduism;
  Buddhism, 178–179 *and illus.*, 262; Jainism,
  174, 177–178, 254, 261; toleration for, 177,
  183, 184, 188
Indian (Arabic) numerals, 189, 287, 410
Indianization, 192–193; in Java and Sumatra,
  374–375, 379; in Southeast Asia, 370–371
Indian Ocean trade (maritime system), 291,
  378, 414–415; Sri Lanka and, 185; shipbuilding technology and, 191*(illus.)*; regions
  of, 191–192; *Periplus of the Erythraean Sea*
  and, 233; East Africa and, 237, 335, 336; China
  and, 307; Portuguese and, 341, 380, 410; India
  port cities and, 367; Melaka and, 380
Individual, the (individualism): in Greece, 145,
  161, 166; in Rome, 209; in Siam, 377; in
  Renaissance Italy, 409

Indo-European languages, 27, 32. *See also*
  specific language
Indo-Europeans, 27, 60. *See also* Aryans; Celts;
  Germans; Hittites, 27, 38–39, 106,
  109*(illus.)*; Mycenaeans, 76; patriarchy and,
  111; Scythians, 148, 169
Indonesia (Indonesians), 92, 315, 378–380;
  early humans in, 11; in East Africa, 237;
  Aboriginal Australia and, 248; spice trade of,
  291, 415; in Madagascar, 335; Madjapahit
  Empire, 371*(map)*, 375
Indradevi (Khmer woman scholar), 374
Indra (Indian god), 48–49
Indus River, 23, 46, 173
Indus River Valley, 31, 105*(map)*; Alexander
  the Great in, 165, 180; Harappa in, 42–46;
  Islam in, 365, 368
Industry, 415. *See also* Manufacturing; Pottery;
  Textiles (textile industry); Song China,
  307–308; in medieval Europe, 390
Infantry, 359. *See also* Armed forces (soldiers);
  Assyrian, 39; Greek phalanx, 153, 160, 165;
  Etruscan, 203; Roman, 205
Infidels (non-Muslims), 395
Inflation: in Han China, 130; in Persian
  Empire, 151; Roman Empire, 213
Inheritance: Hammurabic code, 41; in Han
  China, 132; in Korea, 139; Matrilineal, 15;
  Muslim women and, 286; patrilineal, in
  Africa, 336; women and, 394; women and
  property, 35, 48, 61, 159
Innocent III, Pope, 396
Inoculation against disease, 308
Inquisition, 396–397
Intellectual life (intellectuals): *See also*
  Culture(s); Ideas; Philosophy (philosophers);
  Political thought; Science(s); writing
  and, 37, 113; in imperial China, 121,
  126–127; Confucianism and, 136, 137; in
  Greece, 71, 145, 158, 164; in Classical
  India, 189, 190, 196; Axial Age, 253, 254;
  in Muslim Spain, 283, 389; Islam and, 284,
  295, 331, 389; in Mongol China, 311; in
  Korea, 321; in Hausa states, 333; Aztec,
  350; Hindu, 363; in medieval Europe,
  399–401
Interest on loans (usury), 41, 393, 395
Intermediate era (600 B.C.E.–600 C.E.), xxii,
  412–423; climate change and society in,
  422–423; disease in, 422; eastern predominance in, 416–418; maritime trade in,
  414–415; Mongol Empire in, 420–422; roots
  of oceanic exploration in, 423; slavery and
  feudalism in, 420; trade and interregional
  contact in, 412, 413*(map)*, 414 *and illus.*;
  universal religions in, 415, 419–420
Inuit Eskimos, 14, 96
Ionian Greeks, 149, 154, 163; rebellion by,
  148, 160
Iran, 32, 35. *See also* Aryans; Persia; Persian
  Empire
Iraq, 33, 39, 223. *See also* Mesopotamia; Mongol
  conquest of, 292; Shi'ite Islam in, 280
Irdabama (Persian businesswoman), 151
Ireland: Celts in, 214; Viking raids in, 388;
  English conquest of, 408
Irene (Byzantine empress), 402
Iron Age, 104, 105*(map)*, 106; in China, 121

217(*map*), 218; climate, 71, 200; Roman expansion into, 205–207, 208(*map*)
Mediterranean Sea trade, 71, 199, 414; of Minoans and Mycenaean Greeks, 75–76; of Phoenicians, 108, 149; of Greeks, 163; of Carthaginians, 204; medieval Europe, 389; slavery and, 392
Megaliths (great stones), 21, 26
Mehmed the Conqueror (Sultan), 295, 408
Mekong River Basin, 91, 92, 192
Mekong River Delta, 378
Melaka, 378–379, 423; as maritime trade hub, 380
Melaka, Straits of, 191, 291, 370, 375
Melanesia (Melanesians), 92, 251
Meleager (Syrian Greek poet), 167
Memphis (Egypt), 59, 63
Men. *See* Fathers; Gender relations; Homosexuality; Marriage; Patriarchy; Sexuality
Menelik (Aksum), 232
Menes (Egypt), 57
Mengzi (Mencius, Chinese philosopher), 124, 126, 130
Mercator projection, xx(*map*)
Merchants (merchant class; traders), 423. *See also* Markets; Trade; Mesopotamian, 35; Phoenician, 76; in China, 87, 88, 120; urban networks and, 107; in India, 50, 173, 182, 185, 188; Silk Road, 119; Ionian, 163; religion and, 136, 263; spread of Buddhism by, 136; Sogdian, 184; in Southeast Asia, 194; Greek, 145, 163, 253; Aksumite, 232; in Arabia, 224; Mesoamerican, 239, 242; Axial Age empires and, 257; in Mecca, 274; foreign, in China, 299; from Italian cities, 293, 294(*illus.*), 394; Arab, 270, 271, 279, 285, 286, 291, 327; in China, 305, 306, 309, 410; Jewish, 295, 303, 389, 414, 415; Chinese, in Southeast Asia, 315, 372; Muslim, 289, 290(*map*), 291, 328–329, 330(*map*), 340, 378; in Japan, 324; African, 331, 334, 340; in Hausa states, 333; Mayan, 342; Aztec, 349–350; foreign, in Melaka, 380; Byzantine, 402; in India, 359, 360, 367; medieval Europe, 389, 392, 393–394, 409–410; Silk Road trade and, 412; stereotypes of, 407
Meroë (Kush), 228–229, 230
Mersu (Egyptian priest), 62
Merv (Persia), 292
Mesa Verde (Anasazi town), 345 *and map,* 346
Mesoamerica, 237–242, 341, 414. *See also* Aztec Empire; Mayas; agriculture in, 20 (*map*); ballgames in, 100, 240, 242, 245, 262; maize in, 342; monumental structures in, 100; North American Indian trade with, 344, 346; Olmecs, 101–102 *and illus.,* 241, 246, 260; population of, 342, 343, 353; Teotihuacan, 239, 241–242 *and illus.;* Toltecs in, 246, 343, 344, 347, 348(*map*)
Mesolithic (Middle Stone Age), 14, 18
Mesopotamia, 27, 31–42. *See also* Babylonia; chronology (5500–330 B.C.E.), 35; creation story in, 6; farmer's almanac from, 22; Hittites, 38–39; irrigation in, 23; Akkadian Empire, 37, 46, 106, 108; trade, 46, 108; chronology (3000–605 B.C.E.), 33; environment of, 32–33; Chaldeans, 37, 39, 73, 74 *and illus.;* craftsmen in, 107; early urbanized

societies in, 32–38; Egypt compared to, 57; irrigation in, 33, 247; Assyrian Empire and, 39; foundations of, 33; law in, 38, 39–41 *and illus.;* religion and literature of, 41–42; slavery in, 35, 37, 41; state development in, 108; Sumerians, 30(*illus.*), 33–37, 104, 110; trading cities in, 108; Seleucids in, 166, 167(*map*), 169, 205
Messenger service. *See* Postal (messenger) system
Messianism, 74, 186
Messina, Sicily, 404
Metallurgy (metalworking), 104. *See also* Bronze; Copper; Gold; Iron industry and tools; Silver; Steel; Tin; in Indus Valley, 46, 105(*map*); deforestation and, 104; in sub-Saharan Africa, 66
Metaphysics, 157. *See also* Philosophy
Methodius (missionary to Slavs), 403
Mexica people, 347
Mexico, 21, 100, 342. *See also* Aztec Empire; Mesoamerica; Olmecs, 101–102 *and illus.,* 241, 246, 260; Teotihuacan in, 239, 241–242 *and illus.;* Pueblo peoples of, 345; Toltecs of, 246, 343, 344, 347, 348(*map*); Valley of, 347
Mexico City, 239
Micronesia (Micronesians), 192, 248, 249 (*map*), 251
Middle class: in China, 87; in cities, 107; Persian, 150; in East African city-states, 336
Middle East, 33, 380. *See also* Arabs; Islam; Mesopotamia; Western (southwestern) Asia; *and specific countries, cultures and empires;* African slaves in, 341; agriculture in, 18; China and, 301(*illus.*); chronology (622–1258 C.E.), 271; Crusades in, 291–292; cultural diversity in, 270; gunpowder in, 293; plague in, 292–293; Islam in, 276, 285, 389; maritime trade of, 359; medieval Europe and, 386; use of term, xx
Middle Kingdom (Egypt), 57, 60
Migration(s) (population movement). *See also* Colonies (colonization); Nomadic peoples; from Africa (100,000 to 10,000 years ago), 9–13, 12(*map*); Indo-European pastoralists, 28(*map*); to Americas, 12(*map*), 95–96; ancient Egyptian, 57; Aryan, 43(*map*), 47; Austronesian, 93, 106, 192, 247; desertification and, 65; from Southeast Asia, 92; of Koreans to Japan, 94, 140; of Greeks, 71, 152, 163; to India, 46, 173; to Madagascar, 191(*illus.*), 192, 237; of Bantu speakers, 67, 68–70 *and map,* 106, 230(*map*), 236–237, 262; Pacific Islander, 248; Classic Age, 262; in Southeast Asia, 370–371, 378; Roman Empire and, 384; of Jews in Europe, 395
Milan (Italy), 389, 392, 396
Miletus (Anatolia), 145, 148, 163
Military, the: *See also* Armed forces; Navy; War (warfare); Weapons and military technology; Malaysian, 16; nomadic pastoralist, 27; Assyrian, 39; Aryan, 49; Egyptian, 67; Chinese, 86; empire and, 108, 263; in imperial China, 126, 129, 130; Greek, 153–154, 155, 159, 161; Alexander the Great, 165; Mauryan India, 180, 183; Carthaginian, 205; Roman, 200, 203, 204,

206, 207, 213 *and illus.;* Kushite, 229; Islamic expansion and, 274, 276, 279, 280; Spanish, 283; Chinese, 303, 309; in Japan, 320, 322; Toltec, 343, 344(*illus.*); English, 408
Military conscription (draft), 16, 17, 214; in Japan, 317, 322
Millet (grain), 65, 234, 236, 337
Millet (nationality) system, 295
Mills: watermills, 308, 390; windmills, 390
Minamoto-no-Yoritomo (Japan), 322
Minerva (Roman goddess), 210
Ming Empire (China), 310, 313–316; Afro-Eurasian world and, 313–315; government and culture, 313; inward turn of, 315–316; Melaka and, 380; Zeng He's voyages in, 314–315 *and map,* 380, 418, 423
Minoan civilization, 71, 72(*map*), 75–76
Minos (Crete), 75
Missile launchers (rockets), 303, 308
Missionaries, 259; Buddhist, 136–137, 183, 185, 261, 300; Christian, 74, 232–233, 261, 324, 341, 380, 385–386, 410; Muslim, 275, 300 (*See also* Islam, conversion to)
Mississippi River Valley, 97–98 *and illus.,* 99; Native cultures in, 345(*map*), 346, 353
Mithraism (mystery religion), 169, 218, 224
Mithra (sun god), 169, 218
Mixcoatl (Toltec ruler), 343
Moche (Peru), 242–243, 260, 342, 423; nobility, 244 *and illus.,* 343
Moctecuzma I (Aztec ruler), 347
Moctecuzma II (Aztec ruler), 349
Mogadishu (East African city-state), 335
Mogao Caves (China), fresco in, 118(*illus.*)
Mogollon Indians of American Southwest, 245, 344–345 *and map,* 423
Mohenjo-Daro (India), 43, 44(*illus.*), 48
Moikeha (Polynesian navigator), 251
Molucca (Maluku) Islands, 379, 380, 415
Mombasa (East African city-state), 335, 338
Monaghan, Patricia (historian), 111
Monarchy. *See* Kingship (emperors; monarchy)
Monasteries. *See* Asceticism; Buddhist monasteries; Christian monasteries
Money, Chinese paper, 305. *See also* Coins (coinage); Currency
Mongols (Mongolian Empire), 186, 315, 368, 420–422; nomadic way of life and, 27; Islam and, 282, 286, 292; Buddhism and, 364; China and, 300, 409; conquest of China by, 309, 310–313, 311(*map*); conquest of Korea by, 317; invasion of Japan by, 321(*map*), 323; Southeast Asia and, 375; heritage of, 421–422; Russia and, 403–404; innovation in Europe and, 408, 422; climate change and, 423
Monogamy, 353, 419
Monophysite theology, 218, 222, 231, 270
Monopoly trade, 126, 309
Monotheism, 113, 369; in Africa, 68, 339; Akhenaten, 60; Arab, 270, 271; Hebrew, 60, 71, 73–74; Islamic, 270, 272, 274, 365; in Zoroastrianism, 151
Monsoon winds, 335
Monte Alban (Zapotec), 241, 342
Monte Verde (Chile), 96, 97
Moon cult, Aztec, 351